Il più accurato ed economico
dizionario tascabile
ITALIANO—INGLESE
INGLESE—ITALIANO
finora pubblicato

È un' opera concepita espressamente
come strumento pratico per tutte le cate-
gorie di pubblico: dagli studenti agli
insegnanti, dai turisti agli uomini di
affari, ai corrispondenti, ai tecnici. Oltre
25.000 voci disposte in ordine alfabetico. Concise ma esaurienti note di
grammatica italiana e inglese. Tavole
dei verbi irregolari delle due lingue.
Pronuncia figurata inglese. Neologismi
tecnici, idiomatici e di gergo. Tavole dei
numerali, dei pesi, delle misure e delle
monete.

Compilato con criteri modernissimi da
esperti filologi, è un volume essenziale,
una guida pratica, indispensabile e di
sommo valore.

The above text appears in English on the back cover.

DIZIONARIO
TASCABILE
MONDADORI
Italiano-Inglese
Inglese-Italiano

DUE VOLUMI IN UNO

Di

Alberto Tedeschi e Carlo Rossi Fantonetti
Con la Collaborazione di SEYMOUR A. COPSTEIN

PUBLISHED BY POCKET BOOKS NEW YORK

MONDADORI'S
POCKET
Italian-English
English-Italian
DICTIONARY

TWO VOLUMES IN ONE

By

Alberto Tedeschi & Carlo Rossi Fantonetti
With the Assistance of SEYMOUR A. COPSTEIN

PUBLISHED BY POCKET BOOKS NEW YORK

The system of indicating pronunciation is used by permission. From THE MERRIAM-WEBSTER POCKET DICTIONARY. Copyright © 1961 by G. & C. Merriam Company, publishers of Merriam-Webster dictionaries.

POCKET BOOKS, a Simon & Schuster division of
GULF & WESTERN CORPORATION
1230 Avenue of the Americas, New York, N.Y. 10020

ISBN: 0-671-46209-1

First Pocket Books printing October, 1959

35   34   33   32   31   30   29

POCKET and colophon are trademarks of Simon & Schuster.

Printed in the U.S.A.

CONTENTS

PART ONE: ITALIAN-ENGLISH

PARTE SECONDA: INGLESE-ITALIANO

MONDADORI'S
POCKET
Italian-English
English-Italian
DICTIONARY

Part One

ITALIAN - ENGLISH

LIST OF ABBREVIATIONS

abbr.	abbreviation	mech.	mechanics
account.	accounting	med.	medicine
adj.	adjective	mil.	military
adv.	adverb	min.	mining
aeron.	aeronautics	mus.	music
agr.	agriculture	myth.	mythology
anat.	anatomy	naut.	nautical
arch.	architecture	nw.	new word
artil.	artillery	obs.	obsolete
astr.	astronomy	onom.	onomatopoeia
auto.	automobile	opt.	optic
bank.	banking	ornith.	ornithology
biol.	biology	paint.	painting
bot.	botany	part.	participle
chem.	chemistry	pass.	passive
coll.	colloquial	pathol.	pathology
comm.	commerce	pers.	personal
comp.	comparative	pharm.	pharmacy
conj.	conjunction	philos.	philosophy
cook.	cooking	photo.	photography
demonstr.	demonstrative	phys.	physics
derog.	derogatory	physiol.	physiology
dial.	dialect	pol.	politics
eccl.	ecclesiastic	pp.	past participle
elec.	electric	pr.	proper name
entom.	entomology	prep.	preposition
exch.	exchange	pron.	pronoun
f.	feminine	rail.	railroad
fam.	familiar	recipr.	reciprocal
fig.	figurative	refl.	reflexive
fin.	finance	rhet.	rhetoric
fort.	fortification	sci.	science
geog.	geography	sup.	superlative
geol.	geology	surg.	surgery
geom.	geometry	t.	transitive
gramm.	grammar	teleph.	telephone
hist.	history	telev.	television
ichthyol.	ichthyology	text.	textile
impers.	impersonal	theat.	theater
indef.	indefinite	typog.	typography
interj.	interjection	univ.	university
interr.	interrogative	U.S.	United States
It.	Italian	v.	verb
journ.	journalism	vi.	intransitive verb
L.	Latin	vr.	reflexive verb
liter.	literary	vt.	transitive verb
m.	masculine	vulg.	vulgar
mach.	machinery	zool.	zoology
math.	mathematics		

ITALIAN PRONUNCIATION

The Italian alphabet consists of 21 letters: *a, b, c, d, e, f, g, h, i, l, m, n, o, p, q, r, s, t, u, v, z* (*j, k, w, x, y* are found only in words of foreign origin).

I. VOWELS

Each Italian vowel has one fundamental sound, which is maintained in diphthongs and triphthongs.
1. **a** as in *star, are* — examples: **amore, casa.**
2. **e** has two distinct sounds: a broad sound similar to *e* in *where* — examples: **festa, messa;** and another almost like *e* in *bet* — examples: **pera, tela.**
3. **o** is sometimes open as *o* in *orb* — examples: **cosa, porta,** and sometimes closed as *o* in *foe* — examples: **dono, sole.**
4. **i** as in *police* — examples: **asilo, riso.**
5. **u** like *u* in *rude,* or *oo* in *food* — examples: **muro, tubo.**

II. CONSONANTS

1. **b** has the same sound as in English.
2. **c** before *a, o, u,* and before consonants has a hard sound similar to the English *k* — examples: **calore, corpo, cura; crosta, clava, acme; chilo, perchè.** Before *e* and *i* **c** is pronounced like English *ch* in *church.*
   When an *i* appears between *c* and *a, c* and *o,* or *c* and *u,* for the purpose of indicating this *ch* sound, the *i* is inaudible — examples: **pancia, ciondolo, ciuffo.** However, when the *i* is stressed it is pronounced — examples: **farmacia, vocio.**
3. **d** and **f** are sounded as in English.
4. **g** before *a, o, u* and before consonants sounds like *g* in *good* — examples: **gallo, gola, gusto; globo, grande; laghetto, ghiro.** Before *e* and *i* **g** is pronounced as in English *general* — examples: **gente, giro.** When *i* is inserted between *g* and *a, g* and *o,* or *g* and *u,* for the purpose of indicating this sound, the *i* is inaudible — examples: **giacca, giostra, giusto.**
   The combination **gn** sounds like the combination *n* and *y* in *can you* — examples: **sognare, dignità, bagno, ignudo.**
   The combination **gl** sounds like the *l* and *y* in *will you,* pronounced rapidly — examples: **foglia, figlie, gigli, consiglio.** In some exceptional cases *g* before *l* sounds hard — examples: **negligenza, glicerina.**
5. **h** has no sound. It is found only in the present indicative of **avere** (*to have*) — **io ho, tu hai, egli ha, essi hanno** — and in certain interjections, such as: **ah!, oh!, ahi!** Otherwise **h** is used only to indicate hard *c* and *g* before *e* and *i.*
6. **l, m, n, p** are sounded as in English.
7. **q** is always followed by *u* and another vowel. It sounds like *qu* in *square* — examples: **quaderno, questo, liquido, quota.**
8. **r** is pronounced as in English, but is more strongly trilled.
9. **s** when it begins a word and is followed by a vowel or an unvoiced consonant sounds hard as in *essence* — examples: **sapere, senno, sicuro, sonno, subito; scopo, sforzo, spazio, rosso, stima.** Between vowels or before a voiced consonant it sounds soft like *s* in *rose* and *z* in *gaze* — examples: **casa, mese, risi, viso; sbaglio, sdegno, sgranare, sleale, smania, snello, sradicare, sviare.**

sce and sci are pronounced like *she* in *shelter* and *shi* in *ship* — examples: **scelta, scivolare.**

scia and scio are pronounced like *sha* and *sho* in *shah* and *show* — examples: **scialle** and **sciocco.**

sciu is pronounced like *chu* in *chute* — example: **asciutto.**

sche and schi sound like *ske* in *sketch* and *ski* in *skit* — examples: **scherzo, schizzo.**

10. t is similar to English *t* in *stun, astonish* — examples: **talpa, telo, tiro, tono, tutto, treno.**

11. v is sounded as in English.

12. z is regularly like English *ts* — examples: **scorza, grazia, scherzo, pazzo.** Very often, however, it sounds like English *dz* — examples: **zanzara, zero, zio, zona, zufolo, mezzo, azzurro.**

Note. Every Italian consonant can be doubled, and is then strongly pronounced — examples: **abbaino, accadere, addetto, affare, agguato, allarme, ammettere, annullare, appena, arresto, assenso, attacco, avvilito, azzurro.**

III. STRESS AND ACCENT

Italian words may be accented on the last, or next to the last, or third from the last syllable. Usually, the accent mark (grave accent) is used only when the stress is to be put on the final vowel — examples: **civiltà, caffè, così, perciò, virtù.** Certain monosyllabic words are written with an accent mark to distinguish between pairs — examples: **dà** (*gives*) — **da** (*from*); **dì** (*day*) — **di** (*of*); **là** (*there*) — **la** (*the*); **lì** (*there*) — **li** (*them*); **sè** (*himself, oneself*) — **se** (*if*).

IV. APOSTROPHE

In Italian, the apostrophe indicates the omission of the last vowel of a word when this is followed by another word beginning with a vowel — examples: *la aria* — **l'aria**; *lo emblema* — **l'emblema**; *lo indice* — **l'indice**; *lo orologio* — **l'orologio**; *lo uccello* — **l'uccello**; *gli inglesi* — **gl'inglesi**; *questo uomo* — **quest'uomo**; *un bello albero* — **un bell'albero.**

V. SYLLABIC DIVISION

Italian words are divided according to the syllables forming them. Except at the beginning of a word, each syllable normally starts with a consonant — examples: **a-ni-ma-le; car-ta; pen-sa-re; la-scia-re.** The vowels of a diphthong generally are not separated — examples: **fià-to, piè-no, suò-no; fiù-me; àu-ra, lài-co, fèu-do.** When, however, the vowels are pronounced separately they are treated as separate syllables — examples: **pa-ù-ra, vi-a, flù-i-do, a-è-re-o, pa-è-se, o-cè-ano.**

Double consonants are always divided — examples: **eb-be, tac-co, ad-di-o, zuf-fa, rag-gio, pal-la, stem-ma, pan-no, tap-po, ac-qua, car-ro, sas-so, pat-to, bev-ve, maz-zo.**

When s is followed by one or more consonants, it belongs to the subsequent syllable — examples: **po-sta, ri-schio, a-spet-to.**

THE NOUN

I. GENDER

Italian nouns are either masculine or feminine. There is no neuter gender Names of things and abstractions are either masculine or feminine.

Masculine gender:

1. Names of male beings are masculine by nature — examples: **uomo** *man*, **ragazzo** *boy*, **fratello** *brother*; **cane** *dog*, **gallo** *cock*, **leone** *lion*.

2. Nouns ending in o are usually masculine — examples: **libro** *book*, **martello** *hammer*, **telefono** *telephone*; **dubbio** *doubt*, **coraggio** *courage*, **odio** *hatred*.

Feminine gender:

1. Names of female beings are feminine by nature — examples: **donna** *woman*, **fanciulla** *girl*, **sorella** *sister*; **cagna** *bitch*, **mucca** *cow*, **gallina** *hen*.
2. Nouns ending in a are usually feminine — examples: **penna** *pen*, **lampada** *lamp*, **finestra** *window*; **speranza** *hope*, **umiltà** *humbleness*, **fermezza** *firmness*.

Exceptions:

1. Some nouns ending in o are feminine — examples: **mano** *hand*, **eco** *echo*.
2. Some nouns ending in a are masculine — examples: **poeta** *poet*, **problema** *problem*, **tema** *theme*.
3. Some nouns are feminine but relate to male beings — examples: **spia** *spy*, **recluta** *recruit*, **sentinella** *sentry*.
4. Some nouns are masculine but relate to female beings — examples: **il soprano** *the soprano*, **il contralto** *the contralto*, **un donnone** *a big woman*.
5. Some nouns ending in a may be either masculine or feminine — examples: **il ginnasta** *the man-gymnast*, **la ginnasta** *the woman-gymnast*.
6. Nouns ending in e may be either masculine or feminine — examples: **leone** *lion* (m.), **fiore** *flower* (m.), **pane** *bread* (m.); **arte** *art* (f.), **luce** *light* (f.), **salute** *health* (f.).

Formation of the feminine:

1. Masculine nouns ending in o or e change o or e to a to form the feminine — examples: **zio** *uncle* = **zia** *aunt*, **signore** *gentleman* = **signora** *lady*, **Carlo** *Charles* = **Carla** *Caroline*.
2. Certain nouns have a special form for the feminine — examples: **attore** *actor* = **attrice** *actress*; **principe** *prince* = **principessa** *princess*; **eroe** *hero* = **eroina** *heroine*.
3. The corresponding feminine word for certain nouns is an entirely different word — examples: **uomo** *man* = **donna** *woman*, **marito** *husband* = **moglie** *wife*, **maiale** *pig* = **scrofa** *sow*.

II. PLURAL OF NOUNS

1. Masculine nouns ending in o form the plural by changing the o to i — examples: **palo** = **pali**, **albero** = **alberi**, **sarto** = **sarti**.
2. Feminine nouns ending in a form the plural by changing the a to e — examples: **scarpa** = **scarpe**, **palla** = **palle**, **donna** = **donne**.
3. Nouns ending in e, whether masculine or feminine, change the e to i — examples: **luce** = **luci**, **serpente** = **serpenti**, **eroe** = **eroi**.
4. Nouns ending in cia and gia have two forms of plural: cie and gie, and ce and ge.

   They end in cie and gie when:
   (a) the stressed i of the singular is also stressed in the plural — examples: **farmacia** = **farmacie**, **bugia** = **bugie**.
   (b) although the i is not stressed, cia and gia are preceded by a vowel — examples: **camicia** = **camicie**, **audàcia** = **audàcie**, **valigia** = **valigie**.

   They end in ce and ge when:
   (a) the i is not stressed and cia and gia are preceded by a consonant — examples: **lància** = **lance**, **bòlgia** = **bolge**.

   Note. There are quite a few exceptions to this rule (**ciliègia** = **ciliege**, **provincia** = **province** and **provincie**), and only by consulting a dictionary can any particular case be settled.
5. The ending io becomes ii if the i is stressed; otherwise it becomes just i — examples: **mormorìo** = **mormorìi**, **zìo** = **zìi**; **stùdio** = **stùdi**, **òzio** = **òzi**.
6. The endings co and go change to chi and ghi if preceded by a consonant — examples: **parco** = **parchi**, **solco** = **solchi**, **fungo** = **funghi**, **gorgo** = **gorghi**. If preceded by a vowel, however, they sometimes change to

chi and ghi and sometimes to ci and gi — examples: parroco = parroci, carico = carichi; asparago = asparagi, dialogo = dialoghi.

7. Masculine nouns ending in ca and ga change to chi and ghi — examples: monarca = monarchi, collega = colleghi.

8. Nouns ending in i, in a consonant, in an accented vowel, as well as monosyllabic nouns, do not change — examples: la crisi = le crisi, l'autobus = gli autobus, la città = le città, il re = i re.

9. Certain nouns form the plural irregularly — examples: uomo = uomini, dio = dei, bue = buoi.

10. There are some masculine nouns that change their gender in the plural and take the ending a — examples: l'uovo (m.) = le uova (f.), il lenzuolo (m.) = le lenzuola (f.), un paio (m.) = due paia (f.).

COMMON ITALIAN SUFFIXES

I. DIMINUTIVES

The following convey an idea of lesser size, niceness and affection:

-ino,	-ina	letto = lettino (a small bed), casa = casina (a tiny house), maestra = maestrina (young teacher)
-etto,	-etta	scarpa = scarpetta (small, light shoe), bimbo = bimbetto (small, lovely child)
-ello,	-ella	birbone = birboncello (naughty boy), finestra = finestrella (small window)
-olo,	-ola	figlio = figliolo (dear son), carezza = carezzuola (light caress)
-uccio,	-uccia	caldo = calduccio (comfortable warmth), bocca = boccuccia (small, nice mouth)

II. AUGMENTATIVES

The following convey an idea of greater size:

-one, -ona   libro = librone (big book), finestra = finestrona or finestrone (large window), porta = portone (huge door)
Note. The feminine form ona is not always used. Feminine nouns very often take the suffix one, which causes them to change their gender — example: donna (f.) = donnone (m.)

III. DEPRECIATIVES

The following convey an idea of something bad, ugly or despicable. Note, however, that a depreciative or ironic connotation is often conveyed by the augmentatives and by many of the diminutive endings.

-accio, -accia	vento = ventaccio (harsh wind), libro = libraccio (bad, mean book), donna = donnaccia (woman of loose morals)
-astro, -astra	poeta = poetastro (poetaster), medico = medicastro (quack doctor)
-ucolo, -ucola	paese = paesucolo (small town, small village)
-onzolo, onzola	medico = mediconzolo (inexperienced doctor, inept doctor)

IV. OTHER SUFFIXES

-aggine	(a) is sometimes equal to English ness: stupidaggine = foolishness; (b) expresses also a particular act: stupidaggine = foolish act, piece of foolishness
-aio	indicates a person who makes, sells, or is in charge of: fornaio = baker, libraio = bookseller, lampionaio = lamplighter
-anza	is used to make abstract nouns: vedovanza = widowhood, arroganza = arrogance

-ata	(a) is sometimes equal to the English suffix *ful*: **cucchiaiata** = spoonful (b) often indicates a blow: **testata** = blow with one's head, **pugnalata** = dagger stab (c) often indicates an action: **sfaticata** = spell of hard work, **cabrata** = zoom of an airplane
-enza	is used to make abstract nouns: **magnificenza** = magnificence, **prepotenza** = overbearance
-ere	indicates a person who makes, sells, or is engaged in a certain profession: **panettiere** = baker, **banchiere** = banker
-eria	(a) denotes a place where something is made or sold: **panetteria** = bakery, **libreria** = bookstore (b) indicates a profession, business, or occupation: **ingegneria** = engineering, **editoria** = publishing (c) is sometimes equal to the English suffixes *ry* and *ness*: **cretineria** = foolery, foolishness
-ero	is an adjective-forming suffix: **ciarliero** = talkative, **guerriero** = warlike, fighting
-eto, -eta	denote a grove or plantation: **agrumeto** = citrus grove, **pineta** = pine forest
-ezza	is used to make abstract nouns: **giovinezza** = youth, **grandezza** = greatness
-ia	(a) is the ending of the names of many arts and sciences: **geologia** = geology (b) is the ending of many abstract nouns: **maestria** = master, **fantasia** = imagination
-iccio	is a suffix meaning *tending to* or *somewhat*: **rossiccio** = reddish, **sudaticcio** = rather wet with perspiration
-issimo	is the ending of the absolute superlative: **bellissimo** = extremely beautiful
-mente	is the adverbial ending attached to the feminine form of the adjective: **estremamente** = extremely, **improvvisamente** = suddenly
-one	(a) is an augmentative suffix (b) is also a suffix to add impressiveness to a word: **giocherellone** = playful person, **piagnucolone** = tearful person, crybaby, **strattone** = strong jerk
-ore	(a) is equal to the English suffixes *or* and *er*: **conquistatore** = conqueror, **rilegatore** = bookbinder (b) may also be used to form adjectives: **regolatore** = regulator *and* regulating, **trasmettitore** = broadcaster *and* broadcasting
-oso	is an adjective-forming suffix which usually means: *having, full of, characterized by*: **roccioso** = rocky, **piovoso** = rainy, **famoso** = famous
-tà	is a suffix forming abstract nouns and is equivalent to the English suffix *ty*: **fraternità** = fraternity, **beltà** = beauty, **eternità** = eternity
-ura	is a suffix forming abstract and also concrete nouns: **bravura** = skill, **calura** = heat, **altura** = highland
-uto	is an adjective-forming suffix meaning *having* or *characterized by*: **barbuto** = bearded, **panciuto** = bigbellied.

THE ARTICLE

Italian articles are either definite or indefinite.

I. DEFINITE ARTICLES

These are **il, lo, la** in the singular forms, and **i, gli, le** in the plural forms.

il and i	are used before masculine nouns beginning with a consonant: **il libro — i libri, il serpente — i serpenti, il maestro — i maestri**

lo and gli   are used:

(a) before masculine nouns beginning with "s impura" (that
is an s followed by a consonant: st, sp, sc, sb): lo stato
— gli stati, lo sparo — gli spari, lo scolaro — gli scolari,
lo sciocco — gli sciocchi, lo sbaglio — gli sbagli

(b) before masculine nouns beginning with z: lo zoppo — gli
zoppi, lo zero — gli zeri

(c) before a masculine noun beginning with a vowel: l'asino
— gli asini, l'esempio — gli esempi, l'italiano — gl'italiani
l'osso — gli ossi, l'urlo — gli urli

Note. The o of lo is dropped before masculine nouns beginning with a vowel, and an apostrophe takes its place; gli
may be changed to gl' only before plural masculine nouns
beginning with i.

la and le   are used before feminine nouns: la mamma — le mamme,
la bambola — le bambole, l'anima — le anime

Note. la is changed into l' before feminine nouns beginning with a vowel. The elision of le is very rarely made
before feminine plural nouns.

II. INDEFINITE ARTICLES

These are un, uno, una.

un   is used before masculine nouns beginning either with a vowel
or with a consonant: un albero, un uomo, un contadino,
un gatto, un dubbio

uno   is used before masculine nouns beginning with "s impura"
and z: uno scoiattolo, uno specchio, uno straccio, uno zingaro,
uno zuccone

una and un'   are used before feminine nouns; una before nouns beginning with a consonant: una dama, una sposa, una farfalla;
un' before nouns beginning with a vowel: un'automobile,
un'eroina, un'opera.

THE PREPOSITION

The commonest Italian prepositions are: di = of, a = to, da = from, by,
in = in, con = with, by, su = on, tra, fra = between, among, per = for,
to, by.

The prepositions *di, a, da, in, con, su* blend with the definite articles *il, lo,
la, i, gli, le* into the following forms:

del, dello, della, dei, degli, delle,	of the
al, allo, alla, ai, agli, alle,	to the
dal, dallo, dalla, dai, dagli, dalle,	from the, by the
nel, nello, nella, nei, negli, nelle,	in the
col, collo (con lo),* colla, coi, cogli, colle,	with the, by the
sul, sullo, sulla, sui, sugli, sulle,	on the

*Note. The preposition con is more frequently found separated from the
definite article because collo also means *neck*, colla also means *glue*, and colle
also means *hill*.

The preposition di expresses the possessive case of the English noun. The
name of the possessor follows the name of the thing possessed — example:
Mary's book = il libro di Maria. The prepositions del, dello, della, dei, degli,

delle also precede nouns taken in the partitive sense — examples: I bought some books = **ho comprato dei libri,** give me some more bread = **dammi dell'altro pane.**

THE ADJECTIVE AND ADVERB

I. THE ADJECTIVE

Agreement:

The adjective in Italian agrees in gender and number with the noun it modifies: **scolaro studioso** (*m., sing.*) — **scolari studiosi** (*m., pl.*) — **scolara studiosa** (*f., sing.*) — **scolare studiose** (*f., pl.*).

Formation of the plural:

Adjectives ending in **o** (masculine) form their plural by changing into **i**: **buono — buoni**; adjectives ending in **e** (both masculine and feminine) change to **i**: **mite — miti**; adjectives ending in **a** change to **e**: **buona — buone.**

Formation of the feminine:

1. Adjectives ending in **o** form their feminine by changing to **a**: **amaro — amara**
2. Adjectives ending in **e** do not alter: **prepotente** (*m.*) — **prepotente** (*f.*)

II. THE ADVERB

Many adverbs are formed by adding **-mente** to the feminine form of the adjective: **certo — certamente**; when the adjective ends in **e** and has its stress on the antepenult, the final **e** is dropped: **facile — facilmente.**

III. COMPARISON OF ADJECTIVES AND ADVERBS

Comparative of inequality:

The comparative of inequality is obtained by placing **più** (more) or **meno** (less) before the positive form of the adjective or the adverb, and **di** or **che** (than) before the second member of the comparison — examples: You are happier than I = **tu sei più felice di me**; as a man he is more lucky than intelligent = **è un uomo più fortunato che intelligente**; it is less nice *or* not so nice = **è meno bello**; you must speak faster = **devi parlare più velocemente.**

Comparative of equality:

The comparative of equality is formed in two ways:

1. **come** — examples: my book is as interesting as yours = **il mio libro è interessante come il tuo**; he spoke as convincingly as his brother = **ha parlato convincentemente come il fratello;**
2. **tanto ... quanto** — examples: my book is as interesting as yours = **il mio libro è tanto interessante quanto il tuo.** This form, however, is now regarded as rather stilted.

Superlative of adjectives and adverbs:

1. *Relative superlative of adjectives* is formed by placing the definite article before the unequal comparative form of the adjective — examples: the largest town in the world = **la più grande città del mondo**; the least kind of my friends = **il meno gentile dei miei amici.**
2. *Absolute superlative of adjectives* is obtained in three ways:
   (a) by adding the suffix **-issimo**: **forte** (strong) = **fortissimo**;
   (b) by placing the adverb **molto** or **assai** before the positive form of the adjective: **forte** = **molto forte, assai forte**;
   (c) by repeating the adjective: **forte** = **forte forte.**

The following adjectives have in addition irregular forms of comparison:

buono (good) **migliore** (better) **ottimo** (very good), **il migliore** (the best)
cattivo (bad) **peggiore** (worse) **pessimo** (very bad), **il peggiore** (the worst)
grande (large) **maggiore** (larger) **massimo** (very large), **il maggiore** (the largest)

piccolo (little)	minore (lesser)	minimo, il minore (the least)
alto (high)	superiore (higher)	supremo, sommo (the highest)
basso (low)	inferiore (lower)	infimo (the lowest)
interno (inside)	interiore (inner)	intimo (innermost)

3. *Absolute superlative of adverbs* is obtained by adding the invariable suffix -issimo to the positive form of the adverb: bene = benissimo, tardi = tardissimo, molto = moltissimo.

Note that the last vowel of the adverb is dropped before the suffix.

Adverbs ending in -mente form the absolute superlative by adding the suffix -issimo to the superlative feminine form of the corresponding adjective: lentissimo = lentissimamente.

Note. The English *than* is translated with di when the second member of comparison is a noun or a pronoun — examples: gold is more expensive than silver = l'oro è più caro dell'argento; he is richer than I = egli è più ricco di me. It is translated with che when the comparison is between two different adjectives or two nouns — examples: he is more handsome than intelligent = egli è più bello che intelligente; there is more bread than meat = c'è più pane che carne.

ITALIAN IRREGULAR VERBS

The superior number after a verb entry indicates that it is conjugated like the model verb in this section bearing the corresponding number. Only the tenses that have irregular forms or spelling changes are given. The irregular forms and spelling changes are shown in bold-face type.

1. ACCENDERE

past	**accesi**, accendesti, **accese**, accendemmo, accendeste, **accesero**
past part.	**acceso**

2. ACCLUDERE

past	**acclusi**, accludesti, **accluse**, accludemmo, accludeste, **acclusero**
past part.	**accluso**

3. ADDURRE

past	**addussi**, adducesti, **addusse**, adducemmo, adduceste, **addussero**
fut.	**addurrò, addurrai, addurrà, addurremo, addurrete, addurranno**
cond.	**addurrei, addurresti, addurrebbe, addurremmo, addurreste, addurrebbero**
past part.	**addotto**

Note. All regular forms derive from the infinitive form adducere.

4. ADEMPIERE

pres. ind.	**adempio, adempi, adempie,** adempiamo, adempite, **adempiono**
pres. sub.	**adempia, adempia, adempia,** adempiamo, adempiate, **adempiano**
imper.	**adempi, adempia,** adempite, **adempiano.**
past	**adempii,** adempisti, **adempì,** adempimmo, adempiste, **adempirono**
past part.	**adempito** *or* **adempiuto**

Note. See also empiere, 52 *and* empire, 53.

5. AFFLIGGERE

past	**afflissi,** affligesti, **afflisse,** affliggemmo, affliggeste, **afflissero**
past part.	**afflitto**

6. ALLUDERE

past	allusi, alludesti, **alluse**, alludemmo, alludeste, **allusero**
past part.	alluso

7. ANDARE

pres. ind.	vado, vai, va, andiamo, andate, vanno
pres. sub.	vada, vada, vada, andiamo, andiate, vadano
imp.	vai *or* va', vada, andiamo, andate, vàdano
fut.	andrò, andrai, andrà, andremo, andrete, andranno
cond.	andrei, andresti, andrebbe, andremmo, andreste, andrebbero

8. ANNETTERE

past	annettei *or* annessi, annettesti, annettè *or* annesse, annettemmo, annetteste, annetterono *or* annessero
past part.	annesso

9. APPARIRE

pres. ind.	apparisco *or* appaio, apparisci *or* appari, apparisce *or* appare, appariamo, apparite, appariscono *or* appàiono
past	apparvi *or* apparii, apparisti, apparve *or* appari *or* apparse, apparimmo, appariste, apparvero *or* apparirono *or* apparsero
pres. sub.	apparisca *or* appaia, apparisca *or* appaia, apparisca *or* appaia, appariamo, appariate, appariscano *or* appaiano
imper.	apparisci *or* appari, apparisca *or* appaia, apparite, appariscano *or* appaiano
past part.	apparso

10. APPENDERE

past	appesi, appendesti, appese, appendemmo, appendeste, appesero
past part.	appeso

11. APRIRE

pres. ind.	apro, apri, apre, apriamo, aprite, àprono
past	aprii *or* apersi, apristi, apri *or* aperse, aprimmo, apriste, aprirono *or* apersero
past part.	aperto

12. ARDERE

past	arsi, ardesti, arse, ardemmo, ardeste, arsero
past part.	arso

13. ASPERGERE

past	aspersi, aspergesti, asperse, aspergemmo, aspergeste, aspersero
past part.	asperso

14. ASSALIRE

pres. ind.	assalgo *or* assalisco, assali *or* assalisci, assale *or* assalisce, assaliamo, assalite, assalgono *or* assaliscono
past	assalii *or* assalsi, assalisti, assali *or* assalse, assalimmo, assaliste, assalirono *or* assalsero
pres. sub.	assalga *or* assalisca, assalga *or* assalisca, assalga *or* assalisca, assaliamo, assaliate, assalgano *or* assaliscano

15. ASSIDERSI

past	mi assisi, ti assidesti, si assise, ci assidemmo, vi assideste, si assisero
past part.	assiso

16. ASSISTERE

past   assistei *or* assistetti, assistesti, assistè *or* assistette, assistem-
      mo, assisteste, assisterono *or* assistettero
past part. assistito

17. ASSOLVERE

past   **assolsi** *or* assolvei *or* assolvetti, assolvesti, **assolse** *or* assol-
      vette, assolvemmo, assolveste, **assolsero** *or* assolvettero
past part. **assolto** *or* assoluto

18. ASSORBIRE

pres.   assorbo *or* assorbisco, assorbi *or* assorbisci, assorbe *or*
      assorbisce, assorbiamo, assorbite, assorbono *or* assorbi-
      scono
past part. assorbito or **assorto**

19. ASSUMERE

past   **assunsi**, assumesti, **assunse**, assumemmo, assumeste,
      assunsero
past part. **assunto**

20. ASSURGERE

past   **assursi**, assurgesti, **assurse**, assurgemmo, assurgeste,
      assursero
past part. **assurto**

21. BERE

pres. ind. bevo, bevi, beve, beviamo, bevete, bevono
imp. ind. bevevo, bevevi, beveva, bevevamo, bevevate, bevevano
past   **bevvi** *or* bevei, bevesti, **bevve** *or* bevè *or* bevette, bevemmo,
      beveste, **bevvero** *or* beverono *or* bevettero
fut.   **berrò, berrai, berrà, berremo, berrete, berranno**
cond.   **berrei, berresti, berrebbe, berremmo, berreste, berrebbero**
pres. sub. beva, beva, beva, beviamo, beviate, bevano
imp. sub. bevessi, bevessi, bevesse, bevessimo, beveste, bevessero
imper.   bevi, beva, bevete, bevano
past part. bevuto
      Note. All regular forms derive from the infinitive form
      bevere.

22. CADERE

past   **caddi**, cadesti, **cadde**, cademmo, cadeste, **caddero**
fut.   **cadrò, cadrai, cadrà, cadremo, cadrete, cadranno**
cond.   **cadrei, cadresti, cadrebbe, cadremmo, cadreste, cadrebbero**

23. CEDERE

past   cedei *or* cedetti, cedesti, cedè *or* cedette, cedemmo, cedeste,
      cederono *or* cedettero

24. CHIEDERE

past   **chiesi**, chiedesti, **chiese**, chiedemmo, chiedeste, **chiesero**
past part. chie_to

25. CHIUDERE

past   **chiusi**, chiudesti, **chiuse**, chiudemmo, chiudeste, **chiusero**
past. part. **chiuso**

26. CINGERE

past   **cinsi**, cingesti, **cinse**, cingemmo, cingeste, **cinsero**
past part. **cinto**

27. COGLIERE

pres. ind.	colgo, cogli, coglie, cogliamo, cogliete, colgono
past	colsi, cogliesti, colse, cogliemmo, coglieste, colsero
pres. sub.	colga, colga, colga, cogliamo, cogliate, colgano
past part.	colto

28. COMPIERE

pres. ind.	compio, compi, compie, compiamo, compite, compiono
past	compii, compisti, compi, compimmo, compiste, compirono
pres. sub.	compia, compia, compia, compiamo, compiate, compiano
imper.	compi, compia, compite, compiano
past part.	compito or compiùto

Note. See also empiere, 52 and empire, 53.

29. COMPRIMERE

past	compressi, comprimesti, compresse, comprimemmo, comprimeste, compressero
past part.	compresso

30. CONOSCERE

past	conobbi, conoscesti, conobbe, conoscemmo, conosceste, conobbero

31. CONQUIDERE

past	conquisi, conquidesti, conquise, conquidemmo, conquideste, conquisero
past part.	conquiso

32. CONTUNDERE

past	contusi, contundesti, contuse, contundemmo, contundeste, contusero
past part.	contuso

33. CONVERGERE

past	conversi or convergei, convergesti, converse or convergè, convergemmo, convergeste, conversero or convergerono
past part.	converso

34. CONVERTIRE

past	convertii, convertisti, convertì, convertimmo, convertiste, convertirono
past part.	convertito

35. COPRIRE

pres. ind.	copro, copri, copre, copriamo, coprite, coprono
past	coprii or copersi, copristi, coprì or coperse, coprimmo, copriste, coprirono or copersero
past part.	coperto

36. CORRERE

past	corsi, corresti, corse, corremmo, correste, corsero
past part.	corso

37. COSTRUIRE

past	costruii or costrussi, costruisti, costruì or costrusse, costruimmo, costruiste, costruirono or costrussero
past part.	costruito or costrutto

38. CRESCERE

past	crebbi, crescesti, crebbe, crescemmo, cresceste, crebbero

39. CUOCERE

pres. ind.	cuocio, cuoci, cuoce, cociamo, cocete, cuociono
imp. ind.	cocevo, cocevi, coceva, cocevamo, cocevate, cocevano
past	cossi, cocesti, cosse, cocemmo, coceste, cossero
fut.	cocerò, cocerai, cocerà, coceremo, cocerete, coceranno
pres. sub.	cuòcia, cuòcia, cuòcia, cociamo, cociate, cuòciano
imp. sub.	cocessi, cocessi, cocesse, cocessimo, coceste, cocessero
cond.	cocerei, coceresti, cocerebbe, coceremmo, cocereste, cocerebbero
imper.	cuoci, cuocia, cocete, cuociano
pres. part.	cocente
past part.	cotto or cociuto

40. DARE

pres. ind.	do, dai, da, diamo, date, danno
imp. ind.	davo, davi, dava, davamo, davate, davano
past	diedi, desti, diede, demmo, deste, diedero
fut.	darò, darai, darà, daremo, darete, daranno
pres. sub.	dia, dia, dia, diamo, diate, diano
imp. sub.	dessi, dessi, desse, dessimo, deste, dessero
cond.	darei, daresti, darebbe, daremmo, dareste, darebbero
imper.	da, dia, date, diano
pres. part.	dando
past part.	dato

41. DECIDERE

past	decisi, decidesti, decise, decidemmo, decideste, decisero
past part.	deciso

42. DEVOLVERE

past	devolvei or devolvetti, devolvesti, devolvè or devolvette, devolvemmo, devolveste, devolverono or devolvettero
past part.	devoluto

43. DIFENDERE

past	difesi, difendesti, difese, difendemmo, difendeste, difesero
past part.	difeso

44. DIRE

pres. ind.	dico, dici, dice, diciamo, dite, dicono
imp. ind.	dicevo, dicevi, diceva, dicevamo, dicevate, dicevano
past	dissi, dicesti, disse, dicemmo, diceste, dissero
fut.	dirò, dirai, dirà, diremo, direte, diranno
pres. sub.	dica, dica, dica, diciamo, diciate, dicano
imp. sub.	dicessi, dicessi, dicesse, dicessimo, diceste, dicessero
cond.	direi, diresti, direbbe, diremmo, direste, direbbero
imper.	di, dica, dite, dicano
pres. part.	dicendo
past part.	detto

Note. All regular forms derive from the infinitive form dicere.

45. DIRIGERE

past	diressi, dirigesti, diresse, dirigemmo, dirigeste, diressero
past part.	diretto

46. DISCUTERE

past	discussi or discutei, discutesti, discusse or discutè, discutemmo, discuteste, discussero or discuterono
past part.	discusso

47. DISTINGUERE

past   distinsi, distinguesti, distinse, distinguemmo, distingueste, distinsero

past part.   distinto

48. DIVIDERE

past   divisi, dividesti, divise, dividemmo, divideste, divisero

past part.   diviso

49. DOLERSI

pres. ind.   mi dolgo, ti duoli, si duole, ci doliamo or dogliamo, vi dolete, si dolgono

past   mi dolsi, ti dolesti, si dolse, ci dolemmo, vi doleste, si dolsero

fut.   mi dorrò, ti dorrai, si dorrà, ci dorremo, vi dorrete, si dorranno

pres. sub.   mi dolga, ti dolga, si dolga, ci doliamo, vi doliate, si dolgano

imp. sub.   mi dolessi, ti dolessi, si dolesse, ci dolessimo, vi doleste, si dolessero

cond.   mi dorrei, ti dorresti, si dorrebbe, ci dorremmo, vi dorreste, si dorrebbero

imper.   duoliti, si dolga, doletevi, si dolgano

pres. part.   dolente

past part.   dolutosi

50. DOVERE

pres. ind.   devo or debbo, devi, deve, dobbiamo, dovete, devono or debbono

past   dovei or dovetti, dovesti, dovè or dovette, dovemmo, doveste, doverono or dovettero

fut.   dovrò, dovrai, dovrà, dovremo, dovrete, dovranno

pres. sub.   deva or debba, deva or debba, deva or debba, dobbiamo, dobbiate, devano or debbano

imper.   devi, deve, dovete, devono

past part.   dovuto

51. EMERGERE

past   emersi, emergesti, emerse, emergemmo, emergeste, emersero

past part.   emerso

52. EMPIERE

another infinitive form for empire, 53, which see for conjugation.

53. EMPIRE

pres. ind.   empio, empi, empie, empiamo, empite, empiono

imp. ind.   empivo, empivi, empiva, empivamo, empivate, empivano

past   empii, empisti, empì, empimmo, empiste, empirono

fut.   empirò, empirai, empirà, empiremo, empirete, empiranno

pres. sub.   empia, empia, empia, empiamo, empiate, empiano

imp. sub.   empissi, empissi, empisse, empissimo, empiste, empissero

cond.   empirei, empiresti, empirebbe, empiremmo, empireste, empirebbero

imper.   empi, empia, empite, empiano

pres. part.   empiente

past part.   empito

54. ERGERE

past	ersi, ergesti, erse, ergemmo, ergeste, ersero
past part.	erto

55. ESAURIRE

past part.	esaurito *or* esausto

56. ESIGERE

past	esigei *or* esigetti, esigesti, esigè *or* esigette, esigemmo, esigeste, esigerono *or* esigettero
past part.	esatto

57. ESIMERE

past	esimei *or* esimetti, esimesti, esimè *or* esimette, esimemmo, esimeste, esimerono *or* esimettero
past part.	*lacking; it is replaced by the forms* esente *and* esentato.

58. ESPELLERE

past	espulsi, espellesti, espulse, espellemmo, espelleste, espulsero
past part.	espulso

59. ESPLODERE

past	esplosi, esplodesti, esplose, esplodemmo, esplodeste, esplosero
past part.	esploso

60. EVADERE

past	evasi, evadesti, evase, evademmo, evadeste, evasero
past part.	evaso

61. FARE

pres. ind.	faccio *or* fo, fai, fa, facciamo, fate, fanno
imp. ind.	facevo, facevi, faceva, facevamo, facevate, facevano
past	feci, facesti, fece, facemmo, faceste, fecero
fut.	farò, farai, farà, faremo, farete, faranno
cond.	farei, faresti, farebbe, faremmo, fareste, farebbero
pres. sub.	faccia, faccia, faccia, facciamo, facciate, facciano
imp. sub.	facessi, facessi, facesse, facessimo, faceste, facessero
imper.	fai *or* fa', faccia, fate, facciano
pres. part.	facente
past part.	fatto
	Note. All regular forms derive from the infinitive form facere.

62. FENDERE

past	fendei *or* fendetti, fendesti, fendè *or* fendette, fendemmo, fendeste, fenderono *or* fendettero
past part.	fesso *or* fenduto

63. FIGGERE

past	fissi, figgesti, fisse, figgemmo, figgeste, fissero
past part.	fitto

64. FLETTERE

past	flettei *or* flessi, flettesti, flettè *or* flesse, flettemmo, fletteste, fletterono *or* flessero
past part.	flesso

65. FONDERE

past	fusi, fondesti, fuse, fondemmo, fondeste, fusero
past part.	fuso

66. FRANGERE

past	fransi, frangesti, franse, frangemmo, frangeste, fransero
past part.	franto

67. FRIGGERE

past	frissi, friggesti, frisse, friggemmo, friggeste, frissero
past part.	fritto

68. GIACERE

pres. ind.	giaccio, giaci, giace, giacciamo *or* giaciamo, giacete, giacciono
past	giacqui, giacesti, giacque, giacemmo, giaceste, giacquero
pres. sub.	giaccia, giaccia, giaccia, giacciamo, giacciate, giacciano
past part.	giaciuto

69. INDULGERE

past	indulsi, indulgesti, indulse, indulgemmo, indulgeste, indulsero
past part.	indulto

70. INFERIRE

past	inferii *or* infersi, inferisti, inferì *or* inferse, inferimmo, inferiste, inferirono *or* infersero
past part.	inferito *or* inferto

71. INSERIRE

past part.	inserito *or* (*rare*) inserto

72. INTRUDERE

past	intrusi, indrudesti, intruse, intrudemmo, intrudeste, intrusero
past part.	intruso

73. LEDERE

past	lesi, ledesti, lese, ledemmo, ledeste, lesero
past part.	leso

74. LEGGERE

past	lessi, leggesti, lesse, leggemmo, leggeste, lessero
past part.	letto

75. MESCERE

pres. ind.	mesco, mesci, mesce, mesciamo, mescete, mescono
past	mescei, mescesti, mescè, mescemmo, mesceste, mescerono
pres. sub.	mesca, mesca, mesca, mesciamo, mesciate, mescano
past part.	mesciuto *or* misto

76. METTERE

past	misi, mettesti, mise, mettemmo, metteste, misero
past part.	messo

77. MORDERE

past	morsi, mordesti, morse, mordemmo, mordeste, morsero
past part.	morso

78. MORIRE

pres. ind.	muoio, muori, muore, moriamo, morite, muoiono
fut.	morirò or morrò, morirai or morrai, morirà or morrà, moriremo or morremo, morirete or morrete, moriranno or morranno
cond.	morirei or morrei, moriresti or morresti, morirebbe or morrebbe, moriremmo or morremmo, morireste or morreste, morirebbero or morrebbero
pres. sub.	muoia, muoia, muoia, moriamo, moriate, muoiano
imper.	muori, muoia, morite, muoiano
past part.	morto

79. MUNGERE

past	munsi, mungesti, munse, mungemmo, mungeste, munsero
past part.	munto

80. MUOVERE

past	mossi, movesti, mosse, movemmo, moveste, mossero
past part.	mosso

81. NASCERE

past	nacqui, nascesti, nacque, nascemmo, nasceste, nacquero
past part.	nato

82. NASCONDERE

past	nascosi, nascondesti, nascose, nascondemmo, nascondeste, nascosero
past part.	nascosto

83. NUOCERE

pres. ind.	nuoccio or noccio, nuoci, nuoce, nociamo, nocete, nuocciono or nocciono
past	nocqui, nocesti, nocque, nocemmo, noceste, nocquero
pres. ind.	noccia, noccia, noccia, nociamo, nociate, nocciano
imper.	nuoci, noccia, nocete, nocciano
past part.	nociuto

84. OFFRIRE

past	offrii or offersi, offristi, offrì or offerse, offrimmo, offriste, offrirono or offersero
past part.	offerto

85. PARERE

pres. ind.	paio, pari, pare, paiamo, parete, paiono
past	parvi, paresti, parve, paremmo, pareste, parvero
fut.	parrò, parrai, parrà, parremo, parrete, parranno
pres. sub.	paia, paia, paia, pariamo, pariate or paiate, paiano
cond.	parrei, parresti, parrebbe, parremmo, parreste, parrebbero
imper.	*lacking*
pres. part.	parvente
past part.	parso

86. PARTIRE

pres. ind.	parto, parti, parte, partiamo, partirte, partono

87. PERDERE

past	persi or perdetti, perdesti, perse or perdette, perdemmo, perdeste, persero or perdettero
past part.	perso or perduto

88. PERSUADERE

past	persuasi, persuadesti, **persuase**, persuademmo, persuadeste, persuasero
past part.	persuaso

89. PIACERE

pres. ind.	piaccio, piaci, piace, piacciamo, piacete, piacciono
past	piacqui, piacesti, piacque, piacemmo, piaceste, piacquero
pres. sub.	piaccia, piaccia, piaccia, piacciamo, piacciate, piacciano
past part.	piaciuto

90. PIANGERE

past	piansi, piangesti, **pianse**, piangemmo, piangeste, piansero
past part.	pianto

91. PIOVERE

past	piovvi, piovesti, piovve, piovemmo, pioveste, piovvero

92. PORGERE

past	porsi, porgesti, **porse**, porgemmo, porgeste, porsero
past part.	porto

93. PORRE

pres. ind.	pongo, poni, pone, poniamo, ponete, pongono
imp. ind.	ponevo, ponevi, poneva, ponevamo, ponevate, ponevano
past	posi, ponesti, pose, ponemmo, poneste, posero
fut.	porrò, porrai, porrà, porremo, porrete, porranno
cond.	porrei, porresti, porrebbe, porremmo, porreste, porrebbero
pres. sub.	ponga, ponga, ponga, poniamo, poniate, pongano
imp. sub.	ponessi, ponessi, ponesse, ponessimo, poneste, ponessero
imper.	poni, ponga, ponete, pongano
pres. part.	ponente
past part.	posto
	Note. All regular forms derive from the infinitive form ponere.

94. POTERE

pres. ind.	posso, puoi, può, possiamo, potete, possono
fut.	potrò, potrai, potrà, potremo, potrete, potranno
cond.	potrei, potresti, potrebbe, potremmo, potreste, potrebbero
pres. sub.	possa, possa, possa, possiamo, possiate, possano
past part.	potuto

95. PREDILIGERE

past	predilessi, prediligesti, **predilesse**, prediligemmo, prediligeste, predilessero
past part.	prediletto

96. PRENDERE

past	presi, prendesti, **prese**, prendemmo, prendeste, presero
past part.	preso

97. PRESCINDERE

past	prescindei *or* prescissi, prescindesti, prescindè *or* prescisse, prescindemmo, prescindeste, prescinderono *or* prescissero
past part.	prescisso
	Note. See also scindere, 121.

98. PREVEDERE
see **vedere, 151**

99. PROFERIRE
past   proferii, proferisti, proferì, proferimmo, proferiste,
                 proferirono
past part.   proferito
                 Note. See **profferire, 100.**

100. PROFFERIRE
past   proffersi, profferisti, profferse, profferimmo, profferiste,
                 proffersero
past part.   profferto

101. PROTEGGERE
past   protessi, proteggesti, protesse, proteggemmo, proteggeste,
                 protessero
past part.   protetto

102. RADERE
past   rasi, radesti, rase, rademmo, radeste, rasero
past part.   raso

103. REDIGERE
past   redassi, redigesti, redasse, redigemmo, redigeste, redassero
past part.   redatto

104. REDIMERE
past   redensi, redimesti, redense, redimemmo, redimeste
                 redensero
past part.   redento

105. REGGERE
past   ressi, reggesti, resse, reggemmo, reggeste, ressero
past part.   retto

106. RENDERE
past   resi, rendesti, rese, rendemmo, rendeste, resero
past part.   reso

107. RESTRINGERE
past part.   ristretto

108. RIDERE
past   risi, ridesti, rise, ridemmo, rideste, risero
past part.   riso

109. RIFLETTERE
past   riflettei *or* riflessi, riflettesti, riflettè *or* riflesse, riflettem-
                 mo, rifletteste, rifletterono *or* riflessero
past part.   riflettuto *or* riflesso

110. RIFULGERE
past   rifulsi, rifulgesti, rifulse, rifulgemmo, rifulgeste, rifulsero
past part.   rifulso

111. RILUCERE
past   rilucei, rilucesti, rilucè, rilucemmo, riluceste, rilucerono,
past part.   *lacking*

112. RIMANERE

pres. ind.	rimango, rimani, rimane, rimaniamo, rimanete, rimangono
past	rimasi, rimanesti, rimase, rimanemmo, rimaneste, rimasero
fut.	rimarrò, rimarrai, rimarrà, rimarremo, rimarrete, rimarranno
cond.	rimarrei, rimarresti, rimarrebbe, rimarremmo, rimarreste, rimarrebbero
pres. sub.	rimanga, rimanga, rimanga, rimaniamo, rimaniate, rimangano
imper.	rimani, rimanga, rimanete, rimangano
past part.	rimasto

113. RISPONDERE

past	risposi, rispondesti, rispose, rispondemmo, rispondeste, risposero
past part.	risposto

114. RODERE

past	rosi, rodesti, rose, rodemmo, rodeste, rosero
past part.	roso

115. ROMPERE

past	ruppi, rompesti, ruppe, rompemmo, rompeste, ruppero
past part.	rotto

116. SALIRE

pres. ind.	salgo, sali, sale, saliamo, salite, salgono
pres. sub.	salga, salga, salga, saliamo, saliate, salgano
imper.	sali, salga, salite, salgano

117. SAPERE

pres. ind.	so, sai, sa, sappiamo, sapete, sanno
past	seppi, sapesti, seppe, sapemmo, sapeste, seppero
fut.	saprò, saprai, saprà, sapremo, saprete, sapranno
cond.	saprei, sapresti, saprebbe, sapremmo, sapreste, saprebbero
pres. sub.	sappia, sappia, sappia, sappiamo, sappiate, sappiano
imper.	sappi, sappia, sappiate, sappiano
pres. part.	sapiente

118. SCEGLIERE

pres. ind.	scelgo, scegli, sceglie, scegliamo, scegliete, scelgono
past	scelsi, scegliesti, scelse, scegliemmo, sceglieste, scelsero
pres. sub.	scelga, scelga, scelga, scegliamo, scegliate, scelgano
imper.	scegli, scelga, scegliete, scelgano
past part.	scelto

119. SCENDERE

past	scesi, scendesti, scese, scendemmo, scendeste, scesero
past part.	sceso

120. SCERNERE

past	scernei or scernetti, scernesti, scernè or scernette, scernemmo, scerneste, scernerono or scernettero
past part.	lacking

121. SCINDERE

past	scissi, scindesti, scisse, scindemmo, scindeste, scissero
past part.	scisso

122. SCOLPIRE

past   scolpii, scolpisti, scolpì, scolpimmo, scolpiste, scolpirono;
poet. sculsi, scolpisti, **sculse**, scolpimmo, scolpiste,
sculsero
past part.   scolpito; *poet.* **sculto**

123. SCORGERE

past   scorsi, scorgesti, **scorse**, scorgemmo, scorgeste, **scorsero**
past part.   scorto

124. SCRIVERE

past   scrissi, scrivesti, **scrisse**, scrivemmo, scriveste, **scrissero**
past part.   scritto

125. SCUOTERE

past   scossi, scotesti, **scosse**, scotemmo, scoteste, **scossero**
past part.   scosso

126. SEDERE

pres. ind.   siedo *or* **seggo, siedi, siede**, sediamo, sedete, **siedono** *or*
seggono
past   sedei *or* sedetti, sedesti, sedè *or* sedette, sedemmo, sedeste,
sederono *or* sedettero
pres. sub.   sieda *or* segga, sieda *or* segga, sieda *or* segga, sediamo,
sediate, **siedano** *or* **seggano**
imper.   siedi, sieda *or* segga, sedete, **siedano** *or* **seggano**

127. SEPPELLIRE

past part.   seppellito *or* **sepolto**

128. SODDISFARE

pres. ind.   soddisfo *or* **soddisfaccio**, soddisfi *or* **soddisfai**, soddisfa *or*
soddisfa, soddisfiamo *or* soddisfacciamo, soddisfate, sod-
disfano *or* soddisfanno
pres. sub.   soddisfi *or* **soddisfaccia**, soddisfi *or* **soddisfaccia**, soddisfi *or*
soddisfaccia, soddisfacciamo, soddisfacciate, soddisfino *or*
soddisfacciano
imper.   soddisfa, soddisfi *or* **soddisfaccia**, soddisfate, soddisfino *or*
soddisfacciano

129. SOLERE

pres. ind.   soglio, suoli, suole, sogliamo, solete, sogliono; *or* sono solito,
sei solito, è solito, siamo soliti, siete soliti, sono soliti
imp. ind.   solevo, solevi, soleva, solevamo, solevate, solevano
fut.   *lacking*
cond.   *lacking*
pres. sub.   soglia, soglia, soglia, sogliamo, sogliate, sogliano
imp. sub.   solessi, solessi, solesse, solessimo, soleste, solessero
past   solei, solesti, solè, solemmo, soleste, solerono (*rare*); *now
most commonly*: fui solito, fosti solito, fu solito, fummo
soliti, foste soliti, furono soliti
imper.   *lacking*
pres. part. *lacking*
past part.   solito

130. SORGERE

past   sorsi, sorgesti, **sorse**, sorgemmo, sorgeste, **sorsero**
past part.   sorto

131. SPANDERE

past   spandei *or* **spansi**, spandesti, spandè *or* **spanse**, spandem-
mo, spandeste, spanderono *or* **spansero**
past part.   spanto *or* spanduto *or* **spanso** (*all rare*); *now most commonly*: **sparso**

132. SPARGERE

past	sparsi, spargesti, **sparse**, spargemmo, spargeste, **sparsero**
past part.	sparso

133. SPARIRE

past	sparii *or* sparvi, sparisti, sparì *or* sparve, sparimmo, spariste, sparirono *or* sparvero

134. SPEGNERE *or* SPENGERE

pres. ind.	spengo, spegni *or* spengi, spegne *or* spenge, spegniamo *or* spengiamo, spegnete *or* spengete, spengono
past	spensi, spegnesti *or* spengesti, spense, spegnemmo *or* spengemmo, spegneste *or* spengeste, spensero
pres. sub.	spenga, spenga, spenga, spegniamo *or* spengiamo, spegniate, *or* spengiate, spengano
imper.	spegni *or* spengi, spenga, spegnete *or* spengete, spengano
past part.	spento

135. STARE

pres. ind.	sto, stai, sta, stiamo, state, stanno
past	stetti, stesti, stette, stemmo, steste, stettero .
fut.	starò, starai, starà, staremo, starete, staranno
cond.	starei, staresti, starebbe, staremmo, stareste, starebbero
pres. sub.	stia, stia, stia, stiamo, stiate, stiano
imp. sub.	stessi, stessi, stesse, stessimo, steste, stessero
imper.	stai *or* sta', stia, state, stiano
past part.	stato

136. STRINGERE

past	strinsi, stringesti, **strinse**, stringemmo, stringeste, **strinsero**
past part.	stretto

137. STRUGGERE

past	strussi, struggesti, **strusse**, struggemmo, struggeste, strussero
past part.	strutto

138. SVELLERE

pres. ind.	svelgo *or* svello, svelli, svelle, svelliamo, svellete, svelgono *or* svellono
past	svelsi, svellesti, svelse, svellemmo, svelleste, svelsero
past part.	svelto

139. TACERE

pres. ind.	taccio, taci, tace, taciamo, tacete, tacciono
past	tacqui, tacesti, tacque, tacemmo, taceste, tacquero
pres. sub.	taccia, taccia, taccia, taciamo, tacciate, tacciano
imper.	taci, taccia, tacete, tacciano

140. TENDERE

past	tesi, tendesti, tese, tendemmo, tendeste, tesero
past part.	teso

141. TENERE

pres. ind.	tengo, tieni, tiene, teniamo, tenete, tengono
past	tenni, tenesti, tenne, tenemmo, teneste, tennero
fut.	terrò, terrai, terrà, terremo, terrete, terranno
cond.	terrei, terresti, terrebbe, terremmo, terreste, terrebbero
pres. sub.	tenga, tenga, tenga, teniamo, teniate, tengano
imper.	tieni, tenga, tenete, tengano

142. TERGERE

past	tersi, tergesti, **terse,** tergemmo, tergeste, **tersero**
past part.	**terso**

143. TINGERE

past	tinsi, tingesti, **tinse,** tingemmo, tingeste, **tinsero**
past part.	**tinto**

144. TOGLIERE

pres. ind.	**tolgo,** togli, toglie, togliamo, togliete, **tolgono**
past	**tolsi,** togliesti, **tolse,** togliemmo, toglieste, **tolsero**
pres. sub.	**tolga, tolga, tolga,** togliamo, togliate, **tolgano**
imper.	togli, **tolga,** togliete, **tolgano**
cond.	toglierei *or* **torrei,** toglieresti *or* **torresti,** toglierebbe *or* **torrebbe,** toglieremmo *or* **torremmo,** togliereste *or* **torreste,** toglierebbero *or* **torrebbero**
fut.	toglierò *or* **torrò,** toglierai *or* **torrai,** toglierà *or* **torrà,** toglieremo *or* **torremo,** toglierete *or* **torrete,** toglieranno *or* **torranno**
past part.	**tolto**

145. TORCERE

past	torsi, torcesti, **torse,** torcemmo, torceste, **torsero**
past part.	**torto**

146. TRARRE

pres. ind.	**traggo,** trai, trae, traiamo, traete, **traggono**
imp. ind.	traevo, traevi, traeva, traevamo, traevate, traevano
fut.	trarrò, trarrai, trarrà, trarremo, trarrete, trarranno
past	trassi, traesti, trasse, traemmo, traeste, trassero
cond.	trarrei, trarresti, trarrebbe, trarremmo, trarreste, trarrebbero
pres. sub.	**tragga, tragga, tragga,** traiamo, traiate, **traggano**
imp. sub.	traessi, traessi, traesse, traessimo, traeste, traessero
imper.	trai, **tragga,** traete, **traggano**
pres. part.	traente
past part.	**tratto.**
	Note. All regular forms derive from the infinitive form **traere.**

147. TRASPARIRE

see **apparire, 9**

148. UDIRE

pres. ind.	**odo, odi, ode,** udiamo, udite, **odono**
fut.	udirò *or* **udrò,** udirai *or* **udrai,** udirà *or* **udrà,** udiremo *o* **udremo,** udirete *or* **udrete,** udiranno *or* **udranno**
pres. sub.	**oda, oda, oda,** udiamo, udiate, **odano**
imper.	**odi, oda,** udite, **odano**
pres. part.	udente *or* **udiente**

149. USCIRE

pres. ind.	**esco, esci, esce,** usciamo, uscite, **escono**
pres. sub.	**esca, esca, esca,** usciamo, usciate, **escano**
imper.	**esci, esca,** uscite, **escano**

150. VALERE

pres. ind.	valgo, vali, vale, valiamo, valete, valgono
past	valsi, valesti, valse, valemmo, valeste, valsero
fut.	varrò, varrai, varrà, varremo, varrete, varranno
cond.	varrei, varresti, varrebbe, varremmo, varreste, varrebbero
pres. sub.	valga, valga, valga, valiamo, valiate, valgano
imper.	vali, valga, valete, valgano
past part.	valso or valuto

151. VEDERE

past	vidi, vedesti, vide, vedemmo, vedeste, videro
fut.	vedrò, vedrai, vedrà, vedremo, vedrete, vedranno
cond.	vedrei, vedresti, vedrebbe, vedremmo, vedreste, vedrebbero
pres. part.	vedente or veggente
past part.	visto or veduto

152. VENIRE

pres. ind.	vengo, vieni, viene, veniamo, venite, vengono
past	venni, venisti, venne, venimmo, veniste, vennero
fut.	verrò, verrai, verrà, verremo, verrete, verranno
cond.	verrei, verresti, verrebbe, verremmo, verreste, verrebbero
pres. sub.	venga, venga, venga, veniamo, veniate, vengano
imper.	vieni, venga, venite, vengano
pres. part.	veniente
past part.	venuto

153. VINCERE

past	vinsi, vincesti, vinse, vincemmo, vinceste, vinsero
past part.	vinto

154. VIVERE

past	vissi, vivesti, visse, vivemmo, viveste, vissero
fut.	vivrò, vivrai, vivrà, vivremo, vivrete, vivranno
cond.	vivrei, vivresti, vivrebbe, vivremmo, vivreste, vivrebbero
past part.	vissuto

155. VOLERE

pres. ind.	voglio, vuoi, vuole, vogliamo, volete, vogliono
past	volli, volesti, volle, volemmo, voleste, vollero
fut.	vorrò, vorrai, vorrà, vorremo, vorrete, vorranno
cond.	vorrei, vorresti, vorrebbe, vorremmo, vorreste, vorrebbero
pres. sub.	voglia, voglia, voglia, vogliamo, vogliate, vogliano
past part.	voluto

156. VOLGERE

past	volsi, volgesti, volse, volgemmo, volgeste, volsero
past part.	volto

NUMERALS

	Cardinal numbers	Numeri cardinali	Ordinal numbers	Numeri ordinali
1	one	uno	first	primo
2	two	due	second	secondo
3	three	tre	third	terzo
4	four	quattro	fourth	quarto
5	five	cinque	fifth	quinto
6	six	sei	sixth	sesto
7	seven	sette	seventh	settimo
8	eight	otto	eighth	ottavo
9	nine	nove	ninth	nono
10	ten	dieci	tenth	decimo
11	eleven	undici	eleventh	undicesimo
12	twelve	dodici	twelfth	dodicesimo
13	thirteen	tredici	thirteenth	tredicesimo
14	fourteen	quattordici	fourteenth	quattordicesimo
15	fifteen	quindici	fifteenth	quindicesimo
16	sixteen	sedici	sixteenth	sedicesimo
17	seventeen	diciassette	seventeenth	diciassettesimo
18	eighteen	diciotto	eighteenth	diciottesimo
19	nineteen	diciannove	nineteenth	diciannovesimo
20	twenty	venti	twentieth	ventesimo
21	twenty-one	ventuno	twenty-first	ventunesimo
22	twenty-two	ventidue	twenty-second	ventiduesimo
23	twenty-three	ventitrè	twenty-third	ventitreesimo
26	twenty-six	ventisei	twenty-sixth	ventiseesimo
30	thirty	trenta	thirtieth	trentesimo
40	forty	quaranta	fortieth	quarantesimo
50	fifty	cinquanta	fiftieth	cinquantesimo
60	sixty	sessanta	sixtieth	sessantesimo
70	seventy	settanta	seventieth	settantesimo
80	eighty	ottanta	eightieth	ottantesimo
90	ninety	novanta	ninetieth	novantesimo
100	one hundred	cento	hundredth	centesimo
1000	one thousand	mille	(one) thousandth	millesimo
10000	ten thousand	diecimila	ten thousandth	decimillesimo
100000	one hundred thousand	centomila	(one) hundred thousandth	cento-millesimo
1000000	one million	un milione	(one) millionth	milionesimo

Note. Venti drops the i in ventuno and in ventotto.

Trenta, quaranta, etc., drop the last a in trentuno, trentotto, quarantuno, quarantotto, etc.

Cento and mille are not preceded by the indefinite article or by the number uno.

Cento is invariable.

Mille has the plural form mila.

Eleven hundred, twelve hundred, etc., are expressed in Italian as mille e cento, mille e duecento, etc.

Ordinal numbers are declined like any other adjective.

ITALIAN—ENGLISH

A

a, ad *prep.* to, at, in, by, for, on.
a'baco *m.* abacus (*pl.* abaci).
abate *m.* abbot, priest.
abbacchiarsi *vr.* to lose courage.
abbacchiato *adj.* dejected.
abbac'chio *m.* lamb (*killed*).
abbacinare *vt.* to dazzle.
abbadessa *f.* abbess.
abbagliante *adj.* dazzling.
abbagliare *vt.* to dazzle, blind; to charm.
abba'glio *m.* mistake, dazzling (*fig.*).
abbaiamento *m.* bark.
abbaiare *vi.* to bark.
abbai'no *m.* dormer, dormer window.
abbandonare *vt.* to abandon, forsake; abbandonarsi *vr.* to abandon oneself, trust (*to*); to relax.
abbandonato *adj.* abandoned.
abbandono *m.* abandonment.
abbarbicarsi *vr.* to cling, stick.
abbassamento *m.* lowering.
abbassare *vt.* to lower: — gli occhi, to cast down one's eyes; abbassarsi *vr.* to lower oneself, stoop.
abbasso *adv.*, *prep.* down, below. *interj.* down with!
abbastanza *adv.* enough.
abbat'tere *vt.* to pull down; to shoot down; to slaughter; abbat'tersi *vr.* to fall; to lose courage.
abbattimento *m.* dejection; demolition.
abbazi'a *f.* abbey; abbacy.
abbeceda'rio *m.* spelling book.
abbellimento *m.* embellishment, decoration.
abbellire *vt.* to embellish, adorn; abbellirsi *vr.* to adorn oneself.
abbeverare *vt.*, abbeverarsi *vr.* to water; to drink.
abbeveratoio *m.* watering place.
abbiadare *vt.* to accustom a horse to oats.
abbicci *m.* alphabet; spelling book.
abbiente *adj.* wealthy.
abbigliamento *m.* attire.
abbigliare *vt.*, abbigliarsi *vr.* to dress.
abbinamento *m.* coupling.
abbinare *vt.* to couple.
abbindolare *vt.* to deceive.
abbisognare *vi.* to need, want.
abboccamento *m.* interview.
abboccare *vt.* to bite; abboccarsi *vr.* to confer (*with*).
abbonamento *m.* subscription: biglietto d'—, season ticket.
abbonare *vt.* to grant a discount (*to*); abbonarsi *vr.* to subscribe.

abbonato *m.* subscriber.
abbondante *adj.* abundant.
abbondantemente *adv.* abundantly.
abbondanza *f.* plentifulness, plenty.
abbondare *vi.* to abound (*in*).
abborda'bile *adj.* accessible, approachable; cheap.
abbordag'gio *m.* boarding (*a boat*).
abbordare *vt.* to board; to accost, approach: — un argomento, to broach a subject.
abborracciare *vt.* to bungle, mess.
abborracciatura *f.* bungle.
abbottonare *vt.* to button.
abbottonatura *f.* fastening.
abbozzare *vt.* to sketch.
abbozzo *m.* sketch.
abbracciare *vt.* to embrace: — una causa, to espouse a cause; — una professione, to enter a profession.
abbrac'cio *m.* embrace, hug.
abbrancare *vt.* to grab; abbrancarsi *vr.* to cling (*to*).
abbreviare *vt.* to shorten, abridge, curtail.
abbreviatura *f.* abridgment.
abbreviazione *f.* abbreviation.
abbrivo *m.* (*naut.*) headway.
abbronzare *vt.*, abbronzarsi *vr.* to bask, tan.
abbronzatura *f.* tan.
abbrunare *vt.* to brown; to drape with black: — le bandiere, to fly at half-mast (*as flags*).
abbrustolire *vt.* to broil, toast, roast.
abbrutimento *m.* stupor.
abbrutire *vt.*, *vi.* abbrutirsi *vr.* to brutalize.
abbularsi *vr.* to darken, dim.
abbuono *m.* allowance, discount.
abburattamento *m.* sifting.
abburattare *vt.* to sift.
abburattatura *f.* sifting; bran.
abdicare *vt.*, *vi.* to abdicate.
abdicazione *f.* abdication.
aberrazione *f.* aberration.
abete *m.* fir tree.
abia'tico *m.* grandchild.
abiettezza *f.* baseness.
abietto *adj.* base, abject, despicable.
abiezione *f.* despicableness; misery.
abigeato *m.* cattle rustling.
a'bile *adj.* able, capable; fit, apt.
abilità *f.* ability, skill.
abilitare *vt.*, abilitarsi *vr.* to qualify.
abilitazione *f.* qualification.
abilmente *adv.* skillfully.
abisso *m.* abyss, chasm, gulf.

1

abita'bile *adj.* habitable.
abita'colo *m.* (*aeron.*) cockpit.
abitante *m.* inhabitant, dweller.
abitare *vt.* to inhabit, occupy. *vi.* to dwell, live (*in*).
abitato *m.* inhabited area. *adj.* inhabited, occupied, lived-in.
abitatore *m.* dweller.
abitazione *f.* abode, residence.
a'bito *m.* suit; dress; (*pl.*) clothes: — **mentale**, habit of mind.
abituale *adj.* usual, habitual.
abitualmente *adv.* usually.
abituare *vt.* to accustom; **abituarsi** *vr.* to become accustomed.
abitu'dine *f.* habit, custom.
abituro *m.* hut, shanty.
abiura *f.* abjuration.
abiurare *vt.* to abjure.
ablativo *m.*, *adj.* ablative.
ablazione *f.* ablation.
abluzione *f.* ablution.
abnegazione *f.* self-denial.
abolire *vt.* to abolish.
abolizione *f.* abolition, repeal.
abolizionismo *m.* abolitionism.
abolizionista *m.* abolitionist.
abominare *vt.* to abominate, loathe.
abominazione *f.* abomination.
abomine'vole *adj.* abominable.
abori'geno *m.* aborigine. *adj.* aboriginal.
aborrire *vt.*, *vi.* to abhor, loathe.
abortire *vi.* to miscarry; to fail.
aborto *m.* abortion, miscarriage.
abrasione *f.* abrasion, scraping off.
abrasivo *m.*, *adj.* abrasive.
abrogare *vt.* to abrogate.
abrogazione *f.* abrogation.
ab'side *f.* apse; apsis (*pl.* apsides).
abuli'a *f.* abulia, aboulia.
abu'lico *adj.* abulic.
abusare *vi.* to abuse, misuse; to take advantage (*of*); overdo: — **nel bere**, to drink to excess.
abusivamente *adv.* improperly.
abusivo *adj.* unwarranted.
abuso *m.* abuse, excess.
aca'cia *f.* (*bot.*) acacia.
acanto *m.* acanthus.
a'caro *m.* mite, acarus.
acca *f.* the letter "h": **non ci capisco un'—**, I cannot make head or tail of it; **non valere un'—**, to be worthless.
accade'mia *f.* academy.
accademicamente *adv.* academically.
accade'mico *m.* academician. *adj.* academic.
accadere *vi.* to happen, occur.
accaduto *m.* case, event: **raccontami l'—**, tell me what happened.
accagliare *vt.*, **accagliarsi** *vr.* to curdle, coagulate.

accalappiacani *m.* dogcatcher.
accalappiamento *m.* snare.
accalappiare *vt.* to ensnare.
accalappiatore *m.* snarer.
accalcare *vt.*, **accalcarsi** *vr.* to crowd, throng, swarm.
accaldarsi *vr.* to get hot.
accaldato *adj.* hot.
accalorarsi *vr.* to get excited.
accampamento *m.* camp, camping, encampment.
accampare *vt.*, *vi.* to camp, encamp: — **diritti su**, to lay claim to; **accamparsi** *vr.* (*mil.*) to encamp.
accanimento *m.* fury, stubbornness.
accanirsi *vr.* to persist; (*foll. by* su, contro) to badger.
accanito *adj.* furious; relentless; stubborn; tenacious; bitter.
accanto *prep.*, *adv.* beside, by, near.
accantonamento *m.* billeting.
accantonare *vt.* to billet; to set aside; **accantonarsi** *vr.* to camp.
accaparramento *m.* cornering.
accaparrare *vt.* to hoard, corner; **accaparrarsi** *vr.* to grab.
accaparratore *m.* hoarder.
accapigliarsi *vr.* to scuffle, come to blows, quarrel.
accappato'io *m.* bathrobe.
accapponare *vt.* to caponize; **accapponarsi** *vr.* to creep: **far accapponare la pelle**, to make one's flesh creep.
accarezzare *vt.* to caress; to cherish.
accartocciare *vt.* to wrap up; **accartocciarsi** *vr.* to curl up.
accasare *vt.*, **accasarsi** *vr.* to marry.
accasciamento *m.* dejection.
accasciare *vt.* to enfeeble; to dishearten, discourage; **accasciarsi** *vr.* to weaken; to lose courage.
accasermare *vt.*, **accasermarsi** *vr.* to quarter, billet.
accatastare *vt.* to heap up.
accattabrighe *m.* brawler.
accattare *vt.* to beg.
accattonag'gio *m.* begging.
accattone *m.* beggar.
accavallamento *m.* overlapping, twist.
accavallare *vt.* to overlap; cross; **accavallarsi** *vr.* to overlap, twist.
accecamento *m.* blinding.
accecante *adj.* blinding.
accecare *vt.* to blind; to dazzle. *vi.* to become blind; **accecarsi** *vr.* to blind oneself.
acce'dere *vi.* to accede; to approach; to enter.
accelerare *vt.*, *vi.* to accelerate, hasten, to speed up.
accelerato *m.* local train. *adj.*, *pp of* accelerare, accelerated: **corso —**, intensive course.

acceleratore *m.* accelerator; throttle.

accelerazione *f.* acceleration; pickup.

accen'dere *vt.*[1] to light; to ignite; **accendersi** *vr.* to light, take fire; to get excited.

accendisi'garo *m.* lighter.

accenditore *m.* lighter.

accennare *vt., vi.* to point at; to outline; to beckon; to hint (*at*).

accenno *m.* hint, allusion.

accensione *f.* firing, ignition.

accentare *vt.* to accent.

accentatura *f.* accentuation.

accento *m.* accent, stress.

accentramento *m.* centralization.

accentrare *vt.* to centralize.

accentratore *m.* centralizer.

accentuare *vt.* to accentuate; to emphasize; **accentuarsi** *vr.* to increase.

accentuazione *f.* accentuation.

accerchiamento *m.* encirclement.

accerchiare *vt.* to encircle, encompass; to surround.

accerta'bile *adj.* verifiable.

accertamento *m.* verification, ascertainment, estimate.

accertare *vt.* to assure; to ascertain; **accertarsi** *vr.* to make sure.

acceso *adj.* alight; hot. *pp.* of accendere, lighted, lit.

accessi'bile *adj.* accessible; reasonable.

accesso *m.* fit, burst; entrance.

accesso'rio *adj.* complementary; **accessori** *m. pl.* fittings.

accetta *f.* ax, hatchet.

accetta'bile *adj.* acceptable.

accettante *m.* acceptor.

accettare *vt.* to accept.   [bill.

accettazione *f.* acceptance; accepted

accetto *adj.* agreeable: **bene —,** welcome; **male —,** unwelcome.

accezione *f.* meaning, case, acceptance.

acchiappare *vt.* (*It. slang*) to catch.

acchito *m.* lead: **di primo —,** at first, at once.

acciaccare *vt.* to crush; to bruise.

acciaccatura *f.* bruise; grace note.

acciacco *m.* infirmity.

acciaieri'a *f.* steelworks.

accia'io *m.* steel.

acciarino *m.* steel; tinderbox.

accidentale *adj.* accidental.

accidentalmente *adv.* accidentally.

accidentato *adj.* paralyzed; uneven.

accidente *m.* accident, mishap; stroke (of apoplexy).

accidenti! *interj.* the deuce!, damn!

acci'dia *f.* laziness, sloth.

accidioso *adj.* lazy, slothful.

accigliarsi *vr.* to frown.

accigliato *adj.* frowning.

accin'gersi *vr.* to gird oneself; to set about.

acciocchè *conj.* so that.

acciottolare *vt.* to cobble.

acciottolato *m.* (*cobbled*) paving.

acciottoli'o *m.* clatter.

acciuffare *vt.* to catch, seize; **acciuffarsi** *vr.* to quarrel.

acciuga *f.* anchovy.

acclamare *vt., vi.* to acclaim.

acclamatore *m.* acclaimer.

acclamazione *f.* acclamation.

acclimatare *vt.* to acclimatize; **acclimatarsi** *vr.* to become acclimatized.

acclimatazione *f.,* acclimatization.

acclive *adj.* steep.

acclu'dere *vt.*[2] to enclose.

accluso *adj.* enclosed: **qui —,** herein enclosed. *pp.* of accludere.

accoccare *vt.* to notch, fit.

accoccolarsi *vr.* to cuddle, squat.

accodarsi *vr.* to follow, line up in file.

accogliente *adj.* cozy, hospitable.

accoglienza *f.* reception, welcome.

acco'gliere *vt.*[3] to receive, welcome; **acco'lito** *m.* acolyte.   [to grant.

accollare *vt.* to lay on; **accollarsi** *vr.* to take upon oneself.

accollato *adj.* high-necked (*as a gown*); high-cut (*as shoes*).

accolta *f.* assembly, gathering.

accoltellare *vt.* to knife.

accolto *adj.* received; granted. *pp.* of accogliere.

accomandante *m.* limited partner, depositor.

accomandata'rio *m.* general partner, unlimited partner.

accoman'dita *f.* limited partnership: **società in —,** joint-stock company.

accomiatare *vt.* to dismiss; **accomiatarsi** *vr.* to take one's leave.

accomodamento *m.* arrangement.

accomodante *adj.* obliging.

accomodare *vt.* to mend; to tidy; to settle; to adapt. *vi.* to suit; **accomodarsi** *vr.* to adapt oneself; to come to an agreement; to sit down; to make oneself comfortable.

accomodatura *f.* mending.

accompagnamento *m.* attendance, escort; accompaniment.

accompagnare *vt.* to accompany, escort; to match: **Dio li fa, poi li accompagna,** birds of a feather flock together; **accompagnarsi** *vr.* to go (*with*); to match.

accompagnatore *m.* escort, companion; accompanist.

accomunare *vt.* to join, associate; to mingle; **accomunarsi** *vr.* to join (*with*).

acconciamente *adv.* properly.

acconciare vt. to prepare for use; to adorn; to attire; to dress the hair of; **acconciarsi** vr. to adorn oneself; to adapt oneself; to dress one's hair.

acconciatura f. attire; hairdo.

acconcio adj. fit, proper.

accondiscen'dere see **condiscendere**.

acconsentire vt. to admit, approve. vi. to acquiesce, agree.

accontentare vt. to please, satisfy; to humor; **accontentarsi** vr. to be content (with).

acconto m. account; retainer; advance.

accoppare vt. to kill; to club.

accoppia'bile adj. matchable.

accoppiamento m. coupling; copulation.

accoppiare vt. to couple, pair; to cross; to yoke; **accoppiarsi** vr. to couple; to mate; to copulate.

accoramento m. grief, sorrow.

accorarsi vr. to grieve (over).

accorato adj. grieved, sorrowful.

accorciamento m. shortening; shrinkage.

accorciare vt., **accorciarsi** vr. to shorten; to shrink.

accordamento m. concordance;'tuning,

accordare vt. to tune; to match; to put in agreement; to reconcile; to grant; **accordarsi** vr. to agree (upon); to match.

accordatore m. (mus.) tuner.

accordatura f. (mus.) tuning.

accordo m. agreement, harmony; concordance.

accor'gersi vr.[4] to perceive, become aware (of), realize.

accorgimento m. device, trick, stratagem.

accor'rere vi. to run, rush.

accortamente adv. shrewdly.

accortezza f. shrewdness.

accorto adj. shrewd, sly, clever.

accosciarsi vr. to squat.

accosta'bile adj. approachable.

accostamento m. approach, comparison.

accostare vt. to approach; to set ajar; to bring near. vi. to stand close; **accostarsi** vr. to approach; to look like.

accosto adj. near. adv., prep. by, close to, near.

accovacciarsi vr. to crouch.

accovonare vt. to sheaf.

accozza'glia f. medley, mixed crowd.

accozzare vt., **accozzarsi** vr. to huddle, assemble.

accozzo m. jumble, medley.

accredita'bile adj. that may be credited.

accreditamento m. crediting.

accreditare vt. to credit; to confirm; to accredit.

accre'scere vt. **accre'scersi** vr. to increase.

accrescimento m. increase.

accucciarsi vr. to crouch.

accudire vi. to attend (to), take care (of).

accumulare vt., **accumularsi** vr. to accumulate.

accumulatore m. storage battery.

accumulazione f. accumulation.

accuratamente adv. accurately.

accuratezza f. accuracy.

accurato adj. accurate, careful.

accusa f. charge; prosecution.

accusare vt. to charge (with); to feel, show: — ricevuta, to acknowledge receipt.

accusativo m., adj. accusative.

accusato m. accused; defendant.

accusatore m. accuser: — pubblico, prosecutor.

acerbamente adv. prematurely; bitterly, mercilessly, sharply.

acerbo adj. unripe; sour; merciless; inexperienced; sharp.

a'cero m. maple.

acer'rimo adj. (superl. of **acre**) cruel, fierce, relentless.

acetato m. (chem.) acetate.

ace'tico adj. acetic.

acetilene f. acetylene.

aceto m. vinegar.

acetone m. acetone.

acetosa f. (bot.) sorrel.

acetosella f. (bot.) wood sorrel.

acidificare vt. to acidify.

acidità f. acidity, sourness.

a'cido m., adj. acid.

aci'dulo adj. acidulous.

a'cino m. (bot.) acinus (pl. acini); grapestone; grape.

acme f. climax.

acne f. acne.

aco'nito m. aconite, wolfsbane.

acqua f. water: — cheta, dissembler; — dolce, soft water; — ossigenata, hydrogen peroxide; fare —, to leak; fare un buco nell'—, to fail.

acquaforte f. aqua fortis; etching.

acquafortista m. etcher.

acqua'io m. sink.

acquaiuolo m. water carrier.

acquamarina f. aquamarine.

acquaplano m. aquaplane.

acquaragia f. turpentine oil.

acqua'rio see **aqua'rio**.

acquartierare vt., **acquartierarsi** vr. to quarter.

acqua'tico adj. aquatic.

acquatinta f. aquatint.

acquattare vt. to hide, shelter; **acquattarsi** vr. to crouch; to hide.

acquavite f. brandy.

acquazzone m. shower.

acquedotto m. aqueduct.

ac'queo adj. watery.

acquerellare vt. to paint with water colors.

acquerellista m. aquarellist.

acquerello m. water color.

acqueru'giola f. drizzle.

acquetare see **acquietare**.

acquiescente adj. acquiescent.

acquiescenza f. acquiescence.

acquietare vt. to appease; **acquietarsi** vr. to calm down.

acquirente m. purchaser.

acquisire vt. to acquire.

acquistare vt. to acquire; to buy; to obtain.

acquisto m. purchase; acquisition: potere d'—, buying power.

acquitrino m. marsh, swamp.

acquitrinoso adj. marshy.

acquolina f. drizzle: far venire l'— in bocca, to make one's mouth water.

acquoso adj. watery.

acre adj. acrid; sour; sharp.

acre'dine f. sourness; acrimony.

acrimo'nia f. acrimony.

acro m. acre.

acro'bata m. acrobat.

acroba'tico adj. acrobatic.

acrobatismo m. acrobatism.

acrobazi'a f. acrobatics, stunt.

acro'coro m. plateau.

acuire vt. to sharpen, whet.

acu'leo m. prickle; sting; quill; thorn; goad, spur.

acume m. acumen, keenness.

acuminare vt. to sharpen.

acuminato adj. pointed, sharp.

acu'stica f. acoustics.

acu'stico adj. acoustic: cornetto —, ear trumpet.

acutamente adv. acutely, sharply.

acutezza f. acuteness, sharpness.

acutizzare vt., **acutizzarsi** vr. to sharpen.

acuto m. high note. adj. acute, sharp; shrill; high-pitched.

ad see **a**.

adagiare vt. to lay, lower (to); **adagiarsi** vr. to lie down.

adagino adv. slowly, gently.

ada'gio m. adage. adv. slowly; softly.

adamantino adj. adamantine.

adami'tico adj. adamitic: in costume —, naked.

Adamo m. pr. Adam.

adatta'bile adj. adaptable.

adattabilità f. adaptableness.

adattamento m. adaptation: spirito d'—, compliance, adaptability.

adattare vt. to adapt, adjust; **adattarsi** vr. to fit, suit; to resign oneself.

adatto adj. fit, suitable, proper, expedient.

addebitare vt. to debit with, charge with.

adde'bito m. debit, charge.

addensamento m. thickening.

addensare vt. to thicken; **addensarsi** vr. to thicken; to crowd, surge.

addentare vt. to bite; (mach.) to mesh, to throw into gear.

addentellare vt. to indent.

addentrarsi vr. to penetrate, make one's way into.

addentro adv. inside.

addestramento m. training.

addestrare vt. to train.

addestratore m. trainer.

addetto m. attaché. adj. assigned, appointed

addi adv. on: — 30 Novembre, on the 30th of November.

addiac'cio m. bivouac; sheepfold.

addietro adv. ago, before; behind.

addi'o m. farewell. interj. good-bye.

addirittura adv. straightway, directly; absolutely, quite.

addirsi vr. to become, suit.

additare vt. to point at.

addivenire vi. to come to.

addizionale adj. additional.

addizionare vt. to add up.

addizione f. addition.

addobbamento m. decoration.

addobbare vt. to adorn, decorate, attire.

addobbatore m. decorator.

addobbo m. decoration; hanging.

addolcimento m. sweetening.

addolcire vt., **addolcirsi** vr. to sweeten; to calm down; to soften.

addolorare vt., **addolorarsi** vr. to grieve.

addolorato adj. grieved: l'Addolorata, Our Lady of Sorrows.

addome m. abdomen.

addomestica'bile adj. tamable.

addomesticamento m. taming.

addomesticare vt. to tame; to refine; to accustom.

addomesticato adj. tame; domesticated.

addominale adj. abdominal. [cated.

addormentare vt. to put to sleep; to benumb; to assuage; **addormentarsi** vr. to fall asleep, go to sleep.

addormentato adj. asleep; benumbed; stupid.

addossare vt. to lay (on), load with; to entrust; to impute; **addossarsi** vr. to take upon oneself; to lean (against).

addosso adv., prep. on, upon, against, near; about (oneself).

addotto adj. alleged; brought. pp. of **addurre**.

addottorare *vt.*, **addottorarsi** *vr.* to graduate.

addurre *vt.*[4] to allege; to bring.

adduttore *m.* (*anat.*) adductor.

adeguamento *m.* proportionment.

adeguare *vt.* to proportion; **adeguarsi** *vr.* to become adequate, adapt oneself.

adeguatamente *adv.* adequately.

adeguato *adj.* adequate, fit, fair.

adem'piere[51] *see* **adempire.**[53]

adempimento *m.* fulfillment; discharge.

adempire *vt.*[53] to accomplish; to fulfill; **adempirsi** *vr.* to come true.

adempiuto *adj.* fulfilled, *pp. of* **adempire.**

adeno'idi *f. pl.* (*med.*) adenoids.

adepto *m.* initiate; affiliate.

aderente *m.* supporter. *adj.* adherent; close-fitting.

aderenza *f.* adherence; (*med.*) adhesion; (*pl.*) connections, "pull."

aderire *vi.* to adhere; to accede (*to*).

adescamento *m.* enticement.

adescare *vt.* to bait, decoy, entice.

adesione *f.* adhesion.

adesivo *adj.* adhesive.

adesso *adv.* now, at present; nowadays: **per —**, for the moment.

adiacente *adj.* adjacent, adjoining.

adiacenze *f. pl.* neighborhood.

adianto *m.* (*bot.*) maidenhair.

adibire *vt.* to adhibit; to set apart; to appropriate; to use (*as, for*).

a'dipe *m.* fat.

adiposità *f.* fatness.

adiposo *adj.* adipose, fat.

adirarsi *vr.* to get angry.

adirato *adj.* angry, mad.

adire *vt.* to apply to (*court*): **— le vie legali**, to take legal steps, to sue.

a'dito *m.* entrance; cause.

adocchiare *vt.* to spot; to eye; to glimpse.

adolescente *m., f., adj.* adolescent.

adolescenza *f.* adolescence.

adombrare *vt.* to shadow; to conceal; to outline; **adombrarsi** *vr.* to bridle; to take umbrage.

Adone *m. pr.* Adonis.

adontarsi *vr.* to take offense.

adoperare, adoprare *vt.* to use, employ; **adoperarsi** *vr.* to endeavor (*to*), strive (*to*).

adora'bile *adj.* adorable, charming.

adorare *vt.* to worship, adore.

adorato *adj.* adored, beloved.

adoratore *m.* worshipper.

adorazione *f.* adoration, worship.

adornare *vt.* to adorn; **adornarsi** *vr.* to adorn oneself.

adorno *adj.* adorned, fine, lovely.

adottante *m.* adopter.

adottare *vt.* to adopt.

adottivo *adj.* adoptive; adopted.

adozione *f.* adoption.

Adria'tico *m., adj.* Adriatic.

adulare *vt.* to flatter, cajole.

adulatore *m.* flatterer.

adulato'rio *adj.* flattering.

adulazione *f.* flattery.

adul'tera *f.* adulteress.

adulterare *vt.* to adulterate.

adulterazione *f.* adulteration.

adulterino *adj.* adulterine.

adulte'rio *m.* adultery.

adul'tero *m.* adulterer. *adj.* adulterous.

adulto *m.* adult. *adj.* grown up.

adunanza *f.* meeting.

adunare *vt.* to assemble; **adunarsi** *vr.* to gather, meet.

adunata *f.* meeting, rally; (*mil.*) muster: **segnale d' —**, bugle call.

adunco *adj.* hooked, crooked.

adunghiare *vt.* to claw.

adusto *adj.* adust, tanned.

aerare *vt.* to air, ventilate.

aerato *adj.* aired, ventilated.

aerazione *f.* aeration, airing.

ae'reo *m.* aircraft; aerial. *adj.* aerial.

aerodina'mico *adj.* aerodynamic; streamlined.

aero'dromo *m.* airfield.

aero'grafo *m.* airbrush.

aerolito *m.* aerolite, aerolith.

aerologi'a *f.* aerology.

aerometri'a *f.* aerometry.

aero'metro *m.* aerometer.

aeromezzo *m.*, **aeromo'bile.** *m.* aircraft.

aeromodello *m.* model plane.

aerona'uta *m.* aeronaut.

aerona'utica *f.* aeronautics, aviation.

aerona'utico *adj.* aeronautic, flying.

aeronave *f.* airship.

aeroplano *m.* airplane.

aeroporto, aeroscalo *m.* airport.

aerorazzo *m.* rocket ship.

aerosilurante *m.* torpedo plane.

aerosta'tico *adj.* aerostatic.

aero'stato *m.* aerostat.

aerotaxi *m.* taxiplane.

aeroterapi'a *f.* aerotherapeutics.

afa *f.* sultriness.

affa'bile *adj.* affable, friendly.

affabilità *f.* affability, friendliness.

affaccendarsi *vr.* to bustle about; to busy oneself (*with*); to fuss.

affaccendato *adj.* busy.

affacciare *vt.* to present at a window; to allege: **— un dubbio**, to raise a doubt; **affacciarsi** *vr.* to show oneself at (*the window, etc.*); to lean out of; to look out (*of*); to look (*over*).

affamare *vt.* to starve.

affamato *m.* starveling. *adj.* starved; greedy, eager (*for*).

affamatore *m.* starver.

affannare *vt.* to worry, pester; **affannarsi** *vr.* to bustle; to fuss; to worry.

affannato *adj.* panting; uneasy.

affanno *m.* breathlessness; uneasiness; sorrow.

affannosamente *adv.* anxiously; pantingly; hurriedly.

affannoso *adj.* anxious; hurried; difficult.

affarac'cio *m.* mess.

affare *m.* business, bargain; affair; matter.

affarismo *m.* mercantilism.

affarista *m.* speculator.

affarone *m.* excellent bargain.

affascinante *adj.* charming.

affascinare *vt.* to charm.

affascinatore *m.*, **affascinatrice** *f.* bewitcher.

affastellare *vt.* to bundle; to heap up.

affaticare *vt.*, **affaticarsi** *vr.* to weary.

affaticato *adj.* weary, exhausted.

affatto *adv.* entirely, quite: niente —, by no means, not at all.

affatturare *vt.* to bewitch.

affermare *vt.* to assert; to affirm; **affermarsi** *vr.* to make a reputation; to prove oneself.

affermativa *f.* affirmative.

affermativamente *adv.* affirmatively.

affermativo *adj.* affirmative.

affermazione *f.* assertion, statement; success.

afferrare *vt.* to grasp; **afferrarsi** *vr.* to cling (*to*).

affettare *vt.* to slice; to affect.

affettatamente *adv.* affectedly.

affettato *adj.* sliced; affected.

affettazione *f.* affectation.

affettivo *adj.* affective.

affetto *m.* affection, love.

affetto *adj.* affected; afflicted (*with*), suffering (*from*).

affettuosamente *adv.* affectionately.

affettuosità *f.* affectionateness.

affettuoso *adj.* affectionate, loving: affettuosi saluti da, love from.

affezionarsi *vr.* to grow fond (*of*).

affezionato *adj.* fond (*of*), devoted.

affezione *f.* affection, love; devotion; disease.

affiancare *vt.* affiancarsi *vr.* to flank.

affiatamento *m.* harmony.

affiatarsi *vr.* to hit it off, get together.

affiatato *adj.* well-integrated.

affibbiare *vt.* to buckle, fasten; to shift (*on*); to deal.

affidamento *m.* confidence, trust; assurance; guaranty: dare —, to be reliable; fare — su, to trust; to rely upon.

affidare *vt.* to commit, entrust (*with*);

affidarsi *vr.* to trust (*to*), depend (*on*).

affievolire *vt.*, **affievolirsi** *vr.* to weaken.

affig'gere *vt.*[63] to affix, post up: — lo sguardo su, to stare at.

affilare *vt.* to whet, sharpen, strop; **affilarsi** *vr.* to thin.

affilata *f.* sharpening, whetting.

affilatura *f.* stropping.

affiliare *vt.*, **affiliarsi** *vr.* to affiliate.

affiliato *m.* affiliate.

affiliazione *f.* affiliation.

affinare *vt.*, **affinarsi** *vr.* to thin; to sharpen; to refine; to improve.

affinché *conj.* that, so that, in order that: — non, lest.

affine *m.* relative.

affinità *f.* kinship; affinity.

affiochire *vt.*, *vi.*; **affiochirsi** *vr.* to weaken, dim.

affioramento *m.* outcrop; emergence.

affiorare *vi.* to surface; to outcrop.

affissare *vt.* to fix; to affix.

affissione *f.* posting.

affisso *m.* poster, bill; frame (*of a door*); sash (*of a window*); (*gramm.*) affix; *adj.* fastened, affixed. *pp. of* affiggere.

affitta'bile *adj.* rentable.

affittaca'mere *m.*, *f.* landlord (*m.*), landlady (*f.*).

affittanza *f.* rent; lease.

affittare *vt.* (*dare in affitto*) to let; (*prendere in affitto*) to rent; to hire.

affitto *m.* lease; rent: dare in —, to let, hire out; prendere in —, to rent; to hire.

affittua'rio *m.* tenant, renter.

affiato *m.* breath; afflatus.

affliggente *adj.* grievous.

afflig'gere *vt.*[5] to afflict; **affliggersi** *vr.* to grieve (*over, for*).

afflitto *adj.* afflicted (*with*); grieved *pp. of* affliggere.

afflizione *f.* affliction, distress.

afflosciarsi *vr.* to sag; to slouch.

affloscire *vt.*, **affloscirsi** *vr.* to soften.

affluente *m.* affluent.

affluenza *f.* concourse, affluence.

affluire *vi.* to flock (*to*), flow (*to*); to pour (*in o*).

afflusso *m.* afflux; concourse.

affogamento *m.* drowning, smothering.

affogare *vt.* to drown, smother; to poach (*eggs*); *vi.* to drown.

affollamento *m.* crowding; crowd.

affollare *vt.*, **affollarsi** *vr.* to crowd, throng.

affondamento *m.* sinking.

affondare *vt.*, *vi.* to sink, submerge; (*naut.*) to drop anchor; **affondarsi** *vr.* to sink.

affondatore *m.* sinker.

afforcare *vi.*, **afforcarsi** *vr.* to moor with two anchors.

affossamento *m.* ditching.

affossare *vt.* to ditch, dig; **affossarsi** *vr.* to sink.

affrancare *vt.* to free, affranchise; to stamp; **affrancarsi** *vr.* to free oneself; to take heart.

affrancatura *f.* postage stamp.

affranto *adj.* weary, broken.

affratellamento *m.* fraternization.

affratellare *vt.*, **affratellarsi** *vr.* to fraternize; to unite, join.

affrescare *vt.* to paint a fresco.

affresco *m.* fresco (*pl.* frescoes).

affrettare *vt.*, **affrettarsi** *vr.* to hasten, hurry, speed.

affrettatamente *adv.* hastily.

affrettato *adj.* hasty, hurried.

affrontare *vt.* to face; **affrontarsi** *vr.* to meet; to come to blows.

affronto *m.* affront, insult.

affumicamento *m.* smoking; curing.

affumicare *vt.* to smoke, soot; to fumigate; to cure (*as meat, etc.*).

affusolare *vt.* to taper.

affusolato *adj.* tapering, slender.

affusto *m.* (*artill.*) carriage.

a'fono *adj.* aphonic; voiceless.

aforisma *m.* aphorism.

afoso *adj.* sultry.

africano *m.*, *adj.* African.

afrodis'iaco *adj.*, *m.* aphrodisiac.

afta *f.* aphta (*pl.* aphtae).

a'gape *f.* agape (*pl.* agapae).

a'gata *f.* agate.

agenda *f.* memorandum book.

agente *m.* agent, broker; detective, policeman.

agenzi'a *f.* agency, branch.

agevolare *vt.* to facilitate.

agevolazione *f.* facility.

age'vole *adj.* facile, easy.

agevolezza *f.* facileness.

agevolmente *adv.* easily.

agganciare *vt.* to hook, clasp; to fasten; (*rail.*) to couple.

aggeg'gio *m.* trifle; gadget; device.

aggettivo *adj.* adjective.

agghiacciare *vt.* to freeze, chill; (*fig.*) to horrify; **agghiacciarsi** *vr.* to freeze, be horrified.

agghindare *vt.* to array; **agghindarsi** *vr.* to array oneself, dress up.

ag'gio *m.* agio, premium.

aggiogare *vt.* to yoke.

aggiornamento *m.* adjournment; bringing up-to-date.

aggiornare *vt.* to adjourn; to bring up-to-date; **aggiornarsi** *vr.* to keep oneself posted, modernize.

aggiotag'gio *m.* dealings in exchange.

aggiramento *m.* cheat; (*mil.*) out-flanking.

aggirare *vt.* to cheat, swindle; (*mil.*) to outflank; **aggirarsi** *vr.* to rove, wander; to deal (*with*): il prezzo si aggira sulle mille lire, the price is about a thousand lire.

aggiudicare *vt.* to adjudge, award; **aggiudicarsi** *vr.* to win.

aggiun'gere *vt.* to add; **aggiungersi** *vr.* to join, be added.

aggiunta *f.* addition; eking piece.

aggiuntare *vt.* to join.

aggiuntivo *adj.* additional.

aggiunto *m.* assistant; (*gramm.*) epithet, adjective. *adj.* added. *pp.* of aggiungere.

aggiustare *vt.* to adjust, fit; to settle; to mend; **aggiustarsi** *vr.* to make oneself comfortable; to adapt oneself; to adorn oneself.

aggiustatore *m.* mender.

aggiustatura *f.* mending.

agglomerare *vt.*, **agglomerarsi** *vr.* to agglomerate.

agglomerato *m.* agglomerate. *adj.* agglomerated; thick.

agglomerazione *f.* agglomeration.

agglutinare *vt.*, **agglutinarsi** *vr.*, to agglutinate.

aggobbire *vt.* to become hunchbacked.

aggomitolare *vt.*, **aggomitolarsi** *vr.* to coil; to cuddle.

aggradare *vi.* to like: non mi aggrada, I don't like it.

aggraffare *vt.* to grab.

aggranchire *vt.* to benumb.

aggrapparsi *vr.* to cling (*to*).

aggravamento *m.* aggravation.

aggravante *f.* aggravating circumstance. *adj.* aggravating.

aggravare *vt.* to make worse; **aggravarsi** *vr.* to grow worse.

aggra'vio *m.* burden.

aggraziare *vt.* to embellish; **aggraziarsi** *vr.* to grow pretty; to ingratiate oneself (*with*).

aggraziato *adj.* graceful.

aggredire *vt.* to attack, assault.

aggregare *vt.* to aggregate; **aggregarsi** *vr.* to join.

aggressione *f.* aggression, assault.

aggressività *f.* aggressiveness.

aggressivo *adj.* aggressive.

aggressore *m.* aggressor, assaulter.

aggricciare *vt.*, **aggricciarsi** *vr.* to freeze; to stiffen.

aggrinzare *vt.*, **aggrinzarsi** *vr.* to wrinkle.

aggrottare *vt.* to contract, pucker; (*agr.*) to embank: — le sopracciglia, to frown.

aggrovigliare *vt.* to entangle; **aggrovigliarsi** *vr.* to get entangled.

aggrumare *vi.*, **aggrumarsi** *vr.* to clot, curdle.

aggruppare vt., **aggrupparsi** vr. to group, assemble.

agguagliare vt. to level, equalize; to compare.

agguantare vt. to catch.

agguato m. ambush.

agguerrire vt. to train, inure to war; **agguerrirsi** vr. to get trained; to set up defenses.

agiatamente adv. comfortably.

agiatezza f. prosperity, wealth: **nell'—**, on easy street.

agiato adj. well-off, well-to-do.

a'gile adj. agile, nimble.

agilità f. agility, nimbleness.

agilmente adv. agilely, nimbly.

a'gio m. ease, comfort; time: **non trovarsi a proprio —**, to be ill at ease.

agire vi. to act; to behave; to work.

agitare vt. to toss, agitate; to stir; to wave; **agitarsi** vr. to toss; to get excited; to agitate (for).

agitato adj. agitated, restless.

agitatore m. agitator.

agitazione f. agitation; disturbance; restlessness.

agli comp. prep. to the, see a prep.

aglia'ceo adj. garlicky.

a'glio m. garlic: **spicchio d' —**, clove [of garlic.

agnellino m. lambkin.

agnello m. lamb.

agnizione f. recognition.

agno'stico adj. agnostic.

ago m. needle; (rail.) point.

agognare vt. to covet.

agonali m. pl. agones.

agone m. agon; combat, fight.

agoni'a f. death struggle; agony, anguish: **in —**, at the point of death.

agoni'stico adj. agonistical.

agonizzante adj. dying.

agonizzare vi. to be dying.

agorafobi'a f. agoraphobia.

agora'io m. needlecase.

agosto m. August.

agra'ria f. agronomics.

agra'rio m. landowner. adj. agrarian.

agreste adj. agrestic, rural.

agretto adj. sourish.

agrezza f. sourness.

agri'colo adj. agricultural.

agricoltore m. farmer.

agricoltura f. agriculture.

agrifo'glio m. holly.

agrimensore m. land surveyor.

agrimensura f. land surveying.

agro (1) m. land, field.

agro (2) m. sourness. adj. sour.

agrodolce adj. bittersweet.

agronomi'a f. agronomy.

agro'nomo m. agronomist.

agrume m. citrus fruit.

agucchiare vi. to stitch.

agu'glia f. spire; magnetic needle.

aguzzare vt. to sharpen.

aguzzino m. jailer; slave driver; torturer.

aguzzo adj. sharp, acuminate.

ah! interj. ah!, aha!

ahi! interj. ouch!, oh!

ahimè! interj. alas!

ai comp. prep. to the, see a prep.

a'ia (1) f. yard; threshing floor: **menare il can per l'—**, to beat about the bush.

a'ia (2) f. governess.

Aia (L') f. The Hague.

a'io m. tutor, preceptor.

ai're m. swing, start; course.

airone m. heron.

aitante adj. sturdy, stalwart.

aiuola f. flower bed.

aiutante m. assistant: **— di campo**, aide-de-camp.

aiutare vt. to help; **aiutarsi** vr. to make shift; to help one another.

aiuto m. help, aid, assistance.

aizzare vt. to goad.

al comp. prep. to the, see a prep.

ala f. wing: **abbassare le ali**, to come down a peg.

alabarda f. halberd.

alabardiere m. halberdier.

alabastro m. alabaster.

a'lacre adj. alacritous; active.

alacrità f. alacrity.

alag'gio m. haulage, towage: **scalo d'—**, slip.

alamaro m. loop; gimp.

alambicco m. alembic.

alano m. boarhound, mastiff.

alare (1) m. andiron.

alare (2) vt. to haul, tow. [span.

alare (3) adj. wing: **apertura —**, wing

alato adj. winged; lofty.

alba f. dawn, daybreak.

albagi'a f. haughtiness, pride.

albanese m., adj. Albanian.

al'batro m. (bot.) arbutus; (ornith.) albatross.

albeggiamento m. dawning.

albeggiare vi. to dawn.

alberare vt. to plant trees; (naut.) to mast.

alberato adj. treed, tree-bordered.

alberatura f. trees; (naut.) masting.

albergare vt., vi. to lodge; to shelter.

albergatore m. hotelkeeper.

alberghiero adj. hotel: **industria alberghiera**, hotel trade.

albergo m. hotel.

al'bero m. tree; (mach.) shaft; (naut.) mast: **— genealogico**, family tree.

albicocca f. apricot.

albicocco m. apricot tree.

albina f. albiness.

albino m. albino. adj. whitish.

albo m. album.

albore m. dawn; whiteness; (pl.) beginning.

albume m. albumen.

albumina f. albumin.

al'cali m. alkali (pl. alkalies).

alcalino adj. alkaline.

alcalo'ide m. alkaloid.

alce f. (zool.) moose, elk.

alchimi'a f. alchemy.

alchimista m. alchemist.

alcione m. halcyon.

al'cole, alcool m. alcohol: — denaturato, methylated spirit.

alcoo'lico adj. alcoholic.

alcoolismo m. alcoholism.

alcoolizzato m. dipsomaniac.

alcova f. alcove.

alcunchè pron. anything.

alcuno adj. any, some, no. pron. anyone, someone, none, nobody, anything, a few, something, nothing.

a'lea f. chance, hazard, risk.

Aleardi, Aleardo, Italian poet and patriot (1812–1878).

aleato'rio adj. aleatory, precarious

aleggiare vi. to flutter; to linger; to hover.

alerone m. (aeron.) aileron.

alesag'gio m. reaming.

alesare vt. to bore, ream.

alesatrice f. reamer.

Alessan'dria d'Egitto f. Alexandria (Egypt).

aletta f. fin; lug.

alettone m. (aeron.) aileron.

alfa (1) f. alpha: dall'— all'omega, from A to Z.

alfa (2) f. (bot.) esparto grass.

alfabeticamente adv. alphabetically.

alfabe'tico adj. alphabetical.

alfabeto m. alphabet.

alfiere m. ensign, standard-bearer; bishop (at chess).

Alfieri, Vittorio, Italian dramatist (1749–1803).

alfine adv. in the end, finally, at last; after all.

alga f. (bot.) seaweed.

al'gebra f. algebra.

alge'brico adj. algebraical.

Algeri f. Algiers.

Algeri'a f. Algeria.

Algerino m., adj. Algerian.

aliante m. (aeron.) glider.

a'libi m. alibi.

alice f. anchovy.

aliena'bile adj. alienable.

alienabilità f. alienability.

alienare vt., alienarsi vr. to alienate.

alienato m. madman.

alienazione f. alienation, madness.

alienista m. alienist.

alieno adj. alien; loath, averse (to).

alimentare (1) adj. alimentary.

alimentare (2) vt. to feed; to fuel; to aliment; to keep up; alimentarsi vr. to feed (on).

alimentari m. pl. foodstuff.

alimenta'rio adj. alimentary: assegno —, alimony.

alimentatore m. feeder.

alimentazione f. feeding; diet.

alimento m. aliment, food; (pl.) alimony.

ali'nea m. section, paragraph.

ali'quota f. quota, share.

aliscafo m hydrofoil boat.

aliseo m. trade wind.

alitare vi. to breathe; to blow.

a'lito m. breath.

alla comp. prep. to the, see a prep.

allacciamento m. linking.

allacciare vt. to lace; to connect; to tie; to link.

allacciatura f. lacing, noose.

allagamento m. flood.

allagare vt. to flood.

allampanare vi. to thin.

allampanato adj. scraggy, thin.

allargamento m. broadening.

allargare vt. to broaden; to spread out; to open; allargarsi vr. to widen, spread.

allarmante adj. alarming, startling.

allarmare vt. to alarm; to startle; allarmarsi vr. to be alarmed; to worry.

allarme m. alarm, warning: cessato—, all clear.

allarmista m. alarmist.

allascare vt., vi. (naut.) to ease.

allato, a lato adv. beside; near.

allattamento m. nursing.

allattare vt. to nurse.

alle comp. prep. to the, see a prep.

alleanza f. alliance.

allearsi vr. to ally (oneself); to join forces.

alleato m. ally. adj. allied.

allegare (1) vt. to allege; to enclose.

allegare (2) vt. to set (teeth) on edge.

allegato m. enclosure.

alleggerimento m. lightening.

alleggerire vt. to lighten; to relieve, mitigate; alleggerirsi vr. to relieve oneself; to put on lighter clothes.

allegori'a f. allegory.

allego'rico adj. allegorical.

allegramente adv. cheerfully.

allegri'a f. merrymaking; cheerfulness, mirth.

allegro adj. cheerful, merry, gay.

allelu'ia m. halleluiah.

allenamento m. training.

allenare vt., allenarsi vr. to train, coach.

allenatore *m.* trainer, coach.

allentare *vt.*, allentarsi *vr.* to slacken, loosen.

allergi'a *f.* allergy.

aller'gico *adj.* allergic.

allessare *vt.* to boil.

allesso *m.* boiled meat. *adj.* boiled.

allestimento *m.* preparation; (*naut.*) fitting out; (*theat.*) production.

allestire *vt.* to set, prepare, get up; (*naut.*) to fit out; (*theat.*) to produce.

allettamento *m.* allurement.

allettante *adj.* alluring.

allettare *vt., vi.* to allure; to attract.

allevamento *m.* breeding; rearing.

allevare *vt.* to rear; to breed; to nurse; to bring up.

allevatore *m.* breeder.

alleviamento *m.* alleviation.

alleviare *vt.* to alleviate.

allibire *vi.* to startle, be astonished.

allietare *vt.* to cheer; allietarsi *vr.* to cheer up, rejoice.

allievo *m.* pupil, disciple: — ufficiale, cadet.

alligatore *m.* alligator.

allignare *vi.* to live; to flourish.

allineamento *m.* alignment.

allineare *vt.*, allinearsi *vr.* to align, range, dress.

allitterazione *f.* alliteration.

allo *comp. prep.* to the, *see* a *prep.*

allocco *m.* owl; simpleton, fool.

allocuzione *f.* address.

allo'dio *m.* allodium.

allo'dola *f.* skylark.

allogare *vt.* to settle; to rent; to marry.

allo'geno *m., adj.* alien.

alloggiamento *m.* lodging, quarters.

alloggiare *vt.* to put up; *vi.* to lodge, stay, live.

allog'gio *m.* lodging, quarters.

allontanamento *m.* removal; dismissal; swerving.

allontanare *vt.* to remove; to send away, dismiss; to estrange; allontanarsi *vr.* to get away, leave; to swerve.

allora *adv.* then, at that time, in that case: — —, just then; di qui —, by that time; fino —, up to then; e —? well?, what then?

allorchè *adv.* when.

alloro *m.* (*bot.*) laurel.

allorquando *adv.* when.

al'luce *m.* hallux, great toe.

allucinare *vt.* to hallucinate; to dazzle.

allucinazione *f.* hallucination.

allu'dere *vi.*[6] to hint (*at*), allude (*to*).

allume *m.* alum.

allumina *f.* alumina.

allumi'nio *m.* aluminum.

allungamento *m.* lengthening.

allungare *vt.* to lengthen; to hand; to dilute: — la mano, to reach; — le braccia, to stretch one's arms; allungarsi *vr.* to lengthen, stretch oneself out; to grow tall.

allungatura *f.* lengthening; eking piece.

allusione *f.* allusion, hint.

allusivo *adj.* allusive.

alluso *pp. of* alludere.

alluvionale *adj.* alluvial.

alluvione *f.* alluvion, flood.

almanaccare *vi.* to fancy, muse.

almanacco *m.* almanac.

almeno *conj.* at least.

alno *m.* (*bot.*) alder.

a'loe *m.* aloe.

alone *m.* halo.

al'paca *f.* alpaca.

alpacca *f.* Britannia metal.

alpe *f.* alp; (*pl.*) le Alpi, the Alps mountains.

alpestre *adj.* alpine.

alpigiano *m.* mountaineer.

alpinismo *m.* alpinism, mountaineering.

alpinista *m.* alpinist, mountaineer.

alpino *adj.* alpine.

alquanto *adj.* some; (*pl.*) several. *adv.* somewhat, to some extent; rather; a little. *pron.* some; (*pl.*) a good many.

alsaziano *m., adj.* Alsatian.

alt *interj.* halt.

altalena *f.* swing; seesaw; alternation.

altalenare *vi.* to seesaw, swing.

altamente *adv.* highly; greatly.

altana *f.* belvedere.

altare *m.* altar.

altarini *m. pl. in the phrase:* scoprire gli —, to let the cat out of the bag.

altea *f.* (*bot.*) althea.

altera'bile *adj.* alterable.

alterabilità *f.* alterableness.

alteramente *adv.* haughtily.

alterare *vt.* to alter; to forge; to distort, misrepresent; alterarsi *vr.* to alter, get angry.

alterato *adj.* altered; forged; drunk.

alterazione *f.* alteration; anger.

altercare *vi.* to quarrel.

alterco *m.* quarrel, fight.

alteri'gia *f.* haughtiness.

alternamente *adv.* alternately.

alternare *vt.*, alternarsi *vr.* to alternate.

alternativa *f.* alternation; alternative.

alternato *adj.* alternate: corrente alternata, alternating current.

alternatore *m.* alternator.

alternazione *f.* alternation.

alterno *adj.* alternate, reciprocal.

altero *adj.* proud, dignified.

altezza *f.* height; width; depth; highness; loftiness.

altezzoso *adj.* haughty.
altic'cio *adj.* tipsy.
altimetri'a *f.* altimetry.
alti'metro *m.* altimeter.
altipiano *m.* plateau.
altisonante *adj.* high-sounding.
altis'simo *adj. sup.* very high: l'Altissimo, the Most High.
altitu'dine *f.* altitude.
alto *m.* height, top: gli alti e bassi della vita, the ups and downs of life; guardare qualcuno dall'—, to look down on someone. *adj.* high, tall; loud, deep: la Camera Alta, the Upper House; l'Alta Italia, Northern Italy. *adv.* high; aloud.
altolocato *adj.* lofty: un uomo —, a bigwig.
altoparlante *m.* loudspeaker.
altresì *adv.* also, too; further.
altrettanto *adj., pron.* as much; (*pl.*) as many; so much; (*pl.*) so many. *adv.* as much, so much; equally, the same.
altri *pron. sing.* another person, somebody else.
altrieri (l') *m., adv.* the day before yesterday.
altrimenti *adv.* otherwise, else.
altro *adj.* other, another, else; more; next; further; previous: dell'—vino, some more wine; quest'altra settimana, next week. *pron. indef.* other, another, else, more: un giorno o l'—, some day or other; non te ne posso dare dell'—, I can't give you any more; l'uno e l'—, both; nè l'uno nè l'—, neither; l'uno o l'—, either; l'un l'—, each other; fra l'—, among other things, by the way; senz'altro!, certainly!; tutt'altro!, on the contrary!
altronde, *see* d'altronde.
altrove *adv.* elsewhere.
altrui *pron. indef. sing.* another's (*pl.*) other people's.
altruismo *m.* unselfishness, altruism.
altruista *adj.* unselfish.
altruistico *adj.* altruistic.
altura *f.* mound, height.
alunno *m.*, **alunna** *f.* pupil.
alveare *m.* hive, beehive.
al'veo *m.* bed, river bed.
alve'olo *m.* alveolus (*pl.* alveoli).
alza'ia *f.* hawser; towpath.
alzare *vt.* to raise, lift; to heave, hoist: — le spalle, to shrug; — il gomito, to drink too much; — le carte, to cut cards; alzarsi *vr.* to rise, get up; to lift.
alzata *f.* raising, lifting: — di terra, embankment; — d'ingegno, brainstorm.
alzato *adj.* risen; raised; up.

ama'bile *adj.* amiable; sweetish.
amabilità *f.* amiability.
amabilmente *adv.* amiably.
amaca *f.* hammock.
amal'gama *m.* amalgam; mixture, blend.
amalgamare *vt.* to amalgamate, blend.
amalgamazione *f.* amalgamation.
amante *m.* lover; *f.* mistress; *adj.* fond.
amanuense *m.* clerk.
amaramente *adv.* bitterly.
amaranto *m.* amaranth.
amarasca *f.* morello.
amare *vt., vi.* to love; to be in love (with); to like, be fond of: amarsi reciprocamente, to love each other.
amareggiare *vt.* to embitter, grieve; amareggiarsi *vr.* to fret, worry, grieve.
amarena *f.* amarelle.
amarezza *f.* bitterness.
amarilli *f.* (*bot.*) amaryllis.
amaro *m.* bitter; bitters. *adj.* bitter.
amaro'gnolo *adj.* bitterish.
amarra *f.* (*naut.*) hawser.
amarrare *vi.* to moor.
amato *m.* **amata** *f.* sweetheart. *adj.* beloved.
amatore *m.* lover; amateur.
amaz'zone *f.* horsewoman; (*myth.*) Amazon.
amba'scia *f.* pant; sorrow.
ambasciata *f.* embassy; errand, message.
ambasciatore *m.* ambassador.
ambasciatrice *f.* ambassadress.
ambedue *adj., pron.* both.
ambidestro *m., adj.* ambidexter.
ambientare *vt.* to accustom; ambientarsi *vr.* to get accustomed.
ambiente *m.* ambient air; sphere; surroundings, environment; room.
ambiguità *f.* ambiguity.
ambiguo *adj.* ambiguous.
am'bio *m.* amble.
ambire *vt.* to covet; *vi.* to aspire (to, after).
am'bito *m.* sphere; bounds.
ambizione *f.* ambition.
ambizioso *adj.* ambitious.
ambo *adj., pron.* both.
ambra *f.* amber.
ambrare *vt.* to amber.
ambrato *adj.* amber.
ambulacro *m.* lobby.
ambulante *adj.* itinerant: venditore —, peddler.
ambulanza *f.* ambulance; first-aid station; (*mil.*) field hospital.
ambulare *vi.* to ambulate.
ambulato'rio *m.* ambulatory; dispensary.
ameba *f.* amoeba.

amenità *f.* amenity, pleasantness; pleasantry.

ameno *adj.* pleasant; jocular.

americano *m., adj.* American.

americanismo *m.* Americanism.

americanizzare *vt.* to Americanize.

ametista *f.* amethyst.

amianto *m.* asbestos.

amica *f.* friend, lady friend, girl friend.

amichevole *adj.* friendly.

Amicis, Edmondo de, Italian traveler and writer, *Cuore* (1846–1908).

amici'zia *f.* friendship: stringere —, to make friends.

amico *m.* friend. *adj.* friendly.

amicone *m.* chum, pal, crony.

amida'ceo *adj.* starchy.

a'mido *m.* starch.

ammaccare *vt.* to bruise, contuse; to batter.

ammaccatura *f.* bruise.

ammaestramento *m.* instruction, teaching, training; lesson.

ammaestrare *vt.* to instruct, teach, train, coach.

ammainare *vt.* to lower.

ammalarsi *vr.* to fall ill.

ammalato *m.* patient, invalid. *adj.* ill, sick.

ammaliare *vt.* to bewitch.

ammaliatore *m.* enchanter. ammaliatrice, *f.* enchantress.

ammanco *m.* leakage, deficit.

ammanettare *vt.* to handcuff.

ammannire *vt.* to dish up.

ammansire *vt.* to tame; to appease; to mollify; ammansirsi *vr.* to become tamed; to sober.

ammantare *vt.* to cloak; ammantarsi *vr.* to mantle oneself, wrap oneself up (*in*).

ammarare *vi.* to alight.

ammassare *vt.* to amass, pile up; ammassarsi *vr.* to gather, pile up.

ammasso *m.* heap, pile, stack.

ammattimento *m.* nuisance.

ammattire *vi.* to go mad: far —, to drive mad.

ammattonato *m.* tile floor.

ammazzare *vt.* to kill; to murder; ammazzarsi *vr.* to commit suicide; to be killed.

ammazzasette *m.* swashbuckler.

ammazzato'io *m.* shambles.

ammenda *f.* amends (*pl.*); fine.

ammenni'colo *m.* adminicle; artifice; quibble; gewgaw.

ammesso *pp. of* ammettere admitted; allowed: — che, supposing that.

ammet'tere *vt.*[76] to admit; to let in; to allow; to acknowledge.

ammezzato *m.* mezzanine.

ammiccare *vi.* to wink.

amministrare *vt.* to handle, manage, administer.

amministrativo *adj.* administrative.

amministratore *m.* manager, administrator; director: — delegato, managing director.

amministrazione *f.* management, administration: cattiva —, mismanagement; consiglio d'—, board of directors.

ammiragliato *m.* admiralty.

ammira'glio *m.* admiral.

ammirare *vt.* to admire.

ammiratore *m.*, ammiratrice *f.* admirer; suitor, wooer; fan.

ammirazione *f.* admiration.

ammissi'bile *adj.* permissible.

ammissione *f.* admission.

ammobiliare *vt.* to furnish.

ammodo *adj.* mannerly, respectable, nice. *adv.* properly.

ammogliarsi *vr.* to get married (*of a man*).

ammogliato *adj.* married (*of a man*).

ammollire *vt.*, ammollirsi *vr.* to soften; to weaken.

ammoni'aca *f.* ammonia.

ammoniacale *adj.* ammoniacal.

ammonimento *m.* warning.

ammo'nio *m.* ammonium.

ammonire *vt.* to warn, admonish.

ammonizione *f.* warning.

ammontare *m.* amount, sum. *vi.* to amount.

ammonticchiare *vt.* to heap.

ammorbare *vt.* to taint.   [soften.

ammorbidire *vt.*, ammorbidirsi *vr.* to

ammortamento *m.* amortization: fondo d'—, sinking fund.

ammortizzare *vt.* to amortize.

ammortizzatore *m.* shock absorber.

ammosciare *vi.*, ammosciarsi *vr.* to sag; to get flabby.

ammucchiare *vt.*, ammucchiarsi *vr.* to heap up.

ammuffire *vi.* to mold.

ammutinamento *m.* mutiny.

ammutinare *vt.* to stir up; ammutinarsi *vr.* to mutiny.

ammutinato *m.* mutineer.

ammutolire *vt.* to strike dumb. *vi.* to become dumb; to be dumbfounded.

amnesi'a *f.* amnesia.

amnisti'a *f.* amnesty.

amnistiare *vt.* to grant amnesty to.

amo *m.* hook: abboccare l'—, to take the bait.

amorale *adj.* amoral, unmoral.

amoralità *f.* amorality.

amore *m.* love, fondness, sake: un — di bambino, a charming baby; per — o per forza, by hook or by crook.

amoreggiare *vi.* to flirt.

amore'vole *adj.* loving, affectionate.

amorfo *adj.* amorphous.

amorosa *f.* sweetheart; actress playing lover's part.

amoroso *m.* sweetheart; actor playing lover's part. *adj.* loving.

amperag'gio *m.* amperage.

ampero'metro *m.* ammeter.

ampiamente *adv.* widely.

ampiezza *f.* wideness, width, ampleness.

am'pio *adj.* wide, ample; roomy.

amplesso *m.* embrace, hug.

ampliamento *m.* amplification.

ampliare *vt.*, **ampliarsi** *vr.* to widen; to increase.

amplificare *vt.* to amplify, extend; to exaggerate.

amplificatore *m.* amplifier; exaggerator.

amplificazione *f.* amplification.

ampolla *f.* cruet; ampulla.

ampolliera *f.* cruet stand.

ampollosamente *adv.* pompously.

ampollosità *f.* pompousness.

ampolloso *adj.* turgid; pompous.

amputare *vt.* to amputate.

amputazione *f.* amputation.

amuleto *m.* amulet.

a'nace *m.* anise; aniseed.

anacoreta *m.* anchorite, hermit.

anacronismo *m.* anachronism.

ana'grafe *f.* register of births, deaths and marriages, Hall of Records.

anagramma *m.* anagram.

analco'lico *adj.* nonalcoholic: **bevande analcoliche**, soft drinks.

anale *adj.* anal.

analfabeta *m.*, *adj.* illiterate.

analfabetismo *m.* illiteracy.

analge'sico *m.*, *adj.* analgesic.

ana'lisi *f.* test; analysis (*pl.* analyses): **— grammaticale**, parsing; **— del sangue**, blood test.

anali'tico *adj.* analytical.

analizzare *vt.* to analyze, test.

analogi'a *f.* analogy.

ana'logo *adj.* analogous.

ananasso *m.* pineapple.

anarchi'a *f.* anarchy; anarchism.

anar'chico *m.* anarchist. *adj.* anarchical.

anastigma'tico *adj.* anastigmatic.

anasto'mosi *f.* anastomosis.

anatema *m.* anathema, curse.

anatomi'a *f.* anatomy.

anato'mico *adj.* anatomical.

a'natra *f.* duck; drake.

anatroc'colo *m.* duckling.

anca *f.* hip, haunch.

ancella *f.* maid, maidservant.

anche *adv.*, *conj.* also, too, even.

anchilosato *adj.* ankylosed.

anchilosi *f.* ankylosis.

an'cora *f.* anchor.

ancora *adv.* again; still; more; longer; even: **— meglio**, still better; **— no, non —**, not yet; **ne vuoi —?**, do you wish any more?.

ancorag'gio *m.* anchorage.

ancorare *vt.*, **ancorarsi** *vr.* to anchor.

ancorchè *conj.* though.

ancorotto *m.* grapnel, kedge.

andamento *m.* course, bent, trend.

andante *m.* (*mus.*) andante. *adj.* cheap.

andare *m.* going; gait: **a lungo —**, in the long run.

andare *vi.* to go; to run, work; to sell; to like; to have to: **ciò andava fatto**, it had to be done; **questo mi va**, I like this; **ne va del nostro onore**, our honor is at stake; **— a male**, to deteriorate; **andarsene**, to go away.

andata *f.* going; departure: **biglietto d'—**, single ticket; **biglietto d'— e ritorno**, return ticket.

andato *adj.*, *pp.* gone: **il tempo —**, the past. *pp.* of **andare**.

andatura *f.* gait; pace, speed.

andazzo *m.* practice, trend (of things).

andirivieni *m.* coming and going; bustle.

an'dito *m.* passage; hall.

androne *m.* lobby.

aned'doto *m.* anecdote.

anelare *vt.*, *vi.* to pant; to yearn (*for*).

ane'lito *m.* breath; panting; yearning.

anellino *m.* ringlet.

anello *m.* ring; curl; link; bow (*of a key*); loop (*of rope, etc.*).

anemi'a *f.* anemia.

ane'mico *adj.* anemic.

anemo'metro *m.* anemometer.

ane'mone *m.* anemone.

anestesi'a *f.* anesthesia.

aneste'tico *m.*, *adj.* anesthetic.

anestetizzare *vt.* to anesthetize.

aneurisma *m.* aneurysm.

anfi'bio *m.*, *adj.* amphibious, amphibian.

anfiteatro *m.* amphitheater.

an'fora *f.* amphora.

anfratto *m.* anfractuosity.

angariare *vt.* to vex.

ange'lico *adj.* angelical.

Angelico, Fra (*Giovanni da Fiesole*), Italian painter (1387-1455).

an'gelo *m.* angel: **— custode**, guardian angel.

angheri'a *f.* vexation.

angina *f.* angina.

angioino *m.*, *adj.* Angevin.

angiporto *m.* blind alley.

anglicano *m.*, *adj.* Anglican.

anglicismo *m.* Anglicism.

anglicizzare *vt.* to Anglicize.

anglosas'sone *m.*, *adj.* Anglo-Saxon.

angolare *adj.* angular, corner.

an'golo *m.* corner; angle; nook.
angoloso *adj.* angular.
an'gora *f.* mohair (*wool*).
ango'scia *f.* anguish, distress.
angosciare *vt.* to distress.
angoscioso *adj.* painful, distressing: **sogno —**, nightmare.
anguilla *f.* eel.
anguina'ia *f.* (*anat.*) groin.
angu'ria *f.* watermelon.
angu'stia *f.* narrowness; distress, misery: **angustie pecuniarie,** financial straits.
angustiare *vt.*, **angustiarsi** *vr.* to worry.
angusto *adj.* narrow.
a'nice *m.* anise; aniseed.
anidride *f.* anhydride: **— carbonica,** carbon dioxide.
anilina *f.* aniline.
a'nima *f.* soul, spirit, mind, being, essence; core, pith; mold (*of a button*); stock (*of a gun*); shaft (*of a column*); sounding board (*of a violin*): **con tutta l'—,** wholeheartedly; **un paese di mille anime,** a village with one thousand inhabitants.
animale *m.*, *adj.* animal.
animalesco *adj.* bestial.
animare *vt.* to animate, enliven; **animarsi** *vr.* to become lively; to take courage; to warm up.
animato *adj.* lively, spirited; animated.
animatore *m.* animator. *adj.* animating.
animazione *f.* animation, excitement, liveliness.
animella *f.* sweetbread.
a'nimo *m.* mind; heart; courage; **grandezza d'—,** magnanimity; **stato d'—,** frame of mind, mood; **avere in — di,** to have a mind to; **perdersi d'—,** to lose courage.
animosamente *adv.* boldly; hostilely.
animosità *f.* animosity; hatred.
animoso *adj.* bold, brave.
anisetta *f.* anisette.
anna *f.* (*coin*) anna.
annacquare *vt.* to water; to dilute.
annaffiare *vt.* to water, sprinkle.
anna fiato'io *m.* sprinkler.
annali *m. pl.* annals.
annaspare *vt.* to reel. *vi.* to grope; to flounder.
annata *f.* a year's time; crop; vintage.
annebbiare *vt.* to befog; to dim; **annebbiarsi** *vr.* to grow foggy; to dim; to blur.
annegamento *m.* drowning.
annegare *vt.* to drown. *vi.* to be drowned; **annegarsi,** *vr.* to drown oneself.

annerimento *m.* blackening.
annerire *vt.*, **annerirsi** *vr.* to blacken; to tarnish.
annessione *f.* annexation.
annesso *m.* annex. *adj.* annexed. *pp.* of **annettere**.
annet'tere *vt.*[8] to annex: **— importanza,** to attach significance.
annichilire *vt.* to annihilate.
annidarsi *vr.* to nestle; to hide, burrow.
annientamento *m.* annihilation.
annientare *vt.* to annihilate.
anniversario *m.*, *adj.* anniversary.
anno *m.* year: **— bisestile,** leap year.
annodare *vt.*, **annodarsi** *vr.* to knot.
annoiare *vt.* to bore, weary; **annoiarsi** *vr.* to become bored, weary.
annona *f.* provisions.
annona'rio *adj.* relating to provisions: **carta annonaria,** ration card.
annoso *adj.* old.
annotare *vt.* to annotate; to note, jot down, scribble.
annotazione *f.* annotation, note.
annoverare *vt.* to count, number, comprise.
annuale *m.* anniversary. *adj.* yearly.
annualità *f.* annuity.
annualmente *adv.* yearly.
annua'rio *m.* yearbook; directory.
annuire *vi.* to nod, assent.
annullamento *m.* annulment.
annullare *vt.* to cancel, annul; to void.
annunciare, annunziare *vt.* to announce; to advertise; to foretell.
annunziatore *m.*, **annunziatrice** *f.* announcer; speaker.
annunziazione *f.* Annunciation.
annun'zio *m.* announcement; omen; advertisement.
Annunzio, Gabriele d' (1864–1938), Italian novelist, dramatist, and poet. Leader of Fiume expedition of 1919–20.
annusare *vt.* to smell, sniff.
annuvolamento *m.* cloudiness.
annuvolare *vt.*, **annuvolarsi** *vr.* cloud, overcast.
ano *m.* anus.
anodino *m.*, *adj.* anodyne; inane.
a'nodo *m.* anode.
anomali'a *f.* anomaly.
ano'malo *adj.* anomalous.
ano'nimo *m.* anonym. *adj.* anonymous: **società anonima,** joint-stock company, corporation.
anormale *adj.* abnormal.
anormalità *f.* abnormality.
ansante *adj.* panting.
ansare *vi.* to pant.
ansia, ansietà *f.* anxiety.

ansimare *vi.* to pant.
ansiosamente *adv.* anxiously.
ansioso *adj.* anxious; uneasy; eager.
antagonismo *m.* antagonism.
antagonista *m.* antagonist, opponent.
antar'tico *m.*, *adj.* antarctic.
antecedente *adj.* antecedent.
antecedenza *f.* antecedence.
antece'dere *vi.* to precede.
antefatto *m.* background, antecedents.
anteguerra *m.* prewar time.
antelucano *adj.* antelucan, before the dawn.
antenato *m.* ancestor.
antenna *f.* (*naut.*) sailyard; (*zool.*) antenna (*pl.* antennae); (*radio*) aerial.
anteporre *vt.* to put before.
anteprima *f.* preview.
anteriore *adj.* earlier; fore, front.
antesignano *m.* forerunner.
antiabbaglianti *m. pl.* (*auto.*) dimmers.
antia'cido *m.*, *adj.* antacid.
antiae'reo *adj.* antiaircraft.
antica'glia *f.* trash, junk.
anticamente *adv.* anciently.
antica'mera *f.* hall, waiting room.
antichità *f.* antiquity; ancient times; antique.
anticiclone *m.* anticyclone.
anticipare *vt.* to anticipate; to advance; to forestall; to hasten.
anticipatamente *adv.* in advance.
anticipazione *f.* advance.
anti'cipo *m.* advance.
antico *adj.* ancient, old; obsolete.
anticristiano *adj.* antichristian.
anticristo *m.* antichrist.
antidiluviano *adj.* antediluvian.
anti'doto *m.* antidote.
anti'fona *f.* antiphon; reprimand: **capire l'—**, to take the hint.
anti'lope *f.* antelope.
antimeridiano *adj.* antemeridian, A. M.
antimilitarismo *m.* antimilitarism.
antimo'nio *m.* antimony.
antinazionale *adj.* antinational.
antincendi *adj.* firefighting: **servizio —**, fire department.
antipasto *m.* hors d'oeuvre.
antipati'a *f.* dislike, antipathy.
antipa'tico *adj.* disagreeable: **egli mi è —**, I don't like him.
antipatriot'tico *adj.* antipatriotic.
anti'podi *m. pl.* antipodes.
antiqua'rio *m.*, *adj.* antique dealer.
antiquato *adj.* old-fashioned, out-antirab'bico *adj.* antirabic. [moded.
antireligioso *adj.* irreligious.
antisala *f.* anteroom.
antisemita *m.* anti-Semite.
antisemitismo *m.* anti-Semitism.
antiset'tico *adj.* antiseptic.
antisociale *adj.* antisocial.

anti'tesi *f.* antithesis (*pl.* antitheses).
antite'tico *adj.* antithetical.
antitossina *f.* antitoxin.
antivigi'lia *f.* the day before the eve.
antologi'a *f.* anthology.
antonoma'sia *f.* antonomasia: **per —**, par excellence.
antracite *f.* anthracite.
antro *m.* den; (*anat.*) antrum.
antropofagi'a *f.* cannibalism.
antropo'fago *m.* cannibal.
antropo'ide *m.*, *adj.* anthropoid.
antropologi'a *f.* anthropology.
antropo'logo *m.* anthropologist.
anulare *m.* ring finger. *adj.* annular.
anzi *adv.*, *conj.* on the contrary; nay; actually; even: **— che**, rather than; **— che no**, rather. *prep.* before.
anzianità *f.* seniority.
anziano *adj.* senior; old, aged.
anzianotto *adj.* elderly.
anzichè *conj.* rather than; instead of.
anzidetto *adj.* afore-mentioned.
anzitutto *adv.* first of all.
aorta *f.* aorta.
apati'a *f.* apathy, indifference.
apa'tico *adj.* apathetic.
ape *f.* bee: **— operaia**, worker.
aperitivo *m.* aperitif.
apertamente *adv.* openly.
aperto *adj.* open; unlocked; broad. *pp. of* aprire.
apertura *f.* opening; hole; (*arch.*) span: **— d'ali**, wingspread.
a'pice *m.* apex, vertex; summit; climax; height.
apicultore *m.* apiarist.
apicultura *f.* apiculture.
Apocalisse *f.* Apocalypse.
apocalit'tico *adj.* Apocalyptical.
apo'crifo *adj.* apochryphal.
apo'fisi *f.* apophysis.
apoge'o *m.* apogee; top.
apoli'tico *adj.* non-party.
apolli'neo *adj.* apollonian.
apologe'tico *adj.* eulogistic.
apologi'a *f.* eulogy, apology.
apo'logo *m.* apologue.
apoplessi'a *f.* apoplexy.
apoplet'tico *adj.* apoplectic.
apostasi'a *f.* apostasy.
apo'stata *m.* apostate.
apostolato *m.* apostolate.
aposto'lico *adj.* apostolical.
apo'stolo *m.* apostle.
apostrofare *vt.*, *vi.* to apostrophize; to address.
apo'strofe *f.* apostrophe.
apo'strofo *m.* apostrophe.
apotema *m.* (*geom.*) apothegm.
apoteosi *f.* apotheosis.
appagare *vt.* to satisfy, gratify; to please; **appagarsi** *vr.* to be content (*with*).

appaiare *vt.*, appaiarsi *vr.* to couple, match.

appallottolare *vt.* to make a ball, pellet; appallottolarsi *vr.* to clot, ball; to roll oneself up.

appaltare *vt.* to contract.

appaltatore *m.* contractor.

appalto *m.* bid, contract.

appannag'gio *m.* appanage.

appannamento *m.* tarnishing; blurring.

appannare *vt.*, appannarsi *vr.* to blur, to steam up.

apparato *m.* decoration, display; (*mach.*) apparatus: — scenico, scenery.

apparecchiare *vt.* to prepare, dress: — la tavola, to lay the table.

apparecchiatura *f.* apparatus.

apparec'chio *m.* apparatus, instrument, set; (*aeron.*) airplane.

apparente *adj.* apparent, seeming.

apparentemente *adv.* seemingly; outwardly.

apparenza *f.* appearance; aspect.

apparire *vi.*⁶ to appear; to seem, look.

appariscente *adj.* showy, flashy.

appariscenza *f.* showiness.

apparizione *f.* apparition.

apparso *pp. of* apparire.

appartamento *m.* apartment, suite.

appartarsi *vr.* to seclude oneself; to withdraw.

appartato *adj.* secluded, lonely.

appartenenza *f.* belonging; membership.

appartenere *vi.*¹⁴¹ to belong; to be a member of.

appartenuto *pp. of* appartenere.

appassionare *vt.* to impassion; to grip; appassionarsi *vr.* to be, grow fond (*of*), take a warm interest (*in*).

appassionatamente *adv.* passionately.

appassionato *m.* amateur; fan. *adj.* passionate; fond (*of*).

appassire *vt.*, *vi.* to dry; appassirsi *vr.* to wither, fade.

appassito *adj.* withered, faded.

appellante *m.* appellant.

appellare *vt.*, *vi.* to name; appellarsi *vr.* to appeal.

appellativo *m.*, *adj.* appellative.

appello *m.* appeal; roll call; call: ricorrere in —, to appeal; fare l'—, to call the roll; fare — a, to appeal to.

appena *adv.*, *conj.* hardly, scarcely; as soon as; just; just ... when, no sooner ... than: non — sarò arrivato, as soon as I arrive; avevo — finito, I had just finished; lo aveva — visto che sparò, he had just seen him when he fired.

appen'dere *vt.*¹⁰ to hang (*up*).

appendice *f.* appendix (*pl. also* appendices): romanzo d'—, serial.

appendicite *f.* appendicitis.

appesantire *vt.* to weigh, burden, overload; appesantirsi *vr.* to grow heavy; to don warmer clothing.

appeso *pp. of* appendere; hung (*up*).

appestare *vt.*, *vi.* to infect, taint; to stink.

appeti'bile *adj.* appetible; desirable.

appetibilità *f.* desirableness.

appetire *vt.* to crave for; *vi.* to be appetizing.

appetito *m.* appetite.

appetitoso *adj.* appetizing.

appetto *prep.* in front (*of*).

appezzamento *m.* plot, lot.

appianare *vt.* to smooth, level; to settle.

appianato'io *m.* roller.

appiattare *vt.*, appiattarsi *vr.* to hide.

appiattire *vt.*, appiattirsi *vr.* to flatten.

appiccare *vt.* to hang up; to hang: — fuoco a, to set on fire; appiccarsi *vr.* to hang oneself; to spread.

appiccatic'cio *adj.* sticky.

appiccicare *vt.* to stick; (*fig.*) to saddle (*with*). *vi.* to be sticky; appiccicarsi *vr.* to stick (*to*).

appiccicatic'cio *adj.* sticky.

appicco *m.* pretext, quibble.

appiè, a piè (di), *prep.* at the foot of: nota — di pagina, footnote.

appiedare *vt.* to dismount.

appieno *adv.* fully.

appigionare *vt.* to let.

appigliarsi *vr.* to cling (*to*).

appi'glio *m.* pretext; opportunity.

appiombo *m.*, *adv.* plumb.

appioppare *vt.* to strike, deal; to palm (*off on*).

appisolarsi *vr.* to doze off.

applaudire *vt.*, *vi.* to applaud.

appla'uso *m.* applause; cheer.

applica'bile *adj.* appliable.

applicabilità *f.* appliableness.

applicare *vt.* to apply; applicarsi *vr.* to apply oneself, devote oneself.

applicato *m.* clerk.

applicazione *f.* application.

appoggiare *vt.* to lay, lean, rest; to support; appoggiarsi *vr.* to lean; (*fig.*) to rely upon.

appoggiato'io *m.* rest, support.

appog'gio *m.* support, prop.

appollaiarsi *vr.* to perch.

apporre *vt.*⁹³ to affix, put.

apportare *vt.* to bring.

apportatore *m.* apportatrice *f.* bearer.

apporto *m.* contribution.

appositamente *see* apposta.

appo'sito *adj.* apposite, proper.

apposizione *f.* apposition.

apposta *adv.* expressly; on purpose; deliberately.

appostamento *m.* ambush.
appostarsi *vr.* to lie in ambush.
appren'dere *vt.*[96] to learn.
apprendista *m.* apprentice.
apprensione *f.* uneasiness; dread.
apprensivo *adj.* apprehensive.
appreso *pp. of* apprendere; learnt.
appressamento *m.* approach.
appressare *vt.* appressarsi *vr.* to approach, draw near.
appresso *prep.* near. *adv.* soon after. *adj.* next.
apprestamento *m.* preparation.
apprestare *vt.,* apprestarsi *vr.* to prepare, set, get ready.
apprettare *vt.* to size.
appretto *m.* size.
apprezza'bile *adj.* appreciable.
apprezzamento *m.* appreciation; judgment.
apprezzare *vt.* to appreciate.
approc'cio *m.* approach, feeler.
approdare *vi.* to land.
approdo *m.* landing.
approfittare *vi.* to profit by; to avail oneself (*of*); to take advantage (*of*); approfittarsi *vr.* to take advantage (*of*); to impose (*upon*).
approfondire *vt.* to deepen; to investigate; approfondirsi *vr.* to deepen; to become conversant (*with*).
approntare *vt.* to prepare, set.
appropriarsi *vr.* to appropriate.
appropriato *adj.* fit, proper.
appropriazione *f.* appropriation: — indebita, embezzlement, graft.
approssimare *vt.,* approssimarsi *vr.* to approximate.
approssimativamente *adv.* approximately.
approssimativo *adj.* approximate.
approssimazione *f.* approximation.
approvare *vt.* to approve (*of*).
approvazione *f.* approval.
approvvigionamento *m.* supply; provisions.
approvvigionare *vt.* to supply (*with*), provision.
appuntamento *m.* appointment, engagement; date.
appuntare *vt.* to sharpen; to fasten, stick, pin.
appuntato *m.* private first class; corporal.
appuntino *adv.* punctiliously.
appuntito *adj.* pointed.
appunto *m.* note; charge; blame; remark. per l'— just, exactly, quite so.
appurare *vt.* to ascertain.
apribottiglia *m.* bottle opener.
aprico *adj.* sunny, open.
aprile *m.* April: primo d'—, All Fools' Day.

apripista *m.* bulldozer.
aprire *vt.,*[11] aprirsi *vr.*[11] to open; to unlock.
aprisca'tola *m.* can opener.
aquario *m.* aquarium; (*astr.*) Aquarius.
aqua'tico *adj.* aquatic.
a'quila *f.* eagle.
aquilino *adj.* aquiline.
aquilone *m.* north wind; kite.
aquilotto *m.* eaglet; air cadet.
ara (*1*) *f.* are (*surface measure*).
ara (*2*) *f.* altar.
arabesco *m.* arabesque.
ara'bico *adj.* Arabic, Arabian.
a'rabo *m.* Arab. *adj.* Arabian.
ara'chide *f.* peanut.
arac'nide *m.* (*zool.*) arachnid.
aragosta *f.* lobster.
aral'dica *f.* heraldry.
aral'dico *adj.* heraldic.
araldo *m.* herald.
aranceto *m.* orange grove.
aran'cia *f.* orange.
aranciata *f.* orangeade.
aran'cio *m.* orange tree.
arancione *m.,* *adj.* orange.
arare *vt.* to plow.
aratro *m.* plow.
aratura *f.* plowing.
arazzo *m.* tapestry, arras.
arbitrag'gio *m.* arbitrage.
arbitrale *adj.* arbitral.
arbitrare *vt.,* *vi.* to arbitrate; to referee; arbitrarsi *vr.* to presume.
arbitrariamente *adv.* arbitrarily.
arbitra'rio *adj.* arbitrary.
arbitrato *m.* arbitration.
arbi'trio *m.* discretion; license: libero —, free will.
ar'bitro *m.* arbitrator; referee.
arboscello *m.* small tree, shrub.
arbusto *m.* shrub.
arca *f.* ark: un'— di scienza, a very learned person.
arca'ico *adj.* archaic.
arcaismo *m.* archaism.
arcan'gelo *m.* archangel.
arcano *m.* mystery. *adj.* mysterious.
arcata *f.* arch.
archeologi'a *f.* archeology.
archeolo'gico *adj.* archeological.
archeo'logo *m.* archeologist.
archetipo *m.* archetype.
archetto *m.* (*mus.*) fiddle bow.
archibu'gio *m.* harquebus.
Archimede *m. pr.* Archimedes.
architettare *vt.* to devise; to plan.
architetto *m.* architect.
architetto'nico *adj.* architectural.
architettura *f.* architecture.
architrave *f.* architrave; lintel.
archiviare *vt.* to file.
archi'vio *m.* archives; (*comm.*) files (*journ.*) "morgue."

archivista *m.* archivist.
arcicontento *adj.* most glad.
arcidia'cono *m.* archdeacon.
arciduca *m.* archduke.
arciduchessa *f.* archduchess.
arciere *m.* archer, bowman.
arcigno *adj.* sulky, sullen.
arcimiliona'rio *m.,* *adj.* multimil-
   lionaire.
arcione *m.* saddlebow.
arcipe'lago *m.* archipelago.
arciprete *m.* archpriest.
arcivescovado *m.* archbishopric.
arcivescovile *adj.* archiepiscopal.
arcive'scovo *m.* archbishop.
arco *m.* (*geom.*) arc; (*hist.*) arch; (*mus.,*
   weapon) bow: **strumenti ad —,**
   strings.
arcobaleno *m.* rainbow.
arcola'io *m.* reel.
arcuare *vt.* to bend, curve.
arcuato *adj.* bent, curved.
ardente *adj.* ardent; burning.
ardentemente *adv.* ardently.
ar'dere *vt., vi.*[13] to burn; to shine.
arde'sia *f.* slate.
ardimento *m.* boldness, daring.
ardimentoso *adj.* bold, daring.
ardire *m.* courage; impudence. *vi.* to
   dare: **come ardite?,** how dare you?
arditamente *adv.* boldly.
ardito *adj.* bold.
ardore *m.* ardor.
ar'duo *adj.* arduous, hard.
a'rea *f.* area; surface; lot.
a'rem *m.* harem.
arena *f.* arena; (*sabbia*) sand.
arena'ria *f.* (*min.*) sandstone.
arengo *m.* assembly, forum.
arenile *m.* sandpit.
arenoso *adj.* arenaceous, sandy.
Aretino, Pietro, Italian satirist
   (1492–1557).
Arezzo, Guido d', Italian reformer of
   music (ca. 990–1050).
ar'gano *m.* capstan.
argentare *vt.* to silver.
argentato *adj.* silver-plated: **volpe
   argentata,** silver fox.
argentatura *f.* silvering.
argen'teo *adj.* silver, silvery.
argenteri'a *f.* silverware.
argentiere *m.* silversmith.
argentina *f.* T-shirt.
argentino (*1*) *m., adj.* Argentine.
argentino (*2*) *adj.* argentine, silver,
   silvery.
argento *m.* silver: **— vivo,** quicksilver.
argentone *m.* German silver.
argilla *f.* clay.
argilloso *adj.* clayey.
arginare *vt.* to stem, dam.
ar'gine *m.* embankment, dam.

argomentare *vt., vi.* to argue.
argomentazione *f.* argumentation.
argomento *m.* argument; subject,
   topic.
argona'uta *m.* argonaut.
arguire *vt.* to infer, surmise.
argutamente *adv.* wittily.
arguto *adj.* witty; shrewd.
argu'zia *f.* witticism; wit; shrewdness.
a'ria *f.* air; tune: **camera d'—,** pneumatic tube; **castelli in —,** castles in
   Spain.
aridità *f.* aridness, dryness.
a'rido *adj.* arid, dry; barren; lifeless;
   parched; unfeeling.
arieggiare *vt.* to air. *vi.* (*foll. by* **a**) to
   look like; to sound like.
ariete *m.* (*zool.*) ram; (*mil.*) batter-
   ing ram; (*astr.*) Aries.
aringa *f.* herring.
arioso *adj.* airy.
Ariosto, Ludovico, Italian poet
   Orlando Furioso (1474–1533).
a'rista *f.* pork chine; (*bot.*) arista.
aristocra'tico *m.* aristocrat. *adj.*
   aristocratic.
aristocrazi'a *f.* aristocracy.
aristote'lico *adj.* Aristotelian.
aritme'tica *f.* arithmetic.
aritme'tico *m.* arithmetician. *adj.*
   arithmetic.
aritmi'a *f.* (*med.*) arrhythmia.
arlecchinata *f.* harlequinade.
Arlecchino *m.* pr. Harlequin.
arma *f.* corps, force, service; weapon,
   arm. *see* **arme.**
arma'dio *m.* wardrobe, cupboard:
   — a muro, closet.
armaiuolo *m.* gunsmith.
armamenta'rio *m.* outfit.
armamento *m.* armament; equipment.
armare *vt.* to arm; (*obs.*) to prop;
   (*naut.*) to equip; **armarsi** *vr.* to
   arm oneself.
armata *f.* army; fleet.
armatore *m.* shipowner.
armatura *f.* armor; framework; scaffolding.
arme *f.* arm, weapon; firearm, gun:
   essere sotto le armi, to be in the
   army; **essere alle prime armi,** to be
   a beginner.
armeggiare *vt.* to fumble; to scheme.
armeno *m., adj.* Armenian.
armento *m.* herd.
armeri'a *f.* armory.
armi'gero *m.* armiger.
armisti'zio *m.* armistice.
armoni'a *f.* harmony.
armo'nica *f.* harmonica.
armo'nico *adj.* harmonical.
armo'nio *m.* harmonium.
armonioso *adj.* harmonious.

armonizzare *vt.*, *vi.* to harmonize.
arnese *m.* implement, tool: **in cattivo —**, down at heel.
ar'nia *f.* beehive.
aroma *m.* flavor; (*pl.*) spices.
aroma'tico *adj.* aromatic.
aromatizzare *vt.* to flavor, spice.
arpa *f.* harp.
arpeg'gio *m.* arpeggio.
arpi'a *f.* harpy.
arpione *m.* hinge; spike.
arpista *m.* harper, harpist.
arrabattarsi *vr.* to endeavor.
arrabbiare *vi.*, **arrabbiarsi** *vr.* to get angry: **fare arrabbiare**, to make angry.
arrabbiato *adj.* angry.
arrabbiatura *f.* rage: **prendersi un'—**, to fly into a passion, lose one's temper.
arraffare *vt.* to snatch.
arrampicarsi *vr.* to climb (*up*).
arrancare *vi.* to limp; to trudge; to row away; to labor.
arrangiare *vt.* to arrange; **arrangiarsi** *vr.* to make shift; to manage.
arrecare *vt.* to bring; to cause.
arredamento *m.* interior decoration; furnishings.
arredare *vt.* to furnish, fit up.
arredatore *m.* interior decorator.
arredo *m.* furniture; fittings; decoration.
arrembag'gio *m.* boarding (*by force*): **andare all'—**, to board.
arrenarsi *vr.* to strand.
arrenato *adj.* stranded; in a deadlock.
arren'dersi *vr.*[106] to surrender.
arrende'vole *adj.* amenable, pliant.
arrendevolezza *f.* compliance.
arreso *pp.* of **arrendersi**.
arrestare *vt.* to stop; to arrest; **arrestarsi** *vr.* to stop, halt.
arresto *m.* arrest; stop, halt.
arretrare *vt.*, *vi.* to w thdraw.
arretrato *m.* arrears, arrearage; back number; *adj.* behindhand; late.
arricchimento *m.* enrichment.
arricchire *vt.* to enrich. *vi.* **arricchirsi** *vr.* to get rich.
arricchito *m.* upstart, parvenu.
arricciare *vt.*, **arricciarsi** *vr.* to curl (*up*); to wrinkle.
arricciatura *f.* curling.
arri'dere *vi.*[111] to smile (*on*); to favor.
arringa *f.* harangue; plea.
arringare *vt.*, *vi.* to harangue.
arrischiare *vt.* to risk; **arrischiarsi** *vr.* to risk, dare.
arrischiato *adj.* risky; rash.
arriso *pp.* of **arridere**.
arrivare *vt.* to reach, arrive, get to; (*fig.*) to go so far (*as*).
arrivato *adj.* arrived, come; successful; **ben —!**, welcome!

arrivismo *m.* scrambling.
arrivista *m.* go-getter, scrambler.
arrivo *m.* arrival, coming.
arroccamento *m.* (*chess*) castling.
arroccare *vt.* to fill the distaff; to castle (*at chess*).
arrochire *vt.* to make hoarse; **arrochirsi** *vr.* to grow hoarse.
arrogante *adj.* arrogant.
arroganza *f.* arrogance.
arrogarsi *vr.* to arrogate to oneself.
arrolamento *m.* enlistment.
arrolare *vt.*, **arrolarsi** *vr.* to enlist.
arrossamento *m.* reddening; rash.
arrossare *vt.*, **arrossarsi** *vr.* to redden.
arrossire *vi.* to blush, flush.
arrostire *vt.*, **arrostirsi** *vr.* to roast; to bask.
arrostitura *f.* roasting.
arrosto *m.*, *adj.* roast: **non c'è fumo senz' —**, there is no smoke without a fire; **molto fumo e poco —**, great cry and little wool.
arrotare *vt.* to whet, sharpen: **— i denti**, to grind one's teeth.
arrotino *m.* grinder.
arrotolare *vt.* to roll up.
arrotondare *vt.* to round.
arrovellarsi *vr.* to fret.
arroventare *vt.* to make red hot; **arroventarsi** *vr.* to become red hot.
aruffapo'poli *m.* ringleader.
arruffare *vt.*, **arruffarsi** *vr.* to tangle, ruffle.
arruffi'o *m.* tangle, jumble.
arruffone *m.* jumbler.
arrugginire *vt.*, *vi.*, **arrugginirsi** *vr.* to rust.
arrugginito *adj.* rusty.
arsella *f.* mussel, clam.
arsenale *m.* arsenal, navy yard.
arse'nico *m.* arsenic.
arsenobenzolo *m.* arsphenamine.
arso *adj.* burnt; dry. *pp.* of **ardere**.
arsura *f.* sultriness; thirst.
artatamente *adv.* artfully.
arte *f.* art; skill; wile.
artefatto *adj.* adulterated; artificial; sophisticated.
arte'fice *m.* artificer, craftsman.
arte'ria *f.* artery; thoroughfare.
arteriosclerosi *f.* arteriosclerosis.
arterioso *adj.* arterial.
artesiano (**pozzo**) *m.* Artesian well.
ar'tico *adj.* arctic.
articolare *vt.*, **articolarsi** *vr.* to articulate.
articolato *adj.* articulate.
articolazione *f.* articulation.
articolista *m.* columnist; free-lancer.
arti'colo *m.* article, item.
artificiale *adj.* artificial, fictitious; **fuochi artificiali**, fireworks.
artificialmente *adv.* artificially.

artificiere *m.* (*mil.*) artificer.
artifi'cio *m.* artifice; wile; guile.
artificioso *adj.* artful, fictitious.
artigiano *m.* artisan, craftsman.
artigliare *vt.* to claw.
artigliere *m.* artilleryman.
artiglieri'a *f.* artillery: pezzo d' — piece of ordnance.
arti'glio *m.* claw; clutch.
artista *m.* artist; player, actor.
arti'stico *adj.* artistic, artistical.
arto *m.* limb.
artrite *f.* arthritis.
artri'tico *adj.* arthritic.
arzigogolare *vi.* to muse; to dream, fancy.
arzigo'golo *m.* cavil, subtlety.
arzillo *adj.* sprightly; hale.
asbesto *m.* asbestos.
a'scaro *m.* askari (*pl.* askaris).
ascella *f.* armpit; (*bot.*) axil.
ascendente *m.* ancestor; ascendancy; (*astr.*) ascendant. *adj.* upward.
ascendenza *f.* ancestry.
ascen'dere *vt.*, *vi.*[119] to ascend, mount; to amount: — al trono, to ascend the throne.
ascensione *f.* ascension, ascent.
ascensore *m.* elevator.
ascesa *f.* ascent.
asceso *pp.* of ascendere.
ascesso *m.* abscess.
asceta *m.* ascetic.
asce'tico *adj.* ascetical.
ascetismo *m.* asceticism.
a'scia *f.* ax.
asciugamano *m.* towel.
asciugante *adj.* drying: carta —, blotting paper.
asciugare *vt.* to dry; to wipe. *vi.*, asciugarsi *vr.* to dry (*up*); to become dry: — gli occhi, to dry one's eyes; — la bocca, to wipe one's mouth.
asciugato'io *m.* towel.
asciugatura *f.* drying.
asciutto *adj.* dry; lean. *adv.* dryly: essere all'—, to be penniless.
ascoltare *vt.*, *vi.* to listen (*to*).
ascoltatore *m.* listener.
ascoltazione *f.* listening; auscultation.
ascolto *m.* listening: prestare —, to listen (*to*).
ascritto *adj.* ascribed. *pp.* of ascrivere.
ascri'vere *vt.*[124] to ascribe; to impute; ascriversi *vr.* to claim.
asepsi *f.* asepsis.
aset'tico *adj.* aseptic.
asfaltare *vt.* to asphalt.
asfalto *m.* asphalt.
asfissi'a *f.* asphyxia.
asfissiante *adj.* asphyxiating.
asfissiare *vt.*, *vi.*, asfissiarsi *vr.* to asphyxiate.

asfodelo *m.* asphodel.
asia'tico *adj.* Asiatic.
asilo *m.* refuge, shelter: — infantile, preschool; kindergarten.
asimmetri'a *f.* asymmetry.
asimme'trico *adj.* asymmetrical.
asinag'gine *f.* foolishness.
asina'io *m.* donkey driver.
asin'crono *adj.* asynchronous.
asineri'a *f.* foolishness, asininity.
asinino *adj.* asinine: tosse asinina, whooping cough.
a'sino *m.* ass, donkey; *f.* asina she-ass.
asma *f.* asthma.
asma'tico *m.*, *adj.* asthmatic.
a'sola *f.* buttonhole.
aspa'rago *m.* asparagus.
asper'gere *vt.*[13] to sprinkle (*with*).
asperità *f.* asperity.
aspersione *f.* aspersion; spraying.
asperso *adj.* sprinkled. *pp.* of aspergere.
asperso'rio *m.* aspergillum.
aspettare *vt.*, *vi.* to wait (*for*), await; to look forward to: far —, to keep waiting; aspettarsi *vr.* to expect; to anticipate.
aspettativa *f.* expectation; leave of absence.
aspetto (*1*) *m.* appearance, look, aspect.
aspetto (*2*) *m.* waiting: sala d'—, waiting room; battuta d'— (*mus.*), bar rest.
a'spide *f.* asp.
aspirante (*1*) *m.* candidate; (*naut.*) midshipman.
aspirante (*2*) *adj.* suction, sucking.
aspirapol'vere *m.* vacuum cleaner.
aspirare *vt.* to inhale; to aspirate; to suck. *vi.* (*foll. by* a) to aspire (*to*, *after*), aim (*at*).
aspiratore *m.* aspirator; vacuum cleaner.
aspirazione *f.* aspiration; intake, aspo *m.* reel.   [suction.
asporta'bile *adj.* removable.
asportare *vt.* to remove, take away; (*surg.*) to extirpate.
asportazione *f.* removal; extirpation.
aspramente *adv.* harshly.
asprezza *f.* harshness; sourness.
aspro *adj.* sour; harsh.
assaggiare *vt.* to taste; to assay.
assag'gio *m.* tasting; sample; test; assay.
assai *adv.* very, much: — meno, much less; — più, much more.
assale *m.* axle.
assalire *vt.*[14] to attack, assail; (*fig.*) to seize.
assalitore *m.* assailant.
assaltare *vt.* to assault.

assalto *m.* attack, assault: **prender d'—,** to take by storm.

assaporare *vt.* to relish.

assassinare *vt.* to murder.

assassi'nio *m.* murder.

assassino *m.* murderer, killer.

asse (*1*) *f.* plank.

asse (*2*) *m.* (*sci.*) axis (*pl.* axes): **— patrimoniale,** estate.

assecondare *vt.* to second.

assediante *m.* besieger.

assediare *vt.* to besiege; to beset.

asse'dio *m.* siege.

assegnamento *m.* allotment; reliance: **fare — su,** to rely upon.

assegnare *vt.* to assign, allow, award.

assegnato, (in porto) freight charges to be paid.

assegnazione *f.* assignation, allotment, appointment, award.

assegno *m.* allowance; check: **contro —,** cash on delivery (*abbr.* c.o.d.).

assemblea *f.* assembly; meeting.

assembramento *m.* gathering.

assennato *adj.* wise, sensible.

assenso *m.* assent, agreement.

assentarsi *vr.* to absent oneself.

assente *adj.* absent; missing; absent-minded: **— dalla città,** out of town.

assenteismo *m.* absenteeism.

assentire *vi.* to assent (*to*).

assenza *f.* absence; lack, want.

assen'zio *m.* absinthe.

asserire *vt.* to assert, state.

asserragliarsi *vr.* to barricade oneself.

asserto *m.* assertion, statement.

assertore *m.* advocate.

asservire *vt.* to subjugate; **asservirsi** *vr.* to submit (*to*).

asserzione *f.* statement.

assessore *m.* assessor, alderman.

assestamento *m.* settlement.

assestare *vt.* to settle; to tidy.

assetare *vt.* to make thirsty.

assetato *adj.* thirsty; eager.

assettare *vi.* to settle; to trim.

assettato *adj.* tidy, trim.

assetto *m.* order, shape; (*naut.*) trimming.

asseverare *vt.* to asseverate.

assicurare *vt.* to make safe; to fasten; to secure; to affirm, assure; (*comm.*) to insure; **assicurarsi** *vr.* to make sure, ascertain; (*comm.*) to insure oneself; to fasten oneself (*to*), hold on (*to*); to secure: **— sulla vita,** to take out life insurance.

assicurato *m., adj.* (*comm.*) insured; **assicurata** *f.* insured letter.

assicuratore *m.* insurer.

assicurazione *f.* assurance; (*comm.*) insurance.

assideramento *m.* frostbite: **morire per —,** to freeze to death.

assiderare *vt.,* **assiderarsi** *vr.* to freeze.

assiderato *adj.* frostbitten.

assi'dersi *vr.*[15] to take one's seat.

assiduamente *adv.* assiduously.

assiduità *f.* assiduity.

assi'duo *adj.* assiduous.

assieme *adv.* together. *prep.* with, together with.

assieparsi *vr.* to crowd.

assillare *vt.* to spur; to worry, badger.

assillo *m.* gadfly; spur, goad; worry.

assimilare *vt.,* **assimilarsi** *vr.* to assimilate.

assimilazione *f.* assimilation.

assioma *m.* axiom.

assioma'tico *adj.* axiomatical.

Assiro *m., adj.* Assyrian.

assisa *f.* uniform; livery.

assise *f.pl.* assizes.

assiso *adj.* seated.

assistente *m., adj.* assistant: **—sociale,** social worker.

assistenza *f.* assistance, aid.

assistenziale *adj.* assistance: **comitato —,** aid committee; **opere assistenziali,** charities; **ente —,** welfare organization.

assis'tere *vt.*[16] to assist, help; to tend, nurse. *vi.* to attend; to be a witness

assito *m.* planking. [(*to*).

asso *m.* ace: **piantare in —,** to leave in the lurch.

associare *vt.* to associate; to consolidate; to make a member (*of*); **associarsi** *vr.* to associate; to share; to join; to subscribe.

associato *m.* partner; subscriber.

associazione *f.* association; partnership; subscription; membership: **— a delinquere,** conspiracy.

assodare *vt.* to solidify, harden; to ascertain; **assodarsi** *vr.* to harden.

assoggettare *vt.* to subdue; **assoggettarsi** *vr.* to submit.

assolato *adj.* sunny.

assoldare *vt.* to hire; to enlist; **assoldarsi** *vr.* to enlist.

assolo, a solo *m.* solo.

assolto *adj.* absolved; acquitted. *pp. of* assolvere.

assolutamente *adv.* absolutely.

assolutismo *m.* absolutism.

assolutista *m.* absolutist.

assoluto *adj.* absolute, dire.

assoluzione *f.* acquittal; (*rel.*) absolution.

assol'vere *vt.*[17] to acquit; to absolve; to forgive.

assomigliante *adj.* resembling.

assomiglianza *f.* resemblance.

assomigliare *vi.* to be like; to look like; to taste like; to sound like; to smell like; **assomigliarsi** *vr.* to resemble each other, be alike.

assommare vt. to add. vi. to amount (to).
assonanza f. assonance.
assonnato adj. sleepy.
assopimento m. drowsiness.
assopirsi vr. to doze off.
assorbente m. absorbent. adj. absorbing: carta —, blotting paper.
assorbimento m. absorption.
assorbire vt.[18] to absorb; to engross; to take up.
assordante adj. deafening.
assordare vt. to deafen, stun.
assortimento m. assortment.
assortire vt. to assort.
assorto pp. absorbed, engrossed. pp. of assorbire.
assottigliare vt. to thin; to sharpen; to reduce; assottigliarsi vr. to thin down; to decrease.
assuefare vt. to inure, accustom; assuefarsi vr. to get accustomed.
assuefazione f. habit.
assu'mere vt.[19] to assume, take; to hire, engage: — informazioni, to make inquiries; assumersi vr. to take upon oneself, undertake.
Assunta f. Assumption Day.
assunto m. theory. pp. of assumere hired; assumed.
assuntore m. contractor.
Assunzione (1) f. Assumption Day.
assunzione (2) f. hiring.
assurdità f. absurdity.
assurdo adj. absurd, preposterous.
assur'gere vt.[20] to rise.
asta f. staff; rod; (naut.) boom; spear; auction; straight stroke.
astante m. bystander.
aste'mio m. teetotaler. adj. abstemious, abstaining.
astenersi vr.[141] to abstain (from); to refrain (from); to forbear.
astensione f. abstention.
asterisco m. asterisk.
asticciuola f. small rod; penholder; rib (of an umbrella).
astigmatismo m. astigmatism.
astinenza f. abstinence.
a'stio m. grudge, hate.
astioso adj. spiteful.
astrale adj. astral.
astrarre vt.[156] to abstract; to divert. vi. to prescind; astrarsi vr. to wander.
astratto m. abstract. adj. abstract; abstracted. pp. of astrarre.
astrazione f. abstraction; abstractedness.
astringente m., adj. astringent.
astro m. star; (bot.) aster.
astrola'bio m. astrolabe.
astrologi'a f. astrology.
astro'logo m. astrologer.

astrona'utica f. space navigation.
astronave f. space ship.
astronomi'a f. astronomy.
astrono'mico adj. astronomical.
astro'nomo m. astronomer.
astrusità f. abstruseness.
astruso adj. abstruse.
astuc'cio m. case, box, container.
astutamente adv. cunningly.
astuto adj. astute, cunning, smart.
astu'zia f. cunning; trick, wile.
ata'vico adj. atavistic.
atavismo m. atavism.
ateismo m. atheism.
ateneo m. athenaeum, university.
ateniese m., adj. Athenian.
a'teo m. atheist.
atlante m. atlas.
atlan'tico m., adj. Atlantic.
atleta m. athlete.
atle'tica f. athletics.
atle'tico adj. athletic.
atmosfera f. atmosphere.
atmosfe'rico adj. atmospheric.
atollo m. atoll.
atomicità f. atomicity.
ato'mico adj. atomic: bomba atomica, atom bomb; energia atomica, atomic power.
a'tomo m. atom: disintegrazione dell'—, atomic fission.
a'tono adj. atonic.
atrio m. entrance hall, hall.
atroce adj. atrocious, awful.
atrocità f. atrocity.
atrofi'a f. atrophy.
atro'fico adj. atrophic.
atrofizzare vt., atrofizzarsi vr. to atrophy.
attaccabottoni m. buttonholer.
attaccabrighe m. quarreler, spitfire.
attaccapanni m. rack.
attaccare vt. to attach, connect; to stick; to seam up; to pin; to hang; to communicate; to hitch; to attack. vi. to stick; to take root; to take; to start: — lite, to quarrel; attaccarsi vr. to stick (to); to be contagious.
attaccatic'cio adj. sticky; tiresome; contagious.
attaccatura f. junction; armhole.
attacchino m. bill poster.
attacco m. attack; joint; (radio) jack; (med.) fit.
attagliarsi vr. to fit, suit.
attanagliare vt. to grip.
attardarsi vr. to linger.
attecchire vi. to take root, stick.
atteggiamento m. attitude.
atteggiarsi vr. to attitudinize; to pose as.
attempato adj. elderly.
attendamento m. camping.

attendarsi *vr.* to camp.

attendente *m.* (*mil.*) orderly.

atten'dere *vt.*, *vi.*[140] to wait (*for*); to await; to attend (*to*); attendersi *vr.* to expect, anticipate.

attendi'bile *adj.* reliable.

attendibilità *f.* reliability.

attenere *vi.*[141] to relate (*to*); attenersi *vr.* to conform (*to*); to stick (*to*): — a, to follow.

attentamente *adv.* attentively.

attentare *vi.* to attempt: — alla vita di una persona, to attempt to kill someone; attentarsi *vr.* to dare; to try.

attentato *m.* attempt (*upon*).

attentatore *m.* infringer; murderer; would-be murderer.

attenti! *interj.* attention!; watch out!: stare sull'—, to stand at attention.

attento *adj.* attentive: stare —, to pay attention; to be careful.

attenuante *f.* (*law*) extenuation.

attenuare *vt.* to attenuate, mitigate.

attenzione *f.* attention, heed: con —, carefully.

atterrag'gio *m.* landing.

atterrare *vt.* to knock down; to fell. *vi.* (*aeron.*) to land.

atterrire *vt.* to frighten; atterrirsi *vr.* to take fright.

attesa *f.* waiting; delay.

atteso *adj.* awaited; expected. *pp.* of attendere.

attesochè *conj.* in consideration of, considering.

attestare *vt.* to certify, state.

attestato *m.* certificate.

attestazione *f.* attestation.

atticciato *adj.* stout.

at'tico *m.* attic, garret.

attiguo *adj.* adjacent, contiguous.

attillato *adj.* tight, fitting.

at'timo *m.* moment, minute.

attinente *adj.* relating, regarding.

attinenza *f.* relation, connection.

attin'gere *vt.*[143] to draw; to get.

attinto *pp.* of attingere.

attirare *vt.* to draw, attract, lure; attirarsi *vr.* to draw upon oneself; to win.

attitu'dine *f.* aptitude, bent.

attivamente *adv.* actively.

attivare *vt.* to activate.

attività *f.* activity; liveliness; (*comm. pl.*) assets.

attivo *m.* (*comm.*) assets. *adj.* active; lively.

attizzare *vt.* to poke, stir (*a fire*).

attizzato'io *m.* poker.

atto (*1*) *adj.* inclined; fit (*for*).

atto (*2*) *m.* act; gesture; action; deed: all'— pratico, practically; tradurre in —, to carry out; far — di

presenza, to put in an appearance; dar —, to acknowledge; prender —, to take note.

atti *m.pl.* proceedings: fare gli —, to prosecute; passare agli —, to file.

atto'nito *adj.* amazed, astonished.

attorcigliare *vt.*, attorcigliarsi *vr.* to twist; to wind.

attore *m.* actor, player; (*law*) plaintiff.

attorniare *vt.* to surround.

attorno *prep.*, *adv.* about, around, round: darsi d'—, to busy oneself; levati d'—!, get out of here!; levarsi uno d'—, to get rid of one.

attracco *m.* moorage, moorings.

attraccare *vt.*, *vi.* to moor.

attraente *adj.* attractive, alluring.

attrarre[146] *see* attirare.

attrattiva *f.* attraction, appeal.

attratto *pp.* of attrarre.

attraversare *vt.* to move across, cross; to go through; to thwart.

attraverso *prep.* through, across. *adv.* wrong; across.

attrazione *f.* attraction, appeal.

attrezzare *vt.* to outfit.

attrezzatura *f.* equipment.

attrezzista *m.* (*theat.*) property man.

attrezzo *m.* implement, tool: — scenico (*theat.*) property, prop.

attribuire *vt.* to ascribe; to allot; — importanza a, to attach importance to; attribuirsi *vr.* to claim.

attributo *m.* attribute.

attribuzione *f.* attribution.

attrice *f.* actress.

attrito *m.* friction; variance.

attrupparsi *vr.* to troop.

attua'bile *adj.* feasible.

attuabilità *f.* feasibility.

attuale *adj.* actual; present, current.

attualità *f.* actuality; current events: essere d'—, to be of topical interest; — cinematografiche, newsreel.

attualmente *adv.* at present; actually.

attuare *vt.* to accomplish, carry out.

attua'rio *m.* actuary.

attuazione *f.* fulfillment, carrying out.

attutire *vt.*, attutirsi *vr.* to deaden, mitigate.

audace *adj.* bold, daring.

audacemente *adv.* boldly, daringly.

auda'cia *f.* boldness, daring.

auditore *m.* listener, auditor; judge.

audito'rio *m.* auditorium; (*radio*) studio.

audizione *f.*, audition, hearing.

auge *m.* summit, apex; (*astr.*) apogee: in —, on top; popular.

augello *m.* bird.

augurale *adj.* auspicious.

augurare *vt.* to wish, bid; to foretell; augurarsi *vr.* to wish, hope.

a'ugure *m.* augur.

augu'rio *m.* wish; omen.

augusteo *adj.* Augustan.

augusto *adj.* august, majestic.

a'ula *f.* hall; room; schoolroom.

a'ulico *adj.* aulic.

aumentare *vt.*, *vi.* to increase, augment; to rise.

aumento *m.* increase; raise; rise.

a'ura *f.* breeze; aura.

a'ureo *adj.* gold, golden.

aure'ola *f.* halo, aureole, glory.

auri'fero *adj.* auriferous: giacimento —, gold field.

aurora *f.* dawn, daybreak: — boreale, aurora borealis.

auscultare *vt.*, *vi.* to auscultate.

auscultazione *f.* auscultation.

ausiliare, ausilia'rio *adj.* auxiliary.

ausilia'ria *f.* Wac (*in the Army*); Wave (*in the Navy*); Wasp (*in the Air Force*).

ausi'lio *m.* help, aid.

auspicare *vt.* to wish, hope for.

auspi'cio *m.* auspice, omen.

austerità *f.* austerity.

austero *adj.* austere.

australe *adj.* austral, southern.

australiano *m.*, *adj.* Australian.

austri'aco *m.*, *adj.* Austrian.

autarchi'a *f.* autarchy.

autenticare *vt.* to authenticate.

autenticazione *f.* authentication.

autenticità *f.* authenticity.

auten'tico *adj.* genuine.

autiere *m.* military driver.

autista *m.* driver.

auto *m.* motorcar, car, automobile.

autoambulanza *f.* ambulance.

autobiografi'a *f.* autobiography.

autoblindata *f.* armored car.

au'tobus *m.* autobus, motorbus, bus.

autocarro *m.* motor truck.

autoclave *f.* autoclave.

autocombustione *f.* self-ignition.

autocrazi'a *f.* autocracy.

autoc'tono *m.* autochthon. *adj.* autochthonous, autochthonal.

autodafè *m.* auto da fè (*pl.* autos da fè).

autodecisione *f.* free will.

autodidatta *m.* self-taught person.

auto'dromo *m.* motordrome.

auto'geno *adj.* autogenous.

autogiro *m.* autogyro.

auto'grafo *m.* autograph. *adj.* autographic.

autolesionista *m.* self-wounder.

autolettiga *f.* (*motor*) ambulance.

automa *m.* automaton, robot.

automaticamente *adv.* automatically.

automa'tico *m.* snap fastener. *adj.* automatic.

automatismo *m.* automatism.

automezzo *m.* motor vehicle.

automo'bile *m.* motorcar, car, automobile: viaggiare in —, to motor. *adj.* automobile.

automobilismo *m.* motoring.

automobilista *m.* (car) driver.

automotrice *f.* Diesel, railroad car.

autonomi'a *f.* autonomy, self-government; (*mach.*) range: — di volo, flight range.

auto'nomo *adj.* autonomous.

autopompa *f.* fire engine.

autopsi'a *f.* autopsy, post-mortem examination.

autopub'blica *f.* taxicab, taxi.

autore *m.* author: diritti d'—, copyright.

autore'vole *adj.* authoritative.

autorimessa *f.* garage.

autoristoro *m.* drive-in, roadhouse.

autorità *f.* authority.

autorita'rio *adj.* authoritative, peremptory, domineering.

autoritratto *m.* self-portrait.

autorizzare *vt.* to authorize.

autorizzazione *f.* authorization.

autoscatto *m.* (*photo.*) automatic releaser.

autoservizi *m.pl.* bus lines.

autostello *m.* motel.

autostop *m.* hitchhike: fare l'—, to hitchhike.

autostrada *f.* motor road, highway, toll road.

autosuggestione *f.* autosuggestion, self-deception.

autotreno *m.* trailer truck.

autovei'colo *m.* motor vehicle.

autrice *f.* authoress.

autunnale *adj.* autumnal.

autunno *m.* autumn, fall.

ava *f.* ancestress.

avallante *m.* guarantor.

avallare *vt.* to guarantee.

avallo *m.* guaranty, endorsement.

avambrac'cio *m.* forearm.

avamposto *m.* outpost.

avanguar'dia *f.* van, vanguard.

avannotto *m.* small fry.

avanti *prep.*, *adv.* forward; before; in front of, ahead: andare —, to go on; avanti!, come on!, go ahead!, come in!; il mio orologio va —, my watch is fast; da ora in —, from now on; più —, farther on; later on.

avantieri *adv.* the day before yesterday.

avanzamento *m.* advancement; promotion.

avanzare *vt.* to advance, put forth; to be creditor of. *vi.* to advance, move forward; to superabound; to be left; avanzarsi *vr.* to move forward; to draw near.

avanzata *f.* advance.

avanzato *adj.* advanced; progressive; left over.

avanzo *m.* remnant, residue; (*math.*) remainder: — **di galera,** jailbird; **d'—,** more than enough.

avari'a *f.*damage; breakdown ;(*comm.*) average.

avariare *vt.* to damage.

avari'zia *f.* avarice, stinginess.

avaro *m.* miser. *adj.* stingy.

avello *m.* tomb.

avena *f.* oats: **farina d'—,** oatmeal.

avere (*1*) *m.* credit, credit side; (*pl.*) possessions.

avere (*2*) *vt.*, *vi.* to have; to get; to own: **aver da dare,** to owe; **aver caldo, freddo, fame, sete,** to be hot, cold, hungry, thirsty; **aver ragione,** to be right; — **30 anni,** to be thirty (years old).

aviatore *m.* pilot, airman; **aviatrice** *f.* aviatrix, airwoman.

aviazione *f.* aviation; Air Force.

avicoltura *f.* aviculture.

avidamente *adv.* greedily.

avidità *f.* greed; eagerness.

a'vido *adj.* greedy; eager.

aviere *m.* (*mil.*) airman.

avioli'nea *f.* air line.

aviotrasportato *adj.* airborne.

avitaminosi *f.* avitaminosis.

avito *adj.* ancestral.

avo *m.* ancestor.

avo'rio *m.* ivory.

avvalersi *vr.* to avail oneself.

avvallamento *m.* sinking.

avvallare *vt.* to hollow; **avvallarsi** *vr.* to sink.

avvalorare *vt.* to confirm, strengthen.

avvantaggiare *vt.* to benefit; to increase; to improve; **avvantaggiarsi** *vr.* to benefit (*by*).

avvedersi *vi.*[161] to perceive, become aware (*of*); to realize.

avvedutezza *f.* shrewdness.

avveduto *adj.* shrewd, sagacious. *pp.* *of* avvedersi.

avvelenamento *m.* poisoning.

avvelenare *vt.* to poison; **avvelenarsi** *vr.* to poison oneself.

avvenimento *m.* event.

avvenire (*1*) *m.* future; prospects.

avvenire (*2*) *vi.*[162] to happen, take place; to chance: **avvenga che può,** come what may.

avventarsi *vr.* to dash; to pounce.

avventatezza *f.* rashness.

avventato *adj.* rash, reckless.

avventi'zio *m.*, *adj.* supernumerary.

avvento *m.* advent, accession.

avventore *m.* customer.

avventura *f.* adventure.

avventurarsi *vr.* to venture.

avventuriera *f.* adventuress.

avventuriere *m.* adventurer.

avventuroso *adj.* adventurous.

avverare *vt.* to verify; **avverarsi** *vr.* to come true; to happen.

avver'bio *m.* adverb.

avversare *vt.* to antagonize.

avversa'rio *m.* foe; opponent.

avversione *f.* aversion, dislike, disinclination.

avversità *f.* adversity, misfortune.

avverso *adj.* adverse, averse, hostile.

avvertenza *f.* caution, thoughtfulness; note, foreword; direction; warning.

avvertimento *m.* caution, warning.

avvertire *vt.* to caution; to warn; to notice, feel, sense.

avvezzare *vt.* to accustom; **avvezzarsi** *vr.* to get accustomed.

avvezzo *adj.* accustomed, used.

avviamento *m.* starting, start, outset; introduction, beginning.

avviare *vt.* to start, set going; to introduce, initiate; **avviarsi** *vr.* to start; to set out.

avvicendamento *m.* alternation; rotation.

avvicendare *vt.*, **avvicendarsi** *vr.* to alternate; to rotate.

avvicinare *vt.*, **avvicinarsi** *vr.* to approach, draw near, accost.

avvilimento *m.* humiliation, dejection.

avvilire *vt.* to humiliate; to degrade; to dishearten, deject; to lower; **avvilirsi** *vr.* to humble oneself; to degrade oneself; to lose courage.

avviluppare *vt.* to wrap up; to entangle; **avvilupparsi** *vr.* to wrap oneself up; to tangle.

avvinazzato *m.* tippler.

avvincente *adj.* fascinating.

avvin'cere *vt.*[163] to bind, tie; to hug; to fascinate.

avvinghiare *vt.* to catch, clutch; **avvinghiarsi** *vr.* to cling.

avvinto *adj.* bound; fascinated. *pp. of* avvincere.

avvi'o *m.* start, beginning.

avvisa'glia *f.* skirmish; hint, symptom.

avvisare *vt.* to inform; to warn.

avvisatore *m.* warner, alarm: — **d'incendio,** fire alarm.

avviso *m.* notice; warning; opinion; caution; poster; advertisement; aviso (*ship*).

avvistare *vt.* to sight, espy.

avvitamento *m.* (*aeron.*) barrel roll; tailspin.

avvitare *vt.* to screw; **avvitarsi** *vr.* to screw; (*aeron.*) to spin in.

avviticchiare *vt.*, **avviticchiarsi** *vr.* to twine (*around*).

avvizzire *vt.*, *vi.* to wither.

avvocatessa f. female lawyer.

avvocato m. lawyer; barrister; solicitor; counsel.

avvocatura f. bar: esercitare l'—, to practice law.

avvol'gere vt.[156] to wrap up; to wind up; **avvolgersi** vr. to wrap oneself up; to wind.

avvolgi'bile f. roller blind.

avvolgimento m. winding.

avvolto adj. wound; twisted. pp. of avvolgere.

avvolto'io m. vulture.

avvoltolare vt. to roll up; **avvoltolarsi** vr. to roll, wallow.

Azeglio, Massimo d', Italian statesman and author (1798–1866).

azienda f. concern, firm, business.

azionare vt. to operate.

aziona'rio adj. (comm.) stock.

azione f. action; (comm.) share; lawsuit.

azionista m. shareholder.

azotare vt. to nitrogenize.

azoto m. nitrogen, azote.

azzannare vt. to tusk, gore.

azzardare vt. to stake; to risk. vi. to dare; **azzardarsi** vr. to venture; to dare.

azzardato adj. risky; rash.

azzardo m. hazard, risk: gioco d'—, gamble, gambling.

azzardoso adj. hazardous, risky.

azzeccagarbugli m. pettifogger.

azzeccare vt. to hit: azzeccarla, to hit the mark.

azzimato adj. dressed up.

az'zimo adj. unleavened, azymous.

azzittire vt. to silence; **azzittirsi** vr. to be quiet.

azzoppare vt. to lame. vi. to become lame.

azzoppato adj. lame.

azzuffarsi vr. to come to blows.

azzurro m., adj. blue, azure.

azzurrognolo adj. bluish.

B

babau m. bugbear, bogy.

babbeo m. fool, dupe.

babbo m. father, dad, daddy.

babbuc'cia f. slipper.

babbuino m. baboon.

babele f. babel.

babe'lico adj. uproarious.

babilonese m., adj. Babylonian.

babilo'nia f. hubbub, babel, confusion.

babordo m. port side.

bacarsi vr. to rot.

bacato adj. rotten; wormeaten.

bacca f. berry.

baccalà m. cod, codfish.

baccanale m. bacchanal, orgy.

baccano m. noise, din, hubbub.

Baccante f. Bacchante.

baccarà m. baccarat.

baccello m. (bot.) pod.

Bacchelli, Riccardo, Italian novelist (1891–).

bacchetta f. rod, wand.

bacchettone m. sanctimonious person, pietist.

Bacco m. Bacchus: per —!, by Jove!

bacheca f. showcase.

bachelite f. bakelite.

bacherozzo m. earthworm.

bachicoltura f. sericulture.

bachicultore m. sericulturist.

baciamano m. hand-kissing.

baciapile m., f. sanctimonious person.

baciare vt. to kiss; **baciarsi** vr. to kiss (one another).

bacillare adj. bacillary.

bacillo m. bacillus (pl. bacilli).

bacinella f. basin; (photo.) tray.

bacino m. basin; dock; reservoir; (anat.) pelvis.

ba'cio m. kiss.

baco m. worm; (da seta) silkworm.

bacologi'a f. sericiculture.

bacte'rio see batte'rio.

bada f. in the phrase: tenere a —, to stave off, to check.

badare vi. to mind; to look (after), tend; to listen: badate! watch out!

badessa f. abbess.

badi'a f. abbey.

badilante m. shoveler, digger.

badile m. shovel.

baffetti m pl. clipped mustache.

baffo m. mustache; whisker: baffi all'amer cana, clipped mustache.

bagaglia'io m. baggage car.

baga'glio m. baggage; luggage.

bagarinag'gio m. (theat.) scalping.

bagarino m. (theat.) scalper.

baga'scia f. harlot, whore.

bagattella f. trifle.

baggianata f. nonsense; foolery.

baggiano m. fool, blockhead.

ba'glio m. (naut.) beam.

bagliore m. gleam, glimmer; dazzle.

bagnante m., f. bather.

bagnare vt. to bathe; to wash; to water; to wet; to soak; **bagnarsi** vr. to get wet; to bathe.

bagnarola f. bathtub.

bagnasciuga m. (naut.) waterline.

bagnino m. lifeguard.

bagno m. bath; bathroom; prison: andare ai bagni, to go to the seaside.

bagnomari'a m. bain-marie, double boiler.

bagordo m. revelry.

ba'ia f. bay; jest; hooting.

baiadera *f.* bayadere.
ba'io *m.*, *adj.* bay (*horse*).
baionetta *f.* bayonet.
ba'ita *f.* mountain hut.
balaustrata *f.* balustrade.
balbettamento *m.* stammering; baby talk.
balbettare *vt.*, *vi.* to stammer.
Balbo, Cesare, Italian writer and statesman (1789–1853).
Balbo, Italo, Italian aviator and politician (1896–1940).
balbu'zie *f.* stammer.
balbuziente *m.*, *f.* stammerer. *adj.* stammering.
balca'nico *adj.* Balkan.
balconata *f.* balcony.
balcone *m.* balcony.
baldacchino *m.* canopy.
baldanza *f.* boldness, arrogance.
baldanzosamente *adv.* boldly.
baldanzoso *adj.* bold, arrogant.
baldo *adj.* bold, fearless.
baldo'ria *f.* revelry.
baldracca *f.* harlot, strumpet.
balena *f.* whale.
balenare *vt.* to flash.
baleniera *f.* whaler, whaleship.
baleno *m.* flash, lightning.
balenot'tera *f.* (*zool.*) rorqual.
balenotto *m.* whale calf.
balestra *f.* crossbow; (*mach.*) leaf spring: foglia di —, spring leaf.
ba'lia *f.* nurse.
bali'a *f.* mercy: in — di, at the mercy of.
ba'lio *m.* foster-father.
bali'stica *f.* ballistics.
bali'stico *adj.* ballistic.
balistite *f.* ballistite.
balla *f.* bale; heap.
balla'bile *m.* dance tune.
ballare *vt.*, *vi.* to dance. *vi.* to shake, be loose.
ballata *f.* ballad.
ballato'io *m.* gallery; perch.
ballerino *m.* dancer, partner; ballerina *f.* dancer; ballerina; ballet girl, partner.
balletto *m.* ballet.
ballo *m.* dance; ball: corpo di —, ballet; tirare in —, to call in question.
ballonzolare *vi.* to hop.
ballottag'gio *m.* second ballot.
balneare *adj.* bathing: stazione —, seaside resort.
baloccarsi *vr.* to toy; to trifle.
balocco *m.* toy, plaything.
balordag'gine *f.* silliness; foolery.
balordo *m.* fool; *adj.* foolish, giddy; phony.
balsa'mico *adj.* balmy, balsamic.
bal'samo *m.* balm, balsam.

bal'tico *adj.* Baltic.
baluardo *m.* bulwark.
baluginare *vi.* to flash.
balza *f.* cliff; flounce.
balzano *adj.* white-footed (*horse*); queer, odd, unpredictable.
balzare *vi.* to jump, leap.
balzello *m.* tax; stalk.
balzo *m.* leap: coglier la palla al —, to seize the opportunity.
bamba'gia *f.* cottonwool.
bambina *f.* child, little girl.
bambina'ia *f.* nursemaid.
bambino *m.* child, little boy, "kid."
bamboc'cio *m.* baby; dolt; puppet.
bam'bola *f.* doll.
bambù *m.* bamboo.
banale *adj.* banal, trivial, commonplace.
banalità *f.* banality, triviality, platitude.
banano *m.*, banana *f.* banana.
banca *f.* bank: biglietti di —, banknotes.
bancarella *f.* stall.
banca'rio *m.* bank clerk. *adj.* bank, banking: assegno —, check.
bancarotta *f.* bankruptcy: far —, to go bankrupt.
banchettare *vi.* to banquet.
banchetto *m.* banquet, feast.
banchiere *m.* banker.
banchina *f.* dock; platform.
banchisa *f.* ice pack, floe.
banco *m.* counter, desk, bench; bank; form, school desk: — degli accusati, dock; — dei testimoni, witness stand; — di prova (*mach.*), test stand; — di coralli, coral reef.
bancogiro *m.* clearing.
banconota *f.* banknote, note.
banda *f.* side; band; stripe; gang.
Bandello, Matteo, Italian writer of novelle (1480–1562).
banderuola *f.* banderole; weathercock.
bandiera *f.* flag, colors (*pl.*), banner: mutar —, to change sides.
bandire *vt.* to announce; to banish, dismiss; to outlaw.
bandista *m.* bandsman.
bandito *m.* bandit, outlaw, gangster. *pp. of* bandire banished, outlawed: corte bandita, open house.
banditore *m.* crier, hawker; auctioneer.
bando *m.* announcement; ban; exile: mettere al —, to banish.
bandoliera *f.* bandoleer.
ban'dolo *m.* skeining thread.
bar *m.* saloon, barroom, bar.
bara *f.* bier.
barabba *adj.* rogue, scoundrel.
baracca *f.* hut.

araccamento *m.* hutment.
araccone *m.* tent (*of a circus*).
araonda *f.* hurly-burly, mess.
arare *vi.* to cheat.
a'ratro *m.* abyss, gulf, chasm.
arattare *vt.* to barter, trade, bargain.
aratto *m.* barter.
arat'tolo *m.* pot; can, canister.
arba *f.* beard; hair; (*bot.*) barb:
farsi la —, to shave; far venire
la —, to bore to death.
arbabie'tola *f.* beet; beetroot.
arbagianni *m.* owl.
arba'glio *m.* dazzle.
arbaramente *adv.* barbarously.
arba'rico *adj.* barbaric.
arba'rie *f.* barbarity.
arbarismo *m.* barbarism.
ar'baro *m.* barbarian. *adj.* barbarous.
arbazzale *m.* curb.
arberini, Francesco, Italian cardinal; founder of Barberini Library
(1597-1679).
arbetta *f.* goatee; fetlock; (*fort.,
naut.*) barbette.
arbiere *m.* barber.
arberi'a *f.* barber shop.
arbino *adj.* poor.
ar'bio *m.* barbel.
arbo'gio *adj.* doting.
arbone *m.* poodle; (*dial.*) vagabond,
bum.
arbuto *adj.* bearded; (*bot.*) barbate.
arca *f.* boat; rowboat; sailboat.
arcac'cia *f.* (*theat.*) box.
arcaiuolo *m.* boatman.
arcamenarsi *vr.* to get along, manage.
arcarizzo *m.* gangway.
arcarola *f.* (*mus.*) barcarole.
arcollante *adj.* reeling, staggering.
arcollare *vi.* to reel, stagger, sway.
ardare *vt.* to harness.
ardatura *f.* harness.
ardo *m.* bard.
ardosso, (a) *adv.* bareback.
arella *f.* stretcher.
argello *m.* (*hist.*) constable.
argi'glio *m.* wattle.
aricentro *m.* barycenter.
arile *m.* barrel, cask, keg.
arilozzo *m.* keg; bull's-eye.
a'rio *m.* barium.
arista *m.* bartender. *f.* barmaid.
ari'tono *m.* baritone.
arlume *m.* gleam, glimmer.
aro *m.* cheat, sharper.
aroccia'io *m.* carter.
aroccino *m.* tilbury; pushcart.
aroc'cio *m.* cart.
arocco *m.*, *adj.* baroque.
aro'grafo *m.* barograph.
aro'metro *m.* barometer.
aronale *adj.* baronial.
aroncino *m.* young baron.

barone *m.* baron.
baronessa *f.* baroness.
baronetto *m.* baronet; Sir.
barosco'pio *m.* baroscope.
barra *f.* bar; rod; (*naut.*) tiller.
barricare *vt.* to barricade; barricarsi
vr. to barricade oneself.
barricata *f.* barricade.
barriera *f.* barrier; (*fig.*) obstacle.
barrire *vi.* to trumpet.
barrito *m.* trumpeting, trumpet.
barroc'cio *see* baroccio.
baruffa *f.* scuffle, fight.
baruffare *vi.* to quarrel.
barzelletta *f.* joke, gag, story.
basalto *m.* basalt.
basamento *m.* base.
basare *vt.* to base, found; basarsi *vr.*
to base oneself, rest.
basco *m.*, *adj.* Basque: berretto —,
beret.
basculla *f.* balance.
base *f.* base; basis, ground.
basetta *f.* whisker.
ba'sico *adj.* (*chem.*) basic.
basilare *adj.* basal, basilar.
basi'lica *f.* basilica.
basi'lico *m.* basil.
basilisco *m.* basilisk.
bassezza *f.* shortness; baseness,
meanness; base action.
basso *m.* low, down; bass: alti e bassi,
ups and downs. *adj.* low; short;
common; shallow.
bassofondo *m.* shoal, shallow: i bassifondi, the underworld.
bassopiano *m.* lowland.
bassorilievo *m.* bas-relief.
bassotto *m.* basset; dachshund.
basta (*1*) *f.* tuck.
basta (*2*) *interj.* stop it!
bastante *adj.* sufficient, enough.
bastardo *m.*, *adj.* bastard; mongrel.
bastare *vi.* to suffice, do, be enough;
to last: così basta, that will do.
baste'vole *adj.* sufficient.
bastimento *m.* ship, vessel.
bastione *m.* bulwark, rampart.
basto *m.* pack saddle.
bastonare *vt.* to cudgel.
bastonata *f.* buffet, blow.
bastonatura *f.* thrashing.
bastone *m.* cane, stick, staff; club;
bat; baton; (*pl., in playing cards*)
clubs: mettere i bastoni fra le ruote
a qualcuno, to put a spoke in
someone's wheel.
batac'chio *m.* clapper, tongue.
batiscafo *m.* bathyscaphe.
batisfera *f.* bathysphere.
batista *f.* batiste, cambric.
batosta *f.* blow; damage; defeat.
batrace *m.* batrachian.
batta'glia *f.* battle, fight.

battagliare *vi.* to fight.
battagliero *adj.* bellicose, warlike.
batta'glio *m.* clapper, tongue.
battaglione *m.* battalion.
battelliere *m.* boatman.
battello *m.* boat.
battente *m.* shutter; knocker. *adj. in the phrase*: **a tamburo —**, right away, pronto.
bat'tere *vt., vi.* to beat, hit; to knock: **— le mani,** to clap; **— i piedi,** to stamp one's feet; **battersi** *vr.* to strike oneself; to fight: **battersela,** to take to one's heels.
batteri'a *f.* battery; *(mus.)* drums; *(sport)* heat.
batte'rico *adj.* bacterial.
batte'rio *m.* bacterium *(pl. bacteria).*
batteriologi'a *f.* bacteriology.
batterio'logo *m.* bacteriologist.
battesimale *adj.* baptismal.
batte'simo *m.* baptism, christening, consecration: **nome di —,** Christian name.
battezzare *vt.* to baptize, christen; to name; to water, add water.
battibecco *m.* squabble, tiff.
batticuore *m.* palpitation.
battimano *m.* applause.
battipanni *m.* clothes beater.
battistero *m.* baptistery.
battistrada *m.* harbinger; *(auto.)* tread.
bat'tito *m.* beat, throb; tick.
battitore *m.* beater; scout.
battuta *f.* beat; witticism, joke; cue; battue; *(mus.)* bar: **— d'arresto,** halt.
battuto *adj.* beaten; wrought: **a spron —,** full speed.
batuf'folo *m.* flock, tuft.
bau'le *m.* trunk: **fare, disfare i bauli,** to pack up, to unpack.
bava *f.* drivel, slaver, slobber.
bavaglino *m.* bib.
bava'glio *m.* gag.
bavarese *m., adj.* Bavarian.
ba'vero *m.* collar.
bavoso *adj.* driveling, slobbery.
bazar *m.* bazaar.
bazza *f.* protruding chin; capital bargain, windfall.
bazze'cola *f.* trifle, fiddlestick.
bazzicare *vt., vi.* to frequent; to consort *(with).*
bazzotto *adj.* soft-boiled.
beare *vt.* to delight; **bearsi** *vr.* to delight *(in).*
beatamente *adv.* blissfully.
beatificare *vt.* to beatify.
beatificazione *f.* beatification.
beatitu'dine *f.* beatitude, bliss.
beato *adj.* blessed, blissful: **— te!** you lucky man!

beccac'cia *f.* woodcock.
beccaccino *m.* snipe.
becca'io *m.* butcher.
beccamorti *m.* gravedigger.
beccare *vt.* to peck; to earn; to catch; **beccarsi** *vr.* to peck each other; to tiff; to get; to catch.
Beccaria, Cesare, Italian economist (1735–1794).
beccheggiare *vt.* to pitch.
beccheg'gio *m.* pitching.
becchime *m.* birdseed.
becchino *m.* gravedigger.
becco (*1*) *m.* beak, bill; burner: **non avere il — di un quattrino,** to be penniless.
becco (*2*) *m.* he-goat; cuckold.
beccuc'cio *m.* spout.
beduino *m., adj.* Bedouin.
befana *f.* white witch; hag; Epiphany.
beffa *f.* mockery; jest.
beffardo *m.* mocker. *adj.* mocking.
beffare *vt.* to mock; **beffarsi** *vr.* to mock *(at).*
beffeggiare *vt.* to ridicule.
bega *f.* trouble; quarrel; litigation.
beghina *f.* sanctimonious woman.
bego'nia *f.* begonia.
belare *vi.* to bleat.
belato *m.* bleat, bleating.
belga *m., f., adj.* Belgian.
bella *f.* sweetheart; final game.
belletto *m.* rouge, cosmetic, makeup.
bellezza *f.* beauty; comeliness: **che —!,** how wonderful!
bel'lico *adj.* war.
bellicoso *adj.* bellicose, belligerent, warlike.
belligerante *m., adj.* belligerent.
belligeranza *f.* belligerency.
bellimbusto *m.* dandy, fop.
Bellini, Vincenzo, Italian composer of operas (1802–1835).
bello *m.* beauty; beau. *adj.* fine, beautiful, handsome, good-looking: **il bel mondo,** the high life; **a bella posta,** on purpose.
belluino *adj.* beastly, ferocious.
belva *f.* wild beast.
belvedere *m.* belvedere; *(naut.)* mizzen-topgallant sail; **carrozza —,** observation car.
Belzebù *m.* Beelzebub.
bemolle *m.* *(mus.)* flat.
benaccetto *adj.* welcome.
benchè *conj.* though, although.
benda *f.* band; bandage.
benda'gio *m.* bandage.
bendare *vt.* to bandage: **— gli occhi a,** to blindfold.
bene *m.* good; love; gift, blessing; possession; welfare: **beni mobili,** chattels; **beni immobili,** real estate; **voler —,** to love. *adv.* well; very;

star —, to be well; star — a uno, to become, suit, one; di — in meglio, better and better.

benedetto *adj.* blessed, holy.

benedire *vt.* to bless.

benedizione *f.* blessing; bliss.

beneducato *adj.* well-bred; polite.

benefattore *m.* benefactor.

benefattrice *f.* benefactress.

beneficare *vt.* to benefit.

beneficenza *f.* charity.

beneficiare *vt.*, *vi.* to benefit.

beneficia'rio *m.* beneficiary; payee. *adj.* beneficial.

beneficiata *f.* benefit performance.

benefi'cio *m.* benefit; profit.

bene'fico *adj.* beneficent.

benemerenza *f.* merit, desert.

beneme'rito *m.* benefactor, supporter. *adj.* well-deserving.

benepla'cito *m.* consent.

benes'sere *m.* welfare; prosperity; well-being, comfort.

benestante *m.* well-to-do person. *adj.* well-to-do, well-off.

benestare *m.* assent; O.K.: dare il —, to approve, to O.K.

benevolenza *f.* benevolence.

bene'volo *adj.* benevolent, kindly.

benfatto *adj.* well-made; shapely.

bengala *m.* Bengal-light, firework.

beniamino *m.* favorite.

benignità *f.* benignity, mildness.

benigno *adj.* benign, favorable; mild.

beninteso *adv.* of course.

benis'simo *adv.* very well, O.K.

bennato *adj.* well-born; well-bred.

benone *adv.* very well.

benpensante *m.* sensible person.

benservito *m.* testimonial, character; dismissal, brushoff.

bensì *conj.* indeed; but; on the contrary: è — venuto, ma non l'ho visto, indeed he came but I did not see him.

benvenuto *m.*, *adj.* welcome: dare il —, to welcome.

benvisto *adj.* liked, popular.

benvoluto *adj.* loved, popular.

benzina *f.* gasoline (*abbr.*: gas).

beone *m.* drunkard, sot, toper.

beota *m.*, *adj.* Boeotian.

bequadro *m.* (*mus.*) natural.

berciare *vi.* to scream.

bere *vt.*[31] to drink; to swallow: darla a — a qualcuno, to take somebody in.

bergamotto *m.*, **bergamotta** *f.* bergamot.

berlina *f.* pillory; berlin; limousine, sedan.

bernoc'colo *m.* swelling, bump; (*fig.*) knack: avere il — della pittura, to have a knack for painting.

berretto *m.*, **berretta** *f.* cap; biretta.

bersagliare *vt.* to bombard; to harass; to badger.

bersa'glio *m.* target, butt: tiro al —, rifle practice.

berta *f.* (*mach.*) pile driver.

bertuc'cia *f.* macaque, pithecus.

bestem'mia *f.* oath, blasphemy.

bestemmiare *vt.*, *vi.* to curse, swear.

be'stia *f.* beast, animal: montare in —, to fly into a passion; — nera, pet aversion.

bestiale *adj.* bestial, beastly, brutish.

bestialità *f.* beastliness; nonsense, bosh.

bestiame *m.* cattle; livestock.

betatrone *m.* betatron.

Betlemme *f.* Bethlehem.

bet'tola *f.* tavern.

betto'nica *f.* betony.

betulla *f.* birch.

bevanda *f.* drink, beverage.

bevatrone *m.* bevatron.

beverag'gio *m.* beverage, drink.

bevi'bile *adj.* potable.

bevitore *m.* drinker.

bevuto *pp.* of bere.

biacca *f.* white lead.

biada *f.* feed; oats; crops.

biancastro *adj.* whitish.

biancheri'a *f.* linen; underwear.

bianchezza *f.* whiteness.

bianco *m.* white; blank; linen; whitewash: di punto in —, all of a sudden. *adj.* white; blank: dare carta bianca, to give carte blanche; notte bianca, sleepless night; carbone —, electricity.

biancore *m.* whiteness.

biancospino *m.* hawthorn.

biascicare *vt.*, *vi.* to mumble.

biasimare *vt.* to blame.

biasime'vole *adj.* reprehensible.

bia'simo *m.* blame, censure.

Bibbia *f.* Bible.

biberon' *m.* feeding bottle, nursing bottle.

bi'bita *f.* drink, beverage.

bi'blico *adj.* Biblical.

biblio'filo *m.* bibliophile.

bibliografi'a *f.* bibliography.

bibliogra'fico *adj.* bibliographic.

biblio'grafo *m.* bibliographer.

biblioteca *f.* library: — circolante, lending library.

biblioteca'rio *m.* librarian.

bicarbonato *m.* bicarbonate.

bicchiere *m.* glass, cup.

bicicletta *f.* bicycle; bike.

biciclo *m.* ordinary, bicycle.

bici'pite *m.* biceps.

bicocca *f.* shanty.

bicolore *adj.* two-colored.

bicon'cavo *adj.* biconcave.

biconvesso *adj.* biconvex.
bidè *m.* bidet.
bidello *m.* school janitor.
bidente *m.* pitchfork.
bidone *m.* can, canister; (*slang*) cheat.
bieco *adj.* oblique; sullen; sinister; wicked, dark.
biella *f.* (*mach.*) connecting rod.
biennale *f.* biennial show. *adj.* biennial.
biennio *m.* two-year period.
bie'tola *f.* beet.
bietta *f.* wedge.
bifase *adj.* diphase, two-phase.
bifocale *adj.* bifocal.
bifolco *m.* farmer; boor.
bi'fora *f.* mullioned window.
biforcarsi *vr.* to bifurcate.
biforcazione *f.* bifurcation.
biforcuto *adj.* bifurcated.
biga *f.* chariot.
bigami'a *f.* bigamy.
bi'gamo *m.* bigamist. *adj.* bigamous.
bighellonare *vt.* to saunter, stroll; to idle.
bighellone *m.* stroller; idler.
bi'gio *m.*, *adj.* gray.
biglietteri'o *m.* booking clerk; conductor.
biglietteri'a *f.* ticket bureau; booking office; (*theat.*) box office.
biglietto *m.* ticket; card; note: — d'andata, one-way ticket; — d'andata e ritorno, round-trip ticket.
bigotta *f.* sanctimonious woman, pietist; (*naut.*) dead-eye.
bigotteri'a *f.* sanctimony.
bigotto *m.* sanctimonious man, pietist.
bilancella *f.* (*naut.*) trawler.
bilan'cia *f.* scales (*pl.*), balance; trawl net; whiffletree.
bilanciare *vt.*, bilanciarsi *vr.* to balance.
bilanciere *m.* balance; balance wheel; cross-beam.
bilan'cio *m.* balance; budget; estimate: — fallimentare, financial statement; fare il —, to balance (*books*).
bilaterale *adj.* bilateral; reciprocal.
bile *f.* bile; rage.
bi'lia *f.* pocket; billiard ball: far —, to pocket a ball.
biliardo *m.* billiards.
biliare *adj.* biliary.
bi'lico *m.* balance, equipoise, equilibrium; fulcrum: in —, poised.
bilingue *adj.* bilingual.
bilione *m.* (*U.S.*) billion; (*Engl.*) milliard.
bilioso *adj.* bilious.
bimba *f.* child; infant; little girl.
bimbo *m.* child; infant; little boy, "kid."

bimensile *adj.* semimonthly.
bimestrale *adj.* bimestrial.
bimestre *m.* two months.
bimotore *m.* twin-engined plane.
bina'rio *m.* track, rails: — morto, siding.
binda *f.* jack, screwjack.
binoc'colo *m.* binoculars (*pl.*)
bino'mio *m.* binomial.
bioc'colo *m.* flake; flock, tuft.
biochi'mica *f.* biochemistry.
bioge'nesi *f.* biogenesis.
biografi'a *f.* biography.
bio'grafo *m.* biographer.
biologi'a *f.* biology.
biolo'gico *adj.* biological.
bio'logo *m.* biologist.
bionda *f.* blonde.
biondo *m.* fawn, yellow; blond man. *adj.* blond, fair; fawn-colored, yellow.
bios'sido *m.* dioxide.
bipartito *adj.* bipartite.
bi'pede *m.* biped. *adj.* bipedal.
biplano *m.* biplane.
birba *f.*, birbante *m.* scoundrel.
birbanteri'a *f.* knavery; trick.
birbonata *f.* knavery.
birbone *m.* rogue.
birichinata *f.* prank, escapade.
birichino *m.* urchin.
birillo *m.* skittle: i birilli, ninepins.
birmano *m.*, *adj.* Burmese.
biroc'cio *m.* cart.
birra *f.* beer, ale.
birra'io *m.* brewer.
birreri'a *f.* alehouse.
bis *adv.* encore; bis: chiedere il —, to request an encore.
bisac'cia *f.* wallet, haversack.
bisa'vola *f.* great-grandmother.
bisa'volo *m.* great-grandfather.
bisbe'tica *f.* shrew.
bisbe'tico *adj.* irritable, peevish.
bisbigliare *vt.*, *vi.* to whisper.
bisbi'glio *m.* whisper.
bisboc'cia *f.* merrymaking; food spree.
bisca *f.* gamblinghouse, hell.
biscaglina *f.* Jacob's ladder.
biscazziere *m.* gamblinghouse operator; marker.
bi'scia *f.* watersnake, snake.
biscottare *vt.* to bake.
biscotto *m.* biscuit.
bisestile *adj.* bissextile: anno —, leap year.
bisettrice *f.* bisector.
bisil'labo *m.* disyllable.
bislacco *adj.* queer, wayward.
bislungo *adj.* oblong.
bismuto *m.* bismuth.
bisnonna *f.* great-grandmother.
bisnonno *m.* great-grandfather.

bisogna f. task, business.

bisognare vi. to be necessary; must, shall; to need,. to want, to be in need of; to be compelled to, to have to.

bisogno m. need, want, necessity.

bisognoso adj. needy, poor.

bisolfuro m. disulphide.

bisonte m. bison.

bissare vt. to call for an encore.

bistecca f. beefsteak.

bisticciare vi., bisticciarsi vr. to quarrel, squabble.

bistic'cio m. squabble; pun.

bistrattare vt. to maltreat.

bistro m. bister, bistre.

bi'sturi m. bistoury.

bisunto adj. greasy.

bitor'zolo m. bump; pimple.

bitume m. bitumen.

bituminare vt. to bituminize.

bivaccare vi. to bivouac (ppr. bivouacking; pass.; pp. bivouacked).

bivacco m. bivouac.

bivalente adj. bivalent.

bi'vio m. crossroad; quandary.

bizantino adj. Byzantine.

bizza f. flare, freak, whim.

bizzarri'a f. oddity, queerness.

bizzarro adj. bizarre, queer.

bizzeffe, (a) adv. in plenty, galore.

bizzoso adj. peevish, whimsical.

blandire vt. to blandish, soothe, cajole.

blandi'zia f. blandishment.

blando adj. bland, subdued.

blasfemo adj. blasphemous.

blasonato adj. noble.

blasone m. coat of arms; blazon.

blaterare vi. to babble.

blatta f. cockroach, black beetle.

blenorragi'a f. blenorrhoea.

bleso adj. lisping.

blindare vt. to armor.

blindato adj. armored, plated.

bloccare vt. to block; to blockade.

blocco m. blocking; blockade; block, lump; pad: in —, in bulk.

blu m., adj. blue.

bluastro adj. bluish.

blusa f. blouse.

boa (1) m. (zool.) boa.

boa (2) f. (naut.) buoy.

boato m. bellow, boom, roar.

bobina f. coil, reel, spool.

bocca f. mouth; muzzle; opening, hole: — da fuoco, ordnance piece; — da incendio, fire hydrant; in — al lupo! good luck!; acqua in —! mum's the word; a — aperta, agape.

boccac'cia f. grimace.

Boccaccio, Giovanni, Italian author and writer of novelle, Decamerone (1313-1375).

boccale m. cup, jug, tankard.

boccaporto m. hatch, hatchway.

boccascena f. apron stage.

boccata f. mouthful; puff.

boccheggiare vi. to gasp, fight for breath; to be dying.

Boccherini, Luigi, Italian composer (1743-1805).

bocchetta f. hole, spout; keyhole.

bocchino m. cigarette holder; (mus.) mouthpiece.

boc'cia f. pot; bowling ball.

bocciare vt. to reject; to bowl.

boccino m. jack.

boc'cio, bocciuolo m. bud.

boc'cola f. earring; (mach.) bush.

bocconcino m. morsel.

boccone m. mouthful; bit, scrap: a pezzi e bocconi, by fits and starts.

bocconi adv. flat on one's face.

bodino m. pudding.

boemo m., adj. Bohemian.

boero m., adj. Boer.

bo'ia m. executioner, hangman.

Boiardo, Matteo Maria, Italian poet (1434?-1494).

boiata f. infamy; trash.

boicottag'gio m. boycottage.

boicottare vt. to boycott.

Boito, Arrigo, Italian composer, Mefistofele (1842-1918).

bol'gia f. hellpit; chaos.

bo'lide m. bolide; racer.

bolina f. (naut.) bowline.

bolla f. bubble; blister; bull (as papal).

bollare vt. to stamp; to brand (with, as).

bollatura f. stamping, branding.

bollente adj. boiling, hot.

bolletta f. bill; receipt; certificate: essere in —, to be stone-broke.

bolletta'rio m. counterfoil-book.

bollettino m. bulletin; report: — meteorologico, weather forecast.

bollire vt., vi. to boil; to simmer.

bollitore m. boiler.

bollo m. stamp: carta da —, stamped paper; marca da —, revenue stamp.

bollore m. boil; boiling point; bubbling; turmoil; ardor.

bolscevico m., adj. Bolshevist.

bolscevismo m. Bolshevism.

bolso adj. broken-winded.

boma f. (naut.) boom.

bomba f. bomb: tornare a —, to return to the point; a prova di —, bombproof; — atomica, atom bomb.

bombardamento m. bombing: aereo da —, bomber.

bombardare vt. to bomb; to bombard.

bombardiere m. gunner; bombardier; bomber.

bombetta f. derby hat.

bom'bola *f.* bottle, cylinder: — di ossigeno, oxygen tank.
bomboniera *f.* candy box.
bompresso *m.* (naut.) bowsprit.
bonac'cia *f.* calm.
bonaccione *m.* good fellow.
bonariamente *adv.* good-naturedly.
bonarietà *f.* good nature, kindliness.
bona'rio *adj.* good-natured, kindly.
boni'fica *f.* reclamation.
bonificare *vt.* to reclaim; to grant a discount of.
bonomi'a *f.* good nature.
bonsenso *m.* sense, good sense.
bontà *f.* goodness; kindness.
bontempone *m.* free liver; jolly good fellow.
bonzo *m.* bonze.
bora *f.* bora.
borace *m.* borax.
borato *m.* borate.
borbottare *vt.*, *vi.* to grumble.
borbotti'o *m.* grumble.
borchia *f.* boss.
bordare *vt.* to hem.
bordata *f.* (naut.) broadside.
bordatura *f.* hem, border.
bordeggiare *vi.* to tack.
bordello *m.* brothel; noise.
borderò *m.* account, list.
bordo *m.* border; board; hem, edge: a —, on board; virare di —, to veer around; — del marciapiede, curb.
bordura *f.* hem, edge.
bo'rea *m.* north wind.
boreale *adj.* boreal, northern.
borgata *f.* hamlet.
borghese *m.*, *adj.* bourgeois; civilian: in —, in civvies; poliziotto in —, plain-clothesman.
borghesi'a *f.* bourgeoisie, middle class.
Borgia, Cesare, Italian cardinal and military leader (1476–1507).
Borgia, Lucrezia, sister and political Contemporary of Cesare (1480–1591).
borgo *m.* hamlet.
borgomastro *m.* burgomaster.
bo'ria *f.* conceit, haughtiness.
bo'rico *adj.* boric.
borioso *adj.* haughty.
boro *m.* (chem.) boron.
borra *f.* flocks; stuffing; hair.
borrac'cia *f.* canteen.
Borromeo, Carlo, Italian cardinal and saint (1538–1584).
borsa *f.* purse, pouch, bag, sack: Borsa Valori, Stock Exchange; — di studio, scholarship.
borsaiuolo *m.* pickpocket.
borseggiare *vt.* to rob, pick (some-body's) pocket.
borseg'gio *m.* pocket-picking.

borsellino *m.* purse, pouch.
borsetta *f.* handbag.
borsista *m.* stock-broker.
bosca'glia *f.* brushwood, bush.
boscaiuolo *m.* woodcutter.
bosco *m.* wood, woods, forest: — ceduo, coppice.
boscoso *adj.* woody.
bosso *m.* box tree; boxwood.
bos'solo *m.* box; boxwood; cartridge case.
bota'nica *f.* botany.
bota'nico *m.* botanist. *adj.* botanic.
bo'tola *f.* trap door.
botta *f.* blow, thump; thrust.
botta'io *m.* cooper.
bottata *f.* thrust, hint.
botte *f.* barrel, cask.
bottega *f.* shop; workshop.
bottega'io *m.* shopkeeper.
botteghino *m.* box office.
Botticelli, Sandro, Italian painter (1447?–1510).
botti'glia *f.* bottle.
bottiglieri'a *f.* wineshop.
bottino *m.* booty, loot.
botto *m.* stroke; toll.
botto, (di) *adv.* suddenly.
bottoncino *m.* small button; stud; bud.
bottone *m.* button; knob; bud: bottoni gemelli, links; attaccare un — a, to buttonhole.
bovaro *m.* cowherd, cowboy.
bove *see* **bue.**
bovino *adj.* bovine.
bozza *f.* sketch; proof; bump; (naut.) stopper.
bozzello *m.* (naut.) block.
bozzetto *m.* sketch, drawing.
boz'zolo *m.* cocoon; lump.
braccare *vt.* to hunt, stalk; to bay.
braccetto, (a), arm in arm: prendere uno a —, to take one's arm.
bracciale *m.* armlet.
braccialetto *m.* bracelet: orologio a —, wrist watch.
bracciante *m.* day laborer.
bracciata *f.* armful; stroke.
braccio *m.* arm; limb; wing; branch; bracket; fathom.
bracciuolo *m.* arm (of a chair).
bracco *m.* hound; setter; pointer.
bracconiere *m.* poacher.
brace *f.* live coal, ember.
braciere *m.* firepan, brazier.
braciuola *f.* chop.
brado *adj.* wild.
bragozzo *m.* (naut.) lugger.
brama *f.* greed; longing.
Bramante, Donato d'Agnolo, Italian architect and painter (1444–1514).
bramare *vt.* to covet.
bramino *m.* Brahmin.

bramire *vi.* to bellow, bell.
bramito *m.* bellow, roar; bell.
bramosi'a *f.* greed.
bramoso *adj.* greedy, covetous.
branca *f.* claw; tentacle; flight; branch.
bran'chia *f.* gill.
brancicare *vt.* to handle.
branco *m.* flock, pack, herd; (*ichthyol.*) shoal, school.
brancolare *vi.* to grope.
branda *f.* cot, folding bed.
brandello *m.* shred, tatter.
brandire *vt.* to brandish.
brando *m.* sword.
brano *m.* shred, tatter; passage.
branzino *m.* bass (fish).
brasile *m.* brazilwood.
brat'tea *f.* bract.
bravac'cio *m.* bully, braggart.
bravata *f.* bluster, brag.
bravo (*1*) *m.* bravo.
bravo (*2*) *adj.* brave; clever, skillful: un — ragazzo, a good, nice boy.
bravura *f.* courage; skill.
brec'cia *f.* breach, gap; breccia; metal.
brefotro'fio *m.* foundling hospital.
bretelle *f.pl.* suspenders.
breve (*1*) *m.* (papal) brief.
breve (*2*) *adj.* short, brief; concise.
brevemente *adv.* briefly.
brevettare *vt.* to patent.
brevettato *adj.* patented.
brevetto *m.* patent; brevet.
brevia'rio *m.* breviary. license.
brevità *f.* shortness, brevity.
brezza *f.* breeze.
bricco *m.* kettle, pot, urn.
bricconata *f.* knavery, roguery.
briccone *m.* rascal, scamp.
bricconeri'a *f.* roguery.
bri'ciola *f.* crumb, bit.
briga *f.* trouble; care; quarrel: attaccar —, to pick a quarrel.
brigadiere *m.* brigadier.
brigantag'gio *m.* brigandage.
brigante *m.* brigand, bandit.
brigantino *m.* (*naut.*) brig.
brigare *vi.* to intrigue.
brigata *f.* party; brigade.
brighella *m.* clown.
bri'glia *f.* bridle; (*pl.*) reins: a — sciolta, full speed.
brigoso *adj.* hard, difficult.
brillamento *m.* firing; husking; glare.
brillante *m.* brilliant, diamond; comic (actor). *adj.* brilliant; shining.
brillantemente *adv.* brilliantly.
brillantina *f.* brilliantine, pomade.
brillare *vt.* to fire, blow up; to husk. *vi.* to shine, sparkle.
brillo *adj.* tipsy, woozy.
brina *f.* hoarfrost, rime.
brinare *vi.* to frost.

brindare *vi.* to toast.
brin'disi *m.* toast.
bri'o *m.* sprightliness, liveliness.
briosamente *adv.* lively, briskly.
brioso *adj.* brisk, lively.
bri'scola *f.* trump.
britan'nico *adj.* British.
bri'vido *m.* shiver, shudder; thrill.
brizzolato *adj.* grizzled.
brizzolatura *f.* grizzling.
brocca *f.* jug, pitcher; (*bot.*) shoot.
broccatello *m.* brocatel.
broccato *m.* brocade.
brocco *m.* twig; iron-sting; jade.
broc'colo *m.* broccoli.
broda *f.* slops; rigmarole.
broda'glia *f.* slops.
brodetto *m.* fish soup.
brodo *m.* broth, soup.
brodoso *adj.* thin, juicy.
brogliazzo *m.* waste book.
bro'glio *m.* intrigue, cabal.
brolo *m.* kitchen garden.
bromo *m.* bromine.
bromuro *m.* bromide.
bronchi *m.pl.* bronchi.
bronchiale *adj.* bronchial.
bronchite *f.* bronchitis.
bron'cio *m.* pout; mettere il —, to pout.
broncopolmonite *f.* bronchopneumonia.
brontolamento *see* brontolio.
brontolare *vi.* to grumble.
brontoli'o *m.* grumbling; rumbling.
brontolone *m.* grumbler.
bronzare *vi.* to bronze.
bronzatura *f.* bronzing.
bron'zeo *adj.* bronzy; tanned.
bronzina *f.* bushing; bearing.
bronzo *m.* bronze: faccia di —, brazen face.
brossura *f.* brochure; unbound book.
brucare *vt.* to graze.
bruciacchiare *vt.* to scorch.
bruciacchiatura *f.* scorching.
bruciante *adj.* burning.
bruciapelo, (a) *adv.* point-blank.
bruciare *vt., vi.* to burn; to sear; to cauterize; bruciarsi *vr.* to burn oneself.
bruciatic'cio *m.* smell of burning.
bruciatura *f.* burning; burn, sear.
bruciore *m.* burning sensation.
bruco *m.* caterpillar, worm.
brughiera *f.* heath.
brulicare *vi.* to swarm.
brulichi'o *m.* swarm, swarming.
brullo *adj.* barren, bare.
bruma *f.* cold weather; mist; (*zool.*) shipworm.
bruna, brunetta *f.* brunette.
Brunelleschi, Filippo, Florentine architect (1377–1446).

brunire *vt.* to burnish, polish; to blue.
brunitura *f.* burnish; blueing.
bruno *m.* brown; brunet. *adj.* brown, dark; swarthy.
Bruno, Giordano, Italian philosopher, burned at the stake (1548–1600).
brusca *f.* horse brush.
bruscamente *adv.* sharply; roughly, curtly, gruffly; abruptly.
brusco *adj.* sharp; sour; rough; curt; gruff; abrupt.
bru′scolo *m.* mote, speck.
brusi′o *m.* hubbub, buzzing.
brutale *adj.* brutal, beastly.
brutalità *f.* brutality.
brutalmente *adv.* brutally.
bruto *m.*, *adj.* brute.
bruttare *vt.* to soil, foul.
bruttezza *f.* ugliness.
brutto *adj.* ugly; bad.
bruttura *f.* ugliness; turpitude.
bubbone *m.* bubo.
bubbo′nico *adj.* bubonic.
buca *f.* hole; pocket: — **delle lettere**, letterbox.
bucaneve *m.* (*bot.*) snowdrop.
bucaniere *m.* buccaneer.
bucare *vt.* to bore, pierce; to puncture: to prick; **bucarsi** *vr.* to prick oneself, be punctured.
bucato *m.* wash, washing.
bucatura *f.* boring; puncture.
buc′cia *f.* peel, rind, skin.
bucherellare *vt.* to riddle.
buco *m.* hole.
buco′lico *adj.* bucolic, pastoral.
Budda *m.* Buddha.
buddismo *m.* Buddhism.
buddista *m.*, *adj.* Buddhist.
budello *m.* bowel, gut, catgut; casing (*for sausages*).
budino *m.* pudding.
bue *m.* ox (*pl.* oxen).
bu′falo *m.* buffalo.
bufera *f.* storm.
buffare *vt.* to huff (*at draughts*).
buffetto *m.* flip of the finger, a puff of wind.
buffo (*1*) *m.* gust.
buffo (*2*) *adj.* funny, droll; comic.
buffonata *f.* buffoonery, jest.
buffone *m.* buffoon, clown.
buffoneri′a *f.* clownery.
bugi′a *f.* lie; taper.
bugiardo *m.* liar. *adj.* false.
bugigat′tolo *m.* cubbyhole.
bugliuolo *m.* bucket, bail.
bugna *f.* boss; (*naut.*) clew.
bu′io *m.* darkness.
bulbo *m.* bulb.
bulboso *adj.* bulbous.
bul′garo *m.* Russia leather. *adj.*, *m.* Bulgarian.
bulinare *vt.* to engrave.

bulino *m.* burin.
bulletta *f.* tack.
bullone *m.* bolt.
buona, (alla) *adv.* plainly; informally. *adj.* plain; informal.
buonamano *f.* tip, gratuity.
Buonarroti, Michelangelo, *see* **Michelangelo**.
buongusta′io *m.* gourmet; connoisseur.
buono *m.* good; bond; coupon: — **postale internazionale,** international reply coupon. *adj.* good; kind, kindly; fit; fine: **alla buona,** plain, plainly; **con le buone o con le cattive,** willy-nilly.
buonsenso *m.* common sense.
buonuscita *f.* good will.
burattare *vt.* to bolt, to sift.
burattina′io *m.* puppet showman.
burattinata *f.* mummery.
burattino *m.* puppet.
buratto *m.* bolter, sifter.
burbanza *f.* arrogance.
burbanzoso *adj.* arrogant.
bur′bero *adj.* churlish, surly; gruff.
burchiello *m.* (*naut.*) lighter.
buricco *m.* donkey.
burla *f.* joke, jest, trick, prank.
burlare *vt.*, *vi.*, **burlarsi** *vr.* to make fun of; to jeer, poke fun at.
burlesco *adj.* burlesque, comic.
burletta *f.* farce.
burlone *m.* jester, joker, prankster.
buro′crate *m.* bureaucrat.
burocra′tico *adj.* bureaucratic.
burocrazi′a *f.* bureaucracy, red tape.
burrasca *f.* storm.
burrascoso *adj.* stormy.
burrifi′cio *m.* dairy.
burro *m.* butter.
burrone *m.* ravine.
burroso *adj.* buttery.
buscare *vt.*, **buscarsi** *vr.* to get; to catch.
busec′chia *f.* casing (*for sausages*); tripe.
busillis *m.* problem, question.
Busoni, Ferruccio Benvenuto, Italian pianist and composer (1866–1924).
bussa *f.* blow; (*pl.*) beating.
bussare *vi.* to knock.
bus′sola (*1*) *f.* compass: **perdere la —** to lose one's head.
bus′sola (*2*) *f.* screen door.
bussolotto *m.* juggler's box: **giuoco dei bussolotti,** hocus-pocus.
busta *f.* envelope; portfolio; case.
busta′ia *f.* corsetmaker.
bustina *f.* small envelope; (*mil.*) cap.
busto *m.* trunk, torso; bust; corset.
butano *m.* butane.
butirroso *adj.* buttery.
buttafuori *m.* (*theat.*) callboy; (*naut.*) outrigger.

buttare vt. to throw, fling, hurl; to squander; to throw away; to secrete; **buttarsi** vr. to throw oneself.

butterato adj. pockmarked.
but'tero (1) m. pockmark; (2) m. herder, cowboy.
buzzo m. belly.

C

ca'bala f. cabbala; swindle; cabal, plot.
cabali'stico adj. cabbalistic.
cabina f. cabin, cab; booth; bathhouse; cockpit (of an airplane); car (of an elevator): — di lusso (naut.), stateroom.
cablogramma m. cable.
cabotag'gio m. cabotage; foreign trade.
cabrare vi. (aeron.) to zoom.
cabrata f. (aeron.) zoom, chandelle.
cacao m. cocoa.
cacare vi. to defecate.
cacasenno m. wiseacre.
cacatoa m. parakeet.
cacca f. ordure; (fig.) dirt.
cac'cia (1) f. hunting; fowling; chase; game.
cac'cia (2) m. (aeron.) fighter; (naut.) destroyer.
cacciagione f. game, venison.
cacciare vt., vi. to go hunting; to chase; to rout; to send away; to thrust, drive in; to throw; **cacciarsi** vr. to thrust oneself, hide oneself: **cacciare un urlo,** to utter a cry, scream.
cacciasommergi'bili m. submarine chaser.
cacciata f. routing.
cacciatora f. hunting jacket.
cacciatore m. hunter, huntsman: — di frodo, poacher.
cacciatorpediniere m. destroyer.
cacciatrice f. huntress.
cacciavite m. screw driver.
cac'cola f. rheum; mucus; grease.
cachi m. khaki, Japanese persimmon. adj. khaki-colored.
cachinno m. cachinnation.
ca'cio m. cheese.
cacofoni'a f. cacophony.
cacofo'nico adj. cacophonous.
cadauno adj. each.
cada'vere m. corpse, body.
cadave'rico adj. cadaverous.
cadente adj. falling; decrepit.
cadenza f. cadence; rhythm.
cadere vi.[22] to fall; to drop; to set.
cadetto m. cadet.
cad'mio m. cadmium.
Cadorna, Luigi, Italian general (1850–1928).
caducità f. transiency, perishableness.
caduco adj. deciduous; transient: **mal —,** falling sickness.

caduta f. fall, crash; downfall.
caduto m. dead. pp. of **cadere,** fallen.
caffè m. coffee; café: — concerto, music-hall.
caffeina f. caffeine.
caffettiera f. coffeepot.
cafone m. boor.
cagionare vt. to cause.
cagione f. cause: a — di, on account of, because of.
cagione'vole adj. sickly.
cagliare vi. to curdle.
ca'glio m. rennet.
cagna f. bitch.
cagnara f. barking; uproar; brawl.
cagnesco adj. doggish: guardare in —, to look askance at.
Caienna, (pepe di) m. cayenne (pepper).
caimano m. caiman.
caino m. (Cain) traitor.
Cairoli, Benedetto, Italian statesman (1826–1889).
cala f. creek; hold.
calabrone m. hornet, bumblebee.
calafatare vt. to calk.
calama'io m. inkpot, inkstand.
calamaro m. cuttlefish.
calamita f. loadstone; magnet.
calamità f. calamity.
calamitare vt. to magnetize.
calamitoso adj. calamitous.
ca'lamo m. (bot.) calamus.
calandra f. (mach.) calender.
calandrare vt. to calender.
calante adj. declining; setting.
calap'pio m. noose; snare.
calare vt. to lower; to strike. vi. to descend (upon); to decline; to set; to drop; to decrease: il — della notte, nightfall; **calarsi** vr. to let oneself down; to dive.
calata f. dropping; lowering; descent; wharf.
calca f. throng, crowd.
calcagno m. heel.
calcara f. limekiln.
calcare vt. to tread (upon); to trample; to press; to force; to stress.
cal'care m. limestone.
calca'reo adj. calcareous.
calce (1) f. lime.
calce (2) f. bottom, foot: in —, at (the) foot.
calcedo'nio m. chalcedony.
calcese m. (naut.) masthead.

calcestruzzo *m.* concrete.
calciare *vi.* to kick.
calciatore *m.* kicker; soccer player.
calcificare *vt.* to calcify.
calcificazione *f.* calcification.
calcina *f.* lime, mortar.
calcinac'cio *m.* plaster rubbish; (*pl.*) ruins, debris, rubble.
calcina'io *m.* lime pit.
calcinare *vt.* to calcine; to lime.
cal'cio (1) *m.* kick; butt, stock; (*sport*) soccer.
cal'cio (2) *m.* (*chem.*) calcium.
calciocianamide *f.* calcium cyanamide.
calco *m.* cast; trace.
calcografia *f.* chalcography.
calcola'bile *adj.* calculable.
calcolare *vt.*, *vi.* to calculate; to reckon; to value; to plan; to rely (*on*).
calcolatore *m.* reckoner; schemer. *adj.* calculating.
calcolatrice *f.* reckoner: macchina —, calculator, calculating machine.
cal'colo *m.* calculation; estimate; guess; plan; calculus (*pl.* calculi).
calcolosi *f.* (*pathol.*) stone.
calcomani'a *f.* decalcomania.
calcopirite *f.* chalcopyrite.
calcotipi'a *f.* copperplate.
calda'ia *f.* boiler.
calda'io *m.* caldron.
caldallessa *f.* boiled chestnut.
caldamente *adv.* warmly.
caldana *f.* flush; infatuation.
caldarrosto *f.* roast chestnut.
caldeggiare *vt.* to favor, support.
caldera'io *m.* coppersmith.
calderone *m.* caldron.
caldo *m.* warmth, heat: aver —, to be hot; fa —, it is warm; tener —, to keep warm. *adj.* warm; hot.
calefazione *f.* calefaction.
caleidosco'pio *m.* kaleidoscope.
calenda'rio *m.* almanac, calendar.
calende *f.pl.* kalends: rimandare alle — greche, to put off till doomsday.
calendimag'gio *m.* May Day.
calesse *m.* calèche, buggy.
calettare *vt.* to mortise.
calibrare *vt.* to calibrate.
ca'libro *m.* caliber; gauge (*fig.*) size.
ca'lice *m.* cup; chalice.
califfo *m.* caliph.
cali'gine *f.* fog, mist, smog.
caliginoso *adj.* foggy, misty.
calla'ia *f.* gap; path.
calle *f.* lane.
calli'fugo *m.* corn plaster.
calligrafi'a *f.* calligraphy, penmanship; handwriting.
calli'grafo *m.* calligrapher.
callista *m.* podiatrist, chiropodist.
callo *m.* corn: fare il — a, to become inured to.

callosità *f.* callosity, callus.
calloso *adj.* corny, horny.
calma *f.* calm; composure.
calmante *m.*, *adj.* sedative.
calmare *vt.* to calm, soothe; calmarsi *vr.* to calm down; to abate.
calmiere *m.* compulsory price ceiling.
calmo *adj.* quiet, still; cool.
calo *m.* decrease; shrinkage.
calomelano *m.* calomel.
calore *m.* heat; warmth; inflammation.
calori'a *f.* calorie, calory.
calori'fero *m.* heater.
calori'fico *adj.* calorific.
caloroso *adj.* warm; calorific.
calo'scia *f.* galosh, overshoe.
calotta *f.* skull cap; cap: — cranica, brainpan, skull.
calpestare *vt.* to trample.
calun'nia *f.* slander, calumny.
calunniare *vt.* to slander.
calunniatore *m.* slanderer.
calunnioso *adj.* slanderous.
calura *f.* heat.
Calva'rio *m.* Calvary.
calvi'zie *f.* baldness.
calvo *adj.* bald.
calza *f.* stocking; sock; hose; wick; fare la —, to knit.
calzare (1) *vt.* to boot; to put on; to wear. *vi.* to fit, suit.
calzare (2) *m.* boot.
calzato'io *m.* shoe horn.
calzatura *f.* footwear (*pl.*).
calzaturifi'cio *m.* shoe factory.
calzerotto *m.* sock.
calzetta'io *m.* hosier.
calzettone *m.* woolen sock.
calzola'io *m.* shoemaker.
calzoleri'a *f.* shoemaker shop.
calzoncini *m.pl.* shorts.
calzoni *m.pl.* trousers; pants; slacks; breeches.
camaleonte *m.* chameleon.
camarilla *f.* camarilla, cabal.
cambiale *f.* bill (*of exchange*), IOU; draft; promissory note; — di favore, accommodation bill.
cambiamento *m.* change.
cambiare *vt.*, *vi.* to change, alter: — vita, to turn over a new leaf; cambiarsi *vr.* to change; to turn into.
cambiavalute *m.* moneychanger.
cam'bio *m.* change, shift; exchange; (*mach.*) gear box, transmission; (*mil.*) relief.
cambri *m.* cambric.
cambusa *f.* galley, caboose.
cambusiere *m.* steward.
came'lia *f.* camellia.
ca'mera *f.* room, chamber; parliament: — di combustione, firebox; —

d'aria, inner tube; — ardente, chapelle ardente.
camerata (*1*) *f.* dormitory.
camerata (*2*) *m.* friend; comrade.
cameratismo *m.* comradeship.
cameriera *f.* maid; waitress.
cameriere *m.* valet, servant; waiter.
camerino *m.* cubbyhole; dressing room; lavatory.
ca'mice *m.* alb; gown.
camiceri'a *f.* shirt shop.
camicetta *f.* blouse.
cami'cia *f.* shirt; chemise; wrapper; (*mach.*) jacket: — di forza, strait jacket.
camicia'io *m.*, **camicia'ia** *f.* shirt maker.
camiciola *f.* sports shirt; T-shirt.
camiciotto *m.* blouse, shirt.
caminetto *m.* fireplace.
camino *m.* chimney.
ca'mion *m.* truck; lorry.
camiona'bile, camionale *f.* highway.
camionetta *f.* pickup truck, jeep.
camionista *m.* truckdriver.
cami'tico *adj.* Hamitic.
camma *f.* (*mach.*) cam.
cammelliere *m.* cameldriver.
cammello *m.* camel.
camme'o *m.* cameo.
camminamento *m.* communication trench.
camminare *vi.* to walk; to stroll.
camminata *f.* walk; gait.
camminatore *m.* walker, stroller.
cammino *m.* way; road; path.
camomilla *f.* camomile.
camorra *f.* Camorra; graft.
camorrista *m.* Camorrist; grafter.
camosciare *vt.* to shammy.
camo'scio *m.* chamois, shammy; suède.
campagna *f.* country, countryside; campaign: artiglieria da —, field artillery.
campagnuola *f.* countrywoman.
campagnuolo *m.* countryman. *adj.* country, rural.
campale *adj.* decisive; pitched.
campana *f.* bell: — di vetro, bell jar.
campanac'cio *m.* cattle bell.
campanaro *m.* bellringer.
campanella *f.* small bell; (*bot.*) bell-flower.
Campanella, Tommaso, Italian philosopher, *City of the Sun* (1568–1639).
campanello *m.* bell.
campanile *m.* steeple, belfry.
campanilismo *m.* localism.
campa'nula *f.* campanula.
campare *vi.* to live.
campata *f.* span.
compato *adj.*: — in aria, farfetched, improbable.

campeggiare *vi.* to stand out; to camp.
campeggiatore *m.*, **campeggiatrice** *f.* camper.
campeg'gio *m.* camping; logwood.
campestre *adj.* rural, country: corsa —, cross-country race.
Campido'glio *m.* capitol.
campionare *vt.* to sample.
campiona'rio *m.* sample book, sample set; pattern book.
campionato *m.* championship; competition.
campione *m.* champion; ace; sample; pattern; specimen: — senza valore, sample of no commercial value.
campionessa *f.* championess.
campo *m.* field; camp; ground; trade, industry: — visivo, range of vision; — d'onda (*radio*), wave band; — di tennis, tennis court; aiutante di —, adjutant; —lungo (*moving pictures*), long shot.
camposanto *m.* churchyard.
camuffamento *m.* disguise.
camuffare *vt.* to disguise; **camuffarsi** *vr.* to disguise oneself.
camuso *adj.* snub-nosed.
canadese *m.*, *adj.* Canadian.
cana'glia *f.* rabble; scoundrel.
canagliata *f.* knavery.
canale *m.* channel; canal; gutter; drain; (*anat.*) duct.
canaletto *m.* gutter; groove.
canalizzare *vt.* to canalize.
canalizzazione *f.* canalization.
canalone *m.* ravine.
ca'napa *f.* hemp.
canapè *m.* settee, sofa.
canapifi'cio *m.* hemp mill.
ca'napo *m.* rope, cable.
cana'pulo *m.* stalk of hemp.
canarino *m.* canary.
cancan *m.* can-can; racket; gossip.
cancella'bile *adj.* erasable.
cancellare *vt.* to cross out; to erase; to wipe out; to cancel; to efface.
cancellata *f.* railing.
cancellatura *f.* erasure.
cancellazione *f.* cancellation.
cancelleri'a *f.* chancellery; stationery.
cancelliere *m.* chancellor; clerk.
cancello *m.* gate, gateway.
canceroso *adj.* cancerous.
cancrena *f.* gangrene.
cancrenoso *adj.* gangrenous.
cancro *m.* cancer; (*astr.*) Cancer.
candeggiare *vt.* to bleach.
candeg'gio *m.* bleaching.
candela *f.* candle; chandelle; spark plug; (*aeron.*) nose dive.
candelabro *m.* chandelier.
candeliere *m.* candlestick.
Candelora *f.* Candlemas.

candelotto m. icicle.
candidato m. candidate.
candidatura f. candidature.
can'dido adj. white; candid; naive.
candire vt. to candy.
candito m. candy. adj. candied.
candore m. whiteness; candor.
cane m. dog, hound; cock (of a gun);
   unskilled person, ass; bad actor,
   "flop": menare il can per l'aia, to
   beat about the bush.
canea f. rabble; hubbub.
canestro m., canestra f. basket.
can'fora f. camphor.
canforare vt. to camphorate.
cangiante adj. changeable; shot: seta
   —, shot silk.
canguro m. kangaroo.
cani'cola f. dog days; (astr.) Dog Star.
canile m. kennel, doghouse.
canino (1) m. canine tooth.
canino (2) adj. canine: tosse canina,
   whooping cough.
cani'zie f. frostiness; old age.
canna f. cane, reed; pipe; pole; barrel
   (of a gun): — da pesca, fishing rod;
   — del camino, flue.
cannella f. cinnamon.
cannello m. pipe; stick, rod: — della
   pipa, pipestem.
canni'bale m., adj. cannibal.
cannicciata f. reed fence.
cannic'cio m. wattle.
cannocchiale m. spyglass, binoculars
   (pl.); field glass; opera glass.
cannonata f. gunshot; (it. slang) hit
   (something excellent).
cannoncino m. small gun, howitzer;
   pleat; sweet roll.
cannone m. gun, cannon; pipe, tube;
   box pleat (of a skirt); (it. slang)
   "smart apple," "corker."
cannoneggiare vt. to cannonade.
cannoniera f. gunboat.
cannoniere m. gunner.
cannuc'cia f. tubule; penholder; pipestem.
can'nula f. (med.) cannula.
canoa f. canoe.
ca'none m. rule, tenet, canon; rent.
cano'nica f. parsonage, presbytery.
canonicato m. canonicate.
cano'nico m. canon. adj. canonical:
   diritto —, canon law.
canonizzare vt. to canonize.
canoro adj. canorous, singing.
Canossa f. Canossa: andare a —, to
   eat humble pie, to get off one's high
   horse.
canottag'gio m. boating, rowing.
canottiera f. undershirt; straw hat.
canottiere m. oarsman, rower.
canotto m. boat: — di gomma, rubber
   raft.

Canova, Antonio, Italian sculptor
   (1757–1822).
canovac'cio m. canvas; dishcloth;
   plot (of a story).
cantante m., f. singer.
cantare vt., vi. to sing; (fig.) to squeal.
canta'ride f. (entom.) cantharis, Spanish fly; (chem.) cantharides.
cantasto'rie m. folk singer.
cantatore m., cantatrice f. singer.
canterano m. chest of drawers.
canterellare vt. to hum, croon.
canterino m., canterina f. songster.
can'tero m. chamber pot.
canticchiare vt. to hum, croon.
can'tico m. canticle, hymn, song.
cantiere m. yard; (naut.) shipyard;
   (mil.) navy yard.
cantilena f. dirge; singsong.
cantina f. cellar; coal cellar; wine
   shop.
cantiniere m. cellarman.
canto (1) m. song; singing; canto.
canto (2) m. corner; side: d'altro —,
   on the other hand; dal — mio, for
   my part; da —, aside.
cantonata f. corner, street corner;
   blunder.
cantone m. corner; (geog.) canton.
cantoniera, (casa) f. roadkeeper's
   house.
cantoniere m. roadkeeper; road mender; (rail.) trackwalker.
cantore m. chorister; singer.
cantori'a f. choir.
Cantù, Cesare, Italian historian
   (1807–1895).
cantuc'cio m. corner; nook.
canuto adj. hoary, white-haired.
canzonare vt. to mock.
canzonato'rio adj. mocking.
canzonatura f. mockery, gibe.
canzone f. song: — in voga, hit song.
canzonetta f. song; canzonet.
canzonettista m. songster.f.songstress.
canzoniere m. songbook.
caolino m. kaolin.
caos m. chaos.
capace adj. capacious, roomy; able,
   clever, capable.
capacità f. capaciousness; capacity;
   cleverness; faculty.
capacitare vt. to persuade; capacitarsi
   vr. to be persuaded.
capanna f. hut, cabin; shanty.
capannello m. shanty; group.
capanno m. bower; cabana; booth.
capannone m. barn; hangar, shed.
caparbietà f. stubbornness.
capar'bio adj. stubborn, opinionated.
caparra f. down payment, deposit;
   retainer.
capatina f. call: dare una — da, to
   drop in on.

capeggiare vt. to lead.

capello m. hair: tre capelli, three hairs; pettinarsi (i capelli), to comb one's hair.

capelluto adj. hairy, long-haired: cuoio —, scalp.

capelve'nere m. maidenhair.

capestro m. halter.

capezzale m. bolster; bedside.

capez'zolo m. nipple; udder.

capido'glio m. sperm whale.

capienza f. capacity.

capigliatura f. hair.

capillare adj. capillary.

capillarità f. capillarity.

capinera f. blackcap.

capire vt. to understand, comprehend; to perceive; to realize. vi. to enter (into).

capitale m., f., adj. capital: peccato —, mortal sin.

capitalismo m. capitalism.

capitalista m. capitalist.

capitalizzare vt. to capitalize. vi. to save.

capitana f. flagship.

capitanare vt. to lead.

capitaneri'a f. harbor office, harbor authority.

capitano m. captain; (naut.) skipper: — di lungo corso, shipmaster; — di porto, harbormaster; — di ventura, condottiere.

capitare vi. to happen, occur: mi è capitato d'incontrarla, I happened to meet her.

capitello m. capital; headband.

capitolare vi. to capitulate.

capitolato m. capitulation.

capitolazione f. capitulation.

capi'tolo m. chapter; article.

capitombolare vi. to tumble.

capitom'bolo m. tumble.

capitone m. big eel.

capo m. head; top; end; (geog.) cape; chief, boss; item: da — a fondo, from top to toe; da —, over again; andare da —, to make a paragraph; — di vestiario, garment; — di un partito, party leader; — d'accusa, charge.

capobanda m. bandmaster; ringleader.

capocac'cia m. master of the hounds.

capoc'chia f. head: a —, foolishly.

capoc'cia m. head, chief, boss.

capoco'mico m. actor-manager.

capocronista m. city editor (U.S.).

capocuoco m. chef, head cook.

Capodanno m. New Year's Day.

capofab'brica m. foreman.

capofami'glia m. head of the family.

capofitto, (a) adv. headlong.

capogiro m. dizziness, vertigo.

capolavoro m. masterpiece.

capoli'nea m. terminus.

capolino m.: far —, to peep (in, out).

capoluogo m. county town, county seat, capital.

capomastro m. builder.

capopezzo m. gunner.

capopo'polo m. demagogue.

caporale m. corporal.

caporeparto m. head of a department; floorwalker.

caporione m. ringleader, chief.

caposaldo m. datum point; stronghold; basis; datum.

caposca'rico m. merry andrew.

caposezione m. head of a department.

caposquadra m. squad chief; foreman.

capostazione m. station master.

caposti'pite m. founder (of a family).

capotare vi. to capsize.

capota'vola m. head of the table.

capotreno m. (rail.) conductor.

capoverso m. paragraph.

capovol'gere vt. to overturn, reverse; capovolgersi vr. to overturn, capsize.

capovolgimento m. overturn.

capovolta f. somersault.

cappa (1) f. vault; mantle; frock; cowl.

cappa (2) f. (naut.) trysail.

cappa (3) f. the letter "k."

cappeggiare vi. (naut.) to lie to.

cappella f. chapel.

cappella'io m. hatter.

cappellano m. chaplain, padre.

cappellata f. hatful.

cappelleri'a f. hat store.

cappelliera f. hatbox.

cappello m. hat; cover, cap; pileus (of a mushroom); heading, caption: — a cilindro, tophat; prender —, to take offense.

cappellotto m. percussion cap.

cap'peri! interj. by Jove!

cap'pero m. (bot.) caper.

cap'pio m. bow; noose.

cappona'ia f. coop.

capponare vt. to caponize.

cappone m. capon.

cappotta f. cape; coif; hood.

cappotto m. overcoat; slam.

cappuccino m. Capuchin; coffee with cream.

capra f. goat.

capra'io m. goatherd.

capretto m. kid.

capriata f. truss.

capric'cio m. whim; fancy; flirtation.

capriccioso adj. whimsical, bizarre; moody; peevish; refractory (of a child).

Capricorno m. Capricorn.

caprifo'glio m. honeysuckle.

caprino adj. caprine, goatish.

capriuola f. caper.

capriuolo m. roebuck.

capro, caprone m. he-goat: **capro espiatorio**, scapegoat.

cap'sula f. capsule; percussion cap.

captare vt. to intercept.

captazione f. detecting.

Capuana, Luigi, Italian novelist, poet, and critic (1839–1915).

capzioso adj. captious.

carabat'tola f. trifle, gimcrack.

carabina f. carbine.

carabiniere m. carabineer.

Caracciolo, Francesco, gallant Neapolitan admiral; sentenced to be hanged by Nelson (1752–1799).

carachiri m. hara-kiri.

caracollare vi. to caracole.

caraffa f. decanter.

caram'bola f. carom.

carambolare vi. to carom.

caramella f. candy, drop; monocle.

caramellare vt. to candy.

caramente adv. dearly.

carato m. carat; share; (naut.) part-ownership.

carat'tere m. character; disposition, nature; handwriting; type; feature; temper: — **corsivo**, italics.

caratterista m. character actor; f. character actress.

caratteri'stica f. characteristic, feature, trait, peculiarity, hallmark.

caratteri'stico adj. characteristic.

caratterizzare vt. to characterize.

caratura f. (comm.) share.

Caravaggio, da, Michelangelo Amerighi, Italian painter (1569–1609).

caravella f. caravel, carvel.

carbona'io m. coalman, coal vendor.

carbonato m. carbonate.

carbon'chio m. carbuncle; smut (in wheat).

carboncino m. charcoal (pencil).

carbone m. coal; carbon: **carbon fossile**, mineral coal; — **di legna**, charcoal.

carbonella f. slack, small coal.

carbo'nico adj. carbonic.

carboniera f. (naut.) collier.

carboni'fero adj. carboniferous.

carbonile m. coal bunker.

carbo'nio m. carbon.

carbonizzare vt., **carbonizzarsi** vr. to carburante m. fuel.   [char.

carburare vt. to carburize.

carburatore m. carburetor.

carburazione f. carburization.

carburo m. carbide.

carcassa f. carcass; framework; ribbing (of a ship); wreck; decrepit person, "fossil"; jalopy.

carcera'rio adj. prison: **guardia carceraria**, prison guard, jailor.

carcerato m. prisoner.

car'cere m., f. prison, jail.

carceriere m. jailer, jailor.

carciofo m. artichoke.

carda f. carding machine.

carda'nico adj. universal: **sospensione cardanica**, gimbals; **giunto —**, universal joint.

cardare vt. to card.

cardatore m. carder.

cardatrice f. carding machine.

cardatura f. carding.

cardellino m. goldfinch.

cardi'aco adj. cardiac: **attacco —**, heart attack.

cardinale m., adj. cardinal.

cardinali'zio adj. cardinalesque.

car'dine m. hinge, pivot.

cardiologi'a f. cardiology.

cardio'logo m. heart specialist.

cardiopalmo m. heart disease.

cardo m. cardoon; teasel.

Carducci, Giosuè, Italian poet and man of letters. Nobel prize in literature, 1906 (1836–1907).

carena f. (naut.) bottom.

carenag'gio m. careen: **bacino di —**, dry dock.

carenare vt. to careen; to fair.

carenatura f. (aeron.) fairing.

carenza f. lack, want.

caresti'a f. famine; dearth.

carezza f. caress; expensiveness.

carezzare vt. to caress, fondle.

carezze'vole adj. fondling, sweet.

cariare vt., **cariarsi** vr. to decay, rot.

caria'tide f. caryatid.

ca'rica f. office, appointment; charge: **tornare alla —**, to try again.

caricamento m. loading; lading.

caricare vt. to lade, burden; to charge; to load; to wind up; to exaggerate; **caricarsi** vr. to burden oneself; to take upon oneself.

caricatore m. loader; magazine (of a pistol); (photog.) cartridge, spool.

caricatura f. caricature; cartoon.

caricaturista m. caricaturist, cartoonist.

ca'rico m. load, burden; charge; lot; trump; cargo. adj. loaded (with); wound up; deep.

ca'rie f. decay, caries.

carino adj. nice, cute, fine; funny.

carità f. charity, love; mercy; alms: **chiedere la —**, to beg.

caritate'vole adj. charitable.

carlinga f. (aeron.) fuselage.

carlona, (alla) adv. carelessly.

carme m. poem.

carmi'nio m. carmine.

carnagione f. complexion.

carnale adj. carnal, lustful.

carname m. carrion, carnage.

carne *f.* meat; flesh.

carne'fice *m.* executioner.

carneficina *f.* slaughter.

carnevale *m.* carnival.

carniere *m.* game bag.

carni'voro *adj.* carnivorous.

carnoso *adj.* fleshy.

caro *adj.* dear; expensive.

Caro, Annibal, Italian poet and translator (1507–1566).

carogna *f.* carrion; (*fig.*) "heel," cad.

carosello *m.* carousel.

carota *f.* carrot.

caro'tide *f.* carotid.

carovana *f.* caravan.

carovaniera *f.* desert trail.

carovaniere *m.* caravaneer.

carovi'veri *m.* high cost of living: indennità per —, high-cost-of-living bonus.

carpa *f.* carp.

Carpaccio, Vittore, Italian painter (1450–1522).

carpentiere *m.* carpenter.

carpire *vt.* to extort; to wheedle.

carponi *adv.* on all fours.

carradore *m.* carter.

carra'ia, carrarec'cia *f.* cartway.

carreggiata *f.* rut; cartway; gauge.

carrelata *f.* (*moving pictures*) dolly shot; boom shot.

carrello *m.* trolley; truck; (*aeron.*) landing gear; (*moving pictures*) dolly.

carretta *f.* cart.

carrettiere *m.* carter.

carretto *m.* pushcart.

carriera *f.* career.

carriola *f.* wheelbarrow.

carrista *m.* tank corpsman.

carro *m.* cart; truck, lorry; (*astr.*) the Great Bear; Wain: — armato, armored car; — funebre, hearse.

carrozza *f.* carriage, coach; cab: — ristorante, dining car; — letto, sleeper.

carrozza'bile *adj.* practicable.

carrozzeri'a *f.* carriage factory; body; — fuori serie, custom-built body.

carrozzina *f.* perambulator.

carrozzino *m.* tilbury; sidecar.

carrozzone *m.* wagon; caravan.

carrubo *m.*, carruba *f.* carob.

carru'cola *f.* pulley.

carta *f.* paper; map; card; — assorbente, blotting paper; — da parati, wallpaper; — moneta, paper money; dare — bianca, to give a free hand.

cartac'cia *f.* waste paper.

carta'io *m.* papermaker.

cartape'cora *f.* parchment.

cartapesta *f.* papier-mâchè.

cartastrac'cia *f.* wastepaper.

carteg'gio *m.* correspondence, letters.

cartella *f.* file, folder; form; certificate, policy; ticket; portfolio; satchel; brief case; sheet: — clinica, chart (*med.*).

cartellino *m.* ticket; label.

cartello *m.* poster; cartel.

cartellone *m.* placard, poster; playbill.

cartiera *f.* papermill.

cartila'gine *f.* cartilage.

cartina *f.* (*pharm.*) dose; leaf.

cartoc'cio *m.* cornet; cornetful.

carto'grafo *m.* cartographer.

cartola'io *m.* stationer.

cartoleri'a *f.* stationery store; stationery.

cartolina *f.* card; post card: — illustrata, picture post card; — vaglia, postal order.

cartomante *m.*, *f.* fortuneteller.

cartoncino *m.* card, cardboard.

cartone *m.* cardboard; pasteboard; cartoon.

cartuc'cia *f.* cartridge.

cartucciera *f.* cartridge box.

Caruso, Enrico, Italian operatic tenor (1873–1921).

casa *f.* house, building; home: — editrice, publishing house; — madre, head office; — di pena, prison; — da gioco, gambling house; fatto in —, homemade.

Casa, della, Giovanni, Italian prelate and poet (1503–1556).

casacca *f.* coat, jacket.

casac cio, (a) *adv.* at random, rashly.

casalingo *adj.* homey; homemade; plain: articoli casalinghi, kitchenware.

casamatta *f.* casemate; bunker.

casamento *m.* building; tenement.

casata *f.* house, lineage.

casato *m.* family name.

cascame *m.* waste.

cascante *adj.* falling, limp.

cascare *vi.* to fall, drop.

cascata *f.* fall, waterfall.

cascina *f.* farm.

casco *m.* helmet; topee.

caseggiato *m.* block; building.

caseifi'cio *m.* cheese dairy.

caseina *f.* casein.

casella *f.* pigeonhole; box, case; cell (*of a beehive*): — postale, Post Office Box (*abb.* P.O.B.).

Casella, Alfredo, Italian composer (1883–1947).

casellante *m.* trackwalker.

casella'rio *m.* filing cabinet.

casello *m.* trackwalker's lodge.

caserma *f.* barracks (*pl.*).

casino *m.* clubhouse; bungalow.

caso *m.* case; chance; event; instance: in — affermativo, in the affirmative;

in — contrario, otherwise; **fare al — di,** to suit; **non fateci —,** never mind; — **mai,** in case; if at all.

casolare *m.* hovel.

casotto *m.* booth, box.

ca'spita!, *interj.* bless me!; you don't say! why!

cassa *f.* case, box; cash; coffin: — **toracica,** chest; — **del violino,** belly; — **di risparmio,** savings bank; **a pronta —,** cash down.

cassaforte *f.* safe.

cassapanca *f.* wooden chest; settle.

cassare *vt.* to quash, cancel.

cassazione *f.* cassation.

cas'sero *m.* quarterdeck.

casseruola *f.* stew pan, casserole.

cassetta *f.* box, case; coachman's seat: — **di sicurezza,** safe deposit box; — **per lettere,** mailbox.

cassetto *m.* drawer.

cassettone *m.* chest of drawers.

cassiera *f.* cashier.

cassiere *m.* cashier; teller.

cassone *m.* coffer; cofferdam.

casta *f.* caste.

castagna *f.* chestnut.

castagno *m.* chestnut tree; chestnut wood. *adj.* chestnut, chestnut-colored.

castano *adj.* chestnut-colored.

castellana *f.* lady of the manor.

castellano *m.* squire.

castello *m.* castle, manor; scaffold: — **di poppa,** quarterdeck; — **di prua,** forecastle; **castell' in aria,** castles in Spain.

castigare *vt.* to punish.

castigato *adj.* severely correct.

Castiglione, Baldassarre, Italian statesman and author (1478–1529).

castigo *m.* punishment.

castità *f.* chastity.

casto *adj.* chaste, pure.

castone *m.* bezel, setting.

castoro *m.* beaver.

castrare *vt.* to castrate.

castrato *m.* mutton. *pp. of* castrare castrated.

castrone *m.* gelding (*horse*); wether (*sheep*).

castroneri'a *f.* blunder; nonsense.

casuale *adj.* fortuitous.

casualmente *adv.* fortuitously, by chance.

casu'pola *f.* hovel, hut.

cataclisma *m.* cataclysm.

catacomba *f.* catacomb.

catafalco *m.* catafalque.

catafa'scio, (a) *adv.* topsy-turvy.

Catalani, Alfredo, Italian composer, *Loreley, Wally* (1854–1893).

catalessi *f.* catalepsy.

cata'lisi *f.* catalysis.

catalizzatore *m.* catalyzer.

catalogare *vt.* to catalogue.

cata'logo *m.* catalogue, list.

catapec'chia *f.* tumble-down house, hovel.

cataplasma *m.* poultice.

catapulta *f.* catapult.

catapultare *vt.* to launch, catapult.

cataratta *see* cateratta.

catarro *m.* catarrh.

catarsi *f.* catharsis.

catasta *f.* heap, pile, stack.

catastale *adj.* cadastral.

catasto *m.* cadastre.

cata'strofe *f.* catastrophe.

catastro'fico *adj.* catastrophic.

catechismo *m.* catechism.

catechizzare *vt.* to catechize.

categori'a *f.* category, class.

categoricamente *adv.* categorically.

catego'rico *adj.* categorical, direct.

catena *f.* chain; bondage; range (*of mountains*): — **di montaggio,** assembly line; **reazione a —,** chain reaction.

catenac'cio *m.* bolt.

catena'ria *f.* catenary.

catenella *f.* chainlet: **punto —,** chain stitch.

cateratta *f.* sluice gate; cataract, waterfall; (*med.*) cataract.

caterva *f.* crowd; heap, pile.

cateto *m.* cathetus (*pl.* catheti).

catinella *f.* water basin.

catino *m.* basin.

ca'todo *m.* cathode.

catramare *vt.* to tar.

catrame *m.* tar.

cat'tedra *f.* desk; cathedra; chair; professorship.

cattedrale *f.* cathedral.

cattedra'tico *adj.* professorial: **parlare con tono —,** to pontificate.

cattivarsi *vr.* to gain, win.

cattive'ria *f.* wickedness; spite.

cattività *f.* captivity.

cattivo *adj.* bad, ill; wicked; evil; naughty; wrong; captive.

cattolice'simo *m.* Catholicism.

catto'lico *m., adj.* Catholic.

cattura *f.* capture, arrest.

catturare *vt.* to capture, seize.

caucciù *m.* caoutchouc, rubber.

ca'usa *f.* cause, motive; (*law*) suit: **a — di,** on account of, because of.

causale *f.* cause. *adj.* causal.

causare *vt.* to cause.

causi'dico *m.* pettifogger.

ca'ustico *adj.* caustic.

cautamente *adv.* cautiously, warily.

cautela *f.* caution, care.

cautelare *vt.* to protect; **cautelarsi** *vr.* to take precautions, provide (*against*).

cauterizzare *vt.* to cauterize.
cauterizzazione *f.* cauterization.
ca'uto *adj.* cautious, wary.
cauzione *f.* security; bail.
cava *f.* quarry; mine.
cavadenti *m.* tooth puller.
cavagno *m.* basket.
Cavalcanti, Guido, Italian poet, friend of Dante (?-1300).
cavalcare *vt.* to ride (*a horse*). *vi.* to ride (*on a horse*).
cavalcata *f.* ride, cavalcade.
cavalcatura *f.* mount, horse.
cavalcavi'a *f.* overpass.
cavalcioni *adv.* astraddle.
cavalierato *m.* knighthood.
cavaliere *m.* rider, horseman; cavalryman; knight; escort; partner: cavalier servente, gallant, escort.
cavalla *f.* mare.
cavalleresco *adj.* chivalrous; knightly: ordine —, Order of Knighthood.
cavalleri'a *f.* cavalry; chivalry; chivalrousness.
cavallerizza *f.* horsewoman.
cavallerizzo *m.* horseman, rider; horsebreaker.
cavalletta *f.* grasshopper.
cavalletto *m.* trestle; easel.
cavallino *m.* colt. *adj.* equine: mosca cavallina, horse fly.
cavallo *m.* horse, knight (*at chess*); horsepower: — a dondolo, hobbyhorse; — di battaglia, fad, pièce de résistance; cavalli di Frisia, chevaux-de-frise.
cavallone *m.* big horse; billow.
Cavallotti, Felice, Italian poet, dramatist and politician (1842-1898).
cavare *vt.* to pull out, draw out; to get; to dig, hollow out: cavar sangue, to bleed; cavarsi la voglia di, to gratify one's desire for; cavarsi d'impiccio, to pull through; cavarsi dai piedi, to get out of the way; cavarsi (uno) d'attorno, to get rid of (one).
cavastivali *m.* bootjack.
cavatappi, cavaturac'cioli *m.* corkscrew.
caverna *f.* cavern, cave.
cavernoso *adj.* cavernous, hollow.
cavezza *f.* halter.
ca'via *f.* guinea pig.
caviale *m.* caviar.
cavic'chio *m.* wooden peg.
cavi'glia *f.* ankle; peg; spoke.
cavillare *vi.* to cavil, quibble.
cavillo *m.* cavil, quibble.
cavilloso *adj.* captious.
cavità *f.* cavity, hollow.
cavo (*1*) *m.* rope, cable, hawser.
cavo (*2*) *m.*, *adj.* hollow.
cavolfiore *m.* cauliflower.
ca'volo *m.* cabbage.

Cavour, di, Emilio Benso, Italian statesman (1810-1861).
cazzeruola *f.* stew pan.
cazzottare *vt.* to punch; cazzottarsi *vr.* to fight.
cazzotto *m.* punch, "sock."
cazzuola *f.* trowel.
ce (*1*) *adv.* there: non — n'è, there is none.
ce (*2*) *pron.* us, to us: egli — lo diede, he gave it to us; — lo dissero, they told us so.
cecamente *adv.* blindly.
Cecchi, Emilio, Italian writer and essayist. *Bitter America, English and American Authors* (1884-   ).
cece *m.* chickpea.
cecità *f.* blindness.
ceco *m.*, *adj.* Czech.
ceco-slovacco *m.*, *adj.* Czechoslovak.
ce'dere *vt.*, *vi.*[28] to cede, yield; to surrender; to transfer; to give in; to sink.
cede'vole *adj.* yielding; soft.
cedi'bile *adj.* transferable: non —, non-transferable.
cedimento *m.* yielding; sinking.
ce'dola *f.* coupon.
cedrata *f.* citron syrup.
cedrina *f.* balm mint, melissa.
cedrino *adj.* citrine.
cedro *m.* citron.
cedrone *m.* wood grouse.
ce'duo (bosco) *m.* coppice.
ceduto *pp.* of cedere.
cefalea *f.* headache.
ce'falo *m.* mullet.
ceffo *m.* snout; ugly face.
ceffone *m.* slap in the face.
celare *vt.*, celarsi *vr.* to hide.
celeber'rimo *adj.* famous, renowned.
celebrare *vt.* to celebrate.
celebrazione *f.* celebration.
ce'lebre *adj.* famous, renowned.
celebrità *f.* fame, renown.
ce'lere *adj.* quick, swift: la "Celere," the flying squad.
celerità *f.* swiftness, speed.
celermente *adv.* quickly, swiftly.
celeste *adj.* heavenly, celestial; skyblue.
celestiale *adj.* heavenly.
ce'lia *f.* jest, joke; fun.
celiare *vi.* to jest, joke.
celibato *m.* celibacy, bachelorhood.
ce'libe *m.* bachelor. *adj.* single.
cella *f.* cell; closet, storeroom.
Cellini, Benvenuto, Italian goldsmith, sculptor and author (1500-1571).
cellofane *f.* cellophane.
cel'lula *f.* cell.
cellulare *m.* jail; police wagon. *adj.* cellular: segregazione —, close confinement.

cellulo'ide f. celluloid.
cellulosa f. cellulose.
cel'tico adj. Celtic, Keltic.
cementare vt. to cement.
cemento m. cement; concrete: —armato, ferroconcrete, reinforced con-
cena f. supper. [crete.
cena'colo m. supper room; the Lord's
Supper; society.
cenare vi. to have supper.
cenciaiuolo m. ragpicker.
cen'cio m. rag, tatter; duster.
cencioso adj. ragged, tattered.
ce'nere f. ash; ashes.
Ceneren'tola f. Cinderella.
cenno m. sign; nod; wave, beck;
gesture; hint; intimation.
ceno'bio m. convent, monastery.
cenobita m. cenobite.
censimento m. census.
censire vt. to take the census of.
censo m. census; income; wealth.
censore m. censor.
censura f. censure; censorship.
censurare vt. to censure.
centa'uro m. centaur; (astr.) Centau-
rus; motorcycle racer.
centellinare vt. to sip.
centena'rio m., adj. centennial; cente-
narian.
cente'simo m. hundredth (part); cent.
adj. hundredth.
centi'grado adj. centigrade.
centigramma m. centigram.
centi'litro m. centiliter.
centi'metro m. centimeter.
cen'tina f. centering; (aeron.) rib.
centina'io m. hundred: a centinaia, by
hundreds.
cento m., adj. a hundred, one hundred:
— volte, a hundred times; uno per
—, one per cent; al — per —, hundred
per cent.
centomila adj. a hundred thousand.
centrale f. main house, head office;
headquarters: — elettrica, power
station; — telefonica, telephone
exchange.
centrale adj. central; middle; head;
main.
centralinista m., f. (teleph.) operator.
centralino m. telephone exchange.
centralità f. centrality.
centralizzare vt. to centralize.
centrare vt. to center; to hit the mark.
centrifugare vt. to centrifuge.
centri'fugo adj. centrifugal.
centri'peto adj. centripetal.
centro m. center; heart, core; bull's-
eye: — attacco, center forward;
andare in — to go downtown.
centuplicare vt. to centuple.
cen'tuplo m. centuplicate. adj. centuple, hundredfold.

centu'ria f. century.
centurione m. centurion.
ceppo m. stump; log; chopping
block; anchor stock; brakeshoe;
stock; (pl.) bonds, chains.
cera f. wax; polish; look, mien: — da
pavimenti, floor wax; — da scarpe,
shoe polish.
ceralacca f. sealing wax.
cera'mica f. ceramics; (pl.) pottery.
ceramista m. ceramist.
cerare vt. to wax.
cerata f. oilcloth.
Cer'bero m. Cerberus; disciplinarian,
martinet.
cerbiatta f. young hind.
cerbiatto m. fawn.
cerbottana f. blow gun.
cerca f. search, quest.
cercare vt. to look for, seek; to ask;
to want. vi. to try, endeavor.
cercatore m. seeker, searcher: —
d'oro, gold prospector.
cer'chia f. circle; circuit; sphere.
cerchiare vt. to rim, hoop.
cerchiatura f. rimming, hooping.
cer'chio m. circle; hoop, ring: — della
morte (aeron.), loop.
cerchione m. felly, wheel rim.
cereale m., adj. cereal.
cerebrale adj. cerebral.
ce'reo adj. waxen; waxy; wan.
cerfo'glio f. chervil.
cerimo'nia f. ceremony, rite.
cerimoniale m., adj. ceremonial.
cerimoniere m. Master of Ceremonies.
cerimonioso adj. ceremonious.
cerino m. wax match; taper.
cernec'chio m. lock, tuft.
cer'nere vt.¹²⁰ to choose, sort.
cèrniera f. hinge; clasp: — lampo,
zipper.
cer'nita f. choice, selection.
cero m. church candle.
cerone m. grease paint, make-up.
cerotto m. plaster.
certamente adv. certainly.
certezza f. certainty.
certificare vt. to certify.
certificato m. certificate.
certo m., adj. certain. adv. certainly.
certi pron.pl. some.
certosa f. charterhouse.
certosino m., adj. Carthusian.
certuno pron.indef. somebody.
ceru'leo adj. cerulean, sky-blue.
cerume m. cerumen, ear wax.
cerussa f. ceruse, white lead.
cerva f. (zool.) hind.
cervelletto m. cerebellum.
cervello m. brain; brains; sense; mind.
cervello'tico adj. absurd, preposterous,
fantastic.
cervicale adj. cervical.

cervice f. nape; cervix; head.
Cervino, (Monte) m. Matterhorn.
cervo m. stag, hart: — **volante**, stag-beetle.
cesa'reo adj. Caesarean: **taglio —**, Caesarean section.
cesellare vt. to chase, (en) grave.
cesellatore m. chaser, (en) graver.
cesellatura f. chasing, graving.
cesello m. burin, graver, chisel.
ceso'ia f. shears, scissors; (mach.) shearing machine.
ce'spite m. tuft; source.
cespo m. tuft.
cespu'glio m. bush, thicket.
cessare vt., vi. to cease, stop, discontinue, quit.
cessazione f. cessation.
cessiona'rio m. assignee.
cessione f. assignment, cession.
cesso m. privy, water closet.
cesta f. basket, hamper.
cestinare vt. to throw into the wastebasket; to reject.
cestino m. wastebasket.
cestista m., f. basketball player.
cesto m. basket, hamper.
ceta'ceo m., adj. cetacean.
ceto m. class, rank: **il basso —**, the lower classes; **il — medio**, the middle classes; **il — superiore**, the upper classes.
cetra f. cithara.
cetriolino m. gherkin.
cetriuolo m. cucumber.
che conj. that, as to, to; for; when, at; like; than; whether: **tanto —**, so much that; **è tempo — tu parta**, it is time for you to leave; **più (meno) —**, more (less) than; **lo stesso —**, the same as; **a meno —**, unless; **non importa — egli venga o no**, it doesn't matter whether he comes or not. pron.rel. who; whom; that; which; when, where; something: **colui —**, he who; **il —**, which; **col —**, wherewith; **al —**, dopo di —, whereupon; **il giorno —**, the day when; **paese — vai**, any place you go; **non c'è di —**, don't mention it; **avere di — andare avanti**, to have enough to get along; **non c'è nessuno — non sappia**, everyone knows. adj., pron.interr.excl. what, how: **— ora è?**, what time is it?; **— peccato!**, what a pity!; **— bello!** how beautiful!
chè conj. because, for, since.
checchè pron.indef. whatever.
checchessi'a pron.indef. anything, everything.
chemioterapi'a f. chemotherapy.
Cherubini, Maria Luigi, Italian composer (1760-1842).

cherubino m. cherub.
chetare vt. to quiet, appease; **chetarsi** vr. to quiet down, subside.
chetichella, (alla) adv. surreptitiously; stealthily; noiselessly.
cheto adj. quiet.
chi pron.rel., demonstr. who; whom; whose; he who (that), him who, he whom; she who, her who, she whom; they who, those who, those whom; whoever, whomever; one who; some: — **è?**, who is he?; **di — parli?**, of whom are you speaking?; **di — è questo libro**, whose book is this?; — **vuol mangiare deve lavorare**, he who (that) wants to eat has got to work; — **sarà mai?**, who (ever) can it be?; **chiedilo a — ti pare**, ask whomever you like; — **lo dice e — no**, some say it some don't; — **di loro?**, which of them?
chiac'chiera f. chatter, hoax; gossip; glibness: **fare quattro chiacchiere con**, to have a chat with.
chiacchierare vi. to chatter; to talk.
chiacchierata f. chat, talk.
chiacchieri'o m. chatter, prattle.
chiacchierone m. chatterbox.
chiama f. roll call.
chiamare vt. to call (for); to send for; to draft; to name; to summon; to ring up: — **in causa**, to bring into court; **chiamarsi** vr. to be called, be named: **come ti chiami?**, what is your name?
chiamata f. call, summons.
chiappa f. buttock.
chiappamosche m. fly trap.
chiappare vt. to catch.
chiara f. glair.
chiaramente adv. clearly; frankly.
chiaretto m. claret.
chiarezza f. clearness.
chiarificare vt. to clarify.
chiarificazione f. clarification.
chiarimento m. explanation.
chiarire vt. to clarify, make clear, clear up; to explain; **chiarirsi** vr. to clear up, become clear.
chiaro m. light; brightness: — **di luna**, moonlight. adj. clear; bright; light; illustrious; fair. adv. clearly; frankly: — **e tondo**, bluntly.
chiarore m. light; glimmer.
chiaroscuro m. light and shade; mezzotint.
chiaroveggente m. wizard. adj. clairvoyant, farsighted.
chiaroveggenza f. clairvoyance, farsightedness.
chiassata f. hubbub, uproar.
chiasso m. noise; uproar.
chiassoso adj. noisy; gaudy.

chiatta *f.* punt, barge.
chiavarda *f.* bolt.
chiave *f.* key; wrench, spanner: — inglese, monkey wrench.
chiavetta *f.* small key; tap.
chia'vica *f.* sewer.
chiavistello *m.* bolt, latch.
chiazza *f.* mottle; spot, stain.
chiazzare *vt.* to mottle; to stain, speck.
chiazzato *adj.* mottled; stained.
chicca *f.* sweet, candy.
chic'chera *f.* cup, barge.
chicchessi'a *pron.indef.* anyone, anybody.
chicchirichì *m.* cock-a-doodle-doo.
chicco *m.* grain; seed, pip: — d'uva, grape; — di caffè, coffee bean; — di grandine, hailstone; — di riso, rice grain.
chiedere *vt., vi.*[24] to ask (*for*), inquire (*about*); to question; to beg (*for*): — scusa, to beg pardon; chiedersi *vr.* to wonder.
chie'rica *f.* tonsure.
chie'rico *m.* minor clerk; clergyman.
chiesa *f.* church.
chiesto *pp.* of chiedere.
chiesuola *f.* (*naut.*) binnacle.
chi'glia *f.* keel.
chilo (*1*) *m.* (*med., biol.*) chyle: fare il —, to take one's siesta.
chilo (*2*) *m.* (*weight*) kilogram.
chilociclo *m.* (*radio*) kilocycle.
chilogramma *m.* kilogram.
chilometrag'gio *m.* kilometrage.
chilome'trico *adj.* kilometrical.
chilo'metro *m.* kilometer.
chilowatt *m.* kilowatt.
chimera *f.* chimera; daydream.
chime'rico *adj.* chimerical.
chi'mica *f.* chemistry.
chi'mico *m.* chemist. *adj.* chemical.
chimono *m.* kimono.
china (*1*) *f.* slope, descent.
china (*2*) *f.* (*bot.*) cinchona.
chinare *vt.* to bend; chinarsi *vr.* to bend, stoop.
chincagliere *m.* knickknack dealer.
chincaglieri'a *f.* knickknacks; curio shop.
chinino *m.* quinine.
chino *adj.* bent, stooping.
chioc'cia *f.* brood hen: fare la —, to brood.
chiocciare *vi.* to cluck.
chiocciata *f.* hatch.
chioc'cio *adj.* hoarse.
chioc'ciola *f.* snail: scala a —, spiral staircase.
chiodare *vt.* to nail.
chiodo *m.* nail; debt; craze: — di garofano, clove.
chioma *f.* hair; mane; coma (*of a comet*); foliage (*of a tree*).

chiomato *adj.* haired; leafy.
chiosa *f.* gloss, note.
chiosare *vt.* to gloss, annotate.
chiosatore *m.* annotator.
chiosco *m.* kiosk; booth; newsstand.
chiostra *f.* enclosure, fence; set (*of teeth*).
chiostro *m.* cloister.
chiotto *adj.* quiet, still.
Chirico, Giorgio di, Italian painter, founder of "metaphysical" painting (1888–   ).
chirografa'rio *adj.* chirographer.
chiro'grafo *m.* chirograph.
chiromante *m.* chiromancer, palmist, crystal gazer.
chiromanzi'a *f.* chiromancy, crystal gazing.
chirurgi'a *f.* surgery.
chirur'gico *adj.* surgical.
chirurgo *m.* surgeon.
chitarra *f.* guitar.
chitarrista *m.* guitarrist.
chiù *m.* horned owl.
chiu'dere *vt., vi.*[29] to close, shut (*up*), lock; to fasten; to enclose; to bar; to seal; to conclude; to stop; to clench (*one's fist*): — un occhio (*fig.*), to wink (at); non — occhio, not to sleep a wink; chiudersi *vr.* to shut, close; to shut oneself up.
chiunque *pron.indef.* whoever, whosoever; whomsoever; anyone, anybody.
chiurlo *m.* curlew.
chiusa *f.* lock, sluice; dam, weir; close, end.
chiusino *m.* lid; manhole.
chiuso *m.* enclosure; fold, pen: al —, indoors. *adj.* shut (*in*), closed; ended, stopped. *pp.* of chiudere.
chiusura *f.* close; closing, shutting; lock; fastening: — ermetica, hermetical sealing; — lampo, zipper.
ci *pron.pers.* us, to us. *pron.refl.* ourselves; each other, one another. *pron.demonstr.* that, it, about it, of it: non — credo, I don't believe it. *adv.* here; there; of it: c'è un po' di pane, there is some bread.
ciabattare *vi.* to shuffle.
ciabattino *m.* cobbler.
ciak *m.* (*moving pictures*) clapper, slate.
cialda *f.* wafer.
cialdone *m.* cone (*as for ice cream*).
cialtrone *m.* draggletail; rascal, "heel."
ciambella *f.* ring-cake; wase.
ciambellano *m.* chamberlain.
ciampicare *vi.* to stumble.
cianamide *m.* cyanamide.
cian'cia *f.* idle talk; gossip.
cianciafru'scola *f.* trifle.

cianciare vi. to chatter.
cianfrusa'glia f. trifle, (pl.) trinkets.
ciani'drico adj. hydrocyanic.
ciano'geno m. cyanogen.
ciano'tico adj. cyanotic.
cianuro m. cyanide.
ciao (It. slang) hello, hi; bye-bye, so long.
ciarla see chiac'chera.
ciarlare vi. to chatter.
ciarlatanata, ciarlataneri'a f. quackery.
ciarlatanesco adj. quackish.
ciarlatano m. charlatan, quack.
ciarliero adj. talkative.
ciarpame m. litter, rubbish.
ciascheduno, ciascuno adj. each. pron. indef. each, each one; everyone, everybody.
cibare vt. to feed; cibarsi vr. to feed on; to live on.
ciba'ria f. food, foodstuff.
cibo m. food; meal.
cibo'rio m. ciborium, pyx.
cicala f. cicada; (fig.) chatterbox; (naut.) anchor ring.
cicalare vi. to babble, prattle.
cicalec'cio m. babbling, prattle.
cicatrice f. scar, cicatrice.
cicatrizzare vt., vi., cicatrizzarsi vr. to cicatrize, heal.
cicatrizzazione f. cicatrization.
cicca f. stump, butt; quid.
ciccare vi. to chew tobacco.
cicchetto m. dram, nip, "shot"; lecture, dressing.
cic'cia f. meat; fat.
ciccione m. fatty.
cicciuto adj. fleshy, plump.
cicer'chia f. chickpea.
cicerone m. guide, cicerone.
ciclamino m. cyclamen.
ciclismo m. cycling.
ciclista m. cyclist.
ciclo m. cycle.
ciclone m. cyclone, tornado.
ciclo'nico adj. cyclonic.
ciclo'pico adj. Cyclopean.
ciclostilare vt. to mimeograph.
ciclostile m. mimeograph, cyclostyle.
ciclotrone m. cyclotron.
cicogna f. stork.
cico'ria f. chicory.
cicuta f. hemlock.
cieco m. blind man; i ciechi, the blind. adj. blind: lanterna cieca, dark lantern; intestino —, caecum; mosca cieca, blindman's buff; alla cieca, blindly.
cielo m. sky; heaven: un fulmine a ciel sereno, a bolt out of the blue; portare ai sette cieli, to praise to the skies.
cifra f. figure; sum, amount; cipher; monogram.

cifrare vt. to code; to mark.
cifra'rio m. cipher, code.
cifrato adj. ciphered, coded.
ci'glio m. eyelash, lash; border, edge; shoulder (of a road).
ciglione m. embankment, bank.
cignale m. wild boar.
cigno m. swan.
cigolare vi. to creak, squeak; to hiss.
cigoli'o m. squeaking, hissing.
cilecca f. misfire.
cilestrino m. sky-blue.
cili'cio m. sackcloth.
cilie'gia f. cherry; bigarreau.
cilie'gio m. cherry tree.
cilindrare vt. to calender; to roll.
cilindrata f. cylinder displacement.
cilin'drico adj. cylindrical.
cilindro m. cylinder; top hat; calender, roller.
cima f. top, summit; apex; vertex; (naut.) rope; (bot.) cyme; (fig.) genius.
Cimabue, Giovanni, early Florentine painter (1240?-1302?).
Cimarosa, Domenico, Neapolitan composer (1749-1801).
cimasa f. cyma, coping.
cime'lio m. relic, antique.
cimentare vt. to provoke, vex; to put to test; cimentarsi vr. to hazard, engage; to venture.
cimento m. ordeal.
ci'mice f. bedbug.
cimiero m. crest.
ciminiera f. smokestack; funnel.
cimitero m. churchyard, cemetery.
cimosa f. selvage; eraser.
cimurro m. distemper, glanders.
cinabro m. cinnabar.
cincilla f. chinchilla.
cincischiare vt., vi. to shred; to babble; to dawdle.
cineasta m. moving picture maker; moving picture fan.
cinegiornale m. newsreel.
cinege'tica f. hounding.
cinema'tica f. cinematics.
cinematografare vt. to film, shoot.
cinematografi'a f. cinematography; moving picture show; film.
cinematogra'fico adj. moving picture.
cinema'tografo m. cinema, moving picture theater, moving pictures (pl.).
cine'reo adj. cinereous, ashen.
cinese m., adj. Chinese.
cineteca f. film library.
cine'tica f. kinetics.
cingallegra f. tomtit.
cin'gere vt.[26] to gird, girdle (with); to crown; to surround; to fold: — d'assedio, to besiege.
cin'ghia f. belt, strap; driving belt.

cinghiale *m*. wild boar.
cinghiata *f*. lash.
cin'golo *m*. belt; girdle; (*mach*.) track.
cinguettare *vi*. to chirp, twitter.
cinguetti'o *m*. chirping, twittering.
ci'nico *m*. cynic. *adj*. cynical.
cini'glia *f*. chenille.
cinismo *m*. cynicism.
cino'filo *m*. dog fancier.
cinquanta *m*., *adj.num*. fifty.
cinquantena'rio *m*. fiftieth anniversary. *adj*. quinquagenarian.
cinquantenne *m*., *adj*. quinquagenarian.
cinquanten'nio *m*. half century.
cinquante'simo *adj.num*. fiftieth.
cinquantina *f*. some fifty: essere sulla —, to be on the verge of fifty; aver passato la —, to be past fifty.
cinque *m*., *num. adj*. five.
cinquecento *m*., *num. adj*. five-hundred: il Cinquecento, the Cinquecento, the 16th century.
cinquina *f*. five, five numbers; (*mil*.) soldier's pay.
cinta *f*. enclosure, fence; girdle; fencing wall.
cinto *m*. belt: — erniario, truss. *pp. of* cingere.
cin'tola *f*. waist; belt.
cintura *f*. belt, girdle; waist: — di salvataggio, lifebelt.
cinturino *m*. belt, strap.
cinturone *m*. belt; Sam Browne belt.
ciò *pron.demonstr*. this, that, it: — che, what; tutto — che, all that; — non di meno, nevertheless; oltre a —, besides, moreover.
ciocca *f*. lock; cluster.
ciocco *m*. log.
cioccolata *f*., *adj*. chocolate.
cioccolatino *m*. chocolate.
ciociaro *m*. a peasant of the Roman country.
cioè *conj*. that is, that is to say, namely, viz.
ciondolare *vt*. to dangle. *vi*. to dangle; to idle, to hang about.
cion'dolo *m*. trinket, pendant.
ciondoloni *adv*. dangling, droopingly, loosely.
cio'tola *f*. bowl, cup.
ciottolato *m*. cobblestone paving.
ciot'tolo *m*. pebble, cobblestone.
ciottoloso *adj*. pebbly, pebbled.
cipi'glio *m*. frown, scowl.
cipolla *f*. onion; bulb.
cipresso *m*. cypress.
ci'pria *f*. powder, face powder.
cipriota *m*., *adj*. Cypriote.
circa *adv*., *prep*. about, approximately, some; concerning, as to.
circense *adj*. circensial.

circe'o *adj*. Circean.
circo *m*. circus.
circolante *m*. currency. *adj*. circulating.
circolare *vi*. to circulate.
circolare *f*., *adj*. circular.
circolarmente *adv*. circularly.
circolato'rio *adj*. circulatory.
circolazione *f*. circulation; traffic.
cir'colo *m*. circle; circumference; club, society; sphere.
circonci'dere *vt*.[41] to circumcise.
circoncisione *f*. circumcision.
circonciso *adj*. circumcised. *pp. of* circoncidere.
circondare *vt*. to surround, encircle.
circonda'rio *m*. district.
circonferenza *f*. circumference.
circonflesso *adj*. circumflex.
circonlocuzione *f*. circumlocution.
circonvallazione *f*. belt line; circular road.
circonvenire *vt*. to circumvent.
circonvenzione *f*. circumvention.
circonvicino *adj*. neighboring.
circonvoluzione *f*. circumvolution.
circoscritto *adj*. circumscribed.
circoscrivere *vt*.[124] to circumscribe.
circoscrizione *f*. circumscription; district.
circospetto *adj*. cautious, wary.
circospezione *f*. circumspection.
circostante *adj*. surrounding.
circostanza *f*. circumstance.
circostanziare *vt*. to detail.
circostanziato *adj*. detailed.
circuire *vt*. to circumvent.
circu'ito *m*. circuit.
circumnavigazione *f*. circumnavigation.
cirene'o *m*. drudge; scapegoat.
ciril'lico *adj*. Cyrillic.
cirro *m*. cirrus (*pl*. cirri); curl.
cirrosi *f*. cirrhosis.
cispa *f*. eye rheum.
cisposità *f*. rheuminess.
cisposo *adj*. rheumy.
cistercense *adj*. Cistercian.
cisterna *f*. cistern, tank.
cisti *f*. cyst.
cistifel'lea *f*. gall bladder.
cistite *f*. cystitis.
citante *m*., *f*. plaintiff.
citare *vt*. to quote, cite; to sue; to serve a summons.
citazione *f*. quotation; summons; subpoena.
cito'fono *m*. intercom, interphone.
citrato *m*. citrate.
ci'trico *adj*. citric.
citrullo *m*. dumbbell.
città *f*. city; town.
cittadella *f*. citadel.
cittadina *f*. small town.

cittadinanza f. citizenship; townspeople.
cittadino m. citizen; townsman. f. townswoman. adj. civic.
ciuco m. donkey, ass.
ciuffo m. lock, tuft; forelock.
ciuffolotto m. bullfinch.
ciurlare vi. to waver: — nel manico, to go back on one's word.
ciurma f. crew.
ciurmadore m. swindler.
ciurma'glia f. mob, rabble.
civetta f. owl; coquette, flirt.
civettare vi. to flirt.
civetteri'a f. coquetry.
civettuolo adj. pretty.
ci'vico adj. civic, municipal.
civile adj. civil; civilized: parte —, plaintiff.
civilista m. solicitor.
civilizzare vt. to civilize.
civilizzatore m. civilizer. adj. civilizing.
civilizzazione f. civilizing; civilization.
civilmente adv. civilly: sposarsi —, to contract civil marriage.
civiltà f. civilization; politeness.
civismo m. civism.
cla'mide f. chlamys (pl. chlamydes).
clamore m. clamor, noise.
clamorosamente adv. clamorously.
clamoroso adj. clamorous.
clandestinamente adv. clandestinely, surreptitiously.
clandestino adj. clandestine: passeggiero —, stowaway.
clangore m. clangor.
clarinetto m. clarinet.
clarino m. clarion.
classe f. class, order, rank; grade: la — media, the middle classes.
clas'sico m. classic. adj. classical.
classi'fica f. score, rating.
classifica'bile adj. classifiable.
classificare vt. to classify.
classificatore m. classifier.
classificazione f. classification.
claudicante adj. limping, lame.
clau'sola f. clause, proviso.
claustrofobi'a f. claustrophobia.
clausura f. seclusion.
clava f. club.
clavicem'balo m. harpsichord.
clavi'cola f. clavicle.
clemente adj. clement, merciful.
clemenza f. clemency, mercy.
clepto'mane m. kleptomaniac.
cleptomani'a f. kleptomania.
clericale m. clericalist. adj. clerical.
clericalismo m. clericalism.
clero m. clergy.
clessidra f. clepsydra.
cliente m. customer, patron; client.
clientela f. custom; practice, clientele.

clima m. climate.
climaterio m. menopause, climacteric.
clima'tico adj. climatic.
cli'nica f. clinic; hospital.
cli'nico m. clinician. adj. clinical.
cli'peo m. carapace; shield.
clistere m. enema, clyster.
cloaca f. sewer.
clora'lio m. chloral.
clorato m. chlorate.
clori'drico adj. hydrochloric.
cloro m. chlorine.
clorofilla f. chlorophyll.
cloroformio m. chloroform.
cloroformizzare vt. to chloroform.
cloromicetina f. chloromycetin.
cloruro m. chloride.
coabitante m., f. fellow tenant.
coabitare vi. to share lodgings.
coadiutore m. coadjutor.
coadiuvare vt. to assist.
coagulare vt., coagularsi vr. to coagulate, curdle, clot.
coagulazione f. coagulation.
coa'gulo m. clot, coagulum.
coalizione f. coalition.
coalizzare vt. to rally.
coartare vt. to coerce.
coartazione f. coercion.
coatto adj. coercive.
cobra m. cobra.
cocaina f. cocaine.
cocca f. notch; bowstring; corner.
coccarda f. cockade.
cocchiere m. coachman; cabman.
coc'chio m. chariot, coach.
coc'cia f. rind; pod; hilt; shell; pate.
coc'cige m. coccyx.
coccinella f. ladybird.
coccini'glia f. cochineal.
coc'cio m. earthen pot; potsherd.
cocciutag'gine f. stubbornness.
cocciuto adj. stubborn.
cocco m. coco; coconut; coccus; darling.
coccodè m. cackle.
coccodrillo m. crocodile.
coccolare vt. to fondle, nestle.
cocente adj. burning.
coco'mero m. watermelon.
cocorita f. parakeet, lovebird.
cocuz'zolo m. crown; peak.
coda f. tail; pigtail; queue; train: — di ratto (naut.), ratline.
codardi'a f. cowardice.
codardo m., adj. coward.
codazzo m. train, retinue.
codeina f. codeine.
codesto see cotesto.
co'dice m. code; codex (pl. codices).
codicillo m. codicil.
codificare vt. to codify.
codino m. short tail; pigtail; (fig.) conformist.

coefficiente m. coefficient.

coercitivo m. coercive, compulsory.

coercizione f. compulsion.

coerede m. coheir. f. coheiress.

coerente adj. consistent, logical.

coerenza f. consistency.

coesione f. cohesion.

coesistenza f. coexistence.

coesi'stere vi. to coexist.

coeta'neo m., adj. coeval, contemporary.

co'fano m. coffer, chest; bonnet.

coffa f. (naut.) top.

cogitabondo adj. cogitative.

cogitare vi. to cogitate.

cogli comp.prep. with, by the. see con.

co'gliere vi.²⁷ to catch; to seize; to gather; to pluck.

cognac m. brandy, cognac.

cognata f. sister-in-law.

cognato m. brother-in-law.

cognizione f. knowledge.

cognome m. surname.

coi comp.prep. with, by the. see con.

coibente adj. nonconducting, insulating.

coimputato m. co-defendant.

coincidenza f. coincidence; (rail.) connection.

coinci'dere vi.⁴¹ to coincide.

coinciso pp. of coincidere.

cointeressare vt. to make a sharer of.

cointeressenza f. share, percentage.

coinvol'gere vt.¹⁰⁶ to involve.

col comp.prep. with, by the. see con.

cola f. (bot.) kola.

colà adv. there.

colabrodo m. colander.

colare vt. to strain, drain; (metal.) to melt. vi. to drip; to flow, leak; to gutter: — a picco, to sink.

colata f. cast; stream.

colato'io m. colander; strainer.

colazione f. breakfast; lunch.

cole'i pron.f. she; her.

coleot'tero m. coleopteron, beetle.

colera m. cholera.

colibrì m. hummingbird.

co'lica f. colic.

co'lico adj. colic.

colino m. strainer.

colite f. (pathol.) colitis.

colla (1) f. glue, paste: — di pesce, isinglass.

colla (2) comp.prep. with, by the. see con.

collaborare vi. to collaborate, cooperate; to contribute (to).

collaboratore m. co-operator; assistant, contributor.

collaborazione f. collaboration, cooperation; contribution.

collaborazionismo m.collaborationism.

collaborazionista m. collaborationist, quisling.

collana f. necklace; series.

collare m. collar; hoop.

collasso m. breakdown, collapse.

collaterale m., adj. collateral.

collaudare vt. to test, try.

collaudatore m. tester; test pilot.

colla'udo m. test.

colle (1) m. hill, hillock.

colle (2) comp.prep. with, by the. see con.

collega m., f. colleague.

collegamento m. connection; linkage: ufficiale di —, li·ison officer.

colleganza f. colleagueship.

collegare vt., collegarsi vr. to connect, join.

collegiale m. schoolboy. f. schoolgirl.

colle'gio m. college, body, board; boarding school: — elettorale, constituency.

Colleoni, Bartolomeo, Venetian condottiere (1400–1475).

col'lera f. anger, rage, wrath: in —, angry.

colle'rico adj. irascible, hot-tempered.

colletta f. collection; collect.

collettivamente adv. collectively.

collettivismo m. collectivism.

collettivista m. collectivist.

collettività f. community.

collettivo adj. collective.

colletto m. collar.

collettore m. collector; manifold.

collezionare vt. to collect.

collezione f. collection.

collezionista m. collector.

colli'dere vi. to collide.

collimare vi. to tally.

collina f. hill, hillock.

collinoso adj. hilled, hilly.

colli'rio m. collyrium, eyewash.

collisione f. collision, crash.

collo (1) m. neck; parcel.

collo (2) comp.prep. with, by the. see con.

collocamento m. placement; investment; employment.

collocare vt. to place; to station; to employ; to invest; to arrange; to sell; to settle; collocarsi vr. to place oneself; to get a situation; to get married.

collo'dio m. collodion.

collo'quio m. interview, talk.

collosità f. glueyness.

colloso adj. sticky, gluey.

collot'tola f. nape.

collusione f. collusion.

colluttazione f. fight, scuffle.

colmare vt. to fill (up); to load (with), overwhelm (with).

colmo *m.* top. *adj.* full, bulging; full to the brim.

colofo'nia *f.* colophony, rosin.

colomba *f.* dove.

colomba'ia *f.* dovecote.

colombo *m.* pigeon.

Colombo, Cristoforo, Genoese navigator, discoverer of America (1446?-1506).

colo'nia *f.* settlement, colony; cologne.

coloniale *adj.* colonial: generi coloniali, spices; casco —, topee.

colo'nico *adj.* farm.

colonizzare *vt.* to colonize.

colonizzatore *m.* colonizer.

colonizzazione *f.* colonization.

colonna *f.* column, pillar, post.

colonnato *m.* colonnade.

colonnello *m.* colonel.

colono *m.* settler; farmer.

coloramento *m.* dyeing.

colorante *m.* dye. *adj.* dyeing.

colorare *vt.* to dye, color; colorarsi *vr.* to color up; to blush.

colorato *adj.* colored; dyed.

colorazione *f.* coloring.

colore *m.* color, hue; paint, dye: uomo di —, colored man, Negro.

colorifi'cio *m.* dye factory.

colorire *see* colorare.

colorito *m.* complexion. *adj.* colored; painted; ruddy.

coloritura *f.* coloring.

coloro *pron.pl.* they; them, those.

colossale *adj.* colossal, huge.

Colosseo *m.* Coliseum.

colosso *m.* colossus, giant.

colpa *f.* fault; guilt.

colpe'vole *m.* culprit. *adj.* guilty.

colpevolezza *f.* guilt.

colpire *vt.* to strike, hit; to impress; to smite; to injure, hurt.

colpo *m.* stroke, blow; knock; shot; coup; hit: — di mano, *coup de main*; — di scena, *coup de théâtre*; — di stato, *coup d'état*; — di grazia, *coup de grâce*, finishing stroke; di —, sharply; far —, to impress, be impressive.

colposo *adj.* guilty (but without malicious intent): omicidio —, manslaughter.

coltellac'cio *m.* chopper, cleaver; (*naut.*) studding sail.

coltellata *f.* cut, stab; knife wound.

coltellina'io *m.* cutler.

coltello *m.* knife; clasp knife: avere il — per il manico, to have the upper hand.

coltivare *vt.* to cultivate.

coltivatore *m.* farmer.

coltivazione *f.* cultivation.

colto (1) caught; gathered. *pp. of* cogliere.

colto (2) *adj.* cultivated, learned.

coltre *f.* coverlet, quilt.

coltro *m.* colter.

coltura *f.* culture.

colubrina *f.* culverin.

colu'i *pron.* he, him.

coma *m.* (*med.*) coma.

comandamento *m.* commandment.

comandante *m.* commander.

comandare *vt., vi.* to command; to order; to be in charge (*of*).

comando *m.* command; order; (*mach.*) control.

comare *f.* housewife; godmother.

comatoso *adj.* comatose.

combaciare *vi.* to tally.

combattente *m.* combatant, fighter. *adj.* fighting: ex —, veteran.

combat'tere *vt., vi.* to fight; to struggle (*against*).

combattimento *m.* fight; battle.

combattivo *adj.* pugnacious.

combinare *vt.* to combine; to settle; combinarsi *vr.* to combine.

combinazione *f.* combination; agreement; chance; arrangement; woman's underdress, slip.

combric'cola *f.* cabal; gang.

comburente *m., adj.* comburent.

combusti'bile *m.* fuel. *adj.* combustible.

combustione *f.* combustion.

combutta *f.* cabal, gang.

come *m., adv.* how; as; like, as good as; as soon as. *conj.* that, how, why; as ... as: — avete detto?, what did you say?; — mai?, how come?

cometa *f.* comet.

comicità *f.* comicalness; ludicrousness.

co'mico *m.* comic, comedian. *adj.* comic, funny.

comi'gnolo *m.* chimneypot; coping.

cominciare *vt., vi.* to begin, start.

comitato *m.* committee.

comitiva *f.* party, company.

comi'zio *m.* meeting.

comme'dia *f.* comedy, play.

commediante *m.* player, actor; shammer. *f.* actress; shammer.

commedio'grafo *m.* playwright.

commemorare *vt.* to commemorate.

commemorativo *adj.* commemorative, memorial.

commemorazione *f.* commemoration.

commenda *f.* Knight-Commandership; (*eccl.*) commendam.

commendare *vt.* to commend.

commendati'zia *f.* credentials (*pl.*).

commendatore *m.* Knight-Commander.

commendevole *adj.* commendable.

commensale *m.* commensal.

commentare *vt.* to comment.

commenta'rio *m.* commentary.
commentatore *m.* commentator.
commento *m.* comment; remark.
commerciale *adj.* commercial.
commerciante *m.* merchant, dealer.
commerciare *vt.* to deal in, negotiate.
vi. to trade.
commer'cio *m.* commerce, trade;
business: — all'ingrosso, wholesale
trade; — al minuto, retail trade.
commesso (*1*) *m.* clerk; shopman: —
viaggiatore, traveling salesman. *f.*
shopgirl.
commesso (*2*) *pp.* of commettere.
commesti'bile *m.*, *adj.* eatable, edible.
commettere *vt.*[76] to join; to fit in; to
order; to intrust; to commit, perform.
committtura *f.* joint; joining.
commiato *m.* leave, departure.
commilitone *m.* comrade.
comminare *vt.* to comminate.
comminato'ria *f.* commination, threat.
commiserare *vt.* to pity.
commiserazione *f.* commiseration,
pity; contempt.
commissariato *m.* commissaryship;
commissariat; police station.
commissa'rio *m.* commissary; inspector; commissar: — di bordo,
purser.
commissionare *vt.* to order.
commissiona'rio *m.* commission agent,
selling agent.
commissione *f.* commission; errand;
committee; order.
commisurare *vt.* to proportion; to
compare; to measure.
committente *m.* buyer; customer.
commodoro *m.* commodore.
commosso *adj.* moved; excited; upset.
pp. of commuovere.
commovente *adj.* touching.
commozione *f.* emotion; agitation.
commuo'vere *vt.*[80]to touch, move;com-
muoversi *vr.* to be moved, touched.
commutare *vt.* to commute.
commutatore *m.* commutator, switch.
comò *m.* chest of drawers, bureau.
comodamente *adv.* comfortably; at
ease; snugly; easily.
comodino *m.* night table.
comodità *f.* comfort; convenience;
opportunity.
co'modo *m.* convenience; ease, comfort; opportunity. *adj.* comfortable,
convenient; commodious; easy.
compaesano *m.* fellow countryman.
compa'gine *f.* assemblage; body.
compagno *m.*, compagna *f.* companion, fellow, mate; comrade; pal,
partner: — di scuola, schoolfellow;
— d'armi, comrade-in-arms. *adj.*
alike, similar.

compagni'a *f.* company; troop; set,
gang: dama di —, (lady) companion.
compana'tico *m.* viand.
comparare *vt.* to compare.
comparativo *m.*, *adj.* comparative.
comparazione *f.* comparison.
compare *m.* companion, chum; godfather; confederate.
comparire *vi.*[9] to appear.
comparizione *f.* appearance in court:
mandato di —, subpoena.
comparsa *f.* appearance; supernumerary, extra; (*law*) appearance before
the court; record.
comparso *pp.* of comparire.
compartecipazione *f.* sharing.
comparte'cipe *adj.* sharing (*in*).
compartimento *m.* compartment.
compassato *adj.* formal, poised, stiff.
compassionare *vt.* to pity.
compassione *f.* pity, compassion.
compassione'vole *adj.* compassionate;
piteous; pitiful.
compasso *m.* compasses (*pl.*).
compati'bile *adj.* consistent; excusable.
compatibilità *f.* compatibility.
compatibilmente *adv.* compatibly.
compatimento *m.* pity; forbearance.
compatire *vt.*[86] to pity; to forbear.
compatriota *m.* compatriot.
compattezza *f.* compactness.
compatto *adj.* compact.
compendiare *vt.* to epitomize, summarize, condense.
compen'dio *m.* epitome, summary,
condensation, digest.
compendioso *adj.* compendious.
compenetra'bile *adj.* penetrable.
compenetrabilità *f.* penetrability.
compenetrare *vt.* to penetrate; com-
penetrarsi *vr.* to impress on one's
mind.
compensa'bile *adj.* rewardable; bal-
anceable; indemnifiable.
compensare *vt.* to compensate; to
reward; to counterbalance; to indemnify.
compensato *m.* plywood.
compensazione *f.* compensation: stanza di —, clearing.
compenso *m.* compensation; reward.
comperare *see* comprare.
competente *m.*, *adj.* expert.
competenza *f.* competence.
competenze *f.pl.* fees.
compe'tere *vi.* to compete; to belong.
competitore *m.* competitor.
competizione *f.* competition, contest,
game.
compiacente *adj.* obliging.
compiacenza *f.* obligingness.
compiacere *vt.* to please; compiacersi
vr. to be pleased; to enjoy; to be so

kind as; to be fond of; to congratulate.

compiacimento m. complacence; pleasure.

compiaciuto adj. pleased.

compian'gere vt.[96] to pity; to lament.

compianto m. complaint; regret. adj. pitied; lamented. pp. of compiangere.

compiegare vt. to enclose.

com'piere vt.[28] to accomplish, fulfill; to perform; to complete: domani compio gli anni, tomorrow is my birthday; ho compiuto 20 anni, I am 20 years old.

compilare vt. to compile, fill.

compilatore m. compiler.

compilazione f. compilation.

compimento m. accomplishment; fulfillment; completion.

compire[53] see compiere.

compitare vt. to spell.

compitezza f. politeness.

com'pito m. task; mission.

compi'to adj. polite; also, pp. of compiere.

compiutamente adv. completely.

compiuto adj. accomplished. pp. of compiere.

compleanno m. birthday.

complementare adj. additional, complemental.

complemento m. complement: ufficiale di —, reserve officer.

complessione f. build, constitution.

complessità f. complexity.

complessivamente adv. on the whole.

complessivo adj. total, aggregate.

complesso m. complex, whole. adj. complex; compound; complicated.

completamente adv. completely.

completamento m. completion.

completare vt. to complete.

completo m. suit. adj. complete.

complicare vt. to complicate; complicarsi, vr. to become complicated, entangled.

complicazione f. complication.

com'plice m., f. accomplice.

complicità f. complicity.

complimentare vt. to compliment, congratulate.

complimento m. compliment.

complimentoso adj. ceremonious.

complottare vi. to plot.

complotto m. plot, conspiracy.

componente adj. component; m. component; member.

componimento m. composition.

comporre vt.[93] to compose; to compound; to arrange, settle; (print.) to set (type); comporsi vr. to consist (of).

comportamento m. behavior.

comportare vt. to bear, tolerate; to allow; to entail; comportarsi vr. to behave.

comporto m. allowance; delay.

composito'io m. composing stick.

compositore m. composer; typesetter.

composizione f. composition; settle-

composta f. compote. [ment.

compostamente adv. composedly.

compostezza f. composure.

composto m. compound. adj. composed; compound. pp. of comporre.

compra f. purchase: andare a fare le compre, to go shopping.

comprare vt. to purchase, buy.

compratore m. buyer.

compraven'dita f. buying and selling.

compren'dere vt.[96] to understand; to realize; to include; to imply.

comprendo'nio m. understanding.

comprensi'bile adj. understandable, intelligible.

comprensione f. understanding, grasp; sympathy.

comprensiva f. perception.

comprensivo adj. understanding; sympathetic; inclusive.

compreso'rio m. reclamation area.

compreso adj. understood; included; aware. pp. of comprendere.

compressa f. compress, pad; tablet.

compressibilità f. compressibility.

compressione f. pressure.

compresso adj. compressed. pp. of comprimere.

compressore m. compressor; supercharger; roller; steamroller.

comprima'rio m. second leading man.

comprim'mere vt.[29] to compress, press; to squeeze; to restrain.

compromesso m. compromise. adj. compromised; involved; endangered; committed.

compromettente adj. compromising; dangerous.

compromet'tere vt. to compromise; to involve; to endanger; compromettersi vr. to commit oneself; to get involved (in).

comproprietà f. joint ownership.

comproprieta'rio m. joint owner.

comprova'bile adj. provable.

comprovare vt. to prove.

compulsare vt. to consult.

compunto adj. demure, contrite.

compunzione f. compunction, demureness.

computa'bile adj. computable.

computare vt. to compute.

computista m. bookkeeper.

computisteri'a f. bookkeeping.

com'puto m. computation.

comunale adj. municipal: palazzo —, town hall.

comunanza *f.* community.
comunardo *m.* Communard.
comune *m.* community; municipality; borough; town hall; main exit; Commune: la Camera dei Comuni, the House of Commons. *adj.* common; usual; vulgar; trite; mutual; joint.
comunella *f.* cabal, gang.
comunemente *adv.* generally.
comunicando *m.* communicant.
comunicante *m.* communicator. *adj.* communicating (*with*).
comunicare *vt.*, *vi.* to communicate; comunicarsi *vr.* to communicate; to spread.
comunicativa *f.* communicativeness.
comunicativo *adj.* communicative.
comunicato *m.* communiqué.
comunicazione *f.* communication; connection; message: mettere in —, to connect; to put in touch; togliere la —, to disconnect.
comunione *f.* communion.
comunismo *m.* communism.
comunista *m.*, *f.*, *adj.* communist.
comunità *f.* community.
comunque *adv.* no matter how; however; anyhow.
con *prep.* with; by; through; in: — tutto che, although; — tutto ciò, nevertheless.
conato *m.* effort; conatus; qualm.
conca *f.* basin, depression; dell; lock; (*anat.*) concha.
concatenamento *m.* linking.
concatenare *vt.* to link.
concatenazione *f.* linking.
conca'usa *f.* joint cause.
concavità *f.* concavity.
con'cavo *m.*, *adj.* hollow.
conce'dere *vt.*[23] to grant.
concentramento *m.* concentration.
concentrare *vt.*, concentrarsi *vr.* to concentrate; to gather.
concentrato *m.* concentrate. *adj.* concentrated.
concentrazione *f.* concentration; condensation.
concen'trico *adj.* concentric.
concepi'bile *adj.* conceivable.
concepimento *m.* conception.
concepire *vt.* to conceive.
conceri'a *f.* tannery.
concer'nere *vt.* to concern.
concertare *vt.* to orchestrate; to arrange, plan; concertarsi *vr.* to agree (*on*).
concertatore *m.* conductor.
concertista *m.* concert performer.
concerto *m.* concert; agreement.
concessiona'rio *m.* agent.
concessione *f.* concession; agency.
concesso *adj.* granted. *pp.of* concedere.

concetto *m.* conception; idea; reputation; meaning.
concettoso *adj.* meaningful.
concezione *f.* conception; idea.
conchi'glia *f.* shell, conch.
conchiu'dere[25] *see* concludere.
con'cia *f.* tanning; processing; seasoning.
conciare *vt.* to tan; to process; to season; to reduce: — per le feste, to beat to a pulp; conciarsi *vr.* to make of oneself.
conciatore *m.* tanner.
concilia'bolo *m.* conventicle.
conciliante *adj.* conciliatory.
conciliare *vt.* to conciliate; to win: — il sonno, to induce sleep; conciliarsi *vr.* to win.
conciliativo *adj.* conciliatory.
conciliatore *m.* peacemaker: giudice —, justice of the peace.
conciliazione *f.* conciliation.
conci'lio *m.* council.
concima'ia *f.* dunghill.
concimare *vt.* to manure.
concime *m.* manure.
concionare *vi.* to harangue.
concione *f.* harangue, speech.
conciossiachè *conj.* inasmuch as.
concisamente *adv.* concisely.
concisione *f.* concision.
conciso *adj.* concise.
concistoro *m.* consistory.
concitare *vt.* to excite, stir.
concitato *adj.* excited; breathless; frantic.
concitazione *f.* excitement.
concittadino *m.* fellow citizen.
conclamare *vt.* to proclaim.
conclave *m.* conclave.
conclu'dere *vt.*, *vi.*[3] to conclude.
conclusionale *f.* record.
conclusione *f.* conclusion.
conclusivo *adj.* conclusive.
concluso *adj.* concluded. *pp. of* concludere.
concomitante *adj.* concomitant.
concomitanza *f.* concomitance.
concordanza *f.* concordance.
concordare *vt.* to arrange; to agree upon. *vi.*to agree; to tally;(*gramm.*) to agree.
concordato *m.* concordat; agreement.
concorde *adj.* concordant.
concordemente *adv.* concordantly, unanimously.
concor'dia *f.* concord, agreement.
concorrente *m.* competitor; entrant; candidate; bidder.
concorrenza *f.* concurrence, attendance; competition; extent.
concor'rere *vi.*[36] to concur; to flock (*to*); to co-operate; to compete; to contribute; to bid.

concorso m. attendance; co-operation; competition, contest; contribution; concurrence: **partecipare a un —**, to enter a contest.

concozione f. concoction.

concretare vt. to actualize; to concretize; to conclude; to accomplish, bring about.

concretezza f. concreteness.

concreto m., adj. concrete, real.

concubina f. concubine.

concubinato m. concubinage.

conculcare vt. to trample on.

concupiscente adj. covetous.

concupiscenza f. covetousness.

concussiona'rio m. extortioner.

concussione f. extortion.

condanna f. conviction, sentence.

condanna'bile adj. condemnable.

condannare vt. to condemn, sentence; to find guilty; to blame.

condannato m. convict. adj., pp. condemned, sentenced.

condebitore m. joint debtor.

condensa'bile adj. condensable.

condensare vt., **condensarsi** vr. to condense; to thicken.

condensato m. condensation. adj., pp. condensed.

condensatore m. condenser.

condensazione f. condensation.

condimento m. condiment.

condire vt. to season, flavor; to dress.

condirettore m. joint manager.

condiscendente adj. condescending; complying.

condiscendenza f. condescension.

condiscen'dere vi. to condescend; to yield (to); to consent.

condisce'polo m. schoolfellow.

condivi'dere vt.[48] to share.

condizionale m., adj. conditional; (gramm.) conditional mood. f. (law) suspended sentence.

condizionare vt. to condition (upon); to trim.

condizionato adj. conditioned.

condizione f. condition; term: **a — che**, provided; **essere in — di**, to be in a position to; **mettere in —**, to enable.

condoglianza f. condolence.

condolersi vr. to condole.

condomi'nio m. joint (house) ownership.

condo'mino m. joint (house) owner.

condonare vt. to forgive, remit.

condono m. remission, pardon.

condotta f. conduct, behavior.

condottiero m. leader; condottiere.

condotto (1) m. duct; flue; pipeline.

condotto (2) pp. of **condurre**.

conducente m. driver.

condurre vt., vi.[3] to conduct, lead;

to drive; to take; to give rise (to); to manage; **condursi** vr. to behave.

conduttore m. conductor; driver; manager.

conduttura f. pipeline.

conduzione f. management; conduction; tenancy.

confabulare vi. to confabulate.

confacente adj. becoming, proper.

confarsi vr.[61] to suit, agree (with).

confederare vt., **confederarsi** vr. to confederate.

confederato m., adj. confederate.

confederazione f. confederation, confederacy.

conferenza f. lecture; conference.

conferenziere m. lecturer.

conferimento m. conferment; bestowal; grant.

conferire vt. to confer, bestow (on, upon). vi. to consult (with); to agree (with).

conferma f. confirmation.

confermare vt. to confirm.

confessa'bile adj. avowable.

confessare vt., **confessarsi** vr. to confess.

confessionale m., adj. confessional.

confessione f. confession.

confesso adj. self-convicted.

confessore m. confessor.

confettare vt. to candy.

confettiere m. confectioner.

confetto m. comfit.

confettura f. jam.

confezione f. manufacture.

confezionare vt. to manufacture, make.

conficcare vt. to drive in; **conficcarsi** vr. to get embedded; to bury oneself.

confidare vt. to confide; to entrust. vi. to rely (on), trust; **confidarsi** vr. to unbosom oneself.

confidente m. confidant. f. confidante. adj. confident.

confidenza f. confidence, trust; familiarity; secret.

confidenziale adj. confidential.

configurazione f. configuration.

confinante adj. bordering, neighboring.

confinare vt. to confine. vi. to border (upon).

confina'rio adj. border.

confinato m. confined prisoner. adj. confined.

confine m. border, frontier; (pl.) boundaries.

confino m. confinement.

confisca f. confiscation.

confiscare vt. to confiscate.

confitto adj. driven in; embedded.

conflagrazione f. outbreak.

conflitto m. conflict, struggle.

confluente m., adj. confluent.

confluenza f. confluence.

confluire vi. to converge.

confon'dere vt.[65] to confuse; to mix up; to mistake; to bewilder; **confondersi** vr. to get confused; to mingle (with); to flounder.

confondi'bile adj. mistakable.

conformare vt., **conformarsi** vr. to conform (to).

conformazione f. conformation.

conforme adj. conformable; true.

conforme a adv. in conformity with, in compliance with.

conformemente adv. conformably, in conformity (with).

conformista m. conformist.

conformità f. conformity.

confortante adj. comforting.

confortare vt. to comfort.

confortatore m. comforter. adj. comforting.

conforte'vole adj. comfortable.

conforto m. comfort, solace; assistance.

confratello m. brother (archaic and Biblical pl. brethren).

confraternità f. brotherhood.

confricare vt. to rub.

confrontare vt. to compare (with, to).

confronto m. comparison.

confusamente adv. confusedly.

confusiona'rio m. jumbler. adj. meddlesome; blundering.

confusione f. confusion.

confuso adj. confused; mixed up.

confuta'bile adj. confutable.

confutare vt. to confute.

confutazione f. confutation.

congedare vt. to dismiss; (mil.) to discharge; **congedarsi** vr. to take one's leave (of).

congedo m. leave; discharge.

congegnare vt. to contrive.

congegno m. contrivance.

congelamento m. congealment.

congelare vt., vi.; **congelarsi** vr. to freeze, congeal.

congelazione f. freezing.

conge'nito adj. congenital, inborn.

conge'rie f. congeries; jumble.

congestionare vt. to congest.

congestione f. congestion.

congettura f. conjecture, guess.

congetturare vt. to conjecture, guess, suppose.

congiun'gere vt.,[79] **congiungersi** vr. to join; to weld: — in matrimonio, to get married.

congiuntamente adv. jointly.

congiuntiva f. conjunctiva.

congiuntivite f. conjunctivitis.

congiuntivo m., adj. subjunctive.

congiunto m. relative. adj. joined, connected; related. pp. of congiungere.

congiuntura f. conjuncture; predicament; emergency.

congiunzione f. junction; conjunction.

congiura f. conspiracy, plot.

congiurare vi. to plot.

congiurato m. conspirator.

conglobare vt. to conglobate.

conglomerare vt. to conglomerate.

conglomerato m., adj. conglomerate.

congratularsi vr. to congratulate.

congratulazione f. congratulation.

congrega f. gang, set, coterie.

congregare vt., **congregarsi** vr. to congregate, assemble.

congregazione f. congregation.

congressista m. congressman.

congresso m. congress.

congruamente adv. congruously.

congruità f. congruity.

con'gruo adj. congruous, adequate.

congua'glio m. balance.

coniare vt. to coin, strike.

coniatore m. coiner, minter.

coniatura f. coinage, minting.

co'nico adj. conical.

coni'fera f. conifer.

conigliera f. warren.

coni'glio m. rabbit.

co'nio m. coinage: di nuovo —, newly-coined.

coniugale adj. conjugal.

coniugare vt. to conjugate.

coniugato adj. conjugate; married.

coniugazione f. conjugation.

co'niuge m. mate, spouse: una coppia di coniugi, a married couple; i coniugi Smith, the Smith couple.

connaturale adj. inborn.

connazionale m. fellow countryman. f. fellow countrywoman.

connessione f. connection.

connesso adj. connected. pp. of connettere.

connessura f. joint.

connet'tere vt.[8] to connect; to link. vi. to reason.

connettivo adj. connective.

connivente adj. conniving.

connivenza f. connivance.

connotato m. feature.

connu'bio m. union, match, wedding.

cono m. cone.

conoc'chia f. distaff.

conoscente m. acquaintance.

conoscenza f. knowledge; acquaintance; consciousness.

cono'scere vt.[30] to know, be acquainted with; **conoscersi** vr. to know oneself; to know each other.

conoscitore m. connoisseur.

conosciuto *adj.* known. *pp. of* **conoscere.**

conqui'dere *vt.*[31] to win, conquer.

conquiso *adj.* conquered, won. *pp. of* **conquidere,**

conquista *f.* conquest.

conquistare *vt.* to conquer, win.

conquistatore *m.* conqueror.

consacrare *vt.* to consecrate.

consacrazione *f.* consecration.

consanguineità *f.* consanguinity.

consangui'neo *m.* kinsman. *f.* kinswoman. *adj.* consanguineous.

consape'vole *adj.* aware.

consapevolezza *f.* consciousness, awareness.

consapevolmente *adv.* consciously.

con'scio *adj.* conscious, aware.

consecutivo *adj.* consecutive.

consegna *f.* delivery; order; watchword; confinement; safekeeping: **dare in —,** to entrust; **ricevere in —,** to be entrusted with.

consegnare *vt.* to deliver.

consegnata'rio *m.* consignee.

conseguente *adj.,* consequent, consistent. *ppr. of* **consequire.**

conseguenza *f.* consequence; result: **in — di,** as a result of.

conseguimento *m.* attainment.

conseguire *vt.* to attain; to acquire. *vi.* to ensue, result.

consenso *m.* consent.

consensuale *adj.* consensual.

consentire *vt.* to allow. *vi.* to agree; to yield.

consenziente *adj.* consentient.

conserto *adj.* folded: **a braccia conserte,** with folded arms.

conserva *f.* preserve, sauce.

conservare *vt.* to preserve, keep; **conservarsi** *vr.* to keep.

conservativo *adj.* conservative.

conservatore *m.* conservator; conservative.

conservato'rio *m.* conservatory.

conservazione *f.* preservation: **stato di —,** state of repair; **istinto di —,** instinct of self-preservation.

consesso *m.* assembly.

considerare *vt.* to consider.

consideratezza *f.* considerateness.

considerato *adj.* considerate; considered: **tutto —,** all in all.

considerazione *f.* consideration.

considere'vole *adj.* considerable.

consiglia'bile *adj.* advisable

consigliare *vt.* to advise; **consigliarsi** *vr.* to consult (*with*).

consigliere *m.* adviser; counselor; director.

consi'glio *m.* advice; counsel; council: **— d'amministrazione,** board of directors.

consi'mile *adj.* similar.

consistente *adj.* substantial, solid.

consistenza *f.* consistence; solidity; worth.

consi'stere *vi.*[16] to consist (*of, in*); to amount (*to*).

consociare *vt.* to syndicate.

consociazione *f.* association, syndicate.

conso'cio *m.* associate; copartner.

consolante *adj.* comforting.

consolare (1) *vt.* to console; **consolarsi** *vr.* to take comfort; to cheer up

consolare (2) *adj.* consular.

consolato *m.* consulate; consulship.

consolatore *m.* consoler.

consolazione *f.* consolation, solace.

con'sole *m.* consul.

consolidamento *m.* consolidation.

consolidare *vt.* to consolidate.

consolidato *m.* funded debt.

consonante *f., adj.* consonant.

consonanza *f.* consonance.

con'sono *adj.* consonant, consistent (*with*).

consore la *f.* sister.

consorte *m., f.* mate, consort.

consorteri'a *f.* clique, clan.

consor'zio *m.* syndicate.

constare *vi.* to consist; to be known (*to*): **mi consta che,** I understand that; **a quanto mi consta,** as far as I know.

constatare, constatazione *see* **costatare, costatazione.**

consueto *adj.* usual, customary.

consuetudina'rio *adj.* customary.

consuetu'dine *f.* custom, habit.

consulente *m.* adviser; consulting physician.

consulta *f.* council: **— araldica,** Heralds' College.

consultare *vt.* to consult; to peruse; **consultarsi** *vr.* to take counsel (*with*).

consultazione *f.* consultation.

consultivo *adj.* advisory.

consulto *m.* consultation.

consulto'rio *m.* dispensary.

consumare *vt.* to consume, waste; to use up; to perpetrate; to consummate; **consumarsi** *vr.* to waste away.

consumato *adj.* consummate.

consumatore *m.* consumer.

consumazione *f.* consummation; refreshment; consumption: **fino alla — dei secoli,** till doomsday.

consumo *m.* consumption.

consuntivo *m.* balance sheet.

consunto *adj.* worn; consumptive.

consunzione *f.* consumption.

conta'bile *m.* accountant.

contabilità *f.* bookkeeping.

contachilo'metri m. speedometer.
contadinesco adj. rustic.
contadino m., f. peasant; farmer.
contado m. country.
contagiare vt. to infect (with).
conta'gio m. contagion.
contagioso adj. contagious, catching.
contagiri m. tachometer.
contagocce m. dropper (as for medicine).
contaminare vt. to contaminate, taint.
contaminazione f. contamination.
contante m. cash, ready money. adj. ready: a contanti, cash down.
contare vt. to count, reckon. vi. to rely (on); to intend; to count, matter.
contatore m. reckoner; meter.
contatto m. contact, touch.
conte m. count; earl.
conte'a f. county; earldom.
conteggiare vt. to compute.
conteg'gio m. reckoning.
contegno m. behavior.
contegnoso adj. grave, dignified.
contemplare vt. to contemplate.
contemplativo adj. contemplative.
contemplazione f. contemplation.
contempo (nel) adv. meanwhile.
contemporaneamente adv. contemporaneously.
contemporaneità f. contemporaneousness.
contempora'neo m., adj. contemporary, contemporaneous.
contendente m. contender; competitor
conten'dere vt.[140] to contest. vi. to contend, fight; contendersi vr. to fight (for).
contenere vt.[141] to contain; contenersi vr. to restrain oneself; to behave.
contentare vt. to please, satisfy; contentarsi vr. to content oneself (with).
contentezza f. joy, gladness.
contentino m. makeweight.
contento adj. glad, pleased.
contenuto m. contents (pl.). adj. contained; repressed.
conteri'a f. glassware; beads (pl.).
conterra'nea f. fellow countrywoman.
conterra'neo m. fellow countryman.
contesa f. contest, strife.
conteso pp. of contendere.
contessa f. countess.
contesta'bile adj. contestable.
contestare vt. to dispute; to deny; to notify.
contestazione f. dispute.
contesto m. context.
contiguità f. contiguity.
conti'guo adj. contiguous.
continentale adj. continental.
continente m. continent.
continenza f. continence.
contingentamento m. quota; rationing,

contingentare vt. to allot; to assign a quota; to ration.
contingente m., contingent; quota. adj. contingent.
contingenza f. contingency.
continuamente adv. unceasingly; always.
continuare vt. to continue; vi. to go on.
continuativo adj. continuative.
continuatore m. continuer.
continuazione f. continuation.
continuità f. continuity.
conti'nuo adj. continuous: di —, continuously, often; corrente continua, direct current.
conto m. reckoning; account; bill: per — di, on behalf of; a buon —, anyway; in fin dei conti, after all; rendersi — di, to realize; estratto —, statement of account.
contor'cere vt.[145] to twist; contor'cersi vr. to twist; to writhe.
contorcimento m. twisting.
contornare vt. to surround (with).
contorno m. contour, outline.
contorsione f. writhing.
contorto adj. twisted.
contrabbandiere m. smuggler.
contrabbando m. contraband.
contrabbasso m. contrabass.
contraccambiare vt. to reciprocate.
contraccambio m. requital.
contraccolpo m. rebound; recoil.
contrada f. road; country.
contraddire vt., vi. to contradict; contraddirsi vr. to contradict oneself; to be inconsistent.
contraddistin'guere vt. to earmark; to characterize.
contraddittore m. contradictor.
contradditto'rio m. debate. adj. contradictory; inconsistent.
contraddizione f. contradiction; inconsistency, discrepancy.
contraente m. party (to a contract).
contrae'rea f. antiaircraft artillery.
contrae'reo adj. antiaircraft.
contraffare vt. to counterfeit; to imitate; to mimic; to simulate.
contraffatto adj. counterfeit; adulterated; distorted.
contraffazione f. forgery; fake.
contrafforte m. buttress; range.
contrammira'glio m. rear admiral.
contrappeso m. counterweight.
contrapporre vt. to oppose; to compare.
contrappo'sto m. opposite, opposed, compared. pp. of contrapporre.
contrappunto m. counterpoint.
contrariamente adv. contrarily.
contrariare vt. to vex; to thwart.
contrarietà f. contrariety.

contra'rio m. contrary, opposite. adj. contrary; unfavorable; averse; aver qualcosa in —, to object (to); in senso —, contrariwise.

contrarre vt.[146] to contract; **contrarsi** vr. to contract, shrink.

contrassegnare vt. to earmark.

contrassegno m. earmark; badge. adv. cash on delivery (abbr. c.o.d.)

contrastante adj. conflicting.

contrastare vt. to oppose. vi. to contrast (with); to quarrel.

contrastato adj. (photog.) contrasty.

contrasto m. contrast; conflict; quarrel.

contrattaccare vt., vi. to counterattack.

contrattacco m. counterattack.

contrattare vt., vi. to bargain.

contrattazione f. negotiation.

contrattempo m. contretemps, "hitch"; (mus.) syncopation.

contratto (1) m. contract.

contratto (2) adj. contracted. pp. of contrarre.

contrattuale adj. contractual.

contravveleno m. antidote.

contravvenire vi. to infringe (upon).

contravvenzione f. violation; fine.

contrazione f. contraction.

contribuente m. taxpayer: — moroso tax delinquent.

contribuire vi. to contribute.

contributo m. contribution.

contribuzione f. contribution.

contristare vt. to afflict.

contrito adj. contrite.

contrizione f. contrition.

contro m. con: il pro e il —, the pros and cons. prep., adv. against; counter: — assegno, cash on delivery.

controbat'tere vt., vi. to contest, argue (against); to answer.

controbilanciare vt. to counterbalance

controcampo m. (moving pictures) reverse shot.

controcassa f. outer case.

controchi'glia f. keelson.

controcorrente f. countercurrent. adv. upstream.

controffensiva f. counteroffensive.

controfigura f. (moving pictures) double, stand-in: — acrobatica, stunt man.

controfiocco m. flying jib.

controfirmare vt. to countersign.

controindicazione f. contraindication.

controllare vt. to control, verify, check; **controllarsi** vr. to control oneself.

controllo m. control, check.

controllore m. controller; conductor.

controluce adv. against the light.

contromarca f. countermark; check.

contromar'cia f. countermarch; reverse.

contromezzana f. mizzen topsail.

controparte f. opponent.

controproposta f. counterproposition.

contror'dine m. countermand.

controsenso m. nonsense, absurdity.

controspionag'gio m. counterespionage.

controvelaccino m. foreroyal.

controvelac'cio m. mainroyal.

controvento adv. windward.

controver'sia f. controversy.

controverso adj. controversial, moot.

contumace adj. defaulting.

contuma'cia f. default; quarantine: giudizio in —, judgment by default.

contume'lia f. contumely, insult.

contundente adj. blunt.

conturbante adj. disturbing.

conturbare vt. to disturb, upset.

contusione f. contusion, bruise.

contuso adj. bruised.

contuttochè conj. although.

contuttociò adv. yet, still.

convalescente m., f., adj. convalescent.

convalescenza f. convalescence.

convalescenzia'rio m. nursing home.

conva'lida f. validation; sanction.

convalidare vt. to validate; to confirm; to sanction.

convegno m. meeting; convention; rendezvous.

convene'vole m. propriety; (pl.) manners, proprieties. adj. fit, proper.

convenevolmente adv. properly.

conveniente adj. convenient; appropriate; cheap; profitable.

convenienza f. advantage; suitability; propriety.

convenire vt.[152] to convene. vi. to assemble; to agree; to admit; to suit; to be convenient: conviene che tu ne vada, you had better go.

conventi'cola f. conventicle.

convento m. convent.

convenuto m. defendant; attendant. adj. agreed (upon); convened. pp. of convenire.

convenzionale adj. conventional.

convenzione f. convention.

convergente adj. convergent.

conver'gere vi.[38] to converge.

conversa f. lay sister.

conversare vt. to converse.

conversazione f. conversation.

conversione f. conversion.

converso m. lay brother.

converso (per) adv. conversely.

converti'bile adj. convertible.

convertibilità f. convertibility.

convertire vt.[54] to convert (to, into); to turn (into); **convertirsi** vr. to be converted (to); to turn (into).

convertito m. convert. adj. converted.

convertitore *m.* converter.
convessità *f.* convexity.
convesso *adj.* convex.
convincente *adj.* convincing.
convin'cere *vt.*[153] to convince, persuade; to convict; **convin'cersi** *vr.* to be (become) convinced.
convincimento *m.* firm belief.
convinto *adj.* persuaded; convicted. *pp. of* convincere.
convinzione *f.* firm belief; conviction.
convitato *m.* guest.
convito *m.* feast, banquet.
convitto *m.* boarding school.
convittore *m.* boarding pupil.
convivente *m.* cohabitant. *adj.* cohabiting.
convivenza *f.* cohabitation, life in common.
convi'vere *vi.*[111] to cohabit, live together.
conviviale *adj.* convivial.
convi'vio *see* convito.
convocare *vt.* to summon.
convocazione *f.* convocation.
convogliare *vt.* to convoy; to channel.
convo'glio *m.* convoy; *(rail.)* train.
convulsamente *adv.* convulsively.
convulsione *f.* convulsion.
convulsivo *adj.* convulsive.
convulso *m.* convulsion. *adj.* convulsive, spasmodic.
cooperare *vi.* to co-operate.
cooperativa *f.* co-operative.
cooperativo *adj.* co-operative.
cooperazione *f.* co-operation.
coordinamento *m.* co-ordination.
coordinare *vt.* to co-ordinate.
coordinatore *m.* co-ordinator.
coordinazione *f.* co-ordination.
coorte *f.* cohort.
copale *see* coppale.
coper'chio *m.* lid, cover.
coperta *f.* cover; coverlet; blanket; rug; bedspread; *(naut.)* deck.
copertina *f.* cover.
coperto *m.* shelter; safety; cover: **al —**, sheltered. *adj.* covered; coated; clothed; hidden. *pp. of* coprire.
copertone *m.* tarpaulin; *(auto.)* tire, shoe.
copertura *f.* covering; cover; coverage; screen.
co'pia *f.* copy; plenty.
copialet'tere *m.* copybook; copying press.
copiare *vt.* to copy.
copiativo *adj.* copying.
copiatore *m.* copyist; plagiarist.
copiatura *f.* copying; plagiarism.
copione *m.* script.
copiosamente *adv.* plentifully.
copioso *adj.* copious, plentiful.
copista *m.* copyist.

copisteri'a *f.* copying office.
coppa *f.* cup, bowl; heart (*in playing cards*); trophy; nap; saveloy.
coppale *m.* copal; patent leather.
coppella *f.* cupel: **oro di —**, pure gold.
coppetta *f.* cupping glass.
cop'pia *f.* couple, pair, brace.
coppiere *m.* cupbearer.
coppo *m.* tile; jar, pitcher.
copribusto *m.* bodice.
copricapo *m.* headgear.
coprifuoco *m.* curfew; blackout.
copripiedi *m.* coverlet, blanket.
coprire *vt.*[35] to cover; to hide; to fill (*an office*); to coat; to clothe: **— di ingiurie**, to revile; **coprirsi** *vr.* to cover oneself (*with*); to put on one's hat.
coprivivande *m.* dish cover. [hat.
copto *m.* Copt; Coptic. *adj.* Coptic.
co'pula *f.* sexual intercourse; *(sci.)* copulation; *(gramm.)* copula.
corag'gio *m.* courage: **farsi —**, to take courage; **fare — a**, to hearten.
coraggiosamente *adv.* bravely.
coraggioso *adj.* courageous, brave.
corale *m.*, *adj.* choral.
coralli'fero *adj.* coralliferous.
corallo *m.* coral.
corame *m.* leather.
Corano *m.* Koran.
corata *f.* lights (*pl.*).
corazza *f.* armor plate; breastplate; *(zool.)* carapace, shell.
corazzare *vt.* to armor; to steel; **corazzarsi** *vr.* to steel oneself.
corazzata *f.* battleship.
corazziere *m.* cuirassier.
corba *f.* basket.
corbelleri'a *f.* nonsense, blunder.
corbez'zolo *m.* arbute.
corbez'zoli! *interj.* by Jove!
corda *f.* rope, cable; halter; chord; *(mus.)* string; *(anat.)* cord: **— di rame**, copper plait; **— di pianoforte**, piano wire; **mostrare la —**, to be threadbare; **dare la — a un orologio**, to wind up a clock.
cordame *m.* rope; cordage.
cordata *f.* (*mountaineering*) roped team.
cordiale *m.* cordial. *adj.* hearty.
cordialità *f.* cordiality.
cordialmente *adv.* cordially.
cordigliera *f.* cordillera.
cordo'glio *m.* grief, sorrow.
cordonata *f.* ramp, gradient.
cordone *m.* cordon; cord; girdle; *(archit.)* stringcourse; curb, curbstone.
core'a *f.* (*med.*) St. Vitus's dance.
Corea *f.* (*geog.*) Korea.
coreg'gia *f.* strap.
Corelli, Arcangelo, Italian violinist (1653–1713).

coreografi'a *f.* choreography.

coreogra'fico *adj.* choreographic.

coreo'grafo *m.* choreographer.

coria'ceo *adj.* coriaceous, tough.

corian'dolo *m.* confetto (*pl.* confetti); (*bot.*) coriander.

coricare *vt.* to lay down; coricarsi *vr.* to lie down; to go to bed; to set.

corindone *m.* corundum.

corin'zio *m.*, *adj.* Corinthian.

corista *m.* chorus singer; chorister; diapason. *f.* chorus girl.

co'rizza *f.* coryza.

cormorano *m.* cormorant.

cornac'chia *f.* crow, rook.

cornamusa *f.* bagpipe.

cornata *f.* butt.

cor'nea *f.* cornea.

cornetta *f.* cornet.

cornetto *m.* little horn; amulet; (*bread*) croissant: — acustico, ear trumpet; — telefonico, receiver.

cornice *f.* frame; cornice.

cornicione *m.* entablature.

cornificare *vt.* to be unfaithful to, to cuckold.

cor'niola *f.* (*bot.*) dogberry; (*min.*) carnelian.

cor'niolo *m.* cornel, dogwood.

corno *m.* horn: corna ramificate, antlers; fare le corna al marito, to cuckold one's husband; portare le corna, to be a cuckold.

cornuto *m.* cuckold. *adj.* horned.

coro *m.* chorus; choir.

corografi'a *f.* chorography.

coro'grafo *m.* chorographer.

coro'ide *f.* choroid.

corolla *f.* corolla.

corolla'rio *m.* corollary.

corona *f.* crown; coronet; corona; rim; wreath; rosary, beads (*pl.*).

coronamento *m.* crowning; fulfillment.

coronare *vt.* to crown; to fulfill.

corona'rio *adj.* coronary.

coronato *adj.* crowned; coronate.

corpetto *m.* waistcoat, vest.

corpo *m.* body; staff; corpus; (*typog.*) size, type; (*mil.*) corps: — di ballo, corps de ballet; — del reato, corpus delicti; spirito di —, esprit de corps; a — morto, rashly.

corporale *adj.* corporal, bodily; physical.

corporativismo *m.* corporative system.

corporativo *adj.* corporative.

corporatura *f.* size, build.

corporazione *f.* corporation.

corpo'reo *adj.* corporeal, bodily.

corpulento *adj.* corpulent, portly.

corpulenza *f.* corpulence.

corpu'scolo *m.* corpuscle.

Corpusdo'mini *m.* Corpus Christi.

corredare *vt.* to equip, provide (*with*); to accompany (*with*); to supplement (*with*).

corredo *m.* outfit; kit; trousseau.

correg'gere *vt.*[105] to correct, amend; to rebuke: — le bozze, to read proofs; correg'gersi *vr.* to correct oneself; to improve.

correg'gia *f.* strap.

Correggio, da, Azzo (*Antonio Allegri*), Italian painter (1494–1534).

correggi'bile *adj.* corrigible.

corregionale *m.* fellow countryman.

correità *f.* complicity.

correlativo *adj.* correlative.

correlazione *f.* correlation.

correligiona'rio *m.* coreligionist.

corrente *f.* current; draft; school; tendency: — del Golfo, Gulf Stream; contro —, upstream; essere al — di, to be acquainted with; mettere uno al — di, to acquaint one with. *adj.* current, running, flowing; instant; middling; circulating; common, prevailing.

correntemente *adv.* currently, fluently.

correntista *m.* depositor.

corre'o *m.* codefendant; corespondent.

cor'rere *vt.*, *vi.*[36] to run; to hurry; to flow; to be current; to circulate: coi tempi che corrono, as times go; corre voce che, there is a rumor that; lasciar —, to bear with it; — i mari, to sail the seas; far — un cavallo, to race a horse.

corresponsa'bile *adj.* jointly responsible; corespondent.

corresponsione *f.* payment.

correttamente *adv.* correctly.

correttezza *f.* correctness.

correttivo *m.*, *adj.* corrective.

corretto *adj.* correct; corrected, right, upright; laced, "spiked" (*as of coffee*). *pp.* of correggere. *adv.* correctly.

correttore *m.* corrector: — di bozze, proofreader.

correzione *f.* correction: — delle bozze, proofreading; casa di —, reformatory.

corrido'io *m.* passage; aisle, corridor.

corridore *m.* racer, competitor.

corriera *f.* stagecoach; motor bus.

corriere *m.* messenger, courier; carrier, forwarder; mail: a volta di —, by return mail.

corrigendo *m.* reformatory boy

corrimano *m.* handrail.

corrispet'tivo *m.* return, requital, reward; consideration.

corrispondente *m.* correspondent. *adj* correspondent, corresponding.

corrispondenza f. correspondence; relation; agreement; reciprocity; mail.

corrispon'dere vt.[113] to allow. vi. to correspond (to, with); to match; to fit; to reciprocate; to answer, fulfill; to comply (with).

corrisposto adj. reciprocated, returned; allowed. pp. of **corrispondere**.

corrivo adj. rash; accommodating; lenient.

corroborante m., adj. corroborative.

corroborare vt. to corroborate, strengthen; to invigorate.

corroborazione f. corroboration.

corro'dere vt.[114] to corrode, to eat (into); **corrodersi** vr. to corrode, to be eaten (into).

corrom'pere vt.[115] to corrupt; to taint; to bribe; **corrom'persi** vr. to corrupt, decay, rot.

corrosione f. corrosion.

corrosivo m., adj. corrosive.

corroso adj. corroded. pp. of **corrodere**.

corrotto adj. corrupt, rotten; corrupted, tainted; bribed. pp. of **corrompere**.

corrucciarsi vr. to get angry; to worry.

corrucciato adj. angry; worried.

corruc'cio m. anger; worry.

corrugare vt., **corrugarsi** vr. to wrinkle, knit: — la fronte, to frown.

corruttela f. corruption; bribing.

corrutti'bile adj. corruptible; bribable.

corruttibilità f. corruptibility; bribability.

corruttore m. corrupter; briber.

corruzione f. corruption; seducement; bribing: prezzo della —, bribe.

corsa f. run; race; trip; (aeron.) taxling; (mach.) stroke: — di andata e ritorno, round trip; prezzo della —, fare; di —, in a hurry; perdere la —, to miss (one's train, one's bus, etc.); di gran —, full speed; sala delle corse, horse (betting) room.

corsaletto m. corselet.

corsaro m. privateer; pirate.

corsi'a f. aisle, passageway; ward; alley; (aeron.) catwalk.

corsiere m. race horse, courser.

corsivo m. (typog.) italics (pl.).

corso (1) m. watercourse; avenue: — d'acqua, watercourse; — del cambio, rate of exchange; capitano di lungo —, shipmaster; avere — legale, to be legal tender; fuori —, withdrawn from circulation; nel — della settimana, during the week; in —, under way; in — di stampa, in the press.

corso (2) pp. of **correre**.

corso (3) m., adj. Corsican.

corso'io adj. running, sliding: nodo —, running knot.

corte f. courtyard; court; retinue; addresses (pl.), courtship: Corte Marziale, court martial; dama di —, lady-in-waiting; fare la — a, to court; tenere — bandita, to keep open house.

cortec'cia f. bark; cortex.

corteggiamento m. courtship.

corteggiare vt. to court, woo.

corteg'gio m. retinue.

corteo m. procession, train; parade: — funebre, funeral train.

corteggiatore m. beau (pl. beaux), wooer.

cortese adj. kind, polite, obliging.

cortesemente adv. kindly, politely; obligingly.

cortesi'a f. politeness; kindness; obligingness: per —, please, if you please.

cortezza f. shortness; lack, want: — di mente, dullness.

cor'tice m. cortex (pl. cortices).

cortigiana f. courtesan.

cortigiano m. courtier.

cortile m. courtyard, court, yard.

cortina f. curtain, screen: — di ferro, Iron Curtain.

cortinag'gio m. canopy.

corto adj. short, brief; wanting; short-witted: — di vista, short-sighted; essere a — di, to be short of; venire alle corte, to get down to brass tacks.

cortometrag'gio m. short; documentary.

corvetta f. corvette.

corvino adj. corvine; raven.

corvo m. crow, raven; (naut.) grappling iron; (mach.) tongs (pl.).

cosa f. thing; matter; work; gadget: che —? what? qualche —, something; nessuna —, nothing; alcuna —, anything; ogni —, everything; per la qual —, therefore.

Cosacco m. Cossack.

coscetto m. leg (of mutton, etc.).

co'scia f. thigh; leg; (arch.) abutment; (mach.) jaw.

cosciale m. cuisse, cuish.

cosciente adj. conscious, aware.

coscienza f. conscience; awareness; uprightness: libertà di —, freedom of conscience, religion.

coscienziosità f. conscientiousness.

coscienzioso adj. conscientious.

coscritto m. recruit. adj. conscript.

coscrizione f. conscription.

così adv., adj. so, thus, this way, like this, like that, such.

osicchè conj. so that.

cosiddetto adj. so-called.

cosiffatto adj. such, of that kind.

cosmesi f. cosmesis.

cosme'tico m., adj. cosmetic.

co'smico adj. cosmic.

cosmo m. cosmos.

cosmografi'a f. cosmography.

cosmologi'a f. cosmology.

cosmopolita m. cosmopolite. adj. cosmopolitan.

coso m. thing, thingumbob, thingummy.

cospar'gere vt.[132] to spread; to sprinkle; to smear.

cosparso adj. besprinkled, sprinkled, besmeared. pp. of cospargere.

cospetto m. presence; view.

cospetto! interj. bless me!

cospi'cuo adj. conspicuous, outstanding; substantial; prominent.

cospirare vi. to conspire, plot.

cospiratore m. conspirator.

cospiratrice f. conspiratress.

cospirazione f. conspiracy.

costa m. rib; slope; coast; back (of a knife); middle nerve (of a leaf).

costà adv. there.

costaggiù adv. down there.

costante adj. constant; loyal; lasting; uniform; steady.

costantemente adv. steadily.

costanza f. constancy; steadiness; loyalty.

costare vi. to cost.

costassù adv. up there.

costata f. chop, cutlet.

costatare vt. to ascertain; to perceive.

costatazione f. ascertainment, verification; discovery.

costato m. chest, ribs (pl.).

costeggiare vt. to coast; to flank; border. vi. to coast (along).

coste'i pron.f. this woman, she.

costellare vt. to spangle.

costellazione f. constellation.

costernare vt. to cause consternation (in), dismay, grieve.

costernazione f. consternation.

costì adv. there.

costiera f. coast, shore.

costiere m. pilot.

costiero adj. coastal: nave **costiera**, coaster.

costipare vt. to constipate; to give (one) a cold; **costiparsi** vr. to become constipated; to catch a cold.

costipazione f. constipation; cold.

costituente adj. constituent.

costituire vt. to constitute; to form; to amount to; to appoint; to assign; **costituirsi** vr. to form, be constituted; to appoint oneself; to give oneself up: **costituirsi parte civile**, to sue.

costitutivo adj. constitutive.

costituzionale adj. constitutional.

costituzione f. constitution, formation; make-up; establishment; appointment.

costo m. cost: — **di produzione,** prime cost; **a nessun —,** by no means.

co'stola f. rib; back.

costoletta f. chop, cutlet.

costoro pron.pl. these people; they; these men; these women.

costoso adj. costly, expensive.

costretto adj. compelled, forced, obliged; pressed. pp. of costringere.

costrin'gere vt.[136] to compel, force; to press, cramp.

costrittore m. constrictor.

costrizione f. compulsion.

costruire vt.[37] to build, construct; (gramm.) to construe.

costruito adj., pp. built; construed.

costrutto m. (gramm.) construction; sense, meaning; point; use.

costruttore m. builder.

costruzione f. construction, manufacture; arrangement; make; building.

costu'i pron.m. this man, he.

costumanza f. custom, habit.

costumare vi. to be usual, customary.

costumatezza f. good manners.

costumato adj. well-behaved; polite.

costume m. custom, habit; costume; fancy dress: — **da bagno,** bathing suit; **buoni costumi,** good morals; **cattivi costumi,** loose morals.

costumista m., f., (theat.) costumer.

costura f. seam.

cotale adj., pron. such.

cotanto see tanto.

cote f. hone.

cotechino m. (a certain) sausage.

cotenna f. pigskin; rind; scalp.

cotesto adj. that (pl. those); such. pron. that one.

co'tica f. pigskin; rind.

cotile'done m. cotyledon.

cotogna f. quince.

cotognata f. quince jam.

cotogno m. quince tree.

cotoletta see costoletta.

cotonato m. cotton cloth.

cotone m. cotton; cottonwool.

cotoneri'e f.pl. cotton goods.

cotoniere m. cotton manufacturer; cotton spinner.

cotoniero adj. cotton.

cotonifi'cio m. cotton mill.

cotonina f. calico.

cotta (1) f. cooking; baking; ovenful; kilnful; infatuation: **prendere una — per,** to fall hard for; **un furfante di tre cotte,** an unmitigated scoundrel.

cotta (2) *f.* (*eccl.*) surplice.
cottimista *m.* pieceworker.
cot'timo *m.* piecework.
cotto *m.* earthenware. *adj.* done; cooked: **poco** —, underdone, rare; **troppo** —, overdone; **innamorato** —, head over heels in love. *pp. of* **cuocere.**
cottura *f.* boiling; roasting; baking; grilling; cooking; ovenful.
coturno *m.* cothurnus (*pl.* **cothurni**), buskin.
cova *f.* brooding; brood.
covare *vt., vi.* to brood, sit (*on*); to harbor, cherish; to smolder (*as embers*).
covata *f.* brood; hatch.
covile *m.* den, lair; couch.
covo *m.* den, lair; burrow.
covone *m.* sheaf (*pl.* **sheaves**).
cozza *f.* cockle.
cozzare *vt., vi.* to butt (*at, against*); to hit (*against*); to clash.
cozzo *m.* butt; clash.
crac *m.* crack; failure; slump.
crampo *m.* cramp.
cra'nico *adj.* cranial: **scatola cranica,** skull.
cra'nio *m.* skull.
cra'pula *f.* crapulence; debauchery.
crapulone *m.* debauchee.
crasso *adj.* crass, gross: **intestino** —, large intestine.
cratere *m.* crater.
cra'uti *m.pl.* sauerkraut.
cravatta *f.* tie, necktie; four-in-hand: — **a farfalla,** bow tie.
creanza *f.* politeness: **mala** —, bad manners, rudeness.
creare *vt.* to create; to appoint.
creativo *adj.* creative.
creato *m.* creation, universe. *adj., pp* created, formed.
creatore *m.* creator.
creatrice *f.* creatrix.
creatura *f.* creature: **povera** —! the poor thing!
creazione *f.* creation.
credente *m., f.* believer.
credenza (1) *f.* belief; faith.
credenza (2) *f.* sideboard.
credenziale *f., adj.* credential.
cre'dere *vt., vi.* to believe; to trust; to think: **fa come credi,** do as you like; **cre'dersi** *vr.* to think oneself.
credi'bile *adj.* credible.
credito *m.* credit; trust; reputation: **a** —, on credit; **istituto di** —, bank.
creditore *m.* creditor.
credo *m.* credo, creed; faith.
credulità *f.* credulity.
cre'dulo *adj.* credulous, gullible.
crema *f.* cream; custard: — **da scarpe,** shoe polish.

cremagliera *f.* (*mach.*) rack: **ferrovia a** —, cog railway.
cremare *vt.* to cremate.
cremato'io *m.* crematory.
cremato'rio *adj.* crematory.
cremazione *f.* cremation.
cre'misi *m., adj.* crimson.
Cremlino *m.* Kremlin.
cremore *m.* cream of tartar.
creolina *f.* creolin.
cre'olo *m., adj.* Creole.
creosoto *m.* creosote.
crepa *f.* crack, crevice, chink.
crepac'cio *m.* cleft; crevasse.
crepacuore *m.* heartbreak.
crepapelle (a) *adv.* excessively: **ridere a** —, to burst with laughter.
crepare *vi.* to crack, split; to burst; "to croak," die; **creparsi** *vr.* to crack, burst.
crepitare *vi.* to crackle.
crepiti'o *m.* crepitation, crackling.
crepu'scolo *m.* twilight.
crescendo *m.* crescendo.
crescente *adj.* growing; increasing; rising.
crescenza *f.* growth.
cre'scere *vt.*[38] to increase, raise; to bring up, breed: **farsi** — **la barba,** to grow a beard. *vi.* to increase, rise; to grow; to be left.
crescione *m.* water cress.
cre'scita, **cresciuta** *f.* growth.
cresciuto *adj.* grown (*up*); increased; bred; developed. *pp. of* **crescere.**
cre'sima *f.* Confirmation.
cresimare *vt.* to confirm.
crespa *f.* wrinkle; ripple.
crespo *m.* crepe. *adj.* crispy, crinkled.
cresta *f.* crest; comb; tuft; bonnet; top; peak.
cresta'ia *f.* (*ladies'*) milliner.
creta *f.* clay.
cretese *m., f., adj.* Cretan.
cretineri'a *f.* idiocy; nonsense.
cretino *m.* cretin; idiot, fool.
cribrare *vt.* to sift.
cribro *m.* sieve.
cricca *f.* clique, gang, coterie.
cricco *m.* jack.
criminale *m., adj.* criminal.
criminalità *f.* criminality.
cri'mine *m.* crime.
criminologi'a *f.* criminology.
crimino'logo *m.* criminologist.
criminoso *adj.* criminal.
crinale *m.* ridge; hairpin.
crine *m.* hair.
criniera *f.* mane; crest.
crino *m.* hair.
crinolina *f.* crinoline.
cripta *f.* crypt.
criptocomunista *m.* fellow traveler.
crisa'lide *f.* chrysalis.

crisantemo *m.* chrysanthemum.
crisi *f.* crisis (*pl.* crises); attack; burst; climax.
crisma *f.* chrism.
Crispi, Francesco, Italian statesman (1819–1901).
cristalleri'a *f.* crystal works; crystalware.
cristalliera *f.* glass case.
cristallino *m.* (*anat.*) crystalline lens. *adj.* crystalline, crystal.
cristallizzare *vt.* to crystallize.
cristallizzazione *f.* crystallization.
cristallo *m.* crystal, glass.
cristiane'simo *m.* Christianity.
cristia'nia *m.* (*sport*) christiania turn, christy.
cristianità *f.* Christendom.
cristiano *m.*, *adj.* Christian.
Cristo *m.pr.* Christ: un povero —, a poor fellow.
crite'rio *m.* criterion; standard; idea; sense; principle; rule.
cri'tica *f.* criticism; critique.
criticare *vt.* to criticize; to review.
cri'tico *m.* critic. *adj.* critical.
criticone *m.* faultfinder.
critto'gama *f.* cryptogam.
crittografi'a *f.* cryptography.
crittogramma *m.* cryptogram.
crivellare *vt.* to sift; to riddle (*with*).
crivello *m.* sieve, riddle.
croato *m.* Croat. *adj.* Croatian.
croccante *adj.* crisp, crackling.
crocchetta *f.* croquette.
croc'chia *f.* chignon, bun.
crocchiare *vi.* to crackle; to cluck.
croc'chio *m.* crackle; cluck; group.
croce *f.* cross; cross-mark: a —, crosswise; a occhio e —, at a rough guess; testa e —, head or tail.
Croce, Benedetto, Italian philosopher and historian (1866–1952).
crocerossina *f.* Red Cross Sister.
crocetta *f.* crosslet.
crocevi'a *f.* crossroads (*pl.*), intersection.
crociata *f.* crusade.
crociato *m.* crusader. *adj.* crossed.
crocic'chio *m.* crossroads (*pl.*), intersection.
crociera *f.* intersection; cruise: volta a —, cross vault.
croci'fera *f.* crucifer.
crocifig'gere *vt.*[63] to crucify
crocifissione *f.* crucifixion.
crocifisso *m.* crucifix. *adj.* crucified. *pp.* of crocifiggere.
croco *m.* crocus, saffron.
crogiolarsi *vr.* to cuddle, bask.
crogiuolo *m.* crucible.
crollare *vt.* to shake; to shrug. *vi.* to fall; to collapse; to break down.
crollo *m.* fall, collapse, breakdown.

croma *f.* (*mus.*) quaver.
cromare *vt.* to plate with chromium.
cromato *m.* chromate. *adj.* chromium-plated.
cromatura *f.* chromium plating.
cromo *m.* chrome, chromium.
cromolitografi'a *f.* chromolithography.
cro'naca *f.* chronicle; report, news.
cro'nico *m.*, *adj.* chronic.
cronista *m.* chronicler; reporter: capo —, city editor.
cronisto'ria *f.* chronicle.
cronologi'a *f.* chronology.
cronolo'gico *adj.* chronological.
cronometrare *vt.* to time.
cronome'trico *adj.* chronometrical.
cronometrista *m.* timekeeper.
crono'metro *m.* stop watch, chronometer.
crosciare *vt.* to shower; to rustle.
crosta *f.* crust; scab, eschar.
crosta'ceo *m.*, *adj.* crustacean.
crostata *f.* pie.
crostino *m.* toast.
croupier *m.* dealer.
cro'talo *m.* rattle; rattlesnake.
crucciare *vt.* to torment; to worry; **cruicciarsi** *vr.* to worry; to get angry; to fret.
cruc'cio *m.* sorrow; worry.
cruciale *adj.* crucial.
cruciverba *m.* crossword puzzle.
crudamente *adv.* crudely, rudely.
crudele *adj.* cruel, ruthless.
crudeltà *f.* cruelty.
crudezza *f.* crudeness, roughness.
crudo *adj.* raw; cruel; b unt; hard; unripe.
cruento *adj.* bloody.
crumiro *m.* scab, strikebreaker.
cruna *f.* needle's eye, eye.
crusca *f.* bran; freckles (*pl.*).
cruschello *m.* middlings (*pl.*).
cruscotto *m.* dashboard; (*aeron.*) control panel.
cubatura *f.* cubature.
cu'bico *adj.* cubic; radice cubica, cube root.
cubi'colo *m.* cubicle.
cubismo *m.* cubism.
cubista *m.*, *adj.* cubist.
cubitale *adj.* cubital; (*anat.*) ulnar: caratteri cubitali, large type.
cu'bito *m.* cubit; (*anat.*) ulna.
cubo *m.* cube. *adj.* cubic.
cuccagna *f.* Cockaigne; windfall: albero della —, greased pole.
cuccetta *f.* berth.
cucchiaiata *f.* spoonful.
cucchiaino *m.* teaspoon.
cucchia'io *m.* spoon.
cucchiaione *m.* ladle.
cuc'cia *f.* couch; doghouse.
cuc'ciolo *m.* puppy, whelp.

cuccù *m.* cuckoo.
cuc'cuma *f.* kettle; coffeepot.
cucina *f.* kitchen; cookery, cuisine; cooking: — economica, kitchen range.
cucinare *vt., vi.* to cook; to dress.
cuciniere *m.* cook.
cucinino *m.* kitchenette.
cucire *vt.* to sew, stitch: macchina per —, sewing machine.
cucirini *m.pl.* sewing threads.
cucitrice *f.* seamstress.
cucitura *f.* seam; sewing.
cu'culo *m.* cuckoo.
cucur'bita *f.* gourd; alembic.
cucurbita'ceo *adj.* cucurbitaceous.
cuf'fia *f.* cap; hood; headset.
cugino *m.,* cugina *f.* cousin.
cui a, di, *etc. rel. pron.* whom, whose, to whom, which, of which, to which.
culatta *f.* breech.
culina'ria *f.* cookery.
culina'rio *adj.* culinary.
culla *f.* cradle.
cullare *vt.* to rock; lull, to fondle.
culminante *adj.* highest, culminating.
culminare *vi.* to culminate.
cul'mine *m.* top, summit.
culo *m.* buttocks; bottom.
culto *m.* worship, cult.
cultore *m.* dilettante, devotee.
cultura *f.* culture; learning.
cumulativo *adj.* cumulative, joint.
cu'mulo *m.* pile, heap; lot; pool; cumulus (*pl.* cumuli).
cuna *f.* cradle.
cu'neo *m.* wedge.
cunetta *f.* ditch; gutter.
cuni'colo *m.* tunnel; adit.
cuo'cere *vt., vi.,³⁹* cuo'cersi *vr.* to cook; to bake; to stew; to boil; to roast; (*fig.*) to sting.
cuoco *m.,* cuoca *f.* cook.
cuo'io *m.* leather.
cuore *m.* heart; soul: amico del —, bosom friend; senza—, heartless; nel — della notte, in the dead of night.
cupezza *f.* gloominess.
cupidi'gia *f.* greed, cupidity.
cu'pido *adj.* greedy, covetous.
Cupido *m.* (*myth.*) Cupid.

cupo *adj.* gloomy; sullen; deep; dark.
cu'pola *f.* dome, cupola.
cura *f.* care; cure, treatment, nursing; remedy; editorship; a — di, edited by.
cura'bile *adj.* curable.
curare *vt.* to take care of, manage; to edit; to treat, nurse; to cure; curarsi *vr.* to subject oneself to medical treatment; to take care of oneself; to care; to take care (*of*).
curaro *m.* curare, curari.
curatela *f.* guardianship; trusteeship.
curativo *adj.* curative, healing.
curato *m.* curate.
curatore *m.* curator; trustee; custodian.
curdo *m., adj.* Kurd.
cu'ria *f.* curia; court of justice.
curialesco *adj.* jurisprudential.
curiosare *vi.* to pry (*into*).
curiosità *f.* curiosity; inquisitiveness; quaintness, oddness; curio.
curioso *m.* onlooker. *adj.* curious; inquisitive; quaint, odd, funny.
curro *m.* roller; (*mach.*) dolly.
cursore *m.* process server; (*mach.*) slider.
curva *f.* curve, bend; camber.
curvare *vt.* to curve, to bend; to camber; curvarsi *vr.* to bend, bow, stoop.
curvatura *f.* curving, bending.
curvo *adj.* curved, bent; stooping.
cuscinetto *m.* small cushion; (*mach.*) bearing; (*fig.*) buffer: — per timbri, pad; — a sfere, ball bearing.
cuscino *m.* cushion; pillow.
cu'spide *f.* cusp.
custode *m.* custodian; guardian; keeper; janitor; watchman; warder.
custo'dia *f.* custody, keeping; guardianship; care; case: agente di —, custodian.
custodire *vt.* to keep, preserve; to watch over; to take care of; to cherish.
cuta'neo *adj.* cutaneous, skin.
cute *f.* skin.
cuticagna *f.* nape; scalp.
cutret tola *f.* wagtail.

D

da *prep.* from; by; to; at; since; as, like; for: — principio, at first; dal principio alla fine, from first to last; un contegno — gentiluomo, a gentlemanlike behavior; — vendere, for sale; — affittare, to let; — parte, aside; — basso, downstairs; auto — turismo, touring car.

dabbasso *adv.* downstairs.
dabbenag'gine *f.* candor; credulity.
dabbene *adj.* upright, honest.
daccanto *prep.* beside, by, close to. *adv.* near, near by.
daccapo *adv.* again, over again; paragraph; (*mus.*) da capo.
dacchè *conj.* since.
dadaismo *m.* dadaism.

dadaista *m.* dadaist.
dado *m.* die (*pl.* dice); cube; (*mach.*) nut; (*obs.*) die (*pl.* dies).
daffare *m.* occupation; bustle: avere un gran —, to be very busy; darsi un gran —, to bustle about.
daga *f.* dagger, dirk.
dagherro'tipo *m.* daguerreotype.
dagli, dai *comp.prep.* from, by the. *see* da.
dài! *interj.* come on now!; hurry up!; go on!
da'ina *f.* doe.
da'ino *m.* deer (*pl.* deer); buck.
dal, dalla *comp.prep.* from, by the. *see* da.
da'lia *f.* dahlia.
dallato *adv.* beside; aside.
dalle, dallo *comp.prep.* from, by the. *see* da.
dal'mata *m., adj.* Dalmatian.
dalto'nico *adj.* color-blind.
daltonismo *m.* daltonism.
d'altronde *adv.* on the other hand; besides, moreover.
dama (*1*) *f.* lady; (*dancing*) partner.
dama (*2*) *f.* checkers: king: **fare** —, to become a king.
damascare *vt.* to damask.
damasco *m.* brocade, damask.
Damasco *f.* (*geog.*) Damascus.
damerino *m.* dandy, fop.
damigella *f.* damsel, maid.
damigiana *f.* demijohn.
danaro *see* denaro.
danaroso *adj.* wealthy.
Dan'dolo, Enrico, admiral and blind doge of Venice (1108?-1205).
danese *m.* Dane; Great Dane. *adj.* Danish.
dannare *vt.* to damn; **dannarsi** *vr.* to damn oneself; to rack oneself; to fret.
dannato *m., adj.* damned.
dannazione *f.* damnation; curse.
danneggiare *vt.* to damage, injure; to impair, harm; to damnify.
danneggiato *m.* victim, loser. *adj.* damaged, harmed; damnified.
danno *m.* damage, injure, harm; loss.
dannoso *adj.* hurtful, harmful.
D'Annunzio, Gabriele, *see* Annunzio.
dante (pelle di) *m.* buckskin.
Dante *see* Alighieri.
dantesco *adj.* Dantean, Dantesque.
dantista *m.* Dantist.
danza *f.* dance, dancing.
danzante *adj.* dancing.
danzare *vt., vi.* to dance.
danzatore *m.*, **danzatrice** *f.* dancer.
dappertutto *adv.* everywhere.
dappiè *adv.* at the foot.
dappoco *adj.* worthless, inept.
dappoi *adv.* afterwards.

dappresso *adv.* closely, close by.
dapprima *adv.* at first; first of all.
dapprinci'pio *adv.* in the beginning, at first.
dardeggiare *vt., vi.* to dart (*at*).
dardo *m.* dart.
dare *vt.*[40] to give; to hand over (*to*); to confer, bestow (*on*), award; to grant; to afford; to produce; to utter; to deal: — torto a, to disagree with; — ragione a, to agree with; — alla luce, to give birth to; — da mangiare a, to feed; — uno schiaffo a, to slap; — una commedia, to produce a play; — la buona notte, to wish good night; — l'addio a, to bid good-bye to; — in affitto, to rent; — in prestito, to lend; — a qualcuno 20 anni di età, to take someone to be twenty; gli diedero 10 anni (di prigione), he was sentenced to ten years' imprisonment. *vi.* to hit; to lead; to look (*upon*): — alla testa, to go to one's head; — allo stomaco, to turn one's stomach; — ai nervi, to irk; — nell'occhio, to strike the eye; darsi *vr.* to give oneself; to surrender oneself; to devote oneself (*to*); to pass oneself off (*as*); to take (*to*): — per vinto, to give up; — pensiero, to take pains, to worry; — il caso, to happen; può —, maybe; darsela a gambe, to take to one's heels.
dare *m.* (*comm.*) debit: il — e l'avere, debit and credit.
dar'sena *f.* dock; boathouse.
data *f.* date: in — d'oggi, under today's date; di — recente, recent; alla — stabilita, on the appointed day; a 30 giorni —, 30 days after date; sino alla — d'oggi, down to date.
datare *vt., vi.* to date: a — da oggi, (starting) from today.
dativo *m., adj.* dative.
dato *m.* datum (*pl.* data). *adj.* given: — che, since, supposing that, provided. *pp.of* dare.
datore *m.* giver: — di lavoro, employer.
dat'tero *m.* date; date palm: — di mare, lithodomus.
dattilografare *vt., vi.* to typewrite, to type.
dattilografi'a *f.* typewriting.
dattilo'grafo *m.*, **dattilo'grafa** *f.* typist.
dattiloscritto *m.* typescript.
d'attorno *adv., prep.* about, round, around: levarsi —, to get out of the way; togliersi qualcuno —, to get rid of someone; darsi —, to busy oneself.

davanti *m.,* *adj.* fore, front. *adv.* in front (of), before.

davanzale *m.* sill, window sill.

davanzo *adv.* enough and to spare.

davvero *adv.* really, indeed: **dire —,** to be in earnest.

dazia'rio *adj.* toll.

daziere *m.* exciseman.

da'zio *m.* excise; custom duty; toll-house: **esente da —,** duty free.

dea *f.* goddess.

debellare *vt.* to conquer; to overcome.

debilitante *adj.* debilitative.

debilitare *vt.* to debilitate.

debilitazione *f.* debilitation.

debitamente *adv.* duly, properly.

de'bito *m.* debt; obligation. *adj.* proper, due.

debitore *m.* debtor.

de'bole *m.* weakness. *adj.* weak, feeble.

debolezza *f.* weakness; feebleness.

debolmente *adv.* weakly; faintly.

debosciato *m.* debauchee. *adj.* debauched.

debuttante *m.* debutant. *f.* debutante. *m., f.* beginner.

debuttare *vi.* to open; to make one's debut.

debutto *m.* opening; debut.

de'cade *f.* ten days; decade.

decadente *m., adj.* decadent.

decadenza *f.* decadence; decline: **— da un diritto,** forfeiture.

decadere *vi.*[22] to decline; to fall: **— da un diritto,** to forfeit a right.

decadimento *m.* decay.

decalcificazione *f.* decalcification.

decalcomani'a *f.* decalcomania.

deca'logo *m.* decalogue.

decampare *vi.* to decamp; to recede.

decano *m.* dean.

decantare *vt.* to praise; to decant.

decapitare *vt.* to behead.

decapitazione *f.* beheading.

dece'dere *vi.*[23] to decease.

deceduto *m., adj.* deceased.

decennale *m., adj.* decennial.

decenne *adj.* decennial; ten years old.

decen'nio *m.* decade.

decente *adj.* decent; fair.

decentramento *m.* decentralization.

decentrare *vt.* to decentralize.

decenza *f.* decency.

decesso *m.* decease, death.

deci'dere *vt., vi.*[41] to decide; **decidersi** *vr.* to make up one's mind, resolve.

deci'duo *adj.* deciduous.

decifrare *vt.* to decipher, decode.

decifrazione *f.* decipherment.

decigrammo *m.* decigram.

deci'litro *m.* deciliter.

de'cima *f.* tithe.

decimale *m., adj.* decimal.

decimare *vt.* to decimate.

decimazione *f.* decimation.

deci'metro *m.* decimeter: **doppio —,** ruler.

de'cimo *m., adj.* tenth.

decimoterzo *adj.* thirteenth.

decina *f.* half a score, ten or so.

decisamente *adv.* decidedly; resolutely; unhesitatingly.

decisione *f.* decision, resolution; resoluteness.

decisivo *adj.* decisive.

deciso *adj.* determined; settled, decided. *pp.of* **decidere.**

declamare *vt., vi.* to declaim, mouth.

declamato'rio *adj.* declamatory, mouthy.

declamazione *f.* declamation.

declinare *vt.* to decline; to declare. *vi.* to decline, sink; to slope; to set.

declinazione *f.* (*gramm.*) declension; (*astr.*) declination.

declino *m.* decline, wane.

decli'vio *m.* declivity, slope.

decollare *vt.* to behead. *vi.* (*aeron.*) to take off.

decollo *m.* (*aeron.*) take-off.

decolorare *vt.* to decolor.

decomporre *vt.,*[93] **decomporsi** *vr.* to decompose.

decomposizione *f.* decomposition.

decomposto *adj.* putrid; decomposed.

decorare *vt.* to decorate.

decorativo *adj.* decorative.

decoratore *m.* decorator.

decorazione *f.* decoration.

decoro *m.* decorum, propriety.

decoroso *adj.* decorous; dignified.

decorrenza *f.* beginning.

decor'rere *vi.*[36] to elapse; to date (from).

decorso *m.* lapse; development; course. *adj.* past.

decotto *m.* decoction.

decrepitezza *f.* decrepitude.

decre'pito *adj.* decrepit.

decrescente *adj.* decreasing.

decre'scere *vi.*[38] to decrease.

decretare *vt.* to decree; to award.

decreto *m.* decree.

decu'bito *m.* decubitus: **piaga da —** bedsore.

decuplicare *vt.* to decuple.

de'cuplo *m., adj.* decuple.

decurtare *vt.* to decurtate; to diminish, curtail; to cut (down).

decurtazione *f.* diminution, curtailment.

de'dalo *m.* labyrinth, maze.

De'dalo *m.pr.* (*myth.*) Daedalus.

de'dica *f.* dedication.

dedicare *vt.* to dedicate; to devote **dedicarsi** *vr.* to devote oneself.

de'dito *adj.* devoted; addicted.

dedizione f. submission; devotion.
dedotto adj. deduced; deducted. pp.of dedurre.
dedurre vt.[8] to deduce; to deduct.
deduttivo adj. deductive.
deduzione f. deduction.
defalcare vt. to deduct.
defalco m. deduction.
defecare vt., vi. to defecate.
defenestrare vt. to throw (one) out of the window; to oust; to dismiss.
defenestrazione f. defenestration.
deferente adj. deferential.
deferenza f. deference.
deferire vt. to commit, submit; to report. vi. to defer (to): — il giuramento, to put (one) on oath.
defezione f. defection, apostasy.
deficiente m. idiot. adj. deficient.
deficienza f. deficiency; shortage.
defini'bile adj. definable.
definire vt. to define; to settle.
definitivamente adv. definitively.
definitivo adj. definitive, final.
definito adj. definite.
definizione f. definition; settlement.
deflagrare vi. to deflagrate.
deflagrazione f. deflagration.
deflazionare vt. to deflate.
deflazione f. deflation.
deflet'tere vi.[54] to swerve; to yield; to recede.
deflorare vt. to deflower.
defluire vi. to flow, run down.
deflusso m. flow; reflux.
deformante adj. deforming.
deformare vt. to deform, disfigure; to twist; deformarsi vr. to become deformed; to get out of shape.
deformazione f. deformation.
deforme adj. misshapen, deformed.
deformità f. deformity.
defraudare vt. to defraud, cheat.
defunta f., **defunto** m., adj. deceased, late, dead.
De Gasperi, Alcide, Italian statesman and postwar premier; leader of the Christian Democratic Party from 1943 (1881–1954).
degenerare vi. to degenerate.
degenerato m., adj. degenerate.
degenerazione f. degeneration.
dege'nere adj. degenerate; unworthy.
degente m., f. patient. adj. bedridden.
degenza f. stay in hospital; confinement to bed.
degli comp.prep. of the. part. some, any. see di.
deglutire vt. to swallow.
deglutizione f. deglutition.
degnamente adv. worthily; deservingly; adequately.
degnare vt., vi., degnarsi vr. to deign, condescend; to stoop.

degnazione f. condescension: con —, patronizingly.
degno adj. deserving, worth; worthwhile; adequate; worthy.
degradante adj. degrading.
degradare vt. to degrade; to debase; to cashier; degradarsi vr. to degrade oneself.
degradazione f. degradation.
degustare vt. to taste.
degustazione f. tasting.
dehl interj. alas!; oh please!
dei m.pl. gods.
dei comp.prep. of the. part. some, any. see di.
deificare vt. to deify.
deità f. deity.
del comp.prep. of the. part. some, any. see di.
delatore m. informer.
delazione f. delation.
Deledda, Grazia, Italian novelist, Nobel prize in literature, 1926 (1875–1936).
de'lega f.de legation; power of attorney.
delegare vt. to delegate; to entrust.
delegato m. delegate: — apostolico, nuncio.
delegazione f. delegation, precinct house.
delete'rio adj. deleterious.
del'fico adj. Delphic, Delphian.
delfino m. (ichthyol.) dolphin.
Delfino m. (hist.) Dauphin.
delibazione f. scrutiny of a foreign sentence.
deli'bera f. adjudication.
deliberare vt. to rule; to resolve (upon); to adjudge. vi. to deliberate.
deliberato adj. deliberate; resolved.
deliberazione f. resolution; determination; deliberation.
delicatamente adv. delicately, softly.
delicatezza f. delicacy; tactfulness.
delicato adj. delicate; soft; tactful.
delimitare vt. to delimit.
delimitazione f. delimitation.
delineare vt. to delineate, outline.
delinquente m., f., adj. criminal.
delinquenza f. criminality.
delin'quere vi. to offend, sin.
deli'quio m. swoon: cadere in —, to swoon, to faint.
delirante adj. delirious, raving.
delirare vi. to rave, to be delirious.
deli'rio m. delirium; wild excitement: andare in —, to become delirious.
delitto m. crime; offense; murder.
delittuoso adj. criminal.
deli'zia f. delight.
deliziare vt. to delight, charm; deliziarsi vr. to delight (in).

delizioso adj. delicious, delightful.

della, delle, dello comp.prep. of the. part. some, any. see **di**.

del pari adv. likewise.

del resto conj. as to the rest; besides; anyway.

delucidare vt. to trace.

delucidazione f. elucidation.

deludente adj. disappointing.

delu'dere vt.[6] to disappoint.

delusione f. disappointment.

deluso adj. disappointed. pp.of deludere.

deluso'rio adj. disappointing.

demagogi'a f. demagogy.

demago'gico adj. demagogic.

demagogo m. demagogue.

demandare vt. to commit.

dema'nio m. demesne.

demarcazione f. demarcation

demarrare vi. (aeron.) to alight.

demente m., adj. lunatic, insane.

demenza f. insanity, madness.

deme'rito m. demerit.

demiurgo m. demiurge.

democra'tico m. democrat. adj. democratic.

democrazi'a f. democracy.

democristiano adj. Christian Democratic.

demografi'a f. demography.

demolire vt. to demolish, tear down.

demolitore m. demolisher.

demolizione f. demolition.

de'mone m. demon.

demoni'aco adj. demoniacal, fiendish.

demo'nio m. devil, demon; fiend.

demoralizzare vt. to dispirit, deject; demoralizzarsi vr. to lose heart.

demoralizzazione f. dejection.

denaro m. money; (pl. in playing cards) diamonds; penny: — contante, cash; — spicciolo, change.

denaturato adj. methylated.

denicotinizzare vt. to denicotinize.

denigrare vt. to denigrate, defame; to traduce; to criticize.

denigratore m. denigrator.

denigrazione f. denigration.

denominare vt. to denominate, name.

denominatore m. denominator. adj. denominative.

denominazione f. denomination.

denotare vt. to denote.

densità f. density, thickness.

denso adj. dense, thick.

dentale f., adj. dental.

dentato adj. toothed; dentate: ruota dentata, cogwheel.

dentatura f. set of teeth.

dente m. tooth (pl. teeth); tusk; cog; notch: — di forchetta, prong; — dell'ancora, fluke; mal di denti, toothache; mettere i denti, to cut

teeth; mi battono i denti, my teeth are chattering; parlare fuori dei denti, to speak out.

dentellare vt. to indent, notch.

dentello m. notch; dentil; scallop.

den'tice m. dentex.

dentiera f. denture; rack.

dentifri'cio m. toothpaste.

dentista m. dentist.

dentizione f. dentition.

dentro adv. in, within; inside: essere —, to be in prison; mettere —, to pull in; in —, inward. prep. within; inside: — di sè, inwardly.

denudare vt. to denude, strip; denudarsi vr. to strip.

denun'cia f. denunciation; complaint; charge, statement.

denunciante m., f. complainant.

denunciare vt. to denounce; to state; to bring a charge against; to lodge a complaint against.

denunciatore see denunciante.

denutrito adj. undernourished.

denutrizione f. undernourishment.

deodorante m., adj. deodorant.

deodorare vt. to deodorize.

depauperare vt. to impoverish.

depennare vt. to expunge.

deperi'bile adj. perishable.

deperimento m. decay; wasting.

deperire vi. to decline, waste (away); to deteriorate.

depilare vt. to depilate.

depilato'rio m., adj. depilatory.

depilazione f. depilation.

deplorare vt. to deplore, regret; to blame; to complain of.

deplorevole adj. deplorable.

deporre vt.[93] to lay (down); to place; to dismiss, dethrone; to depose; to deposit. vi. to testify, depose; (chem.) to settle: — la speranza, to give up hope.

deportare vt. to deport, exile.

deportato m. deportee, exile.

deportazione f. deportation.

deporto m. (bank.) backwardation (British).

depositare vt. to deposit.

deposita'rio m. depositary.

depo'sito m. deposit; sediment; storage; warehouse; (mil.) depot; pledge; keeping: — bagagli (rail.), cloakroom.

deposizione f. deposition.

deposto adj. deposed; laid down. pp.of deporre.

depravare vt. to deprave, pervert.

depravato adj. depraved, degenerate.

depravazione f. depravation.

deprecare vt. to deprecate.

depredare vt. to depredate.

depressione f. depression.

depresso *adj.* depressed; lowered; weak. *pp.of* deprimere.

deprezzamento *m.* depreciation.

deprezzare *vt.* to depreciate.

deprimente *adj.* depressing; gloomy.

depri'mere *vt.*[29] to depress.

depurare *vt.* to depurate, purify.

depurativo *m.*, *adj.* depurative.

depuratore *m.* depurator; cleaner.

deputare *vt.* to depute, delegate, appoint.

deputato *m.* deputy; representative.

deputazione *f.* deputation; delegation.

deragliamento *m.* derailment.

deragliare *vi.* to derail.

derelitto *m.*, *adj.* derelict.

deretano *m.* buttocks, rump.

deri'dere *vt.* to ridicule, mock.

derisione *f.* derision, mockery.

deriso *adj.* ridiculed, mocked. *pp.of* deridere.

deriso'rio *adj.* derisive, mocking.

deriva *f.* drift, leeway: andare alla —, to drift, go adrift.

derivare *vt.* to derive; to deviate. *vi.* to derive, come (*from*); to ensue; to make leeway.

derivato *m.*, *adj.* derivative.

derivazione *f.* derivation, shunt: — telefonica, telephone extension.

dermatologi'a *f.* dermatology.

dermato'logo *m.* dermatologist.

dermo'ide *f.* leatheroid.

de'roga *f.* infringement; exception.

derogare *vt.* to derogate, depart (*from*); to transgress.

derrate *f.pl.* foodstuff.

derubare *vt.* to rob.

De Sanctis, Francesco, Italian essayist, man of letters and patriot (1817-1883).

desco *m.* table; mess.

descrittivo *adj.* descriptive.

descri'vere *vt.*[124] to describe.

descrizione *f.* description.

deser'tico *adj.* desert.

deserto *m.* desert, wilderness. *adj.* desert, lonely, empty, vacant.

desiderare *vt.* to desire, wish (*for*); to long (*for*); to want; to recommend: farsi —, to make oneself wanted.

deside'rio *m.* wish, desire; longing, lust.

desideroso *adj.* eager, desirous.

designare *vt.* to designate.

designazione *f.* designation.

desinare *n.* dinner.

desinare *vi.* to dine.

desinenza *f.* desinence.

desi'stere *vi.* to desist (*from*), cease, stop; to give up.

desolante *adj.* disheartening, distressing.

desolare *vt.* to desolate; to grieve, distress.

desolato *adj.* desolate; sorrowful, distressed.

desolazione *f.* desolation, grief.

de'spota *m.* despot.

destare *vt.* destarsi *vr.* to wake (*up*), awaken, stir.

destinare *vt.* to destine; to assign, allot; to appoint; to address; to intend (*for*).

destina'rio *m.* addressee.

destinazione *f.* destination.

destino *m.* destiny, fate; lot; destination.

destituire *vt.* to dismiss, remove.

destituito *adj.* destitute; devoid; dismissed, removed.

destituzione *f.* dismissal, removal.

desto *m.* awake; quick; shrewd.

destra *f.* right, right side; right hand.

destreggiarsi *vr.* to maneuver, manage, make shift.

destrezza *f.* dexterity.

destriero *m.* steed; charger.

destrina *f.* dextrin.

destro *adj.* right; skillful, clever. *m.* opportunity; right-handed blow, right.

destrorso *adj.* clockwise; dextrorse.

destro'sio *m.* (*chem.*) dextrose.

desu'mere *vt.*[19] to draw, take (*from*); to deduce.

desunto *pp.of* desumere.

detenere *vt.*[141] to hold; to detain.

detentore *m.* holder.

detenuto *m.* prisoner. *pp.of* detenere, held, detained.

detenzione *f.* keeping; imprisonment.

detergente *m.*, *adj.* detergent.

deter'gere *vt.*[142] to cleanse, deterge.

deteriorare *vt.*, *vi.*; deteriorarsi *vr.* to deteriorate.

deterioramento *adj.* determining.

determinante *adj.* determining.

determinare *vt.* to determine; to cause; determinarsi *vr.* to resolve (*upon*); to arise.

determinatezza *f.* determinedness.

determinativo *adj.* (*gramm.*) definite.

determinatore *m.* determinant.

determinazione *f.* determination.

detersivo *m.*, *adj.* detersive.

detesta'bile *adj.* detestable, hateful.

detestare *vt.* to detest, hate.

detonare *vi.* to detonate.

detonatore *m.* detonator.

detonazione *f.* detonation, report (*of a gun*), pop.

detrarre *vt.*[145] to detract, subtract.

detratto *adj.* detracted, subtracted.

detrattore *m.* decrier.

detrazione *f.* deduction.

detrimento *m.* detriment.

detrito *m.* fragment, debris.

detronizzare vt. to dethrone.
detta f.: a — di, according to.
dettagliante m. retailer.
dettagliare vt. to detail; to retail.
detta'glio m. detail; retail
dettame m. dictate, precept, tenet.
dettare vt. to dictate; to suggest: — legge, to lay down the law.
dettato m. dictation.
dettatura f. dictation: scrivere sotto —, to write from dictation.
detto m. word; saying. adj. said; named; above-mentioned, aforesaid: — fatto! immediately! pp.of dire.
deturpare vt. to disfigure; to mar.
deturpazione f. disfigurement.
devastare vt. to devastate, ravage.
devastatore m. ravager. adj. ravaging.
devastazione f. devastation, ravage.
deviare vt. to deviate, turn aside. vi. to deviate, swerve, depart (from), derail.
deviatore m. switchman.
deviazione f. deviation; shift, detour; (naut.) deflection.
devoluto pp.of devolvere.
devol'vere vt.⁴² to devolve; to appropriate.
devoto adj. devout, pious; devoted, faithful, loyal.
devozione f. devotion.
di prep. of, 's; by; with; than; from, out, out of; to, on, about; at, after; in: è più alto — te — due dita, he is taller than you by two inches; lavorare — cervello, to work with one's brains; essere — Milano, to be from Milan; un poco —, some, any; qualcosa — buono, something good; niente — buono, nothing good; un poco — buono, a shady character; soffrir —, to suffer from; piangere — gioia, to cry with joy; — mattina, in the morning; — notte, by night; riempire —, to fill with; nutrirsi —, to feed on; — sopra, upstairs, on top; — sotto, downstairs, below. di after verbs, that, to, at. di adv. form: — passo, at a pace; — gran lunga, by far; — punto in bianco, all of a sudden; — tanto in tanto, now and then. di partitive art. some, any, no.
dì m. day.
diabete m. diabetes.
diabo'tico m., adj. diabetic.
diabo'lico adj. diabolic.
diac'cio adj. ice-cold.
dia'cono m. deacon.
diadema m. diadem, tiara.
dia'fano adj. diaphanous.
diaframma m. diaphragm.

dia'gnosi f. diagnosis.
diagnosticare vt. to diagnose.
diagno'stico m. diagnostician.
diagonale f., adj. diagonal.
diagramma m. diagram.
dialettale adj. dialectal.
dialet'tica f. dialectic; dialectics.
dialet'tico adj. dialectic.
dialetto m. dialect.
dialogare vt. to express in dialogue.
dia'logo m. dialogue.
diamante m. diamond.
diamanti'fero adj. diamantiferous.
diametralmente adv. diametrically.
dia'metro m. diameter.
dia'mine! interj. the deuce!
diana f. reveille; tocsin.
dianzi adv. a short time ago.
diapositiva f. transparency, slide.
dia'ria f. expenses (pl.).
dia'rio m. diary, journal.
diarrea f. diarrhea.
diaspro m. jasper.
dia'stole f. diastole.
diatermi'a f. diathermy.
diatriba f. diatribe; debate.
diavolac'cio m. devil; chap.
diavoleri'a f. deviltry.
diavole'rio m. uproar, hubbub.
diavoletto m. devilkin, imp.
dia'volo m. devil, fiend. interj. the devil!: un buon —, a good chap; fare il — a quattro, to try hard, to put oneself out.
Diaz, Armando, Duca della Vittoria, Italian general, commander in chief of the Italian Army from 1917 to 1919 (1861–1928).
dibat'tere vt. to debate, discuss; dibat'tersi vr. to struggle; to writhe.
dibattimento m. trial; debate.
dibat'tito m. debate, dispute.
diboscare vt. to deforest.
di botto adv. suddenly.
dicastero m. department, office.
dicembre m. December.
diceri'a f. rumor, hearsay.
dichiarare vt. to declare, state; to appoint; dichiararsi vr. to declare, proclaim oneself.
dichiarato adj. professed.
dichiarazione f. declaration, statement.
diciannove m., adj. nineteen.
diciannove'simo m., adj., nineteenth.
diciassette m., adj. seventeen.
diciassette'simo m. adj. seventeenth.
diciotte'simo m. adj. eighteenth.
diciotto m., adj. eighteen.
dicitura f. wording; inscription.
didascali'a f. caption; subtitle.
didat'tica f. didactics.
didat'tico adj. didactic; educational, instructional.

didentro m., adv. inside.
dieci m., adj. ten.
diecimila m., adj. ten thousand.
diecina see decina.
die'resi f. dieresis (pl. diereses).
diesis m. (mus.) sharp.
dieta f. diet: a —, on a diet.
diete'tica f. dietetics.
dietro prep., adv. behind; after, along; andare — a, to follow; portarsi —, to bring along.
difen'dere vt.[43] to defend, guard; **difen'dersi** vr. to defend oneself; to protect oneself (against); to get along.
difensiva f. defensive.
difensivo adj. defensive.
difensore m. defender, pleader; avvocato —, counsel for the defense.
difesa f. defense; plea; pleading: legittima —, self-defense (as|a legal plea).
difeso pp.of difendere.
difettare vi. to lack, be wanting (in); to be short (of).
difettivo adj. defective.
difetto m. defect, fault, flaw, blemish; lack; shortcoming: far —, see difettare.
difettoso adj. defective, faulty.
diffalcare vt. to deduct.
diffalco m. deduction.
diffamare vt. to slander.
diffamatore m. slanderer.
diffamato'rio adj. slanderous.
diffamazione f. slander.
differente adj. different.
differenza f. difference: a — di, unlike.
differenziale m., adj. differential.
differenziare vt. to differentiate.
differire (1) vt. to defer, postpone.
differire (2) vi. to differ (from).
difficile adj. difficult, hard; unlikely.
difficilmente adv. hardly.
difficoltà f. difficulty; trouble.
difficoltoso adj. difficult, hard.
diffida f. notice; warning.
diffidare vt. to give notice to, warn: — a comparire, to summon. vi. to mistrust.
diffidente adj. mistrustful, suspicious.
diffidenza f. mistrust.
diffon'dere vt.[65] to diffuse, spread; to broadcast; **diffon'dersi** vr. to spread; to enlarge (upon).
difforme adj. unlike.
diffrazione f. diffraction.
diffusamente adv. diffusely.
diffusione f. diffusion; spreading; circulation (of papers, books, etc.); (radio) broadcast.
diffusivo adj. diffusive.
diffuso adj. diffused; widespread. pp.of diffondere.

diffusore m. spreader; (elec.) light globe; (mach.) choke tube.
difilato adv. straight, straightaway.
difte'rico adj. diphtheritic.
difterite f. diphtheria.
diga f. dam, dike.
digerente adj. digestive.
digeri'bile adj. digestible.
digerire vt. to digest; (fig.) to stand.
digestione f. digestion.
digestivo m., adj. digestive.
digitale f. (bot.) digitalis. adj. (anat.) digital: impronte digitali, fingerprints.
digiunare vi. to fast.
digiunatore m. faster.
digiuno m fast: a —, on an empty stomach. adj. empty; (fig.) unacquainted: essere — di, to be totally ignorant of, unacquainted with.
dignità f. dignity.
dignita'rio m. dignitary.
dignitoso adj. dignified
digradare vi. to slope; to fade.
digressione f. digression.
digrignare vt. to gnash.
digrossare vt. to trim; to rough-cast.
diguazzare vt. to beat, whip; vi. to dabble, splash.
dilagare vi. to spread.
dilaniare vt. to|tear to pieces (as flesh).
dilapidare vt. to squander.
dilatabilità f. dilatability.
dilatare vt., **dilatarsi** vr. to dilate, expand.
dilatazione f. dilatation.
dilato'rio adj. dilatory.
dilavare vt. to wash away.
dilazionare vt. to put off, delay; (comm.) to extend.
dilazione f. respite; extension.
dileggiare vt. to scoff at.
dileg'gio m. scoff.
dileguarsi vr. to vanish.
dilemma m. dilemma; quandary.
dilettante m. amateur.
dilettantesco adj. amateurish.
dilettare vt. to entertain; **dilettarsi** vr. to delight (in); to dabble (in).
dilette'vole adj. entertaining.
diletto (1) m. pleasure, delight.
diletto (2) m., adj. beloved, darling.
diligente adj. diligent.
diligenza (1) f. diligence.
diligenza (2) f. stagecoach.
diluire vt. to dilute.
dilungare vt. to lengthen, delay; **dilungarsi** vr. to linger.
diluviare vi. to shower, pour.
dilu'vio m. flood, downpour, deluge: il Diluvio Universale, the Flood.
dimagrare, dimagrire vt. to thin. vi. to grow thin.

dimane *f.* dawn; the next day.

dimani *see* domani.

dimenare *vt.* to toss; to whip; to wag; **dimenarsi** *vr.* to toss, fidget.

dimensione *f.* dimension, size.

dimenticanza *f.* oversight; negligence; omission.

dimenticare *vt., vi.*, **dimenticarsi** *vr.* to forget; to neglect, omit.

dimenticato'io *m.* oblivion.

dimen'tico *adj.* forgetful, oblivious.

dimesso *adj.* modest, humble; shabby. *pp.of* dimettere.

dimestichezza *f.* familiarity.

dimet'tere *vt.*[76] to dismiss; **dimet'tersi** *vr.* to resign (*from*).

dimezzare *vt.* to halve.

diminuire *vt., vi.* to diminish, reduce; to abate, decrease; to shorten; to subside; to ebb.

diminutivo *m., adj.* diminutive.

diminuzione *f.* diminution, decrease.

dimissiona'rio *adj.* resigning.

dimissioni *f.pl.* resignation: dare le —, to resign.

dimora *f.* abode, home, residence.

dimorante *adj., ppr.* dwelling, residing.

dimorare *vi.* to live, reside, stay.

dimostrante *m., f.* rioter.

dimostrare *vt., vi.* to show; to demonstrate: — 20 anni, to look twenty; **dimostrarsi** *vr.* to prove, show oneself.

dimostrativo *adj.* demonstrative.

dimostrazione *f.* demonstration.

dina'mica *f.* dynamics.

dina'mico *adj.* dynamic; energetic.

dinamismo *m.* dynamism; energy.

dinamitardo *m.* dynamiter.

dinamite *f.* dynamite.

di'namo *f.* dynamo; generator.

dinamo'metro *m.* dynamometer.

dinanzi *prep.* before; in front (*of*); in the presence (*of*). *adv.* on the front.

dinasti'a *f.* dynasty.

dina'stico *adj.* dynastic.

dindo *m.* turkey cock.

diniego *m.* denial; refusal.

dinoccolato *adj.* disjointed; gangling; listless.

dinosa'uro *m.* dinosaur.

dintorni *m.pl.* surroundings; neighborhood.

dintorno *adv., prep.* around, about, round.

Dio *m.* God; Lord: come — vuole, anyhow; — volesse! would to God! — non voglia, God forbid! grazia di —, plenty, abundance; quando — volle¡ arrivammo eventually we arrived.

dio'cesi *f.* diocese.

diodo *m.* (*radio*) diode.

diottri'a *f.* diopter.

dipanare *vt.* to wind off (*into skeins*); to reel; to unravel.

dipartimento *m.* department.

dipartirsi *vr.* to depart (*from*); to swerve (*from*).

dipartita *f.* departure; demise.

dipendente *m.* subordinate. *adj.* dependent, subservient.

dipendenza *f.* subservience; annex: essere alle dipendenze di uno, to be in one's employ.

dipen'dere *vi.*[10] to depend (*on, upon*); to rest (*with*); to derive; to be subject (*to*); to be up (*to*).

dipeso *pp.of* dipendere.

dipin'gere *vt.*[36] to paint: — a olio, to paint in oil; **dipin'gersi** *vr.* to paint oneself.

dipinto *m.* painting, picture. *adj.* painted. *pp.of* dipingere.

diploma *m.* diploma, degree.

diplomare *vt.*, **diplomarsi** *vr.* to graduate (*in*).

diploma'tico *m.* diplomat. *adj.* diplomatic.

diplomato *m.* graduate.

diplomazi'a *f.* diplomacy.

dipoi *adj.* following.

diporto *m.* pastime; pleasure; sport.

dipresso (a un) *adv.* about, more or less.

diradare *vt.*, **diradarsi** *vr.* to rarefy, thin, disperse; to make, become, less frequent.

diramare *vt.* to circulate, issue; **diramarsi** *vr.* to branch off.

diramazione *f.* branching out; ramification; (*rail.*) siding; branch.

dire *vt., vi.*[44] to tell, say; to speak; to call; to celebrate (*Mass*): dite davvero? are you in earnest? voler —, to mean; un si dice, a mere rumor; per sentito —, by hearsay; vale a —, that is to say; dirsela con uno, to get along with one; o per meglio —, or rather.

direttamente *adv.* directly.

direttis'simo *m.* express (train).

direttiva *f.* direction, guidance.

direttivo *adj.* directive, leading.

diretto *m.* (*rail.*) fast train; (*boxing*) straight blow. *adj.* direct; straight; managed; directed; aiming; addressed; bound; meant; fast; through. *pp.of* dirigere.

direttore *m.* manager; director; conductor; managing editor (*of a paper*); principal (*of a school*).

diretto'rio *m.* (*hist.*) Directory; (*pol.*) executive.

direttrice *f.* directress, manageress; headmistress (*of a school*); (*geom.*) directrix. *adj.* leading, guiding:

ruote direttrici, guiding wheels (of a car).

direzione f. direction, way; management, managing board; lead; steering.

dirigente m. executive. adj. managerial.

diri'gere vt.[45] to direct; to manage; to address; to aim; (mus.) to conduct; to guide, lead; to turn; diri'gersi vr. to make, head (for); to be bound to; to address oneself (to).

dirigi'bile m. airship.

dirimpetto adv., prep. opposite, in front (of).

diritta f. right, right hand, right side.

diritto (1) m. right, title, claim; tax, duty, fee; law: — penale, criminal law; — d'autore, copyright.

diritto (2) m. right side, face. adj. straight; right; canny; upright; erect. adv. directly, straight; rigar —, to behave. see dritto.

dirittura f. straightness, uprightness: — d'arrivo (horse racing) home stretch.

dirizzone m. whim; blunder: prendere un —, to fly off at a tangent.

diroccato adj. crumbled, dilapidated.

dirottamente adv. copiously, heavily: piangere —, to weep one's eyes out.

dirotto (a) see dirottamente.

dirozzare vt. to rough-hew, improve; to civilize.

dirupato adj. steep; craggy.

dirupo m. cliff, crag.

disabbigliare vt., disabbigliarsi vr. to undress.

disabitato adj. uninhabited; empty.

disabituare vt. to disaccustom.

disaccordo m. disagreement, variance.

disadatto adj. unfit (for).

disadornare vt. to disadorn.

disadorno adj. unadorned; bare; plain.

disaffezionare vt. to disaffect; disaffezionarsi vr. to become disaffected.

disaffezione f. disaffection.

disage'vole adj. uncomfortable; hard.

disagiare vt. to inconvenience, trouble.

disagiato adj. uncomfortable; straitened.

disa'gio m. discomfort; uneasiness.

disalberare vt. (naut.) to dismast.

disamare vt. to stop loving.

disameno adj. unpleasant.

disa'mina f. scrutiny; criticism.

disaminare vt. to sift, weigh.

disamorare vt. to estrange; to deter (from); disamorarsi vr. to become disaffected; to tire (of).

disamorato adj. disaffected.

disancorare vt. to up anchor. vi. to weigh anchor.

disanimare vt. to dishearten.

disappetenza f. lack of appetite.

disapprovare vt. to disapprove (of).

disapprovazione f. disapproval.

disappunto m. disappointment.

disarcionare vt. to unseat.

disarmare vt. to disarm; (naut.) to unrig.

disarmo m. disarmament.

disarmoni'a f. discord; dissonance.

disarmo'nico adj. inharmonious.

disarticolare vt. to disarticulate.

disastro m. disaster: — ferroviario, railroad accident.

disastroso adj. disastrous.

disattento adj. inattentive; careless.

disattenzione f. inattention; carelessness.

disavanzo m. deficit.

disavveduto adj. inadvertent, heedless.

disavventura f. misadventure.

disavvezzare vt. to wean, cure.

disavvezzo adj. unused.

disborso m. disbursement.

disboscare vt. to disforest.

disbrigare vt. to settle, dispatch; disbrigarsi vr. to get rid of.

disbrigo m. dispatch; settlement.

discacciare see scacciare.

disca'pito see scapito.

disca'rico m. exculpation; extenuation: testimone a —, witness for the defense.

discaro adj. unwelcome, unpleasant.

discendente m. descendant, offspring. adj. descending, sloping.

discendenza f. descent; offspring.

discen'dere vt.,[119] vi. to descend, go down, come down; to slope (down); to slant; to fall, drop; to land; to alight (from a train, etc.): — a un albergo, to put up at a hotel; — da cavallo, to dismount.

disce'polo m. disciple, pupil.

discer'nere vt.[120] to discern.

discerni'bile adj. discernible.

discernimento m. discernment; discrimination.

discesa f. descent; slope, grade; fall; dropping; landing; decline: strada in —, sloping road; prezzi in —, falling prices.

dischiodare vt. to unnail.

dischiu'dere see schiu'dere.

dischiuso see schiuso.

discinto adj. scantily dressed; slovenly.

disciogliere see scio'gliere.

disciolto see sciolto.

disciplina f. discipline.

disciplinare (1) vt. to discipline.

disciplinare (2) adj. disciplinary.

disciplinatamente adv. orderly; obediently.

disciplinato adj. orderly; obedient.

disco *m.* disk, disc; discus; record; (*rail.*) signal: — microsolco, micro-groove record.

disco'bolo *m.* discus thrower.

di'scolo *m.* rogue; imp.

discolpa *f.* vindication, defense.

discolpare *vt.* to exculpate, vindicate; discolparsi *vr.* to exculpate oneself; to apologize (*for*).

discono'scere *vt.*[30] to deny, gainsay.

discontinuità *f.* discontinuity.

disconti'nuo *adj.* discontinuous.

discordante *adj.* discordant, dissonant.

discordanza *f.* disagreement; dissonance.

discordare *vt.* to discord, disagree; to differ (*from*).

discorde *adj.* discordant, conflicting.

discor'dia *f.* discord, dissension: pomo della —, bone of contention.

discor'rere *vi.*[36] to talk, speak: e via discorrendo, and so forth.

discorsivo *adj.* discursive.

discorso *m.* speech; talk; conversation; address: cambiare —, to switch to another subject.

discostare *see* scostare.

discosto *adj.* detached. *adv.*, *prep.* far, away: poco — da, not far from.

discoteca *f.* record library, collection.

discre'dito *m.* discredit.

discrepanza *f.* discrepancy.

discretamente *adv.* discreetly; fairly; rather; moderately.

discretezza *f.* discreetness.

discreto *adj.* discreet; fair; good enough.

discrezionale *adj.* discretional.

discrezione *f.* discretion: arrendersi a —, to surrender at discretion.

discriminare *vt.* to discriminate.

discriminazione *f.* discrimination.

discussione *f.* argument, discussion; debate.

discusso *adj.* debated; controversial *pp.of* discutere.

discu'tere *vt.*, *vi.*[46] to discuss, debate; to argue.

discuti'bile *adj.* debatable, questionable.

disdegnare *vt.*, *vi.* to disdain, scorn.

disdegno *m.* disdain, scorn.

disdegnoso *adj.* scornful.

disdetta (*1*) *f.* misfortune, ill luck.

disdetta (*2*) *f.* notice.

disdice'vole *adj.* unseemly.

disdire *vt.*[44] to cancel; to countermand; to give notice of. *vi.* to contradict oneself; to be unbecoming (*to*); disdirsi *vr.* to contradict oneself, be inconsistent.

disdoro *m.* shame; detriment.

disegnare *vt.*, *vi.* to draw, outline; to plan.

disegnatore *m.* draftsman; designer; cartoonist.

disegno *m.* drawing; outline; plan; scheme: — di legge, bill.

diseguale *etc. see* disuguale.

disellare *vt.* to unsaddle.

diseredare *vt.* to disinherit.

diseredato *m.* beggar. *adj.* poor, wretched. *pp.* disinherited.

disertare *vt.*, *vi.* to desert.

disertore *m.* deserter.

diserzione *f.* desertion.

disfacimento *m.* disintegration; ruin.

disfare *vt.*[61] to undo; to defeat; to pull down; to ruin, destroy; to untie (*a knot*); to melt; disfarsi *vr.* to melt; to decay, go to pieces; to get rid (*of*); to come undone, untied.

disfatta *f.* defeat.

disfattismo *m.* defeatism.

disfattista *m.* defeatist.

disfatto *adj.* broken; defeated; melted; decayed; untied.

disfavore *m.* disfavor; detriment.

disfida *f.* challenge.

disfunzione *f.* dysfunction.

disgelare *vt.*, *vi.*, disgelarsi *vr.* to thaw.

disgelo *m.* thaw, thawing.

disgiun'gere *vt.*,[78] disgiun'gersi *vr.* to disjoin, separate.

disgiunto *adj.* separate, disjoined. *pp.of* disgiungere.

disgra'zia *f.* misfortune, ill luck; accident; blow; disaster; disfavor: — volle che, as ill luck would have it; portar —, to bring bad luck.

disgraziatamente *adv.* unfortunately.

disgraziato *m.* wretch. *adj.* unfortunate; unlucky.

disgregamento *m.* disintegration.

disgregare *vt.*, disgregarsi *vr.* to disintegrate, dissolve; to crumble.

disguido *m.* miscarriage (*failure to arrive*).

disgustare *vt.* to disgust, displease; disgustarsi *vr.* to sicken; to fall off.

disgusto *m.* disgust, dislike; distaste.

disgustoso *adj.* disgusting.

disidratare *vt.* to dehydrate.

disillu'dere *vt.* to disillusion.

disillusione *f.* disappointment.

disilluso *adj.* disillusioned; disappointed.

disimparare *vt.* to unlearn, forget.

disimpegnare *vt.* to extricate; to redeem; to dispatch, perform.

disimpegno *m.* disengagement; redemption; performance.

disincagliare *vt.* (*naut.*) to set afloat; to free, disentangle.

disincantare *vt.* to disenchant.

disincantato *adj.* disenchanted.

disincantamento *m.* disenchantment

disinfestare *vt.* to fumigate.

disinfestazione f. fumigation.
disinfettante m., adj. disinfectant.
disinfettare vt. to disinfect.
disinfezione f. disinfection.
disinfiammare vt. to soothe, salve, relieve.
disingannare vt. to undeceive.
disinganno m. disillusion; disappointment.
disinnestare vt. (mach.) to declutch; (elec.) to disconnect.
disintegrare vt. to disintegrate; to split (an atom).
disintegrazione f. disintegration; fission (of an atom).
disinteressarsi vr. to take no interest (in).
disinteressatamente adv. disinterestedly, unselfishly.
disinteressato m. disinterested, unbiased; unselfish.
disinteresse m. disinterestedness; unselfishness; indifference.
disinvolto adj. unconstrained, easy.
disinvoltura f. unconstraint; ease; unconcern.
disistima f. disesteem.
disistimare vt. to disesteem.
dislivello m. drop; unevenness.
dislocamento m. (naut.) displacement; (mil.) posting.
dislocare vt. (naut.) to displace; (mil.) to post.
dislocazione f. (naut., geol.) displacement; removal; transportation; posting.
dismisura (a) f. measurelessly.
disobbediente adj. disobedient.
disobbedienza f. disobedience.
disobbedire vt., vi. to disobey.
disobbligarsi vr. to repay an obligation.
disoccupato m., adj. unemployed.
disoccupazione f. unemployment.
disonestà f. dishonesty; fraud.
disonestamente adv. dishonestly.
disonesto adj. dishonest, immoral.
disonorante adj. dishonorable.
disonorare vt. to dishonor, disgrace; disonorarsi vr. to dishonor oneself, disgrace oneself.
disonore m. dishonor, disgrace, shame, ignominy; essere il — di, to be the shame of; essere un — per, to be a shame to.
disonore'vole adj. dishonorable, disgraceful.
disopra m. top, upper side; upper (of a shoe); upper hand. adj. upper. adv. on, upon, over; above; upstairs: al — delle proprie possibilità, beyond one's possibilities.
disordinare (1) vt. to mess up, disarrange.

disordinare (2) vi. to indulge oneself.
disordinatamente adv. untidily; confusedly, haphazardly.
disordinato adj. disorderly, untidy, messy; unruly.
disor'dine m. disorder; confusion, mess; riot: in —, in a mess.
disorganizzare vt. to disorganize.
disorganizzazione f. disorganization.
disorientamento m. bewilderment.
disorientare vt. to mislead, lead astray; to bewilder; to mix up; disorientarsi vr. to get mixed up; to lose one's bearings.
disorientato adj. confused, bewildered.
disormeggiare vt. to unmoor.
disossare vt. to ossify.
disotto m. bottom, lower part. adj. lower. adv. below; downstairs: al — di, underneath.
dispac'cio m. dispatch.
disparato adj. disparate, heterogeneous.
disparere m. variance.
di'spari adj. odd; uneven.
disparità f. disparity; difference; discrepancy; dissimilarity; unevenness.
disparte (in) adv. apart, aside.
dispen'dio m. expense; waste.
dispendioso adj. expensive; wasteful.
dispensa f. distribution; dispensation; pantry; installment.
dispensare vt. to dispense, distribute; to exempt, exonerate (from); dispensarsi vr. to excuse oneself (from); to beg off.
dispensa'rio m. dispensary.
dispensatore m. dispenser.
dispensiere m. steward.
dispepsi'a f. dyspepsia.
dispep'tico m., adj. dyspeptic.
disperare vt., vi. to despair (of), give up all hope (of); far —, to drive to despair; disperarsi vr. to be in despair.
disperatamente adv. desperately.
disperato adj. desperate; hopeless.
disperazione f. despair: per —, in despair.
disper'dere vt.,[67] disper'dersi vr. to scatter.
dispersione f. dispersion.
dispersivo adj. dispersive.
disperso adj. lost, missing; scattered. pp. of disperdere.
dispetto m. vexation, spite.
dispettosamente adv. spitefully.
dispettoso adj. spiteful.
dispiacente adj. sorry.
dispiacere (1) m. sorrow, grief; regret.
dispiacere (2) vi.[88] to dislike; to displease; to mind, regret, be sorry (for): mi dispiace per voi, I am sor-

ry for you; se non vi displace, if
you do not mind; quel quadro non
mi dispiace, I rather like that
picture.
displu'vio *m.* watershed; slope.
disponente *m.* testator. *f.* testatrix.
disponi'bile *adj.* available; free;
vacant.
disponibilità *f.* availability; assets.
disporre *vt.*[93] to arrange; to settle. *vi.*
to dispose, order: — di, to com-
mand, have at one's disposal;
disporsi *vr.* to place oneself; to get
ready, be about (*to*).
dispositivo *m.* purview; device.
disposizione *f.* disposition; disposal;
arrangement; leaning, bent; order,
direction; provision.
disposto *adj.* disposed; arranged; willing. *pp.of* disporre.
dispo'tico *adj.* despotic.
dispotismo *m.* despotism.
dispregiativo *adj.* derogatory.
dispre'gio *m.* contempt, defiance.
disprezza'bile *adj.* contemptible; negligible.
disprezzare *vt.* to despise, scorn.
disprezzo *m.* contempt, scorn.
di'sputa *f.* dispute, debate; quarrel.
disputare *vt.* to contend (*for*). *vi.* to
fight for; to fight, quarrel.
disquisizione *f.* dissertation.
dissaldare *vt.* to unsolder.
dissanguare *vt.,* dissanguarsi *vr.* to
bleed.
dissanguato *m.* bloodless: morire —,
to bleed to death.
dissapore *m.* disagreement, grudge.
disseccare *vt.,* disseccarsi *vr.* to desiccate, dry (*up*); to wither.
dissellare *vt.* to unsaddle.
disseminare *vt.* to disseminate, scatter.
dissennato *adj.* mad, insane.
dissenso *m.* disagreement; dissension.
dissenteri'a *f.* dysentery.
dissentire *vi.* to disagree (*with*).
dissenziente *m., adj.* dissentient.
disseppellire *vt.*[127] to exhume, disinter.
dissertare *vi.* to dissertate.
dissertazione *f.* dissertation.
disservi'zio *m.* disorganization; disservice.
dissestare *vt.* to get (*one*) into trouble; to unsettle; dissestarsi *vr.* to
get into trouble; to unsettle; to run
into debt; to go bankrupt.
dissestato *adj.* in debt; bankrupt.
dissesto *m.* financial crisis: subire un
— finanziario, to go bankrupt.
dissetante *m.* quencher. *adj.* quench-
ing.
dissetare *vt.,* dissetarsi *vr.* to quench,
slake (*one's*) thirst.

dissezione *f.* dissection.
dissidente *m., adj.* dissident.
dissidenza *f.* dissidence.
dissi'dio *m.* disagreement, conflict.
dissigillare *vt.* to unseal.
dissi'mile *adj.* unlike.
dissimulare *vt.* to dissimulate, dissemble; dissimularsi *vr.* to conceal
oneself, hide.
dissimulatore *m.* dissembler.
dissimulazione *f.* dissimulation.
dissipare *vt.* to dissipate; to disperse,
scatter; to dispel; to squander.
dissipatezza *f.* dissipation.
dissipato *adj.* dissipated, dissolute;
dispelled.
dissipatore *m.* dissipator, squanderer.
dissociare *vt.,* dissociarsi *vr.* to dis-
sociate.
dissociazione *f.* dissociation.
dissodare *vt.* to harrow.
dissolto *pp.of* dissolvere.
dissolutezza *f.* dissoluteness.
dissoluto *adj.* dissolute.
dissoluzione *f.* dissolution; dissoluteness.
dissolvente *m., adj.* dissolvent.
dissolvenza *f.* (*motion pictures*) dissolve: — in apertura, fade-in; — in
chiusura, fade-out.
dissol'vere *vt.,* dissol'versi *vr.*[17] to
dissolve, melt.
dissonanza *f.* dissonance.
dissotterrare *vt.* to disinter, exhume.
dissuadere *vt.*[88] to dissuade, deter.
dissuaso *pp.of* dissuadere.
dissuggellare *vt.* to unseal.
distaccamento *m.* detachment.
distaccare *vt.* to detach; to unfasten;
to remove; to separate; (*mach.*) to
disconnect; to distance; to outstrip; distaccarsi *vr.* to fall off
sever; to part (*from*); to differ.
distacco *m.* detachment; separation
departure; difference; advantage
distante *adj.* distant, far; remote;
aloof. *adv.* far, away.
distanza *f.* distance; interval; — focale, focal length; tenere a —, t
keep at a distance; a — di un mese
with an interval of a month; in —
in the distance; controllo a —
remote control.
distanziare *vt.* to distance, outstrip.
distare *vi.* to be distant: quanto dista
la casa dalla strada?, how far is i
from the house to the road?; l
casa dista un miglio dal confine
the house is a mile from the border
disten'dere *vt.*[140] to spread, lay out
stretch; to lay down; to stretc
out; to relax; disten'dersi *vr.* t
spread, stretch; to lie (*down*); t
open; to relax.

distensione f. relaxation, pacification.
distesa f. expanse; spread; (aeron.) wingspread: **suonare a —** to ring a full peal.
disteso adj. spread out, stretched out; relaxed: **cadere lungo —**, to fall flat.
distillare vt., vi. to distill.
distillato m. distillate.
distilla'io m. distiller.
distillatore m. distiller.
distillazione f. distillation.
distilleri'a f. distillery.
di'stilo adj. (archit.) distyle.
distin'guere vt.[47] to distinguish; to discern; to mark; **distin'guersi** vr. to distinguish oneself; to stand out; to excel.
distinta f. note, slip, list, detail.
distintamente adv. distinctly, clearly: **— vi salutiamo**, we are respectfully yours.
distintivo m. badge. adj. distinctive, distinguishing.
distinto adj. distinguished; different; separate; clear; **un uomo —**, a man of distinction. pp.of distinguere.
distinzione f. distinction.
disto'gliere vt.[144] to distract, divert; to dissuade, deter; **distogliersi** vr. to distract oneself; to be diverted.
distolto pp.of distogliere.
distor'cere vt.[145] to distort.
distorsione f. distortion; dislocation.
distrarre vt.[146] to distract; to divert (one's attention, a sum); to amuse; **distrarsi** vr. to distract, divert oneself; to wander, be inattentive; to amuse oneself.
distrattamente adv. casually; absentmindedly; inattentively.
distratto adj. absent, absent-minded; inattentive.
distrazione f. heedlessness, absentmindedness; oversight; inattention; entertainment; misappropriation.
distretto m. district.
distrettuale adj. district: **procuratore —**, district attorney.
distribuire vt. to distribute; to deal out; to spread; to deliver (mail); to circulate (papers).
distributivo adj. distributive.
distributore m. distributor; slot machine: **— di benzina**, gasoline pump.
distribuzione f. distribution; allotment; sharing; delivery.
districare vt. to disentangle, extricate; to free; **districarsi** vr. to disentangle oneself.
distrug'gere vt.[137] to destroy; to waste.
distruttivo adj. destructive.

distrutto adj. destroyed. pp.of distruggere.
distruttore m. destroyer.
distruzione f. destruction.
disturbare vt. to disturb, trouble; to annoy; to interfere with; **disturbarsi** vr. to trouble (oneself).
disturbato adj. troubled; unwell.
disturbatore m. disturber; nuisance.
disturbo m. trouble; annoyance; (radio) static.
disubbidiente adj. disobedient.
disubbidienza f. disobedience.
disubbidire see disobbedire
disuguaglianza f. inequality; unevenness; unlikeness; disagreement.
disuguale adj. different; uneven.
disumano adj. brutish, inhuman.
disunione f. disunion.
disunire vt., **disunirsi** vr. to disunite, disjoin.
disunito adj. disunited, disjointed.
disusato adj. unused; obsolete.
disuso m. disuse; desuetude: **in —**, obsolete.
disu'tile adj. useless; harmful.
ditale m. thimble; fingerstall.
ditata f. fingermark.
ditirambo m. dithyramb.
dito m. finger; toe (of foot); finger breadth, digit: **mostrare a —**, to point at; **legarsela al —**, to have it in for.
ditta f. concern, firm, house.
dittatore m. dictator.
dittato'riale adj. dictatorial.
dittatura f. dictatorship.
dittongo m. diphthong.
diure'tico m., adj. diuretic.
diurno adj. diurnal, daytime.
diuturno adj. diuturnal; unrelenting.
diva f. goddess; diva; star.
divagare vt. to divert; to amuse. vi. to wander (from the subject); **divagarsi** vr. to amuse oneself; to relax.
divagazione f. digression, rambling.
divampare vi.to flare up, blaze; to rage.
divano m. divan, couch, sofa.
divaricare vt. to divaricate, spread apart.
diva'rio m. difference, discrepancy.
divedere vi.: **dare a —**, to pretend; to give to understand.
divel'lere vt.[138] to uproot, tear off.
divelto adj. uprooted, torn off. pp.of divellere.
divenire, diventare vi.[152] to become, get; to grow; to turn (into): **diventare pazzo**, to go insane; **far diventare pazzo**, to drive (one) crazy.
diver'bio m. quarrel, argument.
divergente adj. divergent.
divergenza f. divergence; disagreement.

diver'gere vi.[33] to diverge; to swerve.
diversamente adv. differently; otherwise.
diversificare vt. to diversify.
diversione f. diversion.
diversità f. difference; unlikeness; variety.
diversivo m. diversion; pastime.
diverso adj. different; various; distinct. adv. differently. **diversi** adj. pl. several, various.
divertente adj. amusing.
divertimento m. amusement, fun.
divertire vt. to amuse, entertain; **divertirsi** vr. to amuse oneself, have fun: divertirsi alle spalle di, to make fun of.
divezzare vt. to wean.
dividendo m. dividend.
divi'dere vt.[48] to divide; to part, separate; to share; to split; **divi'dersi** vr. to separate; to part company (with).
divieto m. prohibition: — di transito, no thoroughfare; — di sosta, no parking.
divinamente adv. divinely.
divinare vt. to divine; to foresee; to foretell.
divinatore m. diviner, prophet. adj. prophetic.
divinato'rio adj. divinatory, prophetic.
divinazione f. divination.
divincolamento m. struggling; writhing, wriggling.
divincolare vt. to twist, writhe; **divincolarsi** vr. to struggle; to writhe; to wriggle.
divinità f. divinity; deity.
divinizzare vt. to deify.
divino adj. divine; heavenly; wonderful.
divisa f. dress; uniform; motto, device; coat of arms; parting; currency.
divisamento m. design.
divisare vt., vi. to plan; to intend, mean; to determine.
divisi'bile adj. divisible.
divisionale adj. divisional.
divisione f. division; separation; partition; department.
divisionismo m. pointillism.
divisionista m. pointillist.
divismo m. (moving pictures) star system; idolizing of stars.
diviso adj. divided; separated. pp.of **dividere**.
divisore m. divisor.
diviso'rio m. partition. adj. dividing, separating.
divo m. star, lead. adj. divine.
divorare vt. to devour, gobble up; to squander.

divoratore m. devourer. adj. devouring
divorziare vi. to divorce: — dalla moglie (dal marito), to divorce one's wife (one's husband).
divorziata f. divorcée.
divorziato m. divorcé. adj. divorced
divulgare vt. to divulge; **divulgarsi** vr to spread.
divulgatore m. divulger.
divulgazione f. divulgation.
divulsione f. divulsion.
diziona'rio m. dictionary: — geografico, gazetteer.
dizione f. diction; wording; pronunciation.
do m. (mus.) do, C.
doc'cia f. showerbath, douche: fare la —, to take a shower.
docente m. docent, teacher.
docenza f. docentship.
do'cile adj. docile; tame.
docilità f. docility, tameness.
documentare vt. to document.
documenta'rio m. documentary film — di viaggi, travelogue. adj. documental.
documentazione f. documentation.
documento m. document, paper.
dodecafoni'a f. mus. twelve-tone system.
dodecasil'labo m. dodecasyllable.
dodicenne adj. twelve years old.
dodice'simo m., num. adj. twelfth.
do'dici m., adj. twelve.
dodicimila m., num. adj. twelve thousand.
doga f. stave.
dogana f. customs; duty; custom house, custom office: esente da — duty free.
doganale adj. customs: bolla —, bill of entry; unione —, customs union
doganiere m. customs agent.
doge m. doge.
do'glia f. pain, ache, pang, throe.
dogma m. dogma.
dogma'tico adj. dogmatic.
dogmatismo m. dogmatism.
dogmatizzare vi. to dogmatize.
dolce m. sweet. adj. sweet; mild clima —, mild climate; ferro — soft iron; acqua —, fresh water — pendio, gentle slope; consonant —, soft consonant.
dolcemente adv. sweetly; gently softly.
dolcezza f. sweetness; mildness; kindness: — mia! my darling!
dolciastro adj. sweetish.
dolciastro adj. sweetish.
dolcificare vt. to sweeten.
dolciume m. sweetmeat, candy.
dolente adj. grieved; aching; sad sorry; mournful: i dolenti, th mourners.

dolere vi. to ache, hurt, cause pain: mi duole per voi, I am sorry for you; dolersi vr. to be sorry, regret; to complain; to lament.
dolicoce'falo adj. dolichocephalic.
dol'laro m. dollar.
dolo m. fraud; malice.
dolomite f. dolomite.
dolomi'tico adj. dolomitic.
dolorante adj. aching.
dolorare vi. to ache; to suffer.
dolore m. pain, ache; sorrow, grief.
dolorosamente adv. painfully.
doloroso adj. painful; deplorable.
doloso adj. fraudulent; malicious: incendio —, arson; omicidio —, murder.
doma'bile adj. tamable.
domanda f. question; request; application; (comm.) demand: fare una —, to ask a question.
domandare vt. to ask (for). vi. to ask (about), inquire (about); domandarsi vr. to ask oneself, wonder.
domani m. morrow; (fig.) future. adv. tomorrow: — l'altro, the day after tomorrow; — a otto, a week from tomorrow; a —, till tomorrow.
domare vt. to tame; to break; to subdue, suppress.
domatore m. tamer; horsebreaker.
domatrice (1) f. tamer.
domatrice (2) f. break, brake (carriage frame for breaking in horses).
domattina adv. tomorrow morning.
dome'nica f. Sunday.
domenicale adj. Sunday.
domenicano m., adj. Dominican.
dome'stica f. maid, servant.
dome'stico m. servant, valet. adj. domestic, household; tame: utensili domestici, kitchenware; lavori domestici, housework, chores.
domiciliare (1) adj. domiciliary.
domiciliare (2) vt. to domicile; domiciliarsi vr. to settle (at, in).
domici'lio m. domicile; residence: consegna a —, home delivery.
dominante adj. dominant; prevailing, predominant.
dominare vt. to dominate, rule over; to overlook; to master. vi. to rule (over); to prevail (over, against); dominarsi vr. to restrain, control oneself.
dominatore m. ruler, master; winner, conqueror (in games). adj. ruling, domineering.
dominazione f. rule, domination.
Domineddi'o m. the Lord, God.
domi'nio m. possession, dominion; rule, power: — pubblico, public property; — di sè, self-control.

domo adj. tamed; beaten.
donare (1) vt. to donate; to bestow (upon), present (one with).
donare (2) vi. to suit, become.
donata'rio m. donee.
Donatello, Italian sculptor, David in Florence (1386-1466).
donatore m. donor.
donazione f. donation; transfer.
Don Chisciotte m.pr. Don Quixote.
donchisciottesco adj. quixotic.
donde adv. where from, from where, from which.
dondolare vt., vi. to swing, sway, rock, shake, oscillate; dondolarsi vr. to swing, sway, rock; to idle.
dondoli'o m. swinging, swaying.
don'dolo m. swing, pendulum: cavallo a —, rocking horse.
Donizetti, Gaetano, Italian operatic composer, Lucia di Lammermoor, Elisir d'amore (1797-1848).
donna f. woman (pl. women); wife (pl. wives); (as a title, before Christian names of women) Lady; queen (in playing cards): — di servizio, maid.
donnac'cia f. woman of the town.
donnaiuolo m. lady-killer.
donnesco m. womanly, womanlike.
donnina f. little woman; flirt.
don'nola f. weasel.
dono m. gift, present.
donzella f. damsel.
donzello m. page.
dopo prep. after: — di che..., whereupon; — tutto, after all. adv. after, afterwards; then; later, later on; next.
dopodomani adv. the day after tomorrow.
dopoguerra m. postwar period.
doppiag'gio m. (motion pictures) dubbing.
doppiamente adv. doubly; deceitfully.
doppiare vt. to double; (naut.) to double, go round; (motion pictures) to dub.
doppiato m. (motion pictures) dubbing. adj. dubbed.
doppiere m. candelabrum, (pl. candelabra), candelabra.
doppietta f. double-barreled gun.
doppiezza f. duplicity.
dop'pio m. double; peal (of bells): ti darò il —, I will give you twice as much. adj. double; twice as great; paired: giacca a — petto, doublebreasted coat; — senso, double entendre; colonne doppie, paired pillars. adv. double, twofold.
doppione m. double, duplicate, replica.
dorare vt. to gild.

dorato adj. gilt. pp. gilded.
doratore m. gilder.
doratura f. gilding.
Doria, Andrea, Genoese statesman and admiral (1468–1560).
dormicchiare vi. to doze.
dormiente m. sleeper. adj. sleeping.
dormiglione m. slugabed, sleepyhead.
dormire vi. to sleep: andare a —, to go to bed; dormirci sopra, to sleep on it.
dormito′rio m. dormitory.
dormive′glia m. doze.
dorsale f. ridgeline. adj. back, dorsal: spina —, backbone.
dorso m. back.
dosag′gio m. dosage.
dosare vt. to dose.
dosatura f. dosage.
dose f. dose, quantity.
dosso m. back: mettersi in —, to put on; togliersi di —, to take off; (fig.) to get rid of.
dotare vt. to provide with a dowry; to endow (with); to furnish, equip (with).
dotato adj. endowed; equipped (with); complete (with); gifted.
dotazione f. endowment; outfit; (mil.) equipment: dare in —, to equip (with).
dote f. dowry; endowment; gift; talent.
dotto (1) m. scholar. adj. learned.
dotto (2) m. duct.
dottore m. doctor; physician.
dottoressa f. doctor, lady doctor.
dottrina f. doctrine; catechism.
dove adv. where; wherever; while: di (da) —, where ... from, where-from, whence; dove? where? di —, where ... from.
dovere (1) m. duty; task; obligation: sentire il — di, to feel bound to; farsi un — di, to make a point of; i miei doveri a, my regards to.
dovere (a) (2) adv. properly
dovere (3) vt.[50] to owe (to). vi. must, to be compelled (bound, forced, obliged) to, to have to; to be to; shall; should, ought to; si deve sperare che, it is to be hoped that; non avreste dovuto partire, you should not have left; dovreste vergognarvi, you ought to be ashamed; il treno deve arrivare alle quattro, the train is due (to arrive) at four.
doveroso adj. dutiful, fair.
dovi′zia f. plenty, abundance.
dovizioso adj. plentiful, rich.
dovunque adv. wherever, anywhere; everywhere.
dovuto m. due adj. due; fair; proper. pp.of dovere.

dozzina (1) f. dozen: alla —, by the dozen; di (da) —, cheap.
dozzina (2) f. board: stare a —, to board (at, with); tenere a —, to board.
dozzinale adj. cheap.
dozzinante m. boarder.
draconiano adj. draconian, drastic.
draga f. dredge.
dragag′gio m. dredging.
dragamine m. minesweeper.
dragare vt. to dredge.
dra′glia f. (naut.) stay.
drago m. dragon.
dragona f. sword knot.
dragone m. dragon; dragoon.
dramma (1) m. drama; play; tragedy
dramma (2) f. (1/8 ounce) dram; (coin) drachma.
drammaticità f. tragicalness.
dramma′tico adj. dramatic, tragic: attore, autore —, tragedian; attrice drammatica, tragedienne.
drammatizzare vt. to dramatize.
drammaturgo m. playwright.
drappeggiare vt. to drape.
drappeg′gio m. drape, fold.
drappella f. pennon.
drappello m. platoon.
drapperi′a f. drapery.
drappo m. silk cloth; drape.
dra′stico adj. drastic.
drenag′gio m. drainage.
drenare vt. to drain.
dribblare vt. (sport) to dribble.
dritta f. right, right hand; (naut.) starboard.
dritto m. right side, face: (It. slang) clever person, "old fox"; — di poppa, sternpost. see diritto for other meanings, adj., adv.
drizza f. (naut.) hoisting rope.
drizzare vt. to straighten; to erect: — le orecchie, to prick up one's ears; drizzarsi vr. to straighten (up).
droga f. drug; spice, spices.
drogare vt. to drug; to spice.
drogheri′a f. grocery.
droghiere m. grocer.
dromeda′rio m. dromedary.
drupa f. drupe.
dualismo m. dualism; antagonism.
dub′bio m. doubt; misgiving: mettere in —, to doubt, question. adj. dubious; doubtful, uncertain; unreliable.
dubbioso adj. doubtful; dubious; uncertain; irresolute.
dubitare vi. to doubt: — di, to mistrust; to suspect; non —, to have no doubt (about).
dubitativo adj. dubitative.
duca m. duke.
ducato m. duchy; (coin) ducat.

duce m. leader.
duchessa f. duchess.
duchessina f. young duchess.
duchino m. young duke.
due m., num.adj. two: — **volte,** twice; **tutt'e** —, both; — **volte tanto,** twice as much.
duecente'simo m., num.adj. two hundredth.
duecento m., num.adj. two hundred: **il Duecento,** the 13th century.
duellante m. duellist.
duellare vi. to duel. [lenge.
duello m. duel: **sfidare a** —, to challenge.
duemila m., num.adj. two thousand.
duetto m. duet.
duna f. down, dune.
dunque conj. then; well.
duode'cimo num.adj. twelfth.
duodeno m. duodenum.
duolo m. sorrow, grief.
duomo m. cathedral; dome.
duplicare vt. to duplicate.
duplicato m., adj. duplicate.
duplicatore m. duplicator; (radio) doubler.
du'plice adj. twofold, double: **in — copia,** in duplicate.
duplicità f. duplicity.
duplo m., adj. double.
dura f. (bot.) durra, sorghum.

dura'cino adj. clingstone.
durallumi'nio m. duralumin.
duramente adv. hard; harshly, sharply; bitterly.
durante prep. during; in the course of; for; in the process of: — **tutto l'anno,** throughout the year. ppr.of **durare** lasting, during: **vita natural** —, during one's lifetime; forever, for good.
durare vt. to endure, bear. vi. to last; to continue, go on; to wear well: — **fatica a,** to find it hard to.
durata f. duration: **per tutta la — di,** throughout (the).
duraturo adj. lasting, durable: **essere** —, to last long.
dure'vole see duraturo.
durezza f. hardness, toughness; harshness, roughness.
duro adj. hard, tough; firm; solid; strong; rigid, stiff; harsh, callous: — **di comprendonio,** slow-witted; — **d'orecchio,** hard of hearing; **tener** —, to stick to it, hold out; **a muso** —, boldly.
durone m. callosity.
Duse, Eleonora, famous Italian tragedienne (1859–1924).
dut'tile adj. ductile.
duttilità f. ductility.

E

e, ed conj. and: **tutti e due,** both (of them); **tutti e tre,** the three of them.
ebanista m. cabinetmaker.
ebanite f. ebonite, vulcanite.
e'bano m. ebony.
ebbene conj. well, well then.
ebbrezza f. intoxication.
ebbro adj. inebriated, drunk, intoxicated.
ebdomada'rio m., adj. weekly.
e'bete adj. dull, stupid.
ebetu'dine f. hebetude; dullness.
ebollizione f. boiling, ebullition.
ebra'ico m. Hebrew. adj. Hebraic.
ebrea f. Jewess. [Jewish.
ebreo m. Hebrew, Jew. adj. Jewish, Hebrew.
ebro, etc. see ebbro.
bur'neo adj. eburnine, ivory.
ecatombe f. massacre, hecatomb.
eccedente adj. exceeding, extra.
eccedenza f. excess, surplus.
ecce'dere vt., vi. to exceed, go beyond; to surpass, be beyond; to exaggerate, go too far.
eccellente adj. excellent.
eccellenza f. excellence; Excellency: **per** —, par excellence.

eccel'lere vi. to excel.
eccelso adj. surpassing; highest; sublime; exalted.
eccentricità f. eccentricity.
eccen'trico m., adj. eccentric.
eccepi'bile adj. exceptionable.
eccepire vt. to object (to), except.
eccessivamente adv. excessively, exceedingly, to excess.
eccessivo adj. excessive.
eccesso m. excess: — **di bagaglio,** excess baggage; **all'**—, to excess, excessively.
ecce'tera adv. and so on, and so forth; etcetera (abb.: etc.).
eccetto prep. except, but: **tutti — uno,** all but one.
eccetto che conj. except that; provided (that); unless.
eccettuare vt. to except, exclude.
eccettuato adj. excepted.
eccezionale adj. exceptional; unusual; unwonted: **in via** —, as an exception.
eccezionalmente adv. exceptionally.
eccezione f. exception: **ad — di,** with the exception of, excepting; **uno scrittore di** —, an outstanding writer.

ecchi'mosi *f.* ecchymosis, bruise.
ecci'dio *m.* slaughter, massacre.
eccita'bile *adj.* excitable.
eccitabilità *f.* excitability.
eccitamento *m.* excitement.
eccitante *adj.* stimulating; exciting, thrilling.
eccitare *vt.* to excite, stir up, arouse, stimulate; to thrill; eccitarsi *vr.* to get excited, be thrilled.
eccitazione *f.* excitement, thrill.
ecclesia'stico *m.* clergyman. *adj.* ecclesiastical.
ecco *adv.* here, there, that's; well: eccomi, here I am; eccoli qua (là), here (there) they are; — fatto!, that's done!
eccome *adv.* "and how!", indeed!
echeggiare *vi.* to echo; to resound; to reverberate.
eclet'tico *adj.* eclectic; versatile.
eclissare *vt.* to eclipse; to outshine; eclissarsi *vr.* to be eclipsed; to steal away; to disappear.
eclissi *f.* eclipse.
ec'loga *f.* eclogue.
eco *m., f.* (*pl. always m.*) echo: far —, to echo.
economato *m.* stewardship.
economi'a *f.* economy; saving; thrift; (*pl.*) savings: — domestica, housewifery; fare —, to economize; per — di tempo, to save time.
economicamente *adv.* economically.
econo'mico *adj.* economic; thrifty; cheap: bilancia economica, monetary standard.
economista *m.* economist.
economizzare *vt., vi.* to economize, save.
eco'nomo *m.* steward. *adj.* thrifty.
eczema *m.* eczema.
ed *conj. see* e.
E'den *m.* Eden.
e'dera *f.* ivy.
edi'cola *f.* shrine; newsstand.
edificante *adj.* edificatory, edifying.
edificare *vt.* to build; (*fig.*) to edify.
edificatore *m.* builder; (*fig.*) edifier. *adj.* building; (*fig.*) edificatory.
edificazione *f.* building; (*fig.*) edification.
edifi'cio, edifi'zio *m.* building; edifice.
edile *m.* mason. *adj.* building: perito —, masterbuilder.
edili'zia *f.* building.
edili'zio *adj.* building.
e'dito *adj.* published, issued.
editore *m.* publisher. *adj.* publishing.
editori'a *f.* publishing trade.
editoriale *m.* editorial. *f.* publishing firm. *adj.* publishing; editorial.
editrice *f.* publishing house. *adj., f.* publishing.

editto *m.* edict.
edizione *f.* edition; publication: — straordinaria, extra (*edition*).
edonismo *m.* hedonism.
edonista *m.* hedonist.
edoni'stico *adj.* hedonistic.
edotto *adj.* acquainted (*with*); aware.
educanda *f.* schoolgirl, inmate (*of boarding school*).
educandato *m.* boarding school for girls.
educare *vt.* to educate; to polish; to teach; to train; to raise, bring up; educarsi *vr.* to train, educate oneself.
educativo *adj.* educative.
educato *adj.* well-bred; polite; educated; trained.
educatore *m.* educator; teacher; tutor. *adj.* educatory.
educazione *f.* education, training; instruction, schooling; politeness; breeding, manners.
edulcorare *vt.* to edulcorate.
efebo *m.* ephebe.
efe'lide *f.* freckle.
efeme'ride, effeme'ride *f.* ephemera (*pl.* ephemerides).
effeminatezza *f.* effeminacy.
effeminato *adj.* effeminate, womanish.
efferatezza *f.* cruelty, savageness.
efferato *adj.* ferocious, savage.
effervescente *adj.* effervescent.
effervescenza *f.* effervescence.
effettivamente *adv.* actually; really, in fact, as a matter of fact.
effettivo *m.* cash, amount; (*mil.*) effective. *adj.* actual, real; effective: socio —, active member.
effetto *m.* effect; result, outcome; consequence; impression; promissory note; article (*of clothing*); (*mach.*) action; (*pl.*) effects, property: mandare ad —, to carry out; fare l'— di, to give the impression of; di grande —, impressive; far —, to make a sensation, to be impressive; to work; a doppio —, double-acting; in —, in fact, actually.
effettua'bile *adj.* effectible, feasible.
effettuare *vt.* to effect, bring about, accomplish, carry out; to perform, to make; effettuarsi *vr.* to be effected, accomplished; to come true; to take place.
efficace *adj.* efficacious, effectual.
efficacemente *adv.* efficaciously.
effica'cia *f.* efficacy, effectiveness; efficiency.
efficiente *adj.* efficient.
efficienza *f.* efficiency.
effigiare *vt.* to portray, represent.
effi'gie *f.* effigy, image, portrait.

effi'mero *adj.* ephemeral, short-lived, fleeting.

efflu'vio *m.* effluvium; fragrance.

effrazione *f.* breaking, housebreaking.

effusione *f.* effusion; effusiveness.

effusivo *adj.* (geol.) effusive.

egemoni'a *f.* hegemony.

egemo'nico *adj.* hegemonic.

e'gida *f.* aegis; sponsorship.

egiziano, egi'zio *m.*, *adj.* Egyptian.

egli *pron.pers.* he.

e'gloga *f.* eclogue.

egocen'trico *m.*, *adj.* egocentric.

egocentrismo *m.* egocentricity.

egoismo *m.* selfishness; egoism.

egoista *m.*, *f.* selfish person.

egoisticamente *adv.* selfishly, egoistically.

egoi'stico *adj.* selfish, egoistical.

egotismo *m.* egotism.

egotista *m.* egotist.

egregiamente *adv.* excellently.

egre'gio *adj.* excellent; (derog.) egregious: — signore, (beginning of letter) Dear sir; all'— signor X.Y. (addressing a letter), Mr. X.Y.

eguale, *etc. see* uguale.

ehi! *interj.* hey!

ehm! *interj.* hem!

ei *pron.pers.* he; they.

Einaudi, Luigi, Italian economist and statesman (1874-   ).

elaborare *vt.* to elaborate, work out.

elaboratezza *f.* elaborateness.

elaborato *adj.* elaborate; labored.

elaborazione *f.* elaboration.

elargire *vt.* to lavish (on).

elargizione *f.* bestowal; gift.

elasticità *f.* elasticity, resiliency; nimbleness.

ela'stico *m.* elastic, rubber band. *adj.* elastic, resilient; nimble.

elce *m.*, *f.* holm oak, ilex.

elefante *m.* elephant.

elegante *adj.* elegant, graceful; stylish, smart (as a garment); well-dressed; fashionable.

elegantemente *adv.* elegantly.

elegantone *m.* dandy.

eleganza *f.* elegance; stylishness, smartness.

eleg'gere *vt.*[74] to elect, choose, appoint.

elegi'a *f.* elegy.

elementare *adj.* elementary, primary; (phys.) elemental.

elemento *m.* element; factor.

elemo'sina *f.* alms: chiedere l'—, to beg.

elemosinare *vi.* to beg (for alms).

elencare *vt.* to list; to enumerate.

elenco *m.* list, roll; directory.

elettivo *adj.* elective.

eletto *m.* nominee; elect: gli eletti di Dio, the elect. *adj.* elected; elect; chosen; choice. *pp.of* eleggere.

elettorale *adj.* electoral: operazioni elettorali, polls.

elettore *m.* elector, voter.

elettricamente *adv.* electrically.

elettricista *m.* electrician.

elettricità *f.* electricity.

elet'trico *adj.* electric, electrical.

elettrificare *vt.* to electrify.

elettrificazione *f.* electrification.

elettrizzare *vt.* to electrify; to thrill.

elettrocalamita *f.* electromagnet.

elettrocardio'grafo *m.* electrocardiograph.

elettrocardiogramma *m.* electrocardiogram.

elet'trodo *m.* electrode.

elettro'lisi *f.* electrolysis.

elettroli'tico *adj.* electrolytic.

elettrone *m.* electron.

elettro'nico *adj.* electronic: microscopio —, electron microscope; valvola elettronica, electron tube.

elettrotec'nica *f.* electrical technology.

elettrotec'nico *m.* electrician. *adj.* electrical.

elettroterapi'a *f.* electrotherapy.

elettrotreno *m.* electric train.

elevamento *m.* lifting; elevation.

elevare *vt.* to elevate, lift; to exalt; to erect, raise; elevarsi *vr.* to rise; to improve, elevate oneself.

elevatezza *f.* highness; loftiness.

elevato *adj.* elevated, lofty, high; exalted.

elevatore *m.* elevator, hoist.

elevazione *f.* elevation: — a potenza (math.), involution.

elezione *f.* election, choice, appointment; poll.

e'lica *f.* (geom.) helix (pl. helices, helixes); (naut.) screw; (aeron.) propeller: — a passo variabile, variable-pitch propeller.

elicoidale *adj.* helicoidal.

elicoplano *m.* cyclogiro.

elicot'tero *m.* helicopter.

eli'dere *vt.*[48] to elide.

eliminare *vt.* to eliminate; eliminarsi *vr.* to be eliminated; to eliminate one another.

eliminato'ria *f.* (sport) trial heat.

eliminazione *f.* elimination.

e'lio *m.* helium.

eliografi'a *f.* heliography.

elio'grafo *m.* heliograph.

elioterapia *f.* insolation, treatment by sunbaths.

eliotro'pio *m.* heliotrope.

elisabettiano *m.*, *adj.* Elizabethan.

elisione *f.* elision.

elisir *m.* elixir: — di lunga vita, elixir vitae.

eliso *pp.of* **elidere.**
e'litra *f.* elytron (*pl.* elytra).
ella *pron.pers.* she.
elle *f.* l: fatto a —, L-shaped.
ellisse *f.* (*geom.*) ellipse.
ellissi *f.* (*gramm.*) ellipsis (*pl.* ellipses).
ellit'tico *adj.* elliptical.
elmetto *m.* helmet.
elmo *m.* helmet, helm.
elogiare *vt.* to praise, commend.
elo'gio *m.* eulogy; praise: **ti faccio i miei elogi,** I congratulate you.
eloquente *adj.* eloquent.
eloquenza *f.* eloquence.
elo'quio *m.* enunciation, delivery.
elsa *f.* hilt.
elucubrazione *f.* lucubration; musing.
elu'dere *vt.*⁶ to elude, evade, dodge.
elusivo *adj.* elusive.
eluso *pp.of* **eludere.**
elve'tico *m.*, *adj.* Helvetian.
elzeviro *m.* leading literary article; (*typog.*) Elzevir.
emaciato *adj.* emaciated, gaunt.
emanare *vt.* to issue; to diffuse. *vi.* to emanate, issue (*from*); to spring.
emanazione *f.* emanation.
emancipare *vt.* to emancipate; **emanciparsi** *vr.* to emancipate oneself.
emancipazione *f.* emancipation.
emarginare *vt.* to caption.
ematoma *m.* hematoma.
embargo *m.* embargo: **mettere l'— su,** to embargo.
emblema *m.* emblem, symbol.
emboli'a *f.* embolism.
em'bolo *m.* embolus.
em'brice *m.* roof tile.
embrionale *adj.* embryonic; rudimentary, undeveloped.
embrione *m.* embryo.
emendamento *m.* amendment; improvement.
emendare *vt.* to amend; to improve; **emendarsi** *vr.* to amend, reform.
emergenza *f.* emergence; emergency.
emer'gere *vi.*⁵¹ to emerge; to surface; to issue, come out.
eme'rito *adj.* emeritus; (*derog.*) egregious.
emersione *f.* emersion: **in —,** afloat.
emerso *adj.* emersed. *pp.of* **emergere.**
eme'tico *m.*, *adj.* emetic.
emet'tere *vt.*⁷⁶ to emit, send forth, issue; to utter.
emiciclo *m.* hemicycle.
emicra'nia *f.* migraine, headache.
emigrante *m.*, *f.*, *adj.* emigrant.
emigrare *vi.* to emigrate; to migrate.
emigrato *m.* emigrant: **— politico,** refugee.
emigrazione *f.* emigration; migration.
eminente *adj.* eminent, outstanding.
eminentemente *adv.* eminently.

eminenza *f.* eminence.
emisfero *m.* hemisphere.
emissa'rio *m.* emissary; drain; effluent.
emissione *f.* emission (*of bonds, etc.*); radio broadcast.
emittente *m.* issuer; broadcasting station, broadcaster. *adj.* emissive; broadcasting.
emofili'a *f.* hemophilia.
emolliente *m.*, *adj.* emollient.
emolumento *m.* emolument, fee.
emorragi'a *f.* hemorrhage.
emorro'idi *f.pl.* hemorrhoids.
emosta'tico *adj.* hemostatic: **laccio —,** tourniquet.
emoteca *f.* blood bank.
emotività *f.* emotivity.
emotivo *adj.* emotional.
emottisi *f.* hemoptysis.
emozionante *adj.* thrilling.
emozione *f.* thrill; emotion; turmoil; suspense.
em'piere⁵³ *see* **empire.**
empietà *f.* impiety, meanness.
em'pio *m.*, *adj.* impious, unholy; cruel.
empire⁵³ *vt.*, **empirsi** *vr.* to fill.
empi'rico *m.*, *adj.* empiric.
empirismo *m.* empiricism.
e'mpito (*1*) *m.* fit, spell, drive.
empito (*2*) *pp.of* **empire.**
empo'rio *m.* emporium, department store.
emulare *vt.* to emulate.
emulatore *m.* emulator.
emulatrice *f.* emulatress.
emulazione *f.* emulation.
emulsionare *vt.* to emulsify.
emulsione *f.* emulsion.
encefalite *f.* encephalitis.
enci'clica *f.* encyclical.
enciclopedi'a *f.* encyclopedia.
enciclope'dico *a.* encyclopedic.
enciclopedista *m.* encyclopedist.
encomia'bile *adj.* praiseworthy.
encomiare *vt.* to commend, praise.
enco'mio *m.* encomium, eulogy.
endecasil'labo *m.* hendecasyllable.
ende'mico *adj.* endemic.
endocardite *f.* endocarditis.
endo'crino *adj.* endocrine.
endovenoso *adj.* intravenous.
energe'tico *adj.* (*med.*) tonic.
energi'a *f.* energy; (*elec.*) power.
energicamente *adv.* energetically.
ener'gico *adj.* energetic.
energu'meno *m.* energumen.
en'fasi *f.* emphasis; pomposity.
enfaticamente *adv.* emphatically; pompously.
enfa'tico *adj.* pompous, declamatory.
enfiagione *f.* swelling.

enfiare vt., vi., **enfiarsi** vr. to swell, inflate.

enfiato adj., pp. swollen.

enfisema m. emphysema.

enfiteusi f. emphyteusis.

enigma, enimma m. enigma, riddle.

enimmatico adj. enigmatical.

enimmista m. riddler; puzzler.

enne'simo adj. nth.

eno'logo m. oenologist.

enorme adj. enormous, huge.

enormità f. enormity.

ente m. being, entity; institution; office, agency: — statale, government agency.

enterite f. enteritis.

enteroclisma m. enema.

entità f. entity; consequence.

entrambi pron.pl. both: potete andare —, you can go, both of you; mi piacciono —, I like them both.

entrante adj. next.

entrare vi. to enter, get in, go in, come in: — in una casa, to enter a house; — nell'esercito, to enter the army; — in carica, to take office; — in possesso, to take possession (of); il 3 nel 9 entra 3 volte, 3 goes into 9,3 times; voi non c'entrate! it is no business of yours! questo non c'entra, that is beside the point.

entrata f. entrance; admittance; income: — in vigore, enforcement; imposta sull'—, income tax.

entratura f. entrance; entree.

entro prep., adv. in, within, inside: — la casa, indoors.

entroterra m. hinterland.

entusiasmare vt. to fill with enthusiasm, enthuse; **entusiasmarsi** vr. to become enthusiastic, enthuse.

entusiasmo m. enthusiasm.

entusiasta m., f. enthusiast.

entusia'stico adj. enthusiastic.

enumerare vt. to enumerate.

enumerazione f. enumeration.

enunciare vt. to enunciate.

enunciazione f. enunciation.

epa f. belly.

epa'tico adj. hepatic.

epatite f. hepatitis.

e'pica f. epic; epic poetry.

epicentro m. epicenter.

e'pico adj. epic, epical.

epicureo m., adj. epicurean.

epidemi'a f. epidemic.

epide'mico adj. epidemic.

epider'mico adj. epidermal; (fig.) skin deep.

epider'mide f. epidermis.

epifani'a f. Epiphany.

epi'grafe f. epigraph.

epigramma m. epigram.

epilessi'a f. epilepsy.

epilet'tico m., adj. epileptic.

epi'logo m. epilogue.

episcopato m. episcopate.

episo'dico adj. episodical.

episo'dio m. episode.

epi'stola f. epistle.

epistolare adj. epistolary.

epistola'rio m. letters.

epitaf'fio m. epitaph.

epite'lio m. epithelium.

epi'teto m. epithet.

epi'tome f. epitome.

epizoo'tico adj. epizoötic.

e'poca f. epoch, era, age, period, time: una scoperta che ha fatto —, an epoch-making discovery.

epopea f. epopée.

eppure adv. still; nevertheless; yet, however.

epurare vt. to purify; to purge.

epurazione f. purge, purging.

equamente adv. equitably.

equa'nime adj. equanimous.

equanimità f. equanimity.

equatore m. equator, the Line.

equazione f. equation.

equestre adj. equestrian: circo —, circus.

equidistante adj. equidistant.

equilibrare vt. to balance, poise.

equilibrato adj. level-headed.

equili'brio m. equilibrium, balance, equipoise.

equilibrismo m. acrobatics.

equilibrista m. equilibrist.

equino adj. equine.

equino'zio m. equinox.

equipaggiamento m. equipment, outfit.

equipaggiare vt. to equip, fit out; (naut.) to man; to rig.

equipag'gio m. equipage; (naut.) crew.

equiparare vt. to compare (with); to equalize, equate.

equipollente adj. equipollent.

equità f. equitableness, fairness.

equitazione f. riding.

equivalente m., adj. equivalent.

equivalenza f. equivalence.

equivalere vi. to be equivalent (to), amount (to).

equivoca'bile adj. equivocal.

equivocare vi. to misunderstand; to equivocate.

equi'voco m. misunderstanding; ambiguous term. adj. equivocal; ambiguous, shady.

equo adj. equitable, fair.

era f. era.

era'rio m. Treasury, Revenue.

erba f. grass; herb: — benedetta, herb bennet; — medica, lucerne; — mala, weed; scrittore in —, writer in embryo.

erbac'cia f. weed.
erbaggi m.pl. vegetables.
erbiven'dolo m. greengrocer.
erbi'voro adj. herbivorous.
erborista m. herbalist.
erboso adj. grassy, turfy.
Er'cole m. Hercules.
ercu'leo adj. Herculean.
erede m. heir. f. heiress.
eredità f. inheritance; heredity.
ereditare vt., vi. to inherit (from).
ereditarietà f. hereditariness.
eredita'rio adj. hereditary.
ereditiera f. heiress.
eremita m. hermit.
e'remo m. hermitage.
eresi'a f. heresy.
ere'tico m., adj. heretic.
eretto adj. erect; upright; erected, built. pp.of erigere.
erezione f. erection.
ergastolano m. life convict.
erga'stolo m. life sentence; life imprisonment.
er'gere vt.[54] to raise; er'gersi vr. to raise oneself, rise; to straighten.
ergo adv. (Latin) therefore.
ergon m. erg.
e'rica f. heather.
eri'gere vt.[46] to erect, build, raise; eri'gersi vr. to set up (for).
eritema m. erythema.
eritreo m., adj. Eritrean.
erma f. herma (pl. hermae).
ermafrodito m., hermaphrodite. adj. hermaphroditic.
ermellino m. ermine.
ermeticamente adv. hermetically.
erme'tico adj. hermetic; airtight.
ermetismo m. (philos.) hermetics; obscureness.
er'nia f. hernia, rupture.
ernia'rio adj. hernial: cinto —, truss.
eroe m. hero
erogare vt. to distribute; to deliver.
erogazione f. distribution; output.
ero'ico adj. heroic.
eroico'mico adj. heroicomic.
eroina f. heroine.
eroismo m. heroism.
erom'pere vi.[115] to flow forth.
erosione f. erosion.
ero'tico adj. erotic.
erotismo m. eroticism.
er'pete m. herpes.
erpicare vt. to harrow.
er'pice m. harrow.
errabondo adj. nomadic, vagrant.
errante adj. wandering, errant: cavaliere errante, knight-errant.
errare vi. to wander, ramble; to sin; to err, be mistaken; to be wrong.
erratacor'rige f. (typog.) errata.
errato adj. wrong, fallacious.

erroneamente adv. erroneously; by mistake; wrongly.
erro'neo adj. erroneous; wrong.
errore m. error, fault, mistake; oversight, slip: — di stampa, misprint; — di calcolo, misreckoning; — di traduzione, mistranslation; — giudiziario, miscarriage of justice; essere in —, to be mistaken; indurre in —, to mislead; salvo —, errors excepted.
erta f. ascent, slope.
ertal, (all') interj. beware!: stare —, to be on the look out.
erto adj. steep, sloping; pp.of ergere.
erudire vt. to educate; erudirsi vr. to learn.
erudizione f. learning.
eruttare vt., vi. to erupt.
eruttazione f. eructation, belch.
eruttivo adj. eruptive.
eruzione f. eruption.
esacerbare vt. to exacerbate, embitter; to exasperate.
esagerare vt., vi. to exaggerate.
esagerato adj. exaggerated; excessive.
esagerazione f. exaggeration.
esagitare vt. to frenzy.
esa'gono m. hexagon.
esalare vt., vi. to exhale: — l'ultimo respiro, to breathe one's last.
esalazione f. exhalation; fume.
esaltare vt. to exalt; to extol; esaltarsi vr. to get excited.
esaltato m. crank; fanatic; adj. exalted; fanatic; crazy.
esaltazione f. exaltation; excitement.
esame m. examination; inspection; scrutiny; perusal; test: — di coscienza, self-examination; — di collaudo, test: — di riparazione, make-up; — della vista, sight-test; prendere in —, to take into consideration.
esa'metro m. hexameter.
esaminare vt. to examine; to inspect; to scrutinize; to peruse; to test; to weigh, consider.
esaminatore m. examiner.
esangue adj. bloodless.
esa'nime adj. inanimate, lifeless.
esasperante adj. maddening.
esasperare vt. to exasperate, drive (one) crazy.
esasperazione f. exasperation.
esattamente adv. exactly; quite so!
esattezza f. exactitude; accuracy.
esatto adj. exact; accurate; punctual; pp.of esigere.
esattore m. collector.
esattori'a f. collector's bureau.
esaudire vt. to grant; to comply with; to satisfy.
esauriente adj. exhaustive.

esaurimento *m.* exhaustion: — nervoso, nervous breakdown.

esaurire *vt.*[55] to exhaust; to use up; to enervate; **esaurirsi** *vr.* to be exhausted, used up, sold out; to wear off.

esaurito *adj.* exhausted; used up; sold out; out of print; *pp. of* esaurire.

esausto *adj.* exhausted.

esautorare *vt.* to deprive of authority; to discredit.

esazione *f.* collection, exaction.

esborso *m.* disbursement.

esca *f.* bait; enticement; tinder, touchwood: dare — a, to foment; to invite.

escandescenze *f.pl.* fit of temper, burst of rage: dare in —, to fly off the handle.

escavatore *m.*, **escavatrice** *f.* excavator, digger.

eschimese *m.* Eskimo.

escire *see* uscire.

esclamare *vi.* to exclaim, cry out.

esclamativo *adj.* exclamatory: punto —, exclamation mark.

esclamazione *f.* exclamation.

esclu'dere *vt.*[2] to exclude.

esclusione *f.* exclusion; exception: a — di, with the exception of.

esclusiva *f.* exclusive; privilege; sole right.

esclusivamente *adv.* exclusively, solely.

esclusivista *m.* sole agent.

esclusivo *adj.* exclusive: agente —, sole agent.

escluso *adj.* excluded; excepted; *pp. of* escludere.

escogitare *vt.* to devise, think out.

escoriare *vt.* to excoriate.

escoriazione *f.* excoriation.

escremento *m.* excrement.

escrescenza *f.* excrescence.

escursione *f.* excursion, tour.

escursionista *m.* excursionist.

escussione *f.* examination (*of a witness*).

esecrare *vt.* to execrate.

esecrazione *f.* execration.

esecutivo *m.*, *adj.* executive.

esecutore *m.* executor; executioner; (*mus.*) performer.

esecuzione *f.* execution; performance; make; actuation: mettere in —, to carry out.

eseguire *vt.* to execute, effect, carry out; to fulfill, discharge; to perform, make.

esem'pio *m.* example, instance; pattern, specimen, model: per —, for instance.

esemplare *m.* exemplar; sample; pattern; specimen; copy; *adj.* exemplary.

esemplificare *vt.* to exemplify, illustrate.

esentare *vt.* to exempt.

esente *adj.* exempt, free.

esenzione *f.* exemption.

ese'quie *f.pl.* obsequies.

esercente *m.* merchant, dealer: — cinematografico, film exhibitor. *adj.* practicing.

esercire *vt.* to keep, run.

esercitare *vt.* to exercise, train; to practice, disharge, perform; to carry on; **esercitarsi** *vr.* to train (*oneself*), practice.

esercitazione *f.* exercise, practice; training; (*mil.*) drill.

eser'cito *m.* army.

eserci'zio *m.* exercise, training; drill; practice, discharge, performance; shop; management; — finanziario, financial year; — provvisorio, interim management.

esibire *vt.* to exhibit, display; to offer; to produce; **esibirsi** *vr.* to exhibit, show (*oneself*); to show off.

esibizione *f.* show, exhibition.

esigente *adj.* exacting; demanding.

esigenza *f.* exigency; need, demand; pretension.

esi'gere *vt.*[56] to collect; to exact; to ask; to require; to call for; to demand; to want.

esigi'bile *adj.* collectible; exigible.

esiguità *f.* exiguity.

esiguo *adj.* scanty, meager; thin.

esilarante *adj.* exhilarating.

esilarare *vt.* to exhilarate.

e'sile *adj.* thin, lean; weak.

esiliare *vt.* to exile.

esiliato *m.* exile; *adj.* exiled.

esi'lio *m.* exile.

esi'mere *vt.*[57] to exempt, dispense (*from*); **esimersi** *vr.* to exempt oneself (*from*): esimersi da, to avoid, shun.

esi'mio *adj.* eminent, prominent.

esistente *adj.* existent; extant.

esistenza *f.* existence; life.

esistenze *f.pl.* stock on hand.

esistenzialismo *m.* existentialism.

esistenzialista *m.* existentialist.

esi'stere *vi.* to exist; to live; to be.

esita'bile *adj.* salable.

esitante *adj.* hesitant.

esitare (1) *vi.* to hesitate, waver; to pause.

esitare (2) *vt.* to dispose of, sell.

esitazione *f.* hesitation.

e'sito *m.* result, outcome; sale.

esiziale *adj.* fatal, deadly.

e'sodo *m.* exodus.

eso'fago *m.* esophagus.

esonerare *vt.* to exonerate; to exempt; to dismiss.

eso'nero *m.* exoneration, exemption; dispensation; dismissal.

Esopo *m.pr.* Aesop.

esorbitante *adj.* exorbitant.

esorbitare *vi.* to exceed.

esorcismo *m.* exorcism.

esordiente *m.,* beginner; debutant. *f.* beginner; debutante.

esor'dio *m.* debut.

esordire *vi.* to begin, start; to make one's debut; to open.

esortare *vt.* to exhort, urge.

esortazione *f.* exhortation.

esoso *adj.* stingy; greedy.

eso'tico *adj.* exotic.

espan'dere *vt.,* espan'dersi *vr.* to expand, spread.

espansione *f.* expansion; effusion.

espansionismo *m.* expansionism.

espansionista *m.* expansionist.

espansività *f.* effusiveness.

espansivo *adj.* effusive; expansive.

espatriare *vi.* to expatriate oneself; to emigrate.

espa'trio *m.* expatriation.

espediente *m.* expedient; shift; stratagem; device; vivere di espedienti, to live by one's wits.

espel'lere *vt.*[58] to expel, eject; to oust, dismiss.

esperienza *f.* experience; experiment.

esperimento *m.* experiment, trial.

esperto *m.* expert; connoisseur. *adj.* experienced; expert, skillful.

espettorare *vi.* to expectorate.

espiare *vt.* to expiate, atone for; to serve.

espiato'rio *adj.* expiatory: capro —, scapegoat.

espiazione *f.* expiation.

espletare *vt.* to dispatch, carry out.

esplicare *vt.* to explicate; to explain; to practice.

esplicativo *adj.* explanatory.

esplicitamente *adv.* explicitly.

espli'cito *adj.* explicit.

esplo'dere *vt.,* *vi.*[59] to explode, burst; to fire (*at*); to burst out.

esplorare *vt.* to explore; (*telev.*) to scan.

esplorativo *adj.* exploratory.

esploratore *m.* explorer; scout.

esplorazione *f.* exploration; (*telev.*) scanning.

esplosione *f.* explosion: — a catena, chain detonation.

esplosivo *m.,* *adj.* explosive.

esploso *pp.of* esplodere.

esponente *m.* exponent.

esporre *vt.*[93] to expose; to display, exhibit; to subject; to expound, set forth, explain; esporsi *vr.* to expose oneself (*to*); to run the risk (*of*).

esportare *vt.* to export.

esportatore *m.* exporter.

esportazione *f.* exportation, export.

esposi'metro *m.* (*photo.*) exposure meter.

espositore *m.* exhibitor.

esposizione *f.* exhibition; display; exposition, explanation; exposure.

esposto *m.* complaint; statement; *adj.* exposed, exhibited; *pp.of* esporre.

espressamente *adv.* expressly.

espressione *f.* expression.

espressionismo *m.* expressionism.

espressivo *adj.* expressive.

espresso *m.* express; *adj.* explicit; expressed; *pp.of* esprimere.

espri'mere *vt.*[29] to express; to utter; espri'mersi *vr.* to express oneself.

espropriare *vt.* to expropriate; to dispossess; to condemn (*as real property*).

espro'prio *m.* expropriation.

espugnare *vt.* to conquer.

espulsione *f.* expulsion; ejection; dismissal; banishment.

espulso *adj.* expelled, ejected; *pp.of* espellere.

espulsore *m.* ejector.

espurgare *vt.* to expurgate.

esquimese *see* eschimese.

essa *demonstr.pron. f.* it; (*pl.*) they; *pers.pron.* (*fam.*) she; (*pl.*) they; her; (*pl.*) them.

essenza *f.* essence.

essenziale *m.,* *adj.* essential.

es'sere (*1*) *m.* being, creature; condition; existence.

es'sere (*2*) *vi.,* *va.* to be; (*foll. by pass.,* *refl.,* *recipr. verbs*) to have; to belong (*to*): sia questo sia quello, both this and that; sia che ... sia che, whether ... or; sia come sia, be it as it may; comunque sia, however it may be; così sia, so be it; c'è, there is; siete voi? is it you? siamo noi, it is we; se io fossi in voi, if I were you; chi c'è? who is there? che c'è di nuovo? what is new? chi è stato? who was it? che cosa sarà di noi? what will become of us? due anni or sono, two years ago.

essiccare *vt.* to desiccate, dry; essiccarsi *vr.* to dry up.

essiccazione *f.* desiccation.

esso *demonstr.pron. m.* it; (*pl.*) they; *pers.pron.* (*fam.*) he; (*pl.*) they; him; (*pl.*) them.

est *m.* east: dell'—, eastern; verso l'—, eastward.

e'stasi *f.* ecstasy, rapture.

estasiare *vt.* to enrapture, delight; estasiarsi *vr.* to delight, be enraptured.

estate *f.* summer.

esta'tico *adj.* ecstatic.

estempora'neo *adj.* extemporaneous, impromptu, offhand.

esten'dere *vt.*[140] to extend; to lengthen; to expand, spread; to increase; esten'dersi *vr.* to extend, stretch out; to spread.

estensione *f.* extension, extent; range; surface, area; expanse; development; lengthening.

estensivo *adj.* extensive.

estenso (per) *adv.* in full.

estensore *m.* recorder; (*pl.*) stretchers.

estenuante *adj.* enervating; oppressive.

estenuare *vt.* to enervate.

estenuazione *f.* exhaustion.

e'steri *m.pl.* (*chem.*) esters.

esteriore *adj.* exterior, outer.

esteriorità *f.* exteriority.

esteriormente *adv.* outside, outwardly.

esternamente *adv.* externally, outwardly, outside.

esternare *vt.* to manifest.

esterno *m.* outside; day pupil; (*motion pictures*) exterior; *adj.* external, exterior, outer, outside.

e'stero *m.* foreign countries; (*pl.*) foreign affairs: all'—, abroad; dall'—, from abroad; *adj.* foreign.

esterrefatto *adj.* dumbfounded.

estesamente *adv.* extensively.

esteso *adj.* wide; widespread: per —, in full.

esteta *m.* aesthete.

este'tica *f.* aesthetics.

esteticamente *adv.* aesthetically.

este'tico *adj.* aesthetical.

estimatore *m.* estimator; admirer.

e'stimo *m.* survey.

estin'guere *vt.*[47] to extinguish, put out; to slake; estin'guersi *vr.* to go out; to become extinct; to die, pass away.

estingui'bile *adj.* extinguishable.

estinto *m.* deceased; *adj.* extinguished; extinct; deceased; *pp. of* estinguere.

estintore *m.* extinguisher.

estirpare *vt.* to extirpate; to uproot, eradicate; to extract.

estirpatore *m.* (*agr.*) weeder.

estivo *adj.* summer.

estol'lere *vt.* to extol.

estor'cere *vt.*[145] to extort.

estorsione *f.* extortion.

estorto *adj.* extorted; *pp.of* estorcere.

estradare *vt.* to extradite.

estradizione *f.* extradition.

estra'neo *m.* stranger; *adj.* extraneous; strange; alien; unrelated.

estrarre *vt.*[146] to extract; to pull out; to draw (*out*); to dig out.

estrattivo *adj.* extractive.

estratto *m.* extract; estreat; abstract; excerpt; offprint: — di conto, statement of account; *adj.* extracted; abstracted; *pp.of* estrarre.

estrazione *f.* extraction; extirpation; digging; drawing (*by lot*): — di radice, (*math.*) evolution.

estremamente *adv.* extremely.

estremità *f.* extremity; end; verge.

estremo *m.* extreme, highest degree or point; end, extremity; *adj.* extreme, last; farthest; excessive; utmost: all'—, extremely; sino al limite —, to the limit.

estro *m.* whim; inspiration; fancy, imagination; impulse.

estromet'tere *vt.*[75] to oust; to exclude.

estroso *adj.* freakish; fantastic.

estua'rio *m.* estuary.

esuberante *adj.* exuberant.

esuberanza *f.* exuberance.

esulare *vi.* to emigrate; to be alien (*to*): — da, to exceed.

esulcerare *vt.* to exasperate.

e'sule *m., f.* exile; refugee, displaced person.

esultante *adj.* exultant.

esultanza *f.* exultation.

esultare *vi.* to exult.

esumare *vt.* to exhume.

esumazione *f.* exhumation.

età *f.* age: — dell'oro, the Golden Age; nel fiore dell'—, in the prime of life; in — minore, underage; in — maggiore, of age; raggiungere l'— maggiore, to come of age; un uomo in —, an elderly man.

e'tere *m.* ether.

ete'reo *adj.* ethereal.

eternamente *adv.* eternally, forever.

eternare *vt.* to make eternal.

eternità *f.* eternity.

eterno *adj.* eternal, everlasting: in —, forever.

eteroge'neo *adj.* heterogeneous.

e'tica *f.* ethics.

etichetta (1) *f.* tag, label, sticker: mettere l'— a, to label.

etichetta (2) *f.* etiquette.

e'tico (1) *adj.* consumptive.

e'tico (2) *adj.* ethical.

etile *m.* ethyl.

eti'lico *adj.* ethylic.

etilismo *m.* alcoholism.

etimologi'a *f.* etymology.

etisi'a *f.* phthisis.

et'nico *adj.* ethnic, ethnical.

etrusco *m., adj.* Etruscan.

etta'gono *m.* heptagon.

ette *m.* nothing; anything: mancò un —, it was touch and go.

etto, ettogrammo *m.* hectogram.

etto'litro *m.* hectoliter.

etto'metro m. hectometer.
ettowatt m. one hundred watts.
eucalipto m. eucalyptus.
eufemismo m. euphemism.
eufori'a f. euphoria, elation.
eufo'rico adj. elated.
eunuco m. eunuch.
europeo m., adj. European.
eutanasia f. euthanasia.
evacuare vt., vi. to evacuate; to vacate.
evacuazione f. evacuation.
eva'dere vt.[60] to evade; to deal with, settle: — una lettera, to reply to a letter; vi. to evade, escape.
evange'lico adj. evangelical.
evangelista m. evangelist.
Evangelo m. Gospel, Evangel.
evaporare vt., vi. to evaporate.
evaporazione f. evaporation.
evasione f. evasion; escape: dare —, to reply (to).
evasivamente adv. evasively.
evasivo adj. evasive, elusive; noncommittal.
evaso m. runaway, fugitive; adj. evaded, escaped; pp.of evadere.
evasore m. dodger.
evenienza f. occurrence, contingency: per ogni —, just in case.

evento m. event, occurrence; development.
eventuale adj. eventual; possible.
eventualità f. eventuality; event, occurrence: nell'— che, in the event of.
eventualmente adv. in case; anyway.
evidente adj. evident, obvious.
evidentemente adv. evidently.
evidenza f. evidence, obviousness: mettere in —, to point out; mettersi in —, to make oneself conspicuous.
evirare vt. to emasculate.
evita'bile adj. avoidable.
evitare vt. to avoid; to shun, dodge; to spare; to prevent (from); to refrain (from).
evo m. age, time, era: Evo Antico, ancient times; Evo Moderno, modern era.
evocare vt. to evoke, conjure.
evoluto adj. developed; civilized; broad-minded; pp. evolved.
evoluzione f. evolution.
evol'versi vr. to evolve, develop.
evviva m. cheer; interj. long live!; hooray!: gridare —, to cheer.
ex pref. ex, former, past.
eziandi'o adv. also; moreover.

F

fa (1) adj. ago.
fa (2) m. (mus.) fa, F: — diesis, F sharp.
fabbisogno m. necessities (pl.), requirement; demand.
fab'brica f. building; factory, mill, plant, works; manufacture: prezzo di —, cost price.
fabbricante m. manufacturer, maker.
fabbricare vt. to build; to manufacture; to make; to fabricate.
fabbricato m. building; pp. built, manufactured, made.
fabbricazione f. manufacture; manufacturing; make.
fabbro m. smith, blacksmith.
faccenda f. business, matter, thing: faccende domestiche, household chores.
faccetta f. facet; side.
faccettare vt. to facet, to cut in facets.
facchino m. porter; drudge; boor.
fac'cia f. face; look; page; side: in — a, in front of, opposite, in the presence of; visto di —, as seen from the front; — tosta, effrontery, brass.
facciale adj. (anat.) facial.
facciata f. front, façade.
face f. torch; light.

faceto adj. facetious.
face'zia f. joke, witticism.
fachiro m. fakir.
fa'cile adj. easy; facile; likely; prone, ready; liable: aver la parola —, to have a glib tongue; facili costumi, loose morals.
facilità f. facility, ease.
facilitare vt. to facilitate; to aid.
facilitazione f. facility.
facilmente adv. easily; likely.
facinoroso m. rioter; adj. riotous.
facoltà f. faculty; ability, aptitude; power; right; authority; permission; capability: — di scelta, option, election.
facoltativo adj. optional; elective.
facoltoso adj. wealthy, affluent.
facon'dia f. eloquence.
facondo adj. eloquent, voluble.
fag'gio m. beech.
fagiano m. pheasant.
fagiolino m. string bean.
fagiuolo m. bean: andare a —, to suit, to please.
fagotto m. bundle; (mus.) bassoon: far —, to pack off.
faina f. stone marten.
falange f. phalanx.

falce *f.* scythe, sickle; crescent (*of moon*).
falciare *vt.* to scythe, mow.
falciatrice *f.* mowing machine.
falcidiare *vt.* to cut down.
falco *m.* hawk.
falcone *m.* falcon.
falconiere *m.* falconer.
falda *f.* brim (*of a hat*); flap (*of a garment*); tail (*of a coat*); snowflake; slope; slice; layer.
falegname *m.* carpenter.
falena *f.* moth.
Faliero, Marino, Doge of Venice (1274–1355).
falla *f.* leak.
fallace *adj.* fallacious, misleading.
fallare *vi.* to err, make a mistake.
fallimentare *adj.* bankrupt; (*fig.*) disastrous.
fallimento *m.* bankruptcy; (*fig.*) failure.
fallire *vt.* to miss; *vi.* to fail, be unsuccessful; to go bankrupt.
fallito *m.* bankrupt; failure; *adj.* bankrupt; unsuccessful.
fallo (1) *m.* fault, mistake, flaw; sin: senza —, without fail; cogliere in —, to catch red-handed; mettere un piede in —, to take a wrong step.
fallo (2) *m.* phallus (*pl.* phalli).
falò *m.* bonfire.
falsare *vt.* to alter; to distort; to misconstrue.
falsariga *f.* ruling; pattern.
falsa'rio *m.* forger, counterfeiter.
falsificare *vt.* to forge, counterfeit.
falsificazione *f.* falsification, forgery, counterfeiting, adulteration; misrepresentation.
falsità *f.* falseness; untruth, falsehood; duplicity.
falso *m.* untruth; forgery; *adj.* false; forged, counterfeit; wrong, mistaken; sham: essere nel —, to be mistaken; giurare il —, to perjure oneself.
fama *f.* fame, notoriety, renown; reputation; rumor, report.
fame *f.* hunger; famine; longing: avere —, to be hungry; patire la —, far morire di —, to starve; sciopero della —, hunger strike; lungo come la —, slow as molasses in January.
fame'lico *adj.* hungry, famished.
famigerato *adj.* notorious.
fami'glia *f.* family: sentirsi in —, to feel at home.
familiare *m.* familiar; relative; *adj.* familiar; friendly; domestic, homelike: un ambiente —, a homelike atmosphere.

familiarità *f.* familiarity.
familiarizzare *vt.* to familiarize; **familiarizzarsi** *vr.* to become familiar (*with*); to get used (*to*).
famoso *adj.* famous, renowned.
fanale *m.* lamp; light, headlight; beacon; lamppost.
fana'tico *m.*, *adj.* fanatic.
fanatismo *m.* fanaticism.
fanatizzare *vt.*, *vi.* to make, or become fanatic.
fanciulla *f.* little girl; girl.
fanciullesco *adj.* childish.
fanciullezza *f.* childhood.
fanciullo *m.* boy; *adj.* as a boy.
fando'nia *f.* humbug; fib.
fanfara *f.* brass band; fanfare.
fanfaronata *f.* fanfaronade, brag.
fanfarone *m.* braggart.
fanghi'glia *f.* mire.
fango *m.* mire, mud.
fangosità *f.* muddiness.
fangoso *adj.* muddy, miry.
fannullone *m.* loafer, idler.
fanone *m.* whalebone.
fantaccino *m.* foot soldier.
fantascienza *f.* science fiction.
fantasi'a *f.* fantasy, imagination; whim, fancy; mind.
fantasioso *adj.* fanciful.
fantasma *m.* ghost, phantom.
fantasmago'rico *adj.* phantasmagoric.
fantasticare *vi.* to daydream; to dream; to wander.
fantasticheri'a *f.* reverie, daydream.
fanta'stico *adj.* fantastic; imaginary; (*fam.*) wonderful, great.
fante *m.* infantryman; jack (*in playing cards*).
fanteri'a *f.* foot, infantry.
fantesca *f.* housemaid.
fantino *m.* jockey.
fantoc'cio *m.* puppet; figurehead.
fantoma'tico *adj.* ghostly.
farabutto *m.* cad, "heel."
faraglione *m.* cliff.
faraona *f.* guinea hen.
Faraone *m.* Pharaoh.
faraone *m.* faro.
farcire *vt.* to stuff.
fardello *m.* bundle; burden.
fare (1) *vt.*,[61] *vi.* to do; to make; to act; to work; to manufacture; to gather; to form; to play; to be: to practice; to get; to cause; to order; to say: — del male a, to harm, hurt; — debiti, to run into debt; — il callo, to get accustomed (*to*); — la parte di Macbeth, to play Macbeth; — da mangiare, to cook; che mestiere fai? what is your trade? faccio il falegname, I am a carpenter; — benzina, to fuel; — compassione, to stir pity; — paura,

to frighten; — le carte, to deal cards; non fa nulla, it doesn't matter; — al caso di, to suit; — da testimone, to act as a witness; — il nome di, to mention the name of; a far tempo da, dating from; — lo stupido, to behave as a fool; non — lo sciocco! don't be a fool! — un bagno, to take a bath; — una domanda, to ask a question; — domanda di, to file for; —fuoco contro, to fire at; — uno scherzo a, to play a trick upon; — silenzio, to keep silent; — visita, to pay a visit (to); — coraggio a, to enhearten; — attenzione, to pay attention; — la calza, to knit; — caso a, to notice; non farci caso! never mind! — la coda, to queue up; fa caldo (freddo), it is hot (cold); — finta di, to pretend; far venire il medico, to call the doctor; far fare qualcosa, to have something done; far fare qualcosa a uno, to have one do something; far aspettare, to keep waiting; far vedere, to show; far sapere, to let (one) know; — tardi, to be late; — presto, to hurry; — fronte ai propri impegni, to meet one's obligations; — a pugni, to fight; to clash; — a meno di, to do without, dispense with; non potei — a meno di dirglielo, I couldn't help telling him; — in modo che, to see that, manage; lascia — a me, leave it to me; faresti meglio ad andare, you had better go; che tempo fa? how is the weather?; come si fa a dirglielo? how can we tell him? cammin facendo, while walking; — fagotto, to pack up; — fiasco, to fail, be unsuccessful; — l'indiano, to act the fool; far pari e patta, to get even (with); farla in barba a, to outwit; farsi vr. to be done; to be made; to become; to get, grow, turn; to move; farsi vecchio, to grow old; si fa tardi, it is getting late; si fa notte, night is falling; farsi avanti, to step forward; farsi incontro, to meet; farsi male, to hurt oneself; farsi il nodo alla cravatta, to tie one's necktie; farsi il segno della croce, to make the sign of the cross; farsi la barba, to shave (oneself); farsi fare la barba, to have a shave; farsi capire, to make oneself understood; farsi pregare, to want to be coaxed; farsi coraggio, to take courage, to be brave.

fare (2) m. manners (pl.), behavior; style; beginning: una casa sul —

della nostra, a house like ours; sul — del giorno, at daybreak; sul — della notte, at nightfall; tra il dire e il — c'è di mezzo il mare, easier said than done, "there's many a slip."

farfalla f. butterfly.
farfugliare vi. to mumble.
farina f. meal, flour.
faringe f. pharynx.
faringite f. pharyngitis.
fariseo m. Pharisee.
farmaci'a f. pharmacy; drugstore.
farmacista m. chemist.
far'maco m. remedy.
farneticare vi. to rave.
faro m. beacon, light; lighthouse.
farra'gine f. farrago; medley.
farraginoso adj. motley, medley.
farsa f. farce.
farsesco adj. farcical.
farsetto m. doublet; jersey, sweater.
fascetta f. band; girdle.
fa'scia f. band; belt; bandage; (pl.) swaddling bands (for infants); (pl. mil.) puttees.
fasciame m. (naut.) timbers.
fasciare vt. to wrap; to swaddle (as an infant); to bandage, dress.
fasciatura f. bandaging; dressing.
fasci'colo m. dossier; number, issue; pamphlet; (anat.) fascicle.
fascina f. fagot, fascine.
fascinatore m. fascinator.
fa'scino m. charm, glamour.
fa'scio m. bundle, beam (of light); (hist.) fasces (pl.).
fascismo m. fascism.
fascista m., adj. fascist.
fase f. phase; stage.
fastello m. fagot.
fasti m.pl. rise:—e nefasti, rise and fall.
fasti'dio m. trouble, worry; dislike, distaste; nuisance; dare — a, to irk; to annoy.
fastidioso adj. irksome, annoying.
fasto m. pomp; display.
fastoso adj. sumptuous, gorgeous.
fata f. fairy.
fatale adj. fatal; inevitable.
fatalismo m. fatalism.
fatalista m. fatalist.
fatalità f. fatality, fate.
fatato adj. fairy, fairylike.
fatica f. exertion, effort, toil; fatigue; exhaustion; difficulty: a —, scarcely, hardly; with difficulty; uomo di —, hand laborer, odd-job man; animale da —, beast of burden.
faticare vi. to toil, drudge.
faticoso adj. hard, tiring, wearisome; toilsome.
fati'dico adj. fatidic; fateful, prophetic.

fato *m.* fate, destiny, lot.

fatta *f.* sort, kind.

fattac'cio *m.* crime.

fattezze *f.pl.* features.

fatti'bile *adj.* feasible; possible.

fattivo *adj.* active, practical.

fatto (*1*) *m.* fact, deed; business, affair, thing; point; matter, feat; act: **badare ai fatti propri**, to mind one's own business; **venire al —**, to come to the point; **passare alle vie di —**, to resort to violence; **cogliere sul —**, to catch red-handed; **dire a uno il — suo**, to give one a piece of one's mind; **sapere il — proprio**, to know what's what.

fatto (*2*) *adj.* done, made; accomplished; fit; grown-up, ripe; shaped: **giorno —**, broad daylight; **a notte fatta**, in the dead of night; **a conti fatti**, when all is said and done. *pp.of* fare.

fattore *m.* maker; factor; steward; farmer.

fattori'a *f.* farm.

fattorino *m.* messenger; runner.

fattrice *f.* (*zool.*) dam.

fattucchiera *f.* sorceress, witch.

fattura *f.* invoice, itemized bill; make; workmanship, form.

fatturare *vt.* to adulterate; to invoice; to charge.

fa'tuo *adj.* vain; fatuous: **fuoco —**, will-o'-the-wisp.

fa'uci *f.pl.* jaws.

fauna *f.* fauna.

fauno *m.* faun, satyr.

fausto *adj.* auspicious.

fautore *m.* supporter, advocate.

fava *f.* bean.

favella *f.* speech; idiom; language.

favilla *f.* spark.

favo *m.* honeycomb; (*med.*) favus.

fa'vola *f.* fable; tale; fairy tale; humbug: **la — della città**, the talk of the town.

favolosità *f.* fabulousness.

favoloso *adj.* fabulous.

favore *m.* favor; kindness; aid, help: **prezzo di —**, reduced price; **entrata di —**, complimentary admission; **a — di**, in favor of; **col — della notte**, under cover of night; **per —**, please; **cambiale di —**, accommodation bill.

favoreggiamento *m.* abetting.

favoreggiare *vt.* to aid; to abet.

favoreggiatore *m.* abettor.

favore'vole *adj.* favorable.

favorevolmente *adv.* favorably.

favorire *vt.* to favor; to second; to encourage, further; to oblige (*with*); to help, assist, aid; to be conducive to; to protect: **favorite da questa parte!** this way, please!; **favorite uscire!** out you go!; **volete favorirmi quel libro?** would you mind handing me that book?; **volete —?** won't you partake?; **mi dispiace di non poter favorirti**, I am sorry to disoblige you.

favoritismo *m.* favoritism.

favorito *m.*, *adj.* favorite.

fazione *f.* faction; watch.

fazioso *adj.* factious, riotous.

fazzoletto *m.* kerchief; handkerchief.

febbra'io *m.* February.

febbre *f.* fever; temperature.

febbricitante *adj.* feverish.

febbrile *adj.* feverish.

fec'cia *f.* dregs (*pl.*); rabble: **fino alla —**, to the bitter end.

feci *f.pl.* feces, excrement.

fe'cola *f.* starch, fecula.

fecondare *vt.* to fecundate.

fecondazione *f.* fecundation: **— artificiale**, artificial insemination.

fecondità *f.* fecundity.

fecondo *adj.* fecund, prolific.

fede, *f.* faith; confidence, trust; belief; wedding ring: **prestar — a**, to give credit to; **— di nascita**, birth certificate.

fedele *m.* believer; follower, adherent. *adj.* faithful, loyal, true: **i fedeli**, believers, churchgoers; the fold.

fedelmente *adv.* faithfully.

fedeltà *f.* faithfulness, loyalty.

fe'dera *f.* pillowcase.

federalismo *m.* federalism.

federalista *m.* federalist.

federazione *f.* federation.

fedi'frago *m.* traitor.

fedina (*1*) *f.* whisker.

fedina (*2*) *f.* certificate, record.

fe'gato *m.* liver; (*fig.*) courage.

felce *f.* fern.

felceta *f.* fernery.

feldspato *m.* feldspar.

felice *adj.* happy, glad; lucky; felicitous.

felicemente *adv.* happily.

felicità *f.* happiness, bliss.

felicitarsi *vr.* to congratulate: **— con uno per**, to congratulate one on.

felicitazione *f.* congratulation.

felino *m.*, *adj.* feline.

felpa *f.* plush.

felpato *adj.* plushy.

feltrare *vt.* to felt.

feltro *m.* felt.

feluca *f.* cocked hat.

fem'mina *f.* female.

femminile *m.*, *adj.* feminine.

femminilità *f.* femininity.

femminismo *m.* feminism.

femminista *m.*, *f.*, *adj.* feminist.

fe'more *m.* femur.

fendente *m.* slash.

fen'dere *vt.*⁰² to split, cleave; to plow (*waters*): — la folla, to elbow one's way through the crowd; fen'dersi *vr.* to cleave, split.

fenditura *f.* cleft, split.

fenduto *pp.of* fendere.

fenice *f.* (*myth.*) phoenix.

fe'nico (acido) *m.* phenol.

fenicot'tero *m.* flamingo.

fenolo *m.* phenol.

fenomenale *adj.* phenomenal; (*fig.*) grand, great, wonderful.

feno'meno *m.* phenomenon (*pl.* phenomena): sei un —! you are just great!

ferale *adj.* ominous, tragic.

fe'retro *m.* coffin.

fe'ria *f.* holiday, vacation; (*eccl.*) weekday.

feriale *adj.* working: giorno —, working day, weekday.

ferimento *m.* wounding.

ferire *vt.* to wound; to hurt: — l'orecchio, to grate on the ear; ferirsi *vr.* to wound oneself; to get wounded.

ferita *f.* wound, injury.

ferito *adj.* wounded.

ferito'ia *f.* loophole.

feritore *m.* wounder.

ferma *f.* enlistment.

fermacarte *m.* paperweight.

ferma'glio *m.* clasp; buckle; clip.

fermamente *adv.* steadfastly.

fermare *vt.* to stop, arrest, check; to fasten, fix, halt; to interrupt, discontinue; to stop up, block; fermarsi *vr.* to stop, halt; to cease; to pause; to stay.

fermata *f.* stop; station; halt; pause.

fermentare *vi.* to ferment.

fermentazione *f.* fermentation.

fermento *m.* ferment; excitement.

fermezza *f.* firmness.

Fermi, Enrico, Italian physicist, Nobel Prize in physics 1938 (1901-1954).

fermo *m.* stop, catch, stop-switch; arrest; distress, distraint. *adj.* firm, steady; still, motionless: terra ferma, firm land; punto —, full stop, period; — in posta, general delivery; tener —, to hold fast; tener per —, to take for granted.

feroce *adj.* ferocious, wild, savage; ruthless.

fero'cia *f.* ferociousness.

ferragosto *m.* mid-August holiday.

ferra'io (fabbro) *m.* blacksmith.

ferramenta *f.pl.* hardware.

ferrato *adj.* shod; iron-fitted; conversant (*with*): strada ferrata, railroad; essere — in, to be well versed in.

fer'reo *adj.* iron (*also fig.*).

ferriera *f.* ironworks; iron mine.

ferro *m.* iron; tool, implement; sword: — grezzo, pig iron; — chirurgico, surgical instrument; — da calza, knitting needle; — da cavallo, horseshoe; venire ai ferri corti, to come to close quarters.

ferrovi'a *f.* railroad: — sotterranea, subway.

ferrovia'rio *adj.* railroad.

ferroviere *m.* railroadman.

fer'tile *adj.* fertile, productive.

fertilità *f.* fertility.

fertilizzante *m.* fertilizer.

fertilizzare *vt.* to fertilize.

fervente *adj.* hot, fervent.

fer'vere *vi.* to be intense; to rage.

fer'vido *see* fervente.

fervore *m.* heat, fervor.

fervorino *m.* lecture.

fesseria *f.* (*vulgar It. slang*) nonsense; blunder, boner.

fesso *m.* crack; (*vulgar It. slang.*) dolt, sucker. *adj.* cracked; stupid: far —, to play for a sucker. *pp.of* fendere.

fessura *f.* crack.

festa *f.* feast; holiday; saint's day; birthday; party; festival: far la — a, to make away with; far — a, to welcome; guastare la —, to spoil sport; augurare le buone feste, to give the compliments of the season; conciare uno per le feste, to beat one black and blue.

festante *adj.* merry; cheering.

festeggiamento *m.* celebration.

festeggiare *vt.* to celebrate; to welcome; to applaud.

festino *m.* party, banquet.

festività *f.* festivity, festival.

festivo *adj.* festive: giorno —, holiday.

festone *m.* festoon.

festosamente *adv.* merrily; heartily.

festosità *f.* gaiety; heartiness.

festoso *adj.* hearty, warm; merry.

festuca *f.* straw, blade.

fetente *adj.* stinking.

fetic'cio *m.* fetish.

feticismo *m.* fetishism.

fe'tido *adj.* fetid, stinking.

feto *m.* foetus.

fetore *m.* fetor, stench.

fetta *f.* slice: a fette, sliced.

fettuc'cia *f.* tape; ribbon.

fettuccine *f.pl.* noodles.

feudale *adj.* feudal.

feudata'rio *m.*, *adj.* feudatory.

fe'udo *m.* feud; fief.

fiaba *f.* fairy tale.

fiacca *f.* sluggishness; weakness: batter —, to idle.

fiaccare *vt.* to break, crush, smash; to weary, weaken.

fiacchera'io *m*. cabdriver.

fiacchezza *f*. sluggishness; weariness; weakness.

fiacco *adj*. sluggish, lazy; weak.

fiac'cola *f*. torch.

fiala *f*. phial, vial.

fiamma *f*. flame, blaze, flare; (*naut*.) pennant; badge: ritorno di —, backfire; — ossidrica, welding blowpipe.

fiammante *adj*. blazing; scarlet; gaudy: nuovo —, brand-new.

fiammata *f*. blaze; bonfire.

fiammeggiante *adj*. blazing.

fiammeggiare *vi*. to flame, blaze; to sparkle.

fiammi'fero *m*. match.

fiammingo *m*. Fleming; Flemish; (*zool*.) flamingo. *adj*. Flemish.

fiancata *f*. flank, side.

fiancheggiare *vt*. to border; to flank; to aid, support.

fiancheggiatore *m*. supporter.

fianco *m*. side, flank; hip: prestare il — alle critiche, to invite criticism; a — di, beside; di —, sideways.

fiasca *f*. flask.

fiaschetteri'a *f*. wineshop.

fiasco *m*. flask; fiasco, failure.

fiata *f*. (*archaic*) time.

fiatare *vi*. to breathe; to speak.

fiato *m*. breath: tirare il —, to take breath; avere il — grosso, to pant, to breathe hard; bere d'un —, to drink in a gulp; senza —, breathless, out of breath; strumenti a —, wind instruments.

fib'bia *f*. buckle.

fibra *f*. fiber.

fibroso *adj*. fibrous.

ficcanaso *m*. busybody.

ficcare *vt*. to thrust, drive (*in*, *into*); to throw: — il naso in, to poke one's nose into; ficcarsi *vr*. to thrust oneself; to intrude (*upon*); to hide.

fico *m*. fig; fig tree: un — secco! "nuts!"

ficodin'dia *m*. prickly pear.

fidanzamento *m*. engagement.

fidanzarsi *vr*. to become engaged.

fidanzata *f*. fiancée, sweetheart.

fidanzato *m*. fiancé, sweetheart. *adj*. engaged (*to be married*).

fidare *vi*. to trust (*in*), rely (*on*, *upon*); fidarsi *vr*. to rely (*upon*): fidarsi a, to risk, venture, dare; fidarsi di, to trust, rely upon.

fidato *adj*. trustworthy, faithful, reliable.

fidente *adj*. confident.

fido *m*. trusty; (*comm*.) credit. *adj*. faithful, trusty.

fidu'cia *f*. confidence, trust, reliance; belief, faith; hope.

fiducia'rio *m*., *adj*. fiduciary.

fiducioso *adj*. confident, trustful.

fiele *m*. bile, gall.

fienile *m*. hayloft.

fieno *m*. hay.

fiera (*1*) *f*. wild beast.

fiera (*2*) *f*. fair; trade exhibition; market.

fierezza *f*. pride.

fiero *adj*. proud; cruel; sharp.

Fie'sole, da, Giovanni, *see* Angelico.

fie'vole *adj*. feeble.

fifa *f*. (*It. slang*) scare; cowardice.

fifone *m*. coward, softy.

fi'garo *m*. barber; bolero.

fig'gere *vt*.[63] to drive in; to fix: figgersi in capo, to take into one's head.

fi'glia *f*. daughter.

figliare *vt*., *vi*. to bring forth.

figliastra *f*. stepdaughter.

figliastro *m*. stepson.

fi'glio *m*. son: aver figli, to have sons, children.

figlioc'cia *f*. goddaughter.

figlioc'cio *m*. godson.

figliolanza *f*. brood, children.

figliuola *f*. daughter; girl.

figliuolo *m*. son; boy.

figura *f*. figure; face; features; character; court card.

figurac'cia *f*. bad figure; blunder.

figurante *m*., *f*. supernumerary; figurant (*m*.), figurante (*f*.).

figurare *vt*. to figure; to represent; to symbolize. *vi*. to pretend; to figure; to appear; to be present; figurarsi *vr*. to imagine.

figurato *adj*. figurative; illustrated.

figurazione *f*. figuration.

figurina *f*. figurine.

figurinista *m*., *f*. costume designer.

figurino *m*. fashion plate: rivista di figurini, fashion magazine.

figuro *m*. scoundrel: un losco —, a shady character.

figurone *m*. success, hit.

fila *f*. line, row; (*theat*.) tier; queue; list: fuoco di —, enfilading fire; far la —, to queue up; tre notti di —, three nights running.

filaccioso *adj*. thready, fibrous.

filamento *m*. filament.

filanda *f*. spinnery.

filantropi'a *f*. philanthropy.

filan'tropo *m*. philanthropist.

filare (*1*) *vt*., *vi*. to spin; to run; to run away; (*naut*.) to sail; to flirt; to shadow: fila! scat!

filare (*2*) *m*. row, line.

filastrocca *f*. rigmarole.

filateli'a *f*. philately.

filate'lico *m*. philatelist. *adj*. philatelic.

filato *m*. yarn. *adj*. spun; consistent.

filato'io *m.* spinning machine; spinnery.

filatura *f.* spinning; spinnery.

filettare *vt.* to fillet; (*mach.*) to thread.

filettatura *f.* filleting; thread.

filetto *m.* fillet; (*mil.*) stripe; snaffle; thread (*of a screw*).

filiale *f.* branch. *adj.* filial.

filiazione *f.* filiation.

filibustiere *m.* filibuster; swindler.

filiera *f.* (*mach.*) wiredrawer.

filiforme *adj.* threadlike.

filigrana *f.* filigree; thread mark.

fillos'sera *f.* phylloxera.

film *m.* film, moving picture show: — in bianco e nero, black and white film; — a colori, color film.

filmare *vt.* to film.

filo *m.* thread, wire; string; edge: — d'erba, blade of grass; — a piombo, plumbline; telegrafo senza fili, wireless telegraph; passare a fil di spada, to sword; con un — di voce, in a thin voice; dar — da torcere, to be a hard nut to crack; per — e per segno, in full detail.

filobus *m.* trolley bus.

filodramma'tico *m.* amateur actor.

filo'logo *m.* philologist.

filone *m.* lode, vein; loaf (*of bread*).

filosofi'a *f.* philosophy.

filoso'fico *adj.* philosophical.

filo'sofo *m.* philosopher.

filovi'a *f.* trolley bus line.

filtrare *vt.* to filter, strain. *vi.* to leak, filter.

filtro *m.* filter; philtre.

filugello *m.* silkworm.

filza *f.* string; dossier.

finale *m.* finale; (*typog.*) tailpiece. *f.* (*sport*) final trial. *adj.* final.

finalista *f.* (*sport*) finalist.

finalità *f.* finality; end.

finalmente *adv.* finally; at last.

finanche *adv.* even.

finanza *f.* finance; finanze *f. pl.* treasury; (*fam.*) money.

finanziamento *m.* backing.

finanziare *vt.* to finance; to back.

finanziariamente *adv.* financially.

finanzia'rio *adj.* financial; fiscal.

finanziatore *m.* backer.

finanziere *m.* financier.

finchè *conj.* till, until, as long as, as far as, while.

fine (*1*) *f.* end, close; limit, verge; conclusion, outcome: fare una brutta —, to go to the dogs; senza —, endless; alla —, at last; eventually; alla fin —, after all.

fine (*2*) *m.* end, object, purpose, aim: andare a buon —, to come off; (*of an IOU*) to be honored.

fine (*3*) *adj.* choice, fine; nice; refined; delicate; thin; cunning.

finestra *f.* window.

finestrino *m.* window; peephole.

finezza *f.* nicety; delicacy; refinement; shrewdness; kindness.

fin'gere *vt.*,²⁶ *vi.* to feign, pretend, simulate; fingersi *vr.* to feign (*oneself*), simulate, pretend to be.

finimenti *m.pl.* harness.

finimondo *m.* the end of the world; hurly-burly.

finire *vt.* to finish, end; to get over. *vi.* to finish, end, come to an end; to be over; to die; to turn into; to wind up: dove andremo a —? where shall we wind up?; dove è andato a — il mio libro? wherever is my book?; finirla, to stop it.

finito *adj.* finished; over; complete; broken; (*gramm.*) finite: farla finita, to cut it off; fatto e —, downright.

finitura *f.* finish.

finlandese *m.* Finlander, Finn. *adj.* Finnish.

fino *adj.* thin; subtle; fine, pure; delicate; keen, quick.

fino (a) *prep.* until, till; as far as, so far as; up to, down to; as much as; even.

finoc'chio *m.* fennel.

finora *adv.* till now, up to this time; hitherto, yet, so far.

finta *f.* pretense, fake; feint: far — di, to feign, pretend to; far — che, to make as if.

fintantochè *see* finchè.

finto *adj.* feigned, simulated; sham, mock; false, artificial.

finzione *m.* pretense, make-believe; fiction; hypocrisy; sham.

fi'o, *m.* penalty.

fioccare *vi.* to snow; to fall; to pour in: fiocca, it is snowing.

fiocco *m.* bow; tassel; flock; flake (*of snow*); (*naut.*) jib: roba coi fiocchi, first-rate stuff.

fio'cina *f.* harpoon.

fioco *adj.* feeble; dim.

fionda *f.* sling, slingshot.

fiora'ia *f.* flower girl.

fiora'io *m.* florist, horticulturist.

fiordaliso *m.* (*bot.*) iris.

fiore *m.* flower, blossom, bloom; (*pl., in playing cards*) clubs; fior di farina, patent flour; il fior —, the pick, the cream, the chosen few; un fior di birbante, a downright rascal; un fior di galantuomo, a man of honor; fior di quattrini, big money; nel fior degli anni, in the prime of life; a fior di pelle, skin-deep.

fiorente *adj.* blooming; flourishing.

fiorentino m., adj. Florentine.
fioretto m. foil; (rel.) vow.
fiorino m. florin.
fiorire vt. to flower; to embellish. vi. to bloom, blossom, flower; to flourish; to effloresce.
fiorista m. florist.
fiorito adj. flowery.
fioritura f. flowering.
fiorone m. early fig; rosette.
fiotto m. gush, rush.
firma f. signature; name.
firmamento m. firmament, sky.
firmare vt. to sign.
firmata'rio m. signer.
fisarmo'nica f. accordion.
fiscale adj. fiscal: avvocato — (official) prosecutor.
fischiare vt., vi. to whistle, hiss; to buzz; to hoot.
fischiettare vt., vi. to whistle.
fischietto m. whistle.
fi'schio m. whistle; hiss; hoot.
fisco m. treasury.
fi'sica f. physics.
fi'sico m. physicist; constitution; build, physique. adj. physical.
fi'sima f. whim; nonsense.
fisiologi'a f. physiology.
fisiolo'gico adj. physiological.
fisionomi'a, fisonomi'a f. countenance, appearance; physiognomy.
fisionomista m. physiognomist: poco —, (fam.) not good at remembering faces.
fiso adj. fixed. adv. fixedly.
fissag'gio m. (photo.) fixing.
fissamente adv. fixedly.
fissare vt. to fix; to fasten; to stick; to gaze (at), stare (at); to agree; to secure, book; fissarsi vr. to stick; to settle down; to set one's mind (on).
fissato adj. fixed; deranged. m. (fam.) "crank."
fissatore m. fixer, fixative.
fissazione f. fixation; delusion.
fis'sile adj. fissionable.
fissità f. fixity, steadiness.
fisso adj. fixed, steady; firm; regular.
fi'stola f. fistula.
fitta f. stitch, sharp pain.
fitti'zio adj. fictitious.
fitto (1) m. lease; rent.
fitto (2) m., adj. thick: a capo —, headlong.
fitto (3) adj. driven in. pp.of figgere.
fiumana f. stream, flow.
fiume m. river; (fig.) flow.
fiutare vt. to smell, sniff; to scent.
fiuto m. smell, scent.
fiac'cido adj. flabby, flaccid.
flacone m. vial, bottle.
flagello m. scourge; plague.

flagrante adj. flagrant: in —, red-handed.
flanella f. flannel.
flan'gia f. flange.
fla'uto m. flute.
fle'bile adj. feeble, weak; thin.
flemma f. phlegm, coolness.
flemma'tico adj. phlegmatic, cool, self-possessed.
flessi'bile adj. flexible.
flesso pp.of flettere.
flessuoso adj. flexuous.
flet'tere vt.[64] to flex.
flora f. flora.
Flora, Francesco, Italian author and essayist (1891-).
floreale adj. floral.
flo'rido adj. florid; flourishing.
flo'scio adj. flabby; soft.
flotta f. fleet; navy.
flotti'glia f. flotilla.
fluente adj. flowing.
fluido m., adj. fluid.
fluire vi. to flow.
fluorescente adj. fluorescent.
fluori'drico adj. hydrofluoric.
fluoro m. fluorine.
fluoruro m. fluoride.
flussione f. fluxion.
flusso m. flux, flow.
flutto m. wave.
fluttuante adj. fluctuating; floating.
fluttuare vi. to fluctuate.
fluttuazione f. fluctuation; flutter.
fluviale adj. fluvial, river.
fobi'a f. phobia.
foca f. seal; sealskin.
focac'cia f. cake, bun; rendere pan per —, to pay in one's own coin.
foca'ia (pietra) f. flint.
focale adj. focal.
foce f. mouth.
fochista m. stocker.
focola'io m. (pathol.) focus; (fig.) hot-bed.
focolare m. hearth, fireside; home; furnace.
focoso adj. fiery; high-spirited.
fo'dera f. lining; case.
foderare vt. to line; to cover (with); to upholster.
foderato adj. lined.
fo'dero m. scabbard, sheath.
foga f. dash, heat; vehemence.
Fogazzaro, Antonio, Italian novelist, Piccolo Mondo Antico (1842-1911).
fog'gia f. shape; manner; pattern, fashion.
foggiare vt. to shape, fashion.
fo'glia f. leaf (pl. leaves); petal, foil; oro in foglie, gold leaf; mangiare la —, to get wise.
fogliame m. foliage.
fo'glio m. sheet; newspaper.

fogna f. drain, sewer.
fognatura f. sewerage.
fo'laga f. coot.
folata f. blast, gust.
folgorare vt. to strike down; (fig.) to paralyze. vi. to flash.
fol'gore f. thunderbolt.
folla f. crowd, throng; host.
folle m., f. lunatic; (mach.) neutral. adj. insane: in — (mach.) in neutral.
follemente adv. madly.
folletto m. goblin.
folli'a f. madness, lunacy; folly.
folto m., adj. thick.
fomentare vt. to foment.
fonda, (alla) f. at anchor.
fon'daco m. store; warehouse.
fondale m. bottom; (theat.) back cloth.
fondamenta f.pl. foundation.
fondamentale adj. fundamental.
fondamentalmente adv. fundamentally, basically.
fondamento m. foundation; ground; (pl.) elements.
fondare vt. to found; to build (up); to establish; to base, ground; fondarsi vr. to ground, rest (upon); to rely (on).
fondatezza f. groundedness.
fondato adj. well-founded; legitimate.
fondatore m. founder.
fondazione f. foundation.
fon'dere vt.,[65] fon'dersi vr. to melt; to blend.
fonderi'a f. foundry, smeltery.
fondina f. holster; soup plate.
fonditore m. melter, smelter.
fondo m. bottom; fund; end; ground; background; property, land; (pl.) grounds, dregs; funds, money: — dei calzoni, seat; — di cassa, cash on hand; fondi di magazzino, unsold stocks; bassi fondi, shallows; slums; dar — a, to exhaust; in —, after all. adj. deep.
fone'tica f. phonetics.
fone'tico adj. phonetic.
fono'grafo m. phonograph.
fonogramma m. phonogram.
fontana f. fountain.
fontaniere m. water gauger.
fonte f. spring; fountain; source: sapere da — accreditata, to know from a reliable source.
fonte battesimale m. (baptismal) font.
forag'gio m. fodder, forage.
fora'neo adj. rural; outer.
forare vt. to hole, bore; to punch (a ticket); to puncture (a tire).
foratura f. boring; puncture.
for'bici f.pl. scissors; (zool.) pincers.
forbire vt. to furbish, polish; forbirsi vr. to wipe oneself.
forbito adj. polished; lofty.

forca f. fork, pitchfork; gallows: mandare sulla —, to send to the devil; fare la — a, to cross, thwart.
forcella f. fork; hairpin.
forchetta f. fork.
forchettata f. forkful.
forchettone m. carving fork.
forcina f. hairpin.
for'cipe m. forceps (pl.).
forcone m. pitchfork.
forcuto adj. forked.
forense adj. forensic.
foresta f. forest.
forestale adj. forestal: guardia —, forester.
foresteri'a f. guest chambers.
forestiero m. stranger; foreigner; guest. adj. foreign.
for'fora f. dandruff.
for'gia f. forge, smithy.
forgiare vt. to forge.
foriero adj. forerunning.
forma f. form, shape; outline; mold; way, manner; last (for shoes); hat block; cheesecake.
formag'gio m. cheese.
formale adj. formal.
formalità f. formality.
formalizzarsi vr. to take exception (to), be shocked (at).
formalmente adv. formally.
formare vt. to form; to shape, mold; to train; formarsi vr. to form; to grow.
formato m. shape; size; format. adj. formed, shaped, molded; made; grown; developed.
formazione f. formation; (aeron.) flight.
formica f. ant.
formica'io m. anthill; swarm.
formichiere m. anteater.
formicolare vi. to swarm (with); to creep.
formicoli'o m. creeping sensation; swarming.
formida'bile adj. formidable.
formoso adj. stalwart; (f.) buxom.
for'mula f. formula.
formulare vt. to formulate.
formula'rio m. formulary.
fornace f. furnace; kiln.
forna'io m. baker.
fornello m. stove, kitchen range; pipe bowl; chamber (of a mine).
fornire vt. to furnish, supply (with); to cater to; to equip (with); to endow (with).
fornitore m. purveyor; tradesman; dealer; caterer; chandler.
fornitura f. supply.
forno m. furnace; kiln; oven; bakery; (theat.) empty house, poor attendance, absent treatment: al —, baked.

foro (*1*) *m.* hole.

foro (*2*) *m.* forum; bar; jurisdiction.

forse *m.* doubt: mettere in —, to doubt, question. *adv.* perhaps, maybe; probably.

forsennato *m.* maniac.

forte *m.* fort; strong point, forte; sourness. *adj.* strong; sturdy; proficient; firm, steady; brave; loud; sour; heavy: prestar man —, to help; è più — di me, I can't stand it; I can't help it. *adv.* hard, strongly; loudly; fast.

fortemente *adv.* strongly; deeply; highly; loudly; hard.

fortezza *f.* strength; fortress.

fortificare *vt.* to fortify.

fortificazione *f.* fortification.

fortino *m.* blockhouse, outpost.

fortis'simo *adj.sup.* most powerful; extremely loud.

fortu'ito *adj.* fortuitous.

fortuna *f.* luck; chance, lot; success; fortune, property; **campo di —**, emergency landing field; **atterraggio di —,** forced landing; **per —,** luckily.

fortunale *m.* storm, tempest.

fortunatamente *adv.* fortunately, luckily.

fortunato *adj.* lucky; happy; successful.

fortunoso *adj.* eventful; stormy.

forun'colo *m.* furuncle, boil.

foruncolosi *f.* furunculosis.

forza *f.* strength, power, might; force; violence: — pubblica, police; a —, by force, agire per —, to act in spite of oneself; a — di, by dint of; per forza! of course!; per amore o per —, by hook or by crook; di prima —, first-rate.

forzare *vt.* to force; to compel; to break open; to strain: — un blocco, to run a blockade.

forzatamente *adv.* by compulsion, perforce; unwillingly.

forzato *m.* convict. *adj.* forced; broken open; compulsory: lavori forzati, penal servitude.

forziere *m.* safe.

forzoso *adj.* forced, compulsory.

forzuto *adj.* strong, sinewy.

Foscari, Francesco, Doge of Venice (1373–1457).

foschi'a *f.* mist, fog.

fosco *adj.* dark, gloomy, dim.

Foscolo, Ugo, Italian poet and patriot, *I Sepolcri* (1778–1827).

fosforescente *adj.* phosphorescent.

fosfo'rico *adj.* phosphoric.

fo'sforo *m.* phosphorus.

fosfuro *m.* phosphide.

fossa *f.* pit, hole; grave: **del senno di**

poi son piene le fosse, hindsight is easier than foresight.

fossato *m.* ditch.

fossetta *f.* dimple.

fos'sile *m.*, *adj.* fossil: **carbon —,** mineral coal.

fossilizzare *vt.,* **fossilizzarsi** *vr.* to fossilize.

fosso *m.* ditch.

fotoelettrico *adj.* photoelectric.

fotoge'nico *adj.* photogenic.

fotografare *vt.* to photograph.

fotografi'a *f.* photograph, photo; photography; snapshot.

fotogra'fico *adj.* photographic.

foto'grafo *m.* photographer.

fotogramma *m.* still; frame.

fotoincisione *f.* photogravure.

fotolitografi'a *f.* photolithography.

fotometri'a *f.* photometry.

fotome'trico *adj.* photometric.

foto'metro *m.* photometer, exposure meter.

fra (*1*) *prep.* in, within; between; among; amid: — l'altro, by the way; — sè, to oneself.

fra (*2*) *see* frate.

frac *m.* tails.

fracassare *vt.,* **fracassarsi** *vr.* to smash, shatter, crash.

fracasso *m.* crash; racket.

fra'dicio *adj.* rotten; sodden: **ubriaco —,** blind drunk.

fra'gile *adj.* fragile, brittle; frail.

fragilità *f.* brittleness, frailty.

fra'gola *f.* strawberry.

fragore *m.* din, rattle.

fragoroso *adj.* noisy.

fragorosamente *adv.* noisily.

fragrante *adj.* fragrant.

fragranza *f.* fragrance.

frainten'dere *vt.* to misunderstand, get wrong.

frammassone *m.* freemason.

frammassoneri'a *f.* freemasonry.

frammenta'rio *adj.* fragmentary.

frammento *m.* fragment, scrap.

frana *f.* landslide, landslip.

franare *vt.* to slide, crumble.

francamente *adv.* frankly.

Francesca, della, Piero, Umbrian painter (1406?–1492).

francese *m.* Frenchman; French (language). *f.* Frenchwoman. *adj.* French.

francesismo *m.* gallicism.

franchezza *f.* frankness.

franchi'gia *f.* franchise; leave: in — duty-free; post-free.

franco (*1*) *adj.* frank, open; outspoken; firm: porto —, free port; — di porto, free delivery.

franco (*2*) *m.* (*coin*) franc.

francobollo *m.* postage stamp, stamp.

frangente *m.* breaker; emergency; difficulty.

frangere *vt.*[66] **fran'gersi** *vr.* to break.

fran'gia *f.* fringe.

frangiflutti *m.* breakwater.

franto *pp.of* frangere.

franto'io *m.* oilpress; oil mill.

frantumare *vt.*, **frantumarsi** *vr.* to shatter, smash, crush.

frantumi *m.pl.* fragments, smithereens: andare in —, to shatter.

frapporre *vt.* to interpose, insert; **frapporsi** *vr.* to interfere, intrude.

frasa'rio *m.* language, jargon.

frasca *f.* branch: **saltare di palo in —**, to ramble, speak desultorily.

frase *f.* phrase, sentence: **—fatta**, commonplace.

fraseologi'a *f.* phraseology.

fras'sino *m.* ash, ash tree.

frastagliare *vt.* to slit; to make jagged.

frastagliato *adj.* slit, split, indented, jagged; uneven.

frastornare *vt.* to disturb.

frastuono *m.* din, racket.

frate *m.* friar, monk, brother.

fratellanza *f.* brotherhood; brotherliness.

fratellastro *m.* half-brother.

fratello *m.* brother; **fratelli** *pl.* brothers; (*friars*) brethren: **fratelli di latte**, foster brothers; **fratelli gemelli**, twins; **fratelli siamesi**, Siamese twins.

fraternità *f.* fraternity.

fraternizzare *vi.* to fraternize.

fraterno *adj.* fraternal, brotherly.

fratricida *m.* fratricide.]*adj.* fratricidal.

fratrici'dio *m.* fratricide.

fratta *f.* bush; hedge.

fratta'glie *f.pl.* pluck.

frattanto *adv.* meanwhile.

frattempo, (nel) *adv.* meanwhile.

frattura *f.* fracture; breach.

fratturare *vt.*, **fratturarsi** *vr.* to fracture, break.

fraudolento *adj.* fraudulent.

fraudolenza *f.* fraudulence.

frazionamento *m.* fractionization.

frazionare *vt.* to fractionize.

faziona'rio *adj.* fractional.

frazione *f.* fraction; hamlet.

frec'cia *f.* arrow, dart; hand (*of a watch*); pointer; needle (*of a compass*).

frecciata *f.* thrust; gibe.

freddamente *adv.* coldly.

freddare *vt.* to kill.

freddezza *f.* coldness.

freddo *m.* cold; cold weather. *adj.* cold, chilly; unemotional; **avere, fare —**, to be cold; **a —**, deliberately; **sangue —**, courage; **a sangue —**, cold-bloodedly.

freddoloso *adj.* chilly, sensitive to cold, cold-blooded.

freddura *f.* funny story; pun.

freddurista *m.* punster.

fregagione *m.* rubbing, massage.

fregare *vt.* to rub; (*It. slang*) to cheat, lick; to outwit, outdo; (*school jargon*) to pluck; **fregarsene** (*It. slang*), not to care a rap.

fregata *f.* frigate; (*ornith.*) frigate-bird; (*It. slang*) cheat, plant, crooked deal.

fregiare *vt.* to decorate.

fre'gio *m.* frieze, decoration.

frego *m.* line, stroke.

fre'gola *f.* rut; breeding time; (*fig.*) lust.

fremente *adj.* quivering, throbbing, thrilled.

fre'mere *vi.* to quiver; to shudder, shake; to thrill, be thrilled; to fume, fret: **— dal desiderio di,** to long for.

fre'mito *m.* thrill; shudder.

frenare *vt.* to brake; to control; to check, curb, restrain; **frenarsi** *vr.* to control oneself, check oneself.

frenata *f.* check, braking.

frenatore *m.* brakeman.

frenatura *f.* braking.

frenello *m.* (*naut.*) tiller line.

frenesi'a *f.* frenzy; craze.

freneticamente *adv.* frenziedly, wildly.

frene'tico *adj.* frenzied.

fre'nico *adj.* (*anat.*) phrenic.

freno *m.* brake; control, check, restraint: **tenere a —,** to keep in check; **stringere i freni** (*fig.*), to rein in; **mordere il —,** to champ at the bit.

frequentare *vt.* to frequent; to patronize; to attend; to associate with.

frequentatore *m.* patron, customer; constant visitor.

frequente *adj.* frequent; **di —,** frequently: **polso —,** throbbing pulse.

frequenza *f.* frequency; attendance.

fresa *f.* fraise, countersink.

fresare *vt.* to fraise, to countersink.

fresatrice *f.* milling machine.

fresatura *f.* fraising.

freschezza *f.* freshness.

fresco *m.* cool, coolness. *adj.* fresh; cool: **far —,** to be cool; **stai —,** now you are in for it!; forget it!

Frescobaldi, Girolamo, Italian organist and composer (1583–1644).

frescura *f.* coolness.

fretta *f.* haste, hurry: **aver —,** to be in a hurry; **fate in —!** hurry up!

frettolosamente *adv.* hastily.

frettoloso *adj.* hasty; rash.

fria'bile *adj.* friable.

friabilità *f.* friability.

frig'gere *vt.*[67] to fry. *vi.* to fry; to hiss; to sizzle; to fret; to fume.

frigidezza, frigidità *f.* frigidity.

fri'gido *adj.* frigid.

fri'gio *m.*, *adj.* Phrygian.

frignare *vi.* to whimper.

frigori'fero *m.* refrigerator.

fringuello *m.* chaffinch.

frinire *vi.* to chirp.

frittata *f.* omelet: far la — (*fig.*), to make a mess of it.

frittella *f.* fritter.

fritto *adj.* fried, *pp. of* friggere.

frittura *f.* fry.

frivolezza *f.* frivolity.

fri'volo *adj.* frivolous, trifling.

frizione *f.* rubbing, massage; (*mach.*) clutch; friction.

frizzante *adj.* sparkling, racy.

frizzare *vt.* to sparkle.

frizzo *m.* witticism.

frodare *vt.* to cheat, swindle.

frode *f.* swindle, cheat.

frodo *m.* smuggling: cacciar di —, to poach; cacciatore di —, poacher.

fro'gia *f.* nostril (*of a horse*).

frollo *adj.* high; tender: pasta frolla, puff paste.

fronde *f.pl.* foliage.

frondoso *adj.* leafy.

frontale *adj.* frontal.

fronte (1) *f.* forehead; front, façade: far — a, to face; to meet; corrugare la —, to frown; di — a, facing; opposite.

fronte (2) *m.* front: dietro front! about face!;—a destra! right face!

fronteggiare *vt.* to face; to meet; to cope (*with*).

frontespi'zio *m.* title page.

frontiera *f.* frontier, border.

fron'zolo *m.* bauble, gewgaw.

frotta *f.* crowd, swarm; flock.

frot'tola *f.* fib, humbug.

frugale *adj.* spare, meager; frugal.

frugalità *f.* frugality.

frugare *vt.*, *vi.* to search, rummage.

fru'golo *m.* imp.

fruire *vt.* to enjoy.

frullare *vt.* to beat, whip. *vi.* to flutter; to whirl.

frullino *m.* whisk:— elettrico, blender, mixer.

frumento *m.* wheat.

frumentone *m.* maize.

frusciare *vi.* to rustle.

frusci'o *m.* rustle, rustling.

frusta *f.* whip; scourge; lash.

frustare *vt.* to whip, lash; to wear; frustarsi *vr.* to wear.

frustata *f.* lash.

frustino *m.* riding whip.

frusto *adj.* worn; threadbare.

frustrare *vt.* to frustrate.

frutta *f.* (*sing.*, *coll.*, *pl.*) fruit, fruits.

fruttare *vt.* to yield, produce, bring. *vi.* to bring profit, pay.

frutteto *m.* orchard.

frutticultore *m.* fruit grower.

fruttiera *f.* fruit dish.

frutti'fero *adj.* fructiferous; interest-bearing; profitable.

fruttificare *vi.* to fructify; to yield profit.

fruttiven'dolo *m.* fruiterer.

frutto *m.* fruit; result; profit.

fruttuoso *adj.* fruitful, profitable; successful.

fu *adj.* late (*deceased*).

fucilare *vt.* to shoot.

fucilata *f.* rifle shot; rifle report.

fucilazione *f.* execution (*by shooting*).

fucile *m.* gun; rifle.

fuciliere *m.* rifleman.

fucina *f.* forge, smithy.

fuc'sia *f.* fuchsia.

fuga *f.* flight, escape; leak; leakage; (*mus.*) fugue.

fugace *adj.* fleeting; passing.

fugare *vt.* to put to flight, rout; to dispel.

fugge'vole *adj.* fleeting.

fuggevolmente *adv.* fleetingly.

fuggiasco *m.*, *adj.* fugitive, runaway.

fuggifuggi *m.* stampede.

fuggire *vt.* to avoid; to escape. *vi.* to flee, run away, take flight; to fly, speed (*away*, *along*).

fulcro *m.* fulcrum (*pl.* fulcra); (*fig.*) pivot.

fulgente *adj.* fulgent, shining.

ful'gido *adj.* refulgent, shining.

fulgore *m.* refulgence, sparkle.

fulig'gine *f.* soot.

fuligginoso *adj.* sooty.

fulmicotone *m.* guncotton.

fulminante *adj.* fulminant.

fulminare *vt.* to strike (*by lightning*); to fulminate; to flash. *vi.* to thunder; fulminarsi *vr.* to burn out.

ful'mine *m.* thunderbolt, lightning, flash: un — a ciel sereno, a bolt out of the blue.

fulmi'neo *adj.* lightning-swift; sudden; flashing.

fulvo *adj.* tawny.

fumaiuolo *m.* funnel, smokestack.

fumante *adj.* smoking; steaming.

fumare *vt.*, *vi.* to smoke; to steam; to fume.

fumata *f.* smoke; smoke signal.

fumatore *m.* smoker.

fumetti *m.pl.* strips, comics.

fumigare *vi.* to smoke; to steam.

fumista *m.* stove repairer; (*liter.*) mystificator.

fumisteri'a *f.* (*liter.*) mystification.

fumo *m.* smoke; vapor, steam; smoking. **fumi** *pl.* fumes.

fumoso *adj.* smoky.

funambolismo *m.* rope dancing.

funam'bolo *m.* rope dancer; aerialist.

fune *f.* rope; cable.

fu'nebre *adj.* funeral.

funerale *m.* funeral.

funera'rio *adj.* funeral.

fune'reo *adj.* funereal, dismal.

funestare *vt.* to sadden; to ruin.

funesto *adj.* ominous, fatal, tragic; baneful.

funga'ia *f.* mushroom bed; swarm.

fun'gere *vi.* to act, serve (*as*).

fungo *m.* fungus; mushroom.

fungosità *f.* fungosity.

fungoso *adj.* fungous.

funicolare *f.* funicular railway.

funivi'a *f.* telpher.

funzionamento *m.* working.

funzionare *vi.* to work, run, operate; to act (*as*).

funziona'rio *m.* official, executive.

funzione *f.* function; office, duty; (*eccles.*) service.

fuoco *m.* fire; fireplace; heat; focus: **fuochiartificiali**, fire works; — **fatuo**, will-o'-the-wisp; **far** — (**contro**), to fire (*at*); **mettere a** —, to focus.

fuorchè *prep.* except.

fuori *prep.* out, beyond, off. *adv.* out, outside, off; abroad; — **servizio**, off duty; out of commission; — **gioco**, offside; — **di sè**, beside oneself; **il di** —, the outside; **all'infuori di**, except.

fuoribordo *m.* outboard-motor boat. *adv.* outboard.

fuoruscito *m.* refugee.

furbacchione *m.* slyboots.

furberi'a *f.* cunning; subtlety.

furbi'zia *f.* cunning, cleverness.

furbo *adj.* sly, cunning.

furente *adj.* furious.

fureri'a *f.* company headquarters.

furetto *m.* (*zool.*) ferret.

furfante *m.* knave; racketeer.

furfanteri'a *f.* knavery, racketeering.

furgoncino *m.* van.

furgone *m.* wagon.

fu'ria *f.* fury, wrath; vehemence; hurry: **andare su tutte le furie**, to fly off the handle; **aver** —, to be in a hurry; **in fretta e** —, hurry-scurry; **a** — **di**, by dint of.

furibondo *adj.* furious, wild

furiere *m.* quartermaster.

furiosamente *adv.* furiously.

furioso *adj.* furious, wild: **pazzo** —, raving lunatic.

furore *m.* fury, wrath; vehemence; frenzy: **far** —, to make a hit; to be the rage.

furoreggiare *vi.* to be the rage.

furtivamente *adv.* stealthily.

furtivo *adj.* stealthy, surreptitious.

furto *m.* theft, larceny: — **con scasso**, housebreaking.

fuscello *m.* twig; (*fig.*) slip.

fusciacca *f.* sash.

fusello *m.* bobbin; axle spindle.

fusi'bile *m.* fuse. *adj.* fusible.

fusione *f.* fusion, melting; casting; blending; (*comm.*) amalgamation.

fuso (*1*) *m.* spindle; distaff; shaft; shank: — **orario**, time zone; **far le fusa**, to purr.

fuso (*2*) *adj.* fused; melted; blended; cast. *pp.* of **fondere**.

fusoliera *f.* (*aeron.*) fuselage.

fustagno *m.* fustian.

fustella *f.* hollow punch.

fustigare *vt.* to flog; to scourge.

fustigazione *f.* scourging.

fusto *m.* trunk, stalk; shaft; bar; frame; barrel, cask; (*It. slang*) burly young fellow, "husky"; boy friend.

futile *adj.* futile, trifling.

futilità *f.* futility; trifle.

futurismo *m.* futurism.

futurista *m.*, *adj.* futurist.

futuro *m.* future. *adj.* future, coming, to come: **il** — **presidente**, the president to be.

G

gabbamondo *m.* swindler.

gabbano *m.* gaberdine, frock.

gabbare *vt.* to cheat, impose upon.

gab'bia *f.* cage; (*naut.*) top: **vela di** —, main topsail.

gabbiano *m.* gull.

gabbiere *m.* (*naut.*) topman.

gabbo *m.* fun: **pigliare a** —, to make fun of; to make light of.

gabella *f.* (*fiscal*) duty.

gabellare *vt.* to palm off (*on*).

gabelliere *m.* exciseman.

gabinetto *m.* cabinet; laboratory; consulting room; study, den; closet, water closet: — **di lettura**, reading room; — **da bagno**, bathroom.

gaffa *f.* (*naut.*) gaff, hook.

gagà *m.* (*It. slang*) fop, dandy, dude.

gaggi'a *f.* (*bot.*) acacia, mimosa.

gagliardetto *m.* pennon.

gagliardi'a *f.* stalwartness.

gagliardo *adj.* powerful; stalwart.

gaglioffo *m.* knave, rascal.

gaiamente *adv.* gaily.

gaiezza *f.* gaiety.

gaio *adj.* gay, merry; gaudy.

gala *f.* gala; frill.

galalite *f.* casein plastic.

galante *adj.* courtly, flattering: **donna —**, wanton.

galanteri'a *f.* courtliness; flattery; beauty; daintiness.

galantina *f.* galantine.

galantuomo *m.* honest man, gentleman; (*fig.*) fellow.

galas'sia *f.* galaxy.

galateo *m.* politeness, manners; treatise on good manners.

galena *f.* (*min.*) galena; (*radio*) crystal.

galenista *m.* (*med.*) Galenist.

galeone *m.* galleon.

galeotto *m.* convict; galley slave.

galera *f.* (*naut.*) galley; jail; (*fig.*) hell: **pezzo di —**, jailbird.

Galilei, Galileo, great Italian astronomer and philosopher, *Dialogo sopra i due massimi sistemi* (1564-1642).

galla *f.* (*bot.*) gall.

galla, (a) *adv.* afloat: **venire a galla,** to come to the surface.

galleggiamento *m.* floating.

galleggiante *m.* float; *adj.* buoyant, floating.

galleggiare *vi.* to float.

galleri'a *f.* gallery; tunnel; (*theat.*) balcony: **prima —**, dress circle; **seconda —**, balcony.

gallese *m.* Welshman. *f.* Welshwoman; Welsh (*language*). *adj.* Welsh.

galletta *f.* hardtack.

galletto *m.* cockerel; (*mach.*) wing bolt: **fare il —**, to swagger.

gallina *f.* hen: **zampe di — (***fig.***),** scrawls.

gallo (1) *m.* cock, rooster: **fare il —**, to strut.

gallo (2) *m.* Gaul.

gallone (1) *m.* chevron, stripe.

gallone (2) *m.* gallon.

galoppare *vi.* to gallop.

galoppata *f.* gallop.

galoppato'io *m.* riding (*ground*).

galoppatore *m.* galloper.

galoppino *m.* runner; errandboy; canvasser.

galoppo *m.* gallop.

galo'scia *f.* galosh, overshoe.

Galvani, Luigi, Italian discoverer of galvanism (1737-1798).

galva'nico *adj.* galvanic.

galvanizzare *vt.* to galvanize.

galvano *m.* (*typ.*) electrotype.

galvanopla'stica, *f.* galvanoplasty, electrotyping.

galvanopla'stico *adj.* galvanoplastic.

gamba *f.* leg: **darsela a gambe,** to show a clean pair of heels; **andare a gambe levate,** to fall head over heels; **prendere sotto —**, to make light of; **essere in —**, to be all right, to be a "corker."

gambale *m.* legging; puttee.

gamberetto *m.* shrimp.

gam'bero *m.* crawfish: **fare come i gamberi,** to go backwards.

gambo *m.* stem, stalk; shaft.

gamella *f.* (*mil.*) messtin.

gamma *f.* gamut; gamma.

gana'scia *f.* jaw.

gan'cio *m.* hook; clasp; grapple.

ganga *f.* gangue.

gan'ghero *m.* hinge: **uscire dai gangheri,** to fly off the handle.

gan'glio *m.* ganglion (*pl.* ganglia).

ganzo *m.* paramour, lover, beau.

gara *f.* competition, contest; match, race; **fare a —**, to vie.

garante *m.* guarantor, guarantee.

garantire *vt.* to guarantee; to assure; to promise.

garanzi'a *f.* guaranty; security.

garbare *vi.* to suit, please: **non mi garba,** I don't like.

garbatamente *adv.* politely.

garbatezza *f.* politeness.

garbato *m.* polite; graceful.

garbo *m.* politeness; grace; shape, fashion.

garbu'glio *m.* tangle; mess.

gareggiare *vi.* to vie, compete.

garetta *f.* sentrybox.

garetto *m.* hock; ankle.

garganella *f.* gullet: **bere a —**, to gulp down.

gargarismo *m.* gargling; gargle.

gargarizzare *vt.*, **gargarizzarsi** *vr.* to gargle.

gargarozzo *m.* throat.

Garibaldi, Giuseppe, Italian patriot and general; leader of the expedition of *The Thousand* (1807-1882).

garitta *f.* sentrybox.

garo'fano *m.* pink, carnation: **chiodi di —**, cloves.

garrese *m.* withers (*pl.*).

garretto *see* garetto.

garrire *vi.* to warble; to wave (*as flags*).

garrito *m.* warble.

gar'rulo *adj.* garrulous.

garza *f.* gauze.

garzare *vt.* to teasel.

garzo *m.* teasel.

garzone *m.* shopboy; stableboy.

gas *m.* gas, vapor; firedamp.

gasificare *vt.* to gasify.

gasista *m.* gasfitter, gasman.

gas(s)o'geno *m.* gazogene.

gas(s)o'metro *m.* gasometer, gas holder.

gas(s)oso *adj.* gassy.

ga'strico *adj.* gastric.

gastronomi'a *f.* gastronomy.

gatta *f.* she-cat, tabby; puss; — **ci cova**, something is brewing.

gattamorta *f.* unfeeling woman.

gatto *m.* cat, tomcat.

gatton gattoni *adv.* on all fours; stealthily.

gattopardo *m.* serval.

gaudente *m.*, *adj.* epicurean.

gau'dio *m.* joy, happiness.

gavetta *f.* messtin: **venire dalla —**, to rise from the ranks, to be a self-made man.

gazza *f.* magpie.

gazzarra *f.* uproar; riot.

gazzella *f.* gazelle.

gazzetta *f.* gazette.

gazzettino *m.* bulletin; newsmonger.

gelare *vt.*, *vi.* to freeze: **mi si gela il sangue**, my blood runs cold.

gelata *f.* frost.

gelateri'a *f.* ice-cream parlor.

gelatiera *f.* ice-cream freezer.

gelatiere *m.* ice-cream vendor.

gelatina *f.* jelly; aspic; *(chem.)* gelatine.

gelatinoso *adj.* gelatinous.

gelato *m.* ice cream. *adj.* frozen.

gelidamente *adv.* icily.

ge'lido *adj.* icy, ice-cold.

gelo *m.* frost; frostiness.

gelone *m.* chilblain.

gelosi'a *(1)* *f.* jealousy.

gelosi'a *(2)* *f.* blind, shutter (*of a window*).

geloso *adj.* jealous.

gelso *m.* mulberry.

gelsomino *m.* jasmine.

gemebondo *adj.* moaning, plaintive.

gemello *m.*, *adj.* twin; **gemelli** *pl.* cuff links, studs; *(astr.)* **Gemini**, the Twins.

ge'mere *vi.* to groan, moan.

ge'mito *m.* moan; howl.

gemma *f.* gem; *(bot.)* bud.

gendarme *m.* gendarme.

genealogi'a *f.* pedigree, genealogy.

genealo'gico *adj.* genealogical.

generale *m.*, *adj.* general: **— di Brigata**, brigadier general; **— di Divisione**, major general; **— di Corpo d'Armata**, lieutenant general; **— d'Armata**, general; **in —**, generally; as a rule.

generalità *f.* generality: **le —**, the personal data.

generalizzare *vt.*, *vi.* to generalize.

generalmente *adv.* generally; as a rule.

generare *vt.* to generate.

generatore *m.* generator.

generazione *f.* generation.

ge'nere *m.* kind, sort; genus; gender: **il — umano**, mankind; **generi diversi**, assorted articles: **generi alimentari**, foodstuff; **in —**, generally speaking; as a rule.

gene'rico *m.* *(theat.)* utility man. *adj.* generic; vague.

ge'nero *m.* son-in-law.

generosità *f.* generosity.

generoso *adj.* generous.

ge'nesi *f.* genesis.

gene'tica *f.* genetics.

genetli'aco *m.* birthday.

gengiva *f.* gum.

gengivale *adj.* gingival.

geni'a *f.* breed; covey.

geniale *adj.* ingenious; clever.

genialità *f.* ingeniousness, cleverness; genius.

genialo'ide *m.* man of unfulfilled, undisciplined, genius.

geniere *m.* *(mil.)* engineer.

ge'nio *(1)* *m.* genius (*pl.* geniuses) genius (*pl.* genii); talent, gift: **andare a —**, to be to one's liking.

ge'nio *(2)* *m.* *(mil.)* corps of engineers municipal engineering department

genitivo *m.*, *adj.* genitive.

genitore *m.*, **genitrice** *f.* parent; **genitori**, parents.

genna'io *m.* January.

genta'glia *f.* scum, rabble.

gente *f.* people, folk; folks; race.

gentildonna *f.* lady, gentlewoman.

gentile *m.* gentile, pagan. *adj.* kind nice; soft; polite: **il gentil sesso** the fair sex.

Gentile, Giovanni, Italian philosopher and politician (1875–1943).

gentilezza *f.* kindness; politeness favor; gracefulness; obligingness **per —**, if you please, if you don' mind.

gentili'zio *adj.* nobiliary; armorial.

gentilmente *adv.* kindly.

gentiluomo *m.* gentleman; nobleman

genuflessione *f.* genuflection.

genuflesso *adj.* kneeling.

genuflet'tersi *vr.* to kneel down.

genuino *adj.* genuine, real.

genziana *f.* gentian.

geografi'a *f.* geography.

geogra'fico *adj.* geographical.

geo'grafo *m.* geographer.

geologi'a *f.* geology.

geolo'gico *adj.* geological.

geo'logo *m.* geologist.

geo'metra *m.* land surveyor.

geometri'a *f.* geometry,

geome'trico *adj.* geometric.

gera'nio *m.* geranium.

gerarca *m.* hierarch; leader.

gerarchi'a *f.* hierarchy.

gerar'chico *adj.* hierarchical.

gerente *m.* manager, operator; editor

gerenza *f.* management; editorship.

gergo *m.* jargon, slang.

gerla *f.* basket.
germano (*1*) *m.* brother-german. *adj.* german.
germano (*2*) *m.* (*ornith.*) mallard.
germe *m.* germ; seed; embryo.
germinare *vt.*, *vi.* to germinate.
germogliare *vt.*, *vi.* to shoot, sprout; (*fig.*) to issue.
germo'glio *m.* sprout, bud.
gerogli'fico *m.* hieroglyph.
gerun'dio *m.* gerund.
gessare *vt.* to plaster; to chalk.
gesso *m.* chalk; (*chem.*) gypsum; plaster; plaster cast.
gessoso *adj.* chalky, plastery.
gesta *f. pl., sing.* exploit, deed, a-chievement.
gestante *f.* woman in childbirth.
gestazione *f.* gestation.
gesticolare *vi.* to gesticulate.
gestione *f.* management.
gestire *vi.* to operate, manage, run. *vi.* to gesticulate, gesture.
gesto *m.* gesture; attitude.
gestore *m.* operator; (*rail.*) traffic manager.
Gesù *m.* Jesus.
gesuita *m.* Jesuit.
gettare *vt.* to throw, cast, fling; to toss; to shoot; to send forth; gettarsi *vr.* to throw, fling oneself; to rush; to flow (*out, into*): gettarsi in ginocchio, to fall on one's knees.
gettata *f.* jetty; cast; layer.
gettato *adj.* thrown; wasted.
get'tito *m.* flow; revenue, income.
getto *m.* throw, throwing; spurt, gush; jet; shoot; cast, casting; ejecta (*pl.*); discharge: di —, at a stretch; a — continuo, uninter-ruptedly.
gettone *m.* counter, chip; check; tag.
ghepardo *m.* cheetah.
gheri'glio *m.* kernel.
gherlino *m.* (*naut.*) warp.
gherminella *f.* stratagem, trick; mischief.
ghermire *vt.* to clutch; to seize.
gherone *m.* gusset.
ghetta *f.* spat, gaiter; (*mil.*) legging.
ghiac'cia'ia *f.* icebox.
ghiac'cia'io *m.* glacier.
ghiacciare *vt.*, *vi.* ghiacciarsi *vr.* to freeze: sentirsi ghiacciare il sangue, to feel one's blood run cold.
ghiacciata *f.* iced drink.
ghiacciato *adj.* frozen; icy; iced.
ghiac'cio *m.* ice; frost: farsi di —, to freeze. *adj.* icy.
ghiacciuolo *m.* icicle; flaw (*in a gem*).
ghia'ia *f.* gravel.
ghianda *f.* (*bot.*) acorn.
ghianda'ia *f.* (*ornith.*) jay.
ghiera *f.* ferrule.

ghigliottina *f.* guillotine; sash.
ghigliottinare *vt.* to guillotine.
ghigna *f.* (*evil*) face.
ghignare *vi.* to grin, sneer.
ghigno *m.* grin, smirk.
ghinea *f.* guinea.
ghin'gheri, (in) *adv.* in gorgeous attire, dressed up.
ghiotto *adj.* gluttonous; eager (*for*); appetizing.
ghiottone *m.* glutton.
ghiottoneri'a *f.* gluttony; dainty, deli-cacy.
ghiozzo *m.* miller's thump.
ghirba *f.* skin.
ghiribizzo *m.* whim, freak.
ghirigoro *m.* flourish, curlicue.
ghirlanda *f.* garland, wreath.
Ghirlandaio, il (*Domenico di Tommaso Bigordi*) Florentine painter (1449–1494).
ghiro *m.* dormouse (*pl.* dormice).
ghisa *f.* cast iron.
già *adv.* already; once, formerly, pre-viously: il caso — citato, the above (*mentioned*) case; eh, già! of course!
giacca *f.* jacket, coat.
giacchè *conj.* since, as; for.
giacchetta *f.* jacket.
giacente *adj.* in abeyance; unclaimed.
giacenza *f.* abeyance; unsold stock; demurrage.
giacere *vi.*[68] to lie; to be situated; to find oneself.
giaci'glio *m.* bed, cot.
giacimento *m.* layer, bed.
giacinto *m.* hyacinth.
giaciuto *pp.of* giacere.
Giacosa, Giuseppe, Italian dramatist and poet, *Come le foglie, Partita a scacchi* (1847–1906).
giaculato'ria *f.* prayer.
giada *f.* (*min.*) jade.
giaguaro *m.* jaguar.
gialappa *f.* jalap.
giallastro *adj.* yellowish.
giallo *m.*, *adj.* yellow: libro —, thriller, "whodunit."
giammai *adv.* never.
gianniz'zero *m.* Janizary; (*fig.*) par-tisan, follower; papal officer.
giapponese *m.*, *adj.* Japanese.
giara *f.* jar.
giardinag'gio *m.* gardening.
giardinetta *f.* station wagon.
giardiniera *f.* woman gardener; jar-diniere; wagonette; mixed salad.
giardiniere *m.* gardener.
giardino *m.* garden: — zoologico, zoo; — d'infanzia, kindergarten.
giarrettiera *f.* garter.
giavellotto *m.* javelin.
gibbosità *f.* gibbosity.
gibboso *adj.* gibbous, humped.

giberna f. cartridge box; (pl.) cartridge belt.

gigante m., adj. giant.

gigantesco adj. gigantic, giant.

gigione m. (theat.) "ham."

gi'glio m. lily; fleur-de-lis.

gilè m. waistcoat, vest.

ginecologi'a f. gynecology.

gineco'logo m. gynecologist.

ginepra'io m. (fig.) mess, scrape.

ginepro m. (bot.) juniper.

ginestra f. broom, genista.

ginevrino m., adj. Genevan.

gingillare vi., **gingillarsi** vr. to trifle, idle, dawdle.

gingillo m. toy; trifle; trinket.

ginna'sio m. junior high school; grammar school; gymnasium.

ginnasta m. gymnast, athlete.

ginna'stica f. gymnastics.

gin'nico adj. gymnastic.

ginocchiera f. kneelet.

ginoc'chio m. knee: in —, on one's knees; sino alle ginocchia, kneedeep; knee-high.

ginocchioni adv. on one's knees.

Gioberti, Vincenzo, Italian philosopher and statesman, Del Primato morale e civile degl' Italiani (1801-1852).

giocare vt., vi. to play; to bet, stake; to gamble; to outwit; **giocarsi** vr. to wager, stake; to lose.

giocata f. stake, bet; game; play.

giocatore m. player; gambler.

giocat'tolo m. plaything, toy.

giocherellare vi. to play, trifle (with); to toy (with).

giochetto m. pastime; trick; walkover.

gioco see **giuoco**.

giocoliere m. juggler.

giocondo adj. merry, gay.

giocoso adj. jocose, jocular; comic.

gioga'ia f. dewlap; mountain range.

giogo m. yoke; crest, ridge.

gio'ia f. joy, delight; happiness; jewel; darling: che —! how wonderful!, I'm so happy!

gioielleri'a f. jewelry; jeweler's shop.

gioielliere m. jeweler; goldsmith.

gioiello m. jewel.

gioioso adj. joyful.

gioire vi. to rejoice (at, in).

Giolitti, Giovanni, Italian statesman (1842-1928).

giornala'io m. newsdealer; newsboy.

giornale m. newspaper; journal; (comm.) daybook: — di bordo, log; — radio, newscast, news broadcast.

giornaletto m. tabloid.

giornaliero m. day laborer. adj. daily.

giornalismo m. journalism.

giornalista m. journalist, newspaper-

man, columnist: — pubblicista, free lance.

giornali'stico adj. journalistic.

giornalmente adj. daily.

giornata f. day; day's work; day wages: vivere alla —, to live from hand to mouth; in —, before night; today.

giorno m. day: sul far del —, at daybreak; di —, by day; al — d'oggi, nowadays; un — sì e l'altro no, every other day.

giostra f. tournament; merry-go-round.

Giotto (Giotto di Bondone), great Florentine painter and architect (1276?-1337).

giovamento m. advantage, avail; solace; aid.

giovane m. young man, boy, youth. f. young woman, girl; youth: i giovani, young people. adj. young; junior.

giovanetta f. girl.

giovanetto m. boy, lad.

giovanile adj. youthful: opera —, early work.

giovanotto m. young man; bachelor; (naut.) sailor lad.

giovare vi. to help; to be useful, of use; to be good (for); **giovarsi** vr. to avail oneself (of); to profit (by).

giovedì m. Thursday.

giovenca f. heifer.

gioventù f. youth.

giove'vole adj. advantageous.

gioviale adj. jovial, hearty.

giovialità f. heartiness.

giovinastro m. scamp, wastrel.

giovincello m. lad, stripling.

gio'vine see **giovane**.

giovinezza f. youth.

giradischi m. record player.

giraffa f. giraffe.

giran'dola f. girandole; pinwheel.

girante m. (comm.) endorser.

girare vt. to turn; to travel over; to round; (comm.) to endorse; (moving pictures) to shoot. vi. to turn; to revolve, rotate; to whirl; to walk about; **girarsi** vr. to turn, turn around.

girarrosto m. spit.

girasole m. sunflower.

girata f. turn; (comm.) endorsement.

girata'rio m. (comm.) endorsee.

giravolta f. turning; pirouette.

girellare vt. to loaf; to walk around.

gire'vole adj. revolving.

girino m. tadpole.

giro m. turn, round; walk; drive; ride; tour; circle; circulation: mettere in — voci, to spread rumors; nel — di un anno, in a year's time;

prendere in — uno, to pull one's leg; a — di posta, by return (mail); — d'affari, (comm.) turnover.

gironzare, gironzolare vi. to loiter, loaf.

girosco'pio m. gyroscope.

girotondo m. ring-around-a-rosy.

girotta f. weathercock.

girovagare vi. to roam, wander.

giro'vago m., adj. vagrant: mercante —, peddler, hawker.

gita f. excursion; tour, trip.

gitano m., adj. gypsy

gitante m. excursionist.

giù adv. down; off: buttar — una persona (fig.), to blacken a person's character; mandar —, to swallow; — di lì, su per —, approximately; — le mani! hands off!; buttarsi —, to jump down; to lose heart.

giubba f. jacket, coat.

giubbetto m. jacket: — di salvataggio, life belt.

giubilante adj. jubilant.

giubilare vt. to superannuate, pension off. vi. to jubilate, exult.

giubileo m. jubilee.

giu'bilo m. jubilation, joy, glee.

giucco m. fool. adj. foolish.

Giuda m. Judas.

giuda'ico adj. Judaic.

giudeo m., Jew. adj. Jewish, Judean.

giudicare vt., vi. to judge; to consider, deem.

giu'dice m. judge; justice; referee: — conciliatore, justice of the peace; — istruttore, coroner.

giudizia'rio adj. judicial.

giudi'zio m. judgment; sentence, verdict; sense, wisdom; opinion: il giorno del —, doomsday; chiamare in —, to summon before court.

giudizioso adj. sensible, wise.

giugno m. June.

giulivo adj. gay, joyful.

giullare m. jester.

giumenta f. mare.

giunca f. (naut.) junk.

giunchi'glia f. jonquil.

giunco m. reed, rush.

giun'gere vt.[79] to join. vi. to come (to); to arrive: — a, to reach; to go so far as; mi giunge nuovo, this is news to me.

giungla f. jungle.

giunta (1) f. addition; makeweight: per —, moreover; to boot.

giunta (2) f. junta; committee; council.

giuntare see aggiuntare.

giunto (1) m. coupling, joint; universal joint.

giunto (2) pp. of giungere.

giuntura f. juncture; joint.

giuoco m. play, game; joke, trick, jest; pleasure, fun; gambling: (mach.) clearance; — di prestigio, sleight of hand; — di parole, pun; — di Borsa, stockjobbing; pigliarsi — di, to make fun of; mettere in —, to stake; fare il doppio —, to play both ends against the middle.

giuramento m. oath, pledge.

giurare vt., vi. to swear, take an oath: giurarla a, to swear revenge upon.

giurato m. juryman. adj. sworn.

giuri'a f. jury; committee.

giuri'dico adj. juridical.

giurisdizione f. jurisdiction.

giurisprudenza f. jurisprudence.

giurista m. jurist.

giusta prep. in conformity with.

giustamente adv. rightly; exactly; fitly.

giustezza f. justness; fitness; accuracy.

giustifica'bile adj. justifiable.

giustificare vi. to justify; giustificarsi vr. to justify oneself, excuse oneself.

giustificativo m. (comm.) voucher. adj. justificatory.

giustificato adj. justified; just.

giustificazione f. justification; extenuation; excuse.

giusti'zia f. justice; law.

giustiziare vt. to execute, put to death.

giustiziere m. executioner; avenger.

giusto m. just man; just reward; right price; due. adj. just, right, fair; proper; exact; correct: il — mezzo, the golden mean. adv. just, right, exactly: giusto, giusto, just in time; giust'appunto! exactly!

glabro adj. smooth; shaved.

glaciale adj. icy, glacial.

gladiatore m. gladiator.

gla'dio m. sword.

glan'dola f. gland.

gli art.m.pl. the. pron.pers. him, to him; (fam.) (to) them.

glicerina f. glycerin.

gli'cine f. wistaria.

gliela compound pron. her (it) to him, her (it) to her, her (it) to them.

gliele, glieli them to him, them to her. glielo him (it) to him, him (it) to her.

gliene compound pron. (to) him some (or some to him), (to) her some (or some to her), of it to him (her): — diedi, I gave him (her) some, — parlai, I spoke of it to him (her).

globale adj. total, aggregate.

globalmente adv. altogether.

globo m. globe; eyeball.

glo'bulo m. globule, corpuscle.

glo'ria f. glory; fame.

gloriarsi *vr.* to pride oneself (*on*); to boast, glory (*in*).

glorificare *vt.* to glorify.

glorioso *adj.* glorious.

glossare *vt.* to gloss.

glossa'rio *m.* glossary.

glot'tide *f.* glottis.

gluco'sio *m.* glucose.

glu'teo *m.* buttock.

glu'tine *m.* gluten.

gnocco *m.* dumpling.

gnomo *m.* gnome.

gnorri: far lo —, to play possum.

gobba *f.* hunch, hump.

gobbo *m.* hump; humpback. *adj.* humpbacked: naso —, crooked nose.

goc'cia *f.* drop, bead; luster (*of a chandelier*): somiglianti come due gocce d'acqua, as like as two peas.

gocciolare *vi.* to drip, trickle.

gocciolato'io *m.* dripstone.

godere *vt.*, *vi.* to enjoy, take pleasure (*in*); to benefit (*by*); to rejoice; **godersi** *vr.* to enjoy: godersela, to revel; to have a good time.

godimento *m.* enjoyment, pleasure; fruition.

goffo *adj.* clumsy, awkward.

gogna *f.* pillory.

gola *f.* throat; gluttony; longing; gorge; flue; drain: preso alla —, hard-pressed.

Goldoni, Carlo, the greatest Italian dramatist and writer of comedies (in Venetian dialect) (1707–1793).

goletta *f.* schooner.

golfo *m.* gulf.

Golgi, Camillo, Italian physician, Nobel Prize 1906 (1844–1926).

goliardo *m.* university student.

golosità *f.* gluttony.

goloso *m.* glutton. *adj.* gluttonous, greedy; sweet-toothed.

go'mena *f.* cable, hawser.

gomitata *f.* nudge: farsi largo a gomitate, to elbow one's way.

go'mito *m.* elbow: far di —, to nudge; a —, elbow-shaped.

gomi'tolo *m.* ball (of thread).

gomma *f.* rubber; elastic; gum; eraser; tire: — di ricambio, spare tire.

gommato *adj.* gummed.

gommoso *adj.* gummy; sticky.

gonfalone *m.* gonfalon.

gonfaloniere *m.* gonfalonier.

gonfiare *vt.*, *vi.* to inflate; to pump; to exaggerate; **gonfiarsi** *vr.* to swell, puff.

gonfiatura *f.* inflation; swelling; exaggeration.

gon'fio *adj.* inflated, swollen.

gonfiore *m.* swelling.

gongolante *adj.* elated.

gongolare *vi.* to rejoice (*at*), be elated.

gonio'metro *m.* goniometer, protractor.

gonna *f.* skirt: — scampanata, flared skirt.

gonnella *f.* skirt; underskirt, petticoat.

gonnellino *m.* kilt.

gonzo *m.* fool, dolt.

gora *f.* millpond.

gorgheggiare *vi.* to warble.

gorgo *m.* whirlpool.

gorgogliare *vi.* to gurgle; to bubble.

gorgogli'o *m.* gurgling; bubbling.

gota *f.* cheek; chap.

go'tico *m.*, *adj.* Gothic.

gotta *f.* (*pathol.*) gout.

gottazza *f.* (*naut.*) scoop.

gottoso *adj.* gouty.

governante *m.* ruler, governor. *f.* nurse; governess; housekeeper.

governare *vt.* to govern, rule; to lead; to tend; (*naut.*) to steer.

governativo *adj.* governmental.

governatorato *m.* governorship.

governatore *m.* governor; mayor.

governo *m.* government; rule: — della casa, housekeeping.

Gozzi, Carlo, Italian dramatist and novelist, *L'amore delle tre melarance* (1720–1806).

gozzo *m.* goiter; crop (*of a bird*).

gozzovi'glia *f.* debauch, spree.

gozzovigliare *vi.* to debauch, go on a spree.

gracchiare *vi.* to croak.

gracidare *vi.* to croak; cluck.

gra'cile *adj.* thin; weak; ailing.

gradassata *f.* swagger, swashbuckling.

gradasso *m.* braggart, boaster, swashbuckler.

gradatamente *adv.* gradually.

gradazione *f.* gradation; proof.

grade'vole *adj.* agreeable.

gradimento *m.* satisfaction; liking; approval.

gradinata *f.* stoop, flight (*of stairs*); tiers (*of seats*), balcony.

gradino *m.* step.

gradire *vt.* to like; to accept, welcome; to appreciate.

gradito *adj.* agreeable, pleasant, welcome, congenial.

grado *m.* degree, stage; level, rank; position: a gradi, by degrees; essere in — di, to be able to; mettere uno in — di, to enable one to; di buon —, willingly.

graduale *adj.* gradual.

gradualmente *adv.* gradually.

graduare *vt.* to grade, graduate.

graduato *m.* noncommissioned officer. *adj.* graduated.

graduato'ria f. classification; score.

graffa see grappa (1).

graffetta f. (fam.) paper clip.

graffiare vt. to scratch.

graffiatura f. scratch; graze.

graf'fio m. scratch; grapnel.

grafi'a f. writing, spelling.

gra'fico m. chart; blueprint. adj. graphic.

gragnuola f. hail; shower.

grama'glie f.pl. weeds; mourning.

gramigna f. weed.

gramma'tica f. grammar.

grammatura f. weight (in grams).

grammo m. gram.

grammo'fono m. gramophone.

gramo adj. wretched; bad; poor.

gran see grande.

grana (1) f. grain; texture.

grana (2) m. Parmesan cheese.

grana (3) f. (It. slang) trouble; money, "dough": piantare grane, to make trouble; andare in cerca di grane, to look for trouble.

grana'glie f.pl. cereals.

grana'io m. granary, barn.

granata (1) f. broom.

granata (2) f. (artil.) grenade.

granatiere m. grenadier.

granato m. pomegranate.

grancassa f. bass drum.

gran'chio m. crab; (fig.) blunder.

grandangolare adj. wide-angle: obiettivo —, wide-angle lens.

grande m. great man; adult; grandee. adj. great; big, large; tall, lofty, high; grown-up; long; wide; broad; grand: fare il —, to show off; in —, on a large scale.

grandemente adv. very, very much; greatly, highly; strongly.

grandezza f. greatness; bigness; surface, extent; capacity; width; size; loftiness: mania di —, delusion of grandeur.

grandinare vi. to hail.

grandinata f. hailstorm.

gran'dine f. hail.

grandiosità f. grandiosity, grandness.

grandioso adj. grandiose, grand.

granello m. grain; seed; speck.

granita f. sherbet.

granito m. granite.

grano m. grain, corn; wheat; bead; bit; grain (unit of measure): (It. slang) money, "dough": — saraceno, maize; — d'orzo, barleycorn; un — d'uva, a grape.

granoturco m. Indian corn, maize.

granulare adj. granular.

granulare vt. to granulate.

gra'nulo m. granule.

grappa (1) f. cramp; brace, bracket.

grappa (2) f. brandy.

grappetta f. staple (for binding books); (surg.) metal stitch.

grap'polo m. bunch, cluster.

grassatore m. highwayman.

grassazione f. robbery.

grassetto m. (typ.) boldface.

grassezza f. fatness; stoutness.

grasso m. fat; grease: giorno di —, meat day. adj. fat, stout; plentiful; greasy, fatty; lewd: martedì —, Shrove Tuesday.

grata f. grating.

gratella f. grill, gridiron.

gratic'cio m. trellis.

grati'cola f. grill, gridiron; grate; graticule.

gratifica see gratificazione.

gratificare vt. to gratify; to reward.

gratificazione f. bonus, gratuity.

gratile m. (naut.) boltrope.

gratitu'dine f. gratitude.

grato adj. grateful, thankful; pleasant, agreeable.

grattacapo m. trouble, worry.

grattacielo m. skyscraper.

grattare vt. to scratch, scrape; to grate; (fam.) to steal. vi. to grate; grattarsi vr. to scratch (oneself).

grattu'gia f. grater.

grattugiare vt. to grate.

gratuitamente adv. free; gratuitously.

gratu'ito adj. free; gratuitous; unasked for.

gravame m. tax; duty; burden; complaint.

gravare vt. to load, burden (with); vi. to weigh (upon).

grave adj. heavy; grievous; stern; serious; weighty; grave, austere; dangerous; deep, low (in pitch).

gravemente adv. heavily; sternly; seriously; dangerously; deeply.

graveolente adj. stinking.

gra'vida f., adj. pregnant.

gravidanza f. pregnancy.

gra'vido adj. pregnant, fraught.

gravità f. gravity; heaviness; seriousness; dignity; depth (of a sound).

gravitare vi. to revolve (about); to weigh; to gravitate.

gravitazione f. gravitation.

gravoso adj. burdensome; unpleasant.

gra'zia f. grace; charm; favor; privilege; permission; mercy; pardon: senza garbo nè —, shapeless; troppa — Sant'Antonio, it never rains but it pours!; nell'anno di —..., in the year of our Lord ...

graziare vt. to pardon.

gra'zie! interj. thank you!, thanks!

grazioso adj. pretty, graceful; gracious; free.

greca f. fret, Greek fret; tunic.

greco *m.* Greek. *adj.* Greek, Grecian.

grega'rio *m.* follower; serviceman.

gregge *m.* herd, flock.

greg'gio *see* grezzo.

grembiale, grembiule *m.* apron; (*auto.*) drip pan.

grembo *m.* lap: in — alla famiglia, in one's family's bosom; — materno, womb.

gremire *vt.* to overcrowd, fill.

gremito *adj.* overcrowded (*with*).

grep'pia *f.* crib, manger.

gres *m.* sandstone; stoneware.

greto *m.* gravel bank.

grettezza *f.* narrow-mindedness; stinginess.

gretto *adj.* narrow-minded; stingy.

greve *adj.* heavy.

grezzo *adj.* raw, coarse; unrefined.

gridare *vi.*, *vi.* to cry, cry out, shout; to yell; to bellow; to scream; to scold.

grido *m.* cry, shout, yell, squeal, scream: di —, famous; l'ultimo — della moda, the height of fashion.

grifagno *adj.* predatory; fierce.

grifo *m.* snout; gryphon.

grifone *m.* gryphon; griffon.

grigiastro *adj.* grayish.

gri'gio *adj.* gray.

gri'glia *f.* grate; gridiron; grid.

grilletto *m.* trigger.

grillo *m.* cricket; (*fig.*) whim, fancy.

grimaldello *m.* picklock.

grin'fia *f.* claw, clutch.

grinta *f.* grim countenance.

grinza *f.* wrinkle; crease.

grinzoso *adj.* wrinkly; creasy.

grippag'gio *m.* (*mach.*) seizing.

grippare *vi.* (*mach.*) to seize.

griselle *f.pl.* (*naut.*) ratlines.

grissino *m.* bread stick.

grisù *m.* firedamp.

gromma *f.* tartar.

gronda *f.* eaves (*pl.*).

gronda'ia *f.* gutter.

grondante *adj.* pouring, dripping.

grondare *vt.*, *vi.* to shed, pour (*out*), drip; to be drenched: — sangue, to bleed.

groppa *f.* back; horseback.

groppata *f.* curvet, buck.

groppo *m.* knot; lump.

groppone *m.* back, shoulders.

grossa *f.* (*12 dozen*) gross (*pl.* gross).

grossezza *f.* thickness; bulk, size; coarseness.

grossista *m.* wholesaler.

grosso *m.* gross, main, bulk. *adj.* big, bulky; thick; swollen; large; coarse; hard: mare —, rough sea; il dito —, the big toe; un pezzo — (*fig.*) a bigwig; caccia grossa, big-game hunting; fare la voce grossa,

to raise one's voice; to storm; sbagliare di —, to be grossly mistaken.

grossolanità *f.* coarseness; boorishness.

grossolano *adj.* coarse; boorish.

grotta *f.* grotto, cave.

grottesco *adj.* grotesque.

groviera *m.* gruyère.

grovi'glio *m.* tangle, snarl.

gru *f.* crane.

gruc'cia *f.* crutch; perch; hanger.

gruera *m.* gruyère.

grufolare *vi.* to grub, snout.

grugnire *vi.* to grunt.

grugnito *m.* grunt.

grugno *m.* snout.

grulleri'a *f.* foolishness.

grullo *m.* fool. *adj.* foolish.

grumo *m.* clot.

gruppetto *m.* cluster; small group.

gruppo *m.* group, set.

gruz'zolo *m.* hoard, savings.

guadagnare *vt.*, guadagnarsi *vr.* to earn, gain; to get; to win; to reach; to look better.

guadagnato *adj.* earned, gained; deserved: tanto di —, so much the better.

guadagno *m.* earning; earnings; gain, advantage; profit; winnings.

guadare *vt.* to ford.

guado *m.* ford.

gua'ina *f.* case; scabbard, sheath.

gua'io *m.* trouble, scrape; accident, mishap; inconvenience; damage: il tuo — è che..., the trouble with you is that...

guaire *vi.* to yelp; to whine.

guaito *m.* yelp; whine.

gualcire *vt.* to crumple.

gualdrappa *f.* saddlecloth.

guan'cia *f.* cheek.

guanciale *m.* pillow.

guanta'io *m.* glover.

guantiera *f.* tray.

guanto *m.* glove: gettare (raccogliere) il —, to fling down (to take up) the gauntlet; calzare come un —, to suit to a turn.

guantone *m.* mitten, boxing glove.

guardaboschi *m.* forester.

guardacac'cia *m.* gamekeeper.

guardacoste *m.* coast guard.

guardafili *m.* lineman.

guardali'nee *m.* (*sport*) linesman.

guardaportone *m.* doorkeeper.

guardare *vt.*, *vi.* to eye; to look (*at, on, upon, up, etc.*); to look after; to guard; to look out, mind; to see to it (*that*): — la realtà, to face facts; non — in faccia a nessuno, to make no distinctions; guarda, guarda! well, well!; guardarsi *vr.*

to look at each other; to abstain, forbear (*from*); to avoid; to beware.

guardaroba *f.* wardrobe; closet; cloakroom.

guardarobiera *f.* seamstress; check girl.

guardarobiere *m.* cloakroom attendant.

guardasala *m.* warden.

guardasigilli *m.* attorney general.

guar'dia *f.* watch, lookout; watchman; guard, policeman; flyleaf: **turno di —**, watch; **cambio della —**, relief; **— medica**, emergency hospital, first-aid station.

guardiamarina *m.* ensign: **allievo —**, midshipman.

guardiano *m.* watchman; keeper.

guardina *f.* guardroom.

guardingo *adj.* wary, cautious.

guarigione *f.* recovery.

guarire *vt.* to heal, cure; to rid;|*vi.* to recover (*from*); to get rid (*of*).

Guarneri, Giuseppe Antonio, Italian violinmaker (1683–1745).

guarnigione *f.* garrison.

guarnire *vt.* to trim; to adorn; to equip; to garnish; (*naut.*) to rig.

guarnizione *f.* trimming; garnish; (*mach.*) packing.

guascone *m.* Gascon.

guastafeste *m.* kill-joy, spoilsport.

guastare *vt.* to spoil; to destroy, wreck; to mar; to taint, infect; (*mach.*) to put out of gear; **guastarsi** *vr.* to spoil, get spoiled; to rot, decay; (*mach.*) to get out of gear; to quarrel; to become overcast.

guastatore *m.* (*mil.*) commando.

guasto *m.* damage; breakdown. *adj.* spoiled; wrecked; rotten, decayed; (*mach.*) out of gear.

guatare *vt.* to watch; to look askance at.

guazza *f.* dew.

guazzabu'glio *m.* medley; mess.

guazzare *vi.*, *vi.* to wallow.

guazzetto *m.* stew.

guer'cio *m.* squint-eyed.

guernire *see* **guarnire**.

guerra *f.* war; warfare.

guerrafonda'io *m.* warmonger.

Guerrazzi, Francesco Domenico, Italian author and patriot, *Beatrice Cenci* (1804–1873).

guerreggiare *vi.* to fight.

guerresco *adj.* warlike.

guerriero *m.* warrior. *adj.* warlike; martial; bellicose.

guerri'glia *f.* irregular war, skirmish.

guerrigliero *m.* guerrilla.

gufo *m.* owl.

gu'glia *f.* spire, pinnacle.

gugliata *f.* needleful.

Guicciardini, Francesco, Italian historian (1483–1540).

guida *f.* guide; guidance; leadership; guidebook; directory; driving; (*mach.*) slide: **— interna, sedan; —a destra, (a sinistra)**, right- (left)hand drive.

guidare *vt.*, *vi.* to guide; to lead; to drive; (*naut.*) to steer.

guidatore *m.*, **guidatrice** *f.* driver.

guiderdone *m.* reward.

Guido d'Arezzo, Italian reformer of music (990–1050).

guidoslitta *f.* bobsleigh.

guinza'glio *m.* leash.

guisa *f.* way, guise: **a — di**, as; **in — che**, so that.

guitto *m.* (*theat.*) stroller, "barnstormer."

guizzare *vi.* to dart; to swim; to flash.

guizzo *m.* dart; flash.

gu'scio *m.* case; pod; shell.

gustare *vt.*, *vi.* to taste, try; to enjoy; to relish.

gusto *m.* taste; enjoyment; pleasure, relish.

gustoso *adj.* tasty, palatable; amusing, funny.

guttaperca *f.* gutta-percha.

gutturale *f.*, *adj.* guttural, rasping.

H

han'gar *m.* hangar, shed.

ha'rem *m.* harem.

havaiano *m.*, *adj.* Hawaiian.

hennè *m.* henna.

hertziano *m.* Hertzian: **onda hertziana**, hertzian wave.

hòi! *interj.* ah! (*to express surprise*); alas! (*to express sorrow*).

honorem, (ad) (*L.*) honorary, *honoris causa.*

hurrà *interj.* hurrah: **lanciare degli —**, to hurrah.

I

iato *m.* (*gramm.*) hiatus.

iattanza *f.* braggadocio.

iattura *f.* calamity.

ibe'rico *adj.* Iberian.

i'brido *m.*, *adj.* hybrid.

ica'stico *adj.* truthlike, lifelike.

iconoclasta *m.* iconoclast.

iconografi'a *f.* iconography.

idalgo *m.* hidalgo.
Iddio *see* Dio.
idea *f.* idea, notion; opinion: neanche per —! not in the least!
ideale *m., adj.* ideal.
idealismo *m.* idealism.
idealista *m.* idealist.
idealizzare *vt.* to idealize.
ideare *vt.* to conceive, imagine; to devise; to plan.
ideatore *m.* inventor, deviser.
iden'tico *adj.* identical.
identificare *vt.* to identify; identificarsi *vr.* to identify oneself.
identificazione *f.* identification.
identità *f.* identity.
ideogramma *m.* ideograph.
ideologi'a *f.* ideology.
idi *m., f.pl.* ides.
idilli'aco *adj.* idyllic.
idil'lio *m.* idyl; romance.
idioma *m.* idiom, language.
idiosincrasi'a *f.* allergy.
idiota *m.* idiot; *adj.* idiotic.
idiotismo *m.* idiom; idiocy.
idiozi'a *f.* idiocy.
idolatrare *vt.* to idolize, worship.
i'dolo *m.* idol.
idoneità *f.* fitness; aptitude.
ido'neo *adj.* qualified; suitable, fit (*for*).
idrante *m.* hydrant.
idrau'lica *f.* hydraulics.
idrau'lico *m.* plumber; *adj.* hydraulic.
i'drico *adj.* hydric.
idrocarburo *m.* hydrocarbon.
idro'filo *adj.* hydrophilous: cotone —, absorbent cotton.
idrofobi'a *f.* hydrophobia.
idro'fobo *adj.* hydrophobic; (*fig.*) rabid.
idrogenare *vt.* to hydrogenate.
idrogenazione *f.* hydrogenation.
idro'geno *m.* hydrogen.
idro'pico *adj.* dropsical.
idroplano *m.* hydroplane, seaplane.
idroscalo *m.* seaplane airport.
idroscivolante *m.* hydroplane.
idrovolante *m.* seaplane.
idro'vora *f.* water pump.
iella *f.* bad luck.
iena *f.* hyena.
iera'tico *adj.* hieratic.
ieri *adv.* yesterday: l'altro —, the day before yesterday; — sera, last night.
iettatore *m.* bird of ill omen; (*fam.*) hoodoo.
iettatura *f.* evil eye; (*fam.*) hoodoo.
igiene *f.* hygiene; sanitation.
igie'nico *adj.* hygienic; sanitary.
ignaro *adj.* unaware, ignorant.
igna'via *f.* sluggishness.
ignavo *adj.* sluggish.

igno'bile *adj.* ignoble.
ignomi'nia *f.* ignominy.
ignominioso *adj.* ignominous.
ignorante *m.* ignoramus, philistine; *adj.* ignorant; illiterate.
ignoranza *f.* ignorance.
ignorare *vt.* not to know; to be unaware of; to ignore.
ignoto *adj.* unknown.
ignudo *adj.* bare, naked.
il *def. art. m.sing.* the.
i'lare *adj.* cheerful, hilarious.
ilarità *f.* hilarity; laughter.
i'lice *f.* ilex, holm oak.
i'lio *m.* ilium (*pl.* ilia).
illanguidire *vt.* to enfeeble; *vt., vi.* to weaken.
illazione *f.* illation; inference, surmise.
ille'cito *adj.* illicit, unlawful.
illegale *adj.* illegal, unlawful.
illegalità *f.* unlawfulness.
illegi'bile *adj.* illegible.
illegit'timo *adj.* illegitimate.
illeso *adj.* unhurt, unharmed, uninjured, safe and sound.
illetterato *m., adj.* illiterate.
illibato *adj.* irreproachable, pure.
illimitato *adj.* unlimited, boundless.
illogicità *f.* illogicalness.
illo'gico *adj.* illogical, absurd.
illu'dere *vt.*[6] to delude, beguile, "kid"; illu'dersi *vr.* to delude, "kid" oneself.
illuminare *vt.* to light up; (*fig.*) to enlighten; illuminarsi *vr.* to light up.
illuminato *adj.* lit; (*fig.*) enlightened.
illuminazione *f.* light, lighting; illumination; (*fig.*) enlightenment.
illusione *f.* delusion; illusion: farsi illusioni, to delude oneself.
illusionismo *m.* legerdemain; (*philos.*) illusionism.
illusionista *m.* conjurer, juggler; (*philos.*) illusionist.
illuso *m.* optimist; dreamer; *adj.* deluded; deceived. *pp. of* illudere.
illuso'rio *adj.* illusory; illusive; deceptive.
illustrare *vt.* to illustrate.
illustrato *adj.* illustrated: cartolina illustrata, picture post card.
illustratore *m.* illustrator; cartoonist.
illustrazione *f.* illustration, picture; drawing; cartoon.
illustre *adj.* illustrious, distinguished.
imbacuccare *vt.*, imbacuccarsi *vr.* to wrap (up).
imbaldanzire *vi.* to embolden; imbaldanzirsi *vr.* to grow bold.
imballag'gio *m.* packing; wrapping paper.
imballare *vt.* to pack (up); imballarsi *vr.* (*of motors*) to race.

imballatore *m.* packer.

imballo *m.* packing.

imbalsamare *vt.* to embalm; to stuff (*animals*).

imbalsamatore *m.* embalmer; stuffer, taxidermist.

imbambolato *adj.* hazy; dull; drowsy; stunned.

imbandierare *vt.* to flag.

imbandire *vt.* to decorate (*the table*).

imbarazzante *adj.* embarrassing, uncomfortable; bewildering.

imbarazzare *vt.* to obstruct, encumber; to embarrass, hinder.

imbarazzato *adj.* obstructed; embarrassed, uneasy; constipated.

imbarazzo *m.* encumbrance; uneasiness; difficulty; embarrassment; constipation.

imbarcadero *m.* landing stage.

imbarcare *vt.* to embark; imbarcarsi *vr.* to embark, sail; to board a ship; to engage (*in*).

imbarcazione *f.* embarkation; boat, craft.

imbarco *m.* embarkation; shipping; loading.

imbardare *vi.* (*aeron.*) to yaw.

imbardata *f.* (*aeron.*) yaw.

imbastardire *vt.* to adulterate; *vi.*, imbastardirsi *vr.* to degenerate.

imbastire *vt.* to baste; to sketch; to start, set up, organize.

imbastitura *f.* basting.

imbat'tersi *vr.* to stumble (*upon*), come (*across*).

imbatti'bile *adj.* undefeatable; unsurpassable.

imbattuto *adj.* undefeated; unsurpassed.

imbavagliare *vt.* to gag.

imbeccare *vt.* to feed; to prompt; to coach.

imbeccata *f.* beakful; (*fig.*) prompting, cue.

imbecillag'gine *f.* foolishness.

imbecille *m.*, *adj.* imbecile.

imbecillità *f.* imbecility.

imbelle *adj.* pusillanimous.

imbellettare *vt.*, imbellettarsi *vr.* to rouge (*oneself*).

imberbe *adj.* beardless.

imbestialire *vt.* to madden; imbestialirsi *vr.* to go berserk.

imbe'vere *vt.* to steep (*in*); (*fig.*) to imbue (*with*); imbe'versi *vr.* to soak (*with*); (*fig.*) to become imbued (*with*).

imbevuto *adj.* soaked; (*fig.*) imbued.

imbiancare *vt.* to whiten; to whitewash; to bleach; *vi.* to whiten.

imbianchino *m.* whitewasher, house painter.

imbianchire *vi.* to whiten.

imbizzarrirsi *vr.* to bolt.

imboccare *vt.* to put into the mouth; to prompt; to enter (*as a road*).

imboccatura *f.* inlet, mouth, entrance; mouthpiece; bit (*of a horse*).

imbocco *see* imboccatura.

imbonimento *m.* claptrap.

imbonire *vt.* to allure; to soothe.

imbonitore *m.* crier, showman.

imboscare *vt.* to corner; imboscarsi *vr.* (*mil.*) to shirk (conscription).

imboscata *f.* ambush.

imboscato *m.* (*mil.*) slacker, shirker.

imboschire *vi.* to plant or grow woods.

imbottigliare *vt.* to bottle (*up*).

imbottire *vt.* to pad; to stuff.

imbottita *f.* quilt.

imbottitura *f.* padding.

imbracciare *vt.* to level (*a gun*).

imbrancare *vt.* to herd; imbrancarsi *vr.* to consort (*with*).

imbrattare *vt.*, imbrattarsi *vr.* to sully, soil.

imbrattatele *m.* dauber.

imbrigliare *vt.* to bridle.

imbroccare *vt.* to hit: imbroccarla, to hit the mark; to succeed.

imbrodare *vt.*, imbrodarsi *vr.* to sully: chi si loda s'imbroda, self-praise is no recommendation.

imbrogliare *vt.* to tangle; to cheat, swindle; imbrogliarsi *vr.* to get mixed up; to get involved.

imbro'glio *m.* mess, tangle; fraud.

imbroglione *m.* swindler.

imbronciarsi *vr.* to pout; to sulk.

imbronciato *adj.* sulky.

imbrunire *vi.* to grow dark: all'—, at nightfall.

imbruttire *vt.* to uglify; *vi.* to grow ugly (*or* uglier).

imbucare *vt.* to mail (*a letter*).

imburrare *vt.* to butter.

imbuto *m.* funnel.

imitare *vt.* to imitate; to mimic.

imitatore *m.* imitator.

imitazione *f.* imitation.

immacolato *adj.* immaculate.

immagazzinare *vt.* to store.

immaginare *vt.* to imagine; to conceive (*of*); to guess, figure; immaginarsi *vr.* to imagine, figure.

immagina'rio *adj.* imaginary.

immaginativa *f.* imagination.

immaginazione *f.* imagination.

imma'gine *f.* image.

immaginoso *adj.* imaginative.

immalinconire *vt.* to sadden.

immanca'bile *adj.* unfailing; certain; usual.

immancabilmente *adv.* without fail.

immane *adj.* huge, gigantic, great.

immangia'bile *adj.* inedible.

immarcesci'bile *adj.* undecayable.
immatricolare *vi.*, immatricolarsi *vr.* to matriculate.
immatricolazione *f.* matriculation; (*univ.*) initiation.
immaturità *f.* immaturity.
immaturo *adj.* immature, unripe; untimely.
immedesimare *vt.* to identify (*with*); immedesimarsi *vr.* to identify oneself (*with*).
immediatamente *adv.* immediately.
immediatezza *f.* immediateness.
immediato *adj.* immediate.
immemora'bile *adj.* immemorial.
imme'more *adj.* forgetful.
immensità *f.* immensity; (*fig.*) lot.
immenso *adj.* immense; huge.
immer'gere *vt.*[51] to dip, immerse; immergersi *vr.* to immerge, plunge.
immeritato *adj.* undeserved.
immersione *f.* immersion: linea d'—, waterline.
immet'tere *vt.*[76] to let in.
immigrante *m.*, *adj.* immigrant.
immigrare *vi.* to immigrate.
immigrazione *f.* immigration.
imminente *adj.* impending; forthcoming.
imminenza *f.* imminence.
immischiare *vt.* to involve; immischiarsi *vr.* to meddle (*with*).
immiserire *vt.* to impoverish.
immissa'rio *m.* affluent.
immissione *f.* immission, introduction
immo'bile *m.* house; (*pl.*) real estate; *adj.* motionless, still; immovable.
immobiliare *adj.* real, landed: agente —, realtor.
immobilità *f.* immobility.
immobilizzare *vt.* to immobilize; immobilizzarsi *vr.* to become motionless.
immolare *vt.* to immolate.
immondezza'io *m.* dump.
immondi'zia *f.* filth; garbage.
immondo *adj.* filthy.
immorale *adj.* immoral.
immoralità *f.* immorality.
immortalare *vt.* to immortalize, make eternal.
immortale *m.*, *adj.* immortal.
immortalità *f.* immortality.
immoto *adj.* motionless.
immune *adj.* immune; uninjured; exempt (*from*).
immunità *f.* immunity.
immunizzare *vt.* to immunize (*against*).
immuta'bile *adj.* immutable.
immutato *adj.* unchanged.
imo *m.* bottom; *adj.* lowermost.
impacchettare *vt.* to parcel.
impacciare *vt.*, *vi.* to hinder, hamper; to trouble.

impacciato *adj.* awkward, clumsy; uneasy, uncomfortable.
impac'cio *m.* hindrance; trouble: essere d'—, to be in the way.
impacco *m.* compress.
impadronirsi *vr.* to grasp, seize, take possession (*of*).
impaga'bile *adj.* priceless.
impaginare *vt.* (*typog.*) to set up as (or make up into) pages.
impaginatore *m.* pager.
impaginazione *f.* (*typog.*) make-up.
impagliare *vt.* to wicker; to straw; to stuff (*as animals*).
impalato *adj.* (*fig.*) stiff.
impalcatura *f.* scaffolding; frame.
impallidire *vi.* to pale, turn pale.
impalpa'bile *adj.* impalpable.
impanare *vt.* (*cook.*) to bread; (*mach.*) to thread.
impantanare *vt.*, impantanarsi *vr.* to swamp.
impaperarsi *vr.* to blunder, flounder.
impappinarsi *vr.* to blunder, stammer.
imparare *vt.* to learn: — a memoria, to learn by heart.
impareggia'bile *adj.* imcomparable.
imparentarsi *vr.* to become related; to marry.
im'pari *adj.* odd; unequal; unfit (*for*).
impartire *vt.* to impart.
imparziale *adj.* impartial, unbiased.
imparzialità *f.* impartiality.
impassi'bile *adj.* impassive; unmoved.
impassibilità *f.* impassiveness.
impastare *vt.* to knead; to impaste; to paste.
impastatrice *f.* kneading machine.
impasto *m.* dough; mixture.
impastoiare *vt.* to fetter.
impataccare *vt.* to besmear.
impaurire *vt.* to scare; impaurirsi *vr.* to get scared.
impaurito *adj.* scared, afraid.
impa'vido *adj.* fearless.
impaziente *adj.* impatient; eager.
impazientirsi *vr.* to lose one's patience; to get angry.
impazienza *f.* impatience; eagerness.
impazzare *vi.* to go mad; to run riot.
impazzata *f.* folly: all'—, madly.
impazzire *vi.* to go mad, become insane; to run riot: fare —, to drive mad.
impazzito *adj.* crazed, mad.
impecca'bile *adj.* faultless.
impeciare *vt.* to tar.
impedimento *m.* hindrance; obstacle; illness; trouble.
impedire *vt.* to prevent; to avoid; to hinder; to obstruct; to stop.
impegnare *vt.* to pawn, pledge; to bind; to engage; to retain; im-

pegnarsi *vr.* to promise, undertake (*to*); to bind oneself.

impegnativo *adj.* binding; challenging.

impegno *m.* engagement; pledge, promise; care; obligation.

impegolarsi *vr.* (*fig.*) to get involved.

impelagarsi *vr.* to involve oneself, get in trouble.

impellente *adj.* impellent, urging.

impellicciare *vt.* to fur; to veneer.

impellicciatura *f.* veneering.

impenetra'bile *adj.* impenetrable.

impenetrabilità *f.* impenetrableness; (*phys.*) impenetrability.

impenitente *adj.* unrepenting; confirmed.

impennaggi *m.pl.* (*aeron.*) tail vanes.

impennare *vt.* (*aeron.*) to zoom; impennarsi *vr.* to rear; (*fig.*) to rear up; (*aeron.*) to zoom, nose up.

impennata *f.* rearing; (*aeron.*) zoom.

impensato *adj.* unexpected; unforeseen.

impensierire *vt.* impensierirsi *vr.* to worry.

imperante *adj.* ruling; (*fig.*) prevailing.

imperare *vi.* to rule (*over*); (*fig.*) to prevail.

imperativo *m.*, *adj.* imperative.

imperatore *m.* emperor.

imperatrice *f.* empress.

impercetti'bile *adj.* imperceptible.

imperdona'bile *adj.* unpardonable.

imperfetto *m.* imperfect (*tense*); *adj.* imperfect, faulty.

imperfezione *f.* imperfection, fault, flaw.

imperiale *m.* imperial; upper deck (*of a bus, etc.*); *adj.* imperial.

imperialismo *m.* imperialism.

impe'rio *m.* rule, authority.

imperiosità *f.* imperiousness.

imperioso *adj.* imperious, domineering.

imperituro *adj.* immortal; eternal.

imperi'zia *f.* unskillfulness.

imperlare *vt.* to bead; to dew.

impermalire *vt.* to offend, hurt, vex; impermalirsi *vr.* to sulk: impermalirsi di, per, to resent.

imperma'bile *m.*, *adj.* waterproof.

impermeabilità *f.* impermeability.

imperniare *vt.* to pivot; imperniarsi *vr.* to hinge.

impero *m.* empire.

imperscruta'bile *adj.* inscrutable.

impersonale *adj.* impersonal.

impersonare *vt.* to impersonate.

imperter'rito *adj.* undaunted.

impertinente *adj.* impertinent, pert.

impertinenza *f.* impertinence.

imperturba'bile *adj.* imperturbable.

imperturbabilità *f.* imperturbability, composure.

imperversare *vi.* to storm, rage; to run riot.

imper'vio *adj.* impervious.

im'peto *m.* rush; impact; impulse; vehemence; transport.

impetrare *vt.* to impetrate.

impettito *adj.* strutting; stiff.

impetuosità *f.* impetuosity.

impetuoso *adj.* impetuous; rash.

impiallacciare *vt.* to veneer.

impiallacciatura *f.* veneering.

impiantare *vt.* to found, establish; to set up.

impiantito *m.* floor.

impianto *m.* establishment: setting up; plant, outfit.

impiastrare, impiastricciare *vt.* to besmear; to daub.

impiastro *m.* plaster; poultice; (*fig.*) bore.

impiccagione *f.* hanging.

impiccare *vt.* to hang.

impiccato *adj.* hanged.

impicciare *vt.* to hinder; impicciarsi *vr.* to meddle (*with*).

impic'cio *m.* hindrance nuisance; trouble.

impiccione *m.* busybody.

impiccolire *vt.* to reduce, lessen.

impiegare *vt.* to employ; to use, apply; to invest; to spend: ci impiegherò tre giorni, it will take me three days; impiegarsi *vr.* to employ oneself, find a job.

impiegati'zio *adj.* clerical.

impiegato *m.* employee, clerk.

impiego *m.* employment, job; use, application.

impietosire *vt.* to stir pity, touch; impietosirsi *vr.* to relent, feel touched; to feel sorry (*for*).

impietrire *vt.*, *vi.* to petrify.

impigliare *vt.* to entangle; impigliarsi *vr.* to get entangled.

impigrire *vt.* to enervate make lazy; *vi.* to grow lazy.

impinguare *vt.*, *vi.*, impinguarsi *vr.* to fatten.

impinzare *vt.*, impinzarsi *vr.* to cram, stuff (*oneself*).

impiombare *vt.* to lead; to plumb, seal; to stop (*teeth*).

impiombatura *f.* leading, lead seal; stopping.

implaca'bile *adj.* implacable.

implicare *vt.* to implicate, involve; to imply.

impli'cito *adj.* implicit.

implorare *vt.* to entreat.

implorazione *f.* entreaty.

implume *adj.* featherless.

impolverare *vt.* to make dusty; impolverarsi *vr.* to get dusty.

impolverato *adj.* dusty.

impomatare vt. to pomade.
impondera'bile adj. imponderable.
imponente adj. imposing, stately; powerful.
imponenza f. imposingness, stateliness; powerfulness.
impopolare adj. unpopular.
impopolarità f. unpopularity.
imporre vt.[93] to impose, force upon; to call for: — un nome, to give a name (to); — rispetto, to command respect; imporsi vr. to prevail (upon); to be imperative; to inspire awe; to win.
importante m. (the) essential, (main) point; adj. important.
importanza f. importance, consequence: darsi —, to look big.
importare (1) vt. to import (goods).
importare (2) vt. to imply, involve; to call for; vi.impers. to matter; to be necessary, essential; to care: non importa! it does not matter; non me ne importa, I don't care.
importatore m. importer.
importazione f. import, importation.
importo m. amount, cost.
importunare vt. to importune, nag, tease.
importuno m. bore; adj. importunate; irksome.
imposizione f. imposition.
impossessarsi see impadronirsi.
impossi'bile adj. impossible.
impossibilità f. impossibility.
imposta (1) f. shutter.
imposta (2) f. duty, tax.
impostare vt. to start, begin; to post, mail; to attune (one's voice); to lay (a ship).
impostazione f. starting; laying; mailing.
impostore m. impostor.
impostura f. imposture.
impotente m. impotent; adj. impotent; powerless; helpless.
impotenza f. impotence.
impoverimento m. impoverishment.
impoverire vt. to impoverish; impoverirsi vr. to grow poor, go to seed.
impratica'bile adj. impracticable.
impraticabilità f. impracticability.
impratichire vt. to train; to familiarize (with); impratichirsi vr. to get trained; to become conversant, familiar (with).
imprecare vi. to curse.
imprecazione f. imprecation, oath.
imprecisione f. vagueness; inaccuracy.
impreciso adj. vague; inaccurate.
impregiudicato adj. unprejudiced.
impregnare vt. to impregnate, saturate, imbue (with), soak, steep (in).

imprendi'bile adj. impregnable; elusive.
imprenditore m. contractor.
impreparato adj. unprepared; unaware.
impreparazione f. unpreparedness.
impresa f. enterprise; deed; company.
impresa'rio m. contractor; (theat.) impresario, manager: — di pompe funebri, undertaker.
imprescindi'bile adj. indispensable; unavoidable.
impressiona'bile adj. impressionable.
impressionante adj. striking; awesome; frightful.
impressionare vt. to impress; to disturb; to shock, strike; (photo.) to expose; impressionarsi vr. to be impressed or disturbed; to become afraid.
impressione f. impression.
impressionismo m. impressionism.
impresso adj. printed; engraved. pp. of imprimere.
imprevedi'bile adj. unforeseeable.
impreveduto adj. unforeseen; unexpected.
imprevidente adj. improvident.
imprevidenza f. improvidence.
imprevisto adj. unexpected, unforeseen.
imprigionare vt. to imprison.
impri'mere vt.,[29] imprimersi vr. to impress.
improba'bile adj. unlikely.
improbabilità f. unlikelihood.
improbità f. improbity.
im'probo adj. hard; dishonest.
improduttivo adj. unproductive; unprofitable.
impronta f. impression, print, mark; footprint: impronte digitali, fingerprints.
improntare vt. to characterize; impress.
improntitu'dine f. impudence.
imprope'rio m. insult.
impropi'zio adj. unfavorable.
impropriamente adv. improperly; loosely.
improprietà f. impropriety.
impro'prio adj. improper; unsuitable.
improroga'bile adj. undelayable.
improv'vido adj. improvident.
improvvisamente adj. suddenly; unexpectedly.
improvvisare vt. to improvise; to ad-lib; improvvisarsi vr. to turn (out).
improvvisata f. surprise.
improvvisato adj. ex tempore.
improvvisatore m. improviser.
improvvisazione f. extemporization, improvisation, ad lib.

improvviso m. (mus.) impromptu; adj.
sudden: all'—, suddenly.
imprudente adj. imprudent; rash.
imprudenza f. imprudence, rashness.
impudente adj. impudent, pert.
impudenza f. impudence.
impudici'zia f. shamelessness.
impu'dico adj. shameless, brazen, immodest.
impugnare vt. to grip, wield; to
impugn.
impugnatura f. grip, handle; hilt.
impulsività f. impulsiveness.
impulsivo adj. impulsive, rash.
impulso m. impulse, impact; urge;
drive; motive; (phys.) impulsion:
dare — a, to promote.
impunemente adv. safely.
impunità f. impunity.
impunito adj. unpunished.
impuntarsi vr. to insist (on), persist
(in), set one's mind (on, to); to stop
short; to stutter.
impuntigliarsi vr. to persist (in), set
one's mind (on, to).
impuntura f. stitching, sewing.
impurità f. impurity.
impuro adj. impure; tainted.
imputare vt. to ascribe, impute; to
charge (with).
imputato m. defendant; a dj. accused.
imputazione f. imputation; charge.
imputridire vi. to rot.
in prep. in, at; to; within; into; with,
by; inside; on, upon; against:
eravamo — tre, we were three.
ina'bile adj. inept; unqualified.
inabilità f. inability, disability.
inabilitare vt. to disable; to disqualify.
inabilitazione f. disqualification.
inabissare vt., inabissarsi vr. to sink.
inabita'bile adj. uninhabitable.
inabitabilità f. uninhabitability.
inabitato adj. uninhabited.
inaccessi'bile adj. inaccessible.
inaccetta'bile adj. inacceptable.
inacidire vi. to sour.
inacidito adj. sour.
inadatto see disadatto.
inadeguato adj. inadequate.
inadempiente adj. unfulfilling.
inafferra'bile adj. unseizable; elusive.
inalazione f. inhalation.
inalberare vt. to hoist; inalberarsi vr.
to rear up.
inaltera'bile adj. inalterable.
inalterato adj. unaltered.
inamidare vt. to starch.
inammissi'bile adj. inadmissible; preposterous.
inamovi'bile adj. irremovable; steadfast.
inane adj. inane; futile.

inanellato adj. curly; ringleted;
beringed.
inanimato adj. lifeless.
inappagato adj. ungratified.
inappella'bile adj. unappellable.
inappetenza f. inappetence.
inapprezza'bile adj. inappreciable.
inappunta'bile adj. faultless; dapper.
inarcare vt., inarcarsi vr. to arch,
camber: inarcare le sopracciglia, to
raise one's eyebrows.
inargentare vt. to silver.
inaridire vt. to dry, parch; vi., inaridirsi vr. to dry up.
inaridito adj. dry; hardened.
inarriva'bile adj. unattainable; superlative.
inaspettato adj. unexpected.
inasprimento m. exacerbation.
inasprire vt. to embitter; to aggravate; to exacerbate; to sharpen;
inasprirsi vr. to grow bitter; to
sharpen.
inastare vt. to hoist: — una baionetta,
to fix a bayonet.
inattacca'bile adj. unassailable.
inatteso adj. unexpected.
inattivo adj. inactive, inert.
inaudito adj. unheard-of; incredible.
inaugurale adj. inaugural, opening:
viaggio —, maiden voyage.
inaugurare vt. to inaugurate, open.
inaugurazione f. inauguration, open-
inavveduto adj. rash. [ing.
inavvertenza f. inadvertence.
inavvertitamente adv. heedlessly; unintentionally; carelessly.
inavvertito adj. unnoticed.
incagliare vt. to hinder; to strand; to
get stuck; (mach.) to jam; incagliarsi vr. to strand; to jam; to run
aground; to become stuck.
inca'glio m. hindrance; jamming.
incalcola'bile adj. incalculable.
incallire vt., incallirsi vr. to harden.
incallito adj. hardened, inveterate.
incalzante adj. pressing.
incalzare vt., vi. to press, chase; to
urge.
incamerare vt. to confiscate, sequester.
incamminare vt. to start; to set going;
to direct; incamminarsi vr. to set
out (for); to start walking.
incanalare vt. to canalize.
incancella'bile adj. ineffaceable.
incancrenire vi. to gangrene.
incandescente adj. incandescent.
incandescenza f. incandescence.
incannare vt. to wind, spool.
incantare vt. to charm, enchant;
incantarsi vr. to become spellbound;
to jam, get stuck.
incantato adj. spellbound; enchanted,
magic; jammed, stuck.

incantatore m. enchanter.
incantatrice f. enchantress.
incante'simo m. spell, charm.
incante'vole adj. charming; delightful.
incanto (1) m. enchantment, magic:
d'—, wonderfully.
incanto (2) m. auction: vendere all'—,
to sell at auction.
incanutire vi. to hoar.
incanutito adj. hoary.
incapace m., adj. incapable.
incapacità f. inability, incapacity.
incaponirsi see ostinarsi.
incappare vi. to stumble (on, upon);
to incur, run into.
incappucciare vt. to hood.
incapricciarsi vr. to take a fancy (to).
incarcerare vt. to imprison.
incaricare vt. to entrust (with), charge
(with); incaricarsi vr. to charge
oneself (with), see to it, attend (to).
incaricato m. deputy, messenger: —
d'affari, chargé d'affaires.
inca'rico m. task, errand; office, duty;
mission: per — di, in behalf of.
incarnare vt. to incarnate, embody.
incarnato m. complexion; adj. incarnate.
incarnazione f. incarnation.
incarnito adj. ingrown.
incartamento m. dossier, file.
incartapecorito adj. parchmentlike.
incartare vt. to wrap in paper.
incasellare vt. to pigeonhole.
incassare vt., vi. to box; to cash, collect, bring in; to fit (in); (boxing) to
take it.
incasso m. collection; receipts.
incastellatura f. frame.
incastonare vt. to set.
incastrare vt. to infix; to insert; to
fit (in, together); to mortise; to
embed; incastrarsi vr. to get embedded, jam; to squeeze (into).
incastro m. fitting together; socket;
groove; mortise; inlaid work.
incatenare vt. to chain.
incatramare vt. to tar.
incautamente adv. rashly.
incauto adj. rash, incautious.
incavallatura f. roof truss.
incavare vt., incavarsi vr. to hollow,
cave in.
incavato adj. hollow.
incavatura f. hollow.
incavo m. hollow, cavity.
ince'dere vi. to stride.
incendiare vt. to set on fire; incendiarsi
vr. to take fire.
incendia'rio m. arsonist; adj. incendi-
ary.
incen'dio m. conflagration, fire: —
doloso, arson; pompa da —, fire
engine.

incenerire vt. to incinerate, burn to
ashes.
incensamento m. (fig.) flattery.
incensare vt. to incense; (fig.) to
flatter.
incensatore m. flatterer.
incenso m. incense.
incensurato adj. blameless; crimeless.
incentivo m. incentive.
inceppare vt., inceparsi vr. to jam.
incerata f. oilcloth.
incertezza f. uncertainty, doubt.
incerto adj. uncertain, dubious;
doubtful; unsteady.
incespicare vi. to stumble.
incessante adj. steady, unceasing.
incesto m. incest.
incetta f. cornering.
incettare vt. to corner.
incettatore m. cornerer.
inchiesta f. inquiry, investigation.
inchinare vt. to bend; inchinarsi vr. to
bow; to submit.
inchino m. bow; curtsy.
inchiodare vt. to nail; to rivet (as
one's eyes); to hammer.
inchiostrare vt. to ink.
inchiostro m. ink.
inciampare vi. to stumble (over); to
bump (into); to chance (upon).
inciampo m. hitch, hindrance.
incidentale adj. incidental.
incidentalmente adv. incidentally; by
the way.
incidente m., adj. incident.
inci'dere vt.[41] to engrave; to etch;
(surg.) to incise.
incinta adj.f. pregnant.
incipiente adj. incipient.
incipriare vt., incipriarsi vr. to powder
(oneself).
incirca, (all') adv. about.
incisione f. incision; notch; engraving, etching.
incisivo m. incisor (tooth); adj. in-
cisive.
incisore m. engraver, etcher.
incitamento m. incitement.
incitare vt. to urge, stimulate, incite.
incivile adj. uncivilized; boorish.
incivilire vt., incivilirsi vr. to civilize.
inclemente adj. merciless; inclement.
inclemenza f. mercilessness; inclem-
ency.
inclinare vt., vi. to incline, bend, lean,
tilt; inclinarsi vr. to lean, bend; to
incline; to slant.
inclinazione f. inclination; slope;
bent; talent; tendency.
incline adj. inclined, bent.
inclu'dere vt.[3] to include.
incluso adj. included.
incoerente adj. incoherent, inconsistent.

incoerenza *f.* incoherence, inconsistency.

inco'gliere *vi.*[37] to befall.

inco'gnita *f.* (*math.*) unknown quantity; (*fig.*) uncertainty.

inco'gnito *m.* incognito; *adj.* incognito; unknown: **viaggiare in —**, to travel incognito.

incollare *vt.* to paste, stick, glue; to gum; **incollarsi** *vr.* to stick (*to*).

incollatura *f.* sticking; (*turf*) neck.

incollerirsi *vr.* to get angry.

incollerito *adj.* angry.

incolore *adj.* colorless.

incolpa'bile *adj.* accusable.

incolpabilità *f.* innocence.

incolpare *vt.* to accuse (*of*), charge (*with*), blame (*for*).

incolto *adj.* uncultivated; unlearned.

inco'lume *adj.* unhurt, uninjured.

incolumità *f.* safety.

incombente *adj.* impending.

incombenza *f.* errand, task.

incom'bere *vi.* to impend; to be incumbent (*upon*); to be up to.

incominciare *vt.*, *vi.* to begin, start.

incommensura'bile *adj.* incommensurable.

incomodare *vt.* to inconvenience, disturb; **incomodarsi** *vr.* to bother.

inco'modo *m.* inconvenience; *adj.* inconvenient, bothersome; uncomfortable.

incompara'bile *adj.* incomparable, matchless.

incompati'bile *adj.* incompatible, inconsistent, incongruous.

incompatibilità *f.* incompatibility, inconsistency, incongruity.

incompetente *m.*, *adj.* incompetent.

incompetenza *f.* incompetence.

incompiuto *adj.* unfinished.

incompleto *adj.* incomplete.

incomposto *adj.* disorderly; unseemly, unbecoming, unmannerly.

incomprensi'bile *adj.* incomprehensible, unintelligible.

incomprensione *f.* incomprehension, lack of understanding.

incompreso *adj.* misunderstood.

inconcepi'bile *adj.* inconceivable.

inconcilia'bile *adj.* irreconcilable.

inconcludente *adj.* inconclusive.

inconcusso *adj.* unshaken, firm.

incondizionato *adj.* unconditional.

inconfessa'bile *adj.* unavowable.

inconfessato *adj.* unavowed.

inconfuta'bile *adj.* unconfutable.

incongruente *adj.* inconsistent.

incongruenza *f.* inconsistency.

incongruità *f.* incongruity.

incon'gruo *adj.* incongruous.

inconsape'vole *adj.* unconscious, unaware.

incon'scio *m.*, *adj.* unconscious.

inconsiderato *adj.* rash.

inconsistente *adj.* flimsy.

inconsistenza *f.* flimsiness.

inconsueto *adj.* unusual.

inconsulto *adj.* unadvised, rash.

incontaminato *adj.* unpolluted.

incontentabile *adj.* insatiable; hard to please.

incontesta'bile *adj.* incontestable.

incontrare *vt.* to meet, encounter; to meet with; to find; **incontrarsi** *vr.* to meet; to agree.

incontrastato *adj.* undisputed.

incontro (1) *m.* meeting, encounter; rendezvous; match, game, fight.

incontro (2) *prep.* towards, to; opposite: **andare — a metà strada**, to meet halfway; **andare — a guai**, to be in for trouble.

inconveniente *m.* inconvenience, contretemps, hitch; shortcoming.

incoraggiamento *m.* encouragement.

incoraggiante *adj.* encouraging.

incoraggiare *vt.* to encourage.

incorniciare *vt.* to frame.

incoronare *vt.* to crown.

incoronazione *f.* coronation.

incorporare *vt.*, **incorporarsi** *vr.* to incorporate; to annex.

incorpo'reo *adj.* incorporeal.

incorreggi'bile *adj.* incorrigible.

incor'rere *vi.*[36] to incur, suffer.

incorrutti'bile *adj.* incorruptible.

incosciente *m.*, *adj.* irresponsible; unconscious; inanimate.

incoscienza *f.* irresponsibility; unconsciousness.

incostante *adj.* inconstant, changeable; unsteady; fickle.

incostanza *f.* inconstancy, changeableness; fickleness.

incredi'bile *adj.* incredible.

incredulità *f.* incredulity.

incre'dulo *m.* skeptic, unbeliever; *adj.* skeptical, unbelieving.

incrementare *vt.* to foster.

incremento *m.* increment.

increscioso *adj.* disagreeable; deplorable, regrettable.

increspare *vt.*, **incresparsi** *vr.* to ripple; to wrinkle; to crisp.

incriminare *vt.* to incriminate.

incriminato *adj.* incriminated; (*fig.*) offending.

incrinare *vt.*, **incrinarsi** *vr.* to crack, flaw.

incrinatura *f.* crack, flaw.

incrociare *vt.* to cross; to fold; *vi.* (*naut.*) to cruise; **incrociarsi** *vr.* to cross.

incrociato *adj.* crossed: **parole incrociate**, crossword puzzle; **punto —**, cross-stitch.

incrociatore *m.* cruiser.
incro'cio *m.* crossing; cross; cross-roads.
incrolla'bile *adj.* unshakable.
incrostare *vt.* to incrust; to inlay; incrostarsi *vr.* to become incrusted.
incrostazione *f.* incrustation.
incruento *adj.* bloodless.
incubatrice *f.* incubator.
incubazione *f.* incubation.
in'cubo *m.* nightmare, incubus.
incu'dine *f.* anvil.
inculcare *vt.* to inculcate (*on, upon*), to impress (*on, upon*).
incuneare *vt.* to wedge.
incura'bile *m., adj.* incurable.
incurante *adj.* heedless.
incu'ria *f.* neglect.
incuriosire *vt.* to make curious, intrigue; incuriosirsi *vr.* to become curious.
incuriosito *adj.* intrigued, curious.
incursione *f.* raid, incursion: — aerea, air raid.
incurvare *vt.,* incurvarsi *vr.* to bend, stoop; to curve.
incurvatura *f.* incurvation.
incustodito *adj.* unwatched, unguarded.
incu'tere *vt.*⁴⁶ to rouse, command: — terrore, to strike with terror.
in'daco *m.* indigo.
indaffarato *adj.* busy, bustling.
indagare *vt., vi.* to investigate.
indagatore *m.* investigator; *adj.* searching.
inda'gine *f.* investigation, inquiry.
indebitamente *adv.* unduly.
indebitare *vt.* to burden with debts; indebitarsi *vr.* to run into debt.
inde'bito *adj.* undue.
indebolimento *m.* enfeeblement.
indebolire *vt.* to weaken; indebolirsi *vr.* to weaken; (*fig.*) to fade.
indecente *adj.* indecent.
indecenza *f.* indecency, shame.
indecifra'bile *adj.* indecipherable.
indecisione *f.* indecision, hesitation.
indeciso *adj.* uncertain; irresolute.
indecoroso *adj.* indecorous, unseemly.
indefesso *adj.* unrelenting, indefatigable.
indefini'bile *adj.* indefinable; vague.
indegnità *f.* shamefulness; shame; disgrace; indignity.
indegno *adj.* unworthy; disgraceful.
indelicatezza *f.* indelicacy.
indelicato *adj.* indelicate.
indemoniato *adj.* possessed.
indenne *adj.* undamaged.
indennità *f.* indemnity.
indennizzare *vt.* to indemnify.
indennizzo *m.* indemnity, compensation.

indescrivi'bile *adj.* indescribable.
indeterminato *adj.* indeterminate.
indi *adv.* then; afterwards; hence.
indianista *m.* Indologist.
indiano *m., adj.* Indian.
indiavolato *adj.* frenzied; spirited; excessive.
indicare *vt.* to indicate; to show; to point out; to point at.
indicativo *m., adj.* indicative.
indicato *adj.* fit, suitable; advisable.
indicatore *m.* indicator; gauge; pointer; directory.
indicazione *f.* indication; direction; pointer.
in'dice *m.* index; catalogue; sign; pointer; forefinger: mettere all'—, to place on the (*prohibited*) index.
indici'bile *adj.* inexpressible.
indietreggiare *vi.* to back, fall back, draw back; to withdraw, give way; to shrink.
indietro *adv.* back; backward; backwards; behind; behindhand: il mio orologio è — di tre minuti, my watch is three minutes slow.
indifeso *adj.* defenseless, unprotected.
indifferente *m., adj.* indifferent: egli (ciò) mi è —, he (this) is nothing to me, I can take him (it) or leave him (it).
indifferenza *f.* indifference.
indi'geno *m., adj.* native.
indigente *m., adj.* poor.
indigenza *f.* poverty.
indigestione *f.* indigestion.
indigesto *adj.* indigestible; uncongenial; boresome.
indignare *vt.* to make indignant; to incense, shock; indignarsi *vr.* to become indignant, be outraged.
indignato *adj.* indignant, outraged.
indignazione *f.* indignation.
indimentica'bile *adj.* unforgettable.
indipendente *m., adj.* independent.
indipendentemente *adv.* independently (*of*).
indipendenza *f.* independence.
indire *vt.* to call; to fix.
indirettamente *adv.* indirectly.
indiretto *adj.* indirect.
indirizzare *vt.* to address; to direct.
indirizzo *m.* address; direction; turn; bent.
indisciplina *f.* indiscipline, lack of discipline.
indisciplinato *adj.* unruly.
indiscreto *adj.* indiscreet, inquisitive.
indiscrezione *f.* indiscretion; blunder.
indiscusso *adj.* undisputed.
indiscuti'bile *adj.* indisputable.
indiscutibilmente *adv.* indisputably, unquestionably.
indispensa'bile *adj., m.* indispensable.

indispettire *vt.* to peeve; **indispettirsi** *vr.* to get sore.

indisporre *vt.* to indispose; to disgust, annoy, vex.

indisposizione *f.* indisposition.

indisposto *adj.* indisposed, ill.

indissolu'bile *adj.* indissoluble.

indistinto *adj.* indistinct, dim, vague.

indistrutti'bile *adj.* indestructible.

indisturbato *adj.* unmolested.

indi'via *f.* endive.

individuale *adj.* individual.

individualmente *adv.* individually.

individuare *vt.* to individuate; to single out; to spot.

indivi'duo *m.* individual; fellow, "guy," man.

indivisi'bile *adj.* indivisible; (*fig.*) inseparable.

indiviso *adj.* undivided.

indizia'rio *adj.* circumstantial.

indiziato *m.*, *adj.* suspect.

indi'zio *m.* clue, symptom.

indo'cile *adj.* unruly, indocile.

in'dole *f.* disposition, temper; character, nature.

indolente *adj.* indolent, lazy.

indolenza *f.* indolence, laziness.

indolenzimento *adj.* aching.

indolenzire *vi.* to ache; **indolenzirsi** *vr.* to become sore.

indolenzito *adj.* aching.

indoma'bile *adj.* untamable; indomitable.

indomani *m.* morrow: all'—, on the morrow, the following day.

indo'mito *adj.* indomitable.

indorare *vt.* to gild: — la pillola, to sugar-coat the pill.

indorato *adj.*, *pp.* gilt.

indoratore *m.* gilder.

indoratura *f.* gilding.

indossare *vt.* to wear; to don, put on.

indossatrice *f.* model, mannequin.

indosso *adv.* on: avere, mettere —, to have (to put) on.

indotto *m.* (*elec.*) rotor; *adj.* induced. *pp.* of indurre.

indovinare *vt.* to guess; to foresee; to imagine: indovinarla, to guess right; to hit the mark.

indovinato *adj.* felicitous, effective.

indovinello *m.* riddle, puzzle.

indovino *m.* diviner; fortuneteller.

indubbiamente *adv.* certainly.

indub'bio *adj.* certain.

indugiare *vi.* to delay, linger; to hesitate; to dwell (*upon*).

indu'gio *m.* delay: rompere gli indugi, to stop being hesitant, to make up one's mind and take decisive action.

indulgente *adj.* indulgent, lenient.

indulgenza *f.* indulgence, leniency.

indul'gere *vi.*[69] to be indulgent (*to*); to allow; to indulge (*in*).

indulto *m.* pardon; indult.

indumento *m.* garment; (*pl.*) clothes.

indurimento *m.* hardening.

indurire *vt.*, *vi.* to harden.

indurre *vt.*[8] to induce; to lead; to persuade; **indursi** *vr.* to bring oneself (*to*).

indu'stria *f.* industry; manufacture.

industriale *m.* manufacturer, industrialist; *adj.* industrial.

industrializzare *vt.* to industrialize.

industrializzazione *f.* industrialization.

industriarsi *vr.* to endeavor (*to*); to make shift.

industrioso *adj.* industrious; enterprising, energetic.

induttivo *adj.* inductive.

induttore *m.* inductor.

induzione *f.* induction.

inebetire *vt.*, *vi.* to dull.

inebetito *adj.* dazed, stupefied.

inebriare *vt.* to inebriate, intoxicate.

ineccepi'bile *adj.* unexceptionable.

ine'dia *f.* starvation.

ine'dito *adj.* unpublished.

ineducato *adj.* ill-bred, rude.

ineffa'bile *adj.* ineffable.

inefficace *adj.* ineffectual.

ineffica'cia *f.* inefficacy.

ineguaglianza *see* disuguaglianza.

ineguagliato *adj.* unequaled.

ineguale *see* disuguale.

inelutta'bile *adj.* ineluctable, inevitable.

inenarra'bile *adj.* unspeakable, untellable.

inerente *adj.* inherent.

inerenza *f.* inherence.

inerme *adj.* unarmed, defenseless.

inerpicarsi *vr.* to clamber.

inerte *adj.* inert; idle.

iner'zia *f.* inertness; inertia; idleness.

inesattezza *f.* inaccuracy; mistake.

inesatto *adj.* inaccurate, inexact.

inesaudito *adj.* ungranted.

inesauri'bile *adj.* inexhaustible.

inescusa'bile *adj.* inexcusable.

inesigi'bile *adj.* uncollectible.

inesistente *adj.* inexistent.

inesistenza *f.* inexistence.

inesora'bile *adj.* inexorable.

inesperienza *f.* inexperience.

inesperto *adj.* inexperienced, unskilled.

inesplica'bile *adj.* inexplicable.

inesplorato *adj.* unexplored.

inesploso *adj.* unexploded.

inesprimi'bile *adj.* unexpressible.

inespugna'bile *adj.* impregnable.

inespugnato *adj.* unconquered.

inestima'bile *adj.* inestimable, priceless.

inestingui'bile *adj.* inextinguishable, unquenchable.

inestrica'bile *adj.* inextricable.

inettitu'dine *f.* ineptitude.

inetto *adj.* inept; worthless.

inevaso *adj.* unanswered.

inevita'bile *m.*, *adj.* inevitable.

ine'zia *f.* trifle.

infagottare *vt.* to muffle up.

infaili'bile *adj.* infallible.

infallibilità *f.* infallibility.

infamante *adj.* disgraceful.

infamare *vt.* to disgrace; to slander.

infame *adj.* infamous; distasteful.

infa'mia *f.* infamy, disgrace.

infangare *vt.* to muddy; to bespatter; infangarsi *vr.* to become muddy; (*fig.*) to degrade oneself.

infante *m.* infant, baby; Infante (*royal prince of Spain*).

infantici'dio *m.* infanticide.

infantile *adj.* infantile; childish.

infan'zia *f.* infancy, childhood.

infarcire *vt.* to stuff (*with*), cram.

infarinare *vt.* to flour, dredge; infarinarsi *vr.* to get covered with flour; to powder (*oneself*).

infarinatura *f.* (*fig.*) smattering.

infarto *m.* infarction; (*popularly*) heart disease.

infastidire *vt.* to annoy, irk; to irritate; infastidirsi *vr.* to fret, feel annoyed.

infatica'bile *adj.* tireless.

infatti *adv.* in fact; indeed; that's it.

infatuare *vt.* to infatuate; infatuarsi *vr.* to become infatuated.

infatuazione *f.* infatuation.

infa'usto *adj.* unfortunate, inauspicious, ominous.

infecondo *adj.* infecund, barren.

infedele *m.* infidel; *adj.* unfaithful.

infedeltà *f.* unfaithfulness; infidelity.

infelice *m.* wretch; *adj.* unhappy, miserable; unlucky; unfortunate.

infelicità *f.* unhappiness, misery.

inferiore *m.* inferior, subordinate; *adj.* inferior; lower.

inferiorità *f.* inferiority.

inferire *vt.*[70] to infer.

infermeri'a *f.* infirmary.

infermiera *f.* nurse.

infermiere *m.* (male) nurse.

infermità *f.* infirmity, disease.

infermo *m.* patient; *adj.* ill, sick.

infernale *adj.* infernal.

inferno *m.* hell, inferno: mandare all'—, to consign to the devil.

inferocire *vt.* to fiercen; to madden.

inferocito *adj.* infuriated.

inferriata *f.* grating.

infervorarsi *vr.* to warm up.

infervorato *adj.* excited, fervid.

infestare *vt.* to infest.

infettare *vt.* to infect; infettarsi *vr.* to become infected.

infettivo *adj.* infectious.

infetto *adj.* infected, tainted.

infezione *f.* infection.

infiacchire *vt.*, *vi.*, infiacchirsi *vr.* to weaken.

infiamma'bile *adj.* inflammable.

infiammare *vt.* to inflame; infiammarsi *vr.* to become inflamed.

infiammato'rio *adj.* inflammatory.

infiammato *adj.* aflame; inflamed (*with*).

infiammazione *f.* inflammation.

infido *adj.* treacherous.

in fieri *adv.* (*L.*) pending; to come, to become.

infierire *vi.* to rage: — su, to harass.

infig'gere *vt.*[63] to infix, drive (*into*).

infilare *vt.* to insert; to slip; to thread (*a needle*); to string (*beads*); infilarsi *vr.* to slip into: infilarsi un vestito, to slip one's dress on, to step into a dress.

infilata *f.* string; row.

infiltrarsi *vr.* to infiltrate; to leak (*into*).

infiltrazione *f.* infiltration.

infilzare *vt.* to string; to pierce through.

infilzata *f.* string.

in'fimo *adj.* lowest, basest.

infine *adv.* after all; at last; well.

infingardo *m.* sluggard; *adj.* sluggish.

infinità *f.* infinity; infinitude.

infinitamente *adv.* infinitely; (*fig.*) awfully.

infinite'simo *m.* infinitesimal.

infinito *m.* infinite; (*gramm.*) infinitive; *adj.* infinite.

infino (a) *see* fino (a).

infinocchiare *vt.* to fool.

infioccare *vt.* to tassel.

infiorare *vt.* to flower; to embellish.

infirmare *vt.* to invalidate.

infischiarsi *vr.* not to care (*about*); to make light (*of*).

infisso *m.* fixture; *adj.* infixed.

infittire *vt.*, *vi.* to thicken.

inflazione *f.* inflation.

inflessi'bile *adj.* inflexible, unbending.

inflessibilità *f.* inflexibility.

inflessione *f.* inflection.

inflig'gere *vt.*[5] to inflict.

influente *adj.* influential.

influenza *f.* influence; influenza, flu.

influenzare *vt.* to influence, sway.

influire *vi.* to act (*on*): — su, to affect.

influsso *m.* influence.

infocare *vt.* to make red-hot; to incandesce; infocarsi *vr.* to become red-hot.

infocato *adj.* incandescent, red-hot.

infognarsi *vr.* to plunge; to get involved.

infoltire *vi.* to thicken.
infondato *adj.* groundless.
infon'dere *vt.* to infuse, inspire, instill.
inforcare *vt.* to fork; to mount (*on*):
— **gli occhiali**, to put on one's glasses.
informare *vt.* to shape; to inspire; to inform, advise; to acquaint (*with*); **informarsi** *vr.* to inquire (*about*); to conform (*to*).
informativo *adj.* informative.
informatore *m.* informer.
informazione *f.* information; tip.
informe *adj.* shapeless.
infornare *vt.* to put into an oven.
infornata *f.* batch.
infortunato *adj.*, *m.* casualty.
infortu'nio *m.* accident.
infossare *vt.* to hollow, cave; to bury; **infossarsi** *vr.* to sink, hollow, cave in.
infossato *adj.* sunken; buried; caved-in.
infradiciare *vt.*, **infradiciarsi** *vr.* to make sodden; to rot.
inframmettente *m.* busybody; *adj.* meddlesome.
inframmettenza *f.* meddlesomeness.
infran'gere *vt.*,[68] **infran'gersi** *vr.* to break, shatter, crush.
infrangi'bile *adj.* infrangible; shatterproof.
infranto *adj.* broken, shattered.
infrarosso *m.*, *adj.* infrared.
infrazione *f.* infringement.
infreddatura *f.* cold.
infreddolirsi *vr.* to chill.
infreddolito *adj.* chilly.
infrequenza *f.* infrequency.
infruttuoso *adj.* unprofitable, unfruitful; useless.
infuriare *vi.* to rage; **infuriarsi** *vr.* to flare up; to get angry.
infuriato *adj.* furious.
infusione *f.* infusion.
infuso *m.* infusion; *adj.* infused.
ingabbiare *vt.* to encage.
ingaggiare *vt.* to engage, enlist.
ingag'gio *m.* engagement; (*mil.*) enlistment.
ingagliardire *vt.*, *vi.*; **ingagliardirsi** *vr.* to strengthen.
ingannare *vt.* to deceive, mislead; to while away (*time*); to ward off (*hunger*, *sleep*); **ingannarsi** *vr.* to deceive oneself, fool oneself; to be mistaken.
ingannatore *m.* deceiver; *adj.* deceitful.
inganne'vole *adj.* deceitful, misleading.
inganno *m*; deception; fraud: **trarre in —**, to deceive.

ingarbugliare *vt.*, **ingarbugliarsi** *vr.* to tangle; to jumble.
ingegnarsi *vr.* to endeavor; to make shift.
ingegnere *m.* engineer.
ingegneri'a *f.* engineering.
ingegno *m.* genius, talent.
ingegnosità *f.* ingeniousness.
ingegnoso *adj.* ingenious.
ingelosire *vt.* to make jealous. *vi.*, **ingelosirsi** *vr.* to become jealous.
ingemmare *vt.* to gem; to bejewel; *vi.* (*bot.*) to bud.
ingenerare *vt.* to engender.
ingeneroso *adj.* ungenerous, illiberal.
ingente *adj.* very great; very heavy.
ingentilire *vt.*, *vi.*, **ingentilirsi** *vr.* to refine; to soften.
ingenuamente *adv.* naïvely.
ingenuità *f.* naïveness, artlessness.
inge'nuo *adj.* naïve, artless.
ingerenza *f.* connection; interference.
ingerire *vt.* to ingest; **ingerirsi** *vr.* to meddle (*with*).
ingessare *vt.* to plaster; to cast.
ingessatura *f.* plastering; cast.
Inghilterra *f.* England.
inghiottire *vt.* to swallow.
inghirlandare *vt.* to wreathe.
ingiallire *vt.*, *vi.* to yellow.
ingiallito *adj.* yellowed, faded.
ingigantire *vt.* to exaggerate, amplify. *vi.* to become enormous.
inginocchiarsi *vr.* to kneel (*down*).
inginocchiato'io *m.* kneeler.
ingioiellare *vt.* to bejewel.
ingiù *adv.* downwards, down.
ingiun'gere *vt.*,[79] to enjoin, order.
ingiunzione *f.* injunction; order.
ingiu'ria *f.* insult, abuse, slight; injury.
ingiuriare *vt.* to abuse, revile.
ingiurioso *adj.* insulting, reviling.
ingiustamente *adv.* unfairly; wrongly.
ingiustificato *adj.* unjustified; unwarranted.
ingiusti'zia *f.* injustice; wrong.
ingiusto *adj.* unjust; unfair; wrong.
inglese *m.* Englishman; *f.* Englishwoman; English, (the) English language. *adj.* English, British: **andarsene all'—**, to take French leave.
inglorioso *adj.* inglorious.
ingoiare *see* inghiottire.
ingoiatore *m.* swallower.
ingolfarsi *vr.* to plunge (*into*); to involve oneself.
ingollare *vt.* to gulp (*down*).
ingolosire *vt.* to make greedy, tempt. **ingolosirsi** *vr.* to become gluttonous; to be tempted.
ingombrante *adj.* cumbersome.
ingombrare *vt.* to encumber; to obstruct; to clutter.

ingombro *m.* encumbrance; *adj.* cluttered, encumbered (*with*).

ingommare *vt.* to gum; to stick.

ingordi'gia *f.* greed.

ingordo *m.* glutton. *adj.* greedy.

ingorgamento *m.* obstruction.

ingorgare *vi.*, **ingorgarsi** *vr.* to clog, choke up.

ingorgo *m.* obstruction: — **stradale,** traffic jam.

ingoverna'bile *adj.* ungovernable.

ingozzare *vt.* to gobble; to cram.

ingranag'gio *m.* gear; gearing.

ingranare *vt.* to throw into gear; *vi.* to engage; (*fam.*) to go, succeed.

ingrandimento *m.* enlargement; (*photo.*) blow-up: **lente d'—,** magnifying glass.

ingrandire *vt.*, *vi.* to enlarge; to grow; to increase; (*opt.*) to magnify; (*photo.*) to enlarge; **ingrandirsi** *vr.* to enlarge, increase; to expand.

ingrassare *vt.* to fatten; to grease. *vi.* to fatten, grow fat.

ingratitu'dine *f.* ingratitude.

ingrato *m.* ingrate; *adj.* ungrateful; unpleasant; thankless.

ingraziarsi *vr.* to ingratiate oneself (*with*).

ingrediente *m.* ingredient.

ingresso *m.* entrance; admittance; entry.

ingrossamento *m.* bulge; swelling; increase.

ingrossare *vt.* to enlarge, make bigger; to increase; to swell; *vi.*, **ingrossarsi** *vr.* to enlarge, grow bigger; to increase; to swell.

ingrosso, (all') *adv.* (*by*) wholesale.

inguainare *vt.* to sheathe.

inguari'bile *adj.* incurable.

in'guine *m.* groin.

ingurgitare *vt.* to ingurgitate.

inibire *vt.* to inhibit.

inibizione *f.* inhibition.

inido'neo *adj.* unfit, unqualified.

iniettare *vt.* to inject.

iniettato *adj.* injected: — **di sangue,** bloodshot.

iniettore *m.* injector.

iniezione *f.* injection, needle.

inimicare *vt.* to estrange (*from*); **inimicarsi** *vr.* to estrange from oneself; to fall off.

inimici'zia *f.* enmity; hatred.

inimita'bile *adj.* inimitable.

inimmagina'bile *adj.* unimaginable.

inintelligi'bile *adj.* unintelligible.

ininterrotto *adj.* uninterrupted.

iniquità *f.* iniquity.

iniquo *adj.* iniquitous; wicked; unfair.

iniziale *f., adj.* initial.

iniziare *vt.* to begin, start; to initiate (*into*).

iniziativa *f.* initiative; enterprise: **mancare d'—,** to lack initiative.

iniziato *m., adj.* initiate.

iniziatore *m.* initiator.

iniziazione *f.* initiation.

ini'zio *m.* beginning: **sin dall'—,** from the beginning.

innaffiare *vt.* to water; to sprinkle.

innaffiato'io *m.* watering pot, sprinkler.

innalzare *vt.* to raise, elevate, lift; to erect; to exalt; **innalzarsi** *vr.* to rise; to elevate oneself; to tower.

innamorare *vt.* to charm, fascinate; **innamorarsi** *vr.* to fall in love (*with*).

innamorato *m.*, **innamorata** *f.* sweetheart, lover. *adj.* in love (*with*); (*fig.*) fond (*of*).

innanzi *prep., adv.* before; in front of; ahead; on, forward: **tirare —,** to get along; **d'ora —,** from now on; **— tutto,** first of all; **— tempo,** prematurely.

innato *adj.* inborn, native.

innega'bile *adj.* undeniable.

inneggiare *vt.*, *vi.* to exalt; to cheer.

innesco *m.* primer.

innestare *vt.* (*med.*) to inoculate (*with*); to insert; (*bot., surg.*) to graft; (*mach.*) to engage.

innesto *m.* (*med.*) inoculation; (*bot., surg.*) graft; (*mach.*) coupling, clutch.

inno *m.* hymn; anthem.

innocente *m.* innocent; *adj.* innocent, guiltless; harmless; candid.

innocenza *f.* innocence, candor.

inno'cuo *adj.* innocuous, harmless.

innominato *adj.* unnamed; nameless.

innovatore *m.* innovator; *adj.* innovating.

innovazione *f.* innovation, novelty.

innumere'vole *adj.* numberless.

inoculare *vt.* to inoculate.

inoculazione *f.* inoculation.

inodoro *adj.* odorless, inodorous.

inoffensivo *adj.* inoffensive, harmless.

inoltrare *vt.* to forward; **inoltrarsi** *vr.* to advance.

inoltre *adv.* besides, moreover.

inoltro *m.* forwarding.

inondare *vt.* to flood.

inondazione *f.* inundation, flood.

inoperosità *f.* idleness.

inoperoso *adj.* idle.

inopinatemente *adv.* unexpectedly.

inopinato *adj.* unexpected, sudden.

inopportunità *f.* inopportuneness; untimeliness.

inopportuno *adj.* inopportune, untimely.

inoppugna'bile *adj.* indisputable.

inorgoglire *vt.* to elate; *vi.*, **inorgo-**

glirsi *vr.* to become elated; to pride oneself (*upon*).

inorridire *vt.* to horrify; *vi.* to be horrified, shudder.

inorridito *adj.* horrified.

inospitale *adj.* inhospitable

inosservante *adj.* remiss; non observant.

inosservanza *f.* remissness, nonobservance.

inosservato *adj.* unnoticed.

inossida'bile *adj.* inoxidizable; stainless.

inquadrare *vt.* to frame; to arrange; (*moving pictures*) to frame; (*mil.*) to rank, marshal; **inquadrarsi** *vr.* to be framed; (*fig.*) to conform, adjust (*to*).

inqualifica'bile *adj.* despicable.

inquietante *adj.* disquieting.

inquietare *vt.* to worry; to irk; to trouble; **inquietarsi** *vr.* to get angry.

inquieto *adj.* worried, uneasy; fretful; angry; impatient, restless.

inquietu'dine *f.* uneasiness, worry; restlessness; fretfulness.

inquilino *m.* lodger, tenant.

inquinare *vt.* to pollute.

inquirente *adj.* investigating.

inquisitore *m.* inquisitor.

inquisizione *f.* inquisition.

insabbiare *vt.* to sand; (*fig.*) to put aside, pigeonhole; **insabbiarsi** *vr.* to cover oneself with sand; (*fig.*) to go native.

insaccare *vt.* to sack; (*fig.*) to cram, stuff.

insalata *f.* salad.

insalubre *adj.* unhealthy, insalubrious.

insalutato *adj.* unsaluted: andarsene — ospite, to take French leave.

insana'bile *adj.* irremediable.

insanguinare *vt.* to stain with blood, make gory; **insanguinarsi** *vr.* to stain oneself with blood.

insanguinato *adj.* gory, bloody.

insano *adj.* mad, insane.

insaponare *vt.* to soap; to lather.

insaporire *vt.* to flavor.

insaputa, (all') *adv.* unknown (*to*).

insazia'bile *adj.* insatiable.

inscenare *vt.* to stage.

inscindi'bile *adj.* unseverable.

inscri'vere *etc. see* iscrivere.

insecchire *vt., vi.* to dry up.

insediamento *m.* induction (*into*).

insediare *vt.* to install; **insediarsi** *vr.* to install oneself; to settle.

insegna *f.* insigne (*pl.* insignia); flag; sign, signboard; emblem; coat of arms.

insegnamento *m.* teaching; education; doctrine, tuition.

insegnante *m.,f.* teacher; *adj.* teaching.

insegnare *vt.* to teach; to show.

inseguimento *m.* chase, pursuit.

inseguire *vt.* to pursue.

inseguitore *m.* pursuer.

insellare *vt.* to saddle.

insellatura *f.* saddle.

insenatura *f.* inlet, creek.

insensatag'gine *f.* nonsensicalness; nonsense, folly.

insensatezza *see* insensataggine.

insensato *m.* fool; *adj.* foolish; nonsensical; rash.

insensi'bile *adj.* insensible; unfeeling; imperceptible.

insensibilità *f.* insensibility.

insepara'bile *adj.* inseparable.

insepolto *adj.* unburied.

inserire *vt.[1]* to insert; to enclose; **inserirsi** *vr.* to enter (*into*).

inserto *m.* dossier.

inservi'bile *adj.* unserviceable, useless.

inserviente *adj.* attendant.

inserzione *f.* insertion; advertisement, "ad."

inserzionista *m.* advertiser.

insetticida *m.* insecticide; *adj.* insecticidal.

insetto *m.* insect.

insi'dia *f.* snare; ambush; danger.

insidiare *vt.* to endanger, undermine.

insidioso *adj.* insidious; tricky.

insieme *m.* (the) whole; ensemble: nell'—, on the whole; *adv., prep.* together (*with*); at the same time, simultaneously.

insigne *adj.* distinguished, eminent.

insignificante *adj.* insignificant.

insignire *vt.* to confer upon.

insincero *adj.* insincere.

insindaca'bile *adj.* undisputable.

insinuante *adj.* insinuating.

insinuare *vt.* to insinuate, hint; to insert; **insinuarsi** *vr.* to insinuate oneself, creep (*in*).

insinuazione *f.* insinuation, hint, innuendo.

insi'pido *adj.* insipid.

insipienza *f.* insipience.

insistente *adj.* insistent; steady.

insistenza *f.* insistence.

insi'stere *vi.* to insist (*on*); to dwell (*upon*).

in'sito *adj.* inborn, inherent.

insoddisfatto *adj.* dissatisfied.

insofferente *adj.* intolerant.

insofferenza *f.* intolerance.

insoffri'bile *adj.* unbearable.

insolazione *f.* sunstroke.

insolente *m.,f., adj.* insolent.

insolentire *vt.* to insult, abuse.

insolenza *f.* insolence; insult.

inso'lito *adj.* unusual, uncommon.

insolu'bile *adj.* insoluble.

insoluto *adj.* unsolved; unpaid.

insolvenza *f.* insolvency.
insolvibilità *f.* insolvency.
insomma *adv.* finally; in short, in a word; after all.
insonda'bile *adj.* unfathomable.
insonne *adj.* sleepless.
inson'nia *f.* sleeplessness.
insonnolito *adj.* drowsy, sleepy.
insopporta'bile *adj.* unbearable.
insor'gere *vi.*[139] to rise, rebel; to arise: far —, to rouse.
insormonta'bile *adj.* insuperable.
insorto *m., adj.* insurgent, rebel.
insospetta'bile *adj.* above suspicion.
insospettire *vt.* to make suspicious; insospettirsi *vr.* to become suspicious.
insospettito *adj.* suspicious.
insosteni'bile *adj.* unsustainable.
insozzare *vt.* to sully.
insperato *adj.* unhoped for; unexpected.
inspessimento *m.* thickening.
inspessire *vt.*, inspessirsi *vr.* to thicken.
inspirare *vt.* to inhale.
inspirazione *f.* inhalation.
insta'bile *adj.* unstable, unsteady; fickle.
instabilità *f.* unsteadiness.
installare *vt.* to install; to establish, set up. installarsi *vr.* to settle.
installazione *f.* installation.
instancabile *adj.* untiring.
instaurare *vt.* to establish.
instaurazione *f.* establishment.
instillare *see* istillare.
instradare *vt.* to direct, guide; to coach.
insù *adv.* upwards, up.
insubordinato *m., adj.* insubordinate.
insubordinazione *f.* insubordination.
insuccesso *m.* failure, fiasco.
insudiciare *vt.* to dirty.
insufficiente *adj.* insufficient.
insufficienza *f.* insufficiency.
insulare *adj.* insular.
insulina *f.* insulin.
insulsag'gine *f.* silliness; nonsense.
insulso *adj.* insipid, vapid, insignificant.
insultante *adj.* insulting, abusive.
insultare *vt.* to insult, abuse.
insulto *m.* slight, insult; (*pl.*) abuse.
insupera'bile *adj.* insuperable; unsurpassable.
insuperato *adj.* unsurpassed.
insuperbire *vt., vi.*, insuperbirsi *vr.* to swell (*with pride*).
insurrezione *f.* insurrection.
insussistente *adj.* flimsy.
intabarrare *vt.* to wrap up (*in a cloak*).
intaccare *vt.* to notch; to injure; to gnaw: — un capitale, to draw upon a capital.

intaccatura *f.* notch.
intagliare *vt.* to intaglio; to engrave; to carve.
inta'glio *m.* intaglio; indentation.
intangi'bile *adj.* intangible.
intangibilità *f.* intangibility.
intanto *adv.* meanwhile; for the time being.
intarsiare *vt.* to inlay.
intarsiato *adj.* inlaid.
intar'sio *m.* inlaying.
intasare *vt., vi.*, intasarsi *vr.* to choke, clog.
intasatura *f.* obstruction.
intascare *vt.* to pocket.
intatto *adj.* intact, untouched.
intavolare *vt.* to board, plank: — una conversazione, to start a conversation; — trattative, to open up negotiations.
integer'rimo *adj.* blameless, righteous.
integrale *adj.* integral; unabridged.
integrante *adj.* integrant, integrating.
integrare *vt.* to complete, integrate.
integrazione *f.* integration.
integrità *f.* integrity.
in'tegro *adj.* whole, complete; honest, upright.
intelaiatura *f.* framing; frame.
intelletto *m.* intellect, understanding.
intellettuale *m., adj.* intellectual.
intellettualità *f.* intellectuality.
intelligente *adj.* intelligent; clever; smart.
intelligenza *f.* intelligence; cleverness; intellect.
intelligi'bile *adj.* intelligible.
intemerata *f.* reprimand.
intemerato *adj.* unblemished.
intemperante *adj.* intemperate.
intemperanza *f.* intemperance.
intempe'rie *f. pl.* inclement weather.
intempestività *f.* untimeliness.
intempestivo *adj.* untimely.
intendente *m.* manager; superintendent.
intendenza *f.* intendancy, superintendence.
inten'dere *vt.*[140] to intend (*to*), mean; to understand; to hear: far —, to give to understand; — a rovescio, to misunderstand; non — ragioni, not to listen to reason; inten'dersi *vr.* to understand each other; to be conversant (*with*), be well versed (*in*); to get along (*with*), agree: s'intende! of course!
intendimento *m.* understanding; purpose.
intenditore *m.* expert; connoisseur: a buon — poche parole, a word to the wise is sufficient.
intenerire *vt.*, intenerirsi *vr.* to soften.
intensamente *adv.* intensely.

intensificare *vt.*, **intensificarsi** *vr.* to intensify, increase.

intensità *f.* intensity.

intenso *adj.* intense.

intentare *vt.* to institute, bring (*action against*).

intentato *adj.* unattempted.

intento (*1*) *m.* intent; aim; intention: **con l'— di,** with a view to.

intento (*2*) *adj.* intent.

intenzionale *adj.* intentional, deliberate.

intenzionato *adj.* determined; willing; **ben' (mal') —,** well- (ill-) intentioned.

intenzione *f.* intention; design, view, mind.

intepidire *vt.* to make tepid; to warm (*anything cold*); to cool (*anything hot*); **intepidirsi** *vr.* to get tepid; to warm up; to cool down.

interamente *adv.* wholly.

intercalare *m.* recurring word; refrain; *adj.* intercalary.

intercalare *vt.* to intercalate, interpolate.

intercape'dine *f.* air space, hollow space; gap; cavity.

interce'dere *vi.*[33] to intercede (*with*).

intercessione *f.* intercession.

intercettare *vt.* to intercept.

intercomunale *adj.*, *f.* (*teleph.*) long-distance (call).

intercor'rere *vi.* to elapse; to intervene.

interdetto *adj.* disabled; nonplussed.

interdire *vt.* to interdict, forbid; to incapacitate.

interdizione *f.* interdiction.

interessamento *m.* interest, concern; co-operation.

interessante *adj.* interesting: **in stato —,** pregnant.

interessare *vt.* to interest; to concern, regard; *vi.* to be of interest (*to*); to matter; **interessarsi** *vr.* to take an interest (*in*); to concern oneself (*with*); to take care (*of*), attend (*to*).

interessato *m.* interested party: **a tutti gli interessati,** to all concerned; *adj.* interested; greedy; biased.

interesse *m.* interest; advantage; care, concern; importance.

interessenza *f.* percentage.

interferenza *f.* interference.

interferire *vi.* to interfere.

interfogliare *vt.* to interleave.

interiezione *f.* interjection.

interinale *adj.* interim.

interinato *m.* interim office.

interino *m.* substitute; *adj.* temporary.

interiora *f.pl.* entrails.

interiore *m.* inside, interior; *adj.* inside, inner, interior.

interli'nea *f.* interline; (*typog.*) lead.

interlineare *vt.* to interline; (*typog.*) to lead.

interlineatura *f.* (*typog.*) leading.

interlocutore *m.* interlocutor.

interloquire *vi.* to chime in.

interlu'dio *m.* interlude.

intermedia'rio *m.* intermediary, go-between; (*comm.*) middleman; *adj.* intermediate, intermediary.

interme'dio *adj.* middle, intermediate.

intermezzo *m.* intermission, interval.

intermina'bile *adj.* endless.

intermittente *adj.* intermittent.

intermittenza *f.* intermittence.

internamente *adv.* internally.

internamento *m.* internment.

internare *vt.* intern; **internarsi** *vr.* to penetrate (*into*).

internato *m.* internee; *adj.* interned.

internazionale *adj.* international.

internazionalizzare *vt.* to internationalize.

interno *m.* inside, interior; inland; intern; (*moving pictures*) set, interior; *adj.* inside, internal; interior, inner: **commercio —,** home trade; **alunno —,** boarder.

intero *see* intiero.

interpellanza *f.* interpellation.

interpellare *vt.* to consult; to interpellate; to question.

interplaneta'rio *adj.* interplanetary.

interpolare *vt.* to interpolate.

interpolazione *f.* interpolation.

interporre *vt.*,[91] **interporsi** *vr.* to interpose.

interposto *adj.* interposed: **interposta persona,** go-between, intermediary.

interpretare *vt.* to interpret; (*theat.*) to play, act; (*mus.*) to perform.

interpretazione *f.* interpretation; (*theat.*) acting; (*mus.*) performance.

inter'prete *m.* interpreter; actor, player; performer.

interpunzione *f.* punctuation.

interrare *vt.* to inter.

interregno *m.* interregnum.

interrogare *vt.* to question.

interrogativo *m.* question; *adj.* interrogative: **punto —,** interrogation mark.

interrogato'rio *m.* examination; questioning. *adj.* interrogatory.

interrogazione *f.* interrogation; question, query.

interrom'pere *vt.* to interrupt; **interrompersi** *vr.* to interrupt oneself; to cease, stop.

interruttore *m.* interrupter; (*elec.*) switch.

interruzione *f.* interruption.

intersecare *vt.*, **intersecarsi** *vr.* to intersect.

intersezione f. intersection.
intersti'zio m. interstice.
interurbana, (chiamata) f. (teleph.) long-distance call.
intervallo m. interval; gap.
intervenire vi. to intervene; to interfere; to attend; (surg.) to operate.
intervento m. intervention; interference; attendance; (surg.) operation.
intervista f. interview.
intervistare vt. to interview.
intervistatore m. interviewer.
intesa f. agreement; entente.
inteso adj. agreed, understood: **non darsene per —,** to take no notice, not to take the hint.
intestare vt. to head, caption; to inscribe, register; **intestarsi** vr. to take into one's head.
intestato adj. headed, captioned, inscribed, entered (in the name of); determined, dogged; (law) intestate.
intestazione f. heading.
intestinale adj. intestinal.
intestino m., adj. intestine.
intiepidire see intepidire.
intiero m. whole; adj. whole, complete; entire: **per —,** wholly, completely, fully.
intimamente adv. intimately; inside; at heart.
intimare vt. to order; to enjoin: **— la resa a,** to summon to surrender.
intimazione f. order; injunction; notice.
intimidazione f. intimidation.
intimidire vt. to abash; **intimidirsi** vr. to feel abashed.
intimidito adj. bashful.
intimità f. intimacy.
in'timo m. soul, heart; adj. intimate, deep; inmost.
intimorire vt. to frighten; **intimorirsi** vr. to get frightened.
intin'gere vt.[143] to dip.
intingolo m. gravy, sauce.
intinto pp. of intingere.
intirizzire vt. to benumb; to stiffen.
intirizzito adj. numb; stiff.
intisichire vi. to wither.
intitolare vt. to title; to dedicate; to name; **intitolarsi** vr. to be titled; to be named (after).
intollera'bile adj. intolerable.
intollerante adj. intolerant.
intolleranza f. intolerance.
intonacare vt. to plaster.
into'naco m. plaster.
intonare vt. to intone; to tone; to tune; **intonarsi** vr. to harmonize (with).
intonato adj. tuned; in tune (with).
intonazione f. intonation; tune.

intonso adj. uncut.
intontire vt. to stun, dull.
intoppare vt., vi. to stumble (on).
intoppo m. hindrance.
intorbidare, intorbidire vt., **intorbidarsi** vr. to muddy; to blur.
intorno prep., adv. around, about, round: **togliersi uno d'—,** to get rid of one.
intorpidimento m. numbness, torpor.
intorpidire vt. to benumb, make torpid; **intorpidirsi** vr. to get benumbed.
intossicare vt. to poison.
intossicazione f. poisoning.
intraduci'bile adj. untranslatable.
intralciare vt. to hinder.
intral'cio m. hindrance.
intramezzare vt. to intersperse, alternate.
intransigente m., adj. intransigent.
intransigenza f. intransigence.
intransitivo m., adj. intransitive.
intrappolare vt. to entrap.
intraprendente adj. enterprising.
intraprendenza f. enterprise, daring, initiative.
intrapren'dere vt. to start; to undertake; to engage in.
intratta'bile adj. unmanageable; peevish.
intrattenere vt. to entertain; **intrattenersi** vr. to linger; to dwell (upon).
intravedere vt.[151] to glimpse, catch a glimpse of.
intravisto pp. of intravedere.
intrecciare vt. to intertwine; to plait: **— rapporti,** to establish relations; **— le dita,** to lace one's fingers. **intrecciarsi** vr. to intertwine; to crisscross.
intrec'cio m. plaiting, interlacement; plot (as of a novel).
intre'pido adj. fearless, intrepid.
intricare vt., **intricarsi** vr. to tangle.
intricato adj. tangled, intricate, complicated.
intrico m. tangle, intricacy.
intri'dere vt.[48] to soak (with), steep (in).
intrigante m. intriguer; adj. crafty, meddlesome.
intrigare vi. to plot, intrigue; **intrigarsi** vr. to meddle (with).
intrigo m. plot, intrigue.
intrin'seco m. intrinsicality; core; heart, inside; intimate friend; adj. intrinsic, inherent; intimate.
intriso adj. steeped (in), soaked (with): **— di sangue,** imbrued with blood. pp. of intridere.
intristire vi. to degenerate, sour; to wither, droop, waste away.
introdotto pp. of introdurre.
introdurre vt.[3] to introduce, insert; to show in; to slip; to thrust (into); to

import; introdursi vr. to introduce oneself; to slip (into); to penetrate.

introduttivo adj. introductory.

introduzione f. introduction; preface; (mus.) overture.

introitare vt. to cash.

introito m. gains, returns.

intromet'tere vt. to intromit, insert, introduce; to interpose; intromettersi vr. to intrude, interpose, interfere, meddle (with).

intromissione f. intrusion.

intronare vt. to stun; to deafen.

introspezione f. introspection.

introva'bile adj. not to be found.

introverso m., adj. introvert.

intru'dere vt.[92] intru'dersi vr. to intrude.

intrufolarsi vr. to intrude (in), wriggle in.

intru'glio m. hodgepodge.

intrusione f. intrusion.

intruso m. intruder.

intuire vt. to guess; to perceive by intuition; to sense.

intuitivo adj. intuitive; instinctive.

intu'ito m. insight, intuition.

intui'to adj. sensed; intuitive. pp. of intuire.

intuizione f. intuition.

inturgidire vi. to swell.

inumano adj. inhuman.

inumare vt. to inhume.

inumazione f. inhumation.

inumidire vt., inumidirsi vr. to moisten, wet.

inurbano adj. inurbane, rude.

inusato adj. unwonted; obsolete.

inusitato adj. unusual.

inu'tile adj. useless; pointless; vain.

inutilità f. uselessness.

inutilizzato adj. unused; discarded.

inutilmente adv. uselessly, in vain.

invadente adj. meddlesome.

invadenza f. meddlesomeness.

inva'dere vt.[90] to invade.

invaghirsi vr. to fall in love (with); (fig.) to take a liking (to).

invalere vi.[160] to prevail; to spread.

invalica'bile adj. impassable.

invalida'bile adj. voidable.

invalidare vt. to void; to invalidate, nullify.

invalidazione f. invalidation.

invalidità f. invalidity; infirmity.

inva'lido m. invalid; disabled man: piccolo —, crippled child; adj. invalid; null, void; disabled, crippled.

invalso adj. prevailing.

invano adv. in vain, vainly.

invaria'bile adj. invariable.

invariato adj. unchanged; unvaried.

invasato adj. possessed.

invasione f. invasion.

invaso adj. invaded.

invasore m. invader; adj. invading.

invecchiamento m. aging.

invecchiare vt., vi. to age; to make (one) look older; to grow old.

invece adv. instead (of); on the contrary.

inveire vi. to rail (at).

invelenire vt. to envenom; (fig.) to embitter. invelenirsi vr. to grow venomous; (fig.) to sour, to get exacerbated.

invendi'bile adj. unsalable.

invendicato adj. unavenged.

invenduto adj. unsold.

inventare vt. to invent, devise; to create; to fabricate (as lies).

inventariare vt. to inventory.

inventa'rio m. inventory.

inventiva f. inventiveness.

inventivo adj. inventive.

inventore m. inventor.

invenzione f. invention; fabrication.

inverecon'dia f. immodesty.

inverecondo adj. immodest.

invernale adj. winter; wintry.

inverno m. winter: a metà —, in midwinter.

invero adv. indeed, truly.

inverosimiglianza f. unlikelihood, implausibility.

inverosi'mile adj. unlikely, improbable.

inversamente adv. inversely.

inversione f. inversion.

inverso adj. inverse, reverse; opposite.

invertire vt. to invert, reverse.

invertitore m. inverter.

investigare vt. to investigate.

investigativo adj. investigative.

investigatore m. investigator; detective.

investigazione f. investigation.

investimento m. collision; accident, running down; investment.

investire vt. to invest (with); to invest; to attack; to knock against; to run down; to assail (with); investirsi vr. to become conscious (of); to collide; to attack one another: — della propria parte, to merge into one's role.

investitura f. investiture.

inveterato adj. inveterate, ingrained.

invetriata f. glass frame.

invettiva f. invective.

inviare vt. to send.

inviato m. messenger; envoy; correspondent (of a newspaper).

invi'dia f. envy: fare —, to stir envy.

invidia'bile adj. enviable.

invidiare vt. to envy.

invidioso adj. envious; m. envier, envious person.

invigorire vt., vi., **invigorirsi** vr. to strengthen, invigorate.

invinci'bile adj. invincible.

invi'o m. sending, forwarding; mailing (of letters); shipment (of goods); remittance (of money).

inviola'bile adj. inviolable.

inviolato adj. inviolate.

inviperire vt., **inviperirsi** vr. to get sore.

inviperito adj. sore, enraged.

invischiare vt. to lime.

invisi'bile adj. invisible.

inviso adj. disliked.

invitante adj. inviting.

invitare vt. to invite, ask.

invitato m. guest; adj. invited.

invito m. invitation; request.

invitto adj. unvanquished.

invocare vt. to invoke; to entreat; to solicit.

invocazione f. invocation.

invogliare vt. to tempt, entice; to induce, move; **invogliarsi** vr. to bring oneself (to), be induced; to take a fancy (for, to).

involare vt. to abduct; **involarsi** vr. to flee, run away; to disappear; to elope.

invol'gere vt.[156] to wrap up, envelop.

involontariamente adv. unintentionally, unwittingly.

involonta'rio adj. unintentional.

involto (1) m. bundle.

involto (2) pp. of involgere.

invo'lucro m. case; shell; envelope.

involuto adj. involved; involute.

involuzione f. involution.

invulnera'bile adj. invulnerable.

inzaccherare vt., **inzaccherarsi** vr. to muddy; to spatter.

inzeppare vt. to wedge; to fill.

inzuccherare vt. to sugar.

inzuccherato adj. sugared.

inzuppare vt. to soak.

io pers.pron. I: — stesso, I myself; m. I, self; (sci.) ego: il mio —, my own self.

iodato adj. iodized.

io'dio m. iodine.

ioduro m. iodide.

ione m. (sci.) ion.

ionizzare vt. to ionize.

iosa, (a) adv. in plenty, galore.

iota m. iota; jot.

iper'bole f. (rhet.) hyperbole; (math.) hyperbola.

iperbo'lico adj. hyperbolical.

ipercri'tico adj. hypercritical.

ipernutrizione f. overnourishment.

ipersensi'bile adj. hypersensitive.

ipersensibilità f. hypersensitiveness.

ipertensione f. hypertension.

ipertrofi'a f. hypertrophy.

ipertro'fico adj. hypertrophic.

ipnosi f. hypnosis.

ipno'tico adj. hypnotic.

ipnotismo m. hypnotism.

ipnotizzare vt. to hypnotize.

ipnotizzatore m. hypnotizer.

ipocloridri'a f. (gastric) hypoacidity.

ipocondri'a f. hypochondria.

ipocondri'aco m., adj. hypochondriac.

ipocrisi'a f. hypocrisy.

ipo'crita m. hypocrite.

ipo'crito adj. hypocritical.

ipoder'mico adj. hypodermic.

ipogeo m. hypogeum.

iposolfito m. hyposulphite.

ipoteca f. mortgage.

ipotecare vt. to mortgage, hypothecate.

ipoteca'rio adj. mortgage.

ipotenusa f. hypotenuse.

ipo'tesi f. hypothesis (pl. hypotheses); theory, conjecture, surmise: nella migliore delle ipotesi, at best; nella peggiore delle ipotesi, if the worst comes to the worst.

ipote'tico adj. hypothetical.

ip'pica f. horse racing, turf.

ip'pico adj. turf.

ippocampo m. sea horse.

ippocastano m. horse chestnut.

ippodromo m. race track.

ippopo'tamo m. hippopotamus.

iprite f. mustard gas.

ipso facto adv. (L.) pronto, right away.

ira f. wrath, fury, rage.

iracon'dia f. wrathfulness.

iracondo adj. wrathful.

irasci'bile adj. irascible, irritable.

irascibilità f. irascibleness, irritably.

irato adj. angry.

ire vi. to go.

i'reos m. (bot.) iris, German iris.

iridato adj. iridescent.

i'ride f. rainbow; (anat., bot.) iris.

iridescente adj. iridescent.

iridescenza f. iridescence.

iri'dio m. iridium.

irlandese m., adj. Irish.

ironi'a f. irony.

iro'nico adj. ironical.

iroso adj. wrathful, angry.

irradiare vt., vi. to irradiate; **irradiarsi** vr. to radiate.

irradiazione f. irradiation.

irraggiungi'bile adj. unattainable.

irragione'vole adj. unreasonable.

irragionevolezza f. unreasonableness.

irrancidire vi. to (grow) rank.

irrazionale adj. irrational.

irrazionalità f. irrationality.

irreale adj. unreal.

irrealtà f. unreality.

irreconcilia'bile adj. irreconcilable.

irrecusa'bile adj. irrecusable.

irredento *adj.* unredeemed: **una re-gione irredenta**, an irredenta (*It.*).

irrefrena'bile *adj.* unrestrainable.

irrefuta'bile *adj.* irrefutable.

irreggimentare *vt.* to regiment.

irregolare *m.*, *adj.* irregular.

irregolarità *f.* irregularity.

irreligioso *adj.* irreligious.

irremissi'bile *adj.* irremissible.

irremovi'bile *adj.* firm; adamant; stubborn.

irrepara'bile *adj.* irreparable.

irreperi'bile *adj.* not to be found, elusive.

irreprensi'bile *adj.* irreproachable.

irrequietezza *f.* restlessness.

irrequieto *adj.* restless.

irresisti'bile *adj.* irresistible.

irresoluto *adj.* irresolute.

irresponsa'bile *adj.* irresponsible.

irretire *vt.* to ensnare.

irrevoca'bile *adj.* irrevocable.

irriconosci'bile *adj.* unrecognizable.

irri'dere *vt.*[108] to scoff at.

irriduci'bile *adj.* irreducible; stubborn.

irriflessivo *adj.* rash, thoughtless.

irrigare *vt.* to irrigate.

irrigazione *f.* irrigation.

irrigidimento *m.* stiffening.

irrigidire *vt.*, *vi.*, **irrigidirsi** *vr.* to stiffen.

irri'guo *adj.* well-watered.

irrimedia'bile *adj.* irremediable.

irrisione *f.* mockery, scorn.

irriso *pp.* of **irridere**.

irriso'rio *adj.* derisive; paltry.

irrita'bile *adj.* irritable.

irritabilità *f.* irritability.

irritante *adj.* irritating.

irritare *vt.* to irritate; **irritarsi** *vr.* to chafe; to become irritated *or* inflamed.

irritazione *f.* irritation.

irriverente *adj.* irreverent.

irriverenza *f.* irreverence.

irrobustire *vt.*, **irrobustirsi** *vr.* to strengthen.

irrom'pere *vi.*[115] to burst (*in*).

irrorare *vt.* to sprinkle, spray.

irrotto *pp.* of **irrompere**.

irruente *adj.* rash, impetuous.

irruenza *f.* impetuosity.

irruzione *f.* irruption: **fare —**, to burst (*in*).

irsuto *adj.* hirsute, shaggy.

irto *adj.* bristling, bristly.

iscritto *m.* member; entrant (*in a contest*); *adj.* inscribed, entered, recorded. *pp.* of **iscrivere**.

iscri'vere *vt.*[124] to inscribe; to enter, record; to enroll; **iscri'versi** *vr.* to enter, join.

iscrizione *f.* inscription; entry; admission.

islandese *m.* Icelander; *adj.* Icelandic.

i'sola *f.* island, isle.

isolamento *m.* isolation; (*elec.*) insulation.

isolano *m.* islander.

isolante *adj.* isolating; (*elec.*) insulating.

isolare *vt.* to isolate; (*elec.*) to insulate; **isolarsi** *vr.* to seclude oneself.

isolato *m.* block; *adj.* isolated; (*elec.*) insulated.

isolatore *m.* insulator.

isolazionismo *m.* isolationism.

isolazionista *m.* isolationist.

isoletta *f.* islet.

isolotto *m.* islet.

iso'topo *m.* isotope; *adj.* isotopic.

ispettorato *m.* inspectorate; inspectorship.

ispettore *m.* inspector. [ship.

ispettrice *f.* inspectress.

ispezionare *vt.* to inspect.

ispezione *f.* inspection.

i'spido *adj.* shaggy, hispid.

ispirare *vt.* to inspire (*with*); to influence; **ispirarsi** *vr.* to draw inspiration (*from*); to conform oneself

ispirazione *f.* inspiration. [(*to*).

issare *vt.* to hoist.

istanta'nea *f.* (*photo.*) snapshot.

istanta'neo *adj.* instantaneous.

istante (*1*) *m.* instant, moment: **sull'—, all'—**, at once, instantly; **da un — all'altro**, any moment; **in the twinkling of an eye**.

istante (*2*) *m.* petitioner.

istante (*3*) *adj.* impending, imminent.

istanza *f.* instance; application; petition.

iste'rico *m.*, *adj.* hysteric.

isterilire *vt.* to sterilize; *vi.* to become sterile.

isterismo *m.* hysteria.

istigare *vt.* to instigate.

istigatore *m.* instigator.

istigazione *f.* instigation.

istillare *vt.* to instill.

istintivamente *adv.* instinctively.

istintivo *adj.* instinctive.

istinto *m.* instinct.

istituire *vt.* to institute.

istituto *m.* institute.

istitutore *m.* institutor; tutor.

istitutrice *f.* governess.

istituzione *f.* institution.

istmo *m.* isthmus.

istoriare *vt.* to adorn a story (*with historical figures*).

istoriato *adj.*, *pp.* storied.

i'strice *m.*, *f.* porcupine.

istrione *m.* ham (*actor*).

istruire *vt.*[37] to teach; to coach; to educate; to instruct; (*mil.*) to drill; (*law*) to institute; **istruirsi** *vr.* to learn; to study.

istruito adj. learned, educated; enlightened.
istrumento m. instrument.
istruttivo adj. instructive.
istruttore m. instructor, coach.
istrutto'ria f. inquest.
istrutto'rio adj. preliminary.
istruzione f. instruction; education; teaching; learning; direction.
istupidire vt. to dull.
italiano m., adj. Italian.
iterare vt. to iterate.
itinera'rio m. itinerary.

ito pp. of ire, gone.
itteri'zia f. jaundice.
ittiolo m. ichthyol.
ittiologi'a f. ichthyology.
iu'gero m. juger, jugerum.
iugulare (1) adj. jugular.
iugulare (2) vt. to strangle; (fig.) to dupe.
iugulato'rio adj. (fig.) iniquitous.
iuniore m., adj. junior.
iuta f. jute.
iutifi'cio m. jute factory.
ivi adv. there.

K

kaki adj. khaki.
kan m. khan.
kapoc m. kapok.
kedivè m. Khedive.

kimono m. kimono.
kola f. (bot.) kola.
kummel m. kummel.
kursaal m. kursaal.

L

la (1) definite article sing. f. her; neuter it.
la (2) pron. sing. f. her; neuter it.
la (3) m. (mus.) la, A: dare il "la," to give the pitch.
là adv. there: andare troppo in —, to go too far; l'al di —, the hereafter; farsi in —, to move aside; al di — di, beyond, across; più in —, further.
labbro m. lip.
la'bile adj. weak, changeable.
labirinto m. labyrinth, maze.
laborato'rio m. workshop; laboratory.
laboriosità f. laboriousness.
laborioso adj. laborious.
lacca f. lacquer.
laccare vt. to lacquer.
laccatura f. lacquering.
lacchè m. footman, lackey.
lac'cio m. noose; snare; shoelace.
lacerante adj. rending.
lacerare vt. to lacerate; to tear (up); to rend; lacerarsi vr. to tear.
lacerazione f. laceration.
la'cero adj. torn; tattered.
lacerto m. sinew.
laco'nico adj. laconic.
la'crima f. tear; drop.
lacrimale adj. lachrymal.
lacrimare vi. to shed tears, weep; to water.
lacrime'vole adj. lamentable.
lacrimo'geno adj. lachrymatory: gas —, tear gas.
lacrimoso adj. tearful.
lacuale adj. of or growing in lakes.
lacuna f. gap; blank.
lacustre adj. of or growing in lakes.
laddove conj. while; adv. (there) where.

ladresco adj. thievish.
ladro m. thief, burglar, robber.
ladrone m. highwayman.
ladrun'colo m. pilferer.
laggiù adv. down there, yonder.
lagnanza f. complaint.
lagnarsi vr. to complain (of).
lagno see lamento.
lago m. lake.
la'grima, etc. see lacrima, etc.
laguna f. lagoon.
lai m.pl. lamentations.
la'ico m. layman; adj. laic.
la'ido m. ugly, foul.
lama (1) f. blade.
lama (2) m. (zool.) llama.
lambiccare vt. to distill: lambiccarsi il cervello, to rack one's brains.
lambicco m. alembic, still.
lambire vt. to lick; to lap.
lamella f. scale; lamella.
lamentanza f. complaint.
lamentare vt. to lament, regret; lamentarsi vr. to complain (about); to moan.
lamentazione f. lamentation.
lamente'vole adj. lamentable; whining.
lamento m. moan; complaint.
lamentoso adj. doleful.
lametta f. (little) blade: — da rasoio, razor blade.
lamiera f. sheet metal; sheet iron: — ondulata, corrugated iron.
la'mina f. lamina; plate.
laminare vt. to laminate, roll.
laminato'io m. rolling mill.
lam'pada f. lamp.
lampada'rio m. chandelier, luster.

lampadina f. bulb: — tascabile, flashlight, torch.

lampante adj. glaring, evident.

lampeggiante adj. flashing.

lampeggiare vi. to lighten; (fig.) to flash; (auto.) to blink.

lampeggiatore m. (auto.) blinker.

lampioncino m. lantern; Chinese lantern.

lampione m. street lamp.

lampo m. lightning flash: cerniera —, zip fastener; guerra —, blitzkrieg.

lampone m. raspberry.

lana f. wool: guanti di —, woolen gloves.

lancetta f. (surg.) lancet; hand (of a watch); pointer (of a gauge).

lan'cia f. lance, spear; (naut.) launch.

lanciabombe m. howitzer.

lanciafiamme m. flame thrower.

lanciarazzi m. rocket launcher.

lanciare vt. to throw, fling, pitch, hurl; (fig.) to launch; to cast, set; to bring out; to advertise; **lanciarsi** vr. to throw, fling, hurl oneself; to launch: lanciarsi col paracadute, to bail out.

lanciasiluri m. torpedo tube.

lanciatore m. thrower; (baseball) pitcher.

lanciere m. lancer, lance.

lancinante adj. lancinating.

lan'cio m. throwing; leap, jump; (baseball) pitch: — del peso, shot-putting.

landa f. moor, heath.

languente adj. languishing.

languidezza f. languidness.

lan'guido adj. languid.

languire vi. to languish, pine (away); to flag; to pine (for).

languore m. languor; faintness.

lanifi'cio m. woolen mill.

lanoso adj. woolly.

lanterna f. lantern.

lanu'gine f. down.

lanuto adj. woolly.

lanzichenecco m. lansquenet.

laonde adv. therefore.

lapalissiano adj. obvious: osservazione lapalissiana, truism.

laparatomi'a f. laparatomy.

lapidare vt. to lapidate, stone.

lapida'rio adj. lapidary.

la'pide f. tablet: — sepolcrale, tombstone.

lapillo m. lapillus (pl. lapilli).

lapis m. pencil: — per labbra, lipstick.

lappone m., adj. Lappic, Lapponian.

lapsus (calami, linguae) m. slip (of the pen, of the tongue).

lardellare vt. to lard.

lardo m. lard, bacon.

largheggiare vi. to give freely; to abound (in, with).

larghezza f. width, breadth; plenty; liberality: — di vedute, broadmindedness.

largire vt. to bestow (upon).

largizione f. bestowal.

largo m. width, breadth; room; square, circus; (naut.) offing: far —, to make room; farsi —, to elbow one's way; prendere il —, (naut.) to sail out to sea; (fig.) to run away; al — di, off; in lungo e in —, far and wide; adj. broad, wide, extensive; open; liberal: di manica larga, lenient, generous.

la'rice m. larch.

laringe f. larynx.

larva f. larva (pl. larvae).

larvatamente adv. disguisedly.

larvato adj. disguised.

lasagna f. noodle.

lasciapassare m. pass, safe-conduct.

lasciare vt. to leave; to abandon, quit; to omit; to let, allow; to stop: — in eredità, to will, bequeath; — cadere, to drop; **lasciarsi** vr. to let oneself, allow oneself; (reciprocal) to part, to quit each other: — andare, to let oneself go; — sfuggire una parola, to let slip a word.

la'scito m. bequest, legacy.

lasci'via f. lust.

lascivo adj. lustful.

lassativo m., adj. aperient, laxative.

lasso m. lapse (of time).

lassù adv. up there.

lastra f. plate; pane; slab.

lastricare vt. to pave.

lastricato m. pavement; adj. paved.

la'strico m. pavement: ridursi sul —, to come upon the parish; essere sul —, to be on one's uppers.

lastrone m. slab.

latente adj. latent.

laterale adj. lateral, side.

lateri'zio m., adj. brick.

latifondista m. landowner.

latifondo m. large landed estate.

latino m., adj. Latin: vela latina, lateen sail.

latitante m. absconder; adj. absconding.

latitanza f. hiding: darsi alla —, to abscond.

latitu'dine f. latitude.

lato (1) m. side; part; face; viewpoint: a —, aside; a — di, beside.

lato (2) adj. broad: in senso —, broadly speaking.

latore m. bearer.

latrare vi. to bark.

latrato m. bark.

latrina f. lavatory, privy.
latta f. tin.
latta'ia f. milkmaid.
latta'io m. milkman.
lattante m. suckling; adj. sucking.
latte m. milk.
lattemiele m. whipped cream.
lat'teo adj. milky: **Via Lattea, Milky Way**.
latteri'a f. dairy.
lat'tice m. (bot.) latex.
latticini m.pl. dairy products.
lattiginoso adj. milky, lacteous.
lattiven'dolo m. milkman.
lattoniere m. tinsmith.
lattuga f. lettuce.
la'urea f. degree, doctorate: **prendere la —**, to graduate, to take one's doctorate.
laurearsi vr. to graduate.
laureato m. graduate; adj. graduated.
la'uro m. laurel.
la'uto adj. sumptuous, large.
lava f. lava.
lavabiancheri'a m. washing machine.
lava'bile adj. washable.
lavabo m. washstand.
lavacro m. washing.
lavag'gio m. washing: **— a secco**, dry cleaning.
lavagna f. slate; blackboard.
lavamano m. washstand.
lavanda (1) f. (bot.) lavender.
lavanda (2) f. (med.) lavage.
lavanda'ia f. laundress.
lavanda'io m. laundryman.
lavanderi'a f. laundry.
lavandino m. sink.
lavapiatti m. scullion.
lavare vt. to wash: **— a secco**, to dry-clean; **lavarsi** vr. to wash (oneself).
lavata f. wash, washing: **— di capo**, wigging, scolding.
lavativo m. enema; (It. slang) bore; faultfinder, fusser; loafer, "bum."
lavato'io m. washtub, laundry.
lavatrice f. washwoman: **washing machine**.
lavatura f. washing: **— a secco**, dry cleaning; **— di piatti**, dishwater.
lavorante m. workman; f. workwoman.
lavorare vt., vi. to work: **— la terra**, to till land; **— di fantasia**, to fabricate.
lavorativo adj. working, work: **giornata lavorativa**, workday.
lavorato adj. worked; wrought; manufactured.
lavoratore m. worker, workman.
lavoratrice f. working woman.
lavorazione f. manufacturing, working; make: **— della terra**, tillage; **— a catena**, assembly line process.

lavori'o m. bustle; (fig.) plotting.
lavoro m. work, labor: **— in legno**, woodwork; **lavori forzati**, penal servitude.
lazzarone m. lazybones; "heel," cad.
lazzo m. jest, banter.
le (1) definite article pl.f. the.
le (2) pron.sing.f. her, to her.
le (3) deferential pron.m., f. (to) you: **Le assicuro, signore, che è così**, I assure you, sir, that it is so.
le (4) pron.pl.f. them: **— vedemmo a Roma**, we saw them in Rome.
leale adj. loyal; fair.
lealmente adv. loyally; fairly.
lealtà f. loyalty; fairness.
lebbra f. leprosy.
lebbrosa'rio m. leper house, leprosarium.
lebbroso m. leper; adj. leprous.
leccapiedi m. toady, bootlicker.
leccarda f. dripping pan.
leccare vt. to lick; (fig.) to flatter; **— le scarpe (a)**, to bootlick; **leccarsi** vr. to lick (oneself); to polish oneself.
leccata f. lick, licking.
leccato adj. (fig.) affected; sophisticated; "corny"; sleek.
lec'cio m. holm oak, ilex.
leccorni'a f. dainty, delicacy.
le'cito m. right. adj. licit, permissible.
lo'dere vt.[73] to damage, injure.
lega f. union, league.
legac'cio m. string.
legale m. lawyer; adj. legal, lawful, legitimate: **medicina —**, medical jurisprudence.
legalità f. legality.
legalita'rio adj. legalistic.
legalizzare vt. to legalize; to authenticate.
legalmente adv. legally, lawfully.
legame m. bond, tie, link; connection.
legamento m. binding, tying, linkage; ligature; (anat.) ligament.
legare vt. to bind, tie (up); to fasten; (surg.) to ligate; (law) to bequeath; **legarsi** vr. to bind, tie oneself; to unite, combine.
legata'rio m. legatee.
legato m. (eccl.) legate; (law) legacy; adj. tied (up), fastened; bound.
legatore m. bookbinder; (law) legator.
legatori'a f. bindery.
legatura f. binding; ligature.
legazione f. legation.
legge f. law; act: **progetto di —**, bill.
leggenda f. legend; caption.
leggenda'rio adj. legendary.
leg'gere vt.[74] to read.
leggerezza f. lightness; nimbleness; fickleness; levity, thoughtlessness.
leggermente adv. lightly; thoughtlessly; slightly.

leggero see leggiero.
leggiadri'a f. grace, loveliness.
leggiadro adj. graceful, lovely.
leggi'bile adj. readable.
leggiero adj. light; nimble; fickle; lightheaded, thoughtless; slight: **alla leggiera**, superficially.
leggi'o m. bookstand; music stand.
legiona'rio m., adj. legionary.
legione f. legion.
legislativo adj. legislative.
legislatore m. legislator.
legislatura f. term of office; legislature.
legislazione f. legislation.
legit'tima f. legitim.
legittimare vt. to legitimate.
legittimità f. legitimacy.
legit'timo adj. legitimate, legal, lawful: **— proprietario**, lawful owner.
legna f. firewood: **fare —**, to cut wood.
legna'ia f. woodshed.
legname m. timber, lumber.
legnata f. cudgel blow.
legno m. wood.
legnoso adj. ligneous, woody.
legule'io m. pettifogger.
legume m. legume.
lei sing.pron. she; her.
lei deferential appellative pron. you.
lembo m. edge, border; patch, strip.
lemme lemme adv. leisurely.
lena f. breath, wind; vigor, energy, zest.
len'dine m. nit.
lenire vt. to allay.
lenitivo m., adj. lenitive.
lenoci'nio m. pandering; artifice.
lenone m. pander, pimp.
lentamente adv. slowly.
lente f. lens, glass: **— d'ingrandimento**, magnifying glass.
lentezza f. slowness; sluggishness.
lentic'chia f. lentil.
lentig'gine f. freckle.
lentigginoso adj. freckly.
lento adj. slow; loose; tardy.
lenza f. line: **pescare con la —**, to angle.
lenzuolo m. sheet.
Leonardo da Vinci see Vinci.
Leoncavallo, Ruggiero, Italian composer, *I Pagliacci* (1858-1919).
leone m. lion; (astr.) Leo.
leonessa f. lioness.
Leopardi, Giacomo, greatest Italian poet of the 19th century (1798-1837).
leopardo m. leopard.
lepidezza f. humor; witticism.
le'pido adj. witty.
leporino adj. leporine: **labbro —**, harelip.

lepre f. hare.
leprotto m. leveret.
ler'cio adj. filthy, dirty.
lerciume m. filth, dirt.
le'sina f. awl.
lesinare vt. to grudge; vi. to be stingy.
lesione f. injury, lesion.
lesivo adj. harmful (to).
leso adj. damaged: **parte lesa** (law), plaintiff; **lesa maestà**, lese majesty. pp. of ledere.
lessare v. to boil.
les'sico m. lexicon, dictionary.
lesso m. boiled meat; adj. boiled.
lesto adj., adv. swift: **— di mano**, light-fingered.
lestofante m. swindler.
letale adj. lethal, deadly.
letama'io m. dunghill.
letame m. litter; manure.
letargi'a f. lethargy.
letar'gico adj. lethargic: **encefalite letargica**, sleeping sickness.
letargo m. lethargy.
leti'zia f. gladness, joy.
let'tera f. letter: **belle lettere**, belles lettres.
letterale adj. literal.
lettera'rio adj. literary.
letterata f. literary woman.
letterato m. litterateur.
letteratura f. literature.
lettiera f. bedstead; litter.
lettiga f. stretcher; sedan chair.
letto (1) m. bed: **— a una piazza**, single bed; **— a due piazze**, double bed.
letto (2) pp. of leggere.
lettore m. **lettrice** f. reader.
lettura f. reading.
leva f. (mach.) lever; (mil.) draft, levy; class: **esser di —**, to be due for drafting.
levante m. Levant; East.
levantino m., adj. Levantine.
levare vt. to raise, lift (up); to take (off, away), remove; to pull (out); to take, subtract: **da 9 levo 4, I take 4 from 9; — l'ancora**, to weigh anchor; **— le tende**, to break camp; **levarsi** vr. to rise; to get out (of); to take off, remove: **— uno d'attorno**, to get rid of one.
levata f. rising; withdrawal; collection (of mail): **— di scudi**, hue and cry.
levatac'cia f. early rising.
levato'io (ponte) m. drawbridge.
levatrice f. midwife.
levatura f. understanding.
levigare vt. to smooth.
levigatezza f. smoothness.
levigato adj. smooth.

levità f. levity.
levriere m. greyhound.
lezione f. lesson; lecture; reading.
lezioso adj. lackadaisical, affected.
lezzo m. stink, stench.
li (1) pron.pl. them: — odio, I hate them; guardateli, look at them.
li (2) definite article m.pl. (archaic) the.
lì (3) adv. there, over there: giù di —, thereabout; — per —, at first, at once; essere — per, to be on the verge of.
liana f. liane, liana.
libbra f. pound.
libecciata f. southwester.
libec'cio m. southwest wind.
libello m. libel.
libel'lula f. dragonfly.
liberale m., adj. liberal.
liberalità f. liberality.
liberamente adv. freely.
liberare vt. to free, set free; to release; to rescue; to rid (of); liberarsi vr. to free oneself; to get rid (of).
liberatore m. liberator, deliverer; rescuer; adj. rescuing.
liberazione f. release, liberation, deliverance.
liberismo m. free trade.
liberista m. free trader.
li'bero adj. free; exempt; vacant.
libertà f. freedom, liberty: — provvisoria, parole; mettere in —, to set free; to dismiss; mettersi in —, to make oneself comfortable.
libertina'gio m. libertinism, license, licentiousness.
libertino m., adj. libertine, rake.
libi'dine f. lustfulness, lust.
libidinoso adj. lustful.
libra'io m. bookseller.
librarsi vr. to poise; to hover, soar.
libreri'a f. bookstore; bookcase, bookshelf.
libretto m. booklet; (mus.) libretto: — di banca, bankbook, passbook.
libro m. book: — mastro, ledger.
licenza f. license, licentiousness; license, permission; leave, furlough; degree, diploma: in —, on furlough.
licenziamento m. dismissal.
licenziare vt. to dismiss; to graduate; (typog.) to pass; licenziarsi vr. to resign; to take one's leave; to graduate.
licenziosità f. licentiousness.
licenzioso adj. licentious.
liceo m. high school.
licitazione f. auction sale.
lido m. shore; land.
lieto adj. glad; merry.
lieve adj. slight; light; mild.
lievemente adv. slightly; lightly.

lievitare vt. to leaven; vi. to yeast.
lie'vito m. leaven, yeast.
li'gio adj. true, abiding.
lignag'gio m. lineage.
lilla m., adj. lilac.
lima f. file.
limaccioso adj. muddy, miry.
limare vt. to file; to polish.
limatura f. filing; filings (pl.).
limbo m. limbo.
limitare (1) vt. to confine, limit; to restrict; to bound; limitarsi vr. to confine oneself; to check oneself.
limitare (2) m. threshold.
limitato adj. restricted, limited; narrow (minded); meager.
limitazione f. limitation.
li'mite m. limit, bound; boundary: passare i limiti (fig.), to go too far.
limi'trofo adj. limitrophe, adjacent.
limo m. slime, mud.
limonata f. lemonade.
limone m. lemon.
limpidezza, limpidità f. limpidness.
lim'pido adj. limpid.
lince f. lynx.
linciag'gio m. lynching.
linciare vt. to lynch.
lindezza f. neatness.
lindo adj. neat.
lindura f. neatness.
li'nea f. line: a grandi linee, in outline.
lineamento m. feature.
lineare adj. linear.
lineetta f. dash; hyphen.
linfa f. (anat.) lymph; (bot.) sap.
lingotto m. ingot.
lingua f. tongue; language; strip (of land): mala —, backbiter.
linguacciuto adj. gossipy; m. gossip.
linguag'gio m. language.
linguetta f. small tongue; clip.
linifi'cio m. flax spinnery.
linimento m. liniment.
lino m. flax.
linosa f. linseed.
linotipista m. linotypist.
liquefare vt., liquefarsi vr. to liquefy, melt.
liquefazione f. liquefaction.
liquidare vt. to liquidate; to settle (an account); to sell out.
liquidazione f. liquidation; settlement (of an account); clearance sale: prezzi di —, bargain prices.
li'quido m., adj. liquid: denaro —, cash.
liquiri'zia f. licorice.
liquore m. liquor; liqueur.
lira f. lira (Italian coin); (mus.) lyre: — sterlina, pound (sterling).
li'rica f. lyric; lyric poetry; (mus.) opera.
li'rico adj. lyrical; (mus.) operatic.

lirismo *m.* lyricism.
lisca *f.* shive; fishbone.
lisciare *vt.* to smoothe; to "soft-soap"; **lisciarsi** *vr.* to smoothen.
li'scio *adj.* smooth, sleek: **passarla liscia,** to go scot free.
lisci'via *f.* lye.
liso *adj.* threadbare; frayed.
lista *f.* stripe, band; list, note; bill; — **delle vivande,** bill of fare; — **elettorale,** slate.
listare *vt.* to stripe.
listello *m.* listel.
listino *m.* list; price list; market letter.
litani'a *f.* litany.
litantrace *m.* lithanthrax.
lite *f.* quarrel; lawsuit.
litigante *m.* quarreler; (*law*) litigant.
litigare *vi.* to quarrel.
liti'gio *m.* quarrel.
litigioso *adj.* quarrelsome.
litorale *m.,* *adj.* littoral.
litro *m.* liter.
liturgi'a *f.* liturgy.
liuta'io *m.* lutemaker, lutist.
liuto *m.* lute.
livella *f.* level.
livellamento *m.* leveling.
livellare *vt.* to level.
livellatore *m.* leveler; *adj.* leveling.
livellazione *f.* leveling.
livello *m.* level; dumpy level: **passaggio a —,** level crossing, grade crossing.
li'vido *m.* bruise; *adj.* livid, lurid.
lividura *f.* bruise.
livore *m.* grudge, spite.
livrea *f.* livery.
lizza *f.* lists (*pl.*), competition, contest: **entrare in —,** to enter the lists.
lo (*1*) *definite article m.sing.* the.
lo (*2*) *pers.pron.m.sing.* it, him: **egli —è,** he is; — **so,** I know (*it*).
lob'bia *f.* fedora (*hat*).
lobo *m.* lobe.
locale *m.* room; resort; (*pl.*) premises; (*rail.*) local train: — **notturno,** night club; *adj.* local.
località *f.* locality, spot.
localizzare *vt.* to localize; to circumscribe.
locanda *f.* inn.
locandiera *f.,* **locandiere** *m.,* innkeeper.
locare *vt.* to rent.
locata'rio *m.* tenant.
locatore *m.* lessor.
locazione *f.* lease.
locomotiva *f.* locomotive, engine.
locomotore *m.* electric locomotive; *adj.* locomotor.
locomozione *f.* locomotion: **mezzi di —,** transportation.

lo'culo *m.* loculus; burial niche.
locusta *f.* locust.
locuzione *f.* locution.
loda'bile *adj.* praiseworthy.
lodare *vt.* to praise; to commend.
lode *f.* praise; commendation.
lode'vole *adj.* commendable.
lodo *m.* arbitrament.
logaritmo *m.* logarithm.
log'gia *f.* loggia: — **massonica,** masonic lodge.
loggiato *m.* loggia, gallery.
loggione *m.* (*upper*) gallery; the gallery gods.
lo'gica *f.* logic.
lo'gico *adj.* logical; natural.
logi'stico *adj.* logistic.
lo'glio *m.* darnel.
logoramento *m.* wear, wearing.
logorare *vt.* to wear (out, down, away); to fray; to spoil; **logorarsi** *vr.* to wear (*oneself*) out; to fray, become frayed.
logori'o *m.* wear and tear.
lo'goro *adj.* worn (out, down); frayed, threadbare.
lombag'gine *f.* lumbago.
lombo *m.* sirloin; (*anat.*) loin.
lombrico *m.* earthworm.
Lombroso, Cesare, Italian psychiatrist (1836–1909).
londinese *m.* Londoner; cockney; *adj.* Londonese.
longa'nime *adj.* forbearing.
longanimità *f.* forbearance.
longarone *m.* (*aeron.*) longeron, spar; (*auto.*) longitudinal member.
longevità *f.* longevity.
longevo *adj.* longevous; long-lived.
longitudinale *adj.* longitudinal, lengthwise.
longitu'dine *f.* longitude.
lontanamente *adv.* remotely, far.
lontananza *f.* farness, remoteness, distance; absence: **in —,** at a distance.
lontano *adj.* far, distant, remote, away; *adv.* far, afar: **venire di —,** to come from afar.
lontra *f.* otter.
lonza *f.* loin; (*zool.*) ounce.
loquace *adj.* talkative.
loquacità *f.* talkativeness.
loquela *f.* speech: — **facile,** glibness.
lordare *vt.* to dirty.
lordo *adj.* dirty; (*comm.*) gross.
lordume *m.* filth, dirt.
loro *pron.pl.m., f.* they; them, to them: **ero da — quando accadde,** I was at their house when it happened. *deferential appellative pron. pl.* you: — **desiderano il caffè?** would you like to have some coffee? *poss.adj.* their. *poss.pron.* theirs.

losanga f. diamond, lozenge, rhomb.
losco adj. short-sighted; one-eyed; sinister, shady.
loto m. mud; (bot.) lotus.
lotta f. struggle, fight; (sport) wrestling: — libera, catch-as-catch-can; esser in —, to be at war.
lottare vi. to fight, struggle; to strive; (sport) to wrestle.
lottatore m. fighter; wrestler.
lotteri'a f. lottery; sweepstakes.
lotto m. number lottery; area, lot.
lozione f. lotion.
lu'brico adj. lubricous; lubricious, slippery.
lubrificante m., adj. lubricant.
lubrificare vt. to lubricate.
lubrificazione f. lubrication.
lucchetto m. padlock.
luccicare vt. to glitter.
luccichi'o m. glitter, sparkle.
luc'cio m. pike.
luc'ciola f. firefly; glowworm: mostrare lucciole per lanterne, to pull the wool over one's eyes.
luce f. light; window; mirror; (arch.) span: dare alla —, to give birth to.
lucente adj. bright, shining.
lucentezza f. brightness, gloss.
lucerna f. lamp.
lucerna'rio m. skylight.
lucer'tola f. lizard.
lucidare vt. to polish, shine; to gloss; to trace (drawings).
lucidatore m. polisher.
lucidatrice f. polisher: — per pavimenti, floor polisher.
lucidatura f. polishing; shine.
lucidità f. lucidity.
lu'cido m. shine, gloss; polish; shoe polish; tracing; adj. shining, glossy; (fig.) lucid: carta lucida (photo.), glossy paper.
luci'gnolo m. wick.
lucrare vt. to gain.
lucro m. lucre.
lucroso adj. lucrative.
ludi'brio m. mockery; laughing stock.
lue f. lues, syphilis.
lue'tico adj. luetic.
lu'glio m. July.
lu'gubre adj. lugubrious, somber.
lui pron.m.sing. he; him.
lumaca f. snail.
lume m. light; lamp; candle: perdere il — degli occhi, to get blind with rage.
lumeggiare vt. to outline.
lumicino m. lamplet: al —, on one's last legs.
luminare m. luminary.
lumina'ria f. illumination.
lumino m. lamplet, night lamp.
luminosità f. luminosity.
luminoso adj. luminous, bright.

luna f. moon: — di miele, honeymoon; al chiaro di —, by moonlight; avere la —, to have the blues.
lunare adj. lunar.
luna'rio m. almanac: sbarcare il —, to make both ends meet.
luna'tico adj. moody.
lunedì m. Monday.
lunetta f. (archit.) lunette.
lungag'gine f. delay.
lungamente adv. long, lengthily.
lunghezza f. length; span.
lungi adv. far.
lungo m. length: per il —, lengthwise; per — e per largo, far and wide; andare per le lunghe, to drag; adj. long; lengthy; tall; slow; diluted, thin: a —, long, lengthily; a — andare, in the long run; a gran lunga, by far; prep. along: — le rive, along the banks.
luogo m. place, spot, site; room; way: — comune, commonplace; aver —, to take place; dar — a, to give rise to; in — di, in lieu of; in qualche —, somewhere; in qualunque —, anywhere, wherever; in nessun —, nowhere; in primo — . . . e in secondo —, for one thing . . . and secondly.
luogotenente m. lieutenant; deputy; vice regent.
lupa f. she-wolf.
lupanare m. brothel.
lupino m. (bot.), adj. lupine.
lupo m. wolf (pl. wolves): — mannaro, (pathol.) lycanthrope, werewolf; (fig.) big bad wolf; — di mare, seadog; in bocca al lupo! good luck!
lup'polo m. hops.
lu'rido adj. filthy, foul.
lusco adj. dim-sighted: tra — e brusco, in the twilight.
lusinga f. flattery; delusion.
lusingare vt. to flatter; to entice; to deceive.
lusinghiero adj. flattering; promising; satisfactory.
lussare vt. to dislocate.
lussazione f. dislocation.
lusso m. luxury; display: di —, luxurious, de luxe.
lussuoso adj. luxurious; expensive.
lussureggiante adj. luxuriant.
lussu'ria f. lustfulness, lust.
lussurioso adj. lustful.
lustrare vt. to polish; to shine.
lustrascarpe m. bootblack.
lustrino m. tinsel.
lustro (1) m. luster; polish, sheen; distinction; adj. glossy, shining.
lustro (2) m. lustrum (five years).
lutto m. mourning; sorrow, grief; loss.
luttuoso adj. mournful, sad.

M

ma *conj.* but; yet, still; why!; who knows?: — no! why, no!; dov'è? ma! where is he?, who knows?; — che! you don't say!; nonsense!

ma'cabro *adj.* macabre, grisly.

macaco *m.* macaque; (*fig.*) dolt.

maccherone *m.* macaroni.

mac'chia (*1*) *f.* stain, spot; speckle; blemish: — solare, sunspot; senza —, spotless, blameless.

mac'chia (*2*) *f.* woodland; bush: darsi alla —, to become an outlaw; stampare alla —, to print clandestinely.

macchiare *vt.* to stain; to speckle, spray; macchiarsi *vr.* to stain oneself, get stained (*with*): macchiarsi d'un reato, to commit a crime.

macchietta *f.* caricature; character; (*theat.*) comedian, mimicker.

macchiettare *vt.* to speckle.

macchiettista *m.* (*paint.*) cartoonist; (*theat.*) comedian, mimicker.

mac'china *f.* machine, engine; car, automobile: — per scrivere, typewriter; — da presa, — fotografica, camera; andare in — (*auto.*) to go by car; (*typog.*) to go to press.

macchinale *adj.* mechanical.

macchinalmente *adv.* mechanically.

macchinare *vt., vi.* to plot.

macchina'rio *m.* machinery.

macchinazione *f.* machination, plot.

macchinista *m.* engineer; stagehand.

macchinoso *adj.* complicated, heavy.

macchiolina *f.* speck.

macedo'nia *f.* fruit cup.

macella'io *m.* butcher.

macellare *vt., vi.* to butcher.

macellazione *f.* butchering.

macelleri'a *f.* butcher shop.

macello *m.* shambles; massacre, slaughter.

macerare *vt., macerarsi *vr.* to macerate.

macerazione *f.* maceration.

mace'rie *f.pl.* ruins, debris.

ma'cero *m.* macerator.

Machiavelli, Niccolò, Italian political writer and statesman, *Il Principe* (1469–1527).

machiavel'lico *adj.* Machiavellian.

machiavellismo *m.* Machiavellism.

macigno *m.* boulder.

macilento *adj.* emaciated.

ma'cina *f.* millstone.

macinacaffè *m.* coffee mill.

macinapepe *m.* pepper mill.

macinare *vt.* to grind.

macinato *adj.* milled, ground.

macinatura, macinazione *f.* grinding.

macinino *m.* mill; (*fig.*) rattletrap, "jalopy."

maciullare *vt.* to crush.

madama *see* signora.

madamigella *see* signorina.

ma'dia *f.* kneading trough; bread bin.

ma'dido *adj.* wet, damp.

Madonna *f.* Madonna; lady.

madornale *adj.* huge, enormous; (*fig.*) preposterous, gross.

madre *f.* mother; (*anat.*) mater; counterfoil; stub: casa — (*comm.*), head office.

madreggiare *vi.* to take after one's mother.

madrepa'tria *f.* mother country.

madreperla *f.* mother-of-pearl.

madreperla'ceo *adj.* nacreous.

madreselva *f.* honeysuckle.

madrevite *f.* female screw.

madrigale *m.* madrigal.

madrigna *f.* stepmother.

madrina *f.* godmother.

maestà *f.* majesty.

maestosità *f.* stateliness, majesty.

maestoso *adj.* majestic, stately.

maestra (*1*) *f.* teacher, mistress.

maestra (*2*) *f.* (*naut.*) mainsail.

maestrale *m.* northwester.

maestranza *f.* workmen (*pl.*).

maestri'a *f.* skill, mastery.

maestro *m.* master; teacher, schoolmaster; conductor: colpo da —, master stroke; *adj.* master; main: strada maestra, main road.

ma'fia *f.* mafia; (*fig.*) swagger.

maga *f.* sorceress.

magagna *f.* fault, flaw; trouble.

magari! *interj.* would to God!; *adv.* perhaps, possibly: — ci fossi andato! I wish I had gone there!

magazzinag'gio *m.* storage.

magazziniere *m.* warehouseman.

magazzino *m.* warehouse; store; magazine.

magenta *m.* magenta.

maggese *m., adj.* fallow.

mag'gio *m.* May.

maggiolino *m.* cockchafer.

maggioranza *f.* majority.

maggiorare *vt.* to majorate, augment, increase.

maggiorazione *f.* majoration.

maggiordomo *m.* butler; majordomo.

maggiore *m.* elder; ancestor; (*mil.*) major; *adj.* major; greater; greatest; larger; largest; main; bigger;

biggest; older, oldest; elder, eldest:
altar —, high altar; stato —, staff;
per forza —, perforce; essere in età
—, to be of age; andare per la —,
to be "tops."

maggiorenne *m.* major; *adj.* of age.

maggiorente *m.* notable.

maggiormente *adv.* the more; more.

magi′a *f.* magic.

ma′gico *adj.* magic, magical.

magistero *m.* mastery; teaching;
(*pharm.*) magistery.

magistrale *adj.* magisterial; masterly.

magistralmente *adv.* masterly.

magistrato *m.* magistrate.

magistratura *f.* magistracy.

ma′glia *f.* stitch; loop; link; vest;
coat of mail: lavorare a —, to
knit.

maglieri′a *f.* underwear; pull-overs
and sweaters.

maglietta *f.* undervest.

maglifi′cio *m.* knitwear factory.

ma′glio *m.* hammer; drop hammer.

maglione *m.* jersey.

magna′nimo *adj.* magnanimous.

magnano *m.* locksmith.

magnate *m.* magnate, tycoon.

magne′sia *f.* magnesia.

magne′sio *m.* magnesium.

magnete *m.* magnet; magneto.

magne′tico *adj.* magnetic.

magnetizzare *vt.* to magnetize.

magneto′fono *m.* tape recorder.

magnificare *vt.* to exalt.

magnificenza *f.* magnificence; wonder.

magni′fico *adj.* magnificent.

magno *adj.* great: Magna Carta,
Magna Charta; Carlo Magno,
Charlemagne; aula —, assembly
hall, auditorium.

mago *m.* wizard, magician, sorcerer.

magone *m.* gizzard; (*fig.*) sorrow.

magra *f.* low water; dearth.

magrezza *f.* thinness; scantiness.

magro *adj.* lean; meager fare: giorno di
—, fast day; *adj.* lean; thin; gaunt;
meager, scanty, poor; paltry.

mai *adv.* never; ever: come —?
how come?

maiale *m.* pig, swine; pork.

maio′lica *f.* majolica.

maionese *f.* mayonnaise.

mais *m.* Indian corn, maize.

maiu′scolo *adj.* capital.

malaccorto *adj.* awkward; rash.

malacreanza *f.* boorishness.

malafede *f.* bad faith.

malaffare *m.* turpitude: donna di —,
whore; gente di —, scum.

malage′vole *adj.* difficult.

malagra′zia *f.* ungraciousness.

malalin′gua *f.* backbiter.

malamente *adv.* badly; awkwardly.

malandato *adj.* in a bad way; in dis-
repair; battered.

malandrino *m.* ruffian, knave.

mala′nimo *m.* ill will, malice.

malanno *m.* calamity, mishap; disease, illness; ill luck.

malapena, (a) *adv.* hardly.

malatic′cio *adj.* sickly.

malato *m.* patient; *adj.* sick, ill: esser
— di cuore, to have a bad heart.

malatti′a *f.* disease, illness, complaint.

malauguratamente *adv.* unfortunately, unluckily.

malaugurato *adj.* damned; unfortunate, unlucky.

malaugu′rio *m.* ill omen; ill luck.

malavita *f.* underworld.

malavo′glia *f.* unwillingness; slothfulness: di —, reluctantly.

malcaduco *adj.* epileptic.

malcapitato *m.*, *adj.* unfortunate.

malcon′cio *adj.* battered: uscirne —,
to come out the worse for wear.

malcontento *m.* malcontent; dissatis-
faction; disappointment; *adj.* dissatisfied; disappointed.

malcostume *m.* bad practice; immorality.

maldestro *adj.* clumsy.

maldicente *m.*, *f.* slanderer; gossip;
adj. slanderous, gossipy.

maldicenza *f.* slander; gossip.

male *m.* evil, ill; sin; illness, disease;
swoon; harm, injury, damage; ache,
pain; sorrow; misfortune, mishap:
mal di testa, headache; — di cuore,
heart disease; — di mare, seasickness; farsi —, to get hurt; far — a,
to hurt; andare a —, to fall through;
to rot; voler — a, to hate; aversela
a —, to take offense (*at*); che —
c′è? what's wrong with it?; non
c′è — (it is) not bad; meno — I so
much the better!; thank heaven!
adv. bad, badly, ill, wrong: dire —
di, to speak ill of; restare —, to be
disappointed, to feel humiliated;
riuscir —, to be a failure, fail, turn
out wrong; stare —, to be in a bad
way; sentirsi —, to feel sick; to
feel faint; il rosso vi sta—, red does
not become you; capir —, to misunderstand.

maledetto *adj.* damned; hellish: sia
—I curse him!; *pp.* of maledire.

maledire *vt.*[44] to curse.

maledizione *f.* malediction, curse.

maleducato *m.* boor; *adj.* ill-bred, rude.

malefatta *f.* mischief, sin.

malefi′cio *m.* sorcery; curse.

male′fico *adj.* evil, maleficent.

malerba *f.* weed.

males′sere *m.* malaise; discomfort;
uneasiness.

malevolenza *f.* malevolence.
male'volo *adj.* malevolent.
malfamato *adj.* ill-famed.
malfatto *m.* mischief; *adj.* ill-done; misshapen.
malfattore *m.* criminal.
malfermo *adj.* unsteady, faltering, tottering.
malfido *adj.* unreliable; tricky.
malgarbo *m.* ungraciousness.
malgoverno *m.* misrule.
malgrado *prep.*, *adv.* despite, in spite of: **mio —**, against my will; **— ciò,** nevertheless.
mali'a *f.* charm.
maliarda *f.* witch; enchantress, vamp.
malignare *vi.* to malign.
malignità *f.* malignity.
maligno *adj.* malignant; pernicious.
malinconi'a *f.* melancholy, sadness.
malinco'nico *adj.* melancholy, sad.
malincuore, (a) *adv.* unwillingly, reluctantly.
malintenzionato *m.* evildoer; *adj.* evil-minded.
malinteso *m.* misunderstanding; *adj.* misunderstood: **orgoglio —,** misplaced pride.
mali'zia *f.* malice; trick; cunning.
malizioso *adj.* malicious; mischievous, quizzical.
mallea'bile *adj.* malleable; (*fig.*) manageable.
malle'olo *m.* malleolus.
mallevadore *m.* surety: **farsi —,** to stand surety (*for*).
malleveri'a *f.* suretyship.
mallo *m.* husk.
malmenare *vt.* to manhandle.
malmesso *adj.* down at heel, seedy.
malnato *m.* wastrel; *adj.* loutish.
malo *adj.* bad, wicked, evil: **a mal partito,** on one's beam-ends; **prendere in mala parte,** to take amiss.
maloc'chio *m.* evil eye.
malora *f.* ruin.
malore *m.* swoon; disease.
malsano *adj.* unhealthy, unwholesome.
malsicuro *adj.* unsteady; unsafe.
malta *f.* mortar; mud.
maltempo *m.* bad weather.
malto *m.* malt.
maltolto *m.* ill-gotten property.
maltrattamento *m.* maltreatment.
maltrattare *vt.* to maltreat.
malumore *m.* ill-humor; spleen; discontent; discord: **essere di —,** to sulk, be sulky, be in a bad temper.
malva *f.* mallow.
malva'gio *adj.* wicked.
malvagità *f.* wickedness.
malvasi'a *f.* malmsey.
malversazione *f.* embezzlement.

malvisto *adj.* unpopular, hated.
malvivente *m.* criminal.
malvolentieri *adv.* unwillingly.
malvolere *m.* malice.
mamma *f.* mother; **ma: — mia!** dear me!
mammalucco *m.* Mameluke; (*fig.*) simpleton, dolt.
mammella *f.* breast, mamma (*pl.* mammae).
mammi'fero *m.*, *adj.* mammalian.
manata *f.* slap; handful.
manca *f.* left hand; left.
mancante *adj.* failing, lacking, missing, wanting.
mancanza *f.* lack, want; default, gap; shortcoming; fault; blunder: **sentir la — di,** to miss.
mancare *vt.* to miss; *vi.* to fail, miss, be lacking; to run short; to blunder, slip; to stay away (*from*); to be missing; to take; to want, be in need (*of*); to die: **— a un appuntamento,** to miss an appointment; **— alla promessa,** to break one's promise; **manca il tempo di,** there is no time to; **quanto ti manca per finire?,** how long will it take you to get through?; **mancano tre minuti alle quattro,** it is three minutes to four; **ci mancherai,** we shall miss you; **sentirsi — il respiro,** to stifle; **poco mancò che mi vedesse,** I just missed being seen by him.
mancato *adj.* unsuccessful; passed away (deceased); uneffected: **— omicidio,** attempted murder; **mancata esecuzione,** non-performance.
manche'vole *adj.* faulty, wanting.
manchevolezza *f.* shortcoming.
man'cia *f.* gratuity, tip; reward.
manciata *f.* handful.
mancina *f.* left hand, left.
mancino *adj.* left-handed; (*fig.*) treacherous, underhanded.
manco *adv.* not even: **— a dirlo,** of course.
mandamento *m.* jurisdiction.
mandante *m.* (*law*) principal.
mandare *vt.* to send; to dispatch; to forward: **— a chiamare,** to send for; **— a dire,** to send word; **— a monte,** to throw overboard; **— a picco,** to sink; **— a quel paese,** to send to Jericho.
mandarino *m.* mandarin; (*bot.*) tangerine.
mandata *f.* batch; turn (*of the key*): **chiudere a doppia —,** to double-lock.
mandata'rio *m.* mandatary.
mandato *m.* warrant; mandate; order; mission: **— di pagamento,** payment voucher.

mandi'bola f. mandible, jaw.
mandolino m. mandolin.
man'dorla f. almond.
mandorlato m. nougat, almond cake.
man'dorlo m. almond tree.
man'dria f. herd.
mandriano m. herdsman.
mandrino m. (mach.) mandrel.
manegge'vole, maneggia'bile adj. wieldy, manageable; kindly, docile.
maneggiare vt. to handle; to manage; to use.
maneg'gio m. handling, use; machination; manège.
maneggione m. factotum; meddler.
manesco adj. violent, brutal.
manetta f. hand lever; handcuff.
manette f.pl. handcuffs.
manforte f. aid.
manganello m. cudgel.
man'gano m. calender; mangonel.
mangerec'cio adj. edible.
mangeri'a f. graft, swindle.
mangiapane m. idler, wastrel.
mangiapreti m. anticlerical.
mangiare vt., vi. to eat (up); to have one's meals; to eat away; to graft: — pane a tradimento, to eat the bread of idleness; — con gli occhi, to devour with one's eyes.
mangiata f. gorge, meal.
mangiato'ia f. manger, crib.
mangiatore m. (hearty) eater.
mangime m. food; fodder; birdseed.
mangione m. glutton.
mangiucchiare vt., vi. to nibble (at).
mangusta f. mongoose.
mani'a f. mania; hobby; craze.
mani'aco m. eccentric; adj. crazy.
ma'nica f. sleeve; band, gang: — a vento, wind cone; di — larga, broadminded; di — stretta, stingy, narrow-minded; è un altro paio di maniche, it is another matter.
Ma'nica, (La) f. The Channel.
manicaretto m. titbit, treat (to eat).
manichino m. manikin; model; cuff.
ma'nico m. handle; stick.
manico'mio m. mental hospital.
manicotto m. muff.
manicure f. manicure, manicurist.
maniera f. way, manner; politeness; kind, sort; behavior; style: un'-opera di —, a manneristic work; in nessuna —, by no means.
manierato adj. affected, conventional.
manierismo m. mannerism.
maniero m. manor house.
manifattura f. manufacture; manufacturing; manufactory, plant.
manifestare vt. to manifest, show; to reveal; **manifestarsi** vr. to manifest oneself, prove.

manifestazione f. manifestation; demonstration.
manifestino m. little poster; throwaway.
manifesto m. poster, placard; manifesto; adj. manifest, clear, plain.
mani'glia f. handle.
manigoldo m. scoundrel, cad.
Manin, Daniele, Italian patriot and statesman (1804–1857).
manipolare vt. to manipulate, handle.
manipolazione f. manipulation.
mani'polo m. handful; maniple; band.
maniscalco m. blacksmith.
manna f. manna.
manna'ia f. ax; knife (of the guillotine).
mannaro, (lupo) m. werewolf; "big bad wolf."
mano f. hand; side, way; power, control; care, custody; workmanship; touch; handwriting; coat (of paint); lead (at cards); — d'opera, labor; stringere la — a, to shake hands with; chiedere la — a, to propose to; starsene con le mani in —, to idle; fare man bassa, to loot; avere le mani in pasta, to know the ropes; tenere — a, to abet; venire alle mani, to come to blows; essere di —, to have the lead (in a game); a —, by hand; con le mani nel sacco, red-handed; a portata di —, within one's reach, near at hand; a — a — che arrivano, as they arrive.
manodo'pera f. labor.
manomesso adj. tampered with.
mano'metro m. manometer, gauge.
manomet'tere vt. to tamper with.
manomissione f. tampering (with).
manomorta f. mortmain.
mano'pola f. gauntlet; handgrip; button; knob (of a radio, etc.).
manoscritto m. manuscript.
manovale m. laborer.
manovella f. crank, winch.
manovra f. maneuver; operation.
manovrare vt. to maneuver; to operate; to handle.
manovratore m. operator; driver.
manrove'scio m. backhander.
mansalva, (a) adv. unrestrainedly, immoderately.
mansione f. duty, function, capacity.
mansueto adj. tame, meek.
mansuetu'dine f. tameness, meekness.
Mantegazza, Paolo, Italian anthropologist (1831–1910).
Mantegna, Andrea, Italian painter, engraver (1431–1506).
mantella f. cloak.
mantellina f. mantlet, cape.
mantello m. cloak; (zool.) coat.

mantenere vt.[141] to keep, maintain; to support, provide for; to keep (to); mantenersi vr. to keep; to last: mantenersi col proprio lavoro, to earn one's living.

mantenimento m. preservation; maintenance, support; keeping.

mantenuta f. kept woman, "gold digger."

mantenuto m. gigolo, gagger. adj. supported; preserved.

man'tice m. bellows (pl.); hood (of a carriage).

manto m. mantle; (fig.) cloak.

manuale m. handbook; adj. manual.

manu'brio m. handle; handlebar; dumbbell.

manufatto m. ware; adj. handmade.

manuten'golo m. accomplice; (law) accessory, abettor.

manutenzione f. maintenance; up-keep; servicing.

Manuzio, Aldo (Teobaldo Mannucci), Italian printer, designer of the italic type (1450–1515).

manza f. heifer.

manzo m. steer; beef.

Manzoni, Alessandro, Italian novelist and poet, I Promessi Sposi (1785–1873).

maomettano m., adj. Mohammedan.

mappa f. map.

mappamondo m. terrestrial globe.

marachella f. mischief, fault.

maragià m. maharajah.

maramaldo m. traitor.

marasma m. marasmus; (fig.) chaos.

maratona f. marathon race.

maratoneta m. marathoner.

marca f. brand; mark; trademark: — da bollo, revenue stamp.

marcare vt. to mark; to score; to emphasize, stress.

marcato adj. marked; stressed.

marchesa f. marchioness.

marchese m. marquis, marquess.

marchiano adj. gross, glaring.

marchiare vt. to brand.

mar'chio m.brand; trademark; stamp.

mar'cia (1) f. march; (auto.) gear: — indietro, reverse gear; mettersi in —, to start, set out.

mar'cia (2) f. pus.

marciapiede m. sidewalk; platform (of a railroad station).

marciare vi. to march.

mar'cio m. rot, rotten matter; adj. rotten, decayed; corrupted: aver torto —, to be all in the wrong; a — dispetto di, in spite of.

marcire vi. to putrefy, rot, decay; to suppurate: — nell'ozio, to waste away in idleness.

marcita f. marsh.

marciume m. rot, rottenness.

marco m. mark.

Marconi, Guglielmo, Italian electronics pioneer and inventor of wireless telegraphy, Nobel Prize in physics, 1909 (1874–1937).

marconigramma m. radiogram.

marconista m. wireless operator.

mare m. sea; seaside: — grosso, rough sea; — interno, inland waters; — magno, watery waste, (fig.) jumble; mal di —, seasickness; tenere il —, to be seaworthy; buttare a —, to throw overboard; un — di gente, a lot of people.

marea f. tide: alta (bassa) —, high (ebb) tide.

mareggiata f. tidal wave.

maremoto m. seaquake.

marena f. amarelle.

marengo m. (coin) napoleon.

maresciallo m. marshal; warrant officer.

maretta f. choppy sea.

margarina f. margarine.

margherita f. daisy.

marginare vt. to marginate.

marginatura f. margination.

mar'gine m. margin; border, edge.

marina f. navy; sea; shore, beach; (paint.) . marine, seascape: — mercantile, merchant marine.

marina'io m. sailor, mariner.

marinare vt. to marinate, pickle: — la scuola, to play truant.

marinaresco adj. sailorly.

marinaro m. sailor; adj. maritime.

marinato adj. pickled.

Marinetti, Filippo Tommaso, Italian writer and poet, founder of futurism (1876–1944).

marino adj. marine, sea.

marioleri'a f. knavery.

marionetta f. puppet.

maritale adj. marital.

maritalmente adv. maritally: vivere —, to cohabit.

maritare vt. to marry; maritarsi vr. to get married.

maritata f. married woman.

marito m. husband: ragazza da —, eligible girl.

marit'timo m. seafarer; adj. maritime, marine, sea.

mariuolo m. scoundrel, rascal.

marma'glia f. riffraff, rabble.

marmellata f. jam: — di arance, marmalade.

marmista m. marbler.

marmitta f. kettle: — di scappamento, exhaust box, muffler.

marmo m. marble.

marmoc'chio m. brat, bantling.

marmo'reo adj. marmoreal.

marmorizzare vt. to marble.
marmotta f. marmot; sluggard.
marna f. marl.
marocca f. trash.
marocchino m., adj. Moroccan; m. morocco (leather).
maroso m. billow, sea.
marra f. hoe; fluke (of an anchor).
marrano m. marrano; (fig.) cad.
marrone m. chestnut; adj. maroon, brown.
marsigliese m., adj. Marseillais; f. Marseillaise.
marsina f. dress coat, "tails."
martedì m. Tuesday.
martellare vt., vi. to hammer; to throb.
martellata f. hammer blow.
martello m. hammer.
martinello, martinetto m. jack.
martingala f. martingale.
Martini, Ferdinando, Italian statesman and author (1841-1928).
Martini, Simone, Italian painter (1283?-1344).
martinicca f. brake.
mar'tire m. martyr.
marti'rio m. martyrdom; torment.
martirizzare vt. to martyrize.
mar'tora f. marten.
martoriare vt. to torture.
marzapane m. marzipan.
marziale adj. martial, warlike.
marziano m., adj. Martian.
marzo m. March.
mas m. torpedo boat.
Masaccio (Tommaso Guidi), Italian painter (1401-1428).
Masaniello (Tommaso Aniello), Neapolitan insurgent (1620-1647).
Mascagni, Pietro, Italian composer, Cavalleria Rusticana (1863-1945).
mascalzonata f. knavery.
mascalzone m. scoundrel, cad.
mascella f. jaw.
mascellare m., adj. maxillary.
ma'schera f. mask; usher (m.), usherette (f.):— antigas, gas mask; ballo in —, fancy-dress ball, masquerade party.
mascheramento m. camouflage.
mascherare vt., mascherarsi vr. to mask; (mil.) to camouflage.
mascherata f. masquerade.
mascherina f. little mask; masker; toecap; (theat.) usherette.
maschiac'cio m. romp.
maschietta f. tomboy; "bobby soxer."
maschile m. masculine; adj. male, masculine, manly.
ma'schio m. male; son, boy; (mech.) shaft (as of a key, etc.); adj. male, manly.
mascolino adj. masculine.

masnada f. gang, mob.
masnadiere m. highwayman.
massa f. mass; bunch; (elec.) ground: in —, en masse.
massacrante adj. (fig.) toilsome.
massacrare vt. to massacre, butcher.
massacro m. massacre.
massaggiare vt. to massage.
massaggiatore m. masseur.
massaggiatrice f. masseuse.
massag'gio m. massage.
massa'ia f. housewife.
massello m. ingot, block.
masseri'a f. farm.
masseri'zie f.pl. household goods.
massicciata f. road ballast.
massic'ciom. (geog.) massif; adj. massive; compact; stocky.
mas'sima f. maxim, rule; proverb.
mas'simo m. maximum, most, top: al —, at most; al — della velocità, at top speed. adj. maximum; greatest; best; highest; extreme, top: peso — (boxing), heavyweight fighter.
masso m. boulder.
massone m. freemason.
massoneri'a f. freemasonry.
masso'nico adj. masonic.
mastello m. (wooden) tub; bucket.
masticare vt. to chew, masticate; to mumble: — veleno, to feel sore.
masticazione f. mastication.
ma'stice m. mastic.
mastino m. mastiff.
ma'stio m. keep.
mastodonte m. mastodon.
mastodon'tico adj. mammoth, huge.
mastro m. master; ledger.
matassa f. skein.
matema'tica f. mathematics.
matema'tico m. mathematician; adj. mathematical: avere la certezza matematica che, to be dead sure that.
materassa'io m. mattress maker.
materasso m. mattress.
mate'ria f. matter; substance; subject; ground; pus; material: — prima, raw material.
materiale m. materiel, material; adj. material; bulky; rough.
materialmente adv. materially; absolutely.
maternità f. maternity, motherhood; maternity hospital.
materno adj. motherly, maternal: lingua materna, mother tongue.
matita f. pencil: — a sfera, ball point pen.
matriarcato m. matriarchy.
matrice f. matrix; counterfoil; stub.
matricida m., f. matricide.
matrici dio m. matricide.

matri'cola f. freshman; register; roll: numero di —, serial number.

matricolato adj. matriculated; arrant: furbo —, old fox.

matrigna f. stepmother.

matrimoniale adj. matrimonial: letto —, double bed.

matrimo'nio m. marriage; wedding.

matrina f. godmother.

matrizzare see madreggiare.

matrona f. matron.

matta f. madwoman; joker (playing card).

mattacchione m. joker; jester.

mattana f. madness: farsi prender dalla —, to lose one's temper.

mattato'io m. shambles.

Matteotti, Giacomo, Italian socialist, murdered by fascists (1885-1924).

matterello m. rolling pin.

mattina f. morning.

mattinata f. morning; (theat.) matinée.

mattiniero adj. early-rising: essere —, to be an early riser.

mattino m. morning: di buon —, early in the morning.

matto m. madman: un mezzo —, a madcap; adj. mad, insane: farsi matte risate, to roar with laughter; andare — per, to be crazy about; — da legare, mad as a hatter.

matto'ide m. madcap.

mattonato m. tile floor.

mattone m. brick; bore: — cavo, air brick.

mattonella f. tile.

mattutino adj. matutinal, morning.

maturare vt., vi. to ripen.

maturazione f. ripening.

maturità f. maturity, ripeness.

maturo adj. ripe, mature: — esame, due consideration.

mausoleo m. mausoleum.

mazurca f. mazurka.

mazza f. cane; cudgel; mace; sledge (hammer).

mazzata f. cudgel blow; blow.

mazziere m. macer.

Mazzini, Giuseppe, Italian patriot and revolutionist (1805-1872).

mazzo m. bunch, cluster; bundle; pack (of cards); bouquet.

mazzolino m. posy.

mazzuolo m. mallet.

me pers.pron. I; me, myself: è più giovane di —, he is younger than I; tra — e —, within myself; in quanto a —, as to me; secondo—, in my opinion.

meandro m. meander, labyrinth.

mecca'nica f. mechanics.

meccanicamente adv. mechanically.

mecca'nico m.mechanician, mechanic; adj. mechanical.

meccanismo m. mechanism; gear: aver il — guasto, to be out of gear.

meccanizzare vt. to mechanize.

mecenate m. patron (of the arts).

mecenatismo m. patronage (of the arts).

meco compound pron. with me; to me.

meda'glia f. medal.

medaglione m. medallion.

mede'simo m., adj. same; self: io —, I myself; egli —, he himself.

me'dia f. average: fare (avere, sostenere) la — di, to average.

media'nico adj. mediumistic.

mediano m. (sport) halfback; adj. mean, middle.

mediante prep. by means of, through.

mediatore m. mediator; (comm.) middleman, broker.

mediazione f. mediation; (comm.) brokerage.

me'dica, (erba) f. lucerne.

medicamento m. remedy.

medicamentoso adj. medicinal.

medicare vt. to dress, medicate.

medicastro m. quack (doctor).

medicazione f. medication; treatment; dressing.

medichessa see dottoressa.

Me'dici, de, Alessandro, first duke of Florence, assassinated (1510-1537).

Me'dici, de, Cosimo, Il Vecchio, chief of the Florentine Republic (1389-1464).

Me'dici, de, Cosimo I, Il Grande, first grand duke of Tuscany (1519-1574).

Me'dici, de, Giulio, Clement VII, Pope 1523-34 (1478-1534).

Me'dici, de, Lorenzo, Il Magnifico, Florentine ruler and patron of the arts (1449-1492).

Me'dici, de, Caterina, queen of Henry II of France (1519-1589).

medicina f. medicine; remedy.

medicinale m. medicament, remedy; adj. healing, medicinal.

me'dico m. physician, doctor; general practitioner: — chirurgo, surgeon; — condotto, parish doctor.

medievale adj. medieval.

me'dio m. middle finger; adj. middle; mean; average; medium.

mediocre adj. mediocre, ordinary.

mediocrità f. mediocrity.

medioevale adj. medieval.

Medioevo m. Middle Ages.

meditabondo adj. thoughtful.

meditare vt., vi. to meditate; to muse (upon), ponder (over); to plan.

meditato adj. deliberate.

meditazione f. meditation.

Mediterra'neo m., adj. Mediterranean.

medusa *f.* jellyfish; (*myth.*) Medusa.
mefi'tico *adj.* mephitic.
mega'fono *m.* megaphone.
megalo'mane *m.* megalomaniac.
megalomani'a *f.* delusion of grandeur, megalomania.
megera *f.* Megaera; (*old*) hag.
me'glio *m., f.* best: alla —, anyhow; avere la —, to win, have the best of it; *adj.* better, best; *adv.* better; rather: faresti — ad andare, you had better go; di bene in —, better and better; tanto —! so much the better!
mela *f.* apple; quince.
melagrana *f.* pomegranate.
melanconi'a *see* malinconi'a.
melanzana *f.* eggplant, aubergine.
melaran'cia *f.* orange.
melassa *f.* molasses, treacle.
melato *adj.* honeyed.
meienso *adj.* silly.
melitense *adj.* Maltese: febbre —, Malta fever.
melli'fluo *adj.* mellifluous.
melma *f.* mud, mire.
melmoso *adj.* muddy, miry.
melo *m.* apple tree.
melodi'a *f.* melody.
melo'dico *adj.* melodic.
melodioso *adj.* melodious.
melodramma *m.* melodrama.
melodramma'tico *adj.* melodramatic.
melograno *m.* pomegranate (tree).
melone *m.* melon.
membrana *f.* membrane.
membratura *f.* frame.
membro *m.* limb; member.
memora'bile *adj.* memorable.
memorando *adj.* memorable.
memorandum *m.* memorandum; notebook.
me'more *adj.* mindful, unforgetful, grateful.
memo'ria *f.* memory; recollection; souvenir; note; memorial; memoir: imparare a —, to memorize, learn by heart.
memoriale *m.* memorial.
mena *f.* intrigue, machination.
menabò *m.* (*typog.*) dummy copy.
menadito, (a) *adv.* perfectly; inch by inch.
menare *vt.* to lead; to take; to deal; to bring: menar le mani, to resort to violence, to come to blows; — calci, to kick; — il can per l'aia, to beat about the bush.
menda *f.* blemish, flaw.
mendace *adj.* mendacious.
menda'cio *m.* falsehood.
mendicante *m.* beggar.
mendicare *vt., vi.* to beg.

mendicità *f.* beggary: ricovero di —, poorhouse.
mendico *m.* pauper, beggar.
menestrello *m.* minstrel.
menimpipo *m.* devil-may-care.
meninge *f.* meninx.
meningite *f.* meningitis.
menisco *m.* meniscus.
meno *m.* less, least; (*math.*) minus (sign): parlare del più e del —, to talk about the weather; per lo —, at least; *adj.* lesser; lower, inferior; fewer; *adv.* less, least; except, but; (*math.*) minus: le tre — un quarto, a quarter to three; venir —, to faint; to break one's word; to fail; fare a — di, to dispense with; to abstain from; non potei fare a — di dirlo, I couldn't help saying it; a — che non, unless; in men che non si dica, before you can say Jack Robinson.
menomamente *adv.* by no means, by any means.
menomare *vt.* to lessen; to impair.
menomazione *f.* diminution; impairment.
me'nomo *adj.* least.
Menotti, Ciro, Italian patriot (1798–1831).
Menotti, Gian Carlo, Italian composer in U.S. *Il medium*, *Il console* (1911–).
mensa *f.* table; (*mil.*) mess; Eucharist: — aziendale, company cafeteria; — universitaria, faculty cafeteria.
mensile *m.* (*monthly*) salary; monthly allowance; *adj.* monthly.
mensilità *f.* monthly payment; installment.
mensilmente *adv.* monthly.
men'sola *f.* bracket, console.
menta *f.* mint.
mentale *adj.* mental: alienazione —, insanity.
mentalità *f.* mentality.
mente *f.* mind; intellect; understanding; memory: imparare a —, to learn by heart; a — fredda, in cold blood; malato di —, lunatic.
mentecatto *m., adj.* lunatic.
mentire *vi.* to lie, tell lies.
mentito *adj.* false: sotto mentite spoglie, in disguise.
mentitore *m.* liar.
mento *m.* chin.
mentolo *m.* menthol.
men'tore *m.* mentor, counselor.
mentre *conj., adv.* while: in quel —, just then.
menù *m.* menu, bill of fare.
menzionare *vt.* to mention.
menzione *f.* mention: degno di —, worth mentioning.

menzogna *f.* falsehood, lie.

menzognero *adj.* false; deceitful.

meravi'glia *f.* wonder; surprise, amazement: far —, to surprise; far meraviglie, to work wonders; fare le meraviglie, to feign surprise; a —, wonderfully.

meravigliare *vt.* to surprise, astonish; meravigliarsi *vr.* to be surprised (*at, to*); to wonder (*at*).

meraviglioso *adj.* wonderful.

Mercadante, Saverio, Italian composer (1795-1870).

mercante *m.* merchant, trader, dealer: fare orecchio da —, to turn a deaf ear.

mercanteggiare *vi.* to trade, barter, deal; to bargain.

mercantile *adj.* mercantile.

mercanzi'a *f.* merchandise, goods (*pl.*); commodities (*pl.*).

mercato *m.* market, store: a buon —, cheap, cheaply: far — di, to barter away.

merce *f.* goods (*pl.*); commodities (*pl.*).

mercè *f.* mercy, thanks: — sua, thanks to him; alla — di, at the mercy of.

mercena'rio *m., adj.* mercenary.

merceologi'a *f.* commodity research.

merceri'a *f.* notions (*tapes, pins, buttons, etc.*); notions store; haberdashery.

mercerizzare *vt.* to mercerize.

mercia'io *m.* haberdasher.

mercimo'nio *m.* illicit barter.

mercoledì *m.* Wednesday.

mercu'rio *m.* quicksilver; mercury.

merenda *f.* snack, bite: questo c'entra come i cavoli a —, that is beside the point.

meretrice *f.* prostitute.

meridiana *f.* sundial.

meridiano *m., adj.* meridian.

meridionale *m.* Southerner; *adj.* southern, south.

meridione, (il) *m.* the South, Southern Italy.

merig'gio *m.* noon, midday. [Italy.

meringa *f.* meringue.

meritare *vt.*, meritarsi *vr.* to be worth, deserve; to win.

meritato *adj., pp.* deserved.

merite'vole *adj.* deserving, worthy, worth: — di fiducia, trustworthy; — di essere letto, worth reading.

me'rito *m.* merit, desert; worth; credit; subject; proficiency: render —, to reward; to give credit (*to*); per — di, thanks to.

merito'rio *adj.* meritorious.

merlatura *f.* battlements.

merletto *m.* lace (*pl.* lace).

merlo *m.* blackbird; (*fig.*) dolt; (*fort.*) battlement.

merluzzo *m.* codfish, cod.

mero *adj.* mere.

mesata *f.* month; month's wages.

me'scere *vt.*[75] to pour out.

meschineri'a, meschinità *f.* meanness; stinginess.

meschino *adj.* poor; weak; mean, cheap; stingy.

me'scita *f.* pouring; bar, saloon.

mescolanza *f.* mixture, blend.

mescolare *vt.* to mix (*up*), mingle; to blend; to stir; to shuffle (*playing cards*); mescolarsi *vr.* to mix, mingle, blend.

mese *m.* month; monthly salary: mi pagarono tre mesi, they paid me three months' wages.

messa (1) *f.* (*eccl.*) mass: — cantata, high mass; requiem.

messa (2) *f.* putting, placing, laying; stake, bet; — a punto, setup; (*mach.*) truing, tuning; — in opera, installation; — in marcia (*auto.*), starter; — in piega, finger wave; — in scena, staging; — a fuoco (*photo.*), focus, focusing.

messaggeri'a *f.* forwarding agency; shipping office.

messaggiero *m.* messenger.

messag'gio *m.* message, dispatch.

messale *m.* missal.

messe *f.* crop, harvest.

messere *m.* gentleman, sir; mister.

Messi'a *m.* Messiah.

messo *m.* messenger; ambassador. *adj.* put; placed; dressed: mal —, down at heel. *pp. of* mettere.

mestare *vt.* to stir.

mestatore *m.* intriguer, meddler; (*pol.*) ringleader.

mestierante *m.* craftsman; potboiler.

mestiere *m.* occupation, trade; metier; housework.

mesti'zia *f.* sadness.

mesto *adj.* sad.

me'stola *f.* ladle.

me'stolo *m.* wooden ladle.

mestruazione *f.* menstruation.

me'struo *m.* menses (*pl.*).

meta *f.* aim, object, end, goal.

metà *f.* half (*pl.* halves); middle; wife, "better half": fare a —, to go fifty-fifty, to go shares.

metafi'sica *f.* metaphysics.

metafi'sico *m.* metaphysician; *adj.* metaphysical.

meta'fora *f.* metaphor.

metal'lico *adj.* metallic.

metalli'fero *adj.* metalliferous.

metallizzare *vt.* to metallize.

metallo *m.* metal.

metallurgi'a *f.* metallurgy.

metallur'gico *m.* metallurgist; steelworker; *adj.* metallurgical.

metamor'fosi *f.* metamorphosis (*pl.* metamorphoses).

metano *m.* (*chem.*) methane.

metanodotto *m.* natural gas pipeline.

metapsi'chica *f.* metapsychics.

Metastasio (*Pietro Antonio Domenico Bonaventura Trapassi*), Italian poet and dramatist (1698–1782).

mete'ora *f.* meteor.

meteorismo *m.* tympanites, meteorism.

meteorite *f.* meteoroid; meteorite.

meteorografi'a *f.* meteorography.

meteorologi'a *f.* meteorology.

meteorolo'gico *adj.* meteorologic: bollettino —, weather forecast.

metic'cio *m.* mestizo, half-breed; *adj.* half-breed.

meticoloso *adj.* meticulous, painstaking, finicky.

metile *m.* methyl.

meti'lico (alcool) *m.* methyl alcohol, methanol.

meto'dico *adj.* methodical.

me'todo *m.* method.

metrag'gio *m.*, metratura *f.* length in meters.

me'trica *f.* metrics.

me'trico *adj.* metrical, metric.

metro *m.* meter; measure; (*fig.*) yardstick.

metro'poli *f.* metropolis.

metropolitana *f.* subway.

metropolitano *m.* policeman; *adj.* metropolitan.

met'tere *vt.*[75] to put, place; to lay; to charge; to use, employ; to compare; to suppose: ci ho messo tre ore, it took me three hours; — un freno a, to check; — la luce elettrica, to install electricity; — radici, to take root; — i denti, to cut one's teeth; — giudizio, to reform; — a tacere, to hush up; — a disagio, to make uneasy; — a parte di un segreto, to let a secret; — fuori combattimento, to knock out; — in rilievo, to emphasize, stress; — in scena, to stage, produce.

met'tersi *vr.* to put, place oneself; to begin, start; to put on: — a letto, to go, take, to bed; — a sedere, to sit down; — in cammino, to set out, start walking; — in vista, to make oneself conspicuous; — in urto con, to fall out with.

Meucci, Antonio, Italian physicist (1809–1889).

mezzadro *m.* metayer, sharecropper.

mezzaluna *f.* crescent; chopping knife; (*fort.*) lunette.

mezzana *f.* procuress; (*naut.*) mizzen.

mezzanino *m.* mezzanine.

mezzano *m.* pimp. *adj.* middle, mean.

mezzanotte *f.* midnight.

mezzo (*1*) *m.* way; means: mezzi di trasporto, means of transportation.

mezzo (*2*) *m.* middle; half; nel (bel) —, in the (very) middle; togliersi di —, to get out of the way; andarci di —, to get involved; *adj.* half; middle; *adv.* half; almost: le tre e —, half past three.

mezzodi, mezzogiorno *m.* midday, noon; south.

mezzuc'cio *m.* expedient, ruse.

mi (*1*) *pers.pron.* me, to me, at me; (*refl.*) myself, to (at) myself: ec'comi, here I am.

mi (*2*) *m.* (*mus.*) mi, E.

miagolare *vi.* to mew, miaow.

miagoli'o *m.* mewing.

mica (*1*) *f.* (*min.*) mica.

mica (*2*) *f.* crumb.

mica (*3*) *adv.* (*not*) at all, ever; never.

mic'cia *f.* fuse.

Michelac'cio *m.* loafer.

Michela'ngelo (*Buonarroti Michelangelo*), Italian painter, sculptor, architect, poet; chief works as a painter: *Sacra Famiglia, Giudizio Universale*; as a sculptor: *Pietà, Davide, Mosè, Tombe Medicee*; as an architect: *Dome of San Pietro* (1475–1564).

mi'cia *f.* she-cat, pussy.

micidiale *adj.* deadly.

mi'cio *m.* tomcat.

micro'bio, mi'crobo *m.* microbe.

microce'falo *m.* microcephalus; *adj.* microcephalous.

micro'fono *m.* microphone.

microfotografi'a *f.* photomicrography.

microsco'pico *adj.* microscopic.

microsco'pio *m.* microscope.

microsolco *adj.* microgroove.

midolla *f.* crumb.

midollo *m.* marrow; medulla; pith; spinal cord: bagnato fino al —, drenched, soaked.

miele *m.* honey.

mie'tere *vt.* to mow; (*fig.*) to reap.

mietitore *m.* harvester.

mietitrice *f.* harvester; (*mach.*) reaping machine.

mietitura *f.* harvesting; harvest.

miglia'io *m.* thousand.

mi'glio (*1*) *m.* mile.

mi'glio (*2*) *m.* (*bot.*) millet.

miglioramento *m.* improvement.

migliorare *vt.* to improve, better: — un primato, to break a record; *vi.* to improve, get better.

migliore *m.*, *adj.* better; best: — di, better than; il —, the best.

migliori'a *f.* improvement.

Migliorini, Bruno, Italian lexicographer, *Lingua contemporanea, La lingua nazionale, Conversazioni sulla lingua italiana, Appendice al Dizionario moderno* di A. Panzini (1896–).

mignatta *f.* leech.

mi'gnolo *m.* little finger; little toe.

migrare *vi.* to migrate.

migratore *m.,* *adj.* migrant.

migrazione *f.* migration.

miliarda'rio *m.* millionaire; owner of milliards.

millardo *m.* milliard.

miliare, (pietra) *f.* milestone.

miliona'rio *m.* millionaire.

milione *m.* million.

milione'simo *adj.* millionth.

militante *adj.* militant.

militare (1) *m.* soldier; *adj.* military.

militare (2) *vi.* to serve (*in the army*); *(fig.)* to militate.

militaresco *adj.* soldierly.

militarismo *m.* militarism.

militarizzare *vt.* to militarize.

mi'lite *m.* militiaman: Milite Ignoto, Unknown Soldier.

mili'zia *f.* militia; (*pl.*) army.

millanta *adj.* a thousand; (*fig.*) a great many.

millantare *vt.* to vaunt, boast.

millantatore *m.* boaster.

millanteri'a *f.* brag, boast.

mille *m.,* *adj.* a (or one) thousand: -cento, -duecento, ecc., eleven hundred, twelve hundred, etc.

millena'rio *m.,* *adj.* millenary.

millen'nio *m.* millennium.

millepiedi *m.* millipede.

mille'simo *adj.* thousandth.

milligramma *m.* milligram.

milli'metro *m.* millimeter.

milza *f.* spleen.

mime'tico *adj.* mimetic.

mimetismo *m.* (*zool.*) mimicry.

mimetizzare *vt.* to camouflage.

mimetizzazione *f.* camouflage.

mi'mica *f.* mimicry.

mimo *m.* mime.

mina *f.* mine; lead (*of a pencil*).

minac'cia *f.* threat, menace.

minacciare *vt., vi.* to threaten (*with*).

minaccioso *adj.* threatening.

minare *vt.* to mine; to undermine.

minatore *m.* miner; coal miner.

minato'rio *adj.* threatening.

minchionare *vt.* to ridicule; to take in.

minchionatura *f.* banter; deception.

minchione *m.* simpleton, "goof."

minchioneri'a *f.* nonsense; "goofiness."

minerale *m.* mineral; ore; *adj.* mineral.

minera'rio *adj.* mining.

minestra *f.* soup.

mingherlino *adj.* spare, thin.

Minghetti, Marco, Italian statesman and author (1818–1886).

miniatura *f.* miniature.

miniera *f.* mine.

minimamente *adv.* at all, by any (no) means, in the least.

minimizzare *vt.* to belittle.

mi'nimo *m.,* *adj.* least, minimum; (*the*) smallest; (*the*) lowest; (*the*) shortest.

mi'nio *m.* minium, red lead.

ministeriale *adj.* ministerial, cabinet.

ministero *m.* ministry, office, department; cabinet: Ministero degli Esteri, Department of State; Pubblico Ministero, Public Prosecutor.

ministro *m.* minister, secretary (*of state*); ambassador; (*eccl.*) minister.

minoranza *f.* minority.

minorare *vt.* to disable.

minorato *adj.* disabled.

minorazione *f.* disablement; diminution.

minore *m.* minor; youngest (*son*), junior; *adj.* less, lesser, minor; minimum, least; smaller; smallest; lower; lowest; shorter; shortest; younger; youngest: di — età, under age.

minorenne *m.* minor; *adj.* under-age.

minorità *f.* minority.

minuetto *m.* minuet.

minu'scola *f.* small letter.

minu'scolo *adj.* small; (*typog.*) lower case; (*fig.*) diminutive.

minuta *f.* rough copy.

minuta'glia *f.* trifles; "small fry."

minuteri'e *f.pl.* smallware.

minuto (1) *m.* minute: — primo, minute; — secondo, second; spaccare il —, to keep time to the minute.

minuto (2) *m.* (*comm.*) retail.

minuto (3) *adj.* minute, small.

minu'zia *f.* trifle.

minuzioso *adj.* minute, finical.

mio *poss.adj.* my; *poss.pron.* mine; *m.* my own (*money*): i miei, my parents, my family, my folks.

mi'ope *m.* short-sighted person. *adj.* myopic, short-sighted.

miopi'a *f.* myopia, myopy.

mira *f.* sight; aim, target; design, plan: prendere di —, to aim at; (*fig.*) to make a target of.

mirabile *adj.* admirable.

mirabi'lia *f.pl.* wonders: dir —, to speak highly (*of*).

miracolato *m.* one miraculously restored to health.

mira'colo *m.* miracle; wonder.

miracoloso *adj.* miraculous.

mirag'gio *m.* mirage.

mirare *vt.* to look at; *vi.* to sight (*at*), take aim; to aim (*at*).

miri'ade *f.* myriad.

mirino *m.* sight; (*photo.*) finder.

mirra *f.* myrrh.

mirtillo *m.* whortleberry.

mirto *m.* myrtle.

misantropi'a *f.* misanthropy.

misan'tropo *m.* misanthropist.

miscela *f.* mixture; blend.

miscelare *vt.* to mix.

miscella'nea *f.* miscellany.

mi'schia *f.* tussle, fray; (*sport*) scrimmage.

mischiare *see* mescolare.

miscono'scere *vt.*[30] to gainsay; to disregard.

misconosciuto *adj.* unappreciated; disregarded; misunderstood.

miscredente *m.* unbeliever.

miscu'glio *m.* medley; mixture; concoction.

misera'bile *m.* wretch; *adj.* unhappy, wretched; despicable.

miseramente *adv.* poorly; piteously.

miserando, misere'vole *adj.* pitiable.

mise'ria *f.* poverty, destitution; woe; trifle; meanness; want, dearth.

misericor'dia *f.* mercy.

misericordioso *adj.* merciful.

mi'sero *adj.* miserable; meager; stingy; mean; pinched; piteous.

miser'rimo *superl.adj.* extremely miserable (meager, *etc.*).

misfatto *m.* misdeed, crime.

miso'gino *m.* misogynist.

mis'sile *m.*, *adj.* missile: — telecomandato, guided missile.

missiona'rio *m.* missionary.

missione *f.* mission.

missiva *f.*, *adj.* missive.

misterioso *adj.* mysterious.

mistero *m.* mystery.

misticismo *m.* mysticism.

mi'stico *m.*, *adj.* mystic.

mistificare *vt.* to mystify, hoodwink.

mistificatore *m.* mystifier, cheat.

mistificazione *f.* mystification, trick.

misto *m.* mixture. *adj.* mixed: scuola mista, coeducational school.

mistura *f.* mixture.

misura *f.* measure; size; tape measure; moderation, composure; step, action: oltrepassare la —, to go too far.

misurare *vt.* to measure; to try on; to gauge; to weigh; to deal; to judge; to estimate; misurarsi *vr.* to measure oneself; to contend.

misurato *adj.* measured; scanty; moderate; cautious.

misuratore *m.* gauger, measurer; meter.

misurazione *f.* measurement.

mite *adj.* mild; kindly; meek.

mitezza *f.* mildness, meekness.

mi'tico *adj.* mythical.

mitigare *vt.* to allay, mitigate; mitigarsi, *vr.* to abate.

mito *m.* myth.

mitologi'a *f.* mythology.

mitolo'gico *adj.* mythological.

mitra *f.* mitre; submachine gun.

mitra'glia *f.* grapeshot.

mitragliare *vt.* to machine-gun.

mitragliatore *m.* machine gunner: fucile —, submachine gun.

mitragliatrice *f.* machine gun.

mitragliere *m.* machine gunner.

mittente *m.* sender.

mo' *m.* (abbr. of modo) way: a — di, by way of; as; a — d'esempio, for instance.

mo'bile (1) *m.* piece of furniture; (*pl.*) furniture.

mo'bile (2) *adj.* movable; portable; variable; fickle, inconstant.

mobi'lia *f.* furniture.

mobiliere *m.* furniture maker.

mobilità *f.* mobility; changeableness.

mobilitare *vt.* to mobilize.

mobilitazione *f.* mobilization.

moca *m.* mocha.

moc'cio *m.* snivel, snot.

moccioso *m.* sniveler, brat.

moc'colo *m.* candle stump; curse.

moda *f.* fashion: di —, fashionable.

modalità *f.* modality; (*pl.*) procedure.

modanatura *f.* molding.

modella *f.* model.

modellare *vt.* to model, mold; to pattern (*after*).

modello *m.* model; pattern, specimen.

moderare *vt.* to moderate, temper; to restrain; moderarsi *vr.* to moderate, restrain oneself.

moderatezza *f.* soberness; restraint.

moderato *m.*, *adj.* moderate.

moderazione *f.* moderation.

modernità *f.* modernity.

modernizzare *vt.* to modernize.

moderno *m.*, *adj.* modern.

mode'stia *f.* modesty.

modesto *adj.* modest; moderate.

mo'dico *adj.* cheap, reasonable.

modi'fica *f.* alteration.

modificare *vt.* to modify, alter.

modificazione *f.* modification.

Modigliani, Amedeo, Italian painter (1884–1920).

modista *f.* milliner.

modisteri'a *f.* millinery.

modo *m.* way, manner; means; behavior, ways (*pl.*); (*gramm.*) mood: essere a —, to be well-mannered; di — che, so that; in — da, so as; oltre —, beyond measure; in certo qual —, somehow; per — di dire, so to speak.

modulare vt. to modulate.

modulatore m. modulator: — di frequenza, (radio) modulator tube.

modulazione f. modulation.

mo'dulo m. model, standard; form, blank; (arch.) module.

mo'gano m. mahogany.

mog'gio m. bushel.

mo'gio adj. crestfallen; downhearted.

mo'glie f. wife; bride.

moina f. blandishment, guile.

mola f. grindstone; millstone.

molare (1) m., adj. molar.

molare (2) vt. to grind; to bevel.

molato adj. ground; beveled.

mole f. mass, bulk; pile; size.

mole'cola f. molecule.

molecolare adj. molecular.

molestare vt. to irk, annoy, tease.

mole'stia f. trouble; uneasiness.

molesto adj. irksome, troublesome.

molla f. (mach.) spring.

mollare vt. to loosen; to let go; to drop. vi. to give in, yield: — gli ormeggi, to cast off.

molle (1) f.pl. tongs.

molle (2) adj. soft; flabby; wet; weak.

molleggiare see molleggio.

molleggiare vi. to spring, be resilient.

molleg'gio m. suspension.

mollettone m. Canton flannel.

mollezza f. softness; weakness.

mollica f. crumb.

mollificare vt. to soften.

mollo adj. damp: mettere a—, to steep.

mollusco m. mollusk.

molo m. wharf, pier.

molte'plice adj. manifold.

molti'plica f. multiplication; chain gearing.

moltiplicando m. multiplicand.

moltiplicare vt., moltiplicarsi vr. to multiply.

moltiplicatore m. multiplier.

moltiplicazione f. multiplication.

moltitu'dine f. multitude.

molto (1) m. much, a great deal; molti pl. many.

molto (2) adj. much; great; long: per — tempo, for a long time; — tempo fa, long ago; molti pl. many.

molto (3) adv. greatly, very; a great deal; (followed by adj., adv., ppr.) very; (followed by pp., comp.) much.

moltis'simo adv. very much; m., a great deal; adj. very much; very great; very long; moltissimi pl. very many.

momentaneamente adv. temporarily; just now.

momenta'neo adj. momentary; fleeting.

momento m. moment; opportunity; importance: dal — che, since; a momenti, almost; shortly, any moment.

mo'naca f. nun.

monacale adj. monachal.

mo'naco m. monk.

monarca m. monarch.

monarchi'a f. monarchy.

monastero m. monastery.

mona'stico adj. monastic.

moncherino m. stump.

monco adj. maimed; incomplete, unfinished; one-armed.

moncone m. stump.

Mondadori, Arnoldo, leading Italian publisher (1889-   ).

mondana f. fancy woman.

mondanità f. worldliness.

mondano adj. worldly; earthly.

mondare vt. to clean; to cleanse; to hull; to weed.

mondariso m. rice weeder.

mondiale adj. world-wide, world.

mondina see mondariso.

mondo (1) m. world; earth: l'altro —, the world beyond; caschi il —! come what may!; mettere al —, to bring forth.

mondo (2) adj. clean; pure; free (from).

monella f. romp; "bobby-soxer."

monelleri'a f. prank, mischief.

monello m. urchin, imp.

moneta f. coin, piece; money; change.

monetare vt. to coin.

moneta'rio m. monetary.

monile m. necklace.

mo'nito m. warning.

monitore m. monitor.

monna f. lady; (zool.) pithecus.

mono'colo m. one-eyed man; monocle.

monofase adj. single-phase.

monogami'a f. monogamy.

monografi'a f. monograph.

monogramma m. monogram.

monolito m. monolith.

mono'logo m. monologue.

monopat'tino m. scooter.

monoplano m. monoplane.

monopo'lio m. monopoly.

monopolizzare vt. to monopolize.

monosil'labo m. monosyllable.

monoti'pia f. monotype.

monotipista m. monotyper.

monotoni'a f. monotony.

mono'tono adj. monotonous.

monsignore m. (eccl.) Monsignor; (archaic) Your (His) Lordship.

monsone m. monsoon.

monta f. covering; stud; jockey.

montaca'richi m. freight elevator.

montag'gio m. (mach.) assemblage; (moving pictures) editing, montage.

montagna *f.* mountain; pile, heap:
montagne russe, roller coaster.

montagnola *f.* mound.

montagnoso *adj.* mountainous.

Montale, Eugenio, Italian poet
(1896-).

montanaro *m.* mountaineer.

montano *adj.* mountain.

montante *m.* amount; step; post;
(*boxing*) uppercut; (*aeron.*) strut;
adj. rising, mounting.

montare *vt.* to mount, climb; to set;
(*mach.*) to assemble; to fit up; to
frame; (*zool.*) to cover; to whip
(*cream*); to stage (*a show*); to edit
(*a moving-picture film*); *vi.* to
mount; to rise; to swell: — su un
treno, to board a train; — in bestia,
to fly off the handle; montarsi *vr.* to
swell; to work oneself up.

montatore *m.* assembler.

montatura *f.* assembling; setting; (*fig.*)
hocus-pocus;"hokum"; "ballyhoo."

montavivande *m.* lift, dumbwaiter.

monte *m.* mount, mountain; heap,
pile: — di pietà, pawnbroking
establishment; andare a —, to end
in smoke; mandare a —, to throw
overboard; to call off.

Montessori, Maria, Italian educator
(1870-1952).

Monteverdi, Claudio, Italian composer
(1567-1643).

montone *m.* ram; mutton.

montuoso *adj.* mountainous.

montura *f.* uniform.

monumentale *adj.* monumental.

monumento *m.* monument;⁝memorial.

mora (*1*) *f.* (*law*) arrearage.

mora (*2*) *f.* blackberry; mulberry;
brambleberry.

mora (*3*) *f.* Negro woman; brunette.

morale (*1*) *f.* moral; morality, morals.

morale (*2*) *m.* morale: il — delle
truppe, the morale of the troops;
giù di —, downhearted; su di —, in
high spirits.

morale (*3*) *adj.* moral.

moralista *m.* moralist.

moralità *f.* morality; character.

moralizzare *vt.*, *vi.* to moralize.

moralmente *adv.* morally.

morato'ria *f.* moratorium.

Moravia, Alberto (*Alberto Pincherle*),
Italian novelist (1907-).

morbidezza *f.* softness.

mor'bido *adj.* soft; delicate.

morbillo *m.* measles.

morbo *m.* illness, disease; plague.

morboso *adj.* morbid.

mor'chia *f.* oil dregs.

mordace *adj.* mordant, mordacious.

mordente *m.* mordant; (*fig.*) bite;
vim, "zing."

mor'dere *vt.*,⁷⁷ *vi.* to bite; to sting: —
il freno, to champ at the bit.

mordicchiare *vt.* to nibble (*at*).

morena *f.* moraine.

morente *adj.* dying; (*fig.*) fading.

moresco *adj.* Moorish, Moresque.

moretta *f.* brunette; Negro girl.

moretto *m.* brunet; Negro boy.

morfina *f.* morphine, morphia.

morfologi'a *f.* morphology.

morgana'tico *adj.* morganatic.

mori'a *f.* high mortality.

moribondo *m.*, *adj.* moribund.

morigerato *adj.* temperate, moderate,
sober, subdued.

morire *vi.*⁷⁸ to die; to die away: — di
noia, to be bored to death.

morituro *adj.* dying, doomed.

mormorare *vt.*, *vi.* to murmur; to
grumble; to rustle; to gossip.

mormori'o *m.* murmur; grumble;
whisper; rustle.

moro (*1*) *m.* mulberry tree.

moro (*2*) *m.* Moor; Negro; brunet.
adj. dark, swarthy.

morosità *f.* insolvency.

moroso (*1*) *adj.* insolvent: contribuente
—, tax delinquent.

moroso (*2*) *m.*, morosa *f.* (*colloq.*)
sweetheart, lover.

morsa *f.* vise; (*naut.*) davit.

morsetto *m.* clamp.

morsicare *vt.* to bite.

morsicatura *f.* bite; sting.

morso (*1*) *m.* bite; sting; morsel; bit,
snaffle.

morso (*2*) *pp.* of mordere.

morta'io *m.* mortar; trench gun.

mortale *m.* mortal. *adj.* mortal, deadly, fatal: salto —, somersault.

mortalità *f.* mortality.

mortalmente *adv.* mortally; deadly.

mortaretto *m.* firecracker.

morte *f.* death.

mortella *f.* myrtle.

mortificante *adj.* mortifying.

mortificare *vt.* to mortify, snub.

mortificato *adj.* abashed, crestfallen.

mortificazione *f.* mortification, shame.

morto *m.* dead (*man*); deceased;
corpse; dummy (*at bridge and other
games*); *adj.* dead, deceased: a
corpo —, headlong; natura morta,
still life. *pp.* of morire.

morto'rio *m.* funeral; gloom.

mosa'ico *m.* mosaic; *adj.* Mosaic.

mosca (*1*) *f.* fly; gadfly; imperial: una —
bianca, one in a million; — cieca,
blindman's buff.

moscatello *m.* muscatel.

moscato *m.* muscat: noce moscata,
nutmeg.

moscerino *m.* gnat.

moschea *f.* mosque.

moschettiere *m.* musketeer.
moschetto *m.* musket, rifle.
moschettone *m.* clasp, slip hook.
moschicida *adj.* fly-killing: **carta —,** flypaper.
mo'scio *adj.* flabby.
moscone *m.* bluebottle fly.
mossa *f.* move, movement; gesture: **essere sulle mosse,** to be about (*to*).
mossiere *m.* starter (*in a race*).
mosso *adj.* moved; stirred; lively: **mare —,** rough sea. *pp. of* muovere.
mostarda *f.* mustard.
mosto *m.* must.
mostra *f.* exhibition; show; display; show window; pretense: **mettersi in —,** to show off; **far — di,** to pretend to.
mostrare *vt.* to show, exhibit; to point out; to disclose; to pretend: **— la corda,** to be threadbare; **mostrarsi** *vr.* to show; to reveal oneself; to prove; to feign.
mostriciat'tolo *m.* little monster; freak.
mostrine *f.pl.* collar insignia.
mostro *m.* monster.
mostruoso *adj.* monstrous.
mota *f.* mud, mire.
motivare *vt.* to explain; to motivate; to justify; to cause, occasion.
motivato *adj.* grounded (*on*); justified.
motivazione *f.* allegation, motivation.
motivo *m.* motive, reason, cause; ground; motif; tune: **— per cui,** therefore; **a — di,** owing to.
moto *m.* motion, movement; exercise; riot; urge, impulse; *f.* motorcycle.
motocarrozzetta *f.* sidecar.
motobarca *f.* motorboat.
motocicletta *f.* motorcycle.
motociclismo *m.* motorcycling.
motociclista *m.* motorcyclist.
motociclo *m.* motorcycle.
motofurgone *m.* motorcycle truck.
motona'uta *m.* motorboatman.
motonau'tica *f.* boat racing.
motonave *f.* motor ship.
motopescherec'cio *m.* motor fishing boat.
motore *m.* motor, engine: **— a reazione,** jet engine.
motoretta *f.* motor scooter.
motorista *m.* motorist; mechanician.
motorizzare *vt.* to motorize.
motoscafo *m.* motor launch, motorboat.
motrice *f.* driving car; *adj.* motive.
motteggiare *vt.* to mock; *vi.* to banter.
motteg'gio *m.* jest, mockery.
motto *m.* motto; slogan; saying; witticism.
movente *m.* motive, reason.
movenza *f.* movement.

movi'bile *adj.* movable.
movimentato *adj.* lively, animated; eventful; checkered.
movimento *m.* movement; motion; traffic; bustle.
mozione *f.* motion.
mozzare *vt.* to lop (*off*), sever; to cut.
mozzicone *m.* stump; butt.
mozzo (1) *m.* stableboy; (*naut.*) sailor boy.
mozzo (2) *m.* hub (*of a wheel*); boss (*of a screw propeller*).
mozzo (3) *adj.* severed: **fiato —,** panting breath; **coda mozza,** dock.
mucca *f.* cow.
muc'chio *m.* heap, pile, mass; crowd; stack.
mucillag'gine *f.* mucilage.
muco *adj.* mucus.
mucosa *f.* mucous membrane.
muffa *f.* must, mold.
muffire *vi.* to grow musty.
muffito *adj.* musty, moldy.
muffoso *adj.* musty, moldy; (*fig.*) fusty.
muflone *m.* mouflon.
mugghiare *vi.* to bellow, low; to howl; to roar.
mug'gine *m.* mullet.
muggire *see* mugghiare.
muggito *m.* low, bellow.
mughetto *m.* lily of the valley.
mugna'io *m.* miller.
mugolare *vi.* to yelp; to moan.
mugoli'o *m.* yelping, moan.
mugo'lio *m.* pine tar.
mulattiera *f.* mule track, pack road.
mulattiere *m.* muleteer.
mulatto *m.*, *adj.* mulatto.
muliebre *adj.* womanly, feminine.
mulinello *m.* whirligig; whirlwind; whirlpool.
mulino *m.* mill; watermill: **— a vento,** windmill.
mulo *m.* mule.
multa *f.* fine.
multare *vt.* to fine.
multicolore *adj.* multicolored, motley.
mul'tiplo *m.*, *adj.* multiple.
mum'mia *f.* mummy.
mummificare *vt.*, **mummificarsi** *vr.* to mummify.
mun'gere *vt.* to milk; (*fig.*) to sponge.
municipale *adj.* municipal.
munici'pio *m.* municipality; town hall.
munificenza *f.* munificence.
muni'fico *adj.* munificent.
munire *vt.* to provide, equip, furnish, supply (*with*); **munirsi** *vr.* to provide oneself (*with*).
munizione *f.* ammunition.
munto *pp. of* mungere.
muo'vere *vt.* to move; to displace; to stir (*up*); to drive, lead; to

prompt, urge; to raise; *vi.* to go; to come; to move; to advance: — incontro a qualcuno, to go to meet someone; muoversi *vr.* to move; to stir; to act; to leave.

mura *f.pl.* walls (*of a city*).

mura'glia *f.* wall, rampart.

murale *adj.* mural.

murare *vt.* to wall; to immure.

murata *f.* (*naut.*) bulwark.

muratore *m.* bricklayer.

muratura *f.* bricklaying: lavoro in —, brickwork.

murena *f.* moray.

muro *m.* wall: mettere con le spalle al —, to corner; — del suono, sound barrier.

musa *f.* Muse, inspiration.

mu'schio *m.* musk; moss.

muscolare *adj.* muscular.

mu'scolo *m.* muscle, sinew.

muscoloso *adj.* muscular, brawny.

museo *m.* museum.

museruola *f.* muzzle.

mu'sica *f.* music; score; band.

musicale *adj.* musical.

musicalità *f.* musicalness.

musicante *m.* musician.

musicare *vt.* to (*set to*) music.

musicista *m.* musician.

muso *m.* muzzle; snout, face; nose: mettere il —, to pout; avere il —, to sulk.

musone *m.* sulker.

musoneri'a *f.* sullenness, sulkiness.

mus'sola *f.* (*muslin*) delaine.

mussolina *f.* muslin.

Mussolini, Benito (*il Duce*), Italian fascist premier and dictator (1883–1945).

mussulmano *see* musulmano.

mustacchi *m.pl.* mustache.

mustela *f.* stone marten.

musulmano *m.*, *adj.* Moslem.

muta *f.* change; shift; outfit; pack (*of hounds*); relay (*of horses*); set of sails.

mutamento *see* cambiamento.

mutande *f.pl.* drawers (*clothing*).

mutandine *f.pl.* trunks, shorts.

mutare, mutarsi *see* cambiare, cambiarsi.

mute'vole *adj.* changeable; variable; fickle.

mutilare *vt.* to mutilate, maim.

mutilato *m.* cripple; *adj.* mutilated, maimed.

mutilazione *f.* mutilation, maiming, mayhem.

mutismo *m.* muteness, dumbness, silence.

muto *m.* mute; *adj.* dumb, mute; silent; speechless; voiceless: scena muta, dumbshow.

mu'tria *f.* sulk; "crust," "nerve."

mu'tua *f.* medical aid center.

mutuare *vt.* to borrow; to lend.

mu'tuo *m.* loan; *adj.* mutual.

N

nababbo *m.* nabob.

nac'chera *f.* castanet.

nafta *f.* naphtha; diesel oil.

naftalina *f.* naphthalene.

na'ia *f.* cobra; (*It. slang*) military life, service.

na'iade *f.* naiad, waternymph.

nailon *m.* nylon.

nanerot'tolo *m.* dwarf.

nanna *f.* sleep: fare la —, to sleep.

nano *m.*, *adj.* dwarf.

napoletano *m.*, *adj.* Neapolitan.

nappa *f.* tassel.

narciso *m.* daffodil, narcissus.

narcosi *f.* narcosis; anesthesia.

narco'tico *m.*, *adj.* narcotic.

narcotizzare *vt.* to narcotize; to anesthetize.

nare, narice *f.* nostril.

narrare *vt.* to recount, narrate, relate.

narrativa *f.* fiction.

narrativo *adj.* narrative, fiction.

narratore *m.* narrator; storyteller.

narrazione *f.* narration; story.

nasale *adj.* nasal.

nascente *adj.* rising, springing; arising; sprouting.

na'scere *vi.*[61] to be born; to spring, sprout; to derive; to originate, proceed; to rise: far —, to give birth to; — con la camicia, to be born with a silver spoon in one's mouth.

na'scita *f.* birth; extraction, descent.

nascituro *m.* child to be born; *adj.* to be born.

nascon'dere *vt.*[62] to conceal, hide; to mask; to screen; to disguise; nascon'dersi *vr.* to hide.

nascondi'glio *m.* hideout; lair.

nascostamente *adv.* hiddenly; stealthily; secretly.

nascosto *adj.* concealed, hidden; underhand; secret: di —, secretly; stealthily. *pp. of* nascondere.

nasello *m.* whiting.

naso *m.* nose: con un palmo di —, like a duck in thunder.

nastrino *m.* badge, ribbon.

nastro *m.* ribbon, band, strip, tape: metro a —, tapeline; sega a —, bandsaw.

natale (*I*) *m.* birth; birthday: **avere i natali a**, to be born in; **dare i natali a**, to be the birthplace of.

Natale (*2*) *m.* Christmas.

natale (*3*) *adj.* native.

natalità *f.* natality; birth rate.

natali'zio *adj.* natal; Christmas; *m.* birthday.

natante *m.* craft; *adj.* floating.

natato'ia *f.* flipper.

natato'rio *adj.* natatorial, swimming.

na'tica *f.* buttock.

nati'o *adj.* native.

natività *f.* nativity, birth.

nativo *m.*, *adj.* native.

nato *adj.* born; arisen, risen. *pp. of* **nascere.**

natta *f.* wen.

natura *f.* nature: **pagare in —**, to pay in kind.

naturale *adj.* natural; pure; genuine: **di grandezza —**, life-size; **al —**, true to nature.

naturalezza *f.* naturalness; spontaneity.

naturalizzare *vt.*, **naturalizzarsi** *vr.* to naturalize.

naturalizzazione *f.* naturalization.

naturalmente *adv.* naturally; by nature; of course.

naufragare *vi.* to shipwreck; to sink; to fail, wreck.

naufra'gio *m.* shipwreck.

nau'frago *m.* shipwreck survivor; (*fig.*) outcast.

nau'sea *f.* nausea: **aver la —**, to feel sick.

nauseabondo, nauseante *adj.* sickening, disgusting.

nauseare *vt.* to sicken, nauseate, disgust.

nauseato *adj.* disgusted (*with*), sick.

nau'tica *f.* nautics.

nau'tico *adj.* nautical.

nau'tilo *m.* nautilus.

navale *adj.* naval, navy.

navata *f.* nave; aisle.

nave *f.* ship, boat, vessel: **— cisterna, tanker; — traghetto,** ferryboat; **— portaerei,** aircraft carrier.

navetta *f.* shuttle.

navicella *f.* (*naut.*) bark; (*aeron.*) nacelle.

naviga'bile *adj.* navigable.

navigante *m.*, *f.* navigator, seafarer; *adj.* sailing.

navigare *vi.* to navigate, sail, voyage.

navigato *adj.* experienced.

navigatore *m.* navigator.

navigazione *f.* navigation: **— aerea,** aviation, flying.

navi'glio *m.* craft; canal; fleet; merchant marine.

nazionale *f.* national team; *adj.* national.

nazionalità *f.* nationality.

nazionalizzare *vt.* to nationalize.

nazionalizzazione *f.* nationalization.

nazione *f.* nation.

Nazzareno *m.*, *adj.* Nazarene.

ne (*I*) *adv.* from there, therefrom; from here.

ne (*2*) *pron. particle* his, of (*about*) him; her, of (*about*) her; its, of (*about*) it; their, of (*about*) them.

ne (*3*) *partitive pron.* any, some, none.

ne (*4*) (*pleonastic, not to be translated*): **me — vado,** I am going away; **va del mio onore,** my honor is at stake.

nè *neg.conj.* neither, nor: **non poteva — leggere — scrivere,** he could neither read nor write; **non lo vidi più, — mi dispiacque,** I never saw him again, nor did I regret it; **— l'uno — l'altro,** neither.

neanche *see* **nemmeno.**

neb'bia *f.* fog; mist; haze.

nebbione *m.* thick fog, sop.

nebbioso *adj.* foggy.

nebulizzare *vt.* to atomize.

nebulizzatore *m.* atomizer.

nebulosa *f.* (*astr.*) nebula.

nebuloso *adj.* nebulous, hazy.

necessa'rio *m.* necessary, necessity, necessaries (*pl.*); *adj.* necessary; essential, requisite; due.

necessità *f.* necessity, need, want.

necessitare *vt.* to necessitate, need; *vi.* to be necessary; to call (*for*).

necro'foro *m.* gravedigger.

necrologi'a *f.* obituary.

necrolo'gio *m.* necrology, obituary.

necrosi *f.* necrosis.

necrotizzare *vt.* to necrose.

nefandezza *f.* nefariousness.

nefando *adj.* nefarious, unspeakable.

nefasto *adj.* ominous; unfortunate.

nefrite *f.* (*pathol.*) nephritis; (*min.*) nephrite.

negare *vt.* to deny.

negativa *f.* negative, denial; (*photo.*) negative.

negativamente *adv.* negatively.

negativo *adj.* negative.

negato *adj.* denied; unfit; untalented: **essere — alla musica,** to have no bent for music.

negazione *f.* denial, negation; (*gramm.*) negative: **essere la — di** (*fig.*), to have no talent for; to be the opposite of.

neghittoso *adj.* slothful.

negletto *adj.* neglected.

negli *comp.prep. in the. see* **in.**

negligente *adj.* negligent, careless.

negligenza *f.* negligence, neglect, remissness.

negoziante *m.* shopkeeper; dealer.

negoziare *vt.* to negotiate, transact; *vi.* to trade (*in*); to deal (*in*).

negoziato *m.* negotiation.

negoziatore *m.* negotiator.

nego'zio *m.* shop; bargain, transaction.

negra *f.* Negro woman; Negro.

negriero *m.* slave trader, slaver; (*fig.*). slavedriver.

negro *m.* Negro; (*fig.*) ghost writer; *adj.* Negro, black.

nei, nel, nella, nelle, nello *comp.prep.* in the. *see* in.

nembo *m.* (*rain*) cloud; storm.

ne'mesi *f.* nemesis.

nemico *m.* enemy, foe; *adj.* enemy, hostile (*to*), averse (*to*).

nemmanco, nemmeno *conj.* not even, not either, neither: — per sogno! by no means!

ne'nia *f.* dirge.

neo *m.* mole; flaw, blemish.

neologismo *m.* neologism.

neomicina *f.* neomycin.

ne'on *m.* neon: scritta, insegna al —, neon sign.

neonato *m.*, **neonata** *f.* newborn child; *adj.* newborn.

nepote *see* nipote.

neppure *see* nemmanco.

nequi'zia *f.* iniquity.

nerastro *adj.* blackish.

nerbata *f.* scourging.

nerbo *m.* sinew; lash, scourge; strength, vigor.

nerboruto *adj.* sinewy, brawny.

neretto *m.* (*typog.*) boldface.

nerezza *f.* blackness.

nero *m.* black; blackness; *adj.* black, dark: pane —, brown bread.

nerofumo *m.* lampblack.

Nerone *m.* (*hist.*) Nero.

nervatura *f.* nervation.

nervo *m.* nerve; tendon, sinew: avere i nervi, to be peevish, irritable.

nervosamente *adv.* nervously, irritably.

nervosismo *m.* nervousness, irritableness.

nervoso *m.* ill humor; *adj.* nervous; irritable; peevish.

nesci *m.* know-nothing: fare il —, to pretend to know nothing.

ne'spola *f.* medlar; (*colloq.*) blow.

ne'spolo *m.* medlar tree.

nesso *m.* link, connection.

nessuno *adj.* no; *pron.* nobody, no one, none; any, anybody, anyone: nessuna cosa, nothing; in nessun luogo, nowhere; a nessun patto, by no means.

nettamente *adv.* cleanly; markedly; utterly; clearly.

nettapenne *m.* penwiper.

nettapipe *m.* pipe cleaner.

nettare *vt.* to clean, cleanse.

net'tare *m.* nectar.

nettezza *f.* cleanliness; neatness: — urbana, garbage collection service.

netto *adj.* clean; net; clear; marked.

neutrale *m.*, *adj.* neutral.

neutralità *f.* neutrality.

neutralizzare *vt.* to neutralize.

ne'utro *m.*, *adj.* neuter; neutral.

neutrone *m.* neutron.

neva'io *m.* snowfield.

neve *f.* snow.

nevicare *vi.* to snow.

nevicata *f.* snowfall.

nevischio *m.* sleet.

nevoso *adj.* snowy.

nevralgi'a *f.* neuralgia.

nevrasteni'a *f.* neurasthenia.

nevraste'nico *m.*, *adj.* neurasthenic.

nevvero? isn't it (so)?

nib'bio *m.* (*ornith.*) kite.

nic'chia *f.* niche, recess.

nicchiare *vi.* to hesitate, be reluctant.

nichel, niche'lio *m.* nickel.

nichelare *vt.* to nickel, nickelplate.

nichelato *adj.* nickel-plated.

nicotina *f.* nicotine.

nicta'lopo *m.* hemeralope.

nidiata *f.* nestful; brood.

nidificare *vi.* to build a nest.

nido *m.* nest: — d'infanzia, nursery school.

niente *m.* nothing, naught; trifle: far finta di —, to feign indifference; non fa —, it does not matter; *adj.* no: una ferita da —, a slight wound; un uomo da —, a good-for-nothing; *indef.pron.* nothing; anything; *adv.* nothing, not at all.

nientemeno *adv.* nothing less (*than*); no less (*than*); fancy!

Nievo, Ippolito, Italian novelist, poet and patriot, *Le confessioni di un ottuagenario* (1831–1861).

Nilo *m.* (*geog.*) Nile.

ninfa *f.* nymph.

ninfea *f.* (*bot.*) waterlily.

ninnananna *f.* lullaby.

nin'nolo *m.* trinket, trifle.

nipote *m.*, *f.* nephew (*m.*), niece (*f.*); grandchild (*m.*, *f.*), grandson (*m.*), granddaughter (*f.*).

nipotino *m.* little nephew; grandchild.

nippo'nico *adj.* Japanese.

nitidezza *f.* clearness.

ni'tido *adj.* clear; distinct; nitid.

nitore *m.* brightness, polish.

nitrato *m.* nitrate.

nitrire *vi.* to neigh.

nitrito (*1*) *m.* neigh, whinny.

nitrito (*2*) *m.* (*chem.*) nitrite.

nitro m. (chem.) saltpeter.
nitrocellulosa f. nitrocellulose.
nitro'geno m. nitrogen.
Nitti, Francesco Saverio, Italian statesman and economist (1868–1953).
niuno see nessuno.
ni'veo adj. snow-white; niveous.
no adv. no, not: dir di —, to say no; se —, otherwise.
no'bile m. nobleman; f. noblewoman; adj. noble: piano —, second story.
nobiliare adj. nobiliary.
nobilitare vt. to ennoble; to exalt.
nobiltà f. nobility; nobleness.
nocca f. knuckle.
nocchiero m. pilot, steersman.
nocciola see nocciuola.
noc'ciolo m. (fruit) stone: il — della questione, the heart of the matter.
nocciuola f. hazelnut; adj. hazel.
nocciuolo m. hazel.
noce f. walnut; walnut tree: — moscata, nutmeg.
nociuto pp. of nuocere.
nocivo adj. harmful, detrimental.
nocumento m. damage, harm.
nodo m. knot: un — in gola, a lump in one's throat; — scorsoio, noose.
nodoso adj. knotty, gnarly.
noi pers.pron. we; us.
no'ia f. boredom; weariness; trouble: prendere a —, to get tired of; dar — a ,to molest, badger, irk.
noioso adj. boresome, tedious; irksome; m. bore.
noleggiare vt. to hire; to rent; to charter (as a ship).
noleggiatore m. hirer; charterer; freighter.
noleg'gio m. hire; rent; chartering: contratto di —, charter party.
nolente adj. unwilling: volente o —, willy-nilly.
nolo m. hire; (naut.) freight: contratto di —, charter party.
no'made m. nomad; adj. nomadic.
nome m. name; (gramm.) noun; fame, repute: — di battesimo, Christian name; senza —, nameless; a — di, in behalf of.
nomea f. reputation.
nomi'gnolo m. nickname.
no'mina f. appointment; reputation.
nominale adj. nominal.
nominalmente adv. nominally.
nominare vt. to name, call; to mention; to elect; to appoint.
nominativo m. (gramm.) nominative (case); name; adj. nominative.
non adv. not, no; pref. non: un — so che, something (indefinable).
nonagena'rio m. nonagenarian.
nonage'simo adj. ninetieth.

noncurante adj. heedless, careless.
noncuranza f. carelessness, unconcern.
nondimeno adv. nevertheless, still, yet.
nonna f. grandmother.
nonno m. grandfather.
nonni m.pl. grandparents.
nonnulla m. nothing, trifle.
nono adj. ninth.
nonostante prep. in spite of, despite, notwithstanding: ciò —, nevertheless, yet, still, however; — che, although.
nonpertanto prep. still, yet.
nonplusultra m. the ultimate, ne plus ultra.
nonsenso m. nonsense.
nontiscordardimè m. forget-me-not.
nord m. North.
nor'dico m. Northerner; adj. north, northern.
norma f. rule, regulation: di —, as a rule; a — di, in compliance with; per vostra —, for your guidance.
normale f. perpendicular line; adj. normal; ordinary.
normalità f. normality.
normalizzare vt. to normalize.
normalmente adv. normally.
normo'grafo m. lettering guide.
norvegese m., adj. Norwegian.
nosoco'mio m. hospital.
nossignora adv. no, madam.
nossignore adv. no, sir.
nostalgi'a f. homesickness; nostalgia; longing.
nostal'gico adj. homesick; nostalgic.
nostrano adj. home; national; regional.
nostro adj. our; poss.pron. ours.
nostromo m. boatswain.
nota f. note; mark; memorandum; list; bill, invoice: note caratteristiche, fitness report; degno di —, noteworthy; prima — (comm.), waste book.
nota'bile m., adj. notable.
nota'io m. notary (public); lawyer.
notare vt. to note; to jot down, scribble; to notice; to remark: farsi —, to make oneself conspicuous.
notarile adj. notarial.
notaro see notaio.
note'vole adj. remarkable, considerable, notable, noteworthy.
notevolmente adv. remarkably; considerably.
noti'fica see notificazione.
notificare vt. to notify; to serve (as a summons).
notificazione f. notification; service (of a writ).
noti'zia f. (piece of) news; (pl.) news, report; notice; knowledge; reference.

notizia'rio *m.* news report; (*radio*) newscast; (*cinema*) newsreel.

noto *m.* the known; *adj.* known; famous; notorious.

notoriamente *adv.* notoriously.

notorietà *f.* renown, notoriety.

noto'rio *adj.* well known; notorious.

nottam'bulo *m.* night wanderer, noctambulist.

nottata *f.* night: fare —, to burn the midnight oil.

notte *f.* night; night time; darkness: — bianca, sleepless night; sul far della —, at nightfall; di —, by (*at*) night.

nottetempo *adv.* by night.

not'tola *f.* (*zool.*) bat; (*mach.*) latch.

notturno *m.* (*mus.*) nocturne; *adj.* nightly, nocturnal.

novanta *m., adj.* ninety.

novantenne *m., f., adj.* nonagenarian.

novante'simo *m., adj.* ninetieth.

novantina *f.* some ninety: sulla —, about ninety.

nove *m., adj.* nine: fare la prova del —, to cast out nines.

novecentista *m.* modernist.

novecento *m., adj.* nine hundred; *m.* twentieth century.

novella *f.* short story; (*archaic*) news.

novelliere *m.* storyteller, short-story writer.

novellino *m.* beginner, tyro; *adj.* inexperienced, green.

novelli'stica *f.* story-telling; fiction.

novello *adj.* new; tender: sposi novelli, newlyweds.

novembre *m.* November.

novena'rio *adj.* nine-syllabled.

no'vero *m.* number, class.

novis'simo *adj.* quite new.

novità *f.* novelty; innovation; news: — librarie, teatrali, new books, plays.

noviziato *m.* novitiate, apprenticeship.

novi'zio *m.* novice; apprentice; beginner, tyro.

nozione *f.* notion; knowledge; cognition; rudiment.

nozze *f.pl.* wedding; marriage.

nube *f.* cloud.

nubifra'gio *m.* rainstorm; downpour.

nu'bile *f.* maiden; *adj.* unmarried.

nuca *f.* nape, scruff.

nucleare *adj.* nuclear.

nu'cleo *m.* nucleus (*pl.* nuclei); group; squad, force.

nudismo *m.* nudism.

nudista *m.* nudist.

nudità *f.* nudity, nakedness.

nudo *m.* nude; *adj.* naked, bare; stripped (*of*).

nu'golo *m.* cloud; swarm.

nulla *m.* nothingness. *see* niente.

nullaosta *m.* visa, "okay": dare il — per, to visa, "okay."

nullatenente *m.* unpropertied person.

nullità *f.* worthlessness; nullity; voidness, nonentity, (a) nobody.

nullo *adj.* worthless; null, void; no; *pron.* none, no one.

nume *m.* deity, god.

numerale *m., adj.* numeral.

numerare *vt.* to number.

numerato *adj., pp.* numbered.

numerazione *f.* numeration.

numericamente *adv.* numerically.

nume'rico *adj.* numerical.

nu'mero *m.* number, numeral, figure; (*theat.*) act, scene; number, issue (*of a newspaper, etc.*): — legale, quorum; due di —, two and no more.

numeroso *adj.* numerous; (*pl.*) several.

numisma'tica *f.* numismatics.

numisma'tico *m.* numismatist; *adj.* numismatic.

nunziatura *f.* nunciature.

nun'zio *m.* nuncio, papal envoy.

nuo'cere *vi.*[83] to be detrimental (*to*): — a, to damage, injure, harm; non tutto il male vien per —, every cloud has its silver lining.

nuociuto *pp.* of nuocere.

nuora *f.* daughter-in-law.

nuotare *vi.* to swim.

nuotatore *m.* swimmer.

nuoto *m.* swimming.

nuova *f.* news.

nuovamente *adv.* once more; again, afresh.

nuovo *adj.* new; novel; unusual; unused; fresh: di —, again, anew, afresh; rimettere a —, to renovate; — di zecca, brand-new.

nutrice *f.* nurse; wet nurse.

nutriente *adj.* nourishing, rich.

nutrimento *m.* nourishment, food.

nutrire *vt.* to nourish, nurture; to feed; (*fig.*) to harbor, cherish; nutrirsi *vr.* to feed (*on*).

nutritivo *adj.* nutritious.

nutrito *adj.* well-fed; (*fig.*) sustained.

nutrizione *f.* nutrition; nourishment.

nu'vola *f.* cloud.

nu'volo *m.* storm cloud; swarm.

nuvolosità *f.* cloudiness.

nuvoloso *adj.* cloudy, overcast.

nuziale *adj.* wedding, bridal, nuptial: cerimonia —, wedding.

O

o, od *conj.* or, either; else, otherwise.
o'asi *f.* oasis (*pl.* oases).
obbedire *see* ubbidire.
obbiettare *see* obiettare.
obbligare *vt.* to compel, force; obbligarsi *vr.* to undertake; to bind oneself; to guarantee (*for*).
obbligatis'simo *adj.* deeply indebted.
obbligato *adj.* forced, bound; obliged.
obbligato'rio *adj.* mandatory, compulsory.
obbligazione *f.* obligation; (*comm.*) debenture, bond.
ob'bligo *m.* obligation; duty; compulsion; condition: avere l'— di, to be under the obligation to, to have to.
obbro'brio *m.* opprobrium, shame, infamy; (*fig.*) eyesore.
obbrobrioso *adj.* opprobrious.
obelisco *m.* obelisk.
oberato *adj.* burdened (*with*).
obesità *f.* obesity.
obeso *adj.* obese.
o'bice *m.* howitzer.
obiettare *vt.* to argue (*against*).
obiettività *f.* objectivity, impartiality.
obiettivo *m.* lens, objective; aim, object. *adj.* objective, unbiased.
obiezione *f.* objection.
obito'rio *m.* mortuary, morgue.
oblazione *f.* donation.
obliare *vt.* to forget.
obli'o *m.* oblivion.
obli'quo *adj.* oblique, slanting.
obliterare *vt.* to obliterate.
oblò *m.* porthole.
oblungo *adj.* oblong.
o'bolo *m.* mite, contribution; alms.
oca *f.* goose (*pl.* geese); (*male*) gander: pelle d'—, gooseflesh; far venire la pelle d'—, to give the creeps.
occasionale *adj.* occasional; chance.
occasione *f.* occasion; circumstance; opportunity, chance; pretext: in — di, in the occurrence of.
occhia'ia *f.* eyesocket; dark ring: aver le occhiaie, to have dark rings under one's eyes.
occhiala'io *m.* optician.
occhialetto *m.* lorgnette.
occhiali *m.pl.* spectacles, glasses: — da sole, sunglasses.
occhialoni *m.* goggles.
occhialuto *adj.* bespectacled.
occhiata *f.* glance.
occhiatac'cia *f.* glare.
occhieggiare *vi.* to glance.
occhiello *m.* eyelet, eye; buttonhole; (*typog.*) flyleaf.

occhietto *m.* small eye: far l'— a, to wink at.
oc'chio *m.* eye; sight; look, glance; shrewdness; bud: averne fin sopra gli occhi, to be fed up (*with*); perdere d'—, to lose sight of; tenere d'—, to keep an eye on; a — e croce, at a rough guess; a colpo d'—, at a glance; a perdita d'—, as far as the eye can reach; a quattr'occhi, in private; con la coda dell'—, out of the corner of one's eye; a vista d'—, visibly.
occhiolino *see* occhietto.
occidentale *adj.* western, occidental, west.
occidente *m.* west, occident.
occi'pite *m.* occiput.
occlusione *f.* occlusion.
occorrente *m.* necessities (*pl.*); materials (*pl.*); *adj.* necessary.
occorrenza *f.* need; event, occurrence: all'—, if need be, in case.
occor'rere (1) *vi.,³⁶ impers.* to be necessary; must, shall, ought to; to want, be in need of: occorre che io, I must; occorrerebbe che noi, we should; mi occorre, I want, need.
occor'rere (2) *see* accadere.
occorso *pp.* of occorrere.
occultamento *m.* concealment; suppression.
occultare *vt.* to conceal; to suppress.
occultismo *m.* occultism.
occulto *adj.* occult, hidden.
occupante *m.*, *f.* occupier, occupant.
occupare *vt.* to occupy; to take possession of; to employ: — una carica, to hold an office; — il proprio tempo, to spend one's time; occuparsi *vr.* to occupy oneself (*with*, *in*); to mind; to find an occupation; to take care (*that*, *of*); to be interested (*in*).
occupato *adj.* engaged, occupied, busy (*with*); taken, occupied (*as a seat*).
occupazione *f.* occupation; trade; employment, situation.
ocea'nico *adj.* oceanic.
oce'ano *m.* ocean.
ocra *f.* ocher.
oculare *m.*, *adj.* ocular: testimone —, eyewitness.
oculatezza *f.* shrewdness.
oculato *adj.* wise; careful; wary.
oculista *m.* oculist.
od *see* o.
odalisca *f.* odalisque.
ode *f.* ode.
odiare *vt.* to hate.
odierno *adj.* today's; present, current.

o'dio *m.* hatred.
odioso *adj.* hateful; loathsome.
Odissea *f.* Odyssey; (*fig.*) vicissitudes (*pl.*); ordeal.
odontoiatra *m.* odontologist.
odontoiatri'a *f.* odontology.
odontoia'trico *adj.* odontological.
odorac'cio *m.* stink.
odorare *vt., vi.* to smell; to scent: — di, to smell like, to smack of.
odorato *m.* smell; scent.
odore *m.* smell, odor; scent; (*pl.*) seasoning herbs, spice.
odoroso *adj.* fragrant, sweet-smelling, odorous.
offen'dere *vt.*[43] to offend; to abuse; to hurt; **offen'dersi** *vr.* to take offense (*at*); to be hurt.
offensiva *f.* offensive, attack.
offensivo *adj.* offensive, rude.
offerente *m.* offerer; bidder: **il miglior —**, the highest bidder.
offerta *f.* offer; proposal; bid; offering; gift; (*comm.*) tender.
offerto *pp. of* offrire.
offesa *f.* offense; resentment; wrong.
offeso *adj.* offended; hurt. *pp. of* offendere.
officiare *vi.* to officiate.
officina *f.* workshop, works.
offrire *vt.*[64] to offer, tender; to afford. **offrirsi** *vr.* to offer (*oneself*); to volunteer.
offuscamento *m.* obfuscation.
offuscare *vt.* to obfuscate; to blur, dim; to outshine; **offuscarsi** *vr.* to darken, dim.
oftalmi'a *f.* ophthalmia.
oftal'mico *adj.* ophthalmic.
oggettività *f.* objectivity; impartiality.
oggettivo *adj.* objective; unbiased.
oggetto *m.* object; thing; article; subject: **complemento —**, direct object.
oggi *m., adv.* today; nowadays: **dall'— al domani**, overnight; — **come —**, at present; — **a otto**, today week; **da — in poi (in avanti)**, from now on, henceforth.
oggidì, oggigiorno *adv.* nowadays.
ogiva *f.* ogive.
ogivale *adj.* ogival.
ogni *indef.adj.* any; each; every: — **tanto**, (every) now and then; — **due giorni**, every other day; **per — dove** everywhere.
ogniqualvolta *conj.* whenever.
Ognissanti *m.* All-Saints Day.
ognora *adv.* always.
ognuno *pron.* everyone, everybody, each, each one.
ohimè! *interj.* alas!
oibò! *interj.* ah!, fie!
olà! *interj.* hallo!

olandese *m.* Dutch; Dutchman; *f.* Dutchwoman; *adj.* Dutch.
oleandro *m.* oleander.
olea'rio *adj.* oil.
oleifi'cio *m.* oil mill.
oleografi'a *f.* oleography.
oleosità *f.* oiliness.
oleoso *adj.* oily.
olezzare *vi.* to smell sweet.
olezzo *m.* perfume, fragrance.
olfatto *m.* (*sense of*) smell; scent.
oliare *vt.* to oil.
oliera *f.* cruet.
oligarchi'a *f.* oligarchy.
olimpi'ade *f.* Olympiad.
olim'pico *adj.* Olympian, Olympic: **calma olimpica**, imperturbable composure.
olimpio'nico *m.* (*sport*) Olympian; *adj.* Olympic.
Olimpo *m.* Olympus.
o'lio *m.* oil: — **di ricino**, castor oil; **sott'—**, in oil; **liscio come l'—**, smooth; — **di fegato di merluzzo**, cod-liver oil.
oliva *f.* olive.
olivastro *adj.* olivaceous; swarthy.
oliveto *m.* olive grove.
olivo *m.* olive (*tree*).
olla *f.* olla, earthen pot.
olmo *m.* elm tree, elm.
oloca'usto *m.* holocaust.
olo'grafo *adj.* holograph.
oltraggiare *vt.* to outrage; to insult.
oltrag'gio *m.* outrage; offense; abuse; ravage.
oltraggioso *adj.* outrageous; insulting.
oltranza *f.* uttermost: **lotta ad —**, fight to the finish.
oltre *prep.* beyond, past; more than: — **che**, besides; *adv.* on, ahead; far; farther, further, longer: **troppo —**, too far; **non posso andare più —**, I can't go any further.
oltremare *m.* ultramarine; *adv.* overseas: **terre d'—**, overseas lands.
oltremodo *adv.* exceedingly.
oltrepassare *vt.* to go beyond (*past*); to exceed; to surpass; to overstep.
oltretomba *m.* (*the*) beyond.
omaccione *m.* burly man.
omag'gio *m.* homage; present; (*pl.*) compliments: **copia in —**, complimentary copy.
ombelico *m.* navel, umbilicus.
ombra *f.* shadow; shade; umbrage.
ombreggiare *vt.* to shade.
ombreggiatura *f.* shading.
ombrella *f.* (*bot.*) umbel. *see* ombrello.
ombrella'io *m.* umbrella maker.
ombrellino *m.* parasol.
ombrello *m.* umbrella.
ombrellone *m.* beach umbrella.

ombrosità *f.* shadiness; umbrageousness; skittishness.

ombroso *adj.* shady; umbrageous; skittish.

omelia *f.* homily.

omeopa'tico *m.* homeopathist; *adj.* homeopathic.

ome'rico *adj.* Homeric.

o'mero *m.* (*anat.*) humerus.

omertà *f.* code of silence.

omesso *adj.* left out, omitted. *pp. of* **omettere.**

omet'tere *vt.*[76] to leave out, omit; to forget; to skip.

ometto *m.* little man.

omicida *m.* homicide, murderer; *adj.* homicidal, murderous.

omici'dio *m.* homicide, murder.

omino *m.* little man.

omissione *f.* omission.

om'nibus *m.* omnibus, bus.

omoge'neo *adj.* homogeneous.

omologare *vt.* to homologate; to probate.

omologazione *f.* homologation; probation.

omonimi'a *f.* homonymy.

omo'nimo *m.* namesake; *adj.* homonymous.

omosessuale *m.*, *adj.* homosexual.

onagro *m.* onager.

on'cia *f.* (*weight*) ounce.

onda *f.* wave; billow, breaker: **lunghezza d'—,** wave length; **andare in —,** to go on the air.

ondata *f.* wave.

onde *adv.* whence; *pron.* of which; for which; by which, whereby; *conj.* in order to, so that; wherefore.

ondeggiamento *m.* waving; swaying; wavering.

ondeggiante *adj.* waving; swaying; wavering.

ondeggiare *vi.* to undulate; to wave; to sway, swing; to waver.

ondina *f.* (*myth.*) undine.

ondoso *adj.* wavy; undulatory.

ondulare *vt.* to wave; *vi.* to undulate.

ondulato *adj.* wavy; scalloped: **cartone —,** corrugated paper.

ondulato'rio *adj.* undulatory.

ondulazione *f.* waving, undulation: **— permanente,** permanent wave.

o'nere *m.* onus, burden.

oneroso *adj.* onerous, heavy.

onestà *f.* honesty; fairness.

onesto *adj.* honest; fair; moderate; decent, respectable.

o'nice *f.* onyx.

onnipossente, onnipotente *adj.* omnipotent, almighty.

onnipotenza *f.* almightiness.

onnipresente *adj.* omnipresent.

onnisciente *adj.* omniscient.

onni'voro *adj.* omnivorous.

onoma'stico *m.* name day.

onomatopea *f.* onomatopoeia.

onomatope'ico *adj.* onomatopoeic.

onora'bile *adj.* honorable.

onorabilità *f.* honorableness.

onoranza *f.* honor; celebration.

onorare *vt.* to honor; to be an honor to; **onorarsi** *vr.* to take pride (*in*); to be proud (*of, to*).

onora'rio *m.* fee; *adj.* honorary.

onorato *adj.* honored; honorable; decent.

onore *m.* honor; (*pl. in card games*) honors: **l'— del mento,** the beard; **partita d'—,** duel; **serata d'—,** gala night; **fare — a un impegno,** to meet an obligation; **a — del vero,** to tell the truth.

onore'vole *adj.* honorable.

onorificenza *f.* honor; decoration.

onori'fico *adj.* honorific.

onta *f.* disgrace, shame: **ad — di, in spite of.**

ontano *m.* (*bot.*) alder.

onusto *adj.* laden (*with*).

opacità *f.* opacity.

opaco *adj.* opaque, dim, dull.

opale *m.* opal.

o'pera *f.* work; act, deed; (*mus.*) opera: **Opera Pia,** charitable institution; **mano d'—,** labor; **messa in —,** installation; **per — di,** through.

opera'ia *f.* workwoman: **ape —,** worker (*bee*).

opera'io *m.* workman, worker, laborer; machinist: **— specializzato,** skilled workman; **capo —,** foreman; *adj.* working.

operare *vt.*, *vi.* to act; to work; to perform; (*surg.*) to operate (*upon*); **farsi —,** to undergo an operation.

operato *m.* action; behavior; *adj.* operated; fancy (*of a cloth or pattern*).

operatore *m.* operator; (*moving pictures*) cameraman.

operato'rio *adj.* operative; (*surg.*) surgical: **sala operatoria,** surgery.

operazione *f.* operation; (*comm.*) transaction.

operetta *f.* operetta.

operista *m.* opera composer.

operoso *adj.* operose, hard-working.

opifi'cio *m.* works, factory.

opimo *adj.* fat, rich.

opinare *vi.* to deem, judge.

opinione *f.* opinion, view.

oppia'ceo, oppiato *m.*, *adj.* opiate.

op'pio *m.* opium.

oppio'mane *m.*, *f.* opium addict.

opponente *m.*, *adj.* opponent.

opporre vt.⁹³ to oppose; opporsi vr. to oppose; to object.

opportunista m. opportunist.

opportunità f. fitness; advisability; expediency; opportunity.

opportuno adj. fit, suitable, advisable; timely: a tempo —, in due time.

oppositore m. opponent.

opposizione f. opposition; argument: fare — a, to object to.

opposto m., adj. opposite, contrary; opposed. pp. of opporre.

oppressione f. oppression; choking sensation.

oppresso adj. oppressed, overwhelmed; depressed. pp. of opprimere.

oppressore m. oppressor.

opprimente adj. oppressive.

opprimere vt.²⁹ to oppress; to overwhelm; to choke; to press; to depress.

oppugnare vt. to oppugn.

oppugnazione f. confutation.

oppure conj. or; else.

optare vi. to opt, make one's choice: — per, to choose.

opulento adj. opulent.

opulenza f. opulence.

opu'scolo m. pamphlet; booklet.

opzione f. option.

ora (1) f. hour; time; è — di, it is time to; che — è? what time is it?; non vedere l'— di, to look forward to, to be eager to; ore piccole, late hours; a quest'—, at this time; by now; di — in —, hourly; any time; di buon'—, early; a tarda —, late; alla buon'—! at last!

ora (2) adv. see adesso.

ora'colo m. oracle.

o'rafo m. goldsmith.

orale adj. oral; verbal.

oramai adv. now; by this time; already.

orango, orangutan' m. orangutan.

ora'rio m. hours (pl.), time; timetable, schedule: — d'ufficio, office hours; in —, on schedule, punctual; adj. hourly, per hour; fuso —, time zone.

oratore m. speaker, orator.

orato'ria f. oratory; eloquence.

orato'rio m. oratory; (mus.) oratorio. adj. oratorical.

orazione f. oration; prayer.

orbare vt. to bereave.

orbe f. orb, sphere, globe.

orbene adv. well now, well.

or'bita f. orbit; eye socket; sphere, range: con gli occhi fuori dall'—, popeyed.

orbo adj. blind; bereft: botte da orbi, thrashing blows.

orche'stra f. orchestra; band: direttore d'—, conductor, bandleader.

orchestrale m., f. musician, performer. adj. orchestral.

orchestrare vt. to orchestrate.

orchestrazione f. orchestration.

orchidea f. orchid.

or'cio m. jar.

orco m. ogre.

orda f. horde.

ordigno m. contrivance.

ordinale m., adj. ordinal.

ordinamento m. regulation.

ordinanza f. ordinance; (mil.) orderly: uniforme d'—, regimentals.

ordinare vt. to order; to arrange, straighten up; to ordain; to prescribe; ordinarsi vr. (mil.) to draw up; (eccl.) to become ordained.

ordinariamente adv. usually.

ordina'rio m. ordinary; professor; adj. ordinary; cheap.

ordinato adj. trim; orderly; (eccl.) ordained.

ordinazione f. (comm.) order; (med.) prescription; (eccl.) ordination: su —, to order.

or'dine m. order; class, rank; warrant: — d'idee, train of ideas; parola d'—, password; di prim'—, first class.

ordire vt. to weave: — un complotto, to plot, devise a plot.

ordito (1) m. (text.) warp.

ordito (2) pp. of ordire.

orec'chia see orecchio.

orecchietta f. auricle (of the heart).

orecchino m. earring.

orec'chio m. ear; hearing; dog-ear (of a page): fare — da mercante, to turn a deaf ear (to); mettere una pulce nell'— a, to put a doubt in (someone's) mind.

orecchioni m.pl. (med.) mumps.

ore'fice m. goldsmith.

oreficeri'a f. goldsmithery; goldsmith's shop.

or'fano m., or'fana f. orphan; adj. orphaned: — di padre, fatherless; — di madre, motherless.

orfanotro'fio m. orphanage.

organetto m. barrel organ.

orga'nico m. list, roll; staff (as of an office). adj. organic.

organino m. barrel organ.

organismo m. organism; system.

organista m. organist.

organizzare vt. to organize; to set up; to form.

organizzatore m. organizer.

organizzazione f. organization.

or'gano m. organ.

orgasmo m. excitement; anxiety; frenzy; (physiol.) orgasm, climax.

or'gia f. orgy.

orgia'stico adj. orgiastic.

orgo'glio m. pride; dignity.
orgoglioso adj. proud; dignified.
orientale m. oriental; adj. eastern, east, oriental.
orientamento m. orientation; bearing; bent, attitude.
orientare vt. to orient; **orientarsi** vr. to orient oneself, find one's bearings; to turn (towards).
oriente m. East: estremo, medio, vicino —, Far, Middle, Near East.
orifi'zio m. orifice, hole.
ori'gano m. origan.
originale m. original; manuscript; queer fish; adj. original; eccentric, queer.
originalità f. originality; eccentricity.
originare vt. to originate; to cause; vi. to originate, arise.
originariamente adv. originally; formerly.
origina'rio adj. original; native (of).
ori'gine f. origin; source; beginning; birth; extraction: dare — a, to occasion, give rise (to).
origliare vi. to eavesdrop.
origliere m. pillow.
orina f. urine.
orinale m. chamber pot.
orinare vi. to urinate.
orinato'io m. urinal.
oriundo adj. native (of): — francese, of French origin.
orizzontale adj. horizontal.
orizzontare see orientare.
orizzonte m. horizon; (fig.) prospect: giro d'—, survey.
Orlando m. (hist.) Roland: montare sul cavallo d'—, to mount one's high horse.
Orlando, Vittorio Emanuele, Italian statesman and premier (1860–1952).
orlare vt. to hem, edge; to rim.
orlatore m., **orlatrice** f. hemmer.
orlatura f. rimming, hemming.
orlo m. edge, margin, verge; rim; brim; brink; hem: — a giorno, hemstitch.
orma f. footprint; trace, track; mark: ritornare sulle proprie orme, to retrace one's steps.
ormai adv. now, by now; such being the situation; already.
ormeggiare vt., vi.; **ormeggiarsi** vr. to moor.
ormeg'gio m. moorings.
ormone m. hormone.
ormo'nico adj. hormonic.
ornamentale adj. ornamental.
ornamento m. ornament.
ornare vt. to adorn, deck.
ornato m. ornamental design; ornament; adj. ornate, decked, adorned.
ornito'logo m. ornithologist.

ornitorinco m. ornithorhynchus, duckbill.
oro m. gold; money; (pl.) gold works: — zecchino, fine gold; febbre dell'—, gold rush; d'—, golden; libro d'—, roll of honor.
orologeri'a f. watchmaking; watchmaker's shop.
orologia'io m. watchmaker.
orolo'gio m. clock; watch: — da polso, wrist watch: il mio — è avanti (indietro) di 3 minuti, my watch is 3 minutes fast (slow).
oro'scopo m. horoscope.
orpello m. tinsel.
orrendo adj. horrible, hideous, ghastly.
orri'bile adj. horrible, awful, dreadful.
or'rido m. gorge, ravine; adj. horrid, dreadful, hideous, ghastly.
orripilante adj. terrifying; loathsome.
orrore m. horror: fare —, to strike with horror, to be hideous.
orsacchiotto m. bear cub; Teddy bear.
Orsini, Felice, Italian patriot, who attempted to assassinate Napoleon III (1819–1858).
orso m. bear.
orsù interj. come on!
ortag'gio m. vegetable.
orta'glia f. truck garden.
orten'sia f. hydrangea.
ortica f. nettle.
ortica'ria f. nettle rash.
orti'colo adj. horticultural.
orticultore m. truck gardener.
orto m. truck garden: — botanico, botanic garden; non è la via dell'—, it is no bed of roses.
ortodosso adj. orthodox.
ortografi'a f. orthography.
ortogra'fico adj. orthographic.
ortolano m. gardener; greengrocer.
ortope'dico m. orthopedist; adj. orthopedic.
orza f. (naut.) bowline.
orzaiuolo m. stye, sty.
orzare vi. (naut.) to luff.
orzata (1) f. (naut.) luff.
orzata (2) f. orgeat.
orzo m. barley.
osannare vt. to hosanna.
osare vt., vi. to dare, venture.
oscenità f. obscenity.
osceno adj. obscene.
oscillante adj. oscillating, swinging.
oscillare vi. to swing, oscillate; to waver; to fluctuate.
oscillazione f. oscillation, sway, fluctuation.
oscuramento m. darkening: — antiaereo, blackout.
oscurare vt. to darken; to dim; to outshine; **oscurarsi** vr. to darken; to dim; to grow cloudy.

oscurità f. darkness, obscurity; dimness.

oscuro adj. dark; dim, gloomy; obscure.

ospedale m. hospital.

ospedaletto m. hospital station.

ospitale adj. hospitable.

ospitalità f. hospitality.

ospitare vt. to entertain; to house, shelter, accommodate.

o'spite m. guest, visitor.

ospi'zio m. hospice: — di mendicità, poorhouse; — di trovatelli, foundling hospital.

ossatura f. frame.

os'seo adj. osseous, bony.

ossequente adj. observant (of); respectful: — alle leggi, law-abiding.

ossequiare vt. to pay one's respects to; to honor.

osse'quio m. homage, respect; obedience, compliance; (pl.) regards.

ossequioso adj. deferential; respectful; obsequious.

osservante adj. observant (of).

osservanza f. observance; deference; compliance.

osservare vt. to observe; to notice; to watch; to point out, remark; to obey; to comply (with); far — una legge, to enforce a law.

osservatore m. observer; adj. observant, alert.

osservato'rio m. observatory.

osservazione f. observation; remark; comment.

ossessionante adj. obsessive, haunting.

ossessionare vt. to obsess, haunt; to harass.

ossessione f. obsession; nightmare.

ossesso m. demoniac; adj. possessed.

ossi'a conj. or; that is.

ossida'bile adj. oxidizable.

ossidante adj. oxidizing.

ossidare vt., **ossidarsi** vr. to oxidize.

ossidazione f. oxidization.

os'sido m. oxide.

ossi'drico adj. oxyhydrogen: cannello —, oxyhydrogen blowpipe.

ossigenare vt. to oxygenate; to peroxide (hair).

ossigenato adj. oxygenated: bionda ossigenata, a peroxide blonde; acqua ossigenata, (hydrogen) peroxide.

ossi'geno m. oxygen.

osso m. bone; stone (of a fruit): — di seppia, cuttlebone; — sacro, sacrum; un — duro, a hard nut to crack; avere le ossa rotte (fig.), to be bone-tired; bagnato sino alle ossa, wet through; in carne e ossa, in flesh and blood.

ossuto adj. bony.

ostacolare vt. to hinder; to interfere with; to obstruct.

osta'colo m. obstacle, hindrance; (sport) hurdle.

ostag'gio m. hostage.

ostare vi. to be in opposition (to); to prevent (from): nulla osta a, no objection to. see nullaosta.

oste m. innkeeper: fare i conti senza l'—, to reckon without one's host.

osteggiare vt. to antagonize, oppose, be averse to.

ostello m. mansion; inn; hostel.

ostensi'bile adj. ostensible.

ostenso'rio m. ostensory.

ostentare vt. to affect, to show off, display; to feign.

ostentato adj. affected; ostentatious.

ostentazione f. ostentation; show, display.

osteri'a f. public house; (fam.) "joint."

ostessa f. landlady.

oste'trica f. midwife.

ostetri'cia f. obstetrics.

oste'trico m. obstetrician; adj. obstetrical.

o'stia f. wafer: — consacrata, host.

o'stico adj. distasteful; hard.

ostile adj. hostile; averse.

ostilità f. hostility; aversion: le — (mil.) hostilities.

ostinarsi vr. to insist, persist (in); to be stubborn (about).

ostinato adj. obstinate, stubborn; steady.

ostinazione f. obstinacy, stubbornness.

ostracismo m. ostracism: dar l'— a, to ostracize.

o'strica f. oyster.

ostrica'io m. oysterer.

ostruire vt. to obstruct, stop; ostruirsi vr. to become obstructed, to clog.

ostruzione f. obstruction.

ostruzionismo m. obstructionism.

otite f. otitis.

otorinolaringoiatra m. otolaryngologist.

otre m. skin (bag).

ottaedro m. octahedron.

otta'gono m. octagon.

ottanta m., adj. eighty.

ottantenne m., f., adj. octogenarian.

ottante'simo m., adj. eightieth.

ottantina f. fourscore, some eighty: essere sull'—, to be about eighty.

ottava f. octave.

ottavo m., adj. eighth; octavo.

ottemperare vi. to submit (to): — a, to obey; to fulfill; to abide (by).

ottenebrare vt. to befog.

ottenere vt.[141] to obtain, get; to attain, reach; to extract.

ottenuto pp. of ottenere.

ot'tica f. optics.

ot'tico *m.* optician; *adj.* optic.
ottimismo *m.* optimism.
ottimista *m.* optimist.
ot'timo *m., adj.* excellent; optimum.
otto *m., adj.* eight: oggi a —, within a week; in quattro e quattr'—, in the twinkle of an eye; — volante, roller coaster.
ottobre *m.* October.
ottomana *f.* ottoman.
Ottomano *m., adj.* Ottoman.
ottoname *m.* brassware.
ottone *m.* brass.
ottuagena'rio *m., adj.* octogenarian.
ottun'dere *vt.*³² to blunt.
otturamento *see* otturazione.
otturare *vt.* to obturate, stop, fill; **otturarsi** *vr.* to clog.
otturatore *m.* (*photo.*) shutter; (*artil.*) breechblock.
otturazione *f.* stopping; obstruction.
ottusità *f.* obtuseness.
ottuso *adj.* obtuse; blunt. *pp. of* ottun'dere.

ova'ia *f.* ovary.
ovale *m., adj.* oval.
ovatta *f.* wadding.
ovattare *vt.* to wad; to muffle.
ovazione *f.* ovation.
ove *adv.* where; when. *conj.* if; in case.
o'vest *m.* west.
ovile *m.* fold, sheepfold.
ovino *adj.* ovine: gli ovini, sheep.
ovi'paro *adj.* oviparous.
ovo *m.* egg.
o'volo *m.* egg-shaped mushroom.
o'vulo *m.* ovule.
ovunque *see* dovunque.
ovvero *conj.* or.
ovviamente *adv.* obviously; of course.
ovviare *vi.* to obviate.
ov'vio *adj.* obvious; evident.
oxfordiano *m., adj.* Oxonian.
oziare *vi.* to idle, loiter.
o'zio *m.* idleness, laziness; leisure.
oziosità *f.* slothfulness; idle talk.
ozioso *m.* idler, dawdler; *adj.* idle.
ozono *m.* ozone.

P

pacare *vt.* to appease.
pacatezza *f.* collectedness, quietness.
pacato *adj.* collected, quiet.
pacca *f.* slap.
pacchetto *m.* package, small parcel.
pac'chia *f.* gorge; (*fig.*) windfall.
pacchiano *adj.* boorish; garish.
pacco *m.* package; bundle; parcel.
paccotti'glia *f.* cheap stuff, trinketry.
pace *f.* peace; quiet, stillness; rest: lasciare in —, to leave alone.
pachiderma *m.* pachyderm.
paciere *m.* peacemaker.
pacificamente *adv.* peacefully.
pacificare *vt.* to pacify; to reconcile; **pacificarsi** *vr.* to quiet; to make one's peace.
pacificatore *m.* peacemaker.
pacificazione *f.* pacification.
paci'fico *adj.* peaceful, peaceable, peaceloving; out of question.
Pacinotti, Antonio, Italian physicist, discoverer of principle of dynamo (1841-1912).
pacioccone *m.,* **pacioccona** *f.* chubby-faced person; easygoing person.
padella *f.* pan, frying pan; bedpan: dalla — nella brage, out of the frying pan into the fire.
padiglione *m.* pavilion; stand; lodge.
padre *m.* father; (*pl.*) forefathers.
padreggiare *vi.* to take after one's father.
padrino *m.* godfather; second (*in a duel*).
padrona *f.* mistress; owner; landlady.

padronale *adj.* proprietorial; private.
padronanza *f.* mastery, command, possession; proprietorship; masterfulness: — di una lingua, command of a language; — di se stesso, self-possession, self-control.
padrone *m.* master, boss, owner, proprietor: — di casa, landlord.
padroneggiare *vt.* to master, dominate; **padroneggiarsi** *vr.* to keep one's self-control.
padule *m.* marsh.
paesag'gio *m.* landscape.
paesana *f.* countrywoman.
paesano *m.* villager; peasant; fellow countryman; *adj.* rural, country; local.
paese *m.* country; village; hamlet; country, land: mandare a quel —, to send to Jericho.
paf!, paf'fete! *interj.* bang!, wham!
paffuto *adj.* chubby.
paga *f.* pay, reward, wages.
paga'bile *adj.* payable.
paga'ia *f.* paddle.
pagamento *m.* payment; cover.
pagane'simo *m.* heathenism, paganism.
Paganini, Nicolò, Italian violinist, composer (1782-1840).
pagano *m., adj.* heathen; pagan.
pagante *m.* payer; *adj.* paying.
pagare *vt.* to pay; to pay for; to reward: far —, to make (*one*) pay; to charge; farsi —, to get paid.
pagato *adj.* paid.

pagatore *m.* payer.

pagella *f.* school report, report card.

pag'gio *m.* page.

pagherò *m.* promissory note, IOU.

pa'gina *f.* page; leaf: prima —, front page.

pa'glia *f.* straw: coda di —, uneasy conscience; fuoco di —, short-lived passion.

pagliacciata *f.* clownery, farce.

pagliac'cio *m.* clown.

paglia'io *m.* strawstack; straw barn.

paglieric'cio *m.* paillasse.

paglierino *adj.* pale yellow.

paglietta *f.* straw hat, boater.

pagliuzza *f.* straw.

pagnotta *f.* loaf (*pl.* loaves).

pago *adj.* satisfied, content (*with*).

pa'io *m.* pair; couple.

Paisiello, Giovanni, Italian composer (1741–1816).

paiuolo *m.* cauldron.

pala *f.* shovel; paddle (*of a water wheel*); blade (*of a propeller, of an oar*); vane, sail (*of a windmill*): — d'altare, altarpiece.

paladino *m.* paladin; champion.

palafitta *f.* pile, palafitte.

palafreniere *m.* groom.

palanca *f.* copper coin; ‖(*naut.*) gang-plank.

palanco *m.* (*naut.*) tackle.

palandrana *f.* gaberdine.

palata *f.* shovelful: a palate, in plenty.

palatino *m.*, *adj.* palatine.

palato *m.* palate.

Palazzeschi, Aldo, Italian novelist and poet (1885–   ).

Palazzi, Fernando, Italian lexicographer and novelist, *Novissimo dizionario della lingua italiana* (1884–   ).

palazzina *f.* villa.

palazzo *m.* mansion; palace: — municipale, town hall.

palchetto *m.* shelf; (*theat.*) box.

palco *m.* scaffold; planking, flooring; (*theat.*) box; stand; bandstand.

palcosce'nico *m.* stage.

palesare *vt.* to manifest; to disclose; to show; palesarsi *vr.* to reveal oneself, prove (*to be*).

palese *adj.* evident; known.

palesemente *adv.* openly; obviously.

palestra *f.* gymnasium.

Palestrina, da, Giovanni Pierluigi, Italian composer (1526–1594).

paletta *f.* shovel; pallet; paddle (*of a paddle wheel*); blade (*of a ventilating fan, etc.*).

paletto *m.* picket; peg; bolt.

pa'lio *m.* cloak; race: essere in —, to be at stake.

palissandro *m.* rosewood.

palizzata *f.* fence, palisade.

palla *f.* ball; bullet; sphere: — a nuoto, water polo; cogliere la — al balzo, to jump at the opportunity.

pallacanestro *f.* basketball.

Palla'dio, Andrea, Italian architect (1518–1580).

palleggiare *vt.*, *vi.* to dribble (*in soccer*); to toss: palleggiarsi le responsabilità, to shift responsibilities on one another, to "pass the buck."

palleg'gio *m.* dribbling (*in soccer*); tossing (*in tennis*).

palliativo *m.*, *adj.* palliative.

pal'lido *adj.* pale, wan; faint.

pallina *f.* small ball; marble.

pallino *m.* red ball (*in billiards*); jack (*in bowls*); shot (*for a shotgun*); polka dot; (*coll.*) hobby, craze, bee in the bonnet: avere il — di, to be "nuts" about.

pallone *m.* balloon; ball, soccer: un — gonfiato, a "stuffed shirt."

pallore *m.* pallor.

pallot'tola *f.* pellet; bullet.

pallottoliere *m.* abacus.

palma *f.* palm.

palmare *adj.* clear, evident.

palmi'zio *m.* palm.

palmo *m.* palm; span: restare con un — di naso, to be baffled; a — a —, inch by inch.

palo *m.* pole, post, stake; pile.

palombaro *m.* diver.

palombo *m.* (*ornith.*) wood pigeon; (*ichthyol.*) dogfish.

palpa'bile *adj.* palpable; evident.

palpare *vt.* to handle, finger; (*med.*) to palpate.

pal'pebra *f.* eyelid: batter le palpebre, to blink.

palpeggiare *see* palpare.

palpitante *adj.* throbbing; aflutter: di — attualità, topical, newsmaking.

palpitare *vi.* to throb; to pine.

palpitazione *f.* palpitation; throb, throbbing.

pal'pito *m.* throb; beat; anxiety.

paltò *m.* greatcoat.

palude *f.* marsh.

paludoso *adj.* marshy.

palustre *adj.* paludal.

pam'pino *m.* vine tendril; vine leaf.

panacea *f.* panacea.

pa'nama *m.* panama hat.

panca *f.* bench, settee.

pancetta *f.* potbelly; bacon.

panchetto *m.* footstool.

panchina *f.* bench.

pan'cia *f.* belly, paunch.

panciera *f.* bellypiece; girdle.

panciolle, (stare in) to idle away time in comfort.

panciotto *m.* waistcoat, vest.

panciuto *adj.* potbellied; bulging.
pane *m.* bread; loaf; cake; ingot; worm (*of a screw*): dire — al —, to call a spade a spade; **pan per focaccia,** tit for tat.
panegi'rico *m.* panegyric.
panetteri'a *f.* bakery.
panettiere *m.* baker.
panetto *m.* cake.
panfi'lio, pan'filo *m.* yacht.
pa'nia *f.* lime; (*fig.*) snare.
pa'nico *m.*, *adj.* panic.
paniere *m.* pannier: **rompere le uova nel —,** to queer (*one's*) pitch.
panificazione *f.* breadmaking.
panifi'cio *m.* bakery.
panino *m.* roll (*of bread*): — imbottito, sandwich.
panna *f.* cream; breakdown, car trouble: **rimanere in —,** to have a breakdown.
pannello *m.* panel.
panni'colo *m.* membrane, tissue.
panno *m.* cloth; **panni** *pl.* clothes.
pannoc'chia *f.* corncob.
pannolino *m.* diaper.
panorama *m.* panorama, view.
panora'mico *adj.* panoramic.
pantaloni *see* calzoni.
pantano *m.* bog, quagmire.
pantera *f.* panther.
panto'fola *f.* slipper.
pantomima *f.* pantomime; sham.
panzana *f.* fib, hoax.
Panzini, Alfredo, Italian novelist and lexicographer, *Dizionario Moderno delle parole che non si trovano nei dizionari comuni* (1863–1939).
paonazzo *m.*, *adj.* purple.
papà *m.* papa, pa, dad, daddy.
Papa *m.* pope.
papale *adj.* papal.
papalina *f.* skullcap.
papalino *adj.* papal.
papato *m.* papacy.
papa'vero *m.* poppy, papaver: **alto—,** "big shot."
pa'pera *f.* goose; (*theat.*) "fluff"; blunder.
pa'pero *m.* gander; gosling.
Papini, Giovanni, Italian novelist and essayist (1881–1956).
pappa *f.* pap; soup; food.
pappa'fico *m.* (*naut.*) topgallant.
pappagallo *m.* parrot.
pappagor'gia *f.* double chin.
pappare *vt.* to gorge, gobble, wolf.
pappataci *m.* gnat.
pappina *f.* pap; poultice.
para *f.* crepe rubber.
para'bola *f.* parable; (*geom.*) parabola.
parabordo *m.* (*naut.*) buffer, bumper.
parabrezza *m.* windshield.
paracadutare *vt.* to parachute.

paracadute *m.* parachute: **lanciarsi col —,** to bail out.
paracadutista *m.* parachutist.
paracarro *m.* curbstone.
parac'qua *m.* umbrella.
paradisi'aco *adj.* heavenly.
paradiso *m.* heaven, paradise: — terrestre, garden of Eden.
paradossale *adj.* paradoxical.
paradossa *m.* paradox.
parafa *f.* paraph.
parafango *m.* mudguard.
parafare *vt.* to paraph, to initial.
paraffina *f.* paraffin.
para'frasi *f.* paraphrase.
paraful'mine *m.* lightning rod.
parafuoco *m.* firescreen.
paraggi *m.pl.* neighborhood.
paragonare *vt.* to compare (*with*).
paragone *m.* comparison: **pietra di —,** touchstone.
para'grafo *m.* paragraph.
para'lisi *f.* paralysis, palsy.
parali'tico *m.*, *adj.* paralytic.
paralizzare *vt.* to paralyze.
parallela *f.* parallel.
parallelo *m.*, *adj.* parallel.
paralume *m.* lampshade.
paramano *m.* wristband.
paramento *m.* vestment; hanging.
paranco *m.* (*naut.*) tackle.
paraninfo *m.* pander.
parano'ico *m.*, *adj.* paranoiac.
paraocchi *m.pl.* blinkers.
parapetto *m.* parapet; bulwark; railing.
parapi'glia *m.* hurly-burly, melee.
parapiog'gia *m.* umbrella.
parare *vt.*, *vi.* to adorn, drape, hang; to stop, parry; to catch; to shield, protect; to keep off; **pararsi** *vr.* to deck oneself: **pararsi dinanzi a uno,** to loom before one, to confront one.
parasole *m.* parasol, sunshade.
parassita *f.* parasite.
parastatale *adj.* government-controlled.
parata *f.* catch; parry; (*mil.*) parade.
parati'a *f.* (*naut.*) bulkhead.
parato *m.* drape; (*pl.*) drapery; wallpaper.
paraurti *m.* bumper.
paravento *m.* screen.
Parca *f.* (*myth.*) Parca; Death: **le Parche,** the Fates, the Parcae.
parcare *vt.* to park.
parcella *f.* bill.
parcheg'gio *m.* parking lot; parking.
parco (*1*) *m.* park.
parco (*2*) *adj.* sparing, frugal.
parec'chio *adj.* a good deal (*of*); a long time; **parecchi** *pl.* several, a good many; **parecchio** *pron.* a good deal of it; (*pl.*) several; **parecchio** *adv.* a good deal, enough.

pareggiare vt. to equalize; to equal; to level, even; to balance; to square; — un conto, to square an account; — il bilancio, to balance the budget; vi. (in games) to tie, break even.

pareg'gio m. equalization; balance; (sport) tie: raggiungere il —, (comm.) to balance the budget, (sport) to end in a tie.

parentado m. kinsfolk; relatives.

parente m., f. relative, relation, kin.

parentela f. relationship; kinsfolk.

paren'tesi f. parenthesis (pl. parentheses); bracket: fra — (fig.), by the way, incidentally.

parere (1) vi.[85] to seem; to look (like); to sound (like); to feel (like); to taste (like); to smell (like); to like; to appear; to deem, think: che te ne pare? what do you think of it?; mi pare di sì, I think so.

parere (2) m. opinion, mind; judgment; advice.

parete f. wall.

par'golo m. baby.

pari m. peer, like, equal, match: i propri pari, one's likes; senza —, matchless; da — a —, on a level footing; adj. equal, even, level; like; same; equivalent; tantamount; up to, fit; smooth; balanced: essere — e patta, to be quits; saltare a piè — (fig.), to skip altogether; al — di, as, like, as much as; alla — con, on a par with; del —, likewise; titoli alla —, bonds pa'ria m. pariah, outcast. [at par.

parificare see pareggiare.

parigino m., adj. Parisian.

pari'glia f. pair; couple; team (of horses): rendere la —, to give tit for [tat.

parimenti adv. likewise.

Parini, Giuseppe, Italian poet, Il giorno (1729–1799).

parità f. parity, equality.

parlamentare (1) m. parliamentarian; (mil.) parleyer; adj. parliamentary; civil.

parlamentare (2) vi. to parley.

parlamento m. parliament; congress.

parlante adj. talking; lifelike.

parlantina f. glibness.

parlare vt., vi. to speak; to talk: — fra sé e sé, to speak to oneself; — del più e del meno, to talk about the weather; — a quattr'occhi, to talk in private; far — di sé, to make oneself talked about; se ne è fatto un gran —, there has been a lot of talk about it.

parlata f. speech, way of speaking; pronunciation.

parlatore m. speaker, talker, orator.

parlato'rio m. parlatory.

parlottare vi. to confabulate.

parmigiano m., adj. Parmesan.

parodi'a f. parody.

parodiare vt. to parody; to mimic.

parola f. word; speech; promise, pledge: — d'ordine, password; parole incrociate, crossword puzzle, puzzles; giuoco di parole, pun; essere di —, to be as good as one's word; venire a parole, to have words (with); a buon intenditor poche parole, a word to the wise is enough; è una —! no sooner said than done!

parolac'cia f. nasty word; abuse.

parola'io m. wordmonger.

parossismo m. paroxysm; climax.

parricida m. parricide; adj. parricidal.

parrici'dio m. parricide.

parrocchetto m. fore-topsail; foretopmast.

parroc'chia f. parish.

parrocchiano m. parishioner.

par'roco m. parson, vicar.

parrucca f. wig, periwig.

parrucchiere m. wigmaker; hairdresser; barber.

parrucchino m. partial wig; scratch (wig).

parsimo'nia f. parsimony.

parso pp. of parere.

partac'cia f. scene.

parte f. part; portion, share; member; place; side, hand; direction; role; party: — civile, plaintiff; da un po' di tempo a questa —, for some time past; in —, partly; in ogni —, everywhere, on all sides; da —, aside; da qualche (altra) —, somewhere (else); da queste parti, hereabouts; da una — all'altra, through, from side to side; d'altra —, on the other hand; prendere in mala —, to take amiss; far le due parti in commedia, to play both ends against the middle; mettere a — d'un segreto, to let into a secret; da ambe le parti, on both sides.

partecipante m., adj. participant: i partecipanti a una gara, the contestants.

partecipare vt. to notify, announce; vi. to participate, share (in); to take part (in); to partake (of): — a una riunione, to attend a meeting.

partecipazione f. participation, sharing; announcement, card.

parte'cipe adj. partaking, sharing.

parteggiare vi. to side (with); to take sides (with).

partente m. leaver, departer.

partenza f. departure, leaving; (naut.) sailing; (aeron.) take-off; (sport) start: punto di —, starting point.

particella f. particle.
partici'pio m. participle.
parti'cola f. (eccl.) Host.
particolare m. detail, particular; adj. particular; peculiar; private: segni particolari, distinguishing features; in —, especially.
particolareggiato adj. detailed.
particolarità f. peculiarity; partiality.
particolarmente adv. particularly.
partigiana f. partisan.
partigianeri'a f. partisanship; partiality.
partigiano m., adj. partisan; member of underground resistance.
partire vi., partirsi vr. to leave, start, set out, depart; to sail; to go away, quit; to move; to begin: a — da oggi, (as) from today; far — un colpo, to fire a shot.
partita f. (sport) match; (account.) entry: — a carte, card game; — di merce, stock, lot; — doppia, double entry; — di caccia, hunting party.
partitivo m., adj. partitive.
partito m. alternative, choice; resolution; advantage; catch; (pol.) party: prendere un —, to make up one's mind; ridursi a mal —, to go to the dogs; mettere il cervello a —, to reform; prendere — per, to take one's stand for; trarre — da, to make the best of.
partitura f. (mus.) score.
partizione f. partition.
parto m. parturition, delivery, childbirth: doglie 1 —, throes.
partoriente adj. parturient.
partorire vt., vi. to bring forth; to give birth to; to produce.
parvenza f. appearance, semblance, shadow.
parziale adj. partial; unfair; biased.
parzialità f. partiality.
parzialmente adv. partially.
pa'scere vt., vi. to graze; to pasture; to feed; pa'scersi vr. to feed (on).
pascià m. pasha.
pasciuto adj. fed: ben —, well-fed.
Pascoli, Giovanni, Italian poet and critic (1855-1912).
pascolare see pascere.
pa'scolo m. pasture, grassland; pasturage; food.
Pasqua f. Easter: contento come una —, happy.
pasquale adj. Easter; paschal.
passa'bile adj. passable.
passag'gio m. passage; passageway; way; crossing; traffic; lapse; interchange: — a livello, grade crossing; vietato il —, no thoroughfare; ospite di —, transient (guest).
passamaneri'a f. ribandry.

passamano m. riband.
passamontagna m. woollen helmet.
passante m. passerby (pl. passers-by); strap.
passaporto m. passport.
passare vt. to pass; to go beyond, through; to cross; to run through; to exceed, surpass; to pierce; to spend (one's time); to hand (over); to experience, undergo. vi. to move on, proceed; to pass; to fade; to elapse; to stop, cease; to enter, get in; to pass muster; to pass (for), go (for); to call (on, upon, at): — per le armi, to put to death; — a miglior vita, to pass away; — sopra a, to overlook, wink at; passarsela bene (male), to be well (badly) off; passarsela liscia, to go scot free.
passatempo m. pastime.
passatista m. misoneist, old fogy.
passato m. past: — prossimo, present perfect; — remoto, past indefinite; adj. past, previous, former; withered, faded; overripe; gone by: l'anno —, last year.
passato'ia f. carpet strip, runner.
passeggiare vi. to walk; to stroll.
passeggiata f. stroll, walk; excursion; drive.
passeggiero m. passenger; adj. passing.
passeg'gio m. promenade: andare a —, to take a walk, stroll.
passerella f. footbridge; (naut.) gangplank.
pas'sero, passerotto m. sparrow.
passi'bile adj. liable (to), subject (to).
passiflora f. passionflower.
passionale m., adj. passional, temperamental.
passione f. passion; suffering; craze.
passività f. passivity; (comm.) liabilities (pl.).
passivo m. (gramm.) passive; (comm.) liabilities, debts; debit, debit sides (in bookkeeping); adj. passive.
passo (1) m. step, pace, gait, tread; passage; pass; (moving pictures) width, pitch: fare due passi, to take a walk; fare il — secondo la gamba, to cut the coat according to the cloth; — —, leisurely.
passo (2) adj. dried; faded, withered: uva passa, raisins.
pasta f. paste; dough; pastry, cake, cookie: di buona —, good-natured; aver le mani in —, to know the ropes.
pasteggiare vi. to feed (on): — a birra, to drink beer at one's meals.
pastello m. pastel.
pastetta f. batter; (coll.) shady business, hocus-pocus.

pasticca *f.* tablet.
pasticceri'a *f.* confectionery; pastry.
pasticciere *m.* confectioner; pastry cook.
pasticcino *m.* cake, bun.
pastic'cio *m.* pie; pudding; *(fig.)* jumble, mess, fix, scrape; pastiche.
pasticcione *m.* bungler, muddler.
pastifi'cio *m.* macaroni factory.
pasti'glia *f.* tablet, tabloid.
pasto *m.* meal: **vino da —**, table wine.
pasto'ia *f.* hobble, fetter; pastern.
pastone *m.* mash.
pastorale *m., adj.* pastoral.
pastore *m.* shepherd; pastor.
pastorella *f.* shepherdess.
pastori'zia *f.* sheep raising.
pastorizzare *vt.* to pasteurize.
pastoso *adj.* mellow.
pastrano *m.* greatcoat.
pastura *f.* pasture.
patacca *f.* coin; badge; stain.
patata *f.* potato: **— americana**, sweet potato.
patatrac! *m. (onomatopoeic)* bang! crash!
patella *f.* limpet.
patema *f.* anxiety, distress.
patentato *adj.* licensed; *(fig.)* downright, regular.
patente *f.* patent; license; *adj.* patent, plain, glaring.
paterec'cio *m.* whitlow.
paternale *f.* reprimand; *adj.* paternal.
paternità *f.* paternity.
paterno *adj.* paternal, fatherly.
pate'tico *adj.* pathetic.
patibolare *adj.* criminal, forbidding.
pati'bolo *m.* gallows, scaffold.
patimento *m.* torment; suffering.
pa'tina *f.* patina; film; gloss; furring *(of the tongue)*.
patinare *vt.* to patinate; to gloss.
patinato *adj.* patinated: **carta —**, plate paper.
patire *vi., vi.*[86] to suffer *(from)*; to endure, bear; to undergo: **— la fame**, to starve; **— di**, to suffer from; **— il freddo (il caldo)**, to be sensitive to cold (to heat).
patito *adj.* sickly, gaunt.
patologi'a *f.* pathology.
patolo'gico *adj.* pathological.
patos *m.* pathos.
pa'tria *f.* country, fatherland.
patriarca *m.* patriarch.
patriarcale *adj.* patriarchal.
patricida *see* parricida.
patrigno *m.* stepfather.
patrimo'nio *m.* fortune; estate, patrimony; property.
pa'trio *adj.* patrial; paternal; **patria potestà**, parental right.
patriota *m.* patriot.

patriot'tico *adj.* patriotic.
patriottismo *m.* patriotism.
patri'zio *m., adj.* patrician.
patrizzare *see* padreggiare.
patrocinare *vt.* to sponsor, favor, support; to plead.
patrocinatore *m.* sponsor; pleader.
patroci'nio *m.* sponsorship; legal assistance.
patronato *m.* patronage; foundation *(for charitable purposes, etc.)*.
patronessa *f.* patroness.
patroni'mico *m., adj.* patronymic.
patrono *m.* patron saint; counsel.
patta *f.* flap: **essere pari e —**, to be quits.
patteggiare *vt., vi.* to negotiate; to bargain, come to terms.
pattinag'gio *m.* skating.
pattinare *vi.* to skate.
pattinatore *m.* skater.
pat'tino *m.* skate; *(aeron.)* skid; *(mach.)* block; shoe, skid *(of a brake)*.
patto *m.* agreement; pact, compact; condition, term: **a — che**, provided.
pattu'glia *f.* patrol.
pattugliare *vi.* to patrol.
pattuire *see* patteggiare.
pattuito *adj.* agreed *(upon)*.
pattume *m.* garbage.
pattumiera *f.* dustbin.
patur'nie *f.pl.* sulks.
paura *f.* fear, dread; fright, scare: **aver — di**, to be afraid of; **far —**, to frighten; **da far —**, fearful.
pauroso *adj.* fearful; coward; shy.
pa'usa *f.* pause; *(mus.)* rest.
paventare *vt., vi.* to fear; to be afraid *(of)*.
pavesare *vt.* to array, dress.
pavese *f.* shield; *(naut.)* hoist.
pa'vido *m., adj.* coward.
pavimentare *vt.* to pave; to floor.
pavimentazione *f.* paving; flooring.
pavimento *m.* floor.
pavone *m.* peacock.
pavoneggiarsi *vr.* to strut, swagger.
pazientare *vi.* to be patient; to bear *(with)*.
paziente *m., adj.* patient.
pazienza *f.* patience: **far scappare la —**, to drive mad; **pazienza!** all right!, never mind!
pazzesco *adj.* crazy, preposterous.
pazzi'a *f.* madness, lunacy; folly: **far pazzie per**, to go crazy for.
pazzo *see* matto.
pecca *f.* flaw; shortcoming.
peccaminoso *adj.* sinful.
peccare *vi.* to sin *(against)*; to err.
peccato *m.* sin: **che —!** what a pity!, too bad!
peccatore *m.* sinner.
peccatuc'cio *m.* peccadillo.

pec'chia f. bee.
pecchione m. drone.
pece f. pitch: — greca, rosin.
pechinese m., adj. pekingese.
pe'cora f. sheep; (fig.) yes man.
pecora'io m. shepherd.
pecorella f. sheep; cielo a pecorelle, fleecy sky.
pecorino m. Roman cheese; adj. sheep.
peculato m. peculation; embezzlement.
peculiare adj. peculiar.
peculiarità f. peculiarity.
pecu'lio m. savings.
pecu'nia f. money.
pecunia'rio adj. pecuniary.
pedag'gio m., toll.
pedagogi'a f. pedagogics.
pedago'gico adj. pedagogic.
pedagogo m. pedagogue.
pedalare vi. to pedal.
pedale m. pedal; treadle.
pedaliera f. pedals; (mus.) pedal keyboard; (aeron.) rudder bar.
pedalina f. treadle printing press.
pedana f. platform; carpet.
pedante m. pedant; adj. pedantic.
pedanteri'a f. pedantry.
pedantesco adj. pedantic.
pedata f. kick; footprint.
pedestre adj. pedestrian; commonplace.
pediatra m., f. pediatrician.
pediatri'a f. pediatrics.
pedicure m., f. chiropodist.
pedilu'vio m. footbath.
pedina f. man (at checkers); pawn (at chess).
pedinare vt. to follow, shadow, tail.
pedis'sequo adj. literal; servile.
pedivella f. pedal crank.
pedone m. pedestrian.
pedun'colo m. peduncle.
pegamo'ide f. pegamoid.
peg'gio m., f. worst; adv. worse: tanto —, so much the worse; di male in —, from bad to worse; — che, di, worse than.
peggioramento m. worsening.
peggiorare vt., vi. to worsen; to change for the worse; to get worse.
peggiore adj. worse; worst: — di, worse than.
pegno m. pledge; pawn; token; forfeit.
pel comp. prep. for the. see per.
pe'lago m. open sea; (fig.) tangle.
pelame m. hair, coat.
pelare vt. to peel, pare; to pluck; to fleece; pelarsi vr. to peel off; to grow bald.
pelata f. bald spot; baldness.
pelato adj. peeled; hairless, bald.
pellame m. skins, hides.

pelle f. skin; hide; peel, rind: — d'uovo, mull; amici per la —, fast friends; non stare più nella —, to jump out of one's skin; far la — a uno, "to bump someone off."
pellegrinag'gio m. pilgrimage.
pellegrinare vi. to make a pilgrimage; to wander.
pellegrino m. pilgrim.
pelletteri'a f. leatherware.
pellicano m. pelican.
pellicceri'a f. furriery.
pellic'cia f. fur; coat; fur coat.
pelliccia'io m. furrier.
pellicciotto m. fur jacket.
Pellico, Silvio, Italian patriot and writer, Le mie prigioni (1789-1854).
pelli'cola f. film.
pellirossa m. redskin, Indian.
pelo m. hair; pile (of a carpet, etc.); fur; hairbreadth: di primo —, green; — dell'acqua, water surface; avere il — sullo stomaco, to be unscrupulous; cercare il — nell' uovo, to split hairs; per un —, almost, by a hairbreadth; non aver peli sulla lingua, to be outspoken.
peloso adj. hairy: carità pelosa, charity with strings attached.
peltro m. pewter.
pelu'ria f. fuzz, down.
pena f. punishment, penalty; pain, ache; distress; pity; trouble, pains: a mala —, barely, hardly; scontare una —, to serve a sentence; (non) valere la pena, (not) to be worth (while).
penale f. penalty; adj. penal, criminal.
penalista m. criminal lawyer.
penalità f. penalty.
penalizzare vt. to penalize.
penare vi. to suffer; to find it difficult.
pencolare vi. to totter; to waver.
penda'glio m. pendant.
pendente m. pendant, eardrop; adj. hanging (down); leaning; pending.
pendenza f. inclination, slope, slant; controversy; liability: la questione è ancora in —, the matter is still pending.
pen'dere vi.[10] to hang; to lean; to slope, slant; to be pending; to incline.
pendice f. slope, declivity, slant.
pen'dola f. clock.
pen'dolo m. pendulum.
pen'dulo adj. dangling.
penetrante adj. penetrating.
penetrare vt., vi. to pierce; to penetrate; to enter; to fathom.
penetrazione f. penetration.
penicillina f. penicillin.

peni'sola f. peninsula.
penitente m., f., adj. penitent.
penitenza f. penance; penitence; penalty.
penitenzia'rio m. penitentiary.
penna f. feather; pen: — d'oca, quill; — stilografica, fountain pen; — a sfera, ball point pen.
pennac'chio m. plume, tuft; panache.
pennaiuolo m. hack writer.
pennellare vt. to touch; to brush.
pennellata f. stroke of the brush.
pennello m. brush: fare (stare) a —, to do (to suit) to a turn.
pennino m. nib, steel pen.
pennone m. pennant; yard.
pennuto m. bird; adj. feathered.
penombra f. dimness, half light.
penoso adj. painful, distressing.
pensante adj. thinking: i ben pensanti, right-minded people.
pensare vt., vi. to think; to conceive; to intend; to mean; to conceive, suppose; to devise, think up; to take care (of), see (that); to mind: pensa agli affari tuoi! mind your own business!; dar da —, to worry, perplex.
pensata f. thought; brainstorm.
pensato adj. deliberate; weighed.
pensatore m. thinker.
pensiero m. thought; mind; idea, conception; intention, mind; opinion; worry, care: stare in —, to be worried; sopra —, lost in thought; absentminded; darsi — per, to worry about.
pensieroso adj. thoughtful; worried.
pen'sile adj. hanging: giardino —, roof garden.
pensilina f. shelter, shed; marquee.
pensionante m., f. boarder, lodger, paying guest.
pensionare vt. to pension (off).
pensionato m. pensioner; boarding school; adj. pensioned.
pensione f. pension; boarding house: stare a —, to board (at); tenere a —, to board; — completa, room and board.
pensoso adj. thoughtful, pensive.
penta'gono m. pentagon.
pentagramma m. (mus.) staff; (geom.) pentagram.
Pentecoste f. Whitsunday.
pentimento m. repentance; qualm.
pentirsi vr. to repent (of); to change one's mind (about); to be sorry (for): — di, to regret.
pentito adj. repenting; reformed.
pen'tola f. pot: qualcosa bolle in —, something is brewing.
pentolino m. small pot; pannikin; kettle.

penul'timo m., adj. last but one, penultimate.
penu'ria f. dearth, penury.
penzolare vi. to dangle, hang.
penzoloni adv. danglingly, adangle.
peo'nia f. peony.
pepato adj. peppery; stinging.
pepe m. pepper.
peperone m. (bot.) pepper.
pepita f. (min.) nugget.
pepsina f. pepsin.
per prep. for, by; to; on; from; out of, on account of; through; during, along; towards; in, into; in favor of; as; about to; per: — natura, by nature; — modo di dire, so to speak; — tutta la città, throughout the town; stavo — parlare, I was about to speak; — lo più, mostly; — lo meno, at least; — di più, moreover.
pera f. pear; (fig.) pate.
perbene adj. nice; decent; adv. nicely.
percalle m. percale.
percentuale f. percentage, percent; commission; rate.
percepi'bile adj. perceptible.
percepire vt. to perceive; to get; to earn; to feel; to catch.
percetti'bile adj. perceptible.
percettibilità f. perceptibility.
percettiva f. perceptivity.
percettivo adj. perceptive.
percezione f. perception.
perchè conj. why?; because; so that; for, as, since; m. why, reason.
perciò conj. therefore, so; that's why.
percome m. wherefore: il perchè e il —, the whys and wherefores.
percorrenza f. distance; way; range.
percor'rere[36] vt. to run along, cover; to run through, across; to travel over.
percorso (1) pp. of percorrere.
percorso (2) m. route, course, way; distance.
percossa f. blow, stroke.
percosso pp. of percuo'tere.
percuo'tere vt.[125] to strike, hit; to beat.
percussione f. percussion.
percussore m. firing pin.
perdente m. loser; adj. losing.
per'dere vt., vi.[97] to lose; to miss; to leak; to waste; to ruin: — di vista, to lose sight of; perdersi vr. to get lost: — d'animo, to lose heart.
perdifiato, (a) adv. breathlessly; madly.
perdigiorno m. idler.
perdinci! interj. good Lord!; by Jove!, "gee!"
per'dita f. loss; waste; discharge; leakage; damage: a — d'occhio, as far as the eye can reach.

perditempo *m.* waste of time.
perdizione *f.* perdition.
perdonare *vt.*, *vi.* to forgive; to excuse, pardon.
perdono *m.* forgiveness, pardon.
perdurare *vi.* to last; to persist.
perdutamente *adv.* desperately; madly.
perduto *adj.* lost; done for.
peregrinare *vi.* to wander, ramble.
peregrinazione *f.* wandering.
peregrino *adj.* unusual, far-fetched; peculiar; peregrine.
perenne *adj.* perennial; everlasting; continuous, steady.
perentorio *adj.* peremptory.
perequazione *f.* equalization.
perfetto *adj.* perfect; utter; downright.
perfezionamento *m.* perfecting; improvement.
perfezionare *vt.* to perfect; to complete; to improve; **perfezionarsi** *vr.* to become perfect; to improve; to become proficient.
perfezione *f.* perfection: **alla —,** perfectly.
perfidia *f.* perfidy; wickedness.
perfido *adj.* perfidious; wicked; nasty, foul.
perfino *adv.* even.
perforante *adj.* perforating.
perforare *vt.* to perforate, pierce.
perforatore *m.* perforator.
perforatrice *f.* punch, perforator; (*mach.*) boring machine; drilling machine; rock drill.
perforazione *f.* perforation.
pergamena *f.* parchment.
pergamo *m.* pulpit.
pergolato *m.* pergola, arbor.
Pergolesi, Giovanni Battista, Italian composer (1710–1736).
pericolante *adj.* unsafe; tottering.
pericolo *m.* danger, peril, jeopardy; threat; risk; (*fig.*) chance.
pericoloso *adj.* dangerous.
periferia *f.* outskirts (*pl.*).
perifrasi *f.* periphrasis.
perimetrale *adj.* surrounding.
perimetro *m.* perimeter.
periodicità *f.* periodicity.
periodico *m.* periodical; *adj.* periodic.
periodo *m.* period; time; cycle; sentence.
peripezia *f.* vicissitude.
periplo *m.* periplus.
perire *vi.* to perish, die.
periscopio *m.* periscope.
peristilio *m.* peristyle.
peritarsi *vr.* to hesitate.
perito (1) *m.* expert: **— agrimensore,** land surveyor; **— settore,** medical examiner.

perito (2) *adj.* dead.
peritoneo *m.* peritoneum.
peritonite *f.* peritonitis.
perizia *f.* skill; expertness; expert's report, estimate, survey; examination.
periziare *vt.* to appraise, estimate; to survey.
perla *f.* pearl.
perlaceo *adj.* pearly.
perlifero *adj.* pearl-bearing.
perlina *f.* seed pearl; bead.
perlustrare *vt.* to reconnoiter; to scout; to patrol.
perlustrazione *f.* reconnaissance, patrolling.
permaloso *adj.* touchy.
permanente *f.* permanent wave; *adj.* permanent.
permanenza *f.* permanence; stay.
permanere *vi.* to remain, linger; to go on.
permanganato *m.* permanganate.
permeare *vt.* to permeate.
permesso *m.* permission; permit; leave, license; leave of absence; furlough. *adj.* permitted, allowed: **è permesso?** may I (*come in*)?
permettere *vt.* to permit, allow; to suffer; **permettersi** *vr.* to take the liberty of; to allow oneself to; **permettersi il usso di,** to afford.
permuta *f.* permutation; barter.
permutare *vt.* to barter.
pernacchia *f.* (*vulg.*) "raspberry."
pernice *f.* partridge.
perniciosa *f.* (*med.*) pernicious malaria.
pernicioso *adj.* pernicious.
pernio, perno *m.* pivot, pin.
pernottamento *m.* overnight stop.
pernottare *vi.* to stay overnight.
pero *m.* pear tree.
però *conj.* but; yet. still; therefore.
perorare *vt.*, *vi.* to plead.
perorazione *f.* peroration.
perpendicolare *f.*, *adj.* perpendicular.
perpendicolo *m.* plummet: **a —,** perpendicularly.
perpetrare *vt.* to perpetrate.
perpetua *f.* parson's housekeeper.
perpetuare *vt.* to perpetuate.
perpetuità *f.* perpetuity.
perpetuo *adj.* perpetual; everlasting: **moto —,** perpetual motion.
perplessità *f.* perplexity.
perplesso *adj.* perplexed.
perquisire *vt.* to search.
perquisizione *f.* search.
persecutore *m.* persecutor.
persecuzione *f.* persecution.
perseguire *vt.* to pursue; to follow; to prosecute.
perseguitare *vt.* to persecute, harass; to pester.

perseverante *adj.* persevering.
perseveranza *f.* perseverance.
perseverare *vi.* to persevere.
persiana *f.* shutter.
per'sico *m.* (*ichthyol.*) perch.
persino *adv.* even.
persistente *adj.* persistent.
persistenza *f.* persistence.
persi'stere *vi.* to persist.
perso *adj.* lost; wasted: **a tempo —,** in one's spare time. *pp.* of **perdere.**
persona *f.* person; fellow; body; size: **— fisica,** natural person; **— giuridica,** artificial person; **di —,** in person, personally.
personag'gio *m.* personage; character.
personale *m.* body, figure; personnel, staff; *adj.* personal.
personalità *f.* personality; (*pl.*) authorities.
personalmente *adv.* personally; in person.
personificare *vt.* to personify.
personificazione *f.* personification, embodiment.
perspicace *adj.* perspicacious, keen.
perspica'cia *f.* perspicacity, keenness.
persuadere *vt.* [88] to persuade.
persuasione *f.* persuasion.
persuasiva *f.* persuasiveness.
persuasivo *adj.* persuasive.
persuaso *adj.* persuaded; satisfied. *pp.* of **persuadere.**
pertanto *conj.* therefore: **non —,** nevertheless.
per'tica *f.* perch; pole.
pertinace *adj.* pertinacious.
pertina'cia *f.* pertinacity.
pertinente *adj.* pertinent; belonging.
pertinenza *f.* pertinence.
pertosse *f.* whooping cough.
pertu'gio *m.* hole, opening.
perturbare *vt.* to perturb.
perturbatore *m.* perturber.
perturbazione *f.* disturbance.
Perugino, il (*Pietro Vannucci*), Italian painter (1446–1523).
perva'dere *vt.* to pervade.
pervenire *vi.* to arrive (*at*).
perversione *f.* perversion.
perversità *f.* perversity, wickedness.
perverso *adj.* perverse, wicked.
pervertimento *m.* perversion.
pervertire *vt.* to pervert; **pervertirsi** *vr.* to go astray.
pervicace *adj.* obstinate; perverse.
pervica'cia *f.* obstinacy; perverseness.
pervinca *f.* (*bot.*) periwinkle.
pesa *f.* weighbridge; weighing.
pesalet'tere *f.* letter scales.
pesante *adj.* heavy; tiresome.
pesantezza *f.* heaviness; weight.
pesare *vt.,* *vi.* to weigh.
pesatrice *f.* weighing device.

pesatura *f.* weighing.
pesca (1) *f.* peach.
pesca (2) *f.* fishing; catch; fishery: **— alla lenza,** angling.
pescag'gio *m.* (*naut.*) draught.
pesca'ia *f.* dam.
pescare *vt.* to fish; to find, fish (*up, out*); *vi.* (*naut.*) to draw: **— alla lenza,** to angle; **— nel torbido,** to fish in troubled waters.
pescatore *m.* fisher, angler.
pesce *m.* fish: **non saper che pesci pigliare,** to be in a quandary, not to know which way to turn; **— d'aprile,** April-fool joke.
pescecane *m.* shark; profiteer, parvenu.
pescherec'cio *m.* fishing boat.
pescheri'a *f.* fish market.
peschiera *f.* fishpond.
pesciven'dolo *m.* fishmonger.
pesco *m.* peach tree.
peso *m.* weight; load, burden; (*turf*) paddock: **— massimo** (*boxing*), heavyweight; **sollevare di —,** to lift bodily; **lancio del —,** shot-put.
pessimismo *m.* pessimism.
pessimista *m.* pessimist.
pes'simo *superl.adj.* worst; very bad.
pesta *f.* footprint; track.
pestare *vt.* to pound; to trample; to stamp; to batter.
peste *f.* plague; pest.
pestello *m.* pestle.
pesti'fero *adj.* pestiferous.
pestilenza *f.* pestilence; stench.
pestilenziale *adj.* pestilential, stinking.
pesto *m.* Genoese sauce; *adj.* crushed, battered: **buio —,** pitch dark; **occhi pesti,** black-ringed eyes; **ossa peste,** aching bones; **carta pesta,** papier-mâché.
pe'talo *m.* petal.
petardo *m.* petard; hand grenade.
petente *m.* petitioner.
petizione *f.* petition.
peto *m.* breaking of wind.
petonciano *m.* aubergine, egg plant.
Petrocchi, Policarpo, Italian lexicographer, *Novo dizionario universale della lingua italiana* (1852–1902).
petroliera *f.* (*naut.*) tanker.
petroli'fero *adj.* petroliferous: **zona petrolifera,** oil field.
Petrolini, Ettore, Italian comedian and playwright (1886–1936).
petro'lio *m.* petroleum; oil; kerosene: **pozzi di —,** oil wells.
pettegolare *vi.* to gossip.
pettegolezzo *m.* rumor, gossip.
pette'golo *m.* gossip; *adj.* gossipy.
pettinare *vt.* to comb; **pettinarsi** *vr.* to comb one's hair.

pettinatrice *f.* hairdresser.
pettinatura *f.* coiffure, hairdo.
pet'tine *m.* comb.
pettiniera *f.* comb case; dressing table.
pettirosso *m.* robin.
petto *m.* breast; chest: **a doppio —,** double-breasted; **— di camicia,** shirt front; **prendere di —,** to face up to.
pettorale *m.* breast strap; *adj.* pectoral.
pettorina *f.* stomacher.
pettoruto *adj.* strutting.
petulante *adj.* petulant, testy.
petulanza *f.* petulance.
pezza *f.* patch; piece; bolt (*of goods*): **— da piedi,** foot wrapper; **— giustificativa,** voucher; **da lunga —,** for a long while.
pezzato *adj.* spotted; dapple.
pezzatura *f.* length (*of goods*); dapple.
pezzente *m.* beggar.
pezzo *m.* piece; chunk; part, portion; fragment; tract: **un — grosso,** a bigwig; **un — fa,** long ago; **a pezzi e bocconi,** by fits and starts; **pezzi di ricambio,** spare parts.
pezzuola *f.* diaper; handkerchief.
piacente *adj.* attracting.
piacere (1) *m.* pleasure; joy; amusement; will, liking; favor: **per —** please; **mi fa —,** I am glad (*of it*).
piacere (2) *vi.*[89] to like; to love; to win; to be admired: **mi piace il mare,** I like the sea.
piace'vole *adj.* pleasant; agreeable; nice.
piacevolezza *f.* pleasantness; agreeableness; witticism.
piacimento *m.* pleasure, liking.
piaga *f.* fester, sore; evil, plague; bore.
piagare *vt.* to fester.
piaggeri'a *f.* flattery.
piaggiare *vt.* to flatter, blandish.
piaggiatore *m.* flatterer, "yes man."
piagnisteo *m.* wailing, whine.
piagnone *m.* weeper.
piagnucolare *vi.* to whimper.
piagnucolone *m.* whimperer, crybaby.
piagnucoloso *adj.* tearful, whimpering.
pialla *f.* plane.
piallac'cio *m.* veneer.
piallare *vt.* to plane.
piallatrice *f.* (*mach.*) planer.
piallatura *f.* planing.
piana *f.* plain.
pianeggiante *adj.* level.
pianella *f.* slipper; tile.
pianerot'tolo *m.* landing.
pianeta *m.* (*astr.*) planet; (*eccl.*) chasuble.
pian'gere *vt.*, *vi.* [90] to weep, cry, shed tears: **— miseria,** to pretend poverty.

pianino *m.* barrel organ.
pianissimo *adv.* very slowly; very softly.
pianista *m.* pianist.
piano (1) *m.* plain; plan, project; level; footing; surface, plane; story, floor; layer; (*mus.*) piano; (*geom.*) plane; (*moving pictures*) shot; (*aeron.*) stabilizer, vane: **primissimo,** primo, mezzo **—** (*moving pictures*), close up, full shot, medium shot; **— inclinato,** cant; **piani di coda** (*aeron.*), tail vanes.
piano (2) *adj.* plane, level; flat; plain, clear.
piano (3) *adv.* slowly; softly.
pianoforte *m.* piano: **— a coda,** grand piano.
pianola *f.* pianola.
pianoro *m.* plateau.
pianta *f.* plant; tree; map; payroll (*of employees*); sole (*of a foot, shoe, etc.*): **di sana —,** wholly, all over again.
piantagione *f.* plantation.
piantare *vt.* to plant; to drive in; to fix; to place, put; (*fam.*) to abandon, jilt: **— chiodi** (*fig.*), to make debts; **— grane,** to make trouble; **— in asso,** to give the slip to; to leave in the lurch; **piantarsi** *vr.* to plant oneself; (*recipr.*) to part.
piantato *adj.* planted: **ben —,** well-knit, brawny, sturdy.
piantatore *m.* planter.
pianterreno *m.* ground floor.
pianticella *f.* plantlet.
pianto *m.* weeping; *adj.* lamented. *pp.* of piangere.
piantonare *vt.* to watch.
piantone *m.* (*bot.*) shoot; (*mil.*) orderly; sentry.
pianura *f.* plain.
piastra *f.* plate; piaster (*coin*).
piastrella *f.* tile.
piatire *vi.* to litigate.
piattaforma *f.* platform: **— girevole,** turntable; **— di lancio,** springboard.
piattino *m.* small plate; saucer; dainty.
piatto *m.* dish. plate; scale; (*mus.*) cymbal: **— forte,** *pièce de résistance*; *adj.* flat.
piat'tola *f.* crab-louse; bore.
piazza *f.* square; place; clearing; (*comm.*) market: **— d'armi,** drill ground; **fare — pulita,** to make a clean sweep.
piazzaforte *f.* stronghold.
piazzale *m.* esplanade.
piazzare *see* collocare, **piazzarsi** *vr.* (*turf, etc.*) to place: **il favorito si è piazzato,** the favorite was placed.

piazzata f. scene; row, brawl.
piazzato adj. (turf, etc.) placed, to place.
piazzista m. (comm.) salesman.
piazzuola f. emplacement.
picca f. spike; spite; spade (in playing cards): per —, out of spite.
piccante adj. piquant; risqué.
piccare vi. to sparkle; **piccarsi** vr. to insist; to plume oneself (on).
piccato adj. piqued.
picchè m. (textiles) piqué.
picchetto m. stake; (mil.) picket; piquet: di —, on guard duty.
picchiare vt. to hit, beat, knock, strike. vi. to knock; to tap; (aeron.) to dive; **picchiarsi** vr. to strike oneself; (recipr.) to come to blows.
picchiata f. blow; (aeron.) dive.
picchiatore m. dive bomber; (boxing) puncher.
picchiettare vt. to drum; to speckle, spot.
picchiettato adj. spotted.
picchietti'o m. drumming.
pic'chio m. knock; woodpecker.
piccina f. child, little girl.
piccineri'a f. meanness.
piccino m. child, baby; adj. tiny; mean.
picciona'ia m. dovecot; (theat.) upper gallery; gallery gods.
piccione m. pigeon.
picciuolo m. stem, stalk.
picco m. peak: a —, perpendicularly; andare (mandare) a —, to sink.
pic'cola f. little girl, baby.
piccolezza f. smallness; trifle.
pic'colo m. boy, kid; adj. little, small, short; trivial; narrow; mean: in —, on a small scale.
piccone m. pick, pickax.
piccozza f. hatchet.
Pico della Mirandola, Italian humanist (1463–1494).
pidocchieri'a f. stinginess; meanness.
pidoc'chio m. louse; miser.
pidocchioso adj. lousy; stingy.
piede m. foot (pl. feet); bottom: sui due piedi, right away, offhand; in punta di piedi, on tiptoe; saltare a piè pari, to skip altogether; tenere i piedi in due staffe, to play both ends against the middle.
piedestallo m. pedestal.
piega f. fold; crease; pleat: prendere una buona (cattiva) —, to take a good (bad) turn.
piegamento m. folding; flexion.
piegare vt. to fold (up); to bend, bow; to tame; vi. to lean; to turn; **piegarsi** vr. to fold, bend; to yield.
piegatura f. folding; fold; crook.
pieghettare vt. to plait.

pieghe'vole m. folder; adj. folding; pliable, pliant; yielding.
piego see plico.
piena f. swell; flood; crowd; fullness: in —, swollen.
pienezza f. fullness, plenitude.
pienamente adv. fully.
pieno m. top, height; bloom; fill: fare il —, to fuel; in —, full; squarely; smack; adj. full; crammed; crowded: a pieni voti, by absolute majority; with flying colors.
pietà f. pity, mercy; piety: far —, to stir pity.
pietanza f. viand, main course.
pietismo m. pietism.
pietista m. pietist.
pietosio adj. merciful; wretched; pitiful.
pietra f. stone: — da affilare, whetstone, hone; — dello scandalo, shame.
pietrificare vt. to petrify.
pietrina f. flint (for lighters).
pietrisco m. rubble, metal.
pievano m. parson, curate.
pieve f. parish.
piffera'io m. fifer.
pif'fero m. fife.
pigiama m. pajamas.
pi'gia pi'gia m. crowd, press.
pigiare vt. to press, crush; **pigiarsi** vr. to crowd; to squeeze.
pigiatrice f. (mach.) presser, press.
pigiatura f. pressing.
pigionante m., f. tenant.
pigione f. rent: prendere a —, to rent; dare a —, to let.
pigliare see pren'dere.
pi'glio (1) m. mien, countenance.
pi'glio (2) m. hold: dar di — a, to lay hold of.
pigmentazione f. pigmentation.
pigmento m. pigment.
pigmeo m., adj. Pygmy, pygmy.
pigna f. pine cone; (obs.) dome.
pignatta f. pot.
pignoleri'a f. fastidiousness, fussiness, meticulousness.
pignolo m. (bot.) pine nut; (fig.) fussy man.
pignone m. embankment; (mach.) pinion.
pignoramento m. distraint.
pignorare vt. to distrain.
pigolare vi. to peep.
pigoli'o m. peeping, chirping.
pigri'zia f. laziness; sluggishness.
pigro adj. lazy; sluggish.
pila f. heap; pile; baptismal font; battery; basin: — atomica, atomic pile; — a secco, dry battery.
pilastro m. pillar.

Pilato m. (hist.) Pilate: **da Erode a —,** from pillar to post.

pillac'chera f. splash.

pil'lola f. pill, pillule.

pilone m. pylon: **— d'ormeggio,** mooring tower.

piloro m. pylorus.

pilota m. pilot; driver.

pilotag'gio m. pilotage.

pilotare vt. to pilot; to drive; to steer.

piluccare vt. to pluck.

pinacoteca f. picture gallery.

pineta f. pine wood, pinery.

pin'gue adj. fat; substantial, rich; big.

pingue'dine f. fatness.

pinguino m. penguin.

pinna f. fin; rubber flipper (for skin divers).

pinna'colo m. pinnacle.

pino m. pine.

pinoc'chio, pinolo m. pine nut.

pinta f. pint.

Pinturicchio, il (Bernardino Betti), Italian painter (1454-1513).

pinza f., **pinze** f.pl. pincers, pliers.

pinzetta f. tweezers (pl.).

pinzimo'nio m. (oil, salt, and pepper) dressing.

pio adj. pious; merciful; charitable.

pioggerella f. drizzle.

piog'gia f. rain; shower.

piolo see **piuolo.**

piombare vt. to lead; to plumb, seal; vi. to fall, drop; to pounce (on); to dive (upon).

piombatura f. lead coating; sealing.

piombino m. plummet, plumb bob.

piombo m. lead; bullets: **a —,** perpendicularly; **filo a —,** plumb line; **coi piedi di —,** cautiously.

pioniere m. pioneer.

pioppo m. poplar.

piorrea f. pyorrhea.

piovana, (acqua) f. rain water.

piovasco m. squall.

piovente m. slope (of a roof).

pio'vere vi.[91] to rain; to pour: **— a catinelle,** to rain cats and dogs.

piovigginare vi. to drizzle.

piovigginoso adj. drizzling.

piovoso adj. rainy.

piovra f. octopus.

pipa f. pipe.

pipare vi. to smoke a pipe.

pipata, pipatina f. pipe; pipeful.

pipistrello m. bat.

pipita f. hangnail; (veterinary) pip.

pira f. pyre, funeral pile.

pira'mide f. pyramid.

Pirandello, Luigi, Italian novelist and dramatist, Sei personaggi in cerca d'autore, Il fu Mattia Pascal, Nobel Prize, 1934 (1867-1936).

Piranesi, Giambattista, Italian engraver (1720-1778).

pirata m. pirate.

pirateggiare vt., vi. to pirate.

pirateri'a f. piracy.

pi'rica, (pol'vere) f. gunpowder.

pirite f. pyrites.

piroetta f. pirouette.

piroettare vi. to pirouette.

piroga f. pirogue, piragua.

piro'scafo m. steamer, ship.

pirotec'nico adj. pyrotechnic.

Pisano, Andrea (Andrea da Pontedera), Italian sculptor (1270?-1348).

Pisano, Giovanni, Italian sculptor (1245-1314).

pi'scia f. (vulg.) urine.

pisciare vi. (vulg.) to urinate.

pisciato'io m. (vulg.) urinal.

piscina f. swimming pool.

pisello m. pea.

pisolare vi. to doze, nap.

pisolino, pi'solo m. nap.

pista f. track; race course; (aeron.) runway.

pistac'chio m. pistachio.

pistillo m. pistil.

pistola f. pistol, gun.

pistolettata f. pistol shot.

pistolotto m. lecture; peroration.

pistone m. piston.

pitago'rico adj. Pythagorean: **tavola pitagorica,** multiplication table.

pitale m. chamberpot.

pitoccare vi. to beg, to be miserly.

pitoccheri'a f. beggary; stinginess.

pitocco m. beggar; miser.

pitone m. python.

pit'tima f. plaster; bore.

pittore m. painter.

pittoresco adj. picturesque.

pittrice f. painter (female).

pittura f. painting; paint.

pitturare vt., vi. to paint.

più m. most: **i —,** most people; **il — delle volte,** more often than not; **dal — al meno,** more or less; adj. more; several; adv. more (than); most; longer; plus: **non —,** no more, any more; **mai —,** never again, by no means; **non ho — che un vestito,** I have but one suit left; **credersi da — di,** to think oneself superior to; **sempre —,** more and more; **sempre — in alto,** higher and higher; **tutt'al —,** at most; **per lo —,** mainly, mostly; **— in là,** further on, later on; **per di —,** in addition; **tanto — che,** the more so as.

piuma f. feather.

piumac'cio m. feather pillow.

piumag'gio m. plumage.

piumino *m.* down quilt; powder puff; feather duster; "slug."

piumoso *adj.* feathery.

piuolo *m.* peg: **scala a piuoli**, ladder.

piuttosto *adv.* rather (*than*); instead.

piva *f.* bagpipe: **con le pive nel sacco**, disappointed.

pizzardone *m.* policeman, "flatfoot," "cop."

pizzica'gnolo *m.* pork butcher.

pizzicare *vt.*, *vi.* to pinch, nip; to sting, prick; to itch; (*mus.*) to pluck.

piz'zico *m.* pinch.

pizzicore *m.* itch.

pizzicotto *m.* pinch, nip.

pizzo *m.* lace; Vandyke beard; peak.

placare *vt.* to appease, pacify; to allay, soothe; **placarsi** *vr.* to calm down; to subside.

placca *f.* plaque; spot.

placcare *vt.* to plate: **— in oro**, to gold-plate.

pla'cido *adj.* placid.

plafone *m.* ceiling, plafond.

plaga *f.* region.

plagiare *vt.*, *vi.* to plagiarize.

plagia'rio *m.* plagiarist.

pla'gio *m.* plagiarism.

planare *vi.* to volplane, glide; to level off.

plan'cia *f.* planchet; (*naut.*) bridge.

planimetri'a *f.* planimetry; (*arch.*) layout, blueprint.

plasma *m.* plasma.

plasmare *vt.* to mold, shape.

pla'stica *f.* plastic, plastic art; (*surg.*) skin grafting.

plasticità *f.* plasticity.

pla'stico *m.* modeler; model; *adj.* plastic.

pla'tano *m.* plane tree.

platea *f.* pit, orchestra, parquet; audience.

plateale *adj.* vulgar, plebeian, common.

platinare *vt.* to platinize; to bleach (*hair*).

platinato *adj.* platinized; bleached: **bionda platinata**, platinum blonde.

pla'tino *m.* platinum.

plaudire *vi.* to applaud.

plausi'bile *adj.* plausible.

pla'uso *m.* applause; praise.

pleba'glia *f.* mob, rabble.

plebe *f.* common people, populace.

plebeo *m.*, *adj.* plebeian.

plebiscito *m.* plebiscite.

plena'rio *adj.* plenary.

plenilu'nio *m.* full moon.

plenipotenzia'rio *m.*, *adj.* plenipotentiary.

ple'tora *f.* plethora.

pleto'rico *adj.* plethoric.

plettro *m.* plectrum.

pleurite *f.* pleurisy.

plico *m.* folder, cover; letter.

plotone *m.* platoon: **— d'esecuzione**, firing squad.

plum'beo *adj.* leaden.

plurale *m.*, *adj.* plural.

plu'rimo *adj.* plural.

plusvalore *m.* excess value.

pluto'crate *m.* plutocrat.

pneuma'tico *m.* (*pneumatic*) tire; tube; *adj.* pneumatic: **posta pneumatica**, pneumatic dispatch.

po' *see* poco.

pochezza *f.* littleness, smallness.

pochis'simo *adj.*, *adv.* very little; very seldom; very cheap; **pochissimi** *pl.* very few.

poco *m.* little; **pochi** *m.pl.* few (people): **con quel po' po' di patrimonio**, with such a fortune; *adj.* little; some, any; small; scarce; short; *adv.* little; a little (while); slightly; some, any; cheap, cheaply: **— fa**, a few moments ago; **fra —**, soon, in a short time; **per —**, almost, nearly; **— più — meno**, more or less; **né punto né —**, not at all; **a — a —**, little by little; **un bel po' di**, a good deal of; **un altro —**, some more, a little longer; **da —**, cheap; **da — tempo**, not long ago; **— prima, dopo**, shortly before, after.

podere *m.* farm.

poderoso *adj.* powerful, mighty.

podestà *m.* mayor.

podismo *m.* foot racing.

podista *m.* foot racer.

poema *m.* (*long*) poem.

Poerio,Carlo, Italianstatesman (1803–1867).

poesi'a *f.* poetry; poem.

poeta *m.* poet.

poetessa *f.* poetess.

poe'tico *adj.* poetic, poetical.

poggiare *vt.* to lay, rest; *vi.* to rest (*upon*); to move; (*naut.*) to move leeward.

pog'gio *m.* knoll.

poggiuolo *m.* balcony.

poi *adv.* after, afterwards; then; later (*on*); next: **d'ora in —**, from now on; **d'allora in —**, since then; **prima o —**, sooner or later.

poiana *f.* (*ornith.*) buzzard.

poichè *conj.* since; for, as; when; after; as soon as.

polacco *m.* Polish (*language*); Pole; *adj.* Polish.

polare *adj.* polar: **stella —**, polestar.

polarizzare *vt.* to polarize; to focus.

polarizzatore *m.* polarizer.

polca *f.* polka.

pole'mica f. polemic; controversy.
polemista m. polemicist.
polemizzare vi. to argue, polemize.
polentina f. poultice.
poliambulanza f. dispensary.
poli'cromo adj. polychrome.
polifase adj. (elec.) multiphase.
poligami'a f. polygamy.
poli'gamo m. polygamist; adj. polygamous.
poliglotta m., adj. polyglot.
poli'gono m. polygon: — di tiro, shooting range.
poliomielite f. poliomyelitis, infantile paralysis.
po'lipo m. polyp.
politeama m. theater.
politec'nico m. polytechnic; (univ.) engineering institute; adj. polytechnic.
poli'tica f. politics; policy.
politicante m. politician.
poli'tico adj. political; politic: uomo —, politician.
polizi'a f. police: agente di —, policeman, officer.
Poliziano, Angelo, Italian humanist (1454–1494).
poliziesco adj. police: romanzo —, detective story.
poliziotto m. policeman; detective.
po'lizza f. policy; draft; certificate: — di carico, bill of lading; — di pegno, pawn ticket.
polla f. spring.
polla'io m. poultry yard.
pollame m. poultry.
pollanca, pollastra, pollastrella, f. pullet, hen.
pollastro m. cockerel; (fam.) chicken.
polleri'a f. poultry shop.
pol'lice m. thumb (of the hand); big toe (of the foot); inch.
pol'line m. (bot.) pollen.
polliven'dolo m. poulterer.
pollo m. chicken, fowl; dupe: conoscere i propri polli, to be nobody's fool.
polmone m. lung: — d'acciaio, pulmotor.
polmonite f. pneumonia. [motor.
polo m. pole (of the earth, of a magnet, etc.); (sport) polo.
Polo, Marco, Italian traveler in Asia, author of Il Milione (1254?–1324).
polpa f. pulp.
polpac'cio m. (anat.) calf.
polpastrello m. finger tip.
polpetta f. croquette.
polpettone m. hash.
polpo m. (zool.) octopus.
polposo adj. pulpy, fleshy, meaty.
polsino m. cuff.
polso m. wrist; pulse; wristband; nerve, will.

polti'glia f. pulp; mud.
poltrire vi. to idle.
poltrona f. armchair, easy chair; (theat.) orchestra seat, pit stall.
poltroncina f. (theat.) orchestra seat (in the last rows).
poltrone m. lazybones.
poltroneri'a f. laziness.
pol'vere f. dust; (chem.) powder: — da sparo, gunpowder; orologio a —, sand glass.
polveriera f. powder magazine.
polverina f. powder.
polverino m. sand; sandbox; (min.) slack.
polverizzare vt., **polverizzarsi** vr. to pulverize.
polverizzatore m. pulverizer; sprayer.
polverizzazione f. pulverization.
polverone m. dust cloud.
polveroso adj. dusty.
pomata f. pomade; ointment.
pomellato adj. dappled.
pomello m. cheekbone.
pomeridiano adj. (in the) afternoon, P. M.
pomerig'gio m. afternoon.
po'mice f. pumice (stone).
pomidoro see pomodoro.
pomo m. apple; knob; pommel: pomo della discordia, bone of contention.
pomodoro m. tomato.
pompa (1) f. pomp; display: impresario di pompe funebri, undertaker.
pompa (2) f. (mach.) pump.
pompare vt. to pump.
pompelmo m. grapefruit.
pompiere m. fireman.
pomposo adj. pompous, solemn.
Ponchielli, Amilcare, Italian composer (1834–1886).
ponderare vt. to weigh, ponder.
ponderatezza f. caution.
ponderato adj. careful, cautious.
ponderoso adj. ponderous; weighty.
pondo m. weight, burden.
ponente m. west.
Pontano, Giovanni, Italian statesman, historian and poet (1426–1503).
ponte m. bridge; scaffold; (naut.) deck: — aereo, air lift.
ponte'fice m. pontiff, pope.
ponticello m. footbridge; bridge (of a fiddle, etc.).
pontiere m. pontonier.
pontifi'cio adj. papal.
pontile m. landing stage; pier.
pontone m. pontoon.
ponzare vi. to labor; to cogitate.
popolano m., adj. plebeian.

popolare (1) *adj.* popular: posti popolari, "bleachers."

popolare (2) *vt.* to people; popolarsi *vr.* to become populated.

popolarità *f.* popularity.

popolazione *f.* population.

po'polo *m.* people.

popoloso *adj.* populous.

popone *m.* melon.

poppa *f.* (*anat.*) breast; (*naut.*) stern, poop: col vento in —, before the wind.

poppante *m.* suckling.

poppare *vi.* to suckle.

poppato'io *m.* nursing bottle.

porca *f.* (*agr.*) ridge; (*zool.*) sow.

porca'io *m.* swineherd; pigsty.

porcellana *f.* porcelain, china.

porcellino *m.* piggy: — d'India, guinea pig.

porcello *m.* pig.

porcheri'a *f.* dirt; trash; dirty trick; obscenity.

porchetta *f.* roast pig.

porcile *m.* sty, pigsty.

porco *m.* pig, swine; pork.

porcospino *m.* porcupine.

por'fido *m.* porphyry.

por'gere *vt.*[92] to hand; to hold out; to offer.

poro *m.* pore.

porosità *f.* porosity.

poroso *adj.* porous.

por'pora *f.* purple; (*med.*) purpura.

Por'pora, Niccolò, Italian composer (1686–1766).

porporato *m.* cardinal.

porporina *f.* purpurin.

porporino *adj.* purple.

porre *vt.*[92] to put, place; to suppose; to pay (*attention*).

porro *m.* (*bot.*) leek; (*path.*) wart.

porta *f.* door; doorway; gate; (*sport*) goal.

Porta, Carlo, Italian poet in Milanese dialect (1776–1821).

Porta, della, Giambattista, Italian physicist (1538–1615).

portabagagli *m.* porter; rack.

portabandiera *m.* standard-bearer, ensign.

porta'bile *adj.* portable.

portacatino *m.* basin stand.

portace'nere *m.* ash tray.

portaceste *m.* (*theat.*) property man.

portacil'pria *m.* vanity case, compact.

portae'rei *f.* aircraft carrier.

portaferiti *m.* stretcher-bearer.

portafiori *m.* flower stand; flowerpot.

portafo'glio *m.* pocketbook; wallet; (*fin.*, *pol.*) portfolio.

portafortuna *m.* talisman.

portagioielli *m.* jewel case.

portale *m.* portal.

portalet'tere *m.* postman.

portamento *m.* carriage, bearing; behavior.

portamonete *m.* purse.

portante *adj.* carrying: piano —, supporting surface.

portantina *f.* sedan-chair.

portaor'dini *m.* messenger, courier.

portapenne *m.* penholder.

portare *vt.* to bring; to fetch; to take (*away*); to carry; to wear; to move; to drive; to lead; portarsi *vr.* to bring, take along; to behave.

portaritratti *m.* frame.

portasciugamani *m.* towel horse, towel rack.

portasigarette *m.* cigarette case.

portasi'gari *m.* cigar case.

portaspilli *m.* pincushion.

portata *f.* reach; power, strength; capacity; range; (*naut.*) tonnage; lifting power (*of a crane*); carrying capacity (*of a truck*); purport; scope; course, dish: a — di mano, within one's reach.

porta'tile *adj.* portable.

portato *m.* result; *adj.* worn; inclined.

portatore *m.* bearer.

portavasi *m.* (*naut.*) cradle-bar.

portavoce *m.* speaking tube; megaphone; spokesman, mouthpiece.

portello *m.* wicket; porthole.

portento *m.* wonder, marvel.

portentoso *adj.* wonderful.

porticato *m.* porch, gallery, piazza.

por'tico *m.* portico; porch.

portiera *f.* portiere; portress; door (*of an automobile*).

portiere *m.* doorkeeper, doorman; janitor; (*sport*) goalkeeper.

portina'ia *f.* portress.

portina'io *see* portiere.

Portinari, Beatrice, Florentine lady, immortalized by Dante, who made her the central figure of his *Divina Commedia* (? –1290).

portineri'a *f.* janitor's lodge.

porto (1) *m.* carriage; postage: franco di —, carriage free; — d'arme, license to carry arms.

porto (2) *m.* harbor, port, haven: — franco, free port; condurre a buon —, to bring off.

porto (3) *m.* port (*wine*).

porto (4) *pp.of* porgere.

portoghese *m.*, *adj.* Portuguese; "gate crasher."

portone *m.* gate, portal.

porzione *f.* portion, share.

posa *f.* posture; attitude, pose; pause; rest; (*photo.*) time exposure: senza —, endlessly.

posace'nere *m.* ash tray.

posamine *m.* minelayer.

posapiano *m.* slow coach.

posapiedi *m.* footrest.

posare *vt.* to lay (*down*); to rest; *vi.* to rest; to lie; to pose; **posarsi** *vr.* to place oneself; to (*come to*) rest; to alight.

posata *f.* knife fork and spoon.

posato *adj.* sedate; placed, laid.

posato'io *m.* rest; perch, roost.

posatore *m.* poseur.

po'scia *adv.* then, afterwards.

poscritto *m.* postscript.

posdatare *vt.* to postdate.

posdomani *adv.* the day after tomorrow.

positiva *f.* (*photo.*) positive.

positivo *m.* positive; *adj.* positive, practical, matter-of-fact: **di —**, for sure.

posizione *f.* position; posture, attitude; condition; location: **prendere — per (contro)**, to take one's stand for (*against*).

posporre *vt.* to postpone, put off; to subordinate.

posposto *pp.* of **posporre**.

possa, possanza *f.* strength, power, vigor.

possedere *vt.* to own, possess; to have; to master.

possedimento *m.* possession; estate.

possente *adj.* powerful, mighty.

possessivo *m.*, *adj.* possessive.

possesso *m.* possession.

possessore *m.* possessor, owner; holder.

possi'bile *adj.* possible: **fare il —**, to do one's level best.

possibilità *f.* possibility; opportunity; chance; power; means.

possibilmente *adv.* possibly; if possible.

possidente *m.* man of property; *m.*, *f.* landowner.

posta *f.* mail, post; post office; stake; size: **— aerea**, air mail; **fermo in —**, general delivery; **spese di —**, postage; **stare alla —**, to lie in ambush; **a — per**, expressly for; **a (bella) —**, on purpose.

postale *m.* mail boat; *adj.* postal, mail, post.

postare *vt.* to establish, post.

postazione *f.* emplacement.

postbel'lico *adj.* postwar.

posteggiare *vt.* to park.

posteg'gio *m.* stand; parking lot.

po'steri *m.pl.* posterity.

posteri'a *f.* general store.

posteriore *adj.* posterior, hind, back.

posteriormente *adv.* posteriorly; later.

posterità *f.* posterity.

postic'cio *adj.* provisional; artificial; false.

posticipare *vt.* to postpone.

posticipato *adj.* postponed; deferred; on delivery.

postiglione *m.* postillion.

postilla *f.* note, apostil.

postillare *vt.* to annotate.

postino *m.* postman.

posto (*1*) *m.* place; spot; room; seat; job, situation: **— di medicazione**, first-aid station; **— di polizia**, police station; **automobile a due posti**, two-seater; **tenere la lingua a —**, to hold one's tongue; **mettere a —**, to tidy up, to straighten up.

posto (*2*) *pp.* of **porre**.

postochè *conj.* supposing that; provided; since.

postremo *adj.* last.

postri'bolo *m.* brothel.

postulante *m.* petitioner.

postulato *m.* postulate.

po'stumo *m.* aftermath; sequel; *adj.* posthumous.

pota'bile *adj.* drinkable.

potare *vt.* to prune, lop.

potassa *f.* potash.

potas'sio *m.* potassium.

potatura *f.* pruning, lopping.

potentato *m.* potentate.

potente *adj.* powerful, mighty; influential.

potenza *f.* power, might; strength; **in —**, potentially.

potenziale *m.*, *adj.* potential.

potenzialmente *adv.* potentially.

potere (*1*) *m.* power: **il quarto —**, the fourth estate; **cadere in — di**, to fall into the hands of.

potere (*2*) *vi.*[94] can, may; to be able; to be allowed: **non posso**, I cannot; **posso andare?** may I go?; **avrebbe potuto scrivere**, he could have written; **può darsi che**, it may be that; **non posso far altro che andare**, I cannot but go; **non posso fare a meno di pensare**, I can't help thinking; **non poterne più**, to be fed up; to be exhausted; **a più non posso**, with might and main.

potestà *f.* power, authority: **patria —**, *patria potestas*.

po'vero *m.* pauper; beggar; *adj.* poor; needy; scanty, meager; late (*dead*): **— me!** woe is me!

povertà *f.* poverty; poorness, scantiness.

pozione *f.* potion, draft.

pozza *f.* puddle, pool.

pozzan'ghera *f.* puddle.

pozzo *m.* well; pit; (*min.*) shaft: **— petrolifero**, oil well; **— nero**, cesspool.

pramma'tica *f.* custom: **di —**, customary; obligatory, *de rigueur.*

pranzare *vi*. to dine.
pranzo *m*. dinner; banquet: **sala da —**, dining room.
prassi *f*. praxis, procedure.
prateri′a *f*. prairie.
pra′tica *f*. practice; experience; skill; habit; matter, business; dossier, file;apprenticeship;training;(*naut*.) pratique: **far le pratiche per**, to take steps to.
pratica′bile *adj*. practicable; (*theat*.) practical.
praticamente *adv*. practically.
praticante *m*. apprentice; practitioner; *adj*. practicing.
praticare *vt*. to practice; to perform; to frequent; to associate with: — **buoni prezzi**, to charge low prices; — **un′apertura**, to open a gap.
praticità *f*. practicalness.
pra′tico *adj*. practical; experienced, practiced: **all′atto —**, in practice.
praticone *m*. empiric.
prato *m*. meadow.
pravo *adj*. wicked.
pream′bolo *m*. preamble.
preannunziare *vt*. to announce; to forebode.
preannun′zio *m*. warning; foreboding.
preavvertire, preavvisare, *vt*. to forewarn.
preavviso *m*. notice; warning.
prebenda *f*. prebend.
preca′rio *adj*. precarious.
precauzione *f*. precaution; caution.
prece *f*. prayer.
precedente *m*. precedent: **senza —**, unprecedented; *adj*. previous, preceding, former.
precedentemente *adv*. previously.
precedenza *f*. priority, precedence: **in —**, previously.
prece′dere *vt.*, *vi*. to precede: **farsi — da**, to send ahead.
precetto *m*. precept; rule; principle; writ, warrant.
precettore *m*. tutor, teacher.
precipitare *vt.*, *vi*. to precipitate; to drop, fall down, crash; **precipitarsi** *vr*. to precipitate oneself; to rush, dash; (*aeron*). to fall, crash.
precipitato *m*. precipitate; *adj*. precipitate, hasty; rash.
precipitazione *f*. rashness; haste, hurry; precipitation.
precipitoso *adj*. precipitate; precipitous; rash.
precipi′zio *m*. precipice; ruin: **a —**, precipitously, precipitately.
preci′puo *adj*. chief, main.
precisa′mente *adv*. precisely.
precisare *vt*. to determine; to specify; to stress.
precisione *f*. precision, accuracy.

preciso *adj*. precise, accurate; exact; like, alike: **alle dieci precise**, at ten (*o′clock*) sharp.
preclu′dere *vt.*[2] to preclude.
precluso *pp. of* precludere.
precoce *adj*. precocious; premature, untimely.
preconcetto *m*. preconception; bias, prejudice; *adj*. preconceived.
preconizzare *vt*. to preconize, predict.
precor′rere *vt*. to forerun.
precursore *m*. precursor, forerunner.
preda *f*. prey; booty.
predare *vt*. to plunder.
predecessore *m*. predecessor.
predella *f*. dais; footboard.
predellino *m*. footboard.
predestinare *vt*. to predestine; to doom.
predestinato *adj*. predestinate; fated.
predetto *adj*. aforesaid. *pp. of* predire.
pre′dica *f*. sermon; lecture.
predicare *vt.*, *vi*. to preach.
predicato *m*. predicate.
predicatore *m*. preacher.
predicazione *f*. preaching.
predicozzo *m*. lecture.
prediletto *m.*, *adj*. favorite. *pp. of* prediligere.
predilezione *f*. predilection.
predili′gere *vt.*[95]to prefer, like best.
predire *vt.*[44] to foretell.
predisporre *vt.*[93] to predispose; to bias; to prearrange.
predisposizione *f*. predisposition; prearrangement.
predisposto *pp. of* predisporre.
predizione *f*. prediction.
predominante *adj*. predominant; prevailing.
predominare *vt.*, *vi*. to predominate (*over*); to prevail.
predomi′nio *m*. predominance; supremacy.
predone *m*. marauder.
prefazione *f*. preface, introduction.
preferenza *f*. preference: **a — di**, rather than; **di —**, preferably.
preferi′bile *adj*. preferable.
preferire *vt*. to prefer, like better; to choose.
preferito *m.*, *adj*. favorite.
prefetto *m*. prefect.
prefettura *f*. prefecture.
prefig′gere *vt.*[63] to prefix, fix in advance; **prefiggersi** *vr*. to set one′s mind (*on*)
prefisso (*1*) *m*. prefix.
prefisso (*2*) *pp. of* prefiggere.
pregare *vt*. to pray; to beg; to entreat: **farsi —**, to deny oneself; **vi pregol** please!
prege′vole *adj*. valuable; good.
preghiera *f*. prayer; request; entreaty.

pregiarsi vr. to have the honor to.

pregiatis'simo superl.adj. priceless: — Signore, Dear Sir.

pregiato adj. valued, valuable: **la vostra pregiata lettera del,** your favor of.

pre'gio m. esteem; virtue; quality; merit; value, worth: **tenere in —,** to value.

pregiudicare vt. to prejudice; to be prejudicial to; to jeopardize.

pregiudicato m. man with a police record.

pregiudiziale f. exception; adj. prejudicial.

pregiudi'zio m. prejudice; bias; detriment: **essere di —,** to be detrimental (to).

pregno adj. filled (with); pregnant.

prego, please; not at all.

pregustare vt. to foretaste; to anticipate.

preisto'rico adj. prehistoric.

prelato m. prelate.

prelazione f. pre-emption.

prelevamento m. draft: — **in scoperto** (bank.), overdraft.

prelevare vt. to draw, take away; to withdraw; to pick up.

prelibato adj. delicious, dainty.

prelievo see prelevamento.

preliminare m., adj. preliminary.

prelu'dere vi.[6] to prelude.

prelu'dio m. prelude.

preluso pp. of preludere.

prematuro adj. premature, untimely.

premeditare vt. to premeditate, to design.

premeditato adj. premeditated.

pre'mere vt., vi. to press; to push; to squeeze; to weigh (upon); to urge; to insist (on); to be important; to mean a lot.

premessa f. preliminary; foreword; premise.

premet'tere vt. to premise.

premiare vt. to award a prize to; to reward.

premiato m. prize winner; adj. prize-winning, rewarded.

premiazione f. prize awarding.

pre'mio m. prize; trophy; reward; premium; bonus: **monte premi,** win-pool.

pre'mito m. contraction.

premolare m., adj. premolar.

premonizione f. premonition.

premunire vt. to safeguard: **premunirsi** vr. to take precautions.

premura f. care; solicitude; urgency; haste: **aver —,** to be in a hurry; **di —,** hastily, in a hurry.

premurosamente adv. solicitously; readily.

premuroso adj. solicitous, considerate.

pren'dere vt., vi.[96] to take; to catch; to steal; to get; to begin; to hold; to turn: — **alle proprie dipendenze,** to engage; — **le mosse (da),** to start (from); — **sonno,** to go off to sleep; — **quota,** to climb; — **terra,** to land; **pren'dersi** vr. to take, catch, seize, get; to secure: — **a pugni,** to come to blows, to fight; **prendersela a male (calda),** to take amiss (to heart); **prendersela con uno,** to lay the blame on one, to take it out on one.

prenome m. Christian name, given name.

prenotare vt. to book, engage, reserve.

prenotazione f. booking, reservation.

pren'sile adj. prehensile.

preoccupare vt., **preoccuparsi** vr. to worry.

preoccupato adj. preoccupied; worried, anxious.

preoccupazione f. preoccupation; worry, anxiety.

preparare vt. to prepare; to organize; to arrange: — **la tavola,** to lay the table; — **il terreno,** to pave the way; **prepararsi** vr. to prepare (for); to get ready.

preparativo m. preparation.

preparato m. preparation, compound; adj. prepared; ready.

preparato'rio adj. preparatory.

preparazione f. preparation.

preponderante adj. preponderant; prevailing.

preponderanza f. preponderance.

preporre vt.[93] to put, place before; to put in charge (of).

preposizione f. preposition.

preposto m. parson, vicar; adj. in charge of. pp. of preporre.

prepotente m. bully; adj. overbearing; overwhelming.

prepotenza f. outrage; arrogance.

prerogativa f. prerogative.

presa f. taking, seizing, hold, grasp; (elec.) plug jack: — **d'aria,** air shaft; — **di tabacco,** pinch; **essere alle prese con,** to be struggling with; **far —,** to take; **macchina da —** (moving pictures), camera.

presa'gio m. presage, premonition.

presagire vt. to presage.

pre'sbite m. presbyope; adj. presby-opic, long-sighted, far-sighted.

presbite'rio m. presbytery.

prescelto adj. chosen, preferred.

prescienza f. prescience.

prescin'dere vi.[97] to prescind: — **da,** to disregard, leave aside.

prescritto m. prescript. adj. prescribed; prescript. pp. of prescrivere.

prescri'vere vt.[124] to prescribe.
prescrizione f. prescription.
presenta'bile adj. presentable.
presentare vt. to present; to show, exhibit; to offer; to introduce; to propose:—la propria candidatura a, to run for; presentarsi vr. to present, introduce oneself; to report; to show oneself, appear; to arise; to look; to promise:—a un esame, to appear for an examination; si presentò il destro per, an opportunity offered itself to.
presentatore m. introducer; (theat.) host, showman.
presentazione f. presentation; introduction.
presente (1) m. present (time); (gramm.) present (tense); bystander; present: i presenti, those present; the on-lookers; esclusi i presenti, present company excepted.
presente (2) adj. present: tener —, to bear in mind; essere — a se stesso, to have all one's wits about one; presente! here!
presentemente adv. at present.
presentimento m. foreboding.
presentire vt., vi. to presage, foresee, feel.
presenza f. presence: — di spirito, presence of mind; far atto di —, to put in an appearance.
presenziare vt., vi. to attend; to be present (at).
presepe, prese'pio m. manger; crèche.
preservare vt. to preserve.
preservativo m. preservative; contraceptive sheath; adj. preservative.
pre'side m. president; principal (of a school).
presidente m. president; chairman: Presidente del Consiglio (dei Ministri), premier.
presidenza f. presidency; chairmanship.
presidenziale adj. presidential.
presidiare vt. to garrison.
presi'dio m. garrison.
presie'dere vt., vi. to preside (over); to be in charge (of).
preso adj. taken, seized; busy. pp. of prendere.
pressa f. press.
pressante adj. pressing.
pressappoco adv. about, thereabout; more or less; approximately.
pressare vt. to press; to urge.
pressi m.pl. neighborhood, vicinity.
pressione f. pressure.
presso prep. near, by; beside; at, in; with; care of (abb.: c/o): — un amico, at a friend's; godere di

popolarità — i propri allievi, to enjoy popularity with one's pupils; essere impiegato —, to work with; adv. near, nearby; about.
pressochè adv. almost, nearly.
prestabilire vt. to pre-establish, fix in advance.
prestabilito adj. pre-established, appointed.
prestanome m. figurehead.
prestante adj. personable.
prestanza f. personableness.
prestare vt. to lend: — aiuto, to give help; — attenzione, to pay attention; — fede, to believe, trust; — giuramento, to swear an oath; — servizio, to work (with, in, for); farsi —, to borrow; prestarsi vr. to lend oneself (itself); to volunteer; to help.
prestato adj. lent. [to help.
prestatore m. lender: — d'opera, worker.
prestazione f. service; (sport) performance.
prestidigitatore m. juggler.
presti'gio m. prestige; influence: giuoco di —, legerdemain.
pres'tito m. loan: dare a —, to lend; prendere a —, to borrow.
presto adj. quick, ready; adv. early, soon; quickly: far —, to make haste; è — detto, it is sooner said than done; — o tardi, sooner or later; al più —, as soon as possible; ben —, very soon.
pre'sule m. archbishop.
presu'mere vt., vi.[19] to presume, suppose.
presumi'bile adj. presumable.
presumibilmente adv. presumably.
presuntivo m. (comm.) budget; adj. presumptive.
presunto adj. presumptive; supposed; alleged. pp. of presumere.
presuntuoso adj. conceited.
presunzione f. presumption; conceit.
presupporre vt. to presuppose.
presupposto m. assumption.
prete m. priest; clergyman; (fam.) bedwarmer.
pretendente m. pretender, claimant; suitor.
preten'dere vt., vi.[140] to exact, demand; to charge; to claim; to pretend; to maintain; to ask; to be hard to please.
pretenzioso adj. pretentious.
preterintenzionale adj. unintentional.
prete'rito m. (the) past; m., adj. (gramm.) preterit.
pretesa f. pretension; claim; pretense.
preteso adj. claimed; alleged. pp. of pretendere.

pretesto m. pretext, excuse, pretense.
pretore m. judge.
prettamente adv. genuinely.
pretto adj. genuine, pure; undiluted.
pretura f. court of first instance.
prevalente adj. prevailing.
prevalenza f. predominance; supremacy.
prevalere vi.[150] to prevail (over, against), to win.
prevalso pp. of prevalere.
prevaricatore m. grafter, embezzler.
prevaricazione f. graft.
prevedere vt.[98] to foresee; to anticipate.
prevedi'bile adj. foreseeable.
prevenire vt. to forestall; to anticipate; to warn, forewarn; to prevent, avoid.
preventivare vt. to estimate; to appropriate.
preventivo m. estimate; tender; budget; adj. preventive.
prevenuto m. (law) defendant; adj. forewarned; prevented; biased, prejudiced.
prevenzione f. prevention; prejudice.
previdente adj. provident. [bias.
previdenza f. foresight: — sociale, social security; fondo di —, reserve fund.
pre'vio adj. previous: — accordo, subject to an agreement.
previsione f. prevision, anticipation; forecast; expectation.
previsto adj. expected: più del —, more than was expected. pp. of prevedere.
prevosto m. parson, vicar.
prezioso adj. precious; valuable: fare il —, to deny oneself.
prezze'molo m. parsley.
prezzo m. price; cost.
prezzolare vt. to hire.
prezzolato adj. hired, bribed.
prigione f. jail, prison.
prigioni'a f. imprisonment.
prigioniero m. prisoner, captive.
prillare vi. to whirl, spin.
prima (1) prep. before; rather (than). adv. before; earlier; beforehand; first; once, formerly: sulle prime, at first; quanto —, shortly, soon; non è più quello di —, he is no longer what he used to be.
prima (2) f. (rail.) first class; first grade (in a school); (theat.) opening, première; (auto.) first speed.
prima'rio m. chief physician; adj. primary; initial.
primatista m. champion, record holder.
primato m. supremacy; (sport) record, championship.

primavera f. spring, springtime.
primaverile adj. spring.
primeggiare vi. to excel.
primitivo m., adj. primitive.
primi'zia f. first fruit; novelty; (journ.) advance copy, beat, "scoop."
primo adj. first, initial, early; next: minuto —, minute; materia prima, raw material; per prima cosa, first of all; sulle prime, at first; a tutta prima, at first blush; pron. (the) first (one); (the) former.
primoge'nito m., adj. first-born; eldest.
primogenitura f. primogeniture.
primordiale adj. primeval.
primordi m. pl. beginning, origins.
pri'mula f. primrose.
principale m. employer, boss; adj. principal, main, chief: sede —, head office.
principalmente adv. chiefly.
principato m. principality.
prin'cipe m. prince.
principesco adj. princely.
principessa f. princess.
principiante m., f. beginner.
principiare see cominciare.
princi'pio m. beginning, start; principle: in —, sul —, da —, at first; per —, on principle.
priorato m. priorate.
priore m. prior.
priorità f. priority.
prisma m. prism.
privare vt. to deprive; privarsi vr. to deprive oneself; privarsi di, to give up.
privatamente adv. privately.
privatista m. private-school student.
privativa f. monopoly; patent (right); sole (right); tobacco shop.
privato m. private citizen; adj. private; pp. of privare, deprived, bereft.
privazione f. privation; loss; deprivation.
privilegiare vt. to privilege; to grant.
privilegiato m. favorite; adj. privileged.
privile'gio m. privilege; advantage.
privo adj. destitute; lacking (in); wanting (in).
pro (1) m. advantage, avail; good; benefit; profit: a che —? what is the use?; il — e il contro, the pros and cons.
pro (2) prep. in favor of, for.
proba'bile adj. probable, likely.
probabilità f. probability, likelihood; chance.
probabilmente adv. probably.
probato'rio adj. probative, probatory.
problema m. problem.

probo *adj.* upright, honest.

probo'scide *f.* proboscis; trunk (*of an elephant*).

procac'cia *m.* rural postman.

procace *adj.* forward, bold; buxom.

proce'dere *vi.* to proceed; to go, move on; to behave; to derive, originate: **non luogo a —**, no cause of action; **modo di —**, conduct, behavior.

procedimento *m.* proceeding; proceedings; process.

procedura *f.* procedure.

procella *f.* storm, tempest.

processare *vt.* to try.

processione *f.* procession, parade.

processo *m.* process; trial; lawsuit.

processuale *adj.* trial.

procinto *m.*: **essere in — di**, to be about to.

proclama *m.* proclamation; manifesto.

proclamare *vt.* to proclaim.

proclamazione *f.* proclamation.

proclive *adj.* prone, liable.

procrastinare *vt., vi.* to procrastinate.

procreare *vt., vi.* to procreate, generate.

procura *f.* proxy; power of attorney; prosecutor's office: **per —**, by proxy.

procurare *vt.* to procure, get; to try to; to manage, see to it that; to cause; to give; **procura che il lavoro sia fatto bene**, see to it that the work is done well; **procurarsi** *vr.* to obtain, acquire, get, secure; to catch.

procuratore *m.* attorney.

proda *f.* bank; edge.

prode *m.*, *adj.* gallant.

prodezza *f.* feat, exploit; gallantry, daring.

prodigalità *f.* prodigality.

prodigare *vt.* to dispense, lavish; to bestow (*upon*); to give; **prodigarsi** *vr.* to try; to go out of one's way.

prodi'gio *m.* prodigy, wonder.

prodigioso *adj.* prodigious, miraculous; wonderful.

pro'digo *m.* spendthrift; *adj.* prodigal, extravagant.

prodito'rio *adj.* traitorous.

prodotto *m.* product; produce; result. *adj.* produced. *pp. of* **produrre**.

pro'dromo *m.* portent, symptom.

produrre *vt.*[3] to produce; to yield, bear; to generate; to create; to engender, cause; to exhibit; **prodursi** *vr.* to happen; to form; to perform: **prodursi una ferita**, to wound oneself.

produttivo *adj.* productive; fruitful.

produttore *m.* producer; (*comm.*) canvasser.

produzione *f.* production, output; creation; (*comm.*) canvassing.

proe'mio *m.* proem, preface.

profanare *vt.* to profane, desecrate.

profanazione *f.* profanation.

profano *m.* layman; *adj.* lay, uninformed; profane, ignorant, not sacred.

proferire *vt.*[99] to utter.

proferto *pp. of* **proferire**.

professare *vt.* to profess; **professarsi** *vr.* to profess oneself.

professionale *adj.* professional; occupational.

professione *f.* profession; calling: **attore di —**, professional actor.

professionista *m.* professional.

professore *m.* professor.

profeta *m.* prophet.

profe'tico *adj.* prophetic.

profetizzare *vt., vi.* to prophesy.

profezi'a *f.* prophecy.

profferire *vt.*[100] to offer.

profferta *f.* offer.

profferto *pp. of* **profferire**.

profi'cuo *adj.* profitable.

profilare *vt.* to delineate; to hem; **profilarsi** *vr.* to loom.

profilassi *f.* prophylaxis.

profilato *m.* (*metal.*) section iron.

profilo *m.* profile; outlook; angle.

profittare *vi.* to benefit (*by*).

profitte'vole *adj.* profitable.

profitto *m.* profit; profits, returns; benefit; advantage.

proflu'vio *m.* flow, overflow; plenty.

profondamente *adv.* deeply: **dormire —**, to sleep soundly.

profon'dere *vt.* to squander; to lavish (*on*); **profon'dersi** *vr.* to be profuse (*in, of*).

profondità *f.* depth, deep.

profondo *adj.* deep, profound: **poco —**, shallow.

pro'fugo *m.* refugee, displaced person; *adj.* fugitive.

profumare *vt.* to perfume, scent; **profumarsi** *vr.* to put on perfume.

profumatamente *adv.* handsomely; dearly.

profumato *adj.* sweet-smelling; scented.

profumeri'a *f.* perfumery.   [ed.

profumo *m.* perfume, scent; fragrance: **avere — di**, to smell of.

profusione *f.* profusion: **a —**, profusely, in plenty.

proge'nie *f.* progeny, breed.

progenitore *m.* ancestor.

progettare *vt.* to plan.

progettista *m.* draftsman, planner, blueprinter.

progetto *m.* plan, project, schema; layout, blueprint: **— di legge**, bill (*proposed law*).

programma *m.* program; prospectus; plan; schedule: — **politico**, platform.

progredire *vi.* to advance, progress; to improve.

progredito *see* evoluto.

progressione *f.* progression.

progressista *m.*, *adj.* progressive.

progressivo *adj.* progressive.

progresso *m.* progress; improvement; development.

proibire *vt.* to forbid, prohibit.

proibitivo *adj.* prohibitive.

proibito *adj.* forbidden: — **fumare**, no smoking; — **l'ingresso**, no admittance.

proibizione *f.* prohibition.

proiettare *vt.*, *vi.* to project; to cast; to show; **proiettarsi** *vr.* to be projected; to fall.

proiet'tile *m.* missile; bullet, slug.

proiettore *m.* searchlight; projector.

proiezione *f.* projection; moving picture show.

prole *f.* offspring, issue.

proletariato *m.* proletariat.

proleta'rio *m.*, *adj.* proletarian.

proli'fico *adj.* prolific.

prolisso *adj.* prolix, long-winded.

pro'logo *m.* prologue.

prolungamento *m.* prolongation, extension; lengthening.

prolungare *vt.* to prolong, lengthen; to postpone; **prolungarsi** *vr.* to extend, continue; to speak at length.

promemoria *m.* memorandum.

promessa *f.* promise.

promesso *adj.* promised: **i promessi sposi**, the betrothed. *pp. of* promettere.

promettente *adj.* promising.

promet'tere *vt.*[76] to promise.

prominente *adj.* prominent.

promi'scuo *adj.* promiscuous: **scuola promiscua**, coeducational school.

promonto'rio *m.* promontory.

promotore *m.* promoter; *adj.* promotive, supporting.

promozione *f.* promotion.

promulgare *vt.* to promulgate.

promulgazione *f.* promulgation.

promuo'vere *vt.* to promote; to further; to organize.

pronipote *m.*, *f.* great-grandchild; grandnephew (*m.*), grandniece (*f.*).

prono *adj.* prone, prostrate.

pronome *m.* pronoun.

pronosticare *vt.* to prognosticate; to forebode; to predict.

prono'stico *m.* forecast; prediction; omen: **formulare un —**, to make a prediction.

prontamente *adv.* promptly, readily.

prontezza *f.* promptness, readiness; quickness.

pronti, (a) *adv.* (*comm.*) cash.

pronto *adj.* ready, prompt, quick; *interj.* pronto! (*teleph.*), hello!; a **pronta cassa**, cash.

prontua'rio *m.* handbook: — **dei conti fatti**, (ready) reckoner.

pronun'cia, pronun'zia *f.* pronunciation, accent, speech.

pronunziare *vt.* to pronounce; to utter; to deliver; **pronunziarsi** *vr.* to pronounce, pass judgment.

pronunziato *adj.* pronounced.

propaganda *f.* propaganda; advertising; canvassing.

propagandista *m.* propagandist; canvasser.

propagare *vt.*, **propagarsi** *vr.* to propagate, spread.

propag'gine *f.* ramification.

propalare *vt.* to spread, divulge.

propen'dere *vi.* to incline (*to*), be inclined (*to*); to tend (*to*).

propensione *f.* inclination, bent.

propenso *adj.* inclined, prone.

propinare *vt.* to administer (*to*); to palm off (*on*).

propin'quo *adj.* near, related.

propiziare *vt.*, **propiziarsi** *vr.* to propitiate,

propi'zio *adj.* propitious; favorable.

proponente *m.*, *adj.* proponent.

proponi'bile *adj.* proposable.

proponimento *m.* plan; resolution.

proporre *vt.*[93] to propose; to suggest; to propound; **proporsi** *vr.* to intend, mean; to resolve.

proporzionare *vt.* to proportion.

proporzione *f.* proportion; ratio; dimension, size.

propo'sito *m.* purpose, design; resolution; plan; object; subject: **in —**, on the subject; **a —**, by the way; opportunely; **a — di**, in regard to, about: **di —**, deliberately; **fuor di —**, out of place, out of turn; **rispondere a —**, to answer to the point.

proposizione *f.* clause; sentence.

proposta *f.* proposal; offer.

proposto *pp. of* proporre.

propriamente *adv.* exactly: — **detto**, proper.

proprietà *f.* property; possession; ownership; peculiarity; propriety: — **letteraria**, copyright; — **immobiliare**, real estate.

proprieta'rio *m.* owner; proprietor; man of property; landowner; landlord.

pro'prio *m.* one's own (*property, etc.*): **lavorare in —**, to be on one's own; *adj.* own, one's own; his; her; very;

of one's own; proper, appropriate, suitable; peculiar: vero e —, regular; *adv.* just, exactly; really: — bello, really fine; **proprio?** really?; — io (lui, noi), I myself (he himself, we ourselves).

propugnare *vt.* to advocate.

propugnatore *m.* advocate.

propulsione *f.* propulsion.

propulsore *m.* propeller; *adj.* propelling.

prora *f.* prow, bow.

pro'roga *f.* delay, respite; (*comm.*) extension.

prorogare *vt.* to put off, postpone; to extend.

prorom'pere *vi.* to burst (*out*); to break forth: — in lagrime, to burst into tears; — in una risata, to burst out laughing.

prosa *f.* prose; (*theat.*) drama; **compagnia (stagione) di —,** theatrical company (season).

prosa'ico *adj.* prosaic.

prosce'nio *m.* proscenium: **palco di —,** stage box.

proscio'gliere *vt.* to acquit (*of*); to clear (*from, of*).

prosciugare *vt.* to dry; to drain; **prosciugarsi** *vr.* to dry (up.)

prosciutto *m.* ham.

proscritto *m.* exile; *adj.* banished, exiled.

proscrivere *vt.* to proscribe, banish.

prosecuzione *f.,* **proseguimento** *m.* continuation.

proseguire *vt., vi.* to go on, continue.

prose'lito *m.* proselyte.

prosopopea *f.* self-importance.

prosperare *vi.* to prosper, thrive.

prosperità *f.* prosperity.

pro'spero *adj.* prosperous.

prosperoso *adj.* prosperous; healthy.

prospettare *vt.* to expound; to outline.

prospettiva *f.* perspective; prospect; view.

prospetto *m.* prospect; front view; table; diagram.

prossimamente *adv.* shortly, soon.

prossimità *f.* proximity, nearness.

pros'simo *m.* neighbor; fellow creatures. *adj.* next; near (*at hand*); coming: **passato (trapassato) —,** present (past) perfect.

prostituire *vt.* to prostitute; **prostituirsi** *vr.* to prostitute oneself.

prostituta *f.* prostitute.

prostituzione *f.* prostitution.

prostrare *vt.* to prostrate.

prostrazione *f.* prostration.

protagonista *m.* protagonist; hero (*m.*), heroine (*f.*): **la parte del (della) —,** the leading role.

proteg'gere *vt.*[101] to protect; to shelter; to preserve; to defend, guard.

proteina *f.* (*chem.*) protein.

proten'dere *vt.,* **proten'dersi** *vr.* to stretch out; to lean (*out*).

proteso *adj.* outstretched.

protesta *f.* complaint; protestation.

protestare *vt., vi.* to protest; to complain; to assert, aver.

protesto *m.* protest; notice of dishonor.

protettivo *adj.* protective.

protetto *m.* favorite, protégé; *adj.* protected. *pp. of* proteggere.

protettorato *m.* protectorate.

protettore *m.* protector; patron.

protezione *f.* protection.

protezionismo *m.* protectionism.

protezionista *m.* protectionist.

proto *m.* foreman; printer.

protocollo *m.* protocol.

protoplasma *m.* protoplasm.

proto'tipo *m.* prototype; personification.

protrarre *vt.*[146] to protract; to delay; to defer, postpone.

protratto *pp. of* protrarre.

protuberante *adj.* protuberant, bulging.

protuberanza *f.* protuberance, bulge.

prova *f.* proof; evidence; attempt; trial, test; fitting; essay; examination; ordeal; token; (*theat., mus.*) rehearsal: — **generale,** dress rehearsal; **periodo di —,** tryout; **in —,** on trial; **sapere per —,** to know by experience; **a — di bomba,** bombproof.

provare *vt.* to try; to test; to attempt; to experience; to taste; to feel; to prove; to show; to try on; (*theat., mus.*) to rehearse; **provarsi** *vr.* to try, attempt; to endeavor; to dare; to try on (*as a garment*).

provato *adj.* tried.

proveniente *adj.* coming (*from*).

provenienza *f.* provenience, origin, source.

provenire *vi.* to come (*from*); to derive (*from*).

provento *m.* proceeds, profit; income.

proverbiale *adj.* proverbial: **essere —,** to be a byword.

prover'bio *m.* proverb.

provetta *f.* test tube.

provetto *adj.* masterly.

provin'cia *f.* province.

provinciale *m., adj.* provincial.

provino *m.* (*chem.*) test tube; (*moving pictures*) screen test.

provocante *adj.* provoking; enticing.

provocare *vt.* to provoke; to excite; to cause, arouse; to entice.

provocatore *m.* provoker; *adj.* provoking: **agente —**, *agent provocateur.*

provocato'rio *adj.* provocative.

provocazione *f.* provocation; defiance.

provvedere *vt.*[151] to provide (*with*), supply (*with*); to store up; *vi.* to provide (*for*); to attend (*to*); **provvedersi** *vr.* to provide onself (*with*).

provvedimento *m.* provision; measure, step.

provvidenza *f.* providence; windfall.

provvidenziale *adj.* providential.

prov'vido *adj.* provident.

provvigione *f.* provision; (*comm.*) commission.

provviso'rio *adj.* temporary, provisional.

provvista *f.* provision; supply.

provvisto *pp. of* provvedere.

prozi'a *f.* great-aunt.

prozi'o *m.* great-uncle.

prua *f.* prow, bow.

prudente *adj.* prudent; cautious; wise; advisable.

prudenza *f.* prudence, caution.

pru'dere *vi.* to itch.

prugna *f.* plum.

prugno *m.* plum tree.

pruno *m.* thorn, bramble.

prurito *m.* itch, itching.

pseudo'nimo *m.* pseudonym; pen name.

psicana'lisi *f.* psychoanalysis.

psicanalista *m.* psychoanalyst.

psichiatra *m.* psychiatrist.

psichiatri'a *f.* psychiatry.

psicologi'a *f.* psychology.

psicolo'gico *adj.* psychologic.

psico'logo *m.* psychologist.

psicopa'tico *adj.* psychopathic.

psicosi *f.* psychosis, scare: **— di guerra,** war scare.

pubblicamente *adv.* publicly.

pubblicare *vt.* to publish, issue; to spread.

pubblicazione *f.* publication: **pubblicazioni matrimoniali,** marriage banns.

pubblicista *m.* free lance.

pubblicità *f.* publicity; advertising; advertisement.

pubblicita'rio *adj.* advertising: **annuncio —**, advertisement, ad.

pub'blico *m.* public; audience; *adj.* public: **forza pubblica,** police; **debito —**, national debt.

Puccini, Giacomo, Italian composer, *La Bohème, Tosca, Madame Butterfly* (1858–1924).

pudici'zia *f.* modesty; bashfulness.

pudico *adj.* modest; bashful.

pudore *m.* decency, modesty; restraint; shame.

puerile *adj.* childish.

puerilità *f.* childishness.

pugilato *m.* boxing.

pugilatore, pu'gile *m.* boxer, prizefighter.

pu'glia *f.* counter; stake.

pugnace *adj.* pugnacious.

pugnalare *vt.* to stab.

pugnalata *f.* stab.

pugnale *m.* dagger.

pugno *m.* fist; punch, blow; fistful: **di proprio —**, with one's own hand; **fare a pugni,** to fight; to clash; **avere in —**, to have in one's grasp.

pula *f.* chaff.

pulce *f.* flea.

Pulci, Luigi, Italian poet (1432–1484).

pulcino *m.* chick.

puledra *f.* filly.

puledro *m.* colt, foal.

puleg'gia *f.* (*mach.*) pulley.

pulire *vt.* to clean, cleanse; to wipe; to polish: **— a secco,** to dry-clean; **pulirsi** *vr.* to clean oneself.

pulito *adj.* clean; cleaned: **farla pulita,** to go scot-free; **— a secco,** dry-cleaned.

pulitura *f.* cleaning.

pulizi'a *f.* cleanliness; cleaning.

pullulare *vi.* to swarm; (*bot.*) to pullulate; to spring.

pul'pito *m.* pulpit.

pulsante *m.* (push) button.

pulsare *vi.* to pulsate, beat; to throb.

pulvi'scolo *m.* haze.

pulzella *f.* maid.

puma *m.* cougar.

pungente *adj.* pungent, stinging; sharp.

pun'gere *vt.*[79] to prick, sting.

pungiglione *m.* sting.

pungolare *vt.* to goad, prod, spur.

pun'golo *m.* goad; prod; spur.

punire *vt.* to punish.

punizione *f.* punishment; penalty.

punta *f.* point; top, summit, peak; end, tip; bit, tinge; top chuck (*of veal, etc.*): **cane da —**, pointer; **a —**, pointed; **in — di piedi,** on tiptoe; **sulla — delle dita,** at one's fingertips; **fare la —**, to sharpen.

puntale *m.* ferrule.

puntare *vt.* to point; to direct; to aim (*at*); to level (*at*), train (*on*); to wager, stake: **— i piedi,** to make a stand; *vi.* to make (*for*); to push (*toward*); to wager.

puntata *f.* thrust; part, installment; stake: **pubblicare a puntate,** to serialize.

punteggiare *vt., vi.* to dot; (*gramm.*) to punctuate.

punteggiatura *f.* dotting; (*gramm.*) punctuation.

punteggio *m.* score.

puntellare vt. to prop.
puntello m. prop.
punteruolo m. punch; awl.
puntiglio m. punctilio; pique; obstinacy.
puntiglioso adj. punctilious; stubborn.
puntina f. tackle: — da disegno, thumbtack; — per grammofono, phonograph needle.
puntino m. dot: a —, properly, nicely.
punto (1) m. point; period; dot; stitch; place, spot; stage; detail: — fermo, full stop; **due punti**, colon: — **e virgola**, semicolon; — **esclamativo (interrogativo)**, exclamation (question) mark; **di tutto —**, completely; **di — in bianco**, suddenly; **riportare buoni punti**, to get good marks; **dare dei punti a uno**, to outdo one; **far —**, to stop; **fare il —** (naut.), to shoot the sun; **fare il — di**, to sum up; **vincere ai punti**, to win by a decision.
punto (2) adj. at all: **non ho — voglia di**, I have no wish at all to; adv. by no means, not at all.
punto (3) pp. of pungere.
puntuale adj. punctual.
puntualità f. punctuality.
puntura f. puncture, prick; sting; stitch; injection.
puntuto adj. pointed.
punzecchiare vt. to prick; to goad; to tease.
punzecchiatura f. sting; bite; jest.
punzonare vt. to punch.
punzonatrice f. punch press.
punzone m. punch.
pupat'tola f. doll.
pupazzo m. puppet.
pupilla f. pupil (of the eye).
pupillo m., **pupilla** f. ward; pupil.
puramente adv. purely; merely.

purchè conj. provided (that).
purchessi'a adv. any, any ... whatever.
pure adv., conj. also, too; even; yet, still; only; likewise, as well (as); by all means: **pur di vederti**, just to see you; **fate pure!, dite pure!** go ahead!
purè m. purée.
purezza f. pureness, purity.
purga f., **purgante** m. purge.
purgare vt. to purge; to expurgate; **purgarsi** vr. to purge oneself.
purgato'rio m. purgatory.
purificare vt. to purify, cleanse.
purità m. purity, pureness.
puritano m., adj. Puritan.
puro adj. pure; clear, clean; mere, sheer; chaste, innocent.
purosangue m. thoroughbred.
purpu'reo adj. purple (red).
purtroppo adv. unfortunately.
purulento adj. purulent.
pus m. pus, purulent matter.
pusilla'nime m. coward; adj. cowardly.
pu'stola f. pustule, pimple.
putativo adj. putative.
putife'rio m. hullabaloo: **scoppierà un —**, there will be the devil to pay; **costare un —**, to be expensive or "sky high."
putrefare vi., **putrefarsi** vr. to putrefy, rot.
putrefazione f. putrefaction.
putrella f. I-girder, I-beam.
pu'trido adj. putrid, rotten.
puzza see puzzo.
puzzare vi. to stink; to smell (of).
puzzo m. stink, stench, smell.
puz'zola f. (zool.) skunk.
puzzolente adj. stinking.
puzzone m. (It. slang) "skunk."
puzzonata f. (It. slang) trash; underhand trick, bad joke.

Q

qua adv. here: **di — e di là**, on both sides; **per di —**, this way; **ecco qua!** here!; **da due giorni in —**, for the past two days; **da quando in —?** since when?
quaderno m. copybook; booklet.
quadra f. (naut.) square sail.
quadragena'rio m., adj. quadragenarian.
quadrage'simo adj. fortieth.
quadran'golo m. quadrangle.
quadrante m. quadrant; face (of a watch).
quadrare vt., vi. to square (with); to satisfy, please.
quadrato m. square; (naut.) ward-

room; (boxing) ring: **elevare al —** (math.), to square; adj. square; solid, strong-minded.
quadratura f. squaring; quadrature.
quadrello m. square tile.
quadreri'a f. picture gallery.
quadrettato adj. checkered.
quadretto m. small picture; checker.
quadricromi'a f. process printing; color type.
quadrifo'glio m. four-leaf clover.
quadrimestre m. four months.
quadrimotore m. four-engine plane.
quadri'vio m. quadrivium; crossroads.
quadro m. painting, picture; sight, view; square; table; (mil.) cadre,

list; (*mach.*) board; (*theat.*) scene;
(*moving pictures*) frame: — plastico,
tableau vivant; — murale, bulletin board; *adj.* square; quadri
m. pl. diamonds (*in playing
cards*).
quadruplicare *vt.*, **quadruplicarsi** *vr.*
to quadruple.
qua'druplo *m.*, *adj.* quadruple.
quaggiù *adv.* down here.
qua'glia *f.* quail.
quagliare *vt.* to curdle.
qualche *adj.* some, any; a few.
qualcheduno *see* qualcuno.
qualcosa *f.* something, anything.
qualcuno, qualcuna *pron.* someone,
somebody, some, anyone, anybody,
any.
quale *adj.* which, what; as, same;
just as; il quale, i quali (*pl.*) *rel.
pron.* who, whom; which; del
quale, dei quali, whose; of whom;
of which; al quale, ai quali, to
whom: il quadro al quale sto
lavorando, the picture I am working at.
quale?, quali? *interr.pron.* what?;
which?, which one?
quali'fica *f.* qualification; grade,
mark, score (*in a game*).
qualificare *vt.* to qualify.
qualità *f.* quality; gift, good point;
kind, sort: di prima —, first-rate.
qualora *adv.* in case, if; provided.
qualsiasi, qualunque *indef.adj.* any,
whatever; ordinary, indifferent:
qualsiasi cosa, whatever.
quando *conj.* when; while; if; whenever: da —, (ever) since; da
—? since when?; di — in —, from
time to time, now and then.
quantità *f.* quantity.
quantitativo *m.* quantity; *adj.* quan-
titative.
quanto *adj.*, *pron.*, *adv.* how; how
much; as, what; all (*that*) that,
pl. how many; as many: tanto —,
as much as; tanti quanti, as many
as; tutti quanti, all of them; (all)
those who, whom, which; —
tempo, how long; quanta distanza,
how far; quante volte? how often?;
— a, as to; — prima, very soon;
per — possibile, as far as possible;
— più posso, as much as I can;
— più ... tanto più, the more ...
the more; — meno ... tanto meno,
the less ... the less; per — egli
facesse, try as he might.
quantunque *conj.* though, although.
quaranta *m.*, *adj.* forty.
quarantena *f.* quarantine.
quarantenne *m.*, *adj.* quadragenarian; *adj.* forty years old.

quarantesimo *m.*, *adj.* fortieth.
quarantina *f.* some forty: esser sulla
—, to be about forty.
quarantotto *m.*, *adj.* forty-eight;
(*fig.*) mess.
quare'sima *f.* Lent.
quartetto *m.* quartet.
quartiere *m.* quarter; district; flat,
apartment; barracks: lotta senza
—, war to the knife.
quarto *m.* fourth; quarter: le tre
meno un —, a quarter to three;
le tre e un —, a quarter past three;
le tre e tre quarti, a quarter to
four; *adj.* fourth.
quarzo *m.* quartz.
quasi *adv.* almost, nearly; about; as
if; close to: — —, almost; — —
parto, I have half a mind to leave;
direi —, I dare say.
Quasimodo, Salvatore, Italian poet
(1901–   ).
quassù *adv.* up here.
quatto *adj.* cowering, crouching:
— —, quietly; stealthily.
quattordicenne *adj.* fourteen years
old.
quattordice'simo *m.*, *adj.* fourteenth.
quattor'dici *m.*, *adj.* fourteen.
quattrino *m.* farthing; quattrini *pl.*
money, "dough": non aver il
becco d'un —, to be penniless.
quattro *m.*, *adj.* four: fare — passi, to
take a stroll; fare — salti, to do
some dancing; dirne — a uno, to
give one a piece of one's mind;
farsi in —, to spare no effort; in
— e quattr'otto, in the twinkling
of an eye; a quattr'occhi, in private.
quattrocento *num.adj.* four hundred:
il —, the fifteenth century.
quattromila *adj.* four thousand.
quegli *pron.m.sing.* that man.
quegli, quei *pron.*, *adj.m.pl.* those,
see quel.
quel, quello *adj.m.*, **quella** *adj.f.*
that; *pron.m.*, *f.* that one; the
former; quelli *pron.*, *adj.m.pl.*,
quelle *pron.*, *adj.f.pl.* those; the
ones: — che, the one (ones) who;
the one (ones) whom, the one (ones)
that; what; è per quello che, that
is why; non è più quello, he is not
the same any more.
quer'cia *f.* oak: di —, oak, oaken.
querela *f.* complaint.
querelante *m.* plaintiff.
querelare *vt.* to sue.
que'rulo *adj.* querulous.
quesito *m.* problem, question; quiz.
questi *see* questo.
questionare *vi.* to quarrel.
questiona'rio *m.* questionnaire; form.

questione *f.* question, matter; problem; quarrel.

questo *adj.m.*, **questa** *adj.f.* this; *pron.m.*, *f.* this one; the latter; **questi** *pron.m.sing.* this, this fellow; he; *pron.m.pl.* these; these people; **questi** *adj.m.pl.*, **queste** *adj.f.pl.* these: **è per questo che,** that is why; **e con questo?** so what?; **quest'ultima (ultimo),** the latter.

questore *m.* superintendent of police.

que'stua *f.* alms collection.

questura *f.* police headquarters.

questurino *m.* plain-clothes man, "flatfoot," "cop."

queto *see* **quieto.**

qui *adv.* here: — **vicino,** close by, hereabout; **di** —, this way; hence; from here; **fin** —, so far; **di** — **a tre anni,** in three years.

quiescenza *f.* quiescence; superannuation.

quietanza *f.* receipt.

quietanzare *vt.* to give a receipt.

quietare *vt.* to quiet; **quietarsi** *vr.* to quiet down.

quiete *f.* quiet, stillness.

quieto *adj.* quiet, still, peaceful.

quindi *adv.* therefore; then; hence.

quindicenne *adj.* fifteen years old.

quindice'simo *m.,* *adj.* fifteenth.

quin'dici *m.,* *adj.* fifteen: — **giorni,** a fortnight.

quindicina *f.* some fifteen; fortnight; semimonthly pay.

quindicinale *m.,* *adj.* fortnightly.

quinquennale *adj.* quinquennial: **piano** —, five-year plan.

quinta *f.* (*theat.*) wing, tormentor; (*mus.*) quint; (*fencing*) quinte; (*educ.*) fifth grade: **dietro le quinte,** behind the scenes.

quintale *m.* quintal.

quinterno *m.* quinternion.

quintessenza *f.* quintessence.

quinto *m.,* *adj.* fifth.

Quirinale *m.* Quirinal.

quisqui'lia *f.* trifle.

quitanza *see* **quietanza.**

quivi *adv.* there; here.

quota *f.* share; quota; installment; elevation; (*aeron.*) height: **prender** —, to climb; **volare ad alta (bassa)** —, to fly high (low).

quotare *vt.* to quote; **quotarsi** *vr.* to subscribe.

quotato *adj.* (*exch.*) quoted; valued, esteemed.

quotazione *f.* quotation.

quotidiano *m.* daily (*paper*); *adj.* daily.

quoto, quoziente *m.* quotient.

R

rabar'baro *m.* rhubarb.

rabberciare *vt.* to patch (*up*).

rab'bia *f.* rabies; anger: **far** —, to make angry.

rabbino *m.* rabbi.

rabbioso *adj.* rabid, mad; angry.

rabbonire *vt.* to pacify; **rabbonirsi** *vr.* to quiet down.

rabbrividire *vi.* to shudder.

rabbuffo *m.* rebuke.

rabbuiarsi *vr.* to cloud, darken.

rabdomante *m.* diviner.

rabdomanzi'a *f.* divination.

raccapezzare *vt.* to gather; **raccapezzarsi** *vr.* to find one's bearings.

raccapricciante *adj.* horrific, blood-curdling, lurid.

raccapric'cio *m.* horror.

raccattare *vt.* to pick up.

racchetta *f.* racket (*as in tennis*): — **da neve,** snowshoe.

rac'chio *adj.* (*It. slang*) ugly, ratty; poor, atrocious, crummy: **piuttosto** —, no great shakes.

racchiona *f.* (*It. slang*) clock-stopper, "bust."

racchiu'dere *vt.* to contain.

racco'gliere *vt.*[27] to gather (*up*); to collect; to assemble; to pick up;

to reap: — **la sfida,** to take up the gauntlet; **racco'gliersi** *vr.* to gather, assemble; to concentrate.

raccoglimento *m.* concentration, meditation.

raccoglitore *m.* collector; folder.

raccolta *f.* gathering; collection; harvest; **chiamare a** —, to rally.

raccolto *m.* crop, harvest; *adj.* gathered, collected; engrossed. *pp.* of **racco'gliere.**

raccomanda'bile *adj.* recommendable: **poco** —, shady.

raccomandare *vt.* to recommend; **raccomandarsi** *vr.* to recommend oneself; to entreat.

raccomandata *f.* registered letter.

raccomandato *m.* protégé; *adj.* recommended; registered.

raccomandazione *f.* recommendation; entreaty; registration; connection, "in."

raccontare *vt.* to tell; to relate.

racconto *m.* story; tale; narration; report, recital.

raccorciare *see* **accorciare.**

raccordare *vt.* to connect, joint.

raccordo *m.* link, connection; (*rail.*) siding.

rachi'tico *adj.* rachitic, rickety.
racimolare *vt.* to glean, gather; to scrape together.
rada *f.* roadstead.
radar *m.* radar.
radazza *f.* (*naut.*) swab.
raddobbare *vt.* (*naut.*) to repair.
raddolcire *vt.*, raddolcirsi *vr.* to sweeten; to soften, mollify.
raddoppiare *vt.*, raddoppiarsi *vr.* to double, redouble.
raddrizzare *vt.* to straighten; raddrizzarsi *vr.* to straighten (*up*).
radente *adj.* grazing.
ra'dere *vt.*[102] to graze, shave: — al suolo, to level with the ground; radersi *vr.*, to shave.
radiare *vt.* to expel; to disbar.
radiatore *m.* radiator.
radiazione *f.* radiation; expulsion.
ra'dica *f.* brierwood, brier.
radicale *m., f., adj.* radical.
radicalmente *adv.* radically.
radicare *vt.*, radicarsi *vr.* to root.
radice *f.* root.
ra'dio *f.* radius; radium; radio, wireless: stazione —, broadcasting station; giornale —, news broadcast.
radioamatore *m.* radio amateur, "ham."
radioascoltatore, radioauditore *m.* radio listener.
radioattivo *adj.* radioactive.
radiocomandato *adj.* remote-controlled.
radiocomando *m.* remote control.
radiodiffondere *vt.* to broadcast.
radiodiffusione *f.* broadcasting.
radiofaro *m.* radio beacon.
radiofoni'a *f.* radiophony.
radiofo'nico *adj.* wireless: trasmissione radiofonica, broadcast, radio program.
radiografi'a *f.* radiography.
radiologi'a *f.* radiology.
radio'logo *m.* radiologist.
radioonda *f.* radio wave.
radioscopi'a *f.* radioscopy.
radioso *adj.* radiant.
radiotelecomando *m.* remote control.
radiotelefoni'a *f.* radiotelephony, radio.
radiotele'fono *m.* radiotelephone: — portatile, walkie-talkie.
radiotelegrafi'a *f.* radiotelegraphy, wireless.
radiotelegra'fico *adj.* wireless.
radiotelegrafista *m.* wireless operator.
radiotelegramma *m.* radiotelegram.
radioterapi'a *f.* radiotherapy.
radiotrasmissione *f.* broadcast.
radiotrasmittente *f.* broadcasting station; *adj.* broadcasting.

rado *adj.* rare; scattered; thin; sparse: di —, rarely, seldom; non di —, often, frequently.
radunare *vt.*, radunarsi *vr.* to assemble, gather, collect; to rally.
raduno *m.* meeting, gathering, rally.
radura *f.* glade.
Raffaello Sanzio, Italian painter, sculptor and architect; one of the greatest of artists, his works, numerous and varied, included frescoes, cartoons, madonnas, portraits, easel pictures, drawings, besides sculpture and architectural designs (1483–1520).
raffazzonare *vt.* to botch; to patch up.
rafferma *f.* (*mil.*) re-enlistment.
raffermo *adj.* stale.
raf'fica *f.* squall; gust; volley.
raffigurare *vt.* to recognize; to represent.
raffinare *vt.* to refine.
raffinatezza *f.* refinement.
raffineri'a *f.* refinery.
raf'fio *m.* hook.
rafforzare *vt.* to strengthen.
raffreddamento *m.* cooling.
raffreddare *vi.* to cool; raffreddarsi *vr.* to grow cold; to catch a cold.
raffreddore *m.* cold.
raffrontare *vt.* to compare.
raffronto *m.* comparison.
raganella *f.* tree-frog; rattle.
ragazza *f.* girl; maid.
ragazzata *f.* escapade.
ragazzo *m.* boy; lad.
raggiante *adj.* radiant; beaming.
raggiera *f.* halo of rays; corona.
rag'gio *m.* ray; beam; (*geom.*) radius; spoke (*of a wheel*): — d'azione, range; — di sole, sunbeam.
raggirare *vt.* to swindle, cheat.
raggiro *m.* trick.
raggiun'gere *vt.*[79] to overtake; to reach; to attain; to rejoin; to strike.
raggiunto *pp. of.* raggiungere.
raggomitolare *vt.* to coil, roll up; raggomitolarsi *vr.* to coil up; to roll oneself up, curl up.
raggranellare *vt.* to collect, scrape together.
raggrinzare, raggrinzire *vt., vi.*, raggrinzarsi, raggrinzirsi *vr.* to wrinkle.
raggrumare *vt.*, raggrumarsi *vr.* to clot.
raggruppamento *m.* grouping.
raggruppare *vt.* to collect, group; raggrupparsi *vr.* to rally.
ragguagliare *vt.* to compare; to inform.
raggua'glio *m.* comparison; information; report.
ragguarde'vole *adj.* considerable.
ragionamento *m.* reasoning.

ragionare vi. to reason; to discuss; to talk (over).

ragionato adj. logical.

ragione f. reason; right; ratio; motive: — sociale, style; — per cui, therefore; aver —, to be right; aver — di qualcuno, to get the better of somebody; dar — a qualcuno, to admit that somebody is right; to side with somebody; farsi una —, to resign oneself; rendersi — di, to satisfy oneself about; render di pubblica —, to make known.

ragioneri'a f. accountancy.

ragione'vole adj. reasonable; sensible.

ragioniere m. certified public accountant; bookkeeper.

ragliare vi. to bray.

ragliata f., **ra'glio** m. bray.

ragnatela f. spiderweb, web.

ragno m. spider.

rallegramento m. congratulation.

rallegrare vt. to cheer, gladden; **rallegrarsi** vr. to cheer up; to congratulate.

rallentare vt., vi. to slacken; to loosen; to lessen; to slow down.

rallentatore m. (moving pictures) slow motion.

ramanzina f. reprimand, lecture.

ramare vt. to coat with copper.

ramarro m. green lizard.

ramazza f. broom.

rame m. copper.

ramerino m. (bot.) rosemary.

ramificare vi., **ramificarsi** vr. to branch off; to branch out.

ramificazione f. branching.

ramingo adj. wandering, roving.

rammaricarsi vr. to regret, be sorry; to complain.

ramma'rico m. regret, sorrow.

rammendare vt. to darn.

rammendatrice f. darner.

rammendo m. darn, darning.

rammentare vt. to remind; to remember; **rammentarsi** vr. to remember; to recall.

rammodernare vt. to modernize; to refashion.

rammollimento m. softening.

rammollire vt., **rammollirsi** vr. to soften.

rammollito m. softy, weakling.

ramo m. branch; trade: un — di pazzia, a streak of madness.

ramoscello m. twig.

rampa f. ramp; flight (of stairs).

rampicante m. creeper; adj. creeping.

rampino m. hook; prong; quibble.

rampogna f. reprimand.

rampollo m. scion; child.

rampone m. harpoon, grapple.

rana f. frog.

ran'cido m. rankness; adj. rancid, rank.

ran'cio m. (mil.) mess.

rancore m. rancor, grudge.

randa f. (naut.) gaff.

randa'gio adj. wandering; stray.

randello m. cudgel.

ranella f. (mach.) washer.

rango m. rank, standing.

rannicchiarsi vr. to crouch.

ranno m. lye.

rannuvolarsi vr. to cloud, darken.

ranoc'chio m., **ranoc'chia** f. frog.

rantolare vi. to sound the death rattle; to groan.

ran'tolo m. death rattle; groan.

rapa f. (bot.) turnip.

rapace m. bird of prey; adj. rapacious, greedy.

rapacità f. rapacity, greed.

rapare vt. to shave (one's) hair.

rapato adj. shaven-headed.

rapè m. rappee.

ra'pida f. rapid.

rapidamente adv. swiftly.

rapidità f. swiftness.

ra'pido m. express (train); adj. rapid, swift.

rapimento m. rapture; abduction, kidnapping.

rapina f. robbery, plunder: uccello di —, bird of prey; — a mano armata, armed robbery, holdup.

rapinare vt., vi. to plunder, rob.

rapinatore m. robber; holdup man.

rapire vt. to take away; to abduct, kidnap; to enrapture.

rapitore m. kidnapper.

rappacificare vt. to reconcile; **rappacificarsi** vr. to make up, become reconciled.

rappezzare vt. to patch (up).

rappezzo m. patch.

rapporto m. report; statement; relation, connection; intercourse; proportion; (math., mach.) ratio: chiamare a —, to summon; andare a —, to report (to); mettersi a —, to ask for a hearing; in rapporti d'amicizia, on friendly terms.

rappren'dere, **rappren'dersi** vr.[96] to coagulate; to curdle.

rappresa'glia f. retaliation.

rappresentante m. representative; agent; delegate.

rappresentanza f. agency; delegation.

rappresentare vt. to represent; to play, act, perform; to exhibit.

rappresentativo adj. representative.

rappresentazione f. representation; performance; exhibition; description.

rappreso pp. of **rapprendere**.

rapsodi'a f. rhapsody.

raramente adv. seldom.

rarefare vt., rarefarsi vr. to rarefy.

rarefatto adj. rarefied.

rarità f. rarity; curio.

raro adj. rare; unusual: rare volte, seldom, rarely.

rasare vt. to smooth; to shave; to mow; rasarsi vr. to shave (oneself).

raschiare vt. to scrape; to erase; to scratch.

raschietto m. eraser.

ra'schio m. irritation; scratching.

rasentare vt. to graze; to brush, scrape; to border upon: — il codice, to sail close to the wind.

rasente prep. close to.

raso (1) m. satin.

raso (2) adj. shaven; short; even, level; brimful: fare tabula rasa, to make a clean sweep (of). pp. of radere.

raso'io m. razor; safety razor.

raspa f. rasp; scraper; (It. slang) a popular dance.

raspare vt. to rasp; to pinch; to scratch about.

rassegna f. review.

rassegnare vt. to resign: — le dimissioni, to resign; rassegnarsi vr. to resign oneself; to submit; to surrender.

rassegnazione f. resignation, patience.

rasserenare vt., rasserenarsi vr. to clear up, brighten (up).

rassettare vt. to tidy up.

rassicurare vt. to reassure.

rassodare vt., rassodarsi vr. to harden.

rassomigliare see assomigliare.

rastrellamento m. roundup.

rastrellare vt. to rake; to round up; to dredge.

rastrelliera f. rack, crib.

rastrello m. rake.

rastremare vt. to taper.

rata f. installment.

rateale adj., ratealmente adv. by installments.

rati'fica f. ratification.

ratificare vt. to ratify.

ratto (1) m. abduction, kidnapping.

ratto (2) m. rat.

ratto (3) adj. quick; adv. quickly.

rattoppare see rappezzare.

rattrappire vt., vi., rattrapplrsi vr. to contract, shrink.

rattristante adj. saddening.

rattristare vt., rattristarsi vr. to sadden.

rauce'dine f. hoarseness.

rauco m. hoarse.

ravanello m. radish.

ravizzone m. rape.

ravvedersi vr.[151] to repent; to reform.

ravveduto adj. penitent, reformed. pp. of ravvedersi.

ravviare vt., ravviarsi vr. to tidy up: — i capelli, to comb (one's) hair.

ravvicinamento m. reapproachment; reconciliation.

ravvicinare vt. to reapproach; to reconcile; ravvicinarsi vr. to become reconciled.

ravvisare vt. to recognize.

ravvivare vt. to revivify, reanimate; to enliven; to stir (up); ravvivarsi vr. to revive, brighten up.

ravvol'gere see avvolgere.

ra'yon m. rayon.

raziocl'nio m. ratiocination; reason; sense.

razionale adj. rational.

razionamento m. rationing.

razionare vt. to ration.

razlone f. ration; portion.

razza f. race; breed; kind: di — pura, thoroughbred; che — di, what a.

razzi'a f. raid; insect powder.

razziale adj. racial.

razziare vt., vi. to raid.

razziatore m. raider.

razzismo m. racism, racialism.

razzista m. racist, racialist.

razzo m. rocket; spoke: — interplanetario, space ship.

razzolare vi. to scratch about.

re m. king.

reagire vi. to react.

reale adj. real; royal.

realismo m. realism.

realista m. realist; royalist.

reali'stico adj. realistic.

realizzare vt. vi. to realize, accomplish, carry through; to convert into money, sell, cash, gain, to produce, make; realizzarsi vr. to come true.

realizzazione f. realization; accomplishment; production.

realizzo m. conversion into money, sale.

realmente adv. really, indeed.

realtà f. reality.

reame m. realm, kingdom.

reato m. crime.

reattore m. reactor; (aeron.) jet plane.

reazionario m., adj. reactionary.

reazione f. reaction; jet propulsion: a —, jet-propelled.

reb'bio m. prong.

recalcitrante adj. recalcitrant.

recapitare vt. to deliver, hand.

reca'pito m. office; delivery; address.

recare vt. to bring, carry; to bear; to convey, take; recarsi vr. to go, betake oneself.

rece'dere vi.[25] to recede.

recensione f. review.

recensire vt. to review.

recensore *m.* reviewer.
recente *adj.* recent, new.
recentemente *adv.* recently.
recesso *m.* recess.
recettività *f.* receptivity.
recettivo *adj.* receptive.
reci'dere *vt.*⁴¹ to cut off; to excise.
recidiva *f.* relapse.
recidivo *m.* relapser, repeater; *adj.* relapsing, tending to fall back into old habits.
recin'gere *vt.*²⁶ to enclose, fence in.
recinto *m.* enclosure; play pen; corral; *adj.* enclosed, fenced in. *pp. of* recingere.
recipiente *m.* container.
reciprocità *f.* reciprocity.
reci'proco *adj.* reciprocal, mutual.
reciso *adj.* cut off; determined, resolute. *pp. of* recidere.
re'cita *f.* recital, performance.
recitare *vt.* to recite; to play, act; to perform.
recitazione *f.* recitation; acting.
reclamante *m.* complainant.
reclamare *vt.* to claim, demand, ask for; *vi.* to complain, protest.
re'clame *f.* advertising; ballyhoo.
reclami'stico *adj.* advertising.
reclamo *m.* complaint.
reclinare *vt.*, reclinarsi *vr.* to recline; to bend.
reclusione *f.* reclusion; imprisonment.
recluso *m.* recluse; prisoner, convict; *adj.* recluse.
recluso'rio *m.* prison, penitentiary.
re'cluta *f.* recruit.
reclutamento *m.* recruiting; levy, draft.
reclutare *vt.* to recruit, enlist.
recon'dito *adj.* hidden.
recriminare *vt.* to recriminate.
recriminazione *f.* recrimination.
recrudescenza *f.* recrudescence.
recuperare *vt.* to recover.
redarguire *vt.* to scold, reproach.
redatto *adj.* drawn up, written. *pp. of* redigere.
redattore *m.* editor.
redazione *f.* compilation; editorial department; editorial staff; newspaper offices.
redditi'zio *adj.* profitable, paying.
red'dito *m.* income, revenues.
redento *pp. of* redimere.
redentore *m.* redeemer: il Redentore, the Saviour.
redenzione *f.* redemption.
redi'gere *vt.*¹⁰³ to draw up, compile, compose.
redi'mere *vt.*¹⁰⁴ to redeem; to ransom; to free; redi'mersi *vr.* to redeem oneself; to reform.
redimi'bile *adj.* redeemable.

re'dine *f.* rein.
redivivo *adj.* returned to life, raised from the dead; *m.* revenant.
re'duce *m., adj.* veteran: — da un viaggio, back from a journey.
refe *m.* thread.
referen'dum *m.* poll.
referenza *f.* reference, information; (*pl.*) testimonials, characters.
referto *m.* (medical) report.
refetto'rio *m.* refectory.
refezione *f.* refection.
refratta'rio *adj.* refractory; impervious; unruly; fireproof.
refrigerante *m.* refrigerator, freezer; *adj.* refrigerating.
refrigerazione *f.* refrigeration.
refrige'rio *m.* relief, comfort.
refurtiva *f.* stolen goods, booty.
refuso *m.* (*typog.*) misprint.
refutare *vt.* to refute.
rega'glie *see* rigaglie.
regalare *vt.* to present (one, with); to make a present of.
regale *adj.* regal; kingly; queenly.
regali'a *f.* gratuity.
regalità *f.* royalty.
regalmente *adv.* regally.
regalo *m.* present, gift.
regata *f.* regatta, boat race.
reggente *m.* regent.
reggenza *f.* regency.
reg'gere *vt.*¹⁰⁵ to support, bear, carry; to hold up; to manage; to govern, rule; (*gramm.*) to require; *vi.* to stand, resist; to last; to endure: — al confronto, to bear comparison (with); — alla prova, to stand the test; reg'gersi *vr.* to hold; to stand, hold up.
reg'gia *f.* royal palace.
reggicalze *m.* girdle.
reggimento *m.* regiment.
reggipetto *m.* brassière.
regi'a *f.* régie; (moving pictures) direction; (theat.) production.
regina *f.* queen.
re'gio *adj.* royal.
regione *m* region, district.
regista *m.* (theat.) producer; (moving pictures) director.
registrare *vt.* to record, register; to enter.
registratore *m.* recorder: — di cassa, cash register.
registrazione *f.* registration; (comm.) entry.
registro *m.* register; ledger; organ stop; watch regulator.
regnante *adj.* reigning, dominant.
regnare *vi.* to reign; to rule; to prevail.
regno *m.* kingdom; reign.

re'gola f. rule; example; moderation; guidance; order; diet: **di —,** as a rule; **in —,** in order.

regolamentare adj. prescribed, regulation.

regolamento m. settlement; regulations, rules.

regolare (1) adj. regular.

regolare (2) vt. to regulate; to adjust; to settle; to rule; **regolarsi** vr. to conduct oneself, behave; to proceed.

regolarità f. regularity.

regolarizzare vt. to regularize.

regolarmente adv. regularly.

regolatezza f. regulation, moderation.

regolato adj. regular, moderate.

regolatore m. regulator; adj. regulating.

regoli'zia f. licorice.

re'golo m. ruler.

regredire vi. to relapse, regress.

regresso m. relapse, regression.

reietto m., adj. outcast; castaway.

reintegrare vt. to reinstate, restore; to compensate.

reità f. guilt, guiltiness.

reiterare vt. to reiterate, repeat.

relativamente adv. relatively, comparatively: **— a,** with regard to.

relativo adj. relative; comparative: **— a,** concerning, pertaining.

relatore m. reporter; speaker.

relazione f. relation, connection; report, account.

relegare vt. to relegate.

religione f. religion.

religioso m. clergyman; adj. religious.

reli'quia f. relic; vestige.

reliquia'rio m. reliquary.

relitto m. wreck.

remare vi. to row.

rematore m. rower, oarsman.

reminiscenza f. reminiscence.

remissione f. remission; forgiveness: **senza —,** unremittingly.

remissivo adj. submissive.

remo m. oar: **— sensile,** sweep.

re'mora f. delay; hindrance.

remoto adj. remote, distant.

rena f. sand.

ren'dere vt.[106] to render; to make, do; to give back; to reciprocate; to bring, yield; to convey; vi. to pay, bring profit: **— merito,** to reward, give credit; **— grazie,** to thank; **— lode,** to praise; **— conto di,** to answer for; **— pan per focaccia,** to give tit for tat; **ren'dersi** vr. to make oneself; to become: **rendersi conto di,** to realize.

rendiconto m. report.

rendimento m. efficiency; yield; profit.

ren'dita f. income.

rene m. kidney.

reni f.pl. loins.

Reni, Guido, Italian painter (1575–1642).

renitente adj. reluctant, renitent: **— alla leva,** draft delinquent.

renitenza f. reluctance.

renna f. reindeer.

reo m. culprit; adj. guilty.

reparto m. department; (mil.) unit.

repellente adj. repellent, repulsive.

repel'lere vt. to repel.

repenta'glio m. jeopardy: **a —, in** jeopardy.

repente adj. sudden: **di —,** suddenly.

repentino adj. sudden.

reperi'bile adj. to be found.

reperire vt. to find (out).

reperto m. (law) exhibit.

reperto'rio m. repertory; (theat.) repertoire, stock.

re'plica f. reply; repetition; replica; (theat.) performance.

replicare vt. to reply, answer back; to repeat.

repressione f. repression.

represso adj. repressed; suppressed; stifled. pp.of reprimere.

reprimenda f. reprimand.

repri'mere vt.[29] to repress, suppress; to stifle.

re'probo m., adj. reprobate.

repub'blica f. republic.

repubblicano m., adj. republican.

repulisti m. clean sweep.

repulsione f. repulsion.

repulsivo adj. repulsive.

reputare vt., vi. to deem, consider; to think.

reputazione f. reputation.

re'quie f. rest; peace.

requisire vt. to requisition.

requisito m. requisite, qualification; adj. requisitioned.

requisito'ria f. denunciation; (law) summing-up.

requisizione f. requisition.

resa f. surrender; yield; return.

rescin'dere vt.[121] to rescind.

rescisso pp. of rescindere.

resezione f. resection.

residente m., adj. resident.

residenza f. residence; residency.

residuati m.pl. surplus.

resi'duo m. residue.

re'sina f. resin.

resipiscenza f. resipiscence.

resistente adj. resisting, strong, fast.

resistenza f. resistance; endurance; opposition; (pol.) underground.

resi'stere vi.[16] to resist: **— a,** to endure, stand; to oppose.

reso pp. of rendere.

resoconto m. report, relation.

Respighi, Ottorino, Italian composer (1879-1936).

respingente m. buffer.

respin'gere vt. to repel; to reject; to pluck: — al mittente, return to sender.

respirare vt., vi. to breathe.

respirazione f. breathing.

respiro m. breath; delay; respite.

responsa'bile adj. responsible: **direttore** —, managing editor.

responsabilità f. responsibility.

responso m. response; diagnosis.

ressa f. press, crowd.

resta f. awn, beard; fishbone; string.

restante m. residue; adj. remaining.

restare see rimanere.

restaurare vt. to restore, repair.

restaurazione f. restoration.

restauro m. restoration, repair.

resti'o adj. reluctant.

restituire vt. to return, give back; to restore.

restituzione f. restitution, return; restoration.

resto m. remainder, residue, rest; change; remains: del —, besides, after all.

restrin'gere vt.,[107] restrin'gersi vr. to narrow; to lessen; to shrink; to condense.

restrittivo adj. restrictive.

restrizione f. restriction.

resurrezione f. resurrection.

retag'gio m. heritage.

retata f. netful; roundup.

rete f. net; snare; reticule; (sport) goal: — metallica, wire mesh; — ferroviaria, railroad system.

reticella f. small net; reticule; hair net; (rail.) rack.

reticente adj. reticent.

reticenza f. reticence.

reticolato m. network; (mil.) barbed-wire fence.

re'tina f. (anat.) retina.

retino m. (typog.) screen.

reto'rica f. rhetoric.

reto'rico adj. rhetorical.

retribuzione f. pay, reward.

retro adv. behind: vedi —, turn over, please; m. verso, back.

retroattivo adj. retroactive.

retrobottega f. back room (of a shop).

retroca'rica f. breech-loading.

retroce'dere vt.[23] to demote; vi. to draw back; to retreat.

retrocesso pp. of retrocedere.

retrodatare vt. to antedate.

retro'grado m. old fogy, "back number"; adj. fogyish; backward.

retroguar'dia f. rearguard.

retromar'cia f. reverse (gear); backing.

retrospettiva f. retrospective show; revival.

retrospettivo adj. retrospective.

retrovi'e f.pl. (mil.) districts behind the lines.

retta (1) f. (geom.) straight line.

retta (2) f. tariff; terms.

retta (3) f. heed: dare —, to heed; to listen.

rettamente adv. straightforwardly.

rettangolare adj. rectangular.

rettan'golo m. rectangle.

retti'fica f. alteration, amendment; (mach.) honing; honing machine, grinder.

rettifica'bile adj. rectifiable.

rettificare vt. to rectify, alter, amend.

rettifilo m. straight.

ret'tile m. reptile.

rettili'neo m., adj. straight.

rettitu'dine f. uprightness.

retto (1) adj. right; upright.

retto (2) m. (anat.) rectum.

retto (3) pp.of reggere.

rettore m. rector; principal.

re'uma, reumatismo m. rheumatism.

reverendo adj. reverend; m. padre.

reverente adj. reverent, respectful.

reverenza see riverenza.

revisione f. revision; (mach.) overhaul.

revisionare vt. (mach.) to overhaul.

revisore m. reviser; proofreader.

re'voca f. revocation, repeal.

revocare vt. to revoke.

revolver m. revolver, gun.

revolverata f. gunshot.

riabilitare vt. to rehabilitate.

riabilitazione f. rehabilitation.

riaccen'dere vt., riaccen'dersi vr. to relight, rekindle.

riaccompagnare vt. to escort back. see accompagnare.

riaccostarsi vr. to draw near again; to make up.

riacquistare vt. to recover.

riaddormentarsi vr. to go back to sleep.

riaffermare vt. to reaffirm.

rialzare vt. to heighten; to lift up, raise; rialzarsi vr. to get up again; to pick oneself up.

rialzista m. (exch.) bull.

rialzo m. rise, rising: giocare al —, to bull the market.

riammogliarsi vr. to remarry.

riandare vt.[7] to recall, reminisce; vi. to go back.

rianimare vt. to reanimate.

riapertura f. reopening.

riapparire vi.[6] to reappear.

riaprire vt.[11] riaprirsi vr. to reopen.

riarmare vt., vi. to rearm.

riarmo m. rearmament.

riarso adj. dry; thirsty.

riascoltare *vt.* to relisten.
riassettare *vt.* to rearrange.
riassetto *m.* rearrangement.
riassicurare *vt.* to reinsure.
riassicurazione *f.* reinsurance.
riassorbire *vt.*[18] to reabsorb.
riassumere *vt.*[19] to summarize; to re-engage.
riassunto *m.* synopsis; summing up.
riassunzione *f.* re-engagement.
riattaccare *vt.* to refasten; to start afresh; (*mil.*) to attack again; riattaccarsi *vr.* to readhere; to go back (*to*).
riattare *vt.* to repair.
riattivare *vt.* to reactivate.
riattraversare *vt.* to recross.
riavere *vt.* to get back, recover; riaversi *vr.* to come to oneself.
riavvicinamento *see* ravvicinamento.
riavvicinare *vt.* to reapproach; to compare; to reconcile; riavvicinarsi *vr.* to reapproach; to become reconciled.
ribadire *vt.* to clinch; (*mach.*) to rivet.
ribalderi'a *f.* knavery. [rivet.
ribaldo *m.* knave, rascal.
ribalta *f.* lid; (*theat.*) apron stage: luci della —, footlights.
ribaltamento *m.* capsizing.
ribaltare *vt.*, ribaltarsi *vr.* to capsize.
ribaltone *m.* lurch.
ribassare *vt.* to lower, reduce; *vi.* to go down.
ribassista *m.* (*exch.*) bear.
ribasso *m.* fall, decline; discount, reduction: giocare al —, to bear the market; in —, in decline.
ribat'tere *vt.* to rivet; to smooth; to refute; to drive back; *vi.* to retort; to answer back.
ribattezzare *vt.* to rebaptize.
ribattino *m.* rivet.
ribellarsi *vr.* to rebel.
ribelle *m.*, *adj.* rebel.
ribellione *f.* rebellion.
ribes *m.* gooseberry.
riboccare *vt.* to overflow.
ribollire *vt.* to reboil; *vi.* to reboil; (*fig.*) to seethe (*with*).
ribrezzo *m.* disgust, horror.
ributtante *adj.* revolting, repulsive.
ributtare *vt.*, *vi.* to repel; to throw back again; to revolt.
ricacciare *vt.* to drive back.
ricadere *vi.*[22] to fall down; to fall again; to relapse.
ricaduta *f.* relapse.
ricalcare *vt.* to tread upon; to transfer (*as drawings*).
ricamare *vt.* to embroider.
ricamatrice *f.* embroiderer.
ricambiare *vt.* to return, reciprocate; to repay.

ricam'bio *m.* return, exchange: pezzo (ruota) di —, spare part (wheel); malattie del —, metabolic diseases.
ricamo *m.* embroidery.
ricapitolare *vt.* to sum up, recapitulate.
ricaricare *vt.* to reload (*as a gun*); to wind up again (*as a watch*).
ricattare *vt.* to blackmail.
ricattatore *m.* blackmailer.
ricatto *m.* blackmail.
ricavare *vt.* to draw, extract; to obtain.
ricavato, ricavo *m.* proceeds.
riccamente *adv.* richly.
ricchezza *f.* wealth, riches; richness; fortune.
riccio (*1*) *m.* (*zool.*) hedgehog: — di mare, sea urchin.
riccio (*2*) *m.* curl; *adj.* curly.
ric'ciolo *m.* curl.
ricciuto *adj.* curly.
ricco *adj.* rich; wealthy: nuovo —, nouveau riche.
ricerca *f.* research, investigation, inquiry; (*comm.*) demand: alla — di, in search of.
ricercare *vt.* to search for; to seek; to investigate; to hunt.
ricercatezza *f.* affectation; sophistication.
ricercato *adj.* affected; sophisticated; (*comm.*) in demand; popular.
ricercatore *m.* searcher; researcher.
ricetta *f.* recipe; prescription.
ricetta'colo *m.* receptacle.
ricettare *vt.* to receive (stolen goods), "fence."
ricetta'rio *m.* book of prescriptions; cook book.
ricettatore *m.* fence, receiver.
ricettazione *f.* fencing, receiving.
ricettivo *adj.* receptive.
ricetto *m.* refuge: dar —, to shelter.
rice'vere *vt.* to receive; to get; to greet: — cordialmente, to welcome.
ricevimento *m.* reception, party.
ricevitore *m.* receiver: — del registro, registrar; — postale, postmaster.
ricevitori'a *f.* post office.
ricevuta *f.* receipt.
ricezione *f.* (*radio*) reception.
richiamare *vt.* to recall; to call again; to draw; to reprove: — l'attenzione, to draw attention; — alla memoria, to remind; — in vita, to restore to life; — all'ordine, to take to task; — alle armi, to call to the colors, draft.
richiamato *m.* redrafted soldier.
richiamo *m.* call; admonition; cross-reference mark; (*mil.*) redraft.
richiedente *m.* applicant.
richie'dere *vt.*[24] to apply for; to require; to ask; to ask again.

richiesta f. request; application; (comm.) demand.

richiesto pp. of richiedere: essere molto —, to be in great demand.

richiu'dere vt.[25] to shut again.

ri'cino, (olio di) m. castor oil.

ricognitore m. (aeron.) scout plane.

ricognizione f. recognition; (mil.) reconnaissance; identification.

ricollegare vt. to connect; **ricollegarsi** vr. to be connected.

ricolmo adj. full; brimful.

ricominciare vt., vi. to recommence, start afresh.

ricomparire vi.[9] to reappear.

ricomparsa f. reappearance.

ricompensa f. reward.

ricompensare vt. to reward.

ricomperare see ricomprare.

ricomporre vt.[93] to recompose; to reassemble; **ricomporsi** vr. to recover oneself.

ricomposto pp. of ricomporre.

ricomprare vt. to buy again; to buy back.

riconciliare vt. to reconcile; **riconciliarsi** vr. to be (or become) reconciled.

riconciliazione f. reconciliation.

ricondurre vt.[3] to bring back; to take back.

riconferma f. reconfirmation.

riconfermare vt. to reconfirm.

riconfortare vt. to comfort; give solace.

ricongiun'gere vt.[79] **ricongiun'gersi** vr. to reunite.

riconoscente adj. grateful.

riconoscenza f. gratitude.

ricono'scere vt.[30] to recognize; to acknowledge; to identify; to admit: farsi —, to make oneself known; **ricono'scersi** vr. to recognize oneself; to declare oneself; to recognize each other; — colpevole, to plead guilty.

riconosci'bile adj. recognizable.

riconoscimento m. recognition; acknowledgment; identification;

riconquista f. reconquest. [avowal.

riconquistare vt. to reconquer.

riconsegnare vt. to redeliver, give back, return.

ricoperto adj. covered (with); coated (with).

ricopertura f. covering; coating.

ricopiare vt. to copy (again); to copy fair.

ricopiatura f. copying; copy.

ricoprire vt.[35] to cover; to coat.

ricordare vt., vi.; **ricordarsi** vr. to remember; to recollect; to remind; to mention.

ricordo m. memory; recollection.

ricorreg'gere vt.[105] to recorrect.

ricorrente adj. recurrent.

ricorrenza f. recurrence; anniversary; festivity.

ricor'rere vi.[36] to resort; to have recourse; to turn; to appeal; to recur.

ricorso (1) m. recourse; appeal.

ricorso (2) pp. of ricorrere.

ricostituente m., adj. tonic.

ricostituire vt. to reconstitute; to reestablish; **ricostituirsi** vr. to be reconstituted; to recover.

ricostruire vt.[37] to rebuild; to reconstruct.

ricostruzione f. rebuilding; reconstruction; rehabilitation.

ricotta f. fresh curd cheese resembling cottage cheese.

ricoverare vt. to shelter; **ricoverarsi** vr. to take shelter.

rico'vero m. shelter, refuge: — di mendicità, poorhouse.

ricreare vt. to recreate; to relieve; to entertain; **ricrearsi** vr. to recreate oneself; to amuse oneself.

ricreazione f. recreation.

ricre'dersi vr. to change one's mind, think better of it.

ricre'scere vi.[38] to grow again.

ricucire vt. to sew again; to sew up.

ricuperare vt. to recover.

ricu'pero m. recovery.

ricurvo adj. bent; crooked.

ricusare vt. to refuse; to reject.

ridacchiare vi. to giggle.

ridare vt.[40] to give back.

ridda f. roundelay; (fig.) confusion.

ridente adj. laughing; bright, pleasant.

ri'dere vi.[108] to laugh (at); — sotto i baffi, to laugh up one's sleeve; farsi — dietro, to make a fool of oneself; per —, for fun; **ridersela** di, to scorn; not to care (about).

ridestare vt., **ridestarsi** vr. to wake, wake up.

ridetto pp. of ridire.

ridicolag'gine f. nonsense; trifle; ridiculousness.

ridi'colo m. ridicule; adj. ridiculous, paltry: mettere in —, to ridicule.

ridipin'gere vt.[26] to repaint.

ridire vt.[44] to repeat: trovare da — su, to find fault with; non ho nulla da —, I have no objection

ridiscen'dere vt., vi.[119] to redescend.

ridivenire, ridiventare vi.[152] to become again.

ridonare vt. to give back again.

ridondante adj. redundant.

ridorare vt. to regild.

ridosso: a — di, against.

ridotta f. (mil.) redoubt.

ridotto m. (theat.) foyer; adj. reduced; pp. of ridurre: mal —, in a bad way.

riduci'bile adj. reducible.

ridurre vt.³ to reduce; to drive, bring; to adapt; **ridursi** vr. to reduce oneself; to shrink.

riduttore m. reducer.

riduzione f. reduction; adaptation; arrangement; rebate, discount.

riec'co adv. here he, she, it, is (they are) again: **riec'comi!** here I am again!

riecheggiare vt., vi. to reverberate; to remind.

riedificare vt. to rebuild.

rieducare vt. to re-educate.

riemer'gere vi.⁵¹ to re-emerge.

riempire vt.⁵¹ to fill (in); to stuff; to cram; **riempirsi** vr. to fill up; to cram oneself: **riempirsi di,** to get filled, covered, spattered with.

riempimento m. filling.

riempitivo m., adj. expletive; filling.

rientrante adj. receding.

rientranza f. recess.

rientrare vi. to re-enter; to return; to sink; to shrink; to recede; to be included: — **in sè,** to come to one's senses.

riepilogare vt., vi. to recapitulate.

riepi'logo m. recapitulation.

riesaminare vt. to re-examine.

rievocare vt. to reminisce; to commemorate.

rievocazione f. reminiscence; commemoration.

rifacimento m. remaking; manipulation; adaptation; treatment.

rifare vt.⁶¹ to remake, do again; to retrace; to imitate; to indemnify, make good for; **rifarsi** vr. to start, move (from); to recoup.

rifatto pp. of **rifare**: **villano** —, upstart.

riferimento m. reference.

riferire vt. to relate, report; to refer; **riferirsi** vr. to refer; to concern.

rifermentare vi. to ferment again.

riffa f. lottery: **di** — **o di raffa,** by hook or by crook.

rifilare vt. to palm off (on, upon); to report; to deal.

rifinire vt. to finish, trim.

rifinitura f. finish.

rifiorire vi. to reflourish.

rifischiare vt. to report.

rifiutare vt., vi. to refuse; to decline; to deny; to reject; **rifiutarsi** vr. to refuse, decline.

rifiuto m. refusal; refuse, rubbish; garbage.

riflessione f. reflection; consideration; meditation.

riflessivo adj. thoughtful; (gramm.) reflexive.

riflesso m. reflection, reflex; adj. reflected; reflex.

riflet'tere vt.¹⁰⁹ to reflect, cast back; to show, reveal; vi. to ponder, think (over): **senza —,** rashly; **riflet'tersi** vr. to reflect, be reflected.

riflettore m. searchlight, flood light; reflector.

rifluire vi. to ebb.

riflusso m. reflux; ebb.

rifocillare vt., **rifocillarsi** vr. to refresh.

rifon'dere vt.⁶⁵ to melt again; to repay.

riforma f. reform; reformation; (mil.) discharge for military ineptitude.

riformare vt. to reform; to amend; (mil.) to discharge for military ineptitude.

riformato adj. reformed, amended; (mil.) discharged for military ineptitude.

riformatore m. reformer.

riformato'rio m. reformatory.

riformista m. reformist.

rifornimento m. supply; refill.

rifornire vt. to supply (with); to replenish; **rifornirsi** vr. to supply oneself (with): **rifornirsi di carburante,** to refuel.

rifran'gere vt.⁸⁶ to refract; **rifran'gersi** vr. to be refracted.

rifratto pp. of **rifrangere**.

rifrazione f. refraction.

rifrig'gere vt.⁶⁷ to fry again; to hackney.

rifritto adj. hackneyed.

rifuggire vi.: — **da,** to abhor, shun.

rifugiarsi vr. to take refuge; to take shelter.

rifu'gio m. shelter, refuge; haunt, den: — **alpino,** mountain hut.

riful'gere vi.¹¹⁰ to shine.

rifusione f. remelting; repayment.

rifuso pp. of **rifon'dere**.

riga f. line; row; stripe; ruler: **a righe,** striped.

riga'glie f. pl. giblets.

riga'gnolo m. gutter.

rigare vt. to rule; to streak: — **diritto,** to behave.

rigato adj. ruled; striped; streaked.

rigattiere m. second-hand dealer.

rigatura f. ruling; striping.

rigenerare vt., **rigenerarsi** vr. to regenerate.

rigettare (1) vt., vi. to vomit.

rigettare (2) vt. to reject; to repel.

righello m. ruler.

righina f. thin stripe; pin stripe.

rigidezza, rigidità f. stiffness; rigor; strictness; austerity.

ri'gido adj. rigid, stiff; unbending; strict, severe; rigorous.

rigirare vt., vi. to turn again, over; to surround, gird; to turn; **rigirarsi** vr. to turn around.

rigo'glio m. bloom.

rigonfio m. swelling. adj. swollen.

rigore m. rigor; strictness: **di —**, obligatory; **a — di termini**, strictly speaking.

rigoroso adj. rigorous, strict.

rigovernare vt., vi. to tidy up; to curry; to do the dishes.

riguadagnare vt. to earn again; to recover, recoup.

riguardare vt. to look again; to check; to revise; to regard, concern: **per quanto mi riguarda**, as far as I am concerned; **riguardarsi** vr. to take care of oneself.

riguardo m. regard, respect; consideration; care: **— a**, with regard to; **mancare di — a**, to be disrespectful to.

riguardoso adj. considerate, respectful.

rigurgitare vi. to regurgitate; to overflow.

rigur'gito m. regurgitation; backwash.

Rigutini, Giuseppe, Italian lexicographer, author together with P. Fanfani of *Il vocabolario della lingua parlata* (1830-1903).

rilanciare vt. to fling again; to fling back; (poker) to raise.

rilan'cio m. return; (poker) raise.

rilasciare vt. to free, release; to grant; **rilasciarsi** vr. to relax; to slacken.

rila'scio m. release; granting.

rilassamento m. slackening; relaxation.

rilassare vt., **rilassarsi** vr. to relax; to slacken; to weaken.

rilassatezza f. laxity.

rilassato adj. lax; relaxed.

rilegare vt. to rebind.

rilegato adj. bound; rebound.

rilegatore m. bookbinder.

rilegatura f. binding.

rileg'gere vt.[74] to reread.

rilento, (a) adv. slowly.

rilevante adj. relevant; substantial.

rilevare vt. to notice; to point out; to emphasize; to relieve; to take over; to buy; to survey: **— il calco di**, to cast.

rilevata'rio m. purchaser, buyer.

rilevato adj. in relief.

rilievo m. relief; remark; survey: **di —**, prominent, outstanding; **mettere in —**, to emphasize.

rilucente adj. shining.

rilu'cere vi.[111] to shine, glitter.

riluttante adj. reluctant.

riluttanza f. reluctance.

rima f. rhyme.

rimandare vt. to send back; to reject; to defer, postpone, put off; to refer.

rimando m. postponement; (sport) return; (mach.) intermediate control: **di —**, in one's turn.

rimaneggiamento m. rearrangement.

rimaneggiare vt. to rearrange; to alter.

rimanente m. remainder; adj. remaining.

rimanenza f. remainder.

rimanere vi.[112] to remain, stay; to stop; to be left: **— della propria opinione**, to stick to one's opinion; **mi rimangono due dollari**, I have two dollars left; **— di stucco**, to be dumfounded; **— male**, to be crestfallen, to be abashed, to be disappointed; **— d'accordo**, to agree; **— a letto**, to keep to one's bed; **— alzato**, to stay up.

rimangiare vt. to eat again: **rimangiarsi la parola**, to go back on one's word.

rimarcare vt. to remark, notice.

rimarche'vole adj. remarkable.

rimare vt., vi. to rhyme.

rimarginare vi. to heal.

rima'rio m. rhyming dictionary.

rimaritarsi vr. to get married again.

rimasto pp.of rimanere.

rimasu'glio m. remains.

rimatore m. rhymer.

rimbalzare vi. to rebound, bounce.

rimbalzo m. rebound, bouncing.

rimbambimento m. dotage.

rimbambinire, rimbambire vi. to become a dotard.

rimbambito m. dotard.

rimbeccare vt. to retort.

rimbecillimento m. dotage.

rimboccare vt. to tuck up.

rimbombare vi. to thunder, resound, boom.

rimbombo m. boom, loud noise.

rimborsare vt. to reimburse, repay.

rimborso m. repayment, reimbursement.

rimboschire vt. to reforest.

rimbrottare vt. to scold, reprove.

rimbrotto m. reprimand.

rimediare vt. to remedy; to repair.

rime'dio m. remedy; cure; help: **non c'è —**, it can't be helped.

rimembranza f. remembrance.

rimenare vt. to stir.

rimeritare vt. to reward.

rimescolare vt. to stir.

rimessa (1) f. carriage house; garage.

rimessa (2) f. remittance.

rimesso pp.of rimettere.

rimestare vt. to stir.

rimet'tere vt.[76] to put (lay, set) again, or back; to give back; to send back; to postpone, defer; to send; to remit, forgive; to entrust; to vomit: **rimetterci**, to lose, to be the loser; **— a nuovo**, to renovate; **rimet'tersi** vr. to put, place oneself again or back; to start afresh or again; to resume; to put on again; to recover, get better; to trust (to), rely (upon); **— in viaggio**, to resume one's journey; **— a sedere**, to resume one's seat; **— in piedi**, to stand up again; to pick oneself up.

rimirare vt. to contemplate, watch.

rimminchionire vt., vi. to grow dull, stupid.

rimodernare vt. to renovate.

rimonta f. vamping (of shoes).

rimontare vt., vi. to remount, go up; to go back (to); (mach., etc.) to reassemble; to vamp: **— la corrente**, to go upstream.

rimorchiare vt. to tow.

rimorchiatore m. tug, tugboat.

rimor'chio m. trailer: **a —**, in tow; **autocarro con —**, trailer truck.

rimor'dere vt.[77] (fig.) to prick, give remorse. [morse.

rimorso m. remorse.

rimosso pp.of rimuovere.

rimostranza f. expostulation.

rimozione f. removal.

rimpannucciare vt. to fit out again; **rimpannucciarsi** vr. to rig oneself up again.

rimpastare vt. (fig.) to re-form.

rimpasto m. re-forming: **— ministeriale**, reconstitution of the ministry.

rimpatriare vt., vi. to repatriate.

rimpa'trio m. repatriation.

rimpian'gere vt.[90] to regret, be sorry.

rimpianto (1) m. regret.

rimpianto (2) pp.of rimpiangere.

rimpiattare vt. to hide, conceal; **rimpiattarsi** vr. to hide oneself.

rimpiattino m. hide and seek.

rimpiazzare vt. to replace.

rimpicciolire vt. to lessen, make smaller; vi. to lessen; to become smaller.

rimpinzare vt. to stuff (with), cram; **rimpinzarsi** vr. to cram oneself.

rimproverare vt. to reproach, blame; to scold; **rimproverarsi** vr. to blame oneself, repent.

rimpro'vero m. reproach, reproof; reprimand.

rimuginare vt. to muse, ruminate.

rimunerare vt. to reward.

rimunerativo adj. remunerative.

rimunerazione f. reward.

rimuo'vere vt.[86] to remove.

rina'scere vi.[81] to be reborn; to grow up again; to revive: **sentirsi —**, to feel greatly relieved; **far —**, to revive.

rinascimento m. revival; Renaissance.

rina'scita f. revival, rebirth.

rincagnato adj. snub.

rincalzare vt. to tuck (in, up).

rincalzo m. reinforcement, support.

rincantucciarsi vr. to withdraw (into a corner).

rincarare vt., vi. to increase in price: **— la dose**, (fig.) to add a nail to one's coffin.

rincaro m. rise in prices.

rincasare vi. to return home.

rinchiu'dere vt.[25] to shut up; to inclose.

rinchiuso adj. shut up; hidden: pp. of rinchiudere.

rincitrullire vt., vi. to dull.

rincominciare see ricominciare.

rincorare vt. to encourage, cheer; **rincorarsi** vr. to take courage; to cheer up.

rincor'rere vt.[36] to pursue, run after.

rincorsa f. run.

rincre'scere vi.[38] to be painful: **mi rincresce per**, I am sorry for; **se non vi rincresce**, if you do not mind.

rincrescimento m. regret.

rincrudire vt. to aggravate; to embitter; vi. to grow (to get, to become) worse.

rinculare vi. to recoil; to fall back; to withdraw.

rinculo m. recoil.

rinfacciare vt. to reproach, throw in one's face.

rinfocolare vt. to inflame, rekindle.

rinfoderare vt. to sheathe.

rinforzare vt., **rinforzarsi** vr. to strengthen.

rinforzo m. reinforcement.

rinfrancare vt. to reanimate, strengthen; **rinfrancarsi** vr. to buck up.

rinfrescare vt. to cool, freshen; to restore. vi., **rinfrescarsi** vr. to freshen, refresh; to grow cool.

rinfresco m. refreshments; party.

rinfusa, (alla) adv. pell-mell.

ringalluzzire vt. to elate; **ringalluzzirsi** vr. to become elated.

ringhiare vi. to snarl, growl.

ringhiera f. balustrade, railing; banisters.

rin'ghio m. snarl, growl.

ringhioso adj. snarly.

ringhiottire vt. to swallow up again.

ringiovanire vt. to rejuvenate, make younger; to make (one) look younger; vi. to become younger; to become young again.

ringoiare see ringhiottire.

ringraziamento m. thanks; thanksgiving.

ringraziare vt. to thank (for).

rinnegare vt. to disown; to forswear.

rinnegato m., adj. renegade.

rinnovamento m. renewal; renovation; revival; reawakening.

rinnovare vt. to renew; to renovate; **rinnovarsi** vr. to renew; to recur, be repeated.

rinnovo m. renewal.

rinoceronte m. rhinoceros.

rinomanza f. renown, fame.

rinomato adj. renowned, famous.

rinsaldare vt. to strengthen; to starch.

rinsavire vi. to return to reason; to sober down.

rintanarsi vr. to burrow; to hide, hide oneself; to retire.

rintocco m. toll, knell.

rintracciare vt. to trace, find.

rintronare vt. to stun, deafen.

rintuzzare vt. to repel; to repress, suppress.

rinun'cia, rinun'zia f. renunciation.

rinunciare, rinunziare vt., vi. to renounce; to relinquish; to give up; to resign.

rinvangare vt. to rake up.

rinvenire vt. to find; to find out; vi. to come to oneself.

rinviare vt. to send back; to defer; to adjourn.

rinvigorire vt. to strengthen, reinvigorate.

rinvi'o m. postponement, adjournment.

rio (1) m. brook, creek.

rio (2) adj. guilty; wicked.

rioccupare vt. to reoccupy.

rione m. district, quarter, section; neighborhood.

riordinare vt. to rearrange; to trim, put in order; to reorganize.

riorganizzare vt. to reorganize.

riorganizzazione f. reorganization.

riottoso adj. refractory, riotous; quarrelsome.

ripa f. bank, quay.

ripagare vt. to pay again; to repay, reward.

riparare vt. to protect; to shelter; to repair, mend; to redress, make good for; to repeat (an examination); vi. to remedy; to take refuge, repair; **ripararsi** vr. to take shelter.

riparazione f. repair; fixing; reparation: **esame di —**, make-up examination.

riparo m. remedy; shelter; protection, cover.

ripartire (1) vi. to leave again, start again; to resume one's journey.

ripartire (2) vt. to divide, subdivide; to distribute; to split.

ripartizione f. division; allotment; distribution.

ripassare vt. vi. to repass, pass again; to call again; to brush up; to finish, polish; (mach.) to overhaul: **— la parte** (theat.), to go over one's lines.

ripasso m. review; (mach.) overhaul.

ripensare vi. to think again (of); to think over: **ci ripenserò**, I will think it over; **ora che ci ripenso**, now that I think of it.

ripercosso pp. of ripercuotere.

ripercuo'tere, ripercuo'tersi vr.[125] to rebound; to reverberate: **— su**, to affect.

ripercussione f. repercussion.

ripescare vt. to fish out; to catch, find again.

ripetente m. repeater (pupil).

ripe'tere vt. to repeat; to report; **ripe'tersi** vr. to repeat oneself; to happen again; to recur.

ripetitore m. repeater; coach.

ripetizione f. repetition; coaching: **orologio, arma a —**, repeater; **dare — a**, to coach; **prendere — da**, to coach with, to take lessons with.

ripetutamente adv. repeatedly.

ripiano m. shelf; ledge; landing.

ripicco m. pique.

ri'pido adj. steep, precipitous.

ripiegamento m. refolding; retreat.

ripiegare vt. to refold; to fold; to bend (again). vi. to retreat, withdraw; **ripiegarsi** vr. to fold; to bend, stoop.

ripiego m. expedient, remedy.

ripienezza f. repletion; surfeit.

ripieno m. stuffing; adj. full.

ripigliare vt. to take again.

ripiombare vi. to fall again; to fall back.

ripopolare vt. to repopulate.

riporre vt.[93] to put back; to put away; to hide; to place: **— la propria fiducia in**, to trust.

riportare vt. to bring again; to bring back; to take back; to report; to get.

riporto m. amount carried forward; (exch.) contango.

riposante adj. restful.

riposare vt. to lay again or back; to put down again: **far —**, to rest; vi. to rest; to sleep; **riposarsi** vr. to rest.

riposato adj. relaxed; quiet; rested.

riposo m. rest, repose; calm; relaxation: **— festivo**, holyday; **buon —! sleep well!; questa sera —** (theat.), no performance tonight; **riposo!** (mil.), stand at easel; **collocare a —**, to superannuate.

riposti'glio m. closet; hiding place.

riposto adj. hidden, secret. pp. of riporre: **mal —**, misplaced.

ripren'dere vt.⁹⁶ to take again; to get back; to recover; to resume; to reprove; (moving pictures) to shoot: — fiato, to pause for breath; vi. to start again; to go on; ripren'dersi vr. to recover; to catch oneself up.

ripresa f. resumption; recovery; revival; (sport) round; pickup (of a motor); (moving pictures) shooting.

ripresentare vt. to present again; ripresentarsi vr. to present oneself again.

ripreso pp.of riprendere. [again.

ripristinare vt. to restore.

ripri'stino m. restoration.

riprodotto pp.of riprodurre.

riprodurre vt.³ to reproduce; riprodursi vr. to reproduce; to recur.

riproduzione f. reproduction.

ripromet'tersi vr.⁷⁶ to anticipate; to intend, mean, propose (to).

riproporre vt.⁹³ to propose again; riproporsi vr. to mean, intend, propose (to); to arise again.

riprova f. new proof, confirmation.

riprovare vt., vi. to try again; to experience again; to censure; riprovarsi vr. to try again.

riprovazione f. reprobation.

riprove'vole adj. blamable.

ripubblicare vt. to republish.

ripudiare vt. to repudiate; to disown.

ripugnante adj. loathsome, repugnant.

ripugnanza f. loathing, repugnance; aversion: aver — a, to be loath to.

ripugnare vt., vi. to disgust, be repugnant, to make or feel sick.

ripulire vt. to clean again; to clean up; to polish; ripulirsi vr. to tidy (oneself) up.

ripulitura f. cleaning.

ripulsa f. repulse.

ripulsivo adj. repulsive.

riputazione f. reputation.

riquadro m. square.

risacca f. surf.

risa'ia f. rice field.

risaiuolo m., risaiuola f. rice reaper.

risalire vt.¹¹⁶ to go up again, ascend again: — la corrente, to go upstream; vi. to go up again, go back; to date from.

risaltare vi. to stand out; to project: far —, to set forth, to emphasize.

risalto m. relief; prominence; emphasis.

risanare vt. to heal, cure; to reclaim; to reform; vi. to recover.

risapere vt.¹¹⁷ to know, come to know.

risaputo adj. known, well-known.

risarcimento m. compensation, indemnification.

risarcire vt. to compensate, indemnify (for).

risata f. (burst of) laughter.

riscaldamento m. heating.

riscaldare vt. to heat, warm (up); riscaldarsi vr. to warm up, warm oneself; to get excited.

riscattare vt. to ransom; to redeem.

riscatto m. ransom; redemption.

rischiarare vt. to clarify, make clear; to enlighten, light up; rischiararsi vr. to clear up, get clear; to brighten: rischiararsi la voce, to clear one's throat.

rischiare vt., vi. to run the risk of; to risk.

ri'schio m. risk; danger; daring.

rischioso adj. risky, dangerous.

risciacquare vt. to rinse.

risciaquatura f. rinsing; rinsing water.

riscontrare vt. to collate; to check; to find; to notice.

riscontro m. collation; checking; test; reply: — d'aria, current (of air).

riscossa f. insurrection; redress.

riscossione f. collection.

riscosso pp.of riscuotere.

riscri'vere vt.¹²⁴ to rewrite; to write again.

riscuo'tere vt.¹²⁵ to collect; to shake; to rouse; to win. riscuo'tersi vr. to start; to catch oneself up.

risentimento m. resentment.

risentire vt. to hear again; to listen to again; to feel (again); to experience; to show the effects, signs, traces of.

risentirsi vr. to suffer (from): risentirsi di, to resent; si risenti della sfaticata, the hard work told on him.

risentito adj. angry, resentful.

riserbare, see riservare.

riserbo m. discretion, reservedness.

riserva f. reservation; reserve: uomini di —, reserves (mil.).

riservare vt. to reserve; to set aside; riservarsi vr. to reserve oneself; to reserve to oneself, secure; to purpose.

riservatezza f. reservedness.

riservato adj. reserved; unobtrusive; private, confidential.

risguardo m. (typog.) flyleaf.

risie'dere vi. to reside.

risi'pola f. erysipelas.

risma f. ream; quality, kind.

riso (1) m. rice.

riso (2) m. laughing, laugh, laughter.

riso (3) pp.of ridere.

risolare vt. to resole.

risolatura f. resoling.

risolino m. little laugh, giggle.

risollevare vt. to raise again; to lift up again.

risolto pp.of risolvere.

risolutezza f. resolution.

risoluto adj. resolute; determined.
risoluzione f. resolution; solution; rescission: **prendere una —**, to make up one's mind.
risol'vere vt.[17] to resolve upon, decide; to solve; to rescind; **risol'versi** vr. to dissolve; to resolve (upon), decide; to end (in).
risonante adj. resonant.
risonanza f. resonance.
risonare vi. to resound, echo, reverberate, ring; to resonate.
risor'gere vi.[130] to rise again.
risorgimento m. revival, renaissance; (cap.) the movement for political unity in Italy in the 19th century.
risorsa f. resource.
risorto adj. reborn, resuscitated.
risparmiare vt. to save, spare; **risparmiarsi** vr. to spare oneself; to refrain from.
risparmiatore m. saver.
rispar'mio m. saving.
rispecchiare vt. to reflect.
rispedire vt. to send again or back; to forward.
rispetta'bile adj. respectable, decent; considerable.
rispettabilità f. respectability, decency.
rispettare vt. to respect: **farsi —**, to make oneself respected; **un uomo che si rispetti**, a self-respecting man.
rispettivamente adv. respectively.
rispettivo adj. respective; one's own.
rispetto m. respect; regard: **con — parlando**, excuse the word; **mancare di — a**, to be disrespectful to.
rispettoso adj. respectful.
risplendente adj. shining.
risplen'dere vi. to shine; to glitter, sparkle.
rispon'dere vt., vi.[113] to answer, reply; to correspond; to meet, come up (to); to answer (for): **— picche**, to say no, to turn down.
risposarsi vr. to marry again.
risposta f. answer, reply: **con — pagata**, with reply prepaid.
risposto pp.of **rispondere**.
rissa f. fray, fight.
rissare vi. to fight.
rissoso adj. quarrelsome, troublesome.
ristabilire vt. to re-establish; to restore; **ristabilirsi** vr. to recover.
ristagnare vi. to stagnate.
ristampa f. reprint.
ristampare vt. to reprint.
ristare vi. to pause.
ristorante m. restaurant.
ristorare vt. to refresh.
ristoratore m. restaurant.
ristoro m. refreshment; relief; rest.

ristrettezza f. narrowness; narrow-mindedness; straits.
ristretto adj. narrow; restricted, limited; reduced. pp.of **restringere**: **— di mente**, narrow-minded; **brodo —**, consommé.
risuc'chio m. swirl.
risultanza f. result, issue.
risultare vi. to result; to follow, ensue; to arise; to appear; to come out; to turn out: **da quel che mi risulta**, as far as I know; **mi risulta che**, I understand that.
risultato m. result; outcome.
risurrezione f. resurrection.
risuscitare vt. to resuscitate, revive; vi. to resuscitate, return to life.
risvegliare vt. to wake (up); to rouse, arouse; **risvegliarsi** vr. to wake up.
risve'glio m. awakening; revival.
risvolto m. lapel (of a coat); cuff (of sleeves); pleat (of trousers).
ritagliare vt. to clip (off), cut (out, off).
rita'glio m. snip; (newspaper) clipping: **— di tempo**, odd moment, spare time.
ritardare vt. to delay; to put off; to retard; vi. to be late; to be slow (as a watch).
ritardata'rio m. laggard; defaulter; latecomer.
ritardato adj. delayed; overdue.
ritardo m. delay; slowness: **essere in —**, to be late.
ritegno m. discretion; restraint; qualm.
ritemprare vt. to strengthen; (metal.) to retemper; **ritemprarsi** vr. to strengthen, harden.
ritenere (1) vt.[141] to check, detain; withhold: **— a memoria**, to commit to memory.
ritenere (2) vt., vi.[141] to deem; to think; to believe; to consider; **ritenersi** vr. to consider oneself.
ritentare vi. to try again.
ritirare vt. to withdraw; to take back; to collect; **ritirarsi** vr. to withdraw; to retreat; to retire; to go home; to shrink; to give up.
ritirata f. retreat; watercloset; (mil.) taps.
ritirato adj. retired; secluded.
ritiro m. withdrawal; collection; retreat: **in —**, retired.
ritmato adj. measured; rhythmical.
rit'mico adj. rhythmical.
ritmo m. rhythm, measure; dance music, "swing."
rito m. rite; ceremony: **essere di —**, to be the (very) thing, to be de rigueur.
ritoccare vt. to retouch.

ritoccatura, f. **ritocco** m. retouch; finishing touch; change; improvement.

ritor'cere vt. to twist, twine; to retort; **ritor'cersi** vr. to twist; to recoil (on).

ritornare vt. to return, give back; vi. to return; to go back; to come back; to recur: — **in sè,** to come to oneself.

ritornello m. refrain.

ritorno m. return; recurrence: **far** —, to go back; **esser di** —, to be back; — **di fiamma,** backfire.

ritorsione f. retaliation.

ritorto adj. twisted.

ritradurre vt. to retranslate.

ritrarre vt.[146] to withdraw; to portray, represent; to draw, gain; **ritrarsi** vr. to withdraw, retreat.

ritrattare vt. to retract; to withdraw; to portray; **ritrattarsi** vr. to recant.

ritrattazione f. retraction.

ritrattista m. portrait painter.

ritratto (1) m. portrait, picture, image.

ritratto (2) pp.of **ritrarre**.

ritrito adj. stale, hackneyed.

ritrosi'a f. demureness; reluctance.

ritroso adj. demure, coy; reluctant: **a** —, backward.

ritrovamento m. finding, discovery.

ritrovare vt. to find (again); to meet again; to discover; **ritrovarsi** vr. to find oneself; to meet again; to get one's bearings.

ritrovato m. discovery; device; adj. found again; rediscovered.

ritrovo m. meeting; haunt: — **notturno,** night club.

ritto see **diritto**.

rituffare vt., **rituffarsi** vr. to replunge.

riunione f. meeting, gathering.

riunire vt. to reassemble; to gather; to rejoin; to bring together; **riunirsi** vr. to reunite; to gather; to come together; to unite.

riuscire vi.[149] to get out again; to get to; to succeed (in); to turn out; to be proficient; to be; to prove: **non — a nulla,** to get nowhere; **non** —, to fail.

riuscita f. result, outcome: **buona** —, success; **cattiva** —, failure.

riuscito adj.: — **bene,** successful; satisfactory; — **male,** unsuccessful; unsatisfactory.

riva f. shore; bank; waterfront.

rivale m., adj. rival.

rivaleggiare vi. to rival.

rivalersi vr [150] to take it out (on): — **di,** to retaliate upon.

rivalità f. rivalry.

rivalsa f. retaliation; (fin.) redraft.

rivalso pp.of **rivalere**.

rivalutare vt. to revalorize.

rivalutazione f. revalorization.

rivangare vt. to rake up.

rivedere vt.[151] to see again; to examine; to correct, revise; to go over; (mach.) to overhaul: — **le bozze,** to read proofs; — **le bucce a,** to pick to pieces.

riveduto adj. revised.

rivelare vt. to reveal, disclose; **rivelarsi** vr. to reveal oneself; to prove.

rivelatore m. revealer; (radio, etc.) detector; adj. revealing; telltale.

rivelazione f. revelation; disclosure.

riven'dere vt. to resell: — **al minuto,** to retail.

rivendicare vt. to vindicate; to claim.

rivendicazione f. vindication; claim.

riven'dita f. resale; shop.

rivenditore m. retailer; reseller.

rivendu'gliolo m. huckster.

river'bero m. reverberation; reflection.

riverente adj. reverent; respectful.

riverenza f. reverence; curtsy, bow.

riverire vt. to revere, venerate; to pay one's respects to.

riverniciare vt. to repaint.

riversare vt. to pour again or back; to pour down; to lay (on); **riversarsi** vr. to flow (into), pour (into); to invade.

riversi'bile adj. reversible.

riverso adj. on one's back.

rivestimento m. covering, lining, coating.

rivestire vt. to dress again; to cover (with); to line (with); to upholster; to hold (as an office).

riviera f. coast; Riviera.

rivin'cere vi. to win again; to win back.

rivin'cita f. revenge; return game or match.

rivista f. review; magazine; (mil.) parade; (theat.) musical comedy, revue.

rivisto pp.of **rivedere**.

rivi'vere vt., vi. to live again; to resurrect; to revive.

rivo m. stream; brook.

rivolere vt. to want back.

rivol'gere vt. to turn; to direct; to address; **rivol'gersi** vr. to turn (back); to address oneself; to turn (to), apply (to).

rivolgimento m. change; disturbance; upheaval.

rivolta f. insurrection; revolt.

rivoltante adj. disgusting, revolting.

rivoltare vt. to turn (over) again, turn back; to turn inside; to reverse, turn inside out; to upset, disgust: — **un indumento,** to turn a garment; **rivoltarsi** *vr.* to turn back; to toss; to revolt; to feel sick.

rivoltato *adj.* turned (*out*); turned inside out: **colletto** —, turndown collar.

rivoltella *f.* revolver.

rivoltellata *f.* revolver shot.

rivoltoso *m.* rioter; *adj.* rebellious.

rivoluzionare *vt.* to revolutionize.

rivoluziona'rio *m.*, *adj.* revolutionary.

rivoluzione *f.* revolution.

rivulsivo *adj.* revulsive.

rizzare, rizzarsi see **drizzare, drizzarsi.**

roano *m.*, *adj.* roan.

roba *f.* stuff; belongings: — **da poco,** cheap stuff; trifles; — **da chiodi!** things beyond description!, how preposterous!, incredible!

robi'nia *f.* (*bot.*) locust tree.

robustezza *f.* robustness.

robusto *adj.* robust, sturdy.

rocca *f.* rock; fortress; distaff.

roccaforte *f.* stronghold.

rocchetto *m.* reel, spool.

roc'cia *f.* rock; cliff.

roccioso *adj.* rocky.

roco *adj.* hoarse.

rodag'gio *m.* running in: **mettere un automobile in** —, to run a car in.

ro'dere *vt.*[114] to gnaw; to corrode: — **il freno,** to champ at the bit; **un osso duro da** —, a hard nut to crack; **ro'dersi** *vr.* to be gnawed or eaten; to fret: — **le unghie,** to bite one's nails.

rodimento *m.* gnawing; worry.

ro'dio *m.* (*metal.*) rhodium.

roditore *m.* rodent.

rododendro *m.* rhododendron.

rodomonte *m.* swashbuckler.

rogato'ria *f.* rogatory commission.

rog'gia *f.* gutter.

ro'gito *m.* instrument, deed.

rogna *f.* scab, mange.

rognone *m.* kidney (*as food*).

rognoso *adj.* mangy.

rogo *m.* pyre, stake.

romanesco *m.* Roman dialect.

romano *m.*, *adj.* Roman: **fare alla romana,** to go Dutch treat.

romanticismo *m.* romanticism.

romantico *adj.* romantic, sentimental.

romanza *f.* song; romance, ballad.

romanzare *vt.* to novelize.

romanzesco *adj.* romantic, adventurous; extraordinary.

romanziere *m.* novelist.

romanzo *m.* novel.

rombante *adj.* roaring.

rombare *vi.* to roar.

rombo *m.* thunder, roar; (*geom.*) rhomb, diamond.

romeno *m.*, *adj.* Rumanian.

romito *adj.* secluded, lonely.

rom'pere *vt.*[115] to break; to shatter: — **le scatole a,** to pester; **rom'persi** *vr.* to break (*up*); to shatter.

rompicapo *m.* puzzle.

rompicollo *m.* madcap: **a** —, rashly.

rompighiaccio *m.* icebreaker.

rompisca'tole *m.* nuisance, pest.

ron'cola *f.* pruning knife.

ronda *f.* rounds, watch; patrol.

ron'dine, rondinella *f.* swallow.

rondone *m.* swift.

ronfare *vi.* to snore.

ronzare *vi.* to hum, buzz.

ronzino *m.* jade.

ronzi'o *m.* humming, buzzing.

rosa *f.* rose. *m.* pink; *adj.* pink, rose-colored.

Rosa, Salvator, Italian painter and poet (1615–1673).

ro'saio *m.* rosebush.

rosario *m.* beads, rosary.

rosato *adj.* rosy.

ro'seo *adj.* rose-colored, rosy.

roseto *m.* rose garden, rosary.

rosicante *m.*, *adj.* rodent.

rosicchiare *vt.* to nibble, gnaw.

rosmarino *m.* rosemary.

Rosmini, Antonio, Italian philosopher (1797–1855).

roso *adj.* gnawed; eaten. *pp.of* rodere.

rosolare *vt.* to brown, broil; **rosolarsi** *vr.* to get brown.

rosoli'a *f.* German measles.

rospo *m.* toad.

rossetto *m.* rouge; lipstick.

Rossi, Pellegrino, Italian statesman (1787–1848).

rossic'cio *adj.* reddish.

Rossini, Gioacchino Antonio, Italian composer, *Il Barbiere di Siviglia* (1792–1868).

rosso *m.* red: — **d'uovo,** yolk; *adj.* red: **diventar** —, to redden, blush.

rossore *m.* redness; blush, flush; erythema, rash.

rosticceri'a *f.* cookshop, grill.

rostro *m.* rostrum (*pl.* rostra).

rota'bile *f.* highroad: **materiale** —, (*rail.*) rolling stock.

rota'ia *f.* rail.

rotare *vi.* to rotate, revolve.

rotativa *f.* (*typog.*) rotary press.

rotato'rio *adj.* rotatory.

rotazione *f.* rotation; **movimento di** —, rotatory motion.

roteare *vi.* to circle: **far** — **la spada,** to flourish one's sword.

rotella *f.* small wheel; roller; caster; (*anat.*) kneecap.

rotocalco *m.* rotogravure.

rotolare *vt.*, *vi.* to roll; **rotolarsi** *vr.* to roll; to welter.

ro'tolo *m.* roll: **andare (mandare) a rotoli,** to go (to send) to ruin.

rotolone m. tumble.
rotonda f. terrace.
rotondità f. roundness.
rotondo adj. round.
rotta f. rout; (naut., aeron.) course, route: essere in — con, to be at odds with; a — di collo, at break-neck speed; from bad to worse; far — per, to sail for; ufficiale di —, navigator.
rottame m. fragment; wreckage; wreck: rottami di ferro, scrap iron.
rotto adj. broken; out of gear; inured. pp.of rompere.
rottura f. break; breakage; crack; breaking off; cessation; breach.
ro'tula f. kneecap.
rovello m. anger, rage.
rovente adj. red-hot; poignant.
ro'vere m. oak.
rovesciamento m. overturn.
rovesciare vt. to overturn, overthrow, upset; to turn inside out; to pour; to spill; rovesciarsi vr. to overturn, to capsize; to fall; to flow, dis-charge (into); to spill.
rove'scio m. reverse; wrong side; back; opposite, contrary; down-pour; downfall, overthrow; lap, lapel; adj. reverse, inverse, wrong side out; upside down: a —, wrong; alla rovescia, upside down.
roveto m. bramble bush.
rovina f. ruin.
rovinare vt. to ruin; to spoil, wreck; vi. to ruin; to crumble (down); rovinarsi vr. to ruin oneself; to get [spoiled.
rovini'o m. clatter.
rovinoso adj. ruinous.
rovistare vt., vi. to rummage.
rovo m. bramble.
rozzo adj. rough, clumsy.
ruba f.: andare a —, to sell like hot-cakes.
rubacchiare vt., vi. to pilfer.
rubacuori m. ladykiller.
rubare vt. to steal; to rob: — sul peso, to give short measure; — a man salva, to loot.
ruberi'a f. theft, robbery, graft, fraud.
rubicondo adj. ruddy, rubicund.

rubinetto m. tap.
rubino m. ruby.
ru'brica f. directory; column (in a newspaper, etc.)
rude adj. rough, rude, tough.
ru'dere m. ruin.
rudimentale adj. rudimentary.
rudimento m. rudiment.
ruffiana f. procuress, go-between.
ruffiano m. pander, pimp, go-between.
ruga f. wrinkle.
rug'gine f. rust: aver della — con, to harbor a grudge against.
rugginoso adj. rusty.
ruggire vi. to roar.
ruggito m. roar, roaring.
rugiada f. dew.
rugoso adj. wrinkled; ridged; rugose.
ruilare vi. to roll; (aeron.) to taxi.
rulli'o m. roll; rub-a-dub.
rullag'gio m. (aeron.) taxiing: pista di —, runway.
rullo m. roll.
rumeno m., adj. Rumanian.
ruminante m., adj. ruminant.
ruminare vi. to ruminate.
rumore m. noise; rumor.
rumoreggiare vi. to rumble; to riot.
rumorosamente adv. noisily.
rumoroso adj. noisy.
ruolo m. roll, list; number, class; roster: insegnante di —, regular teacher.
ruota f. wheel; spread (of a peacock's tail): seguire a —, to follow closely.
rupe f. rock, cliff.
rurale adj. rural, farm.
ruscello m. brook.
russare vi. to snore.
russo m., adj. Russian.
rusticano adj. rustic.
ru'stico m. farmhouse; adj. rustic.
rutilante adj. shining, rutilant.
ruttare vi. to belch.
rutto m. belch.
ruvidezza, ruvidità f. roughness; harshness.
ru'vido adj. rough, harsh; coarse.
ruzzolare vi. to roll; to tumble down.
ruzzolone m. tumble, fall.
ruzzoloni adv. tumblingly.

S

sa'bato m. Saturday.
sab'bia f. sand.
sabbioso adj. sandy.
sabotag'gio m. sabotage.
sabotare vt. to sabotage.
sabotatore m. saboteur.
sacca f. bag, satchel; pocket.
saccarina f. saccharine.
saccaro'sio m. saccharose.

saccente m. sciolist, wiseacre; adj. presumptuous.
saccheggiare vt. to sack, plunder.
saccheg'gio m. sack, plunder.
sacchetto m. small bag.
sacco m. sack, bag; plunder; heap, lot: con le mani nel —, redhanded; con la testa nel —, harum-scarum; colazione al —, picnic; mettere nel — (fig.), to outwit.

saccoc'cia *f.* pocket.
sacerdote *m.* priest.
sacerdotessa *f.* priestess.
sacerdo'zio *m.* priesthood.
sacramento *m.* sacrament.
sacra'rio *m.* sacrarium; sanctuary.
sacresti'a *f.* sacristy, vestry.
sacrificare *vt.*, *vi.* to sacrifice; sacrificarsi, *vr.* to sacrifice oneself.
sacrifi'zio *m.* sacrifice; privation.
sacrile'gio *m.* sacrilege.
sacri'lego *adj.* sacrilegious, impious.
sacrista *f.* sexton.
sacro *adj.* sacred, holy: osso — (*anat.*), sacrum.
sacrosanto *adj.* sacrosanct, sacred.
sa'dico *m.*, sadist; *adj.* sadistic.
sadismo *m.* sadism.
saetta *f.* dart; thunderbolt.
saettare *vt.*, *vi.* to shoot, dart.
sagace *adj.* sagacious, shrewd.
saga'cia, sagacità *f.* sagacity.
saggezza *f.* wisdom.
saggiamente *adv.* wisely.
saggiare *vt.* to try, test.
saggiatore *m.* assayer.
sag'gio (1) *m.* sage, wise man; *adj.* sage, wise, judicious.
sag'gio (2) *m.* essay; trial, test; specimen, sample; (*fin.*) rate.
sa'gola *f.* (*naut.*) halyard.
sa'goma *f.* mold; shape; outline.
sagomare *vt.* to mold, shape.
sagrato *m.* churchyard.
sagrestano *m.* sexton.
sagresti'a *f.* sacristy, vestry.
sa'io *m.* sackcloth; (*eccl.*) frock.
sala (1) *f.* hall, room; — operatoria, operating room.
sala (2) *f.* (*mach.*) axletree.
salace *adj.* spicy; salacious.
salamandra *f.* salamander.
salame *m.* sausage, salami.
salamelecco *m.* salaam; (*pop.*) toadying greeting.
salamo'ia *f.* pickle.
salare *vt.* to salt.
salariato *m.* wage earner.
sala'rio *m.* wages, pay.
salassare *vt.* to bleed.
salasso *m.* bloodletting; extortion.
salato *m.* salami; *adj.* salted.
salatura *f.* salting.
saldamente *adv.* firmly.
saldare *vt.* to solder; to weld; to settle, pay up; to receipt.
saldatura *f.* soldering.
saldezza *f.* firmness.
saldo (1) *adj.* firm; resolute.
saldo (2) *m.* (*comm.*) balance; receipt.
sale *m.* salt; wit.
salgemma *m.* rock salt.
sa'lice *m.* willow tree.
saliente *m.*, *adj.* salient.

saliera *f.* saltcellar.
salina *f.* saltern, salt pond.
salino *adj.* salty, saline.
salire *vt.*, *vi.*[116] to rise; to mount; to ascend, climb; to go up.
saliscendi *m.* latch.
salita *f.* ascent; slope; rise, increase.
saliva *f.* saliva.
salma *f.* corpse.
salmastro *adj.* brinish.
salmeri'a *f.* (*mil.*) pack train; pack transport group *or* unit.
salmo *m.* psalm.
salmodiare *vi.* to psalmodize.
salmone *m.* salmon.
salnitro *m.* saltpeter.
salone *m.* hall.
salottino, salotto *m.* parlor, drawing room, sitting room.
salpare *vi.* to weigh anchor, sail.
salsa *f.* sauce.
salsamenta'rio *m.* pork butcher.
salse'dine *f.* saltiness, brininess.
salsic'cia *f.* sausage.
salsiera *f.* sauceboat.
salso *adj.* briny, salt, salty.
saltare *vt.* to jump, jump over; to skip. *vi.* to spring, leap; to vault; to explode, pop: far —, to blast; far — la mosca al naso, to put one's back up; gli è saltato il ticchio, he got a notion to; — all'occhio, to be evident, apparent, patent.
saltatore *m.* hurdle racer; hurdler.
saltellare, salterellare *vi.* to hop, skip.
saltimbanco *m.* tumbler, acrobat; mountebank.
salto *m.* jump, leap, bound: fare un — mortale, to perform a somersault.
saltua'rio *adj.* desultory, fitful.
salubre *adj.* salubrious, wholesome.
saluma'io, salumiere *m.* pork butcher.
salume *m.* salt meat; salami.
salumeri'a *f.* pork-butcher's shop.
salutare (1) *vt.* to salute; to greet; to say good-bye (hello) to.
salutare (2) *adj.* healthy.
salute *f.* health; welfare; safety; salvation: bere alla — di uno, to drink one's health.
saluto *m.* salute; greeting.
salva *f.* salvo (*pl.* salvoes).
salvacondotto *m.* safe-conduct.
salvadana'io *m.* moneybox.
salvagente *m.* life preserver; platform, (*traffic*) island.
salvaguardare *vt.* to safeguard, protect. [tect.
salvaguar'dia *f.* safeguard.
salvamento *m.* rescue; safety.
salvare *vt.* to save, rescue; salvarsi *vr.* to save oneself: — da, to avoid.
salvatag'gio *m.* rescue: barca di —, lifeboat; cintura di —, life belt.

salvatore *m.* rescuer, savior.

salvazione *f.* salvation.

salve! *interj.* hail!, hello!

Salve'mini, Gaetano, Italian historian (1873–1957).

salvezza *f.* safety; salvation; escape.

sal'via *f.* (*bot.*) sage.

salvietta *f.* napkin; towel.

salvo *adj.* safe, secure: in —, in safety; rubare a man salva, to plunder; *prep.*, *adv.* except, excepted, barring, but.

sambuco *m.* elder tree.

San *adj.* (*contr.* of Santo) Saint.

sanare *vt.* to cure, heal; to reclaim; to remedy; to settle.

sanato'rio *m.* sanatorium, sanitarium.

sancire *vt.* to ratify, sanction.

Sanctis, de, Francesco, Italian critic (1817–1883).

san'dalo *m.* sandal; sandalwood.

sandolino *m.* kayak, flatboat.

sangue *m.* blood: — freddo, self-possession; a — freddo, in cold blood; spargimento di —, bloodshed; farsi cattivo —, to fret.

sanguigno *adj.* sanguine, bloody; red.

sanguinante *adj.* bleeding.

sanguinare *vi.* to bleed.

sanguina'rio *adj.* murderous; bloodthirsty.

sanguinolento *adj.* sanguinolent.

sanguinoso *adj.* bloody; mortal.

sanguisuga *f.* leech; bloodsucker.

sanità *f.* soundness; sanity; medical department; (*mil.*) medical corps.

sanita'rio *m.* doctor; *adj.* sanitary.

Sannazzaro, Jacopo, Italian poet (1458–1530).

sano *adj.* sound; healthy; wholesome; whole.

Sansovino, Andrea (*Andrea Contucci*), Italian sculptor (1460–1529).

Sansovino, Jacopo (*Jacopo Tatti*), Italian architect and sculptor (1486–1570).

santabar'bara *f.* (*naut.*) powder room.

santarellina *f.* plaster saint.

santificare *vt.* to sanctify.

santis'simo *m.* the Holy Host; *adj.* most sacred.

santità *f.* holiness, sanctity.

santo *m.* saint: non sapere più a che — votarsi, not to know which way to turn; non essere uno stinco di —, not to be much of a saint; *adj.* sainted; holy, sacred; blessed: tutto il — giorno, all day long; tutti i santi giorni, day in, day out.

santua'rio *m.* sanctuary, shrine.

sanzionare *vt.* to sanction.

sanzione *f.* sanction.

sapere (1) *vt.*, *vi.*[117] to know; to be able; to be acquainted with; to be aware of, realize; to taste (*of*); to smell (*of*); venire a —, to get to know, to learn; — a menadito, to have at one's finger's tips; saperla lunga, to know a thing or two; — nuotare (scrivere) bene, to be good at swimming (writing); non volerne più — di, to be through with, to want no part of.

sapere (2) *m.* knowledge; learning.

sa'pido *adj.* sapid, savory.

sapiente *m.* sage, scholar; *adj.* learned, wise.

sapientone *m.* wiseacre, know-it-all.

sapienza *f.* learning; wisdom.

sapona'ria *f.* soapwort.

saponata *f.* soapsuds, soaping.

sapone *m.* soap.

saponetta *f.* soap cake.

sapore *m.* savor, taste, relish.

saporitamente *adv.* relishingly: ridere —, to laugh heartily; dormire —, to sleep soundly.

saporito *adj.* savory; witty, salty.

saracinesca *f.* sluice, floodgate; rolling shutter (*of a shop, etc.*).

sarcasmo *m.* sarcasm.

sarca'stico *adj.* sarcastic.

sarchiare *vt.* to weed.

sarchiatrice *f.* weeder.

sarco'fago *m.* sarcophagus.

sardella *f.* pilchard.

sardina *f.* sardine.

sardo *m.*, *adj.* Sardinian.

sardo'nico *adj.* sardonic, jeering.

Sarpi, Paolo, Italian philosopher and historian (1552–1623).

sarta *f.* dressmaker, tailoress.

sar'tia *f.* (*naut.*) shroud.

sartiame *m.* shrouds (*pl.*).

sarto *m.* tailor.

Sarto, del, Andrea, Florentine painter (1486–1531).

sartori'a *f.* tailor's shop; dressmaker's shop.

sassaiuola *f.* shower of stones; stone fight.

sassata *f.* stoneshot: prendere a sassate, to stone.

sasso *m.* stone; cobble; rock: restar di —, to stand aghast.

sasso'fono *m.* saxophone.

sassolino *m.* pebble.

sata'nico *adj.* satanic.

satel'lite *m.* satellite.

sa'tira *f.* satire.

sati'rico *adj.* satiric, satirical.

sa'tiro *m.* satyr.

saturare *vt.* to saturate; to imbue, soak (with); (*chem.*) to charge: — il mercato, to glut the market; saturarsi *vr.* to become saturated.

saturazione *f.* saturation.

saturnismo *m.* lead poisoning.

sa'turo *adj.* saturated; soaked.

sa'uro *adj.* chestnut, sorrel.

sa'vio *m.* sage; *adj.* wise.

Savonarola, Girolamo, Italian religious reformer (1452–1498).

saziare *vt.* to sate; to satisfy; to cloy; saziarsi *vr.* to sate oneself.

sazi età *f.* satiety.

sa'zio *adj.* sated, full.

sbadatag'gine *f.* inattention; oversight; carelessness; heedlessness.

sbadato *adj.* inattentive; careless.

sbadigliare *vi.* to yawn.

sbadi'glio *m.* yawn.

sbagliare *vt.*, *vi.* to make mistakes in; to miss: — strada, to take the wrong way; sbagliarsi *vr.* to be wrong, be mistaken, make a mistake.

sbagliato *adj.* wrong; mistaken.

sba'glio *m.* mistake; blunder; fault.

sbalestrare *vt.* to fling; to pack off.

sballare *vt.* to unpack, unbale: sballarle grosse (*fig.*), to talk big.

sballato *adj.* (*fig.*) foolish, wild.

sballottare *vt.* to toss.

sbalordimento *m.* astonishment.

sbalordire *vt.* to amaze, startle, astound; to bewilder; *vi.* to be astonished, bewildered.

sbalorditivo *adj.* amazing.

sbalzare *vt.* to overthrow, cast out; to dismiss: — di sella, to unhorse.

sbalzo *m.* leap, spring: — di temperatura, sudden change of temperature; lavoro a —, relief work.

sbancare *vt.* to clean out.

sbandamento *m.* disbandment, dispersion; (*naut.*) list, heel; (*auto.*) swerve, skid.

sbandare *vt.* to disband; *vi.* (*naut.*) to heel, list; (*auto.*) to swerve; sbandarsi *vr.* to disband, scatter.

sbandata *f.* swerve, skid; (*naut.*) list.

sbandato *m.* straggler.

sbaragliare *vt.* to rout.

sbara'glio *m.* rout; (*fig.*) jeopardy: mettere allo —, to jeopardize.

sbarazzare *vt.* to rid; to clear away; sbarazzarsi *vr.* to get rid.

sbarazzino *m.* wag.

sbarbare *vt.*, sbarbarsi *vr.* to shave: farsi —, to get shaved.

sbarbatello *m.* youngster, lad.

sbarcare *vt.*, *vi.* to disembark; to unload; to land: — il lunario, to make both ends meet.

sbarcatoio *m.* landing place, pier.

sbarco *m.* landing; unloading: truppe da —, landing troops.

sbarra *f.* bar; tiller (*of a rudder*).

sbarramento *m.* barrage; blockade.

sbarrare *vt.* to bar, obstruct; to hinder; to block up; to open wide (*as*

one's eyes): — un assegno, to stop a check.

sbarrato *adj.* blocked; wide open: con occhi sbarrati, with eyes wide open.

sbatacchiare *vt.* to strike; to slam, bang.

sbat'tere *vt.* to shake; to fling, toss; to slam (*as a door*); *vi.* to bang: — uova, to whip eggs; — le ali, to flap the wings.

sbattuto *adj.* shaken, tossed; haggard, emaciated; whipped.

sbavare *vt.*, *vi.* to drivel, slaver; (*metal.*) to trim.

sbavatura *f.* drivel; (*metal.*) burr.

sbellicarsi *vr.*: — dalle risa, to split one's sides with laughter.

sbendare *vt.* to unbandage.

sberleffo *m.* wry face, mocking grimace.

sbiadire *vi.* to fade, lose color.

sbiadito *adj.* faded, drab.

sbiancare *vt.* to whitewash; to bleach; *vi.* to whiten; to grow pale.

sbieco *adj.* slanting.

sbigottimento *m.* dismay.

sbigottire *vt.* to dismay; *vi.* to be dismayed.

sbigottito *adj.* dismayed.

sbilanciare *vt.* to unbalance; (*fig.*) to unsettle; to upset; sbilanciarsi *vr.* to lose one's balance; (*fig.*) to commit oneself.

sbilan'cio *m.* (*comm.*) deficit.

sbilenco *adj.* crooked, twisted.

sbirciare *vt.* to glance at; to peer in.

sbizzarrirsi *vr.* to satisfy one's fancy.

sbloccare *vt.* to free; to loosen, unjam.

sbobba *f.* slop.

sboccare *vi.* to flow (*into*); to open (*into*).

sboccato *adj.* foul; foul-tongued.

sbocciare *vi.* to blossom, bloom.

sbocco *m.* outlet; way out.

sbocconcellare *vt.* to nibble; to nick.

sbollire *vi.* (*fig.*) to calm down.

sbor'nia *f.* intoxication: prendere la —, to get drunk.

sborsare *vt.* to disburse, pay.

sborso *m.* disbursement; payment.

sbottare *vi.* to blurt out, burst out.

sbottonare *vt.* to unbutton; sbottonarsi *vr.* to unbutton one's clothes; (*fig.*) to break one's reserve, open up.

sbozzare *vt.* to rough-hew.

sbracciarsi *vr.* to tuck up one's sleeves; to strive; to flail one's arms.

sbracciato *adj.* bare-armed.

sbraitare *vi.* to shout, bawl.

sbranare *vt.* to tear to pieces.

sbreccare *vt.* to nick.

sbrecciare *vt.* to gap.

sbren'dolo *m.* rag, tatter.

sbriciolare *vt.*, sbriciolarsi *vr.* to crumble.

sbrigare *vt.* to dispatch; sbrigarsi *vr.* to hurry up, make haste.

sbrigativo *adj.* cavalier, offhand; hasty, summary; businesslike.

sbrigliare *vt.* to unbridle.

sbrigliato *adj.* unbridled; lively.

sbrindellato *adj.* in rags.

sbrodolare *vt.*, *vi.* to slobber.

sbrogliare *vt.*, sbrogliarsi *vr.* to disentangle.

sbruffare *vt.* to squirt.

sbruffo *m.* sprinkle; bribe.

sbruffone *m.* braggart.

sbucare *vi.* to come out, issue, emerge.

sbucciare *vt.* to peel; to shell; sbucciarsi, *vr.* to skin oneself.

sbudellare *vt.* to disembowel.

sbuffare *vi.* to puff; to pant, gasp.

sbuffo *m.* puff: maniche a —, puffed sleeves.

scab'bia *f.* scabies, itch.

scabro *adj.* rough; rugged.

scabroso *adj.* scabrous; delicate; risqué.

scacchiera *f.* chessboard; draughtsboard.

scacchiere *m.* chessboard; (*mil.*) sector: Cancelliere dello Scacchiere, Chancellor of the Exchequer.

scacciamosche *m.* flyflap.

scacciapensieri *m.* (*mus.*) jew's harp.

scacciare *vt.* to drive away, oust; to expel; to dispel.

scaccino *m.* sexton, sacristan.

scacco *m.* chessman; square; scacchi *pl.* (*game*) chess: giocare a scacchi, to play chess; — matto, checkmate; tessuto a scacchi, checkered cloth; subire uno —, to suffer a defeat; tenere in —, to hold at bay; vedere il sole a scacchi, to be in prison.

scadente *adj.* inferior, cheap, poor.

scadenza *f.* maturity: cambiale a breve (a lunga) —, short- (long-) dated bill; a breve —, on short notice.

scadere *vi.*[22] to come due; to fall due; to expire; to decline, fall off.

scaduto *adj.* due, overdue; expired; outmoded. *pp.of* scadere.

scafandro *m.* diving suit.

scaffale *m.* shelf, bookcase.

scafo *m.* hull.

scagionare *vt.* to exculpate, excuse; scagionarsi *vr.* to exculpate oneself.

sca'glia *f.* scale; chip; spangle, fragment.

scagliare *vt.* to throw, fling, hurl; scagliarsi *vr.* to fling oneself; to dash.

scaglionare *vt.* to echelon.

scaglione *m.* echelon; unit.

scala *f.* staircase; (*mus.*) scale: — a piuoli, portatile, ladder; — a chiocciola, spiral staircase.

Scala, della, Can Grande, Prince of Verona, patron of Dante (1291–1329).

scalandrone *m.* gangway.

scalare *vt.* to scale, escalade, climb; to deduct.

scalata *f.* escalade.

scalatore *m.* climber, cragsman.

scalcagnato *adj.* down at heel, seedy.

scalciare *vi.* to kick.

scalcinato *adj.* (*fig.*) shabby.

scaldabagno *m.* water heater, geyser.

scaldare *vt.* to heat, warm; scaldarsi *vr.* to get warm; (*fig.*) to warm up; to get excited.

scalea *f.* flight of steps, stairway.

scaletta *f.* narrow stairway; ladder; (*moving pictures*) treatment.

scalfire *vt.* to scratch, graze.

scalfittura *f.* graze, scratch.

scalinata *f.* stairway, stoop.

scalino *m.* step.

scalmana *f.* cold: prendere una — per, to take a fancy to.

scalmanarsi *vr.* to bustle; to make a fuss, to warm up.

scalmo *m.* thole, tholepin.

scalo *m.* landing place, pier: — merci, freight station; fare — a, to touch at; volo senza —, nonstop flight.

scalogna *f.* (*bot.*) scallion; (*fam.*) bad luck.

scaloppina *f.* collop.

scalpellare *vt.* to chisel.

scalpellino *m.* stonecutter.

scalpello *m.* chisel.

scalpicci'o *m.* patter; shuffling of feet.

scalpitare *vi.* to paw.

scalpiti'o *m.* pawing.

scalpore *m.* bustle, fuss; sensation.

scaltrezza *f.* shrewdness, cunning.

scaltrire *vt.*, scaltrirsi *vr.* to smarten.

scaltro *adj.* cunning, shrewd, sly.

scalzare *vt.* to hoe; to dislodge; to demolish; to undermine; to oust.

scalzo *adj.* barefoot.

scambiare *vt.* to exchange; to mistake.

scambie'vole *adj.* mutual.

scam'bio *m.* exchange; (*rail.*) switch, points: libero —, free trade.

scamiciato *m.* ragamuffin; firebrand; *adj.* shirtless, in one's shirt sleeves.

scamosciato *adj.* chamois-dressed.

scampagnata *f.* excursion.

scampanare *vi.* to peal, chime.

scampanato *adj.* flaring.

scampanellare *vi.* to ring the bell.

scampanellata f. loud ring, prolonged ring.
scampani'o m. toll.
scampare vt. to rescue, save; vi. to escape, avoid: **scamparla bella,** to escape by the skin of one's teeth; **Dio ci scampi!** God forbid!
scampo m. safety; escape.
scam'polo m. remnant.
scanalare vt. to groove.
scanalatura f. groove.
scancellare see **cancellare**.
scandagliare vt. to sound.
scanda'glio m. sounding lead.
scandalizzare vt. to scandalize, shock; **scandalizzarsi** vr. to be shocked.
scan'dalo m. scandal.
scandaloso adj. scandalous.
scandire vt. to scan; to spell.
scannare vt. to slaughter, butcher.
scannato'io m. shambles.
scanno m. bench.
scansafatiche m. loafer.
scansare vt. to avoid, shun; **scansarsi** vr. to get out of the way, step aside; to duck.
scansi'a f. shelf; bookcase.
scansione f. (telev.) scanning.
scanso m. avoiding, avoidance: a — **di malintesi,** to avoid any misunderstanding.
scantinare vi. to go astray.
scantinato m. basement.
scantonamento m. turning (of the corner).
scantonare vt. to round off; vi. to turn the corner.
scanzonato adj. flippant; jaunty.
scapaccione m. slap.
scapestrato m. libertine, rake.
scapigliare vt. to dishevel.
scapigliato adj. disheveled; (fig.) giddy.
scapitare vi. to lose.
sca'pito m. damage; detriment.
sca'pola f. shoulder blade.
scapolare vt., vi. to escape, avoid.
sca'polo m. bachelor.
scappamento m. escapement (of a spring); exhaust (of a motor): **marmitta di —,** muffler.
scappare vi. to fly away, run away, escape: **lasciarsi — un'occasione,** to miss an opportunity; **mi scappò la pazienza,** I lost my patience.
scappata f. escape; close call; slip.
scappato'ia f. expedient, shift.
scappellata f. unhatting.
scappellotto m. slap in the head.
scapricciarsi see **sbizzarrirsi**.
scarabat'tole f.pl. odds-and-ends.
scarabeo m. beetle.
scarabocchiare vt., vi. to blot, smudge; to scribble.

scaraboc'chio m. scrawl; blot.
scarac'chio m. spit.
scarafag'gio m. cockroach.
scaramanzi'a f. exorcism.
scaramuc'cia f. skirmish.
scaraventare vt. to hurl, fling; **scaraventarsi** vr. to dash.
scarcerazione f. release (from prison).
scarcerare vt. to release from prison; to set free.
scardinare vt. to unhinge.
Scarfoglio, Eduardo, Italian writer and journalist (1860–1917).
sca'rica f. discharge; volley; shower (of blows).
scaricabarili m.: **fare a —,** to lay the blame upon one another, to shift responsibilities.
scaricare vt. to unload, discharge; **scaricarsi** vr. to discharge oneself; to relieve oneself; to run down (as a watch); to flow into (as a river).
scaricatore m. unloader; dockman, longshoreman.
sca'rico m. discharge; unloading; (comm.) transfer: **tubo di —,** wastepipe; adj. discharged, unloaded (as a gun); down, run-down (as a watch): **un capo —,** a scatterbrain.
Scarlatti, Domenico, Italian composer (1683–1757).
scarlattina f. scarlet fever.
scarlatto adj. scarlet.
scarmigliato adj. disheveled.
scarnificare vt. to scarify.
scarnire vt. to thin, make lean.
scarno adj. meager; thin.
scarpa f. shoe.
Scarpa, Antonio, Italian anatomist and surgeon (1747–1832).
scarpata f. bluff, cliff; scarp.
scarrozzare vt. to cart about; to take for a ride.
scarrozzata f. drive, ride.
scarseggiare vi. to lack, be scarce.
scarsella f. pocket; purse.
scarsità f. shortness; dearth.
scarso adj. scanty, short (of).
scartabellare vt. to ruffle.
scartafac'cio m. scratch pad; (pl.) papers.
scartamento m. discarding, rejecting; (rail.) gauge.
scartare vt. to discard; to reject; to unwrap; vi. to swerve.
scartata f. swerve.
scarto m. discarding, rejecting; discard; litter, rubbish; swerve: **merce di —,** cheap stuff.
scartocciare vt. to unpack, unwrap.
scartof'fie f.pl. papers.
scassare vt. to break; to grub up, plow up; to uncase.
scassatura f. breaking.

scassinare vt. to pick the lock of, break open, crack.
scassinatore m. picklock; burglar: — di casseforti, safecracker.
scassinatura f. lockpicking, cracking.
scasso m. lockpicking; (ag.) grubbing: furto con —, burglary.
scatenamento m. unchaining.
scatenare vt. to unchain; to foment; to provoke, kindle: — una guerra, to kindle a war; **scatenarsi** vr. to burst out; to fling oneself (against).
scatenato adj. wild, unruly.
sca'tola f. box; tin, can: **carne in** —, canned meat; **caratteri di** —, large types; **rottura di scatole,** nuisance; **rompere le scatole a,** to pester.
scatolame m. canned food.
scattare vi. to spring; to go off; to burst (with anger): — **in piedi** (sull'attenti), to spring to one's feet (to attention); far —, to release; to click.
scatto m. spring, start; dash; (fig.) outburst, spurt; click: **di** —, abruptly; **a scatti,** jerkily.
scaturi'gine f. source, spring.
scaturire vi. to spring, gush; to derive.
scavalcare vt. to unhorse; to climb over; to outrun, outstrip; (fig.) to steal a march (upon).
scavallare vi. to frolic.
scavamento m. excavation.
scavare vt. to excavate, dig.
scavatore m. digger; miner.
scavatrice f. digger; power shovel, excavator.
scavezzacollo m. scamp; playboy.
scavezzare vt. to break; to lop; **scavezzarsi** vr. to break.
scavo m. excavation.
scazzottare see cazzottare.
sce'gliere vt.[118] to choose, select, sort out.
scelleratag'gine, scelleratezza f. wickedness; crime.
scellerato m. villain; adj. wicked.
scellino m. shilling.
scelta f. choice; selection; option: **di prima** —, choice.
scelto adj. choice; chosen; selected. pp. of scegliere.
scemare vi. to diminish, drop.
scemenza f. silliness; foolery.
scemo m. fool, idiot; adj. foolish.
scempiag'gine f. foolishness.
scem'pio (1) m. fool; adj. silly; single.
scem'pio (2) m. slaughter; havoc.
scena f. scene: **colpo di** —, coup de théâtre; **messa in** —, stage setting, production; **mettere in** —, to set up, to produce, to stage.
scena'rio m. scenery; scenario, screenplay.

scenarista m. scenarist; script writer.
scenata f. row, scene.
scen'dere vt., vi.[119] to get down, descend; to slope down; to flow down, run down; to fall; to drop; to dismount: — **a patti,** to come to terms, to bargain.
scendiletto m. bedside carpet.
sceneggiare vt. to write a scenario.
sceneggiatura f. screenplay, script.
scenografia f. scene painting.
sceno'grafo m. scene designer, scene painter.
sceriffo m. sheriff.
scer'nere vt.[120] to discern; to select.
scervellarsi vr. to rack one's brains.
scervellato m. scatterbrain.
scesa see discesa.
sceso pp. of scendere.
scespiriano adj. Shakespearean.
scetticismo m. skepticism.
scet'tico m., adj. skeptic.
scettro m. scepter.
scevro adj. free, exempt.
scheda f. card; form.
scheda'rio m. card index; file.
scheg'gia f. splinter.
scheggiare vt., **scheggiarsi** vr. to splinter.
schele'trico adj. skeletal.
sche'letro m. skeleton; frame.
schema m. schema (pl. schemata); summary, outline; plan, blueprint.
schema'tico adj. schematic.
scherma f. fencing.
scherma'glia f. skirmish.
schermare vt. to screen.
schermirsi vr. to defend oneself; to dodge; to make shift.
schermitore m. fencer.
schermo m. screen: — panoramico, wide screen.
schernire vt. to mock, deride.
scherno m. sneer, mockery.
scherzare vi. to play; to joke, jest; to trifle (with).
scherzo m. joke, jest; trick; practical joke: — di natura, freak of nature; fare uno — a, to play a trick on.
scherzoso adj. playful.
schettinare see pattinare.
schiacciamento m. crushing.
schiaccianoci m. nutcrackers.
schiacciante adj. overwhelming.
schiacciapatate m. ricer.
schiacciare vt. to crush; to overwhelm.
schiaffeggiare vt. to slap.
schiaffo m. slap, smack; insult.
schiamazzare vi. to squawk; to clamor.
schiamazzo m. noise, hubbub; squawking.
schiantare vt. to break, fell; **schiantarsi** vr. to break; to burst: **schiantarsi dalle risa,** to split one's sides with laughter.

schianto m. crash, clap; pang: **di —,** suddenly; crash.

Schiaparelli, Giovanni Virginio, Italian astronomer (1835-1910).

schiappa f. splinter; (fig.) bungler.

schiarimento m. elucidation.

schiarire vt. to make clear; to lighten (as a shade); **schiarirsi** vr. to clear; to brighten; to fade, become lighter: **schiarirsi la voce,** to clear one's throat.

schiatta f. race, breed, issue.

schiattare vi. to burst (with).

schiavista m. slave trader: **Stati schiavisti,** slave states.

schiavitù f. slavery; bondage.

schiavo m., **schiava** f. slave.

schidionata f. spitful; spadeful.

schidione m. spit, broach.

schiena f. back.

schienale m. back.

schiera f. line, group; crowd; (mil.) rank.

schieramento m. drawing up; ranks; cordon.

schierare vt., **schierarsi** vr. to draw up; to side (with).

schietto adj. frank, straightforward; genuine; undiluted; adv. frankly.

schifare vt. to despise; to loathe; **schifarsi** vr. to be averse (to).

schifato adj. disgusted.

schifezza f. horror; shame.

schifiltoso adj. fastidious.

schifo (1) m. disgust; shame: **fare —,** to be disgusting; to make sick.

schifo (2) m. (naut.) skiff.

schifosità f. loathsomeness; horror.

schifoso adj. disgusting; filthy.

schioccare vt. to snap (one's fingers); to crack (a whip); to smack (one's lips).

schiocco m. snap; crack; smack. see schioccare.

schiodare vt. to unnail.

schioppettata f. shot, gunshot.

schioppo m. gun, shotgun.

Schipa, Tito, Italian tenor (1890-).

schiu'dere vt.[25] to open; **schiudersi** vr. to open; to part; (bot.) to expand.

schiuma f. froth, foam; (metal.) dross; scum; (min.) meerschaum: **pipa di —,** meerschaum; **aver la — alla bocca,** to foam at the mouth.

schiumare vt. to scum; vi. to foam, froth.

schiuso adj. open. pp.of schiudere.

schivare vt., vi. to avoid, shun.

schivo m. bashful, shy.

schizzare vt. to splash; to bespatter; to sketch; vi. to gush, squirt: **— via,** to dart away; **— faville,** to spark; **— veleno,** to vent one's spite.

schizzetto m. syringe; squirt.

schizzinoso adj. squeamish; fastidious.

schizzo m. splash; squirt, jet; sketch.

sci m. ski.

sci'a f. wake; track.

scia'bola f. saber.

sciacallo m. jackal.

sciacquare vt. to rinse; **sciacquarsi** to rinse oneself: **— la bocca,** to rinse one's mouth, (fig.) to get (it) off one's chest.

sciacquatura f. rinsing.

sciacqui'o m. splash.

sciagura f. disaster; misfortune.

sciagurato m. wretch; adj. unlucky; unfortunate; wretched.

scialacquare vt. to squander.

scialare vi. to squander.

scialbo adj. pale, wan; dim.

scialle m. shawl.

scialo m. show; waste; lavishness.

scialuppa f. launch.

sciamannato adj. slovenly.

sciamare vi. to swarm.

sciame m. swarm; host.

sciampagna m. champagne.

sciancato m., adj. crippled, lame.

sciarada f. charade.

sciare vi. to ski.

sciarpa f. scarf; (mil.) sash.

sciatore m., **sciatrice** f. skier.

sciatteri'a f. slovenliness; inelegance.

sciatto adj. slovenly; unpolished.

sci'bile m. knowledge.

scientemente adv. knowingly.

scienti'fico adj. scientific.

scienza f. science; knowledge.

scienziato m. scientist.

scilingua'gnolo m. (anat.) frenum of the tongue: **aver lo — sciolto,** to have a glib tongue; **perdere lo —,** to dry up.

scim'mia f. ape, monkey.

scimmiesco adj. monkeyish, apish.

scimmiottare vt. to mimic, ape.

scimpanzè m. chimpanzee.

scimunito m. dolt.

scin'dere vt.[121] to separate.

scintilla f. sparkle, spark.

scintillante adj. sparkling.

scintillare vi. to sparkle.

scintilli'o m. sparkling.

sciocchezza f. silliness, foolishness, nonsense; mistake, folly.

sciocco m. fool, dolt; adj. silly.

scio'gliere vt.[144] to dissolve; to untie; to undo; to loosen; to free, release; to resolve, solve; to melt; to dilute; to disband; to break up: **— un voto,** to fulfill a vow; **— le vele,** to unfurl the sails; **sciogliersi** vr. to dissolve; to untie oneself; to get loose; to release oneself; to melt; to be disbanded; to break up.

scioglilin'gua *m.* tongue twister.
scioglimento *m.* dissolution; end, issue.
sci'oli'na *f.* ski wax.
sciolta *f.* diarrhea.
scioltezza *f.* nimbleness; ease; fluency.
sciolto *adj.* untied; loose; free; easy. *pp.of* sciogliere.
scioperante *m.* striker.
scioperare *vi.* to strike, be on strike.
scioperato *m.* loafer; *adj.* lazy.
scio'pero *m.* strike: fare —, to strike; in —, on strike.
sciorinare *vt.* to display.
sciovinismo *m.* chauvinism.
sciovinista *m.* chauvinist.
scipito *adj.* dull, insipid.
scirocco *m.* southeast wind, sirocco.
sciroppo *m.* syrup, sirup.
scisma *m.* schism.
scisma'tico *adj.* schismatic.
scissione *f.* scission; split.
scisso *adj.* parted, split; separated. *pp.of* scindere.
sciupare *vt.* to spoil; to damage; to squander; to waste.
sciupato *adj.* spoiled; run down.
sciupi'o *m.* waste, wastage.
sciupone *m.* waster; squanderer.
scivolare *vi.* to slip; to slide, glide: — d'ala, to sideslip; — di coda, to skid.
scivolata *f.* slide.
scivolone *m.* slip.
scoccare *vt.*, *vi.* to shoot, dart; to strike (*as hours*): — un bacio, to throw a kiss.
scocciante *adj.* (*fam.*) boring.
scocciare *vi.* to break; (*fam.*) to bore, bother.
scocciatore *m.* (*fam.*) bore.
scocciatura *f.* (*fam.*) nuisance.
scodella *f.* porringer, bowl.
scodellare *vt.* to dish up.
scodinzolare *vi.* to wag the tail.
scogliera *f.* cliffs; reef.
sco'glio *m.* rock; (*fig.*) facer, stumbling block.
scoiat'tolo *m.* squirrel.
scolara *f.* schoolgirl, pupil.
scolare *vt.*, *vi.* to drain, drip.
scolaresca *f.* schoolchildren.
scolaro *m.* schoolboy, pupil.
scola'stico *adj.* scholastic; educational.
scolato'io *m.* drain; drainer.
scolatura *f.* draining; dripping; dregs.
scollacciato *adj.* (*fig.*) licentious; risqué.
scollare (1) *vt.* to unglue; scollarsi *vr.* to come off.
scollare (2) *vt.* to trim off at the neck.
scollato *adj.* décolletté; unglued.
scollatura *f.* neckhole.

scollo *see* scollatura.
scolo *m.* drainage; drip, dripping; (*pathol.*) gonorrhea.
scolopendra *f.* centipede.
scolorare *vt.* to discolor.
scolorire *vi.*, scolorirsi *vr.* to lose color; to grow pale.
scolpare *vt.* to exculpate; scolparsi *vr.* to exculpate oneself; to apologize.
scolpire *vt.*[122] to sculpture; to engrave; (*fig.*) to impress.
scolpito *pp.of* scolpire.
scolta *f.* sentry, watch.
scombussolare *vt.* to upset.
scommessa *f.* wager, bet; stake.
scommesso *pp.of* scommettere.
scommet'tere (1) *vt.*[76] to wager, bet.
scommet'tere (2) *vt.*[76] to disconnect, disjoin.
scommettitore *m.* bettor.
scomodare *vt.* to disturb, trouble, inconvenience; scomodarsi *vr.* to trouble (*oneself*); to take (the) trouble.
scomodità *f.* uncomfortableness, inconvenience.
sco'modo *adj.* uncomfortable, inconvenient.
scompaginare *vt.* to upset, disarrange; (*typog.*) to break up.
scomparire *vi.*[9] to disappear.
scomparsa *f.* disappearance; death.
scomparso *adj.* disappeared, vanished; missing; deceased. *pp.of* scomparire.
scompigliare *vt.* to upset; to tangle; to tousle.
scompi'glio *m.* confusion; disorder; bustle, fuss; hurly-burly.
scompisciarsi *vr.*: — dalle risa, to split one's sides with laughter.
scomporre *vt.*[93] to decompose, disintegrate; (*fig.*) to discompose, ruffle; (*math.*) to resolve; scomporsi *vr.* to be discomposed.
scomposto *adj.* uncomely, unseemly. *pp.of* scomporre.
scomu'nica *f.* excommunication.
scomunicare *vt.* to excommunicate.
scomunicato *m.*, *adj.* excommunicate.
sconcertante *adj.* disconcerting.
sconcertare *vt.* to disconcert, upset, trouble, baffle.
sconcerto *m.* disconcertion.
sconcezza *f.* obscenity.
scon'cio *m.* shame; *adj.* obscene, indecent; filthy, nasty.
sconclusionato *adj.* rambling.
sconcordanza *f.* disagreement.
scondito *adj.* unflavored.
sconfessare *vt.* to disavow.
sconfig'gere *vt.*[63] to defeat.
sconfinamento *m.* trespass.

sconfinare vi. to trespass (on).
sconfinato adj. unlimited.
sconfitta f. defeat.
sconfitto adj. beaten, defeated. pp.of sconfiggere.
sconfortante adj. distressing.
sconfortare vt. to distress.
sconforto m. dejection, distress.
scongiurare vt. to implore; to avoid.
scongiuro m. exorcism: fare gli scongiuri, to touch wood.
sconnesso adj. disconnected. pp.of sconnettere.
sconnet'tere vt.[8] to disconnect.
sconosciuto m. stranger; adj. unknown; obscure.
sconquassare vt. to shatter, smash.
sconquasso m. smash.
sconsacrare vt. to desecrate.
sconsideratezza f. inconsiderateness; thoughtlessness; rashness.
sconsiderato adj. inconsiderate; thoughtless; rash.
sconsiglia'bile adj. inadvisable.
sconsigliare vt. to discourage (from), dissuade (from).
sconsigliato adj. unadvised, rash.
sconsolato adj. disconsolate, sad.
scontare vt. (comm.) to discount; to atone (for); to serve (as a term of imprisonment).
scontato adj. atoned for; served; foregone; (fin.) discounted.
scontentare vt. to discontent.
scontento m., adj. discontent.
scontista m. discounter.
sconto m. discount; reduction; allowance.
scontrarsi vr. to meet (with); to come to blows; to collide.
scontrino m. check, ticket; receipt.
scontro m. collision; (mil.) engagement.
scontroso adj. morose, pouty.
sconveniente adj. unbecoming, unseemly; indecent.
sconvenienza f. unbecomingness, unseemliness; indecency.
sconvol'gere vt.[186] to upset.
sconvolgimento m. upsetting.
sconvolto adj. upset. pp.of sconvolgere.
scopa f. broom.
scopare vt. to sweep.
scoperchiare vt. to uncover.
scoperta f. discovery.
scoperto adj. uncovered; open; bare; unsheltered; (account.) overdrawn, unpaid: allo ——, in the open; a carte scoperte, openly. pp. of scoprire.
scopo m. aim, purpose, object; use.
scoppiare vi. to burst, explode; to break out: —— in lagrime, to burst

into tears; —— in riso, to burst out laughing.
scoppiettare vi. to crackle.
scoppietti'o m. crackling.
scop'pio m. burst, bursting, explosion; outbreak.
scop'pola f. blow.
scoprimento m. uncovering; detecting, finding out.
scoprire vt.[35] to uncover; to strip; to unlid, lay open; to unveil; to reveal; to discover, find out: —— gli altarini, to let the cat out of the bag; scoprirsi vr. to uncover; to denude oneself; to take off one's hat; to reveal oneself; to discover oneself.
scopritore m. discoverer.
scoraggiamento m. depression.
scoraggiante adj. discouraging.
scoraggiare vt. to discourage; scoraggiarsi vr. to be (to get) discouraged.
scoramento m. discouragement.
scorbu'tico m., adj. scorbutic.
scorbuto m. scurvy.
scorciatoia f. short cut.
scorcio m. foreshortening, perspective; close.
scordare (1) vt., scordarsi vr. to forget.
scordare (2) vt. (mus.) to put out of tune, untune.
scordato adj. out of tune, untuned.
scoreggia f. (vulg.) breaking of wind.
scoreggiare vi. (vulg.) to break wind.
scor'gere vt.[123] to perceive; to descry; to discern.
sco'ria f. slag, scum, dross.
scornato adj. crestfallen.
scorno m. shame, disgrace.
scorpacciata f. bellyful.
scorpione m. scorpion.
scorrazzare vi. to ramble; to ride about.
scor'rere vt.[36] to scour; to run over; vi. to run; to flow; to go by; to glide; to run smoothly.
scorreria f. incursion, raid.
scorrettezza f. incorrectness; impropriety; (sport) foul play.
scorretto adj. incorrect; improper.
scorrevole adj. smooth-running; fluent; sliding.
scorrevolezza f. smoothness; fluency.
scorribanda f. incursion, raid.
scorsa f. glance.
scorso adj. last, past.
scorso'io, (nodo) m. running knot.
scorta f. convoy; provision; escort; chaperon.
scortare vt. to convoy; to escort; to chaperon.
scortecciare vt. to strip off bark.
scortese adj. impolite, unkind, rude.
scortesi'a f. impoliteness; rudeness.

scorticare vt. to skin; to fleece.
scorticatura f. excoriation, scratch.
scorto pp.of **scorgere**.
scorza f. bark; rind; outside.
scosceso adj. steep; sloping.
scossa f. shake; shock; jerk: — tel-lurica, tremor; — elettrica, electric shock.
scosso pp.of **scuotere**.
scossone m. jolt.
scostare vt. to thrust aside, remove; **scostarsi** vr. to step aside; to get off the way; to draw away.
scostumato adj. licentious.
scotennare vt. to scalp.
scotta f. (naut.) sheet.
scottante adj. scalding, burning; sore.
scottare vt., vi. to burn, scald; to sting; **scottarsi** vr. to burn oneself.
scottata, scottatura f. scald, burn.
scotto (1) m. bill, score.
scotto (2) adj. overdone, overcooked.
scovare vt. to run to earth; to find, fish out, unearth.
sco'volo m. (artil.) swab.
scozzese m. Scotsman, Scotswoman; adj. Scots, Scottish.
scozzonare vt. to break in.
scranna f. chair, seat.
screanzato m. boor; adj. unmannerly.
screditare vt. to discredit.
scre'dito m. discredit, disgrace.
scremare vi. to skim.
screpolare vi., **screpolarsi** vr. to crack, chap.
screpolatura f. crack, chap.
screziare vt. to variegate, marble.
screziato adj. variegated, marbled.
scre'zio m. tiff.
scribacchiare vt. to scribble, scrawl.
scribacchino m. scribbler.
scricchiolare vi. to creak.
scricchioli'o m. creaking.
scrigno m. jewel case.
scriminatura f. parting (of the hair).
scritta f. inscription; notice.
scritto m. writing; adj. written. pp.of **scrivere**.
scritto'io m. writing desk.
scrittore m. writer, author.
scrittura f. writing; handwriting; deed; entry; (theat.) engagement, contract.
scritturale m. clerk, copyist.
scritturare vt. (theat.) to engage.
scrivani'a f. desk, table.
scrivano m. clerk.
scrivente m. writer.
scri'vere vt.[134] to write, write down.
scroccare vt. to sponge.
scrocco m. sponging.
scroccone m. sponger.
scrofa f. sow.
scrollare vt. to shake.

scrollata f. shake: — di spalle, shrug.
scrosciante adj. pelting; thunderous (as applause).
scrosciare vi. to shower, pelt; to thunder (as applause).
scro'scio m. shower; burst; clap.
scrostare vt. to scratch, rub off, peel; **scrostarsi** vr. to peel.
scroto m. scrotum.
scru'polo m. scruple; painstaking.
scrupoloso adj. scrupulous.
scrutare vt. to scan, search (into).
scrutatore m. investigator; scrutineer; adj. inquisitive.
scruti'nio m. scrutiny.
scucire vt. to seamrend, unseam; **scucirsi** vr. to rip.
scucitura f. seam-rent.
scuderi'a f. stable.
scudetto m. badge.
scudiere, scudiero m. esquire; groom.
scudisciare vt. to lash.
scudisciata f. lash.
scudi'scio m. lash, whip.
scudo m. shield; escutcheon; far da — a, to shield.
scugnizzo m. Neapolitan urchin.
sculacciare vt. to spank.
sculacciata f., **sculaccione** m. spank.
scultore m. sculptor.
scultrice f. sculptress.
scultura f. sculpture.
scuoiare vt. to skin.
scuola f. school: i problemi della —, educational problems.
scuo'tere vt.[125] to shake; to rouse; to toss, jerk about; **scuo'tersi** vr. to rouse.
scure f. ax, hatchet.
scuriosare see **curiosare**.
scurire vt. to darken.; **scurirsi** vr. to grow dark, darken.
scuro m. dark; shutter; adj. dark, dim; obscure; swarthy.
scurrile adj. scurrilous.
scusa f. excuse; apology; pretext: chiedere —, to apologize.
scusante f. excuse; extenuation.
scusare vt. to excuse; to forgive, par-don; to justify; **scusarsi** vr. to apologize (for); to justify oneself (for).
sdaziare vt. to clear.
sdebitarsi see **disobbligarsi**.
sdegnare vt. to disdain, scorn; to abhor; **sdegnarsi** vr. to be outraged.
sdegnato adj. outraged.
sdegno m. indignation; disdain.
sdegnoso adj. disdainful, scornful; haughty.
sdentato adj. toothless.
sdilinquire vt. to weaken, enervate; **sdilinquirsi** vr. to soften; to go mawkish.

sdoganare *vt.* to clear (*at customs*).

sdolcinato *adj.* mawkish; affected.

sdoppiare *vt.* to undouble; to split.

sdraiare *vt.*, **sdraiarsi** *vr.* to stretch out.

sdra'io, (sedia a) *f.* chaise longue, deck chair.

sdrucciolare *vi.* to slip, slide.

sdrucciole'vole *adj.* slippery.

sdruc'ciolo *m.* slide; *adj.* (*gramm.*) proparoxytonal.

sdrucciolone *m.* slipping.

sdrucire *vt.* to seamrend, rip; **sdrucirsi** *vr.* to rip.

sdrucito *adj.* ripped; threadbare.

sdrucitura *f.* rent, rip.

se *m.* if; *conj.* if; whether; provided; in case, providing: — **pure, anche** —, even if, even though; — **non altro**, at least; — **non che**, but (it so happens that); — **mai**, if at all; in case; if by any chance.

sè *pron.refl.* oneself; himself, herself, itself; themselves: **fare da** —, to do by oneself; **fuori di** —, beyond oneself; **ritornare in** —, to come to one's senses; **fra** — **e** —, within oneself; — **stesso**, — **medesimo**, oneself.

sebbene *conj.* though, although.

sebo *m.* sebum, tallow, grease.

secca *f.* sandbank.

seccamente *adv.* dryly.

seccante *adj.* boring; annoying.

seccare *vt.*, *vi.* to dry (*up*); to bore, annoy; to bother; **seccarsi** *vr.* to dry (*up*); to be annoyed.

seccatore *m.* bore, nuisance.

seccatura *f.* nuisance, trouble.

secchia *f.* pail, bucket.

secco *adj.* dry; lean; hard; sharp; *adv.* dryly, curtly.

secer'nere *vt.* to secrete.

seco *pron.* with him; with her; with them; with oneself.

secolare *adj.* secular; centuried.

se'colo *m.* century; age.

seconda, (a) *adv.* favorably: — **di**, according to

secondare *vt.* to second.

seconda'rio *adj.* secondary.

secondino *m.* warder.

secondo *m.* second; (*naut.*) second mate; *adj.* second; *prep.*, *adv.* according to, in accordance with, in compliance with; after: — **me**, in my opinion; **verrai? Secondo!** are you coming? It depends!

secondoge'nito *m.*, *adj.* second-born.

secrezione *f.* secretion.

se'dano *m.* celery.

sedare *vt.* to calm, appease.

sedativo *m.*, *adj.* sedative.

sede *f.* residence; (*eccl.*) see.

sedentario *adj.* sedentary.

sedere (1) *vt.*[126] **sedersi** *vr.* to sit (*down*); to take one's seat; to be situated; to be sitting.

sedere (2) *m.* backside, rump.

se'dia *f.* chair.

sedicenne *adj.* sixteen years old.

sedicente *adj.* pretended, alleged, self-proclaimed.

sedice'simo *m.*, *adj.* sixteenth.

se'dici *m.*, *adj.* sixteen.

sedile *m.* seat, bench.

sedimento *m.* sediment; dregs.

sedizione *f.* sedition.

sedizioso *adj.* seditious, turbulent.

sedotto *pp.of* **sedurre**, alluring.

seducente *adj.* seducing, alluring.

sedurre *vt.*[a] to seduce; to charm.

seduta *f.* sitting, session; meeting: — **stante**, right away, on the spot.

seduto *adj.* sitting. *pp.of* **sedere**

seduttore *m.*, **seduttrice** *f.* seducer.

seduzione *f.* seduction, charm.

sega *f.* saw.

se'gala, se'gale *f.* rye.

segaligno *adj.* (*fig.*) wiry.

Segantini, Giovanni, Italian painter (1858–1899).

segare *vt.* to saw; to mow.

segatura *f.* sawing; sawdust.

seg'gio *m.* seat; chair; see.

seg'giola *see* **sedia**.

seggiovi'a *f.* chair lift.

segheri'a *f.* sawmill.

seghettato *adj.* serrate; toothed.

segmento *m.* segment.

segna'colo *m.* mark, sign.

segnalare *vt.* to signal; to indicate; to point out; **segnalarsi** *vr.* to distinguish oneself.

segnalato *adj.* distinguished; great.

segnalazione *f.* s gna'ing; indication: — **stradale**, traffic signal.

segnale *m.* signal; sign; call: — **d'allarme**, alert, warning signal.

segnale'tico *adj.* anthropometric.

segnalibro *m.* bookmark.

segnali'nee *m.* (*sport*) linesman.

segnare *vt.* to mark; to note, jot down; to record; to sign; to indicate; to point out; to score.

segnatasse *m.* postage-due stamp.

segno *m.* sign, mark; token; trace; track; vestige; symptom; limit, boundary; target; aim; **per filo e per** —, in detail.

sego *m.* tallow.

segregare *vt.* to segregate.

segregazione *f.* segregation; seclusion.

segretamente *adv.* secretly.

segreta'rio *m.*, **segreta'ria** *f.* secretary.

segreteri'a *f.* secretary's office.

segretezza *f.* secrecy.

segreto *m.* secret; secrecy; *adj.* secret; hidden; reticent.

seguace *m.* follower; disciple.

seguente *adj.* following, next.

segu'gio *m.* bloodhound; private detective.

seguire *vt.*, *vi.* to follow; to continue, go on; to shadow; to comply with.

seguitare *see* continuare.

se'guito *m.* continuation; sequel; following; succession; retinue: di —, without interruption; in —, afterwards, later on; in — a, following, as a result of.

sei *m.*, *adj.* six.

selce *f.* flint stone.

selciato *m.* pavement.

selettivo *adj.* selective.

selettività *f.* selectivity.

selezionare *vt.* to select, sort out.

selezione *f.* selection, choice; digest.

sella *f.* saddle.

sella'io *m.* saddler.

sellare *vt.* to saddle.

seltz *m.* seltzer.

selva *f.* forest, wood.

selvaggina *f.* game.

selvag'gio *m.*, *adj.* savage.

selva'tico *adj.* wild; untamed.

sema'foro *m.* semaphore; traffic lights.

sembiante *m.*, **sembianza** *f.* look, aspect.

sembrare *see* parere (I).

seme *m.* germ, seed; source.

semente *f.* seed.

semenza *f.* seed, seeds; origin.

semenza'io *m.* seedbed; hotbed.

semestrale *adj.* half-yearly, semi-annual.

semestre *m.* half year; semester.

semiaperto *adj.* half-open.

semi'as'se *m.* (*mach.*) axle shaft.

semicer'chio *m.* semicircle.

semichiuso *adj.* half-closed.

semicu'pio *m.* sitz bath.

semidi'o *m.* demigod.

se'mina, seminagione *f.* sowing.

seminare *vt.* to sow; to scatter.

semina'rio *m.* seminary.

seminarista *m.* seminarist.

seminato *m.*: uscire dal —, to digress.

seminatore *m.* sower.

seminatrice *f.* sower; seeding machine.

seminterrato *m.* basement.

seminudo *adj.* half-naked.

semioscurità *f.* half-darkness.

semiri'gido *adj.* semiflexible; semirig-id.

semise'rio *adj.* serio-comic.

semisfera *f.* hemisphere.

semivivo *adj.* half-dead.

se'mola *f.* bran; freckles.

semovente *adj.* self-propelled.

sempiterno *adj.* everlasting.

sem'plice *adj.* simple; easy; plain; unsophisticated; mere; single: soldato —, private, serviceman.

semplicemente *adv.* simply, merely.

sempliciotto *m.* halfwit.

semplicità *f.* simplicity.

semplificare *vt.* to simplify.

sempre *adv.* always; at all times: per —, forever; — più, more and more; — meno, less and less.

sempreché *conj.* provided (that).

sempreverde *m.*, *adj.* evergreen.

se'napa, se'nape *f.* mustard.

senapismo *m.* mustard poultice, mustard plaster.

senato *m.* senate; senate house.

senatore *m.* senator.

senile *adj.* senile.

senilità *f.* senility.

seniore *m.*, *adj.* senior, elder.

senno *m.* wisdom: perdere il —, to go mad; fuor di —, insane; del — di poi son piene le fosse, hindsight is easier than foresight.

sennonché *conj.* but, except that.

seno *m.* bosom; breast; cove.

sensale *m.* broker, middleman.

sensato *adj.* sensible, reasonable.

sensazionale *adj.* sensational; lurid.

sensazione *f.* feeling; sensation.

sensi'bile *adj.* sensitive; considerable; substantial; sensible.

sensibilità *f.* sensibility; sensitiveness; sensitivity.

sensibilmente *adv.* considerably.

sensitivo *adj.* sensitive.

senso *m.* sense; feeling; meaning; way, direction: — pratico, practicalness; buon —, common sense; doppio —, *double-entendre*; strada a — unico, one-way street; — vietato, no thoroughfare; privo di —, meaningless; privo di sensi, unconscious; perdere i sensi, to swoon; riprendere i sensi, to come to.

sensuale *adj.* sensual.

sensualità *f.* sensuality.

sentenza *f.* maxim; sentence; judgment; verdict: sputar sentenze, to dogmatize, pontificate.

sentenziare *vt.*, *vi.* to lay down the law; to rule; to pontificate.

sentenzioso *adj.* sententious.

sentiero *m.* path.

sentimentale *adj.* sentimental; mawkish; "corny."

sentimentalismo *m.* sentimentalism.

sentimento *m.* feeling; sentiment; sense.

sentina *f.* (*naut.*) bilge.

sentinella *f.* sentinel, sentry.

sentire *vt.*, *vi.* to feel; to hear; to learn; to smell of: — parlare di, to hear about; **per sentito dire,** by hearsay; **stare a —,** to listen to; **sentirsi** *vr.* to feel: **sentirsela,** to feel like it.

sentitamente *adv.* heartily, sincerely.

sentito *adj.* heartfelt; hearty, sincere; **per — dire,** by hearsay. *pp.of* sentire.

sentore *m.* feeling; inkling; scent, smell.

senza *prep.* without: **senz'altro,** immediately; (*fig.*) say no more.

senzapa'tria *m.* renegade.

senzatetto *m.* homeless person.

separare *vt.,* **separarsi** *vr.* to separate; to part.

separato *adj.* separate; disjoined.

separazione *f.* separation; parting.

sepolcrale *adj.* sepulchral.

sepolcreto *m.* cemetery.

sepolcro *m.* sepulcher, grave.

sepolto *adj.* buried. *pp.of* seppellire.

sepoltura *f.* burial; grave.

seppellire *vt.*[127] to bury; to hide; **seppellirsi** *vr.* to hide, bury (*oneself*).

sep'pia *f.* (*ichthyol.*) cuttlefish; (*paint.*) sepia: **osso di —,** cuttlebone.

seppure *conj.* even if; supposing that.

sequela *f.* sequence, series.

sequenza *f.* sequence.

sequestrare *vt.* to seize, distrain; to suppress; to seclude.

sequestrata'rio *m.* sequestrator.

sequestro *m.* distraint; suppression: **— di persona,** unlawful detention.

sera *f.* evening; night.

sera'fico *adj.* seraphic.

serafino *m.* seraph.

serale *adj.* evening, nightly.

Serao, Matilde, Italian novelist (1856–1927).

serata *f.* evening; evening performance; evening party, soirée.

serbare *vt.* to preserve, keep: **— rancore a,** to bear a grudge against.

serbato'io *m.* reservoir, tank.

serbo *m.:* **in serbo,** in store.

serenata *f.* serenade.

serenità *f.* serenity.

sereno *m.* serene; *adj.* serene, clear, cloudless.

sergente *m.* sergeant.

seriamente *adv.* earnestly, seriously.

se'rie *f.* series, set, succession; line, row: **di —,** current, standard; **fuori —,** custom built.

serietà *f.* earnestness, seriousness; trustworthiness.

se'rio *adj.* serious, earnest; trustworthy, reliable; grave: **sul —, in** earnest; really.

sermone *m.* sermon; lecture.

serpa *f.* coach box.

serpe *m.,* *f.* serpent, snake.

serpeggiare *vi.* to wind; to creep.

serpente *m.* snake, serpent.

serpentina *f.* coil; serpentine.

serpentino *m.* worm; serpentine.

ser'qua *f.* dozen; lot, lots.

serra *f.* greenhouse, hothouse.

serrafilo *m.* (*elec.*) contact plug screw.

serra'glio *m.* menagerie; seraglio.

serrama'nico, (coltello a) *m.* clasp-knife.

serramenti *m.pl.* window *or* door frames.

serranda *see* saracinesca.

serrare *vt.* to shut, close; to lock (*up*); to tighten; to press: **— i pugni,** to clench one's fists; **— le file,** to close ranks.

serrato *adj.* close; compact; concise.

serratura *f.* lock.

serva *f.* woman servant, maid.

servente *m.,* *f.* servant; (*mil.*) gunner.

servi'bile *adj.* serviceable, useful.

servi'gio *m.* favor, service.

servile *adj.* servile, obsequious.

servilismo *m.* servility, servileness.

servire *vt.* to serve; to help; *vi.* to serve; to be of use, help: **non serve,** it is no use; **servirsi** *vr.* to help oneself: **— da,** to patronize; **servirsi di,** to use; to avail oneself of; to help oneself (*to food, etc.*).

servitore *m.* servant.

servitù *f.* servants; servitude, bondage, slavery.

serviziale *m.* clyster, enema.

servizie'vole *adj.* obliging, helpful.

servi'zio *m.* service; favor; outfit, set: **mezzo —,** part-time service; **donna a mezzo —,** part-timer; **in —,** on duty; **fuori —,** off duty.

servo *m.* manservant, valet; slave.

servofreno *m.* brake booster.

servomotore *m.* servomotor.

sessanta *m.,* *adj.* sixty.

sessante'simo *m.,* *adj.* sixtieth.

sessantina *f.* some sixty.

sessione *f.* session.

sesso *m.* sex: **il — debole, il gentil —,** the fair sex.

sessuale *adj.* sexual.

sestante *m.* sextant.

sesto *m.,* *adj.* sixth.

se'stuplo *m.,* *adj.* sextuple.

seta *f.* silk.

setacciare *see* stacciare.

setac'cio *m.* sieve, crib.

setaiuolo *m.* silk merchant.

sete *f.* thirst; craving; longing: **aver —,** to be thirsty; **aver — di,** to thirst for.

seteri'a *f.* silk goods; silk factory.

setifi'cio *m.* silk factory, silk mill.

se'tola *f.* hair; bristle.

setta f. sect; faction.

settanta m., adj. seventy.

settante'simo m., adj. seventieth.

settantina f. some seventy.

setta'rio m., adj. sectarian.

sette m., adj. seven.

settembre m. September.

settentrionale m. northerner; adj. north, northern.

settentrione m. north.

setticemi'a f. septicemia.

settice'mico adj. septicemic.

set'tico m., adj. septic.

settimana f. week; weekly wages.

settimanale m., adj. weekly.

settimino m. seven month's child.

set'timo m., adj. seventh.

settore m. sector; branch; department.

severamente adv. sternly, harshly.

severità f. sternness, strictness.

severo adj. strict, stern.

sevi'zia f. cruelty.

seviziare vt. to torture.

seviziatore m., **seviziatrice** f. torturer.

sezionare vt. to cut up, dissect.

sezione f. section; department.

sfaccendato m. idler, loafer.

sfaccettatura f. faceting.

sfacchinare vi. to drudge.

sfacchinata f. tour de force; grind.

sfacciatag'gine f. impudence, "brass."

sfacciato adj. impudent; shameless.

sfacelo m. breakdown, collapse, ruin.

sfacimento m. ruin, decay.

sfaldare vt. to scale, flake off; **sfaldarsi** vr. to foliate; to scale off, flake off.

sfamare vt. to satiate; **sfamarsi** vr. to appease one's hunger.

sfare vt. to undo; to melt; **sfarsi** vr. to become undone; to melt; to decay.

sfarzo m. display; pomp; luxury.

sfarzosità f. gorgeousness.

sfarzoso adj. gorgeous; dazzling.

sfasare vt., vi. to throw; to go out of phase.

sfasciamento m. collapse, smashing.

sfasciare (1) vt. to unswathe; to unbandage.

sfasciare (2) vt. to smash; **sfasciarsi** vr. to smash, collapse.

sfatare vt. to explode, discredit.

sfaticato m. idler; bum; adj. lazy.

sfavillante adj. sparkling, glittering.

sfavillare vi. to glitter, sparkle.

sfavore m. disfavor.

sfavore'vole adj. unfavorable; averse.

sfebbrato adj. recovered from a fever.

sfegatato adj. passionate.

sfera f. sphere; hand (of a clock, etc.); globe; (mach.) ball.

sferico adj. spherical.

sferrare vt. to unshoe (as a horse); to deliver (as a blow).

sferruzzare vi. to knit away.

sferza f. scourge, lash, whip.

sferzare vt. to scourge, whip, lash.

sferzata f. lash.

sfiancare vt. to wear out, overwork; **sfiancarsi** vr. to tire, overwork oneself.

sfiatarsi vr. to talk oneself hoarse.

sfiatato adj. out of breath; worn out.

sfiatato'io m. vent.

sfibbiare vt. to unfasten.

sfibrare vt. to unfiber; to enervate.

sfida f. challenge.

sfidante m. challenger; adj. challenging.

sfidare vt. to challenge, dare; to brave.

sfidu'cia f. mistrust; pessimism: **voto di —**, vote of no confidence.

sfiduciato adj. disheartened.

sfigurare vt. to disfigure; vi. to cut a poor figure.

sfigurato adj. disfigured.

sfilacciare vt. to ravel; **sfilacciarsi** vr. to fray.

sfilacciato adj. frayed.

sfilacciatura f. fray; fraying.

sfilare vt. to unthread; to unstring (as pearls); vi. to defile, file off; **sfilarsi** vr. to get unthreaded, unstrung; to take off (as a garment).

sfilata f. parade, defiling: **— di modelli**, fashion parade.

sfinge f. sphinx.

sfinimento m. exhaustion.

sfinire vt. to wear out, exhaust.

sfinito adj. exhausted, worn out.

sfintere m. sphincter.

sfiorare vt. to graze; to touch lightly on; to skim.

sfiorire vi. to fade; to wither.

sfitto adj. untenanted.

sfocare vt. (photo.) to soft-focus.

sfocato adj. blurred.

sfociare vi. to debouch (into).

sfoderare vt. to unline; to unsheathe; to draw; to display.

sfogare vt. to vent, give vent to: **— la collera su**, to take it out on; **sfogarsi** vr. to vent oneself; to unbosom oneself.

sfogato'io m. vent, outlet.

sfoggiare vt. to flaunt, display.

sfog'gio m. display, show, parade.

sfo'glia f. foil; puff paste; paste; sole.

sfogliare vt. to unleaf, pluck; to leaf through (a book); to exfoliate; **sfogliarsi** vr. to shed leaves, petals; to exfoliate.

sfogliata f. puff paste.

sfogo m. vent; outburst; outlet; (med.) eruption, rash.

sfolgorante adj. blazing.

sfolgorare *vi.* to blaze.

sfolgori'o *m.* blazing.

sfollagente *m.* truncheon, club.

sfollamento *m.* evacuation.

sfollare *vt.*, *vi.* to evacuate.

sfondamento *m.* unbottoming; breaking through.

sfondare *vt.* to unbottom, stave in; to break, smash; to break through.

sfondato *adj.* bottomless; smashed: **ricco —**, rolling in riches.

sfondo *m.* background.

sfondone *m.* blunder.

sforacchiare *vt.* to riddle.

sforbiciare *vt.* to scissor.

sfòrmare *vt.* to deform, pull out of shape; **sformarsi** *vr.* to lose one's shape.

sformato *adj.* shapeless.

sfornare *vt.* to take out of the oven.

sfornire *vt.* to deprive.

sfornito *adj.* destitute; unprovided, out of; lacking.

sfortuna *f.* ill *or* bad luck; misfortune.

sfortunatamente *adv.* unluckily; unfortunately.

sfortunato *adj.* unfortunate; unlucky; unhappy.

Sforza, Carlo, Italian statesman (1872–1952).

Sforza, Francesco, Duke of Milan, Italian warrior (1401–1466).

Sforza, Muzio Attendolo, Italian condottiere (1369–1424).

Sforza, Ludovico (*Ludovico il Moro*), Duke of Milan (1451–1508).

sforzare *vt.* to strain, urge, force; **sforzarsi** *vr.* to endeavor, strive.

sforzato *adj.* forced.

sforzo *m.* effort; exertion.

sfracassare *see* fracassare.

sfracellare *vt.* to smash, shatter; **sfracellarsi** *vr.* to get smashed.

sfrangiare *vt.* to ravel.

sfrangiatura *f.* raveling.

sfrattare *vt.* to evict; to give notice to.

sfratto *m.* notice to quit, eviction.

sfrecciare *vi.* to speed, dart, whizz.

sfregamento *m.* rubbing.

sfregare *vt.* to rub.

sfregiare *vt.* to disfigure; to slash.

sfregiato *m.* scarface; *adj.* scarfaced; disfigured.

sfre'gio *m.* gash; scar; slash; (*fig.*) disgrace, affront.

sfrenato *adj.* unrestrained.

sfrondare *vt.* to trim (*off*); to lop.

sfrontatezza *f.* effrontery, cheek.

sfrontato *adj.* impudent, brazen.

sfruttamento *m.* exploitation.

sfruttare *vt.* to exploit; to sponge on; to take advantage of.

sfruttatore *m.* exploiter; sponge, parasite: **— di donne**, gigolo.

sfuggire *vt.* to avoid; to shun; *vi.* to escape; to slip away (*from*); to elude; to evade: **mi sfugge il suo nome**, I can't recall his name; **lasciarsi — un'occasione**, to miss an opportunity.

sfuggita, (di, alla) *loc.adv.* in passing, cursorily; hastily; stealthily: **vedere di —**, to catch a glimpse of.

sfumare *vi.* to vanish, evaporate.

sfumato *adj.* lost, evaporated; shaded.

sfumatura *f.* shade, nuance.

sfumino *m.* stump.

sfuriata *f.* outburst; scolding.

sgabello *m.* stool.

sgabuzzino *m.* closet.

Sgambati, Giovanni, Italian composer (1841–1914).

sgambettare *vi.* to toddle; to kick; to frisk about.

sgambetto *m.* trip; jump; caper.

sganasciarsi *vr.*: **— dalle risa**, to laugh oneself silly.

sganciare *vt.* to unhook.

sgangherare *vt.* to unhinge.

sgangheratamente *adv.* immoderately, rudely.

sgangherato *adj.* unhinged; (*fig.*) immoderate, rude.

sgarbato *adj.* unmannerly, rude.

sgarbo *m.*, **sgarberi'a** *f.* rudeness, affront.

sgargiante *adj.* gaudy, flashy, showy.

sgarrare *vi.* to go wrong.

sgattaiolare *vi.* to slip away.

sgavazzare *vi.* to debauch.

sgelare *vt.*, *vi.* to thaw, melt.

sgelo *m.* thaw.

sghembo *m.* slant; *adj.* slanting, aslant.

sgherro *m.* bravo.

sghignazzare *vi.* to guffaw.

sghignazzata *f.* guffaw.

sghimbe'scio : **di —**, awry, askew.

sghiribizzo *m.* freak, whim.

sgobbare *vt.* to work hard, drudge.

sgobbone *m.* fag.

sgocciolare *vi.* to drip, trickle.

sgocciolatura *f.* drip.

sgoc'ciolo *m.* dripping: **essere agli sgoccioli**, to be at an end.

sgolarsi *vr.* to shout oneself hoarse.

sgomberare, **sgombrare** *vt.* to clear out *or* up; to quit; *vi.* to clear out; to move.

sgom'bero, **sgombro** *m.* clearance; moving; *adj.* clear (*from*), free (*from*); empty.

sgombro *m.* mackerel.

sgomentare *vt.* to dismay; **sgomentarsi** *vr.* to become dismayed; to l ose courage.

sgomento *m.* dismay; *adj.* dismayed.

sgominare *vt.* to rout, overthrow.

sgonfiare vt. to deflate; **sgonfiarsi** vr. to get, become deflated.

sgon'fio adj. deflated, flat.

sgor'bia f. gouge.

sgor'bio m. scrawl, stain, daub.

sgorgare vi. to gush, spurt.

sgozzare vt. to slaughter; to cut the throat of.

sgrade'vole adj. disagreeable, unpleasant.

sgradire vt. to dislike.

sgradito adj. unwelcome.

sgraffignare vt. to steal, pilfer.

sgrammaticato adj. ungrammatical.

sgranare vt. to shell; to husk, hull: — il rosario, to tell one's beads; — gli occhi, to stare, open one's eyes.

sgranchire vt., **sgranchirsi** vr. to stretch (one's limbs).

sgranocchiare vt. to crunch.

sgrassare vt. to degrease.

sgravare vt. to lighten, relieve; **sgravarsi** vr. to relieve oneself; to give birth (to).

sgra'vio m. lightening; relief.

sgraziato adj. gawky, awkward.

sgretolamento m. crumbling.

sgretolare vt., **sgretolarsi** vr. to crumble.

sgridare vt. to scold, reprove.

sgridata f. scolding, reprimand.

sgroppata f. buck.

sguaiatag'gine f. coarseness, vulgarity.

sguaiato adj. coarse, loose, vulgar.

sguainare vt. to unsheathe, draw.

sgualcire vt. to wrinkle, crumple.

sgualdrina f. strumpet.

sguardo m. look, glance.

sguarnire vt. to untrim; to dismantle.

sguat'tera f. scullery maid.

sguat'tero m. scullery boy.

sguazzare vi. to splash, wallow.

sguinzagliare vt. to unleash, let loose.

sgusciare vt. to husk, hull; vi. to slip (away, in, out).

si refl.pron. oneself; himself; herself; itself; themselves. indef.pron. one; people, they: **non — sa mai**, one never knows; **— capisce!** of course!; **— vede che**, it is evident that. recipr. pron. each other, one another.

sì (1) adv. yes: **un giorno — e l altro no**, every other day.

sì (2) adv. see **così**.

sia ... sia conj. whether ... or; both ... and.

sibilante adj. sibilant, hissing.

sibilare vt. to sibilate; to whizz, hiss.

sibilla f. sibyl.

sibillino adj. sibylline.

si'bilo m. hiss, hissing.

sica'rio m. hired assassin.

sicchè conj. so that; so.

siccità f. dryness, drought.

siccome adv., conj. as, since.

sicumera f. self-assurance.

sicura f. safety bolt; safety stop.

sicuramente adv. certainly; safely.

sicurezza f. safety; certainty: **pubblica —**, police; **uscita di —**, emergency exit; **spillo di —**, safety pin.

sicuro (1) m. safety: **al —**, on the safe side, in safety; **andare sul —**, to play safe, to take no chances.

sicuro (2) adj. safe, secure; sure, certain; reliable; bold; firm, steady: **a colpo —**, with no risks; adv. (also **di —**) sure, certainly.

siderurgi'a f. siderurgy.

siderur'gico m. ironman; steelworker; adj. siderurgical.

sidro m. cider.

siepe f. hedge.

siero m. serum; whey.

siesta f. siesta, afternoon nap.

siffatto adj. such.

sifi'lide f. syphilis.

sifone m. siphon.

sigara'ia f. cigar seller; cigarette girl.

sigara'io m. cigar seller; cigarmaker.

sigaretta f. cigarette.

si'garo m. cigar.

sigillare vt. to seal.

sigillo m. seal.

sigla f. monogram, cipher, abbreviation, initials; (radio and telev.) signature, theme.

siglare vt. to initial.

significare vt. to mean; to express, signify.

significativo adj. significant.

significato m. meaning.

signora f. lady; madam; Mrs.; wife.

signore m. gentleman; Sir; Mr.; master; owner; lord: **Nostro Signore**, Our Lord; **fare il —**, to be on Easy Street.

signori'a f. seigniory; domain; Lordship; Ladyship: **la Signoria Vostra**, Your Lordship or Ladyship.

signorile adj. (m.) gentlemanly; (f.) ladylike; lordly; refined; lavish; luxurious.

signorilità f. distinction.

signorina f. young lady; miss.

signorino m. young gentleman; master.

signorotto m. lordling; squire.

silenziatore m. silencer; muffler.

silen'zio m. silence, quiet; (mil.) taps.

silenzioso adj. silent, quiet; noiseless.

sil'fide f. sylph.

si'lice f. silex, flint.

sil'laba f. syllable.

sillaba'rio m. spelling book.

silo'fono m. (mus.) xylophone.

silograf'ia f. xylography.

siluramento m. torpedoing; dismissal, firing.

silurante f. destroyer, torpedo boat.

silurare vt. to torpedo; to cashier, dismiss, fire.

siluro m. torpedo.

silvestre adj. sylvan.

simboleggiare vt., vi. to symbolize.

simbo'lico adj. symbolical.

simbolis'mo m. symbolism.

sim'bolo m. symbol.

similare adj. similar.

similarità f. similarity.

si'mile m. like; fellow creature; adj. like, alike, similar; such.

similitu'dine f. similitude; simile.

similmente adv. likewise.

similoro m. pinchbeck.

simmetri'a f. symmetry.

simme'trico adj. symmetrical.

Simoni, Renato, Italian playwright and critic (1875-1954).

simpamina f. benzedrine.

simpati'a f. liking; favor; sympathy: attirarsi la — di, to make oneself liked by.

simpa'tico adj. nice, pleasant; congenial: inchiostro —, sympathetic ink.

simpatizzante m. sympathizer.

simpatizzare vi. to sympathize (with); to hit it off (with); to become friends.

simpo'sio m. banquet.

simulare vt. to feign, simulate.

simulatore m. simulator; fraud.

simulazione f. simulation.

simulta'neo adj. simultaneous.

sincerarsi vr. to make sure.

sincerità f. sincerity.

sincero adj. sincere; genuine; loyal.

sincronizzare vt., vi. to synchronize, time.

sin'crono adj. synchronous.

sindacale adj. syndical.

sindacalismo m. syndicalism.

sindacalista m., f. syndicalist.

sindacare vt. to criticize; to dispute.

sindacato m. syndicate; (pol.) trade union, labor union.

sin'daco m. mayor; (comm.) auditor.

sinecura f. sinecure, walkover.

sinfoni'a f. symphony.

sinfo'nico adj. symphonic.

singhiozzare vi. to sob.

singhiozzo m. sob; hiccup.

singolare adj. singular; odd, strange; striking; single.

singolarità f. singularity.

sin'golo adj. single.

singulto see singhiozzo.

sinistra f. left, left hand; left wing.

sinistramente adv. sinisterly.

sinistrato m. damage sufferer.

sinistro m. accident, disaster; (boxing) left; adj. left; sinister.

sinistrorso adj. counterclockwise.

sino see fino (a).

sino'nimo m. synonym.

sinora see finora.

sinovite f. synovitis.

sintassi f. syntax.

sin'tesi f. synthesis.

sinte'tico adj. synthetical; concise.

sintetizzare vt. to synthesize.

sin'tomo m. symptom, sign.

sintoni'a f. syntony.

sintonizzare vt. to tune in (on).

sinuoso adj. sinuous, winding.

sipa'rio m. curtain.

sirena f. mermaid; siren, hooter; foghorn; (fam.) vamp.

siringa f. syringe; syringa.

siringare vt. to syringe.

si'smico adj. seismic.

sistema m. system.

sistemare vt. to arrange; to settle; sistemarsi vr. to settle.

sistema'tico adj. systematic.

sistemazione f. arrangement, settlement; situation, employment.

sito m. place, spot; adj. situated.

situare vt. to place.

situazione f. situation; position.

slabbrare vt. to jag; slabbrarsi vr. to become jagged.

slacciare vt. to unlace, undo; to untie; to unfasten; to unbutton; slacciarsi vr. to get untied, loose; to untie; to unbutton.

sladinare vt. (mach.) to run in.

slanciare vt. to throw; to thin out, taper; to streamline; slanciarsi vr. to rush; to venture; to get (more) slender.

slanciato adj. slim, slender.

slan'cio m. rush, impetus; enthusiasm, warmth: prendere lo —, to take the start.

slargare see allargare.

slattare vt. to wean.

slavato adj. wan, colorless.

sleale adj. disloyal, unfair, treacherous.

slealtà f. disloyalty.

slegare vt. to untie, unbind; slegarsi vr. to become untied, to get free.

slegato adj. untied; (fig.) disconnected.

slitta f. sled, sledge, sleigh.

slittare vi. to skid, slip, slide.

slogamento m., slogatura f. dislocation.

slogare vt. to dislocate; slogarsi vr. to become dislocated: slogarsi un braccio, to dislocate one's arm.

sloggiare vt. to dislodge; to oust, eject, remove; vi. to quit, move.

smacchiare vt. to scour, clean.

smacco *m.* affront, shame.

smagliante *adj.* dazzling, bright.

smagliare *vt.* to ravel; **smagliarsi** *vr.* to run, ravel.

smagliatura *f.* run; ladder.

smagrire *see* dimagrire.

smaliziare *vt.*, **smaliziarsi** *vr.* to make wise.

smaliziato *adj.* worldlywise.

smaltare *vt.* to enamel, glaze.

smaltatura *f.* enameling.

smaltire *vt.* to digest; to recover from (*drunkenness*); (*comm.*) to sell out.

smalto'io *m.* sewer, drain.

smalto *m.* enamel.

smanceri'a *f.* fuss.

smangiare *vt.* to eat away; **smangiarsi** *vr.* to corrode; to fret.

sma'nia *f.* frenzy; craze, passion.

smanioso *adj.* eager.

smaniare *vi.* to rave.

smantellare *vt.* to dismantle.

smargiasso *m.* bully, blusterer.

smarrimento *m.* bewilderment, dismay; miscarriage; loss.

smarrire *vt.* to lose; to mislay; **smarrirsi** *vr.* to get lost; to become dismayed; to go astray.

smascellarsi *vr.*: — dalle risa, to split one's sides with laughter.

smascherare *vt.*, **smascherarsi** *vr.* to unmask.

smembramento *m.* dismemberment.

smembrare *vt.* to dismember.

smemoratag'gine *f.* forgetfulness; lack of memory.

smemorato *adj.* forgetful; absent-minded.

smentire *vt.* to disprove; to deny; to refute; to give the lie to; to belie; **smentirsi** *vr.* to belie oneself.

smentita *f.* denial, refutation; dismeraldo *m.* emerald.   [proval.

smerciare *vt.* to sell; to sell out.

smer'cio *m.* sale.

smergo *m.* (*ornith.*) cormorant.

smerigliare *vt.* to emery; to grind.

smerigliato *adj.* emeried; ground *or* frosted (*as glass*).

smeri'glio *m.* emery.

smerlare *vt.* to scallop.

smerlo *m.* scallop.

smesso *adj.* cast-off. *pp. of* smettere.

smet'tere *vt.*, *vi.*[76] to cease, stop, give up: — un vestito, to cast off a suit; smettila! stop it!

smezzare *see* dimezzare.

smidollato *m.* softy; *adj.* weakly.

smilzo *adj.* slim, slender, thin.

sminuire *vt.* to belittle.

sminuzzare *vt.* to mince.

smistamento *m.* distribution; (*rail.*) shunting.

smistare *vt.* to distribute; (*rail.*) to shunt.

smisurato *adj.* immense, enormous.

smobilitare *vt.* to demobilize.

smobilitazione *f.* demobilization.

smoccolare *vt.* to snuff; *vi.* to swear.

smodato *adj.* immoderate.

smontare *vt.* to dismount; to unhorse; to disassemble; to damp; to flatten; *vi.* to dismount, alight; to fade; **smontarsi** *vr.* to cool down.

smor'fia *f.* wry face, grimace.

smorfiosa *f.* coquette.

smorfioso *adj.* mawkish.

smorto *adj.* pale, wan.

smorzare *vt.* to abate; to appease; to extinguish; to quench; to tone down; **smorzarsi** *vr.* to abate; to go out.

smosso *adj.* loose. *pp. of* smuovere.

smozzicare *vt.* to break; to clip.

smozzicato *adj.* broken.

smunto *adj.* haggard; faded.

smuo'vere *vt.*[8] to move; to displace; (*agr.*) to till; to remove; to budge; to deter; **smuoversi** *vr.* to budge.

smussare *vt.* to blunt; to bevel.

snaturare *vt.* to distort; to misrepresent.

snaturato *adj.* vicious, unnatural.

snebbiare *vt.*, **snebbiarsi** *vr.* to clear(*up*).

snellezza *f.* slenderness; nimbleness.

snello *adj.* slender; nimble; lively.

snervante *adj.* enervating.

snervare *vt.* to enervate; **snervarsi** *vr.* to break down; to weaken.

snidare *vt.* to drive out; to unburrow.

snobismo *m.* snobbery.

snocciolare *vt.* to cough up.

snodare *vt.* to untie, loosen, undo; **snodarsi** *vr.* to get untied; to wind.

snodo *m.* (*mach.*) joint, knuckle.

snudare *vt.* to bare; to unsheathe.

soave *adj.* sweet; mild.

soavità *f.* sweetness, softness.

sobbalzare *vi.* to start; to jolt.

sobbalzo *m.* start; jolt.

sobbarcarsi *vr.* to take upon oneself; to shoulder.

sobborgo *m.* suburb, outskirt.

sobillare *vt.* to instigate, stir up.

sobillatore *m.* instigator.

sobrietà *f.* temperance.

so'brio *adj.* temperate, sober; quiet.

socchiu'dere *vt.* to half-shut; to set ajar.

socchiuso *adj.* ajar.

soccom'bere *vi.* to succumb.

soccor'rere *vt.*[36] to succor, help; *vi.* to occur.

soccorso (*1*) *pp. of* soccorrere.

soccorso (*2*) *m.* succor, help, assistance, aid: pronto —, first aid; uscita di —, emergency exit.

sociale *adj.* social: **capitale —**, permanent capital; **ragione —**, style.

socialismo *m.* socialism.

socialista *m.* socialist.

società *f.* society; company; partnership; association; club: **— in accomandita, — a responsabilità limitata,** limited liability company; **— anonima,** corporation, joint stock company.

socie'vole *adj.* companionable.

so'cio *m.* associate; member; partner.

sociologi'a *f.* sociology.

socio'logo *m.* sociologist.

soda *f.* soda.

sodali'zio *m.* society; guild; association; brotherhood.

soddisfacente *adj.* satisfactory.

soddisfare *vt.*[128] to satisfy; to gratify; to please; to grant; to discharge.

soddisfatto *adj.* satisfied; gratified; pleased; content. *pp.of* **soddisfare.**

soddisfazione *f.* satisfaction; gratification.

so'dio *m.* sodium.

sodisfare *see* **soddisfare.**

sodo *adj.* compact, firm; fast; hard; *adv.* hard; soundly.

sodomi'a *f.* sodomy.

sodomita *m.* sodomite.

sofà *m.* sofa, davenport.

sofferente *adj.* suffering; sickly.

sofferenza *f.* suffering, pain.

soffermarsi *vr.* to linger.

sofferto *pp.of* **soffrire.**

soffiare *vt., vi.* to blow: **soffiarsi il naso,** to blow one's nose.

sof'fice *adj.* soft.

soffietto *m.* bellows (*pl.*); hood (*of a carriage*); puff, write-up (*journ.*)

sof'fio *m.* blowing; puff; blast; breath: **— al cuore,** heart murmur.

soffione *m.* blowpipe; fumarole.

soffitta *f.* attic, garret.

soffitto *m.* ceiling.

soffocamento *m.* stifling, suffocation.

soffocante *adj.* suffocating.

soffocare *vt., vi.* to stifle, smother, suffocate, choke; to hush up.

soffocato *adj.* stifled; muffled.

soffocazione *f.* suffocation.

sof'foco *m.* sultriness, oppression.

soffon'dere *vt.*[65] to suffuse (*with*).

soffregare *vt.* to rub.

soffrig'gere *vt.* to fry slightly.

soffrire *vt., vi.*[84] to suffer (*from*); to undergo; to endure, bear.

soffuso *adj.* suffused (*with*). *pp.of* **soffondere.**

sofista *m.* sophist.

sofi'stico *adj.* sophistical; fault-finding, fastidious.

soggettista *m.* script writer.

soggettivo *adj.* subjective.

soggetto *m.* subject; matter; topic; person; scenario, story: **cattivo —,** rascal, scamp; *adj.* subject: **andar — a,** to be subject *or* liable to.

soggezione *f.* subjection; respect, awe; uneasiness: **incutere —, to command respect, to awe.

sogghignare *vi.* to sneer.

sogghigno *m.* sneer.

soggiacere *vi.*[68] to be liable (*to*); to succumb.

soggiogare *vt.* to subdue, subjugate; (*fig.*) to enthrall.

soggiornare *vi.* to stay, sojourn.

soggiorno *m.* stay, sojourn: **stanza di —,** living room.

soggiun'gere *vt.* to add; *vi.* to remark, reply.

soggiuntivo *adj.* subjunctive.

so'glia *f.* threshold.

so'gliola *f.* sole.

sognare *vt., vi.* to dream: **— a occhi aperti,** to daydream.

sognatore *m.* dreamer.

sogno *m.* dream; reverie: **nemmeno per —,** by no means.

so'ia *f.* soybean, soya.

sola'io *m.* lumber room; garret.

solamente *adv.* only; solely; merely.

solare *adj.* solar.

sola'rio *m.* solarium; sunroom.

solati'o *adj.* sunny.

solatura *f.* soling.

solcare *vt.* to furrow.

solco *m.* furrow.

soldatesco *adj.* soldierlike, soldierly.

soldato *m.* soldier: **— semplice,** private; **— scelto,** private first class; **andare —,** to join the army.

soldo *m.* farthing, penny; money; pay: **non avere un —,** to be penniless; **al — di,** in the pay of.

sole *m.* sun; sunshine: **levar del —,** sunrise; **tramonto del —,** sunset; **cura di —,** heliotherapy; **alla luce del —,** in the daylight, openly.

soleggiare *vt.* to sun.

soleggiato *adj.* sunny.

solenne *adj.* solemn.

solennità *f.* solemnity.

solennizzare *vt.* to solemnize.

solere *vi.*[129] to be accustomed (*to*), be wont (*to*); to use.

solerte *adj.* industrious, diligent.

solerzia *f.* diligence.

soletta *f.* inner sole; ceiling.

soletto *adj.* alone, lonely.

solfa *f.* gamut.

solfanello *m.* match.

solfara, solfatara *f.* sulphur mine.

solfato *m.* sulphate.

solfeggiare *vi.* (*mus.*) to sol-fa.

solferino *m.* purplish, solferino.

solfo *see* **zolfo.**

solfo'rico *adj.* sulphuric.
solfuro *m.* sulphide.
solidale *adj.* joint, solidary; loyal (*to*).
solidarietà *f.* solidarity; loyalty, sympathy.
solidificare *vt.* to solidify.
solidità *f.* solidity; fastness.
so'lido *adj.* solid, firm; fast (*as colors*): in —, jointly.
solilo'quio *m.* soliloquy, monologue.
solino *m.* collar.
solista *m.*, *f.* soloist.
solitamente *adv.* usually; as a rule.
solita'rio *m.* solitary, hermit; solitaire *or* patience (*card game*); solitaire (*a gem set by itself*); *adj.* solitary, lonely, secluded: verme —, tapeworm.
so'lito *adj.* usual; used, accustomed: al —, as usual; di —, usually, as a rule; essere —, to use. *pp.of* solere.
solitu'dine *f.* loneliness, solitude.
sollazzare *vt.* to amuse; sollazzarsi *vr.* to enjoy oneself.
sollazzo *m.* amusement, sport.
sollecitare *vt.* to request, solicit; to hasten.
sollecitazione *f.* solicitation.
solle'cito *m.* pressure, solicitation; *adj.* quick; prompt; solicitous.
sollecitu'dine *f.* diligence; promptness; solicitude, concern.
solleone *m.* dog days.
solleticare *vt.* to tickle; to flatter.
solle'tico *m.* tickling; excitement: fare il — a, to tickle.
sollevamento *m.* lifting.
sollevare *vt.* to lift, raise; to heave, hoist; to cause; to stir up; to alleviate, relieve; sollevarsi *vr.* to rise, get up; to lift; (*aeron.*) to take off; to be *or* feel relieved.
sollevazione *f.* sedition, riot, revolt.
sollievo *m.* relief, comfort.
sollu'chero *m.*: andare in —, to be in seventh heaven.
solo *m.* (the) only one: da — a —, in private; *adj.* alone; lonely; only; single, one; sole: da sè —, by oneself; *adv.* only.
solsti'zio *m.* solstice.
soltanto *see* solamente.
solu'bile *adj.* soluble.
solutore *m.* solver.
soluzione *f.* solution.
solvente *m.*, *adj.* solvent.
solvi'bile *adj.* reliable, solvent.
solvibilità *f.* reliability, solvency.
soma *f.* load, burden; weight.
somaro *m.* donkey, ass.
somigliante *adj.* resembling, like.
somiglianza *f.* resemblance.
somigliare *vi.* to resemble, be like.
somma *f.* amount, sum; addition.

sommare *vt.* to add (*up*), total; *vi.* to amount to.
somma'rio *m.*, *adj.* summary.
sommato *adj.*: tutto —, on the whole.
sommer'gere *vt.*[51] to submerge; to flood; sommergersi *vr.* to sink; (*naut.*) to submerge.
sommergi'bile *m.* submarine; *adj.* submersible.
sommerso *pp.of* sommergere.
sommessamente *adv.* in a subdued voice; softly.
sommesso *adj.* soft, subdued.
somministrare *vt.* to administer.
somministrazione *f.* administration.
sommità *f.* summit; top.
sommo *m.* top, summit; master talent; *adj.* highest, extreme, top: per sommi capi, summarily.
sommossa *f.* riot, rising.
sommosso *pp.of* sommuovere.
sommovimento *m.* disturbance.
sommozzatore *m.* (*naut.*) diver, frogman.
sommuo'vere *vt.*[80] to excite, stir up.
sonagliera *f.* collar of bells.
sona'glio *m.* rattle, bell.
sonare *vt.*, *vi.* to sound; to ring; to play; to strike (*hours as a clock*); aver 60 anni sonati, to be on the wrong side of sixty.
sonata *f.* ring, peal; (*mus.*) sonata.
sonatore *m.* player.
sonda *f.* probe, sound; sounding line: pallone —, pilot balloon.
sondag'gio *m.* sounding.
sondare *vt.* to sound; to probe.
soneri'a *f.* alarum, alarm.
sonetto *m.* sonnet.
sonnacchioso *adj.* drowsy, sleepy.
sonnambulismo *m.* sleepwalking.
sonnam'bulo *m.*, sonnam'bula *f.* sleepwalker.
sonnecchiare *vi.* to doze.
sonnellino *m.* doze, nap.
sonni'fero *m.* soporific, narcotic.
sonno *m.* sleep: aver —, to be sleepy; prendere —, to drop off.
sonnolento *adj.* sleepy, drowsy.
sonnolenza *f.* drowsiness.
sonorità *f.* sonorousness.
sonorizzazione *f.* sound recording.
sonoro *adj.* sonorous, sounding: film —, sound film; colonna (onda) sonora, sound track (wave).
sontuoso *adj.* sumptuous.
soperchieri'a *see* sopruso.
sopire *vt.* to appease, calm.
sopore *m.* drowsiness.
sopori'fero *m.*, *adj.* soporific.
sopperire *vi.* to provide (*for*).
soppesare *vt.* to weigh (*in one's hand*).
soppiantare *vt.* to oust, supplant.
soppiatto, (di) *adv.* stealthily.

sopporta'bile adj. bearable.
sopportare vt. to bear, support; to endure, stand; to tolerate.
sopportazione f. forbearance, endurance; tolerance.
soppressione f. suppression, abolition.
soppri'mere vt.[29] to suppress; to abolish; to omit; to kill.
soppresso pp.of sopprimere.
sopra m. upper side; prep. on, upon; over; above; beyond; about: **al di — di,** above; **— pensiero,** lost in thought; **passar — a,** to pass over; adv. above, over; upstairs; overhead: **il piano di —,** the upper floor; **andare di —,** to go upstairs; **dormirci —,** to sleep on it; **pensarci —,** to think it over.
sopra'bito m. overcoat.
sopracci'glio m. eyebrow, brow.
sopraccoperta f. coverlet; cover, wrapper (of a book).
sopraffare vt. to overpower, overwhelm; to overcome.
sopraffazione f. overpowering, oppression, tyranny.
sopraffino adj. first-rate, excellent.
sopraggitto m. overcast stitch.
sopraggiun'gere vi. to come up, arrive; to occur, happen.
sopraintendente, soprintendente m. superintendent.
soprainten'dere vi. to superintend.
sopraluogo m. survey, inspection.
sopralzo m. (building) addition.
soprammercato, (per) adv. moreover, to boot.
soprammo'bile m. knickknack.
soprannaturale m., adj. supernatural.
soprannome m. nickname.
soprannominare vt. to nickname.
soprannu'mero, (in) adv. in excess, extra.
soprappassag'gio m. overpass.
soprappensiero adv. absent-minded y
soprappiù m. extra.
soprapprezzo m. additional price.
soprascarpa f. overshoe.
soprascritta f. address.
soprassalto m. start: **di —,** with a start; suddenly.
soprassedere vi. to wait; to bide one's time: **— a,** to delay; to suspend.
soprassoldo m. extra pay.
soprastante adj. overhanging; overhead, above.
soprastare see sovrastare.
soprattassa f. additional tax.
soprattutto adv. above all; mainly.
sopravanzare vt. to surpass, excel; vi. to project, jut out; to be left.
sopravanzo m. surplus.
sopravvalutare vt. to overrate.
sopravvenire see sopraggiungere.

sopravvento m. upper hand, advantage; adv. (naut.) windward.
sopravvissuto m. survivor.
sopravvivenza f. survival, surviving.
sopravvi'vere vi. to survive: **— a,** to outlive.
soprosso m. (surg.) exostosis.
sopruso m. offense; outrage.
soqquadro, (a) adv. topsy-turvy.
sorba f. sorb, sorb apple.
sorbetto m. ice cream.
sorbire vt. to sip; **sorbirsi** vr. (fam.) to put up with, endure.
sorbo m. sorb, service tree.
sor'cio m. mouse (pl. mice).
sor'dido adj. sordid.
sordina f. (mus.) mute, sordino: **mettere la —,** to muffle; **in —,** softly; stealthily.
sordità f. deafness.
sordo m. deaf man; adj. deaf; dull; hollow, muffled: **fare il —,** to turn a deaf ear.
sordomuto m. deaf-mute; adj. deaf and dumb.
sorella f. sister.
sorellastra f. half-sister; stepsister.
sorgente f. source, spring.
sor'gere vi.[130] to rise, arise; to spring up: **far — un dubbio,** to raise a doubt.
sormontare vt. to surmount.
sornione m. slyboots; adj. sly.
sorpassare vt. to run past, pass; to surpass; to outdo, excel.
sorpassato adj. old-fashioned, obsolete.
sorpasso m. overtaking.
sorprendente adj. astonishing.
sorpren'dere vt.[96] to surprise, astonish; to catch: **— la buona fede di,** to steal a march on.
sorpresa f. surprise: **di —,** unawares; by surprise.
sorpreso adj. surprised. pp.of sorprendere.
sorreg'gere vt.[105] to support.
sorretto pp.of sorreggere.
sorridente adj. smiling.
sorri'dere vi.[108] to smile: **mi sorride l'idea di,** I look forward to; **questa idea non mi sorride,** this idea does not appeal to me.
sorriso (1) m. smile.
sorriso (2) pp.of sorridere.
sorsata f. gulp, draft.
sorseggiare vt., vi. to sip.
sorso m. draft; drop: **bere d'un —,** to gulp down; **bere a piccoli sorsi,** to sip.
sorta f. kind, sort.
sorte f. lot, destiny, fate; luck, fortune; chance: **tirare a —,** to cast lots; **toccare in —,** to fall to one's lot.

sorteggiare vt. to draw (by lot): — un premio, to draw a prize.

sorteg'gio m. drawing of lots.

sortile'gio m. sortilege, sorcery.

sortire vt. to get, obtain; to give, yield; vi. to be drawn (by lot); to go out, get out.

sortita f. (mil.) sally.

sorto pp.of sorgere.

sorvegliante m. inspector; caretaker, keeper; watchman; overseer.

sorveglianza f. surveillance; supervision.

sorvegliare vt. to oversee; to watch, watch over; **sorvegliarsi** vr. to control oneself; to watch one another.

sorvolare vi. to fly over; to pass over.

so'sia m. double.

sospen'dere vt.[10] to suspend; to hang; to interrupt, discontinue, stop; to defer, put off, adjourn.

sospensione f. suspension; suspense: — cardanica, gimbals.

sospenso'rio adj. suspensory; m. athletic supporter.

sospeso adj. suspended, hanging; in abeyance; pending: ponte —, suspension bridge; con l'animo in —, in suspense. pp.of sospendere.

sospettare vt., vi. to suspect.

sospetto m. suspicion; suspect; adj. suspect, suspicious.

sospettoso adj. suspicious.

sospin'gere vt.[26] to drive, push.

sospinto adj. pushed, driven: ad ogni pie' —, at every moment. pp.of sospingere.

sospirare vt. to long for; vi. to sigh.

sospirato adj. longed for.

sospiro m. sigh.

sossopra adv. upside down, topsy-turvy.

sosta f. halt, stay; rest; truce; pause; warehousing.

sostantivo m., adj. substantive.

sostanza f. substance; matter; gist; fortune: in —, in short; altogether.

sostanzioso adj. substantial.

sostare vi. to pause; to stop; to cease.

sostegno m. prop, support.

sostenere vt.[141] to support, sustain; to suffer; to stand; to undergo; to maintain: — una parte, to play a role; **sostenersi** vr. to support oneself; to lean (on); to support each other.

sostenitore m. supporter.

sostentamento m. sustenance.

sostentare vt. to support; **sostentarsi** vr. to support oneself.

sostenuto adj. aloof; stiff; (comm.) steady; (mus.) sustained.

sostituire vt. to substitute.

sostituto m. substitute.

sostituzione f. substitution.

sottacere vt.[139] to withhold, hold back.

sottaceti m.pl. pickles.

sottana f. petticoat; skirt; cassock, soutane.

sottecchi adv. surreptitiously.

sotterfu'gio m. subterfuge.

sotterra adv. underground.

sotterra'nea f. subway.

sotterra'neo m. cave, vault; adj. underground, subterranean.

sotterrare vt. to bury.

sottigliezza f. thinness; subtlety.

sottile adj. thin, slender; subtle.

sottilizzare vt. to subtilize; to quibble.

sottinten'dere vt. to imply.

sottinteso m. matter of course, thing implied; adj. implied, understood, implicit.

sotto adv., prep. under, underneath; beneath, below: al piano di —, downstairs; sott'olio, in oil; — mano, handy; — voce, in a low voice; prendere — gamba, to make light of.

sottobicchiere m. coaster.

sottobosco m. underbrush.

sottoc'chio adv. under one's eyes.

sottochiave adv. under lock and key.

sottocoperta f., adv. (naut.) below.

sottocuta'neo adj. subcutaneous.

sottogola f. chin strap; throatlatch.

sottolineare vt. to underscore; to emphasize, lay stress on.

sottomano m. writing pad; adv. underhand.

sottomarino m., adj. submarine.

sottomesso adj. submissive. pp.of sottomettere.

sottomet'tere vt.[76] to subdue, subjugate, subject; to conquer; **sottomet'tersi** vr. to submit; to yield.

sottomissione f. submission.

sottopassag'gio m. underpass.

sottoporre vt.[93] to submit; to subject; to put; **sottoporsi** vr. to submit; to undergo.

sottoposto m. subordinate. pp.of sottoporre.

sottoprodotto m. by-product.

sottoscritto m., adj. undersigned. pp. of sottoscri'vere.

sottoscrittore m. subscriber.

sottoscri'vere vt., vi.[124] to subscribe (to), underwrite; to sign; **sottoscriversi** vr. to sign.

sottoscrizione f. subscription.

sottosegreta'rio m. undersecretary.

sottosopra adv. upside down; topsy-turvy.

sottostante adj. lying below, lower.

sottostare vi.[135] to lie below; to submit; to give in.

sottosuolo m. underground.
sottotenente m. second lieutenant; (navy) ensign.
sottoterra adv. underground.
sottoti'tolo m. subtitle; caption.
sottovalutare vt. to underrate.
sottovento adv. leeward.
sottoveste f. undergarment; waistcoat.
sottovoce adv. in a low voice, softly.
sottrarre vt.[146] to subtract; to steal; to deduct; to rescue, save; to snatch; **sottrarsi** vr.: **sottrarsi a**, to escape, evade; to shirk.
sottratto pp.of sottrarre.
sottrazione f. subtraction, deduction; theft.
sottufficiale m. noncommissioned officer.
sovente adv. frequently, often.
soverchiante adj. overwhelming.
soverchiare vt. to overflow; to surpass; to overwhelm.
sover'chio m. surplus, excess; adj. [excessive.
sovra see sopra.
sovrabbondante adj. superabundant.
sovrabbondanza f. superabundance.
sovrabbondare vi. to superabound.
sovraccaricare vt. to overburden.
sovracca'rico m. overweight; adj. overburdened.
sovrana f. sovereign.
sovranità f. sovereignty.
sovrano m. sovereign; adj. sovereign; paramount.
sovrappopolare vt. to overpopulate.
sovrapporre vt.[93] to superimpose (on, upon); to overlay; **sovrapporsi** vr. to be superimposed: **sovrapporsi a**, to overlap; to overwhelm, outdo.
sovrapposizione f. superimposition.
sovrapproduzione f. overproduction.
sovrastante adj. overhanging; impending; overhead, above.
sovrastare vt., vi.[135] to overhang; to impend; to tower (over); to crown; to surpass, excel.
sovreccitare vt. to overexcite.
sovreccitazione f. overexcitement.
sovrimposta f. additional tax.
sovrumano adj. superhuman.
sovvenire vt. to help, assist; **sovvenirsi** vr.: **sovvenirsi di**, to recall, remember.
sovvenzionare vt. to subsidize.
sovvenzione f. subvention, subsidy.
sovversivo m. (pol.) extremist; adj. subversive.
sovvertimento m. subversion.
sovvertire vt. to subvert.
sozzo adj. filthy, foul.
sozzura f. filth.
spaccamontagne m. braggart.
spaccare vt., **spaccarsi** vr. to cleave, split, crack.

spaccato m. section; adj. split, cleft.
spaccatura f. split, crack, crevice.
spacciare vt. to sell off; to palm off; to pass off (as counterfeit notes); to spread; to dispatch; **spacciarsi** vr. to set up as.
spacciato adj. past cure.
spacciatore m. seller: — di monete false, passer of counterfeit money,
spac'cio m. sale; shop. [layer,
spacco m. split; crack.
spacconata f. brag.
spaccone m. braggart, boaster.
spada f. sword: passare a fil di —, to put to the sword; **difendere a — tratta**, to defend doggedly.
spadaccino m. swordsman.
spadroneggiare vi. to boss.
spaesato adj. out of one's element.
spaghetto m. (coll.) fear: avere un bello —, to be in a blue funk; (pl.) spaghetti.
spagnoletta f. cigarette; spool; peanut.
spagnolo m. Spaniard; adj. Spanish.
spago m. string, twine.
spaiare vt. to unpair, unspan.
spalancare vt., **spalancarsi** vr. to open wide, to throw open.
spalancato adj. wide open.
spalare vt. to shovel.
spalatore m. shoveler.
spalla f. shoulder; (mus.) second violin; (theat.) "stooge." spalle pl. shoulders, back: con le spalle al muro, cornered; voltare le spalle a, to turn one's back upon; cogliere alle spalle, to attack from the rear; stringersi nelle spalle, to shrug.
Spallanzani, Lazzaro, Italian naturalist (1729–1799).
spallata f. shouldering.
spalleggiare vt. to back, support.
spaletta f. retaining wall; jamb.
spalliera f. back (of a chair, etc.); head (of a bed); trellis (for plants).
spallina f. epaulette; shoulder strap; shoulder loop.
spalluc'cia f.: far spallucce, to shrug.
spalmare vt. to smear; to spread.
spanare vt. to mar or strip out the thread (of a screw).
spanciata see scorpacciata.
span'dere vt.[131] to spread; to diffuse; to scatter; to send forth; to shed: spendere e —, to squander; **spandersi** vr. to spread.
spanna f. span.
spannare vt. to skim.
spappolare vt., **spappolarsi** vr. to crush, squash, pulp.
sparadrappo m. plaster.
sparare vt., vi. to shoot (at), fire (at); to discharge: spararle grosse, to draw the long bow, tell a tall tale.

sparato m. shirtfront.

sparatore m. shooter.

sparato'ria f. shooting.

sparecchiare vt. to clear away.

spareg'gio m. disparity, deficit.

spar'gere vt.[132] to spread; to diffuse; to scatter; to shed; **spargersi** vr. to spread.

spargimento m. spreading, scattering: — di sangue, bloodshed.

spargitore m. spreader.

sparigliare vt. to unmatch.

sparire vi.[133] to disappear; far —, to conceal; to steal.

sparizione f. disappearance.

sparlare vi.: — di, to slander.

sparo m. shot; report.

sparpagliare vt., **sparpagliarsi** vr. to scatter.

sparso adj. scattered: ordine —, extended order. pp.of **spandere** and **spargere**.

spartiac'que m. watershed.

spartire vt. to share, divide; to part, split: non aver nulla da — con, to have nothing in common with.

spartito m. (mus.) score.

spartizione f. division, sharing.

sparto m. esparto.

sparuto adj. gaunt.

sparviere, sparviero m. hawk.

spasimante m. lover, wooer.

spasimare vi. to agonize, writhe (with); to long (for): — per, to be head over heels in love with.

spa'simo m. pang, spasm.

spasmo'dico adj. spasmodic.

spassionato adj. unbiased; dispassionate.

spasso m. toy, pastime; fun: per —, for fun; andare a —, to go for a walk; mandare a —, to send packing; trovarsi a —, to be out of a job.

spassoso adj. amusing, droll.

spato m. (min.) spar.

spa'tola f. spatula; slapstick.

spaurac'chio m. scarecrow; bugaboo.

spaurire vt. to frighten.

spavalderi'a f. boldness; defiance.

spavaldo adj. bold; impudent.

spaventare vt. to frighten, scare; **spaventarsi** vr. to take fright, be scared.

spavente'vole adj. frightful, dreadful.

spavento m. fright, fear, terror.

spaventoso adj. dreadful.

spaziale adj. space.

spaziare (1) vi. to rove, wander about; to soar.

spaziare (2) vt. to space.

spaziatura f. spacing.

spazientirsi see **impazientirsi.**

spa'zio m. space; room; extent; area; surface; distance; interval.

spazioso adj. spacious, large, wide, roomy.

spazzacamino m. chimney sweeper.

spazzamine m. minesweeper.

spazzaneve m. snowplow.

spazzare vt. to sweep (away, off).

spazzatura f. sweeping; sweepings.

spazzatura'io, spazzino m. sweeper, scavenger, dustman, garbageman.

spazzettone m. floor brush.

spaz'zola f. brush.

spazzolare vt. to brush; **spazzolarsi** vr. to brush oneself.

spazzolino m. toothbrush; nailbrush.

spazzolone see **spazzettone.**

specchiarsi vr. to look at oneself (in the mirror, in a reflecting surface); to be reflected.

specchiera f. looking glass, mirror.

specchietto m. hand mirror; schedule.

spec'chio m. mirror; looking glass; pattern; form, schedule, prospectus: — d'acqua, water surface.

speciale adj. special, peculiar.

specialista m. specialist.

specialità f. speciality; peculiarity; specialty: — farmaceutiche, proprietary medicines.

specializzare vt., **specializzarsi** vr. to specialize.

specialmente adv. especially.

spe'cie f. kind, sort, species: sotto — di, under pretense of; (in) —, especially; far —, to surprise.

speci'fica f. detailed note.

specificare vt. to specify.

speci'fico m., adj. specific.

specillo m. (surg.) probe, sound.

specioso adj. specious.

spe'cola f. observatory.

speculare vt., vi. to speculate.

speculativo adj. speculative.

speculatore m. speculator: — al rialzo, bull; — al ribasso, bear.

speculazione f. speculation.

spedire vt. to dispatch; to send; to ship, forward.

speditamente adv. expeditiously.

speditezza f. expeditiousness.

spedito adj. prompt; quick; easy.

speditore m. forwarder, sender.

spedizione f. expedition; consignment; sending, forwarding; dispatch: corpo di —, expeditionary force.

spedizioniere m. carrier, forwarding agent; shipping agent.

spe'gnere vt.[134] to extinguish, put out; (elec.) to switch out; to quench; **spe'gnersi** vr. to go out; to fade, fail; to die; to die away.

spelacchiare vt. to strip (of hair); (fig.) to fleece; **spelacchiarsi** vr. to lose one's hair.

spelacchiato *adj.* mangy, hairless.

spelare *vt.* to make bald; **spelarsi** *vr.* to become bald.

spelato *adj.* bald.

spellare *vt.* to skin; **spellarsi** *vr.* to get skinned; to peel.

spellatura *f.* excoriation.

spelonca *f.* cave, den.

spendaccione *m.* spendthrift.

spen'dere *vt., vi.*[10] to spend.

spenderec'cio *adj.* prodigal.

spen'gere *see* spegnere.

spennacchiare *vt.* to unfeather; to pluck; to fleece.

spennare *see* spennacchiare.

spennellare *vt.* to touch.

spensieratezza *f.* lightheartedness.

spensierato *adj.* carefree.

spento *adj.* extinguished, put out; dead; lifeless. *pp.of* spegnere.

spenzolare *see* penzolare.

speranza *f.* hope; expectation: **di belle speranze,** promising.

speranzoso *adj.* hopeful, confident.

sperare *vt., vi.* to hope (for); to expect; to trust: — **in bene,** to hope for the best; **speriamo in Dio,** in God we trust.

sper'dere *vt.*[87] to scatter, disperse; **sper'dersi** *vr.* to disperse; to get lost, go astray.

sperduto, sperso *adj.* lost. *pp.of* sperdere.

sperequazione *f.* disproportion.

spergiurare *vt.* to perjure oneself.

spergiuro *m.* perjurer; perjury.

spericolato *m.* daredevil; *adj.* reckless.

sperimentale *adj.* experimental.

sperimentare *vt.* to experiment, test, try.

sperimentato *adj.* experienced.

speronare *vt.* to ram.

sperone *m.* spur; abutment; ram.

sperperare *vt.* to squander.

sperperatore *m.* squanderer.

sper'pero *m.* waste, squandering.

sperso *see* sperduto.

sperticato *adj.* exaggerated, excessive.

spesa *f.* expenditure; expense; cost, charge: **andare a far la —,** to go out marketing; **fare le spese di,** to be the victim of; **fare le spese di una conversazione,** to be the main subject of a conversation.

spesato *adj.* supported.

speso *adj.* spent. *pp.of* spendere.

spessire *vt.,* **spessirsi** *vr.* to thicken.

spesso *adj.* thick: **spesse volte,** often; *adv.* frequently, often.

spetta'bile *adj.* respectable: — **Ditta,** Gentlemen, Dear Sirs.

spetta'colo *m.* sight, spectacle; show, performance: **dare — di sè,** to make a fool of oneself.

spettacoloso *adj.* spectacular, sensational; gorgeous; grand.

spettanza *f.* due: **essere di — di,** to belong to; to concern.

spettare *vi.* to belong (to); to be up (to); to be one's turn.

spettatore *m.* spectator; bystander: **gli spettatori,** the audience.

spettegolare *vi.* to gossip.

spettinare *vt.* to tousle; **spettinarsi** *vr.* to ruffle one's hair.

spettinato *adj.* tousled.

spettrale *adj.* ghostly, spectral: **analisi —,** spectrum analysis.

spettro *m.* ghost; *(phys.)* spectrum.

speziale *m.* chemist; druggist.

spe'zie *f.pl.* spices, spicery.

spezieri'a *f.* grocery; drugstore.

spezzare *vt.,* **spezzarsi** *vr.* to break.

spezzatino *m.* stew.

spezzettare *vt.* to mince.

spezzone *m.* bomb stick.

spi'a *f.* spy; informer, "stool pigeon."

spiacciare *vt.* to crush, pulp.

spiacente *adj.* sorry; unpleasant.

spiacere *see* dispiacere (2).

spiace'vole *adj.* unpleasant.

spiag'gia *f.* shore; beach.

spianare *vt.* to smooth; to level; to settle; to raze, demolish: — **un fucile contro,** to level a gun at; — **la pasta,** to roll out dough; — **la strada,** to pave the way for.

spianata *f.* esplanade.

spianato'ia *f.* smoothing board.

spianato'io *m.* rolling pin.

spiano, (a tutto) *adv.* profusely, abundantly; with a will.

spiantato *m. (coll.)* destitute; lame duck, have-not; *adj.* penniless.

spiare *vt.* to spy.

spiattellare *vt.* to blurt out.

spiazzo *m.* plaza; clearing.

spiccare *vt.* to detach; to pick: — **un balzo,** to jump up; — **il volo,** to fly away; — **tratta,** to draw a bill; *vi.* to stand out; to excel.

spiccato *adj.* marked; conspicuous.

spic'chio *m.* clove; slice.

spicciare, spicciarsi *see* sbrigare.

spicciativo *see* sbrigativo.

spiccicare *vt.* to detach; to pronounce.

spic'cio *adj.* expeditious, quick.

spicciolata, (alla) *adv.* little by little, a few at a time: **entrare (uscire) alla —,** to straggle in (out).

spic'cioli *m.pl.* change, money.

spic'ciolo *adj.* small.

spicco *m.* relief; prominence: **fare —,** to stand out.

spiedo *m.* spit.

spiegamento *m.* spreading out; *(mil.)* deployment.

spiegare vt. to explain; to unfold, spread out, lay out; to display; to unfurl (as sails); (mil.) to deploy; **spiegarsi** vr. to explain oneself; to make oneself understood; to unfurl (as a flag).

spiegato adj. explained; spread out; open; unfurled; unfolded: **a voce spiegata**, in a full voice.

spiegazione f. explanation.

spiegazzare vt. to rumple; to batter.

spietato adj. pitiless, ruthless.

spifferare vt. to speak out; to report; to blow.

spif'fero m. draft (of air).

spiga f. ear (of corn).

spigato adj. herringbone.

spighetta f. braid.

spigliatezza f. ease, promptness.

spigliato adj. easy, prompt.

spigo m. (bot.) lavender.

spigolare vt. to glean.

spigolatura f. gleaning.

spi'golo m. corner, corner edge.

spilla f. pin, brooch.

spillare vt. to broach, tap; to pierce: — danaro a, to squeeze money out of.

spilla'tico m. pin money.

spillo m. pin: — di sicurezza, safety pin.

spillone m. hatpin.

spilluzzicare vt. to nibble.

spilorceri'a f. niggardliness.

spilor'cio m. miser; adj. stingy.

spilungone m. lanky fellow.

spina f. thorn; (elec.) plug: — dorsale, spine; — di pesce, fishbone; a — di pesce, herringbone.

spina'cio m. spinach.

spinato, (filo) m. barbed wire.

spin'gere vt.[26] to push, shove; to drive; to propel; **spin'gersi** vr. to push, make one's way; to advance.

spino m. thorn.

spinone m. griffon.

spinoso adj. thorny.

spinta f. push; thrust; impulsion.

spintero'geno m. (mach.) (ignition) distributor.

spinto adj. excessive; risqué. pp.of spingere.

spintone m. push, shove, thrust.

spionag'gio m. espionage.

spioncino m. peephole.

spione m. spy, "stool pigeon."

spiovente m. slope; adj. drooping.

spira f. spire, coil.

spira'glio m. crack, fissure, airhole; gleam.

spirale f., adj. spiral.

spirare vt., vi. to blow; to expire, die; to issue, send forth, exhale: **allo — di un mese**, by the end of a month.

spiritato adj. possessed, crazy; wild.

spiri'tico adj. spiritualistic: **seduta spiritica**, seance.

spiritismo m. spiritualism.

spi'rito m. spirit; soul; ghost; tendency; virtue; faculty; wit; inspiration, impulse; spirits: — di sacrificio, abnegation, self-denial; — di corpo, esprit de corps; lampada a —, vapor lamp; fare dello —, to crack jokes.

spiritosag'gine f. witticism, crack.

spiritoso adj. witty; alcoholic.

spirituale adj. spiritual.

spiritualità f. spirituality.

spiz'zico, (a) adv. little by little; by fits and starts.

splendente adj. bright, shining.

splen'dere vi. to shine, sparkle.

splen'dido adj. splendid, glorious.

splendore m. splendor; grandeur.

spoc'chia f. haughtiness.

spocchioso adj. haughty.

spodestare vt. to dispossess; to dethrone; to oust.

spoetizzare vt. to disgust.

spo'glia f. spoil: — di guerra, spoils of war.

spogliare vt. to undress; to strip; to despoil; to plunder; **spogliarsi** vr. to undress; to give up; to deprive oneself; to get rid (of).

spogliarello m. "strip tease."

spogliato'io m. dressing room.

spogliazione f. dispossession; pillaging.

spo'glio m. castoff; scrutiny; perusal. adj. stripped; bare.

spola f. shuttle.

spoletta f. shuttle; fuse.

spolmonarsi vr. to talk one's head off; to shout oneself hoarse.

spolpare vt. to unflesh; to despoil.

spolverare vt. to dust.

spolveratura f. dusting; brushing; smattering.

spolverina f. duster; overall.

spolverino m. duster; sandbox.

spol'vero m. pounce; dusting; smattering.

sponda f. bank; edge; side.

sponsali see sposalizio.

spontaneità f. spontaneity.

sponta'neo adj. spontaneous.

Spontini, Gaspare, Italian composer (1774–1851).

spopolare vt. to depopulate; vi. (coll.) to make a hit; **spopolarsi** vr. to become depopulated.

spopolato adj. depopulated.

spora'dico adj. sporadic.

sporcaccione m. filthy person.

sporcare vt. to dirty, soil; **sporcarsi** vr. to dirty oneself, get dirty.

sporci'zia f. dirt, filth; dirtiness.

sporco adj. dirty, foul.

sporgente adj. jutting, protuberant.

sporgenza f. jut, projection, protuberance.

spor'gere vt.⁹⁵ to thrust out; to lodge (a complaint); vi. to jut; to protrude; **spor'gersi** vr. to lean out.

sport m. sport; game: per —, for pleasure.

sporta f. shopping bag: **un sacco e una** —, a lot; **dirne un sacco e una** — **a,** to abuse profusely.

sportello m. wicket; door; window.

sportivo m. sportsman; adj. sporting, sportsmanlike.

sporto m. jut, projection; adj. outstretched. pp.of sporgere.

sposa f. bride; wife.

sposali'zio m. wedding.

sposare vt. to marry, wed; to embrace; vi., **sposarsi** vr. to marry, get married.

sposo m. bridegroom; husband.

spossare vt. to exhaust, prostrate.

spossatezza f. exhaustion, weakness.

spossato adj. weary; worn-out.

spostamento m. displacement, shifting; change.

spostare vt. to shift, move; to displace; to change; to bring; **spostarsi** vr. to shift, move.

spranga f. bar, crossbar, bolt.

sprangare vt. to bar, bolt.

sprazzo m. flash; splash.

sprecare vt. to waste, squander.

spreco m. squandering, waste.

sprege'vole adj. despicable.

spregiare vt. to despise.

spregiativo adj. disparaging.

spre'gio m. contempt, scorn.

spregiudicatezza f. broadmindedness.

spregiudicato adj. broadminded; unprejudiced, unbiased.

spre'mere vt. to squeeze, press; to wring: **spremersi il cervello,** to rack one's brain.

spremuta f. squash.

sprezzante adj. contemptuous.

sprezzare see disprezzare.

sprigionare vt. to exhale; to emit; **sprigionarsi** vr. to burst out.

sprimacciare vt. to plump up.

sprizzare vt. to sprinkle; to radiate; vi. to spring out.

sprofondare vt., vi., **sprofondarsi** vr. to sink, cave in.

sprolo'quio m. rigmarole.

spronare vt. to spur, goad; to urge.

sprone m. spur; (naut.) ram; a — battuto, full speed.

sproporzionato adj. disproportionate.

sproporzione f. disproportion.

spropositare vi. to blunder.

spropositato adj. blundering; (fig.) enormous, disproportionate, huge.

spropo'sito m. blunder; mistake: a —, at random; out of turn: **costare uno** —, to cost a fortune.

sprovvista, (alla) adv. unawares, unexpectedly.

sprovvisto adj. unprovided; lacking (in).

spruzzare vt. to spray, sprinkle.

spruzzatore m. sprayer.

spruzzo m. sprinkle; splash.

spudorato adj. impudent, shameless.

spugna f. sponge; (coll.) drunkard.

spugnatura f. sponge bath.

spugnoso adj. spongy.

spulciare vt. to free from fleas; (fig.) to scrutinize.

spuma f. foam, froth.

spumante m. champagne; adj. foaming, sparkling.

spumare vi. to foam, froth.

spumeggiante see spumante.

spumeggiare see spumare.

spumoso adj. foamy, frothy.

spuntare vt. to blunt; to clip, trim; to unpin; (comm.) to check, tick (off); vi. to appear, turn up; to grow; to peep out; to rise; to dawn; to spring; to cut (as teeth): **spuntarla,** to win out; **spuntarsi** vr. to blunt, become blunt; to get unpinned; to unfasten.

spuntino m. snack.

spunto m. cue; start; opening.

spurgare vt. to purge; vi. to discharge.

spurgo m. discharge.

spu'rio adj. spurious.

sputacchiera f. spittoon.

sputac'chio m. spit, spittle.

sputare vt., vi. to spit.

sputo m. spit, spittle.

squadra f. (geom.) square; (aeron.) squadron; (mil.) squad; gang, crew; (sport) team.

squadrare vt. to square.

squadri'glia f. squadron.

squagliare vt., **squagliarsi** vr. to melt: **squagliarsela** (coll.), to beat it, to take a powder.

squali'fica f. disqualification.

squalificare vt. to disqualify.

squal'lido adj. dreary, squalid.

squallore m. dreariness, squalor.

squalo m. shark.

squama f. scale.

squamare vt. to scale.

squarciagola, (a) adv. at the top of one's voice.

squarciare vt. to rend, tear apart; **squarciarsi** vr. to rend, tear.

squar'cio m. rent, tear, gash; (liter.) passage; rift.

squartare vt. to quarter, chop.

squartatore m. chopper.
squassare vt. to shake.
squattrinato m. pauper; adj. penniless.
squilibrato m. lunatic; adj. unbalanced, mad.
squili'brio m. want of balance; disparity; — mentale, insanity.
squillante adj. ringing.
squillare vi. to blare, ring.
squillo m. blare, ring.
squisito adj. exquisite.
squittire vi. to yelp, squeak.
sradicare vt. to uproot.
sragionare vi. to ramble; to talk nonsense.
sregolatezza f. disorder, intemperance, debauchery.
sregolato adj. intemperate.
stabbiuolo m. sty, pigsty.
sta'bile m. building; adj. stable, steady; permanent.
stabilimento m. establishment; factory, works, mill.
stabilire vt. to establish; to rule; to state; to decide; to settle; stabilirsi vr. to settle (down).
stabilità f. steadiness.
stabilizzatore m. stabilizer.
stabilizzare vt. to stabilize.
staccare vt. to detach; to separate; to pull off, tear away; (mach.) to disconnect; to take down (from); vi. to contrast; staccarsi vr. to become detached; to fall off; to part (from).
stacciare vt. to sift, sieve.
stac'cio m. sieve.
staccionata f. fence.
stacco see spicco.
stadera f. steelyard.
sta'dio m. stadium; stage, phase.
staffa f. stirrup: perder le staffe, to fly off the handle; tenere il piede in due staffe, to run with the hare and hunt with the hounds.
staffetta f. estafette: corsa a —, relay race.
staffiere m. groom, lackey.
staffilare vt. to lash.
staffilata f. lash.
staffile m. stirrup leather; whip.
stagionale adj. seasonal.
stagionare vt., vi. to season, ripen.
stagionato adj. seasoned; ripe.
stagliarsi vr. to stand out.
stagione f. season.
stagnante adj. stagnant.
stagnare vt. to tin; to solder; to stanch. vi. to stagnate.
stagnino m. tinsmith.
stagno m. tin; pond, pool; adj. tight, watertight; airtight.
sta'io m. bushel.
stalattite f. stalactite.

stalla f. stable.
stalliere m. stableman, groom.
stallo m. stall, seat.
stallone m. stallion.
stamane, stamattina adv. this morning.
stambecco m. ibex.
stamberga f., **stambugio** m. den, hole.
stame m. (bot.) stamen; thread.
stampa f. print; printing; press: in corso di —, on press; errore di —, misprint; stampe raccomandate, registered printed matter; godere di una buona (cattiva) —, to have a good (bad) reputation.
stampare vt. to print; to publish; to impress.
stampatello m. block letters.
stampato m. (printed) form; adj printed.
stampatore m. printer.
stampatrice f. printing press; press.
stampella f. crutch.
stamperi'a f. printing house.
stampi'glia f. stamp.
stampigliare vt. to stamp.
stampigliatura f. stamping.
stampino m. stencil.
stampo m. stamp; (fig.) kind, sort; mold.
stanare vt. to unburrow; to find out.
stancare vt. to tire, fatigue, weary; to annoy; to bore; stancarsi vr. to grow tired; to weary.
stanchezza f. tiredness, weariness.
stanco adj. tired (of), weary (of).
standardizzato adj. standard.
stanga f. bar; shaft.
stangata f. blow with a bar.
stanghetta f. bow (of spectacles).
stanotte adv. tonight, this night; last night.
stante adj. being: seduta —, on the spot; a sè —, apart; prep. on account of: — che, since, as.
stanti'o adj. stale.
stantuffo m. piston; plunger.
stanza f. room, chamber: essere di —, to be stationed; — di compensazione, clearinghouse.
stanziamento m. appropriation.
stanziare vt. to appropriate.
stanzino m. closet; lumber room.
stappare vt. to uncork.
stare vi.[135] to stand; to be; to stay; to lie; to sit; to go on, keep; to live; to last; to be up to; to be in proportion to: — sdraiato, to lie; — seduto, to be sitting; — zitto, to keep silent; — in piedi, to stand; tutto sta nella sua decisione, everything depends upon his decision; — per, to be about to; — alzati sino a

tardi, to sit up late; — **dietro a,** to keep an eye upon; to court; — **bene (male)**, to be well (ill); to be well (badly) off; **questo vestito ti sta bene**, this dress becomes you; **ti sta bene!** it serves you right!; **come stai?** how are you?; **starci**, to agree; to go shares; **lasciar —,** to leave alone; **non — in sè,** to be beside oneself.

starna f. gray partridge.

starnazzare vi. to flutter.

starnutare, starnutire vi. to sneeze.

starnuto m. sneeze, sneezing.

stasera adv. tonight.

stasi f. stasis.

statale adj. governmental: **impiegato —,** government official.

sta'tico adj. static, statical.

statista m. statesman.

stati'stica f. statistics.

stativo m. base (of a microscope).

stato (1) m. state; condition; status: — **civile**, registrar's office; **in — interessante**, pregnant; **colpo di —,** coup d'état; **uomo di —,** statesman; — **maggiore**, army staff; — **d'assedio**, martial law.

stato (2) pp.of stare and of essere.

sta'tua f. statue.

statua'rio m., adj. statuary.

statura f. stature, height.

statuto m. statute, constitution; (comm.) articles of association.

stavolta adv. this time.

stazionare vi. to stay, station.

staziona'rio adj. stationary.

stazione f. depot, station; stop; resort: — **balneare**, seaside resort.

stazza f. displacement.

stazzare vt. to gauge; to have a displacement of.

stazzonare vt. to crumple.

stecca f. stick; rib (of an umbrella); cue (for billiards); (mus.) false note; carton (of cigarettes).

steccato m. paling, palisade; rails.

stecchetto m.: **stare a —,** to stint (oneself); **tenere a —,** to keep on a meager pittance.

stecchino m. toothpick.

stecchito adj. lank: **morto —,** stark dead.

stecco m. (dry) twig.

stecconata f. stockade; fence.

stella f. star: — **di mare**, starfish; **chiaror di stelle**, starlight; **stelle filanti**, shooting stars; confetti.

stellare adj. stellar; radial.

stellato adj. starry, star-spangled.

stelletta f. starlet; asterisk: **portare le stellette** (It. Army), to be in the army.

stelloncino m. paragraph.

stelo m. stem, stalk.

stemma m. coat of arms.

stemperare vt. to dilute; to melt; **stemperarsi** vr. to melt.

stendardo m. standard.

sten'dere vt.,¹⁴⁰ to spread; to relax; to draw up; to hang; to stretch out; **sten'dersi** vr. to spread; to lie down; to stretch; to relax.

stenodattilo'grafo m., **stenodattilo'grafa** f. stenographer.

stenografare vt. to take in shorthand.

stenografato adj. shorthand.

stenografi'a f. shorthand.

stenogra'fico adj. shorthand.

steno'grafo m. stenographer.

stentare vt., vi. to halt; to starve; to be hardly able (to); to find it hard (to); to demur, be unwilling (to).

stentato adj. stunted; halting.

stento m. privation; hardship; toil: **vivere di stenti**, to starve; **a —,** hardly; with difficulty; stuntedly.

stento'reo adj. stentorian.

steppa f. steppe.

sterco m. dung.

stereoscopi'a f. stereoscopy.

stereosco'pico adj. stereoscopic.

stereotipato adj. stereotyped; stilted.

stereotipi'a f. stereotype.

stereo'tipo adj. stereotypic.

ste'rile adj. sterile, barren.

sterilire see isterilire.

sterilità f. sterility.

sterilizzare vt. to sterilize.

sterlina f. pound (sterling).

sterminare vt. to exterminate.

sterminato adj. immense, boundless.

sterminatore m. exterminator.

stermi'nio m. extermination.

sternutare, sternutire vi. to sneeze.

sterpo m. offshoot, weed.

sterrare vt. to dig up.

sterratore m. navvy, digger.

sterro m. digging.

sterzare vt., vi. to swerve.

sterzata f. swerve.

sterzo m. steering gear; steering wheel; handle bar.

steso pp.of stendere.

stesso adj. same; self; very: **io —,** I myself; **noi stessi**, we ourselves; **se —,** oneself, one's self; **il giorno —,** that very day; **fa lo —,** it makes no difference.

stesura f. drawing up.

stetosco'pio m. stethoscope.

sti'a f. coop.

stigmatizzare vt. to stigmatize.

stilare vt. to draw up.

stile m. style; stylet, dagger.

stilizzare vt. to stylize.

stilla f. drop.

stillare vt., vi. to ooze, exude, drip.

stillici'dio *m.* dripping; stillicidium.
stilo *m.* style.
stilogra'fica, (penna) *f.* fountain pen.
stima *f.* estimate; esteem.
stimare *vt.* to estimate, appraise; to esteem; to consider, deem.
stimatore *m.* appraiser.
stimolante *m.*, *adj.* stimulant.
stimolare *vt.* to stimulate.
sti'molo *m.* stimulus.
stinco *m.* shinbone, shin.
stin'gere *vt.*, stin'gersi *vr.*[143] to fade.
stinto *adj.* faded. *pp.of* stingere.
stipare *vt.*, stiparsi *vr.* to crowd, throng; to jam.
stipendiare *vt.* to salary; to hire.
stipen'dio *m.* salary, stipend.
sti'pite *m.* jamb; stem.
stipo *m.* cabinet.
stipulare *vt.* to stipulate.
stiracchiare *vt.*, *vi.* to stretch; to strain; to bargain, haggle; stiracchiarsi *vr.* to stretch (*oneself*).
stiracchiato *adj.* farfetched.
stirare *vt.* to stretch; to iron, press; stirarsi *vr.* to stretch (*oneself*).
stiratrice *f.* ironer; laundress.
stiratura *f.* ironing.
stireri'a *f.* laundry shop.
stiro, (ferro da) *m.* (*pressing*) iron.
stirpe *f.* birth; race; issue.
stitichezza *f.* constipation.
sti'tico *adj.* constipated.
stiva *f.* hold.
stivale *m.* boot.
stivare *vt.* to stow.
stivatore *m.* stevedore, longshoreman.
stizza *f.* vexation, anger.
stizzire *vt.* to irk, annoy; to peeve; stizzirsi *vr.* to get angry, flare up.
stizzito *adj.* cross, angry.
stizzoso *adj.* testy, peevish.
stoccafisso *m.* stockfish.
stoccata *f.* thrust; touch.
stoffa *f.* cloth, stuff, material.
stoicismo *m.* stoicism.
sto'ico *m.* stoic; *adj.* stoical.
stola *f.* stole.
sto'lido *adj.* stolid.
stoltezza *f.* foolishness, silliness.
stolto *m.* fool; *adj.* foolish, silly.
stomacare *vt.* to disgust, sicken.
stomache'vole *adj.* loathsome, disgusting.
sto'maco *m.* stomach: dar di —, to vomit; avere il pelo sullo —, to be utterly unscrupulous.
stonare *vi.* to be out of tune; to jar; to "fluff."
stonato *adj.* out of tune; jarring.
stonatura *f.* dissonance; jarring note.
stoppa *f.* tow; (*naut.*) oakum.
stoppac'cio *m.* wadding, wad.
stop'pia *f.* stubble.

stoppino *m.* wick.
storcere *vt.*[145] storcersi *vr.* to twist; to twitch; to sprain.
stordimento *m.* daze, dizziness.
stordire *vt.* to stun, daze; stordirsi *vr.* to dull one's senses.
storditag'gine *f.* heedlessness; mistake, oversight.
stordito *m.* fool, numskull; *adj.* dull, scatterbrained; heedless.
sto'ria *f.* history; story, tale; pretext: fare un sacco di storie, to quibble a lot; to kick up a row.
sto'rico *adj.* historical.
storiella *f.* short story; lie, fib; joke.
storione *m.* sturgeon.
stormire *vi.* to rustle.
stormo *m.* flight; flock; swarm; (*aeron.*, *mil.*) wing: comandante di —, wing commander.
stornare *vt.* to ward off; to divert; to misapply; (*comm.*) to transfer, adjust; to cancel.
stornello *m.* refrain, ditty.
storno (1) *m.* (*ornith.*) starling.
storno (2) *m.* (*comm.*) transfer; cancellation.
storpiare *vt.* to maim; to mar.
stor'pio *m.* cripple; *adj.* crippled.
storta *f.* sprain; (*chem.*) retort.
storto *adj.* crooked; askew, awry; twisted; wrong; misshapen; *adv.* awry; the wrong way: avere gli occhi storti, to be squint-eyed. *pp. of* storcere.
stortura *f.* twist; incongruity.
stovi'glie *f.pl.* pottery, earthenware.
stra- *pref.* over: stramaturo, overripe; straricco, excessively rich.
stra'bico *adj.* squinting, squint-eyed.
strabiliante *adj.* astonishing.
strabiliare *vi.* to be amazed: far —, to amaze.
strabismo *m.* squint, strabismus.
straboccare *vi.* to overflow.
strabocche'vole *adj.* overflowing.
strabuzzare *see* stralunare.
stracaricare *vt.* to overload.
straca'rico *adj.* overladen.
stracca, (alla) *adv.* lazily; halfheartedly.
straccali *m.pl.* suspenders.
straccare *see* stancare.
stracciare *vt.* to rend, tear; stracciarsi *vr.* to tear.
stracciato *adj.* in rags, torn.
strac'cio *m.* rag, tatter.
straccione *m.* ragged man, scarecrow.
stracco *adj.* tired.
stracotto *m.* stew; *adj.* overdone.
stracuo'cere *vt.* to overdo (*as meat*).
strada *f.* road; street; way; course: — maestra, highroad; mettersi su una brutta —, to go astray; met-

tere fuori di —, to throw off the track.

stradale m. avenue. adj. road: **carta** —, road map; **fondo** —, roadbed; **illuminazione** —, street lighting; **incidente** —, traffic accident; **polizia** —, traffic police; **regolamento** —, traffic regulations; **targa** —, street marker.

Stradella, Alessandro, Italian composer (1645–1682).

Stradivari, Antonio (*Antonius Stradivarius*), Italian violinmaker (1644–1737).

strafalcione m. blunder.

strafare vi. to overdo.

straforo, (di) adv. surreptitiously, stealthily; underhandedly.

strafottente adj. cocky, unconcerned; bumptious.

strafottenza f. unconcern; bumptiousness.

strage f. massacre; (*fig.*) plenty.

stragrande adj. enormous.

stralciare vt. to lop off; to cancel; to pigeonhole.

stral'cio m. (*agr.*) lopping: **vendita a** —, bargain sale.

strale m. dart, arrow.

strallo m. (*naut.*) stay.

stralunare vt. to roll; to open (*one's eyes*) wide.

stralunato adj. wild-eyed.

stramazzare vi. to fall heavily, drop.

stramazzo m. paillasse.

stramberi'a f. oddity, quaintness.

strambo adj. odd, queer, quaint.

strame m. litter.

strampalato adj. preposterous, absurd.

stranezza f. queerness.

strangolamento m. strangling.

strangolare vt. to strangle, throttle; to suffocate.

strangolatore m. strangler.

straniare vt. to estrange; **straniarsi** vr. to estrange oneself.

straniero m. foreigner, alien. adj. foreign, alien.

strano adj. strange, queer, odd.

straordina'rio adj. extraordinary; wonderful; unusual; (*comm.*) overtime: **lavoro** —, overtime work; **fare gli straordinari,** to work overtime.

strapagare vt. to overpay.

strapazzare vt. to misuse; to upbraid; to crumple; to scramble (*as eggs*); **strapazzarsi** vr. to overtask one's strength; to wear oneself out.

strapazzata f. reproof, rebuke.

strapazzo m. fatigue, excess.

strapieno adj. full up, overfull.

strapiombare vi. to jut out.

strapiombo m. drop, sheer drop: **a** —, sheer, sheerly.

strapotente adj. overpowerful.

strapotenza f. overpower.

strappare vt. to tear; to snatch; to pluck; to wrench; to extort; to pull: — **le lacrime,** to stir pity; — **il cuore,** to wring one's heart; **strapparsi** vr. to tear; to tear oneself away (*from*): **strapparsi i capelli,** to tear one's hair.

strappo m. pull, wrench; rent, tear strain: — **muscolare,** muscular strain; **a strappi,** jerkily; **fare uno** — **alla regola,** to stretch a point.

strapuntino m. jump seat, bucket seat.

straricco adj. immensely rich, rolling in riches.

straripamento m. overflowing.

straripare vi. to overflow.

strascicare vt. to shuffle; to drag; to drawl.

stra'scico m. sequel; train; aftermath.

strascinare vt. to drag.

stra'scino m. dragnet, trawl.

stratagemma m. stratagem.

stratega m. strategist.

strategi'a f. strategy.

strate'gico adj. strategic: **posizione strategica,** vantage point.

strato m. layer; stratum; stratus; film: — **sensibile** (*photo.*), sensitive surface.

stratosfera f. stratosphere.

stratosfe'rico adj. stratospheric.

strattone m. jerk, pull.

stravagante m., adj. eccentric; whimsical; moody.

stravaganza f. oddity, eccentricity; vagary.

stravec'chio adj. very old.

stravin'cere vi. to triumph, to vaunt.

straviziare vi. to debauch.

stravi'zio m. intemperance, debauch.

stravol'gere vt.[166] to roll, twist.

stravolto adj. twisted; troubled.

straziante adj. heart-rending.

straziare vt. to tear, torture; to grate on; to make a mess of; to rend, wring: — **una lingua,** to murder a language.

straziato adj. torn, stricken: **col cuore** —, heart-stricken.

stra'zio m. torture, torment.

strega f. sorceress, witch.

stregare vt. to bewitch.

stregone m. wizard, sorcerer.

stregoneri'a f. witchcraft.

stregua f. rate, proportion: **alla stessa** —, by the same token; **alla** — **di,** as, the same as.

stremare vt. to exhaust.

strenna f. present, gift.

stre'nuo adj. vigorous, strenuous.

strepitare *vi.* to roar, shout, thunder.
stre'pito *m.* uproar; din, roar; hit: far — (*fig.*), to make a hit.
strepitoso *adj.* uproarious; sensational.
streptomicina *f.* streptomycin.
stretta *f.* tightening; hold, grasp, grip; pang: — di mano, handshake; una — al cuore, a pang in one's heart; mettere alle strette, to drive into a corner.
strettamente *adv.* tightly; strictly.
stretto (1) *m.* (geog.) straits.
stretto (2) *adj.* narrow; tight, close; strict; stingy: pugno —, clenched fist. *pp.of* stringere.
stretto'ia *f.* straits.
stria *f.* stria; stripe; furrow.
striare *vt.* to stripe, streak.
stricnina *f.* strychnine.
stridente *adj.* jarring, strident, sharp.
stri'dere *vi.* to screech, squeak; to shriek; to clash, jar.
stridore *m.* screeching.
stri'dulo *adj.* piercing, shrill.
strigare *vt.* to disentangle.
stri'glia *f.* currycomb.
strigliare *vt.* to curry; to rebuke.
strillare *vi.* to shriek, scream.
strillo *m.* scream, shriek, cry.
strillone *m.* newsboy, newsman.
striminzito *adj.* scrubby, stunted.
strimpellare *vt.* to thrum.
strinare *vt.* to singe.
stringa *f.* shoelace.
stringato *adj.* terse, concise.
stringente *adj.* urgent; severe; cogent.
string'ere *vt.*[136] to tighten; to press, clench; to grip; to shorten; to narrow; to squeeze; *vi.* to be tight: — un patto, to make an agreement; — d'assedio, to besiege; il tempo stringe, there is no time to be lost; stringersi *vr.* to draw near, get close; to tighten; to narrow; to shorten: stringersi nelle spalle, to shrug.
stri'scia *f.* strip, band: a strisce, striped.
strisciante *adj.* creeping; fawning, cringing: un essere —, a toady, a "softsoaper."
strisciare *vt.* to shuffle; to drag; to raze; to fawn upon, flatter; *vi.* to crawl, creep: — coi piedi, to shuffle one's feet.
strisciata *f.* rub; track; flattery.
stri'scio *m.* graze: di —, grazingly.
striscione *m.* festoon.
stritolare *vt.* to smash, crush.
strizzare *vt.* to wring, squeeze.
strizzata *f.* wring, squeeze; wink.
strofa, strofe *f.* strophe.
strofinac'cio *m.* floorcloth; duster; wiper.

strofinare *vt.* to rub; to wipe; strofinarsi *vr.* to rub.
strofini'o *m.* rubbing, friction.
strombazzare *vt.* to flaunt; to divulge; to "ballyhoo."
strombettare *vi.* to toot.
stroncare *vt.* to break; to pull to pieces; to censure, slash.
stroncatura *f.* slashing criticism, slash.
stropicciare *vt.* to rub; to scrub.
strozza *f.* throttle, throat.
strozzare *vt.* to throttle, strangle; to choke; (*fig.*) to fleece.
strozzatura *f.* narrowing.
Strozzi, Giambattista (*Filippo II*), Florentine statesman (1488–1538).
strozzinag'gio *m.* usury.
strozzino *m.* usurer, loan shark.
strug'gere *vt.*[137] to melt; to consume, eat up; to torment; strug'gersi *vr.* to melt; to pine (*for, with*); to languish, waste away: struggersi in lacrime, to melt into tears; struggersi d'invidia, to burst with envy.
struggimento *m.* melting; pining; anxiety; torment.
strumento *m.* instrument; tool: strumenti a fiato (*mus.*), winds; strumenti ad arco, strings.
strusciare *vt.* to wear out; to rub.
strutto (1) *m.* lard.
strutto (2) *pp.of* struggere.
struttura *f.* structure, frame.
struzzo *m.* ostrich.
stuccare *vt.* to stucco; to putty; to fill up; to surfeit; stuccarsi *vr.* to grow weary, grow sick.
stuccatura *f.* plastering; filling.
stucche'vole *adj.* sickening; boring.
stucco *m.* stucco, plaster; putty: rimanere di —, to be nonplussed.
studente *m.* student.
studentesco *adj.* student, student-like.
studentessa *f.* girl student.
studiare *vt.* to study; to examine; to scrutinize, observe; — legge, to read, study, for the bar; studiarsi *vr.* to endeavor, try.
studiato *adj.* accurate; studied; deliberate; forced.
stu'dio *m.* study; studio; office.
studioso *m.* scholar; *adj.* studious.
stufa *f.* stove; conservatory.
stufare (1) *vt.* to bore, tire; stufarsi *vr.* to get bored, tired.
stufare (2) *vt.* to stew.
stufato *m.* stew, stewed meat.
stufo *adj.* sick, tired; bored.
stuo'ia *f.* mat, matting.
stuoino *m.* doormat.
stuolo *m.* troop, multitude.

stupefacente *m.* drug, dope: **dedito agli stupefacenti**, drug-addicted; *adj.* stupefying; astonishing.

stupefare *vt.* to stupefy; to astonish.

stupefatto *adj.* astonished, surprised, amazed. *pp.of* stupefare.

stupefazione *f.* astonishment.

stupendo *adj.* stupendous, wonderful.

stupidag'gine *f.* foolishness, silliness; nonsense.

stupidamente *adv.* foolishly.

stupidità *f.* stupidity, silliness.

stu'pido *m.* fool: **fare lo —**, to make a fool of oneself; **non fare lo —!** don't be a fool!; *adj.* stupid, silly.

stupire *vt.* to astonish; **stupirsi** *vr.* to be astonished, wonder (*at*).

stupore *m.* astonishment, amazement; (*med.*) stupor.

stuprare *vt.* to rape.

stupro *m.* rape, violation.

stura *f.:* **dare la — a**, to uncork; to set off, start.

sturare *vt.* to uncork.

stuzzicadenti *m.* toothpick.

stuzzicante *adj.* stimulating.

stuzzicare *vt.* to stimulate, stir; to tease: **stuzzicarsi i denti**, to pick one's teeth.

su *prep.* on, upon; over; above; about; against; after: **sul mezzogiorno**, about noon; **sulla cinquantina**, about fifty; **sul serio**, in earnest; **sui due piedi**, right away, offhand; *adv.* up, over; upstairs; overhead: **tirar —**, to bring up, rear; **venir —**, to grow; **in —**, up; **all'insù**, upturned; **più —**, higher; **— per giù**, approximately, more or less.

sua *see* suo.

suadente *adj.* persuasive, coaxing.

subac'queo *adj.* subaqueous, underwater: **pescatore, nuotatore —**, skin diver; **fucile —**, speargun.

subaffittare *vt.* to sublet.

subaffitto *m.* sublease.

subalterno *m.*, *adj.* subaltern, subordinate.

subbu'glio *see* scompiglio.

subcosciente *m.*, *adj.* subconscious.

sub'dolo *adj.* shifty, deceitful.

subentrare *vi.:* **— a**, to succeed.

subire *vt.* to undergo; to suffer; *vi.* to bear with it.

subissare *vt.* to ruin; to overcome: **— di fischi**, to boo; **— d'applausi**, to applaud enthusiastically.

subisso *m.* ruin: **un — di**, plenty of; **un — d'applausi**, a roar of applause.

subita'neo *adj.* sudden; unexpected.

su'bito *adj.* sudden; *adv.* at once, right away; soon: **— dopo**, soon after.

sublimato *m.*, *adj.* sublimate.

sublime *adj.* sublime.

subodorare *vt.* to suspect; to get an inkling of.

subordinare *vt.* to subordinate.

subordinato *m.*, *adj.* subordinate.

subornare *vt.* to bribe.

substrato *m.* substratum.

suburbano *adj.* suburban.

subur'bio *m.* suburbs.

succeda'neo *m.* substitute, ersatz; *adj.* succedaneous.

succe'dere *vi.*[23] to ensue, happen, occur: **— a**, to follow; to succeed.

successione *f.* succession: **tasse di —**, inheritance taxes.

successivo *adj.* following; next.

successo (1) *m.* success; hit; outcome.

successo (2) *pp.of* succedere.

successore *m.* successor.

succhiare *vt.* to suck (*up*); (*fig.*) to put up with.

succhiello *m.* gimlet.

succinto *adj.* succinct; concise.

succo *m.* juice; sap; (*fig.*) gist.

succosamente *adv.* pithily, substantially.

succoso *adj.* juicy; sappy.

suc'cubo *m.* succubus; *adj.* (*fig.*) slave (*to*).

succulento *adj.* succulent, juicy.

succursale *f.* branch (office), agency.

su'cido *see* sudicio.

sud *m.* south.

sudamericano *adj.* South American.

sudafricano *adj.* South African.

sudare *vt.*, *vi.* to sweat, perspire; to exude; to toil: **— freddo**, to be in a cold sweat; **— sette camicie**, to be hard put to it; to strive hard.

suda'rio *m.* shroud.

sudata *f.* sweat, sweating.

sudato *adj.* sweating.

suddetto *adj.* above-mentioned.

sud'dito *m.* subject.

suddivi'dere *vt.*[48] to subdivide, break up.

suddivisione *f.* subdivision.

suddiviso *pp.of* suddividere.

sud-est *m.* southeast.

sudiceri'a *f.* dirtiness; indecency.

su'dicio *adj.* dirty, filthy; obscene.

sudiciume *m.* dirt, filth.

sudore *m.* sweat, perspiration: **madido di —**, wet with perspiration.

sud-ovest *m.* southwest.

sufficiente *m.*, *adj.* enough; sufficient.

sufficienza *f.* sufficiency: **a —**, enough; **con aria di —**, patronizingly.

suffisso *m.* suffix.

suffragare *vt.* to support; to corroborate.

suffragetta *f.* suffragette.

suffra'gio *m.* suffrage; approval.
suffumi'gio *m.* fumigation.
suggellare *vt.* to seal; to seal up.
suggello *m.* seal.
suggerimento *m.* suggestion.
suggerire *vt.* to suggest; to prompt.
suggeritore *m.* (*theat.*) prompter.
suggestiona'bile *adj.* suggestible.
suggestionare *vt.* to hypnotize; to influence.
suggestione *f.* suggestion.
suggestivo *adj.* suggestive.
su'ghero *m.* cork; cork tree.
sugli *comp.prep.* on the. *see* su.
sugna *f.* lard; grease.
sugo *m.* juice; gravy: — di pomidoro, tomato sauce; senza — (*fig.*), idle, empty, pointless, dull.
sugoso *see* succoso.
sui *comp.prep.* on the. *see* su.
suicida *m.* suicide; *adj.* suicidal.
suicidarsi *vr.* to commit suicide.
suici'dio *m.* suicide.
suino *m.* swine; *adj.* swinish: carne suina, pork meat.
sul *comp. prep.* on the. *see* su.
sulfamide, sulfami'dico *m.* sulfanilamide: i sulfamidici, sulfa drugs.
sulla, sulle, sullo *prep.* on the. *see* su.
sullodato *adj.* above (*mentioned*).
sunteggiare *vt.* to epitomize, condense.
sunto *m.* epitome, summary, condensation.
suo *poss.adj.* his; her; its; *poss.pron.* his; hers; the one belonging to it: un amico —, a friend of his (hers).
suo'cera *f.* mother-in-law; (*fig.*) termagant.
suo'cero *m.* father-in-law.
suola *f.* sole.
suolo *m.* ground, soil; floor: precipitare al — (*aeron.*), to crash.
suonare, suonatore, *etc. see* sonare.
suono *m.* sound: muro del —, sound barrier.
suora *f.* nun, sister.
superallenamento *m.* over-training.
superamento *m.* overcoming.
superare *vt.* to surpass; to overcome; get over; to negotiate; to exceed; to get the better of; to pass; to outrun; to outspeed; to climb over; to leave behind: — se stesso, to excel oneself: — una curva (*auto.*), to negotiate a turn.
super'bia *f.* haughtiness; conceit: montare in —, to put on airs.
superbioso *adj.* haughty, conceited.
superbo *adj.* proud; haughty; conceited, contemptuous; superb.
supereterodina *f.* superheterodyne.
superficiale *adj.* superficial; slight; cursory.
superficialità *f.* superficiality.

superfi'cie *f.* surface; area:— portante, airfoil; salire alla —, to surface.
super'fluo *m.* surplus; *adj.* superfluous; unnecessary; needless.
superfortezza *f.* superfortress: — volante, flying superfortress.
superiora *f.* mother superior.
superiore *m.* superior; *adj.* superior; higher; above; upper; excellent: ufficiale —, ranking officer; scuola —, high school.
superiorità *f.* superiority.
superlativo *m., adj.* superlative.
superlavoro *m.* overwork.
superso'nico *adj.* supersonic.
super'stite *m.* survivor; *adj.* surviving.
superstizione *f.* superstition.
superstizioso *adj.* superstitious.
superuomo *m.* superman.
supino *m., adj.* supine, on one's back.
suppellet'tili *f.pl.* fittings; furniture.
suppergiù *adv.* nearly; just about; more or less.
supplementare *adj.* supplementary, additional, extra; auxiliary.
supplemento *m.* supplement, addition; extra.
supplente *m., f.* deputy, substitute.
sup'plica *f.* petition; entreaty.
supplicante *m.* petitioner, suppliant; *adj.* suppliant.
supplicare *vt.* to implore, entreat, beg, beseech.
suppliche'vole *adj.* imploring, beseeching.
supplire *vt.* to substitute, take the place of; *vi.* to provide (*for*); to make up (*for*): — a, to substitute.
suppli'zio *m.* torture; torment; punishment, execution: — di Tantalo (*fig.*), tantalization.
supporre *vt., vi.*[93] to suppose; to surmise.
supporto *m.* support, prop; bearing; bracket.
supposizione *f.* supposition, surmise.
supposta *f.* (*med.*) suppository.
supposto *m.* supposition; *adj.* supposed. *pp.of* supporre.
suppurare *vi.* to suppurate.
suppurazione *f.* suppuration.
supremazi'a *f.* supremacy.
supremo *adj.* supreme.
surclassare *vt.* to outclass.
surrealismo *m.* surrealism.
surrealista *m., adj.* surrealist.
surrenale *adj.* suprarenal.
surriscaldare *vt.* to overheat.
surrogato *m.* substitute, ersatz.
suscetti'bile *adj.* susceptible; receptive; touchy.
suscettibilità *f.* susceptibility; receptivity; touchiness.

suscitare *vt.* to raise; to stir (*up*); to provoke; to inspire.

susina *f.* plum.

susseguente *adj.* subsequent.

susseguire *vi.* to succeed, follow.

sussi'dio *m.* subsidy; allowance: — militare, separation allowance.

sussiego *m.* primness; aloofness.

sussistenza *f.* validity; subsistence; livelihood; (*mil.*) Quartermaster Corps.

sussi'stere *vi.* to subsist; to exist; to hold good; to last.

sussultare *vt.* to start, jump, quake.

sussulto *m.* start, jump, quake.

sussulto'rio *adj.* sussultorial.

sussurrare, susurrare *vt.*, *vi.* to whisper; to murmur.

sussurratore *m.* murmurer.

sussurri'o *m.* whispering.

susurro *m.* murmur, rustle; whisper.

sutura *f.* suture.

suturare *vt.* to suture.

svagare *vt.* to distract, divert (*one's attention*); to amuse, entertain; to relax; svagarsi *vr.* to distract oneself, divert oneself; to enjoy oneself; to relax, take some recreation.

svagatezza *f.* absent-mindedness.

svagato *adj.* absent-minded; inattentive.

svago *m.* recreation; entertainment.

svaligiamento *m.* robbery.

svaligiare *vt.* to rob; to clean out.

svaligiatore *m.* robber, burglar.

svalutare *vt.* to depreciate.

svalutato *adj.* depreciated.

svalutazio'ne *f.* depreciation.

svanire *vi.* to vanish; to fade (*away, out*); to evaporate.

svanito *adj.* vanished; muddled, addled.

svantag'gio *m.* drawback; disadvantage.

svantaggioso *adj.* unfavorable; detrimental.

svaporare *vi.* to evaporate.

svariato *adj.* varied; svariati *pl.* various, several.

svarione *m.* blunder; (*typog.*) misprint.

svasare *vt.* to flare (*as a skirt*).

svasato *adj.* flaring.

sva'stica *f.* swastika.

svecchiare *vt.* to renew.

sve'glia *f.* waking up; alarm clock; (*mil.*) reveille.

svegliare *vt.*, svegliarsi *vr.* to wake (*up*), awaken, stir.

svegliarino *m.* prompter.

sve'glio *adj.* awake; quick-witted; lively; shrewd.

svelare *vt.* to unveil; to reveal, disclose; svelarsi *vr.* to reveal oneself.

svel'lere *see* divellere.

sveltezza *f.* quickness.

sveltire *vt.* to quicken; to make more self-confident; sveltirsi *vr.* to quicken; to become self-confident.

svelto (1) *adj.* quick; nimble; slender, quick-witted, smart; *adv.* quickly, fast.

svelto (2) *pp. of* svellere.

svenare *vi.* to bleed; svenarsi *vr.* to open one's veins; to bleed.

sven'dere *vt.* to undersell; to dispose of.

svene'vole *adj.* mawkish, spoony.

svenevolezza *f.* mawkishness.

svenimento *m.* swoon, faint.

svenire *vi.*[152] to swoon, faint.

sventagliare *vt.* to fan.

sventagliata *f.* fanning; volley.

sventare *vt.* to avert; to thwart.

sventatag'gine, sventatezza *f.* heedlessness, carelessness.

sventato *m.* scatterbrain; *adj.* heedless.

sven'tola *f.* fire fan; slap; (*boxing*) swing.

sventolare *vt.* to flutter; to wave; to fan; *vi.* to fly, flutter; sventolarsi *vr.* to fan oneself.

sventoli'o *m.* fluttering.

sventramento *m.* disembowelment; demolition.

sventrare *vt.* to eviscerate; to disembowel; to demolish, dismantle.

sventura *f.* misfortune; mishap.

sventurato *m.* wretch; *adj.* unlucky, unfortunate.

svenuto *adj.* unconscious, in a swoon. *pp. of* svenire.

sverginare *vt.* to deflower.

svergognare *vt.* to put to shame.

svergognato *adj.* shameless, impudent; abashed.

svergolare *vi.* to twist; (*aeron.*) to warp.

svernare *vi.* to winter.

sverniciare *vt.* to unpaint.

svestire *vt.* to undress; svestirsi *vr.* to undress (*oneself*).

svettare *vt.* to pollard; *vi.* to waver, sway; to soar.

Svevo, Italo (*Ettore Schmitz*), Italian novelist of German father (1861–1928).

svezzare *vt.* to wean; to cure.

sviare *vt.* to deviate; to avert; to lead astray, mislead; sviarsi *vr.* to go astray.

svignar'sela *vi.* to slip away, steal away; to "beat it," decamp.

svilire *vt.* to depreciate; to lower.

svillaneggiare *vt.* to treat rudely, insult, snub, knock about.

sviluppare *vt.* to develop; to increase. *vi.*, svilupparsi *vr.* to develop; to grow; to spread; to thrive; to branch out.

sviluppo *m.* development; growth; increase: età dello —, age of puberty.

svincolare *vt.* to free, disengage; to redeem; to clear; **svincolarsi** *vr.* to free oneself, disengage oneself.

svin'colo *m.* clearing.

svisare *vt.* to misrepresent; to alter.

sviscerare *vt.* to eviscerate; to exhaust, examine thoroughly.

sviscerato *adj.* ardent, passionate.

svista *f.* oversight.

svitare *vt.* to unscrew.

svogliatezza *f.* listlessness.

svogliato *adj.* listless, lazy.

svolazzante *adj.* flitting.

svolazzare *vi.* to flutter.

svolazzo *m.* flourish, curlicue.

svol'gere *vt.*[156] to unwind; to undo, unroll; to develop; to perform, carry out, be engaged (*in*), discharge; **svol'gersi** *vr.* to unroll, unfold; to happen, occur, take place.

svolgimento *m.* development; performance; discharge; treatment.

svolta *f.* turn; corner; turning-point.

svolto *pp.of* svolgere.

svoltare *vi.* to make a turn; to turn.

svotare *vt.*, **svotarsi** *vr.* to empty.

T

tabacca'io *m.* tobacconist.

tabaccare *vi.* to snuff.

tabaccheri'a *f.* tobacco store, cigar store.

tabacchiera *f.* snuffbox.

tabacco *m.* tobacco: — da fiuto, snuff.

tabarro *m.* tabard.

tabella *f.* table; schedule; list.

taberna'colo *m.* tabernacle.

tabù *m.* taboo.

ta'bula *f.:* far — rasa, to make a clean sweep (*of*).

tacca *f.* notch; nick: di mezza —, middle-sized; mediocre.

taccagneri'a *f.* stinginess.

taccagno *m.* miser; *adj.* stingy.

taccheggiatore *m.*, **taccheggiatrice** *f.* shoplifter.

taccheg'gio *m.* shoplifting.

tacchino *m.* turkey.

tac'cia *f.* blemish, fault; charge; fame.

tacciare *vt.* to accuse (*of*), charge (*with*).

tacco *m.* heel (*of a shoe*): alzare i tacchi, to take to one's heels.

taccone *m.* patch.

taccuino *m.* notebook.

tacere *vt.*[139] to withhold, omit; *vi.* to keep silent, be silent, hold one's tongue; to stop (*talking*); to say nothing: far —, to silence; **tacete!** shut up!

tachi'metro *m.* tachometer; speedometer.

tacitare *vt.* to silence; to indemnify; to pay (*off*).

ta'cito *adj.* tacit, silent; implied.

taciturno *adj.* taciturn; sullen.

taciuto *pp.of* tacere.

tafano *m.* gadfly; oxfly.

tafferu'glio *m.* fray, scuffle, fight.

taffettà *m.* taffeta; court plaster.

ta'glia (*1*) *f.* levy, tribute; ransom; reward.

ta'glia (*2*) *f.* stature; size.

tagliaborse *m.* pickpocket.

tagliaboschi, taglialegna *m.* woodman, woodcutter.

tagliacarte *m.* paper knife.

tagliamare *m.* (*naut.*) breakwater.

tagliando *m.* coupon.

tagliare *vt.* to cut; to clip; to sever; to split; to cross; *vi.* to cut: — la strada a uno, to stand in one's way; — i panni addosso a, to slander; — i viveri, to cut off supplies; — la corda, to "vamoose"; farsi — i capelli, to have one's hair cut; **tagliarsi** *vr.* to cut oneself.

tagliatelle *f.pl.* noodles.

tagliatore *m.* cutter.

taglieggiare *vt.* to ransom.

tagliente *adj.* cutting; sharp.

taglierina *f.* paper cutter.

ta'glio *m.* cut, cutting; clipping; rent, fissure; edge (*of a blade*); denomination (*of banknotes*); fit, style; harvest: — di stoffa, piece of cloth; arma da —, edged weapon; di —, edgeways.

taglione *m.:* legge del —, law of retaliation.

tagliuola *f.* trap, snare.

tagliuzzare *vt.* to mince.

ta'lamo *m.* nuptial bed.

talare, (abito) *m.* soutane.

talchè *adv.* so that.

talco *m.* talc; talcum powder.

tale *adj.*, *pron.* such; like, similar; same; certain: — il padre — il figlio, like father like son; è — quale il mio, it is just like mine; una tal qual paura, a certain fear; nella — città, in such and such town; il — dei tali, Mr. So and So; un —, a "guy"; quei tali che, those (*people*) who; è — quale era, it is just as it was; — quale lo vedi, such as you see it.

talento *m.* talent, ability: **a vostro —,** at your will.

talismano *m.* talisman, charm.

tallire *vi.* to sprout.

tallone *m.* heel.

talmente *adv.* so much, so, so very.

talora *adv.* sometimes.

talpa *f.* mole; (*fig.*) dullard.

taluno *adj., pron.* someone.

talvolta *adv.* sometimes.

tamarindo *m.* tamarind.

tambureggiare *vi.* to drum.

tamburello *m.* tambourine.

tamburino *m.* tambourine; drummer.

tamburo *m.* drum; drummer; barrel (*of a watch*): **a — battente,** instantly.

tamerice *m.* tamarisk.

Tamigi *m.* Thames.

tampoco, (nè) *adv.* neither, not even.

tamponare *vt.* to stop, tampon, plug.

tampone *m.* stopper, tampon.

tana *f.* lair, hole, den.

tana'glia *f.* pincers, nippers, tongs (*all pl.*); tenaille.

tanfo *m.* stench.

tangente *f.* share; (*geom.*) tangent; *adj.* tangent.

tan'gere *vt.* to touch; to concern.

tan'ghero *m.* bumpkin, boor.

tangi'bile *adj.* tangible.

tantino *m.* bit, little bit.

tanto (*1*) *adj., pron.* so much, as much; much; enough, sufficient; **tanti** *pl.* so (as) many; many; many people: **— denaro quanto ne vuoi,** as much money as you want; **cinquanta e tante lire,** fifty odd lire; **da — tempo,** for quite a while; **— vale restar a casa,** we might as well stay at home; **due volte tanti,** twice as many.

tanto (*2*) *adv.* so, such; so much; as; both ... and: **è — caro!** he is such a dear!; **è — bella quanto buona,** she is as beautiful as she is good; **— l'Italia quanto l'Inghilterra,** both Italy and England; **— più che,** (all) the more so as; **una volta —,** once in a while; **di — in —,** now and then; **— per fare qualcosa,** just to.

tanto (*3*) *m.* (a) given quantity, (a) given amount: **un — per cento,** a percentage.

tapino *m.* wretch; *adj.* wretched.

tappa *f.* stop, halting place; stage; leg.

tappabuchi *m.* (*fig.*) stopgap.

tappare *vt.* to cork, plug; to stop (*up*); to shut; **tapparsi** *vr.* to shut oneself (*up*); **tapparsi il naso,** to stop one's nose.

tappeto *m.* carpet, rug: **— verde,** green cloth; **mettere al —,** to knock out.

tappezzare *vt.* to tapestry; to paper; to upholster.

tappezzeri'a *f.* tapestry; wallpaper; upholstery.

tappezziere *m.* upholsterer; paperhanger; decorator.

tappo *m.* stopper; bung; cork; plug.

tara *f.* tare; disease; stigma, brand.

tarare *vt.* to tare; to adjust.

tarato *adj.* branded; stigmatic.

tarchiato *adj.* thickset, stocky.

tardare *vt., vi.* to delay; to be late.

tardi *adv.* late: **sul —,** at a late hour; **più —,** later; **al più —,** at the latest; **far —,** to be late.

tardivo *adj.* tardy; late; slow.

tardo *adj.* tardy; slow; slow-witted; late.

targa *f.* shield; plate; number plate, license plate; trophy: **— stradale,** street marker.

targare *vt.* (*auto.*) to register.

targatura *f.* (*auto.*) registration.

tariffa *f.* rates, tariff.

tarlarsi *vr.* to get worm-eaten.

tarlato *adj.* worm-eaten.

tarlo *m.* woodworm; moth.

tarma *f.* moth.

tarmare *vi.*, **tarmarsi** *vr.* to get motheaten.

tarmato *adj.* moth-eaten.

tarocchi *m.pl.* tarot.

tarpare *vt.* to clip.

tartagliare *vi.* to stammer, stutter.

tartaruga *f.* tortoise; turtle.

tartassare *vt.* to badger; to mangle.

tartina *f.* sandwich.

Tartini, Giuseppe, Italian violinist and composer, *Il trillo del diavolo* (1692–1770).

tartufo *m.* truffle.

tasca *f.* pocket: **rompere le tasche a,** to bother; **averne piene le tasche di,** to be fed up with.

tasca'bile *adj.* pocket.

tascapane *m.* pouch, haversack.

tassa *f.* tax; duty; fee.

tassa'metro *m.* taximeter.

tassare *vt.* to assess; to tax.

tassativamente *adv.* positively.

tassativo *adj.* positive, absolute.

tassazione *f.* assessment, taxation.

tassello *m.* dowel.

tassi *m.* taxi.

tasso (*1*) *m.* (*zool.*) badger.

tasso (*2*) *m.* (*bot.*) yew tree.

tasso (*3*) *m.* rate (*of interest*).

Tasso, Torquato, Italian poet, *La Gerusalemme Liberata* (1544–1595).

Tassoni, Alessandro, Italian poet and critic, *La secchia rapita* (1565–1635).

tastare *vt.* to finger, feel; (*med.*) to palpate: **— il terreno,** to feel one's way.

tastiera f. keyboard.
tasto m. fingering; touch; (mus., mach.) key: — telegrafico, tapper; un — delicato, a sore subject.
tastoni, (a) adv. gropingly.
tat'tica f. tactic, tactics; policy.
tat'tico m. tactician; adj. tactical.
tatto m. touch, feeling; tact.
tatuag'gio m. tattoo.
tatuare vt. to tattoo.
taumaturgo m. thaumaturgist.
taurino adj. bull-like, taurine.
taverna f. tavern, public house.
taverniere m. publican.
ta'vola f. table; plank; plate; board: — pitagorica, multiplication table; — reale, backgammon; — calda, cafeteria.
tavolac'cio m. plank bed.
tavolata f. tableful.
tavolato m. planking; plank wall; (geog.) plateau.
tavoletta f. small board; tablet; bar (of chocolate, etc.).
tavoliere m. chessboard; cardtable; (geog.) tableland.
tavolino m. small table.
ta'volo m. table.
tavolozza f. palette.
tazza f. cup, mug.
te pers.pron. you (fam.sing.); particle, (to) you.
tè m. tea.
teatrale adj. theatrical, stage.
teatro m. theater; playhouse; stage; drama: — dell'opera, opera house; — lirico, opera; — di prosa, drama, — di posa (moving pictures), studio.
teca f. case; (bot., anat.) theca.
tec'nica f. technique; technics.
tec'nico m. expert; technician; adj. technical.
teco pers.pron. with you; (poet.) with thee.
tedesco m., adj. German.
tediare vt. to bore; tediarsi vr. to get bored.
te'dio m. tedium, weariness.
tedioso adj. tedious, boring.
tegame m. pan.
te'glia f. bakepan.
te'gola f. tile; (fig.) brickbat.
te'golo m. tile.
teiera f. teapot.
tela f. linen, cloth; canvas; painting; (theat.) curtain: — di iuta, burlap; — greggia, canvas; — incerata, oilcloth; — di ragno, cobweb.
tela'io m. loom; frame, framework; (text.) loom; (auto.) chassis; sash (as of a window).
telearma f. guided missile.
teleca'mera f. telecamera.
telecomandato adj. remote-controlled.

telecomando m. remote control.
telecomunicazione f. telecommunication.
telecro'naca f. telecast.
telefe'rica f. telpherage; telpher; telpherway.
telefonare vt. to telephone, phone.
telefonata f. telephone call.
telefo'nico adj. telephonic; telephone.
telefonista m., f. telephone operator.
tele'fono m. telephone, phone: — interno, interphone; chiamare uno al —, to call one up.
telefoto f. telephotograph.
telege'nico adj. telegenic.
telegiornale m. telenewscast.
telegrafare vt. to telegraph, wire, cable.
telegrafi'a f. telegraphy.
telegra'fico adj. telegraphic: indirizzo —, cable address.
telegrafista m., f. telegraph operator.
tele'grafo m. telegraph; telegraph office: — senza fili, radiotelegraph.
telegramma m. telegram, wire; cable: — lettera, lettergram.
tele'metro m. telemeter; (photo.) rangefinder.
teleobbiettivo m. telephoto lens.
telepati'a f. telepathy.
telepa'tico adj. telepathic.
teleproietto m. robot bomb, rocket-propelled bomb.
telesco'pio m. telescope.
telescrivente f. teletypewriter, teleprinter.
telespettatore m. televiewer.
teletrasmet'tere vt. to telecast.
televisionare vt. to telecast; to televise.
televisione f. television, TV.
televisivo adj. television, TV.
televisore m. televisor.
tellu'rico adj. telluric.
telo m. piece of cloth, sheet: telo da tenda, shelter half.
telone m. (theat.) curtain; (moving pictures) screen.
tema (1) m. theme; subject.
tema (2) f. see timore.
temerarietà see temerità.
temera'rio m. daredevil; adj. reckless.
temere vt., vi. to fear, be afraid (of); to dread.
temerità f. rashness.
temi'bile adj. redoubtable.
tem'pera f. (metal.) temper.
temperamatite m. pencil sharpener.
temperamento m. mitigation; temperament, disposition.
temperante adj. temperate, moderate.
temperanza f. temperance, sobriety.
temperare vt. to temper; to moderate; to sharpen (as a pencil).

temperatura *f.* temperature.
temperino *m.* penknife.
tempesta *f.* storm; tempest.
tempestare *vt.* to storm (*with blows*);
vi. to storm: — di domande, to pelt
with questions.
tempestato *adj.* spangled, studded
(with).
tempestivo *adj.* timely, seasonable.
tempestoso *adj.* tempestuous, stormy.
tem'pia *f.* temple.
tem'pio *m.* temple.
tempo *m.* time; weather; (*gramm.*)
tense; (*moving pictures*) part: fare a
— per, to be in good time to; aver
fatto il proprio —, to have seen
one's days; da (molto) —, for
(quite) a while; col —, in time; —
fa, some time ago; molto — prima,
long before; a — perso, in one,s
spare moments; a suo —, in due
time; previously; in questi ultimi
tempi, lately; per —, early; a far
— da, dating from.
temporale *m.* storm; *adj.* secular.
tempora'neo *adj.* transitory, temporary.
temporeggiare *vi.* to temporize, procrastinate; to stall.
temporeggiatore *m.* temporizer.
tempra *f.* make, disposition; (*metal.*)
temper.
temprare *vt.* to temper; to harden; to
inure; **temprarsi** *vr.* to get inured;
to harden.
tenace *adj.* tenacious, stubborn.
tena'cia *f.* tenacity.
tena'glia *f. see* tana'glia.
tenda *f.* curtain; tent; awning.
tendenza *f.* inclination, tendency.
tendenzioso *adj.* tendentious.
ten'der (*rail.*) tender.
ten'dere *vt.*[140] to stretch (*out*); to hold
out, hand; to tighten; to prepare,
set; *vi.* to tend; to aim, drive (*at*);
to incline (*to*): — le orecchie, to
strain one's ears; — un arco, to
draw a bow.
tendina *f.* blind; window curtain.
ten'dine *m.* tendon.
te'nebre *f.pl.* obscurity, darkness.
tenebroso *adj.* obscure, dark, gloomy;
shady.
tenente *m.* lieutenant.
tenere *vt.*[141] to hold; to keep; to sustain; to wear; to contain; to stand;
to follow; to observe; to make; to
consider, think; *vi.* to be valid; to
hold, resist: — posto, to take room;
la via da —, the way to be followed;
— un discorso, to make, deliver
a speech; — per amico, to consider
a friend; — a mente, to bear in
mind; — d'occhio, to keep an

eye on; — a battesimo, to be
(one's) godfather *or* godmother;
— dietro a, to follow; — le parti
di, to stand up for; — per una
squadra (*sport*), to root for a team;
— conto di, to consider; — duro,
to hold on; **tenerci**, to be keen (*on*);
tenersi *vr.* to keep (*oneself*); to refrain, keep (*from*); to stick to:
tenersi per mano, to hold hands.
tenerezza *f.* tenderness, fondness;
softness.
te'nero *adj.* tender; loving, fond; soft.
te'nia *f.* tapeworm, taenia.
tenore *m.* tenor; standard; purport.
tensione *f.* tension; stress, strain.
tenta'colo *m.* tentacle.
tentare *vt., vi.* to try, attempt; to
tempt; to endeavor; to touch; to
feel.
tentativo *m.* attempt.
tentatore *m.* tempter; *adj.* tempting.
tentazione *f.* temptation.
tentennare *vt.* to shake; *vi.* to vacillate; to waver; to totter, stagger.
tentoni, (a) *adv.* gropingly.
te'nue *adj.* thin, slender; tenuous:
intestino —, small intestine.
tenuta *f.* uniform; capacity; estate,
farm: in alta —, in full dress; a —
d'acqua, watertight.
tenuta'rio *m.* operator.
tenuto *adj.* bound; obliged. *pp.of*
tenere.
teologi'a *f.* theology.
teo'logo *m.* theologian.
teorema *m.* theorem.
teore'tico *adj.* theoretic.
teori'a *f.* theory; row, procession.
teoricamente *adv.* in theory.
teo'rico *adj.* theoretical.
te'pido *adj.* lukewarm, tepid.
tepore *m.* warmth.
teppa *f.* underworld.
teppista *m.* hoodlum, tough.
terape'utico *adj.* therapeutic.
terapi'a *f.* therapeutics.
ter'gere *vt.*[142] to wipe (*off, away*); to
polish; to clean.
tergicristallo *m.* windshield wiper.
tergiversare *vi.* to stall; to quibble.
tergo *m.* back: a —, behind; overleaf.
termale *adj.* thermal.
terme *f.pl.* thermae; thermal springs;
bathing establishment; spa.
ter'mico *adj.* thermic.
terminare *see* finire.
terminazione *f.* end, close; termination, ending.
ter'mine *m.* term, limit; boundary;
end: avere —, to end; a rigor di
—, strictly speaking; in altri termini,
in other words.
terminologi'a *f.* terminology.

termo'foro *m.* thermophore.

termo'metro *m.* thermometer.

ter'mos *m.* Thermos (*trademark*), vacuum bottle.

termosifone *m.* heating plant; radiator.

termo'stato *m.* thermostat.

terna *f.* tern.

terno *m.* tern; *adj.* triple.

terra *f.* earth; land; ground, soil; floor: scendere a —, to land; essere a —, to be downcast; to be on one's uppers.

terracotta *f.* earthenware; terracotta.

terra'glia *f.*, terra'glie *f.pl.* pottery, earthenware.

terrapieno *m.* embankment.

terraza *f.*, terrazzo *m.* balcony; terrace.

terremotato *m.* earthquake victim *or* survivor.

terremoto *m.* earthquake.

terreno *m.* ground; soil; land: preparare il —, to pave the way; tastare il —, to throw out feelers; *adj.* earthly; worldly: piano —, ground floor, first floor (*U.S.*).

ter'reo *adj.* ghastly; pale; wan, ashen.

terrestre *adj.* terrestrial; land, earthly.

terri'bile *adj.* dreadful, terrible.

terribilmente *adv.* awfully, dreadfully.

terrificante *adj.* appalling, terrific.

terrificare *vt.* to appall, terrify.

terrina *f.* tureen.

territoriale *m.*, *adj.* territorial.

territo'rio *m.* territory.

terrone *m.*, *adj.* (*It.slang*) Southerner.

terrore *m.* dread, terror.

terrorismo *m.* terrorism.

terrorista *m.* terrorist.

terrorizzare *vt.* to terrorize.

terso *adj.* terse, polished; clear. *pp.of* tergere.

terzaruolo *m.* (*naut.*) reef.

terzetto *m.* triplet; trio.

terzo *m.*, *adj.* third.

terzul'timo *m.*, *adj.* last but two.

tesa *f.* brim (*of a hat*).

teschio *m.* skull.

tesi *f.* thesis (*pl.* theses).

teso *adj.* tight, taut, strained. *pp.of* tendere.

tesoreri'a *f.* treasure, treasury.

tesoriere *m.* treasurer.

tesoro *m.* treasure; treasury: far di, to treasure; buono del —, bond.

tes'sera *f.* card, ticket.

tesseramento *m.* rationing.

tesserare *vt.* to ration; to give a membership card to.

tesserato *m.* ration card holder; (*polit.*) cardholder.

tes'sere *vt.* to weave.

tes'sile *m.*, *adj.* textile.

tessitore *m.*, tessitrice *f.* weaver.

tessitura *f.* weaving; weaving mill.

tessuto *m.* fabric, cloth; tissue.

testa *f.* head: essere in —, to have the lead; colpo di —, plunge; mettere la — a partito, to reform; battere in — (*of a motor*), to ping; non saper dove battere la —, to be at one's wit's end; rompersi la —, to rack one's brains; to have the worst of it.

testamento *m.* testament, will.

testardag'gine *f.* stubbornness.

testardo *m.* stubborn.

testata *f.* head, headpiece; top; heading; blow with the head.

teste *m.* witness.

testè *adv.* a short time ago; just now.

testificare *vt.*, *vi.* to testify.

testimone *m.* witness; best man (*at a wedding*): — oculare, eyewitness.

testimonianza *f.* witness; evidence.

testimoniare *vt.*, *vi.* to serve as a witness; to testify, depose.

testimo'nio *m.* witness; best man (*at a wedding*).

testo *m.* text; contents.

testuale *adj.* verbatim.

testug'gine *f.* turtle, tortoise.

te'tano *m.* tetanus.

tetra'gono *adj.* tetragonal; resistant, unshaken (*by*).

tetro *adj.* gloomy, dark, bleak.

tetto *m.* roof.

tetto'ia *f.* shed; marquee.

ti *pers.pron.* you, to you; yourself.

tibia *f.* (*anat.*) shinbone.

ticchetti'o *m.* ticking.

tic'chio *m.* whim, fancy.

tie'pido *adj.* tepid, lukewarm.

Tie'polo, Giambattista, great Venetian painter (1696–1770).

tifo *m.* typhus: fare il — per (*sport*), to root for.

tifoidea *f.* typhoid fever.

tifone *m.* typhoon.

tifoso *m.* fan; (*sport*) rooter; *adj.* typhous.

ti'glio *m.* lime tree, lime.

tiglioso *adj.* fibrous; sinewy; tough.

tignola, tignuola *f.* moth.

tigrato *adj.* streaked, striped; tabby.

tigre *f.* tiger.

timbrare *vt.* to stamp.

timbratura *f.* stamping; postmarking.

timbro *m.* stamp; timbre (*of sounds*).

timidezza *f.* shyness, timidity.

ti'mido *adj.* timid, bashful, shy.

timone *m.* rudder, helm: — di profondità (*aeron.*), elevator.

timoneggiare *vt.* to steer.

timoniere *m.* steersman, helmsman

timorato *adj.* pious.

timore m. fear, dread; awe.
timoroso adj. timid, timorous.
tim'pano m. eardrum; kettledrum.
tinca f. (ichthyol.) tench.
tinello m. breakfast room.
tin'gere vt.[143] to dye; to paint; to stain: **tingersi i capelli**, to dye one's hair.
tino m. tub, vat.
tinozza f. tub; bathtub.
tinta f. dye; hue, color; tinge.
tinteggiare vt. to tinge.
tintinnare vi. to tinkle; to clink.
tintinni'o m. tinkling; clinking.
tinto pp.of **tingere.**
tintore m. dyer; dry cleaner.
Tintoretto, il (Iacopo Robusti), Italian painter (1518–1594).
tintori'a f. dyeing; dyehouse; dry cleaner's shop.
tintura f. tincture; dye; dyeing: — **di iodio**, iodine.
ti'pico adj. typical.
tipo m. type, model, standard; specimen; fellow, guy.
tipografi'a f. printing house; typography.
tipogra'fico adj. typographic, printing.
tipo'grafo m. typographer, printer.
tipo'metro m. (typog.) em scale, pica rule, line gauge.
tirag'gio m. draught, drawing.
tirali'nee m. ruling pen.
tiranni'a f. tyranny.
tiran'nico adj. tyrannical.
tiran'nide f. tyranny.
tiranno m. tyrant.
tirante m. brace; trace (of a harness); (mach.) stag rod, drag link.
tirapiedi m. underling, man Friday.
tirare vt. to draw, pull; to stretch; to take in; to move; to trace; to fling hurl; to shoot; (typog.) to print; vi. to pull; to tend; to blow; to shoot (at): — **su**, to bring up; — **una somma**, — **le somme**, to sum up; — **calci**, to kick; — **pugni**, to punch; — **su le maniche**, to roll up one's sleeves; — **le cuoia**, to kick the bucket; — **avanti**, to get along; — **di scherma**, to fence; **tirarsi** vr. to draw: — **indietro**, to draw back; — **su**, to get up, rise; — **un colpo di rivoltella**, to shoot oneself.
tirata f. pull, draw; stretch; tirade.
tirato adj. taut; drawn; stingy.
tiratore m. marksman, shot, shooter: **franco** —, sniper.
tiratura f. printing; circulation.
tirchieri'a f. stinginess.
tir'chio m. miser; adj. stingy.
tiretto m. drawer.
tiritera f. rigmarole.

tiro m. draft; pull; shooting; shot; fire; range; trick; team (of horses): — **a segno**, rifle range; shooting gallery; **a** —, within one's reach; — **alla fune**, tug of war; **cavallo da** —, draft horse.
tiroci'nio m. apprenticeship.
tisana f. ptisan.
tisi f. consumption, phthisis.
ti'sico adj. consumptive; stunted.
titillare vt. to titillate, tickle.
titino m., adj. (pol.) Titoist.
titolare m. owner; holder; adj. regular.
ti'tolo m. title; heading, caption; qualification; claim, right; stock, bond; insult; (text.) count; (chem.) titer: — **di studio**, diploma, degree; scholastic titles; **a** — **di**, as a.
titubante adj. hesitating, irresolute.
titubanza f. perplexity, diffidence.
titubare vi. to waver, hesitate.
Tiziano (Tiziano Vecellio), one of the greatest Italian painters, head of the Venetian school (1477–1576).
tizio m. fellow, guy.
tizzo, tizzone m. firebrand.
to' (interj.) here! take this! well! why!
toccare vt. to touch; to concern; to call at; vi. to happen, befall; to be up (to); to have (to); to belong (to); to be awarded; to be one's turn: — **sul vivo**, to sting to the quick; — **con mano**, to make sure; **gli estremi si toccano**, extremes meet; **mi tocca obbedire**, I have to obey.
toccasana m. cure-all, panacea.
tocco (1) m. touch; stroke; one o'clock.
tocco (2) adj. crackbrained, touched.
tocco (3) m. chunk; toque, mortarboard.
toga f. gown; toga.
to'gliere vt.[144] to take away or off; to remove; to subtract: — **il saluto a**, to cut; — **dalla testa**, to get out of (one's) head; — **di mezzo**, to get rid of; **ciò non toglie che egli sia benvoluto**, this does not prevent him from being popular; — **d'impaccio**, to help out of a scrape; **to'gliersi** vr. to get off; to take off; to deprive oneself: — **la vita**, to commit suicide; — **di mezzo**, to get out of the way.
toh see **to'.**
tolda f. deck.
toletta f. toilette; attire; watercloset; dressing room; dressing table.
tollera'bile adj. tolerable.
tollerante adj. tolerant.
tolleranza f. endurance, tolerance.
tollerare vt. to endure, tolerate.
tolto pp. of **togliere.**
toma'ia f. vamp, upper.

tomba f. tomb, grave.

tombino m. road manhole; drain well.

tom'bola f. tombola; fall, tumble.

tom'bolo m. lace pillow: **merletto a —**, pillow lace.

Tommaseo, Nicolò, Italian lexicographer, novelist and patriot, *Dizionario dei sinonimi, Dizionario della lingua italiana* (1802–1874).

tomo m. volume, tome.

to'naca f. frock; (*eccl.*) cassock.

tonalità f. tonality.

tonante *adj.* thundering.

tonare *see* **tuonare**.

tondeggiante *adj.* roundish.

tondino m. (*iron*) rod.

tondo m. round; plate; (*typog.*) roman; *adj.* round, circular: **chiaro e —**, straight, outspokenly.

tonfo m. thud; splash.

to'nico m., *adj.* tonic.

tonificare *vt.* to invigorate.

tonnara f. tunny snare.

tonnellag'gio m. tonnage.

tonnellata f. (*Kg.* 1016) long ton; (*Kg.* 907) short ton; (*Kg.* 1000) metric ton.

tonno m. tunny.

tono m. tone; hue; tune; pitch: **darsi —**, to give oneself airs.

tonsilla f. tonsil.

tonsura f. tonsure.

Tonti, Lorenzo, Italian banker in France (*living in* 1653).

tontina f. tontine.

tonto *adj.* silly, dull.

topa'ia f. rats' nest; hovel.

topa'zio m. topaz.

to'pica f. blunder, *faux pas.*

topo m. mouse; rat: **— di biblioteca**, bookworm.

topografi'a f. topography.

topo'grafo m. topographer.

Topolino m. Mickey Mouse.

toporagno m. shrewmouse.

toppa (*1*) f. lock.

toppa (*2*) f. patch.

torace m. thorax.

torba f. peat.

tor'bido *adj.* turbid, murky, muddy; troubled; shady; m. trouble, disorder: **pescare nel —**, to fish in troubled waters.

tor'cere *vt.*[145] to twist, wring: **— il naso (la bocca)**, to make a wry face; **dar del filo da —**, to cause a great deal of trouble; **tor'cersi** *vr.* to writhe, twist; to squirm.

torchiare *vt.* to press.

torchietto m. (*photo.*) printing frame.

tor'chio m. press.

tor'cia f. torch.

torcicollo m. stiff neck.

tordo m. thrush.

torello m. young bull; (*naut.*) garboard.

torio *see* **tuorlo**.

torma f. crowd, swarm; herd.

tormenta f. blizzard, snowstorm.

tormentare *vt.* to torment; **tormentarsi** *vr.* to torment oneself; to worry.

tormento m. torment; agony, pain.

tornaconto m. profit, benefit.

tornare *vi.* to return; to go back; to come back; to start afresh; to recur: **— a bomba**, to return to the point; **— indietro**, to get back; **— a onore**, to do (one) credit; **— comodo**, to suit, to be of use; **— amici**, to be friends again.

tornasole m. (*chem.*) litmus.

torneo m. tournament.

tor'nio m. lathe, turning lathe.

tornire *vt.* to turn; to shape, polish.

tornitore m. turner.

torno (*1*) m. period, length (*of time*).

torno (*2*) *prep., adv.* round, about: **torno torno**, all around; **togliersi uno di —**, to get rid of one.

toro m. bull; (*astr.*) Taurus.

torpe'dine f. torpedo.

torpediniera f. destroyer escort, torpedo-boat destroyer.

torpedo f. (*auto.*) torpedo.

torpedone m. motor coach, bus.

tor'pido *adj.* torpid; drowsy.

torpore m. torpor, drowsiness.

torre f. tower; steeple.

torreggiare *vi.* to tower.

torrente m. torrent, stream.

torretta f. turret; conning tower (*of a submarine*).

Torricelli, Evangelista, Italian physicist, inventor of barometer (1608–1647).

tor'rido *adj.* torrid.

torrione m. keep.

torrone m. nougat.

torsione f. torsion, twist.

torso m. (*anat.*) trunk, torso.

tor'solo m. stump, stalk; core.

torta f. cake, tart, pie.

torto (*1*) m. wrong; injury; injustice; fault: **aver —**, to be wrong; **a — o a ragione**, rightly or wrongly.

torto (*2*) *adj.* twisted. *pp.of* **torcere**.

tor'tora f. turtledove.

tortuoso *adj.* tortuous; crooked; winding.

tortura f. torture.

torturare *vt.* to torture; **torturarsi** *vr.* to torment oneself.

torvo *adj.* grim, surly, stern.

tosare *vt.* to shear.

Toscanini, Arturo, Italian conductor (1867–1957).

toscano m., *adj.* Tuscan.

tosse *f.* cough: — **asinina**, whooping cough.

tos'sico *m.* poison; *adj.* toxic.

tossina *f.* toxin.

tossire *vi.* to cough.

tostare *vt.* to roast; to toast.

Tosti, Francesco Paolo, Italian composer (1846-1916).

tosto (*1*) *adv.* soon, immediately.

tosto (*2*) *adj.* compact, firm; bold: **faccia tosta,** cheek, impudence.

totale *m., adj.* total.

totalità *f.* totality, entirety, whole.

totalita'rio *adj.* totalitarian.

totalizzare *vt.* to totalize.

totalizzatore *m.* pari mutuel, betting machine.

to'tano *m.* cuttlefish.

totocal'cio *m.* soccer pool.

tova'glia *f.* tablecloth.

tovagliolo *m.* napkin.

tozzo *m.* bit, morsel; *adj.* stocky, squat.

tra *see* fra.

trabac'colo *m.* (*naut.*) lugger; (*fig.*) "jalopy."

traballante *adj.* tottering, shaky.

traballare *vi.* to reel, stagger, totter; to jolt.

trabic'colo *m.* warming pan; (*fig.*) "jalopy."

traboccante *adj.* overflowing.

traboccare *vi.* to overflow.

trabocchetto *m.* pitfall, trap.

tracagnotto *adj.* stocky, squat.

tracannare *vt.* to gulp down, swill.

traccia *f.* trace, track, trail; mark, impression; footprint; sketch, outline.

tracciare *vt.* to trace, sketch; to draw, mark out; to outline.

tracciato *m.* tracing, outline; lay.

trachea *f.* windpipe, trachea.

tracolla *f.* baldric: **a** —, baldric-wise.

tracollo *m.* breakdown; (*exch.*) slump; fall.

tracotante *adj.* overbearing.

tracotanza *f.* arrogance.

tradimento *m.* treason; treachery: **a** —, treacherously; unawares; **mangiar pane a** —, to eat the bread of idleness.

tradire *vt.* to betray; to deceive; **tradirsi** *vr.* to give oneself away.

traditore *m.* traitor, betrayer.

traditrice *f.* traitress.

tradizionale *adj.* traditional.

tradizione *f.* tradition.

tradotta *f.* troop train.

tradotto *pp.of* tradurre.

tradurre *vt.*[a] to translate; to convey; to take: — **alle carceri,** to take to jail; — **in pratica,** to put into practice; **tradursi** *vr.* to result (*in*), turn out.

traduttore *m.* translator.

traduzione *f.* translation.

traente *m.* (*comm.*) drawer.

trafelato *adj.* panting, breathless.

trafficante *m.* dealer, trader.

trafficare *vi.* to trade, traffic.

traf'fico *m.* traffic; trade.

trafig'gere *vt.*[63] to transfix, stab.

trafila *f.* drawplate; series; routine; red tape.

trafilare *vt.* to wiredraw.

trafiletto *m.* paragraph; (*journ.*) box.

trafitto *pp.of* trafiggere.

trafittura *f.* stitch.

traforare *vt.* to bore; to openwork.

traforo *m.* piercing; tunnel; openwork.

trafugare *vt.* to steal.

trage'dia *f.* tragedy.

traghettare *vt.* to ferry.

traghetto *m.* ferryboat.

tra'gico *adj.* tragic.

tragitto *m.* route, course; journey.

traguardo *m.* winning post, finish line; aim: **tagliare il** —, to break the tape.

traietto'ria *f.* trajectory.

trainare *vt.* to tow, drag.

tra'ino *m.* sledge; tow; train.

tralasciare *vt., vi.* to interrupt; to cease; to omit, fail; to give up; to abstain (*from*).

tral'cio *m.* vine shoot, shoot.

tralic'cio *m.* trellis; ticking.

tralice, (in) *adv.* askance.

tralignare *vi.* to degenerate.

tram *m.* streetcar.

trama *f.* weft, woof; plot.

trama'glio *m.* dragnet.

tramandare *vt.* to hand down.

tramare *vt., vi.* to plot.

trambusto *m.* bustle; fuss.

tramesti'o *m.* bustle.

tramezza *f.* partition.

tramezzino *m.* sandwich.

tramezzo *m.* partition.

tra'mite: per il — di, through.

tramog'gia *f.* hopper.

tramontana *f.* northwind; north: **perdere la** —, to lose one's bearings.

tramontare *vi.* to set, go down; to decline; to end.

tramontato *adj.* faded; vanished; outmoded; forgotten.

tramonto *m.* setting; sunset; end.

tramortire *vt.* to stun, knock on the head.

tramortito *adj.* stunned.

trampoliere *m.* (*ornith.*) stilt.

trampolino *m.* springboard.

tram'polo *m.* stilt.

tramutare *vt.* to transform; **tramutarsi** *vr.* to turn (*into*).

tramvi'a *f.* streetcar line.

trancia f. shears; slice.

tranello m. trap, snare.

trangugiare vt. to swallow up.

tranne prep. save, except.

tranquillare, tranquillizzare vt. to pacify, quiet (down); **tranquillarsi, tranquillizzarsi** vr. to calm down.

tranquillità f. tranquillity, calm.

tranquillo adj. tranquil, quiet, calm: **sta'** —, don't worry; **lasciar** —, to leave alone.

transatlan'tico m. liner; adj. transatlantic.

transatto pp.of transigere.

transazione f. arrangement; compromise.

tran'sfuga m. deserter.

transi'gere vi.[56] to compromise; to bargain; to stretch a point.

transitare vi. to pass or move (across, through, over).

tran'sito m. transit, traffic.

transito'rio adj. transitory.

transizione f. transition.

tran tran m. routine.

tranvai m. streetcar, tramcar.

tranvia f. streetcar line.

tranviere m. streetcar man.

trapanare vt. to drill; to trephine.

trapanazione f. drilling; trephination.

tra'pano m. drill; trephine.

trapassare vi. to pierce (through).

trapasso m. passage; transfer; death.

trapelare vi. to ooze; to leak out.

trape'zio m. trapezium; trapeze.

trapiantare vt. to transplant.

trapiantarsi vr. to emigrate.

trapianto m. transplantation.

trap'pola f. trap, snare; rattletrap.

trapunta f. quilt.

trapuntare vt. to quilt.

trapunto adj. quilted.

trarre vt.[146] to draw; to throw; to get: — **in salvo**, to rescue; — **in inganno**, to deceive; — **un sospiro**, to heave a sigh; — **d'impaccio**, to get (one) out of a scrape; **trarsi** vr. to draw (back, out, aside).

trasalire vi. to start.

trasandato adj. careless; slovenly.

trasbordare vt. to transship, transfer.

trasbordo m. transshipment, transfer.

trascendentale adj. transcendental.

trascen'dere vt.[119] to transcend, exceed; vi. to exaggerate; to fly off the handle.

trascinare vt. to drag; to stir up, carry away, enthuse; **trascinarsi** vr. to drag oneself.

trasco'rere vt.[96] to spend, pass; vi. to go by; to elapse.

trascorso m. peccadillo; slip of the pen; adj. elapsed, gone by. pp.of **trascorrere**.

trascrivere vt. to transcribe.

trascrizione f. transcription.

trascura'bile adj. negligible.

trascurare vt. to neglect; to disregard; to omit; **trascurarsi** vr. not to take care of oneself.

trascuratezza f. carelessness; negligence; slovenliness.

trascurato adj. careless, negligent; neglected; slovenly.

trasecolare vi. to marvel, wonder.

trasecolato adj. astonished, nonplussed.

trasferi'bile adj. transferable.

trasferimento m. removal; transfer; move.

trasferire vt. to move, remove; to transfer. **trasferirsi** vr. to move (to).

trasferta f. mission; expenses.

trasforma'bile adj. transformable; (auto.) convertible.

trasformare vt. to transform; **trasformarsi** vr. to transform oneself; to turn (into).

trasformatore m. transformer.

trasformazione f. transformation.

trasformista m. transformist.

trasfusione f. transfusion.

trasgredire vt. to transgress.

trasgressione f. transgression.

trasgressore m. transgressor.

traslazione f. removal; translation.

traslocare vt., vi. to move.

trasloco m. move; household removal.

trasmet'tere vt. to transmit; (radio) to broadcast.

trasmettitore m. transmitter.

trasmigrare vi. to transmigrate.

trasmigrazione f. transmigration.

trasmissione f. transmission; (radio) broadcasting; (mach.) drive, gear: — **idraulica**, fluid drive; — **del pensiero**, thought transference.

trasmittente f. broadcasting station; adj. transmitting; (radio) broadcasting.

trasognato adj. dazed, stupefied.

trasparente adj. transparent, clear.

trasparenza f. transparence.

trasparire vi.[147] to appear through; to be transparent; to beam; to reveal oneself.

trasparso pp.of **trasparire**.

traspirare vi. to perspire.

traspirazione f. perspiration.

trasporre vt.[95] to transpose.

trasportare vt. to transport, convey; to carry; to translate; to postpone; to transpose.

trasporto m. transport; transportation, conveyance; freighter; transfer.

trasposto pp.of **trasporre**.

trastullarsi *vr.* to amuse oneself; to toy; to idle.

trastullo *m.* plaything; fun.

trasudare *vi.* to transude, ooze.

trasversale *f.* transverse; cross street; *adj.* transversal.

trasverso *adj.* transverse.

trasvolare *vi.* to fly (*across*).

trasvolata *f.* flight.

trasvolatore *m.* flyer.

tratta *f.* pull, jerk; (*comm.*) draft; leg (*of a journey*); (*slave*) trade: — **delle bianche,** white slavery.

trattabile *adj.* tractable; open to offer.

trattamento *m.* treatment; refreshment; party; board; wages, salary.

trattare *vt.* to treat, deal with; to handle; to transact; **trattarsi** *vr.* to treat oneself; to be (*a question of*).

trattativa *f.* negotiation.

trattato *m.* treatise; treaty.

trattazione *f.* treatment.

tratteggiare *vt.* to hatch; to delineate, trace, outline; to sketch.

tratteg'gio *m.* hatching.

trattenere *vt.* to keep, hold; to restrain; to check; to withhold; to deduct; **trattenersi** *vr.* to stay, remain; to linger (*on*); to refrain (*from*).

trattenimento *m.* entertainment; party.

trattenuta *f.* deduction; checkoff.

trattino *m.* hyphen, dash.

tratto (*1*) *m.* stroke; pull, jerk; stretch, distance; way; while; part; passage; manner, bearing; gesture; feature: — **di spirito,** witticism; **disegnare a** —, to hatch; **a un** —, suddenly; **di** — **in** —, now and then.

tratto (*2*) *pp.of* **trarre.**

trattore (*1*) *m.* restaurateur, landlord.

trattore (*2*) *m.* tractor, caterpillar.

trattori'a *f.* restaurant.

trattrice *f.* tractor.

tra'uma *m.* trauma, shock.

travagliare *vt.* to trouble; to torment; *vi.* to toil.

trava'glio *m.* labor, toil; trouble, worry.

travasare *vt.* to pour off.

travaso *m.* (*pathol.*) effusion.

trave *f.* beam.

travedere *vt.* to glimpse; *vi.* to see wrongly; to dote (*on*).

traveg'gole *f.:* aver le —, to see things.

traversa *f.* transverse; crossway; (*rail.*) tie.

traversale *adj.* transversal.

traversare *vt.* to cross.

traversata *f.* passage, crossing.

traversi'a *f.* misfortune, trial.

traversina *f.* (*rail.*) tie; (*Brit.*) sleeper.

traverso *adj.* transverse, cross, oblique; awry: **via traversa** (*fig.*), artful dodge; **di** —, across; wrong; the wrong way; askance.

traversone *m.* (*fencing*) traverse; (*fort.*) traverse trench; (*sport*) cross.

travestimento *m.* disguise.

travestire *vt.* to disguise; **travestirsi** *vr.* to disguise oneself.

traviare *vt.* to mislead; to corrupt; lead astray.

travisare *vt.* to distort, alter.

travolgente *adj.* forcible, driving; (*fig.*) enormous, roaring.

travol'gere *vt.* to overturn, upturn; to overthrow; to sweep away; to take by storm.

trazione *f.* traction.

tre *m.,* *adj.* three.

treb'bia *f.* flail.

trebbiare *vt.* to thresh.

trebbiatrice *f.* thresher.

trebbiatura *f.* threshing.

trec'cia *f.* plait; pigtail.

trecento *card.num.* three hundred.

tredice'simo *m.,* *adj.* thirteenth.

tre'dici *m.,* *adj.* thirteen.

tre'gua *f.* truce; rest; respite.

tremante *adj.* trembling, shivering.

tremare *vi.* to tremble, shake; to quiver, shiver.

tremebondo *adj.* trembling, quaking.

tremendo *adj.* tremendous, dreadful.

trementina *f.* turpentine.

tre'mito *m.* trembling, shaking.

tremolare *vi.* to tremble; to flicker.

treno (*1*) *m.* train: — **di lusso,** train de luxe; — **accelerato,** local train; — **belvedere,** observation train, astradome train.

treno (*2*) *m.* train, retinue: — **di vita,** way of life.

trenta *m.,* *adj.* thirty.

trente'simo *m.,* *adj.* thirtieth.

trentina *f.* some thirty: **essere sulla —,** to be about thirty.

trepidare *vi.* to be anxious, fret.

trepidazione *f.* trepidation.

treppiede *m.* trivet; tripod.

tresca *f.* intrigue; love affair.

tre'spolo *m.* trestle.

trian'golo *m.* triangle.

tribolare *vt.* to trouble, harass; *vi.* to labor; to have trouble.

tribolato *adj.* afflicted, distressed.

tribolazione *f.* tribulation; ordeal.

tri'bolo *m.* trouble, trial, ordeal.

tribù *f.* tribe.

tribuna *f.* tribune; rostrum; grandstand: — **stampa,** press gallery, press row.

tribunale *m.* tribunal, court (*of law*).

tributare *vt.* to bestow.

tributa'rio *m.*, *adj.* tributary.

tributo *m.* tribute; tax.

tricheco *m.* walrus.

triciclo *m.* tricycle.

tricolore *m.*, *adj.* tricolor.

tricorno *m.* tricorne, cocked hat.

tricromi'a *f.* colortype.

triennale *adj.* triennial; *f.* triennial exhibition.

trifase *adj.* three-phase.

trifo'glio *m.* clover, trefoil.

tri'fola *f.* truffle.

trige'mino *adj.* trigeminous; trigeminal.

tri'glia *f.* (*ichthyol.*) mullet: fare l'occhio di — a, to ogle.

trillare *vi.* to trill; to ring, peal.

trillo *m.* trill; ring, peal.

trilogi'a *f.* trilogy.

Trilussa (*Carlo Alberto Salusti*), Italian poet in Roman dialect (1873–1950).

trimestrale *adj.* quarterly.

trimestre *m.* quarter.

trimotore *m.* trimotored plane.

trina *f.* lace.

trinca *f.* (*naut.*) gammon: nuovo di —, brand new.

trincare *vt.* to gulp down, swill.

trincea *f.* trench.

trincerarsi *vr.* to entrench oneself.

trincetto *m.* shoemaker's knife.

trinchettina *f.* (*naut.*) fore-topmast staysail.

trinchetto *m.* (*naut.*) foremast.

trinciante *adj.* carving knife, carver.

trinciare *vt.* to cut up; to carve: — giudizi, to pontificate.

trinciato *m.* smoking tobacco.

trinità *f.* trinity.

trionfale *adj.* triumphal.

trionfante *adj.* triumphant, exulting

trionfare *vi.* to triumph (*over*).

trionfatore *m.* triumpher; winner.

trionfo *m.* triumph; trump card.

triplicare *vt.* to triplicate, triple, treble.

tri'plice *adj.* threefold, triple: in —, copia, in triplicate.

triplo *adj.* triple.

trippa *f.* tripe; belly.

tripudiare *vi.* to exult.

tripu'dio *m.* exultancy.

trisa'vola *f.* great-great-grandmother.

trisa'volo *m.* great-great-grandfather.

triste *adj.* sad, sorrowful; gloomy.

tristezza *f.* sadness, sorrow.

tristo *adj.* wicked; base; mean.

tritacarne *m.* meat grinder, masticator.

tritare *vt.* to mince; to hash.

tritatutto *m.* triturator.

trito *adj.* minced, trite, stale.

tritolo *m.* (*chem.*) trinitrotoluene.

trit'tico *m.* triptych.

triturare *vt.* to triturate, hash, mince.

trivella *f.* drill, auger, wimble.

trivellare *vt.* to bore, wimble.

triviale *adj.* low, vulgar.

trivialità *f.* vulgarity.

tri'vio *m.* crossroad; trivium: da —, vulgar.

trofeo *m.* trophy.

troglodita *m.* troglodyte.

tro'ia *f.* sow; (*vulg.*) whore.

tromba *f.* trumpet; (*mil.*) bugle; (*auto.*) horn; (*anat.*) tube: — delle scale, stairwell; — marina, waterspout; — d'aria, whirlwind.

trombare *vt.* to beat; to reject.

trombetta *f.* trumpet.

trombettiere *m.* trumpeter.

trombone *m.* trombone.

troncare *vt.* to truncate; to cut off; to break off; to discontinue; to interrupt.

tronchesino *m.* nipper.

tronco *m.* trunk; log; (*rail.*) section, siding: — di cono, truncated cone; *adj.* truncate: licenziare in —, to "fire," "sack."

troncone *m.* stump.

troneggiare *vi.* to tower.

tron'fio *adj.* smug, self-conceited.

trono *m.* throne.

tropicale *adj.* tropical.

tro'pico *adj.* tropic.

troppo *adj.*, *adv.* too; too much; too long; excessively; quite; troppi *m. pl.* too many.

frota *f.* trout.

trottare *vi.* to trot.

trotterellare *vi.* to trot along; to toddle.

trotto *m.* trot: al —, at a trot; corsa al —, trotting race.

trot'tola *f.* top, whip top.

trovare *vt.* to find; to discover, find out; trovarsi *vr.* to find oneself; to lie; to be; to meet.

trovarobe *m.* property man.

trovata *f.* invention; trick; idea; "gimmick."

trovatello *m.* foundling.

truccare *vt.* to make up; to disguise; to prearrange, rig (*as a game*); truccarsi *vr.* to make up one's face.

truccato *adj.* made up; disguised: incontro —, prearranged match, setup.

truccatore *m.* dresser, make-up man.

trucco *m.* trick; deceit; make-up.

truce *adj.* fierce, grim; cruel.

trucidare *vt.* to slay, kill.

tru'ciolo *m.* shaving, chip.

truculento *adj.* truculent.

truculenza *f.* truculence.

truffa *f.* cheat, swindle: — all'americana, confidence trick.

truffare vt. to cheat, swindle.
truffatore m. cheat, cheater: — all'americana, confidence man.
truo'golo m. trough.
truppa f. troop; rank and file.
tu pers.pron. you (sing.); (poet.) thou.
tuba f. tophat; (mus.) tuba.
tubare vi. to coo.
tubatura, tubazione f. piping, pipes, pipeline.
tubercolosa'rio see sanatorio.
tubercolosi f. tuberculosis.
tubercoloso adj. tuberculous; m. consumptive.
tu'bero m. tuber.
tubo m. pipe, tube; duct.
tubolare adj. tubular.
tuffare vt., **tuffarsi** vr. to plunge, dive.
tuffo m. plunge, dive: sentire un — al cuore, to feel one's heart jump.
tufo m. tufa.
tuga f. (naut.) shelter deck.
tugu'rio m. doghole, hovel.
tulipano m. tulip.
tumefarsi vr. to tumefy.
tumefazione f. tumefaction.
tu'mido adj. tumid.
tumore m. tumor.
tumulare vt. to bury.
tumulazione f. burial.
tu'mulo m. tumulus.
tumulto m. tumult; uproar, riot.
tumultuoso adj. tumultuous.
tu'nica f. tunic; gown, robe.
tuo adj.poss. your; (poet.) thy; poss. pron. yours; (poet.) thine: i tuoi, yours; your people.
tuonare vi. to thunder; to roar.
tuono m. thunder; roar.
tuorlo m. yolk.
turac'ciolo m. stopper; cork.
turare vt. to tappare.
turba f. crowd; mob, rabble.
turbamento m. agitation; commotion; uneasiness.
turbante m. turban.
turbare vt. to trouble, disturb; to touch; to upset; to worry; turbarsi vr. to be disturbed; to become uneasy.
turbina f. turbine.
turbinare vi. to whirl; to eddy.

tur'bine m. whirl, whirlwind, eddy; hurricane.
turbinoso adj. whirling; tumultuous.
turboe'lica f. jet-prop engine.
turbolento adj. turbulent.
turbolenza f. turbulence.
turbolocomotiva f. turbomotive.
turbonave f. turbo-electric liner.
turboreattore m. turbojet.
turchese m. turquoise.
turchino m., adj. dark blue.
turco m. Turk; Turkish (language); adj. Turkish: bestemmiare iome un —, to swear like a trooper; fumare come un —, to smoke like a chimney.
tur'gido adj. turgid, swollen, full.
turismo m. tourism: auto da —, touring car.
turista m. tourist.
turi'stico adj. tourist, touristic.
turlupinare vt. to swindle, hoodwink.
turlupinatura f. swindle.
turno m. turn, shift; duty: fare a —, to take turns.
turpe adj. filthy, base, shameful.
turpilo'quio m. foul language.
tuta f. overall.
tutela f. guardianship; protection, defense.
tutelare vt. to protect, defend; adj. tutelary.
tutore m., **tutrice** f. guardian.
tuttavia adv. still, yet, nevertheless, however.
tutto (1) m. everything; whole.
tutto (2) adj. all; whole; tutti m. pl. every.
tutto (3) pron. all, everything. tutti m. pl. all; everybody, everyone.
tutto (4) adv. quite, all, wholly; fully; deeply: essere tutt'uno, to be the same (thing); in — e per —, completely; da per —, everywhere; a tutt'oggi, so far; tutt'a un tratto, all of a sudden; del —, quite, at all; tutt'altro, on the contrary; tutt'altro che, far from; tutt'al più, at most.
tuttora adv. still.
tzigano m., adj. gipsy.

U

ubbi'a f. delusion, whim.
ubbidiente adj. obedient, dutiful.
ubbidienza f. obedience.
ubbidire vt., vi. to obey.
ubbriacare, ubbriaco see ubriacare, ubriaco.
ubertoso adj. fertile, fruitful.
ubicazione f. location, emplacement.
ubiquità f. ubiquity, omnipresence.

ubriacare vt. to make drunk, intoxicate; ubriacarsi vr. to get drunk.
ubriachezza f. drunkenness.
ubriaco adj. drunk, intoxicated.
ubriacone m. drunkard.
uccelliera f. aviary, birdcage.
uccello m. bird: — di bosco, fugitive.
Uccello, Paolo (Paolo di Dono), Italian painter (1397–1475).

ucci'dere *vt.*[41] to kill, slay; to shoot; **uccidersi** *vr.* to kill oneself; to commit suicide.

uccisione *f.* killing, slaughter.

ucciso *m.* victim; *adj.* killed, slain. *pp.of* uccidere.

uccisore *m.* killer, slayer.

udienza *f.* hearing, interview; session.

udire *vt.*, *vi.*[148] to hear; to listen (*to*).

udito (1) *pp.of* udire.

udito (2) *m.* hearing.

udito'rio *m.* audience.

ufficiale *m.* officer; official: — **giudiziario**, process server, bailiff; — **di rotta**, navigator; — **pagatore**, paymaster; *adj.* official.

ufficiare *vi.* to officiate.

uffi'cio *m.* office; bureau; function, duty: **d'—, ex officio; buoni uffici,** services.

ufficioso *adj.* officious; semiofficial; overkind.

uffi'zio *m.* (*rel.*) office.

ufo, (a) *adv.* for a thank-you, free.

ug'gia *f.* aversion, dislike: **prendere in —,** to take a dislike to.

uggiolare *vi.* to whimper.

uggioso *adj.* depressing, gloomy.

u'gola *f.* uvula; throat.

uguaglianza *f.* equality.

uguagliare *vt.* to equal; to make even; to equalize.

uguale *adj.* equal; like; same.

ul'cera *f.* ulcer.

ulcerazione *f.* ulceration.

uliva *f.* olive.

ulivo *m.* olive tree.

ulteriore *adj.* ulterior, further, later.

ultimamente *adv.* lately, of late.

ultimare *vt.* to finish, complete.

ul'timo *adj.* last; latest; final; utmost: **da —,** finally; **in —,** in the end; **fino all '—,** to the last.

ultra *adv.*: **il non plus —,** the acme; the ultimate.

ultrarosso *adj.* infrared.

ultrasuono *m.* supersonant.

ultraso'nico *adj.* supersonic.

ultravioletto *adj.* ultraviolet.

ululare *vi.* to howl.

ululato *m.* howl, howling.

umane'simo *m.* humanism.

umanista *m.* humanist.

umanità *f.* humanity; mankind.

umanita'rio *m.*, *adj.* humanitarian.

umano *adj.* human; humane.

umettare *vt.* to moisten.

umidità *f.* dampness, moisture.

umidic'cio *adj.* dampish.

u'mido (1) *m.*, *adj.* damp.

u'mido (2) *m.* stew, ragout.

u'mile *adj.* humble.

umiliante *adj.* humiliating.

umiliare *vt.* to humble; **umiliarsi** *vr.* to humble oneself.

umiliazione *f.* humiliation.

umiltà *f.* humility, humbleness.

umore *m.* humor; mood, temper.

umorismo *m.* humor.

umorista *m.* humorist.

umori'stico *adj.* humoristic, comic.

un *see* uno.

una'nime *adj.* unanimous.

unanimità *f.* unanimity.

uncinare *vt.* to hook, grapple.

uncinetto *m.* crotchet; crochet.

uncino *m.* hook; clasp.

undice'simo *adj.* eleventh.

un'dici *m.*, *adj.* eleven.

Ungaretti, Giuseppe, most prominent contemporary Italian poet (1888–).

un'gere *vt.*[26] to grease, oil.

un'ghia *f.* nail; claw, talon; hoof.

unguento *m.* ointment, pomade.

u'nico *adj.* unique, only, sole, single, one: **l'—,** the only one.

unificare *vt.* to unite; to unify.

uniformare *vt.* to make uniform; **uniformarsi** *vr.* to conform (*to*), comply (*with*).

uniforme *f.*, *adj.* uniform.

uniformità *f.* uniformity.

unilaterale *adj.* unilateral, one-sided.

unione *f.* union, conjunction; unity.

unire *vt.*, **unirsi** *vr.* to unite, join: — **in matrimonio,** to marry.

uni'sono *m.* unison: **all'—,** in unison; simultaneously.

unità *f.* unity; unit.

unita'rio *m.*, *adj.* unitarian.

unito *adj.* united, joined: **a tinta unita,** plain.

universale *adj.* universal: **giudizio —,** final judgment.

università *f.* university.

universita'rio *m.* university *or* college student; *adj.* university.

universo *m.* universe.

uni'voco *adj.* univocal.

un, uno, una *indef.art.* a, an; one; **uno m. una** *f. adj.* one: **marciare per —,** to march in single file; *indef.pron.* one: **l'— l'altro,** each other.

unto (1) *m.* grease; *adj.* greasy.

unto (2) *pp.of* ungere.

untuoso *adj.* unctuous; greasy.

unzione *f.* unction.

uomo *m.* man: — **fatto,** grown man; **come un sol —,** with one accord.

uopo *m.*: **all'—,** if necessary.

uovo *m.* egg.

uragano *m.* hurricane.

ura'nio *m.* uranium.

urbane'simo *m.* urbanism.

urbanistica *f.* town planning.

urbanità *f.* urbanity, politeness.

urbano *adj.* urban; urbane, polite.
urgente *adj.* pressing, urgent.
urgenza *f.* urgency; hurry.
ur'gere *vt.* to urge, press; *vi.* to be [urgent.
urina, *etc. see* orina *etc.*
urlare *vi.* to shout, howl, yell.
urlo *m.* shout, cry, yell, howl.
urna *f.* urn; ballot box.
urrà *interj.* hurra, hooray.
urtare *vt.* to knock against, push; to irk, annoy; **urtarsi** *vr.* to quarrel, fall out; to collide, clash; to be vexed.
urto *m.* clash; shock, impact, collision; tiff.
usanza *f.* custom, habit, practice.
usare *vt.* to use, employ; to show; *vi.* to be accustomed to, be in the habit of; to be fashionable; to be the custom; to make use (*of*): **usarsi**, to be in use, be in vogue, be the fashion.
usato *adj.* used; usual; second-hand, worn out.
usciere *m.* usher, porter; bailiff, process server.
u'scio *m.* door; entrance.
uscire *vi.*[149] to get out (*of*), issue; to go out; to come out; to flow out; to be issued; to escape: **— di senno,** to go insane; **— di strada,** to go astray.
uscita *f.* exit, way out; outlet; getting out; witticism, crack; (*comm.*)

expenditure, disbursement; issue: **dazio di —,** export duty; **in libera —,** off duty.
uscito *pp.of* uscire.
usignuolo *m.* nightingale.
uso *m.* use; custom, usage: **fuori —,** obsolete; out of commission; *adj.* accustomed, used.
ustionare *vt.* burn, scorch.
ustione *f.* burn.
usuale *adj.* usual; common.
usufruire *vi.* to benefit (*by*); to avail oneself: **— di,** to enjoy.
usufrutto *m.* usufruct.
usufruttua'rio *m.* usufructuary.
usura *f.* usury; wear and tear: **a —,** with usury.
usura'io *m.* usurer, moneylender, loanshark.
usurpare *vt.* to usurp.
usurpatore *m.* usurper.
utensile *m.* implement, tool.
utente *m.* user.
u'tero *m.* uterus.
u'tile *m.* profit, gain; *adj.* useful.
utilità *f.* utility; use; usefulness.
utilita'ria *f.* baby car.
utilizzare *vt.* to utilize; to use.
utilizzazione *f.* utilization.
uva *f.* grape: **— passa,** raisin; **— spina,** gooseberry.
uxoricida *m.* uxoricide (*agent*).
uxorici'dio *m.* uxoricide (*act*).
uz'zolo *m.* caprice, whim, fancy.

V

vacante *adj.* vacant, empty.
vacanza *f.* holiday, vacation.
vacca *f.* cow.
vaccaro *m.* cowboy.
vacchetta *f.* cowhide.
vaccinare *vt.* to vaccinate.
vaccinazione *f.* vaccination.
vaccino *m.,* *adj.* vaccine.
vacillamento *m.* wavering.
vacillante *adj.* wavering; flickering.
vacillare *vi.* to waver, vacillate.
va'cuo *adj.* vacuous, empty.
vagabondag'gio *m.* vagrancy; wandering.
vagabondare *vi.* to wander, rove.
vagabondo *m.* wanderer, vagrant; tramp. *adj.* vagabond, wandering.
vagamente *adv.* vaguely.
vagare *vi.* to wander, ramble.
vagheggiare *vt.* to cherish.
vagire *vi.* to wail.
vagito *m.* wail.
va'glia (*1*) *m.* money order: **— bancario,** check; **— telegrafico,** telegraph money order.

va'glia (*2*) *f.* good standing, worth.
vagliare *vt.* to sift.
va'glio *m.* sieve: passare al **—,** to sift.
vago *adj.* vague; pretty.
vagone *m.* car, coach; truck: **— letto** (ristorante), sleeping (dining) car.
va'io *m.* miniver; *adj.* dark grey.
vaiuolo *m.* smallpox.
valanga *f.* avalanche.
valente *adj.* clever, skillfull.
valenti'a *f.* cleverness, skill, ability.
valenza *f.* (*chem.*) valence.
valere *vi.*[149] to be worth; to deserve; to be equal to; to be valid; to succeed; to be of avail; to be equivalent to: **vale a dire,** that is to say, namely; **— la pena,** to be worth while; **farsi —,** to push oneself forward, to assert oneself; **far —,** to enforce; **non valsero i suoi sforzi,** his efforts were of no avail; **tanto valeva che,** we might as well; **valersi** *vr.* to avail oneself.
vale'vole *adj.* valid; good.
valicare *vt.* to pass; to cross.
va'lico *m.* pass; ford.

validità *f.* validity, effectiveness.

va'lido *adj.* effective; good; valid; able-bodied.

valigetta *f.* small bag, satchel.

vali'gia *f.* suitcase, portmanteau.

vallata, valle, *f.* valley.

valletto *m.* page, valet; bellboy.

valore *m.* value, worth, price; braveness; gallantry: campione senza —, sample parcel, no commercial value sample.

valorizzare *vt.* to increase the value of; to enhance; to improve.

valoroso *adj.* brave; valiant.

valso *pp. of* valere.

valuta *f.* value; money.

valutare *vt.* to value; to appraise; to reckon; to estimate.

valutazione *f.* valuation, estimation.

val'vola *f.* valve; (*radio*) tube, valve; val'zer *m.* waltz. [(*elec.*) fuse.

vampa *f.* flame, blaze.

vampata *f.* burst of flame.

vampiro *m.* vampire.

vanaglorioso *adj.* vainglorious.

vaneggiare *vi.* to rave, be delirious.

vane'sio *adj.* vain, foppish.

vanga *f.* spade.

vangare *vt.* to spade, dig.

vangelo *m.* gospel; gospel truth.

vani'glia *f.* vanilla.

vanilo'quio *m.* idle talk.

vanità *f.* vanity.

vanitoso *adj.* vain, conceited.

vano *m.* room; opening; *adj.* vain, useless.

vantag'gio *m.* advantage; (*sport*) odds: essere in —, to have the lead.

vantaggioso *adj.* advantageous, profitable; favorable.

vantare *vt.* to praise; to boast (*of*); vantarsi *vr.* to boast, brag; to pride oneself (*on*).

vanteri'a *f.* boast.

vanto *m.* boast; pride.

van'vera, (a) *adv.* at random.

Vanvitelli, Luigi, Neapolitan architect (1700–1773).

vapore *m.* vapor; steam; steamship: a tutto —, full speed; cavallo —, horsepower.

vaporiera *f.* steam engine.

vaporizzare *vt.* to vaporize.

vaporizzatore *m.* vaporizer.

vaporosità *f.* vaporosity.

vaporoso *adj.* vaporous, airy.

varare *vt.* to launch: — una legge, to have an act passed.

varcare *vt.* to cross, pass.

varco *m.* passage, gap, way: attendere al —, to lie in wait (*for*).

varechina *f.* varec, kelp.

varia'bile *adj.* variable, unsteady, fickle.

variante *f.* variant; *adj.* varying.

variare *vt.*, *vi.* to vary.

variato *adj.* varied; various; changed.

variazione *f.* variation; change.

variegato *adj.* variegated.

varietà *f.* variety.

vari *m.pl.*, varie *f.pl.* several.

va'rio *adj.* various; different.

variopinto *adj.* multicolored.

varo *m.* (*naut.*) launch.

Vasari, Giorgio, Italian painter, architect and historian: builder of *Palazzo degli Uffizi* in Florence; author of *Le Vite* (1511–1574).

vasca *f.* basin; tub; pond; pool.

vascello *m.* vessel; ship.

vaselina, vasellina *f.* vaseline.

vasellame *m.* pottery.

vaso *m.* pot, vessel; vase.

vassallo *m.* vassal.

vasso'io *m.* tray.

vastità *f.* roominess; vastness; wideness; expanse.

vasto *adj.* roomy; wide; large, vast.

vate *m.* prophet; poet.

vaticinare *vt.* to prophesy.

vatici'nio *m.* prophecy, prediction.

ve, vi *m.*, *f.*, *pron.* you, to you. *adv.* there; here.

vec'chia *f.* old woman, old lady.

vecchia'ia, vecchiezza *f.* old age, oldness.

vec'chio *m.* old man; *adj.* old; elder: più —, older; il più —, the oldest; i vecchi, old people.

vece *f.* stead, place: in sua —, in his stead, in his place; fare le veci di, to act as.

vedere *vt.*, *vi.*[151] to see: ci vedo poco, I can see little; — di, to try to; non — l'ora di, to be anxious to; non poter — uno, to hate the sight of one; a mio modo di —, in my opinion; vedersi *vr.* to see oneself; (*recipr.*) to see one another; to meet: vedersi costretto a, to be forced to.

vedetta *f.* lookout; sentry; (*theat.*) star.

ve'dova *f.* widow.

vedovanza *f.* widowhood.

ve'dovo *m.* widower.

veduta *f.* sight, view.

veduto *pp.of* vedere.

veemente *adj.* vehement.

veemenza *f.* vehemence.

vegetale *m.*, *adj.* vegetable.

vegetare *vi.* to vegetate.

vegetazione *f.* vegetation.

ve'geto *adj.* vigorous.

vegetominerale, (acqua) *f.* lead water.

veggente *m.*, *f.* seer.

ve'glia *f.* wake; sitting up; watch; night party, revels.

vegliardo m. old man.
vegliare vt., vi. to be awake; to wake; to sit up; to watch, watch over.
veglione m. masked ball, fancy-dress ball.
vei'colo m. vehicle.
vela f. sail: far —, to sail; a gonfie vele, full sail; (fig.) very well.
velac'cio m. main topgallant sail.
velare vt. to veil; to conceal, disguise; velarsi vr. to veil oneself; to become veiled.
vela'rio m. (theat.) curtain.
velato adj. veiled; sheer.
velatura f. (naut.) sails; dimness; veiling.
veleggiare vt., vi. to sail.
veleno m. poison; venom.
velenoso adj. poisonous, venomous.
ve'lico adj. sailing.
veliero m. sailing ship.
velina f. flimsy: carta —, tissue paper; copia in —, carbon copy.
veli'volo m. aircraft, aeroplane.
velleità f. velleity.
vellicare vt. to tickle, titillate.
velloso adj. hairy, shaggy.
vellutato adj. velvety.
velluto m. velvet.
velo m. veil.
veloce adj. quick, fast, speedy, swift.
velocemente adv. swiftly, speedily.
veloci'pede m. velocipede.
velocista m. (sport) sprinter.
velocità f. speed; velocity: eccesso di —, speeding.
vena f. vein; lode; mood.
venale adj. venal.
venalità f. venality.
venato adj. veined, variegated.
venato'rio adj. venatorial, hunting.
venatura f. veining.
vendem'mia f. vintage.
vendemmiare vt. to gather grapes.
ven'dere vt. to sell; ven'dersi vr. to sell oneself; to be sold: quel libro si vende bene, that book sells well.
vendetta f. revenge, vengeance.
vendicare vt. to avenge; vendicarsi vr. to avenge oneself; to retaliate (against).
vendicativo adj. revengeful.
vendicatore m. avenger; adj. avenging.
ven'dita f. sale; shop.
venditore m., venditrice f. seller; dealer: — ambulante, hawker, peddler.
venefi'cio m. poisoning.
vene'fico adj. poisonous.
venera'bile, venerando adj. venerable.
venerare vt. to worship, venerate.
venerazione f. veneration.
venerdì m. Friday: mancare di un —, to have a screw loose.

Ve'nere f. Venus.
vene'reo adj. venereal.
venire vi.[151] to come; to turn out; — alle mani, to come to blows; — a parole, to have words; — su bene, to grow up well; far — il medico, to send for the doctor; — meno, to faint; to fail; — bene, to succeed, turn out well; — in mente, to occur; — a sapere, — a conoscenza di, to learn, hear.
venoso adj. venous.
venta'glio m. fan: a —, fanlike.
ventata f. gust.
vente'simo adj. twentieth.
venti m., adj. twenty.
venticello m. breeze.
ventilare vt. to winnow; to ventilate; to air.
ventila'tore m. ventilator, fan.
ventilazione f. ventilation.
ventina f. some twenty.
vento m. wind.
ven'tola f. fire fan; lampshade.
ventosa f. sucking disk; (med.) cupping glass.
ventoso adj. windy.
ventre m. belly, abdomen, womb: correre — a terra, to run at full speed; giacere — a terra, to lie flat on one's face.
ventriera f. belt.
ventrilo'quio m. ventriloquism.
ventri'loquo m. ventriloquist; adj. ventriloquous.
ventura f. fortune, luck, chance: alla —, at random.
venturo adj. next; future, coming.
venuta f. coming, arrival.
venuto (1) m. comer: il nuovo —, the newcomer; adj. come: — da, from.
venuto (2) pp. of venire.
verace adj. truthful.
veracità f. truthfulness.
veramente adv. truly; really, indeed; as a matter of fact.
veranda f. veranda.
verbale m. minutes, official report; adj. verbal.
verbena f. verbena, vervain.
verbo m. verb; word.
verbosità f. verbosity, prolixity.
verboso adj. verbose, prolix.
verdastro adj. greenish.
verde adj. green: al —, penniless; ridere —, to laugh on the wrong side of one's mouth.
verdeggiante adj. verdant.
verderame m. verdigris.
verdetto m. verdict.
Verdi, Giuseppe, the greatest Italian operatic composer, Nabucco, I Lombardi alla Prima Crociata, Rigoletto, Il Trovatore, La Tra-

viata, I Vespri Siciliani, La Forza del Destino, Aida, Falstaff (1813–1901).

verdo'gnolo *adj.* greenish.

verdura *f.* vegetables.

verecon'dia *f.* pudency, modesty.

verecondo *adj.* modest, bashful.

verga *f.* rod; cane; bar.

Verga, Giovanni, Italian novelist, *I Malavoglia, Vita dei Campi, Novelle Rusticane* (1840–1922).

vergare *vt.* to write.

vergato *adj.* ruled: **carta vergata,** ruled paper.

verginale *adj.* virgin, maidenly.

ver'gine *f.* virgin, maid; *adj.* virgin; free (*from*).

verginità *f.* virginity.

vergogna *f.* shame; bashfulness.

vergognarsi *vr.* to be ashamed: **vergognatevil** shame on you!

vergognoso *adj.* shameful, disgraceful; shy, bashful.

veridicità *f.* veracity, genuineness.

veri'dico *adj.* veracious, true, genuine.

veri'fica *f.* verification; inspection; examination; overhaul.

verificare *vt.* to verify; to check; to audit (*as an account*); **verificarsi** *vr.* to happen.

verismo *m.* realism.

verista *m.* realist; *adj.* realistic.

verità *f.* truth, verity, actuality: **in —,** really, actually, as a matter of fact.

veritiero *adj.* truthful, veracious.

verme *m.* worm: **— solitario,** tapeworm.

vermi'glio *m., adj.* vermilion.

vernice, *f.* varnish, paint; glaze; polish; patent leather; varnishing day.

verniciare *vt.* to varnish, paint.

vero *m.* truth, reality; *adj.* true, real, veritable, genuine: **(non è) —?** isn't it?; **dal —,** from nature, from life.

verone *m.* balcony.

Veronese, Paolo (*Paolo Cagliari*), Italian painter (1528–1588).

verosimiglianza *f.* likelihood.

verosi'mile *adj.* likely, probable.

Verrazzano, Giovanni, Florentine navigator (1485?–1528).

verricello *m.* windlass.

verro *m.* boar.

Verrocchio, del, Andrea, Italian sculptor and painter (1435–1488).

verruca *f.* wart.

versamento *m.* pouring; payment; (*bank.*) deposit.

versante *m.* side, slope.

versare *vt.* to pour; to spill, shed; to pay; (*bank.*) to deposit: **— in gravi**

condizioni, to be in serious condition; **versarsi** *vr.* to pour (*into*); to spill.

versa'tile *adj.* versatile.

versatilità *f.* versatility.

versato *adj.* spilled; versed, skilled, proficient (*in*).

versione *f.* translation; version.

verso (*I*) *m.* verse, line; note, song, cry, hoot; sense, direction; way, means; verso; reverse: **versi liberi,** vers libre, free verse.

verso (*2*) *prep.* towards, to; about.

ver'tebra *f.* vertebra.

vertebrale *adj.* vertebral: **colonna —,** spine.

vertenza *f.* quarrel, question.

ver'tere *vi.* to be about, regard.

verticale *f., adj.* vertical.

ver'tice *m.* vertex, apex, top.

verti'gine *f.* giddiness, dizziness, staggers, vertigo: **avere le vertigini,** to be giddy; **dare le vertigini,** to make dizzy.

vertiginoso *adj.* dizzy; mad; breathtaking.

verza *f.* cabbage.

verziere *m.* vegetable market.

vescica *f.* bladder.

vescicante *m.* vesicant.

vescovado *m.* bishopric.

ve'scovo *m.* bishop.

vespa *f.* wasp.

vespa'io *m.* hornets' nest; (*med.*) favus.

vespasiano *m.* public urinal.

ve'spero *m.* evening.

vespertino *adj.* evening; vespertine.

vespro *m.* vesper; evening.

Vespucci, Amerigo, Florentine navigator; from his two voyages, 1499 and 1501, the two Americas derive their name (1451–1512).

vessare *vt.* to harass, wrong.

vessazione *f.* injustice, oppression.

vessillo *m.* flag.

vesta'glia *f.* dressing gown.

veste *f.* dress, gown; capacity; appearance: **— da camera,** dressing gown; **in — di,** as; **vesti** *pl.* clothes.

vestia'rio *m.* clothes: **oggetti di —,** garments.

vesti'bolo *m.* lobby, vestibule.

vesti'gio *m.* sign, trace, vestige.

vestire *vt., vi.* to dress; to wear; to clothe: **— la penne del pavone,** to put on borrowed plumes; **vestirsi** *vr.* to dress (oneself) **— da,** to disguise oneself (*as*).

vestito *m.* dress; suit; clothes; *adj.* dressed: **— da festa,** in one's Sunday best.

veterano *m., adj.* veteran.

veterina'rio *m., adj.* veterinary.

veto *m.* veto: mettère il **—** a, to veto.

vetra'io *m.* glass manufacturer; glass-blower; glazier.

vetrata *f.* glass window; glass door; glass partition: **—** a colori, stained glass window.

vetrato *adj.:* carta vetrata, sandpaper.

vetreri'a *f.* glass works.

vetrificare *vt., vi.* to vitrify.

vetrina *f.* show window; shop window; glass case.

vetrinista *m., f.* window dresser.

vetriolo *m.* vitriol.

vetro *m.* glass; pane, windowpane: **—** colorato, stained glass; **—** smerigliato, ground glass.

vetroso *adj.* glassy, vitreous.

vetta *f.* summit, top.

vettova'glie *f.pl.* victuals, food.

vettura *f.* carriage; coach; cab: in **—**, signori! all aboard, please!; lettera di **—**, carriage note.

vetturetta *f.* baby carriage.

vetturino *m.* cabman, driver.

vetusto *adj.* ancient, old.

vezzeggiare *vt.* to fondle, cuddle.

vezzeggiativo *m.* endearing term; diminutive.

vezzo *m.* bad habit; habit; fondling; charm; necklace.

vezzoso *adj.* graceful, pretty.

vi (*1*) *pron.* you, to you.

vi (*2*) *adv.* here, there: eccovi infine! there you are at last!

via (*1*) *f.* street; road; way: **—** d'uscita, way out; per **—** diplomatica, through diplomatic channels; venire a vie di fatto, to come to blows; vie legali, legal steps; la Via Lattea, the Milky Way; dare il **—**, to start; per vie traverse, by roundabout means; la Via Crucis, the Way of the Cross.

via (*2*) *adv.* away, off: via! go away!, go!; ma via! now come!; e così **—**, and so on; **—** che vengono, as they come; in **—** di favore, as a favor; per **—** di, on account of.

viadotto *m.* viaduct.

viaggiare *vi.* to travel.

viaggiatore *m.*, **viaggiatrice** *f.* traveler; passenger: **—** di comercio, commesso **—**, salesman.

viag'gio *m.* trip, journey, voyage, travel: **—** di piacere, tour; **—** d'andata, outward journey; **—** d'andata e ritorno, round trip.

viale *m.* avenue.

viandante *m.* wayfarer, pedestrian, passer-by.

via'tico *m.* viaticum.

viavai *m.* coming and going; bustle; swarm.

vibrante *adj.* vibrant, quivering

vibrare *vt.* to hurl; *vi.* to vibrate, quiver: **—** un colpo, to deal (strike) a blow.

vibrato *adj.* concise; energetic.

vibrazione *f.* vibration.

vica'rio *m.* vicar.

vice- *pref.* vice, assistant, deputy.

vice-direttore *m.* assistant director; assistant editor; assistant manager.

vicenda *f.* alternation; vicissitude; case; event, occurrence: a **—**, reciprocally, one another; in turn.

vicende'vole *adj.* reciprocal, mutual.

vicepresidente *m.* vice president, vice chairman.

vicerè *m.* viceroy.

viceversa *adv.* vice versa, conversely; on the contrary.

vicinanza *f.* nearness, closeness, vicinity; imminence; vicinanze (*pl.*) neighborhood.

vicinato *m.* neighborhood; neighbors.

vicino *m.* neighbor; *adj.* near, adjoining; neighboring; like, resembling; *adv.* near, near by, near at hand, close by: da **—**, at close quarters.

vicino, (a) *prep.* near, by, beside, close to.

vicissitu'dine *f.* vicissitude; event.

Vico, Giambattista, Italian philosopher, author of *Scienza Nuova*, by which he became the father of the modern philosophy of history (1668–1744).

vi'colo *m.* lane, alley.

vidimare *vt.* to authenticate; to sign; to visa.

vidimazione *f.* authentication, signature, visa.

vieppiù *adv.* more and more.

vietare *vt.* to forbid.

vietato *adj.* forbidden: **—** il transito, no thoroughfare; sosta vietata, no parking.

vieto *adj.* stale; trite; obsolete.

vigente *adj.* operative, current.

vi'gere *vi.* to be in force.

vigilante *adj.* vigilant, watchful, alert.

vigilanza *f.* vigilance, watchfulness.

vigilare *vt.* to watch, guard; *vi.* to be on guard; to keep watch.

vi'gile *m.* policeman: **—** del fuoco, fireman; *adj.* vigilant, watchful; wary.

vigi'lia *f.* eve; watch; fast, vigil.

vigliaccheri'a *f.* cowardice.

vigliacco *m.*, *adj.* coward; dastard; cad, "heel."

vigna *f.*, **vigneto** *m.*, vineyard.

vignetta *f.* vignette, cartoon.

vignettista *m.* vignettist, cartoonist.

vigogna *f.* vicuña.

vigore *m.* vigor, strength, force: in —, in force; entrare in —, to take effect.

vigori'a *f.* vigor, strength.

vigoroso *adj.* vigorous, strong.

vile *m.* coward; *adj.* cowardly; vile, mean; cheap, low.

vilipen'dere *vt.*[10] to despise; to insult.

vilipen'dio *m.* contempt; insult.

vilipeso *adj.* despised. *pp. of* vilipendere.

villa *f.* villa, country house, cottage.

villag'gio *m.* village.

villanata *f.* slight, snub, insult.

Villani, Giovanni, Italian historian (1280?-1348).

villani'a *f.* rudeness, uncivility; insult.

villano *m.* peasant, countryman; boor; *adj.* rude.

villanzone *m.* boor.

villeggiante *m.* vacationist, vacationer.

villeggiare *vi.* to vacation.

villeggiatura *f.* summer vacation: luogo di —, summer resort.

villino *m.* cottage.

villoso *adj.* hairy, shaggy.

viltà *f.* cowardice; meanness.

viluppo *m.* tangle.

vi'mine *m.* osier, withe, wicker.

vina'io *m.* wine merchant.

vincente *m.* winner; *adj.* winning.

vin'cere *vt.*, *vi.*[153] to win, gain; to vanquish; to beat, defeat; to overcome, master; vincersi *vr.* to master oneself.

Vinci, da, Leonardo, celebrated painter, sculptor and architect of the Florentine school; extraordinarily versatile, he distinguished himself in engineering as well as art; his most important works as a painter, *Il Cenacolo, La Gioconda* ("*Mona Lisa*"), *La Vergine delle Rocce, San Giovanni Battista, La Battaglia di Anghiari* (cartoon); he also wrote a *Trattato della pittura* and *Del moto e misura dell'acqua* (1452-1519).

vin'cita *f.* winning; winnings.

vincitore *m.* winner; conqueror.

vincolare *vt.* to bind; to engage; to entail; vincolarsi *vr.* to bind oneself; to engage (for).

vin'colo *m.* bond, tie, link.

vino *m.* wine.

vinto *adj.* conquered; vanquished; won; overcome: darsi per —, to give in *or* up. *pp. of* vincere.

viola (1) *f.* : — mammola, violet; — del pensiero, pansy; *adj.* violet, purple.

viola (2) *f.* (*mus.*) viola.

violacciocca *f.* wallflower.

viola'ceo *adj.* violet=blue; cyanotic.

violare *vt.* to violate.

violazione *f.* violation, infringement: — di domicilio, housebreaking.

violentare *vt.* to force; to rape.

violento *adj.* violent.

violenza *f.* violence: — carnale, rape.

violetta *f.* violet.

violetto *m.*, *adj.* violet.

violinista *m.*, *f.* violinist; fiddler.

violino *m.* violin; fiddle.

viot'tolo *m.* path.

vi'pera *f.* viper.

virag'gio *m.* (*naut.*) tacking; (*aeron.*) yaw; (*photo.*) toning.

virare *vi.* (*naut.*) to tack; (*aeron.*) to yaw; (*photo.*) to tone.

virata *f.* (*naut.*) tacking; (*aeron.*) yaw, turn.

virginale *adj.* maidenly, virginal.

vir'gola *f.* comma.

virgolette *f.pl.* quotation marks, inverted commas.

virgulto *m.* shoot; shrub.

virile *adj.* virile, manly; manful.

virilità *f.* manliness, virility; manhood.

virtù *f.* virtue; property.

virtuale *adj.* virtual.

virtuosismo *m.* virtuosity, stunt.

virtuoso *m.* virtuoso; *adj.* virtuous.

virulento *adj.* virulent.

virulenza *f.* virulence.

vi'scere *f.pl.* viscera; bowels; heart of hearts; entrails, innermost recesses.

vischio *m.* mistletoe; birdlime.

vi'scido *adj.* viscid, clammy.

viscosa *f.* viscose.

viscoso *adj.* viscous, clammy; viscose.

visi'bile *adj.* visible; obvious.

visibi'lio *m.* lot, heap, great deal: mandare in —, to enrapture; andare in —, to become enraptured.

visibilità *f.* visibility.

visiera *f.* visor; eyeshade; peak.

visiona'rio *m.*, *adj.* visionary.

visione *f.* vision: prender —, to examine; prima — first showing (*of a moving picture*).

visita *f.* visit, call; examination; inspection; caller: marcar — (*mil.*) to report sick.

visitare *vt.* to visit; to pay a visit; to call on.

visitatore *m.*, visitatrice *f.* visitor.

visivo *adj.* visual: facoltà visiva, sight.

viso *m.* face; features (*pl.*) far buon — a cattiva sorte, to put a good face on it; a — aperto, boldly, frankly, directly.

visone *m.* mink.

vispo *adj.* brisk, lively.

vissuto *adj.* lived; worldly-wise. *pp. of* vivere.

vista f. sight; eyes; view; landscape: far — di, to feign, pretend; persone in —, prominent people; punto di —, standpoint, opinion; a — d'occhio, apace.

vistare vt. to visa, sign.

visto (1) m. visa; approval.

visto (2) adj. seen: ben —, popular; mal —, disliked; — che, since, as. pp.of vedere.

vistoso adj. showy; considerable, large.

visuale f. view; adj. visual.

vita f. life; living, livelihood; lifetime; (anat.) waist: condannato a —, sentenced for life; — natural durante during one's lifetime; for-

vitale adj. vital. [ever.

vitalità f. vitality.

vitali'zio m. life annuity; adj. for life: pensione vitalizia, life pension.

vitamina f. vitamin.

vite (1) f. vine.

vite (2) f. screw; (aeron.) barrel roll; tail spin.

vitello m. calf, veal: — marino, seacalf.

vitellone m. young bullock; (coll.) "drugstore cowboy."

vitic'cio m. tendril.

vit'reo adj. vitreous.

vit'tima f. victim; casualty.

vitto m. food; board.

vitto'ria f. victory, victoria (carriage): cantar —, to crow.

Vittorio Emanuele I, King of Sardinia, 1802–21 (1759–1824).

Vittorio Emanuele II, first king of Italy, 1861–78 (1820–1878).

Vittorio Emanuele III, son of Umberto I, King of Italy, 1900–46 (1869–1947).

vittorioso adj. victorious.

vituperare vt. to vituperate.

vitupe'rio m. ignominy, shame; insult.

viuzza f. narrow street, lane.

viva! see vivere.

vivacchiare vi. to get along somehow, to live from hand to mouth.

vivace adj. lively, brisk; quick; bright.

vivacità f. vivacity, liveliness; quickness; brightness.

vivaddio! interj. by God!, so help me God!

vivagno m. selvage, selvedge.

viva'io m. hatchery.

vivamente adv. deeply, keenly; strongly; warmly.

vivanda f. food.

vivente adj. living, alive.

vi'vere (1) vt., vi.[154] to live; to enjoy one's life; to last: viva! hurrah!, long live!; sul chi vive, on the alert.

vi'vere (2) m. existence, living.

vi'veri m.pl. victuals, food, provisions; supplies: tagliare i —, to cut off (one's) allowance.

vivezza f. liveliness; brightness.

vi'vido adj. vivid, lively.

vivificare vt. to vivify.

vivisezione f. vivisection.

vivo m. living man; core: pungere sul —, to sting to the quick; una descrizione al —, a lifelike description; adj. alive; living; lively; strong; sharp, keen; bright: a viva forza, by main force; a viva voce, by word of mouth; farsi —, to show up; to let hear about oneself; vivi auguri, best wishes.

viziare vt. to spoil; to corrupt.

vi'zio m. vice; fault; bad habit; flaw.

vizioso adj. vicious; corrupt; profligate.

vizzo adj. withered.

vocabolario m. dictionary; vocabulary.

voca'bolo m. term; word; entry.

vocale f. vowel; adj. vocal.

vocazione f. vocation, calling; aptness.

voce f. voice; term, word; entry, item; rumor: — bianca, soprano voice; a —, by word of mouth; a —Jalta, aloud; ad una —, in unison; non aver — in capitolo, to cut no ice; dare sulla — a, to contradict; to rebuke.

vociare vi. to bawl.

vociferare vi. to vociferate, shout: si vocifera, it is being rumored.

voga f. vogue, fashion; (naut.) rowing.

vogare vt. to row.

vogata f. row, rowing.

vogatore m. rower, oarsman; rowing machine.

voglia f. wish, desire; will, willingness; intention; craving, longing; birthmark: ho — di, I feel like; non ne ho —, I don't feel like it; di buona —, willingly; di mala —, reluctantly.

voglioso adj. desirous. [ly.

voi pers.pron. you: — stesso, yourself; — stessi, yourselves.

volano m. shuttlecock; (mach.) flywheel.

volante m. (steering) wheel; adj. flying.

volantino m. throwaway, leaflet.

volare vi. to fly.

volata f. flight; run: — finale (sport), homestretch; final dash; di —, in a hurry; full speed; at once.

vola'tile adj. volatile; flying; m. winged animal.

volatilizzare vt., vi., volatilizzarsi vr. to volatilize.

volatore m. flyer; adj. flying.

volente adj. willing: — o nolente, willy-nilly.

volenteroso adj. zealous; dedicated; willing.

volentieri adv. willingly.

volere (1) m. see volontà.

volere (2) vt., vi.[155] to want; to wish, like; to ask, require; to will, command; to intend (to): voglio che tu, I want you to; vorrei avere, I wish I had; vorrei essere, I wish I were; ci vuole coraggio per, it takes courage to; — bene a, to love; voler male a, to hate; — dire, to mean; parla vuoi l'italiano vuoi l'inglese, he speaks both Italian and English; — è potere, where there is a will there is a way.

volgare adj. vulgar, coarse, low.

volgarità f. vulgarity, coarseness.

volgarizzare vt. to vulgarize.

vol'gere (1) m. turning; course; space: il — degli avvenimenti, the course of events; nel — di pochi anni, within a few years.

vol'gere (2) vt., vi.[156] to turn; to elapse; to go by: — alla fine, to draw to an end; — in fuga, to put to flight; vol'gersi vr. to turn.

volgo m. common people.

voliera f. aviary.

volitivo adj. determined, strong-willed.

volo m. flight, flying: prendere il —, to take to flight; — a vela, gliding; — librato, volplane.

volontà f. will: forza di —, will power.

volonta'rio m. volunteer; adj. voluntary.

volonteroso see volenteroso.

volontieri see volentieri.

volpe f. fox; vixen; (bot.) mildew.

volpino adj. foxy.

volpone m. (fig.) old fox.

volta (1) f. time; turn; vault: una —, once; due volte, twice; tre volte, thrice, three times; rare volte, seldom; a mia —, in my turn; una — tanto, for once; una — ogni tanto, once in a while; di — in — each time; il più delle volte, mostly; spesse volte, often; chiave di —, keystone; partire alla — di Roma, to set out for Rome; gli diede di — il cervello, he went mad; a — di corriere, by return of post.

volta (2) m. (elec.) volt.

Volta, Alessandro, Italian physicist, inventor of the voltaic pile (1745-1827).

voltafac'cia m. volte-face.

voltag'gio m. (elec.) voltage.

volta'ico adj. (elec.) voltaic.

voltare vt., vi. to turn; to translate; voltarsi vr. to turn; to change; to rebel.

voltata f. turn, turning.

volteggiare vt. to turn; to hover; to vault, circle.

volteg'gio m. vaulting.

volto m. face.

volto adj. turned; looking (on, towards); devoted. pp.of volgere.

voltura f. transfer.

volu'bile adj. fickle, changeable.

volubilità f. fickleness.

volume m. volume; mass, bulk.

voluminoso adj. voluminous.

voluta f. volute, scroll, coil.

voluto adj. artificial; farfetched; intentional. pp.of volere.

voluttà f. delight; voluptuousness.

voluttua'rio adj. superfluous, luxury.

voluttuoso adj. voluptuous.

vo'mere m. plowshare.

vo'mico adj. emetic: noce vomica, vomit nut, nux vomica.

vomitare vt., vi. to vomit: aver voglia di —, to feel sick; far venire la voglia di —, to make sick.

vomitivo adj. emetic, disgusting.

vo'mito m. vomit.

von'gola f. mussel.

vorace adj. voracious; greedy.

voracità f. voracity; greediness.

vora'gine f. gulf, chasm, abyss.

vor'tice m. vortex; whirl; whirlpool; whirlwind.

vorticoso adj. vortical, whirling.

vostro poss. adj. your, of yours; poss. pron. yours.

votag'gine f. emptiness.

votante m. voter; adj. voting.

votare vt., vi. to devote; to approve, pass; to vote; votarsi vr. to devote oneself: non sapere a che santo votarsi, not to know which way to turn.

votato adj. approved, passed; devoted, doomed.

votazione f. voting, poll; marks (pl.).

votivo adj. votive.

voto m. vow; wish; prayer; mark; vote: far voti, to pray; scheda di —, ballot paper; a pieni voti, with full marks, with flying colors.

vulca'nico adj. volcanic.

vulcanizzare vt. to vulcanize.

vulcanizzazione f. vulcanization.

vulcano m. volcano.

vulnera'bile adj. vulnerable.

vulnerabilità f. vulnerability.

vuotare vt. to empty: — il sacco (fig.), to make a clean breast of it; vuo-tarsi vr. to empty.

vuoto m. empty space, gap; (phys.)

vacuum, void: andare a —, to fail, come to nothing; a —, to no purpose; assegno a —, un-covered check; — di cassa, deficit; — d'aria (aeron.), air pocket; adj. empty; vain, void.

X

X *L. and Gr. letter.* x: raggi x, X rays.
xenofobi'a f. xenophobia.
xeno'fobo m. xenophobe.
Xeres m. sherry (wine).
xilofonista m. xylophone player.

xilo'fono m. xylophone.
xilografi'a f. xylograph; xylography.
xilogra'fico adj. xylographic.
xilo'grafo m. xylographer.

Z

zabaione m. eggnog.
Zacconi, Ermete, famous Italian stage actor (1857-1948).
zaffare vt. to bung; to tampon.
zaffata f. whiff.
zaffatura f. bunging; tamponment.
zafferano m. saffron.
zaffiro m. sapphire.
zaffo m. bung; tampon.
zaga'glia f. assagai.
za'gara f. orange blossom.
za'ino m. knapsack.
zampa f. paw, leg: zampe di gallina, crow's feet; zampe di mosca, scrawls.
zampettare vi. to toddle.
zampillare vi. to gush, spring, spout.
zampillo m. spurt.
zampogna f. bagpipe.
zampognaro m. bagpiper.
zampone m. pig's trotter.
zan'gola f. churn.
zanna f. tusk, fang.
zannata f. snap.
zanzara f. mosquito.
zanzariera f. mosquito net.
zappa f. hoe: darsi la — sui piedi, to cut the ground from under one's own feet.
zappare vt., vi. to hoe, dig.
zappatore m. hoer, digger.
zat'tera f. raft.
zavorra f. ballast; dregs, trash.
zavorrare vt. to ballast.
zaz'zera f. mane, long hair.
zebra f. zebra.
zebrato adj. zebra-striped.
zecca f. mint: nuovo di —, brand new.
zecchino m. sequin: oro di —, pure gold.
zef'firo m. breeze, light wind.
zelante adj. zealous, overhelpful.
zelatore m. zealot; supporter.
zelo m. zeal.
zenit m. zenith.
zen'zero m. ginger.
zeppa f. wedge.
zeppo adj. chock-full, crammed (with); overcrowded.

zerbino m. doormat.
zerbinotto m. dandy.
zero m. zero, cipher, nought; 0; nothing, naught: — via —! absolutely nothing.
zeta f. zee, zed.
zia f. aunt.
zibaldone m. commonplace-book.
zibellino m. sable.
zibetto m. zibet.
zibibbo m. raisin.
zigano m., adj. gypsy.
zi'gomo m. cheekbone.
zigrinato adj. shagreened; knurled.
zigrino m. shagreen.
zimarra f. robe, cloak.
zimbello m. laughingstock.
zincare vt. to zinc.
zinco m. zinc.
zincografi'a f. zincography.
zinco'grafo m. zincographer.
Zingarelli, Nicola, Italian lexicographer and essayist, *Vocabolario della lingua italiana* (1860-1935).
zingaresco adj. gypsyish.
zin'garo m. gypsy.
zinzino m. little bit.
zio m. uncle.
zi'polo m. spigot.
zirlare vi. to warble.
zirlo m. warbling.
zitella f. maid, old maid.
zittire vt., vi. to hiss.
zitto adj. silent: star —, to keep silent; zitto! shut up!; zitti! quiet!
zizza'nia f. darnel: seminar —, to sow the seeds of dissension.
zoc'colo m. clog; hoof; (archit.) socle; dado.
zodi'aco m. zodiac.
zolfanello m. sulphur match.
zolfara f. sulphur mine.
zolfo m. sulphur.
zolla f. clod; sod, turf; lump (of sugar).
zolletta f. lump (of sugar).
zona f. zone, area; stripe.
zonzo, (a) adv. strolling: andare a — to stroll.

zoo'filo m. zoöphilist; adj. zoöphilous.

zoolo'gico adj. zoölogical: giardino —, zoölogical garden, zoo.

zootec'nico adj. zoötechnic: patrimonio —, livestock.

zoppicante adj. limping, halting.

zoppicare vi. to limp, halt.

zoppo m. lame person; adj. lame, limping; wobbling.

zo'tico m. boor; adj. boorish.

zoticone m. boor, lout, rustic.

zucca f. gourd, pumpkin; pate: non aver sale in —, to be shallow-brained.

zuccata f. bump with the head.

zuccherare vt. to sugar.

zuccheriera f. sugar basin.

zuccherifi'cio m. sugarworks.

zuccherino m. sweet; adj. sugary.

zuc'chero m. sugar.

zuccheroso adj. sugary.

zucchino m. Italian vegetable marrow, cocozelle, zucchini.

zuccone m. dunce.

zuffa m. scuffle, fight.

zufolare vt., vi. to whistle.

zu'folo m. whistle; pipe.

zuppa f. soup.

zuppiera f. tureen.

zuppo adj. wet, drenched.

zuzzurullone m. hobbledehoy.

Parte Seconda

INGLESE - ITALIANO

ABBREVIAZIONES

abbr.	abbreviazione	*med.*	medicina
aeron.	aeronautica	*metall.*	metallurgia
agg.	aggettivo	*meteor.*	meteorologia
agr.	agricoltura	*mil.*	militare
am.	americano	*min.*	mineralogia
anat.	anatomia	*mus.*	musica
arch.	architettura	*n.*	nome
art. indef.	articolo indefinito	*naut.*	nautica
artigl.	artiglieria	*ornit.*	ornitologia
auto.	automobile	*ott.*	ottica
avv.	avverbio	*part.*	participio
biol.	biologia	*pass.*	passato, passivo
bot.	botanica	*pat.*	patologia
chim.	chimica	*pers.*	personale
comm.	commercio	*pitt.*	pittura
comp.	comparativo	*pl.*	plurale
cong.	congiunzione	*pp.*	participio passato
dimonstr.	dimonstrativo	*ppr.*	participio presente
ecc.	et cetera	*pref.*	prefisso
eccl.	ecclesiastico	*prep.*	preposizione
edil.	edilizia	*pret.*	preterito
elett.	elettricità	*pron.*	pronome
f.	femminile	*recipr.*	reciproco
fam.	familiare	*rel.*	relativo
ferr.	ferrovia	*rif.*	riferito
fis.	fisica	*rifl.*	riflessivo
fot.	fotografia	*sch.*	scherma
fr.	francese	*scherz.*	scherzenole
gen. pl.	genitivo plurale	*seg.*	seguente
geog.	geografia	*spec.*	speciale
geom.	geometria	*sprezz.*	sprezzante
giorn.	giornale	*S.U.*	Stati Uniti
giur.	giurisprudenza	*sup.*	superlativo
gramm.	grammatica	*t.*	transitivo
impers.	impersonale	*teat.*	teatro
indef.	indefinito	*tec.*	tecnico
ing.	ingegneria	*telef.*	telefono
Ingh.	Inghilterra	*tip.*	tipografia
ingl.	inglese	*T.V.*	televisione
inter.	interiezione	*univ.*	universita
interrog.	interrogativo	*v.*	verbo
intr.	intransitivo	*vet.*	veterinario
ittiol.	ittiologia	*vi.*	verbo intransitivo
m.	maschile	*vr.*	verbo riflessivo
mat.	matematica	*vt.*	verbo transitivo
mecc.	meccanica	*zool.*	zoologia

PRONUNCIA INGLESE FIGURATA

I simboli fonetici usati per la pronuncia figurata di questo vocabolario sono quelli del MERRIAM-WEBSTER POCKET DICTIONARY, 14a edizione, aprile 1955.

Accentazione:

L'accento principale è indicato con un segno pesante ('), e l'accento secondario con un segno leggiero (').

Voci senza pronuncia figurata:

Per alcune voci derivate da altre mediante l'aggiunta dei suffissi -er, -est, -ing, -ish, -less, -like, -ness, -ship, e per altre composte di due voci reperibili separatamente, a volte è stata omessa la pronuncia figurata. Si tratta di casi in cui la pronuncia della voce derivata o composta è assolutamente regolare, e può essere appresa studiando la pronuncia figurata della voce base o delle singole voci componenti.

ā corrisponde al dittongo *ei* di *sei*, con la *i* a volte più marcata, a volte meno.

â è simile alla precedente, ma con una pronuncia molto rapida, tale da non far quasi sentire la *i*.

â ha un suono che sta tra il dittongo *ea* e il dittongo *ei*, con una pronuncia molto fusa delle due vocali. Non ha equivalente in italiano.

ă ha un suono che sta tra la *a* e la *e*, con maggior tendenza verso la *e*. Non ha corrispondente in italiano.

ă corrisponde alla *a* italiana, ma con un suono molto meno marcato.

ä corrisponde alla *a* italiana.

á ha un suono tra la *a* e la *e*, con maggiore tendenza verso la *a*. Non ha equivalente in italiano.

á corrisponde alla *a* italiana, ma è molto meno udibile.

b si pronuncia come in italiano.

ch si pronuncia come la *c* dolce italiana di *cena*.

d si pronuncia come in italiano, ma con un suono più pastoso, puntando la lingua contro l'interno delle gengive; è quasi uguale alla *d* siciliana di *bedda* (bella).

dū corrisponde approssimativamente alla sillaba *giu* di *giusto*.

ē corrisponde alla *i* italiana di *vita*.

ę si pronuncia, più o meno, *ia* come in *stia*, ma la *a* è quasi impercettibile. Non ha equivalente italiano.

è corrisponde alla *i* di *vita*, ma con un suono molto più breve.

ĕ corrisponde alla *e* stretta italiana di *dentro*.

ě è simile alla precedente, ma molto meno udibile, sino a diventare quasi muta. Non ha equivalente italiano.

ẽ è una *e* strettissima, in certo modo affine alla *eu* francese. Non ha corrispondente italiano.

f si pronuncia come in italiano.

g ha sempre il suono della *g* aspra italiana di *gomma*.

gz suona come sonerebbe in italiano il gruppo di consonanti *ghs*, con la *s* dolce.

h si pronuncia, in principio di parola, quasi sempre aspirata.

ī si pronuncia *ai* come in *mai*.

ĭ corrisponde a una *i* molto breve.

ĭ corrisponde approssimativamente alla *i* italiana, ma anch'essa è molto breve.

j corrisponde alla *g* dolce di *gente*.

iii

k	corrisponde alla *c* aspra italiana di *canto*.
ks	suona come in italiano, con la *s* aspra.
kw	corrisponde al *qu* italiano di *quanto*.
l	suona come in italiano
m	suona come in italiano.
n	suona come in italiano.
ng	corrisponde, più o meno, alla *ng* di *sangue*, ma la *g*, quando è in fine di parola, è molto meno udibile.
ō	si pronuncia *ou*, ma con la *u* piuttosto debole. Non ha equivalente in italiano.
ŏ	si pronuncia come la *o* italiana di *Napoli*.
ô	si pronuncia approssimativamente come la *o* italiana di *ciò*.
ŏ̀	è una *o* estremamente aperta, che sconfina quasi nella *a*. Non ha corrispondente italiano.
ŏ̆	assomiglia molto alla precedente, ma è più breve.
ŏ̥	sta a indicare che si può pronunziare *o* come ŏ, o come ô
oi	si pronuncia come in italiano, ma con la *i* molto più debole.
ōō	si pronuncia come la *u* italiana di *frutto*.
ŏŏ	si pronuncia come la *u* italiana, ma molto più breve.
ou	si pronuncia come la *au* italiana di *paura*, ma con la *u* più breve.
p	si pronuncia come in italiano.
r	si pronuncia come la *r* italiana, piegando però la punta della lingua verso la cima del palato. Ne risulta un suono molto sordo, che non ha corrispondente italiano.
s	si pronuncia come la *s* aspra in italiano.
sh	si pronuncia come l' *sc* italiano di *scena*.
t	si pronuncia come in italiano, ma con un suono più pastoso, puntando la lingua contro l'interno delle gengive.
th	si pronuncia come la *s* aspra italiana, mettendo però la punta della lingua tra i denti.
th	si pronuncia come la *s* dolce italiana, mettendo però la punta della lingua tra i denti.
tŭ	si pronuncia approssimativamente come *ciù* in *ciarla*. Non ha corrispondente italiano.
ū	si pronuncia approssimativamente come *iù* in *fiume*.
û	assomiglia alla precedente, ma la *i* è molto meno udibile.
û	si pronuncia come la *eu* francese, o la *oeu* lombarda.
ŭ	assomiglia alla *a* italiana, ma è un suono che sta tra la *a* e la *o*. Non ha equivalente italiano.
ŭ	assomigilia alla precedente, ma è molto meno udibile.
ü	corrisponde alla *u* francese e lombarda.
v	si pronuncia come in italiano.
w	si pronuncia come la *u* italiana di *uomo*.
y	si pronuncia come la *i* italiana di *ieri*.
z	si pronuncia come la *s* dolce di *rosa*.
zh	si pronuncia come la *j* francese di *joli*. Non ha corrispondente italiano.
'	indica che la vocale non si pronuncia.

Pronuncia della s del plurale:

1. La s del plurale è aspra quando la parola termina per consonante sorda— *f, k, p, t, th*: cliffs, books, caps, mats, lengths.

2. La s del plurale è dolce quando la parola termina per vocale (ivi compresa la *y*, che diventa ies), o per consonante sonora — *b, d, g, l, m, n, ng, th, v, w,*: cries, robes, beds, rags, girls, terms, tins, songs, breathes, dives, blows.

3. La s che si aggiunge alle parole terminanti in *ce, dge, ge, se*, e la es che si aggiunge alle parole terminanti in *ch, sh, ss, si* leggono entrambe *is*, con la *s* dolce: faces, judges, fringes, roses, churches, ashes, kisses.

IL SOSTANTIVO

I. GENERE DEL SOSTANTIVO

In inglese sono maschili i nomi di persona o animale di sesso maschile, e femminili i nomi di persona o animale di sesso femminile. Femminili sono pure considerati le nazioni, le navi, gli aeroplani e le automobili. Ogni altro nome in genere è neutro. L'articolo definito the vale per tutti i generi, sia al singolare, sia al plurale.

Formazione del femminile:

Quando non esistano forme distinte per il maschile e il femminile — es: uncle, *zio* = aunt, *zia* — il femminile si forma come segue:

1. con l'aggiunta di alcuni suffissi:

   -ess   poet = poetess; prince = princess
   -trix   aviator = aviatrix; creator = creatrix

2. facendo precedere al nome talune definizioni:

   woman   writer = woman writer
   lady   doctor = lady doctor
   girl   friend = girl friend

3. per i nomi di animali, facendo precedere la definizione:

   she   bear = she bear

II. PLURALE DEL SOSTANTIVO

1. Generalmente, si forma aggiungendo una s al singolare: book = books.
2. I sostantivi terminanti in *ch* (pronunziata come *c* dolce), *o*, *ss*, *sh*, *x*, *z*, prendono al plurale il suffisso es: church = churches; hero = heroes; kiss = kisses; brush = brushes; box = boxes; buzz = buzzes.
3. I sostantivi terminanti in *ch* aspra (pronunziata come *k*) prendono al plurale la s semplice: monarch = monarchs.
4. I sostantivi terminanti in *y* preceduta da consonante hanno il plurale in ies: family = families. Se la *y* è preceduta da vocale, il plurale si forma normalmente: day = days.
5. I sostantivi terminanti in *fe* e certi sostantivi terminanti in *f* hanno il plurale in ves: life = lives; leaf = leaves.
6. Alcuni sostantivi terminanti in *is* hanno il plurale in es: crisis = crises; axis = axes. Altri, terminanti in *um*, lo hanno in a: medium = media; serum = sera o serums.
7. Un certo numero di sostantivi ha il plurale irregolare: man = men; woman = women; mouse = mice; louse = lice; tooth = teeth; foot = feet; ox = oxen.

L'AGGETTIVO

L'aggettivo è invariabile nel numero e nel genere. Normalmente, si colloca davanti al sostantivo: a rainy day = *una giornata piovosa*; a big cup of coffee = *una gran tazza di caffè*; a witty man = *un uomo spiritoso*; green pastures = *verdi pascoli*.

I. COMPARATIVO E SUPERLATIVO

Comparativo di maggioranza e superlativo:

1. Sebbene non vi sia una regola severa e assoluta, in genere gli aggettivi monosillabi, gli aggettivi accentati sull'ultima sillaba e alcuni bisillabi formano il comparativo di maggioranza con l'aggiunta del suffisso -er, e il superlativo con l'aggiunta del suffisso -est. Tuttavia, quando tali aggettivi terminano per *e* muta, si aggiunge solo, rispettivamente, -r e -st:

   es: tall (alto)   taller (più alto)   the tallest (il più alto)
   nice (grazioso)   nicer (più grazioso)   the nicest (il più grazioso)

polite (educato) politer (più educato) the politest (il più educato)
narrow (stretto) narrower (più stretto) the narrowest (il più stretto)

2. Gli aggettivi terminanti per consonante preceduta da vocale raddoppiano la consonante:
    fat (grasso)   fatter (più grasso)   the fattest (il più grasso)

3. Gli aggettivi terminanti in y cambiano la y in i:
    happy (felice)   happier (più felice)   the happiest (il più felice)

4. In tutti gli altri casi, l'aggettivo è preceduto da more e most:
    intelligent, in-   more intelligent, più   the most intelligent, il più
      telligente   intelligente   intelligente.

5. I seguenti aggettivi hanno una forma irregolare:

good, well	better	best
bad, ill	worse	worst
little	less, lesser	least
far	farther, further	farthest, furthest
much	more	most
old	older, elder	oldest, eldest

Superlativo assoluto:

Si forma anteponendo very e, a volte, most, all'aggettivo:
    happy (felice)   very happy opp.   most happy (felicissimo)

Comparativo e superlativo di minoranza:

Si formano anteponendo all'aggettivo less e least:
    happy (felice)   less happy (meno   the least happy (il meno
                    felice)   felice)

Comparativo di eguaglianza:

Si forma con gli avverbi as ... as davanti agli aggettivi:
    he is as poor as you are = è povero come te,
e con as much ... as davanti ai nomi:
    as much money as you want = tanto denaro quanto ne vuol.

L'AVVERBIO

La maggioranza degli avverbi inglesi si forma aggiungendo all'aggettivo il suffisso -ly: great = greatly; nice = nicely; eternal = eternally.

Irregolarità:

1. Gli aggettivi terminanti in -ble cambiano solo la e in y: possible = possibly.
2. Gli aggettivi terminanti in -ic prendono il suffisso -ally: specific = specifically.
3. Gli aggettivi terminanti in -ll prendono solo la y: full = fully.
4. Gli aggettivi terminanti in -ue perdono la e: true = truly.
5. Gli aggettivi terminanti in y cambiano la y in i: happy = happily.

Comparativo e superlativo:

Come gli aggettivi, anche gli avverbi formano il comparativo e il superlativo con gli avverbi more, most, very, e con i suffissi -er e -est:

boldly	more boldly	most boldly	very boldly
generously	more generously	most generously	very generously
soon	sooner	soonest	very soon

I seguenti hanno forme irregolari di comparativo e superlativo:

well	better	best	very well
badly, ill	worse	worst	very badly
little	less	least	very little
much	more	most	very much
far	farther, further	farthest, furthest	very far

PRINCIPALI SUFFISSI INGLESI

-dom	indica dominio, giurisdizione, stato, condizione, ecc.: **kingdom** = regno, reame; **martyrdom** = martirio; **boredom** = noia; **freedom** = libertà.
-ed, -d	è il suffisso del passato e participio passato dei verbi regolari: **I handed** = io porsi; **handed** = posto; **I loved**, io amai; **loved** = amato.
-ee	indica la persona che riceve o subisce l'azione: **addressee** = destinatario; **draftee** = coscritto.
-eer	indica mestiere, occupazione o professione: **engineer** = macchinista, ingegnere; **cannoneer** = cannoniere; **auctioneer** = banditore d'asta.
-en	(*a*) terminazione del participio passato di numerosi verbi irregolari: **fallen, broken, shaken.**
	(*b*) suffisso che indica *fatto di*: **golden** = dorato, d'oro; **wooden**, ligneo, di legno.
	(*c*) terminazione dei verbi che indica l'azione di *rendere*: **whiten** = imbiancare, rendere bianco; **darken** = oscurare, rendere oscuro.
-er	(*a*) indica mestiere, occupazione o professione: **baker** = fornaio, panettiere; **trainer** = allenatore; **lawyer** = avvocato.
	(*b*) indica la persona che compie una determinata azione: **player** = giocatore; **talker** = chi parla, parlatore.
	(*c*) indica residenza, cittadinanza: **islander** = isolano; **New Yorker** = newyorchese.
	(*d*) è il suffisso per la formazione del comparativo degli aggettivi e degli avverbi (*vedi più sopra*).
-ess	si usa per formare il femminile di certi sostantivi: **poet** = **poetess; count** = **countess.**
-est	è il suffisso per la formazione del superlativo (*vedi più sopra*).
-fold	suffisso che significa *volte*: **twofold** = due volte; **manyfold** = molte volte, più volte.
-ful	(*a*) suffisso che equivale a *pieno di*: **hopeful** = speranzoso; **careful** = attento, prudente, guardingo;
	(*b*) indica abitudine, tendenza: **forgetful** = smemorato.
	(*c*) indica la quantità che una cosa può contenere o di cui è piena: **spoonful** = cucchiaiata; **cartful** = carrettata.
-hood	indica stato, condizione, carattere, gruppo: **motherhood** = maternità; **falsehood** = falsità; **brotherhood** = confraternita.
-ician	indica professione o specialità in un determinato ramo: **musician** = musicista; **electrician** = elettricista; **beautician** = specialista in cure di bellezza.
-ie	suffisso per formare taluni diminutivi: **dog** = **doggie; bird** = **birdie; Gerald** = **Gerrie.**
-ing	(*a*) suffisso per la formazione del participio presente e del gerundio: **love** = **loving**, amare, amando.
	(*b*) si usa per formare anche taluni aggettivi: **drinking water** = acqua potabile; **washing machine** = lavatrice meccanica.
	(*c*) si usa per la sostantivazione del verbo: **understanding** = il comprendere, comprensione, l'intendere, intesa.
-ish	(*a*) si usa per formare taluni aggettivi di nazionalità; **English** = inglese; **Spanish** = spagnolo.
	(*b*) indica caratteristica, tendenza, somiglianza: **boyish** = fanciullesco; **childish** = infantile, puerile; **whitish** = bianchiccio; **bookish** = libresco.
-less	indica assenza: **childless** = senza figli; **penniless** = senza soldi, spiantato; **endless** = senza fine, interminabile.
-like	indica somiglianza: **childlike** = simile a un bambino, fanciullesco, infantile; **lifelike** = al naturale.
-ly	(*a*) suffisso avverbiale: **slow** = **slowly; happy** = **happily; possible** = **possibly.**

vii

          (b) aggiunto a certi sostantivi, indica caratterstica: **mother** = **motherly**, materno; **friend** = **friendly**, da amico, amichevole, cordiale; **man** = **manly**, da uomo, virile, mascolino.

          (c) aggiunto a sostantivi di tempo indica periodicità: **day** = **daily**, quotidiano, ogni giorno; **week** = **weekly**, settimanale, settimanalmente.

-ness serve a formare i sostantivi astratti: **good** = **goodness**, bontà; **red** = **redness**, rossore; **tall** = **tallness**, altezza.

-ship   (a) serve a formare certi sostantivi astratti: **friend** = **friendship**, amicizia.

          (b) indica abilità particolare, bravura: **horseman**, cavallerizzo= **horsemanship**, abilità equestre.

          (c) indica titoli, cariche, uffici, ecc: **professor** = **professorship**, carica di professore, cattedra; **chairman** = **chairmanship**, presidenza, carica di presidente; **lord** = **lordship**, signoria.

-some si aggiunge a taluni sostantivi per indicare il grado notevole cui giunge la cosa, o la qualità espressa dal sostantivo: **burden**, peso = **burdensome**, pesante, gravoso; **fear**, paura = **fearsome**, pauroso, spaventoso; **life**, vita = **lifesome**, vivace, arzillo.

-th si usa per formare gli aggettivi ordinali: **five** = **fifth**, quinto; **ten** = **tenth**, decimo.

-ty è la terminazione di moltissimi sostantivi astratti: **continuity** = continuità; **liberty** = libertà; **beauty** = bellezza, beltà.

-ward(s) indica, negli aggettivi e avverbi, direzione: **homeward** = verso casa; **downward** = verso il basso, discendente.

-ways, -wise esprimono maniera, direzione, posizione, ecc.: **edgewise** = di lato; **sideways** = di lato, di traverso; **lengthwise** = per il lungo.

-y   (a) corrisponde alla terminazione italiana *ia*: **biology** = biologia; **glory** = glòria; **victory** = vittoria.

          (b) come suffisso è diminutivo: **dog** = **doggy**, cagnolino.

          (c) in taluni casi indica presenza, abbondanza: **rock**, roccia = **rocky**, roccioso, duro come la roccia; **hair**, capelli = **hairy**, capelluto, irsuto.

          (d) esprime anche tendenza, somiglianza: **rosy** = rosato, roseo, tendente al rosa.

VERBI IRREGOLARI INGLESI

I GRUPPO

Infinito		Passato	Part. passato
(to) beat	battere	beat	beat, beaten
» burst	scoppiare	burst	burst
» cast	gettare	cast	cast
» cost	costare	cost	cost
» cut	tagliare	cut	cut
» hit	colpire	hit	hit
» hurt	ferire	hurt	hurt
» knit	far la calza	knit	knit
» let	lasciare, locare	let	let
» put	mettere	put	put
» rid	liberare	rid	rid
» set	posare	set	set
» shed	versare	shed	shed
» shred	tagliuzzare	shred	shred
» shut	chiudere	shut	shut
» slit	fendere	slit	slit
» spit	sputare	spit	spit
» split	spaccare, dividere	split	split
» spread	spandere	spread	spread
» sweat	sudare	sweat (sweated)	sweat (sweated)
» thrust	spingere	thrust	thrust

II GRUPPO

(Nota: i verbi contrassegnati da una R si coniugano anche regolarmente)

Infinito		Passato	Part. passato
(to) abide	dimorare	abode	abode
» bend	piegare	bent	bent
» bereave	orbare	bereft	bereft
» beseech	implorare	besought	besought
» bind	legare	bound	bound
» bleed	sanguinare	bled	bled
» breed	generare, allevare	bred	bred
» bring	portare	brought	brought
» build	costruire	built	built
» burn	bruciare	burnt (R)	burnt (R)
» buy	comperare	bought	bought
» catch	afferrare	caught	caught
» cleave	fendere	cleft	cleft
» cling	aggrapparsi	clung	clung
» creep	strisciare	crept	crept
» deal	trattare	dealt	dealt
» dig	scavare	dug (R)	dug (R)
» dream	sognare	dreamt (R)	dreamt (R)
» dwell	abitare	dwelt (R)	dwelt (R)
» feed	nutrire	fed	fed
» feel	sentire	felt	felt
» fight	combattere	fought	fought
» find	trovare	found	found
» flee	fuggire	fled	fled
» fling	lanciare	flung	flung
» get	acquisire	got	got (gotten)
» gild	dorare	gilt	gilt
» gird	cingere	girt	girt
» grind	macinare	ground	ground
» hang	impiccare	hung	hung (hanged)
» hear	udire	heard	heard
» hold	tenere	held	held
» keep	conservare	kept	kept
» kneel	inginocchiarsi	knelt (R)	knelt (R)
» lay	deporre	laid	laid
» lead	guidare	led	led
» leave	lasciare	left	left
» lend	prestare	lent	lent
» light	accendere, illuminare	lit (R)	lit (R)
» lose	perdere	lost	lost
» make	fare	made	made
» mean	significare	meant	meant
» meet	incontrare	met	met
» pay	pagare	paid	paid
» read	leggere	read	read
» rend	lacerare	rent	rent
» say	dire	said	said
» seek	cercare	sought	sought
» seethe	bollire, fremere	sod (R)	sod (R) (sodden)
» sell	vendere	sold	sold
» send	mandare	sent	sent
» shine	brillare	shone	shone
» shoe	calzare, ferrare	shod	shod
» shoot	sparare	shot	shot
» shrink	ritrarsi	shrank (shrunk)	shrunk (shrunken)
» sit	sedere	sat	sat

Infinito		Passato	Part. passato
(to) sleep	dormire	slept	slept
» slide	slittare	slid	slid (slidden)
» sling	lanciare, appendere	slung	slung
» slink	svignarsela	slunk	slunk
» smell	fiutare	smelt	smelt
» spend	spendere	spent	spent
» spill	versare	spilt (R)	spilt (R)
» spin	filare	spun (span)	spun
» stand	stare in piedi	stood	stood
» stick	attaccare, attaccarsi	stuck	stuck
» sting	pungere	stung	stung
» stink	puzzare	stank (stunk)	stunk
» strike	colpire	struck	struck (stricken)
» string	infilare	strung	strung
» sweep	scopare	swept	swept
» swing	pendere	swung	swung
» teach	insegnare	taught	taught
» tell	dire	told	told
» think	pensare	thought	thought
» weep	piangere	wept	wept
» win	vincere	won	won
» wind	attorcigliare	wound	wound
» work	lavorare	wrought (R)	wrought (R)
» wring	torcere	wrung	wrung

III GRUPPO

Infinito		Passato	Part. passato
(to) awake	svegliare, svegliarsi	awoke (R)	awaken (awoke)
» be		was	been
» bear	portare	bore	borne (born)
» begin	cominciare	began	begun
» bid	ordinare	bade (bid)	bidden (bid)
» bite	mordere	bit	bitten (bit)
» blow	soffiare	blew	blown
» break	rompere	broke	broken
» chide	sgridare	chid (R)	chidden (chid) (R)
» choose	scegliere	chose	chosen
» come	venire	came	come
» crow	cantare (del gallo)	crew	crowed
» dare	osare	durst (R)	dared
» do	fare	did	done
» draw	disegnare	drew	drawn
» drink	bere	drank	drunk
» drive	guidare	drove	driven
» eat	mangiare	ate	eaten
» fall	cadere	fell	fallen
» fly	volare	flew	flown
» forsake	abbandonare	forsook	forsaken
» freeze	gelare	froze	frozen
» give	dare	gave	given
» go	andare	went	gone
» grow	crescere	grew	grown
» hew	potare	hewed	hewn (R)
» hide	nascondere	hid	hidden (hid)
» know	sapere, conoscere	knew	known
» lade	caricare	laded	laden
» lie	giacere	lay	lain
» mow	mietere	mowed	mown (R)
» ride	cavalcare	rode	ridden (rode)
» ring	suonare	rang	rung
» rise	alzarsi, sorgere	rose	risen

Infinito		Passato	Part. passato
(to) rive	spaccare	rived	riven
» run	correre	ran	run
» see	vedere	saw	seen
» shake	scuotere	shook	shaken
» shear	tosare	shore (R)	shorn (R)
» show	mostrare	showed (shew)	shown (shewn)
» sing	cantare	sang	sung
» sink	affondare	sank (sunk)	sunk
» slay	uccidere	slew	slain
» smite	percuotere	smote	smitten
» sow	seminare	sowed	sown (R)
» speak	parlare	spoke	spoken
» spring	balzare, scaturire	sprang	sprung
» steal	rubare	stole	stolen
» stride	camminare a lunghi passi	strode	stridden
» strive	sforzarsi	strove	striven
» swear	giurare, imprecare	swore	sworn
» swell	gonfiarsi	swelled	swollen (R)
» swim	nuotare	swam	swum
» take	prendere	took	taken
» tear	stracciare	tore	torn
» thrive	prosperare	throve	thriven
» throw	gettare	threw	thrown
» tread	camminare, calpestare	trod	trodden (trod)
» wear	indossare	wore	worn
» weave	tessere	wove	woven
» write	scrivere	wrote	written

PRINCIPALI PESI E MISURE INGLESI

Pesi (avoirdupois):

Dram (dragma) 1/16 di libbra	= gr.	1,17718
Ounce (oncia)	= »	28,3495
Pound (libbra)	= Kg.	0,4535926
Stone	= »	6,350
Quarter (quarto)	= »	12,6956
Hundredweight	= »	50,8009
Long ton (tonnellata)	= »	1016,018
Short ton	= »	907,2

Pesi (troy-weight):

Grain (grano)	= gr.	0,064798
Pennyweight (1/20 di oncia)	= »	1,55517
Ounce (oncia t.)	= »	31,1035
Pound (libbra t.)	= Kg.	0,37324

Misure di lunghezza:

Inch (pollice)	= cm.	2,539954
Foot (piede)	= m.	0,3047944
Yard (jarda) = 3 piedi	= »	0,914383
Fathom = 2 jarde	= »	1,828766
Pole, rod (pertica) = jarde 5,1/4	= »	5,—
Furlong = jarde 220	= »	201,64
Mile (miglio) = jarde 1760	= »	1609,347
Nautical mile (miglio marittimo)	= »	1853,248

Misure di superficie:

Square inch (pollice quadrato)	= cm.²	6,451366
» foot (piede quadrato)	= m.²	0,0929
» yard (jarda quadrata)	= m.²	0,836097
Rod (jarde 230,1/4)	= m.²	25,291939
Rood (1.210 jarde quadrate)	= are	10,116775
Acre (4.840 jarde quadrate)	= ha.	0,404687
Square mile (miglio quadrato)	= Km.²	2,588881

Monete, banconote e denominazioni monetarie degli Stati Uniti d'America:

(Nota: il Dollaro è indicato dal simbolo $; il cent [centesimo di $] da una **c.**)

Mill	=	1/10 di c.
Cent (anche Penny)	=	1/100 » $.
Nickel	=	5 c.
Dime	=	10 c.
Quarter	=	25 c.
Half dollar	=	50 c.
Dollar	=	100 c.

Banconote in corso:

$ 1, 2, 5, 10, 20, 50, 100, 500, 1000, 5.000, 10.000.

INGLESE-ITALIANO

A

a (ā) prima lettera dell'alfabeto; (*mus.*) la. A 1 di prima classe; di primo ordine.

a (ā) *art.indef.* uno, una: what a ..., che razza di ...; che ...; such a ..., un simile ..., un tale....

aback (á·băk') *avv.* all'indietro: taken —, colto alla sprovvista.

abaft (á·bằft') *avv.* da poppa. *prep.* dietro a, a poppavia.

abandon (á·băn'dŭn) *n.* abbandono. *vt.* abbandonare, cedere, lasciare, rinunciare a, desistere. —ed *agg.* abbandonato; dissoluto. —ment *n.* umiliazione.

abash (á·băsh') *vt.* intimidire, umiliare. —ed *agg.* intimidito, umiliato.

abate (á·bāt') *vt.* mitigare, abbassare, diminuire, attenuare. *vi.* diminuire; calmarsi. —ment *n.* diminuzione, indebolimento; sconto.

abbey (ăb'ĭ) *n.* abbazia.

abbot (ăb'ŭt) *n.* abate.

abbreviate (ă·brē'vĭ·āt) *vt.* abbreviare, accorciare.

abbreviation *n.* abbreviazione.

abdicate (ăb'dĭ·kāt) *vt.* abdicare, rinunciare a.

abdomen (ăb·dō'měn) *n.* addome; basso ventre.

abduct (ăb·dŭkt') *vt.* rapire, asportare.

abduction *n.* ratto, rapimento.

aberration (ăb'ĕr·ā'shŭn) *n.* aberrazione; mancanza.

abet (á·bĕt') *vt.* favoreggiare. [zione.

abeyance (á·bā'ăns) *n.* stasi: in —, in sospeso, pendente.

abhor (ăb·hôr') *vt.* aborrire. —rence *n.* orrore, avversione.

abide (á·bīd') *vi.* attenersi; soggiornare; tollerare; resistere; essere fedele.

ability (á·bĭl'ĭ·tĭ) *n.* abilità, estro.

abject (ăb'jěkt) *agg.* abietto, vile.

ablaze (á·blāz') *agg.* in fiamme, splendente.

able (ā'b'l) *agg.* capace, abile, in grado di: —-bodied, robusto.

ably (ā'blĭ) *avv.* abilmente.

abnormal (ăb·nôr'măl) *agg.* anormale.

aboard (á·bōrd') *avv.* a bordo: to go —, imbarcarsi; all —! signori in carrozza!

abode (á·bō'd) *n.* abitazione, dimora.

abolish (á·bŏl'ĭsh) *vt.* abolire, annullare.

abolition (ăb'ō·lĭsh'ŭn) *n.* abolizione.

abominable (á·bŏm'ĭ·náb'l) *agg.* abominevole, infame.

abortion (á·bôr'shŭn) *n.* aborto.

abound (á·bound') *vi.* abbondare.

abounding *agg.* abbondante.

about (á·bout') *prep.* intorno, circa, riguardo a, sul punto di. *avv.* quasi, più o meno: to bring —, provocare; to be — to, stare per, essere sul punto di; to face —, voltarsi; — one's person, indosso.

above (á·bŭv') *prep.*, *avv.* al disopra, sopra, in alto, in cima; a monte di: — all, soprattutto; —-mentioned, suddetto.

aboveboard (á·bŭv'bōrd') *avv.* lealmente, apertamente.

abrasion (ăb·rā'zhŭn) *n.* abrasione, logoramento.

abreast (á·brĕst') *avv.* di fronte, a fianco a fianco, in linea.

abridge (á·brĭj') *vt.* abbreviare, compendiare.

abroad (á·brōd') *avv.* fuori; all'estero; all'esterno; in circolazione: to spread —, divulgare.

abrupt (ăb·rŭpt') *agg.* improvviso; brusco; precipitoso; ripido. —ly *avv.* bruscamente, improvvisamente.

abscess (ăb'sĕs) *n.* accesso.

absence (ăb'sĕns) *n.* assenza; distrazione; mancanza.

absent (ăb'sĕnt) *agg.* assente: —-minded, distratto. *vt.* (ăb·sĕnt') to — oneself, assentarsi, allontanarsi.

absolute (ăb'sō·lūt) *agg.* assoluto. —ly, *avv.* assolutamente.

absolution (ăb'sō·lū'shŭn) *n.* assoluzione.

absolve (ăb·zŏlv') *vt.* assolvere; svincolare.

absorb (ăb·zôrb') *vt.* assorbire. —ent *n.*, *agg.* assorbente.

absorption (ăb·zôrp'shŭn) *n.* assorbimento, l'essere assorto.

abstain (ăb·stān') *vi.* astenersi.

abstemious (ăb·stē'mĭ·ŭs) *agg.* astemio, temperante.

abstinence (ăb'stĭ·nĕns) *n.* astinenza.

abstract (ăb·străkt') *vt.* sottrarre; separare, staccare; riassumere. *n.* (ăb'străkt) estratto, riassunto; (*comm.*) estratto conto. *agg.* (anche

1

ăb·străkt′) astratto. —ion n. astrazione. —ed agg. distratto. —ly avv. astrattamente, distrattamente.

abstruse (ăb·strōōs′) agg. astruso, oscuro.

absurd (ăb·sûrd′) agg. assurdo. —ity n. assurdità.

abundance (á·bŭn′dăns) n. abbondanza; prosperità.

abundant (á·bŭn′dănt) agg. abbondante.

abuse (á·būz′) vt. insultare, ingiuriare; maltrattare; abusare di. n. (á·būs′) abuso, insulto.

abusive (á·bū′sĭv) agg. ingiurioso, abusivo.

abut (á·bŭt′) vi. sfociare, sboccare.

abysmal (á·bĭs′măl) agg. abissale, insondabile.

abyss (á·bĭs′) n. abisso.

academic (ăk′á·děm′ĭk) agg. accademico, universitario.

academy (á·kăd′ě.mĭ) n. accademia.

accede (ăk·sēd′) vi. accedere, consentire, assentire.

accelerate (ăk·sĕl′ĕr.āt) vt. accelerare.

acceleration (-ā′shŭn) n. accelerazione.

accelerator (ăk·sĕl′ĕr.ā′tĕr) n. acceleratore.

accent (ăk′sĕnt) vt. accentare, accentuare. n. accento, tono.

accentuate (ăk·sĕn′tŭ.āt) vt. accentuare, intensificare.

accept (ăk·sĕpt′) vt. accettare, accogliere, gradire, approvare. —able agg. accettabile, ammissibile. —ance n. accettazione; approvazione; (comm.) cambiale. —or n. (comm.) accettante.

access (ăk′sĕs) n. accesso, entrata. —ible agg. accessibile; abbordabile.

accessory (ăk·sĕs′ŏ·rĭ) agg. accessorio. n. complice: — before the fact, complice; — after the fact, favoreggiatore.

accident (ăk′sĭ·dĕnt) n. incidente, sciagura; contrattempo: by —, per caso. —al agg. accidentale, fortuito. —ally avv. casualmente.

acclaim (á·klām′) vt. acclamare, applaudire.

acclamation (ăk′lá·mā′shŭn) n. acclamazione.

acclimatize (á·klī′má·tīz) vt. acclimare, acclimatare.

accommodate (á·kŏm′ō·dāt) vt. accomodare, aggiustare; ospitare, alloggiare; contenere; fornire; favorire: to — oneself, adattarsi.

accommodating agg. accomodante, conciliante.

accommodation; (—dā′shŭn) n. accomodamento; agevolazione, aiuto; alloggio: — bill, cambiale di favore.

accompaniment (á·kŭm′pánĭ·mĕnt). n. accompagnamento.

accompanist (-ĭst) n. accompagnatore.

accompany (á·kŭm′pá·nĭ) vt. accompagnare.

accomplice (á·kŏm′plĭs) n. complice.

accomplish (á·kŏm′plĭsh) vt. compiere, realizzare, terminare, effettuare. —ed agg. compiuto; perfetto; compito. —ment n. compimento, impresa, prodezza, merito, qualità; (pl.) cognizioni, nozioni.

accord (á·kŏrd′) vt. accordare, concedere, conciliare. n. accordo, accomodamento, consenso: of one's own —, spontaneamente; with one —, simultaneamente, di comune accordo. —ance n. accordo, conformità. —ing agg. conforme: — as, a seconda che; — to, a seconda di, secondo, a detta di, in conformità di. —ingly avv. pertanto, di conseguenza; conformemente, in conformità.

accordion (á·kŏr′dĭ·ŭn) n. fisarmonica.

accost (á·kŏst′) vt. accostare, abbordare.

account (á·kount′) (1) n. conto, calcolo; versione, resoconto: on — of, a causa di; by all accounts, a detta di tutti; of no —, di nessun valore, di nessuna importanza; to turn to —, approfittare di, trarre profitto da; on no —, per nessun motivo.

account (á·kount′) (2) vt. contare, valutare, stimare: to — for, render conto di, giustificare, rispondere di. —able agg. responsabile, spiegabile. —ant n. contabile. —ing n. contabilità.

accredit (á·krĕd′ĭt) vt. accreditare.

accrue (á·krōō′) vi. accumularsi.

accumulate (á·kū′mŭ.lāt) vt. accumulare, ammucchiare. vi. accumularsi, ammucchiarsi.

accumulation n. accumulazione, ammasso.

accumulator n. accumulatore.

accuracy (ăk′û.rá.sĭ) n. accuratezza, esattezza, precisione.

accurate (ăk′û.rĭt) agg. accurato, giusto, esatto, sicuro, preciso.

accursed (á·kûr′sĕd; á·kûrst′) agg. maledetto, malaugurato.

accusation (ăk.û.zā′shŭn) n. accusa.

accuse (á·kūz′) vt. accusare.

accuser n. accusatore.

accustom (á·kŭs′tŭm) vt. abituare: to — oneself, abituarsi, ambientarsi.

ace (ās) n. asso; campione (sportivo, ecc.): within an — of, a un pelo da.

ache (āk) n. male, dolore. vi. dolere, soffrire.

aching (āk'ing) *agg.* dolorante.

achieve (á·chēv') *vt.* eseguire, conseguire, realizzare, ottenere: to — fame, farsi una fama. —ment *n.* successo, affermazione, realizzazione; prodezza.

acid (ăs'ĭd) *n.*, *agg.* acido. —ity *n.* acidità.

ack-ack (ăk'ăk) *n.* cannone antiaereo; artiglieria antiaerea.

acknowledge (ăk·nŏl'ĕj) *vt.* riconoscere, confessare: to — receipt, accusare ricevuta.

acknowledgment *n.* riconoscimento, ringraziamento, cenno di ricevuta.

acorn (ā'kôrn) *n.* ghianda.

acoustics (á·kōōs'tĭks) *n.* acustica.

acquaint (á·kwānt') *vt.* informare, mettere al corrente, far sapere: to be acquainted with, conoscere, sapere; to get acquainted with, to — oneself with, fare la conoscenza di, rendersi edotto di. —ance *n.* conoscenza; conoscente.

acquiesce (ăk'wĭ·ĕs') *vi.* acconsentire, assentire. —nce *n.* acquiescenza, arrendevolezza.

acquire (á·kwīr') *vt.* acquistare, ottenere; imparare.

acquisition (ăk'wĭ·zĭsh'ŭn) *n.* acquisto.

acquit (á·kwĭt') *vt.* assolvere, prosciogliere: to — oneself well, fare una buona figura.

acquittal *n.* assoluzione.

acre (ā'kēr) *n.* acro.

acrobat (ăk'rō·băt) *n.* acrobata.

across (á·krôs') *prep.* attraverso; dirimpetto a, di là di; *avv.* dirimpetto; trasversalmente: to come —, imbattersi in.

act (ăkt) *vt.*, *vi.* agire; comportarsi; recitare, rappresentare, sostenere una parte; funzionare: to — as, fungere da. —ing *n.* rappresentazione, recitazione. —ion *n.* azione, fatto; causa; funzionamento. —ive *adj.* attivo, svelto. —ivity. (-ĭv'ĭ·tĭ) *n.* attività.

actor (ăk'tēr) *n.* attore.

actress (ăk'trĕs) *n.* attrice.

actual (ăk'tū·ăl) *agg.* attuale; reale, effettivo. —ity (ăk'tū·ăl'ĭ·tĭ) *n.* realtà, attualità. —ly *avv.* realmente, effettivamente, addirittura.

acumen (á·kū'mĕn) *n.* acume.

acute (á·kūt') *agg.* aguzzo; acuto; perspicace.

Adam's apple (ăd'ămz ăp''l) *n.* pomo d'Adamo.

adamant (ăd'á·mănt) *agg.* duro, saldo, inflessibile.

adapt (á·dăpt') *vt.* adattare. —ation *n.* adattamento.

add (ăd) *vt.* aggiungere, sommare, aumentare.

addict (á·dĭkt') —ed *agg.* dedito a: drug addict, tossicomane.

addition (á·dĭsh'ŭn) *n.* aggiunta, addizione: in — to, oltre a. —al *agg.* addizionale, supplementare.

addleheaded (ăd'lhĕd'ĕd) *agg.* stolto.

address (á·drĕs') *vt.*, *vi.* indirizzare; apostrofare, rivolgere la parola a; rivolgersi a. *n.* indirizzo; discorso; destrezza: to pay one's addresses to, corteggiare.

addressee (ăd'rĕs·ē') *n.* destinatario.

adept (ăd'ĕpt) *n.* esperto, specialista.

adequate (ăd'ē·kwĭt) *agg.* proporzionato, sufficiente, all'altezza di.

adhere (ăd·hēr') *vi.* aderire; attenersi a.

adherence (-hēr'ĕns) *n.* aderenza.

adhesion (ăd·hē'zhŭn) *n.* adesione.

adhesive (-sĭv) *agg.* adesivo, vischioso, gommato: — tape, cerotto.

adjacent (á·jā'sĕnt) *agg.* adiacente.

adjective (ăj'ĕk·tĭv) *n.* aggettivo.

adjoin (á·join') *vt.* confinare con, essere attiguo a. —ing *agg.* attiguo.

adjourn (á·jûrn') *vt.* aggiornare, rinviare; sospendere. *vi.* tresferirsi. —ment *n.* aggiornamento, rinvio.

adjunct (ăj'ŭngkt) *agg.* aggiunto, accessorio. *n.* aggiunta, appendice.

adjust (á·jŭst') *vt.* aggiustare, adattare, regolare: to — oneself, adattarsi, conformarsi. —ment *n.* accomodamento, regolamento.

ad-lib (ăd'lĭb) *vt.*, *vi.*, improvvisare (un discorso, ecc.); *n.* improvvisazione; *agg.* improvvisato.

administer (ăd·mĭn'ĭs·tēr) *vt.* amministrare, gestire; governare; somministrare.

administration (ăd·mĭn'ĭs·trā'shŭn) *n.* amministrazione, governo.

administrative (ăd·mĭn'ĭs·trā'tĭv) *agg.* amministrativo.

administrator (ăd·mĭn'ĭs·trā'tēr) *n.* amministratore.

admirable (ăd'mĭ·rá·b'l) *agg.* ammirevole.

admirably *avv.* mirabilmente.

admiral (ăd'mĭ·răl) *n.* ammiraglio.

admiration (ăd'mĭ·rā'shŭn) *n.* ammirazione.

admire (ăd·mīr') *vt.* ammirare.

admirer (ăd·mīr'ēr) *n.* ammiratore.

admission (ăd·mĭsh'ŭn) *n.* ammissione, confessione; ingresso; entrata; entratura.

admit (ăd·mĭt') *vt.* ammettere, far entrare; confessare. —tance *n.* accesso, entrata, ammissione: no —, vietato l'ingresso.

admonish (ăd·mŏn'ĭsh) *vt.* ammonire, esortare, redarguire.

admonition (ăd'mŏ·nĭsh'ŭn) *n.* ammonizione, reprimenda.

ado (á·dōō') *n.* azione, trambusto, difficoltà.

adolescence (ăd'ō·lĕs'ĕns) *n.* adolescenza.

adolescent *n.*, *agg.* adolescente.

adopt (á·dŏpt') *vt.* adottare.

adoption (á·dŏp'shŭn) *n.* adozione.

adorable (á·dōr'á·b'l) *agg.* adorabile.

adoration (ăd'ō·rā'shŭn) *n.* adorazione.

adore (á·dōr') *vt.* adorare.

adorn (á·dôrn') *vt.* ornare, adornare.

adornment *n.* ornamento.

adrift (á·drĭft') *avv.* alla deriva.

adroit (á·droit') *agg.* destro, accorto.

adulation (ăd'ū·lā'shŭn) *n.* adulazione.

adult (á·dŭlt'; ăd'ŭlt) *n.*, *agg.* adulto.

adulterate (á·dŭl'tĕr·āt) *vt.* adulterare, contraffare, alterare.

adulterer (á·dŭl'tĕr·ẽr) *n.* adultero.

adulteress (á·dŭl'tĕr·ĕs; -ĭs) *n.* adultera.

adultery (á·dŭl'tĕr·ĭ) *n.* adulterio.

advance (ăd·văns') *vt.* avanzare, far avanzare, far progredire, migliorare, promuovere; accelerare; anticipare, pagare in anticipo; rincarare. *vi.* avanzarsi, progredire; anticipare; andare avanti.

advance *n.* progresso, avanzamento; anticipo: to make advances, fare approcci.

advanced *agg.* avanzato, progredito.

advancement *n.* avanzamento, progresso.

advantage (ăd·văn'tĭj) *n.* vantaggio, profitto, interesse: to take — of, approfittare di, trarre profitto da, abusare di. —ous (ăd'văn·tā'jŭs) *agg.* vantaggioso.

advent (ăd'vĕnt) *n.* avvento.

adventure (ăd·vĕn'tŭr) *n.* avventura; caso; impresa.

adventurer (ăd·vĕn'tŭr·ẽr) *n.* avventuriero.

adventuress (ăd·vĕn'tŭr·ĕs) *n.* avventuriera.

adventurous (-tŭr·ŭs) *agg.* avventuroso.

adverb (ăd'vûrb) *n.* avverbio.

adversary (ăd'vẽr·sẽr'ĭ) *n.* avversario.

adverse (ăd·vûrs'; ăd'vûrs) *agg.* avverso, contrario, sfavorevole.

adversity (ăd·vûr'sĭ·tĭ) *n.* contrarietà, ostilità, avversità.

advertise (ăd'vẽr·tīz) *vt.*, *vi.* divulgare, reclamizzare; mettere inserzioni sul giornale. —ment *n.* annuncio, inserzione.

advertiser (ăd'vûr·tīz'ẽr) *n.* divulgatore; inserzionista.

advice (ăd·vīs') *n.* avviso, consiglio.

advisable (ăd·vīz'á·b'l) *agg.* consigliabile, conveniente, opportuno.

advise (ăd·vīz') *vt.* consigliare, avvertire, annunciare. *vi.* consigliarsi.

adviser (ăd·vīz'ẽr) *n.* consigliere.

advocate (ăd'vō·kăt) *n.* propugnatore, sostenitore, difensore, avvocato. *vt.* sostenere, difendere, propugnare.

aerial (ā·ẽr'ĭ·ăl; âr'ĭ·ăl) *agg.* aereo; *n.*, antenna radiofonica.

aerodrome (ā'ẽr·ō·drōm'; âr'ō-) *n.* aerodromo.

aerodynamics (ā'ẽr·ō·dī·năm'ĭks) *n.* aerodinamica.

aeroplane (ā'ẽr·ō·plān'; âr'ō-) *n.* aeroplano, velivolo.

aerosol (ā'ẽr·ō·sŏl) *n.* aerosol.

aesthete (ĕs'thēt) *n.* esteta.

aesthetics (ĕs·thĕt'ĭks) *n.* estetica.

afar (á·fär') *avv.* lontano, in lontananza: from —, da lontano; — off, in distanza.

affable (ăf'á·b'l) *agg.* affabile.

affair (á·fâr') *n.* affare; tresca: love —, relazione amorosa.

affect (á·fĕkt') *vt.* influenzare, commuovere; fingere, ostentare. — **ation** (ăf'ĕk·tā'shŭn) *n.* affettazione. —ed *agg.* influenzato; affettato, ostentato; pretenzioso; commosso. —**ion** (á·fĕk'shŭn) *n.* affezione; amore; attaccamento; propensione. —**ionate** (á·fĕk'shŭn·ĭt) *agg.* affettuoso, affezionato.

affiliate (á·fĭl'ĭ·āt) *vt.* affiliare, adottare. *vi.* affiliarsi, associarsi.

affinity (á·fĭn'ĭ·tĭ) *n.* affinità.

affirm (á·fûrm') *vt.* affermare. —**ative** (á·fûr'má·tĭv) *agg.* affermativo: in the —, affermativamente.

affix (á·fĭks') *vt.* affiggere; apporre.

afflict (á·flĭkt') *vt.* affliggere, tormentare. —ion *n.* afflizione, calamità.

affluence (ăf'lū·ĕns) *n.* ricchezza, abbondanza.

affluent *n.* affluente. *agg.* ricco.

afford (á·fōrd') *vt.* concedere, fornire, accordare, permettere: I cannot — this luxury, non posso permettermi questo lusso.

affront (á·frŭnt') *vt.* affrontare; offendere, insultare. *n.* affronto, insulto.

afield (á·fēld') *avv.* sul campo: far —, molto lontano.

afire (á·fīr') *agg.* in fuoco, in fiamme.

afloat (á·flōt') *agg.* a galla; in navigazione: a rumor is —, corre voce.

afoot (á·fŏŏt') *avv.* a piedi, in movimento; in ballo.

aforesaid (á·fōr'sĕd') *agg.* sudetto, predetto.

afraid (á·frād') *agg.* spaventato, timoroso: to be —, temere.

afresh (á·frĕsh') *avv.* nuovamente; da capo.

after (áf'tĕr) *prep.* dopo, in seguito a; secondo, alla maniera di. *avv.* dopo, secondo, in seguito. *agg.* successivo, ulteriore: **the day — tomorrow,** posdomani. **aftereffect** (áf'tĕr·ĕ·fĕkt') *n.* conseguenza, contraccolpo.

aftermath (áf'tĕr·măth) *n.* postumo, conseguenza.

afternoon (áf'tĕr·nōōn') *n.* pomeriggio.

afterthought (áf'tĕr·thôt') *n.* riflessione postuma o tardiva.

afterward (áf'tĕr·wĕrd) *avv.* dopo, successivamente.

again (á·gĕn) *avv.* ancora, nuovamente: **— and —,** ripetutamente, a più riprese; **now and —,** di tanto in tanto; **as large —,** due volte tanto; **never —,** mai più.

against (á·gĕnst') *prep.* contro, di contro, addosso, in previsione di.

agape (á·gāp') *agg.* a bocca aperta.

age (āj) *n.* età, èra, secolo: **of —,** maggiorenne; **old —,** vecchiaia; **under —,** minorenne. *vt., vi.* invecchiare.

aged *agg.* vecchio; invecchiato; stagionato: **middle —,** di mezza età.

agency (ā'jĕn·si) *n.* azione; mezzo, influsso; agenzia, ente.

agent (ā'jĕnt) *n.* agente, rappresentante.

aggrandize (ăg'răn·dīz) *vt.* ingrandire.

aggravate (ăg'rá·vāt) *vt.* aggravare; provocare, esasperare.

aggregate (ăg'rĕ·gāt) *n.* aggregato, complesso. *agg.* complessivo.

aggression (á·grĕsh'ŭn) *n.* aggressione.

aggressive (á·grĕs'ĭv) *agg.* aggressivo.

aggressor (á·grĕs'ĕr) *n.* aggressore.

aghast (á·gàst') *agg.* sgomento, costernato.

agile (ăj'ĭl) *agg.* svelto.

agility (á·jĭl'ĭ·ti) *n.* agilità.

agitate (ăj'ĭ·tāt) *vt.* agitare, eccitare, smuovere, turbare.

agitation (ăj'ĭ·tā'shŭn) *n.* agitazione.

agitator (ăj'ĭ·tā'tĕr) *n.* agitatore.

ago (á·gō') *avv.* passato: **long —,** molto tempo fa; **two days —,** due giorni or sono.

agog (á·gŏg') *agg.* ansioso, bramoso: **to be all —,** non stare più nella pelle.

agonizing *agg.* angoscioso, lancinante.

agony (ăg'ō·nĭ) *n.* dolore, angoscia; agonia.

agree (á·grē') *vi.* approvare, convenire, acconsentire; concordare; giovare, confarsi a: **I — with you,** sono d'accordo con voi. **—able** *agg.* gradevole, conforme, d'accordo. **—ment** *n.* accordo; convenzione, contratto; armonia.

agricultural (ag'rĭ·kŭl'tůr·ǎl) *agg.* agricolo.

agriculture (ăg'rĭ·kŭl'tůr) *n.* agricoltura.

agriculturist *n.* agricoltore, agronomo.

aground (á·ground') *avv.* in secca.

ahead (á·hĕd') *avv.* avanti, alla testa, in prima fila: **go —! fate pure; — of time,** in anticipo.

aid (ād) *vt.* aiutare, assistere, agevolare. *n.* aiuto, assistenza; collaboratore, aiutante.

ail (āl) *vt.* affliggere. *vi.* soffrire, patire: **what ails you?** che vi piglia? **—ment** *n.* acciacco; indisposizione.

aileron (ā'lĕr·ŏn) *n.* alerone.

aim (ām) *vt.* mirare, dirigere, lanciare, puntare (*un'arma*). *vi.* mirare a, aspirare a, avere per meta. *n.* bersaglio, scopo, mira, aspirazione: **to take —,** mirare. **—less** *agg.* futile. **—lessly** *avv.* futilmente, senza scopo. **—lessness** *n.* futilità, mancanza di scopo.

air (âr) *vt.* arieggiare, sciorinare. *n.* aria, atmosfera; (*fig.*) atteggiamento: **—borne** aviotrasportato; **—conditioning,** aria condizionata; **— cushion,** cuscino pneumatico; **— balloon,** pallone, palloncino; **— bladder,** vescica d'aria; (*ittiol.*) vescica natatoria; **—gun,** fucile ad aria compressa; **—line,** aviolinea; **—liner,** apparecchio di linea; **—mail,** posta aerea; **— pocket,** sacca d'aria, vuoto; **— pump,** pompa pneumatica; **— shaft,** tromba d'aerazione; **— raid,** incursione aerea; **— sleeve, — sock,** manica a vento; **—tight,** impermeabile all'aria. **—ily** *avv.* leggermente, allegramente, con disinvoltura. **—iness** *n.* leggerezza, disinvoltura. **—ing** *n.* ventilazione, passeggiata all'aperto: **to get some —,** prendere una boccata d'aria.

Air Corps *n.* aviazione.

aircraft (âr'kráft') *n.* velivolo.

airdrop (âr'drŏp') *n.* lancio aereo di rifornimenti; lancio aereo di manifestini.

airlift (âr'lĭft') *n.* ponte aereo; *vt.* mandare rifornimenti per aereo (*a una zona bloccata*).

airman (âr'măn) *n.* aviatore.

airplane (âr'plān) *n.* aeroplano.

airport (âr'pōrt') *n.* aeroporto.

airship (âr'shĭp') *n.* dirigibile.

airy (âr'ĭ) *agg.* arioso, aerato; leggero; disinvolto.

aisle (il) *n.* navata (*di chiesa*).

ajar (á·jär') *agg.* socchiuso.

akimbo (á·kĭm'bō) *avv.* con le mani sui fianchi.

akin (à·kǐn') *agg.* affine, imparentato, analogo.

alarm (à·lärm') *vt.* allarmare. *n.* allarme; ansia: — clock, orologio a sveglia. —ing *adj.* allarmante.

alas! (à·lăs') *inter.* ahimè!

albeit (ôl·bē'ǐt) *avv.* benchè.

alcohol (ăl'kō·hôl) *n.* alcole. —ic *agg.* alcolico.

alcove (ăl'kōv) *n.* alcova, nicchia.

alder (ôl'dēr) *n.* ontano.

alderman (ôl'dēr·măn) *n.* assessore municipale.

ale (āl) *n.* birra.

alert (à·lûrt') *agg.* svelto, sveglio, vigile. *n.* allarme; segnale di allarme.

algebra (ăl'jē·brà) *n.* algebra.

alias (ā'lǐ·ăs) *n.* pseudonimo. *avv.* detto, altrimenti detto.

alien (āl'yěn) *n.*, *agg.* straniero, estraneo.

alienate (āl'yěn·āt) *vt.* alienare; estraniare, inimicare.

alienist (āl'yěn·ǐst) *n.* alienista.

alight (à·lǐt') *vi.* scendere (*da un veicolo, ecc.*); atterrare, posarsi.

alike (à·lǐk') *avv.* ugualmente. *agg.* analogo, uguale, somigliante: to be —, assomigliarsi.

alive (à·lǐv') *agg.* vivo, vitale, conscio: — with, pieno di; — to, conscio di; while —, vita natural durante.

all (ôl) *agg.* tutto, tutti: — at once, tutt'a un tratto; — right, benissimo, perfettamente; — clear, (*segnale di*) cessato allarme aereo; not at —, nient'affatto, non c'è di che; — the worse, tanto peggio; to be — in, essere esausto o affranto; —out, totale, radicale, completo; to go — out for, to, buttarsi a corpo morto (*in un'impresa*).

allay (à·lā') *vt.* chetare, mitigare, ammansire.

allegation (ăl'ē·gā'shŭn) *n.* affermazione.

allege (à·lěj') *vt.* affermare, addurre.

allegiance (à·lē'jăns) *n.* fedeltà, obbedienza.

allergic (à·lûr'jǐk) *agg.* allergico; intollerante.

allergy (ăl'ēr·jǐ) *n.* allergia.

alleviate (à·lē'vǐ·āt) *vt.* alleviare, sollevare, lenire.

alley (ăl'ǐ) *n.* vicolo: blind —, vicolo cieco.

alliance (à·lī'ăns) *n.* alleanza.

allied (à·lǐd') *agg.* alleato, parente.

alligator (ăl'ǐ·gā'tēr) *n.* alligatore; (*gergo*) jazzomane.

allocate (ăl'ō·kāt) *vt.* assegnare, destinare, distribuire.

allot (à·lŏt') *vt.* assegnare; spartire.

allow (à·lou') *vt.* permettere; autorizzare, accordare; riconoscere; abbonare; ammettere: to — for, tener conto di. —able *agg.* ammissibile, lecito.

allowance (à·lou'ăns) *n.* assegno fisso; permesso, concessione; pensione; ribasso, sconto: to make — for, tener conto di.

alloy (à·loi') *vt.* fondere. *n.* (ăl'oi) lega metallica.

allude (à·lūd') *vi.* alludere.

allure (à·lūr') *vt.* allettare, adescare, sedurre. —ment *n.* fascino, attrattiva, seduzione.

alluring (à·lur'ǐng) *agg.* attraente, seducente.

allusion (à·lū'zhŭn) *n.* allusione.

ally (ăl·lī') *n.* alleato. *vt.* alleare. *vi.* allearsi.

almanac (ôl'mà·năk) *n.* almanacco, calendario.

almighty (ôl·mǐt'ǐ) *agg.* onnipossente.

almond (ä'mŭnd; ăm'ŭnd) *n.* mandorla. — tree *n.* mandorlo.

almost (ôl'mōst; ôl·mōst') *avv.* quasi, pressochè.

alms (ämz) *n.* elemosina.

aloft (à·lôft') *avv.* in alto, dall'alto.

alone (à·lōn') *agg.* solo, solitario, unico. *avv.* solo, soltanto: to let —, lasciare in pace, lasciar stare.

along (à·lông') *avv.*, *prep.* lungo, accanto, avanti; — with, insieme con; all —, sempre, da un capo all'altro di; to get —, tirare avanti; to get — with, andar d'accordo con; to carry — with one, portare seco; to go — with, andare con.

alongside (à·lông'sǐd') *prep.*, *avv.* accosto (*a*); accanto (*a*).

aloof (à·lōōf') *agg.* riservato, sostenuto, arcigno. *avv.* a distanza, in disparte, in modo sostenuto. —ness *n.* isolamento, sostenutezza, scontrosità.

aloud (à·loud)' *avv.* ad alta voce.

alphabet (ăl'fá·bĕt) *n.* alfabeto.

already (ôl·rĕd'ǐ) *avv.* già.

also (ôl'sō) *avv.* anche, inoltre.

altar (ôl'tēr) *n.* altare.

alter (ôl'tēr) *vt.* alterare, modificare. *vi.* modificarsi. —ation *n.* modifica, cambiamento.

alternate (ôl'tēr·nǐt; ăl'-) *agg.* alternato, alterno. *vi.* (ôl'tēr·nāt) alternare: alternating current, corrente alternata. —ly *avv.* alternativamente.

alternative (ôl·tûr'ná·tǐv; ăl-) *n.* alternativa. *agg.* alternativo.

although (ôl·thō') *cong.* benchè.

altitude (ăl'tǐ·tūd)*n.* altitudine.

altogether (òl'tŏŏ·gĕth'ẽr) *avv.* complessivamente, completamente.

aluminum (á·lū'mĭ·nŭm) *n.* alluminio.

alumnus (á·lŭm'nŭs) *n.* laureato, diplomato; ex allievo.

always (òl'wāz; -wĭz) *avv.* sempre.

am (ăm) *1a pers.sing.ind.pres. di* to be.

amalgamate (á·măl'gá·māt) *vt.* amalgamare. *vi.* amalgamarsi; ambientarsi.

amass (á·măs') *vt.* ammassare, ammucchiare.

amateur (ăm'á·tûr'; ăm'á·tûr; ăm'á·tûr) *n.* dilettante; principiante.

amaze (á·māz') *vt.* stupire, sbalordire. —ment, —dness *n.* meraviglia, sbalordimento.

amazing *agg.* straordinario, sbalorditivo.

ambassador (ăm·băs'á·dẽr) *n.* ambasciatore.

ambassadress (ăm·băs'á·drĕs) *n.* ambasciatrice.

amber (ăm'bẽr) *n.* ambra.

ambergris (ăm'bẽr·grēs; -grĭs) *n.* ambra grigia.

ambient (ăm'bĭ·ĕnt) *agg.* ambiente.

ambiguity (ăm'bĭ·gū'ĭ·tĭ) *n.* ambiguità.

ambiguous (ăm·bĭg'ū·ŭs) *agg.* ambiguo, equivoco.

ambition (ăm·bĭsh'ŭn) *n.* ambizione.

ambitious (ăm·bĭsh'ŭs) *agg.* ambizioso.

amble (ăm'b'l) *n.* ambio.

ambulance (ăm'bū·lăns) *n.* ambulanza.

ambulatory (ăm'bū·lá·tō'rĭ) *n.*, *agg.* ambulatorio.

ambuscade (ăm'bŭs·kād'), ambush (ăm'bŏŏsh) *n.* imboscata.

ameliorate (á·mēl'yō·rāt) *vt.*, *vi.* migliorare.

amelioration *n.* miglioramento.

amenable (á·mē'ná·b'l) *agg.* malleabile. trattabile: — to reason, ragionevole.

amend (á·mĕnd') *vt.* emendare, migliorare. *vi.* emendarsi, correggersi. —ment *n.* emendamento, riforma, modifica.

amends *n.pl.* risarcimento, riparazione.

amenity (á·mĕn'ĭ·tĭ) *n.* amentià. (*pl.*) complimenti, cerimonie.

American (á·mĕr'ĭ·kăn) *n.*, *agg.* americano. —ize *vt.* americanizzare.

amethyst (ăm'ê·thĭst) *n.* ametista.

amiability (ā'mĭ·á·bĭl'ĭ·tĭ), amiableness *n.* cortesia, amabilità.

amiable (ā'mĭ·á·b'l) *agg.* amabile.

amicable (ăm'ĭ·ká·b'l) *agg.* amichevole.

amid (á·mĭd'), amidst (á·mĭdst') *prep.* tra, nel mezzo.

amidships (á·mĭd'shĭps) *avv.* (*naut.*) a mezzanave.

amiss (á·mĭs') *agg.* errato, deplorevole. *avv.* a sproposito, erroneamente: to take —, offendersi per, prendere in malaparte.

amity (ăm'ĭ.tĭ) *n.* amicizia.

ammeter (ăm'mē'tẽr) *n.* amperometro.

ammonia (ă·mō'nĭ·á;- mōn'yá) *n.* ammoniaca.

ammunition (ăm' û·nĭsh'ŭn) *n.* munizione. *vt.* fornire munizioni a. — pouch *n.* giberna.

amnesty (ăm'nĕs·tĭ) *n.* amnistia. *vt.* amnistiare.

among (á·mŭng'), amongst (á·mŭngst') *prep.* tra, in mezzo.

amorous (ăm'ō·rŭs) *adj.* amoroso.

amorphous (á·mòr'fŭs) *agg.* amorfo.

amortize (á·mòr'tĭz; -tĭz) *vt.* ammortizzare. —ment, amortization *n.* ammortamento.

amount (á·mount') *vi.* ammontare, assommare, salire; risolversi. *n.* ammontare, totale, somma, prezzo.

amour (á·mŏŏr') *n.* tresca.

amperage (ăm'pẽr·ĭj) *n.* amperaggio.

amphibian (ăm·fĭb'ĭ·ăn) *n.*, *agg.* anfibio.

amphibious (ăm·fĭb'ĭ·ŭs) *agg.* anfibio.

amphitheater (ăm'fĭ·thē'á·tẽr) *n.* anfiteatro.

ample (ăm'p'l) *agg.* ampio, spazioso, abbondante.

amplification (ăm'plĭ·fĭ·kā'shŭn) *n.* amplificazione.

amplifier (ăm'plĭ·fĭ'ẽr) *n.* amplificatore; altoparlante.

amplify (ăm'plĭ·fĭ) *vt.* ampliare, estendere; esagerare.

amplitude (ăm'plĭ·tūd) *n.* ampiezza.

amputate (ăm'pū·tāt) *vt.* amputare.

amputation (ăm·pū·tā'shŭn) *n.* amputazione.

amuck (á·mŭk') *avv.* freneticamente: to run —, smaniare, imbestialirsi.

amulet (ăm'û·lĕt) *n.* amuleto.

amuse (á·mūz') *vt.* divertire. —ment, *n.* divertimento.

amusing (á·mūz'ĭng) *agg.* divertente.

an (ăn) *art.indef.* un, uno, una.

anachronism (á·năk'rŏ·nĭz'm) *n.* anacronismo.

anal (ā'năl) *agg.* anale.

analgesia (ăn'ăl·jē'zĭ·á; -sĭ·á) *n.* analgesia.

analgesic (-jē'sĭk) *n.*, *agg.* analgesico.

analogous (á·năl'ō·gŭs) *agg.* analogo.

analysis (á·năl'ĭ·sĭs) *n.* analisi.

analytic (ăn'á·lĭt'ĭk), analytical *agg.* analitico.

analyze (ăn'á·lĭz) *vt.* analizzare.

anarchical (ăn·är kĭ·kăl) *agg.* anarchico.

anarchist (ăn'ăr·kĭst) *n.* anarchico.

anarchy (ăn'ăr·kĭ), *n.* anarchia.

anatomical (ăn'ă·tŏm'ĭ·kăl) *agg.* anatomico.

anatomy (ă·năt'ō·mĭ) *n.* anatomia.

ancestor (ăn'sĕs'tĕr) *n.* antenato.

ancestral (ăn·sĕs'trăl) *agg.* atavico, avito.

ancestry (ăn'sĕs'trĭ) *n.* lignaggio, ascendenza.

anchor (ăng'kĕr) *n.* àncora: sheet — (*fig.*), ancora di salvezza; to drop —, gettare l'ancora; to weigh —, levar l'ancora; to ride at —, essere all'ancora.

anchorite (ăng'kŏ·rīt) *n.* anacoreta, eremita.

anchovy (ăn·chŏ'vĭ; ăn'chŏ·vĭ) *n.* acciuga.

ancient (ān'shĕnt) *agg.* antico, vecchio: the ancients, gli antichi.

and (ănd) *cong.* e, ed: — so forth, eccetera, e così via; let us try — do it, cerchiamo di farlo; go — see, andate a vedere.

andiron (ănd'ī'ĕrn) *n.* alare.

anecdote (ăn'ĕk·dŏt) *n.* aneddoto.

anesthesiologist (ăn'ĕs·thē'zĭ·ŏl'ŏ·jĭst) *n.* anestesista.

anesthetic (ăn'ĕs·thĕt'ĭk) *n.*, [*agg.* anestetico.

anew (ă·nū') *avv.* daccapo, di nuovo.

angel (ān'jĕl) *n.* angelo: guardian —, angelo custode.

anger (ăng'ĕr) *n.* collera, stizza. *vt.* incollerire, far arrabbiare.

angle (ăng'g'l) (1) *n.* angolo; prospettiva, punto di vista.

angle (2) *vi.* pescare alla lenza; adescare; presentare (*un argomento, un fatto, ecc.*) sotto un aspetto particolare.

angler (ăng'glĕr) *n.* pescatore.

angling (ăng'glĭng) *n.* pesca alla lenza.

Anglo-Saxon (ăng'glŏ·săk's'n) *n.*, *agg.* anglosassone.

angry (ăng'grĭ) *agg.* collerico, incollerito, irritato: to get —, arrabbiarsi.

anguish (ăng'gwĭsh) *n.* angoscia, dolore. *vt.* angosciare.

angular (ăng'gū·lĕr) *agg.* angolare.

animadversion (ăn'ĭ·măd·vûr'shŭn) *n.* malanimo, rimprovero, censura, critica.

animal (ăn'ĭ·măl) *n.*, *agg.* animale. —cule (ăn'ĭ·măl'kūl) *n.* microrganismo.

animate (ăn'ĭ·māt) *vt.* animare.

animation (ăn'ĭ·mā'shŭn) *n.* animazione.

animosity (ăn'ĭ·mŏs'ĭ·tĭ) *n.* animosità, accanimento.

animus (ăn'ĭ·mŭs) *n.* astio; propensione.

anise (ăn'ĭs) *n.* anice.

ankle (ăng'k'l) *n.* caviglia. —deep *avv.* fino alla caviglia.

annals (ăn'ălz) *n.pl.* annali.

anneal (ă·nēl') *vt.* temprare (*acciaio, ecc.*).

annex (ă·nĕks') *vt.* annettere, unire. *vi.* unirsi. *n.* annesso, fabbricato annesso. —ation *n.* annessione.

annihilate (ă·nī'ĭ·lāt) *vt.* annientare.

Annie Oakley (ăn'ĭ ŏk'lĭ) *n.*, biglietto di favore, ingresso di favore.

annihilation (ă·nī'ĭ·lā'shŭn) *n.* annientamento.

anniversary (ăn'ĭ·vûr'să·rĭ) *n.*, *agg.* anniversario.

annotate (ăn'ō·tāt) *vt.* annotare.

annotation *n.* annotazione.

announce (ă·nouns') *vt.* annunciare, proclamare. —ment *n.* annuncio, partecipazione.

annoy (ă·noi') *vt.* molestare, tormentare, irritare, seccare. —ance *n.* irritazione, molestia, seccatura. —ing *agg.* molesto, noioso.

annual (ăn'ū·ăl) *n.* annuario. *agg.* annuale.

annuity (ă·nū'ĭ·tĭ) *n.* annualità, pensione: life —, vitalizio.

annul (ă·nŭl') *vt.* annullare.

annular (ăn'ū·lĕr) *agg.* anulare.

annunciation (ă·nŭn'sĭ·ā'shŭn) *n.* annuncio, annunciazione.

anoint (ă·noint') *vt.* ungere, consacrare.

anomalous (ă·nŏm'ă·lŭs) *agg.* anomalo.

anomaly (ă·nŏm'ă·lĭ) *n.* anomalia.

anon (ă·nŏn') *avv.* subito: ever and —, di quando in quando.

anonymity (ăn'ŏ·nĭm'ĭ·tĭ) *n.* anonimità, l'anonimo.

anonymous (ă·nŏn'ĭ·mŭs) *agg.* anonimo.

another (ă·nŭth'ĕr) *agg.*, *pron.* un altro: one after —, l'uno dopo l'altro; one—, l'un l'altro, avicenda.

answer (ăn'sĕr) *n.* risposta. *vt.*, *vi.* rispondere, evadere, corrispondere, servire (*allo scopo*). —able *agg.* responsabile.

ant (ănt) *n.* formica. —eater *n.* formichiere. —hill *n.* formicaio.

antagonism (ăn·tăg'ŏ·nĭz'm) *n.* antagonismo.

antagonist (—nĭst) *n.* antagonista.

antagonize (—nīz) *vt.* avversare.

ante (ăn'tē) *n.* (*al poker*) buio.

antecedent (ăn'tē·sēd'ĕnt) *n.*, *agg.* antecedente.

antedate (ăn'tē·dāt'; ăn'tē·dāt') *vt.* antidatare.

antelope (ăn'tē·lŏp) n. antilope.
anterior (ăn·tēr'ĭ·ēr) agg. anteriore.
anteroom (ăn'tē·rōōm') n. anticamera.
anthem (ăn'thĕm) n. inno.
anthology (ăn·thŏl'ō·jĭ) n. antologia.
anthracite (ăn'thrá·sīt) n. antracite.
antiaircraft (ăn'tĭ·âr'kráft') agg. antiaereo, contraereo.
antibiotic (ăn'tĭ·bĭ·ŏt'ĭk) n., agg. an-
tibiotico.
antic (ăn'tĭk) n. buffonata, farsa;
smania.
anticipate (ăn·tĭs'ĭ·pāt) vt. anticipare,
prevedere, prevenire.
anticipation n. anticipazione, previsione; ansia.
anticlimax (ăn'tĭ·klī'măks) n. crollo,
discesa.
antidote (ăn'tĭ·dōt) n. antidoto.
antipathy (ăn·tĭp'á·thĭ) n. antipatia.
antipodes (ăn·tĭp'ōdēz) n.pl. antipodi.
antiquarian (ăn'tĭ·kwâr'ĭ·ăn) n. anti-
quario.
antiquated (ăn'tĭ·kwāt'ĕd) agg. antiquato.
antique (ăn·tēk') n. oggetto antico,
antichità. agg. antico, arcaico. —ly
avv. anticamente.
antiquity (ăn·tĭk'wĭ·tĭ) n. antichità.
antiseptic (ăn'tĭ·sĕp'tĭk) n., agg. an-
tisettico.
antihistamine (ăn'tĭ·hĭs'tá·mēn) n.
antistamina.
antithesis (ăn·tĭth'ĕsĭs) n. antitesi.
antitoxin (ăn'tĭ·tŏk'sĭn) n. antitossina.
antler (ant'lēr) n. corno di cervo.
antonym (ăn'tō·nĭm) n., contrario,
opposto.
anvil (ăn'vĭl) n. incudine.
anxiety (ăng·zī'ĕ·tĭ) n. ansia, inquietudine, premura.
anxious (ăngk'shŭs; ăng'shŭs) agg.
inquieto; sollecito; impaziente,
desideroso.
any (ĕn'ĭ) agg. alcuno, alcuni, qualche, un poco di, del, della, dei,
delle, più: — better, meglio; —
further, più oltre; — man, qualunque uomo; in — case, comunque;
have you — bread? avete del pane?;
you do not know — of my friends,
non conoscete nessuno dei miei
amici; I haven't —, non ne ho.
anybody (ĕn'ĭ·bŏd'ĭ; -bŭd·ĭ), anyone
(ĕn'ĭ·wŭn) n. chiunque, qualcuno,
chicchessia.
anyhow (ĕn'ĭ·hou) avv. comunque, in
qualche modo, alla meglio. cong.
però.
anything (ĕn'ĭ·thĭng) n. qualunque
cosa, qualcosa: not . . . —, non . . .
niente; — but, tutt'altro.
anyway (ĕn'ĭ·wā) avv. in ogni modo,
in tutti i casi, comunque.

anywhere (ĕn'ĭ·hwâr) avv. dovunque,
da qualche parte: not . . . —, non
. . . da alcuna parte; — else, da
qualunque altra parte.
apace (á·pās') avv. rapidamente; a
vista d'occhio.
apart (á·pärt') avv. a parte, in disparte, separatamente: to come —,
dividersi, sfasciarsi; to take —,
smontare, smantellare; to tear —,
disfare, fare a pezzi.
apartheid (á·pärt'hĭt) n. segregazione
razziale.
apartment (á·pärt'mĕnt) n. stanza,
camera; appartamento.
apathetic (ăp'á·thĕt'ĭk) agg. apatico.
apathy (ăp'á·thĭ) n. apatia.
ape (āp) n. scimmia. vt. scimmiottare,
imitare.
aperient (á·pēr'ĭ·ĕnt) n., agg. lassativo.
aperture (ăp'ēr·tūr) n. apertura.
apex (ā'pĕks) n. apice, vertice.
apiece (á·pēs') avv. ciascuno, ognuno,
a testa.
apocryphal (á·pŏk'rĭ·făl) agg. apo-
crifo, falso.
apologetic (á·pŏl'ō·jĕt'ĭk) agg. di
scusa, di giustificazione.
apologize (á·pŏl'ō·jīz) vi. scusarsi,
chiedere perdono.
apology (á·pŏl'ō·jĭ) n. scusa, giustificazione.
apoplexy (ăp'ō·plĕk'sĭ) n. apoplessia.
apostle (á·pŏs''l) n. apostolo.
apostolic (ăp'ŏs·tŏl'ĭk) agg. apostolico.
apostrophe (á·pŏs'trō·fē) n. apostrofo.
appal (á·pôl') vt. sgomentare, impaurire; scandalizzare. —ling agg.
spaventoso, terrorizzante.
apparatus (ăp'á·rā'tŭs) n. apparato,
apparecchio, impianto.
apparel (á·păr'ĕl) n. vestiario, indumenti.
apparent (á·păr'ĕnt; á·pâr'-) agg. visibile, apparente, manifesto: heir
—, erede legittimo. —ly avv. visibilmente, evidentemente; presumibilmente, a quanto pare.
apparition (ăp'á·rĭsh'ăn) n. apparizione.
appeal (á·pēl') vi. appellarsi, fare
appello a; ricorrere in appello;
attrarre. n. appello; attrattiva.
—ing agg. supplichevole; attraente.
appear (á·pēr') vi. apparire, comparire;
sembrare, aver l'aria di. —ance n.
apparizione, apparenza; comparizione.
appease (á·pēz') vt. calmare, pacificare, ammansire, sedare. —ment
n. pacificazione.
appendix (á·pĕn'dĭks) n. appendice.
appertain (ăp'ēr·tān') vi. appartenere,
riguardare.

appetite (ăp'ê·tǐt) *n.* appetito, desiderio.

appetizer (ăp'ê·tīz'ẽr) *n.* aperitivo.

appetizing *agg.* appetitoso.

applaud (ā·plôd') *vt.* applaudire, lodare.

applause (ā·plòz') *n.* plauso, applauso.

apple (ăp''l) *n.* mela: — of the eye, pupilla. — tree *n.* melo.

appliance (ā·plī'ăns) *n.* applicazione; apparecchio, meccanismo: house appliances, elettrodomestici.

applicant (ăp'lǐ·kănt) *n.* postulante; candidato.

application (ăp'lǐ·kā'shŭn) *n.* domanda; richiesta.

apply (ā·plī') *vt.* applicare. *vi.* rivolgersi, richiedere, presentare una domanda; applicarsi: to — to, rivolgersi a; to — for, chiedere, sollecitare; to — on account, accreditare in conto.

appoint (ā·point') *vt.* nominare; designare; stabilire; arredare, ammobiliare. —ment *n.* nomina; decreto; designazione; appuntamento; incarico; arredamento, mobilia.

apportion (ā·pōr'shŭn) *vt.* distribuire, spartire, assegnare. —ment *n.* ripartizione, assegnazione.

appraisal (ā·prāz'ăl) *n.* valutazione, stima.

appraise (ā·prāz') *vt.* stimare, valutare.

appreciable (ā·prē'shǐ·ā·b'l) *agg.* apprezzabile.

appreciate (ā·prē'shǐ·āt) *vt.* capire, apprezzare; valutare; rendersi conto di; gradire.

appreciation (ā·prē'shǐ·ā'shŭn; -sǐ·ā'shŭn) *n.* apprezzamento; giusta valutazione; gradimento; aumento, rialzo (*di prezzo*).

apprehend (ăp'rê·hěnd') *vt.* catturare, arrestare; temere; afferrare, capire.

apprehension (ăp'rê·hěn'shŭn) *n.* apprensione; assimilazione (*di un' idea*); timore; cattura.

apprehensive (ăp'rê·hěn'sǐv) *agg.* timoroso; pronto di mente.

apprentice (ā·prěn'tǐs) *n.* apprendista. *vt.* collocare come apprendista. —ship *n.* apprendistato, tirocinio.

approach (ā·prōch') *n.* accostamento; accesso; impostazione; metodo. *vi.* avvicinarsi; fare approcci. *vt.* accostare, abbordare; raggiungere; somigliare a.

approbation (ăp'rō·bā'shŭn) *n.* approvazione.

appropriate (ā·prō'prǐ·āt') *vt.* assegnare, aggiudicare; stanziare; appropriarsi di. *agg.* (ā·prō'prǐ·ĭt) appropriato, acconcio, proprio.

appropriation (ā·prō'prǐ·ā'shŭn) *n.* appropriazione, assegnazione; stanziamento.

approval (ā·prōōv'ăl) *n.* approvazione: on —, in prova.

approve (ā·prōōv') *vt.* approvare: to — of, essere favorevole a.

approving *agg.* approvativo.

approximate (ā·prŏk'sǐ·mǐt) *agg.* approssimativo. *vt.* (-māt) approssimare, avvicinare. *vi.* approssimarsi. —ly *avv.* approssimativamente.

approximation (ā·prŏk'sǐ·mā'shŭn) *n.* approssimazione.

apricot (ā'prǐ·kŏt; ăp'rǐ-) *n.* albicocca.

April (ā'prǐl) *n.* aprile: — Fools' Day, primo di aprile.

apron (ā'prŭn) *n.* grembiale.

apropos (ăp'rō·pō') *agg.* opportuno; tempestivo. *avv.* a proposito; opportunamente.

apt (ăpt) *agg.* adatto; atto; proclive. —itude, (ăp'tǐ·tūd), —ness *n.* attitudine, capacità, tendenza.

aquacade (ăk'wā·kād) *n.* spettacolo aquatico.

aquarium (ā·kwâr'ǐ·ŭm) *n.* acquario.

aquatic (ā·kwăt'ǐk; -kwŏt'ǐk) *agg.* acquatico.

aqueduct (ăk'wê·dŭkt) *n.* acquedotto.

aqueous (ā'kwê·ŭs) *agg.* acquoso.

Arab (ăr'ăb), **Arabian** (ā·rā'bǐ·ăn) *n.*, *agg.* arabo: street arab, monello.

arbiter (ăr'bǐ·tēr) *n.* arbitro.

arbitrament (ăr·bǐt'rā·měnt) *n.* arbitraggio.

arbitrary (ăr'bǐ·trěr'ǐ) *agg.* arbitrario.

arbitrate (ăr'bǐ·trāt) *vt.*, *vi.* arbitrare.

arbitration *n.* arbitrato.

arbitrator *n.* arbitro; mediatore.

arbor (ăr'bēr) *n.* pergola; (*mecc.*) trave, albero, asse.

arc (ärk) *n.* arco: — lamp, lampada ad arco.

arcade (är·kād') *n.* portico, porticato.

arch (ärch) *n.* arco, volta. *vt.* arcuare, curvare. *vi.* arcuarsi. *agg.* malizioso, astuto. *pref.* arci, super: —criminal, superdelinquente; —foe, nemico giurato; —priest, arciprete.

archaic (är·kā'ĭk) *agg.* arcaico.

archbishop (ärch'bĭsh'ŭp) *n.* arcivescovo. —ric *n.* arcivescovado.

archdeacon (ärch'dē'kŭn) *n.* arcidiacono.

archipelago (är'kǐ·pěl'ā·gō) *n.* arcipelago.

architect (är'kǐ·těkt) *n.* architetto. —ural *agg.* architettonico. —ure *n.* architettura.

archive (är'kǐv) *n.* archivio.

archly (ärch'lǐ) *agg.* maliziosamente.

archway (ärch'wā') *n.* volta, andito.

arctic (ärk'tǐk) *agg.* artico.

ardent (är'dĕnt) *agg.* ardente: — spirits, bevande alcooliche.

ardor (är'dēr) *n.* ardore.

arduous (är'dū̆·ŭs) *agg.* arduo, difficile; impervio.

are (är) *2a pers.pl. di* to be, sei, siete; siamo; (*essi*) sono.

area (ā'rē̆·ā; är'ē̆·á) *n.* area, superficie, zona.

arena (á·rē'nà) *n.* arena: — theater, teatro circolare, teatro a scena centrale.

Argentine (är'jĕn·tīn; -tēn) *n. agg.* argentino.

argue (är'gū) *vt., vi.* discutere, ragionare; denotare, indicare; to — one into, convincere uno a; to — one out of, dissuadere uno da.

argument (är'gu·mĕnt) *n.* argomento, discussione, disputa, tesi.

arid (är'ĭd) *agg.* arido.

arise (á·rīz') *vi.* (*pass.* arose, *pp.* arisen) alzarsi, innalzarsi; sorgere; provenire, derivare.

aristocracy (är'ĭs·tŏk'rá·sĭ) *n.* aristocrazia.

aristocrat (ä·rĭs'tō·krăt; ăr'ĭs·tō·krăt) *n.* aristocratico.

aristocratic *agg.* aristocratico.

arithmetic (á·rĭth'mĕ·tĭk) *n.* aritmetica.

ark (ärk) *n.* arca: Noah's —, l'arca di Noè.

arm (ärm) *n.* braccio; arma; manica; bracciuolo: — in —, a braccetto; coat of arms, stemma. *vt.* armare. *vi.* armarsi.

armament (är'má·mĕnt) *n.* armamento.

armature (är'má·tū̆r) *n.* armatura.

armchair (ärm'châr') *n.* poltrona.

armful (ärm'fŏ͝ol) *n.* bracciata.

armistice (är'mĭ·stĭs) *n.* armistizio.

armlet (ärm'lĕt) *n.* bracciale.

armor (är'mēr) *n.* armatura, corazza; corazzatura; forze corazzate; *vt.* blindare, corazzare. —**ial** *agg.* araldico. *n.* almanacco araldico. —**ed** *agg.* corazzato, blindato: — car, autoblindo.

armory (är'mēr·ĭ) *n.* armeria.

armpit (ärm'pĭt') *n.* ascella.

army (är'mĭ) *n.* esercito; turba.

aroma (á·rō'má) *n.* aroma. —**tic** *agg.* (är'ō·măt'ĭk) aromatico.

arose (á·rōz') *pass. di* arise.

around (á·round') *avv.* intorno, all'intorno. *prep.* intorno a, in giro, tutt'attorno.

arouse (á·rouz') *vt.* svegliare; provocare, irritare. *vi.* svegliarsi, scuotersi.

arraign (á·rān') *vt.* accusare, citare in giudizio.

arrange (á·rānj') *vt., vi.* disporre, combinare; adattare; comporre (*una controversia*). —**ment** *n.* disposizione, organizzazione, accordo: to make arrangements, prender misure, accordarsi.

arrant (är'ănt) *adj.* notorio, famigerato.

array (á·rā') *n.* spiegamento, schiera; esposizione; lista dei giurati: in great —, in pompa magna; in battle —, in ordine di battaglia. *vt.* allineare, schierare; vestire, parare.

arrears (á·rērz') *n.pl.* arretrati, residuo.

arrest (á·rĕst') *n.* arresto, cattura; sospensione. *vt.* arrestare, catturare; fermare, sospendere.

arrival (á·rīv'ăl) *n.* arrivo.

arrive (á·rīv') *vi.* arrivare, giungere.

arrogance (är'ō·găns) *n.* arroganza.

arrogant (är'ō·gănt) *agg.* arrogante.

arrow (är'ō) *n.* freccia. —**head** *n.* punta di freccia.

arsenal (är'sē·năl) *n.* arsenale.

arsenic (är'sē·nĭk) *n.* arsenico.

arson (är's'n) *n.* incendio doloso.

art (ärt) *n.* arte, abilità; Master of Arts, laureato in lettere.

artery (är'tēr·ĭ) *n.* arteria.

artful (ärt'fŏ͝ol; -f'l) *agg.* subdolo, astuto; artificioso.

artichoke (är'tĭ·chōk) *n.* carciofo.

article (är'tĭ·k'l) *n.* articolo; Articles of War, codice militare.

articulate (är·tĭk'ū·lāt) *agg.* articolato; scandito. *vt., vi.* (-āt) articolare, scandire.

articulation *n.* articolazione.

artifice (är'tĭ·fĭs) *n.* artificio, astuzia.

artificial (är'tĭ·fĭsh'ăl) *agg.* artificiale; artificioso, affettato: — insemination, fecondazione artificiale.

artillery (är·tĭl'ẽr·ĭ) *n.* artiglieria.

artisan (är'tĭ·zăn) *n.* artigiano, operaio.

artist (är'tĭst) *n.* artista. —**ic** *agg.* artistico.

artless (ärt'lĕs) *agg.* ingenuo, spontaneo.

as (ăz) *cong.* come, nello stesso modo; poichè, dal momento che: as ... as, tanto ... quanto; — far —, sin dove; sino a; — large —, grande come; — much, altrettanto; — much —, tanto quanto; — yet, sino ad ora; — long —, fintanto che; the same —, lo stesso che; — well, come pure, anche; you can come — well, potete venire anche voi; — if, — though, come se; — soon — possible, il più presto possibile; — it were, per così dire.

asbestos (ăs·bĕs'tŏs; ăz-) *n.* amianto.

ascend (á·sĕnd') *vt., vi.* scalare; elevarsi, salire; risalire (*a*).

ascension (ă·sĕn'shŭn) *n.* ascensione.

ascent (ă·sĕnt') *n.* ascensione, salita; erta.

ascertain (ăs'ĕr·tān') *vt.* appurare, sincerarsi di, verificare.

ascribe (ăs·krīb') *vt.* attribuire; imputare.

ash (ăsh) *n.* cenere. — **colored** *agg.* cinereo. — **tray** *n.* portacenere: **Ash Wednesday**, Mercoledì delle Ceneri.

ash, ash tree *n.* frassino.

ashamed (ă·shāmd') *agg.* vergognoso (*che si vergogna*): to be — of, vergognarsi di.

ashen (ăsh'ĕn) *agg.* cinereo.

ashore (ă·shōr') *avv.* a terra, a riva: **to run** —, arenarsi; **to go** —, sbarcare.

aside (ă·sīd') *avv.* a lato; in disparte, lateralmente; eccetto: — **from,** eccetto, a prescindere da.

ask (ăsk) *vt.* domandare, chiedere; invitare: **to** — **a question,** rivolgere una domanda; **to** — **for,** chiedere, esigere; **to** — **after, about,** chiedere, informarsi di; **to** — **to dinner,** invitare a pranzo.

askance (ă·skăns') *avv.* sospettosamente, con diffidenza, obliquamente: **to look** —, guardare in tralice, con sospetto; disapprovare.

askew (ă·skū') *avv.* di sghimbescio.

asleep (ă·slēp') *agg., avv.* dormiente, addormentato: **to fall** —, addormentarsi.

asparagus (ăs·păr'ă·gŭs) *n.* asparago.

aspect (ăs'pĕkt) *n.* aspetto.

aspersion (ăs·pûr'shŭn; -zhŭn) *n.* aspersione; calunnia.

asphalt (ăs'fôlt; -fălt) *n.* asfalto.

asphyxiate (ăs·fĭk'sĭ·āt) *vt.* asfissiare.

asphyxiation *n.* asfissia.

aspiration (ăs'pĭ·rā'shŭn) *n.* aspirazione.

aspire (ă·spīr') *vi.* aspirare, anelare.

ass (ăs) *n.* asino: **to make an** — **of oneself,** fare una figura barbina.

assail (ă·sāl') *vt.* assalire, aggredire. —**ant** *n.* assalitore.

assassin (ă·săs'ĭn) *n.* assassino. —**ate** *vt.* assassinare.

assault (ă·sôlt') *n.* assalto, grassazione: — **and battery,** vie di fatto. *vt.* aggredire, assaltare.

assay (ă·sā'; ăs'ā) *n.* saggio, prova; verifica. *vt.* saggiare.

assemblage (ă·sĕm'blĭj) *n.* montaggio.

assemble (ă·sĕm'b'l) *vt.* riunire, radunare; montare.

assembly (ă·sĕm'blĭ) *n.* assemblea; montaggio.

assent (ă·sĕnt') *n.* assenso, sanzione. *vi.* assentire, acconsentire.

assert (ă·sûrt') *vt.* asserire, affermare; sostenere; rivendicare. —**ion** *n.* asserzione; r vendicazione.

assess (ă·sĕs') *vt.* assegnare; tassare; multare; calcolare (*l'imponibile*). —**ment** *n.* tassazione, assegnazione.

asset (ăs'ĕt) *n.* vantaggio, qualità: he is an — **to his family,** egli fa onore alla sua famiglia. **assets** *pl.* beni; (*comm.*) attività: **assets and liabilities,** attività e passività.

assiduous (ă·sĭd'ū·ŭs) *agg.* assiduo.

assign (ă·sīn') *vt.* assegnare.

assignation (ăs'ĭg·nā'shŭn) *n.* assegnazione, appuntamento.

assignment (ă·sīn'mĕnt) *n.* assegnazione; missione; designazione; compito.

assimilate (ă·sĭm'ĭ·lāt) *vt.* assimilare, assorbire. *vi.* assimilarsi.

assimilation *n.* assimilazione.

assist (ă·sĭst') *vt.* aiutare. —**ance** *n.* aiuto. —**ant** *n.* aiutante: —**manager,** vice-direttore.

associate (ă·sō'shĭ·āt; -sĭ·āt) *vt.* associare. *vi.* associarsi: **to** — **with,** frequentare. *n.* socio, compare, complice. *agg.* associato, consociato.

association *n.* associazione.

assort (ă·sôrt') *vt.* assortire. *vi.* far comunella. —**ed** *agg.* assortito. —**ment** *n.* assortimento; accolita.

assuage (ă·swāj') *vt.* ammansire; attenuare; soddisfare; placarsi.

assume (ă·sūm') *vt.* ritenere; supporre; presumere; assumere; assumersi; arrogarsi.

assuming *agg.* arrogante, presuntuoso.

assumption (ă·sŭmp'shŭn) *n.* presupposto, supposizione; assunzione.

assurance (ă·shŏŏr'ăns) *n.* assicurazione; affermazione; sicurezza; sicumera.

assure (ă·shŏŏr') *vt.* assicurare.

assuredly (ă·shŏŏr'ĕd·lĭ) *avv.* sicuramente.

asterisk (ăs'tĕr·ĭsk) *n.* asterisco.

astern (ă·stûrn') *avv.* (*naut.*) a poppa.

asthma (ăz'mă·; ăsth'mă) *n.* asma.

astir (ă·stûr') *agg., avv.* in movimento; alzato (*dal letto*).

astonish (ăs·tŏn'ĭsh) *vt.* stupire. —**ing** *agg.* stupefacente, straordinario. —**ment** *n.* stupore, meraviglia.

astound (ăs·tound') *vt.* sbalordire, stordire.

astray (ă·strā') *agg., avv.* fuor della retta via, fuorviato, sbandato: **to go** —, perdersi, smarrirsi; deviare, traviarsi; **to lead** —, sviare, fuorviare, traviare.

astride (ă·strīd') *avv.* a cavalcioni.

astronomer (ăs·trŏn'ŏ·mĕr) *n.* astronomo.

astronomy (ăs·trŏn'ŏ·mĭ) *n.* astronomia.

astute (ăs·tūt') *agg.* astuto.

asunder (á·sŭn'dĕr) *avv.* separatamente, a pezzi, lontano: to tear —, fare a pezzi, separare violentemente.

asylum (á·sī'lŭm) *n.* asilo, rifugio, ospedale: lunatic —, manicomio.

at (ăt; ắt) *prep.* a, al, alla, in: — first, da principio, sulle prime; — hand, a portata di mano; — home, a casa; — last, alla fine, finalmente; — once, subito; — work, all'opera.

ate (āt) *pass. di* to eat.

atheist (ā'thē·ĭst) *n.* ateo.

athlete (ăth'lēt) *n.* atleta.

athletic (ăth·lĕt'ĭk) *agg.* atletico.

athletics (ăth·lĕt'ĭks) *n.* atletica.

Atlantic (ăt·lăn'tĭk) *n.*, *agg.* Atlantico.

atlas (ăt'lås) *n.* atlante geografico.

atmosphere (ăt'mŏs·fẽr) *n.* atmosfera.

atmospheric (ăt'mŏs·fĕr'ĭk) *agg.* atmosferico.

atom (ăt'ŭm) *n.* atomo: — bomb, bomba atomica. —ic, —ical *agg.* atomico. —ize, *vt.* atomizzare, polverizzare. —izer, *n.* atomizzatore, spruzzatore.

atone (á·tōn') *vt.*, *vi.* espiare; riparare; attenuare. —ment *n.* espiazione, riparazione.

atrocious (á·trō'shŭs) *agg.* atroce.

atrocity (á·trŏs'ĭ·tĭ) *n.* atrocità.

atrophic (á·trŏf'ĭk) *agg.* atrofico.

attach (á·tăch') *vt.*, *vi.* attaccare, assicurare; attribuire, annettere; aderire, attaccarsi; sequestrare, requisire. —ment *n.* sequestro; attaccamento; vincolo; affetto; accessorio, parte aggiunta.

attack (á·tăk') *n.* assalto, aggressione; attacco, accesso. *vt.* attaccare, assalire.

attain (á·tān') *vt.* raggiungere, ottenere. *vi.* pervenire, arrivare. —ment *n.* raggiungimento, realizzazione; dote, abilità; successo.

attempt (á·tĕmpt') *n.* tentativo, attentato: — on someone's life, attentato alla vita di qualcuno. *vt.* tentare, provare, attentare.

attend (á·tĕnd') *vt.* assistere, presenziare; servire, scortare. *vi.* prestare attenzione, provvedere (*a*); accudire. —ance *n.* assistenza; presenza; pubblico (*affluenza di spettatori*). —ant *n.* inserviente; accompagnatore, assistente; guardiano; (*teatro*) maschera. *agg.* relativo (*a*), connesso.

attention (á·tĕn'shŭn) *n.* attenzione; premura, cura: to pay —, fare attenzione, badare.

attentive (átĕn'tĭv) *agg.* attento, premuroso.

attest (á·tĕst') *vt.* attestare.

attic (ăt'ĭk) *n.* attico, solaio.

attire (á·tīr') *n.* vestiario. *vt.* vestire, agghindare. *vi.* vestirsi, agghindarsi.

attitude (ăt'ĭ·tūd) *n.* atteggiamento, posa; attitudine.

attorney (á·tûr'nĭ) *n.* procuratore, avvocato: — General, procuratore generale; District —, procuratore distrettuale; power of —, procura.

attract (á·trăkt') *vt.* attrarre. —ion *n.* attrazione. —ive *agg.* attraente, seducente. —iveness *n.* attrattiva, fascino.

attribute *n.* (ăt'rĭ·būt) attributo, qualità. *vt.* (á·trĭb'ūt) attribuire, imputare.

attrition (á·trĭsh'ŭn) *n.* logorio.

auburn (ò'bẽrn) *agg.* castano, rosso Tizianesco.

auction (ôk'shŭn) *n.* asta (*vendita*): to sell by —, vendere all'asta. —eer *n.* banditore.

audacious (ô·dā'shŭs) *agg.* audace.

audacity (ô·dăs'ĭ·tĭ) *n.* audacia.

audible (ô'dĭ·b'l) *agg.* udibile, percettibile.

audience (ô'dĭ·ĕns; ôd'yĕns) *n.* udienza; uditorio, pubblico.

audio (ô'dĭ·ō) *agg.* auditivo, audio.

audit (ô'dĭt) *n.* controllo, verifica (*dei conti*). *vt.* verificare (*i conti*). —or *n.* revisore, sindaco (*di società*).

audition (ô·dĭsh'ŭn) *n.* audizione; *vt.* ascoltare in audizione; *vi.* avere un'audizione, esibirsi in audizione.

auditorium (ô'dĭ·tō'rĭ·ŭm) *n.* sala di udienza *o* di audizione.

auger (ô'gĕr) *n.* succhiello, trivella.

aught (ôt) *pron.* qualcosa: for — I know, per quanto ne so io.

augment (ôg.mĕnt') *vt.*, *vi.* aumentare.

augur (ô'gĕr) *vt.*, *vi.* presagire, vaticinare, predire.

august (ô·gŭst') *agg.* augusto.

August (ô'gŭst) *n.* agosto.

aunt (ănt; ànt) *n.* zia: great —, prozia.

aureomycin (ô'rē·ō·mī'sĭn) *n.* aureomicina.

auspice (ôs'pĭs) *n.* auspicio.

auspicious (ôs·pĭsh'ŭs) *agg.* propizio, favorevole.

austere (ôs·tẽr') *agg.* austero.

austerity (ôs·tĕr'ĭ·tĭ) *n.* austerità; economia obbligatoria.

Austrian (ôs'trĭ·ăn) *n.*, *agg.* austriaco.

autarchy (ô'tär·kǐ) *n.* autarchia.
authentic (ô·thĕn'tǐk) *adj.* autentico.
author (ô'thĕr) *n.* autore.
authoritative (ô·thŏr'ǐ·tā'tǐv) *agg.* autoritario; autorevole.
authority (ô·thŏr'ǐ·tǐ) *n.* autorità: on good —, da fonte auterevole.
authorization *n.* autorizzazione.
authorize (ô'thĕr·īz) *vt.* autorizzare.
automatic (ô'tô·mǎt'ǐk) *agg.* automatico. *n.* pistola automatica. —ally *avv.* automaticamente.
automation *n.* automazione.
automaton (ô·tŏm'á·tŏn) *n.* automa.
automobile (ô'tô·mô·bēl'; -mō'bǐl *or* -bēl) *n.* automobile.
automotive (ô'tô·mō'tǐv) *agg.* automotore.
autonomy (ô·tŏn'ô·mi) *n.* autonomia.
autopilot (ô'tô·pī'lăt) *n.* autopilota, pilota automatico.
autosled (ô'tô·slĕd) *n.* autoslitta.
autumn (ô'tŭm) *n.* autunno. —al (ô·tŭm'năl) *agg.* autunnale.
auxiliary (ôg·zǐl'yá·rǐ) *n.,* *agg.* ausiliario, ausiliare.
avail (á·vāl') *n.* vantaggio, utilità: of no —, inutile; *vt.* valere, giovare: to — oneself of, valersi di. —able *adj.* disponibile.
avalanche (ăv'á·lânch) *n.* valanga.
avarice (ăv'á·rǐs) *n.* avarizia, rapacità.
avaricious (ăv'á·rǐsh'ŭs) *agg.* avaro, cupido.
avenge (á·vĕnj') *vt.* vendicare.
avenger (á·vĕn'jĕr) *n.* vendicatore.
avenue (ăv'ĕ·nū) *n.* viale, corso.
aver (á·vûr') *vt.* asserire.
average (ăv'ĕr·ǐj) *n.* media; (*naut.*) avaria, rischio. *agg.* medio. *vt.* fare *o* sostenere la media di.
averse (á·vûrs') *agg.* avverso; contrario; ostile.
aversion (á·vûr'zhŭn; -shŭn) *n.* contrarietà, avversione.
avert (á·vûrt') *vt.* evitare, schivare; distogliere.
aviary (ā'vǐ·ĕr'ǐ) *n.* uccelliera.
aviation (ā'vǐ·ā'shŭn) *n.* aviazione.
aviator (ā'vǐ·ā'tĕr; ăv'ǐ-) *n.* aviatore.
avid (ăv'ǐd) *agg.* avido.

avocation (ăv'ô·kā'shŭn) *n.* passatempo preferito, occupazione, professione.
avoid (á·void') *vt.* evitare, schivare.
avow (á·vou') *vt.* confessare, ammettere. —al *n.* confessione.
await (á·wāt') *vt.* aspettare.
awake (á·wāk') *vt.* (*pass.* awoke, *pp.* awaked) svegliare. *vi.* svegliarsi. *agg.* sveglio; conscio.
awaken (á·wāk'ĕn) *vt.* svegliare. —ing *n.* risveglio.
award (á·wôrd') *n.* decisione, sentenza, attribuzione; premio; conferimento. *vt.* assegnare, aggiudicare, conferire (*premi, ecc.*).
aware (á·wâr') *agg.* conscio, consapevole.
away (á·wā') *avv.* via, lontano: to do — with, sopprimere; right —, subito, seduta stante; to give oneself —, tradirsi, svelarsi.
awe (ô) *n.* rispetto; sacro timore: to stand in — of, temere. *vt.* imporre rispetto; intimorire; stupire.
awful (ô'fŏŏl, -f'l) *agg.* terribile; solenne, imponente. —ly *avv.* terribilmente; notevolmente, molto.
awhile (ȧ·hwīl') *avv.* momentaneamente, brevemente; un poco; un momento.
awkward (ôk'wĕrd) *agg.* goffo, maldestro; imbarazzante; imbarazzato; scomodo.
awl (ôl) *n.* lesina, punteruolo.
awning (ôn'ǐng) *n.* tenda, riparo.
awoke (á·wōk') *pass. di* awake.
AWOL, awol (ā'wôl) *agg.,* assente senza permesso, assente ingiustificato (*mil.*).
awry (á·rī') *agg.,* *avv.* storto, di sghimbescio.
ax, axe (ăks) *n.* ascia, scure.
axis (ăk'sǐs) *n.* (*pl.* axes) asse (*di rotazione*).
axle (ăk's'l) *n.* assale, asse, sala (*di ruota*); — box, mozzo di ruota.
axletree (ăk's'l trē') *n.* assale.
ay, aye (ā) *avv.* sì, davvero. *n.* voto favorevole, assenso.
azote (ăz'ōt) *n.* azoto.
azure (ăzh'ĕr; ā'zhĕr) *agg.* azzurro. —stone *n.* lapislazzuli.

B

babble (bǎb''l) *n.* balbettìo, chiacchierìo; ciarla. *vi.* balbettare; straparlare; ciarlare. *vt.* far pettegolezzi, divulgare.
babbler *n.* chiacchierone.
babe (bāb) *n.* neonato; (*fam.*) ragazza.
baboon (bȧ·bōōn') *n.* babbuino.

baby (bā'bǐ) *n.* bimbo, creatura; ragazza: — sitter, bambinaia a ore. *vt.* ninnare; coccolare. —ish *agg.* infantile. —hood *n.* infanzia.
bachelor (băch'ĕ·lĕr) *n.* celibe, scapolo: — of arts, diplomato in lettere.

bacillus (bá·sĭl'ŭs) *n.* (*pl.* **bacilli**) bacillo.

back (băk) *n.* schiena, dorso, tergo, parte posteriore; schienale. *agg.* posteriore; arretrato. *avv.* addietro; indietro; di ritorno: **years —**, anni addietro; **to come —**, tornare indietro; **to call —**, richiamare; **to give —**, restituire; **— and forth**, avanti e indietro. *vt.* sostenere, spalleggiare; aiutare; avallare. *vi.* retrocedere, ritirarsi: **to — out, to — down**, ritirarsi.

backbite (băk'bīt) *vt.* denigrare, sparlare (*di*).

backbone (băk'bōn') *n.* colonna vertebrale; fermezza; sostegno.

backer (băk'ēr) *n.* finanziatore; sostenitore.

backfire (băk'fīr') *n.* ritorno di fiamma.

background (băk'ground') *n.* fondo; sfondo; fondale; precedenti (*di una persona*); retroscena; musica di fondo.

backhand (băk'hănd') *n.* dorso della mano; scrittura revesciata; colpo rovescio.

backhanded (băk'hăn'dĕd) *agg.* revescio, a rovescio; indiretto; ironico: **— stroke**, manrovescio.

backing (băk'ĭng) *n.* appoggio; garanzia; scommessa.

backward (băk'wĕrd) *agg.* arretrato, retrogrado. *avv.* (*also* **backwards**) dietro; indietro; a ritroso. **—s** *n.* lentezza; riluttanza; mentalità retrograda.

bacon (bā'kăn; -k'n) *n.* pancetta affumicata.

bacterial (băk·tẽr'ĭ·ăl) *agg.* batterico.

bacteriology (băk·tẽr'ĭ·ŏl'ō·jĭ) *n.* batteriologia.

bad (băd) *agg.* cattivo, malvagio; cagionevole (*in salute*); sfavorevole; dannoso: **— coin**, moneta falsa; **from — to worse**, di male in peggio. **—ly** *avv.* malamente, fortemente; gravemente. **—ness** *n.* cattiveria; cattiva qualità.

bade (băd) *pass. di* **bid**.

badge (băj) *n.* distintivo, insegna, emblema; decorazione.

badger (băj'ẽr) (1) *n.* (*zool.*) tasso.

badger (2) *vt.* tormentare; perseguitare.

baffle (băf''l) *vt.* frustrare; disorientare, sconcertare, confondere.

bag (băg) *n.* borsa, valigia, sacco. *vt.* insaccare, rubare. *vi.* insaccarsi, gonfiarsi.

baggage (băg'ĭj) *n.* bagaglio.

bagpipe (băg'pīp) *n.* cornamusa.

bail (bāl) *n.* libertà provvisoria dietro cauzione; cauzione. *vt.* versare cauzione per scarcerare; (*naut.*) aggottare: **to — out**, lanciarsi col paracadute.

bait (bāt) *vt.* adescare; aizzare. *n.* esca.

bake (bāk) *vt.* cuocere al forno. *vi.* fare il pane; cuocersi, abbrustolirsi.

baker (bāk'ẽr) *n.* fornaio.

bakery (băk'ẽr·ĭ) *n.* panetteria.

baking powder *n.* lievito in polvere.

balance (băl'ăns) *n.* bilancia, equilibrio; (*comm.*) saldo; residuo attivo. *vt.* bilanciare, pesare, equilibrare; soppesare; saldare, pareggiare (*un conto*). *vi.* bilanciarsi, barcamenarsi.

balcony (băl'kŏ·nĭ) *n.* balcone; (*teat.*) balconata, galleria.

bald (bôld) *agg.* calvo; brullo; nudo; squallido, disadorno. **—ness** *n.* calvizie; squallore.

bale (bāl) *n.* balla. *vt.* imballare. **—ful** *agg.* minaccioso, funesto.

balk (bôk) *n.* ostacolo; delusione. *vt.* frustrare, ostacolare; sconcertare. *vi.* esitare, recalcitrare.

ball (bôl) (1) *n.* palla, sfera; gomitolo: **—bearing**, cuscinetto a sfere.

ball (2) *n.* ballo: **—room**, sala da ballo; **— point pen**, penna a sfera.

ballad (băl'ăd) *n.* ballata.

ballast (băl'ăst) *n.* zavorra; pietrisco. *vt.* zavorrare.

balloon (bá·lōōn') *n.* aerostato.

ballot (băl'ŭt) *n.* ballotta, palla *o* scheda (*per votazioni*); voto; **— box**, urna. *vt.*, *vi.* votare.

balm (bäm) *n.* balsamo.

balmy (băm'ĭ) *agg.* balsamico; scriteriato.

balsam (bôl'săm) *n.* balsamo.

bamboo (băm·bōō') *n.* bambù.

ban (băn) *n.* bando, interdizione. *vt.* bandire; vietare; maledire.

banal (bā'năl) *agg.* banale.

band (bănd) (1) *n.* fascia; banda; benda, nastro. *vt.* legare, fasciare. *vi.* imbrancarsi; **—saw**, sega a nastro.

band (2) *n.* banda, orchestra: **— leader**, capobanda. **—stand** *n.* podio dell'orchestra.

bandage (băn'dĭj) *n.* bendaggio. *vt.* bendare, medicare.

bandanna (băn·dăn'á) *n.* fazzolettone colorato.

bandit (băn'dĭt) *n.* bandito, brigante.

bang (băng) *n.* colpo, schianto, tonfo. *vt.* tempestare di colpi; sbattere, percuotere.

bangle (băng'g'l) *n.* braccialetto.

banish (băn'ĭsh) *vt.* bandire, esiliare. **—ment** *n.* bando, esilio.

banister (băn'ĭs·tẽr) *n.* ringhiera.

bank (băngk) (1) *n.* sponda, riva, argine, altura, margine *o* ciglio (*di* *strada*); banco (*di nubi*); (*aeron.*) inclinazione in virata. *vt.* ammucchiare, ammonticchiare; (*aeron.*) inclinare in virata. —ing *n.* arginatura; diga.

bank (2) *n.* banca, banco; panca, sedile, seggio: blood —, banca del sangue; piggy —, salvadanaio. *vt.* depositare in banca: to — upon, contare su. —book *n.* libretto bancario. —er *n.* banchiere. —ing *n.* operazioni bancarie, attività bancaria. *agg.* bancario. —note *n.* banconota.

bankrupt (băngk'rŭpt) *agg.* fallito; rovinato. *vt.* far fallire, rovinare.

bankruptcy (băngk'rŭpt.sĭ) *n.* fallimento, bancarotta.

banner (băn'ẽr) *n.* stendardo, bandiera.

banns (bănz) *n.* pubblicazioni matrimoniali.

banquet (băng'kwĕt) *n.* banchetto.

banter (băn'tẽr) *n.* scherzo. *vt.* scherzare.

baptism (băp'tĭz'm) *n.* battesimo.

baptize (băp.tīz') *vt.* battezzare.

bar (bär) *n.* sbarra; bar, mescita; barriera, ostacolo; tavoletta (*di cioccolata*); tribunale; foro; magistratura; (*legge*) banco (*degli accusati*): called to the —, ammesso a esercitare l'avvocatura; to read for the —, studiare legge. *vt.* sbarrare, impedire, vietare, bloccare.

barb (bärb) *n.* punta di ferro. —ed *agg.* irto di punte, seghettato, spinato: —wire, filo spinato.

barbarian (bär.bâr'ĭ.ăn) *n.* barbaro.

barbarous (bär'bà.rŭs) *agg.* barbaro.

barbecue (bär'bė.kū) *n.* animale arrostito intero; festino all'aperto: to —, mettere allo spiedo (*un animale intero*).

barber (bär'bẽr) *n.* barbiere.

bard (bàrd) *n.* bardo, trovatore.

bare (bâr) *agg.* nudo, scoperto; solo, semplice; squallido, brullo; palese; smobiliato: to lay —, mettere a nudo. *vt.* scoprire; denudare; spogliare, rivelare. —foot *agg.* scalzo. —ly *avv.* a malapena, soltanto. —ness *n.* nudità, squallore.

barfly (bär'flī) *n.* frequentatore di bar.

bargain (bär'gĭn) *n.* baratto, affare, contrattazione: into the —, in soprammercato; — sale, liquidazione. *vt.* mercanteggiare, contrattare: to — for, prevedere.

barge (bärj) *n.* chiatta, barcone.

bark (bärk) *n.* corteccia, scorza; brigantino, veliero; latrato. *vt.* scortecciare, scorticare. *vi.* latrare, abbaiare.

barley (bär'lĭ) *n.* orzo.

barn (bärn) *n.* baracca, granaio. —yard *n.* cortile di fattoria.

barometer (bà.rŏm'ĕ.tẽr) *n.* barometro.

baron (băr'ŭn) *n.* barone; finanziere.

barracks (băr'ăks) *n.pl.* caserma.

barrel (băr'ĕl) *n.* barile, botte; canna (*di arma da fuoco*). *vt.* imbarilare. *vi.* correre a grande velocità, filare.

barren (băr'ĕn) *agg.* nudo, sterile, squallido. —ness *n.* sterilità, squallore.

barricade (băr'ĭ.kăd') *n.* barricata. *vt.* barricare.

barrier (băr'ĭ.ẽr) *n.* barriera, ostacolo.

barring (bär'ĭng) *prep.* eccetto, eccettuato, tranne: — mistakes, salvo errori.

barrister (băr'ĭs.tẽr) *n.* avvocato.

barrow (băr'ō) *n.* barella; carretto.

barter (bär'tẽr) *n.* baratto. *vi.* barattare.

base (bās) (1) *agg.* basso, vile, spregevole. —ness *n.* bassezza.

base (2) *n.* base, fondamento. *vt.* basare. —ment *n.* seminterrato, sotterraneo.

bashful (băsh'fŏŏl; -f'l) *agg.* timido, modesto, pudico. —ness *n.* timidezza.

basic (bās'ĭk) *agg.* basilare, fondamentale; (*chim.*) basico.

basin (bā's'n) *n.* bacile, catinella; bacino.

basis (bā'sĭs) *n.* (*pl.* bases) base, fondamento.

bask (bàsk) *vi.* riscaldarsi; crogiolarsi: to — in the sun, crogiolarsi al sole.

basket (bàs'kĕt) *n.* cesto, paniere. —ball *n.* pallacanestro.

bass (bās) (1) *n.*, *agg.* (*mus.*) basso: double —, contrabbasso. — viol *n.* violone.

bass (bās) (2) *n.* pesce persico.

bassoon (bà.sŏōn') *n.* (*mus.*) fagotto.

bastard (băs'tẽrd) *n.*, *agg.* bastardo; farabutto.

baste (bāst) *vt.* imbastire; bastonare, redarguire; ungere (*la carne durante la cottura*).

bat (băt) (1) *n.* mazza; colpo; baldoria. *vt.*, *vi.* battere; fare il battitore, battere (*al baseball*): not to — an eye, non batter ciglio.

bat (2) *n.* pipistrello; missile radiocomandato.

batch (băch) *n.* infornata; lotto, partita.

bath (bàth) *n.* bagno, stanza da bagno: — house, stabilimento balneare, cabina balneare, bagni pubblici; —robe, accappatoio; —tub, vasca (da bagno).

bathe (bāth) *vt.* bagnare, lavare. *vi.* bagnarsi, fare il bagno.

bather (bāth'ĕr) *n.* bagnante.

battalion (bă·tăl'yŭn) *n.* battaglione.

batter (băt'ĕr) *vt.* battere, tempestare di colpi; logorare; sfigurare: **to — down,** demolire.

battery (băt'ĕr·ĭ) *n.* batteria, accumulatore; percosse; assalto.

battle (băt''l) *n.* battaglia, combattimento. **—field,** *n.* campo di battaglia. **—ship,** *n.* corazzata.

bauble (bô'b'l) *n.* gingillo.

bawdy (bôd'ĭ) *agg.* osceno: **—house,** postribolo.

bawl (bôl) *n.* urlo, schiamazzo. *vi.* urlare, schiamazzare.

bay (bā) (1) *n.* alloro: **—tree,** lauro.

bay (2) *n.* baia, golfo, insenatura: alcova, rientranza: **bomb —,** rastrelliera *o* compartimento delle bombe.

bay (3) *n.* latrato. *vi.* latrare: **at —,** ai ferri corti, con le spalle al muro, in scacco.

bay (4) *agg.* baio.

bayonet (bā'ŏnĕt; -nĭt) *n.* baionetta. *vt.* colpire con baionetta.

bazooka (bà·zōō'kà) *n.* cannone portatile anticarro.

be (bē) *vi.* (*pass.* was, *pl.* were, *pp.* been) essere, esistere, vivere, stare, dovere: **so — it,** così sia; **— that as it may,** comunque sia; **to — well,** star bene; **to — cold (warm, hungry, right, wrong),** aver freddo, (caldo, fame, ragione, torto); **to — ten years old,** avere dieci anni.

beach (bēch) *n.* spiaggia, riva. *vt.* tirare in secca. **—head,** *n.* testa di ponte.

beacon (bē'kŭn; -k'n) *n.* faro, segnalazione luminosa.

bead (bēd) *n.* grano, perlina, goccia, bolla: **to tell one's beads,** sgranare il rosario.

beak (bēk) *n.* becco, beccuccio; sperone (*di nave*); promontorio.

beam (bēm) *n.* trave; timone (*di aratro, ecc.*); raggio (*di luce*); fusto (*dell'ancora*); sorriso; asta (*di bilancia*). *vt.* irradiare. *vi.* sorridere radiosamente, risplendere. **—ing** *agg.* raggiante, sorridente.

beamy (bēm'ĭ) *agg.* luminoso, radioso.

bean (bēn) *n.* fava, fagiolo; chicco, grano: **string—,** fagiolino; **to be full of beans,** essere di ottimo umore.

bear (bâr) *n.* orso; (*borsa*) giocatore al ribasso. *v.* (*pass.* bore, *pp.* borne) reggere, sostenere; sopportare, subire; generare. *vi.* reggere, resistere; svoltare; pesare; avere attinenza, riferirsi; pazientare: **to — oneself,** comportarsi; **to — out,** sostenere,

convalidare; **to — witness,** testimoniare; **to — down,** deprimere; **to — a grudge,** serbare rancore; **— in mind,** tenere a mente; **to — up,** tener duro; **to — upon,** aver attinenza con. **—able** *agg.* sopportabile.

beard (bērd) *n.* barba. *vt.* affrontare, sfidare. **—ed** *agg.* barbuto.

bearer (bâr'ĕr) *n.* portatore, latore.

bearing (bâr'ĭng) *n.* comportamento, portamento, atteggiamento; rapporto, attinenza; orientamento: **ball —,** cuscinetto a sfere; **to lose one's bearings,** disorientarsi; **to get one's bearings,** orientarsi.

beast (bēst) *n.* bestia, animale. **—ly** *agg.* bestiale, orrendo.

beat (bēt) *n.* battito, palpito; itinerario, ronda. *vt.* (*pass.* beat, *pp.* beaten) battere, colpire, martellare; sconfiggere; sferzare: **to — about the bush,** tergiversare, menare il can per l'aia; **to — down,** abbattere, diminuire, sfondare. **—en** *agg.* abbattuto; vinto, battuto; scoraggiato. **—er** *n.* battitore; frullino. **—ing** *n.* battito; percosse, busse; sconfitta.

beatitude (bē·ăt'ĭ·tūd) *n.* beatitudine, felicità.

beau (bō) *n.* spasimante, corteggiatore.

beau idéal (bō'ĭ·dē'ăl) *n.* (*fr.*) bellezza perfetta; ideale perfetto.

beauteous (bū'tē·ŭs) *n.* bello, incantevole.

beautician (bū·tǐsh'ăn) *n.* estetista.

beautiful (bū'tǐ·fŏŏl; -f'l) *agg.* bello.

beautify (bū'tǐ·fī) *vt.* abbellire. *vi.* abbellirsi, truccarsi.

beauty (bū'tǐ) *n.* bellezza: **— spot,** neo.

beaver (bē'vĕr) *n.* castoro; lana di castoro; cappello di feltro castoro.

beaverboard *n.* cartone per tramezze.

became (bē·kām') *pass. di* to become.

because (bē·kôz'; -kŏz') *cong.* perchè: **— of,** a causa di, per.

beck (bĕk) *n.* cenno: **at one's — and call,** a completa disposizione (agli ordini) di uno.

beckon (bĕk'ŭn) *vt., vi.* far cenno; chiamare.

become (bē·kŭm') *vi.* (*pass.* became, *pp.* become) divenire, cominciare a essere, succedere. *vt.* addirsi, attagliarsi, essere degno di.

becoming (bē·kŭm'ĭng) *agg.* acconcio, adatto; che sta bene *o* si addice (*di vestiario, ecc.*)

bed (bĕd) *n.* giaciglio; letto; alveo; fondo (*del mare*); aiuola; giacimento (*min.*): **— and board,** vitto e alloggio; **to take to one's —**, mettersi a letto (*malato*); **to make one's own —, and have to lie in it,** agire di propria testa e sopportarne le conseguenze.

bedbug (bĕd′bŭg′) *n.* cimice.

bedclothes (bĕd′klōᵺz) *n.pl.* coltri.

bedfellow (bĕd′fĕl′ō) *n.* compagno di stanza.

bedlam (bĕd′lăm) *n.* pandemonio.

bedraggle (bĕ.drăg′'l) *vt.* infangare, insozzare. **—d** *agg.* malconcio, infangato.

bedside (bĕd′sīd′) *n.* capezzale.

bedtime (bĕd′tīm′) *n.* ora di coricarsi.

bee (bē) *n.* ape: **to have a — in one's bonnet,** avere una fissazione.

beech (bēch) *n.* faggio.

beechnut (bēch′nŭt′) *n.* faggiuola.

beef (bēf) *n.* manzo (*carne*). **—steak** *n.* bistecca. **— tea** *n.* brodo ristretto.

beehive (bē′hīv′) *n.* alveare.

beeline (bē′līn′) *n.* linea diretta, linea d'aria.

been (bĭn; Ingh. bēn) *pp. di* to be.

beer (bēr) *n.* birra. **—house, —shop** *n.* birreria.

beet (bēt) *n.* barbabietola.

beetle (bē′t'l) *n.* scarafaggio.

befall (bĕ.fôl′) *vt., vi.* (*pass.* **befell,** *pp.* **befallen**) accadere, succedere.

befit (bĕ.fĭt′) *vt.* convenire, addirsi.

before (bĕ.fōr′) *avv., prep.* davanti a, prima di; precedentemente; più avanti di, al cospetto di: **long —,** molto tempo prima.

beforehand (bĕ.fōr′hănd′) *avv.* in anticipo, precedentemente.

befriend (bĕ.frĕnd′) *vt.* aiutare, sostenere, soccorrere.

beg (bĕg) *vt.* pregare, implorare; chiedere. *vi.* elemosinare: **to — leave,** chiedere il permesso, prendersi la libertà; **to — the question,** supporre come vero.

began (bĕ.găn′) *pass. di* to begin.

beget (bĕ.gĕt′) *vt.* (*pass.* **begot,** *pp.* **begot, begotten**) generare, produrre, causare.

beggar (bĕg′ẽr) *n.* mendicante, furfante. *vt.* impoverire, rovinare.

begin (bĕ.gĭn′) *vt., vi.* (*pass.* **began,** *pp.* **begun**) cominciare, iniziare, esordire, accingersi: **to — with,** innanzi tutto, per cominciare. **—ner** *n.* principiante. **—ning** *n.* inizio, esordio, principio, origine.

begot (bĕ.gŏt′) *pass., pp. di* to beget.

beguile (bĕ.gīl′) *vt.* ingannare, adescare.

begun (bĕ.gŭn′) *pp. di* to begin.

behalf (bĕ.häf′) *n.*: **in — of,** in favore di; **on — of,** a nome (*per conto*) di.

behave (bĕ.hāv′) *vi.* comportarsi; **to — oneself,** comportaersi bene.

behavior (bĕ.hāv′yẽr) *n.* condotta, comportamento.

behead (bĕ.hĕd′) *vt.* decapitare.

beheld (bĕ.hĕld′) *pass., pp. di* to behold.

behind (bĕ.hĭnd′) *prep., avv.* dietro; indietro; in arretrato; in ritardo: **— time,** in ritardo. **—hand** *agg.* arretrato, tardo. *avv.* indietro, in arretrato.

behold (bĕ.hōld′) *vt.* (*pass., pp.* **beheld**) contemplare, guardare.

behoove (bĕ.hōōv′) *vi.* convenire, essere acconcio: **it behooves me to go,** conviene che io vada.

being (bē′ĭng) *n.* essere, esistenza: **human —,** essere umano; **for the time —,** per il momento.

belated (bĕ.lāt′ĕd; -ĭd) *agg.* tardivo, fuori orario.

belch (bĕlch) *n.* rutto; eruzione. *vt., vi.* ruttare; eruttare: **to — forth,** vomitare.

belfry (bĕl′frĭ) *n.* campanile.

Belgian (bĕl′jǐ.ắn) *n., agg.* belga.

belie (bĕ.lī′) *vt.* smentire.

belief (bĕ.lēf′) *n.* credenza, convinzione, fede.

believable (bĕ.lēv′à.b'l) *agg.* attendibile, credibile.

believe (bĕ.lēv′) *vt., vi.* credere, ritenere, prestar fede, supporre.

believer *n.* credente, fedele.

belittle (bĕ.lĭt′'l) *vt.* sminuire, svalutare, minimizzare.

bell (bĕl) *n.* campana, campanello; rintocco; calice (*di fiore*): **— buoy,** boa sonora. *vi.* bramire: **to — the cat,** assumersi una responsabilità.

bellboy (bĕl′boi′), **bellhop** (bĕl′hŏp′) *n.* inserviente d'albergo.

belle (bĕl) *n.* bella: **the — of the village,** la bella del paese.

bellflower (bĕl′flou′ẽr) *n.* campanula.

belligerency (bĕ.lij′ẽr.ĕn.sĭ) *n.* aggressività; belligeranza.

belligerent (bĕ.lij′ẽr.ĕnt) *n.* belligerante. *agg.* battagliero, bellicoso.

bellow (bĕl′ō) *n.* muggito. *vi.* muggire, mugghiare; gridare, tuonare.

bellows (bĕl′ōz; -ŭs) *n.pl.* mantice.

belly (bĕl′ĭ) *n.* ventre, pancia.

belong (bĕ.lŏng′) *vi.* appartenere, essere di proprietà (*di*); far parte (*di*). **—ings** *n.pl.* effetti personali; beni; bagaglio.

beloved (bĕ.lŭv′ĕd; bĕ.lŭvd′) *n., agg.* amato, adorato, diletto.

below (bĕ.lō′) *prep.* sotto, al disotto di; a valle di. *avv.* inferiormente, da basso, in basso.

belt (bĕlt) *n.* cinghia, cintura, cinturone, fascia: to hit below the —, infliggere un colpo basso, colpire slealmente. *vt.* cingere; staffilare.

bemoan (bĕ-mōn') *vt.* compiangere, deplorare. *vi.* gemere, addolorarsi.

bemuse (bĕ-mūz') *vt.* confondere, disorientare.

bench (bĕnch) *n.* sedile, panca; seggio; banco di lavoro; tribunale.

bend (bĕnd) *n.* curva, curvatura; inclinazione; (*naut.*) nodo. *vt.* (*pass.* **bent**, *pp.* **bent**, **bended**) piegare, curvare, inclinare, torcere; tendere (*l'arco*); flettere (*le ginocchia*); (*fig.*) adattare, orientare; (*naut.*) ormeggiare, guarnire: to — one's endeavors to, dedicare i propri sforzi a. *vi.* piegarsi, curvarsi, chinarsi, inclinarsi, adattarsi, propendere.

beneath (bĕ-nēth') *avv., prep.* sotto, al disotto, in basso.

benediction (bĕn'ĕ-dĭk'shŭn) *n.* benedizione.

benefactor (bĕn'ĕ-făk'tēr) *n.* benefattore.

beneficence (bĕ-nĕf'ĭ-sĕns) *n.* beneficenza.

beneficent (-sĕnt) *agg.* caritatevole.

beneficial (bĕn'ĕ-fĭsh'ăl) *agg.* benefico, vantaggioso.

benefit (bĕn'ĕ-fĭt) *n.* beneficio, profitto, vantaggio: — performance, spettacolo di beneficenza; — society, società di mutuo soccorso; — night, serata in onore. *vt.* beneficare. *vi.* beneficiare (*di*), trarre vantaggio (*da*); approfittare.

benevolence (bĕ-nĕv'ō-lĕns) *n.* benevolenza, carità.

benevolent *agg.* benevolo, caritatevole.

benign (bĕ-nīn') —**ant** (bĕ-nĭg'nănt) *agg.* benevolo, benigno, affabile.

bent (bĕnt) *agg.* curvato, piegato, propenso; deciso, risoluto. *n.* tendenza, propensione; attitudine; curva. *pass., pp. di* to bend.

benumb (bĕ-nŭm') *vt.* intirizzire, paralizzare; intontire; intorpidire.

benzene (bĕn'zēn; bĕn-zēn') *n.* benzolo.

bequeath (bĕ-kwēth') *vt.* legare, assegnare in eredità.

bequest (bĕ-kwĕst') *n.* legato, lascito.

berate (bĕ-rāt') *vt.* redarguire.

berry (bĕr'ĭ) *n.* bacca, chicco: coffee in the —, caffè in grani.

berserk (bûr'sûrk; bûr-sûrk') *agg.* infuriato: to go —, perdere la testa, abbandonarsi a violenze.

berth (bûrth) *n.* cuccetta, letto; riparo, nicchia; impiego; ormeggio: to give a wide — to, girar largo da, schivare. *vt., vi.* ormeggiarsi, dare *o* prendere alloggio.

beseech (bĕ-sēch') *vt.* (*pass., pp.* besought) supplicare, implorare.

beset (bĕ-sĕt') *vt.* (*pass., pp.* beset) assediare, assillare; ingombrare.

beside (bĕ-sīd') *prep.* accanto a; di fianco a; vicino a; in confronto a; oltre a; all'infuori di: to be — oneself, esser fuori di sè.

besides (bĕ-sīdz') *avv.* d'altronde, per giunta. *prep.* oltre a.

besiege (bĕ-sēj') *vt.* assediare.

besieger *n.* assediante.

besought (bĕ-sôt') *pass., pp. di* to beseech.

best (bĕst) *agg.* (*superl. di* good) (il) migliore, ottimo: at —, tutt'al più; — man, testimone alle nozze; for the —, per il meglio; to do one's —, fare del proprio meglio; to have the — of, avere il sopravvento su; to make the — of, trarre il miglior partito da. *avv.* meglio.

bestow (bĕ-stō') *vt.* elargire, concedere, conferire: to — a favor on, rendere un servigio a.

bet (bĕt) *n.* scommessa, puntata. *vt., vi.* scommettere, puntare, sfidare: you bet! ci puoi scommettere!, eccome!

betake (bĕ-tāk') *vt.* (*pass.* betook, *pp.* betaken): to — oneself, andare, dirigersi.

betatron (bē'tá-trŏn) *n.* betatrone.

betray (bĕ-trā') *vt.* tradire, ingannare; rivelare; trarre in inganno: —al *n.* tradimento. —er *n.* traditore.

betrothed (bĕ-trôtht'; -trŏthd') *agg. n.* fidanzato.

betrothal (bĕ-trôth'ăl) *n.* fidanzamento.

better (bĕt'ēr) *agg.* (*comp. di* good) migliore, meglio: you had —, fareste meglio, vi converrebbe; to get the — of, aver la meglio, *o* il sopravvento su. *avv.* meglio: — and —, di bene in meglio; a change for the —, un cambiamento in meglio; so much the —, tanto meglio; to be —, stare meglio; to get —, migliorare; to think — of it, ripensarci, mutare parere. *vt.* migliorare: to — oneself, migliorare la propria posizione. —ment *n.* miglioramento.

betting *n.* scommessa, puntata.

bettor (bĕt'ēr) *n.* scommettitore.

between (bĕ-twēn') *prep., avv.* tra, fra, nel mezzo, in mezzo: far —, distante, a lunghi intervalli.

beverage (bĕv'ēr-ĭj) *n.* beveraggio, bibita.

bevy (bĕv'ĭ) *n.* stormo; combriccola.

bewail (bĕ-wāl') *vt.* piangere. *vi.* lamentarsi. —ing *n.* lamentazione.

beware (bĕ·wâr') *vi.* guardarsi, diffidare.

bewilder (bĕ·wĭl'dĕr) *vt.* disorientare, confondere, stupire, sconcertare. —ing *agg.* sconcertante. —ment *n.* smarrimento, disorientamento.

bewitch (bĕ·wĭch') *vt.* stregare, incantare, affascinare. —ing *agg.* affascinante, seducente.

beyond (bĕ·yŏnd') *prep.*, *avv.* al di là, oltre, al disopra, più lontano: — my reach, fuori della mia portata.

bias (bī'ăs) *n.* inclinazione, pendenza; diagonale; sbieco; propensione; preconcetto, prevenzione: on the —, di sbieco. *agg.* di sbieco. *vt.* far pendere, influire su, influenzare. —ed, *agg.* prevenuto.

bib (bĭb) *n.* bavaglino, pettorina (*di* grembiule).

Bible (bī'b'l) *n.* bibbia.

biblical (bĭb'lĭ·kăl) *agg.* biblico.

biceps (bī'sĕps) *n.* bicipite.

bicker (bĭk'ĕr) *vi.* bisticciare, discutere.

bicycle (bī'sĭk.'l) *n.* bicicletta.

bid (bĭd) *vt.* (*pass.* bade, *pp.* bidden) ordinare, ingiungere, esortare, offrire: to — farewell, dire addio; it bids fair to, promette di, c'è speranza che. *n.* offerta (*a un'asta*); invito; tentativo; appello.

bidden (bĭd''n) *pp. di* to bid.

bidder *n.* offerente.

bide (bīd) *vt.* aspettare pazientemente: to — one's time, aspettare il momento opportuno.

bier (bĕr) *n.* catafalco, bara.

big (bĭg) *agg.* grande, grosso; ampio, spazioso; importante: to grow bigger, crescere; to act —, darsi delle arie; to talk —, fare il gradasso; — Dipper, Orsa Maggiore; — sister (brother), sorella (fratello) maggiore; — game, caccia grossa; — with child, incinta; —-bellied, panciuto; —-hearted, magnanimo. —ness *n.* grossezza, grandezza, importanza.

bigamist (bĭg'á·mĭst) *n.* bigamo.

bigamy (bĭg'á·mĭ) *n.* bigamia.

bigot (bĭg'ŭt) *n.* fanatico. —ry fanatismo.

bike (bīk) *n.* (*gergo*) bicicletta, bici.

bile (bīl) *n.* bile.

bilge (bĭlj) *n.* sentina.

bill (bĭl) (*1*) *n.* becco (*d'uccello*).

bill (*2*) *n.* conto, fattura, nota; banconota; cambiale; progetto di legge; manifesto: — of exchange, tratta, cambiale; — of fare, lista delle vivande; — of lading, lettera di carico; to draw a —, spiccare tratta; to take up a —, onorare una

cambiale; — of rights, dichiarazione dei diritti; — of sale, atto di vendita. *vt.* aggiudicare; mandare un conto a; annunciare; mettere in programma. —case, —fold *n.* portafoglio, portacarte.

billet (bĭl'ĕt) *vt.* alloggiare, acquartierare.

billiards (bĭl'yĕrdz) *n.* biliardo.

billion (bĭl'yŭn) *n.* bilione, miliardo: (*in U.S.*) un miliardo = mille milioni; (*in G.B.*) un milione di milioni.

billow (bĭl'ō) *n.* onda, cavallone, maroso. *vi.* gonfiarsi, ingrossarsi.

bin (bĭn) *n.* barattolo, bidone; deposito.

bind (bīnd) *vt.* (*pass.*, *pp.* bound) legare, impegnare, assicurare, cingere; rilegare (*libri*). —er *n.* legatore, rilegatore. —ing *n.* rilegatura; bordatura. *agg.* impegnativo, obbligatorio.

biochemistry (bī'ō·kĕm'ĭs.trĭ) *n.* biochimica.

biographer (bī'ŏg'rá.fĕr) *n.* biografo.

biography (bī·ŏg'rá.fĭ) *n.* biografia.

biologist (bī·ŏl'ō·jĭst) *n.* biologo.

biology (bī·ŏl'ō.jĭ) *n.* biologia.

birch (bûrch) *n.* betulla, verga.

bird (bûrd) *n.* uccello. —seed, *n.* becchime. —shot, *n.* pallini da caccia.

birth (bûrth) *n.* nascita, origine, discendenza: to give— to, mettere alla luce, provocare, dar luogo a. —day *n.* compleanno. —mark *n.* voglia, segno caratteristico (*di persona*). —place *n.* luogo di nascita. — rate *n.* natalità. —right *n.* diritto di nascita, diritto ereditario; primogenitura.

biscuit (bĭs'kĭt) *n.* biscotto.

bishop (bĭsh'ŭp) *n.* vescovo.

bison (bī's'n; -z'n) *n.* bisonte.

bit (bĭt) (*1*) *n.* pezzetto, briciola, frammento; attimo: a — more, un po' di più; — by —, a poco a poco; not to care a —, infischiarsene.

bit (bĭt) (*2*) *n.* morso (*di cavallo*); punta di trapano.

bitch (bĭch) *n.* cagna; femmina (*di lupo, ecc.*); strega, donnaccia. *vi.* lagnarsi, brontolare.

bite (bīt) *n.* morso; presa; boccone; puntura (*d'insetto*). *vt.* (*pass.* bit, *pp.* bitten) mordere; rosicchiare; addentare; pungere; corrodere.

biting (bīt'ĭng) *agg.* mordente, mordace.

bitter (bĭt'ĕr) *agg.* amaro; accanito; pungente; severo: to fight to the — end, lottare sino alla morte. —ly *avv.* amaramente, aspramente.

—ness *n.* amarezza. —sweet *agg.* agrodolce.

bitters *n. pl.* liquore amaro, stomatico.

blabber (blăb´ẽr) *vi.* chiacchierare.

black (blăk) *agg.* nero, scuro, cupo; iniquo; negro. *n.* nero; (*comm.*) attivo. *vt.* annerire; lustrare (*scarpe*). —**ball** *n.* palla nera; bocciatura. *vt.* bocciare. —**berry** *n.* mora. —**bird** *n.* merlo. —**board** *n.* lavagna. —**en** *vt.* annerire; scurire; denigrare. —**guard** (blăg´-)*n.* mascalzone. —**lead** *n.* grafite. —**leg** *n.* imbroglione. —**mail** *n.* ricatto. *vt.* ricattare. —**mailer** *n.* ricattatore. — **market,** mercato nero. — **marketeer** *n.* borsanerista. —**ness** *n.* nerezza, tenebra. —**out** *n.* oscuramento; ottenebramento; *vt.* oscurare; ottenebrare; censurare. —smith *n.* fabbro.

bladder (blăd´ẽr) *n.* vescica.

blade (blād) *n.* lama, parte tagliente (*di un utensile*); filo (*d'erba*); pala (*di remo o elica*)

blame (blām) *n.* biasimo, colpa. *vt.* biasimare, attribuire la colpa a, tenere responsabile. —**less** *agg.* innocente, irreprensibile.

blameworthy (blām´wûr´thĭ) *agg.* biasimevole.

blanch (blånch) *vt.* imbianchire, schiarire; mondare; scottare (*nell'acqua bollente*). *vi.* sbiancare, impallidire.

bland (blănd) *agg.* blando, soave, melifluo.—**ishment** *n.* blandizie,lusinga

blank (blăngk) *n.* lacuna; spazio bianco; vuoto; centro (*del bersaglio*); pezzo semilavorato. *agg.* bianco, in bianco; (*fig.*) vuoto, sconcertato; — **form,** modulo in bianco; — **face,** volto inespressivo; — **countenance,** espressione sconcertata; — **verse,** verso sciolto; — **cartridge,** cartuccia a salve.

blanket (blăng´kĕt) *n.* coltre, coperta: **wet** —, guastafeste. *agg.* generale, complessivo, cumulativo.

blare (blår) *n.* fragore; squillo (*di tromba*); nota sgargiante (*di colore*). *vi.* squillare (*di tromba, ecc.*); *vt.* proclamare a gran voce.

blaspheme (blăs·fēm´) *vt., vi.* bestemmiare.

blasphemy (blăs´fē·mĭ) *n.* bestemmia.

blast (blåst) *n.* ventata, raffica di vento; squillo (*di strumento a fiato*); esplosione; bufera; maledizione. *vt.* distruggere; inaridire; far esplodere; far saltare, rovinare. —**furnace** *n.* alto forno. —**pipe** *n.* tubo di scappamento.

blatant (blā´tănt) *agg.* rumoroso; sguaiato; lampante, evidente.

blaze (blāz) *n.* fiamma, fuoco; luce viva, splendore. *vi.* risplendere, ardere, divampare. *vt.* far rifulgare; divulgare, proclamare.

blazer (blāz´ẽr) *n.* giubbetto a colori vivaci.

blazing (blāz´ĭng) *agg.* fiammante, fiammeggiante.

bleach (blēch) *n.* candeggio; decolorante. *vt., vi.* imbiancare, scolorire, schiarire, candeggiare. —**er** *n.* decolorante; candeggiatore; *pl.* posti popolari (*di stadio sportivo*).

bleak (blēk) *agg.* pallido, smorto, squallido, freddo, deprimente.

blear (blēr) *vt.* annebbiare, offuscare (*la vista*).

bleary (blēr´ĭ) *agg.* annebbiato; infiammato; lagrimoso; cisposo.

bleat (blēt) *n.* belato. *vi.* belare.

bled (blĕd) *pass., pp. di* to bleed.

bleed (blēd) *vi.* (*pass., pp.* bled) sanguinare. *vt.* salassare, dissanguare; sfruttare.

blemish (blĕm´ĭsh) *n.* macchia, difetto. *vt.* macchiare, deturpare.

blench (blĕnch) *vi.* impallidire; indietreggiare; titubare. *vt.* imbiancare; far impallidire.

blend (blĕnd) *n.* miscuglio, fusione, miscela. *vt.* mescolare, miscelare, riunire, fondere. *vi.* fondersi, mescolarsi; armonizzare.

bless (blĕs) *vt.* benedire, consacrare; rendere felice. —**ed, blest** *agg.* benedetto, santo: to be — **with,** esser dotato di, aver la fortuna di possedere.

blessing (blĕs´ĭng) *n.* benedizione; felicità, fortuna.

blew (blōō) *pass. di* to blow.

blight (blīt) *n.* rovina; malocchio; calamità; carbonchio; golpe, ruggine (*delle piante*). *vt.* distruggere, rovinare, frustrare. —**er** *n.* (*gergo*) tizio: poor —, povero diavolo.

blimp (blĭmp) *n.* pallone frenato; **Colonel** —, nazionalista conservatore.

blind (blīnd) *agg.* cieco; chiuso; oscuro; alla cieca. *n.* tendaggio, tapparella, persiana; mascheratura; pretesto. *vt.* accecare, bendare gli occhi a; abbagliare; opacare; mascherare:—**man's buff,** mosca cieca.

blinder (blīn´dẽr) *n.* paraocchio (*del cavallo*)

blindly *avv.* ciecamente, alla cieca.

blindness *n.* cecità; (*fig.*) ignoranza.

blindfold (blīnd´fōld) *vt.* bendare gli occhi a. *n.* benda per gli occhi. *agg.* a occhi bendati; irriflessivo.

blink (blĭngk) *n.* strizzata d'occhio; occhiata; barlume. *vi.* ammiccare;

sogguardare, sbirciare; lampeggiare. to — at, chiudere un occhio su. *vt.* evadere, schivare. —er *n.* lampeggiatore; paraocchi.

bliss (blĭs) *n.* felicità, beatitudine.

blister (blĭs'tĕr) *n.* vescica, bolla. *vt.* applicare un vescicante. *vi.* coprirsi di vesciche.

blitz (blĭts) *n.* guerra lampo; bombardamento aereo.

blizzard (blĭz'ĕrd) *n.* tormenta.

bloat (blōt) *vt.* gonfiare, enfiare. *vi.* gonfiarsi.

block (blŏk) *n.* blocco, masso; ceppo; forma (*per cappelli*); manichino (*da parrucchieri*); carrucola, puleggia; (*tip.*) clichè; ostacolo; blocco di case, isolato urbano. *vt.* bloccare, ostacolare, opporsi a; ostruire.

blockade (blŏk-ād') *n.* assedio, blocco navale: to run the —, rompere il blocco. *vt.* bloccare.

blockhead (blŏk'hĕd) *n.* imbecille.

blond (blŏnd) *n.*, *agg.* biondo.

blonde (blŏnd) *n.*, *agg.* bionda.

blood (blŭd) *n.* sangue; parentela; temperamento; razza: in cold —, a sangue freddo, spietatamente; —poisoning, avvelenamento del sangue.

bloodhound (blŭd'hound') *n.* segugio.

bloodless *agg.* esangue; incruento.

bloodshed (-shĕd') *n.* spargimento di sangue.

bloodshot (-shŏt') *agg.* iniettato di sangue.

bloodthirsty (-thûrs'tĭ) *agg.* assetato di sangue, sanguinario.

bloody (blŭd'ĭ) *agg.* sanguinoso; insanguinato; maledetto.

bloom (blōōm) *n.* fiore, fioritura, freschezza. *vi.* fiorire, sbocciare. —ing, —y *agg.* fiorente, fiorito.

blossom (blŏs'ŭm) *n.* fiore, fioritura. *vi.* fiorire, essere in fiore, sbocciare.

blot (blŏt) *n.* macchia, chiazza. *vt.* macchiare, sporcare, scarabocchiare; cancellare; asciugare (con carta assorbente): to — out, cancellare; eliminare; celare alla vista. —ter *n.* carta assorbente; registro, brogliaccio. —ting-paper *n.* carta assorbente.

blotch (blŏch) *n.* pustola; macchia; scarabocchio. *vt.* macchiare.

blouse (blouz; blous) *n.* blusa.

blow (blō) *n.* colpo, ventata, folata; to come to blows, venire alle mani. *vt.*, *vi.* (*pass.* blew, *pp.* blown) soffiare, sbuffare, ansimare; suonare (*uno strumento a fiato*): to — away, spazzar via, dissipare; to — one's nose, soffiarsi il naso; to — out, soffiare, spegnere (*un lume*); to —

out one's brains, farsi saltar le cervella; to — over, dissiparsi, finire in niente; to — up, saltare in aria; (*fot.*) ingrandire. —er *n.* soffiatore; ventilatore, ventola; compressore; gradasso. —pipe *n.* tubo per soffiare il vetro; cerbottana.

blown (blōn) *pp.* di to blow.

bludgeon (blŭj'ŭn) *n.* randello, sfollagente. *vt.* tramortire.

blue (blōō) *n.* blu: to have the blues, avere la malinconia. *agg.* blu, turchino, azzurro; triste, melanconico: to be in a — funk, essere atterrito. *vt.* tingere di blu; (*metal.*) brunire.

bluebell (blōō'bĕl') *n.* giacinto.

bluebottle (blōō'bŏt''l) *n.* fiordaliso.

blueprint (blōō'prĭnt) *n.* cianotipia; progetto; programma d'azione. *vt.* pianificare.

bluff (blŭf) *n.* contrafforte di roccia (*sul mare*); millanteria, vanteria; inganno. *agg.* cordiale; brusco; scosceso.*vt.* millantare, imbrogliare.

bluffer (blŭf'ĕr) *n.* millantatore.

bluish (blōō'ĭsh) *agg.* bluastro.

blunder (blŭn'dĕr) *n.* abbaglio, papera, errore, stordITaggine. *vi.*, *vi.* commettere un errore, una papera.

blunt (blŭnt) *agg.* spuntato, ottuso; grossolano, brusco. *vt.* ottundere, spuntare. —ly *avv.* bruscamente, esplicitamente.

blur (blûr) *n.* macchia. *vt.* macchiare; confondere; offuscare.

blurt (blûrt) *vt.* parlare precipitosamente, rivelare (*un segreto, ecc.*) to — out, parlare storditamente, lasciarsi sfuggire.

blush (blŭsh) *n.* rossore. *vi.* arrossire.

bluster (blŭs'tĕr) *n.* frastuono, trambusto; fanfaronata; bufera; prepotenza. *vi.* infuriare (*degli elementi*); fare il gradasso; lanciar vane minacce. —ing *agg.* tempestoso, rumoroso, spavaldo.

boar (bōr) *n.* verro.

board (bōrd) *n.* tavola, asse; vitto, pensione; consiglio, consesso; scacchiera: above —, franco, a viso aperto; — and lodging, vitto e alloggio; — of directors, consiglio d'amministrazione; free on — (f.o.b.) franco bordo. *vt.* chiudere o coprire con tavole; prendere a pensione; (*naut.*) imbarcarsi su; salire su (*un treno, ecc.*); abbordare. *vi.* essere a pensione. —er *n.* pensionante. —inghouse *n.* pensione per famiglia.

boast (bōst) *vi.* vantarsi, gloriarsi. *vt.* vantare, decantare. *n.* vanteria. —er *n.* spaccone. —ful *agg.* vanaglorioso. —fulness *n.* vanagloria.

boat (bŏt) *n.* barca, canotto, imbarcazione. **—house** *n.* darsena. **—swain** (bō's'n; bŏt'swãn') *n.* nostromo. **—ing** *n.* canottaggio.

bob (bŏb) *n.* cenno del capo; colpetto; piombino; pendente, orecchino; peso (*del pendolo*); romano (*peso mobile di stadera*); taglio (*di capelli*) alla bebè; parrucca a riccioli; coda mozza; esca (*da lenza*); beffa; imbroglio; dondolio, scossa: **to wear a —,** avere i capelli alla bebè. *vt.* dondolare (*il capo, ecc.*): battere. *vi.* oscillare; agitarsi, saltellare: **to — up,** venire a galla, apparire all'improvviso; **to — up and down,** oscillare in su e in giù.

bobbin (bŏb'ĭn) *n.* bobina.

bobby-soxer (bŏb'ĭ-sŏk'sẽr) *n.f.* adolescente, ragazzina.

bode (bŏd) *pass., pp.* di to **bide.**

bodice (bŏd'ĭs) *n.* corpetto, busto.

bodily (bŏd'ĭ-lĭ) *agg.* corporeo, materiale. *avv.* materialmente; in massa; per intero; di peso.

body (bŏd'ĭ) *n.* corpo; gruppo; massa; raccolta; carrozzeria (*d'auto*); fusoliera (*d'aereo*): **in a —,** in massa.

bog (bŏg) *n.* palude, pantano. *vt.* impantanare.

boggle (bŏg''l) *vi.* esitare.

bogus (bō'gŭs) *agg.* finto, contraffatto.

bogy (bō'gĭ) *agg.* spauracchio, spettro.

Bohemian (bō.hē'mĭ.ăn) *n., agg.* boemo; bohemien.

boil (boil) *n.* bollire, ribollire. *vt.* cuocere a lesso, bollire: **to — down,** condensare; ridursi. *n.* ebollizione; foruncolo. **—er** *n.* caldaia.

boisterous (bois'tẽr.ŭs) *agg.* violento, rumoroso, turbolento, vivace, allegro.

bold (bŏld) *agg.* audace, temerario; impudente, sfacciato; chiaro, evidente: **to make — to,** prendersi la libertà di. **—faced** *agg.* impudente, sfrontato; (*tip.*) grassetto. **—ness** *n.* spavalderia, audacia; impudenza.

bolster (bŏl'stẽr) *n.* cuscino, traversino, cuscinetto, supporto. *vt.* reggere, sorreggere, sostenere: **to — up,** dar manforte a.

bolt (bŏlt) (1) *vt.* sprangare, scagliare. *vi.* scappare, spiccare un salto. *n.* catenaccio, chiavistello; fulmine; bullone; salto, balzo; (*naut.*) caviglia: **— upright,** diritto, irrigidito.

bolt (2) *vt.* setacciare, vagliare.

bomb (bŏm) *n.* bomba; bombola, spruzzatore. *vt., vi.* bombardare. **—er** *n.* bombardiere.

bombard (bŏm·bärd') *vt.* bombardare, cannoneggiare. **—ier** *n.* bombardiere. **—ment** *n.* bombardamento.

bombastic (bŏm·băs'tĭk) *agg.* tronfio, ampolloso.

bonanza (bō·năn'zả) *n.* fortuna, prosperità.

bond (bŏnd) *n.* vincolo, impegno, legame; (*comm.*) titolo, azione, obbligazione: **goods in —,** merci in sosta.

bondage (bŏn'dĭj) *n.* schiavitù.

bondholder (bŏnd'hŏld'ẽr) *n.* azionista.

bondman (bŏnd'măn) *n.* servo, schiavo.

bone (bŏn) *n.* osso; vertebra; lisca, stecca di balena; avorio; (*pl.*) ossatura; (*gergo*) dadi da gioco: **— of contention,** pomo della discordia; **to make no bones about it,** parlare esplicitamente, agire senza esitare, non farsi scrupoli; **to have a — to pick with,** avere un conto da regolare con. *vt.* disossare.

bonfire (bŏn'fīr') *n.* falò.

bonnet (bŏn'ĕt) *n.* berretto; (*naut.*) bonetta; (*autom.*) cofano.

bonus (bō'nŭs) *n.* gratifica, indennità, regalia, dividendo, premio.

bony (bŏn'ĭ) *agg.* ossuto, scarno, pieno di lische.

boo (bōō) *vt.* disapprovare con urlacci.

booby (bōō'bĭ) *n.* tonto, sciocco; (*sport*) schiappa. **—trap** *n.* tranello; mina nascosta.

book (bŏŏk) *n.* libro, libretto, registro, quaderno. *vt.* registrare; iscrivere; prenotare (*un posto*); scritturare.

bookcase (bŏŏk'kās') *n.* scaffale.

bookkeeper (bŏŏk'kēp'ẽr) *n.* contabile.

bookkeeping (bŏŏk'kēp'ĭng) *n.* contabilità.

booklet (bŏŏk'lĕt) *n.* opuscolo, libriccino.

bookmaker (bŏŏk'māk'ẽr) *n.* allibratore.

bookmark (bŏŏk'märk) *n.* segnalibro.

bookseller (bŏŏk'sĕl'ẽr) *n.* libraio.

bookshelf (bŏŏk'shĕlf) *n.* scaffale.

bookshop (bŏŏk'shŏp), **bookstore** (-stŏr) *n.* libreria.

bookstall (bŏŏk'stäl') *n.* edicola.

boom (bōōm) (1) *n.* (*naut.*) boma.

boom (bōōm) (2) *n.* rimbombo; boato; rialzo in borsa, risveglio negli affari. *vt.* sviluppare; lanciare (*un prodotto*); *vi.* rimbombare.

boon (bōōn) *n.* beneficio, vantaggio; favore. *agg.* gaio, benigno.

boor (bŏŏr) *n.* zotico. **—ish** *agg.* grossolano.

boost (bōōst) *n.* spinta in su, aiuto. *vt.* dare una spinta in su; aumentare (*i prezzi*).

boot (bōōt) (1) *n.* stivale, scarpa; congedo, licenziamento; recluta della marina: **to give the —,** cacciar via.

boot (bōōt) (2) *n.* profitto, vantaggio: **to —,** per soprammercato. *vi.* servire, giovare.

bootblack (bōōt′blăk) *n.* lustrascarpe.

booth (bōōth) *n.* baracca, sgabuzzino; cabina telefonica *o* di proiezione.

bootlegger (bōōt′lĕg′ĕr) *n.* contrabbandiere di alcool.

boots (bōōts) *n.* facchino d'albergo.

booty (bōō′tĭ) *n.* bottino.

booze (bōōz) *n.* (*gergo*) liquore spiritoso; orgia, sbornia.

border (bôr′dĕr) *n.* margine, orlo, ciglio; confine, frontiera; riva. *vt.* orlare; essere ai margini di, contiguo a; delimitare. *vi.*: **to — on, upon,** essere all'estremo limite di, confinare con, rasentare.

bore (bōr) (1) *vt.* bucare, forare, perforare. *n.* buco, calibro (*d'arma*).

bore (2) *vt.* annoiare, tediare; opprimere. *n.* noia, tedio; seccatore. **—dom** *n.* noia, stanchezza.

bore (3) *pass. di* to bear.

born (bôrn) *agg., pp. di* to bear, nato; innato: **to be —,** nascere, essere nato; **to be — again,** rinascere.

borne (bôrn) *pp. di* to bear.

borough (bŭr′ō) *n.* borgo; capoluogo; comune.

borrow (bŏr′ō) *vt.* farsi prestare, chiedere *o* prendere a prestito.

borrower (bŏr′ō-ĕr) *n.* chi prende a prestito.

bosom (bōōz′ŭm; bōō′zŭm) *n.* petto, seno: **— friend,** amico del cuore.

boss (bôs) *n.* protuberanza; mozzo (*di ruota*); padrone; capo. *vt.* comandare, dominare.

bossy (bôs′ĭ) *agg.* autoritario, dispotico.

botany (bŏt′ā·nĭ) *n.* botanica.

both (bōth) *agg., pron.* entrambi, l'uno e l'altro: **on — sides,** d'ambe le parti; **— of them,** tutti e due; **— this and that,** tanto questo quanto quello. *cong.* del pari. *avv.* ugualmente.

bother (bŏth′ĕr) *vt.* molestare, disturbare, irritare, infastidire, *vi.* preoccuparsi. *n.* seccatura, molestia, inconveniente. **—some** *agg.* seccante, molesto.

bottle (bŏt′'l) *n.* bottiglia. *vt.* imbottigliare.

bottom (bŏt′ŭm) *n.* fondo, base: **to sink to the —,** sprofondare, andare a fondo. *agg.* ultimo, infimo.

boudoir (bōō′dwär) *n.* stanza da letto di una signora.

bough (bou) *n.* ramo d'albero.

bought (bôt) *pass., pp. di* to buy.

boulder (bōl′dĕr) *n.* pietra, masso, roccia.

boulevard (bōō′lĕ·värd; bōōl′ĕ-) *n.* viale; corso.

bounce (bouns) *n.* balzo, rimbalzo; vanteria. *vt.* far saltare, far rimbalzare. *vi.* saltare, balzare, rimbalzare; slanciarsi; vantarsi.

bound (bound) *n.* limite, confine; balzo, salto; rimbalzo. *vt.* limitare, contenere, cintare. *vi.* balzare, saltare. *agg.* rilegato, legato, tenuto (*a*), obbligato, impegnato; diretto (*a*); in partenza (*per*): **— up in,** assorto in; **— to happen,** destinato ad accadere; **I feel — to say,** sento il dovere di dire. *pp. di* to bind.

boundary (boun′dā·rĭ) *n.* limite, frontiera, confine.

boundless *agg.* sconfinato, illimitato.

bountiful (boun′tĭ·fōōl; f'l) *agg.* generoso.

bounty (boun′tĭ) *n.* generosità, liberalità; indennità, gratifica.

bouquet (bōō·kā′) *n.* mazzo di fiori; aroma (*di vini o liquori*).

bourgeois (bōōr·zhwä′; bōōr′zhwä) *n., agg.* borghese.

bout (bout) *n.* colpo; turno, volta; attacco, accesso.

bow (bou) *vt.* piegare, curvare, inclinare: **to — one's head,** chinare il capo. *vi.* piegarsi, curvarsi, inchinarsi, sottomettersi, rassegnarsi. *n.* inchino, riverenza; (*bō*) arco (*per frecce*); archetto (*di violino*); arcione, nodo, nastro, fiocco; (bou) (*naut.*) prora. **—legged** *agg.* (bō-)sbilenco, con le gambe arcuate. **—sprit** (bou-) *n.* bompresso.

bowels (bou′ĕlz) *n.pl.*in testini, budella, viscere.

bower (bou′ĕr) *n.* pergolato.

bowl (bōl) *n.* vaso, coppa, ciotola, vaschetta; palla, boccia. *vt.* far rotolare. *vi.* giocare alle bocce: **to — over,** rovesciare, travolgere.

box (bŏks) (1) *n.* cassa, scatola, cassetta (*anche di vettura*); box (*di scuderia*), palco (*di teatro*); garritta, cabina, banco (*dei giurati o dei testimoni*). *vt.* incassare, mettere in cassa. **—office** *n.* botteghino (*di teatro*).

box (2) *n.* ceffone, pugno. *vi.* fare del pugilato, boxare. *vt.* schiaffeggiare, percuotere. **—er** *n.* pugile. **—ing** *n.* pugilato.

box (3) *n.* (*bot.*) bosso.

boy (boi) *n.* ragazzo, giovinetto; servitorello: **— Scout,** Giovane Esploratore.

boycott (boi′kŏt) *vt.* boicottare.

boyhood (boi'hŏŏd) *n.* infanzia.
boyish (boi'ĭsh) *n.* infantile, giovanile.
brace (brās) *n.* coppia (*al gioco dei dadi, ecc.*); paio; supporto, tirante; trapano; attacco; sospensione (*di un veicolo*); (*pl. in G.B.*) bretelle. *vt.* assicurare, agganciare, rafforzare: **to — up**, farsi forza.
bracelet (brās'lĕt) *n.* braccialetto; manetta.
bracket (brăk'ĕt) *n.* mensola; braccio (*supporto*); parentesi quadra. *vt.* munire di supporto; mettere tra parentesi quadre.
brag (brăg) *vi.* vantarsi, gloriarsi. *vt.* decantare. *n.* vanteria, fanfaronata. **—gart** *n.* fanfarone.
braid (brād) *n.* treccia (*di capelli*); spighetta. *vt.* intrecciare, rifinire, spighettare.
brain (brān) *n.* cervello; intelligenza: **to puzzle (to rack) one's brains**, lambiccarsi il cervello; **—trust**, consiglio di esperti. *vt.* far saltare le cervella a.
brake (brāk) *n.* freno; battitoio. *vt.* frenare. **—man** *n.* frenatore.
bramble (brăm'b'l), *n.* rovo.
bran (brăn) *n.* crusca.
branch (brănch) *n.* ramo, fronda; succursale, filiale; (*ferr.*) diramazione. *vi.* ramificarsi, biforcarsi, diramarsi.
brand (brănd) *n.* tizzone; marchio; stimmata; qualità. *vt.* marcare, marchiare, stigmatizzare. **—new** *agg.* nuovo di zecca.
brandish (brăn'dĭsh) *vt.* brandire.
brandy (brăn'dĭ) *n.* acquavite, cognac.
brash (brăsh) *agg.* avventato, impudente; friabile.
brass (brăs) *n.* ottone; quattrini; alti ufficiali: **as bold as —**, con faccia tosta; **to get down to — tacks**, venire al sodo; **—es**, ottoni (*strumenti musicali*); **— band**, banda (*mus.*).
brassy (brăs'ĭ) *agg.* d'ottone; impudente, sfrontato.
brassière (brá-zĕr') *n.* reggipetto.
brat (brăt) *n.* marmocchio.
bravado (brá-vä'dō) *n.* bravata; spavalderia.
brave (brāv) *agg.* coraggioso, ardito. *vt.* sfidare, affrontare. **—ry** *n.* ardimento.
brawl (brôl) *n.* zuffa, disputa; trambusto. *vi.* litigare.
brawn (brôn) *n.* muscolo, forza muscolare.
bray (brā) *n.* raglio. *vi.* ragliare.
brazen (brā'z'n) *agg.* di ottone; impudente, sfrontato.

breach (brēch) *n.* breccia; violazione, infrazione: **— of promise**, rottura di promessa; **— of trust**, abuso di fiducia. *vt.* far breccia in; infrangere.
bread (brĕd) *n.* pane: **new —**, pane fresco.
breadth (brĕdth) *n.* larghezza; ampiezza; (*tess.*) altezza.
break (brāk) *vt.* (*pass.* **broke**, *pp.* **broken**) rompere, frantumare; interrompere; domare; attutire; violare; rovinare; battere: **to — news**, comunicare notizie (*con delicatezza*); **to — in**, sfondare, irrompere; **to — in upon**, sorprendere; **to — loose**, liberarsi, scatenarsi; **to — up**, sciogliere, disperdere. *vi.* rompere; rompersi, frantumarsi; (*comm.*) fallire; sorgere (*dell'alba*); scoppiare (*di conflitti, ecc.*); declinare, indebolirsi: **to — away**, svincolarsi; **to — down**, battersi; guastarsi (*di auto, ecc.*); classificare, analizzare; **to — up**, separarsi, sciogliersi. *n.* rottura; apertura; interruzione; pausa; possibilità: **to give a — (gergo)**, concedere una possibilità.
breakdown (brāk'doun') *n.* crollo; collasso; incidente, guasto; insuccesso, catastrofe; classificazione, analisi: **nervous —**, esaurimento nervoso.
breaker (brāk'ĕr) *n.* violatore; domatore (*di cavalli*); maroso.
breakfast (brĕk'fást) *n.* prima colazione.
breakwater (brāk'wŏ'tĕr) *n.* tagliamare, diga.
breast (brĕst) *n.* petto, pettorale; seno; cuore, animo: **to make a clean — of it**, confessare tutto, vuotare il sacco. *vt.* affrontare.
breath (brĕth) *n.* respiro, soffio, fiato: **short of —**, ansimante; **out of —**, sfiatato, ansante.
breathe (brēth) *vi., vt.,* respirare; prendere fiato; sbuffare; sussurrare.
bred (brĕd) *pass., pp. di* **to breed**: **well —**, beneducato; **ill —**, maleducato.
breech (brēch) *n.* deretano, parte posteriore; culatta (*di cannone, ecc.*).
breeches (brĭch'ĕz) *n.pl.* brache, calzoni da cavallo.
breed (brēd) *vt.* (*pass., pp.* **bred**) generare, mettere al mondo; allevare; causare. *vi.* moltiplicarsi; nascere; riprodursi. *n.* razza, covata; origine, schiatta. **—er** *n.* allevatore. **—ing** *n.* allevamento; educazione: **good — compitezza**.
breeze (brēz) *n.* brezza.

breezy (brēz'ĭ) *agg.* ventilato; vivace; loquace.

brethren (brĕth'rĕn) *n.pl.* frati; confratelli.

brevity (brĕv'ĭ·tĭ) *n.* brevità, concisione.

brew (brōō) *vt., vi.* preparare (*il tè*); manipolare; fabbricare (*birra, ecc.*); tramare, complottare; fermentare, maturare: **something is brewing**, qualcosa bolle in pentola. **—er** *n.* birraio. **—ery** *n.* fabbrica di birra.

briar (brī'ẽr) *n.* radica; rosa selvatica, rovo; pipa di radica.

bribe (brīb) *n.* regalo (*per corrompere*), "bustarella"; allettamento. *vt.* corrompere, allettare.

bribery (brīb'ẽr·ĭ) *n.* corruzione, subornazione.

brick (brĭk) *n.* mattone. *vt.* mattonare.

bridal (brīd'ăl) *agg.* nuziale. *n.* nozze.

bride (brīd) *n.* sposa, sposina.

bridegroom (brīd'grōōm') *n.* sposo.

bridesmaid (brīdz'mād') *n.* damigella d'onore.

bridesman (brīdz'măn) *n.* testimonio alle nozze.

bridge (brĭj) *n.* ponte, passerella; ponticello (*di strumento a corda*). *vt.* gettare un ponte; congiungere. **—head** *n.* testa di ponte.

bridle (brī'd'l) *n.* briglia, freno; (*naut.*) cavo d'ormeggio. *vt.* imbrigliare, metter la briglia a; frenare. *vi.* drizzare il capo; impennarsi. **—path** *n.* sentiero per cavalli.

brief (brēf) *agg.* breve, conciso, corto. *n.* breve papale; lettera; esposto, memoriale; riassunto; citazione; *vt.* dare le ultime istruzioni (*a un equipaggio militare prima di un'-azione*); mettere al corrente. **—case** *n.* cartella, borsa da avvocato. **—ing** *n.* ultime istruzioni; ragguagli. **—ly** *avv.* brevemente.

brig (brĭg) *n.* brigantino; (*naut.*) prigione.

brigade (brĭ·gād') *n.* brigata: **fire —**, vigili del fuoco.

brigand (brĭg'ănd) *n.* brigante.

bright (brīt) *agg.* chiaro, luminoso; lucido, brillante, scintillante; allegro; bello; intelligente.

brighten (brīt'n) *vt.* rischiarare, illuminare, rallegrare, lucidare, abbellire. *vi.* rischiararsi, brillare; rallegrarsi: **to — up**, rasserenarsi.

brightness (brīt'nĕs) *n.* chiarità, chiarore; luminosità, scintillio; allegria.

brilliance (brĭl'yăns) **brilliancy** (brĭl'yăn·sĭ) *n.* intelligenza; splendore, scintillio.

brilliant (brĭl'yănt) *agg.* intelligente; brillante, splendente.

brim (brĭm) *n.* bordo, orlo (*di recipiente*), ala, tesa (*di cappello*). *vi.*: **to — over**, traboccare.

brine (brīn) *n.* acqua salata, acqua di mare, mare.

bring (brĭng) *vt.* (*pass., pp.* **brought**) portare, recare, condurre; indurre, provocare: **to — forth**, produrre, mettere alla luce; **to — out**, far uscire, far apparire, pubblicare; **to — up**, allevare, educare; **to — up the rear**, chiudere la marcia.

brink (brĭngk) *n.* orlo, limite estremo.

brisk (brĭsk) *agg.* vivace, svelto; sbrigativo; frizzante. **—ly** *avv.* vivacemente. **—ness** *n.* vivacità.

bristle (brĭs'l) *vi.* drizzare il pelo; irrigidirsi; mettersi sulla difensiva. *n.* setola.

bristly (brĭs'lĭ) **bristling** (brĭs'lĭng) *agg.* irto, irsuto.

British (brĭt'ĭsh) *agg.* britannico, inglese.

brittle (brĭt'l) *agg.* fragile, friabile.

broach (brōch) *n.* spiedo; trapano. *vt.* mettere allo spiedo; perforare; affrontare o svolgere (*un argomento*).

broad (brōd) *agg.* largo, ampio, vasto; grossolano, esplicito: **— daylight**, pieno giorno. **—ly** *avv.* esplicitamente, largamente. **—minded** *agg.* spregiudicato; indulgente; di larghe vedute.

broadcast (brōd'kást') *n.* radiodiffusione, trasmissione, emissione; diffusione. *vt.* radiodiffondere, trasmettere; diffondere.

broadcloth (brōd'klŏth') *n.* panno.

broaden (brōd''n) *vi.* allargarsi, estendersi. *vt.* allargare.

broadness *n.* larghezza; volgarità.

broadside (brōd'sīd') *n.* (*naut.*) bordo; bordata.

brocade (brō·kād') *n.* broccato.

broil (broil) *n.* tafferuglio, lite. *vt.* arrostire in graticola. *vi.* abbrustolirsi; fremere d'impazienza.

broke (brōk) *agg.* rovinato; al verde. *pass. di* to break.

broken (brō'kĕn) *agg.* rotto; sconnesso; incerto; interrotto; affranto: **— English**, inglese imperfetto. *pp. di* to break.

broker (brō'kĕr) *n.* mediatore, sensale; agente di cambio.

bronchitis (brŏn·kī'tĭs; brŏng-) *n.* bronchite.

bronco (brŏng'kō) *n.* cavallo selvaggio.

bronze (brŏnz) *n.* bronzo. *agg.* bronzeo. *vt., vi.* bronzare, abbronzare.

brooch (brōch; brōōch) *n.* spilla, spillone.

brood (brōōd) *n.* covata. *vt.* covare; arzigogolare. *vi.* arrovellarsi: **to — on (over)**, meditare su; ruminare.

brooder (brōōd'ĕr) *n.* incubatrice.

brook (brōŏk) *n.* ruscello; *vt.* sopportare.

broom (brōōm) *n.* scopa, saggina. **—stick** *n.* manico di scopa.

broth (brŏth) *n.* brodo.

brothel (brŏth'ĕl; brŏth'-) *n.* postribolo, bordello.

brother (brŭth'ĕr) *n.* fratello.

brotherhood (brŭth'ĕr·hŏŏd) *n.* confraternità, fratellanza.

brother-in-law *n.* cognato.

brotherly (brŭth'ĕr lĭ) *agg.* fraterno.

brought (brôt) *pass., pp. di* to bring.

brow (brou) *n.* ciglio, sopracciglio; fronte; sommità.

browbeat (brou'bēt') *vt.* intimorire.

brown (broun) *agg.* bruno, marrone; scuro; castagno; abbronzato; rosolato. *vt., vi.* brunire; scurire; rosolare; rosolarsi.

browse (brouz) *vt., vi.* brucare, pascolare; leggiucchiare.

bruise (brōōz) *n.* contusione, ammaccatura. *vt.* ammaccare, percuotere, frantumare.

bruiser (brōōz'ĕr) *n.* pugile; gradasso.

brunette (brōō-nĕt') *agg.* bruno. *n.f.* bruna, brunetta.

brunt (brŭnt) *n.* urto; furore.

brush (brŭsh) *n.* spazzola; pennello; coda (*di volpe*); scaramuccia, tafferuglio; colpo di spazzola; (*elett.*) scarica; conduttore volante. *vt.* spazzolare; sfiorare; rasentare: **to — away**, spazzar via; **to — past**, passare alla svelta, rasentare; **to — up**, ripulire; ripassare (*una materia*).

brusque (brŭsk; brōōsk) *agg.* brusco, ruvido.

brutal (brōō'tăl) *agg.* brutale, crudele. **—ity** *n.* brutalità, crudeltà.

brute (brōōt) *n.* bestia, animale, bruto. *agg.* bestiale, irragionevole, selvatico.

brutish (brōōt'ĭsh) *agg.* brutale.

bubble (bŭb''l) *n.* bolla, bollicina; fantasticheria. *vi.* far bollicine: **to — with**, sprizzare.

buck (bŭk) *n.* daino, capriolo; maschio (*di lepre o coniglio*); (gergo, S.U.) dollaro: **— private**, recluta. **to pass the —**, scaricare la responsabilità (*addosso a qualcuno*). *vi.* sgroppare.

bucket (bŭk'ĕt) *n.* secchio: **— seat**, strapuntino.

buckle (bŭk''l) *n.* fibbia. *vt.* allacciare, agganciare; contorcere; accartocciare. **to — down to**, dedicarsi a, accingersi a.

buckram (bŭk'răm) *n.* tela da fusto, garza.

buckshot (buk'shŏt') *n.* pallini da fucile (*per caccia grossa*).

buckwheat (buk'hwēt') *n.* grano saraceno.

bud (bŭd) *n.* germoglio, bocciolo; (*gergo*) amico, compare. *vt.* innestare (*piante*). *vi.* germogliare.

buddy (bŭd'ĭ) *n.* amico, compare.

budge (bŭj) *vi.* muoversi. *vt.* far muovere, smuovere.

budget (bŭj'ĕt; -ĭt) *n.* sacco; bilancio, stanziamento. *vt., vi.* stanziare; fare un bilancio.

buff (bŭf) (1) *n.* pelle di bufalo; pelle nuda. *agg.* marrone chiaro. *vt.* lucidare, tingere color camoscio.

buff (2) *n.* colpo, buffetto: **blindman's —**, mosca cieca. **—er** *n.* respingente (*di vagone, ecc.*); cuscinetto.

buffet (bŏŏ-fā'; bŭ-fā'; bōō-fā') *n.* buffet, ristorante; credenza; (bŭf'ĕt) pugno, ceffone.

buffoon (bŭ-fōōn'; bŭ-) *n.* buffone.

bug (bŭg) *n.* cimice; insetto; difetto: **big —** (*gergo*), pezzo grosso.

bugbear (bŭg'bâr') *n.* spauracchio.

buggy (bŭg'ĭ) *n.* calesse; carrello, vagoncino.

bugle (bū'g'l) *n.* corno da caccia; tromba. *vi.* strombettare.

bugler (bū'glĕr) *n.* trombettiere.

build (bĭld) *vt.* (*pass., pp.* built) costruire; fondare, creare; basare: **to — up one's health**, rimettersi in salute. *n.* struttura; corporatura. **—er** *n.* costruttore. **—ing** *n.* fabbricato, edificio. **buildup** (bĭld'ŭp') *n.* propaganda, soffietto.

bulb (bŭlb) *n.* bulbo, globo; lampadina.

bulge (bŭlj) *n.* protuberanza, gonfiore. *vi.* gonfiarsi, sporgere.

bulgy (bul'jĭ) *agg.* rigonfio.

bulk (bŭlk) *n.* massa, volume, quantità; (*naut.*) carico.

bulkhead (bŭlk'hĕd') *n.* paratia.

bulky (bŭl'kĭ) *agg.* voluminoso, ingombrante.

bull (bŏŏl) (1) *n.* bolla (*papale*).

bull (2) *n.* toro; maschio (*di elefante, ecc.*); (*borsa*) rialzista. *vt.* (*borsa*) giocare al rialzo. **—dog** *n.* molosso. **—fight** *n.* corrida di tori. **—fighter** *n.* torero.

bull's-eye *n.* occhio di bue (*finestrino*); lente convessa; centro del bersaglio.

bulldozer (bŏŏl'dŏz'ĕr) *n.* gradasso, prepotente; (*mecc.*) livellatrice.

bullet (bŏŏl'ĕt) *n.* pallottola.

bulletin (bŏŏl'ĕ·tĭn) *n.* bollettino.

bullion (bŏŏl'yŭn) n. oro o argento in lingotti; frangia d'oro.

bullock (bŏŏl'ŭk) n. manzo (animale).

bully (bŏŏl'ĭ) n. gradasso, prepotente; briccone. agg. magnifico, formidabile. vt. maltrattare; costringere con violenza.

bulwark (bŏŏl'wĕrk) n. contrafforte, parapetto; baluardo.

bum (bŭm) n. vagabondo, pelandrone; scroccone; orgia; gozzoviglia: to go on a —, fare gozzoviglia; to feel —, essere indisposto. vi. vivere di scrocco.

bumblebee (bŭm'b'l-bē') n. calabrone.

bump (bŭmp) n. colpo; bernoccolo. vt. battere, urtare. vi. sbattere (urtare contro qualcosa). —er n. respingente, paraurti. agg. abbondante.

bumptious (bŭmp'shŭs) agg. tronfio, presuntuoso.

bun (bŭn) n. panino; pasticcino.

bunch (bŭnch) n. fascio, mazzo (di fiori, chiavi, ecc.), grappolo. vt. riunire in mazzo. vi. riunirsi, raggrupparsi, far massa.

bundle (bŭn'd'l) n. fagotto, involto, pacco, fascio, ammasso, mucchio (di carte). vt. impaccare, imballare. vi. : to — off (out), uscire frettolosamente; to — up, infagottarsi.

bung (bŭng) n. zaffo, zipolo, tappo; budello (per salami); bugia.

bungalow (bŭng'gà-lō) n. casetta a un piano.

bungle (bŭng'g'l) n. lavoro malfatto. vt. rovinare, guastare, eseguire malamente. vi. lavorare alla carlona.

bungler (bŭng'glĕr) n. incapace, pasticcione.

bunion (bŭn'yŭn) n. gonfiore, protuberanza.

bunk (bŭngk) n. cuccetta, letto; fuga; sciocchezza.

bunker (bŭngk'ĕr) n. (naut.) carbonile; (mil.) casamatta.

bunny (bŭn'ĭ) n. coniglietto; scoiattolino.

buoy (bōō'ĭ; boi) n. boa: life —, salvagente. vt. mantenere a galla; delimitare con boe: to — up, rincuorare. —ancy n. leggerezza; galleggiabilità; gaiezza, esuberanza. —ant agg. galleggiante; allegro; esuberante.

burden (bûr'd'n) n. fardello, carico; peso; soma. vt. caricare, gravare. —some agg. greve, pesante; noioso.

bureau (bū'rō) n. ufficio, studio; comò: travel —, ufficio turistico; weather —, ufficio meteorologico.

bureaucracy (bú-rŏk'rá-sĭ; bû-rō'krá-sĭ) n. burocrazia.

burglar (bûr'glĕr) n. ladro, scassinatore.

burglary (bûr'glá-rĭ) n. furto con scasso.

burial (bĕr'ĭ-ăl) n. sepoltura, inumazione. — ground n. cimitero.

burlap (bûr'lăp) n. tela da sacco.

burlesque (bûr-lĕsk') n. farsa, parodia, spettacolo comico. agg. burlesco.

burly (bûr'lĭ) agg. corpulento, ruvido, bonario.

burn (bûrn) n. bruciatura, ustione. vt. (pass., pp. burnt, burned) bruciare, incendiare; cauterizzare; cuocere (mattoni, ecc.). vi. bruciare, divampare; brillare; scottare. —er n. bruciatore; becco (a gas, ecc.). —ing n. bruciatura; combustione, incendio; infiammazione. agg. ardente, bruciante, rovente. —ing glass n. specchio ustorio.

burnish (bûr'nĭsh) n. brunitura; lucidatura. vt. brunire; lucidare.

burnt (bûrnt) pass., pp. di to burn.

burrow (bûr'ō) n. tana, buca. vi. rintanarsi, nascondersi.

burst (bûrst) n. scoppio, esplosione, impeto, accesso (di collera, ecc.). vt., vi. (pass., pp. burst) far scoppiare, fendere, sfondare, prorompere, traboccare, irrompere; scoppiare, esplodere; sfogarsi: to — open, forzare, sfondare, spalancare; to — into, irrompere in; to — into tears, scoppiare in lagrime.

bury (bĕr'ĭ) vt. (pass., pp. buried) seppellire, sotterrare; sprofondare; nascondere.

bus (bŭs) n. autobus. —man n. conducente d'autobus.

bush (bŏŏsh) n. cespuglio, macchia, boschetto; foresta: to beat about the —, menare il can per l'aia.

bushel (bŏŏsh'ĕl) n. staio.

busily (bĭz'ĭ-lĭ) avv. attivamente, energicamente; con aria affaccendata.

business (bĭz'nĕs) n. affare, affari, commercio; professione, occupazione; compito, missione: mind your own —, badate agli affari vostri; to make it one's —, provvedere, assumersi il compito. —like agg. pratico, sbrigativo, disinvolto; metodico, preciso.

bust (bŭst) n. busto. vi. andare in malora. vt. far saltare, mandare in rovina; (gergo mil.) degradare; domare (un cavallo).

bustle (bŭs'l) n. movimento, trambusto, frastuono, attività, tramestio. vi. darsi attorno, affaccendarsi, affannarsi. vt. sollecitare, stimolare.

busy (bĭz'ĭ) *agg.* occupato; affannato; attivo; movimentato; affaccenda- to. *vt.* : to — oneself, occuparsi, affaccendarsi. —body *n.* ficcanaso.

but (bŭt) *cong.*, *prep.*, *avv.* ma, però, eccetto, salvo, a eccezione di; che non; soltanto, esclusivamente: **no one — you**, nessuno eccetto voi; **— for**, senza, in mancanza di; **— for him**, se non fosse (stato) per lui; **the last — one**, il penultimo; **I can —**, non posso a meno di; **it is — a scratch**, è soltanto un graffio; **all —**, quasi, pressochè; **all — dead**, pressochè morto.

butcher (bŏŏch'ĕr) *n.* macellaio. *vt.* macellare; massacrare; rovinare.

butchery (bŏŏch'ĕr·ĭ) *n.* macello; strage.

butler (bŭt'lĕr) *n.* maggiordomo.

butt (bŭt) *n.* estremità: mozzicone; bersaglio; meta, limite, cornata, testata; calcio (*di fucile, ecc.*): **— end**, estremità; impugnatura; calcio (*d'arma da fuoco*). *vt.*, *vi.* dar testate (o cornate) a; urtare; essere adiacente; congiungere testa a testa: **to — out**, sporgere, sbucare; **to — in**, intromettersi, interloquire.

butter (bŭt'ĕr) *n.* burro. *vt.* imburrare. —cup *n.* ranuncolo. —milk *n.* siero.

butterfly (bŭt'ĕr·flī') *n.* farfalla.

buttocks (bŭt'ŭks) *n.pl.* natiche, dere- tano.

button (bŭt'n) *n.* bottone; pulsante. *vt.* abbottonare.

buttonhole (bŭt'n·hōl') *n.* occhiello, asola. *vt.* fare gli occhielli a; trat- tenere; attaccare un bottone a.

buttonhook (bŭt'n·hŏŏk') *n.* allaccia- bottoni.

buttons *n.* inserviente in livrea.

buttress (bŭt'rĕs) *n.* contrafforte, spe- rone. *vt.* rinforzare; sostenere; av- valorare.

buxom (bŭk'sŭm) *agg.* gagliardo, allegro, esuberante; malleabile; procace.

buy (bī) *vt.* (*pass.*, *pp.* **bought**) com- perare, acquistare; corrompere, subornare: **to — off**, comperare, corrompere; riscattare; **to — out**, liquidare (*un azionista, ecc.*); rile- vare in blocco; **to — over**, corrom- pere; **to — up**, accaparrare.

buyer (bī'ĕr) *n.* compratore, acquiren- te.

buzz (bŭz) *n.* ronzio, brusio; (*gergo*) telefonata. *vi.* ronzare; (*aeron.*) volare a bassissima quota.

buzzard (bŭz'ĕrd) *n.* (*ornit.*) poiana.

by (bī) *prep.* per, di, a, su, presso, accanto, durante, per opera di: **— night**, di notte; **— far**, di gran lunga; **— no means**, per niente affatto; **— dint of**, a forza di; **— the way**, a proposito, tra parentesi; **— tomorrow**, entro domani; **one — one**, a uno a uno. *avv.* presso, vi- cino; via, da parte: **— and large**, complessivamente, tutto, consi- derato; **to stand —**, esser presen- te, tenersi pronto a intervenire; **— and —**, fra poco, di lì a poco; **days gone —**, giorni lontani.

bye-bye (bī'bī) *int.* arrivederci, ciao.

bygone (bī'gŏn') *agg.* passato, andato: **to let bygones be bygones**, mettere una pietra sul passato.

bylaw (bī'lâ') *n.* legge locale, con- suetudine, regolamento.

by-line *n.* occupazione secondaria; (*giorn.*) firma.

byname *n.* soprannome.

bypass *n.* circonvallazione esterna; via secondaria.

bypath (bī'pȧth'), **byroad** (bī'rōd'), **byway** (bī'wā') *n.* strada privata, deviazione, scorciatoia.

by-product *n.* sottoprodotto.

bystander (bī'stăn'dĕr) *n.* astante, spettatore.

byword (bī'wûrd') *n.* proverbio, epi- teto; oggetto di derisione.

C

cab (kăb) *n.* carrozza di piazza; auto- pubblica; cabina (*d'autocarro o di locomotiva*). **—man**, **—driver** *n.* vetturino; autista di piazza.

cabbage (kăb'ĭj) *n.* cavolo, verza.

cabin (kăb'ĭn) *n.* capanna, baracca; cabina: **— class passenger**, pass- eggero di classe cabina.

cabinet (kăb'ĭ·nĕt) *n.* armadietto; gabinetto, studio.

cable (kā'b'l) *n.* gomena; cablogram- ma; cavo. *vt.* ormeggiare; telegra- fare: **— address**, indirizzo telegra- fico. —gram *n.* cablogramma.

cackle (kăk''l) *n.* verso (*della gallina, ecc.*); cicaleccio, chiacchierio. *vi.* chiocciare, ciarlare, blaterare.

cad (kăd) *n.* furfante; buono a nulla.

cadaverous (kȧ·dăv'ĕr·ŭs) *agg.* ca- daverico; scarno; pallidissimo.

caddie (kăd'ĭ) *n.* porta-mazze (*al golf*).

cadence (kā'dĕns) *n.* cadenza.

cadet (kȧ·dĕt') *n.* cadetto.

café (kȧ·fā') *n.* caffè (*ritrovo*), risto- rante: **— society**, frequentatori dei ritrovi eleganti.

cafeteria (kăf'ê·tēr'ĭ·á) *n.* (*S.U.*) mensa, bar-ristorante (*dove il cliente si serve da sè*); tavola calda.

cage (kāj) *n.* gabbia (*anche fig.*) *vt.* mettere in gabbia.

cagey (kāj'ĭ) *agg.* (*gergo*) astuto; cauto.

cake (kāk) *n.* focaccia, pasticcino; pezzo; crosta; grumo: a — of soap, una saponetta. *vi.* indurirsi, consolidarsi, incrostarsi; coagularsi.

calamity (ká·lăm'ĭ·tĭ) *n.* calamità.

calcium (kăl'sĭ·ŭm) *n.* calcio (*metallo*).

calculate (kăl'kû·lāt) *vt.* calcolare, valutare.

calculating machine *n.* macchina calcolatrice.

calculation (-lā'shŭn) *n.* calcolo.

calculus (kăl'kû·lŭs) *n.* calcolo.

calendar (kăl'ĕn·dẽr) *n.* calendario; programma: — month, mese solare.

calender (kăl'ĕn·dẽr) *n.* calandra. *vt.* calandrare.

calf (kăf) *n.* (*pl.* calves [kăvz]) vitello; (*anat.*) polpaccio.

caliber (kăl'ĭ·bẽr) *n.* calibro.

calico (kăl'ĭ·kō) *n.* calicò, cotone stampato.

calipers (kăl'ĭ·pẽrz) *n.pl.* compassi.

calisthenics (kăl'ĭs·thĕn'ĭks) *n. sing.* e *pl.* ginnastica a corpo libero.

call (kôl) *n.* chiamata, appello, grido, richiamo; visita; diritto; eccitamento sessuale, foia: to have no — to, non avere il diritto di. *vt., vi.* chiamare, gridare; convocare, richiamare: to — upon somebody, far visita a qualcuno; to — at a port, fare scalo a un porto; to — for, richiedere; esigere; to — the roll, far l'appello; to — together, radunare; to — up, richiamare alla memoria; convocare; presentare (*un'istanza, un disegno di legge, ecc.*); telefonare a; chiamare alle armi. —er *n.* visitatore.

calling (kôl'ĭng) *n.* professione; vocazione.

callous (kăl'ŭs) *agg.* calloso; insensibile, spietato.

callow (kăl'ō) *agg.* imberbe, inesperto.

callus (kăl'ŭs) *n.* callo; callosità.

calm (käm) *agg.* calmo, quieto. *n.* calma, quiete. *vt.* calmare. *vi.* calmarsi. —ly *avv.* tranquillamente, quietamente. —ness *n.* placidità, calma.

calvary (kăl'vá·rĭ) *n.* calvario.

cam (kăm) *n.* (*mecc.*) camma, eccentrico.

camber (kăm'bẽr) *vt.* arcuare, curvare.

cambric (kām'brĭk) *n.* batista.

came (kām) *pass. di* to come.

camel (kăm'ĕl) *n.* cammello.

camelopard (ká·mĕl'ō·pärd) *n.* giraffa.

camera (kăm'ẽr·á) *n.* macchina fotografica: motion picture —, macchina da presa; candid —, macchina fotografica in miniatura (*per scattare fotografie di nascosto*).

cameraman (-măn) *n.* operatore (*cinematografico*).

camouflage (kăm'ŏŏ·fläzh) *n.* mascheramento, mimetizzazione. *vt.* mascherare, mimetizzare.

camp (kămp) *n.* campo, accampamento. *vi.* accamparsi.

campaign (kăm·pān') *n.* (*mil.* e *pol.*) campagna. *vi.* fare una campagna; fare propaganda.

camphor (kăm'fẽr) *n.* canfora.

can (kăn) (1) *n.* barattolo, lattina, scatoletta, latta, bidone: — opener, apriscatole. *vt.* mettere in scatola: canned food, cibi in scatola.

can (kăn) (2) *v.* ausiliare difettivo (*negativo* cannot; *pass.* could; *non ha infinito nè pp.*) potere, essere in grado di; sapere, essere capace di: I — help you, io posso aiutarvi; I — speak Italian, so parlare l'italiano.

Canadian (ká·nā'd ăn) *n.*, *agg.* canadese.

canal (ká·năl') *n.* canale.

canary (ká·nâr'ĭ) *n.* canarino.

cancel (kăn's'l) *vt.* annullare, disdire, cancellare, revocare. —ation (-ā'shŭn) *n.* cancellazione, annullamento, revoca.

cancer (kăn'sẽr) *n.* cancro.

candid (kăn'dĭd) *agg.* candido, franco, ingenuo: — camera, macchinetta fotografica (*per scattare fotografie di nascosto*).

candidacy (kăn'dĭ·dá·sĭ) *n.* candidatura.

candidate (kăn'dĭ·dāt) *n.* candidato.

candle (kăn'd'l) *n.* candela, lume. —stick *n.* candeliere, candelabro.

candor (kăn'dẽr) *n.* candore, ingenuità.

candy (kăn'dĭ) *n.* candito. *vt.* candire.

cane (kān) *n.* canna, giunco, bastone: — chair, sedia di vimini; — sugar, zucchero di canna.

canine (kā'nĭn) *n.*, *agg.* canino.

canister (kăn'ĭs·tẽr) *n.* scatola di latta, barattolo; (*U.S.*) bidoncino per carburante.

canker (kăng'kẽr) *n.* canchero, cancrena delle piante; tara.

canned (kănd) *agg.* in barattoli: — food, scatolame, cibi in scatola.

cannibal (kăn'ĭ·băl) *n.* cannibale, antropofago.

canniness (kăn'ĭ·nĕs) *n.* astuzia.

cannon (kăn'ŭn) n. cannone; (bili-ardo) carambola. vt., vi. sparare il cannone; far carambola; urtare.

cannonade (kăn'ŭn·ād') n. cannonata. vt. bombardare, cannoneggiare.

canny (kăn'ĭ) agg. astuto, furbo.

canoe (kả·nōō') n. canoa, piroga.

canon (kăn'ŭn) n. canonico; canone (regola), norma, criterio.

canopy (kăn'ō·pĭ) n. baldacchino; volta; (aeron.) tetto (dell'abita-colo).

cant (kănt) (1) n. linguaggio ipocrita; affettazione; gergo; cantilena.

cant (2) (kănt) n. inclinazione. vi. inclinarsi, pendere.

cantaloupe (kăn'tả·lōp) n. melone.

cantankerous (kăn·tăng'kẽr·ŭs) agg. bisbetico.

canteen (kăn·tēn') n. spaccio; borrac-cia.

canter (kăn'tẽr) n. piccolo galoppo.

cantilever (kăn'tĭ·lē'vẽr) n. trave a sbalzo.

canton (kăn'tŏn) n. cantone, regione.

canvas (kăn'vȧs) n. canovaccio, tela; vela: under — (naut.), a vele spie-gate.

canvass (kăn'vȧs) n. dibattito, di-scussione, vaglio; sollecitazione di suffragi; (comm.) raccolta di or-dinazioni. vt. discutere, sollecitare. vi. sollecitare suffragi; (comm.) fare la piazza. —er n. agente elettorale; piazzista; propagandista.

canyon (kăn'yŭn) n. burrone.

caoutchouc (kōō'chŏŏk) n. caucciù; gomma.

cap (kăp) n. berretto, cuffia; (gergo) capsula; calotta. vt. coprire, in-cappucciare; superare, eccellere.

capability (kā'pả·bĭ'lĭ·tĭ) n. capacità, abilità.

capable (kā'pả·b'l) agg. capace, abile.

capacious (kả·pā'shŭs) agg. ampio, capace, vasto, spazioso.

capacity (kả·păs'ĭ·tĭ) n. capacità, veste: in the — of, in veste (in qualità) di.

cape (kāp) (1) n. cappa.

cape (kāp) (2) n. (geog.) capo.

caper (kā'pẽr) n. capriola: to cut capers, fare capriole.

capillary (kăp'ĭ·lẽr'ĭ) agg. capillare.

capital (kăp'ĭ·tăl) n. capitale, patri-monio; (città) capitale; (lettera) maiuscola; (arch.) capitello. agg. maiuscolo; capitale; eccellente, perfetto.

capitalism (kăp'ĭ·tăl·ĭz'm) n. capi-talismo.

capitalist (-ĭst) n.capitalista.

capitalization (-ĭ·zā'shŭn) n. capi-talizzazione.

capitalize (-īz) vt. capitalizzare; scri-vere con la maiuscola.

capitol (kăp'ĭ·tŏl) n. campidoglio.

capitulate (kả·pĭt'ū·lāt) vi. capitolare.

capitulation n. capitolazione.

capon (kā'pŏn) n. cappone.

caprice (kả·prēs') n. capriccio.

capricious (kả·prĭsh'ŭs) agg. capric-cioso, estroso.

capsizal (kăp·sīz'ăl) n. capovolgimen-to.

capsize (kăp·sīz') vt. capovolgere. vi. capovolgersi.

capstan (kăp'stăn) n. argano.

capsule (kăp'sūl) n. capsula; riassun-to, compendio; agg., riassuntivo, compendioso; in miniatura; aero-dinamico; vt. delineare, riassumere.

captain (kăp'tĭn) n. capitano, coman-dante. vt. capitanare.

caption (kăp'shŭn) n. intestazione (di capitolo); didascalia.

captivate (kăp'tĭ·vāt) vt. conquistare; accattivarsi; sedurre; sottomettere.

captivating agg. seducente.

captive (kăp'tĭv) n., agg. prigioniero.

captivity (kăp'tĭv'ĭ·tĭ) n. prigionia.

captor (kăp'tẽr) n. chi eseguisce una cattura.

capture (kăp'tựr) n. cattura. vt. cattu-rare.

car (kär) n. carro; automobile; navi-cella (di aerostato); carrozza, vet-tura, vagone.

caramel (kär'ả·měl) n. caramella.

carat (kär'ăt) n. carato.

caravan (kär'ả·văn) n. carovana; furgone; casa-rimorchio, roulotte.

carbide (kär'bĭd) n. carburo.

carbolic (kär·bŏl'ĭk) agg. fenico.

carbon (kär'bŏn) n. carbone; car-bonio: — paper, cartacarbone.

carbuncle (kär'bŭng'k'l) n. carbon-chio; foruncolo.

carburetor (kär'bū·rā'tẽr) n. carbura-tore.

carcass, carcase (kär'kȧs) n. carcassa, carogna.

card (kärd) (1) n. biglietto; carta da gioco; partecipazione; tessera: in the cards, assai probabile; — index, schedario.

card (kärd) (2) n. carda. vt. cardare.

cardboard (kärd'bōrd') n. cartone.

cardholder (kärd'hōl'dẽr) n. socio (di una biblioteca, ecc.); tesserato.

cardigan (kär'dĭ·găn) n. giubbetto di lana.

cardinal (kär'dĭ·năl) n. cardinale. agg. cardinale; principale, fonda-mentale.

cardsharper (kärd'shär'pẽr) n. baro.

care (kär) n. cura, cautela; preoccupa-zione; sollecitudine; ansietà: to

take — of, aver cura di, fare attenzione a. *vi.* interessarsi; voler bene; curarsi; provvedere; preoccuparsi: **to — for,** interessarsi, di apprezzare, avere simpatia per, voler bene a; **I don't —,** non me ne importa; **I don't — for this,** questo non mi piace.

careen (kȧ·rēn') *vt.* inclinare. *vi.* inclinarsi.

career (kȧ·rēr') *n.* carriera (*in tutte le accez.*) *vi.* correre.

careful (kâr'fŏŏl) *agg.* attento, accurato, prudente, economo; premuroso. **—ly** *avv.* accuratamente. **—ness** *n.* accuratezza, prudenza.

carefree (kâr'frē') *agg.* spensierato.

careless (kâr'lĕs) *agg.* noncurante, sbadato, negligente, indifferente. **—ly** *avv.* sbadatamente, imprudentemente. **—ness** *n.* sbadataggine, indifferenza, negligenza.

caress (kȧ·rĕs') *n.* carezza. *vt.* accarezzare.

caret (kăr'ĕt) *n.* segno d'omissione.

caretaker (kâr'tāk'ẽr) *n.* custode, guardiano; *agg.* interinale, provvisorio, supplente.

careworn (-wôrn') *agg.* angosciato.

carfare (kär'fâr) *n.* denari per il tram; spiccioli.

cargo (kär'gō) *n.* carico mercantile; nave da carico.

caricature (kăr'ĭ·kȧ·tŭr) *n.* caricatura. *vt.* mettere in caricatura.

carmine (kär'mĭn) *n.* carminio.

carnage (kär'nĭj) *n.* carnaio, carneficina.

carnal (kär'năl) *agg.* carnale.

carnation (kär·nā'shŭn) *n.* incarnato; garofano.

carnival (kär'nĭ·văl) *n.* carnevale; festa, baldoria.

carnivorous (kär·nĭv'ō·rŭs) *agg.* carnivoro.

carob (kăr'ŏb) *n.* carrubo, carruba.

carol (kăr'ăl) *n.* canto, canzone, nenia. *vi.* cantare.

carousal (kȧ·rouz'ăl) *n.* baldoria.

carouse (kȧ·rouz') *vi.* far baldoria, schiamazzare.

carousel (kăr'ŏŏ·sĕl') *n.* giostra.

carpenter (kär'pĕn·tẽr) *n.* carpentiere.

carpentry (-trĭ) *n.* carpenteria.

carpet (kär'pĕt; -pĭt) *n.* tappeto. **—bag** *n.* valigia di stoffa.

carport (kär'pōrt') *n.* tettoia-autorimessa.

carriage (kär'ĭj) *n.* carrozza; (*ferr.*) vagone; (*comm.*) trasporto (*di merci*); spese di trasporto; (*fig.*) portamento, condotta.

carrier (kär'ĭ·ẽr) *n.* trasportatore; portaerei: **disease —,** veicolo di malattie.

carrion (kăr'ĭ·ŭn) *n.* carogna.

carrot (kăr'ŭt) *n.* carota.

carrousel *vedi* **carousel**

carry (kăr'ĭ) *vt.*, *vi.* trasportare, portare; avere indosso; condurre; sopportare; conseguire; far votare *o* approvare; (*comm.*) avere in assortimento; fungere da latore *o* da guida; avere una portata di: **to — on,** continuare; **to — out,** compiere, portare a termine, effettuare; **to — oneself,** comportarsi, atteggiarsi; **this gun carries a mile,** questo fucile ha una portata di un miglio; **his voice carries far,** la sua voce porta lontano.

cart (kärt) *n.* carro, carretto, furgone, calesse: **—horse** cavallo da tiro. *vt.* trasportare col carro.

cartilage (kär'tĭ·lĭj) *n.* cartilagine.

carton (kär'tŏn) *n.* cartone; involucro, imballaggio, scatola; stecca (*di sigarette*).

cartoon (kär·tōōn') *n.* disegno, illustrazione, vignetta; cartone animato; caricatura.

cartoonist (kär·tōōn'ĭst) *n.*, caricaturista; disegnatore.

cartridge (kär'trĭj) *n.* cartuccia: **blank —,** cartuccia a salve. **— belt** *n.* cartuccera.

carve (kärv) *vt.* scolpire, intagliare, incidere; scalcare, trinciare.

carver (kärv'ẽr) *n.* intagliatore, cesellatore; scalco; trinciante.

carving (kärv'ĭng) *n.* scultura, intaglio; scalcatura: **— knife,** trinciante.

cascade (kăs·kăd') *n.* cascata. *vi.* riversarsi.

case (kās) (1) *n.* astuccio, involucro, cassa, cassetta.

case (2) *vt.* chiudere, imballare, rivestire, mettere in scatola; (*gergo*) osservare, ispezionare; occuparsi di.

case (kās) (3) *n.* caso, avvenimento, situazione; causa, processo; tesi (*d'accusa, ecc.*).

casement (kās'mĕnt) *n.* finestra, vetrata.

cash (kăsh) *n.* cassa; danaro contante. *vt.* pagare; incassare, scontare (*una cambiale*): **to — in on,** trarre profitto da. **—box** *n.* cassa. **cashier** (kăsh·ẽr') *n.* cassiere. *vt.* espellere, silurare.

casing (kās'ĭng) *n.* involucro, rivestimento, cassa; budello (*per salami*); copertone (*per auto*).

cask (kȧsk) *n.* barile, botte, fusto.

casket (kȧs'kĕt) *n.* cofanetto; (*S.U.*) bara.

cassock (kăs'ŭk) n. (eccles.) tonaca.

cast (kăst) n. lancio, getto; stampo, impronta; fusione; carattere; strabismo; (teatr.) complesso di attori; distribuzione delle parti. vt., vi. lanciare, gettare, scagliare; rivolgere (lo sguardo); spargere; fondere; plasmare; (teatr.) distribuire (le parti), reclutare (attori): to — about, andare in cerca; to be — down, essere abbattuto; to — off, scartare; respingere; mollare gli ormeggi; to — a ballot, votare.

cast iron n. ghisa.

castanets (kăs'tá·nĕts') n. nacchere.

caste (kăst) n. casta, classe: to lose —, disonorarsi, degradarsi.

caster vedi castor (2).

castigate (kăs'tĭ·gāt) vt. castigare, redarguire.

castle (kás''l), n. castello; (scacchi) torre.

castor (kàs'tĕr) (1) n. castoro.

castor (kás'tĕr) (2) n. rotella per mobili; pepaiuola.

castor oil n. olio di ricino.

castrate (kăs'trāt) vt. castrare.

casual (kăzh'û·ăl) agg. casuale, fortuito; distratto; indifferente; saltuario; (di indumenti) sciolto, comodo, sportivo, semplice.

casualty (-tĭ) n. incidente, sinistro; vittima. casualties n.pl. perdite (morti, feriti, dispersi).

cat (kăt) n. gatto, felino; (fig.) creatura perfida; staffile: to let the — out of the bag, scoprire gli altarini.

cataclysm (kăt'á·klĭz'm) n. cataclisma.

catalogue (kăt'á·lôg) n. catalogo. vt. catalogare.

catapult (kăt'á·pult) n. catapulta; (aeron.) catapulta di lancio. vt. catapultare.

cataract (kăt'á·răkt) n. cateratta.

catarrh (ká·tär') n. catarro.

catastrophe (ká·tăs'trō·fê) n. catastrofe.

catch (kăch) n. presa; cattura; trucco, tranello; pesca; bottino; guadagno; colpo; buon partito; gancio; catenaccio: — phrase, frase di richiamo. vt. (pass., pp. caught) prendere, afferrare; raggiungere; sorprendere sul fatto. vi.agganciarsi; impigliarsi; far presa; prender fuoco; dilagare (di malattia, ecc.): to — sight of, scorgere, intravedere; to — up with, mettersi alla pari con; raggiungere. —ing agg. attraente; (med.) contagioso; ricorrente.

catechism (kăt'ê·kĭz'm) n. catechismo.

category (kăt'ê·gō'rĭ) n. categoria.

cater (kā'tĕr) vi. provvedere, servire, procurare svaghi.

caterpillar (kăt'ĕr·pĭl'ĕr) n. bruco; cingolo: — tractor, trattrice a cingoli.

cathedral (ká·thē'drăl) n. cattedrale.

cathode (kăth'ōd) n. catodo.

catholic (kăth'ō·lĭk; kăth'lĭk) n., agg. cattolico. —ism (ká·thŏl'ĭ·sĭz'm) n. cattolicesimo.

cattle (kăt''l) n. bestiame (spec. bovino). —man n. bovaro.

catwalk (kăt'wôk') n. ballatoio, passerella, corsia.

caucus (kô'kŭs) n. comitato elettorale.

caught (kôt) pass., pp. di catch.

cauliflower (kô'lĭ·flou'ĕr) n. cavolfiore.

caulk (kôk) vt. calafatare.

cause (kôz) n. causa, motivo; processo. vt. causare, provocare; indurre: to — anything to be done, far fare qualcosa.

causeway (kôz'wā') n. strada in rialza in terreno paludoso.

caution (kô'shŭn), n. cautela, prudenza; ammonimento; avvertenza. vt. ammonire, mettere in guardia.

cautious (kô'shŭs) agg. prudente, circospetto.

cavalier (kăv'á·lêr') n. cavaliere. agg. altezzoso, sdegnoso; sbrigativo.

cavalry (kăv'ăl·rĭ) n. cavalleria.

cave (kāv) n. cava, caverna; antro; sotterraneo. vt., vi. scavare: to — in, far sprofondare; sprofondare; cedere; sottomettersi.

cavern (kăv'ĕrn) n. caverna. —ous agg. cavernoso.

caviar, caviare (kăv'ĭ·är') n. caviale.

cavity (kăv'ĭ·tĭ) n. cavità.

cease (sēs) vi. cessare, smettere, interrompersi; decedere. vt. interrompere, far cessare. —less agg. incessante.

cedar (sē'dĕr) n. cedro (albero).

cede (sēd) vt., vi. cedere; piegarsi.

ceiling (sēl'ĭng) n. soffitto; prezzo massimo, calmiere.

celebrate (sĕl'ê·brāt) vt. celebrare.

celebrated (-brāt'ĕd) agg. celebrato, celebre.

celebration (-brā'shŭn) n. celebrazione.

celebrity (sê·lĕb'rĭ·tĭ) n. celebrità.

celery (sĕl'ĕr·ĭ) n. sedano.

celestial (sê·lĕs'chăl) n. celestiale, celeste.

celibacy (sĕl'ĭ·bá·sĭ) n. celibato.

cell (sĕl) n. cellula; cella; alveolo; scompartimento.

cellar (sĕl'ĕr) n. cantina, sotterraneo, sottosuolo, scandinato.

cello (chĕl'ō) n. violoncello.

cellophane (sĕl'ō·fān) n. cellofane.

celluloid (sĕl'ū·loid) n. celluloide.

cellulose (sĕl'ū·lōs) n. cellulosa.

cement (sē·mĕnt') n. cemento: reinforced —, cemento armato. vt. cementare, consolidare, rafforzare.

cemetery (sĕm'ē·tĕr'ĭ) n. cimitero.

censor (sĕn'sĕr) n. censore. vt. censurare. —ious (sĕn·sō'rĭ·ŭs) agg. severo, aspro. —ship n. censura.

censure (sĕn'shĕr) n. censura, critica; biasimo. vt. censurare; criticare; biasimare.

census (sĕn'sŭs) n. censimento.

cent (sĕnt) n. centesimo (di dollaro): ten per —, dieci per cento.

centennial (sĕn·tĕn'ĭ·ăl) n. centenario. agg. centenario, secolare.

center (sĕn'tĕr) n. centro. vt., vi. centrare, concentrare. —bit n. trapano.

centigrade (sĕn'tĭ·grād) agg. centigrado.

centipede (sĕn'tĭ·pēd) n. scolopendra.

central (sĕn'trăl) agg. centrale.

centralize (sĕn'trăl·īz) vt. accentrare.

centre vedi center.

centrifugal (sĕn·trĭf'ū·găl) agg. centrifugo.

century (sĕn'tū·rĭ) n. secolo; (S.U.) biglietto da cento dollari.

cereal (sēr'ē·ăl) n., agg. cereale.

ceremonial (sĕr'ē·mō'nĭ·ăl) n., agg. cerimoniale.

ceremonious agg. cerimonioso.

ceremony (sĕr'ē·mō'nĭ) n. cerimonia.

certain (sûr'tĭn) agg. certo, sicuro: for —, sicuramente. —ly avv. certamente. —ty n. certezza.

certificate (sĕr·tĭf'ĭ·kĭt) n. certificato. vt. certificare.

certify (sûr'tĭ·fī) vt. certificare, garantire.

certitude (sûr'tĭ·tūd) n. certezza, sicurezza.

cessation (sĕ·sā'shun) n. cessazione, sospensione.

cession (sĕsh'ŭn) n. cessione.

cesspool (sĕs'pōōl') n. pozzo nero.

cetacean (sē·tā'shăn) n., agg. cetaceo.

chafe (chāf) n. irritazione; riscaldamento; sfregamento. vt. strofinare, logorare per attrito. vi. essere irritato, fremere; dolere; logorarsi.

chaff (chăf) n. burla, scherzo; paglia; rifiuto. vt., vi. beffare, scherzare; sminuzzare.

chaffinch (chăf'ĭnch) n. fringuello.

chafing dish (chāf'ĭng) n. scaldavivande.

chagrin (shă·grĭn') n. angoscia, cruccio.

chain (chān) n. catena: — stitch, punto a catenella; — reaction, reazione a catena. vt. incatenare.

chair (châr) n. sedia, seggio; cattedra: arm—, easy —, poltrona; bath —, carrozzella per invalidi; deck —, sedia a sdraio; rocking —, poltrona a dondolo; sedan —, portantina; — lift, seggiovia.

chairman (châr'măn) n. presidente.

chairmanship n. presidenza.

chalice (chăl'ĭs) n. calice.

chalk (chôk) n. gesso. vt. segnare o scrivere col gesso; imbiancare: to — out, abbozzare.

chalk-talk n. conferenza illustrata (con disegni o cartoni animati).

chalky (chôk'ĭ) agg. gessoso.

challenge (chăl'ĕnj) n. sfida, provocazione; opposizione; (mil.) chi-va-là. vt., vi. sfidare, provocare; impegnare; respingere; lanciare il chi-va-là.

chamber (chām'bĕr) n. camera, stanza, aula.

chambermaid (-mād') n. cameriera.

chamber pot (-pŏt) n. pitale.

chamois (shăm'ĭ) n. camoscio.

champ (chămp) vt. rosicchiare: to — at the bit, mordere il freno.

champion (chăm'pĭ·ŏn) n. campione; paladino. vt. difendere; farsi paladino di.

championship n. campionato.

chance (chans) n. caso, combinazione; sorte; imprevisto; probabilità; rischio: by —, per caso; game of —, gioco di azzardo. vi. accadere per caso. vt. arrischiare, tentare: to — upon, imbattersi in.

chancellor (chàn'sĕ·lĕr) n. cancelliere.

chandelier (shăn'dĕ·lĕr')n.lampadario.

change (chānj) n. mutamento; cambio (di vestiario); fase; cambio, moneta spicciola; variazione: the — of life, la menopausa. vt., vi. cambiare; convertire in danaro spicciolo; modificarsi. —able agg. mutevole.

changer n. cambiavalute.

channel (chăn'ĕl) n. canale, stretto: the English —, la Manica.

chant (chànt) n. canto, cantilena. vt., vi. cantare, salmodiare.

chaos (kā'ŏs) n. caos.

chaotic (kā·ŏt'ĭk) agg. caotico.

chap (chăp) (1) n. screpolatura. vt. screpolare. vi. screpolarsi.

chap (chăp) (2) n. individuo, tipo, tizio: a fine —, un brav'uomo o ragazzo.

chapel (chăp'ĕl) n. cappella.

chaperon (shăp'ĕr·ŏn) n. scorta, accompagnatore o accompagnatrice. vt. scortare.

chaplain (chăp'lĭn) n. cappellano.

chapped (chăpt) agg. screpolato.

chapter (chăp'tĕr) n. capitolo.

char (chär) vt. carbonizzare. vi. carbonizzarsi.

character (kăr'ăk.tĕr) n. carattere; caratteristica; scrittura; benservito; personaggio, tipo caratteristico. —istic (-ĭs'tĭk) agg. caratteristico. n. peculiarità, caratteristica. —ize vt. caratterizzare.

charcoal (chär'kōl')n.carbone di legna.

charge (chärj) n. carico; incarico; gravame, responsabilità; cura; accusa; carica; spesa, addebito: to take — of, incaricarsi di; to be in — of, essere incaricato di, dirigere; under my —, a mie spese; free of —, senza spese, gratis; to give one in —, consegnare uno alla polizia. vt. caricare; saturare; incaricare; accusare; addebitare.

charger (chär'jĕr) n. cavallo da battaglia; vassoio.

chariot (chăr'ĭ.ŭt) n. cocchio.

charitable (chăr'ĭ.tá.b'l) agg. caritatevole.

charity (chăr'ĭ.tĭ) n. carità, elemosina, beneficenza: out of —, per beneficenza.

charlatan (shär'lá.tăn) n. ciarlatano.

charm (chärm) n. fascino, incantesimo; talismano; ciondolo portafortuna. vt. affascinare; stregare; lusingare. —ing agg. affascinante, delizioso.

chart (chärt) n. carta nautica; grafico, statistica; cartella clinica. vt. tracciare, delineare.

charter (chär'tĕr) n. licenza, brevetto: The Great —, la Magna Carta: — member, socio fondatore. vt. concedere una licenza o un privilegio a; noleggiare. — party n. (naut.) contratto di noleggio.

chartered agg. munito di licenza: — accountant (Ingh.), ragioniere.

charwoman (chär'wŏŏm'ăn) n. domestica a ore.

chary (châr'ĭ) agg. prudente; parco.

chase (chās) n. caccia, inseguimento. vt. cacciare; inseguire; scacciare; cesellare, incidere.

chaser n. inseguitore; incisore; (S.U.) bicchiere d'acqua o selz (da bersi dopo un liquore forte), "ammazzaliquore."

chasm (kăz'm) n. voragine, crepaccio.

chaste (chāst) agg. casto; moderato; sobrio. —ness n. castità.

chastise (chăs.tīz') vt. castigare, punire.

chastisement (chăs'tĭz·mĕnt) n. punizione.

chastity (chăs'tĭ.tĭ) n. castità.

chat (chăt) n. chiacchierata, conversazione. vi. chiacchierare.

chattel (chăt'l) n. bene mobile.

chatter (chăt'ĕr) n. chiacchiera, chiacchierata; battito (dei denti); vi. chiacchierare, parlottare, cinguettare, battere i denti. —box n. chiacchierone.

chatty (chăt'ĭ) agg. vaniloquente, chiacchierone.

chauffeur (shō·fûr'; shō'fĕr) n.autista.

cheap (chēp) agg. economico, a buon mercato; di scarso valore; svalutato, deprezzato; spregevole: dirt —, a prezzo irrisorio; to hold —, disprezzare.

cheapen (chēp'ĕn) vt., vi. svilire, deprezzare; mercanteggiare.

cheaply (-lĭ) avv. economicamente, a buon mercato.

cheapness (-nĕs) n. buon mercato, meschinità.

cheat (chēt) n. frode; imbroglione, truffatore; mistificatore. vt., vi. ingannare, imbrogliare, barare.

check (chĕk) n. ostacolo, impedimento, freno; arresto brusco; verifica, controllo; contromarca, scontrino; assegno; quadretto (nel disegno di tessuti, ecc.); (scacchi) scacco: blank —, assegno in bianco; crossed —, assegno barrato. vt. fermare, bloccare, trattenere; moderare; verificare, controllare; dare scacco matto a, tenere in scacco. —book n. libretto d'assegni. —mate n. scacco matto. —room n. guardaroba.

checker (chĕk'ĕr) n. pedina (per scacchi o dama); scacchiera; scacco; ispettore, verificatore.

checkerboard (chĕk'ĕr·bôrd') n. scacchiera.

checkered (chĕk'ĕrd) agg. quadrettato; variato: a — career, una carriera fortunosa.

checkers (chĕk'ĕrz) n. (gioco degli) scacchi.

cheek (chēk) n. guancia, gota; impudenza, faccia tosta.

cheekbone (chēk'bōn') n. zigomo.

cheeky (chēk'ĭ) agg. insolente.

cheer (chēr) n. allegria, animazione; acclamazione, applauso. vt. acclamare; rallegrare, incoraggiare. vi. rasserenarsi, rincuorarsi. —ful agg. allegro. —fully avv. allegramente. —fulness n. allegria. —ily avv. gaiamente. —less agg. triste, cupo. —y agg. gaio, allegro.

cheese (chēz) n. formaggio: cottage —, specie di ricotta.

cheesecake (chēz'kāk') *n.* torta a base di presame e uova; (*gergo*) fotografia di ragazza procace con le gambe in mostra.

chemical (kĕm'ĭ-kăl) *n.* prodotto chimico. *agg.* chimico.

chemist (kĕm'ĭst) *n.* chimico; farmacista.

chemistry (kĕm'ĭs-trĭ) *n.* chimica.

cheque (chĕk) *vedi* check.

cherish (chĕr'ĭsh) *vt.* custodire amorevolmente (*ricordi, ecc.*); curare con affetto; accarezzare, nutrire (*speranze, sentimenti*).

cherry (chĕr'ĭ) *n.* ciliegia. — **tree** *n.* ciliegio.

chess (chĕs) *n.* (gioco degli) scacchi. —**board** *n.* scacchiera. —**men** *n.* pezzi degli scacchi.

chest (chĕst) *n.* petto, torace, cassa, cofano: — **of drawers**, cassettone.

chestnut (chĕs'nŭt) *n.* castagna, castagno. *agg.* castagno, marrone, sauro.

chew (chōō; chū) *n.* masticazione; ciò che si mastica. *vt.* masticare.

chewing gum *n.* gomma da masticare.

chichi (shē'shē) *agg.* (*gergo*) elegante; ricercato; effeminato.

chick (chĭk) *n.* pulcino; bambino.

chicken (chĭk'ĕn) *n.* pollo, pollastra: — **-hearted**, vigliacco; — **-pox**, vaiolo, varicella.

chick-pea (chĭk'pē') *n.* cece.

chide (chīd) *vt.* (*pp.* chid) sgridare, biasimare, redarguire.

chief (chēf) *n.* capo, comandante. *agg.* principale, sommo, supremo. —**ly** *avv.* principalmente, soprattutto.

chiffon (shĭ-fon'; shĭf'on) *n.* velo.

chilblain (chĭl'blān) *n.* gelone.

child (chīld) *n.* (*pl.* **children** [chĭl'-drĕn]) bambino, figlio, figlia: to be with —, essere in stato interessante. —**bearing** *n.* gravidanza. —**birth** *n.* parto. —**hood** *n.* infanzia. —**ish** *agg.* infantile, puerile: to grow —**ish**, rimbambire. —**ishness** *n.* puerilità. —**less** *agg.* senza figli. —**like** *agg.* infantile, spontaneo.

chill (chĭl) *n.* freddo; raffreddamento; brivido; raffreddore. *vt.* raffreddare; raggelare. *vi.* raffreddarsi; raggelarsi.

chilly (chĭl'ĭ) *agg.* freddo, fresco.

chime (chīm) *n.* rintocco; scampanio; armonia. *vt.*, *vi.* scampanare; sonare armoniosamente; risonare; armonizzarsi; essere d'accordo: to — **in**, interloquire; to — **in with**, essere in armonia con, approvare.

chimney (chĭm'nĭ) *n.* camino; fumaiolo.

chin (chĭn) *n.* mento.

china (chī'nà) *n.* porcellana.

Chinese (chī'nēz') *n.*, *agg.* cinese: — **lantern**, lampioncino alla veneziana.

chink (chĭngk) *n.* fessura, crepa, screpolatura.

chip (chĭp) *n.* frammento, scheggia: **potato chips**, patatine fritte. *vt.* tagliuzzare, scheggiare, scorticare, affettare. *vi.* scheggiarsi, scrostarsi: to — **in**, contribuire, dare la propria offerta.

chirp (chûrp) *n.* cinguettio, trillo. *vi.* cinguettare.

chisel (chĭz''l) *n.* scalpello, cesello. *vt.* cesellare; (*gergo*) scroccare; imbrogliare.

chitchat (chĭt'chăt') *n.* chiacchierio.

chivalrous (shĭv'ăl-rŭs) *agg.* cavalleresco.

chivalry (shĭv'ăl-rĭ) *n.* cavalleria.

chloral (klō'răl) *n.* cloralio.

chloride (klō'rīd) *n.* cloruro.

chlorine (klō'rēn) *n.* cloro.

chloroform (klō'rō-fôrm) *n.* cloroformio. *vt.* cloroformizzare.

chlorophyll (klō'rō-fĭl) *n.* clorofilla.

chock (chŏk) *n.* cuneo, bietta, supporto. —**full** *agg.* pieno, colmo.

chocolate (chok'ō-lĭt; chŏk'lĭt) *n.* cioccolata.

choice (chois) *n.* scelta; assortimento. *agg.* scelto; eccellente.

choir (kwīr) *n.* coro.

choke (chōk) *n.* strozzamento, strozzatura; soffocazione; (*mecc.*) regolatore (*d'aria, di carburante, ecc.*). *vt.* soffocare, strangolare; ostruire; colmare; (*mecc.*) togliere aria (*al carburatore*). *vi.* soffocare; ostruirsi.

choler (kŏl'ĕr) *n.* collera, bile.

cholera (kŏl'ĕr-à) *n.* colera.

choose (chōōz) *vt.* (*pass.* chose, *pp.* chosen) scegliere, decidere, volere: to — **to**, preferire: I don't — to do it, non mi va di farlo.

chop (chŏp) *n.* colpo di scure; tran-cio, costoletta. *vt.* tagliare. —**house** *n.* ristorante. —**py** *agg.* screpolato: — **sea**, mare agitato.

choral (kō'răl) *agg.* corale; *n.* (kō-răl'; -räl') corale.

chord (kôrd) *n.* corda; accordo.

chore (chōr) *n.* lavoro, faccenda; *pl.* lavori domestici.

choreography (kō'rē ŏg'rà fĭ) *n.* coreografia.

chorister (kŏr'ĭs-tĕr) *n.* corista.

chorus (kō'rŭs) *n.* coro, corpo di ballo (*nel varietà*); ritornello. — **girl** *n.* corista (*donna*); ballerina di varietà.

chose (chōz) *pass. di* to choose.

hosen (chō'z'n) *pp. di* to choose·

Christ (krīst) *n.* Cristo.

christen (krĭs''n) *vt.* battezzare.

christening (krĭs''n·ĭng) *n.* battesimo.

Christian (krĭs'chăn) *n., agg.* cristiano: — **name**, nome di battesimo.

Christianity (krĭs'chĭ·ăn'ĭ·tĭ; -tĭ·ăn'ĭ-tĭ) *n.* cristianità; cristianesimo.

Christmas (krĭs'măs) *n.* Natale: **Merry —!** buon Natale! **—tide** *n.* periodo natalizio.

Christy (krĭs'tĭ) *n.* (*sci.*) cristiania.

chrome (krōm), **chromium** (krō'mĭ-ŭm) *n.* cromo.

chronic (krŏn'ĭk) *agg.* cronico.

chronicle (krŏn'ĭ·k'l) *n.* cronaca, cronistoria. *vt.* fare la cronaca di; raccontare.

chronicler (-klẽr) *n.* cronista.

chronological (krŏn'ô·lŏj'ĭ·kăl) *agg.* cronologico.

chronology (krŏ·nŏl'ô·jĭ) *n.* cronologia.

chronometer (krŏ·nŏm'ĕ·tẽr) *n.* cronometro.

chrysalis (krĭs'á·lĭs) *n.* crisalide.

chubby (chŭb'ĭ) *agg.* paffuto.

chuck (chŭk) (1) *n.* richiamo della chioccia. *vi.* chiocciare.

chuck (2) *n.* buffetto, colpetto sotto il mento. *vt.* dare un buffetto a; gettare, scaraventare: **to — out**, mettere alla porta, scacciare; **to —** (*athing*) rinunciare a, abbandonare.

chuck (3) *n.* (*mecc.*) mandrino.

chuckle (chŭk''l) *n.* risatina. *vi.* ridacchiare; ridere sotto i baffi.

chum (chŭm) *n.* amico; compagno di stanza.

chump (chŭmp) *n.* ceppo, pezzo di legno; (*gergo*) testa; sciocco.

chunk (chŭngk) *n.* fettona; grosso pezzo.

church (chûrch) *n.* chiesa, tempio. **—man** *n.* ecclesiastico, uomo devoto. **—yard** *n.* cimitero.

churl (chûrl) *n.* zotico, villanzone.

churn (chûrn) *n.* zangola. *vt., vi.* sbattere il latte per fare il burro; spumeggiare (*dei flutti*); scuotere, agitare.

chute (shōōt) *n.* cascata; tromba, scarico; condotto; piano inclinato.

cider (sī'dẽr) *n.* sidro.

cigar (sĭ·gär') *n.* sigaro.

cigarette (sĭg'á·rĕt') *n.* sigaretta: **— case**, portasigarette; **— holder**, bocchino.

cinch (sĭnch) *n.* cinghia da sella; (*gergo*) certezza; impresa facile, giochetto. *vt.* legare strettamente, assicurare con cinghia; (*gergo*) agguantare, accaparrarsi.

cinder (sĭn'dẽr) *n.* tizzone; (*pl.*) ceneri.

Cinderella (sĭn'dẽr·ĕl'á) *n.* Cenerentola.

cinnamon (sĭn'á·mŭn) *n.* cannella.

cipher (sī'fẽr) *n.* cifra; zero; cifrario.

circle (sûr'k'l) *n.* circolo, cerchio, cerchia; (*astr.*) orbita. *vt.* circondare, accerchiare, aggirare. *vi.* rotare.

circuit (sûr'kĭt) *n.* rotazione, circuito; circonferenza, cinta; deviazione.

circuitous (sẽr·kū'ĭ·tŭs) *agg.* sinuoso, indiretto.

circular (sûr'kû·lẽr) *n., agg.* circolare: **— staircase**, scala a chiocciola.

circulate (sûr'kû·lāt) *vt.* diffondere, mettere in circolazione, distribuire; divulgare. *vi.* circolare.

circulation (-lā'shŭn) *n.* circolazione, diffusione.

circumcise (sûr'kŭm·sīz) *vt.* circoncidere.

circumcision (sûr·kŭm·sĭzh'ŭn) *n.* circoncisione.

circumference (sẽr·kŭm'fẽr·ĕns) *n.* circonferenza.

circumflex (sûr'kŭm·flĕks) *agg.* circonflesso.

circumlocution (sûr'kŭm·lō kū'shŭn) *n.* circonlocuzione.

circumscribe (sûr'kŭm·skrīb') *n.* circoscrivere.

circumspect (sûr'kŭm·spĕkt) *agg.* circospetto. **—ion** *n.* circospezione.

circumstance (sûr'kŭm·stăns) *n.* circostanza, condizione; cerimonia, solennità; (*pl.*) situazione economica, posizione.

circumstantial (sûr'kŭm·stăn'shăl) *agg.* particolareggiato; indiziario.

circumvent (sûr'kŭm·vĕnt') *vt.* circuire.

circus (sûr'kŭs) *n.* circo equestre; rotonda.

cistern (sĭs'tẽrn) *n.* cisterna, serbatoio.

citadel (sĭt'á·d'l) *n.* cittadella.

citation (sī·tā'shŭn) *n.* citazione.

cite (sīt) *vt.* citare.

citizen (sĭt'ĭ·zĕn) *n.* cittadino: **fellow —**, concittadino.

citizenship (-shĭp) *n.* cittadinanza.

citron (sĭt'rŭn) *n.* cedro (*frutto*).

citrous, citrus (sĭt'rŭs) *agg.* agrumario: **— grove**, agrumeto.

city (sĭt'ĭ) *n.* città; municipio; centro degli affari (*in grande città*). *agg.* urbano, municipale: **— hall**, municipio; **— council**, giunta comunale; **— editor** (*giorn.*), capocronaca.

civic (sĭv'ĭk) *agg.* civico.

civics (sĭv'ĭks) *n.* diritto politico.

civil (sĭv'ĭl) *agg.* civile; cortese, educato; municipale.

civilian (sĭ·vĭl'yăn) *n., agg.* borghese (*non militare*).

civility (sĭ-vĭl'ĭ-tĭ) n. urbanità, cortesia.
civilization (sĭv'ĭ-lĭ-zā'shŭn; -lĭ-zā'-) n. civiltà, civilizzazione.
civilize (sĭv'ĭ-lĭz) vt. civilizzare, incivilire.
civilized (-lĭzd) agg. civile, incivilito.
clad (klăd) pass., pp. di to **clothe**; agg. vestito, rivestito; placcato: **armor—**, agg, corazzato, blindato.
claim (klām) n. richiesta, pretesa, rivendicazione, diritto; (min.) concessione, zona concessa per lo sfruttamento o rivendicata: **to lay —** to, accampare diritti su. vt. reclamare, pretendere, rivendicare; asserire, affermare. **—ant** n. reclamante; pretendente.
clairvoyance (klâr-voi'ăns) n. chiaroveggenza.
clairvoyant (klâr-voi'ănt) n., agg. chiaroveggente.
clam (klăm) n. mollusco bivalve; (fig.) persona discreta.
clamber (klăm'bēr) vi. arrampicarsi.
clammy (klăm'ĭ) agg. viscido, umidiccio.
clamor (klăm'ēr) n. clamore, frastuono. vi. gridare, far clamori. **—ous** agg. clamoroso, rumoroso.
clamp (klămp) n. morsa; rampone. vt. stringere nella morsa; unire.
clan (klăn) n. tribù; fazione, cricca.
clandestine (klăn-dĕs'tĭn) agg. clandestino.
clang (klăng) n. clangore. vi. risonare. vt. far risonare.
clap (klăp) n. colpo; schiocco; battimani; scoppio (di tuono); manata. vt., vi. colpire; battere (le mani); sbattere (le ali, ecc.); applaudire; dar manate; schiaffare, scaraventare.
claret (klăr'ĕt) n. chiaretto (vino).
clarify (klăr'ĭ-fĭ) vt. chiarificare.
clarinet (klăr'ĭ-nĕt') n. clarinetto.
clash (klăsh) n. cozzo, scontro; frastuono; conflitto, contrasto. vi. urtarsi, cozzare; risonare; essere in conflitto; contrastare. vt. urtare; far risonare.
clasp (klăsp) n. gancio, fermaglio; presa; abbraccio; stretta. vt., vi. agganciare, allacciare; cingere; abbracciare; stringere (la mano): **—knife**, coltello a serramanico.
class (klăs) n. classe; categoria. vt. classificare.
classbook n. registro di classe.
classic (klăs'ĭk) n., agg. classico: **—al scholar**, umanista.
classification (klăs'ĭ-fĭ-kā'shŭn) n. classificazione.
classify (klăs'ĭ-fĭ) vt. classificare.
classmate n. compagno di scuola.

classroom n. aula scolastica.
clatter (klăt'ēr) n. acciottolio, fracasso, vocio, schiamazzo. vi. far fracasso; risonare; blaterare.
clause (klôz) n. clausola; (gramm.) proposizione.
claw (klô) n. artiglio, grinfia; pinza (di crostaceo); taglio (di martello). vt. artigliare, lacerare con gli artigli, graffiare; afferrare; annaspare.
clay (klā) n. argilla, creta: **baked —**, terracotta.
clean (klēn) agg. pulito, puro, lustro; retto, onesto: **to show a — pair of heels**, darsela a gambe, sparire. avv. nettamente, completamente, chiaramente. vt. pulire, purificare: lucidare; smacchiare. **—er** n. pulitore, smacchiatore. **—ing** n. pulizia, lucidatura, smacchiatura. **—liness** (klĕn-) n. nettezza, purezza. **—ly** avv. pulitamente; nettamente. agg. lindo, ordinato. **—ness** n. pulizia, purezza, nitidezza.
cleanse (klĕnz) vt. lavare, pulire, detergere; purificare, purgare, depurare.
cleanser (klĕn'zēr) n. detersivo.
clear (klēr) agg. chiaro, limpido; netto, evidente; innocente; immacolato: **to keep — of**, evitare; **to steer — of**, schivare, girar largo da; **to be in the —**, essere scagionato, essere fuori di sospetto. vt. chiarire, chiarificare; sgomberare; svincolare; guadagnare; discolpare, assolvere; superare (un ostacolo); scagionare, prosciogliere; passare (una barriera doganale, ecc.); (naut.) doppiare. vi. schiarirsi, rasserenarsi; sbarazzarsi. **—ance** n. liberazione; levata (delle lettere); svincolo; sgombero: **—ance sale**, liquidazione. **—ing** n. compensazione; liquidazione dei bilanci; radura. **—inghouse** n. camera di compensazione.
clearness (klēr'nĕs) n. chiarezza.
cleavage (klēv'ĭj) n. fenditura, scissione, sfaldamento.
cleave (klēv) vt. (pass. **clove**, **cleft**, pp. **cloven**, **cleft**) fendere, dividere, sfaldare. vi. fendersi, sfaldarsi.
clef (klĕf) n. (mus.) chiave.
cleft (klĕft) n. fessura. pp. di to **cleave**.
clemency (klĕm'ĕn-sĭ) n. clemenza.
clement (klĕm'ĕnt) agg. clemente.
clench (klĕnch) vt. ribadire; stringere (i denti, il pugno); afferrare.
clergy (klûr'jĭ) n. clero. **—man** n. (pl. **—men**) ecclesiastico, pastore evangelico.
clerical (klĕr'ĭ-kăl) agg. clericale; impiegatizio; sedentario.

clerk (klŭrk) *n*. impiegato, commesso; contabile; cancelliere (*di tribunale*): chief —, capufficio.

clever (klĕv'ẽr) *agg*. abile, bravo; intelligente; astuto. **—ly** *avv*. abilmente; astutamente. **—ness** *n*. abilità; destrezza; disinvoltura.

clew (kloō) *n*. gomitolo; traccia, indizio.

click (klĭk) *n*. scatto, schiocco. *vi*., *vt*. scattare, schioccare; far schioccare. **—ing** *n*. ticchettio.

client (klī'ĕnt) *n*. cliente. **—ele** (klī'-ĕn.tĕl') *n*. clientela.

cliff (klĭf) *n*. roccia, rupe, scarpata.

climate (klī'mĭt) *n*. clima.

climax (klī'măks) *n*. punto culminante, crescendo, apice, crisi risolutiva. *vt*. portare al punto culminante. *vi*. raggiungere il punto culminante.

climb (klĭm) *vt*. scalare, dare la scalata a, salire. *vi*. arrampicarsi; innalzarsi: to — down, ritirarsi, calar le arie. **—er** *n*. scalatore; pianta rampicante.

clime (klĭm) *n*. clima; paese.

clinch (klĭnch) *n*. ribattitura; ribattino; (*pugilato*) corpo a corpo. *vt*. ribadire, stringere. *vi*. avvinghiarsi.

cling (klĭng) *vi*. (*pass*., *pp*. clung) aggrapparsi, attaccarsi, appiccicarsi, aderire, avviticchiarsi.

clinic (klĭn'ĭk) *n*. clinica. **—al** *agg*. clinico.

clink (klĭngk) *n*. tintinnio.

clip (klĭp) *n*. taglio (*di capelli, ecc.*), tosatura; molletta; caricatore (*di arma da fuoco*): paper —, fermaglio, graffetta; to go at a good —, andare a passo rapido, avere un' andatura forte. *vt*. tagliare, tosare, abbreviare. **—per** *n*. tosatore, tosatrice (*macchinetta*); (*naut*.) veliero mercantile veloce; (*aeron*.) aeroplano transatlantico. **—ping** *n*. taglio, tosatura; ritaglio (*di giornale, ecc.*).

cloak (klōk) *n*. mantello, manto; maschera; pretesto. *vt*. ammantare, mascherare. **—room** *n*. guardaroba; (*ferr*.) deposito bagagli. **— -and-dagger** *agg*. (*di romanzi*) di cappa e spada.

clobber (klŏb'ẽr) *vt*. (*gergo*) bastonare; abbattere; tramortire.

clock (klŏk) *n*. orologio (*da muro*), pendola: alarm —, sveglia; it is two o'—, sono le due. **—wise** *agg*. destrorso. **—work** *n*. movimento di orologeria.

clod (klŏd) *n*. zolla, pezzo; tonto.

clodhopper (klŏd'hŏp'ẽr) *n*. aratore; *pl*., scarponi.

clog (klŏg) *n*. pastoia; impedimento; ostruzione; zoccolo. *vt*. impastoiare; ostruire; ostacolare. *vi*. incagliarsi; ostruirsi.

cloister (klois'tẽr) *n*. chiostro.

close (klōz) *n*. fine, chiusura, conclusione; chiostro; recinto; corpo a corpo. *agg*. (klōs) chiuso, stretto; compatto; avaro; male arieggiato, soffocante; esatto; intimo; conciso; discreto; misterioso: — questioning, interrogatorio serrato o minuzioso; — at hand, a portata di mano; — by, vicinissimo. *avv*. vicino, da vicino, strettamente, intimamente. *vt*. (-z) chiudere; terminare, concludere; stringere; serrare le file; togliere (*la seduta*). *vi*. chiudersi, concludere, finire; cicatrizzarsi (*di ferite*): to — in upon, accerchiare.

closely (klōs'lĭ) *avv*. da vicino; strettamente; intimamente; segretamente; attentamente.

closeness (klōs'nĕs) *n*. vicinanza; compattezza, pesantezza (*di atmosfera*).

closing (klōz'ĭng) *n*. chiusura, fine, conclusione.

closet (klŏz'ĕt) *n*. gabinetto; salottino; sgabuzzino; ripostiglio. *vt*. chiudere, rinchiudere; nascondere: to be —ed with, essere in conciliabolo con.

closure (klō'zhẽr) *n*., chiusura, conclusione.

clot (klŏt) *n*. grumo, coagulo. *vi*. coagularsi, raggrumarsi.

cloth (klŏth) *n*. tela, stoffa, panno, drappo; tovaglia; clero.

clothe (klōth) *vt*. (*pass*., *pp*. clad, clothed) vestire, rivestire, coprire, adornare.

clothes (klōthz; *fam*. klōz) *n.pl*. vestiti, indumenti; coltri: plain —, abiti borghesi; suit of —, (vestito) completo. **—line**, *n*. corda per biancheria. **—pin**, *n*. molletta per biancheria.

clothier (klōth'yẽr) *n*. fabbricante di tessuti: ready-made —, negoziante d'abiti fatti.

clothing (klōth'ĭng) *n*. vestiario; coltri.

cloud (kloud) *n*. nuvola, nube; chiazza. *vt*. oscurare; confondere, rendere nebuloso. *vi*. rannuvolarsi, oscurarsi. **—less** *agg*. limpido, sereno, senza nubi.

cloudy (kloud'ĭ) *agg*. nuvoloso, nebuloso.

clout (klout) *n*. scapaccione; mazzata.

clove (klōv) *n*. chiodo di garofano; spicchio.

cloven (klōv''n) *pp*. *di* to cleave.

clover (klō'vẽr) *n.* trifoglio: **to be in
—**, vivere negli agi.
clown (kloun) *n.* buffone, pagliaccio.
cloy (kloi) *vt.* saziare, nauseare.
club (klŭb) *n.* mazza, bastone; circolo, associazione; fiore (*nelle carte
da gioco*). *vt.* bastonare, tramortire.
vi. quotarsi (*versar danaro*); associarsi.
cluck (klŭk) *vi.* chiocciare.
clue (klōō) *vedi* clew.
clump (klŭmp) *n.* massa, blocco;
cespuglio, boschetto. *vt.* ammonticchiare. *vi.* camminare con passo
pesante.
clumsiness (klŭm'zĭ·nĕs) *n.* goffaggine.
clumsy (klŭm'zĭ) *agg.* goffo, maldestro; sgraziato; mal fatto.
clung (klŭng) *pass., pp. di* to cling·
cluster (klŭs'tẽr) *n.* grappolo; mazzo
(*di fiori*); gruppo, sciame, folla. *vi.*
raggrupparsi, formare grappolo. *vt.*
raggruppare.
clutch (klŭch) *n.* stretta, presa; (*pl.*)
grinfie, artigli; (*mecc.*) manicotto
d'accoppiamento; (*auto.*) frizione.
vt., vi. afferrare, stringere, artigliare; aggrapparsi.
clutter (klŭt'ẽr) *n.* fracasso; trambusto; confusione, disordine. *vt.* gettare alla rinfusa; scompigliare. *vi.*
fare baccano; riversarsi in disordine.
coach (kōch) *n.* carrozza; diligenza;
ripetitore, istruttore; allenatore.
vt. istruire, preparare, allenare;
to — with, prendere lezione da.
—man *n.* cocchiere.
coagulate (kō·ăg'ū·lāt) *vi.* coagularsi. *vt.* coagulare.
coagulation (-lā'shŭn) *n.* coagulazione.
coal (kōl) *n.* carbone; tizzone. *vt.*
fornire *o* rifornire di carbone. *vi.*
(*naut.*) far carbone. **—bin** *n.* carbonile. **— oil,** petrolio. **—tar** *n.*
catrame.
coalesce (kō'à·les') *vi.* fondersi, unirsi.
coalition (kō'à·lĭsh'ŭn) *n.* coalizione.
coarse (kōrs) *agg.* grossolano, volgare; grezzo, ruvido.
coarseness (kōrs'nĕs; -nĭs) *n.* volgarità, grossolanità; ruvidezza.
coast (kōst) *n.* costa, litorale. *vt., vi.*
costeggiare, rasentare; scendere
(*un pendio*) in folle (*detto di veicolo*). **—guard** *n.* guardacoste.
—line *n.* costa, litorale.
coat (kōt) *n.* giacca, abito; mantello
(*anche di animale*); copertura, rivestimento, strato, vernice; (*S.U.*)
soprabito; **— of arms,** stemma nobiliare. *vt.* vestire; rivestire; pitturare. **—ing** *n.* tessuto per abito;
rivestimento; strato (*di vernice,
ecc.*); patina.

coax (kōks) (1) *vt., vi.* blandire, adulare, circuire, persuadere.
coax (kō·ăks') (2) (*abbr. di* coaxial
cable) *n.* cavo coassiale.
cob (kŏb) *n.* cigno maschio; pannocchia di granoturco; cavallo da tiro.
cobble (kŏb''l) *n.* ciottolo. *vt.* acciottolare; accomodare, rattoppare.
cobbler (kŏb'lẽr) *n.* ciabattino.
cobweb (kŏb'wĕb') *n.* ragnatela.
cocaine (kō·kān') *n.* cocaina.
cock (kŏk) *n.* gallo; maschio (*di
qualunque uccello*); rubinetto; cane
(*d'arma da fuoco*): **— -and-bull
story,** panzana. *vt., vi.* drizzare,
raddrizzare; armare (*un fucile,
ecc.*). **—ed hat,** tricorno.
cockatoo (kŏk'à·tōō') *n.* cacatoa.
cockerel (kŏk'ẽr·ĕl) *n.* galletto.
cockeye (kŏk'ī) *n.* occhio strabico.
—d *agg.* strabico; (*gergo*) sbilenco;
sciocco, assurdo, scombinato.
cockle (kŏk''l) (1) *n.* loglio (*erba parassita*).
cockle (kŏk''l) (2) *n.* cardio (*frutto di
mare bivalve*).
cockpit (kŏk'pĭt') *n.* (*naut.*) castello
di poppa; (*aeron.*) abitacolo.
cockroach (kŏk'rōch') *n.* scarafaggio.
cocksure (kŏk'shōōr') *agg.* ostinato;
certissimo; presuntuoso.
cocktail (kŏk'tāl') *n.* miscuglio di
liquori; miscuglio di frutti di mare
in salsa serviti in coppa; cavallo
con coda mozza *o* bastardo.
cocky (kŏk'ĭ) *agg.* impudente, sfrontato.
coco (kō'kō) *n.* cocco. **—nut** *n.* noce di
cocoa (kō'kō) *n.* cacao. [cocco.
cocoon (kŏ·kōōn') *n.* bozzolo.
cocozelle (kŏk'ō·zĕl'ĕ) *n.* zucchina.
cod (kŏd) (1) *n.* merluzzo: **- -liver
oil,** olio di fegato di merluzzo.
cod (kŏd) (2) *n.* guscio; (*anat.*) scroto.
coddle (kŏd''l) *vt.* curare, colmar di
premure; coccolare.
code (kōd) *n.* codice; cifrario. *vt.* codificare, tradurre in codice. *agg.*
cifrato.
codicil (kŏd'ĭ·sĭl) *n.* codicillo.
coeducational (school) (kō'ĕd·û·kā'-
shŭn·ăl) *n.* scuola mista.
coefficient (kō'ĕ·fĭsh'ĕnt; kō'ĭ-) *n.*
coefficiente.
coerce (kō·ûrs') *vt.* costringere, forzare, reprimere.
coercion (kō·ûr'shŭn) *n.* coercizione.
coexist (kō'ĕg·zĭst') *vi.* coesistere.
coffee (kŏf'ĭ) *n.* caffè. **— bean,
berry** *n.* chicco di caffè. **— grounds**
n.pl. fondi di caffè. **—house —,shop**
n. caffè (*ritrovo*). **—mill, — grinder**
n. macinino da caffè. **—pot** *n.* caffettiera.

coffer (kŏf'ẽr) *n.* cofano, scrigno, forziere.

coffin (kŏf'ĭn) *n.* bara, cassa da morto.

cog (kŏg) *n.* dente (*d'ingranaggio*). —**wheel** *n.* ruota dentata, ingranaggio, cremagliera.

cogent (kō'jĕnt) *agg.* potente, persuasivo.

cognate (kŏg'nāt) *agg.*, analogo, dello stesso ceppo.

cognition (kŏg·nĭsh'ŭn) *n.* cognizione, conoscenza, contezza.

cohere (kō·hẽr') *vi.* aderire.

coherence (kō·hẽr'ĕns) *n.* coerenza; aderenza.

coherent (-ĕnt) *n.* coerente; aderente.

coign (koin) *n.* (*arch.*) angolo, pietra angolare.

coil (koil) *n.* matassa, bobina, rotolo (*di corda*); spira (*di un rettile*); ciocca (*di capelli*); tumulto, affanno. *vt.* avvolgere, arrotolare. *vi.* arrotolarsi, aggomitolarsi.

coin (koin) *n.* moneta, danaro. *vt.* coniare, batter moneta: **to —words,** coniare vocaboli. —**age** *n.* conio, sistema monetario; invenzione.

coincide (kō·ĭn·sĭd') *vt.* coincidere, concordare. **coincidence** (kō·ĭn'sĭ·dĕns) *n.* coincidenza, concordanza.

coke (kōk) *n.* carbone coke; (*gergo*) cocaina; coca cola.

cold (kōld) *agg.* freddo: **— cream,** crema cosmetica; **to be —,** avere freddo; **fare freddo.** *n.* raffreddore; freddo, raffreddamento. **— -blooded** *agg.* a sangue freddo, insensibile. —**ly** *avv.* freddamente. —**ness** *n.* freddezza.

Coliseum (kŏl'ĭ·sē'ŭm) *n.* Colosseo.

collaborate (kō·lăb'ō·rāt) *vi.* collaborare.

collaboration (-rā'shŭn) *n.* collaborazione.

collaborator (-rā'tẽr) *n.* collaboratore.

collapse (kō·lăps') *n.* caduta; collasso; crollo, catastrofe; abbattimento; sgonfiamento. *vi.* crollare; afflosciarsi; scoraggiarsi. *vt.* far crollare, ribaltare.

collapsible (kō·lăp'sĭ·b'l) *agg.* sgonfiabile; pieghevole; ribaltabile.

collar (kŏl'ẽr) *n.* colletto, collo (*di camicia*), bavero, collare, collana. *vt.* agguantare, catturare, imporre il collare a. —**bone** *n.* clavicola.

collate (kō·lāt') *vt.* raffrontare.

collateral (kō·lăt'ẽr·ăl) *n.*, *agg.* collaterale.

colleague (kŏl'ēg) *n.* collega.

collect (kō·lĕkt') *vt.* raccogliere, riunire, radunare; collezionare; esigere (*incassare*); fare la levata (*della posta*): **to — oneself,** rimettersi, riprendersi. *vi.* adunarsi, raccogliersi; riprendere il dominio di sè. *agg.*, *avv.* in porto assegnato, in assegno. —**ed** *agg.* raccolto; equilibrato, padrone di sè. —**ion** *n.* collezione, raccolta; esazione, incasso; assortimento; levata postale. **-ive** *agg.* collettivo. —**ivism** *n.* collettivismo. —**ivist** *n.* collettivista. —**ivity** *n.* collettività. —**or** *n.* collezionista; raccoglitore; esattore; (*ferr.*) controllore.

college (kŏl'ĕj) *n.* collegio (*di professori, elettori, ecc.*); scuola superiore; università: **medical —,** facoltà di medicina.

collide (kō·lĭd') *vi.* urtarsi, scontrarsi.

collier (kŏl'yẽr) *n.* minatore; carbonaio; (*naut.*) nave carboniera.

collision (kō·lĭzh'ŭn) *n.* collisione, urto, scontro; contrasto (*d'interessi, ecc.*).

collocate (kŏl'ō·kāt) *vt.* collocare.

colloquial (kō·lō'kwĭ·ăl) *agg.* familiare (*di vocaboli*). —**ism** *n.* vocabolo o espressione familiare.

collusion (kō·lū'zhŭn) *n.* collusione, connivenza.

colon (kō'lŏn) *n.* (*gramm.*) due punti; (*anat.*) colon.

colonel (kûr'nĕl) *n.* colonnello.

colonial (kō·lō'nĭ·ăl) *agg.* coloniale.

colonist (kŏl'ō·nĭst) *n.* colono, coloniale.

colonization (kŏl'ō·nĭ·zā'shŭn; -nĭ·zā'-) *n.* colonizzazione.

colonize (kŏl'ō·nīz) *vt.* colonizzare.

colony (kŏl'ō·nĭ) *n.* colonia.

color (kŭl'ẽr) *n.* colore, colorito; apparenza. *pl.* bandiera; colori (*di squadra sport., ecc.*): **fast —,** colore solido; **high —,** colorito accesso; **— -blind,** daltonico. *vt.* colorare, dipingere, tingere; (*fig.*) colorire (*discorsi, ecc.*) *vi.* arrossire, imporporarsi. —**ation** *n.* colorazione, colore. —**ed** *agg.* colorato, di colore: **—ed person,** persona di colore (*non di razza bianca*). —**ful** *agg.* multicolore; vivace; pittoresco. —**ing** *n.* colorazione, coloritura: **—ing matter,** sostanza colorante. —**less** *agg.* incolore.

colossal (kō·lŏs'ăl) *n.* colossale.

colt (kōlt) *n.* puledro; novellino.

column (kŏl'ŭm) *n.* colonna; (*giorn.*) rubrica.

columnist (kŏl'ŭm·nĭst) *n.* (*giorn.*) titolare di una rubrica, giornalista.

coma (kō'mä) *n.* coma, torpore.

comb (kōm) *n.* pettine; striglia; cresta (*del gallo, dell'onda*); favo (*di miele*). *vi.* pettinare, strigliare;

rastrellare. *vi.* frangersi (*delle onde*).

combat (kŏm′băt; kŏm·băt′) *n.* combattimento, lotta: — car, autoblindo. *vt.*, *vi.* combattere, lottare; avversare. —ant *n.*, *agg.* combattente.

combination (kŏm′bĭ·nā′shŭn) *n.* combinazione.

combine (kŏm·bīn′) *n.* consorzio; combriccola. *vt.* combinare, riunire. *vi.* unirsi, accordarsi, coalizzarsi.

combustible (kŏm·bŭs′tĭ·b'l) *n.*, *agg.* combustibile.

combustion (kŏm·bŭs′chŭn) *n.* combustione.

come (kŭm) *vi.* (*pass.* came, *pp.* come) venire, arrivare, giungere; accadere, divenire, riuscire: — what may, avvenga che può; the time to —, l'avvenire; to — about, accadere; to — again, tornare; ripetere. to — against, urtare contro; to — asunder, separarsi, sfasciarsi; to — back, tornare; to — in, entrare; to — into, entrare in possesso di, ereditare; to — of age, diventare maggiorenne; to — off, staccarsi; riuscire, accadere; to — out, uscire; to — to, riprendere i sensi; to — to terms, accordarsi; to — undone, unsewed, disfarsi, scucirsi; to — up with, raggiungere.

comedian (kŏ·mē′dĭ·ăn) *n.* commediante; (attore) comico, buffone.

comedy (kŏm′ĕ·dĭ) *n.* commedia; comica.

comeliness (kŭm′lĭ·nĕs) *n.* bellezza, grazia.

comely (kŭm′lĭ) *agg.* bello, aggraziato.

comet (kŏm′ĕt) *n.* cometa.

comfort (kŭm′fĕrt) *n.* conforto, consolazione; comodità, benessere, sollievo; coltre. *vt.* confortare, incoraggiare. —able *agg.* comodo, confortevole; rilassato. —ably *avv.* comodamente; agiatamente. —er *n.* consolatore; lo Spirito Santo-coltre; sciarpa di lana. —less *agg.* sconfortato, desolato, inconsolabile.

comic (kŏm′ĭk) *n.* comico; comica; (*pl.*) storiella *o* giornale a fumetti. *agg.* comico; a fumetti. —al *agg.* comico, ridicolo.

coming (kŭm′ĭng) *n.* arrivo, venuta, avvento: to be long in —, farsi aspettare; *agg.* veniente, prossimo; (*fam.*) promettente, sulla strada del successo.

comma (kŏm′à) *n.* virgola.

command (kŏ·mànd′) *n.* comando, ordine, autorità; padronanza. *vt.*

comandare, disporre di; incutere (*rispetto*); dominare (*un panorama, ecc.*); aver padronanza di.

commandeer (kŏm′ăn·dēr′) *vt.* requisire.

commander (kŏ·màn′dĕr) *n.* comandante.

commanding (kŏ·mànd′ĭng) *agg.* imponente, autoritario: — officer, ufficiale superiore.

commandment (kŏ·mànd′mĕnt) *n.* comandamento.

commando (kŏ·màn′dō) *n.* formazione di guastatori, commando.

commemorate (kŏ·mĕm′ō·rāt) *vt.* celebrare, commemorare.

commence (kŏ·mĕns′) *vt.*, *vi.* cominciare, esordire. —ment *n.* inizio, esordio, origine; cerimonia per la distribuzione di diplomi.

commend (kŏ·mĕnd′) *vt.* raccomandare, approvare, lodare; affidare. —able *agg.* lodevole, raccomandabile. —ation *n.* elogio, raccomandazione.

comment (kŏm′ĕnt) *n.* commento. *vt.*, *vi.* commentare, chiosare. —ary *n.* commentario. —ator *n.* commentatore.

commerce (kŏm′ûrs) *n.* commercio.

commercial (kŏ·mûr′shăl) *agg.* commerciale. *n.* (*radio, T.V.*, *cinema*) pubblicità, annuncio.

commiserate (kŏ·mĭz′ĕr·āt) *vt.* commiserare, compiangere.

commiseration (-ā′shŭn) *n.* commiserazione.

commissary (kŏm′ĭ·sĕr′ĭ) *n.* commissario; commissariato, ufficio approvvigionamenti; mensa.

commission (kŏ·mĭsh′ŭn) *n.* commissione; provvigione, ordine, incarico; comitato; (*mil.*) nomina (*a ufficiale*); perpetrazione: in — (*naut.*), in assetto di navigazione; out of —, fuori uso, guasto, in disarmo. *vt.* incaricare, autorizzare, affidare un comando a; armare (*una nave*). —ed officer *n.* ufficiale (*munito di nomina*).

commissioner *n.* commissario: — in bankruptcy, giudice delegato (*di fallimento*).

commit (kŏ·mĭt′) *vt.* commettere, fare; affidare, consegnare; rinviare (*a giudizio*): to — oneself, compromettersi; impegnarsi: to — to memory, imparare a memoria; to — suicide, uccidersi.

committee (kŏ·mĭt′ĭ) *n.* comitato, commissione: — of one, delegato unico.

commode (kŏ·mōd′) *n.* cassettone, comodino.

commodious (kŏ·mō'dĭ·ŭs) agg. comodo, spazioso.

commodity (kŏ·mŏd'ĭ·tĭ) n. merce, derrata.

common (kŏm'ŭn) n. comune. (pl.) plebe, (la) massa; refettorio. agg. comune; generale; pubblico; ordinario, volgare, corrente, triviale: — sailor, semplice marinaio; — soldier, soldato semplice. —ly avv. comunemente, solitamente, normalmente. —ness n. ordinarietà, volgarità.

commonplace (kŏm'ŭn·plās') n. luogo comune, banalità. agg. banale, comune.

commonwealth (kŏm'ŭn·wĕlth') n. stato, repubblica, collettività.

commotion (kŏ·mō'shŭn) n. commozione, agitazione, tumulto, disordine.

commune (kŏ·mūn') vi. confabulare, conversare, scambiare idee, intrattenersi: to — with oneself, raccogliersi in meditazione, riflettere. n. (kŏm'ún) comune (divisione amministrativa di territori).

communicate (kŏ·mū'nĭ·kāt) vt. comunicare, far conoscere, partecipare. vi. comunicarsi, comunicare.

communication (kŏ·mū'nĭ·kā'shŭn) n. comunicazione.

communicative (kŏ·mū'nĭ·kā'tĭv) agg. comunicativo.

communion (kŏ·mūn'yŭn) n. comunione.

communism (kŏm'ū·nĭz'm) n. comunismo.

communist (-nĭst) n., agg. comunista.

communistic (-nĭs'tĭk) agg. comunista.

community (kŏ·mū'nĭ·tĭ) n. comunità, collettività: — chest, fondo di beneficenza.

commutation (kŏm'ū·tā'shŭn) n. commutazione: — ticket (ferr.), biglietto d'abbonamento tra città e suburbio.

commute (kŏ·mūt') vt. commutare. vi. viaggiare con biglietto d'abbonamento, fare la spola.

compact (kŏm'păkt) n. patto, contratto, convenzione; portacipria. agg. (kŏm·păkt') compatto, compresso, conciso, serrato. —ness n. compattezza; concisione.

companion (kŏm·păn'yŭn) n. compagno, amico, socio; dama di compagnia. —able agg. socievole. —ship n. amicizia, cameratismo.

companionway (-wā') n. scaletta di piroscafo (che scende sottocoperta).

company (kŭm'pá·nĭ) n. compagnia; società; comitiva; equipaggio: to part —, dividersi, separarsi da.

comparable (kŏm'pá·ráb'l) agg. comparabile.

comparative (kŏm·păr'á·tĭv) agg., n. comparativo.

compare (kŏm·pâr') vt. comparare, confrontare, verificare: to — notes, avere uno scambio di idee; beyond —, senza uguali. vi. rivaleggiare, reggere al confronto.

comparison (kŏm·păr'ĭ·sŭn) n. confronto, paragone, raffronto: beyond —, incomparabile; in — with, in confronto a.

compartment (kŏm·pärt'mĕnt) n. compartimento, suddivisione; scompartimento.

compass (kŭm'pás) n. circonferenza, limite, area, àmbito, portata; (naut.) bussola. —es pl. compasso, compassi.

compassion (kŏm·păsh'ŭn) n. compassione, pietà. —ate (-ĭt) agg. compassionevole, caritatevole. vt. (-āt) compassionare.

compatible (kŏm·păt'ĭ·b'l) agg. compatibile.

compatriot (kŏm·pā'trĭ·ŭt) n. compatriota.

compel (kŏm·pĕl') vt. costringere, obbligare, forzare, imporre.

compelling (kŏm·pĕl'ĭng) agg. imperioso; autorevole; imponente; impellente; irresistibile.

compendious (kŏm·pĕn'dĭ·ŭs) agg. succinto, compatto.

compensate (kŏm'pĕn·sāt) vt. compensare, ricompensare, risarcire.

compensation (-sā'shŭn) n. compensazione; risarcimento, indennità; assicurazione sul lavoro.

compete (kŏm·pēt') vi. competere, rivaleggiare, concorrere.

competence (kŏm'pĕ·tĕns) n. competenza, capacità, attitudine; agiatezza.

competent (-tĕnt) agg. competente, abile, esperto.

competition (kŏm'pĕ·tĭsh'ŭn) n. competizione, gara, concorso; concorrenza.

competitive (kŏm·pĕt'ĭ tĭv) agg. competitivo, di concorrenza.

competitor (kŏm·pĕt'ĭ·tĕr) n. concorrente, rivale.

compilation (kŏm·pĭ·lā'shŭn) n. compilazione.

compile (kŏm·pīl') vt. compilare.

compiler (kŏm·pīl'ĕr) n. compilatore.

complacency (kŏm·plā'sĕn·sĭ) n. compiacenza, compiacimento, soddisfazione.

complacent (kŏm·plā'sĕnt) agg. compiacente, compiaciuto.

complain 44 concern

complain (kŏm·plān′) vi. lagnarsi, dolersi. —ant n. querelante, attore (d'una causa).

complaint (kŏm·plānt′) n. lagnanza, protesta, reclamo; malattia: to lodge a —, presentare un reclamo, sporgere querela.

complaisance (kŏm′plā·zăns) n. compiacenza.

complaisant (-zănt) agg. compiacente.

complement (kŏm′plē·mĕnt) n. complemento. vt. completare.

complete (kŏm·plēt′) agg. completo. vt. completare, terminare. —ly avv. completamente. —ness n. completezza, perfezione.

completion (kŏm·plē′shŭn) n. completamento, perfezionamento; compimento.

complex (kŏm′plĕks) n. complesso; raccolta. agg. (kŏm·plĕks′) complesso, complicato.

complexion (kŏm·plĕk′shŭn) n. complessione, temperamento; colorito, carnagione; aspetto.

complexity (kŏm·plĕk′sĭ tĭ) n. complessità.

compliance (kŏm·plī′ăns) n. acquiescenza, condiscendenza, obbedienza, osservanza: in — with, in conformità di.

complicate (kŏm′plĭ·kāt) vt. complicare.

complicated (-kāt′ĕd) agg. complicato.

complication (-kā′shŭn) n. complicazione.

compliment (kŏm′plĭ·mĕnt) n. complimento, omaggio, ossequio, cortesia, regalo: —s of the season, auguri. vt. complimentare, congratularsi con. —ary agg. lusinghiero; gratuito, in omaggio.

comply (kŏm·plī′) vi. acconsentire, compiacere, ottemperare: to — with a request, accogliere una richiesta.

component (kŏm·pō′nĕnt) n., agg. componente.

compose (kŏm·pōz′) vt., vi. comporre, scrivere, redigere: to — oneself, calmarsi, ricomporsi.

composed (-pōzd′) agg. composto, calmo.

composer (-pōz′ĕr) n. compositore; paciere.

composite (kŏm·pŏz′ĭt) n., agg. composto.

composition (kŏm·pō·zĭsh′ŭn) n. composizione; (comm.) compromesso, accordo.

compositor (kŏm·pŏz′ĭ·tĕr) n. (tip.) compositore.

composure (kŏm·pō′zhĕr) n. calma, equilibrio, imperturbabilità.

compound (kŏm·pound′) n., agg. composto. vt., vi. comporre; mescolare, combinare; transare; accordarsi: to — with one's creditors, ottenere un corcordato.

comprehend (kŏm′prē·hĕnd′) vt. capire, concepire; abbracciare, includere.

comprehensible (-hĕn′sĭ·b'l) agg. comprensibile.

comprehension (-hĕn′shŭn) n. comprensione.

comprehensive (-hĕn′sĭv) agg. comprensivo, inclusivo; esauriente.

compress (kŏm·prĕs′) n. compressa. vt. comprimere. —ion n. compressione.

comprise (kŏm·prīz′) vt. contenere, comprendere, includere.

compromise (kŏm′prō·mīz) n. compromesso, accordo, transazione. vt., vi. compromettere; transare; transigere.

comptroller vedi controller.

compulsion (kŏm·pŭl′shŭn) n. costrizione, coercizione.

compulsory (-sō·rĭ) agg. obbligatorio; coercitivo; irresistibile.

compunction (kŏm·pŭngk′shŭn) n. compunzione, rimorso.

computation (kŏm′pū·tā′shŭn) n. computo, calcolo.

compute (kŏm·pūt′) vt. computare, calcolare.

comrade (kŏm′răd; -rĭd) n. camerata, compagno. —ship n. cameratismo.

concave (kŏn′kāv; kŏn·kāv′) agg. concavo, cavo.

conceal (kŏn·sēl′) vt. nascondere, celare, dissimulare, occultare. —ment n. occultamento, nascondiglio.

concede (kŏn·sēd′) vt. concedere; ammettere, riconoscere; accordare.

conceit (kŏn·sēt′) n. presunzione; concetto, idea; immaginazione. —ed agg. presuntuoso, vanitoso.

conceivable (kŏn·sēv′à·b'l) agg. concepibile.

conceive (kŏn·sēv′) vt. concepire, immaginare, credere.

concentrate (kŏn′sĕn.trāt) vt. concentrare. vi. concentrarsi.

concentration (-trā′shŭn) n. concentrazione: — camp, campo di concentramento.

concept (kŏn′sĕpt) n. concetto.

conception (kŏn·sĕp′shŭn) n. concezione; concetto, idea.

concern (kŏn·sûrn′) n. interesse, cura; preoccupazione, ansia; (comm.) impresa, azienda, ditta, affare: this is no — of mine, questo non mi riguarda. vt. concernere, interessare, riguardare; preoccupare. —ed *agg.* interessato (*a*); preoccupato, in ansia. —ing *prep.* riguardo a.

concert (kŏn'sûrt) *n.* concerto. *vt.* (kŏn·sûrt') concertare. *vi.* concertarsi, accordarsi.

concession (kŏn·sĕsh'ŭn) *n.* concessione.

conciliate (kŏn·sĭl'ĭ·āt) *vt.* conciliare.

conciliation (-ā'shŭn) *n.* conciliazione.

concise (kŏn·sīs') *agg.* conciso. —ness *n.* concisione.

conclude (kŏn·klōōd') *vt.* concludere. *vi.* concludersi, terminare.

conclusion (kŏn·klōō'zhŭn) *n.* conclusione, fine.

conclusive (-sĭv) *agg.* conclusivo, persuasivo.

concoct (kŏn·kŏkt') *vt.* preparare; tramare; architettare. —ion *n.* mescolanza, intruglio; preparazione; macchinazione.

concord (kŏn'kôrd) *n.* concordia, armonia; accordo; concordanza. *vi.* concordare, accordarsi.

concourse (kŏn'kōrs) *n.* concorso, affluenza, affollamento.

concrete (kŏn'krēt; kŏn·krēt') *n.* cemento: reinforced —, cemento armato. *agg.* concreto, solido. *vi.* solidificarsi.

concur (kŏn·kûr') *vi.* concorrere, accordarsi, cooperare. —rence *n.* concorso, consenso, cooperazione. —rent *agg.* concorrente, simultaneo, acquiescente.

concussion (kŏn·kŭsh'ŭn) *n.* trauma: — of the brain, commozione cerebrale.

condemn (kŏn·dĕm') *vt.* condannare, biasimare; espropriare, confiscare. —ation (-nā'shŭn) *n.* condanna.

condensation (kŏn'dĕn·sā'shŭn) *n.* condensazione; riassunto.

condense (kŏn·dĕns') *vt.* condensare; riassumere, compendiare. *vi.* condensarsi.

condenser (kŏn·dĕn'sĕr) *n.* condensatore.

condescend (kŏn'dē·sĕnd') *vi.* accondiscendere. —ence *n.* condiscendenza.

condescension (-sĕn'shŭn) *n.* degnazione, condiscendenza.

condiment (kŏn'dĭ·mĕnt) *n.* condimento.

condition (kŏn·dĭsh'ŭn) *n.* condizione, stato; clausola. *vt.* sistemare a dovere; determinare, limitare, condizionare; rimandare (*uno studente*). —al *agg.* condizionale.

condole (kŏn·dōl') *vi.* condolersi, rammaricarsi. —nce *n.* condoglianza.

condone (kŏn·dōn') *vt.* condonare, perdonare.

conduce (kŏn·dūs') *vi.* condurre *o* contribuire (*a un risultato*), tendere (*verso*).

conducive (-dū'sĭv) *agg.* che contribuisce, tendente, apportatore: — to slumber, che concilia il sonno.

conduct (kŏn'dŭkt) *n.* condotta; direzione, guida. *vt.* (-dŭkt') condurre, dirigere, portare: to — oneself, comportarsi. —ive *agg.* conduttivo. —ivity *n.* conduttività. —or *n.* conduttore, guida; capotreno; direttore d'orchestra.

conduit (kŏn'dĭt; -dōo̯.ĭt) *n.* condotto.

cone (kōn) *n.* cono; (*bot.*) pigna.

confabulate (kŏn·făb'ū·lāt) *vi.* confabulare.

confection (kŏn·fĕk'shŭn) *n.* confezione; confettura, conserva. *vt.* confezionare, preparare. —er *n.* pasticcere. —ery *n.* pasticceria.

confederacy (kŏn·fĕd'ĕr·á·sĭ) *n.* confederazione; lega (*di cospiratori*); associazione a delinquere.

confederate (kŏn·fĕd'ĕr·ĭt) *n.* confederato, alleato; complice, compare. *agg.* confederato, ausiliario. *vi.* confederarsi, associarsi.

confederation (kŏn·fĕd'r·ā'shŭn) *n.* confederazione.

confer (kŏn·fûr') *vt.* conferire, assegna e; accordare. *vi.* conferire (*con*), consultarsi.

conference (kŏn'fĕr·ĕns) *n.* conferenza.

confess (kŏn·fĕs') *vt.* confessare, ammettere. *vi.* confessarsi. —ion *n.* confessione. —ional *n.*, *agg.* confessionale. —or *n.* confessore.

confetti (kŏn·fĕt'ĭ) *n.pl.* coriandoli.

confidant *m.*, confidante *f.* (kŏn'fĭ·dănt'; kŏn'fĭ·dănt) *n.* confidente.

confide (kŏn·fīd') *vt.* confidare; affidare. *vi.* confidarsi; fare affidamento (*su*).

confidence (kŏn'fĭ·dĕns) *n.* fiducia, sicurezza, baldanza; confidenza: — game (trick), truffa all'americana; — ("con") man, truffatore all'americana.

confident (-dĕnt) *agg.* fiducioso, sicuro; baldanzoso. —ial *agg.* confidenziale, riservato. —ly *avv.* fiduciosamente, baldanzosamente.

confine (kŏn'fīn) *n.* confine, limite. *vt.* (-fīn') confinare, rinchiudere, limitare; relegare; delimitare: to — oneself, limitarsi; relegarsi. *vi.* confinare (*con*): —d to bed, costretto a letto. —ment *n.* confino, reclusione; isolamento; parto; degenza: solitary —ment, segregazione cellulare.

confirm (kŏn·fûrm′) *vt.* confermare, convalidare; (*relig.*) cresimare. —ation *n.* conferma, ratifica; cresima. —ed *agg.* inveterato, convinto.

confiscate (kŏn′fĭs·kāt) *vt.* confiscare, requisire.

confiscation (-kā′shŭn) *n.* confisca.

conflagration (kŏn′flá·grā′shŭn) *n.* incendio, conflagrazione.

conflict (kŏn′flĭkt) *n.* conflitto, contrasto, lotta, guerra. *vi.* (-flĭkt′) lottare, contrastare, urtarsi. —ing *agg.* contrastante, contraddittorio.

conform (kŏn·fôrm′) *vt.* conformare. *vi.* conformarsi; ottemperare. —ity *n.* conformità: in — with, conformemente a.

confound (kŏn·found′) *vt.* confondere, scompigliare; devastare; turbare; mandare al diavolo: — you! va al diavolo! ; — it! accidenti!

confront (kŏn·frŭnt′) *vt.* confrontare, raffrontare, paragonare, mettere a confronto, mettere di fronte.

confuse (kŏn·fūz′) *vt.* confondere, imbrogliare, arruffare, disorientare, sconcertare.

confused *agg.* confuso, sconcertato.

confusion (kŏn·fū′zhŭn) *n.* confusione, disordine; imbarazzo, vergogna.

congeal (kŏn·jēl′) *vt.* ghiacciare, congelare, gelare. *vi.* congelarsi.

congenial (kŏn·jēn′yǎl) *agg.* affine; gradevole, simpatico; concorde (*a*).

congest (kŏn·jĕst′) *vt.* congestionare. *vi.* congestionarsi. —ion *n.* congestione; ammasso; ingombro.

conglomeration (kŏn·glŏm′ẽr·ā′shŭn) *n.* conglomerazione, conglomerato.

congratulate (kŏn·grăt′ū·lāt) *vt.* felicitare, congratularsi con: to — oneself, rallegrarsi, compiacersi.

congratulation (-lā′shŭn) *n.* congratulazione.

congregate (kŏng′grē·gāt) *vt.* radunare. *vi.* radunarsi.

congregation (kŏng′grē·gā′shŭn) *n.* congregazione; riunione, assemblea; uditorio.

congress (kŏng′grĕs) *n.* congresso; (*S.U.*) Parlamento. —ional *agg.* di congresso. —man *n.* congressista; (*S.U.*) deputato al Parlamento.

conic (kŏn′ĭk), conical (-ĭ·kǎl) *agg.* conico.

conjecture (kŏn·jĕk′tûr) *n.* congettura. *vt., vi.* congetturare.

conjugate (kŏn′jŏȯ·gāt) *vt.* coniugare.

conjugation (-gā′shŭn) *n.* coniugazione.

conjunction (kŏn·jŭngk′shŭn) *n.* congiunzione.

conjunctive (-tĭv) *n., agg.* congiuntivo.

conjure (kŭn′jẽr; kŏn′-) *vt.* invocare, evocare; fare giochi di prestigio; (kŏn·jŏȯr′) implorare, scongiurare.

conjurer (kŭn′jẽr·ẽr) *n.* mago; prestigiatore.

conk (kŏngk) *vt.* (*gergo*) colpire (*alla testa*), tramortire. *vi.* incepparsi, guastarsi.

connect (kŏ·nĕkt′) *vt.* collegare, associare, unire. *vi.* collegarsi; (*ferr.*) fare coincidenza. —ing rod *n.* biella. —ion *n.* connessione; attinenza; conoscenza; parentela; parente; setta religiosa; coincidenza (*di treni, ecc.*); clientela.

connivance (kŏ·nĭv′ǎns) *n.* connivenza.

connive (kŏ·nĭv′) *vi.* essere connivente, farsi complice.

connoisseur (kŏn′ĭ·sûr′; -sûr′) *n.* competente, intenditore.

conquer (kŏng′kẽr) *vt.* conquistare, vincere, domare, piegare. —or *n.* conquistatore; vincitore.

conquest (kŏng′kwĕst) *n.* conquista, vittoria.

conscience (kŏn′shĕns) *n.* coscienza.

conscientious (kŏn′shĭ·ĕn′shŭs) *agg.* coscienzioso: — objector, obiettore di coscienza.

conscious (kŏn′shŭs) *agg.* conscio, cosciente, edotto. —ly *avv.* consapevolmente, scientemente. —ness *n.* coscienza, percezione, conoscenza: to regain —, riprendere i sensi.

conscript (kŏn′skrĭpt) *n., agg.* coscritto. —ion *n.* coscrizione.

consecrate (kŏn′sē·krāt) *vt.* consacrare, benedire, santificare.

consecration (-krā′shŭn) *n.* consacrazione.

consecutive (kŏn·sĕk′ū·tĭv) *agg.* consecutivo.

consensus (kŏn·sĕn′sŭs) *n.* accordo, concordanza; unanimità.

consent (kŏn·sĕnt′) *n.* consenso, accordo, adesione. *vi.* consentire, aderire.

consequence (kŏn′sē·kwĕns) *n.* conseguenza, risultato, effetto, importanza: it is of no —, non ha importanza.

consequent (-kwĕnt) *n.* conseguenza; (*mat.*) conseguente. *agg.* conseguente. —ly *avv.* conseguentemente, quindi, perciò.

conservation (kŏn′sẽr·vā′shŭn) *n.* conservazione.

conservative (kŏn·sûr′vá·tĭv) *n.* conservatore. *agg.* conservativo; prudente, cauto; tradizionale, tradizionalista.

conservatory (kŏn·sûr′vá·tō′rĭ) *n.* serra; conservatorio musicale.

conserve (kŏn·sûrv') *n.* conserva. *vt.* conservare, preservare, mettere in conserva.

consider (kŏn·sĭd'ẽr) *vt.* considerare, esaminare, valutare. *vi.* riflettere, pensare. —**able** *agg.* considerevole, notevole, importante. —**ableness** *n.* importanza. —**ably** *avv.* considerevolmente, assai.

considerate (kŏn·sĭd'ẽr·ĭt) *agg.* riguardoso, prudente, premuroso. —**ness** *n.* delicatezza; cautela, prudenza; discrezione.

consideration (kŏn·sĭd'ẽr·ā'shŭn) *n.* considerazione; ,esame; riguardo; giudizio, opinione; importanza; ricompensa.

considering *prep.*, *cong.* in vista di, tenendo conto (che, di), dato (che), tutto sommato, visto che.

consign (kŏn·sīn') *vt.* consegnare, affidare. —**ment** *n.* consegna, spedizione; fornitura *o* partita (*di merce*).

consist (kŏn·sĭst') *vi.* consistere, constare (*di*); sussistere; esser compatibile: to — in, of, essere compreso in; consistere di; —**ence**, —**ency** *n.* consistenza, coerenza, compatibilità, solidità. —**ent** *agg.* coerente, compatibile, costante.

consolation (kŏn'sŏl·ā'shŭn) *n.* consolazione.

console (kŏn·sōl') *vt.* consolare.

consolidate (kŏn·sŏl'ĭ·dāt) *vt.* consolidare. *vi.* consolidarsi.

consonant (kŏn'sṓ·nănt) *agg.* armonico, concorde, consono. *n.* (*gramm.*) consonante.

consort (kŏn'sŏrt) *n.* consorte, coniuge, compagno. *vi.* (kŏn·sŏrt'): to — with imbrancarsi con, frequentare, far lega con.

conspicuous (cŏn·spĭk'ū·ŭs) *agg.* cospicuo; evidente, vistoso: to make oneself —, farsi notare.

conspiracy (kŏn·spĭr'ȧsĭ) *n.* cospirazione, congiura.

conspirator (kŏn·spĭr'ȧ·tẽr) *n.* cospiratore, congiurato.

conspire (kŏn·spīr') *vi.* congiurare.

constable (kŏn'stȧ·b'l) *n.* conestabile; poliziotto, agente.

constancy (kŏn'stăn·sĭ) *n.* costanza.

constant (kŏn'stănt) *agg.* costante, scontinuo.

constellation (kŏn'stĕ·lā'shŭn) *n.* costellazione.

consternation (kŏn'stẽr·nā'shŭn) *n.* costernazione.

constipation (kŏn'stĭ·pā'shŭn) *n.* stitichezza, ingombro intestinale.

constituency (kŏn·stĭt'ū·ĕn·sĭ) *n.* complesso degli elettori, circoscrizione.

constituent (-ĕnt) *n.* elemento costituente; elettore. *agg.* costituente.

constitute (kŏn'stĭ·tūt) *vt.* costituire, formare.

constitution (kŏn'stĭ·tū'shŭn) *n.* costituzione. —**al** *agg.* costituzionale. *n.* passeggiata igienica.

constrain (kŏn·strān') *vt.* costringere; comprimere; reprimere, trattenere; imprigionare.

constraint (kŏn·strānt') *n.* costrizione, repressione (*di sentimenti*); imbarazzo, riserbo.

constrict (kŏn·strĭkt') *vt.* comprimere; reprimere, —**or** *n.* costrittore (*muscolo*); (*zool.*) boa.

constriction (kŏn·strĭk'shŭn) *n.* costrizione, restrizione; restringimento.

construct (kŏn·strŭkt') *vt.* costruire; interpretare. —**ion** *n.* costruzione, interpretazione: to put a wrong — -ion on, interpretare male. —**ive** *agg.* costruttivo.

construe (kŏn·strōō') *vt.* interpretare, spiegare, tradurre.

consul (kŏn'sŭl) *n.* console. —**ar** *agg.* consolare. —**ate** *n.* consolato.

consult (kŏn·sŭlt') *vt.* consultare. —**ation** *n.* consultazione, consulto.

consume (kŏn·sūm') *vt.* consumare; sprecare. *vi.* consumarsi; struggersi.

consumer (-sūm'ẽr) *n.* consumatore.

consummate (kŏn·sŭm'ĭt) *agg.* consumato, abile, raffinato. *vt.* (kŏn'sŭ·māt) compiere, consumare.

consumption (kŏn·sŭmp'shŭn) *n.* consumo; consunzione; tisi.

consumptive (kŏn·sŭmp'tĭv) *agg.* logorato; tisico.

contact (kŏn'tăkt) *n.* contatto; rapporto. *vt.* mettere in contatto; accostare, mettersi in comunicazione con. *vi.* prender contatto.

contagion (kŏn·tā'jŭn) *n.* contagio.

contagious (-jŭs) *agg.* contagioso.

contain (kŏn·tān') *vt.* contenere, includere; limitare, reprimere: to — oneself, dominarsi. —**er** *n.* recipiente, involucro, astuccio.

contaminate (kŏn·tăm'ĭ·nāt) *vt.* contaminare.

contamination (-nā'shŭn) *n.* contaminazione.

contango (kŏn·tăng'gō) *n.* (*ingl. borsa*) riporto.

contemplate (kŏn'tĕm·plāt; kŏn·tĕm'plāt) *vt.* contemplare, meditare, progettare, prevedere.

contemplation (kŏn'tĕm·plā'shŭn) *n.* contemplazione; progetto, proposito.

contemporaneous (kŏn·tĕm′pō·rā′nĕ-ŭs), **contemporary**) kŏn·tĕm′pō·rĕr′ĭ) n., agg. contemporaneo; coetaneo.

contempt (kŏn·tĕmpt′) n. disprezzo, sdegno: — of court, offesa alla magistratura. —**ible** agg. spregevole. —**tuous** agg. sprezzante, sdegnoso.

contend (kŏn·tĕnd) vt., vi. contendere; lottare; contestare, obiettare; sostenere, affermare.

content (kŏn·tĕnt′) (1) n. contentezza, soddisfazione: to one's heart's —, a sazietà. agg. contento, soddisfatto. vt. accontentare, soddisfare.

content (kŏn′tĕnt) (2) n. (gen.pl.) contenuto: table of —s, sommario, indice.

contented (kŏn·tĕn′tĕd) agg. soddisfatto.

contention (kŏn·tĕn′shŭn) n. contesa, disputa, dibattito; asserzione: bone of —, pomo della discordia.

contentious (-shŭs) agg. litigioso; controverso.

contest (kŏn′tĕst) n. contesa, controversia; gara. vt., vi. (kŏn·tĕst′) contestare, disputare; lottare, competere.

context (kŏn′tĕkst) n. contesto.

contiguous (kŏn·tĭg′ū·ŭs)agg. contiguo.

continence (kŏn′tĭ·nĕns) n. continenza, moderazione, ritegno.

continent (kŏn′tĭ·nĕnt) (1) agg. moderato; morigerato.

continent (2) n. continente.

continental (-nĕn′t′l) agg. continentale; europeo.

contingency (kŏn·tĭn′jĕn·sĭ) n. contingenza, caso.

contingent (-jĕnt) agg. contingente.

continual (kŏn·tĭn′ū·ăl) agg. continuo. —**ly** avv. continuamente.

continuance (ăns) n. continuazione, continuità; permanenza.

continuation (kŏn·tĭn′ū·ā′shŭn) n. continuazione, seguito.

continue (kŏn·tĭn′ū) vt. continuare, perseverare; rimanere.

continuity (kŏn′tĭ·nū′ĭ·tĭ) n. continuità; (cinema, radio, T.V.) sceneggiatura.

continuous (kŏn·tĭn′ū·ŭs) agg. continuo.

contortion (kŏn·tôr′shŭn) n. contorsione, lussazione.

contour (kŏn′tŏŏr) n. contorno, perimetro.

contraband (kŏn′trȧ·bănd) n. contrabbando.

contract (kŏn′trăkt) n. contratto, convenzione, appalto. vt. (kŏn′trăkt′) contrattare; contrarre; restringere. vi. contrarsi, restringersi; comm.) trattare, contrattare.

contraction (kŏn·trăk′shŭn) n. contrazione; scarsità.

contractor (kŏn·trăk′tĕr; kŏn′trăk-tĕr) n. contraente; imprenditore (edile); appaltatore; fornitore.

contradict (kŏn′trȧ·dĭkt′) vt. contraddire, smentire. —**ion** n. contraddizione, smentita. —**ory** agg. contraddittorio.

contrail (kŏn′trāl′) n. (aeron.) scia di vapore acqueo.

contrary (kŏn′trĕr·ĭ; -trȧ·rĭ) n. (il) contrario. agg. contrario, ostinato. avv. contrariamente, in senso contrario: on the —, al contrario.

contrast (kŏn′trăst) n. contrasto. vt. (kŏn·trăst′) mettere in contrasto, raffrontare. vi. contrastare, essere in contrasto.

contribute (kŏn·trĭb′ūt) vt., vi. contribuire (con); collaborare.

contribution (kŏn′trĭ·bū′shŭn) n. contribuzione; collaborazione.

contributor (kŏn·trĭb′ū·tĕr) n. contributore; collaboratore.

contrite (kŏn·trīt′) agg. contrito.

contrition (kŏn·trĭsh′ŭn) n. contrizione.

contrivance (kŏn·trĭv′ăns) n. meccanismo, invenzione, congegno, piano, artificio.

contrive (kŏn·trīv′) vt. escogitare, trovare il modo di; inventare, progettare; tramare. vi. adoperarsi, arrangiarsi, riuscire (a).

control (kŏn·trōl′) n. controllo, freno, autorità; (pl.) comandi: — panel, quadro di comando; (aeron.) cruscotto. vt. controllare, regolare; dirigere, dominare. —**ler** n. controllore; regolatore.

controversy (kŏn′trō·vûr′sĭ) n. controversia, polemica, disputa.

contumacious (kŏn′tū·mā′shŭs) agg. ostinato, perverso.

contusion (kŏn·tū′zhŭn) n. contusione, ammaccatura.

conundrum (kō·nŭn′drŭm) n. indovinello, enigma.

convalesce (kŏn′vȧ·lĕs′) vi. essere in convalescenza.

convalescence (kŏn′vȧ·lĕs′′ns) n. convalescenza.

convalescent (-ĕnt) n., agg. convalescente: — home, convalescenziario.

convene (kŏn·vēn′) vt. riunire, convocare. vi. riunirsi.

convenience (kŏn·vēn′yĕns) n. convenienza; comodità, comodo.

convenient (-yĕnt) agg. comodo, conveniente. —**ly** avv. comodamente, acconciamente; opportunamente.

convent (kŏn′vĕnt) n. convento.

convention (kŏn·vĕn′shŭn) *n.* convenzione, patto; assemblea. **—al** *agg.* convenzionale; di convenzione; tradizionale; manierato.

converge (kŏn·vûrj′) *vi.* convergere.

conversant (kŏn′vẽr·sănt) *agg.* versato, dotto, edotto: **to be — with**, essere ferrato in, intendersi di.

conversation (kŏn′vẽr·sā′shŭn) *n.* conversazione.

converse (kŏn·vûrs′) (1) *vi.* chiacchierare, intrattenersi.

converse (kŏn′vûrs) (2) *n.*, *agg.* converso, reciproco, contrario.

conversely *avv.* inversamente; viceversa, al contrario.

conversion (kŏn·vûr′zhŭn) *n.* conversione.

convert (kŏn′vûrt) *n.* convertito, neòfito. *vt.* (kŏn·vûrt′) convertire, trasformare; adibire. *vi.* convertirsi, trasformarsi. **—ible** *agg.* trasformabile.

convex (kŏn′vĕks; kŏn·vĕks′) *agg.* convesso.

convey (kŏn·vā′) *vt.* trasportare, portare; esprimere, far capire; trasmettere (*suoni, ecc.*), riferire: **to — thanks**, porgere ringraziamenti.

conveyance (kŏn·vā′ăns) *n.* trasporto; trasmissione, comunicazione; veicolo; passaggio di proprietà.

convict (kŏn′vĭkt) *n.* condannato, galeotto. *vt.* (kŏn·vĭkt′) condannare, dichiarare reo. **—ion** *n.* convinzione, persuasione; convinzione di reità, condanna.

convince (kŏn·vĭns′) *vt.* convincere.

convincing (-vĭn′sĭng) *agg.* convincente.

convocation (kŏn′vō·kā′shŭn) *n.* convocazione.

convoke (kŏn·vōk′) *vt.* convocare.

convoy (kŏn′voi) *n.* convoglio, scorta. *vt.* (kŏn·voi′) convogliare; scortare.

convulsed (kŏn·vulst′) *agg.* convulso, sconvolto; spasmodico.

convulsion (kŏn·vŭl′shŭn) *n.* convulsione; rivolgimento, convulso.

cony, coney (kō′nĭ) *n.* coniglio.

coo (kōō) *vi.* tubare.

cook (kōōk) *n.* cuoco, cuoca, cuciniere. *vt.*, *vi.* cucinare, far cucina; alterare (*la contabilità*), cuocere, far cuocere; manipolare: **to — up a plan**, ordire un piano.

cookery (kōōk′ẽr·ĭ) *n.* culinaria, cucina.

cookie (kōōk′ĭ) *n.* pasticcino.

cooking (kōōk′ĭng) *n.* cucina, culinaria: **— stove**, cucina a gas *o* elettrica; **— utensils**, batteria di cucina.

cookout (kōōk′out′) *n.* spuntino all'aperto, colazione sull'erba.

cool (kōōl) *agg.* fresco; calmo, freddo, impudente. *n.* freddezza, freschezza. *vt.* rinfrescare, raffreddare, calmare. *vi.* calmarsi; raffreddarsi: **to — down**, placarsi. **—er** *n.* ghiacciaia; (*auto.*) radiatore; (*gergo*) galera, cella. **—ness** *n.* freschezza, freddezza, indifferenza, sfacciataggine.

coop (kōōp) *n.* pollaio, stia. *vt.* rinchiudere, imprigionare.

cooper (kōōp′ẽr) *n.* bottaio.

co-operate (kō·ŏp′ẽr·āt) *vi.* cooperare, collaborare, concorrere.

co-operation (-ā′shŭn) *n.* cooperazione.

co-operative (kō·ŏp′ẽr·ā′tĭv) *n.*, *agg.* cooperativo.

co-ordinate (kō·ôr′dĭ·nāt) *agg.* coordinato. *n.* (*mat.*) coordinata. *vt.* (-nāt) coordinare.

co-ordination (-nā′shŭn) *n.* coordinazione.

coot (kōōt) *n.* fòlaga.

cop (kŏp) *n.* (*gergo*) poliziotto: **cops and robbers**, guardie e ladri.

copartner (kō·pärt′nẽr) *n.* socio, consocio.

cope (kōp) *n.* cappa, manto; volta. *vt.*: **to — with**, affrontare, lottare con, sostenere una lotta con, tener testa a: **I can't — with this**, non ce la faccio.

copious (kō′pĭ·ŭs) *agg.* copioso, abbondante.

copper (kŏp′ẽr) *n.* rame, paiolo; (*gergo*) poliziotto.

coppice (kŏp′ĭs), **copse** (kŏps) *n.* boschetto.

'copter (kŏp′tẽr) *n.* elicottero.

copy (kŏp′ĭ) *n.* copia; esemplare (*di volume*); imitazione; numero (*di periodico, ecc.*); materiale (*letterario*): **rough —**, minuta; **true —**, copia conforme. *vt.* copiare, imitare, trascrivere.

copybook (kŏp′ĭ·bŏŏk′) *n.* quaderno.

copyright (kŏp′ĭ·rīt′) *n.* diritto d'autore, proprietà letteraria.

coquetry (kō′kĕ·trĭ) *n.* civetteria.

coquette (kō·kĕt′) *n.* civetta (*ragazza provocante*).

coquettish (kō·kĕt′ĭsh) *agg.* civettuolo, provocante.

coral (kŏr′ăl) *n.* corallo. *agg.* corallino.

cord (kôrd) *n.* cordone, corda, fune; (*pl.*) calzoni a coste: **spinal —**, spina dorsale.

cordial (kôr′jăl) *n.*, *agg.* cordiale. **—ity** *n.* cordialità.

corduroy (kôr′dŭ·roi; -dū-) *n.* tessuto a coste: **corduroys**, calzoni di velluto a coste.

core (kōr) *n.* torsolo (*di frutto*), parte centrale; profondo dell'anima: **rot-**

ten to the —, marcio fino al midollo. *vt.* togliere il torsolo a.

corespondent (kŏ'rĕ·spŏn'dĕnt) *n.* complice, coimputato, correo.

cork (kŏrk) *n.* sughero, turacciolo. *vt.* tappare, mettere il turacciolo a. —screw *n.* cavaturaccioli. — tree *n.* sughera quercia da sughero.

corn (kŏrn) (1) *n.* (*Ingl.*) cereale, grano, frumento; (*S.U.*) granoturco, mais: Indian —, granoturco; —meal, farina di mais. *vt.* salare (*carni, ecc.*); granulare: — beef, manzo salato.

corn (kŏrn) (2) *n.* callo.

corn (3) *n.* (*gergo*) banalità, cose risapute, vecchia trovata (*vedi* corny).

corner (kŏr'nĕr) *n.* angolo; (*comm.*) incetta, accaparramento. *vt.* mettere alle strette, accumulare, accaparrare. — cupboard, cantoniera. —stone *n.* pietra angolare.

cornet (kŏr·nĕt') *n.* cornetta; imbuto di carta; cono (*per gelato*).

cornice (kŏr'nĭs) *n.* cornicione.

corny (kŏr'nĭ) *agg.* banale, di maniera sentimentale, melodrammatico.

coronation (kŏr'ō·nā'shŭn) *n.* incoronazione.

coroner (kŏr'ō·nĕr) *n.* magistrato inquirente.

coronet (kŏr'ō·nĕt) *n.* diadema, corona.

corporal (kŏr'pō·răl) *n.* caporale. *agg.* corporale.

corporation (kŏr'pō·rā'shŭn) *n.* corporazione, società; (*gergo*) pinguedine, pancia.

corps (kŏr) *n.* corpo (*formazione mil.*): air —, aviazione.

corpse (kŏrps) *n.* cadavere.

corpulence (kŏr'pū·lĕns) *n.* corpulenza.

corpulent (-lĕnt) *agg.* corpulento.

corpuscle (kŏr'pŭs·'l) *n.* corpuscolo, cellula; elettrone; globulo (*sanguigno*).

corral (kŏ·răl') *n.* recinto (*per bestiame*).

correct (kŏ·rĕkt') *agg.* corretto, esatto; veritiero. *vt.* correggere, rettificare. —ion *n.* correzione, punizione. —ly *avv.* correttamente, giustamente. —ness *n.* correttezza, esattezza. —or *n.* correttore.

correlate (kŏr'ĕ·lāt) *vi.* essere in correlazione. *vt.* porre in correlazione.

correlation (-lā'shŭn) *n.* correlazione.

correspond (kŏr'ĕ·spŏnd') *vi.* corrispondere, accordarsi; essere in corrispondenza. —ence *n.* corrispondenza. —ent *n.*, *agg.* corrispondente. —ing *agg.* corrispondente.

corridor (kŏr'ĭ·dŏr' -dĕr) *n.* corridoio.

corroborate (kŏ·rŏb'ō·rāt) *vt.* corroborare, convalidare.

corroboration (-rā'shŭn) *n.* convalida, conferma.

corrode (kŏ·rōd') *vt.* corrodere. *vi.* corrodersi.

corrosion (kŏ·rō'zhŭn) *n.* corrosione.

corrosive (-rō'sĭv) *n.*, *agg.* corrosivo.

corrugate (kŏr'ū̇·gāt; kŏr'ŏo-) *vt.* corrugare, ondulare. *vi.* ondularsi: —d iron, lamiera ondulata.

corrupt (kŏ·rŭpt') *agg.* corrotto, marcio, infetto. *vt.* corrompere; guastare. *vi.* corrompersi, marcire. —ion *n.* corruzione, alterazione, decomposizione.

corset (kŏr'sĕt) *n.* busto (*da donna*).

cortisone (kŏr'tĭ·sōn) *n.* cortisone.

corundum (kŏ·rŭn'dŭm) *n.* (*min.*) corindone.

cosmetic (kŏz·mĕt'ĭk) *n.*, *agg.* cosmetico: — surgery, chirurgia estetica.

cosmic (kŏz'mĭk) *agg.* cosmico.

cosmopolitan (kŏz'mō·pŏl'ĭ·tăn) *agg.* cosmopolita.

cost (kŏst) *n.* costo, prezzo, spesa. *vi.* (*pass., pp.* cost) costare.

costive (kŏs'tĭv) *agg.* stitico. —ness *n.* stitichezza.

costliness (kŏst'lĭ·nĕs) *n.* costosità.

costly (kŏst'lĭ) *agg.* costoso, dispendioso.

costume (kŏs'tūm) *n.* costume, vestiario.

cosy *vedi* cozy.

cot (kŏt) (1) *n.* capanna, casetta.

cot (kŏt) (2) *n.* branda, cuccetta.

cottage (kŏt'ĭj) *n.* villino, casetta: —cheese, specie di ricotta; —piano, pianoforte verticale.

cotton (kŏt''n) *n.* cotone.

couch (kouch) (1) *n.* divanetto, letto.

couch (2) *vi.* giacere. *vt.* esprimere: to — in difficult language, esprimere con parole difficili.

cough (kŏf) *n.* tosse: whooping —, tosse asinina. *vi.* tossire: to — up, espettorare; sputare quattrini.

could (kŏod) *pass. di* can.

council (koun'sĭl) *n.* consiglio, concilio: city —, giunta municipale; — board, consiglio d'amministrazione. —lor, —man *n.* consigliere, assessore.

counsel (koun'sĕl) *n.* consiglio, parere; discrezione; avvocato: — for the defense, avvocato difensore; to take — with, consultarsi con; to keep one's —, tacere, mantenere il segreto. *vt.* consigliare. —lor *n.* consigliere, avvocato.

count (kount) (1) *n.* conte.

count (kount) (2) *n.* conto, calcolo; conteggio, scrutinio; capo d'accusa. *vt., vi.* contare, ritenere, tenere in conto, avere importanza, computare: to — out, escludere.

countenance (koun'tĕ·nǎns) n. sembiante, espressione, volto, aria, contegno; approvazione, incoraggiamento: out of —, sconcertato; to give — to, approvare, incoraggiare; to keep one's —, mantenersi serio. vt. incoraggiare, approvare.

counter (koun'tĕr) (1) n. calcolatore; contatore.

counter (2) n. banco (di negozio); gettone (da gioco).

counter (3) avv. contro, contrariamente. vi. parare (al pugilato, ecc.); rispondere a un colpo. vt. ribattere; avversare.

counteract (koun'tĕr·ǎkt') vt. frustrare, neutralizzare, controbilanciare.

counterbalance (koun'tĕr·bǎl'ǎns) n. contrappeso. vt. controbilanciare.

counterfeit (koun'tĕr·fĭt) n. contraffazione, falsificazione. agg. contraffatto, falso, imitato. vt. contraffare, falsificare. —er n. falsario.

countermand (koun'tĕr·mànd) n. contrordine, disdetta. vt. contrordinare, disdire, revocare.

counterpane (koun'tĕr·pān') n. coprilétto.

counterpart (-pärt') n. copia, complemento; sosia.

counterpoint (-point') n. (mus.) contrappunto.

counterpoise (-poiz') n. contrappeso. vt. controbilanciare.

counterrevolution (-rĕv'ō·lū'shǔn) n. controrivoluzione.

countersink (-sĭngk) n. accecatoio, fresa. vt. fresare.

counterweight (-wāt') n. contrappeso.

countess (koun'tĕs) n. contessa.

countless (kount'lĕs) agg. innumerevole.

country (kǔn'trĭ) n. paese, nazione, patria; regione; campagna (zona rurale). —man n. contadino; compaesano: fellow —man, compatriota. —woman n. contadina; compaesana. —side n. campagna.

county (koun'tĭ) n. contea.

couple (kǔp''l) n. coppia, paio. vt. accoppiare; (ferr.) agganciare. vi. accoppiarsi.

coupling (kǔp'lĭng) n. accoppiamento.

coupon (kōō'pŏn) n. biglietto, tagliando, scontrino.

courage (kǔr'ĭj) n. coraggio. —ous (kǔ·rā'jǔs) agg. coraggioso.

courier (kōōr'ĭ·ĕr) n. corriere, messaggero.

course (kōrs) n. corsa; corso (di un fiume, di lezioni, dei cambi, ecc.); serie; percorso, pista; portata (a

tavola); rotta; punto (della bussola): in due —, a tempo debito; of —, naturalmente; a matter of —, una cosa ovvia; — of conduct, comportamento. vi. scorrere; dirigersi, seguire una rotta.

court (kōrt) n. corte, cortile; corte di giustizia; vicolo; autostello: tennis —, campo di tennis. vt. corteggiare, cercare: to — danger, andare in cerca di pericoli.

courteous (kûr'tĕ·ǔs) agg. cortese, educato, amabile.

courtesan (kōr'tĕ·zǎn) n. cortigiana, prostituta.

courthouse (kōrt'hous') n. palazzo di giustizia.

courtly (kōrt'lĭ) agg. raffinato, elegante, cortese.

court-martial (kōrt'mär'shǎl) n. corte marziale. vt. processare davanti alla corte marziale.

courtship (kōrt'shĭp) n. corte, corteggiamento, periodo di fidanzamento.

courtyard (kōrt'yärd') n. cortile.

cousin (kǔz''n) n. cugino, cugina.

cove (kōv) n. baia, caverna; incàvo, nicchia; (gergo) tizio, individuo.

covenant (kǔv'ĕ·nǎnt) n. convenzione, patto, contratto. vt., vi. pattuire, stipulare.

cover (kǔv'ĕr) n. coperchio; copertura; copertina, busta, riparo; tovaglia; pretesto, apparenza; cauzione: under separate —, in plico a parte. vt. coprire, celare; tenere a bada (con un'arma); percorrere; (giorn.) occuparsi di, fare un servizio su. —ing n. copertura. —let n. coperta, coltre.

covert (kǔv'ĕrt) n. rifugio, riparo. agg. (-ĕrt') coperto, nascosto, segreto, velato. —ly, avv. di nascosto, in segreto.

covet (kǔv'ĕt) vt. agognare, desiderare. —ous agg. avido, bramoso.

cow (kou) n. mucca; femmina (di altri mammiferi).

coward (kou'ĕrd) n. codardo, vigliacco. —ice, —liness n. codardia, vigliaccheria. —ly agg. codardo, meschino. avv. vigliaccamente.

cowboy (kou'boi') n. bovaro, buttero.

cower (kou'ĕr) vi. rannicchiarsi (per il terrore); accasciarsi.

cowhide (kou'hīd') n. pelle di mucca; scudiscio.

cowl (koul) n. cappuccio (da frate); cappa (del camino).

coxswain (kŏk's'n; kŏk'swän) n. (naut.) timoniere.

coy (koi) agg. timido, riservato, modesto. —ness n. timidezza, riserbo.

coyote (kī'ōt; kī·ō'tē) *n.* lupo della prateria.

cozy (kō'zĭ) *agg.* comodo; intimo.

crab (krăb) *n.* branchio; (*mecc.*) gru.

crack (krăk) *n.* spaccatura, screpolatura, crepa; detonazione; schianto, schiocco; spuntare (*dell'alba*); (*gergo*) frizzo, spiritosaggine, frottola; *vt.* incrinare, fendere, spaccare; far schioccare (*la frusta*): to — a joke, dire una spiritosaggine. *vi.* spaccarsi, screpolarsi; scricchiolare; schioccare.

crack-brained *agg.* pazzo.

cracker (krăk'ēr) *n.* petardo; biscotto croccante, galletta.

crackle (krăk'l) *n.* crepitio, scricchiolio. *vi.* scricchiolare, crepitare.

crackling *n.* crepitio; ciccioli (*di maiale*).

crack-up (krăk'up') *n.* sfasciamento, caduta (*di un aereo*).

cradle (krā'd'l) *n.* culla; infanzia; (*naut.*) invasatura; (*min.*) setaccio per sabbie aurifere.

craft (kráft) *n.* mestiere, arte, abilità; astuzia, artificio; (*naut.*) imbarcazione, flottiglia di barche; aeroplano.

craftiness (kráft'ĭ·nĕs) *n.* astuzia, furberia.

craftsman (kráfts'măn) *n.* operaio, artigiano; artista.

crafty (kráf'tĭ) *agg.* astuto, abile; subdolo.

crag (krăg) *n.* picco, rocca scoscesa.

cram (krăm) *n.* folla, calca; preparazione affrettata (*in vista di esami*). *vt.* riempire eccessivamente, rimpinzare, affollare, preparare (*agli esami*). *vi.* rimpinzarsi; infarcire la propria mente di cognizioni.

crammer (krăm'ēr) *n.* sgobbone; ripetitore.

cramp (krămp) *n.* crampo; (*tec.*) grappa; (*fig.*) intralcio, ostacolo. *vt.* stringere, serrare; ostacolare; assicurare con grappa. —ed *agg.* scomodo, stretto: —ed writing, scrittura scarabocchiata.

crane (krān) *n.* gru (*uccello e macchina*). *vt.* allungare (*il collo*).

cranium (krā'nĭ·ŭm) *n.* cranio.

crank (krăngk) *n.* manovella; gomito (*di tubo, ecc.*); pedaliera (*di bicicletta*); (*fig.*) pazzoide, originale. *vt.* piegare, curvare; munire di manovella, girare la manovella; avviare (*un motore*) con la manovella; *vi.* serpeggiare.

crankcase (krăngk'kās') *n.* copricatena (*di bicicletta*); carter (*di motori*).

crankshaft (krăngk'shàft') *n.* albero a gomito.

cranny (krăn'ĭ) *n.* crepaccio, fessura.

crape (krāp) *n.* crespo.

crash (krăsh) *n.* schianto, tonfo, colpo, crollo, rovinio, caduta; scoppio; (*comm.*) fallimento. *vt.* distruggere, abbattere. *vi.* crollare fragorosamente; cozzare, urtare (*contro*); (*aeron.*) precipitare, atterrare irregolarmente: to — the gate, intrufolarsi senza biglietto (*a teatro, ecc.*); partecipare a una festa senza esservi invitato.

crass (krăs) *agg.* crasso, grossolano, ottuso.

crate (krāt) *n.* gabbia d'imballaggio.

crater (krā'tēr) *n.* cratere.

cravat (krd·văt') *n.* cravatta, sciarpa.

crave (krāv) *vt.*, *vi.* bramare, desiderare ardentemente, abbisognare di, implorare.

craven (krā'věn) *n.*, *agg.* vigliacco.

craving (krāv'ĭng) *n.* brama, desiderio impellente; sete.

craw (krò) *n.* gozzo (*di uccello*).

crawl (kròl) *n.* strisciamento; vivaio (*di pesci*); crawl (*stile di nuoto*). *vi.* strisciare; trascinarsi; insinuarsi; brulicare (*di*). —ing *agg.* strisciante; brulicante (*di*).

crayon (krā'ŏn) *n.* pastello per disegno. *vt.* disegnare a pastello.

craze (krāz) *n.* pazzia, mania, passione, entusiasmo; moda. *vt.* far impazzire; screpolare. *vi.* impazzire; screpolarsi.

crazy (krā'zĭ) *agg.* pazzo; instabile, precario: to go —, impazzire.

creak (krēk) *n.* scricchiolio, cigolio. *vi.* scricchiolare, cigolare. —ing *n.* cigolio. *agg.* cigolante, scricchiolante.

cream (krēm) *n.* crema, panna; (*il*) meglio, (*il*) fior fiore. —ery *n.* caseificio.

creamy (krēm'ĭ) *agg.* cremoso.

crease (krēs) *n.* piega, grinza. *vt.* raggrinzire, sgualcire. **creasy** *agg.* spiegazzato.

create (krė·āt') *vt.* creare.

creation (krė·ā'shŭn) *n.* creazione; (*il*) Creato.

creative (-tĭv) *agg.* creativo.

creator (-tēr) *n.* creatore.

creature (krē'tŭr) *n.* creatura.

credence (krē'd'ns) *n.* fede, convinzione, credenza.

credentials (krė·děn'shălz) *n.pl.* credenziali.

credible (krěd'ĭ·b'l) *agg.* credibile.

credit (krěd'ĭt) *n.* credito, fiducia; (*fig.*) prestigio, merito; (*pl.*, *cinema*, *T.V.*) titoli di testa: — and debit, dare a avere; that does him —, questo torna a suo onore. *vt.* credere accreditare: **to — with,** ascrivere, attribuire a.

creditable (-á.b'l) *agg.* lodevole.

creditor (-ĭ.tẽr) *n.* creditore.

credulity (krĕ.dū'lĭ.tĭ) *n.* credulità.

credulous (krĕd'ū.lŭs) *agg.* credulo.

creed (krĕd) *n.* credo, fede, culto.

creek (krēk) *n.* ansa, baia; (*S.U.*) fiumicello.

creep (krēp) *n.* strisciamento; pelle d'oca, (*fig.*) brivido: **it gives me the —s,** mi fa venire i brividi. *vi.* (*pass., pp.* **crept**) trascinarsi, strisciare, arrampicarsi: **to feel one's flesh —,** sentirsi accapponare la pelle. **—er** *n.* rettile, verme; pianta rampicante.

crematory (krē'má.tō'rĭ) *n.* forno crematorio.

creole (krē'ōl) *n.,* *agg.* creolo.

crept (krĕpt) *pass., pp. di to* creep.

crescent (krĕs'ĕnt) *agg.* crescente: **— moon,** luna crescente. *n.* quarto di luna; (*fig.*) mezza luna.

cress (krĕs) *n.* crescione.

crest (krĕst) *n.* cresta, crinale, ciuffo di piume, criniera, cimiero, pennacchio; orgoglio.

crestfallen (krĕst'fôl'ĕn) *agg.* abbattuto, scoraggiato, sconcertato, deluso.

cretin (krē'tĭn) *n.* cretino.

crevasse (krĕ.văs') *n.* crepaccio.

crevice (krĕv'ĭs) *n.* fessura, fenditura.

crew (krōō) (1) *pass. di to* crow.

crew (krōō) (2) *n.* ciurma, equipaggio; squadra; combriccola, masnada. **— cut,** capelli a spazzola. **— neck,** scollatura a barchetta.

crib (krĭb) *n.* letto da bambino; mangiatoia, rastrelliera; capanna, casetta; (*fam.*) furterello, plagio; (*gergo*) bigino (*trad. letterale di classici ad uso degli studenti*).

cricket (krĭk'ĕt) *n.* grillo; cricket (*sport*); sgabello. **—er** *n.* giocatore di cricket.

crime (krīm) *n.* delitto, reato.

criminal (krĭm'ĭ.năl) *n.* delinquente *agg.* criminale, colpevole, penale.

crimp (krĭmp) *vt.* arricciare, ondulare.

crimpy (krĭmp'ĭ) *agg.* arricciato.

crimson (krĭm'z'n) *n., agg.* cremisi, rosso vivo.

cringe (krĭnj) *vi.* umiliarsi, sottomettersi, tremare; retrocedere.

cringing (krĭn'jĭng) *n.* servilismo. *agg.* servile; tremebondo, pauroso.

crinkle (krĭng'k'l) *n.* grinza, increspatura. *vt., vi.* raggrinzire; frusciare; serpeggiare; raggrinzirsi.

cripple (krĭp''l) *n.* storpio, zoppo, invalido. *vt.* storpiare, menomare, azzoppare; frustrare, avariare.

crisis (krī'sĭs) *n.* (*pl.* **crises**) crisi.

crisp (krĭsp) *agg.* crespo; ricciuto; croccante; friabile; frizzante (*dell'aria*); acuto; arzillo; efficiente. *vt.* arricciare (*chiome, ecc.*), increspare; *vi.* incresparsi.

criterion (krī.tẽr'ĭ.ŭn) *n.* (*pl.* **criteria**) criterio; valutazione; prova.

critic (krĭt'ĭk) *n.* critico. **—al** *agg.* critico, precario. **—ism** (sĭzm) *n.* critica; censura; recensione.

criticize (krĭt'ĭ.sīz) *vt.* criticare, censurare.

critique (krĭ.tēk') *n.* critica (*la critica*); recensione.

croak (krōk) *n.* gracidìo (*della rana*), gracchio (*del corvo*). *vi.* gracidare, gracchiare; (*gergo*) crepare (*morire*).

crochet (krō.shā') *n.* lavoro all'uncinetto. *vt., vi.* lavorare all'uncinetto. **—** needle *n.* uncinetto.

crock (krŏk) *n.* vaso di terracotta, bacinella. **—ery** *n.* vasellame.

crocodile (krŏk'ō.dīl) *n.* coccodrillo.

Croesus (krē'sŭs) *n.* Creso.

crone (krōn) *n.* vecchia (*donna*).

crony (krō'nĭ) *n.* amico, compare.

crook (krŏŏk) *n.* curva, incavo, gomito (*di tubo, ecc.*); pastorale (*bastone del vescovo*); furfante, imbroglione: **by hook or by —,** con qualunque mezzo. *vt.* curvare. *vi.* curvarsi. **—ed** *agg.* curvo, ricurvo, storto, contorto, tortuoso, disonesto.

croon (krōōn) *n.* canto sommesso. *vt., vi.* canticchiare, cantare in tono sentimentale. **—er** *n.* cantante sentimentale.

crop (krŏp) *n.* raccolto, messi; raccolta; gozzo (*di uccello*); frustino; pelle intera di animale (*conciata*); tosatura; chioma corta. *vt., vi.* mietere, raccogliere, falciare; brucare; tosare; spuntare; seminare.

cropper (krŏp'ẽr) *n.* mietitore, coltivatore; (*fam.*) capitombolo: **to come a —,** fare un capitombolo.

croquet (krō.kā') *n.* (*sport*) pallamaglio.

cross (krŏs) *n.* croce; incrocio (*anche di razze*); crocevia; tormento, calamità. *agg.* trasversale, obliquo; adirato, imbronciato: **— section,** spaccato; gruppo rappresentativo (*di una totalità*); **to be at — purposes,** fraintendersi. *avv.* attraverso, trasversalmente. *vt.* attraversare; segnare con una croce; incrociare; cancellare; barrare (*un assegno*); ostacolare; contrariare; varcare· **to — oneself,** farsi il segno della croce. *vi.* incrociarsi (*incontrarsi*); accoppiarsi; compiere una traversata.

cross-armed (krŏs'ärmd) *agg.* a braccia conserte.

crosscut (krŏs′kŭt′) *n.* scorciatoia.

cross-examination *n.* controinterrogatorio; *(fig.)* subisso di domande.

cross-examine *vt.* sottoporre a controinterrogatorio.

crossing (krŏs′ĭng) *n.* crocicchio, incrocio, passaggio pedonale; traversata *(per mare)*: railroad —, passaggio a livello; river —, guado.

crossroad (krŏs′rōd′) *n.* strada trasversale: to find oneself at the —s, essere a un bivio *o* a una svolta decisiva.

crosswise (krŏs′wĭz′) *avv.* di traverso.

crossword puzzle (krŏs′wûrd′) *n.* cruciverba, parole incrociate.

crotchet (krŏch′ĕt) *n.* uncino; capriccio.

crouch (krouch) *vi.* chinarsi, accovacciarsi, inchinarsi, umiliarsi.

croup (krōōp) *n.* groppa, quarti posteriori *(di un animale)*.

crow (krō) *n.* corvo, cornacchia; canto del gallo: —'s foot, zampe d'oca *(agli angoli degli occhi)*. *vi.* *(pass.* crowed, crew, *pp.* crowed) cantare *(del gallo)*; esultare, cantar vittoria.

crowbar (krō′bär′) *n.* leva di ferro, piede di porco.

crowd (kroud) *n.* folla, massa. *vt.* pigiare, ingombrare. *vi.* affollarsi. —ed *agg.* affollato, stipato, pieno.

crown (kroun) *n.* corona; cima, sommità; cocuzzolo *(del cappello)*. *vt.* coronare, incoronare, sormontare. —ing *n.* incoronazione. *agg.* supremo, ultimo, finale.

crucible (krōō′sĭ·b′l) *n.* crogiolo.

crucifix (krōō′sĭ fĭks) *n.* crocifisso. —ion *n.* crocifissione.

crucify (krōō′sĭ·fī) *vt.* crocifiggere; *(fig.)* angariare; stroncare.

crude (krōōd) *agg.* grezzo; acerbo, rozzo, esplicito. —ness, **crudity** *n.* crudezza, rozzezza.

cruel (krōō′ĕl) *agg.* crudele.

cruelty (krōō′ĕl·tĭ) *n.* crudeltà; sevizie.

cruet (krōō′ĕt) *n.* oliera, ampolla; ampolliera; calice.

cruise (krōōz) *n.* crociera. *vi.* andare in crociera; incrociare.

cruiser (krōō′zĕr) *n.* incrociatore; automobile della polizia munita di radiotelefono.

crumb (krŭm) *n.* briciola. *vt.* sbriciolare.

crumble (krŭm′b′l) *vt.* sbriciolare, sgretolare. *vi.* sbriciolarsi, frantumarsi: to — down, cadere in rovina, franare.

crumple (krŭm′p′l) *vt.* sgualcire. *vi.* sgualcirsi; accasciarsi.

crunch (krŭnch) *vt.* sgranocchiare; frantumare; calpestare rumorosamente.

crusade (krōō·sād′) *n.* crociata. *vi.* combattere *(per)*, essere paladino *(di)*.

crusader (-sād′ĕr) *n.* Crociato.

crush (krŭsh) *n.* folla; pigiatura; schiacciamento; oppressione. *vt.* schiacciare, far scricchiolare, frantumare; gualcire; reprimere: to — in, sfondare. —er *n.* frantoio.

crust (krŭst) *n.* crosta, scorza; *(gergo)* sfacciataggine.

crustacean (krŭs·tā′shǎn) *n.* crostaceo.

crutch (krŭch) *n.* gruccia, stampella.

crux (krŭks) *n.* *(pl.* cruxes *o* cruces [krōō′sēz]) difficoltà, perplessità; indovinello; crisi, punto cruciale.

cry (krī) *n.* grido, richiamo, pianto: a far — from, ben lontano da. *vt.,* *vi.* gridare, urlare, piangere: to — out, ritirarsi; to — down, biasimare; to — for, invocare.

crypt (krĭpt) *n.* cripta. —ic *agg.* occulto, oscuro, misterioso. —ogram *n.* crittogramma. —ography (krĭpt·ŏg′rá·fĭ) *n.* crittografia.

crystal (krĭs′tăl) *n.* cristallo. *agg.* cristallino. —line —line (-lēn′) *agg.* cristallino: crystalline lens, cristallino *(dell'occhio)*.

crystallize (krĭs′tăl·īz) *vt.,* *vi.* cristallizzare.

cub (kŭb) *n.* cucciolo; *(aeron.)* piccolo velivolo da turismo: — reporter, giornalista principiante.

cubbyhole (kŭb′ĭ·hōl) *n.* sgabuzzino.

cube (kūb) *n.* cubo: — root, radice cubica.

cubic (kū′bĭk) *agg.* cubico.

cubism (kūb′ĭz′m) *n.* cubismo.

cubist (kūb′ĭst) *n.* cubista.

cuckold (kŭk′ŭld) *n.* cornuto, becco.

cuckoo (kŏŏk′ōō) *n.* cuculo. *agg.* *(gergo)* matto.

cucumber (kū′kŭm·bĕr) *n.* cetriolo.

cud (kŭd) *n.* bolo alimentare: to chew the —, rimuginare.

cuddle (kŭd′′l) *n.* abbraccio. *vt.* abbracciare. *vi.* abbracciarsi; rannicchiarsi.

cudgel (kŭj′ĕl) *n.* randello, clava. *vt.* bastonare: to — one's brains, lambiccarsi il cervello.

cue (kū) (1) *n.* stecca da biliardo.

cue (kū) (2) *n.* spunto, indicazione, imbeccata, cenno. *vt.* dare lo spunto *o* l'imbeccata a.

cuff (kŭf) *n.* pugno, scapaccione; polsino *(di camicia)*, paramano; risvolto *(dei calzoni)*. *vt.* percuotere.

cull (kŭl) *vt.* cogliere, scegliere.

culpable (kŭl′pá·b′l) *agg.* colpevole.

culprit (kŭl'prĭt) *n.* imputato; colpevole.

cult (kŭlt) *n.* culto.

cultivate (kŭl'tǐ·vāt) *vt.* coltivare.

cultivation (-vā'shŭn) *n.* coltivazione, cultura.

cultivator (-vā'tẽr) *n.* coltivatore.

cultural (kŭl'tŭr·ăl) *agg.* culturale.

culture (kŭl'tŭr) *n.* cultura, istruzione.

cultured (-tŭrd) *agg.* colto.

cumbersome (kŭm'bẽr·sŭm) **cumbrous** (kŭm'brŭs) *agg.* ingombrante, pesante, poco maneggevole.

cumulative (kū'mū·lā'tǐv) *agg.* cumulativo.

cuneiform (kū·nē'ǐ·fôrm) *agg.* cuneiforme.

cunning (kŭn'ĭng) *n.* astuzia. *agg* astuto.

cup (kŭp) *n.* tazza, coppa, cavità.

cupboard (kŭb'ẽrd) *n.* credenza, armadio: — **love**, amore interessato.

Cupid (kū'pĭd) *n.* Cupido.

cupidity (kū·pĭd'ǐ·tǐ) *n.* cupidigia.

cur (kûr) *n.* cane bastardo *o* randagio; *(gergo)* persona spregevole.

curare (kū·rä'rē) *n.* curaro.

curate (kū'rĭt) *n.* curato.

curb (kûrb) *n.* freno, barbazzale *(del cavallo)*; cordone di marciapiede, ciglio di strada. *vt.* reprimere, frenare, dominare.

curd (kûrd) *n.* giuncata, latte rappreso.

curdle (kûr'd'l) *vt.* rapprendere. *vi.* rapprendersi.

cure (kūr) *n.* cura, rimedio. *vt.* guarire, sanare; rimediare; conservare sotto sale.

curfew (kûr'fū) *n.* coprifuoco.

curio (kū'rǐ·ō) *n.* oggetto raro, curiosità.

curiosity (kū'rǐ·ŏs'ǐ·tǐ) *n.* curiosità.

curious (kū'rǐ·ŭs) *agg.* curioso; strano.

curl (kûrl) *n.* ricciolo *(di capelli)*, spirale, ondulazione; piega *(delle labbra)*. *vt.* arricciare, arrotolare. *vi.* arricciarsi, arrotolarsi: to — up, accovacciarsi.

curly (kûr'lĭ) *agg.* ricciuto.

currant (kûr'ănt) *n.* sultanina *(uva)*, ribes.

currency (kûr'ĕn·sĭ) *n.* circolante *(danaro)*; corso legale; valutazione, moda; attualità.

current (kûr'ĕnt) *n.* corrente. *agg.* corrente, in corso, attuale, ammesso.

curry (kûr'ĭ) *vt.* conciare *(pelli)*; strigliare *(un cavallo)*; percuotere: to — **favor**, adulare per ottenere favori.

curse (kûrs) *n.* maledizione, imprecazione; calamità. *vt.* maledire, affliggere. *vi.* imprecare.

cursed (kûr'sĕd; kûrst) *agg.* maledetto; afflitto, malaugurato.

cursive (kûr's v) *agg.* corsivo.

cursory (kûr'sō·rǐ) *agg.* rapido, superficiale.

curt (kûrt) *agg.* brusco, sbrigativo, sgarbato.

curtail (kûr·tāl') *vt.* accorciare, restringere.

curtain (kûr'tǐn) *n.* sipario, tendaggio, tendina; cortina.

curtsy (kûrt'sǐ) *n.* riverenza, inchino.

curve (kûrv) *n.* curva. *vt.* curvare.

curved (kûrvd) *agg.* curvo.

cushion (kŏŏsh'ŭn) *n.* cuscino, guanciale.

cuspidor (kŭs'pǐ·dôr) *n.* sputacchiera.

cuss (kŭs) *n.*, *vi.* *(gergo) vedi* **curse**.

custard (kŭs'tẽrd) *n.* crema di latte e uova.

custody (kŭs'tō·dǐ) *n.* custodia, guardia, arresto, detenzione: to **take into** —, trarre in arresto; to **commit to someone's** —, affidare a qualcuno.

custom (kŭs'tŭm) *n.* usanza, abitudine; clientela. — **house**, ufficio doganale: —**house official**, doganiere. —**made**, *agg.* fatto su ordinazione *o* su misura; *(autom.)* fuori serie.

customary (kŭs'tŭm·ẽr·ǐ) *agg.* consueto, abituale.

customs *n.pl.* dogana.

customer (kŭs'tŭm·ẽr) *n.* cliente, avventore; tipo, individuo.

cut (kŭt) *n.* taglio, linea; fetta, trancio; riduzione, scorciatoia. *vt.(pass., pp.* cut) tagliare; troncare; affettare; ridurre; mettere al bando; togliere il saluto a: to — **back**, ridurre, diminuire; to — **class**, marinare la scuola. *vi.* tagliare *(esser tagliente)*: to — **a poor figure**, fare una figura meschina.

cute (kūt) *agg.* astuto; carino, originale.

cuticle (kū'tǐ·k'l) *n.* cuticola, pellicola.

cutlass (kŭt'lăs) *n.* scimitarra.

cutlery (kŭt'lẽr·ǐ) *n.* coltelleria.

cutlet (kŭt'lĕt) *n.* cotoletta.

cutter (kŭt'ẽr) *n.* tagliatore; *(naut.)* cutter *(canotto a vela)*; *(tec.)* fresa.

cutthroat (kŭt'thrōt') *n.* assassino.

cutting (kŭt'ĭng) *n.* taglio, incisione; ritaglio, frammento. *agg.* tagliente, mordace.

cuttle (kŭt''l), **cuttlefish** *n.* seppia.

cutwater (kŭt'wô·tẽr) *n.* tagliamare.

cyanide (sī'ȧ·nīd) *n.* cianuro.

cybernetics (sī'bĕr·nĕt'ĭks) *n.* cibernetica.

cyclamen (sĭk'lå·mĕn) *n.* ciclamino.

cycle (sī'k'l) *n.* ciclo; bicicletta. *vi.* andare a cicli; andare in bicicletta.

cyclist (sī'klĭst) *n.* ciclista.

cyclone (sī'klōn) *n.* ciclone, uragano.

cyclops (sī'klŏps) *n.* (*pl.* cyclopes [sĭ-klō'pēz]) ciclope.

cyclotron (sī'klŏ·trŏn) *n.* ciclotrone.

cylinder (sĭl'ĭn·dĕr) *n.* cilindro.

cylindrical (sĭl·ĭn'drĭ·kăl) *agg.* cilindrico.

cymbal (sĭm'băl) *n.* piatto (*da orchestra*).

cynic (sĭn'ĭk) *n.*, *agg.* cinico. —al *agg.* cinico. —ism (-sĭzm) *n.* cinismo.

cypress (sī'prĕs) *n.* cipresso.

cyst (sĭst) *n.* (*med.*) cisti.

D

dab (dăb) *n.* colpetto; chiazza. *vt.* sfiorare; cospargere.

dabble (dăb''l) *vt.* umettare, spruzzare, sguazzare: to— in (at) dilettarsi di.

dabbler (dăb'lĕr) *n.* dilettante, inesperto.

dad (dăd), **daddy** (dăd'ĭ) *n.* babbo, babbino.

daffodil (dăf'ō·dĭl) *n.* narciso selvatico.

daft (dăft) *agg.* sciocco, pazzoide.

dagger (dăg'ĕr) *n.* daga, pugnale; (*tip.*) croce: with —s drawn, ai ferri corti.

daily (dā'lĭ) *n.* quotidiano (*giorn.*). *agg.* quotidiano, giornaliero, diurno. *avv.* quotidianamente, di giorno in giorno.

dainty (dān'tĭ) *agg.* fine, delicato, prelibato, raffinato (*di gusti*).

dairy (dâr'ĭ) *n.* latteria, caseificio.

daisy (dā'zĭ) *n.* margherita.

dale (dāl) *n.* valle, valletta.

dally (dăl'ĭ) *vi.* oziare; amoreggiare; attardarsi: to— with danger, scherzare col pericolo.

dam (dăm) (1) *n.* sbarramento, diga, bacino artificiale. *vt.* arginare, bloccare, imbrigliare; munire di diga.

dam (2) *n.* madre (*in rif. ad animali*).

damage (dăm'ĭj) *n.* danno; torto; avaria. *vt.* danneggiare; avariare; nuocere; compromettere. *vi.* subire danni; avariarsi.

dame (dām) *n.* dama; nobildonna; padrona di casa; direttrice di scuola; (*gergo S.U.*) donna.

damn (dăm) *n.* maledizione, imprecazione: I don't give a —! non me ne importa niente; *inter.* maledizione! accidenti! *vt.* maledire, condannare. —ation (nă'shŭn) *n.* dannazione, condanna. —ed (dămd) *agg.* dannato, maledetto, malaugurato.

damp (dămp) *n.* umidità, vapore; abbattimento, scoramento. *agg.* umido; abbattuto. *vt.* inumidire, umet- tare; soffocare; demoralizzare. —en *vt.* inumidire. *vi.* inumidirsi. —er *n.* persona *o* cosa deprimente; regolatore (*di stufa, ecc.*); (*mus.*) sordina. —ness *n.* umidità.

damsel (dăm'zĕl) *n.* damigella.

dance (dáns) *n.* danza, ballo. *vi.*, *vt.* ballare.

dancer (dàn'sĕr) *n.* ballerino, ballerina.

dandelion (dăn·dē·lī'ŭn) *n.* dente-di-leone.

dander (dăn'dĕr) *n.* (*gergo*) collera.

dandruff (dăn'drŭf) *n.* forfora.

dandy (dăn'dĭ) *n.* damerino, elegantone; (*naut.*) jole a vela. *agg.* elegante; (*S.U.*) ottimo, di prim'ordine.

danger (dăn'jĕr) *n.* pericolo. —ous *agg.* pericoloso. —ously *avv.* pericolosamente.

dangle (dăng'g'l) *vt.* far penzolare. *vi.* penzolare; stare alle calcagna (*di qualcuno*).

dank (dăngk) *agg.* umido.

dapper (dăp'ĕr) *agg.* piccolo e attivo; inappuntabile; lindo.

dapple (dăp''l) *n.* chiazza. *agg.* chiazzato, pezzato. *vi.* macchiarsi. —gray *n.* grigio pomellato.

dare (dâr) *vt.* (*pass.* durst, dared, *pp.* dared) sfidare, affrontare. *vi.* osare. *n.* sfida; provocazione.

daredevil (dâr'dĕv''l) *n.*, *agg.* audace, temerario.

daring (dâr'ĭng) *n.* ardimento. *agg.* intrepido, audace.

dark (därk) *n.* oscurità. *agg.* oscuro, cupo, scuro, buio, sinistro, bruno: — horse, cavallo sconosciuto (*che vince inaspettatamente la gara*); candidato politico che vince inaspettatamente le elezioni; — secret, segreto profondo, enigma. —ly *avv.* oscuramente, velatamente. —ness *n.* oscurità. — some *agg.* scuro, tetro.

darken (där'kĕn) *vt.* oscurare, scurire; turbare. *vi.* oscurarsi, rabbuiarsi.

darky (där'kĭ) *n.* (*S.U.*) negro (*sprezz.*).

darling (där'lĭng) *n.* prediletto, tesoro. *agg.* diletto, adorato: my —, mio caro, tesoro mio.

darn (därn) *n.* rammendo, rattoppo: —! acciderba! maledizione! *vt.* rammendare.

dart (därt) *n.* dardo, pungiglione, balzo. *vt.* dardeggiare, scagliare. *vi.* lanciarsi.

dash (dăsh) *n.* impeto; colpo, urto; spruzzo; pennellata (*di colore*); tratto di penna, lineetta. *vt.* scagliare, scaraventare, infrangere; spruzzare. *vi.* rompersi; piombare (*al suolo, ecc.*); slanciarsi: to — by, passare di corsa; to — off a letter, buttar giù una lettera. —**board** *n.* cruscotto. —**ing** *agg.* impetuoso; vistoso, appariscente.

dastard (dăs'tërd) *n.* vigliacco, furfante.

dastardly (-lĭ) *agg.* vile, spregevole.

data (dā'tà) *n.pl.* dati, elementi.

date (dāt) (1) *n.* data; scadenza, termine; (*S.U.*) appuntamento: to bring up to —, aggiornare; up to —, aggiornato, moderno; out of —, antiquato; scaduto. *vt., vi.* datare; dare appuntamento a.

date (dāt) (2) *n.* dattero.

datum (dā'tŭm) *n.* dato.

daub (dôb) *n.* imbratto; crosta (*quadro privo di valore*). *vt.* imbrattare; pitturare malamente.

daughter (dô'tër) *n.* figlia. —**in-law**, nuora.

daunt (dônt) *vt.* intimidire; smorzare (*gli entusiasmi*). —**less** *agg.* intrepido.

davenport (dăv'ĕn-pôrt) *n.* (*S.U.*) divano; (*Ingl.*) scrivania.

davit (dăv'ĭt) *n.* (*naut.*) argano.

dawdle (dô'dl) *vi.* bighellonare; oziare.

dawdler (dô'dlêr) *n.* bighellone.

dawn (dôn) *n.* alba, aurora. *vi.* albeggiare; (*fig.*) balenare (*nella mente*).

day (dā) *n.* giorno, giornata: broad —, pieno giorno; (*Ingl.*) this — week, oggi otto; — after tomorrow, dopodomani; — before yesterday, avantieri; by —, di giorno; by the —, a giornata. to carry the —, riportare la vittoria.

daybook *n.* (*comm.*) libro-giornale.

daybreak *n.* alba.

daydream *n.* fantasticheria, sogno a occhi aperti. *vi.* fantasticare.

daylight *n.* giorno, luce del giorno.

dayroom *n.* (*mil.*) sala di lettura e di ricreazione.

daytime *n.* giorno: in the —, di giorno.

daze (dāz) *n.* stupore, intontimento. *vt.* sbalordire, inebetire.

dazzle (dăz''l) *vt.* abbagliare; stordire; confondere. *n.* bagliore.

deacon (dē'kŭn) *n.* diacono.

deactivate (dē·ăk'tĭ·vāt) *vt.* disattivare, fermare, interrompere; sciogliere (*un ufficio, un reparto, ecc.*); disinnescare.

dead (dĕd) *agg.* morto, estinto; spento (*di fuoco*); sordo (*di suono*); smorto (*di colore*): — body, cadavere; — sleep, sonno profondo; — stop, fermata improvvisa; — certainty, certezza matematica; — letter, lettera non reclamata; cosa antiquata; — loss, perdita assoluta; the — of night, il cuor della notte; the —, i morti. *avv.* completamente. — drunk, ubriaco fradicio; — sure, arcisicuro.

deaden (dĕd''n) *vt.* smorzare, attutire. *vi.* affievolirsi, smorzarsi.

deadlock *n.* punto morto, vicolo cieco.

deadly *agg.* mortale, micidiale.

deadpan (dĕd'păn') *agg.* detto con finta serietà, impassibile, staccato.

deaf (dĕf) *agg.* sordo.

deafen (dĕf'ĕn) *vt.* assordare.

deafening *agg.* assordante.

deafness *n.* sordità.

deal (dēl) *n.* quantità; affare; distribuzione; mano (*al gioco*); politica (*amministrativa*); asse o legno di abete o di pino: a good —, molto; a great —, moltissimo; it is my —, tocca a me; to give a square —, trattare con equanimità. *vt.* (*pass., pp.* dealt) distribuire, ripartire, assestare (*un colpo*). *vi.* agire, fare affari: to — in, occuparsi di, commerciare in; to — with, agire verso, avere a che fare con, vedersela con. —**er** *n.* commerciante; mazziere, croupier. —**ing** *n.* affare, trattativa, condotta.

dealt (dĕlt) *pass., pp. di* to deal.

dean (dēn) *n.* decano, prelato; (*S.U.*) preside di facoltà universitaria.

dear (dēr) *agg.* caro, amabile; costoso: — Sir, egregio signore. dear! dear!, dear me!, santo cielo!

dearly *avv.* caramente; a caro prezzo.

dearth (dûrth) *n.* carestia.

death (dĕth) *n.* morte, fine, trapasso: to beat to —, massacrare. — rate *n.* mortalità. — warrant *n.* ordine d'esecuzione capitale.

deb *vedi* debutante.

debase (dē·bās') *vt.* degradare, abbassare; adulterare, falsificare.

debasing *agg.* degradante.

debatable (dē·băt'á·b'l) *agg.* discutibile, controverso.

debate (dē·bāt') *n.* dibattito, disputa. *vt., vi.* dibattere, discutere, deliberare.

debauch (dē·bôch') *n.* intemperanza.

debenture (dĕ·bĕn'tŭr) n. obbligazione.

debit (dĕb'ĭt) n. debito, addebito; (comm.) dare. vt. addebitare.

debonair (dĕb'ō·nâr') agg. amabile, bonario.

debris (dĕ·brē') n. detriti.

debt (dĕt) n. debito. —or n. debitore.

debut (dā'bū; dâ·bū') n. esordio: to make a —, esordire. —ant n. esordiente (m.). —ante n. esordiente (f.).

decade (dĕk'ād) n. decennio.

decadence (dĕ·kā'dĕns) n. decadenza.

decadent n., agg. decadente.

decalogue (dĕk'à·lŏg) n. decalogo.

decanter (dĕ·kăn'tĕr) n. caraffa.

decay (dĕ·kā') n. decadenza, rovina; decomposizione; carie. vi. decadere, cadere in rovina; guastarsi; cariarsi.

decease (dĕ·sēs') n. decesso. vi. decedere, morire.

deceased n., agg. defunto.

deceit (dĕ·sēt') n. inganno, frode. —ful agg. ingannevole, fraudolento.

deceive (dĕ·sēv') vt. ingannare.

deceiver n. ingannatore.

December (dĕ·sĕm'bĕr) n. dicembre.

decency (dē'sĕn·sĭ) n. correttezza, pudore.

decent (dē'sĕnt) agg. corretto, onesto; buono, cortese.

deception (dĕ·sĕp'shŭn) n. inganno, illusione.

decide (dĕ·sīd') vt. decidere. vi. decidersi; concludere.

decided agg. deciso, risoluto; chiaro.

decimal (dĕs'ĭ·măl) n., agg. decimale.

decipher (dĕ·sī'fĕr) vt. decifrare.

decision (dĕ·sĭzh'ŭn) n. decisione; risolutezza.

decisive (dĕ·sī'sĭv) agg. decisivo; deciso, risoluto.

deck (dĕk) (1) n. (naut.) ponte, tolda; mazzo di carte (da gioco).

deck (dĕk) (2) vt. adornare: to — oneself out, agghindarsi.

declaim (dĕ·klām') vt., vi. declamare.

declaration (dĕk'lá·rā'shŭn) n. dichiarazione.

declare (dĕ·klâr') vt. dichiarare, annunciare, asserire, proclamare. vi. dichiararsi, pronunciarsi.

decline (dĕ·klīn') n. declino, decadenza; deperimento; pendenza; diminuzione (dei prezzi). vt. declinare; rifiutare. vi. pendere, declinare; diminuire (dei prezzi).

declivity (dĕ·klĭv'ĭ·tĭ) n. declivio.

decode (dĕ·kōd') vt. decifrare, tradurre in chiaro (testi in codice).

decompose (dē'kŏm·pōz') vt. decomporre; scomporre. vi. decomporsi, marcire.

decorate (dĕk'ō·rāt) vt. decorare, abbellire, adornare; arredare.

decoration (dĕk'ō·rā'shŭn) n. decorazione; arredamento.

decorative (dĕk'ō·rā'tĭv) agg. decorativo, ornamentale.

decorator (dĕk'ō·rā'tĕr) n. decoratore; arredatore.

decorum (dĕ·kō'rŭm) n. decoro.

decoy (dĕ·koi') n. trappola, esca, uccello da richiamo. vt. adescare, intrappolare.

decrease (dĕ'krēs) n. diminuzione. (-krēs') vt., vi. diminuire.

decree (dĕ·krē') n. decreto, sentenza. vt. decretare.

decrepit (dĕ·krĕp'ĭt) agg. decrepito.

dedicate (dĕd'ĭ·kāt) vt. dedicare, consacrare.

dedicated agg. dedicato; ligio, scrupoloso; consacrato.

dedication (dĕd'ĭ·kā'shŭn) n. dedica, consacrazione; dedicazione.

deduce (dĕ·dūs') vt. dedurre, concludere.

deduct (dĕ·dŭkt') vt. dedurre; sottrarre; diffalcare. —ion n. deduzione; sottrazione; diffalco.

deed (dēd) n. azione, prodezza, impresa; titolo, contratto.

deem (dēm) vt., vi. ritenere, giudicare.

deep (dēp) n. profondità; mare. agg. profondo; scuro, cupo; astuto: — mourning, lutto stretto; to be in — waters, essere in difficoltà; — in debt, affogato nei debiti; — in thought, assorto.

deepen (dēp'ĕn) vt. approfondire, oscurire. vi. divenire più profondo, incupirsi.

deeply avv. profondamente; intensamente; astutamente.

deepness n. profondità; astuzia.

deer (dēr) n. cervo, daino, renna.

deface (dĕ·fās') vt. sfigurare, deturpare; mutilare, cancellare.

defame (dĕ·fām') vt. diffamare.

default (dĕ·fôlt') n. mancanza; insolvenza, morosità; contumacia. vi. essere insolvente; essere contumace; (sport) ritirarsi da una gara. —er n. persona contumace; debitore insolvente; malversatore; (sport) concorrente ritiratosi.

defeat (dĕ·fēt') n. sconfitta, disfatta. vt. sconfiggere, frustrare.

defect (dĕ·fĕkt') n. difetto, imperfezione.

defective (dĕ·fĕk'tĭv) agg. difettoso, insufficiente; difettivo.

defence vedi defense.

defend (dĕ·fĕnd') vt. difendere, proteggere.

defendant (dē·fĕn'dănt) *n.* imputato, convenuto.

defender (dē·fĕn'dẽr) *n.* difensore.

defense (dē·fĕns') *n.* difesa: self- —, legittima difesa. —**less** *agg.* indifeso.

defensive (de·fĕn'sĭv) *n.* difensiva. *agg.* difensivo.

defer (dē·fũr') *vt.* differire, rimandare; deferire. *vi.* temporeggiare: **to —to**, rimettersi al giudizio di.

deference (dĕf'ẽr·ĕns) *n.* deferenza, riguardo.

deferential (dĕf'ẽr·ĕn'shăl) *agg.* riguardoso.

defiance (dē·fī'ăns) *n.* sfida, provocazione; spavalderia: **in — of**, in dispregio a, a dispetto di.

defiant (dē·fī'ănt) *agg.* insolente, provocante; spavaldo.

deficiency (dē·fĭsh'ĕn·sĭ) *n.* deficienza, debolezza; (*comm.*) disavanzo.

deficient (dē·fĭsh'ĕnt) *agg.* insufficiente, deficiente.

deficit (dĕf'ĭ·sĭt) *n.* deficit.

defile (dē·fīl') (1) *n.* gola (*di montagna*).

defile (2) *vi.* sfilare, marciare in parata.

defile (3) *vt.* insudiciare; violare, profanare; corrompere.

define (dē·fīn') *vt.* definire, determinare.

definite (dĕf'ĭ·nĭt) *agg.* determinato, esatto, preciso, definito.

definitely (dĕf'ĭ·nĭt·lĭ) *avv.* definitivamente; assolutamente; senz'altro.

definition (dĕf'ĭ·nĭsh'ăn) *n.* definizione.

definitive (dē·fĭn'ĭ·tĭv) *agg.* definitivo; determinativo.

deflate (dē·flāt') *vt.* sgonfiare.

deform (dē·fôrm') *vt.* deformare, sformare. —**ation** *n.* deformazione, alterazione. —**ed** *agg.* deforme, deformato. —**ity** *n.* deformità.

defraud (dē·frôd') *vt.* defraudare, privare.

defray (dē·frā') *vt.* risarcire, pagare.

defrost (dē·frŏst') *vt.* decongelare; sbrinare (*il frigorifero*).

deft (dĕft) *agg.* abile, destro.

defy (dē·fī') *vt.* sfidare, mettere a dura prova; opporsi a; resistere a.

degeneracy (dē·jĕn'ẽr·à·sĭ) *n.* degenerazione.

degenerate (dē·jĕn'ẽr·ĭt) *n.*, *agg.* degenerato. (-āt) *vi.* degenerare.

degradation (dĕg'rà·dā'shŭn) *n.* degradazione, ignominia.

degrade (dē·grād') *vt.* degradare.

degree (dē·grē') *n.* grado, gradino, livello; diploma, laurea: **to take one's —**, conseguire una laurea, **by —s**, per gradi, a poco a poco.

dehydrate (dē·hī'drāt) *vt.* disidratare.

deign (dān) *vt.*, *vi.* degnare, degnarsi.

deify (dē'ĭ·tĭ) *n.* divinità.

deject (dē·jĕkt') *vt.* scoraggiare.

dejected (dē·jĕk'tĕd) *agg.* scoraggiato, triste.

dejection (dē·jĕk'shŭn) *n.* abbattimento; (*med.*) defecazione.

delay (dē·lā') *n.* ritardo, indugio; rinvio, dilazione. *vt.* ritardare, rimandare. *vi.* indugiare.

delegate (dĕl'ē·gāt) *n.* delegato. *vt.* delegare.

delegation (-gā'shŭn) *n.* delegazione; delega.

delete (dē·lēt') *vt.* cancellare, cassare.

deletion (dē·lē'shŭn) *n.* cancellazione.

deliberate (dē·lĭb'ẽr·ĭt) *agg.* intenzionale; ponderato, misurato, cauto; lento. *vt.*, *vi.* deliberare; ponderare, considerare, discutere. —**ly** *avv.* deliberatamente, intenzionalmente, apposta; lentamente. —**ness** *n.* ponderatezza, prudenza.

deliberation (-ā'shŭn) *n.* deliberazione; riflessione; lentezza.

delicacy (dĕl'ĭ·kà·sĭ) *n.* delicatezza, finezza; leccornia.

delicate (dĕl'ĭ·kĭt) *agg.* delicato.

delicateness (-nĕs) *n.* delicatezza.

delicatessen (dĕl'ĭ·kà·tĕs'ĕn) *n.* (*S.U.*) negozio di specialità alimentari.

delicious (dē·lĭsh'ŭs) *agg.* delizioso.

delight (dē·līt') *n.* gioia, diletto, entusiasmo. *vt.* deliziare, dilettare. *vi.* compiacersi, divertirsi, entusiasmarsi: **to — in**, compiacersi di, essere entusiasta di. —**ed** *agg.* contento, lieto, felice. —**ful** *agg.* delizioso, incantevole.

delineate (dē·lĭn'ē·āt) *vt.* delineare, abbozzare.

delinquency (dē·lĭng'kwĕn·sĭ) *n.* malefatta, colpa; negligenza, manchevolezza.

delinquent (-kwĕnt) *n.* colpevole, responsabile: **tax —**, evasore fiscale.

delirious (dē·lĭr'ĭ·us) *agg.* delirante: **to be —**, delirare, smaniare.

delirium (-ŭm) *n.* delirio.

deliver (dē·lĭv'ẽr) *vt.* liberare, salvare; consegnare, distribuire (*posta*), recapitare; pronunciare (*un discorso*); assestare (*un colpo*); partorire. —**ance** *n.* liberazione; recapito; parto; allocuzione. —**er** *n.* liberatore; latore.

delivery (dē·lĭv'ẽr·ĭ) *n.* consegna; distribuzione postale; liberazione; parto; eloquio.

dell (dĕl) *n.* valletta, conca.

delude (dē·lūd') *vt.* ingannare, illudere; deludere.

delusion 60 depot

delusion (-lū'zhăn) *n.* illusione, inganno, allucinazione.
delusive (-sĭv), delusory (-sŏ·rĭ) *agg.* illusorio, ingannevole.
deluge (dĕl'ûj) *n.* diluvio. *vt.* inondare.
delve (dĕlv) *vt.*, *vi.* frugare, scavare.
demand (dĕ·mȧnd') *n.* richiesta, domanda; esigenza: on —, a richiesta. *vt.* richiedere, domandare; esigere. —ing *agg.* esigente.
demeanor (dĕ·mēn'ẽr) *n.* condotta, comportamento, contegno.
demented (dĕ·mĕn'tĕd) *agg.* demente.
demerit (dĕ·mĕr'ĭt) *n.* demerito.
demigod (dĕm'ĭ·gŏd) *n.* semidio.
demijohn (-jŏn) *n.* damigiana.
demise (dĕ·mīz) *n.* decesso; trapasso di proprietà.
demobilization (dĕ·mō'bĭ·lĭ·zā'shŭn) *n.* smobilitazione.
demobilize (dĕ·mō'bĭ·līz) *vt.* smobilitare.
democracy (dĕ·mŏk'rȧ·sĭ) *n.* democrazia.
democrat (dĕm'ō·krăt) *n.* democratico.
democratic (dĕm'ō·krăt'ĭk) *agg.* democratico.
demolish (dĕ·mŏl'ĭsh) *vt.* demolire.
demolition (dĕ'mō·lĭsh'ŭn) *n.* demolizione.
demon (dē'mŭn) *n.* demonio.
demonstrate (dĕm'ŭn·strāt) *vt.* dimostrare.
demonstration (dĕm'ŭn·strā'shŭn) *n.* dimostrazione.
demonstrative (dĕ·mŏn'strȧ·tĭv) *agg.* dimostrativo; espansivo.
demote (dĕ·mōt') *vt.* retrocedere (*di grado*).
demur (dĕ·mûr') *n.* titubanza. *vi.* titubare, esitare; tergiversare, fare obiezioni.
demure (dĕ·mūr') *agg.* pudico, riservato, compassato.
den (dĕn) *n.* antro, tana, covo; stamberga; (*fam.*) studiolo personale.
denial (dĕ·nī'ăl) *n.* diniego, rifiuto; rinnegazione: self-—, altruismo, abnegazione.
denizen (dĕn'ĭ·zĕn) *n.* abitante; straniero naturalizzato.
denominate (dĕ·nŏm'ĭ·nāt) *vt.* denominare.
denomination (dĕ·nŏm'ĭ·nā'shŭn) *n.* denominazione; comunità, setta; taglio (*di banconota*).
denote (dĕ·nōt') *vt.* denotare, indicare.
denounce (dĕ·nouns') *vt.* denunciare, dichiarare, propalare.
dense (dĕns) *agg.* denso, compatto; folto, fitto; ottuso, stupido.
density (dĕn'sĭ·tĭ) *n.* densità.

dent (dĕnt) *n.* tacca, incavo; dente (*d'ingranaggio*). *vt.* dentellare, fare una tacca a. *vi.* dentellarsi.
dental (dĕn'tăl) *agg.* dentario, odontoiatrico. *n.*, *agg.* (*gramm.*) dentale.
dentist (dĕn'tĭst) *n.* dentista. —ry *n.* odontoiatria.
denunciation (dē·nŭn'sĭ·ā'shŭn) *n.* denuncia, aperta condanna, accusa.
deny (dē·nī') *vt.* negare; rinnegare, smentire, rifiutare: to — oneself, sacrificarsi; far dire che non si è in casa.
deodorize (dē·ō'dẽr·īz) *vt.* deodorare.
deodorizer (dē·ō'dẽr·īz'ẽr) *n.* deodorante.
depart (dĕ·pärt') *vi.* partire; dipartirsi, deviare; derogare. —ed *agg.* defunto: the departed, i defunti.
department (dĕ·pärt'mĕnt) *n.* dipartimento; reparto. — store *n.* (*S.U.*) grande emporio.
departure (dĕ·pär'tûr) *n.* partenza; dipartita; allontanamento; deviazione; deroga.
depend (dĕ·pĕnd') *vi.* dipendere: to — upon, fare affidamento su, credere a; — upon it, potete contarci, statene certo. —able *agg.* fidato, sicuro, attendibile. —ence *n.* dipendenza; subordinazione; fiducia. —ency *n.* dipendenza, edificio aggiunto, territorio annesso. —ent *n.* dipendente, familiare; *agg.* dipendente.
depict (dĕ·pĭkt') *vt.* dipingere, descrivere.
depilate (dĕp'ĭ·lāt) *vt.* depilare.
deplete (dĕ·plēt') *vt.* vuotare, svotare.
deplorable (dĕ·plōr'ȧ·b'l) *agg.* deplorevole.
deplore (dĕ·plōr') *vt.* deplorare.
deploy (dĕ·ploi') *vt.* schierare, spiegare. —ment *n.* schieramento, spiegamento.
depopulate (dĕ·pŏp'û·lāt) *vt.* spopolare. *vi.* spopolarsi.
deport (dĕ·pōrt') *vt.* deportare: to — oneself, comportarsi. —ation *n.* deportazione. —ment *n.* condotta; portamento.
depose (dĕ·pōz') *vt.*, *vi.* deporre; destituire; testimoniare.
deposit (dĕ·pŏz'ĭt) *n.* deposito. *vt.* depositare, deporre; versare.
deposition (dĕp'ō·zĭsh'ŭn) *n.* deposizione.
depositor (dĕ·pŏz'ĭ·tẽr) *n.* depositante, correntista.
depository (dĕ·pŏz'ĭ·tō'rĭ) *n.* deposito, ripostiglio, magazzino; depositario, fiduciario.
depot (dē'pō) *n.* magazzino, deposito; (*S.U.*) stazione ferroviaria.

depravity (dĕ·prăv′ĭ·tĭ) *n.* depravazione.

deprecate (dĕp′rĕ·kāt) *vt.* deprecare, deplorare, disapprovare.

deprecating *agg.* umile, supplichevole; disapprovante, di deplorazione.

depreciate (dĕ·prē′shĭ·āt) *vt.* deprezzare. *vi.* deprezzarsi, perdere di valore.

depreciation (dĕ·prē′shĭ·ā′shŭn) *n.* deprezzamento.

depress (dĕ·prĕs′) *vt.* deprimere; inclinare. **—ed** *agg.* depresso; abbassato. **—ing** *agg.* deprimente. **—ion** (dĕ·prĕsh′ŭn) *n.* depressione; avvallamento; crisi.

deprive (dĕ·prīv′) *vt.* privare; defraudare.

depth (dĕpth) *n.* profondità, spessore: **the — of night**, il cuor della notte; **to be out of one's —**, navigare in acque troppo profonde.

deputation (dĕp′ū·tā′shŭn) *n.* deputazione; delega.

depute (dĕ·pūt′) *vt.* deputare, delegare.

deputy (dĕp′ū·tĭ) *n.* deputato, delegato, sostituto; agente; vicesceriffo.

derail (dĕ·rāl′) *vt.* far deragliare. *vi.* deragliare.

derange (dĕ·rānj′) *vt.* scompigliare, sconvolgere, turbare.

deranged (dĕ·rānjd′) *agg.* scompigliato, disordinato; squilibrato, pazzo.

derby (där′bĭ) *n.* corsa inglese per puledri di tre anni; (dûr′bĭ) gran premio ippico; gara, partita; bombetta (*cappello duro*).

deride (dĕ·rīd′) *vt.* deridere, schernire.

derision (-rĭzh′ŭn) *n.* derisione, scherno.

derisive (-rī′sĭv) *agg.* derisivo, beffardo; risibile.

derive (dĕ·rīv′) *vt., vi.* derivare; trarre, attingere; discendere (*provenire*).

derogation (dĕr′ō·gā′shŭn) *n.* calunnia, diffamazione, denigrazione.

derogatory (dĕ·rŏg′à·tō′rĭ) *agg.* calunnioso, diffamatorio; denigratorio.

derrick (dĕr′ĭk) *n.* gru meccanica; derrick, castello (*di pozzo petrolifero*).

descend (dĕ·sĕnd′) *vt., vi.* scendere, discendere, abbassarsi. **—ant** *n.* discendente.

descent (dĕ·sĕnt′) *n.* discesa, pendio; origine; calata.

describe (dĕ·skrīb′) *vt.* descrivere.

description (dĕ·skrĭp′shŭn) *n.* descrizione; specie, genere: **of all —s**, di tutti i generi.

descriptive (-tĭv) *agg.* descrittivo.

desecrate (dĕs′ē·krāt) *n.* profanare.

desecration (-krā′shŭn) *n.* profanazione.

desert (dĕ·zûrt′) (1) *n.* merito; giusta ricompensa; giusta punizione: **to have one's —s**, avere ciò che si merita.

desert (dĕz′ĕrt) (2) *n., agg.* deserto. *vt.* (dĕ·zûrt′) disertare, abbandonare. *vi.* (*mil.*) disertare. **—er** *n.* disertore. **—ion** *n.* diserzione; abbandono.

deserve (dĕ·zûrv′) *vt.* meritare.

deserving (-zûr′vĭng) *agg.* meritevole, degno.

desiccate (dĕs′ĭ·kāt) *vt.* essiccare. *vi.* essiccarsi.

design (dĕ·zīn′) *n.* disegno, progetto, mira. *vt., vi.* disegnare; ideare, progettare, proporsi; designare: **industrial —**, disegno industriale, estetica del prodotto.

designate (dĕz′ĭg·nāt) *vt.* designare.

designer (dĕ·zīn′ĕr) *n.* disegnatore; progettista; inventore; modellista.

designing (dĕ·zīn′ĭng) *agg.* astuto, subdolo.

desirability (dĕ·zīr′à·bĭl′ĭ·tĭ) *n.* opportunità, convenienza, utilità; desiderabilità.

desirable (dĕ·zīr′à·b′l) *agg.* desiderabile, auspicabile.

desire (dĕ·zīr′) *n.* desiderio; brama. *vt.* desiderare, bramare; augurare, auspicare.

desirous (dĕ·zīr′ŭs) *agg.* desideroso.

desist (dĕ·zĭst′) *vi.* desistere, cessare.

desk (dĕsk) *n.* scrivania; banco.

desolate (dĕs′ō·lĭt) *agg.* desolato, sconfortato; disabitato; squallido. *vt.* desolare, devastare; spopolare; affliggere.

desolation (dĕs′ō·lā′shŭn) *n.* desolazione; sconforto.

despair (dĕ·spâr′) *n.* disperazione. *vt.* disperare, disperarsi. **—ing** *agg.* disperato.

despatch (dĕs·păch′) *vedi* dispatch.

desperate (dĕs′pĕr·ĭt) *agg.* disperato; forsennato, accanito; terribile; gravissimo. **—ly** *avv.* disperatamente; perdutamente; gravemente.

desperation (dĕs′pĕr·ā′shŭn) *n.* disperazione, furore, accanimento.

despicable (dĕs′pĭ·kà·b′l) *agg.* spregevole, ignobile.

despise (dĕ·spīz′) *vt.* disprezzare, sdegnare.

despite (dĕ·spīt′) *n.* dispetto, astio, stizza. *prep.* nonostante, a dispetto di. *vt.* offendere, indispettire. **—ful** *agg.* dispettoso, maligno.

despoil (dĕ·spoil′) *vt.* spogliare.

despondency (dĕ·spŏn′dĕn·sĭ) *n.* abbattimento, sconforto.

despondent (-dĕnt) *agg.* scoraggiato, abbattuto.

despot (dĕs'pŏt) *n.* despota. **—ic**
(-pŏt'ĭc) *agg.* dispotico. **—ism** (dĕs'-)
n. dispotismo.

dessert (dĭ-zûrt') *n.* dolce *o* frutta
(*ultima portata a tavola*).

destination (dĕs't ˏnā'shŭn) *n.* destinazione.

destine (dĕs'tĭn) *vt.* destinare.

destiny (dĕs't ĭ·ni) *n.* destino, fato.

destitute (dĕs'tĭ-tūt) *agg.* povero,
diseredato; privo (*di*).

destitution (-tū'shŭn) *n.* povertà;
abbandono.

destroy (dē-stroi') *vt.* distruggere.

destroyer (-ẽr) *n.* distruttore; (*naut.*)
cacciatorpediniere: **— escort**, cac-
ciasottomarini.

destruction (dē-strŭk'shŭn) *n.* distruzione, rovina.

destructive (-tĭv) *agg.* distruttivo,
deleterio.

desultory (dĕs'ŭl·tō'rĭ) *agg.* saltuario,
intermittente; sconnesso, irregolare.

detach (dē·tăch') *vt.* staccare, isolare.
—ment *n.* distacco, separazione;
indifferenza, imparzialità; (*mil.*)
distaccamento.

detail (dē·tāl') *n.* particolare; rapporto particolareggiato; squadra,
pattuglia: **to go into —**, entrare nei
particolari. *vt.* specificare, riferire;
distaccare (*una pattuglia, ecc.*).

detain (dē·tān') *vt.* trattenere; detenere; arrestare.

detect (dē·tĕkt') *vt.* scoprire, sorprendere; captare, avvertire, sentire.
—ion *n.* scoperta, rivelazione. **—ive**
n. investigatore, agente. **—or** *n.*
(*radio*) rivelatore.

detention (dē·tĕn'shŭn) *n.* detenzione,
arresto, fermo.

deter (dē·tûr') *vt.* trattenere, dissuadere, distogliere, frenare.

detergent (dē·tûr'jĕnt) *agg., n.* detersivo.

deteriorate (dē·tẽr'ĭ·ō·rāt) *vi.* deteriorarsi.

deterioration (-rā'shŭn) *n.* deterioramento.

determination (dē·tûr'mĭ·nā'shŭn) *n.*
determinazione, risolutezza, scadenza, conclusione.

determine (dē·tûr'mĭn) *vt., vi.* determinare, stabilire, decidere, fissare.

determined (-mĭnd) *agg.* risoluto,
deciso.

deterrent (dē·tûr'ĕnt) *n.* remora,
freno.

detest (dē·tĕst') *vt.* detestare.

detour (dē·tŏor') *n.* deviazione, giravolta. *vi.* compiere una deviazione.

detract (dē·trăkt') *vt., vi.* detrarre,
sottrarre, diminuire; svilire, denigrare.

detriment (dĕt'rĭ·mĕnt) *n.* detrimento,
danno.

detrimental (-mĕn'tăl) *agg.* dannoso.

deuce (dūs) *n.* sfortuna; diavolo; due
(*a carte*); 40 pari (*al tennis*).

devastate (dĕv'ŭs·tāt) *vt.* devastare.

devastating *agg.* devastante; straziante; (*gergo S.U.*) sconvolgente; potentissimo.

develop (dē·vĕl'ŭp) *vt.* sviluppare. *vi.*
svilupparsi; risultare. **—er** *n.*
sviluppatore. **—ing**, **—ment** *n.*
sviluppo; crescita; sfruttamento.

deviate (dē'vĭ·āt) *vi.* deviare; divagare. *vt.* sviare, far deviare.

deviation (-ā'shŭn) *n.* deviazione.

device (dē·vīs') *n.* meccanismo, dispositivo; accorgimento, disegno,
espediente, mezzo; astuzia; divisa,
motto.

devil (dĕv'l) *n.* diavolo, demonio: **the
— to pay**, guai in vista. *vt.* tormentare; (*cucina*) arrostire e aromatizzare. **—ish** *agg.* diabolico.

devil-may-care *agg.* temerario.

devilry (dĕv''l·rĭ) *n.* diavoleria.

devious (dē'vĭ·ŭs) *agg.* remoto, fuori
di mano; errante; indiretto, tortuoso; stravagante, bizzarro; tra-
viato.

devise (dē·vīz') *vt.* escogitare, inventare, tramare.

devoid (dē·void') *agg.* privo (*di*),
sprovvisto (*di*), scevro (*di*).

devote (dē·vōt') *vt.* dedicare, consacrare.

devoted (-vōt'ĕd) *agg.* devoto, votato;
predestinato.

devotee (dĕv'ō·tē') *n.* devoto, fanatico.

devotion (dē·vō'shŭn) *n.* devozione;
preghiera.

devour (dē·vour') *vt.* divorare.

devout (dē·vout') *agg.* devoto, pio.

dew (dū) *n.* rugiada. *vt.* irrorare.
—drop *n.* goccia di rugiada. **—worm**
n. lombrico.

dewy (dū'ĭ) *agg.* rugiadoso.

dexterity (dĕks·tĕr'ĭ·tĭ) *n.* destrezza,
abilità.

dexterous (dĕk'stẽr·ŭs) *agg.* destro,
abile, disinvolto. **—ness** *n.* destrezza, abilità.

diabetes (dī'á·bē'tēs) *n.* diabete.

diabetic (-bĕt'ĭk) *agg., n.* diabetico.

diabolic (dī'á·bŏl'ĭk) *agg.* diabolico.

diadem (dī'á·dĕm) *n.* diadema.

diagnose (dī'ăg·nōs') *vt.* diagnosticare.

diagnosis (dī'ăg·nō'sĭs) *n.* diagnosi.

diagonal (dī·ăg'ō·năl) *agg., n.* diagonale.

diagram (dī'á·grăm) *n.* diagramma,
grafico.

dial (dī'ăl) *n.* quadrante (*dell'orologio*);
meridiana; manometro; disco com-

binatore (*del telefono*). *vt.*, *vi.* misurare con un manometro; formare un numero telefonico, chiamare (*per telefono*).

dialect (dĭ.ă'lĕkt) *n.* dialetto.

dialectic (dī'á.lĕk'tĭk) *n.* dialettica.

dialogue (dī'á.lôg) *n.* dialogo. *vt.*, *vi.* dialogare, conversare.

diameter (dī.ăm'ê.tẽr) *n.* diametro.

diamond (dī'á.mŭnd) *n.* diamante; losanga, rombo; (*carte da gioco*) quadro.

diaper (dī'á.pẽr) *n.* pannolino per neonati.

diarrhea (dī'á.rē'á) *n.* diarrea.

dice (dīs) *n.pl.* dadi (*da gioco*). *vi.* giocare ai dadi. *vt.* tagliare a cubetti, quadrettare.

dick (dĭk) *n.* (*gergo*) frustino; (*S.U.*) poliziotto.

dickens (dĭk'ĕnz) *inter.* diavolo, diamine!

dictate (dĭk'tāt) *n.* ordine, dettame, precetto. *vt.*, *vi.* dettare, ordinare.

dictation (dĭk·tā'shŭn) *n.* dettatura; ordine perentorio: to take —, scrivere sotto dettatura.

dictator (dĭk·tā'tẽr) *n.* dittatore. —ship *n.* dittatura.

diction (dĭk'shŭn) *n.* dizione.

dictionary (dĭk'shŭn·ẽr'ĭ) *n.* dizionario.

did (dĭd) *pass.* di to do.

die (dī) (1) *n.* (*pl.* dies [dīz]) calco, stampo, marchio, conio; (*arch.*) dado.

die (dī) (2) *n.* (*pl.* dice [dīs]) dado da gioco; (*fig.*) sorte, alea: the — is cast, il dado è tratto: no dice (*gergo*), niente da fare.

die (dī) (3) *vi.* (*pass.* died, *ppr.* dying, *pp.* dead) morire, spegnersi; smorzarsi, affievolirsi; cessare.

diet (dī'ĕt) *n.* dieta, regime, alimentazione: on a —, a dieta. *vt.* mettere a dieta. *vi.* seguire una dieta. —ary *n.* regime dietetico. *agg.* dietetico. —etics *n.pl.* dietetica.

differ (dĭf'ẽr) *vi.* differire; dissentire. —ence *n.* differenza; divergenza, controversia. —ent *agg.* differente, divergente.

differentiate (dĭf'ẽr.ĕn'shĭ.āt) *vt.*, *vi.* differenziare; differenziarsi, discriminare.

difficult (dĭf'ĭ.kŭlt) *agg.* difficile.

difficulty (dĭf'ĭ.kŭl·tĭ) *n.* difficoltà, imbarazzo.

diffidence (dĭf'ĭ.dĕns) *n.* diffidenza, titubanza, timidezza.

diffident *agg.* diffidente, timido.

diffuse (dĭ.fūs') *agg.* diffuso, prolisso. *vt.* (-fūz') diffondere. *vi.* diffondersi, dilungarsi.

diffusion (-fū'zhŭn) *n.* diffusione, propagazione.

dig (dĭg) *n.* urto, gomitata; punzecchiatura, sarcasmo. *vt.* (*pass.*, *pp.* dug) scavare, frugare: to — up, dissotterrare.

digest (dĭ'jĕst) *n.* digesto; compendio; *vt.*, *vi.* digerire; condensare, riassumere, redigere. —ible *agg.* digeribile. —ion *n.* digestione. —ive *n.*, *agg.* digestivo.

digger (dĭg'ẽr) *n.* scavatore, cercatore; (*mecc.*) scavatrice; (*gergo*) unghia; sgobbone.

diggings *n.pl.* scavi; (*fam.*) alloggio.

dignified (d g'nĭ.fīd) *agg.* dignitoso, solenne.

dignitary (dĭg'nĭ.tẽr'ĭ) *n.* dignitario.

dignity (dĭg'nĭ·tĭ) *n.* dignità.

digress (dĭ·grĕs') dĭ-) *vi.* divagare. —ion (shŭn) *n.* digressione.

dike (dīk) *n.* diga, fossato; (*geol.*) basalto. *vt.* imbrigliare, arginare.

dilapidated (dĭ·lăp'ĭ.dāt'ĕd) *agg.* diroccato, dilapidato.

dilation (dĭ·lā'shŭn) *n.* dilatazione.

dilate (dĭ·lāt') *vt.* dilatare, estendere, ampliare. *vi.* dilatarsi, espandersi.

dilatory (dĭl'á.tō'rĭ) *agg.* lento, dilatorio.

diligence (dĭl'ĭ.jĕns) *n.* diligenza, perseveranza; corriera.

diligent *agg.* diligente.

dilute (dĭ·lūt') *agg.* diluito. *vt.* diluire. *vi.* diluirsi.

dim (dĭm) *agg.* oscuro, vago; pallido, sbiadito; scettico; pessimistico: —sighted *agg.* corto di vista. *vt.* smorzare, offuscare, oscurare, annebbiare, confondere. *vi.* oscurarsi, offuscarsi, indebolirsi (*della luce, ecc.*).

dime (dīm) *n.* moneta da 10 centesimi di dollaro.

dimension (dĭ·mĕn'shŭn) *n.* dimensione.

diminish (dĭ·mĭn'ĭsh) *vt.*, *vi.* diminuire, abbassare, abbassarsi. —ing *agg.* decrescente.

diminution (dĭ·mĭ·nū'shŭn) *n.* diminuzione.

diminutive (dĭ·mĭn'û·tĭv) *agg.* diminutivo; minuscolo, in miniatura.

dimly (dĭm'lĭ) *avv.* vagamente, oscuramente.

dimness (dĭm'nĕs) *n.* oscurità, debolezza (*di vista*), opacità; penombra.

dimple (dĭm'p'l) *n.* fossetta (*spec. del viso*).

din (dĭn) *n.* frastuono, clangore, clamore.

dine (dīn) *vi.* desinare. *vt.* offrire un desinare a.

diner (dīn'ẽr) *n.* chi desina; (*S.U.*) vagone ristorante.

dinghy (dĭng'gĭ) n. dingo, barchetta.
dinginess (dĭn'jĭ·nĕs) n. colore sbiadito; sporcizia; squallore.
dingy (dĭn'jĭ) agg. sbiadito; sporco; squallido.
dining ppr. di to dine: — car, vagone ristorante; — room, sala da pranzo.
dinner (dĭn'ẽr) n. pranzo, desinare: — jacket smoking (vestito da sera).
dint (dĭnt) n. forza, tacca: by — of, a forza di.
diocese (dī'ō·sēs) n. diocesi.
dip (dĭp) n. tuffo, immersione; inclinazione; candela di sego. vt. immergere; intingere; inclinare; salutare (con la bandiera). vi. immergersi, tuffarsi; inclinarsi; abbassarsi.
diphtheria (dĭf·thẽr'ĭ·á) n. difterite.
diphthong (dĭf'thŏng) n. dittongo.
diplomacy (dĭ·plō'má·sĭ) n. diplomazia.
diplomat (dĭp'lō·mbăt) n. diplomatico.
diplomatic (dĭp'lō·măt'ĭk) agg. diplomatico.
dipper (dĭp'ẽr) n. tuffatore; mestolo; uccello acquatico; escavatore; (fot.) vaschetta: the Big Dipper, l'Orsa Maggiore.
dipsomania (dĭp'sō·mā nĭ·á) n. dipsomania; alcoolismo cronico.
dipsomaniac (-ăk) n. dipsòmane; alcoolizzato.
dire (dīr) agg. terribile, tremendo, calamitoso; estremo.
direct (dĭ·rĕkt') agg. diretto; sincero, esplicito: — current, corrente continua; — object, accusativo, complemento oggetto. avv. direttamente, sùbito. vt. dirigere, ordinare, indirizzare; ragguagliare. vi. impartire ordini. —ion n. direzione, istruzione, ordine. —ive agg. direttivo. n. direttiva, ordine, comando. —ly avv. direttamente, immediatamente. —ness n. dirittura, sincerità, modo esplicito. —or n. direttore; (cinema) regista; (comm.) consigliere (di società). —ory n. direttorio; guida (dei telefoni, ecc.); indirizzario.
dirndl (dûrn'd'l) n. vestito alla tirolese (da donna).
dirge (dûrj) n. canto funebre.
dirigible (dĭr'ĭ·jĭ·b'l) n., agg. dirigibile.
dirt (dûrt) n. sudiciume, fango.
dirtiness (dûr'tĭ·nĕs) n. sporcizia, bassezza.
dirty (dûr'ĭ) agg. sudicio, immondo. vt. sporcare.
disability (dĭs'á·bĭl'ĭ·tĭ) n. incapacità, invalidità.

disable (dĭs·ā'b'l) vt. inabilitare, mettere fuori combattimento, interdire.
disadvantage (dĭs'ăd·văn'tĭj) n. svantaggio, inconveniente.
disagree (dĭs'á·grē') vi. dissentire, differire, essere in disaccordo; nuocere: liquor disagrees with me, il liquore mi fa male.
disagreeable (-á·b'l) agg. sgradevole, dannoso.
disagreement (-grē'mĕnt) n. disaccordo, divergenza, contrasto.
disappear (dĭs'á·pẽr') vi. sparire.
disappearance (-áns) n. sparizione.
disappoint (dĭs'á·point') vt. deludere. —ing agg. deludente. —ment n. delusione, disappunto.
disapprobation (dĭs'ăp·rō·bā'shŭn) disapproval n. disapprovazione.
disapprove (dĭs'á·prōōv') vt., vi. disapprovare.
disarm (dĭs·ärm') vt., vi. disarmare.
disarmament (dĭs·är'má·mĕnt) n. disarmo.
disarming agg. disarmante, ingenuo.
disarrange (dĭs'á·rānj') vt. scompigliare, mettere in disordine.
disarray (dĭs'á·rā') n. scompiglio, confusione. vt. scompigliare; spogliare.
disaster (dĭ·zăs'tẽr) n. disastro, catastrofe.
disastrous (-trŭs) agg. disastroso.
disavow (dĭs'á·vou') vt. rinnegare, sconfessare, disapprovare.
disband (dĭs·bănd') vt. sbandare, smobilitare, disperdere. vi. sbandarsi.
disbelieve (dĭs'bḗ·lēv') vt., vi. non credere, essere scettico, mettere in dubbio.
disburden (dĭs·bûr'd'n) vt., vi. alleggerire; sgravare; ilberarsi (di un fardello), sfogarsi.
disburse (dĭs·bûrs') vt. sborsare. —ment n. esborso.
disc vedi disk.
discard (dĭs·kärd') n. scarto. vt. scartare, eliminare.
discern (dĭ·zûrn') vt., vi. discernere, distinguere. —ing agg. accorto, avveduto. —ment n. discernimento.
discharge (dĭs·chärj') n. scarico, scarica (elett., d'arma, ecc.); scarcerazione, proscioglimento; (mil.) congedo; esecuzione (di un incarico); (comm.) quietanza; licenziamento; spurgo. vt. scaricare; licenziare, congedare; emettere; spurgare; eseguire (un incarico); compiere (un dovere); prosciogliere; scarcerare.
disciple (dĭ·sī'p'l) n. discepolo.
discipline (dĭs'ĭ·plĭn) n. disciplina. vt. disciplinare.

disclaim (dĭs·klām') *vt.* declinare (*una responsabilità, ecc.*); smentire; rinunciare (*a un diritto*).

disclose (dĭs·klōz') *vt.* svelare, rivelare.

disclosure (-klō'zhĕr) *n.* rivelazione.

discography (dĭs·kŏg'rd·fĭ) *n.* discografia.

discolor (dĭs·kŭl'ĕr) *vt.* macchiare. *vi.* macchiarsi, scolorirsi.

discomfiture (dĭs·kŭm'fĭ·tûr) *n.* sconfitta, confusione.

discomfort (dĭs·kŭm'fĕrt) *n.* disagio, scomodità. *vt.* incomodare, mettere a disagio.

disconcert (dĭs'kŏn·sûrt') *vt.* sconcertare.

disconnect (dĭs'kŏ·nĕkt') *vt.* dividere, staccare, interrompere, disinnestare. —ed *agg.* sconnesso; incoerente; interrotto.

disconsolate (dĭs·kŏn'sō·lĭt) *agg.* sconsolato.

discontent (dĭs'kŏn·tĕnt') *n.* malcontento, scontentezza. *agg.* scontento, malcontento. *vt.* scontentare. —ed *agg.* insoddisfatto.

discontinue (dĭs'kŏn·tĭn'ū) *vt., vi.* interrompere, far cessare, sospendere; disdire (*un abbonamento*); cessare, interrompersi, smettere.

discord (dĭs'kôrd) *n.* discordia, disarmonia.

discount (dĭs'kount) *n.* sconto, riduzione: — **rate**, (*comm.*) tasso di sconto. *vt.* scontare; ribassare, screditare. *vi.* effettuare uno sconto.

discountenance (dĭs·koun'tĕ·năns) *vt.* disapprovare; scoraggiare, mortificare.

discourage (dĭs·kûr'ĭj) *vt.* scoraggiare; dissuadere.

discouragement (-mĕnt) *n.* scoraggiamento.

discouraging *agg.* demoralizzante.

discourse (dĭs·kōrs') *n.* discorso, dissertazione. *vi.* discorrere, dissertare.

discourteous (dĭs·kûr'tĕ·ŭs) *agg.* scortese.

discourtesy (dĭs·kûr'tĕ·sĭ) *n.* scortesia.

discover (dĭs·kŭv'ĕr) *vt.* scoprire, rivelare.

discoverer (-ĕr·ĕr) *n.* scopritore.

discovery (-ĕr·ĭ) *n.* scoperta.

discredit (dĭs·krĕd'ĭt) *n.* discredito. *vt.* screditare, confutare.

discreet (dĭs·krēt') *agg.* discreto; prudente.

discrepancy (dĭs·krĕp'ăn·sĭ) *n.* discrepanza, contraddizione.

discretion (dĭs·krĕsh'ŭn) *n.* discrezione, prudenza.

discriminate (dĭs·krĭm'ĭ·nāt) *vt., vi.* discriminare, distinguere: **to — against**, fare distinzioni a sfavore di.

discus (dĭs'kŭs) *n.* disco: — **thrower**, *n.* discobolo.

discuss (dĭs·kŭs') *vt., vi.* discutere.

discussion (-kŭsh'ŭn) *n.* discussione.

disdain (dĭs·dān') *n.* sdegno, disprezzo. *vt.* disdegnare, disprezzare. —ful *agg.* sdegnoso.

disease (dĭ·zēz') *n.* malanno, malattia.

diseased (dĭ·zēzd') *agg.* malato.

disembark (dĭs'ĕm·bärk') *vt., vi.* sbarcare.

disembowel (dĭs'ĕm·bou'ĕl) *vt.* sbudellare, sventrare.

disencumber (dĭs'ĕn·kŭm'bĕr) *vt.* sbarazzare, sgombrare.

disengage (dĭs'ĕn·gāj') *vt.* svincolare, sbarazzare; disincagliare; disinnestare.

disentangle (dĭs'ĕn·tăng'g'l) *vt.* liberare, districare.

disfavor (dĭs·fā'vĕr) *n.* sfavore.

disfigure (dĭs·fĭg'ûr) *vt.* sfigurare, deturpare.

disgorge (dĭs·gôrj') *vt.* emettere, riversare; vomitare; sborsare.

disgrace (dĭs·grās') *n.* disonore, sfavore, vergogna. *vt.* disonorare. —ful *agg.* vergognoso, disonorevole.

disgruntle (dĭs·grŭn't'l) *vt.* scontentare, mettere di cattivo umore, irritare.

disguise (dĭs·gīz') *n.* travestimento, inganno: **in —**, camuffato. *vt.* travestire, mascherare.

disgust (dĭs·gŭst') *n.* disgusto. *vt.* disgustare. —ful, —ing *agg.* disgustoso.

dish (dĭsh) *n.* piatto; vivanda. *vt.* scodellare, ammannire, servire.

dishearten (dĭs·här't'n) *vt.* scoraggiare.

disheveled (dĭ·shĕv'ĕld) *agg.* scarmigliato.

dishonest (dĭs·ŏn'ĕst) *agg.* disonesto.

dishonesty (-ŏn'ĕs·tĭ) *n.* disonestà.

dishonor (dĭs·ŏn'ĕr) *n.* disonore. *vt.* disonorare; (*comm.*) non onorare (*un assegno, una cambiale, ecc.*). —able *agg.* disonorevole.

disillusion (dĭs'ĭ·lū'zhŭn) *vt.* disilludere.

disinclination (dĭs·ĭn'klĭ·nā'shŭn) *n.* avversione, contrarietà.

disinclined (dĭs'ĭn·klīnd') *agg.* contrario, restio, poco propenso (*a*).

disinfect (dĭs'ĭn·fĕkt') *vt.* disinfettare. —ant *n.* disinfettante. —ion (-fĕk'shŭn) *n.* disinfezione.

disintegrate (dĭs·ĭn'tĕ·grāt) *vt.* disgregare. *vi.* disgregarsi.

disinterested (dĭs·ĭn'tĕr·ĕs·tĕd) *agg.* indifferente; disinteressato, imparziale.

disjoin (dĭs·join') *vt.* disgiungere.
disjoint (dĭs·joint') *vt.* dislogare, interrompere, guastare (*un meccanismo, ecc.*). *vi.* separarsi, slogarsi, guastarsi.
disk (dĭsk) *n.* disco: — **jockey**, *n.* presentatore radiofonico di dischi.
dislike (dĭs·lĭk') *n.* antipatia, avversione. *vt.* detestare, esser contrario a, provare avversione per, avere in antipatia: **I — it**, non mi piace; **I — him**, mi è antipatico; **to be —d**, essere malvisto.
dislocate (dĭs'lō·kāt) *vt.* slogare. lussare; spostare, scompigliare.
dislocation (-kā'shŭn) *n.* slogatura, lussazione; spostamento.
dislodge (dĭs·lŏj') *vt.* sloggiare, scacciare, spostare.
disloyal (dĭs·loi'ăl) *agg.* sleale, infedele.
dismal (dĭz'măl) *agg.* triste, tetro, squallido.
dismantle (dĭs·măn't'l) *vt.* smantellare.
dismay (dĭs·mā') *n.* sgomento, terrore. *vt.* sgomentare, spaventare.
dismiss (dĭs·mĭs') *vt.* congedare, licenziare, respingere, scacciare: **to — the meeting**, togliere la seduta. **—al** *n.* congedo, licenziamento, rigetto.
dismount (dĭs·mount') *vt.* disarcionare; appiedare; smontare (*togliere dalla montatura, opp. disfare p. es. un meccanismo*). *vi.* smontare (*da cavallo, ecc.*).
disobedience (dĭs'ō·bē'dĭ·ĕns) *n.* disobbedienza.
disobedient (-ĕnt) *agg.* disobbediente.
disobey (dĭs'ō·bā') *vt.* disobbedire.
disoblige (dĭs'o·blīj') *vt.* offendere; essere scortese con; disturbare, importunare.
disobliging *agg.* scortese, scompiacente; importuno.
disorder (dĭs·ôr'dĕr) *n.* disordine; (*med.*) disfunzione, malattia. *vt.* scompigliare. **—ed** *agg.* ammalato (*spec. di mente*). **—ly** *agg.* disordinato; sregolato; turbolento.
disorganization (dĭs·ôr'gằn·ĭ·zā'shŭn) *n.* disorganizzazione.
disorganize (dĭs·ôr'gằn·īz) *vt.* disorganizzare.
disown (dĭs·ōn') *vt.* smentire, sconfessare, rinnegare, ripudiare.
disparage (dĭs·păr'ĭj) *vt.* disprezzare, denigrare.
disparaging *agg.* sprezzante, ingiurioso.
dispassionate (dĭs·păsh'ŭn·ĭt) *agg.* calmo, spassionato.
dispatch (dĭs·păch') *n.* dispaccio; spedizione; diligenza, prontezza. *vt.*

spedire, sbrigare. — **box** *n.* portacarte, custodia.
dispel (dĭs·pĕl') *vt.* dissipare, scacciare.
dispensable (dĭs·pĕn'sả·b'l) *agg.* superfluo.
dispensary (dĭs·pĕn'sả·rĭ) *n.* dispensario.
dispensation (dĭs'pĕn·sā'shŭn) *n.* distribuzione; dispensa, esenzione; provvidenza.
dispense (dĭs·pĕns') *vt.* dispensare; distribuire, somministrare. *vi.* concedere una dispensa: **to — with**, rinunciare a, fare a meno di.
dispenser (dĭs·pĕn'sĕr) *n.* dispensatore; distributore.
dispersal (dĭs·pûr'săl) *n.* dispersione.
disperse (dĭs·pûrs') *vt.* disperdere, spargere, pagliare. *vi.* sparpagliarsi, dissiparsi.
dispirit (dĭs·pĭr'ĭt) *vt.* scoraggiare.
displace (dĭs·plās') *vt.* spostare; soppiantare, destituire; (*naut.*) dislocare, stazzare.
displaced *agg.* spostato: — **person** *n.* profugo.
displacement (dĭs·plās'mĕnt) *n.* spostamento, destituzione; cilindrata (*di un motore*); (*naut.*) stazza, tonnellaggio.
display (dĭs·plā') *n.* esposizione, esibizione, ostentazione, spiegamento (*di truppe*). *vt.* esporre, esibire; ostentare; rivelare.
displease (dĭs·plēz') *vt.* contrariare, spiacere, offendere.
displeasure (dĭs·plĕzh'ĕr) *n.* contrarietà, disapprovazione, dispiacere, sfavore.
disposal (dĭs·pōz'ăl) *n.* disposizione; vendita, realizzo.
dispose (dĭs·pōz') *vt.*, *vi.* disporre: **to — of**, disporre di, sbarazzarsi di, accudire a, eliminare.
disposition (dĭs'pŏ·zĭsh'ŭn) *n.* disposizione; carattere, temperamento.
dispossess (dĭs'pŏ·zĕs') *vt.* defraudare.
disproportion (dĭs'prŏ·pōr'shŭn) *n.* sproporzione. **—ate** (-ĭt) *agg.* sproporzionato.
disprove (dĭs·prōōv') *vt.* confutare, invalidare.
dispute (dĭs·pūt') *n.* disputa. *vt.*, *vi.* disputare, discutere.
disqualify (dĭs·kwŏl'ĭ·fĭ) *vt.* squalificare.
disregard (dĭs'rē·gärd')*n.* noncuranza; dispregio. *vt.* trascurare, tenere in dispregio, non curarsi (*di*).
disreputable (dĭs·rĕp' û·tả·b'l) *agg.* indecoroso, screditato, losco, malfamato, disonorevole.
disrepute (dĭs'rē·pūt') *n.* discredito, disonore.

disrespect (dĭs'rē·spĕkt') n. irriverenza, insolenza. —ful agg. irriverente,
insolente.

disrupt (dĭs·rŭpt') vt. spaccare; separare; distruggere. —ion n. scissione.

dissatisfied (dĭs·săt'ĭs·fīd) agg. malcontento.

dissatisfy (dĭs·săt'ĭs·fī) vt. scontentare,
deludere.

dissect (dĭ·sĕkt') vt. sezionare; esaminare minuziosamente.

dissemble (dĭ·sĕm'b'l) vt., vi. dissimulare, fingere, simulare, nascondere.

dissension (dĭ·sĕn'shŭn) n. dissenso

dissent (dĭ·sĕnt') n. dissenso. vi. dissentire.

dissertation (dĭs'ĕr·tā'shŭn) n. dissertazione; tesi di laurea.

disservice (dĭs·sûr'vĭs) n. disservizio

dissimilar (dĭ(s)·sĭm'ĭ·lēr) agg. dissimile, diverso. —ity (-lăr'ĭ·tĭ) n. diversità.

dissimulate (dĭ·sĭm'ū·lāt) vt., vi. dissimulare, fingere.

dissimulation (dĭ·sĭm'ū·lā'shŭn) n.
dissimulazione, finzione.

dissipate (dĭs'ĭ·pāt) vt. dissipare, sparpagliare. vi. dissiparsi, disperdersi,
traviarsi.

dissipated (-pāt'ĕd) agg. dissoluto.

dissipation (-pā'shŭn) n. dissipazione,
dissolutezza.

dissolute (dĭs''ō·lūt) agg. dissoluto.

dissolution (dĭs'ō·lū'shŭn) n. sfacelo,
dissoluzione; scioglimento.

dissolve (dĭ·zŏlv') vt. dissolvere, sciogliere, separare; distruggere, risolvere, vi. sciogliersi; svanire.

dissuade (dĭ·swād') vt. dissuadere.

distaff (dĭs'tȧf) n. conocchia.

distance (dĭs'tăns) n. distanza. vt.
distanziare.

distant (dĭs'tănt) agg. lontano, distante; riservato.

distantly (dĭs'tănt) avv. lontanamente, vagamente; freddamente; in lontananza.

distaste (ds·tāïst') n. disgusto, avversione, ripugnanza. —ful agg. disgustoso, sgradevole, ostico.

distemper (dĭs·tĕm'pēr) n. (vet.) stran-
guglione; (pitt.) tempera; malu-
more.

distend (dĭs·tĕnd') vt. distendere, dilatare, gonfiare; allentare. vi. distendersi, gonfiarsi.

distil (dĭs·tĭl') vt. distillare. —lation
(-ā'shŭn) n. distillazione. —lery n.
distilleria.

distinct (dĭs·tĭngkt') agg. distinto,
diverso, singolo, netto. —ion n.
distinzione. —ive agg. distintivo,
caratteristico. —ly avv. distintamente, chiaramente.

distinguish (dĭs·tĭng'gwĭsh) vt., vi. distinguere, discernere; far distinzione. —ed agg. distinto, illustre.
—ing agg. peculiare, caratteristico,
distintivo.

distort (dĭs·tôrt') vt. deformare, alterare; torcere, contrarre; falsare.

distract (dĭs·trăkt') vt. distrarre; tormentare, sconvolgere. —ed agg.
sconvolto, disperato. —ion n. disperazione, confusione, pazzia; distrazione (svago): to love to —ion,
amare alla follia. —ing agg. straziante.

distress (dĭs·trĕs') n. dolore, pena;
miseria, difficoltà; sequestro. vt.
affliggere, addolorare; sequestrare:
— signal, segnale di soccorso. —ed
agg. afflitto, infelice, povero.

distribute (dĭs·trĭb'ūt) vt. distribuire.

distribution (dĭs'trĭ·bū'shŭn) n. distribuzione.

district (dĭs'trĭkt) n. distretto, regione,
zona; quartiere (di città).

distrust (dĭs·trŭst') n. sfiducia, diffidenza. vt. diffidare di. —ful agg.
diffidente, sospettoso.

disturb (dĭs·tûrb') vt. disturbare, turbare; mettere in disordine. —ance
n. perturbazione, trambusto, disordine; alterazione mentale o
psichica.

disuse (dĭs·ūs') n. disuso. [psichica.

ditch (dĭch) n. fossato; canale: to
fight to the last —, resistere ad
oltranza. vt., vi. solcare; scavare
fossati; gettare in un fossato; piantare in asso; (aeron.) compiere un
ammaraggio forzato.

dither (dĭth'ĕr) n. (fam.) agitazione,
scombussolamento; tremito; vi.
essere in agitazione, essere scom-
bussolato; tremare.

ditto (dĭt'ō) n. il suddetto, lo stesso.
avv. come sopra.

ditty (dĭt'ĭ) n. canzoncina, stornello.

divan (dĭ'văn) n. divano.

dive (dīv) n. tuffo, immersione; (S.U.)
taverna, bettola: — bomber (aeron.)
picchiatore. vi. tuffarsi, immergersi; (aeron.) scendere in picchiata.

diver (dīv'ĕr) n. tuffatore; palombaro, sommozzatore.

diverge (dĭ·vûrj') vi. divergere.

divergence (-vûr'jĕns) n. divergenza.

divers (dī'vērz) agg. vari, diversi.

diverse (dĭ·vûrs') agg. diverso, differente, variato.

diversion (dĭ·vûr'zhŭn) n. diversione,
deviazione; ricreazione, diversivo.

diversity (dĭ·vûr'sĭ·tĭ) n. diversità,
varietà.

divert (dĭ·vûrt') vt. sviare, deviare;
divertire. —ing agg. divertente, che
distrae.

divide (dĭ·vīd′) *vt.* dividere, separare. *vi.* dividersi, scindersi.

dividend (dĭv′ĭ·dĕnd) *n.* dividendo.

divination (dĭv′ĭ·nă′shŭn) *n.* divinazione.

divine (dĭ·vīn′) *agg.* divino *n.* teologo. *vt.* divinare, predire.

diviner (dĭ·vīn′ẽr) *n.* indovino.

diving (dīv′ĭng) *n.* tuffo; immersione. — **bell** *n.* campana pneumatica. — **dress**, — **suit** *n.* scafandro.

divining rod *n.* bacchetta del rabdomante.

divinity (dĭ·vĭn′ĭ·tĭ) *n.* divinità; teologia.

division (dĭ·vĭzh′ŭn) *n.* divisione; scissione.

divorce (dĭ·vŏrs′) *n.* divorzio. *vt.* divorziare da, ripudiare.

divorcé *m.*, **divorcée** *fem.* (dĭ·vor′sē′) divorziato, divorziata.

divulge (dĭ·vŭlj′) *vt.* divulgare.

dizziness (dĭz′ĭ·nĕs) *n.* vertigine, stordimento.

dizzy (dĭz′ĭ) *agg.* stordito, che ha le vertigini; vertiginoso.

do (dōō) *vt.* (*1a* pers.*sing.pres.* do; *2a* dost; *3a* does; *pl.* do; *pass.* did; *pp.* done; *ppr.* doing) fare, compiere; bastare; preparare, cucinare; to — into, tradurre (*in*); to — out of, defraudare, derubare; to — away with, eliminare, liquidare; to — in, rovinare, ammazzare; to — up, avvolgere, impacchettare, acconciare; riassettare, pulire; to — one's best, fare del proprio meglio; to — the dishes, lavare i piatti; to — one's hair, pettinarsi; this will — me for today, questo mi basta per oggi. *vi.* agire, essere in azione; stare (*di salute*); comportarsi; bastare: to — by, comportarsi verso; how — you —?, come state?; tanto piacere (*di conoscervi*); to make something —, far bastare, accontentarsi di qualcosa; to have to — with, avere a che fare con; to — without, fare a meno di; to well in business, prosperare negli affari; do you like it? vi piace?; I — not know her, non la conosco; — come! suvvia, venite!; — you like this?, vi piace questo?; yes, I —, sì, mi piace.

docile (dŏs′ĭl) *agg.* docile.

dock (dŏk) (1) *n.* coda mozza. *vt.* mozzare; detrarre, ridurre: to — wages, abbassare la paga.

dock (dŏk) (2) *n.* bacino portuario, molo: dry —, bacino di carenaggio; wet —, darsena. *vt.*, *vi.* portare *o* entrare in cantiere, attracca-

re. —**yard** *n.* arsenale, cantiere navale.

dock (dŏk) (3) *n.* banco degli accusati.

docket (dŏk′ĕt) *n.* etichetta; distinta di contenuto; (*giur.*) estratto, verbale; (*S.U.*) ordine del giorno, programma dei lavori.

doctor (dŏk′tẽr) *n.* medico, dottore. *vt.* curare; accomodare, rimediare; adulterare: to — oneself, curarsi, prendere medicine.

doctrine (dŏk′trĭn) *n.* dottrina.

document (dŏk′ū·mĕnt) *n.* documento. *vt.* documentare.

documentary (dŏk′ū·mĕn′tá·rĭ) *agg.* documentario. *n.* film *o*, dramma *o*, libro documentario.

dodder (dŏd′ẽr) *vi.* tremare, vacillare.

dodge (dŏj) *n.* scarto (*brusco movimento*), balzo; espediente, trucco. *vi.* scartare; scantonare; temporeggiare. *vt.* schivare; eludere; (*foto.*) correggere.

doe (dō) *n.* daina; femmina (*dell'antilope, del coniglio e altri animali*).

does (dŭz) *1a* pers.*sing.pres.* di *to* do.

doff (dŏf) *vt.* togliersi (*un indumento, il cappello*).

dog (dŏg) *n.* cane; (*fig.*) tipo, individuo: to go to the dogs, andare in malora; hot —, salsiccia calda. *vt.* braccare; spiare. *avv.* sommamente: —tired, stanco morto. — days *n.pl.* canicola. —face *n.* (*S.U.*) fante, marmittone. —fight *n.* duello aereo. —hole *n.* tana, tugurio. —house *n.* canile: to be in the — (*gergo S.U.*) essere in disgrazia.

dogged (dŏg′ĕd) *agg.* ostinato, accanito. —ness *n.* accanimento.

dogma (dŏg′má) *n.* dogma. —tic *agg.* dogmatico.

doily (doi′lĭ) *n.* tovagliolino, sottocoppa.

doings (dōō′ĭngz) *n.pl.* attività, azione; prodezze; sforzi: great —, gran daffare, gran festa.

dole (dōl) *n.* ripartizione, distribuzione, sussidio (*per disoccupati*). *vt.* (*gen. seg. da* out) distribuire (*a poco a poco*), distribuire per carità; lesinare.

doleful (dōl′fŏŏl) *agg.* dolente, afflitto.

doll (dŏl) *n.* bambola.

dollar (dŏl′ẽr) *n.* dollaro.

dolly (dŏl′ĭ) *n.* bambolina; (*cinema*) carrello.

dolor (dō′lẽr) *n.* dolore.

dolphin (dŏl′fĭn) *n.* delfino; (*naut.*) boa.

dolt (dōlt) *n.* stupido.

domain (dō·mān′) *n.* regno, dominio, proprietà.

dome (dōm) *n.* cupola.

domestic (dṓ·mĕs′tĭk) *n.*, *agg.* domestico.

domesticate (dṓ·mĕs′tĭ·kāt) *vt.* addomesticare, civilizzare, acclimatare.

domicile (dŏm′ĭ·sĭl) *n.* domicilio.

dominant (dŏm′ĭ·nănt) *agg.* dominante, predominante; autoritario.

dominate (dŏm′ĭ·nāt) *vt.*, *vi.* dominare, prevalere, predominare.

domination (-nā′shŭn) *n.* dominazione.

domineer (dŏm′ĭ·nēr′) *vt.*, *vi.* tiranneggiare, far prepotenze. —**ing** *agg.* tirannico, prepotente, tracotante.

Dominican (dṓ·mĭn′ĭ·kăn) *agg.*, *n.* domenicano.

dominion (dṓ·mĭn′yŭn) *n.* dominio, autorità, sovranità; possedimento, colonia autonoma.

don (dŏn) (1) *n.* don; signore; (*Ingl.*) docente *opp.* preside universitario.

don (dŏn) (2) *vt.* indossare; mettersi.

donate (dṓ′nāt) *vt.*, *vi.* donare.

donation (dṓ·nā′shŭn) *n.* donazione, dono.

donator (dṓ′nā·tẽr) *n.* donatore.

done (dŭn) *pp. di* to do: fatto; compiuto; preparato; cucinato, cotto: — **in**, esausto.

donkey (dŏng′kĭ) *n.* asino.

donor (dṓ′nẽr) *n.* donatore.

don't (dōnt) = do not *vedi* to **do.**

doodle (dōō′d'l) *vt.*, *vi.* (S.U.) imbrogliare; disegnare, scarabocchiare. *n.* babbeo; scarabocchio, disegnetto.

doom (dōōm) *n.* giudizio, condanna, sentenza; destino: the voice of —, la tromba del Giudizio Universale. *vt.* condannare, destinare. —**ed** *agg.* condannato; predestinato.

doomsday (dōōmz′dā′) *n.* il giorno del giudizio: till —, fino all'eternità.

door (dōr) *n.* porta, sportello: out of —, fuori, all'aperto. —**mat** *n.* zerbino. —**nail** *n.* borchia. —**way** *n.* soglia, entrata.

dope (dōp) *n.* lubrificante, assorbente; (*aeron.*) vernice impermeabilizzante; (*gergo*) stupefacenti; informazione, ragguaglio; stupido, gonzo: — **fiend**, tossicomane. *vt.* somministrare stupefacenti a, narcotizzare: to — **out**, capire l'antifona, escogitare, dedurre; to — **oneself up**, imbottirsi di medicine.

dormancy (dôr′măn·sĭ) *n.* letargo, torpore.

dormant (dôr′mănt) *agg.* dormiente, assopito, sopito; in letargo; latente, inattivo.

dormer (dôr′mẽr) *n.* abbaino, lucernario.

dormitory (dôr′mĭ·tō′rĭ) *n.* dormitorio.

dormouse (dôr′mous′) *n.* (*pl.* dormice) (*zool.*) ghiro.

dory (dō′rĭ) *n.* barchetta a fondo piatto.

dose (dōs) *n.* dose. *vt.* dosare; somministrare una dose di medicina a.

dossier (dŏs′ĭ·ā) *n.* incartamento; curriculum vitae.

dot (dŏt) *n.* punto, chiazza, pallino: on the —, in punto. *vt.* mettere il punto su, costellare di puntini o pallini.

dotage (dṓt′ĭj) *n.* rimbambimento: in one's —, rimbambito.

dotard (dṓ′tẽrd) *n.* rimbambito.

dote (dōt) *vi.* rimbambire: to — **on, upon**, adorare, essere innamorato o cotto di.

double (dŭb′'l) *agg.* doppio; falso, insincero:— **talk** *n.* frase senza senso, composta di parole astruse. *n.* doppio (*il doppio*), duplicato; ripiegamento, giravolta; sosia; (*teat.*) sostituto; (*cinema*) controfigura; (*ippica*) doppia; *pl.* (*tennis*) doppio. *avv.* doppiamente, al doppio. *vt.* raddoppiare, piegare in due, doppiare. *vi.* raddoppiare (*diventare il doppio*); piegarsi; (*cinema*) fare la controfigura di: to — **up**, piegarsi in due; to — **back**, ritornare sui propri passi.

double-breasted *agg.* a due petti.

double-cross *vt.* tradire. *n.* tradimento; imbroglio.

double-dealer *n.* imbroglione.

doubly (dŭb′lĭ) *avv.* doppiamente.

doubt (dout) *n.* dubbio, sospetto: no —, indubbiamente. *vt.*, *vi.* dubitare (*di*), diffidare (*di*), temere; titubare. —**ful** *agg.* dubbioso, incerto. —**less** *agg.* indubbio. —**lessly** *avv.* indubbiamente.

dough (dō) *n.* pasta; (*gergo*) danaro.

doughnut (dṓ′nŭt′) *n.* frittella.

dour (dōōr) *agg.* aspro, cocciuto.

dove (dŭv) *n.* colomba, piccione.

dovecot (dŭv′kŏt′) *n.* colombaia.

dovetail (dŭv′tāl′) *n.* (*carp.*) coda di rondine (*incastro*). *vt.* unire ad incastro, far combaciare. *vi.* incastrarsi, combaciare; concordare.

dowager (dou′ȧ·jẽr) *n.* vedova usufruttuaria.

down (doun) (1) *n.* piuma, peluria, lanugine.

down (2) *n.* duna, collinetta.

down (3) *avv.* giù, in giù, in basso; in diminuzione, in declino: — **to**, sino a; — **East**, a oriente; — **the street**, in fondo alla strada, giù per la strada; to be — **with flu**, essere a letto con l'influenza; to be — **on one's luck**, attraversare un momento sfortunato; **to get — to work**, mettersi al lavoro; **to pay —**, pagare in contanti. *prep.* giù da, giù per. *agg.* discendente; depresso. *vt.* abbattere, dominare; trangugiare.

downcast (doun'kăst') *agg.* abbattuto: **with — eyes**, a occhi bassi.

downgrade (doun'grād') *n.* declivio, discesa. *vt.*, retrocedere, degradare.

downhearted (-här'tĕd) *agg.* scoraggiato, depresso.

downhill (-hĭl') *agg.* discendente, inclinato. *avv.* in discesa, in pendio.

downpour (-pōr') *n.* scroscio di pioggia.

downright (-rīt') *agg.* netto, assoluto, vero; completo *avv.* completamente, assolutamente.

downstairs (doun'stârz') *avv.* da basso, al piano inferiore, al piano terreno. *n.* pianterreno.

downstream (doun'strēm') *avv.* verso valle, a valle, seguendo la corrente.

downtown (doun'toun') *n.* il centro (*di una città*). *agg.* centrale, del centro. *avv.* in centro, al centro (*di una città*).

downward (doun'wĕrd) *agg.* discendente, inclinato. *avv.* (*anche* **downwards**) in discesa; in declino; in giù, verso valle.

downy (doun'ĭ) *agg.* lanuginoso, soffice.

dowry (dou'rĭ) *n.* dote.

dowser (douz'ĕr) *n.* rabdomante.

doze (dōz) *n.* assopimento. *vi.* assopirsi; sonnecchiare.

dozen (dŭz''n) *n.* dozzina.

drab (drăb) *n.* prostituta. *agg.* di colore morto, sbiadito; monotono.

draft (drăft) *n.* disegno, abbozzo, minuta; sorsata; corrente d'aria; tiraggio; (*naut.*) pescaggio; (*comm.*) tratta, prelevamento; (*med.*) pozione; (*mil.*) leva: **— beer**, birra spillata; **— horse**, cavallo da tiro. *vt.* disegnare, tracciare, redigere (*un progetto, ecc.*); (*mil.*) arruolare; requisire; aspirare (*liquidi*); tirare (*di fornace, ecc.*). **—sman** *n.* disegnatore.

drag (drăg) *n.* (*naut.*) draga (*rete*); (*agr.*) erpice; freno; carrozza a quattro cavalli (*giardiniera*); trazione; arpione; (*gergo*) influenza: **to have —**, essere influente. *vt.* trascinare, tirare; dragare, arare (*dell'ancora*). *vi.* trascinarsi, strisciare.

dragnet (drăg'nĕt') *n.* tramaglio; retata di polizia.

dragon (drăg'ŭn) *n.* drago; (*astr.*) Dragone.

dragonfly (-flī') *n.* libellula.

dragoon (drȧ·gōōn') *n.* dragone (*soldato*). *vt.* ridurre all'obbedienza: **— into**, costringere a.

drain (drān) *n.* canale, scarico, tubazione; perdita; esborso continuo; (*chir.*) drenaggio. *vt.* prosciugare, filtrare, drenare. *vi.* defluire, prosciugarsi. **—age** *n.* scolo, drenaggio.

drake (drāk) *n.* maschio dell'anitra.

drama (drä'mȧ) *n.* dramma; arte drammatica; teatro di prosa. **—tic** *agg.* drammatico. **—tist** *n.* drammaturgo.

dramatize (drăm'ȧ·tīz) *vt.* drammatizzare.

drank (drăngk) *pass.* di **to drink**.

drape (drāp) *n.* drappeggio, tendaggio. *vt.* drappeggiare.

draper (drāp'ĕr) *n.* negoziante in tessuti.

drastic (drăs'tĭk) *agg.* drastico, violento.

draught (drȧft) *vedi* **draft**.

draughts (drȧfts) *n.pl.* dama (*gioco*).

draw (drò) *n.* trazione; attrazione; estrazione (*sorteggio*). *vt.* (*pass.* **drew**, *pp.* **drawn**) tirare, trascinare; disegnare, tracciare; percepire; estrarre; tendere; attingere; **attrarre: to — a sigh**, trarre un sospiro; **to — away**, trascinar via; **to — in**, trascinar dentro, raggirare; **to — lots**, tirare a sorte; **to — out**, indurre a parlare; **to — up**, issare, schierare, redigere. *vi.* esercitare attrazione, attrarre; contrarsi; muoversi; soffiare, tirare (*di canna fumaria, ecc.*): **to — back**, ritrarsi, retrocedere; **to — near**, avvicinarsi; **to — off**, allontanarsi; **to — oneself up**, raddrizzarsi; **to — up**, fermarsi.

drawback (drò'băk') *n.* inconveniente.

drawbridge (drò'brĭj') *n.* ponte levatoio.

drawer (drò'ĕr) *n.* traente; cassetto (*di mobile*); (*pl.*) mutande.

drawing (drò'ĭng) *n.* tiraggio; sorteggio; disegno: **— room**, salotto; (*ferr. S.U.*) scompartimento riservato.

drawl (dròl) *vt., vi.* parlare o dire lentamente, strascicare le parole.

drawn (dròn) *pp.* di **to draw**.

dread (drĕd) *n.* timore, terrore. *agg.* temuto, temibile. *vt.* temere. **—ful** *agg.* atroce, spaventevole.

dream (drēm) *n.* sogno. *vi.* (*pass., pp.* **dreamed**, **dreamt**) sognare; (*fig.*) fantasticare: **to — up**, inventare; escogitare; creare. **—er** *n.* sognatore, visionario.

dreamy (drēm'ĭ) *agg.* sognante, trasognato; chimerico.

dreary (drēr'ĭ) *agg.* squallido, desolato.

dredge (drĕj) *n.* draga. *vt.* dragare.

dregs (drĕgz) *n.pl.* feccia, sedimento, fondo.

drench (drĕnch) *vt.* inzuppare.

dress (drĕs) *n.* vestito, abito: full —, tenuta da cerimonia, alta tenuta; — coat, marsina; (*mil.*) tenuta di gala. — rehearsal, prova generale. *vt.* vestire; medicare (*una ferita*); pettinare; condire; (*mil.*) schierare. *vi.* vestirsi; (*mil.*) allinearsi: to — down, dare una lezione a; to — up, agghindarsi.

dresser (drĕs'ĕr) *n.* (*teat.*) guardarobiere, guardarobiera (*degli attori*): a good —, una persona elegante.

dressing *n.* toletta, abbigliamento, medicazione; (*cucina*) salsa, condimento: — gown, veste da camera; — room, spogliatoio; (*teat.*) camerino; — table, tavolino da toletta.

dressmaker (drĕs'māk'ĕr) *n.* sarta.

drew (drōō) *pass. di* to draw.

dribble (drĭb'l) *n.* goccia, spruzzo. *vt.*, *vi.* sgocciolare, sbavare.

dried (drīd) *pass.*, *pp. di* dry. *agg.* secco, appassito: — fig, fico secco.

drift (drĭft) *n.* corrente, deriva; direzione, corso; significato; rottami (*alla deriva*); monticello (*di neve o sabbia*): — ice, ghiaccio alla deriva. *vi.* andare alla deriva; esser trascinato (*dal vento*); accumularsi. —wood *n.* rottami di legno alla deriva; legna raccogliticcia.

drill (drĭl) *n.* trapano, perforatrice, solco; (*mil.*) esercitazione; seminatrice. *vt.* perforare, trapanare; seminare; istruire, allenare, addestrare.

drily (drī'lĭ) *avv.* seccamente.

drink (drĭngk) *n.* bevanda: to take to —, darsi all'alcool. *vt.*, *vi.* (*pass.* drank, *pp.* drunk) bere: to — in, assorbire, ascoltare attentamente; to — a toast, brindare (*a*); to — down, tranguciare. —able *agg.* bevibile, potabile. —ing water *n.* acqua potabile.

drip (drĭp) *n.* sgocciolìo, stillicidio. *vi.* sgocciolare, grondare.

drive (drīv) *n.* corsa (*in veicolo*); viale, corso; spinta, impulso; tendenza; guida; energia; (*mecc.*) propulsione, trasmissione, trazione. *vt.* (*pass.* drove, *pp.* driven) spingere, azionare; piantare (*chiodi, ecc.*), introdurre; guidare; trasportare (*in auto, ecc.*); costringere: to — away, scacciare; to — back, respingere; to — mad, far impaz-

zire; to — a good bargain, concludere un buon affare. *vi.* andare, dirigersi, correre, guidare, andare in carrozza *o* in auto: what are you driving at? dove (a quale conclusione) volete arrivare?

drive-in *n.* cinema *o* ristorante *o* negozio per automobilisti.

drivel (drĭv'l) *n.* bava, saliva; vaniloquio; insulsaggine. *vi.* sbavare; vaneggiare.

driven (drĭv'ĕn) *pp. di* to drive.

driver (drĭv'ĕr) *n.* guidatore.

driveway (drĭv'wā') *n.* vialetto d'entrata.

driving *n.* guida (*il guidare*). *agg.* propulsore, di propulsione; impetuoso, dinamico: — power, forza motrice; — wheel, ruota motrice.

drizzle (drĭz'l) *n.* pioggerella. *vi.* piovigginare, sgocciolare.

droll (drōl) *agg.* comico, bizzarro.

drone (drōn) *n.* fuco (*maschio dell'ape*); ronzìo; meccanismo telecomandato; (*fig.*) sfruttatore, fannullone. *vi.* ronzare, borbottare.

droop (drōōp) *n.* portamento curvo; abbassamento. *vi.* curvarsi; penzolare, ricadere; afflosciarsi, indebolirsi, languire, deperire.

drop (drŏp) *n.* goccia; caduta, discesa; strapiombo, dislivello; ribasso; abbassamento (*della temperatura*); caramella; pastiglia: letter —, buca delle lettere. *vt.* far cadere; lasciar cadere, abbattere, scaricare; abbandonare (*un'impresa*): to — anchor, gettar l'ancora; to — a curtsey, fare una riverenza; to — a line, scrivere due righe. *vi.* cadere, precipitare, abbattersi; decadere, diminuire; aver termine, gocciolare: to — away, scomparire; to — asleep, addormentarsi; to — behind, restare indietro; to — in, entrare casualmente, dare una capatina; to — off, distaccarsi, allontanarsi, crollare (*di prezzi, ecc.*); to — out, ritirarsi; sparire.

dropsy (drŏp'sĭ) *n.* idropisia.

dross (drŏs) *n.* scoria, rifiuto.

drought (drout) *n.* siccità; arsura, sete.

drove (drōv) (1) *pass. di* to drive.

drove (2) *n.* mandria, gregge, branco.

drover (drō'vĕr) *n.* mandriano.

drown (droun) *vt.*, *vi.* affogare, sommergere; soffocare; annegare.

drowse (drouz) *n.* sopore. *vi.* sonnecchiare, assopirsi.

drowsiness (drou'zĭ-nĕs) *n.* sonnolenza.

drowsy (drou'zĭ) *agg.* sonnolento, sonnacchioso, assonnato.

drubbing (drŭb'ĭng) *n.* bastonatura.

drudge (drŭj) *n.* lavoratore, schiavo. *vi.* sfacchinare.

drug (drŭg) *n.* droga, rimedio, stupefacente, prodotto chimico, narcotico: to be a — on the market, essere invendibile. *vt.* narcotizzare; adulterare; drogare. **—gist** *n.* farmacista. **—store** *n.* farmacia.

drum (drŭm) *n.* tamburo; rullo; cassa; timpano (*dell'orecchio*). *vi.*, *vt.* tamburellare, tambureggiare, ronzare; chiamare a raccolta (*a suon di tamburo*); (*fig.*) inculcare; to — out (*mil.*), espellere, degradare. **—mer** *n.* tamburino, batterista; (*S.U.*) piazzista, propagandista. **—stick** *n.* bacchetta del tamburo.

drunk (drŭngk) *agg.* ubriaco: to get —, ubriacarsi. **—ard** *n.* ubriacone. **—en** *agg.* ubriaco, alcoolizzato.

drunkenness (-nĕs) *n.* ubriachezza.

dry (drī) *agg.* asciutto, arido, secco (*di vino, ecc.*): — dock, bacino di carenaggio; — goods, tessili, tessuti. *vt.* (*pass.*, *pp.* dried) seccare, disseccare, asciugare. *vi.* asciugarsi, seccarsi, inaridirsi: to — up, ammutolire.

dry-clean *vt.* lavare a secco. **—er** *n.* tintore, smacchiatore. **—ing** *n.* lavatura a secco.

dryness (drī'nĕs) *n.* siccità, aridità.

dub (dŭb) *vt.* nominare, qualificare; lisciare; (*cinema*) doppiare. **—bing**, *n.* doppiaggio.

dubious (dū'bĭ.ŭs) *agg.* dubbioso, dubbio, incerto.

duchess (dŭch'ĕs) *n.* duchessa.

duchy (dŭch'ĭ) *n.* ducato.

duck (dŭk) *n.* anitra; tuffo, immersione; tela grossolana; (*pl.*) calzoni di tela; camion anfibio. *vt.* immergere, tuffare; abbassare. *vi.* tuffarsi; abbassarsi; scantonare, schivare il colpo. **—ling** *n.* anatroccolo.

duct (dŭkt) *n.* condotto, canale; (*anat.*) vaso.

dude (dūd) *n.* damerino; cittadino: — ranch, ranch di villeggiatura.

due (dū) *n.* spettanza, debito; tributo, imposta; (*pl.*) quota: to give someone his —, render giustizia a qualcuno. *agg.* dovuto, debito, giusto; scaduto; previsto, voluto: in — time, a tempo debito; to fall —, scadere; to be —, essere in arrivo; essere previsto; scadere.

duel (dū'ĕl) *n.* duello, lotta, contesa.

duet (dū.ĕt') *n.* duetto.

dug (dŭg) *pass.*, *pp.* di *to dig*.

dug *n.* capezzolo, mammella (*di animale*).

duke (dūk) *n.* duca. **—dom** (-dŭm) *n.* ducato.

dull (dŭl) *agg.* sciocco, tardo, ottuso; cupo, fosco; sordo, smorzato (*dei suoni*); triste, noioso: — season, stagione morta; — pain, dolore sordo. *vt.* smussare; rendere opaco, intorpidire, offuscare. *vi.* intorpidirsi; smussarsi. **—ard** *n.* imbecille. **-ness** *n.* ottusità, stupidità, lentezza; stasi, monotonia; opacità.

duly (dū'lĭ) *avv.* debitamente, puntualmente, regolarmente.

dumb (dŭm) *agg.* muto, taciturno; sciocco: — creature, animale; — show, pantomima. **—ness** *n.* mutismo, ottusità.

dumbfound, dumfound (dŭm'found') *vt.* sbalordire, far ammutolire.

dummy (dŭm'ĭ) *n.* muto, fantoccio; uomo di paglia; morto (*al gioco del bridge, ecc.*).

dump (dŭmp) *n.* magazzino; deposito di rifiuti. *vt.* scaricare, vuotare; ammassare; liquidare. **—ing** *n.* vendita a prezzi rovinosi.

dumps *n.pl.* umor nero: in the —, di umor nero.

dun (dŭn) *agg.* marrone grigiastro; cupo. *vt.*, *vi.* importunare o perseguitare (*un debitore*).

dunce (dŭns) *n.* ignorante, sciocco.

dune (dūn) *n.* duna.

dung (dŭng) *n.* letame. *vt.* concimare. **—hill** *n.* concimaia.

dungeon (dŭn'jŭn) *n.* carcere sotterraneo, segreta.

dupe (dūp) *n.* gonzo. *vt.* gabbare.

duplicate (dū'plĭ.kāt) *agg.*, *n.* duplicato: in —, in doppia copia. *vt.* duplicare, copiare.

duplicity (dū.plĭs'ĭ.tĭ) *n.* duplicità, malafede.

durable (dū'rá.b'l) *agg.* durevole.

durance (dū'răns) *n.* prigionia.

duration (dū.rā'shŭn) *n.* continuazione, durata; tempo; esistenza.

duress (dū.rĕs') *n.* coercizione, oppressione, prigionia.

during (dū'rĭng) *prep.* durante.

dusk (dŭsk) *n.* imbrunire, crepuscolo; semi-oscurità.

dusky (dŭs'kĭ) *agg.* scuro, fosco, bruno.

dust (dŭst) *n.* polvere. *vt.* spolverare (*togliere la polvere opp. cospargere di polvere*).

dustbin (dŭst'bĭn') *n.* pattumiera.

duster (dŭs'tĕr) *n.* strofinaccio, spolverina: feather —, piumino.

dustman (dŭst'măn) *n.* spazzino.

dusty (dŭs'tĭ) *agg.* polveroso.

Dutch (dŭch) *agg.*, *n.* olandese: to go — treat, fare alla romana. **—man** *n.* olandese.

dutiful (dū'tĬ·fŏŏl) *agg.* obbediente; rispettoso.

duty (dū'tĬ) *n.* dovere; tassa, imposta; obbligo; mansione: **to do — for, fungere da; — free,** esente da tasse.

dwarf (dwôrf) *n.*, *agg.* nano. *vt.* rimpicciolire; far sfigurare; impedire lo sviluppo di.

dwell (dwĕl) *vi.* (*pass.*, *pp.* **dwelt**) abitare; soffermarsi, dilungarsi. **—er** *n.* abitante. **—ing** *n.* abitazione. **—ing-place** *n.* residenza abituale.

dwelt (dwĕlt) *pass.*, *pp. di* to dwell.

dwindle (dwĬn'd'l) *vi.* diminuire, ridursi.

dye (dī) *n.* tintura, colorante. *vt.* tingere. *vi.* tingersi.

dyer (dī'ĕr) *n.* tintore: **—'s shop,** tintoria.

dying (dī'ĭng) *agg.* morente, supremo.

dyke (dīk) *vedi* dike.

dynamic (dĬ·năm'Ĭk) *agg.* dinamico.

dynamics (dĬ·năm'Ĭks) *n.pl.* dinamica.

dynamite (dī'nά·mīt) *n.* dinamite. *vt.* minare, far saltare.

dynamiter (dī'nά·mīt'ĕr) *n.* dinamitardo.

dynamo (dī'nά·mō) *n.* dinamo.

dynasty (dī'nάs·tĬ) *n.* dinastia.

dysentery (dĬs'ĕn·tĕr'Ĭ) *n.* dissenteria.

dyspepsia (dĬs·pĕp'shά) *n.* dispepsia.

dyspeptic (-tĬk) *agg.*, *n.* dispeptico.

E

each (ēch) *agg.*, *pron.* ciascuno, ogni, ognuno: **— other,** l'un l'altro, a vicenda.

eager (ē'gĕr) *agg.* bramoso, avido; impaziente; premuroso. **—ly** *avv.* avidamente, premurosamente. **—ness** *n.* brama, impazienza, premura, avidità.

eagle (ē'g'l) *n.* aquila.

ear (ēr) *n.* orecchio; (*bot.*) spiga: **to prick up one's —s,** drizzare le orecchie; **to turn a deaf —,** fare orecchio da mercante; **— of corn,** pannocchia; **— of wheat,** spiga; **by —,** a orecchio. **—drop** *n.* orecchino. **—drum** *n.* timpano. **—mark** *n.* marchio di riconoscimento. **—ring** *n.* orecchino (*ad anello*). **—shot** *n.* portata dell'udito. **— trumpet** *n.* cornetto acustico.

earl (ûrl) *n.* conte.

early (ûr'lĬ) *agg.* mattutino; mattiniero; primo; precedente; prematuro, precoce: **— riser,** persona mattiniera. *avv.* presto, di buonora, in anticipo.

earn (ûrn) *vt.* guadagnare, acquistare, meritare.

earnest (ûr'nĕst) *n.* caparra, anticipo. *agg.* **serio, sincero,** zelante: **in —, sul serio; — money,** caparra. **—ly** *avv.* seriamente, premurosamente. **—ness** *n.* serietà, zelo.

earnings (ûr'nĬngs) *n.pl.* guadagni, introiti.

earth (ûrth) *n.* terra.

earthquake (ûrth'kwāk') *n.* terremoto.

earthen (ûrĕth'n) *agg.* di terra.

earthenware (-wâr) *n.* vasellame di terracotta.

earthworm (-wûrm) *n.* bruco.

earthly (-lĬ) *agg.* terrestre, terreno; basso, meschino.

ease (ēz) *n.* comodità, agio, facilità; quiete; disinvoltura; sollievo: **at —,** a proprio agio; **ill at —,** a disagio. *vt.* sollevare, attenuare, calmare; allargare; (*naut.*) allentare, mollare.

easel (ē'z'l) *n.* cavalletto (*da pittore*).

easily (ēz'Ĭ·lĬ) *avv.* facilmente; agevolmente; con disinvoltura.

easiness (-nĕs) *n.* facilità, disinvoltura.

east (ēst) *n.* est, oriente. *agg.* dell'est, orientale: **the East,** l'Oriente; **the Far East,** l'estremo Oriente.

Easter (ēs'tĕr) *n.* Pasqua: **— Sunday,** domenica di Pasqua.

eastern (ēs'tĕrn) *agg.* orientale.

eastward (ēst'wĕrd) *avv.* in direzione est.

easy (ēz'Ĭ) *agg.* facile, comodo; bonario; accomodante; disinvolto; sciolto, scorrevole: **— circumstances,** agiatezza; **— chair,** poltrona; **at an — pace,** pian pianino, lemme lemme; **by — stages,** a piccole tappe; **to take it —,** prendersela con calma. *avv.* comodamente, con calma.

easygoing *agg.* indolente; accomodante, poco esigente; pacifico, pacioso.

eat (ēt) *vt.* (*pass.* **ate,** *pp.* **eaten** [ēt''n]) mangiare; corrodere: **to — breakfast,** fare colazione; **to — dinner,** pranzare; **to — supper,** cenare; **to — one's heart out;** rodersi il cuore, soffrire in silenzio; **to — one's word,** rimangiarsi la parola. *vi.* cibarsi. **—able** *agg.* commestibile. **—er** *n.* mangiatore.

eaves (ēvz) *n.pl.* grondaia.

eavesdrop (ēvz'drŏp') *vi.* origliare.

ebb (ĕb) *n.* marea, risucchio; decadenza. *vi.* defluire, abbassarsi, declinare. **—tide** *n.* bassa marea.

ebony (ĕb'ŭn·ĭ) *n*. ebano.
eccentric (ĕk·sĕn'trĭk) *agg.*, *n*. eccentrico.
ecclesiastic (ĕ·klē'zĭ·ăs'tĭk) *agg.*, *n*. ecclesiastico.
echelon (ĕsh'ĕ·lŏn) *n*. (*mil.*) scaglione; (*aeron.*) formazione; **in the higher —s**, nelle alte sfere.
echo (ĕk'ō) *n*. eco. *vt*. ripetere (*come l'eco*). *vi*. echeggiare, risuonare.
eclectic (ĕk·lĕk'tĭk), *agg*. eclettico.
eclipse (ĕ·klĭps') *n*. eclisse. *vt*. eclissare, superare.
economic (ē'kō·nŏm'ĭk) *agg*. economico.
economics (ē'kō·nŏm'ĭks) *n.pl*. economia, scienze economiche.
economist (ē·kŏn'ō·mĭst) *n*. economista.
economize (ē·kŏn'ō·mīz) *vt*., *vi*. economizzare.
economy (ē·kŏn'ō·mĭ) *n*. economia, parsimonia.
ecstasy (ĕk'stá·sĭ) *n*. estasi.
ecstatic (ĕk·stăt'ĭk) *agg*. estatico, estasiante.
eddy (ĕd'ĭ) *n*. vortice, turbine. *vi*. turbinare.
Eden (ē'd'n) *n*. Paradiso Terrestre.
edge (ĕj) *n*. orlo, margine, filo (*di una lama*), limite estremo, taglio (*di un libro*); tensione: **to take off the —**, smussare, attenuare; **to be on —**, essere nervoso; **to have an —**, avere un piccolo vantaggio *o* superiorità. *vt*. affilare; orlare; rasentare; esasperare; spronare. *vi*. avanzare gradatamente, spostarsi lateralmente. **—ways, —wise** *avv*. di taglio; longitudinalmente; **a mala pena**.
edible (ĕd'ĭ·b'l) *agg*. commestibile.
edifice (ĕd'ĭ·fĭs) *n*. edificio.
edify (ĕd'ĭ·fĭ) *vt*. edificare.
edit (ĕd'ĭt) *vt*. pubblicare, redigere, curare (*un'edizione, ecc.*); (*cinema*) curare il montaggio. **—ing** *n*. (*cinema*) montaggio. **—ion** (ē·dĭsh'ŭn) *n*. edizione. **—or** *n*. redattore; direttore (*di giornale*); curatore (*di un' opera*)· **—orial** *agg*. editoriale; redazionale; *n*. articolo di fondo.
educate (ĕd'ū·kāt) *vt*. educare, istruire.
education (ĕd'ū·kā'shŭn) *n*. educazione; istruzione; pedagogia.
educational (-ăl) *agg*. educativo; pedagogico; della scuola.
educator (ĕd'ū·kā'tĕr) *n*. educatore.
eel (ēl) *n*. anguilla.
eerie *opp*. **eery** (ēr'ĭ) *agg*. irreale, strano, sovrannaturale.
efface (ĕ·fās') *vt*. cancellare: **to — oneself**, stare nell'ombra.

effect (ĕ·fĕkt') *n*. effetto; (*pl.*) effetti, masserizie. **to carry into —**, eseguire, mettere in pratica; **to take —**, entrare in vigore. *vt*. effettuare, compiere. **—ive** *agg*. efficace, effettivo. **—ual** *agg*. efficace, valido.
effeminate (ĕ·fĕm'ĭ·nĭt) *agg*. effeminato.
efficacious (ĕf'ĭ·kā'shŭs) *agg*. efficace.
efficacy (ĕf'ĭ·ká·sĭ) *n*. efficacia.
efficiency (ĕ·fĭsh'ĕn·sĭ) *n*. efficienza, rendimento.
efficient (ĕ·fĭsh'ĕnt) *agg*. efficiente, efficace.
effluvium (ĕ·flōō'vĭ·ŭm) *n*. esalazione.
effort (ĕf'ĕrt) *n*. sforzo. **—less** *agg*. agevole, senza sforzo, passivo.
effrontery (ĕ·frŭn'tĕr·ĭ) *n*. sfacciataggine.
effulgence (ĕ·fŭl'jĕns) *n*. splendore.
effulgent (ĕ·fŭl'jĕnt) *agg*. splendente.
effusion (ĕ·fū'zhŭn) *n*. effusione; emanazione, perdita.
effusive (-sĭv) *agg*. espansivo.
egg (ĕg) (1) *n*. uovo: **bad —** (*gergo*), cattivo soggetto; **boiled —**, uovo a la coque; **hard-boiled —**, uovo sodo.
egg (ĕg) (2) *vt*. spronare, esortare, incitare, indurre.
egghead *n*. (*gergo S.U.*) intellettuale, intellectualoide.
eggplant *n*. melanzana.
ego (ē'gō) *n*. l'io, spirito, personalità. **—ism** *n*. egoismo. **—ist** *n*. egoista. **—tism** *n*. egotismo. **—tist** *n*. egotista.
egress (ē'grĕs) *n*. uscita.
Egyptian (ē·jĭp'shŭn) *agg.*, *n*. egiziano.
eider (ī'dĕr) *n*. (*ornit.*) edrèdone: **—down**, piume di edrèdone; copriletto di piume.
eight (āt) *agg.*, *n*. otto. **eighteen** *agg.*, *n*. diciotto. **—eenth** *agg*. diciottesimo.
eighth (ātth) *agg*. ottavo. *n*. l'ottava parte.
eighty (ā'tĭ) *agg*. ottanta.
either (ē'thĕr) *pron*. l'uno o l'altro; uno dei due; ognuno dei due; **entrambe: I do not see — of them**, non vedo nè l'uno nè l'altro; **on — side**, d'ambe le parti; **in — case**, in entrambi i casi. *cong.*: **— you know him or you do not**, o lo conoscete o non lo conoscete. *avv.* nemmeno: **I do not see him —**, non lo vedo nemmeno io.
eject (ē·jĕkt') *vt*. espellere, emettere.
elaborate (ē·lăb'ō·rĭt) *agg*. accurato, elaborato. *vt*. (-āt) elaborare.
elapse (ē·lăps') *vi*. passare, trascorrere, intercorrere (*del tempo*).

elastic (ĕ·lăs'tĭk) *agg.* elastico.

elated (ĕ·lāt'ĕd) *agg.* fiero; esaltato; euforico.

elation (ĕ·lā'shŭn) *n.* esaltazione; euforia.

elbow (ĕl'bō) *n.* gomito: at one's —, molto vicino; out at —s, in cattivo arnese. *vt.*, *vi.* prendere a gomitate; farsi largo a gomitate: to — one's way, aprirsi il varco a gomitate.

elder (ĕl'dēr) *agg.* maggiore, più vecchio. —**ly** *agg.* anziano, vecchiotto.

eldest (ĕl'dĕst) *agg.* (il) più vecchio, (il) maggiore.

elect (ĕ·lĕkt') *n.*, *agg.* scelto, designato, eletto. *vt.* eleggere, designare, decidere. —**ion** *n.* elezione, scelta.

elector (ĕ·lĕk'tēr) *n.* elettore.

electoral (-ăl) *agg.* elettorale.

electric (ĕ·lĕk'trĭk) *agg.* elettrico: — **meter**, contatore elettrico.

electrician (ĕ·lĕk'trĭsh'ăn) *n.* elettrotecnico.

electricity (ĕ·lĕk'trĭs'ĭ·tĭ) *n.* elettricità.

electrify (ĕ·lĕk'trĭ·fī) *vt.* elettrificare; elettrizzare.

electrocute (ĕ·lĕk'trō·kūt) *vt.* giustiziare con elettrocuzione.

electrode (ĕ·lĕk'trōd) *n.* elèttrodo.

electrolier (ĕ·lek'trō·lēr') *n.* lampadario.

electron (ĕ·lĕk'trŏn) *n.* elettròne. *agg.* elettronico: — **microscope**, microscopio elettronico.

electronics (ĕ·lĕk'trŏn'ĭks) *n.* elettronica.

electrotype (ĕ·lĕk'trō·tīp) *n.* (*tip.*) stereotipia.

elegance (ĕl'ē·găns) *n.* eleganza.

elegant (-gănt) *agg.* elegante.

element (ĕl'ē·mĕnt) *n.* elemento; fattore; (*aeron.*) squadriglia. —**al** *agg.* elementare. —**ary** *agg.* elementare, fondamentale.

elephant (ĕl'ē·fănt) *n.* elefante.

elevate (ĕl'ē·vāt) *vt.* elevare, innalzare, esaltare.

elevated *n.* (S.U.) ferrovia soprelevata. *agg.* elevato.

elevation (-vā'shŭn) *n.* elevazione.

elevator (ĕl'ē·vā'tēr) *n.* elevatore; ascensore; (*aeron.*) timone di profondità.

eleven (ē·lĕv'ĕn) *agg.*, *n.* undici. —**th** *agg.* undicesimo.

elicit (ĕ·lĭs'ĭt) *vt.* estrarre; suscitare; strappare; dedurre; appurare.

eligible (ĕl'ĭ·jĭ·b'l) *agg.* eleggibile; accettabile; conveniente.

eliminate (ĕ·lĭm'ĭ·nāt) *vt.* eliminare.

elimination (-nā'shŭn) *n.* eliminazione.

elk (ĕlk) *n.* (*zool.*) alce.

ellipse (ĕ·lĭps') *n.* (*geom.*) ellisse.

ellipsis (ĕ·lĭp'sĭs) *n.* (*pl.* **ellipses**) (*gramm.*) ellissi.

elm (ĕlm) *n.* (*bot.*) olmo.

elope (ĕ·lōp') *vi.* fuggire (*spec. con l'amante*). —**ment** *n.* fuga romantica.

eloquence (ĕl'ō·kwĕns) *n.* eloquenza.

eloquent (ĕl'ō·kwĕnt) *agg.* eloquente.

else (ĕls) *avv.* altrimenti, oppure. *agg.* altro (*si aggiunge a pron.interr., opp. ai composti di* some, any, no, every): **anybody** —, chiunque altro; **nobody** —, nessun altro; **somebody** —, qualcun altro; **everything** —, qualunque altra cosa; **nothing** —, nient'altro; **anywhere** —, da qualunque altra parte; **nowhere** —, da nessun'altra parte; **what** —?, che altro?; **or** —, altrimenti.

elsewhere (ĕls'hwâr) *avv.* altrove.

elucidate (ĕ·lū'sĭ·dāt) *vt.* spiegare, chiarire.

elucidation (-dā'shŭn) *n.* chiarificazione, delucidazione.

elude (ĕ·lūd') *vt.* eludere, schivare.

emaciated (ē·mā'shĭ·āt'ĕd) *agg.* emaciato, deperito.

emanate (ĕm'á·nāt) *vi.* emanare.

emanation (-nā'shŭn) *n.* emanazione.

emancipate (ē·măn'sĭ·pāt) *vt.* emancipare.

emancipation (-pā'shŭn) *n.* emancipazione.

emasculation (ē·măs'kū·lā'shŭn) *n.* castrazione.

embalm (ĕm·bäm') *vt.* imbalsamare. —**er** *n.* imbalsamatore.

embankment (ĕm·băngk'mĕnt) *n.* diga, argine, terrapieno.

embargo (ĕm·bär'gō) *n.* embargo. *vt.* mettere l'embargo su.

embark (ĕm·bärk') *vt.*, *vi.* imbarcare; imbarcarsi.

embarrass (ĕm·băr'ăs) *vt.* imbarazzare: **financially** —**ed**, a corto di fondi.

embarrassing *agg.* imbarazzante.

embarrassment *n.* imbarazzo, disagio.

embassy (ĕm'bà·sĭ) *n.* ambasciata.

embellish (ĕm·bĕl'ĭsh) *vt.* abbellire, adornare.

ember (ĕm'bēr) *n.* bragia, tizzone.

embezzle (ĕm·bĕz''l) *vt.* appropriarsi fraudolentemente. —**ment** *n.* appropriazione indebita, malversazione.

embezzler (ĕm·bĕz'lēr) *n.* malversatore.

embitter (ĕm·bĭt'ēr) *vt.* amareggiare.

emblem (ĕm'blĕm) *n.* emblema.

embody (ĕm·bŏd'ĭ) *vt.* incorporare; incarnare, personificare; includere. *vi.* incorporarsi.

embolden (ĕm·bōl'dĕn) *vt.* imbaldanzire.

emboss (ĕm·bŏs') *vt.* dare rilievo, scolpire in rilievo.

embrace (ĕm·brās') *n.* abbraccio. *vt.,* *vi.* abbracciare; abbracciarsi.

embrasure (ĕm·brā'zhẽr) *n.* vano (*di porta, finestra, ecc.*); (*fort.*) feritoia.

embroider (ĕm·broi'dẽr) *vt.* ricamare. —er *n.* ricamatore, ricamatrice. —y *n.* ricamo.

embryo (ĕm'brĭ·ō) *n.* embrione.

emcee (ĕm'sē') *n.* (*radio, T.V. = m.c.*, sigla di *Master of Ceremonies*) presentatore (*di un programma*).

emerald (ĕm'ẽr·ᾰld) *n.* smeraldo.

emerge (ē·mûrj') *vi.* emergere.

emergence (ē·mûr'jĕns) *n.* emersione, apparizione imprevista.

emergency (ē·mûr'jĕn·sĭ) *n.* emergenza, crisi: — exit, uscita di sicurezza.

emery (ĕm'ẽr·ĭ) *n.* smeriglio.

emigrate (ĕm'ĭ·grāt) *vi.* emigrare.

eminence (ĕm'ĭ·nĕns) *n.* eminenza, altura.

eminent (-nĕnt) *agg.* eminente, illustre.

emission (ē·mĭsh'ᾰn) *n.* emissione.

emit (ē·mĭt') *vt.* emettere, esalare.

emotion (ē·mō'shᾰn) *n.* emozione; sentimento, moto dell'animo. —al *agg.* emotivo, ipersensibile; riguardante i sentimenti.

emperor (ĕm'pẽr·ẽr) *n.* imperatore.

emphasis (ĕm'fᾰ·sĭs) *n.* enfasi; rilievo.

emphasize (-sĭz) *vt.* ribadire, accentuare, mettere in rilievo.

emphatic (ĕm·făt'ĭk) *agg.* espressivo, deciso, efficace.

emphatically (-ĭ·kᾰl·ĭ) *agg.* energicamente, decisamente.

empire (ĕm'pῑr) *n.* impero.

emplacement (ĕm·plās'mĕnt) *n.* collocazione; (*mil.*) piazzuola.

employ (ĕm·ploi') *n.* impiego: to be in somebody's —, essere impiegato presso *o* alle dipendenze di qualcuno. *vt.* impiegare, usare, utilizzare.

employee (ĕm·ploi'ē) *n.* impiegato.

employer (ĕm·ploi'ẽr) *n.* principale, datore di lavoro.

employment (-mĕnt) *n.* impiego, occupazione: out of —, disoccupato.

emporium (ĕm·pōr'ĭ·ᾰm) *n.* emporio.

empower (ĕm·pou'ẽr) *vt.* autorizzare.

empress (ĕm'prĕs) *n.* imperatrice.

emptiness (ĕmp'tĭ·nĕs) *n.* il vuoto, vacuità.

empty (ĕmp'tĭ) *agg.* vuoto, vacuo, deserto, vano. *vt.* vuotare, scaricare. *vi.* vuotarsi, riversarsi.

emulate (ĕm'ū·lāt) *vt.* emulare; uguagliare.

emulation (ĕm'ū·lā'shᾰn) *n.* emulazione.

enable (ĕn·ā'b'l) *vt.* consentire, mettere in grado (*di*).

enact (ĕn·ăkt') *vt.* decretare, ordinare; recitare (*una parte*).

enamel (ĕn·ăm'ĕl) *n.* smalto. *vt.* smaltare.

enamor (ĕn·ăm'ẽr) *vt.* innamorare.

encamp (ĕn·kămp') *vt.* accampare *vi.* accamparsi. —ment *n.* accampamento.

enchain (ĕn·chān') *vt.* incatenare.

enchant (ĕn·chånt') *vt.* incantare, affascinare. —er *n.* incantatore. —ing *agg.* incantevole. —ment *n.* incantesimo. —ress *n.* incantatrice.

encircle (ĕn·sûr'k'l) *vt.* cingere, aggirare.

enclose (ĕn·klōz') *vt.* rinchiudere, recingere; accludere.

enclosure (-klō'zhẽr) *n.* recinto, spazio cintato; allegato.

encompass (ĕn·kŭm'pᾰs) *vt.* circondare, contenere; (*fam.*) superare in astuzia.

encore (äng·kōr') *int.* bis. *vt.* chiedere il bis (*di*).

encounter (ĕn·koun'tẽr) *n.* incontro; scontro (*combattimento*). *vt.* incontrare, affrontare.

encourage (ĕn·kûr'ĭj) *vt.* incoraggiare. —ment *n.* incoraggiamento.

encouraging *agg.* incoraggiante.

encroach (ĕn·krōch') *vi.* (*seg. da.* on, upon) insinuarsi; sconfinare, invadere; usurpare; rubare tempo (*a*).

encumber (ĕn·kŭm'bẽr) *vt.* ingombrare, gravare, imbarazzare.

encumbrance (-brᾰns) *n.* ingombro, impaccio, gravame; ipoteca.

encyclopaedia (ĕn·sī'klō·pē'dĭ·ᾰ) *n.* enciclopedia.

end (ĕnd) *n.* fine, termine; estremità; scopo, mira; decesso: to be at one's wit's —, non saper dove battere la testa; by the — of, prima della fine di; at the — of one's tether, al limite delle proprie risorse; to make both —s meet, sbarcare il lunario; to stand on —, drizzarsi; to put an — to, mettere fine a; no — of things, un'infinità di cose; odds and —s, cianfrusaglie. *vi., vt.* finire: to — by, finire con *o* per.

endanger (ĕn·dān'jẽr) *vt.* mettere in pericolo, compromettere.

endear (ĕn·dēr') *vt.* rendere caro: to — oneself to, accattivarsi l'affetto di. —ment *n.* blandizie, tenerezza.

endeavor (ĕn·dĕv'ẽr) *n.* sforzo, tentativo, impresa. *vi.* sforzarsi, cercare.

ending (ĕn'dĭng) *n.* conclusione, fine; (*gramm.*) desinenza.

endless (ĕnd'lĕs) *agg.* interminabile.
endorse (ĕn·dôrs') *vt.* attergare; girare; avallare; sottoscrivere, approvare.
endorsee (ĕn'dôr·sē') *n.* giratario.
endorsement (ĕn·dôrs'mĕnt) *n.* girata; avallo; approvazione.
endorser (ĕn·dôr'sẽr) *n.* girante; avallante.
endow (ĕn·dou') *vt.* dotare, munire, corredare (*di*). —**ment** *n.* dotazione; dote, pregio.
endurance (ĕn·dūr'ăns) *n.* sopportazione, resistenza: beyond —, intollerabile.
endure (ĕn·dūr') *vt.*, *vi.* sopportare, tollerare. *vi.* durare, continuare.
endways (ĕnd'wăz'), **endwise** (-wīz') *avv.* in posizione eretta, con l'estremità in su o in fuori; testa a testa.
enema (ĕn'ê·má) *n.* clistere.
enemy (ĕn'ê·mĭ) *n.* nemico.
energetic (ĕn'ẽr·jĕt'ĭk) *agg.* energico, attivo, dinamico.
energy (ĕn'ẽr·jĭ) *n.* energia.
enervate (ĕn'ẽr·vāt) *vt.* snervare, scoraggiare.
enfeeble (ĕn·fē'b'l) *vt.* indebolire.
enfold (ĕn·fōld') *vt.* avvolgere, abbracciare.
enforce (ĕn·fôrs') *vt.* imporre; applicare (*leggi, ecc.*), render esecutivo. —**ment** *n.* coercizione; applicazione (*di un regolamento, ecc.*).
engage (ĕn·gāj') *vt.* ingaggiare, tener occupato; impegnare; prenotare (*un posto*); attirare. *vi.* impegnarsi; imbarcarsi (*in un'impresa*); (*mecc.*) ingranare.
engaged (ĕn·gājd') *agg.* impegnato, occupato; intento (*a*); fidanzato; ingranato.
engagement (-mĕnt) *n.* impegno, obbligo; fidanzamento; (*mil.*) scontro: to keep an —, andare a un appuntamento.
engaging (-ĭng) *agg.* impegnativo; attraente.
engender (ĕn·jĕn'dẽr) *vt.* generare; produrre; provocare.
engine (ĕn'jĭn) *n.* macchina; motore; locomotiva: fire —, pompa da incendio.
engineer (ĕn'jĭ·nēr') *n.* ingegnere; meccanico; macchinista; (*mil.*) geniere. *vt.* architettare. —**ing** *n.* ingegneria.
English (ĭng'glĭsh) *n.*, *agg.* inglese: the —, gli inglesi; in plain —, in parole povere, esplicitamente. —**man** *n.* (*pl.* —men) (*cittadino*) inglese. —**woman** *n.* (*pl.* —women) (*cittadina*) inglese.
engrave (ĕn·grāv') *vt.* incidere, scolpire, imprimere. —**r** *n.* incisore.

—ing *n.* incisione: wood —, silografia.
engross (ĕn·grōs') *vt.* assorbire (*l'attenzione*), occupare: to be —ed, essere assorto. —**ing** *agg.* interessante.
engulf (ĕn·gŭlf') *vt.* inghiottire, sommergere.
enhance (ĕn·hâns') *vt.* accentuare, intensificare, valorizzare.
enigma (ê·nĭg'má) *n.* enigma. —**tical** (-măt'ĭ·kăl) *agg.* enigmatico.
enjoin (ĕn·join') *vt.* ingiungere: to — from, proibire di.
enjoy (ĕn·joi') *vt.* gustare, godere, apprezzare; compiacersi di: to — oneself, divertirsi; to — the use of, usufruire di. —**able** *agg.* gradevole, divertente. —**ment** *n.* godimento, divertimento.
enlarge (ĕn·lärj') *vt.* ampliare, dilatare. *vi.* dilungarsi; ampliarsi.
enlighten (ĕn·līt'n) *vt.* illuminare (*istruire*).
enlist (ĕn·lĭst') *vt.* arruolare, assicurarsi (*l'aiuto di qualcuno*). *vi.* arruolarsi: —ed man (*mil.*) gregario, soldato.
enlistment (-mĕnt) *n.* arruolamento; ferma.
enliven (ĕn·līv'ĕn) *vt.* ravvivare.
enmity (ĕn'mĭ·tĭ) *n.* inimicizia, ostilità.
ennoble (ĕ·nō'b'l) *vt.* nobilitare.
enormity (ê·nôr'mĭ·tĭ) *n.* enormità.
enormous (ê·nôr'mŭs) *agg.* enorme.
enough (ê·nŭf') *n.* sufficienza, quanto basta. *agg.* sufficiente. *avv.* sufficientemente, abbastanza: that is —, così basta; — of it! basta!
enquire (ĕn·kwīr') *vedi* inquire.
enrage (ĕn·rāj') *vt.* infuriare, esasperare.
enrapture (ĕn·răp'tûr) *vt.* estasiare.
enrich (ĕn·rĭch') *vt.* arricchire. —**ment** *n.* arricchimento.
enroll, enrol (ĕn·rōl') *vt.* arrotolare; registrare, iscrivere; arruolare. —**ment** *n.* iscrizione; arruolamento.
ensemble (än·sŏm'b'l) *n.* insieme; complesso.
ensign (ĕn'sīn; ĕn'sĭn) *n.* insegna, bandiera; alfiere; (*marina S.U.*) (ĕn'sĭn) guardiamarina.
enslave (ĕn·slāv') *vt.* asservire, mettere in schiavitù.
ensnare (ĕn·snâr') *vt.* prendere in trappola; sedurre.
ensue (ĕn·sū') *vi.* succedere, verificarsi (*come conseguenza*).
ensure (ĕn·shŏōr') *vt.* assicurare.
entail (ĕn·tāl') *vt.* comportare, imporre; vincolare (*un'eredità*).
entangle (ĕn·tăng'g'l) *vt.* arruffare, complicare, aggrovigliare, impego-

enter   78   ere

lare; coinvolgere. **—ment** *n.* complicazione; groviglio; legame.
enter (ĕn'tĕr) *vt.*, *vi.* entrare, penetrare; iscrivere, registrare; abbracciare (*una professione*): **to — an application,** presentare una domanda; **to — upon a subject,** affrontare un argomento.
enterprise (ĕn'tĕr·prīz) *n.* impresa, prodezza; intraprendenza.
enterprising (-prīz'ĭng) *agg.* intraprendente.
entertain (ĕn'tĕr·tān') *vt.*, *vi.* intrattenere, ricevere; divertire, dare spettacolo; concepire (*una idea*); accarezzare (*speranze*); prendere in considerazione (*una proposta*). **—er** *n.* ospite (*chi ospita*). **—ing** *agg.* divertente. **—ment** *n.* ospitalità; festa, divertimento; spettacolo.
enthrall (ĕn·thrôl') *vt.* asservire; incantare, ammaliare.
enthusiasm (ĕn·thū'zĭ·ăz'm) *n.* entusiasmo.
enthusiast (-ăst) *n.* entusiasta.
enthusiastic (-tĭk) *agg.* entusiastico.
entice (ĕn·tīs') *vt.* adescare, sedurre. **—ment** *n.* seduzione, tentazione.
entire (ĕn·tīr') *agg.* intero, completo. **—ly** *avv.* interamente, completamente. **—ty** (ĕn·tī'rĕ·tĭ) *n.* interezza, totalità.
entitle (ĕn·tī't'l) *vt.* intitolare; dare diritto (*a*): **to be —d to,** aver diritto a *o* il diritto di.
entity (ĕn'tĭ·tĭ) *n.* entità.
entourage (än'tŏŏ·räzh') *n.* ambiente, cerchia.
entrails (ĕn'trēlz) *n.pl.* interiora, viscere.
entrance (ĕn'trăns) (1) *n.* entrata, ingresso; esordio; iscrizione.
entrance (ĕn·trăns') (2) *vt.* incantare, rapire in estasi.
entrap (ĕn·trăp') *vt.* intrappolare.
entreat (ĕn·trēt') *vt.* supplicare.
entreaty (-ĭ) *n.* supplica.
entrench (ĕn·trĕnch') *vt.* trincerare. *vi.* (*seg. da* on, upon) sconfinare, usurpare.
entry (ĕn'trĭ) *n.* entrata, ingresso; iscrizione, registrazione, annotazione: **double —,** partita doppia; **single —,** partita semplice.
enumerate (ē·nū'mĕr·āt) *vt.* enumerare.
enunciate (ē·nŭn'sĭ·āt) *vt.* enunciare.
enunciation (-sĭ·ā'shŭn) *n.* enunciazione.
envelop (ĕn·vĕl'ŭp) *vt.* avvolgere.
envelope (ĕn'vĕ·lōp) *n.* busta, rivestimento.
envenom (ĕn·vĕn'ŭm) *vt.* avvelenare.
enviable (ĕn'vĭ·á·b'l) *agg.* invidiabile.

envious (ĕn'vĭ·ŭs) *agg.* invidioso.
environment (ĕn·vī'rŭn·mĕnt) *n.* ambiente, contorno.
environs (ĕn·vī'rŭnz) *n.pl.* dintorni.
envoy (ĕn'voi) *n.* inviato.
envy (ĕn'vĭ) *n.* invidia. *vt.* invidiare.
epaulet (ĕp'ô·lĕt) *n.* spallina.
ephemeral (ĕ·fĕm'ĕr·ăl) *agg.* effimero, fuggevole.
epic (ĕp'ĭk) *n.* epica. *agg.* epico.
epicure (ĕp'ĭ·kūr) *n.* epicureo. **—an** (-kŭ·rē'ăn) *n.*, *agg.* epicureo.
epidemic (ĕp'ĭ·dĕm'ĭk) *agg.* epidemico.
epidermis (ĕp'ĭ·dûr'mĭs) *n.* epidermide.
epigram (ĕp'ĭ·grăm) *n.* epigramma.
epigraph (ĕp'ĭ·gráf) *n.* epigrafe.
epilogue (ĕp'ĭ·lôg) *n.* epilogo.
episode (ĕp'ĭ·sōd) *n.* episodio.
epistle (ĕ·pĭs''l) *n.* epistola.
epistolary (ĕ·pĭs'tō·lĕr'ĭ) *agg.* epistolare.
epitaph (ĕp'ĭ·tàf) *n.* epitaffio.
epitome (ĕ·pĭt'ô·mĕ) *n.* epitome, compendio.
epoch (ĕp'ŏk) *n.* epoca.
epopee (ĕp'ô·pē') *n.* epopea.
equable (ĕk'wá·b'l) *agg.* uniforme, calmo; equilibrato, equo.
equal (ē'kwăl) *agg.* uguale, pari: **— to,** all'altezza di. *n.* uguale: **our —s,** i pari nostri. *vt.* eguagliare. **—ity** *n.* eguaglianza.
equalize (ē'kwăl·īz) *vt.* uguagliare, pareggiare.
equally (ē'kwăl·ĭ) *avv.* egualmente.
equanimity (ē'kwá·nĭm'ĭ·tĭ) *n.* equanimità.
equation (ē·kwā'zhŭn) *n.* equazione.
equator (ē·kwā'tĕr) *n.* equatore.
equilibrium (ē'kwĭ·lĭb'rĭ·ŭm) *n.* equilibrio.
equinox (ē'kwĭ·nŏks) *n.* equinozio.
equip (ē·kwĭp') *vt.* equipaggiare. **—ment** *n.* equipaggiamento, utensileria.
equitable (ĕk'wĭ·tá·b'l) *agg.* equo, giusto.
equity (ĕk'wĭ·tĭ) *n.* equità, giustizia.
equivalent (ē·kwĭv'á·lĕnt) *n.*, *agg.* equivalente.
equivocal (ē·kwĭv'ô·kăl) *agg.* equivoco, ambiguo.
era (ē'rá) *n.* èra.
eradicate (ē·răd'ĭ·kāt) *vt.* sradicare.
erase (ē·rās') *vt.* cancellare, raschiare.
eraser (ē·rās'ĕr) *n.* raschietto; gomma da cancellare: **blackboard —,** cimosa.
erasure (ē·rā'shĕr) *n.* cancellatura.
ere (âr) *prep.*, *cong.* prima, prima di, piuttosto che. **—long** *avv.* tra poco. **—now** *avv.* prima d'ora, finora, già. **—while** *avv.* poco fa, precedentemente.

erect (ĕr·ĕkt') agg. eretto, elevato. vt. erigere, drizzare, elevare.

ermine (ûr'mĭn) n. ermellino.

erode (ĕ·rōd') vt. corrodere.

erosion (ĕ·rō'zhŭn) n. erosione.

erosive (ĕ·rō'sĭv) agg. erosivo.

err (ûr) vi. errare, smarrirsi.

errand (ĕr'ănd) n. incarico, commissione: — boy, fattorino, galoppino.

errant (ĕr'ănt) agg. errante: knight —, cavaliere errante.

erratic (ĕ·răt'ĭk) agg. erratico; errante; irregolare, stravagante.

erroneous (ĕ·rō'nē·ŭs) agg. erroneo, scorretto.

error (ĕr'ĕr) n. errore, sbaglio; colpa.

ersatz (ĕr·zäts') n., agg. surrogato: — coffee, surrogato di caffè.

erstwhile (ûrst'hwĭl') agg., avv. anticamente.

eruption (ĕ·rŭp'shŭn) n. eruzione.

erysipelas (ĕr'ĭ·sĭp'ĕ·lăs) n. risipola.

escalator (ĕs'kà·lā'tĕr) n. scala meccanica; scala mobile (degli stipendi).

escapade (ĕs'kà·pād') n. scappata, marachella.

escape (ĕs·kāp') n. evasione, fuga (anche di gas, ecc.): to have a narrow —, scamparla bella o per miracolo; fire —, scala di sicurezza; literature of — letteratura d'evasione. vt. sfuggire; evitare. vi. evadere; liberarsi. —ment n. via di scampo; scappamento.

escort (ĕs'kôrt) n. scorta: — carrier, portaerei ausiliaria. vt. scortare.

escutcheon (ĕs·kŭch'ŭn) n. scudo, blasone.

espalier (ĕs·păl'yĕr) n. spalliera (di fiori, ecc.).

esparto (ĕs·pär'tō) n. (bot.) sparto.

especial (ĕs·pĕsh'ăl) agg. speciale. —ly avv. specialmente, soprattutto.

espionage (ĕs'pĭ·ō·nĭj) n. spionaggio.

esplanade (ĕs'plà·nād') n. spianata, passeggiata.

esquire (ĕs·kwĭr') n.: posposto al nome corrisponde a: egregio sig.: John Smith, Esq., egregio sig. J. S.

essay (ĕs'ā) n. saggio, prova. vt. (e·sā') provare.

essence (ĕs'ĕns) n. essenza.

essential (ĕ·sĕn'shăl) agg. essenziale.

establish (ĕs·tăb'lĭsh) vt. stabilire, costituire, consolidare, fondare. —ment n. fondazione; costituzione; sede, casa, stabilimento, istituto.

estate (ĕs·tāt') n. condizione; proprietà, tenuta: real —, beni immobili.

esteem (ĕs·tēm') n. stima, conside razione. vt. stimare, rispettare.

estimable (ĕs'tĭ·mà·b'l) agg. stimabile.

estimate (ĕs'tĭ·māt) n. valutazione, perizia, calcolo, giudizio. vt. valutare, calcolare, stimare.

estimation (-mā'shŭn) n. stima, valutazione.

estrange (ĕs·trānj') vt. alienare, estraniare, inimicarsi.

estuary (ĕs'tū̇·ĕr'ĭ) n. estuario.

etch (ĕch) vt. incidere all'acquaforte. —er n. incisore, acquafortista. —ing n. incisione, acquaforte.

eternal (ĕ·tûr'năl) agg. eterno.

eternity (ĕ·tûr'nĭ·tĭ) n. eternità.

ether (ē'thĕr) n. etere. —eal (ĕ·thēr'ē·ăl) agg. etereo.

ethical (ĕth'ĭ·kăl) agg. etico.

ethics (ĕth'ĭks) n.pl. etica.

ethnology (ĕth·nŏl'ō·jĭ) n. etnologia.

ethyl (ĕth'ĭl) n. etile.

etiquette (ĕt'ĭ·kĕt) n. etichetta.

etymology (ĕt'ĭ·mŏl'ō·jĭ) n. etimologia.

Eucharist (ū'kà·rĭst) n. eucarestia.

eunuch (ū'nŭk) n. eunuco.

European (ū'rō·pē'ăn) n., agg. europeo.

euthanasia (ū'thà·nā'zhĭ·à) n. eutanasia.

evacuate (ĕ·văk'ū̇·āt) vt. evacuare. vi. sfollare.

evacuee (ĕ·văk'ū̇·ē') n. sfollato.

evade (ĕ·vād') vt. eludere, schivare.

evaluate (ĕ·văl'ū̇·āt) vt. valutare.

evaluation (-ā'shŭn) n. valutazione.

evaporate (ĕ·văp'ō·rāt) vt. far evaporare, disidratare. vi. evaporare.

evaporation (-rā'shŭn) n. evaporazione.

evasion (ĕ·vā'zhŭn) n. evasione, scappatoia.

evasive (-sĭv) agg. evasivo.

eve (ēv) n. vigilia: New Year's —, l'ultimo dell' anno, San Silvestro; on the — of, alla vigilia di.

even (ē'věn) agg. pari; uguale; liscio; uniforme; equanime; allo stesso livello: — number, numero pari; — temper, carattere pacifico; to be — with someone, essere alla pari con qualcuno; to get — with, sdebitarsi con; rendere pan per focaccia. avv. persino, anche, proprio: — as, nel momento in cui; — so, eppure, ciò nonostante; — though, anche se, quantunque; not —, neppure, nemmeno. vt. uguagliare, livellare, levigare.

evening (ēv'nĭng) n. sera. agg. serale, da sera.

evenly (ē'věn·lĭ) avv. uniformemente; in parti uguali; pianamente; pacatamente.

evenness (ē'vĕn·nĕs) *n.* uniformità, pacatezza.

event (ē·vĕnt') *n.* evento, eventualità, caso; gara: **in any —**, in ogni caso, comunque; **in the — of**, in caso di. **—ful** *agg.* movimentato, pieno di avvenimenti, fortunoso.

eventual (ē·vĕn'tū·ǎl) *agg.* eventuale, finale. **—ity** (-ǎl'ĭ·tǐ) *n.* eventualità. **—ly** *avv.* finalmente; eventualmente.

ever (ĕv'ẽr) *avv.* sempre; continuamente; mai: **for —, for — and —**, per sempre; **if —**, se mai, se qualche volta; **— after**, da allora in poi; **— so**, tanto, così; **— so much**, moltissimo; **scarcely —**, quasi mai; **more than —**, più che mai; **the finest man I — met**, il miglior uomo che io abbia mai visto.

evergreen (ĕv'ẽr·grēn) *n.*, *agg.* sempreverde.

everlasting (ĕv'ẽr·làs'tǐng) *n.* eternità. *agg.* duraturo, eterno.

evermore (ĕv'ẽr·mōr') *avv.* sempre, per sempre.

every (ĕv'ẽr·ǐ) *agg.* ogni, ciascuno: **— now and then**, di tanto in tanto; **— other**, uno sì, uno no; **— other day**, a giorni alterni. **—body** *pron.* ognuno, tutti. **—day** *agg.* d'ogni giorno, comune, normale. **—one** *pron.* ognuno, tutti. **—thing** *pron.* ogni cosa, tutto. **—where** *avv.* dovunque.

evict (ē·vĭkt') *vt.* espellere, estromettere.

evidence (ĕv'ĭ·dĕns) *n.* evidenza, prova, testimonianza: **to give —**, deporre. *vt.* manifestare, dimostrare.

evident (-dĕnt) *agg.* evidente.

evil (ē'v'l) *n.* male, danno. *agg.* cattivo, funesto, nocivo, maligno: **— eye**, malocchio; **the — one**, il maligno, il diavolo. *avv.* male, dannosamente.

evildoer (ē'v'l·dōō'ẽr) *n.* malfattore.

evince (ē·vĭns') *vt.* manifestare.

evoke (ē·vōk') *vt.* evocare.

evolution (ĕv'ō·lū'shŭn) *n.* evoluzione; (*mat.*) estrazione di radice.

evolve (ē·vŏlv') *vt.* sviluppare. *vi.* evolversi.

ewe (ū) *n.* pecora (*femmina*). **— lamb** *n.* agnella.

ewer (ū'ẽr) *n.* brocca.

exact (ĕg·zăkt') *agg.* esatto, preciso. *vt.* esigere, richiedere. **—ing** *agg.* esigente, gravoso, impegnativo. **—itude**, **—ness** *n.* esattezza. **—ly** *avv.* esattamente.

exaggerate (ĕg·zăj'ẽr·āt) *vt.*, *vi.* esagerare.

exaggeration (-ā'shŭn) *n.* esagerazione.

exalt (ĕg·zôlt') *vt.* esaltare, innalzare. **—ation** *n.* esaltazione. **—ed** *agg.* elevato; esaltato; sommo, altolocato.

examination (ĕg·zăm'ĭ·nā'shŭn) *n.* esame: **competitive —**, esame di concorso; **post-mortem —**, autopsia; **oral —**, esame orale.

examine (ĕg·zăm'ĭn) *vt.* esaminare, interrogare.

examiner (-ĭnẽr) *n.* esaminatore.

example (ĕg·zàm'p'l) *n.* esempio.

exasperate (ĕg·zăs'pẽr·āt) *vt.* esasperare.

exasperation (-ā'shŭn) *n.* esasperazione.

excavate (ĕks'kà·vāt) *vt.* scavare.

excavator (-vā'tẽr) *n.* escavatore.

exceed (ĕk·sēd') *vt.* superare. *vi.* eccedere; eccellere. **—ing** *agg.* eccessivo, straordinario. **—ingly** *avv.* estremamente, eccessivamente: **— well**, benissimo.

excel (ĕk·sĕl') *vt.* superare, battere. *vi.* eccellere. **—lence** (ĕk'sĕ·lĕns), **—lency** *n.* eccellenza; superiorità, perfezione. **—lent** *agg.* eccellente.

except (ĕk·sĕpt') *prep.* eccetto, a eccezione di, tranne, fuorchè. *cong.* eccetto che. *vt.* eccettuare, escludere. *vi.* obiettare, sollevare obiezioni.

excepting *prep. vedi* except.

exception (ĕk·sĕp'shŭn) *n.* eccezione, obiezione: **with the — of**, eccetto, tranne; **to take —**, obiettare; offendersi. **—al** *agg.* eccezionale.

excess (ĕk·sĕs') *n.* eccesso; eccedenza: **to —**, eccessivamente, troppo; **— baggage**, eccedenza di bagaglio.

excessive (-sĕs'ĭv) *agg.* eccessivo.

exchange (ĕks·chānj') *n.* scambio; (*telef.*) centrale; borsa valori: **bill of —**, cambiale; **rate of —**, tasso di scambio; **— broker**, agente di cambio. *vt.* cambiare, scambiare: **to — greetings**, salutarsi.

excise (ĕk'sīz) *n.* imposta indiretta, dazio: **— duty**, dazio.

excitable (ĕk·sīt'à·b'l) *agg.* eccitabile, impressionabile, irascibile.

excite (ĕk·sīt') *vi.* eccitare, agitare, irritare, provocare.

excited (-sīt'ĕd) *agg.* eccitato, sovreccitato, accalorato, concitato: **to get —**, accalorarsi; perdere la calma; entusiasmarsi.

excitedly (-lǐ) *avv.* concitatamente.

excitement (-mĕnt) *n.* eccitazione, sovreccitazione, emozione, agitazione; trambusto.

exciting (-ĭng) *agg.* emozionante; eccitante.

exclaim (ĕks·klām′) *vt.*, *vi.* esclamare.

exclamation (ĕks′klá·mā′shŭn) *n.* esclamazione: — **point**, **punto** esclamativo.

exclude (ĕks·klōōd′) *vt.* escludere.

exclusion (-klōō′zhŭn) *n.* esclusione.

exclusive (ĕks·klōō′sĭv) *agg.* esclusivo, limitativo, rigoroso: — **of**, senza calcolare, eccettuato, escluso.

exclusiveness (-nĕs) *n.* esclusività.

excommunicate (ĕks′kŏ·mū′nĭ·kāt) *vt.* scomunicare.

excommunication (-kā′shŭn) *n.* scomunica.

excoriate (ĕks·kō′rĭ·āt) *vt.* escoriare, scorticare; criticare aspramente.

excoriation (-ā′shŭn) *n.* escoriazione.

excrement (ĕks′krē·mĕnt) *n.* escremento.

excrescence (ĕks·krĕs′ĕns) *n.* escrescenza.

excruciating (ĕks·krōō′shĭ·āt′ĭng) *agg.* tormentoso, straziante.

exculpate (ĕks′kŭl·pāt) *vt.* discolpare.

excursion (ĕks·kûr′zhŭn) *n.* escursione; digressione; (*mecc.*) corsa (*di cilindro*).

excusable (ĕks·kūz′á·b′l) *agg.* scusabile, perdonabile.

excuse (ĕks·kūz′) *n.* scusa, giustificazione. *vt.* scusare; dispensare; congedare: — **mel scusami!**, mi scusi!, scusatemi!

execrable (ĕk′sē·krá·b′l) *agg.* esecrabile, esecrando.

execrate (ĕk′sē·krāt) *vt.* esecrare.

execute (ĕk′sē·kūt) *vt.* eseguire, compiere; applicare (*una sanzione, ecc.*); giustiziare.

execution (ĕk′sē·kū′shŭn) *n.* esecuzione (*anche capitale*); sequestro; adempimento: **to carry into —**, mettere in atto.

executioner (-ẽr) *n.* carnefice.

executive (ĕg·zĕk′û·tĭv) *n.* funzionario, dirigente. *agg.* esecutivo.

executor (ĕg·zĕk′û·tẽr) *n.* esecutore.

exemplar (ĕg·zĕm′plẽr) *n.* esemplare, modello.

exemplary (ĕg·zĕm′plá·rĭ) *agg.* esemplare.

exempt (ĕg·zĕmpt′) *agg.* esente. *vt.* esentare. **—ion** *n.* esenzione.

exercise (ĕk′sẽr·sīz) *n.* esercizio. *vt.* esercitare; preoccupare. *vi.* esercitarsi.

exert (ĕg·zûrt′) *vt.* esercitare, compiere: **to — oneself**, compiere uno sforzo, adoperarsi. **—ion** *n.* sforzo.

exhalation (ĕks′há·lā′shŭn) *n.* esalazione.

exhale (ĕks·hāl′) *vt.*, *vi.* esalare.

exhaust (ĕg·zôst′) *n.* scarico, valvola, scappamento. *vt.* esaurire; vuotare;

fiaccare. *vi.* scaricarsi (*di gas, ecc.*). **—ed** *agg.* esaurito; esausto, sfinito. **—ion** *n.* esaurimento. **—ive** *agg.* esauriente; che esaurisce.

exhibit (ĕg·zĭb′ĭt) *n.* pezzo da esposizione, campione; (*legge*) reperto, documento agli atti. *vt.* esibire, esporre.

exhibition (ĕk′sĭ·bĭsh′ŭn) *n.* esibizione; esposizione, mostra; spettacolo. **—ism** *n.* esebizionismo.

exhilarate (ĕg·zĭl′á·rāt) *vt.* esilarare, rallegrare.

exhilaration (-rā′shŭn) *n.* ilarità.

exhort (ĕg·zôrt′) *vt.* esortare, ammonire. **—ation** *n.* esortazione.

exigency (ĕk′sĭ·jĕn·sĭ) *n.* esigenza.

exigent (-jĕnt) *agg.* esigente.

exile (ĕk′sīl) *n.* esilio; esule. *vt.* esiliare.

exist (ĕg·zĭst′) *vi.* esistere. **—ence** *n.* esistenza: **to be in —**, esistere; **to call into —**, creare, far nascere. **—ent**, **—ing** *agg.* esistente, attuale.

existentialism *n.* esistenzialismo. **existentialist** *n.* esistenzialista.

exit (ĕk′sĭt) *n.* uscita; fine; morte; *v.* (*teat.*) esce. *vi.* uscire.

exodus (ĕk′sŏ·dŭs) *n.* èsodo.

exonerate (ĕg·zŏn′ẽr·āt) *vt.* esonerare, dispensare, assolvere.

exorbitant (ĕg·zôr′bĭ·tănt) *agg.* esorbitante.

exorcise (ĕk′sôr·sīz) *vt.* esorcizzare.

exotic (ĕks·ŏt′ĭk) *agg.* esotico; pittoresco; vistoso.

expand (ĕks·pănd′) *vt.* espandere, dilatare, sviluppare. *vi.* espandersi, dilatarsi, svilupparsi.

expanse (-păns′) *n.* distesa, estensione.

expansion (ĕks·păn′shŭn) *n.* espansione, estensione, dilatazione, sviluppo.

expansive (-sĭv) *agg.* espansivo, diffuso.

expatriate (ĕks·pā′trĭ·āt) *vt.* espatriare.

expect (ĕks·pĕkt′) *vt.*, *vi.* aspettare; prevedere; supporre; sperare; calcolare di: **I — so**, ritengo di sì, spero di sì. **—ation** *n.* attesa, speranza, prospettiva.

expectorate (ĕks·pĕk′tŏ·rāt) *vt.*, *vi.* espettorare.

expedience (ĕks·pē′dĭ·ĕns), **expediency** (-ĕn·sĭ) *n.* convenienza, utilità; solerzia, fretta.

expedient (-ĕnt) *n.* espediente. *agg.* conveniente, utile.

expedition (ĕks′pē·dĭsh′ŭn) *n.* sveltezza, prontezza; spedizione. **—ary** *agg.* (*mil.*) di spedizione.

expel (ĕks·pĕl′) *vt.* espellere.

expend (ĕks·pĕnd′) *vt.* spendere; sborsare; profondere. **—able** *agg.* spendibile; (*mil.*) sacrificabile. **—iture** *n.* spesa, sborso.

expense (ĕks·pĕns′) *n.* spesa, costo.

expensive (-pĕn′sĭv) *agg.* costoso, dispendioso.

experience (ĕks·pēr′ĭ·ĕns) *n.* esperienza. *vt.* provare, subire, patire.

experienced (-ĕnst) *agg.* esperto.

experiment (ĕks·pĕr′ĭ·mĕnt) *n.* esperimento. *vi.* (*seg. da* with) sperimentare. **—al** *agg.* sperimentale.

expert (ĕks′pûrt) *n.* perito, competente. *agg.* (ĕks·pûrt′) esperto. **—ly** *avv.* espertamente, abilmente.

expiate (ĕks′pĭ·āt) *vt.* espiare.

expiation (-ā′shŭn) *n.* espiazione.

expiration (ĕk′spĭ·rā′shŭn) *n.* scadenza, termine, espirazione.

expire (ĕk·spīr′) *vt., vi.* espirare, spirare, scadere, emettere, esalare.

explain (ĕks·plān′) *vt., vi.* spiegare. **—able** *agg.* spiegabile.

explanation (ĕks′plȧ·nā′shŭn) *n.* spiegazione, schiarimento.

explanatory (ĕks·plăn′ȧ·tō′rĭ) *agg.* esplicativo.

explicatory (ĕks′plĭ·kȧ·tō′rĭ) *agg.* esplicativo.

explicit (ĕks·plĭs′ĭt) *agg.* esplicito.

explode (ĕks·plōd′) *vt.* far esplodere; svalutare, demolire (*una teoria*). *vi.* esplodere.

exploit (ĕks′ploit) (1) *n.* prodezza, impresa.

exploit (ĕks·ploit′) (2) *vt.* sfruttare, utilizzare. **—ation** *n.* sfruttamento, utilizzazione.

exploration (ĕks′plō·rā′shŭn) *n.* esplorazione.

explore (ĕks·plōr′) *vt., vi.* esplorare.

explorer (ĕks·plōr′ēr) *n.* esploratore.

explosion (ĕks·plō′zhŭn) *n.* esplosione.

explosive (-sĭv) *n., agg.* esplosivo.

export (ĕks′pōrt) *n.* esportazione. *vt.* (ĕks·pōrt′) esportare. **—ation** *n.* esportazione. **—er** *n.* esportatore.

expose (ĕks·pōz′) *vt.* esporre, scoprire, svelare.

exposé (ĕks′pō·sā′) *n.* (*giorn.*) denuncia, rivelazione (*di uno scandalo*).

exposer (-ēr) *n.* espositore.

exposition (ĕks′pō·zĭsh′ŭn) *n.* esposizione.

expostulate (ĕks′pŏs′tū·lāt) *vi.* protestare, rimostrare.

expostulation (-lā′shŭn) *n.* rimostranza, protesta.

exposure (ĕks·pō′zhēr) *n.* esposizione (*al sole, ecc.*); smascheramento, scandalo; (*fot.*) posa: **— meter** (*fot.*), esposimetro.

expound (ĕks·pound′) *vt.* esporre, divulgare.

express (ĕks·prĕs′) *n.* (*lettera*) espresso; (*treno*) rapido; messaggero: **— company**, società di trasporti. *agg.* apposito, espresso; rapido. *avv.* espressamente; per espresso. *vt.* esprimere; (*S.U.*) spedire per espresso. **—ion** *n.* espressione. **—ive** *agg.* espressivo. **—way** *n.* superautostrada.

expropriate (ĕks·prō′prĭ·āt) *vt.* espropriare.

expulsion (ĕks·pŭl′shŭn) *n.* espulsione.

exquisite (ĕks′kwĭ·zĭt) *agg.* sublime, squisito, raffinato; acuto (*di dolore*).

extant (ĕks′tănt) *agg.* esistente, disponibile, attuale.

extend (ĕks·tĕnd′) *vt.* estendere; prolungare; protrarre, prorogare; tendere; porgere. *vi.* estendersi, protrarsi: **extended play record**, disco a lunga durata.

extension (ĕks·tĕn′shŭn) *n.* estensione, prolungamento; proroga; (*telef.*) derivazione.

extensive (-sĭv) *agg.* vasto, ampio, diffuso. *avv.* ampiamente, diffusamente.

extent (ĕks·tĕnt′) *n.* estensione; grado; punto; portata; limite: **to a great —,** in gran parte; **to a certain —,** sino a un certo punto.

extenuate (ĕks·tĕn′ū·āt) *vt.* attenuare, giustificare.

extenuating *agg.* attenuante.

extenuation (-ā′shŭn) *n.* attenuazione, attenuante.

exterior (ĕks·tēr′ĭ·ēr) *agg.* esteriore, esterno.

exterminate (ĕks·tûr′mĭ·nāt) *vt.* sterminare.

extermination (-nā′shŭn) *n.* sterminio.

external (ĕks·tûr′năl) *n., agg.* esterno, esteriore.

extinct (ĕks·tĭngkt′) *agg.* estinto, scomparso. **—ion** *n.* estinzione, soppressione.

extinguish (ĕks·tĭng′gwĭsh) *vt.* estinguere, spegnere.

extirpate (ĕk′stēr·pāt) *vt.* estirpare, sterminare.

extol (ĕks·tŏl′) *vt.* esaltare, estollere.

extort (ĕks·tôrt′) *vt.* estorcere. **—ion** *n.* estorsione; (*giur.*) concussione.

extra (ĕks′trȧ) *n.* supplemento; edizione straordinaria; avventizio; comparsa. *agg.* supplementare; straordinario; superiore. *avv.* straordinariamente; eccessivamente.

extract (ĕks·trăkt′) *n.* estratto. *vt.* estrarre. **—ion** *n.* estrazione: **of foreign —,** di origine straniera.

extraneous (ĕks·trā'nē·ŭs) *agg.* estraneo.

extraordinary (ĕks·trôr'dĭ·nĕr'ĭ) *agg.* straordinario.

extravagance (ĕks·trăv'á·gáns) *n.* prodigalità.

extravagant (-gánt) *agg.* prodigo; dispendioso; esorbitante (*di prezzo*); eccessivo.

extreme (ĕks·trēm') *n., agg.* estremo. —ly *avv.* estremamente.

extremity (ĕks·trĕm'ĭ·tĭ) *n.* estremità; estremo; punto estremo; eccesso; estremo pericolo; dolore; bisogno.

extremities (-tĭz) *n.pl.* (*le*) estremità; estremi rimedi.

extricate (ĕks'trĭ·kāt) *vt.* districare, liberare.

extrude (ĕks·trōōd') *vt.* espellere. *vi.* sporgere.

exuberance (ĕg·zū'bĕr·áns) *n.* esuberanza.

exuberant (-ánt) *agg.* esuberante.

exude (ĕks·ūd') *vt., vi.* sudare, trasudare.

exult (ĕg·zŭlt') *vi.* esultare. —ance *n.* esultanza. —ant *agg.* esultante.

eye (ī) *n.* occhio; sguardo; mira; cruna (*d'ago*); direzione (*del vento*): in the twinkling of an —, in un batter d'occhio; to catch one's —, colpire l'occhio, destare l'attenzione; to have good eyes, avere buona vista; to keep an — on, tenere d'occhio; to see — to —, essere assolutamente d'accordo; to cry one's eyes out, sciogliersi in lacrime. *vt.* osservare, sbirciare. —ball *n.* bulbo oculare. — bank, banca degli occhi. —brow *n.* sopracciglio. —glass *n.* lente; (*pl.*) occhiali. —let *n.* occhiello. —lashes *n.pl.* ciglia. —lid *n.* palpebra. —shade *n.* visiera. —sight *n.* vista. —sore *n.* bruttura. —tooth *n.* dente canino. —witness *n.* testimone oculare.

F

fable (fā'b'l) *n.* favola.

fabric (făb'rĭk) *n.* tessuto, stoffa; struttura; grana.

fabricate (făb'rĭ·kāt) *vt.* fabbricare; inventare, falsificare.

fabrication *n.* fabbricazione; menzogna, invenzione.

fabulous (făb'ū·lŭs) *agg.* favoloso.

face (fās) *n.* faccia; superficie; apparenza, aspetto, smorfia; facciata; faccetta; quadrante (*d'orologio*): — value, valore nominale; in the — of, davanti a; to lose —, perdere prestigio. to have the — to, aver l'impudenza di; to make faces, fare smorfiacce; to put a good — on a bad business, fare buon viso a cattiva sorte; on the — of it, giudicando dalle apparenze. *vt.* affrontare, sfidare; rivestire; volgere il viso verso, essere esposto a: to — about, fare dietro-front; to — a street, dare su una strada.

facer (fās'ẽr) *n.* sgrugno, pugno sul viso; difficoltà imprevista.

facet (fās'ĕt) *n.* faccetta. *vt.* sfaccettare.

facial (fā'shǎl) *agg.* facciale. [tare.

facilitate (tá·sĭl'ĭ·tāt) *vt.* facilitare, agevolare.

facility (tá·sĭl'ĭ·tĭ) *n.* facilità; destrezza; (*pl.*) agevolazioni; installazioni, attrezzatura.

fact (făkt) *n.* fatto: in —, as a matter of —, effettivamente; to be matter-of-fact, essere positivo *o* sbrigativo.

faction (făk'shŭn) *n.* fazione, intrigo politico.

factious (făk'shŭs) *agg.* fazioso.

factor (făk'tẽr) *n.* fattore, agente.

factory (făk'tō·rĭ) *n.* fabbrica, azienda.

factual (făk'tū·ǎl) *agg.* effettivo, reale, concreto.

faculty (făk'ŭl·tĭ) *n.* facoltà.

fad (făd) *n.* mania.

fade (fād) *vt.* sbiadire; affievolire. *vi.* sbiadire; affievolirsi, svanire. — in *n.* (*cinema*) dissolvenza (*in apertura*).

fag (făg) *n.* lavoro pesante; (*gergo*) sigaretta. —ged *agg.* sfinito, esausto.

fail (fāl) *n.* fallo; mancanza; insuccesso: without —, senza fallo. *vt., vi.* mancare, fallire; indebolirsi; deludere; abbandonare: to — in an examination, essere bocciato a un esame; to — a student, bocciare uno studente; to — to do something, non fare una cosa; don't — to come, non mancare (di venire). —ing *n.* difetto, debolezza, fallimento. *agg.* declinante. *prep.* in mancanza di.

failure (fāl'ũr) *n.* mancanza, difetto, omissione; fallimento, insuccesso, indebolimento, fiasco.

faint (fānt) *agg.* debole, lieve, vago; abbattuto, scoraggiato: — - hearted, timido, codardo. *vi.* affievolirsi; svenire: to — away, perdere i sensi. —ing *n.* svenimento, indebolimento. —ly *avv.* debolmente, vagamente. —ness *n.* debolezza, languore; malore.

fair (fâr) (1) *n.* fiera, mercato, esposizione.

fair (fâr) (2) *agg.* bello, gradevole; favorevole; sereno; biondo; giusto, equo, leale, legittimo: — chance of success, buona probabilità; — complexion, carnagione chiara; — name, reputazione immacolata; — play, comportamento leale; — sex, sesso gentile, sesso debole; — weather, bel tempo. *avv.* onestamente, lealmente, favorevolmente. — dealing *n.* lealtà. — -haired *agg.* biondo di capelli. —ing *n.* (aeron.) carenatura. —ly *avv.* abbastanza; discretamente; onestamente, giustamente. —ness *n.* onestà, equità, giustezza; bellezza; purezza; biondezza.

fairy (fâr'ĭ) *n.* fata. *agg.* fatato. —land *n.* regno delle fate. — tale, racconto di fate.

faith (fâth) *n.* fede, credenza, fiducia; fedeltà: breach of —, mancanza di parola; to keep —, mantenere la parola; to be in bad (good) —, essere in mala (buona) fede. —ful *n.*, *agg.* fedele. —fully *avv.* fedelmente, devotamente: — yours, vostro devotissimo. —fulness *n.* fedeltà. —less *agg.* infedele, miscredente, sleale.

fake (fâk) *n.* contraffazione, falso. *agg.* falso. *vt.*, *vi.* falsificare; fingere, simulare.

falcon (fôl'kŭn) *n.* falcone.

fall (fôl) *n.* caduta; decadenza; fine; declivio; cascata (*d'acqua*); ribasso; abbassamento; autunno. *vi.* (*pass.* fell, *pp.* fallen) cadere; decadere; abbattersi; diminuire; accadere: to — away, deperire; staccarsi; to — asleep, addormentarsi; to — back, retrocedere; to — behind, restare indietro; to — due, scadere; to — foul of, venire in collisione con; to — in love with, innamorarsi di; to — off, staccarsi; diminuire; to — out, litigare; to — short, essere insufficiente; to — through, andare a monte; to — to blows, venire alle mani.

fallen (fôl'ĕn) *pp. di* to fall. *agg.* caduto, degradato, disonorato.

fallible (făl'ĭ·b'l) *agg.* fallibile.

falling (fôl'ing) *n.* caduta, diminuzione, scadenza: — in, infossamento, crollo; — off, caduta; defezione; apostasia. *agg.* cadente: — sickness, epilessia.

false (fôls) *agg.* falso, sleale, finto, simulato. *avv.* falsamente: to play —, ingannare, tradire; —hood *n.* falsità, menzogna. —ness *n.* falsità.

falsies (fôl'sĭz) *n.pl.* (*gergo*) seno finto.

falsify (fôl'sĭ·fĭ) *vt.* falsificare.

falsity (-tĭ) *n.* falsità.

faltboat (fôlt'bōt) *n.* sandolino (*smontabile di tela impermeabilizzata*).

falter (fôl'tĕr) *n.* titubanza, esitazione. *vt.*, *vi.* esitare; incespicare, barcollare; balbettare.

fame (fâm) *n.* fama, gloria, nomea.

famed (fâmd) *agg.* famoso, rinomato.

familiar (fá·mĭl'yĕr) *n.*, *agg.* familiare: to be — with a subject, conoscere bene un argomento, intendersene. —ity *n.* familiarità.

family (făm'ĭ·lĭ) *n.* famiglia: to be in the — way, essere incinta. — name, cognome. — tree, albero genealogico.

famine (făm'ĭn) *n.* carestia.

famish (făm'ĭsh) *vt.* affamare. *vi.* soffrire la fame. —ed *agg.* affamato.

famous (fâ'mŭs) *agg.* famoso, celebre.

fan (făn) (1) *n.* ventaglio, ventilatore, mantice, pala (*di mulino a vento*). *vt.* sventolare, ventilare; (*fig.*) stimolare. *vi.*: to — out, aprirsi a ventaglio.

fan (2) *n.* ammiratore, appassionato, tifoso.

fanatic (fá·năt'ĭk) *n.*, *agg.* fanatico. —al *agg.* fanatico. —ism (-ĭ·sĭz'm) *n.* fanatismo.

fancier (făn'sĭ·ĕr) *n.* amatore, appassionato; allevatore *o* coltivatore.

fanciful (făn'sĭ·fŏŏl) *agg.* fantasioso, capriccioso, originale; immaginario.

fancy (făn'sĭ) *n.* fantasia, capriccio, passione, desiderio: to have a — for, essere invaghito di; to take a — to, incapricciarsi di, affezionarsi a. *agg.* di fantasia, originale; decorativo: — dress, costume (*carnevalesco, ecc.*); — dress ball, ballo in costume. *vt.* immaginare, pensare; prediligere: to — oneself, stimarsi molto; just — the idea! ma guarda un po' che idea!, ma te lo immagini? — goods, tessuti fantasia; — work, ricamo decorativo.

fang (făng) *n.* zanna; dente velenoso (*dei rettili*); radice (*dei denti*).

fantastic (făn·tăs'tĭk) *agg.* antastico, bizzarro.

fantasy (făn'tá·sĭ) *n.* fantasia.

far (fâr) *agg.* lontano, remoto: — cry, grande distanza. *avv.* lontano, a distanza; molto, assai: as — as, fino a; as — as I know, a quanto ne so io; by —, di gran lung ; how —? sin dove? so —, sin qui; — and wide, da tutte le parti; — better, molto meglio; — between, a lunghi intervalli; — off, in lontananza;

thus—, sin qui. —away, agg. lontano, remoto; vacuo, assente. —fetched agg. remoto, improbabile, inverosimile, fittizio; —seeing, —sighted agg. lungimirante, presbite.

farce (färs) n. farsa.

farcical (fär'sĭ-kăl) agg. burlesco.

fare (fâr) n. prezzo (di posto, viaggio, ecc.), corsa (in tassi, ecc.), passeggero; cibo, nutrimento: bill of —, lista delle vivande; car—, n. (costo del) biglietto tranviario. vi. barcamenarsi, campare: to — badly, andar male, essere in cattive condizioni; to — well, andar bene, prosperare.

farewell (fâr'wĕl') n. addio, commiato. agg. d'addio. inter. addio!

farm (färm) n. fattoria. agg. agricolo. vt. coltivare. vi. fare l'agricoltore. —er n. agricoltore, fattore. —ing n. agricoltura. —stead n. fattoria. —yard n. aia.

farrow (făr'ō) vt., vi. figliare.

farther (fär'thĕr) agg. ulteriore, successivo, più lontano, estremo. avv. oltre, inoltre, maggiormente, più lontano, più a lungo.

farthest (fär'thĕst) agg. estremo, più lontano. avv. alla maggior distanza.

fascinate (făs'ĭ-nāt) vt. affascinare.

fascinating agg. affascinante, incantevole.

fascination (-nā'shŭn) n. fascino, attrazione.

fashion (făsh'ŭn) n. moda, foggia, stile, maniera; consuetudine: — plate, figurino; the latest —, l'ultima moda; after a —, in qualche modo, alla meglio; to come into —, diventare di moda. vt. foggiare, adattare, modellare. —able agg. elegante, di moda.

fast (făst) (1) n. digiuno. vi. digiunare.

fast (făst) (2) agg. saldo, sicuro, fedele, costante; profondo (del sonno); solido (di colore); rapido; in anticipo (di orologio); (fam.) dissoluto: — friend, amico fedele; to make —, fissare, chiudere bene; (naut.) ormeggiare. avv. saldamente, fermamente; rapidamente: to hold —, tener duro; to sleep —, dormire profondamente.

fasten (făs''n) vt. attaccare, fissare, assicurare; chiudere. vi. attaccarsi, fissarsi. —er n. fibbia, fermaglio: zip —, cerniera lampo.

fastidious (făs·tĭd'ĭ·ŭs) agg. schizzinoso, difficile (di gusti).

fat (făt) n. grasso. agg. grasso, pingue; untuoso; ricco, fertile. vt., vi. ingrassare.

fatal (fā'tăl) agg. fatale, funesto, mortale. —ity (fȧ·tăl'ĭ·tĭ) n. fatalità. —ly avv. fatalmente.

fate (fāt) n. fato, sorte: The Fates, le Parche.

fateful (fāt'fŏŏl) agg. fatale, decisivo.

father (fä'thĕr) n. padre: father-in-law, suocero. vt. procreare; adottare, assumere la paternità di o la responsabilità di. —hood n. paternità. —land n. patria. —ly agg. paterno. avv. paternamente.

fathom (făth'ŭm) n. unità di lunghezza (circa m. 1,83). vt. sondare, scandagliare.

fatigue (fȧ·tēg') n. stanchezza, fatica; (mil.) corvè; tenuta da fatica; vt. stancare, affaticare.

fatiguing (-tē'gĭng) agg. faticoso.

fatness (făt'nĕs) n. pinguedine; untuosità; ricchezza, fertilità.

fatten (făt''n) vt. ingrassare, impinguare. vi. ingrassarsi, arricchirsi.

fatty (făt'ĭ) agg. grasso, untuoso.

fatuous (făt'ū·ŭs) agg. fatuo, sciocco.

faucet (fô'sĕt) n. rubinetto.

fault (fôlt) n. colpa, difetto, pecca: to a —, eccessivamente, fin troppo; to be at —, essere in colpa. to find — with, trovar da ridire su. —finder n. pignuolo, criticone. —less agg. perfetto, innocente, impeccabile.

faulty (fôl'tĭ) agg. difettoso; colpevole, biasimevole.

favor (fā'vĕr) n. favore; propensione; lettera: to be in — with, essere nelle buone grazie di; to find — with, trovar favore presso; I received your —, ricevetti la vostra stimata lettera. vt. favorire, essere favorevole a; assomigliare a. —able agg. favorevole. —ed agg. favorito: ill-favored, brutto (di persona). —ite n., agg. preferito, favorito. —itism n. favoritismo.

fawn (fôn) n. cerbiatto, capriolo. agg. marrone-chiaro, giallastro.

fawn (2) n. adulazione, inchino servile. vi. far riverenze; far le feste (di animali): to — upon, adulare.

fawning n. adulazione, servilismo. agg. servile.

FBI (ĕf'bē'ī') n. Ufficio Federale Investigativo.

fear (fēr) n. paura, timore. vt. temere. vi. aver paura: never fear! state tranquillo! —ful agg. timoroso; terribile. —less agg. intrepido. —lessness n. intrepidezza. —some agg. spaventoso.

feasible (fē'zĭ·b'l) agg. fattibile, probabile.

feast (fēst) n. festa, festino. vt. festeggiare. vi. far festa; banchettare; bearsi.

feat (fēt) n. prodezza, impresa.

feather (fĕth'ẽr) n. piuma, penna, pennacchio: this is a — in his cap, questo va a onor suo; birds of a —, gente della stessa risma. vt. ornare o imbottire di piume; filare (i remi). vi. metter piume. —less agg. impiume. —y agg. piumato, piumoso, leggerissimo.

feature (fē'tụr) n. lineamento; caratteristica; fisionomia, viso; manifestazione; (S.U.) film principale (nel programma); servizio, articolo speciale (in giornali, ecc.). vt. caratterizzare, delineare, mettere in risalto; (fam.) assomigliare a.

February (fĕb'rŏō-ĕr'ĭ) n. febbraio.

fecund (fē'kŭnd) agg. fecondo.

fed (fĕd) pass., pp. di to feed: to be — up with, essere sazio o stufo di; (fig.) averne fin sopra i capelli.

federal (fĕd'ẽr-ăl) n. federalista; unionista. agg. federale.

federation (fĕd'ẽr-ā'shŭn) n. federazione.

fee (fē) n. onorario; ricompensa; proprietà ereditaria: admission —, prezzo d'entrata, quota, tassa d'iscrizione.

feeble (fē'bl) agg. debole, flebile. —ness n. debolezza.

feebly (-blĭ) avv. debolmente.

feed (fĕd) n. nutrimento, alimentazione, rifornimento. vt. (pass., pp. fed) nutrire, alimentare, rifornire; pascolare. vi. nutrirsi, cibarsi: to — upon, nutrirsi di. —er n. alimentatore; (ferr.) tronco secondario.

feel (fĕl) n. tatto, sensazione tattile: this cloth has a nice —, questo tessuto è gradevole al tatto. vt. (pass., pp. felt) sentire, tastare; ritenere; sondare. vi. sentirsi, frugare; avere una convinzione; (seg. da for, with) provar simpatia o compassione per: to — better, sentirsi meglio; to — one's way, procedere a tastoni; it feels soft, è morbido al tatto; it feels hot in here, fa caldo qua dentro. to — strongly on a subject, avere decise opinioni su un argomento. —er n. antenna (di insetto); tentacolo (di mollusco); sondaggio; approccio. —ing n. sensazione, sentimento, sensibilità: ill —, malanimo, rancore.

feet (fēt) pl. di foot.

feign (fān) vt., vi. fingere, simulare.

felicitate (fē·lĭs'ĭ·tāt) vt. complimentare, congratularsi con.

felicitous (fē·lĭs'ĭ·tŭs) agg. acconcio, felice, opportuno.

felicity (fē·lĭs'ĭ·tĭ) n. felicità.

fell (fĕl) (1) agg. crudele, brutale. vt. abbattere, stroncare.

fell (fĕl) (2) pass. di to fall.

feller (fĕl'ẽr) n. boscaiolo; (gergo) vedi fellow.

fellow (fĕl'ō) n. compagno, collega; membro, socio; docente; ragazzo, tipo, individuo, tizio: a good —, un buon diavolo; poor —! poveraccio! agg. accompagnato, affine, analogo: — citizen, concittadino; — countryman, compatriota; — creature, simile (il nostro simile); — member, consocio; — student, condiscepolo; — sufferer, compagno di sventura; — traveler, compagno di viaggio; (pol.) simpatizzante (spec. per il Comunismo).

fellowship (fĕl'ō-shǐp) n. associazione; solidarietà; borsa di studio; (univ.) docenza.

felon (fĕl'ŭn) n. colpevole, criminale; (med.) patereccio.

felony (fĕl'ō-nĭ) n. reato grave, delitto.

felt (fĕlt) (1) n. feltro. vt. feltrare.

felt (fĕlt) (2) pass., pp. di to feel.

female (fē'māl) n., agg. femmina.

feminine (fĕm'ĭ-nĭn) agg. femminile.

femur (fē'mẽr) n. femore.

fence (fĕns) n. recinto, palizzata, barriera; scherma; (fam.) ricettatore: to be on the —, essere indeciso, non impegnarsi. vt. cintare, proteggere. vi. tirar di scherma.

fencing (fĕn'sǐng) n. recinto; scherma.

fend (fĕnd) vt. parare, schivare. vi. resistere: to — for oneself, ingegnarsi. —er n. parafuoco; paraurti.

fennel (fĕn'ĕl) n. finocchio.

ferment (fûr'mĕnt) n. fermento. vi. fermentare. —ation n. fermentazione.

fern (fûrn) n. felce.

ferocious (fē·rō'shŭs) agg. feroce. —ness n. ferocia.

ferocity (fē·rŏs'ĭ·tĭ) n. ferocia.

ferret (fĕr'ĕt) n. (geol.) furetto, puzzola. vt. stanare: to — out, snidare, scoprire.

ferroconcrete (fĕr'ō-kŏn'krēt) n. cemento armato.

ferrous (fĕr'ŭs) agg. ferroso, di ferro.

ferry (fĕr'ĭ) vt., vi. traghettare. —boat n. nave-traghetto. —man n. traghettatore.

fertile (fûr'tĭl) agg. fertile, fecondo.

fertility (fûr·tĭl'ĭ·tĭ) n. fertilità.

fertilize (fûr'tĭ·līz) vt. fertilizzare.

fertilizer (-līz'ẽr) n. fertilizzante, concime.

fervency (fûr'vĕn·sĭ) n. fervore.

fervent (fûr'vĕnt) agg. fervente. —ly avv. con fervore.

fervid (fûr'vĭd) agg. fervido, ardente.

fervor (fûr'vẽr) n. fervore, ardore.

fester (fĕs'tĕr) *n.* suppurazione, ulcera. *vi.* suppurare, marcire.

festival (fĕs'tĭ-vǎl) *n.* festa, festival. *agg.* festivo.

festive (fĕs'tĭv) *agg.* festivo, festoso.

festivity (fĕs-tĭv'ĭ-tĭ) *n.* festa, allegria.

fetch (fĕch) *vt., vi.* cercare; andare a prendere, andare a chiamare; assestare (*un pugno, ecc.*); cattivare; raggiungere, ottenere. —**ing** *agg.* attraente, piacevole.

fete (fāt) *n.* festa. *vt.* festeggiare.

fetish (fēt'ĭsh) *n.* feticcio.

fetter (fĕt'ĕr) *n.* pastoia. *vt.* impastoiare, ostacolare.

feud (fūd) *n.* contesa; inimicizia; feudo: old —, vecchia ruggine. —**al** *agg.* feudale.

fever (fē'vĕr) *n.* febbre. —**ish** *agg.* febbrile, febbricitante. —**ishly** *avv.* febbrilmente. —**ishness** *n.* stato febbrile.

few (fū) *n., agg.* pochi: a —, alcuni, qualche; a good —, un discreto numero; not a —, non pochi. —**er** *agg.* in minor numero.

fiancé (fē'än-sā') *n.* fidanzato.

fiancée (fē'än-sā) *n.* fidanzata.

fib (fĭb) *n.* frottola. *vi.* mentire. —**ber** *n.* mentitore.

fiber (fī'bĕr) *n.* fibra.

fibrous (-brŭs) *agg.* fibroso.

fickle (fĭk''l) *agg.* volubile, incerto, mobile.

fiction (fĭk'shŭn) *n.* finzione, invenzione; narrativa. —**al** *agg.* narrativo, immaginario.

fictitious (fĭk-tĭsh'ŭs) *agg.* fittizio, immaginario.

fiddle (fĭd''l) *n.* violino: to play second —, essere in sottordine a. *vi.* sonare il violino: to — around (*gergo*), gingillarsi.

fiddler (fĭd'lĕr) *n.* violinista.

fidelity (fī-dĕl'ĭ-tĭ) *n.* fedeltà.

fidget (fĭj'ĕt) *vi.* agitarsi, preoccuparsi, essere irrequieto.

fidgety (-tĭ) *agg.* inquieto, irrequieto.

field (fēld) *n.* campo, (*min.*) giacimento; gruppo (*dei cavalli partecipanti a una corsa*): to take the —, entrare in azione; — artillery, artiglieria da campagna; — glass, binocolo.

fiend (fēnd) *n.* demonio, perfido. —**ish** *agg.* demoniaco, perfido.

fierce (fērs) *agg.* accanito, feroce; ardente. —**ness** *n.* violenza; ardore.

fiery (fī'rĭ) *agg.* infiammato, ardente, focoso, infocato.

fifteen (fĭf'tēn') *n., agg.* quindici. —**th** *n., agg.* quindicesimo, (*il*) quindici (*del mese*).

fifth (fĭfth) *n., agg.* quinto; (*il*) cinque (*del mese*).

fifty (fĭf'tĭ) *n., agg.* cinquanta.

fig (fĭg) *n.*fico.—**tree** *n.* (albero di) fico.

fight (fĭt) *n.* battaglia, lotta, zuffa; combattività, forza, aggressività: to show —, reagire. *vt., vi.* (*pass., pp.* fought) avversare, combattere, lottare: to — it out, lottare sino in fondo, liquidare una disputa; to — one's way through, aprirsi un varco.

fighter (fĭt'ĕr) *n.* combattente, lottatore; (*aeron.*) caccia: prize —, pugile, campione di pugilato.

fighting (-ĭng) *n.* combattimento, lotta. *agg.* combattivo, combattente; da combattimento.

figment (fĭg'mĕnt) *n.* finzione; invenzione.

figurative (fĭg'ūr-á-tĭv) *agg.* figurato, metaforico, simbolico.

figure (fĭg'ūr) *n.* figura; volto; disegno; cifra, numero: — of speech, modo di dire; to be good at figures, essere forte in aritmetica, saper fare i conti bene; to cut a poor —, fare una magra figura. *vt.* figurare, raffigurare, immaginare. *vi.* calcolare; figurare; pensare, ritenere: to — on, far conto su, fidarsi di, avere intenzione di; to — out, decifrare, risolvere, capire.

filament (fĭl'á-mĕnt) *n.* filamento.

filch (fĭlch) *vt.* rubare, rubacchiare.

file (fīl) (1) *n.* lima. *vt.* limare.

file (fīl) (2) *n.* incartamento, schedario, raccolta; schieramento; fila, coda: — card, scheda; single —, fila indiana. *vt.* schedare, passare agli atti, presentare (*un'istanza*). *vi.* sfilare; (*pol.*) porre la propria candidatura.

filial (fĭl'ĭ-ǎl) *agg.* filiale.

filigree (fĭl'ĭ-grē) *n.* filigrana.

fill (fĭl) *n.* sufficienza, sazietà; riempitivo, carica. *vt.* riempire; gonfiare; rifornire, saziare; ricoprire (*una carica*); assolvere (*un compito*); otturare (*un dente*): to — up, completare. *vi.* riempirsi, gonfiarsi.

fillet (fĭl'ĕt) *n.* nastro per capelli, fregio; (*cucina*) filetto.

filling (fĭl'ĭng) *n.* riempimento; otturazione (*di dente*).

filly (fĭl'ĭ) *n.* puledra.

film (fĭlm) *n.* velatura; pellicola, velo, patina. *vt.* velare, coprire con pellicola; (*cinema*) filmare. *vi.* velarsi. — strip, proiezione, film illustrativo *per conferenze, ecc.*).

filter (fĭl'tĕr) *n.* filtro. *vt.* filtrare.

filth (fĭlth) *n.* sudiciume. —**iness** *n.* sporcizia.

filthy (fĭl'thĭ) *agg.* sudicio, immondo.
fin (fĭn) *n.* pinna; *(gergo)* cinque dollari.
final (fī'năl) *agg.* finale, ultimo, definitivo, decisivo. **—ly** *avv.* infine, finalmente, definitivamente.
finance (fĭ·năns') *n.* finanza.
financial (fĭ·năn'shăl) *agg.* finanziario.
financier (fĭn·ăn·sḗr') *n.* finanziere.
financing *n.* finanziamento.
finch (fĭnch) *n.* fringuello.
find (fīnd) *n.* scoperta, ritrovamento. *vt.* (*pass.*, *pp.* found) trovare, scoprire; ritenere, giudicare; **to — out**, scoprire, smascherare; **to — fault with**, trovar a ridire su. **—er** *n.* scopritore; *(fot.)* mirino. **—ing** *n.* scoperta, constatazione; sentenza; *(pl.)* utensili da artigiano.
fine (fīn) (1) *n.* multa, ammenda. *vt.* multare.
fine (fīn) (2) *agg.* bello; fine; delicato; lieve; bravo; perfetto, eccellente: **a — boy,** un bravo ragazzo, un ottimo figliolo; **to have a — time,** divertirsi; **— arts,** belle arti. *avv.* bene: **to feel —,** sentirsi bene *o* benone. **—ly** *avv.* finemente. **—ness** *n.* finezza. **—ry** (fīn'ẽr·ĭ) *n.* ornamenti, vestiario appariscente.
finesse (fĭ·nĕs') *n.* finezza, sottigliezza, astuzia, stratagemma.
finger (fĭng'gẽr) *n.* dito: **middle —,** medio; **ring —,** anulare; **little —,** mignolo. *vt.* maneggiare, tastare. **—board** *n.* tastiera, manico *(di violino).* **—nail** *n.* unghia. **—print** *n.* impronta digitale.
finical (fĭn'ĭ·kăl) finicky (-kĭ) *agg.* minuzioso; affettato; pedante.
finish (fĭn'ĭsh) *n.* fine, conclusione; rifinitura, ornamento; educazione. *vt.* rifinire, terminare. *vi.* finire, aver termine. **—ed** *agg.* finito, rifinito.
fink (fĭngk) *n.* *(gergo)* spia; crumiro.
fir (fûr) *n.* abete.
fire (fīr) *n.* fuoco; incendio; ardore: **to be on —,** essere in fiamme; **to set on —,** incendiare. *vt.* bruciare, incendiare; sparare, far scoppiare; *(fam.)* licenziare. *vi.* incendiarsi; infiammarsi; far fuoco. **—arms** *n.pl.* armi da fuoco. **— block,** *(mil.),*sbarramento di fuoco. **—brand** *n.* tizzone. **— department,** corpo dei pompieri. **— engine,** pompa da incendio, carro dei pompieri; **—escape,** scala di sicurezza. **—fly** *n.* lucciola. **— insurance,** assicurazione incendi. **—man** *n.* pompiere, fochista. **—place** *n.* camino. **—proof** *agg.* incombustibile. **—side** *n.* focolare, focolare

domestico. **—wood** *n.* legna da ardere. **—works** *n.pl.* fuochi d'artificio.
firing (fīr'ĭng) *n.* accensione, sparatoria: **— party, — squad,** plotone d'esecuzione.
firm (fûrm) *n.* ditta, azienda. *agg.* saldo, fermo, forte, risoluto. *avv.* fermamente; risolutamente. **—ly** *avv.* fermamente; solidamente. **—ness** *n.* fermezza; solidità.
firmament (fûr'mȧ·mĕnt) *n.* firmamento.
first (fûrst) *n.*, *agg.* primo: **the very —,** il primissimo. *avv.* prima, da principio, per primo, in primo luogo: **at —,** sulle prime; **— and last,** dal principio alla fine: **—class** *agg.* di prima classe. **—rate** *agg.* di prima categoria, di prim'ordine. **—hand** *agg.*, *avv.* di prima mano.
fisc (fĭsk) *n.* fisco. **—al** *agg.* fiscale.
fish (fĭsh) *n.* pesce: **a queer —,** un tipo ambiguo; **neither — nor fowl,** nè carne nè pesce: **— story,** storia incredibile. *vt.*, *vi.* pescare, frugare. **—bone** *n.* lisca di pesce. **—hook** *n.* amo. **—monger** *n.* pescivendolo. **—er, —erman** *n.* pescatore. **—ery** *n.* pesca, luogo pescoso. **—ing** *n.* pesca: **— rod,** canna da pesca; **to go —,** andare a pesca.
fishy (fĭsh'ĭ) *agg.* pescoso; ambiguo, losco; non convincente.
fission (fĭsh'un) *n.* fissione nucleare. **—able** *agg.* fissile.
fissure (fĭsh'ẽr) *n.* fessura, crepa.
fist (fĭst) *n.* pugno.
fit (fĭt) (1) *n.* accesso, attacco, crisi; capriccio: **by fits and starts,** saltuariamente, irregolarmente.
fit (fĭt) (2) *n.* l'adattarsi *(bene o male):* **this coat is a good —,** questa giacca sta a pennello. *agg.* adatto, conveniente, sano, in forma, idoneo: **— to be tied,** infuriato; **to think —,** ritenere opportuno. *vt.* adattare, rendere idoneo, calzare: **to — out,** equipaggiare. *vi.* convenire, adattarsi; attagliarsi, stare a pennello: **to — in with,** coincidere, concordare.
fitful (fĭt'fŏŏl) *agg.* saltuario, irregolare; capriccioso; intermittente.
fitness *n.* convenienza, idoneità, opportunità; *(sport, ecc.)* forma.
fitting (fĭt'ĭng) *n.* aggiustatura, adattamento, montaggio; prova *(di un vestito);* *(pl.)* arredamento; accessori. *agg.* conveniente, appropriato, opportuno.
five (fīv) *n.*, *agg.* cinque.
fiver (-ẽr) *n.* *(fam.)* banconota da cinque dollari.

fix (fĭks) *n.* difficoltà, imbarazzo; imbroglio, truffa: **in a bad —,** nei guai. *vt.* fissare, assicurare, sistemare, aggiustare, riparare. **—ed** *agg.* fisso, permanente, costante. **—ture** (fĭks'tŭr) *n.* infisso; persona (*o cosa*) installata stabilmente: **electric light fixtures,** impianto elettrico.

flabbiness (flăb'ĭ-nĕs) *n.* flaccidezza.

flabby (flăb'ĭ) *agg.* flaccido.

flag (flăg) (1) *n.* bandiera; bandiera ammiraglia: **— of truce,** bandiera bianca. *vt.*, *vi.* imbandierare, pavesare; segnalare con bandierine. **— officer,** ammiraglio. **—ship** *n.* nave ammiraglia. **—staff** *n.* asta di bandiera. **—stone** *n.* lastra di pietra per pavimentazione.

flag (flăg) (2) *vi.* afflosciarsi, penzolare, indebolirsi, languire; rallentare.

flagellate (flăj'ĕ-lāt) *vt.* flagellare.

flagrant (flā'grănt) *agg.* flagrante, clamoroso.

flair (flâr) *n.* fiuto; istinto; acume; attitudine.

flak (flăk) *n.* artiglieria contraerea.

flake (flāk) *n.* fiocco, scaglia, falda: **corn flakes,** fiocchi di granturco. *vt.* sfioccare. *vi.* sfioccarsi.

flaky *agg.* fioccoso, sfaldato.

flamboyant (flăm-boi'ănt) *agg.* fiammeggiante; risplendente; appariscente, vistoso.

flame (flām) *n.* fiamma, fuoco. *vi.* fiammeggiare, infiammarsi: **to — up** (*opp.* **out**), dare in escandescenze.

flaming (flām'ĭng) *agg.* fiammeggiante, ardente: **— red,** rosso acceso, rosso fiamma.

flange (flănj) *n.* orlo, bordo, flangia.

flank (flăngk) *n.* fianco, lato. *vt.* fiancheggiare.

flannel (flăn'ĕl) *n.* flanella.

flap (flăp) *n.* colpo, battito; lembo, patta (*della tasca*); (*aeron.*) ipersostentatore; subbuglio, panico. *vt.* colpire, battere. *vi.* sbattere, penzolare.

flare (flâr) *n.* bagliore, fiammata; accesso (*di collera*); rifrazione; ampiezza, svasatura. *vt.* esibire, ostentare. *vi.* divampare; essere svasato, allargarsi: **to — up, to — out,** dare in escandescenze.

flaring (-ĭng) *agg.* fiammeggiante, accecante; svasato.

flash (flăsh) *n.* splendore, vampata, lampo; ostentazione: **— of hope,** raggio di speranza; **— of lightning,** lampo, saetta; **— of wit,** tratto di spirito; **in a —,** in un baleno. *vt.* trasmettere con segnalazioni lu-

minose, far lampeggiare; far esplodere; mostrare con ostentazione. *vi.* splendere, avvampare, balenare: **to — by,** passare come un lampo. **— bulb,** (*fot.*) lampada per fotolampo. **— gun,** (*fot.*) sincronizzatore del fotolampo. **—ing** *n.* vampata, splendore. *agg.* splendente. **—light** *n.* lampadina tascabile; (*fot.*) fotolampo.

flashy (flăsh'ĭ) *agg.* sgargiante, vistoso.

flask (flȧsk) *n.* fiasco; borraccia.

flat (flăt) *n.* spianata, superficie piana; palmo (*della mano*); appartamento. *agg.* piatto, piano; sgonfio; appiattito; pari; disteso; uniforme; che ha perso l'effervescenza, insipido; abbattuto; reciso, esplicito; (*mus.*) bemolle; stonato: **— denial,** secco rifiuto, un bel no; **— rate,** cifra tonda; **to be — broke,** essere completamente al verde; **to fall —,** cadere disteso; (*fig.*, *di discorsi, ecc.*) cadere nel vuoto. **—foot** *n.* piede piatto; (*gergo*) poliziotto. **—iron** *n.* ferro da stiro. **—ly** *avv.* fred da mente, recisamente, perentoriamente. **—ness** *n.* uniformità, monotonia, banalità. **—top** *n.* portaerei.

flatten (flăt'n) *vt.* appiattire. *vi.* appiattirsi.

flatter (flăt'ĕr) *vt.* lusingare, adulare. **—er** *n.* adulatore. *agg.* lusinghiero.

flattery (flăt'ĕr-ĭ) *n.* adulazione.

flaunt (flônt) *n.* ostentazione. *vt.* esibire, ostentare.

flavor (flā'vĕr) *n.* aroma, sapore, fragranza. *vt.* aromatizzare, profumare. **—less** *agg.* senza aroma.

flaw (flô) *n.* difetto, pecca; fenditura. **—less** *agg.* perfetto, impeccabile.

flax (flăks) *n.* lino. **—en** *agg.* di lino; biondo-chiaro.

flay (flā) *vt.* scorticare.

flea (flē) *n.* pulce: **a — in one's ear,** un rabbuffo, un'umiliazione.

fled (flĕd) *pass.*, *pp.* di **to flee.**

flee (flē) *vt.* (*pass.*, *pp.* **fled**) evitare, schivare. *vi.* fuggire.

fleece (flēs) *n.* vello. *vt.* tosare; defraudare, spogliare.

fleet (flēt) *n.* flotta; (*Ingl.*) braccio di mare, baia. *agg.* rapido, lesto, agile. **—ing** *agg.* fuggevole.

Flemish (flĕm'ĭsh) *agg.* fiammingo.

flesh (flĕsh) *n.* carne; polpa (*di frutto*): **in the —,** in carne ed ossa; **— color,** incarnato. **—iness** *n.* carnosità; pinguedine. **—less** *agg.* scarno.

fleshy (flĕsh'ĭ) *agg.* carnoso, pingue.

flew (floo) *pass.* di **to fly.**

flexibility (flĕk'sĭ-bĭl'ĭ-tĭ) *n.* flessibilità; duttilità.

flexible (flĕk′sĭ·b′l) *agg.* flessibile.

flicker (flĭk′ẽr) *n.* bagliore, barlume; tremolio, guizzo; vibrazione, battito. *vt.* far vacillare. *vi.* vacillare, vibrare, ondeggiare, svolazzare, guizzare. —ing *n.* tremolio. *agg.* tremolante, vacillante, svolazzante, guizzante.

flier (flī′ẽr) *n.* volatore, aviatore; (*S.U.*) volantino; veicolo veloce.

flight (flīt) *n.* fuga, volo; stormo (*di uccelli*); squadriglia (*di aerei*); sciame (*d'insetti*); rampa (*di scale*): to put to —, mettere in fuga; to take —, prender la fuga.

flighty (flīt′ĭ) *agg.* leggero, volubile.

flimflam (flĭm′flăm′) *n.* mistificazione, truffa. *vt.* imbrogliare, truffare.

flimsiness (-nĕs) *n.* leggerezza, inconsistenza, trasparenza; frivolezza.

flimsy (flĭm′zĭ) *agg.* sottile; trasparente; tenue, lieve; inconsistente, frivolo: — excuse, scusa magra. *n.* velina, copia in carta velina.

flinch (flĭnch) *vi.* ritrarsi, sottrarsi; rattrappirsi, contrarsi (*per il dolore*): without flinching, senza battere ciglio.

fling (flĭng) *n.* lancio, frecciata; tentativo: to have a — at, provare, tentare. *vt.* (*pass.*, *pp.* flung) lanciare, spargere: to — away, respingere, buttar via; to — down, gettare in terra, abbattere; to — open, spalancare; to — shut, chiudere sbattendo; to — out, buttar fuori. *vi.* precipitarsi; dibattersi; imbizzarrirsi (*di cavalli*).

flint (flĭnt) *n.* selce, pietra focaia; pietrina (*di accendisigari*).

flip (flĭp) *n.* colpetto, buffetto, schiocco; sorta di zabaione. *agg.* impertinente. *vt.* spingere a ditate, dare un buffetto. *vi.* muoversi a scatti. —per *n.* pinna, natatoia.

flippancy (flĭp′ăn·sĭ) *n.* impertinenza, leggerezza.

flippant (flĭp′ănt) *agg.* impertinente, leggiero.

flirt (flûrt) *n.* civetta (*donna*); moto brusco. *vt.* sventolare; lanciare bruscamente. *vi.* civettare, "flirtare." —ation *n.* civetteria, amoretto.

flit (flĭt) *n.* guizzo. *vi.* fuggire; svolazzare, volteggiare, volar via.

float (flōt) *n.* galleggiante, salvagente. *vt.* far galleggiare, disincagliare; inondare, irrigare, varare. *vi.* fluttuare, galleggiare. —plane *n.* idrovolante.

flock (flŏk) *n.* gregge, branco; stormo (*di uccelli*); fiocco: — of people,

sciame di gente. *vi.* riunirsi *o* affluire in gruppo; sciamare.

floe (flō) *n.* banchisa.

flog (flŏg) *vt.* frustare, fustigare. —ging *n.* fustigazione.

flood (flŭd) *n.* diluvio, inondazione, alta marea. *vt.* inondare, sommergere: —tide *n.* alta marea.

floodgate (flŭd′gāt) *n.* chiusa.

flooding (flŭd′ĭng) *n.* inondazione; emorragia.

floodlight (flŭd′līt′) *n.* riflettore, proiettore.

floor (flōr) *n.* pavimento; piano (*di casa*); tribuna (*in Parlamento*); limite minimo (*di prezzi, ecc.*): — show, numero di varietà (*in un locale notturno*); to have the —, aver la parola. *vt.* pavimentare; atterrare; ridurre al silenzio.

flop (flŏp) *n.* tonfo, caduta, insuccesso. *vi.* scaraventare. *vi.* stramazzare; sventolare; far fiasco.

florin (flŏr′ĭn) *n.* fiorino.

florist (flō′rĭst) *n.* fioraio, floricultore.

floss (flŏs) *n.* bavella; lanugine.

flounce (flouns) *n.* volante (*di gonna*).

flounder (floun′dẽr) *vt.* dibattersi; impappinarsi.

flour (flour) *n.* farina.

flourish (flûr′ĭsh) *n.* ostentazione; infiorazione; svolazzo (*di scrittura*); mulinello (*col bastone, ecc.*). *vt.* infiorare, fiorire; roteare (*un bastone, ecc.*), brandire. *vi.* fiorire, prosperare; fare svolazzi. —ing *agg.* fiorente.

floury (flour′ĭ) *agg.* farinoso.

flow (flō) *n.* flusso, corrente; facilità di parola. *vi.* scorrere; essere fluente; sgorgare, affluire.

flower (flou′ẽr) *n.* fiore. *vt.* infiorare. *vi.* fiorire: — bed, aiuola.

flowery (flou′ẽr·ĭ) *agg.* fiorito.

flowing (flō′ĭng) *agg.* fluente, scorrente, sciolto (*di eloquio*).

flown (flōn) *pp.* di to fly.

flu (flōō) *n.* influenza.

fluctuate (flŭk′tū·āt) *vi.* fluttuare.

fluctuation (-ā′shŭn) *n.* fluttuazione.

flue (flōō) *n.* gola (*del camino*).

fluency (flōō′ĕn·sĭ) *n.* facilità di parola.

fluent (flōō′ĕnt) *agg.* fluente, facile di parola. —ly *avv.* correntemente, speditamente.

fluff (flŭf) *n.* peluria, lanugine; (*teat.*) papera, stecca. *vi.* deventare lanuginoso; (*teat.*) impaperarsi, steccare.

fluffy (flŭf′ĭ) *agg.* lanuginoso; vaporoso.

fluid (flōō′ĭd) *n.*, *agg.* fluido.

fluke (flōōk) *n.* marra (*dell'ancora*); (*ittiol.*) passera; (*fam.*) colpo di fortuna.

flung (flŭng) *pass.*, *pp. di* to fling.
flunk (flŭngk) *vi.* far fiasco. *vt.* espellere: to — out, abbandonare gli studi; ritirarsi.
flunky (flŭngk'ĭ) *n.* lacchè.
fluorescent (floo˘o˘·rĕs'ĕnt) *agg.* fluorescente. *n.* lampada fluorescente.
flush (flŭsh) *n.* rossore; impeto, vigore; (*poker*) colore; straight *o* royal —, scala reale. *agg.* pari, livellato; prosperoso, abbondante; imporporato; vigoroso: — with, allo stesso livello di, a fior di. *vt.* pareggiare, livellare; arrossare; risciacquare, innaffiare. *vi.* arrossire; crescer di livello; affluire; volar via.
fluster (flŭs'tẽr) *vt.* sconcertare.
flute (floot) *n.* flauto; scanalatura. *vt.* scanalare.
flutter (flŭt'ẽr) *n.* tremito, battito (*di ala*), agitazione, orgasmo; speculazione: in a —, in orgasmo. *vt.* agitare. *vi.* svolazzare, sbattere le ali, agitarsi, vibrare.
flux (flŭks) *n.* flusso; dissenteria.
fly (flī) (1) *n.* (*pl.* flies) mosca.
fly (flī) (2) *n.* volo; traiettoria; finta (*per nascondere i bottoni*); (*tip.*) levafoglio. *vt.* (*pass.* flew, *pp.* flown) sfuggire, evitare; far volare. *vi.* volare; scappare, slanciarsi: to — asunder, rompersi, scoppiare; to — at, lanciarsi su; to — away, scappare, volarsene via; to — off the handle, perdere le staffe. to — into a passion, andare in collera.
flyer *vedi* flier.
flying *agg.* volante: — colors, bandiere spiegate; — ground, aerodromo; — bomb, bomba volante, missile; — saucer, disco volante; — wing (*aeron.*), ala volante, tutt'ala.
flyleaf *n.* guardia (*foglio bianco al principio e alla fine di un libro*).
foal (fōl) *n.* puledro.
foam (fōm) *n.* schiuma. *vi.* spumeggiare, schiumare: — rubber, gommapiuma.
focal (fō'kăl) *agg.* focale.
focus (fō'kŭs) *n.* fuoco (*della lente*). *vt.* mettere a fuoco. —ing *n.* messa a fuoco.
fodder (fŏd'ẽr) *n.* foraggio. [fuoco.
foe (fō) *n.* nemico, avversario.
foetus (fē'tŭs) *n.* feto, embrione.
fog (fŏg) *n.* nebbia; confusione, oscurità. *vt.* annebbiare, offuscare, confondere. *vi.* annebbiarsi, confondersi:—horn *n.* sirena (acustica).
foggy (fŏg'ĭ) *agg.* nebbioso, oscuro.
fogy (fō'gĭ) *n.* barbogio, persona retrograda.
foil (foil) *n.* lamina metallica, amalgama (*degli specchi*); sconfitta,

scacco; risalto; (*scherma*) fioretto. *vt.* frustrare.
fold (fōld) (1) *n.* piega, ripiegatura. *vt.* piegare, avvolgere, stringere, abbracciare: to — one's arms, incrociare le braccia. *vi.* piegarsi; fallire, chiudere i battenti.
fold (fōld) (2) *n.* ovile, recinto.
-fold (3) *suff.*: tenfold, dieci volte, dieci volte tanto; manifold, molteplice, multiforme.
foldboat *vedi* faltboat.
folder (fōl'dẽr) *n.* pieghevole (*stampato*); cartella, raccoglitore; piegatrice.
folding *agg.* pieghevole: — screen, paravento.
foliage (fō'lĭ·ĭj) *n.* fogliame.
folio (fō'lĭ·ō) *n.* folio.
folk (fōk) *n.* gente; popolo; (*pl.*) persone di famiglia: — dance, danza popolare. —lore *n.* folclore; tradizioni popolari; colore locale.
follow (fŏl'ō) *vt.* seguire, inseguire; esercitare (*una professione*): to — suit, seguire l'esempio. *vi.* susseguirsi, derivare di conseguenza. —er *n.* seguace, imitatore; corteggiatore. —ing *n.* seguito. *agg.* seguente.
folly (fŏl'ĭ) *n.* pazzia, sciocchezza.
foment (fō·mĕnt') *vt.* fomentare.
fond (fŏnd) *agg.* appassionato, amante (*di*); affettuoso: — of, affezionato a.
fondle (fŏn'd'l) *vt.* vezzeggiare, accarezzare.
fondly *avv.* teneramente, appassionatamente.
fondness *n.* tenerezza; passione, propensione.
font (fŏnt) *n.* fonte battesimale, acquasantiera; (*tip.*) serie di caratteri.
food (food) *n.* cibo, alimento.
foodstuff (food'stŭf') *n.* commestibili, derrate.
fool (fool) *n.* sciocco, tonto; ingenuo; buffone: All Fools' Day, primo d'aprile; to make a — of oneself, fare una figura da sciocco; to play the —, fare lo sciocco; fare il tonto. *vt.* ingannare, mistificare: to — away, sperperare. *vi.* fare lo sciocco, scherzare. —hardy *agg.* temerario. —ish *agg.* sciocco, stolto. —ishness *n.* stoltezza. —proof *agg.* infallibile, a tutta prova.
foolscap (foolz'kăp') *n.* carta protocollo.
foot (foot) *n.* (*pl.* feet) piede; base (*di colonna*); falda (*di collina*); (*mil.*) fanteria: on —, a piedi; to put one's — in it, fare una papera. *vt.* pagare (*un conto*). *vi.* andare a

piedi, ballare: to — up to, ammontare a. —ball, n. pallone, gioco del calcio. —board n. predellino. —fall n. passo, rumor di passi. —ing n. punto d'appoggio, rapporti, base: to miss one's —, mettere un piede in fallo; on an equal —, su piede di parità; to be on a good — with, essere in buoni rapporti con. —lights n.pl. (teat.) ribalta. —man n. domestico; (mil.) fantaccino. —note n. nota a piè di pagina. —path n. sentiero, passaggio pedonale, marciapiede. —print n. orma. —step n. passo, orma, vestigio. —stool n. sgabello. —way n. passaggio pedonale.

fop (fŏp) n. persona fatua. —**pish** agg. fatuo, affettato, ricercato.

for (fôr) prep. per, a, di: as — him, in quanto a lui; but — him, se non fosse stato per lui; — all that, nonostante ciò; — the present, per adesso. cong. perchè, poichè.

forage (fŏr'ĭj) n. foraggio. vt. saccheggiare. vi. foraggiare.

foray (fŏr'ā) n. incursione, saccheggio, razzia. vt., vi. razziare.

forbad, **forbade** (fôr·băd') pass. di to forbid.

forbear (fôr·bâr') vt. (pass. forbore, pp. forborne) evitare, desistere da, trattenersi da, sopportare. vi. astenersi; esser paziente. —ance n. sopportazione, indulgenza.

forbid (fôr·bĭd') vt. (pass. forbad, forbade, pp. forbidden) vietare, impedire, proibire. —den agg. vietato. —ding n. pauroso (che fa paura); severo, riservato; repellente.

forbore (fôr'bōr') pass. di to forbear.

force (fôrs) n. forza, vigore; validità: in —, in vigore, vigente. vt. forzare, costringere: to — in, sfondare; to — something on, imporre qualcosa a; to — one's way into, entrare con la forza in; to — out, scacciare con la forza, far uscire di forza.

forced (fôrst) agg. forzato, sforzato.

forceful (fôrs'fōōl) agg. forte, possente; violento; energico; efficace.

forceps (fôr'sĕps) n.pl. (chir.) forcipe.

forcible (fôr'sĭ·b'l) agg. coercitivo; efficace, convincente.

forcibly (-blĭ) avv. con forza, per forza, efficacemente, in modo convincente.

ford (fôrd) n. guado. vt. guadare.

fore (fôr) n. parte anteriore. agg. anteriore; (naut.) di prua. avv. a prua; avanti. prep., cong. prima.

forearm n. (fôr'ärm') avambraccio. vt. (-ärm') premunire.

forebear (fôr'bâr) n. (gen. al pl.) antenato.

forebode (fôr·bōd') vt. presagire, predire.

foreboding (-bōd'ĭng) n. presagio, presentimento.

forecast (fôr'kåst) n. presagio, pronostico. vt. (kåst') prevedere, pronosticare.

forefather (fôr'fä'thẽr) n. avo.

forefinger (fôr'fĭng'ẽr) n. dito indice.

forefoot (fôr'fŏŏt') n. piede anteriore (di animale).

forego (fôr·gō') vt., vi. (pass. forewent, pp. foregone) precedere.

foregoing (-gō'ĭng) agg. precedente.

foregone (fôr·gôn') agg. previsto, scontato: — conclusion, conclusione inevitabile, partito preso.

foreground (fôr'ground') n. primo piano (di una visuale).

forehead (fôr'ĕd) n. fronte.

foreign (fŏr'ĭn) agg. straniero, estero, forestiero, estraneo: Foreign Office, Ministero degli Esteri; — to one's nature, estraneo alla propria indole; — trade, commercio con l'estero; —born, nato all'estero. —er n. straniero.

foreleg (fôr'lĕg') n. zampa anteriore.

forelock (fôr'lŏk') n. ciuffo (di capelli): to take time by the —, cogliere il momento opportuno.

foreman (fôr'măn) n. (pl. foremen) capo-operaio, caposquadra; capo dei giurati.

foremost (fôr'mōst) agg. anteriore; primo, principale. avv. in avanti; innanzi tutto.

forename (fôr'nām) n. nome di battesimo.

forenoon (fôr'nōōn') n. mattino, mattinata.

forerun (fŏr·rŭn') vt. precedere, precorrere, presagire. —ner n. araldo, precursore; antenato; presagio.

foresaw pass. di to foresee.

foresee (fôr·sē') vt. (pass. foresaw, pp. foreseen) prevedere.

foresight (fôr'sīt') n. previdenza; mirino (d'arma).

forest (fôr'ĕst) n. foresta. —er n. guardaboschi; abitore della foresta. — ranger, guardia forestale. —ry n. silvicultura.

forestall (fôr·stôl') vt. prevenire; (comm.) accaparrare, incettare.

foretaste (fôr'tåst) n. pregustazione; primo assaggio. vt. pregustare.

foretell (fôr·tĕl') vt. predire.

forethought (fôr'thôt') n. previdenza.

foretold pass. e pp. di to foretell.

forever (fôr·ĕv'ẽr) avv. per sempre; sempre, incessantemente.

forewarn (fŏr'wôrn') vt. preavvisare.

forfeit (fôr'fĭt) n. multa, pena; perdita (di un diritto); confisca. vt. perdere (un diritto).

forgave pass. di to forgive.

forge (fôrj) n. fucina. vt. forgiare, inventare (notizie); alterare, contraffare.

forger (fôr'jĕr) n. falsario. [fare.

forgery (fôr'jĕr·ĭ) n. falso, contraffazione.

forget (fŏr·gĕt') vt., vi. (pass. forgot, pp. forgot, forgotten) dimenticare: to — oneself, perdere il dominio di sè, mancare alla propria dignità.

forgetful (fŏr·gĕt'fŏŏl) agg. dimentico, smemorato. —ness n. oblio, smemorataggine.

forget-me-not n. miosòtide.

forgive (fŏr·gĭv') vt. (pass. forgave, pp. forgiven) perdonare. —ness n. perdono, indulgenza.

forgiving agg. clemente, misericordioso, indulgente.

forgo (fŏr·gō') vt. (pass. forwent, pp. forgone) astenersi da, rinunciare a.

forgot (fŏr·gŏt') pass. di to forget.

forgotten pp. di to forget.

fork (fôrk) n. forchetta; forca; biforcazione; forcella (di ciclo). vt. inforcare. vi. biforcarsi, diramarsi.

forlorn (fŏr·lôrn') agg. afflitto, desolato, sperduto.

form (fôrm) n. forma; figura; formalità; modulo; (Ingl.) banco di scuola, classe (scolastica): blank —, modulo da riempire o in bianco. vt. formare, costituire. vi. concretarsi, prender forma; disporsi.

formal (fôr'măl) agg. formale, formalista; di etichetta. —ity (-măl'ĭtĭ) n. formalità, affettazione: to stand on —, fare cerimonie. —ly avv. formalmente, con formalismo.

formation (fôr·mā'shŭn) n. formazione.

former (fôr'mĕr) agg., pron. precedente, antico, ex, il primo (di due). —ly avv. precedentemente, in passato.

formidable (fôr'mĭ·dá·b'l) agg. formidabile, temibile.

formula (fôr'mū·lá) n. formula.

formulate (-lāt) vt. formulare.

forsake (fŏr·sāk') vt. (pass. forsook, pp. forsaken) abbandonare, disertare.

forsaken (fŏr·sāk'ĕn) agg. abbandonato, desolato. pp. di to forsake.

forsook pass. di to forsake.

fort (fôrt) n. forte, fortezza.

forth (fōrth) avv. avanti, in avanti, fuori; successivamente: from this time —, d'ora in poi; to come —,

venir fuori; and so —, e così via. —coming agg. prossimo, imminente. —right agg. retto, franco, esplicito. avv. immediatamente, esplicitamente. —with avv. sùbito, al più presto.

fortieth (fôr'tĭ·ĕth) n., agg. quarantesimo.

fortification (fôr'tĭ·fĭ·kā'shŭn) n. fortificazione.

fortify (fôr'tĭ·fī) vt. fortificare, rafforzare.

fortifying agg. corroborante, fortificante.

fortitude (fôr'tĭ·tūd) n. coraggio, forza d'animo.

fortnight (fôrt'nīt; -nĭt) n. quattordici giorni: a — ago, due settimane or sono; today — (Ingl.), fra due settimane.

fortress (fôr'trĕs) n. fortezza.

fortuitous (fôr·tū'ĭ·tŭs) agg. fortuito. avv. fortuitamente.

fortunate (fôr'tŭ·nĭt) agg. fortunato, propizio. —ly avv. fortunatamente.

fortune (fôr'tŭn) n. fortuna, sorte; patrimonio: —hunter n. cacciatore di dote; —teller, chiromante.

forty (fôr'tĭ) n., agg. quaranta.

forum (fō'rŭm) n. fòro.

forward (fôr'wĕrd) agg. avanzato; ardente; precoce; impertinente, presuntuoso. avv. avanti, in avanti. vt. spedire, inviare, far proseguire, promuovere, agevolare. —er n. speditore, spedizioniere; promotore.

fossil (fŏs'ĭl) n., agg. fossile.

foster (fŏs'tĕr) vt. allevare, nutrire; promuovere, favorire, incoraggiare, fomentare. — brother, fratello di latte. —child, —ling n. bimbo a balia o adottivo. — father, balio. — mother, balia. — sister, sorella di latte.

fought (fôt) pass. e pp. di to fight.

foul (foul) agg. sporco; immondo; torbido; fetido; infetto; brutto; osceno; (sport) irregolare, scorretto: to fall — of, scontrarsi con, aggredire; — ball, fallo, irregolarità; — play, dolo, condotta sleale o disonesta; (sport) fallo, gioco scorretto (pugilato), colpo proibito. vt. insudiciare; incrostare; speronare; aggrovigliare. —mouthed agg. triviale. —ness n. sporcizia, turpitudine.

found (found) (1) pass., pp. di to find.

found (found) (2) vt. fondare, gettare le basi di; fondere; basare. —ation n. fondazione, fondamenta, fondamento; (cosmetico) base: —garment, bustino per donna; reggicalze.

founder (1) (foun'dĕr) n. fondatore; fonditore.

founder (2) *vt.* affondare, azzoppare (*un cavallo*). *vi.* sprofondare, naufragare; azzopparsi.

foundling (found'ling) *n.* trovatello.

foundry (foun'drĭ) *n.* fonderia.

fountain (foun'tĭn) *n.* fontana, sorgente; serbatoio: — pen, penna stilografica.

four (fōr) *n.*, *agg.* quattro: on all fours, carponi. —score *n.*, *agg.* ottanta.

fourteen (fōr'tēn') *n.*, *agg.* quattordici.

fourth (fōrth) *n.*, *agg.* quarto.

fowl (foul) *n.* pollo, pollame.

fox (fŏks) *n.* volpe. *vi.* dissimulare.

foxhole (fŏks'hōl) *n.* (*mil.*) buca da tiratore, buca-ricovero.

foxy (fŏk'sĭ) *agg.* astuto.

fraction (frăk'shŭn) *n.* frazione.

fracture (frăk'tŭr) *n.* frattura, rottura. *vt.* fratturare, rompere.

fragment (frăg'mĕnt) *n.* frammento.

fragrance (frā'grăns) *n.* fragranza.

fragrant (frā'grănt) *agg.* fragrante.

frail (frāl) *agg.* debole, fragile. —ness, —ty *n.* fragilità.

frame (frām) *n.* cornice, telaio; struttura; corporatura, scheletro; (*fot.*) fotogramma; (*cinema*) inquadratura: — of mind, stato d'animo; — of reference, teoria, opinione, punto di vista; — house, casa con incastellatura di legno. *vt.* costruire, montare, formare; incorniciare; predisporre fraudolentemente (*competizioni, ecc.*); incriminare con false accuse; riuscire. —work *n.* struttura, scheletro; (*edil.*) traliccio; (*mecc., naut.*) ossatura; teoria.

franchise (frăn'chĭz) *n.* franchigia; diritto di voto; esenzione.

frank (frăngk) *n.* franchigia (*postale*). *agg.* franco, sincero. *vt.* esentare, spedire in franchigia. —ly *avv.* francamente. —ness *n.* franchezza.

frankfurter (frăngk'fẽr-tẽr) *n.* salsiccia.

frantic (frăn'tĭk) *agg.* frenetico; pazzo (*di gioia o di dolore*). —ally *avv.* freneticamente.

fraternal (frȧ-tûr'năl) *agg.* fraterno.

fraternity (frȧ-tûr'nĭ-tĭ) *n.* fraternità, confraternita.

fraternize (frăt'ẽr-nīz) *vi.* affratellarsi; fraternizzare.

fraud (frôd) *n.* frode, impostura; impostore. —ulent (frôd'ū-lĕnt) *agg.* fraudolento, doloso.

fraught (frôt) *agg.* carico (*di*): — with danger, pieno di pericoli.

fray (frā) (1) *n.* zuffa, lite, conflitto.

fray (frā) (2) *n.* logoratura. *vt.* logorare. *vi.* logorarsi. —ed *agg.* logoro.

freak (frēk) *n.* capriccio, bizzarria; scherzo di natura; striatura.

freckle (frĕk''l) *n.* lentiggine, efelide. *vi.* divenire lentigginoso.

freckled (frĕk''ld) freckly (frĕk'lĭ) *agg.* lentigginoso.

free (frē) *agg.* libero, indipendente; gratuito; esente; disinvolto; prodigo; esplicito; impudente: — on board (F.O.B.), franco a bordo; — of charge, gratis, gratuito; postage —, franco di porto; to give someone a — hand, lasciare a uno mano libera; to make — with, appropriarsi. *avv.* liberamente; gratuitamente. *vt.* (*pass., pp.* freed) liberare, emancipare, esimere; svincolare. —dom *n.* libertà, indipendenza; disinvoltura; esenzione. —ly *avv.* liberamente, apertamente; gratuitamente; generosamente. —mason *n.* massone; —masonry *n.* massoneria.

freeze (frēz) *vt.* (*pass.* froze, *pp.* frozen) gelare, congelare. *vi.* congelarsi, ghiacciarsi.

freezer (frēz'ẽr) *n.* congelante; frigorifero; cella frigorifera.

freezing (frēz'ĭng) *agg.* gelido, congelante: — point, punto di congelamento.

freight (frāt) *n.* carico mercantile; nolo marittimo, trasporto. *vt.* caricare, trasportare, noleggiare (*una nave*): — car, vagone merci; — train, treno merci. —er *n.* spedizioniere, noleggiatore; vapore mercantile.

French (french) *n.* il francese (*lingua*): the —, i francesi. *agg.* francese: to take — leave, svignarsela; — beans, fagiolini; — window, porta-finestra. —man *n.* francese (*maschio*).

frenzied (frĕn'zĭd) *agg.* frenetico, delirante.

frenzy (frĕn'zĭ) *n.* frenesia, delirio.

frequency (frē'kwĕn-sĭ) *n.* frequenza: — modulation (*radio*), modulazione di frequenza.

frequent (frē'kwĕnt) *agg.* frequente. *vt.* (frē-kwĕnt') frequentare. —ly *avv.* spesso, di frequente.

fresco (frĕs'kō) *n.* affresco. *vt.* affrescare.

fresh (frĕsh) *agg.* fresco, nuovo, recente; inesperto; insolente: — water, acqua dolce.

freshen (frĕsh'ĕn) *vt.* rinfrescare. *vi.* rinfrescarsi.

freshly (frĕsh'lĭ) *avv.* di fresco, recentemente, da poco tempo.

freshman (frĕsh'măn) *n.* novellino; studente del primo anno.

freshness *n.* freschezza; impudenza, insolenza.

fret (frĕt) *n.* erosione; agitazione, inquietudine; tasto (*di strumento a* *corde*); greca, fregio. *vt.* strofinare, logorare, agitare; infastidire; decorare con greca. *vi.* agitarsi, fremere, logorarsi, amareggiarsi. —ful *agg.* agitato, inquieto, impaziente.

friar (frī'ẽr) *n.* frate.

friction (frĭk'shŭn) *n.* attrito, frizione.

Friday (frī'dĭ) *n.* venerdì: Good Friday, Venerdì Santo.

fried (frīd) *pass.*, *pp. di* to fry.

friend (frĕnd) *n.* amico, amica. —less *agg.* senza amici, abbandonato. —liness *n.* bonomia, cordialità. —ly *agg.* amichevole, affabile: friendly society, società di mutuo soccorso. —ship *n.* amicizia.

frigate (frĭg'ĭt) *n.* fregata (*nave*).

fright (frīt) *n.* spavento, orrore.

frighten (frīt''n) *vt.* spaventare. —ed *agg.* spaventato: to become —, spaventarsi.

frightful (frīt'fŏŏl) *agg.* spaventevole, straordinario. —ly *avv.* terribilmente; straordinariamente.

frigid (frĭj'ĭd) *agg.* freddo, frigido, glaciale.

fringe (frĭnj) *n.* frangia; orlo; periferia. *agg.* periferico; secondario. *vt.* orlare, ornare di frange.

frippery (frĭp'ẽr.ĭ) *n.* ostentazione; cianfrusaglie, fronzoli.

frisk (frĭsk) *n.* capriola, sgambetto. *vt.* (*gergo*) perquisire. *vi.* far capriole, sgambettare.

frisky (frĭs'kĭ) *agg.* vivace, allegro.

fritter (frĭt'ẽr) *n.* frittella; frammento, brandello. *vt.* sminuzzare: to — away, sperperare, sparpagliare.

frivolity (frĭ-vŏl'ĭ.tĭ) *n.* frivolezza.

frivolous (frĭv'ō-lŭs) *agg.* frivolo.

frizzle (frĭz''l) *vt.* arricciare, increspare.

fro (frō) *avv.* indietro: to and —, avanti e indietro.

frock (frŏk) *n.* vestito, tunica, saio. — coat, finanziera (*giacca*).

frog (frŏg) (1) *n.* rana, ranocchio: — in the throat, mal di gola, rauco.

frog (frŏg) (2) *n.* alamaro. [cedine.

frogman (frŏg'măn') *n.* sommozzatore, uomo rana.

frolic (frŏl'ĭk) *n.* scherzo, farsa. *vi.* divertirsi, fare allegria. —some *agg.* allegro, giocoso.

from (frŏm) *prep.* da, sin da, per, a causa di: to take something away —, portare via qualcosa a.

front (frŭnt) *n.* fronte; faccia, facciata; sparato (*di camicia*); apparenza; prestanome, paravento. *agg.* frontale, di fronte, anteriore: in — of, davanti a. *vt.*, *vi.* affrontare; guardare su, essere di fronte a; essere esposto (*verso*).

frontier (frŭn'tẽr') *n.* frontiera. *agg.* di frontiera, confinario.

frost (frŏst) *n.* gelo, brina. *vt.* congelare, coprire di brina; smerigliare (*vetri*); candire. —iness *n.* gelo. —ing *n.* cappa per dolci.

frosty (frŏs'tĭ) *agg.* brinato, gelato.

froth (frŏth) *n.* schiuma, spuma. *vi.* spumeggiare, spumare, schiumare: to — at the mouth, schiumare di rabbia.

frown (froun) *n.* cipiglio, sguardo corrucciato. *vi.* aggrottare le sopracciglia, accigliarsi: to — on, upon, essere contrario a, disapprovare. —ing *agg.* accigliato, corrucciato.

froze (frōz) *pass. di* to freeze.

frozen (frō'z'n) *agg.* gelato; congelato; glaciale. *pp. di* to freeze.

frugal (frŏŏ'găl) *agg.* frugale, economo.

fruit (frŏŏt) *n.* frutto, frutta: — tree, albero da frutta. *vt.*, *vi.* fruttare, fruttificare. —ful *agg.* fruttifero. —less *agg.* inutile, improduttivo.

frustrate (frŭs'trāt) *vt.* frustrare.

frustration (frŭs·trā'shŭn) *n.* frustramento, delusione, insuccesso.

fry (frī) *n.* fritto, frittura: small —, frittura minuta. *vt.*, *vi.* (*pass.*, *pp.* fried) friggere. —ing pan, padella.

fuddle (fŭd''l) *vt.* ubriacare, stordire.

fuel (fū'ĕl) *n.* combustibile, carburante. *vt.*, *vi.* rifornire, rifornirsi di carburante.

fugitive (fū'jĭ.tĭv) *n.* fuggiasco. *agg.* fuggevole.

fulfill (fŏŏl-fĭl') *vt.* compiere, adempiere, realizzare, soddisfare. —ment *n.* adempimento, realizzazione.

full (fŏŏl) *agg.* pieno, completo, colmo, abbondante; ampio: at — speed, a gran velocità; in —, al completo, per intero; to the —, al massimo; —-blooded, di pura razza; —-dress, vestito da cerimonia; alta tenuta; —-grown, adulto, maturo; —-fledged, maturo, completo; — stop, punto, punto fermo. *avv.* molto, in pieno, perfettamente: — in the face, in pieno viso; to know — well, sapere benissimo.

fullness (-nĕs) *n.* pienezza, pieno.

fully (fŏŏl'ĭ) *avv.* pienamente, completamente.

fumble (fŭm'b'l) *vt.*, *vi.* maneggiare goffamente; annaspare.

fume (fūm) *n.* esalazione. *vt.* esalare. *vi.* evaporare; fremere (*per la collera*).

fumigate (fū'mĭ.gāt) *vt.* fumigare, disinfettare.

fun (fŭn) *n.* allegria, divertimento, scherzo: to have —, divertirsi; to make — of, farsi beffe di, mettere in ridicolo; **in —,** per scherzo; **full of —,** molto divertito.

function (fŭngk'shăn) *n.* funzione, attribuzione; cerimonia. *vi.* funzionare.

fund (fŭnd) *n.* fondo, riserva: **sinking —,** fondo di ammortamento. *vt.* consolidare.

fundamental (fŭn'dá·měn'tăl) *n.* fondamento. *agg.* fondamentale.

funeral (fū'nĕr·ăl) *n.* funerale. *agg.* funebre, mortuario.

fungus (fŭng'gŭs) *n.* fungo.

funk (fŭngk) *n.* paura, panico: **to be in a blue —,** avere una paura del diavolo.

funnel (fŭn'ĕl) *n.* imbuto; ciminiera.

funny (fŭn'ĭ) *agg.* strano, buffo, faceto: **the funnies** (*giorn.*), i fumetti.

fur (fûr) *n.* pelliccia, pelo; patina (*della lingua*). *vt.* impellicciare, ornare di pelliccia.

furious (fū'rĭ·ŭs) *agg.* furibondo, accanito.

furl (fûrl) *vt.* ammainare, arrotolare. *vi.* arrotolarsi.

furlough (fûr'lō) *n.* licenza: **sick —,** licenza di convalescenza. *vt.* (*mil.*) mandare in licenza.

furnace (fûr'nĭs) *n.* fornace.

furnish (fûr'nĭsh) *vt.* fornire; ammobiliare.

furniture (fûr'nĭ·tûr) *n.* mobilia: **a piece of —,** un mobile.

furrier (fûr'ĭ·ẽr) *n.* pellicciaio.

furrow (fûr'ō) *n.* solco, scìa. *vt.* solcare, arare.

furry (fûr'ĭ) *agg.* peloso; patinoso.

further (fûr'thẽr) *agg.* ulteriore, successivo, più lontano; altro, nuovo: **the — end,** l'estremità. *avv.* inoltre, più avanti, ulteriormente, al di là. *vt.* favorire, assecondare. **—more** *avv.* per di più, d'altronde, inoltre.

furthest (fûr'thĕst) *agg.* estremo, (*il*) più lontano. *avv.* alla massima distanza.

furtive (fûr'tĭv) *agg.* furtivo, evasivo, subdolo.

fury (fū'rĭ) *n.* furore, frenesia, furia.

fuse (fūz) *n.* fusibile; spoletta: **delayed action —,** spoletta a tempo. *vt., vi.* fondere; far esplodere, fondersi.

fuselage (fū'zĕ·lĭj) *n.* fusoliera.

fuss (fŭs) *n.* agitazione inutile, trambusto; faccendone: **to make a —,** agitarsi sproporzionatamente. *vi.* inquietarsi, affannarsi; far confusione.

fussy (fŭs'ĭ) *agg.* meticoloso; inquieto, confusionario, concitato; vistoso.

fustian (fŭs'chăn) *n.* fustagno.

futile (fū'tĭl) *agg.* futile, insignificante.

future (fū'tûr) *n., agg.* futuro, avvenire.

fuze (fūz) *vedi* **fuse.**

fuzz (fŭz) *n.* lanugine, pulviscolo.

fuzzy (fŭz'ĭ) *agg.* lanuginoso; confuso.

G

gab (găb) *n.* parlantina, chiacchiera. *vi.* ciarlare.

gabble (găb'l) *n.* borbottio, discorso confuso. *vi.* borbottare, affastellar parole.

gable (gā'b'l) *n.* (*arch.*) frontone: **— roof,** tetto a due spioventi.

gad (găd) *vi.* bighellonare.

gadfly (găd'flī') *n.* tafano.

gadget (găj'ĕt) *n.* aggeggio, meccanismo.

gag (găg) *n.* bavaglio; scherzo, trovata, improvvisazione; battuta *o* scenetta comica. *vt., vi.* far venire (*o* avere) i conati, dare (*o* avere) la nausea; imbavagliare; improvvisare battute; mistificare. **—man** *n.* comico, improvvisatore.

gage (gāj) *n.* scommessa, pegno. *vt.* scommettere, dare in pegno.

gaiety (gā'ĕ·tĭ) *n.* allegria, gaiezza.

gaily (gā'lĭ) *avv.* allegramente, vivacemente; vistosamente.

gain (gān) *n.* guadagno, vantaggio. *vt.* guadagnare, ottenere, vincere. *vi.* migliorare, fare progressi: **to —**

on, upon, guadagnar terreno su. **—ings** *n.pl.* utili, profitti.

gainsay (gān'sā') *vt.* contraddire.

gait (gāt) *n.* andatura.

galaxy (găl'ak·sĭ) *n.* galàssia, Via Lattea.

gale (gāl) *n.* vento, brezza, bufera.

gall (gôl) *n.* fiele, bile; rovello, stizza. *vt., vi.* irritare, infastidire: **— bladder,** vescica biliare.

gallant (găl'ănt) *n.* eroe; uomo galante, amante, seduttore. *agg.* ardito, nobile; galante. **—ry** *n.* ardimento, nobiltà; galanteria.

gallery (găl'ẽr·ĭ) *n.* galleria, pinacoteca; corridoio.

galley (găl'ĭ) *n.* galera; cucina di nave; (*tip.*) vantaggio: **— proof,** bozza in colonna; **— slave,** galeotto.

gallon (găl'ăn) *n.* gallone (*Ingh.* = litro 4,546; *S.U.* = litro 3,785).

gallop (găl'ŭp) *n.* galoppo. *vi.* galoppare.

gallows (găl'ōz) *n.* forca: **— bird,** pendaglio da forca.

galore (gá·lōr') *n.* abbondanza; *avv.* in abbondanza, a volontà.

galosh (gà·lŏsh') n. caloscia.
gamble (găm'b'l) n. gioco d'azzardo, rischio. vt., vi. giocare d'azzardo, speculare, rischiare, puntare.
gambler (găm'blĕr) n. giocatore.
gambling (găm'blĭng) n. gioco d'azzardo.
gambol (găm'bŭl) n. piroetta, capriola vi. piroettare.
game (găm) n. gioco, partita; cacciagione, selvaggina: to die —, resistere fino in fondo; to make a — of, burlarsi di. agg. di caccia; coraggioso. vi. giocare d'azzardo. — room, sala di ricreazione, sala da gioco.
gamut (găm'ŭt) n. gamma.
gander (găn'dĕr) n. maschio dell'oca.
gandy dancer (găn'dĭ) n. (ferr.) manovale; lavoratore stagionale.
gang (găng) n. banda, associazione a delinquere; squadra (di operai); assortimento (di utensili). vi. raggrupparsi. —ster n. bandito.
gangplank (găng'plăngk') n. (naut.) palanca; scalandrone; plancia di sbarco.
gangrene (găng'grēn) n. cancrena. vt., vi. incancrenire.
gangway (găng'wā') n. passaggio, corridoio; (naut.) passerella, barcarizzo.
gantlet (gŏnt'lĕt) n. bastonatura, fustigazione, tortura: to run the —, affrontare critiche severe.
gaol (jāl) n. carcere.
gap (găp) n. breccia, apertura, fessura, crepaccio; lacuna.
gape (găp; găp; găp) n. squarcio; apertura della bocca, stupore; sbadiglio. vi. aprirsi, essere aperto; aprire la bocca, restare a bocca aperta (per la meraviglia, ecc.): to — at, guardare a bocca aperta.
garage (gà·räzh' [S.U.], găr'ĭj [Ingl.]) n. autorimessa.
garb (gärb) n. vestiario, tenuta. vt. vestire.
garbage (gär'bĭj)n. rifiuti, immondizia.
garden (gär'd'n) n. giardino. vt., vi. coltivare a giardino, darsi al giardinaggio. —er n. giardiniere.
gargle (gär'g'l) n. gargarismo. vt., vi. gargarizzare, gargarizzarsi.
gargoyle (gär'goil) n. garguglia (mascherone da grondaia); (fig.) mascherone.
garish (gär'ĭsh) agg. sgargiante, vistoso.
garland (gär'lănd) n. ghirlanda.
garlic (gär'lĭk) n. aglio.
garment (gär'mĕnt) n. indumento.
garnish (gär'nĭsh) n. guarnizione, contorno. vt. guarnire, adornare.
garret (găr'ĕt) n. soffitta, abbaino.

garrison (găr'ĭ·sŭn) n. guarnigione, presidio: — state, stato militarista. vt. presidiare.
garter (gär'tĕr) n. giarrettiera.
gas (găs) n. gas; benzina: — burner, becco a gas; — stove, fornello a gas; — tar, catrame. —eous agg. gassoso.
gash (găsh) n. squarcio. vt. squarciare.
gasoline (găs'ō·lēn) n. benzina.
gasp (gàsp) n. anelito, fiato sospeso, esclamazione soffocata. vi., boccheggiare, soffocare un'esclamazione: to — for breath, ansimare.
gate (gāt) n. porta, portone, cancello. —way n. andito, portone.
gather (găth'ĕr) vt. raccogliere, cogliere; concludere, dedurre: to — dust, impolverarsi. vi. riunirsi, venire a maturazione (di ascesso). —ing n. riunione, assemblea, raccolta; ascesso.
gaudy (gôd'ĭ) agg. vistoso, sgargiante.
gauge (gāj) n. portata, capacità, misura base; (ferr.) scartamento. vt. misurare, valutare.
gaunt (gônt; gänt) agg. magro, sparuto.
gauntlet (gônt'lĕt) n. manopola: to take up the —, raccogliere una sfida; to throw down the —, lanciare la sfida.
gauze (gôz) n. garza, velo.
gave (gāv) pass. di to give.
gawk (gôk) n. sciocco, persona goffa. vi. fissare con occhi imbambolati.
gawky (gôk'ĭ) agg. goffo, impacciato.
gay (gā) agg. gaio, allegro; vistoso, colorito. —ety n. gaiezza, allegria.
gaze (gāz) n. sguardo fisso. vi. guardare fissamente.
gazelle (gà·zĕl') n. gazzella.
gazette (gà·zĕt') n. gazzetta.
gazetteer (găz'ĕ·tẽr') n. dizionario geografico; giornalista.
gear (gẽr) n. ingranaggio, congegno, meccanismo, innesto (di ingranaggi); (auto) marcia; attrezzatura; equipaggiamento, vestiario; moltiplica (di bicicletta, ecc.): low —, prima; high —, quarta, presa diretta; —shift lever, leva del cambio; in —, ingranato; out of —, disinnestato, guasto; — box, scatola del cambio; — case, copricatena. vt. innestare, ingranare; mettere in movimento; preparare, mettere a punto, organizzare, coordinare: to — up, accelerare, far accelerare. vi. combaciare, ingranarsi; organizzarsi; adattarsi.
gee (jē) inter. santo cielo!, caspita!, mamma mia!

geese (gēs) pl. di goose.
gelatin (jĕl'ȧ·tĭn) n. gelatina.
geld (gĕld) vt. castrare.
gem (jĕm) n. gemma.
gender (jĕn'dẽr) n. (gramm.) genere.
general (jĕn'ẽr·ăl) n., agg. generale.
—ity (-ăl'ĭ·tĭ)n. generalità, maggioranza.
generalize (jĕn'ẽr·ăl·īz) vt., vi. generalizzare.
generally (-lĭ) avv. generalmente; largamente, in genere.
generate (jĕn'ẽr·āt) vt. generare, produrre
generation (jĕn'ẽr·ā'shŭn) n. generazione.
generosity (jĕn'ẽr·ŏs'ĭ·tĭ)n.generosità.
generous (jĕn'ẽr·ŭs) agg. generoso.
genial (jĕn'yăl) agg. cordiale. —ity (-ăl'ĭ·tĭ) n. cordialità.
genius (jĕn'yŭs) n. genio, ingegno.
genocide (jĕn'ō·sīd) n. genocidio; genocida.
genteel (jĕn·tēl') agg. raffinato, elegante, ricercato, distinto.
gentile (jĕn'tĭl) agg., n. gentile (pagano, miscredente).
gentility (jĕn·tĭl'ĭ·tĭ) n. raffinatezza, distinzione.
gentle (jĕn't'l) agg. soave, delicato, docile, dolce, tranquillo; bennato. —man n. (pl. —men) signore, gentiluomo; uomo; —manlike, —manly agg. distinto, ben educato, da gentiluomo. —woman n. (pl. —women) gentildonna. —ness n. mitezza, bontà.
gently (jĕn'tlĭ) avv. dolcemente, delicatamente, cautamente.
gentry (jĕn'trĭ) n. alta borghesia; (fam.) gente.
genuine (jĕn'ū.ĭn) agg. genuino, autentico; sincero.
geographer (jė·ŏg'rȧ·fẽr) n. geografo.
geographical (jė'ō·grăf'ĭ·kăl) agg. geografico.
geography (jė·ŏg'rȧ·fĭ) n. geografia.
geological (jė·ō·lŏj'ĭ·kăl) agg. geologico.
geologist (jė·ŏl'ō·jĭst) n. geologo.
geology (jė·ŏl'ō·jĭ) n. geologia.
geometrical (jė·ō·mĕt'rĭ·kăl) agg. geometrico.
geometry (jė·ŏm'ė·trĭ) n. geometria; configurazione; forma.
geopolitics (jė'ō·pŏl'ĭ·tĭks) n. geopolitica.
geranium (jė·rā'nĭ·ŭm) n. geranio.
geriatrics (jĕr'ĭ·ăt'rĭks) n. geriatria.
germ (jûrm) n. germe.
german (jûr'măn) (1) agg. germano, di primo grado.
German (jûr'măn) (2) n., agg. tedesco.
germinate (jûr'mĭ·nāt) vt., vi. produrre, germinare.

gesticulate (jĕs·tĭk'û·lāt) vi. gesticolare.
gesture (jĕs'tûr) n. gesto. vi. gestire, gesticolare.
get (gĕt) vt., vi. (pass. got, pp. got, gotten) ottenere, acquisire, acquistare, afferrare, procurare, catturare, indurre, generare; arrivare; divenire, farsi, riuscire: to — over, superare (una crisi, ecc.); to — married, sposarsi; to — somebody to, indurre qualcuno a; to — the better of, avere il sopravvento su; to — wind of, avere sentore di; to — ill, ammalarsi; to — old, invecchiare; to — tired, stancarsi; to — even with, pareggiare la partita con; to — off, sfuggire, cavarsela; partire; smontare (da un veicolo); to — away, andarsene, scappare; to — along, barcamenarsi, andar d'accordo; to — out, uscire, andarsene; trapelare (di un segreto); to — rid of, sbarazzarsi di; to — up, alzarsi, salire; to — through, passare; finire; I've got to do it, devo farlo, bisogna che lo faccia; I don't — it, non lo capisco, non ci arrivo; that's what gets me, è questo che mi lascia perplesso o che mi secca o che mi urta.
gewgaw (gū'gô) n. bagattella.
ghastly (gȧst'lĭ) agg. macabro, orrendo; livido, cadaverico.
gherkin (gûr'kĭn) n. cetriolino.
ghost (gōst) n. fantasma, apparizione: The Holy Ghost, lo Spirito Santo; — town (S.U.), città abbandonata; to give up the —, morire, spirare. —like, —ly agg. spettrale. —writer n. (S.U.) negro (autore che lavora per un altro senza figurare).
G.I. (jė'ī') n. (S.U.) militare, soldato. agg. militare, soldatesco.
giant (jī'ănt) n. gigante. agg. gigantesco.
gibbet (jĭb'ĕt; jĭb'ĭt) n. forca. [sco.
gibbon (gĭb'ŭn) n. (zool.) gibbone.
gibe (jīb) n. beffa, sarcasmo.
giddiness (gĭd'ĭ·nĕs) n. vertigine, stordimento; volubilità, frivolezza.
giddy (gĭd'ĭ) agg. stordito; vertiginoso, che dà il capogiro; volubile, frivolo: to feel —, avere le vertigini.
gift (gĭft) n. dono; dote (morale o fisica). —ed agg. dotato, valente.
gigantic (jī·găn'tĭk) agg. gigantesco.
giggle (gĭg''l) n. riso convulso o sciocco. vi. ridere convulsamente o stoltamente.
gild (gĭld) vt. dorare.
gill (jĭl) n. gola, burrone; (ittiol.) (gĭl) branchia; (ornit.) bargigli.
gilt (gĭlt) n. doratura. agg. dorato. —edged securities, titoli solidi.

gimbals (gĭm′bălz) *n. pl.* sospensione cardanica: **gimbal joint**, giunto cardanico.

gimlet (gĭm′lĕt) *n.* succhiello.

gimmick (gĭm′ĭk) (*gergo*) *n.* trucco; espediente, stratagemma.

gin (jĭn) (1) *n.* liquore di ginepro, gin: — mill, bar, spaccio di liquori.

gin (jĭn) (2) *n.* trabocchetto; trappola; elevatore; sgranatrice.

ginger (jĭn′jĕr) *n.* zenzero; (*fig.*) vivacità. — **ale** (*Ingl.* — **beer**), sorta di gazzosa al zenzero.

gingerly (jĭn′jĕr·lĭ) *avv.* cautamente, delicatamente *agg.* cautissimo.

gingham (gĭng′ăm) *n.* rigatino.

gipsy (jĭp′sĭ) *n.* zingaro. *agg.* zingaresco.

giraffe (jĭ·răf′) *n.* giraffa. [sco.

gird (gûrd) *vt.* (*pass.*, *pp.* girded, girt) cingere, circondare: **to — oneself for,** prepararsi a.

girder (gûr′dĕr) *n.* putrella.

girdle (gûr′d'l) *n.* cintura, cinturone; reggicalze. *vt.* cingere, recingere.

girl (gûrl) *n.* ragazza, ragazzina. —**hood** *n.* adolescenza, giovinezza (*di femmina*). —**ish** *agg.* fanciullesco (*di femmina*), da fanciulla.

girt (gûrt) *pass.*, *pp. di* to gird.

girth (gûrth) *n.* circonferenza; sottopancia. *vt.* cingere.

gist (jĭst) *n.* essenza, sostanza.

give (gĭv) *n.* cedevolezza, elasticità. *vt.*, *vi.* (*pass.* gave, *pp.* given) dare, consegnare, porgere, abbandonare; cedere, lasciarsi; retrocedere: **to — away,** regalare; rivelare (*un segreto*); tradire; **to — back,** restituire; **to — birth to,** generare, dare origine a; **to — in,** cedere; **to — off,** emanare, emettere; **to — out,** esaurirsi; distribuire, emettere; **to — up,** rinunciare, arrendersi, desistere; **to — way,** cedere.

given (gĭv′ĕn) *agg.* dato, specificato; dedito, proclive: — **name,** nome di battesimo; — **time,** data ora, ora prestabilita.

giver (gĭv′ĕr) *n.* datore, donatore.

gizzard (gĭz′ĕrd) *n.* ventriglio.

glacial (glā′shǎl) *agg.* glaciale.

glacier (glā′shĕr) *n.* ghiacciaio.

glad (glăd) *agg.* lieto, contento; sgargiante: — **rags** (*gergo*), vestito della festa; **to be only too —,** non chieder di meglio.

gladden (glăd′'n) *vt.* rallegrare.

glade (glād) *n.* radura.

gladiator (glăd′i·ā′tĕr) *n.* gladiatore.

gladly (glăd′lĭ) *avv.* volontieri.

gladness (glăd′nĕs) *n.* contentezza, piacere.

glamorize (glăm′ĕr·īz) *vt.* rendere affascinante, (*cinema*) valorizzare

la bellezza di, rendere affascinante.

glamorous (glăm′ĕr·ŭs) *agg.* affascinante.

glamour (glăm′ĕr) *n.* fascino; magia: — **girl,** maliarda, fatalona.

glance (glàns) *n.* sguardo; bagliore; rimbalzo. *vt.*, *vi.* guardare di sfuggita, dare un'occhiata; balenare; rimbalzare; intravedere.

gland (glănd) *n.* (*anat.*) glandola.

glare (glâr) *n.* bagliore, riverbero, barlume; sguardo intenso, occhiata malevola. *vi.* abbagliare, splendere: **to — at,** guardare con astio, dare un'occhiataccia a.

glaring (glâr′ĭng) *agg.* malevolo; abbagliante, splendente; sfrontato; lampante.

glass (glàs) *n.* vetro; bicchiere; (*pl.* glasses) occhiali, cannocchiale: — **case,** vetrinetta; **looking —,** specchio; **weather —,** barometro. *vt.* rispecchiare; mettere sotto vetro; confezionare in barattoli di vetro. —**blower** *n.* soffiatore di vetro. —**ware** *n.* vetrerie, cristalleria.

glassy (glàs′ĭ) *agg.* vitreo; vetroso.

glaze (glāz) *n.* smaltatura, vernice. *vt.* munire *o* coprire di vetro; smaltare; glassare (*dolci, ecc.*).

glazier (glā′zhĕr) *n.* vetraio.

gleam (glēm) *n.* raggio, barlume, sprazzo di luce. *vi.* brillare, splendere.

glean (glēn) *vt.*, *vi.* spigolare, raccogliere; racimolare.

glee (glē) *n.* gioia, gaiezza, ilarità.

glib (glĭb) *agg.* loquace; disinvolto: — **excuse,** scusa facile.

glide (glīd) *vi.* colare; scivolare, sdrucciolare; (*aeron.*) planare, volare a vela.

glider (glīd′ĕr) *n.* aliante; divanetto a dondolo *o* ad altalena.

gliding (glīd′ĭng) *n.* volo a vela.

glimmer (glĭm′ĕr) *n.* barlume; bagliore. *vi.* risplendere debolmente, baluginare.

glimpse (glĭmps) *n.* lampo; occhiata, colpo d'occhio: **to catch a — of,** intravedere. *vt.* intravedere.

glint (glĭnt) *n.* scintillio, bagliore. *vt.*, *vi.* rifrangere, brillare.

glisten (glĭs′'n) *vi.* luccicare, risplendere.

glitter (glĭt′ĕr) *n.* lustro, scintillio. *vi.* brillare, scintillare, essere vistoso. —**ing** *agg.* scintillante.

gloat (glōt) *vi.* gongolare: **to — over** another's misfortunes, godere delle altrui sventure.

globe (glōb) *n.* globo, sfera.

gloom (glōōm), **gloominess** (glōōm′ĭnĕs) *n.* oscurità, tenebre; tristezza, desolazione, umor nero.

gloomy (glōōm'ĭ) *agg.* oscuro; triste, malinconico; nuvoloso.

glorify (glō'rĭ.fĭ) *vt.* glorificare.

glorious (glō'rĭ.ŭs) *agg.* glorioso, magnifico, radioso, splendido.

glory (glō'rĭ) *n.* gloria, aureola. *vi.* gloriarsi, esultare.

gloss (glŏs) *n.* lucentezza; chiosa, commento. *vt.* lustrare; commentare, chiosare: to — over, adonestare. —ary *n.* glossario. —iness *n.* lustro, splendore; levigatezza.

glossy (glŏs'ĭ) *agg.* liscio; lucido splendente. *n.* (*fot.*) foto su carta lucida.

glove (glŭv) *n.* guanto. *vt.* inguantare.

glover (glŭv'ĕr) *n.* guantaio.

glow (glō) *n.* calore, incandescenza, riflesso; ardore, splendore. *vi.* ardere, rosseggiare, brillare. —ing *agg.* brillante, rosseggiante, lucente, ardente, animato.

glower (glou'ĕr) *vi.* guardare torvamente *o* con occhi torvi.

glowworm (glō'wûrm') *n.* lucciola.

glucose (glōō'kōs) *n.* glucosio.

glue (glōō) *n.* colla. *vt.* incollare.

gluey (glōō'ĭ) *agg.* appiccicoso, colloso.

glum (glŭm) *agg.* arcigno, cupo. —ly *avv.* cupamente.

glut (glŭt) *vt.* saziare, colmare.

gluten (glōō'tĕn) *n.* glutine.

glutton (glŭt''n) *n.* ghiottone, mangione. —ous *agg.* ghiotto.

gluttony (glŭt'nĭ) *n.* ghiottoneria.

G-man (jē'măn') *n.* (*S.U.*) agente federale.

gnarled (närld) gnarly *agg.* nodoso, nocchieruto; perverso.

gnash (năsh) *vt.*, *vi.* stringere *o* digrignare i denti.

gnat (năt) *n.* zanzara, moscerino.

gnaw (nô) *vt.*, *vi.* (*pass.* gnawed, *pp.* gnawed, gnawn) rodere, rosicchiare.

go (gō) *n.* l'andare; vigore; moda; tentativo, successo: to make a — at, provarsi a fare; to make a — of, far andar bene; it's a —! affare fatto!; no —! niente da fare! *vi.* (*pass.* went, *pp.* gone) andare, partire, diventare, camminare, tendere, essere sul punto di, stare per. *vt.* sopportare, tollerare: to — astray, smarrirsi, traviarsi; to — away, andarsene; to — back, tornare; to — back on one's word, rimangiarsi la parola; to — between, interporsi; to — by, passare, scorrere (*del tempo*); regolarsi con; to — down, scendere, mettersi a letto, cadere, declinare; to — in, entrare; to — in for, dedi-

carsi a, intraprendere; to — into, entrare, partecipare, darsi a, addentrarsi (*in un argomento*); to — into mourning, prendere il lutto; to — off, partire, morire, spegnersi; to — on, proseguire; accadere, succedere; to — out, uscire, estinguersi; to — out of one's way to, sforzarsi di; to — over, attraversare, percorrere, esaminare, verificare; to — to sleep, addormentarsi; to — under, tramontare; affogare, affondare; soccombere, essere sopraffatto.

goad (gōd) *n.* pungolo, stimolo. *vt.* stimolare, spronare.

goal (gōl) *n.* meta, mira; (*sport*) porta. —keeper, portiere.

goat (gōt) *n.* capra.

goatee (gō'tē') *n.* barba caprina.

gobble (gŏb''l) *vt.* trangugiare.

gobbledygook (gŏb''l·dĭ·gōōk') (*gergo S.U.*) *n.* paroloni, discorso altisonante e astruso.

gobbler (gŏb'lĕr) *n.* mangione; tacchino.

go-between *n.* intermediario; ruffiano.

goblet (gŏb'lĕt) *n.* coppa.

goblin (gŏb'lĭn) *n.* folletto.

god (gŏd) *n.* dio. —child *n.* figlioccio. —daughter *n.* figlioccia. —dess *n.* dea. —father *n.* padrino. —like *agg.* divino. —ly *agg.* pio, devoto; divino. —mother *n.* madrina. —send *n.* fortuna inattesa. —son *n.* figlioccio.

goggle (gŏg''l) *vi.* stralunare gli occhi: to — at, sbirciare.

goggles (gŏg''lz) *n.pl.* (*fam.*) occhiali.

going (gō'ĭng) *n.* andamento, portamento, andatura; partenza: to be —, andare, andarsene; avere intenzione (*di*); I'm — to tell him, gli dirò..., glielo dirò, *agg.* in movimento, funzionante: a — concern, una ditta avviata.

goiter (goi'tĕr) *n.* (*pat.*) gozzo.

gold (gōld) *n.* oro, danaro. —bricker *n.* scansafatiche. —en *agg.* d'oro, aureo.

goldfinch (gōld'fĭnch) *n.* (*ornit.*) cardellino.

goldfish (gōld'fĭsh) *n.* pesce dorato.

goldsmith (gōld'smĭth) *n.* orefice.

golf (gŏlf) *n.* (*sport*) golf: — course, — links, campo di golf.

golosh *vedi* galosh.

gondola (gŏn'dŏlà) *n.* gondola; (*ferr.*) carro merci scoperto.

gone (gŏn) *agg.* andato, partito; fuggito; spacciato; aggiudicato (*all'asta*): far —, all'estremo; in days

—by, nei tempi passati; — under, rovinato, (*pp. di* to go).

oner (gŏn'ĕr) *n*. (*gergo S.U.*) uomo spacciato.

ong (gŏng) *n*. gong.

ood (gŏod) *n*. bene; felicità; virtù; vantaggio, profitto: for —, per sempre, definitivamente. *agg*. buono; onesto; conveniente; valido, genuino; savio: it is no —, è inutile; — breeding, buona educazione, belle maniere; —bye, addio; Good Friday, Venerdì Santo; —looking, bello; —natured, bonario, affabile.

oodly (gŏod'lĭ) *agg*. bello, buono; considerevole, notevole.

oodness (gŏod'nĕs) *n*. bontà, nobiltà: — knows! sa Iddio!; thank —! grazie a Dio!

oody (gŏod'ĭ) *n*. dolciume.

ook (gŏok) *n*. (*gergo*) roba appiccicosa; robaccia, scarto; sciocchezze; indigeno del Sud Pacifico o del Nord Africa (*sprezz.*)

oose (gōos) *n*. (*pl*. geese) oca; (*fig.*) imbecille, balordo: wild — chase, impresa vana; —flesh *n*. pelle d'oca.

ooseberry (gōoz'bĕr'ĭ; gōos-) *n*. ribes.

ore (gōr) *n*. sangue, sangue coagulato; (*sartoria*) gherone. *vt*. trafiggere con le corna; mettere un gherone a.

orge (gôrj) *n*. gola, fauci; forra. *vt*. trangugiare; ingozzare. *vi*. rimpinzarsi.

orgeous (gôr'jŭs) *agg*. magnifico, sontuoso, fastoso.

ory (gōr'ĭ) *agg*. insanguinato, sanguinoso.

ospel (gŏs'pĕl) *n*. vangelo: — truth, verità sacrosanta.

ossamer (gŏs'à-mĕr) *n*. velo; ragnatela; filo di ragnatela. *agg*. sottile, velato; tenue; frivolo.

ossip (gŏs'ĭp) *n*. pettegolo, pettegola; pettegolezzo. *vi*. spettegolare. —y *agg*. pettegolo.

ot (gŏt) *pass.*, *pp. di* to get.

otten (gŏt''n) *pp. di* to get.

Gothic (gŏth'ĭk) *agg*. gotico; barbarico.

gouge (gouj) *n*. cesello, sgorbia. *vt*. lavorare con la sgorbia, estirpare.

gourd (gōrd) *n*. zucca.

gout (gout) *n*. gotta, podagra.

govern (gŭv'ĕrn) *vt.*, *vi*. governare; (*gramm.*) reggere: to — oneself, dominarsi. —ess *n*. istitutrice, governante. —ment *n*. governo, amministrazione, regime. —mental *agg*. governativo. —or *n*. governatore; (*mecc.*) regolatore; (*gergo*) padre, padrone, "capo."

gown (goun) *n*. veste, gonna, toga: dressing —, veste da camera; night— *n*. camicia da notte.

grab (grăb) *n*. l'arraffare, presa, morsa. *vt*. afferrare, arraffare.

grace (grās) *n*. grazia, garbo; favore. *vt*. ornare, abbellire. —ful *agg*. grazioso, aggraziato, garbato. —fully *avv*. graziosamente, cortesemente. —fulness *n*. grazia. —less *agg*. sgraziato, perverso.

gracious (grā'shŭs) *agg*. clemente, cortese, favorevole.

gradation (grà·dā'shŭn) *n*. gradazione.

grade (grād) *n*. grado, rango; classe (*scolastica*); classificazione; pendenza, declivio: — crossing, passaggio a livello; the grades, la scuola elementare. *vt*. graduare; selezionare; pareggiare

gradual (grăd'û·ăl) *agg*. graduale. —ly *avv*. gradatamente, a poco a poco.

graduate (grăd'û·āt) *n.*, *agg*. laureato, diplomato; graduato. *vt*. graduare; conferire un diploma a. *vt*. graduare; conferire un diploma a. *vi*. diplomarsi, laurearsi.

graduation (grăd'û·ā'shŭn) *n*. graduazione; laurea.

graft (grȧft) (1) *n*. innesto. *vt*. innestare. —er *n*. innestatore.

graft (grȧft) (2) *n*. (*S.U.*) corruzione, mangeria, camorra. *vt.*, *vi*. frodare, prevaricare. —er *n*. prevaricatore.

grain (grān) *n*. grano, chicco; grana, vena (*del marmo*), fibra (*del legno*); filo: against the —, contropelo; di malavoglia.

gram (grăm) *n*. grammo.

grammar (grăm'ĕr) *n*. grammatica: — school, scuola media (*dal 5⁰ all' 8⁰ anno*).

grammatical (grȧ·măt'ĭ·kăl) *agg*. grammaticale.

gramophone (grăm'ŏ·fōn) *n*. grammofono.

granary (grăn'à·rĭ) *n*. granaio.

grand (grănd) *n*. (*gergo, S.U.*) biglietto da mille. *agg*. grande, magnifico, illustre, maestoso, grandioso. —dad *n*. nonno. —child *n*. (*pl*. grandchildren) nipotino, nipotina. —daughter *n*. nipotina. —eur *n*. grandezza, lustro, splendore. —father *n*. nonno. —ma, —mother *n*. nonna. —nephew *n*. pronipote (*maschio*). —ness *n*. grandezza, magnificenza. —niece *n*. pronipote (*femmina*). —son *n*. nipote (*maschio*). —stand *n*. tribuna principale.

grange (grănj) *n*. fattoria, casa colonica; società fra agricoltori.

granite (grăn'ĭt) *n.* granito.

granny (grăn'ĭ) *n.* (*fam.*) nonna.

grant (grȧnt) *n.* concessione, assegnazione. *vt.*, *vi.* accordare, assegnare, permettere, acconsentire, convenire, ammettere, aggiudicare: **granted that**, ammesso che; **to take for granted**, ammettere come assodato, fare affidamento su.

granulate (grăn'ū·lāt) *vt.* granulare. *vi.* divenir granuloso.

grape (grāp) *n.* acino d'uva; (*pl.* **grapes**) uva: **a bunch of grapes**, un grappolo d'uva.

grapefruit (grāp'frōōt') *n.* pompelmo.

grapevine (grāp'vīn) *n.* vigna; diceria, voce; — **telegraph**, comunicazione a distanza (*con tamburi, ecc.*); diffusione di dicerie.

graph (grȧf) *n.* grafico; diagramma; (*mat.*) curva. *vt.* tracciare un grafico. —**ic** *agg.* grafico, descrittivo.

graphite (grăf'īt) *n.* grafite.

graphology (grȧf·ŏl'ō·jĭ) *n.* grafologia.

grapple (grăp'l) *n.* rampone, lotta. *vt.* uncinare, afferrare. *vi.* avvinghiarsi, lottare; andare all'abbordaggio.

grasp (grȧsp) *n.* presa, stretta; percezione; conoscenza: **to be within one's —**, essere a portata di mano; **to have a good — of a subject**, essere padrone di una materia. *vt.* stringere, impugnare, afferrare.

grasping *agg.* avido, taccagno.

grass (grȧs) *n.* erba; —**roots** *n.pl.* (*fig.*), radici, base; zone agricole. —**hopper** *n.* grillo, saltamartino; (*aeron. mil.*) apparecchio di collegamento.

grassy (grȧs'ĭ) *agg.* erboso, verdeggiante.

grate (grāt) *n.* grata, graticola, inferriata, focolare. *vt.* grattugiare, raschiare, munire di grata. *vi.* stridere; irritare, molestare.

grater (grāt'ẽr) *n.* grattugia; raspa.

grateful (grāt'fŏŏl) *agg.* grato; gradevole.

gratification (grăt'ĭ·fĭ·kā'shŭn) *n.* soddisfazione, piacere.

gratify (grăt'ĭ·fī) *vt.* accontentare, far piacere a, soddisfare; gratificare.

gratifying *agg.* gradevole, soddisfacente.

grating (grāt'ĭng) *n.* inferriata. *agg.* irritante, stridente.

gratis (grā'tĭs) *avv.* gratuitamente.

gratitude (grăt'ĭ·tūd) *n.* gratitudine.

gratuitous (grȧ·tū'ĭ·tŭs) *agg.* gratuito.

gratuity (grȧ·tū'ĭ·tĭ) *n.* mancia, gratifica.

grave (grāv) (1) *n.* tomba. —**digger** *n.* affossatore. — **stone** *n.* pietra tombale, lapide.

grave (grāv) (2) *agg.* grave, serio.

grave (grāv) (3) *vt.* incidere; (*naut.* calafatare.

gravel (grăv'ĕl) *n.* ghiaia; (*med.*) calcolosi renale. *vt.* inghiaiare.

graver (grāv'ẽr) *n.* scultore, incisore bulino.

graveyard (grāv'yärd') *n.* cimitero.

gravity (grăv'ĭ·tĭ) *n.* gravità.

gravy (grā'vĭ) *n.* sugo di carne.

gray (grā) *agg.* grigio; brizzolato. —**is** *agg.* grigiastro, grigiognolo. —**nes** *n.* grigiore; color grigio; canizie.

graze (grāz) *n.* escoriazione, graffia tura. *vt.*, *vi.* graffiare, scalfire sfiorare; brucare, pascolare.

grease (grēs) *n.* unto, grasso. *vt.* dar il grasso a, ungere: **to — the palm** ungere le ruote (*fig.*).

greasy (grēs'ĭ) *agg.* grasso, unto, su dicio.

great (grāt) *agg.* grande, considerevole, magnanimo, superiore: **a — deal**, un bel po', molto; **a — many** moltissimi; **a — while**, un bel po di tempo. —**er** *agg.* più grande —**est** *agg.* (il) più grande. —**grandchild** *n.* pronipote. —**granddaughter** *n.* pronipote (*femmina*). —**grandfather** *n.* bisavolo. —**grandmother** *n.* bisavola. —**grandson** *n* pronipote (*maschio*).

greatly *avv.* grandemente, molto oltremodo, generosamente.

greatness *n.* grandezza.

Grecian (grē'shăn) *agg.*, *n.* greco.

greed (grēd) *n.* avidità, cupidigia. —**ily** *avv.* avidamente. —**iness** *n.* cupidigia, avidità.

greedy (grēd'ĭ) *agg.* avido, ingordo.

Greek (grēk) *n.*, *agg.* greco.

green (grēn) *n.* verde; prato; campo di golf; (*pl.*) frasche; verdura. *agg.* verde, verdeggiante; fresco, nuovo, novello, giovane; recente, inesperto: — **light**, segnale verde o di via libera; (*fig.*) benestare, autorizzazione. —**back** *n.* biglietto di banca (*S.U.*). —**grocer** *n.* erbivendolo, fruttivendolo. —**house** *n.* serra. —**ish** *agg.* verdastro. —**ness** *n.* verdezza; freschezza, acerbezza, ingenuità, inesperienza.

greet (grēt) *vt.*, *vi.* salutare: **to — each other**, salutarsi. —**ing** *n.* saluto.

gregarious (grē·gàr'ĭ·ŭs) *agg.* socievole; (*bot.*, *zool.*) gregario.

greige (grāzh) *agg.* greggio (*di colore*).

gremlin (grĕm'lĭn) *n.* (*aeron. scherz.*) folletto maligno degli aviatori.

grenade (grē·nād') *n.* granata: **hand —**, bomba a mano.

grenadier (grĕn'ȧ·dẽr') *n.* granatiere.

grew (groo) *pass. di* to grow.

grey (grā) *vedi* gray.

greyhound (grā'hound') *n.* levriere.

greyish, greyness *vedi* gray.

grid (grĭd) *n.* griglia.

griddle (grĭd''l) *n.* teglia, piastra.

gridiron (grĭd'i'ĕrn) *n.* graticola; impalcatura.

grief (grēf) *n.* dolore, calamità: to come to —, finire male.

grievance (grēv'ăns) *n.* afflizione, torto, pena, ingiustizia.

grieve (grēv) *vt.* affliggere, rattristare. *vi.* affliggersi, addolorarsi.

grievous (grēv'ŭs) *agg.* doloroso; grave; gravoso.

grill (grĭl) *n.* graticola. *vt.* cuocere in graticola, sottoporre a interrogatorio.

grim (grĭm) *agg.* arcigno, torvo; sinistro; implacabile; accanito.

grimace (grĭ-mās') *n.* smorfia, boccaccia. *vi.* fare smorfie *o* boccacce.

grime (grīm) *n.* sudiciume. *vt.* sporcare.

grimy (grīm'ĭ) *agg.* sudicio.

grin (grĭn) *n.* smorfia, sogghigno; sorriso. *vi.* sogghignare, sorridere.

grind (grīnd) *n.* macinazione, smerigliatura; lavoro arduo, preparazione a un esame; sgobbone: daily —, andazzo *o* tran-tran quotidiano. *vt.* (*pass., pp.* ground) macinare, smerigliare, rettificare; affilare; opprimere, tartassare, schiacciare; sonare (*l'organetto*). *vi.* digrignare (*i denti*); frantumarsi, sgobbare; raschiare. —er *n.* arrotino; mola, rettifica; macinino (*per caffè*); dente molare; sgobbone; banditore; (*radio*) scarica; tosto (*panino imbottito*). —stone *n.* mola.

grip (grĭp) *n.* presa, stretta; impugnatura; afflizione; valigetta: to come to grips, venire alle mani. *vt.* afferrare, stringere; impadronirsi di.

gripe (grīp) *n.* presa, grinfia; (*pl.*) crampi, coliche; (*gergo*) malumore, "buschere." *vt.* irritare, seccare. *vi.* borbottare, lagnarsi.

grisly (grĭz'lĭ) *agg.* orrendo, macabro.

grist (grĭst) *n.* grano da macinare; provvista; profitto: to bring the — to the mill, tirar l'acqua al proprio mulino.

grit (grĭt) *n.* sabbia; pietra arenaria; pulviscolo; pertinacia, coraggio. *vt.*, *vi.* macinare; digrignare. —ty *agg.* sabbioso; pertinace.

grizzled (grĭz''ld) *agg.* grigio, brizzolato.

grizzly (grĭz'lĭ) *n.* orso grigio. *agg.* grigiastro.

groan (grōn) *n.* gemito, lamento. *vi.* gemere, lamentarsi.

grocer (grō'sĕr) *n.* droghiere.

grocery (grō'sĕr-ĭ) *n.* drogheria; (*pl.*) droghe e coloniali.

groin (groin) *n.* inguine.

groom (groōm) *n.* palafreniere, stalliere; sposo. *vt.* agghindare; strigliare (*cavalli*); istruire: well-groomed, ben vestito, curato, in ordine. —sman *n.* compare d'anello.

groove (groōv) *n.* scanalatura, solco. *vt.* scanalare.

grope (grōp) *vi.* brancolare, annaspare: to — for, cercare a tastoni.

gropingly (grōp'ĭng-lĭ) *avv.* a tastoni.

gross (grōs) *n.* grossa (*dodici dozzine*); massa. *agg.* grosso, grossolano; lordo: — weight, peso lordo; — ignorance, ignoranza crassa.

grot (grŏt) *n.* grotta.

grotesque (grō-tĕsk') *agg.* grottesco.

grotto (grŏt'ō) *n.* grotta.

grouch (grouch) *n.* malumore, broncio, rovello: to have a — against, avere rancore contro, avercela con. *vi.* essere di malumore, brontolare. —y *agg.* imbronciato, intrattabile.

ground (ground) (1) *pass., pp. di* grind.

ground (ground) (2) *n.* terra, terreno, suolo; motivo, base, fondamento: to break —, arare, scavare; to give —, retrocedere, cedere terreno; to hold one's —, resistere (a piè fermo); — crew (*aeron.*) squadra di manutenzione a terra. *vt.* fondare, basare; far atterrare; far arenare; mettere a terra; atterrare. (*aeron.*) trattenere a terra, non autorizzare al volo. *vi.* basarsi; incagliarsi, arenarsi; (*aeron.*) atterrare: well-ed, benfondato. —floor *n.* piano terreno. —less *agg.* infondato.

grounds *n.pl.* parco; sedimento; sfondo.

groundwork *n.* base.

group (groōp) *n.* gruppo. *vt.*, *vi.* raggruppare, raggrupparsi. —ing *n.* raggruppamento.

grove (grōv) *n.* boschetto.

grovel (grŏv''l) *vi.* strisciare, umiliarsi. —ling *agg.* abbietto, strisciante.

grow (grō) *vt.* (*pass.* grew, *pp.* grown) allevare, coltivare. *vi.* crescere, progredire, aumentare; farsi, diventare; germogliare: to — better, migliorare; to — late, farsi tardi; to — worse, peggiorare; to — into, diventare; to — less, diminuire; to — out of a habit, perdere un'abitudine; to — up, crescere.

growl (groul) *n.* brontolio, ringhio. *vi.* ringhiare, brontolare. —er *n.*

grown (grōn) (*pp. di* to grow), *agg.* cresciuto, sviluppato, fatto: — man, adulto, uomo fatto; — with trees, coperto d'alberi. —up *n.*, *agg.* adulto.

growth (grōth) *n.* crescita, sviluppo; raccolto; evoluzione; vegetazione; tumore, escrescenza.

grub (grŭb) *n.* larva, verme, baco; (*fam.*) cibo.

grudge (grŭj) *n.* rancore; invidia; livore, malevolenza. *vt.* invidiare; lesinare.

grudgingly (grŭj'ĭng·lĭ) *avv.* malvolontieri.

gruesome (grōō'sŭm) *agg.* macabro, lugubre, spaventoso.

gruff (grŭf) *agg.* burbero, brusco.

grumble (grŭm'b'l) *n.* brontolio. *vi.* brontolare, lagnarsi.

grumbler (grŭm'blĕr) *n.* brontolone.

grumpy (grŭmp'ĭ) *agg.* bisbetico.

grunt (grŭnt) *n.* grugnito; brontolio. *vt., vi.* grugnire, borbottare.

G-suit (jē'sūt') *n.* (*aeron.*) tuta a pressione

guarantee (găr'ăn·tē') *n.* garanzia; garante. *vt.* garantire.

guarantor (găr'ănt·ôr) *n.* garante.

guaranty (găr'ăn·tĭ) *n.* garanzia.

guard (ärd) *n.* guardia; difesa, protezione; (*ferr.*) capotreno: on —, in guardia; to be off one's —, essere impreparato (*a un attacco*). *vt.* sorvegliare, proteggere. *vi.* stare in guardia, difendersi, premunirsi.

guarded *agg.* prudente, circospetto.

guardian (gär'dĭ·ăn) *n.* guardiano, tutore: — angel, angelo custode. —ship *n.* tutela, difesa, protezione.

guerrilla (gĕ·rĭl'ă) *n.* guerriglia; franco tiratore, partigiano.

guess (gĕs) *n.* congettura, supposizione: at a rough —, a occhio e croce. *vt., vi.* ritenere, supporre, credere; indovinare. —work *n.* congettura.

guest (gĕst) *n.* ospite (*invitato*).

guffaw (gŭ·fô') *n.* risata sganherata. *vi.* sghignazzare.

guidance (gīd'ăns) *n.* guida, norma; direzione; regola.

guide (gīd) *n.* guida. *vt.* guidare: guided missile, missile telecomandato *o* radiocomandato.

guidebook (gīd'bŏŏk') *n.* guida (*opuscolo*): railroad —, orario ferroviario.

guild (gĭld) *n.* corporazione, associazione. —hall *n.* palazzo municipale.

guile (gīl) *n.* astuzia. —less *agg.* semplice, ingenuo, sincero, candido.

guilt (gĭlt) *n.* colpa, colpevolezza, m sfatto. —less *agg.* innocente. — *agg.* colpevole.

guinea (gĭn'ĭ) *n.* ghinea (*moneta*): - fowl, gallina faraona; — pig, cavi

guise (gīz) *n.* guisa, maniera, app renza: under the — of, camuffa da; col pretesto di.

guitar (gĭ·tär') *n.* chitarra.

gulf (gŭlf) *n.* golfo, baia; gorg abisso.

gull (gŭl) (1) *n.* gabbiano.

gull (gŭl) (2) *n.* gonzo.

gullet (gŭl'ĕt) *n.* gola, strozza.

gullible (gŭl'ĭ·b'l) *agg.* credulone.

gully (gŭl'ĭ) *n.* burrone.

gulp (gŭlp) *n.* sorsata, boccone. *vt.* i ghiottire, ingoiare, trangugiare.

gum (gŭm) (1) *n.* gengiva.

gum (gŭm) (2) *n.* gomma: chewing- gomma da masticare; *vt.* ingomm re. —ming *n.* ingommatura. — tre albero da gomma, eucaliptus.

gun (gŭn) *n.* fucile; cannone; pistol rivoltella; arma da fuoco: big — pezzo grosso, personaggio impo tante. *vt., vi.* prender di mira; da la caccia (*a*); dare tutto gas (*motore*): — license, porto d'arm —boat *n.* cannoniera. —powder, polvere da sparo.

gunner (gŭn'ĕr) *n.* artigliere.

gunsmith (gŭn'smĭth') *n.* armaiolo.

gurgle (gûr'g'l) *n.* gorgoglio. *vi.* go gogliare.

gush (gŭsh) *n.* zampillo; effusion entusiasmo. *vi.* zampillare, sco rere; abbandonarsi a effusioni.

gust (gŭst) *n.* folata, raffica, access d'ira.

gusto (gŭs'tō) *n.* gusto, piacere; e tusiasmo, foga.

gusty (gŭs'tĭ) *agg.* ventoso, impetuos

gut (gŭt) *n.* budello, intestino; (*pl* intestini, ventre; to have —s, (*gerg S.U.*) aver coraggio. *vt.* sventrar vuotare.

gutter (gŭt'ĕr) *n.* grondaia; cunett rigagnolo, solco; (*fig.*) bassifondi.

guy (gī) *n.* individuo, tipo, soggett uomo, ragazzo; fantoccio; (*naut* tirante, catena di sostegno, cavo. v sostenere con tiranti *o* catene burlarsi (*di*).

gymnasium (jĭm·nā'zĭ·ŭm) *n.* palestra

gymnastics (jĭm·năs'tĭks) *n.* ginnast ca.

gypsum (jĭp'sŭm) *n.* gesso.

gypsy (jĭp'sĭ) *vedi* gipsy.

gyrate (jī'rāt) *vi.* girare, turbinare.

gyration (jī·rā'shŭn) *n.* moviment rotatorio, vortice.

gyrene (jī·rēn') *n.* (*gergo mil. S.U.* fante di marina, marine.

H

aberdasher (hăb'ĕr·dăsh'ĕr) *n.* merciaio. —**y** *n.* merceria.

abit (hăb'ĭt) *n.* abitudine, costume, usanza; abito: — **of body**, costituzione fisica; — **of mind**, abito mentale.

abitual (hă·bĭt'ū·ăl) *agg.* abituale.

ack (hăk) *n.* tosse secca; ronzino; carrozza da nolo; intaccatura; scrittore mercenario, scribacchino: —**work**, lavoro letterario mal retribuito. *vt.* tritare, sminuzzare, massacrare, scorticare. *vi.* tossire convulsamente; (*sport*) colpire un avversario (*spec. al polso*).

ackle (hăk''l) *n.* carda (*per fibre tessili*). *vt.* cardare.

ackneyed (hăk'nĭd) *agg.* banale, comune.

ad (hăd) *pass. e pp. di* to have.

ag (hăg) *n.* megera, strega.

aggard (hăg'ĕrd) *agg.* sparuto, smunto, emaciato, spettrale; selvaggio, truce.

aggle (hăg''l) *vi.* mercanteggiare.

ail (hāl)(1) *n.* grandine. *vi.* grandinare.

ail (hāl) (2) *n.* saluto. *inter.* salve! *vt.* salutare, acclamare, chiamare: **to** — **from**, essere oriundo di.

ailstorm (-stôrm') *n.* grandinata.

air (hâr) *n.* capello, capelli, pelo, peli, criniera, setole, peluria (*vegetale*): **to a** —, esattamente, con precisione; **not to turn a** —, non scomporsi; **to split hairs**, sottilizzare, cercare il pelo nell'uovo. —**breadth** *n.*: **to have a hairbreadth escape**, cavarsela per miracolo. —**brush** *n.* spazzola per capelli. —**cut** *n.* taglio di capelli. —**do** *n.* acconciatura, pettinatura. —**dresser** *n.* parrucchiere. —**less** *agg.* calvo, senza peli. —**pin** *n.* forcina per capelli. —**y** *agg.* capelluto, peloso.

ale (hāl) *agg.* robusto, sano, vigoroso. *vt.* trainare, trascinare a forza.

alf (hăf) *n.* (*pl.* **halves** [hăvz]) metà, mezzo: — **as much as**, la metà di; — **an apple**, mezza mela. *agg.* mezzo, incompleto. *avv.* a metà, incompletamente. —**breed** *n.* meticcio. —**brother** *n.* fratellastro. —**done** *agg.* cotto a metà. —**hearted** *agg.* tepido, indifferente. —**mast** *agg.* a mezz'asta (*di bandiera*). —**open** *agg.* semiaperto. —**sister** *n.* sorellastra. —**way** *avv.* a metà (strada). —**witted** *agg.* tonto.

all (hôl) *n.* sala, vestibolo; corridoio; palazzo; refettorio scolastico; aula

(*di palazzo di giustizia*). —**mark** *n.* marchio (*sull'oro o sull'argento*); impronta caratteristica.

hallo! (hă·lōō') *inter.* (*Ingl.*) ohè! (*telef.*) pronto.

hallow (hăl'ō) *vt.* santificare.

Halloween (hăl'ō·ēn') *n.* vigilia dell'Ognissanti.

hallucination (hă·lū'sĭ·nā'shŭn) *n.* allucinazione.

halo (hā'lō) *n.* alone, aureola.

halt (hôlt) *n.* fermata, sosta; zoppicamento. *agg.* zoppo. *vt.* fermare, trattenere. *vi.* fermarsi, trattenersi; zoppicare; esitare.

halter (hôl'tĕr) *n.* cavezza; capestro; bustino (*del prendisole*).

halting *agg.* esitante, vacillante.

halve (hăv) *vt.* dimezzare, spartire in due.

halves (hăvz) *pl. di* half: **to go** —, fare a mezzo.

halyard (hăl'yĕrd) *n.* (*naut.*) drizza.

ham (hăm) *n.* prosciutto; (*teat.*) gigione, istrione; radioamatore. *vi.* (*teat.*) caricare una parte, gigionare.

hamburger (hăm'bûr·gĕr) *n.* polpetta di carne tra due fette di pane.

hamlet (hăm'lĕt) *n.* borgo, villaggio.

hammer (hăm'ĕr) *n.* martello; cane (*di fucile*). *vt.*, *vi.* martellare; tempestare; inculcare.

hammock (hăm'ŭk) *n.* amaca.

hamper (hăm'pĕr) *n.* canestro, cesta; impedimento. *vt.* mettere in imbarazzo, impedire, ostacolare.

hand (hănd) *n.* mano; spanna (*misura*); scrittura; lancetta (*dell'orologio*); operaio; parte, lato: — **in**—, per mano, con la mano in mano; **at** —, a portata di mano; — **to** —, corpo a corpo; **on** —, pronto, disponibile; **on the other** —, d'altro canto, per contro; **second**—, d'occasione; **to be** — **and glove together**, essere come pane e cacio; **to get the upper** —, prendere il sopravvento; **to live from** — **to mouth**, vivere alla giornata; **to show one's** —, rivelare le proprie intenzioni. *vt.* porgere, dare, consegnare: **to** — **down**, aiutare a discendere; **to** — **over**, trasmettere, cedere. —**bag** *n.* valigetta, borsa. —**bill** *n.* manifesto, prospetto, volantino. —**book** *n.* manuale. —**cuff** *n.* manetta; *vt.* ammanettare. —**ful** *n.* manciata. —**made** *agg.* fatto a mano. —**out** *n.* (*gergo S.U.*) elemosina di cibo o vestiario; manifestino o pieghevole pubblicitario; (giorn.) comunicato stampa, dichiarazione ufficiale per la stampa. —shake n. stretta di mano. —writing n. scrittura.

handicap (hăn'dĭ·kăp) n. intralcio, svantaggio, ostacolo. vt. impedire, ostacolare.

handiwork (hăn'dĭ·wûrk') n. lavoro fatto a mano; opera.

handkerchief (hăng'kẽr·chĭf) n. fazzoletto.

handle (hăn'd'l) n. manico; impugnatura (di spada); maniglia (di porta); ansa (di brocca); manovella: to give a —, fornire il destro. vt. maneggiare; trattare; toccare; amministrare. —bar n. manubrio (di bicicletta).

handsome (hăn'sŭm) agg. bello, piacente; elegante; generoso.

handy (hăn'dĭ) agg. abile; comodo, maneggevole; a portata di mano: to come in —, tornare comodo, giungere opportuno.

hang (hăng) vt., vi. (pass., pp. hung, hanged [nel significato d'impiccare]) appendere, attaccare, tappezzare; pendere; abbassare (il capo): to — back, esitare, indugiare; to — on, tenersi avvinto a, dipendere da; penzolare da, essere appeso a; persistere; to — together, accordarsi, tenersi uniti; to — about, bighellonare, aggirarsi. n. modo di stare (di un indumento indosso); maneggio, manovra (di uno strumento); metodo (per risolvere un problema); significato: I don't give a—, non me ne importa un fico. —er n. uncino, gancio, gruccia (per vestiti): —on, seguace; parassita; paper—, tappezziere. —ing n. impiccagione; tappezzeria; tendaggio. agg. sospeso, appeso. —man n. boia. —over n. residuo, sopravvivenza; postumi di sbornia.

hanker (hăng'kẽr) vi.: to — after, bramare. —ing n. desiderio ardente.

haphazard (hăp'hăz'ẽrd) n. caso, agg. casuale. avv. casualmente, a casaccio.

hapless (hăp'lĕs) agg. sfortunato.

happen (hăp'ĕn) vi. avvenire, capitare: I happened to hear, udii per caso; if he happened to come, se per caso egli venisse; to — upon, imbattersi. —ing n. avvenimento.

happily (hăp'ĭ·lĭ) avv. fortunatamente, felicemente.

happiness (hăp'ĭ·nĕs) n. felicità.

happy (hăp'ĭ) agg. felice; contento. —go-lucky agg. spensierato.

harangue (há·răng') n. arringa. vt., vi. arringare, concionare.

harass (hăr'ăs) vt. molestare, tormentare.

harbinger (här'bĭn·jẽr) n. precursore, pioniere; staffetta, messaggiero.

harbor (här'bẽr) n. porto; rifugio, asilo. vt. albergare, alloggiare, ospitare.

hard (härd) agg. duro, tenace; difficile, faticoso; rude, severo: — labor, lavori forzati; — liquor, liquore forte; — luck, sfortuna; — up, al verde, senza quattrini; in — cash, in moneta sonante. avv. duramente, faticosamente, forte, mente: — by, accanto a, vicino, —hearted agg. insensibile, inumano. —working agg. laborioso. —of-hearing agg. duro d'orecchio.

harden (här'd'n) vt. indurire; (metal.) temperare. vi. indurirsi. —ing n. indurimento; (metal.) tempera.

hardihood (här'dĭ·hŏŏd) n. ardimento, audacia; resistenza.

hardly (härd'lĭ) avv. appena, a mala pena, stentatamente; duramente, difficilmente, probabilmente no: — ever, quasi mai.

hardness (härd'nĕs) n. durezza; fermezza; difficoltà; brutalità.

hardship (härd'shĭp) n. fatica; pena, privazione, avversità.

hardware (härd'wâr') n. utensileria, ferramenta.

hardy (här'dĭ) agg. ardito, coraggioso, duro, vigoroso, forte.

hare (hâr) n. lepre. —brained agg. scervellato.

hark (härk) vi. ascoltare: to — back, tornare a bomba.

harlot (här'lŏt) n. prostituta.

harm (härm) n. danno, male, torto: out of harm's way, in salvo. vt. nuocere a, danneggiare. —ful agg. dannoso, nocivo, malefico. —less agg. innocuo.

harmonic (här·mŏn'ĭk) agg. armonico, armonioso.

harmonious (här·mō'nĭ·ŭs) agg. armonico, melodioso.

harmonize (här'mō·nīz) vt., vi. armonizzare, rendere armonioso; mettere d'accordo, andare d'accordo.

harmony (här'mō·nĭ) n. armonia.

harness (här'nĕs) n. bardatura, finimenti (di cavallo): to die in —, morire sul lavoro. vt. bardare; attaccare (a una carrozza).

harp (härp) n. arpa. vi. sonare l'arpa: to — on, upon, insistere su un argomento.

harpoon (här·pōōn') n. rampone, fiocina. vt. fiocinare.

harrow (hăr'ō) n. erpice. vt. erpicare; lacerare, straziare, torturare. —ing *n.* erpicamento, strazio. *agg.* straziante, doloroso.

harry (här'ĭ) *vt.* saccheggiare, devastare; tormentare.

harsh (härsh) *agg.* aspro, rude, agro, duro; roco; discordante. **—ness** *n.* asprezza, severità, discordanza.

hart (härt) *n.* cervo.

harvest (här'věst) *n.* messe, raccolto: **— home,** festa del raccolto. *vt.* mietere, raccogliere. **—er** *n.* mietitore; mietitrice (*macchina*).

hash (hăsh) *n.* carne trita; accozzaglia, mescolanza; manipolazione; confusione. *vt.* triturare.

hasp (hàsp) *n.* fermaglio, lucchetto.

haste (hāst) *n.* fretta, precipitazione: **to make —,** affrettarsi, far presto. *vi.* affrettarsi: **to — away,** andarsene precipitosamente.

hasten (hās'n) *vt.* affrettare, accelerare. *vi.* affrettarsi.

hastily (hās'tĭ.lĭ) *avv.* affrettatamente, frettolosamente.

hasty (hās'tĭ) *agg.* frettoloso, rapido, precipitoso, impulsivo.

hat (hăt) *n.* cappello. **—band** *n.* nastro per cappello.

hatch (hăch) *n.* covata, nidiata; botola, portello; boccaporto. *vt.* covare, incubare, far dischiudere; tramare; tratteggiare (*un disegno*). **—er** *n.* incubatrice.

hatchet (hăch'ět) *n.* scure, ascia, accetta: **to bury the —,** riconciliarsi; **to take up the —,** aprire le ostilità.

hatchway (hăch'wā') *n.* boccaporto.

hate (hāt) *n.* odio. *vt.* odiare, detestare. **—ful** *agg.* odioso, detestabile.

hatred (hā'trĕd) *n.* odio, avversione.

haughtily (hô'tĭ.lĭ) *avv.* altezzosamente, arrogantemente.

haughtiness (hô'tĭ.nĕs) *n.* orgoglio, alterigia.

haughty (hô'tĭ) *agg.* altezzoso, sprezzante, arrogante.

haul (hôl) *n.* rimorchio (*il rimorchiare*); trascinamento, retata (*di pesci*); bottino, guadagno. *vt.* tirare, trascinare, rimorchiare, trasportare: **to — in** (*naut.*); alare; **to — up,** issare; **to — down,** ammainare.

haunt (hônt) *n.* ritrovo, luogo di convegno, rifugio. *vt.* frequentare, bazzicare; ossessionare, perseguitare: **a haunted house,** una casa abitata dagli spettri.

have (hăv) *vt. e aus.* (*pass., pp.* had) avere, possedere: **had he known,** se egli avesse saputo; **I had to go there,** dovetti andarci; **I had better go away,** è meglio che me ne vada; **I will not — it,** non lo permetterò; **to — something done,** far fare

qualche cosa; **to — done with,** finirla con, non aver più a che fare con; **to — on,** indossare; **to — a look at,** dare un'occhiata a.

haven (hā'věn) *n.* porto, rifugio.

havoc (hăv'ŭk) *n.* rovina, devastazione, strage: **to play — with,** devastare.

hawk (hôk) *n.* falco, sparviero. *vt.* portare attorno (*mercanzie*) per vendere.

hawthorn (hô'thôrn) *n.* biancospino.

hay (hā) *n.* fieno. **—loft** *n.* fienile. **—rick, —stack** *n.* mucchio di fieno.

hazard (hăz'ērd) *n.* azzardo, rischio. *vt., vi.* arrischiare, osare, avventurarsi. **—ous** *agg.* azzardato, rischioso.

haze (hāz) *n.* nebbia, bruma; confusione. *vt.* annebbiare, angariare.

hazel (hā'z'l) *n.* nocciuolo. *agg.* di nocciuolo, color nocciuola: **—nut,** nocciuola.

hazy (hā'zĭ) *agg.* nebuloso, nebbioso, annebbiato, opaco, velato: **— notions,** idee poco chiare.

he (hē) (1) *pron.pers.m.* egli, colui: **— who,** colui che.

he (2) *pref.* maschio: **he-elephant,** elefante maschio; **he-goat,** caprone; **a he-man,** un vero uomo.

head (hĕd) *n.* testa, capo; prua; capezzale; sorgente (*di fiume*); punta (*di freccia*); pomo (*di bastone*); testata (*di pagina*): **a —, per —,** a testa, per persona; **— over heels,** perdutamente, a rotoli; **— or tail,** testa o croce; **to come to a —,** maturare; suppurare; risolversi; **to keep one's —,** controllarsi; **to make — against,** far fronte a. *agg.* primo, principale, in capo. *vt.* mettersi alla testa di, capeggiare, dirigere; intestare; affrontare. *vi.* dirigersi. **—ache** *n.* mal di capo, emicrania, (*fig.*) noia, grattacapo, rompicapo. **—dress** *n.* pettinatura, cappellino. **—gear** *n.* copricapo. **—ing** *n.* intestazione, titolo. **—land** *n.* promontorio. **—light** *n.* fanale anteriore. **—line** *n.* intestazione (*di articolo*), titolo (*di libro*). **—long** *avv.* a capofitto, a testa bassa, impetuosamente. **—quarters** *n.* quartier generale; direzione, sede centrale. **—strong** *agg.* testardo. **—way** *n.* progresso, avanzamento: **to make —,** avanzare, progredire. **— wind,** vento contrario.

heady (hĕd'ĭ) *agg.* inebriante.

heal (hēl) *vt.* guarire, cicatrizzare, sanare. **—ing** *n.* guarigione, cicatrizzazione.

health

health (hĕlth) *n.* salute. **—ful** *agg.* sano, salubre. **—fulness** *n.* salubrità, sanità.

healthy (hĕl'thĭ) *agg.* sano, salubre, salutare.

heap (hēp) *n.* mucchio, cumulo, quantità. *vt.* ammucchiare, accumulare.

hear (hḗr) *vt.*, *vi.* (*pass.*, *pp.* **heard**) udire, ascoltare; apprendere: **to —from**, avere notizie da; **to — of** *o* **about**, avere notizie di. **—er** *n.* ascoltatore. **—ing** *n.* udito (*senso*); udienza; ascolto: **within —**, a portata di voce.

heard (hûrd) *pass* e *pp. di to* hear.

hearken (här'kĕn) *vi.* ascoltare.

hearsay (hḗr'sā') *n.* diceria: **by —**, per sentito dire.

hearse (hûrs) *n.* carro funebre.

heart (härt) *n.* cuore, animo; centro; coraggio: **at —**, nell'intimo, in sostanza; **by —**, a memoria; **in one's — of hearts**, nel più profondo del cuore. *vt.* incoraggiare, rincuorare. **—ache** *n.* angoscia. **—break** *n.* crepacuore. **—breaking** *agg.* straziante. **—broken** *n.* angosciato, affranto.

hearten (här't'n) *vt.* incoraggiare, rincuorare.

heartfelt (härt'fĕlt') *agg.* cordiale, spontaneo.

hearth (härth) *n.* focolare; (*fig.*) famiglia.

heartily (här'tĭ.lĭ) *avv.* cordialmente; con slancio; di buon appetito.

heartiness (här'tĭ.nĕs) *n.* cordialità, vigore.

heartless (härt'lĕs) *agg.* spietato, vile.

heart-rending *agg.* straziante.

heartsease (härts'ēz) *n.* pace del cuore; (*bot.*) viola del pensiero.

hearty (här'tĭ) *agg.* sincero, cordiale; robusto, vigoroso; di buon appetito; nutriente; abbondante.

heat (hēt) *n.* calore, caldo; ardore, collera; (*S.U.*) applicazione severa delle leggi, persecuzione dei criminali; pressioni; tensione; (*sport*) prova: **the deciding —**, la prova finale. *vt.*, *vi.* riscaldare, infiammare, riscaldarsi, infiammarsi. **—er** *n.* calorifero, apparecchio di riscaldamento. **—ing** *n.* riscaldamento.

heath (hēth) *n.* brughiera, erica.

heathen (hē'thĕn) *n.*, *agg.* pagano.

heather (hĕth'ĕr) *n.* erica.

heave (hēv) *n.* sforzo, conato; scossa; sollevamento. *vt.* (*pass.*, *pp.* **heaved**) alzare; sollevare, gettare, lanciare, emettere (*un sospiro*); (*naut.*) (*pass.*, *pp.* **hove**) issare, virare. *vi.*

heaven (hĕv'ĕn) *n.* paradiso, cielo. **—ly** *agg.* celeste, celestiale, divino.

heavily (hĕv'ĭ.lĭ) *avv.* pesantemente, penosamente, intensamente.

heaviness (hĕv'ĭ.nĕs) *n.* pesantezza; tristezza; sonnolenza.

heavy (hĕv'ĭ) *agg.* pesante; gravoso; penoso, noioso; triste; difficile: **— water**, acqua pesante; **— rain**, pioggia fitta *o* scrosciante.

heckle (hĕk''l) *n.* carda. *vt.* cardare; tempestare di domande; schernire.

hectic (hĕk'tĭk) *agg.* tisico; febbrile.

hedge (hĕj) *n.* siepe. *vt.* cintare con siepe: **to — a bet**, agire in modo evasivo; **to — in**, rinchiudere, cintare. *vi.* nascondersi, sgattaiolare. **—hog** *n.* istrice. **—hop** *vi.*, *vt.* volare *o* pilotare un apparecchio rasente al suolo.

heed (hēd) *n.* attenzione, diligenza. *vt.*, *vi.* prestare attenzione, badare a. **—less** *agg.* sventato, disattento.

heel (hēl) *n.* tallone, calcagno, tacco; (*gergo*) farabutto, vigliacco; sbandamento: **down at —**, in miseria; **to go head over heels**, andare a gambe all'aria; **to take to one's heels**, darsela a gambe. *vt.*, *vi.* seguire da vicino; ballare sui tacchi; mettere il tacco (*a una scarpa*) *o* il calcagno (*a una calza*); (*naut.*) sbandare.

heifer (hĕf'ĕr) *n.* giovenca.

height (hīt) *n.* altezza, statura; altura; culmine.

heighten (hīt'n) *vt.* innalzare, elevare, accrescere, intensificare. *vi.* innalzarsi, accentuarsi.

heinous (hā'nŭs) *agg.* atroce.

heir (âr) *n.* erede. **—ess** *n.* erede (*f.*), ereditiera.

held (hĕld) *pass.*, *pp. di to* hold.

helicopter (hĕl'ĭ.kŏp'tĕr) *n.* elicòttero.

heliotrope (hē'lĭ.ō.trōp) *n.* (*bot.*) eliotropio.

heliport (hĕl'ĭ.pōrt) *n.* eliporto.

helix (hē'lĭks) *n.* (*pl.* **helices**) elice, spirale, voluta.

hell (hĕl) *n.* inferno; casa da gioco. **—cat** *n.* strega, bisbetica. **—ish** *agg.* infernale.

hello (hĕ.lō') *inter.* salve!, pronto! (*al telefono*): **— -girl**, telefonista (*f.*).

helm (hĕlm) *n.* timone.

helmet (hĕl'mĕt) *n.* elmo; casco; casco coloniale.

helmsman (hĕlmz'măn) *n.* timoniere.

help (hĕlp) *n.* aiuto, assistenza, soccorso, rimedio; aiutante; domestico: **there's no — for it**, è inevitabile.

vt. aiutare, assistere, soccorrere, evitare, rimediare; servire *(cibo)*: how can I — it? che posso farci?; I cannot — saying, non posso fare a meno di dire; to — down, aiutare a discendere; to — out, aiutare ad uscire; to — oneself, aiutarsi; servirsi *(a tavola)*. —er *n.* aiutante, soccorritore. —ful *agg.* utile, servizievole. —ing *n.* aiuto; porzione. —less *agg.* debole, impotente, disperato, incapace, smarrito, irreparabile. —lessly *avv.* debolmente, senza aiuto. —lessness *n.* debolezza, impotenza, irreparabilità.

helter-skelter (hĕl'tĕr-skĕl'tĕr) *avv.* confusamente, frettolosamente.

hem (hĕm) *n.* orlo, bordo. *vt.* orlare; tossicchiare. to — in, circondare, accerchiare.

hemisphere (hĕm'ĭ.sfĕr) *n.* emisfero.

hemlock (hĕm'lŏk) *n.* cicuta.

hemorrhage (hĕm'ŏ.rĭj) *n.* emorragia.

hemp (hĕmp) *n.* canapa.

hemstitch (hĕm'stĭch') *n.* orlo a giorno. *vt.* orlare a giorno.

hen (hĕn) *n.* gallina; femmina *(degli uccelli)*: — party, riunione di sole donne.

hence (hĕns) *avv.* di qui, donde, per questo motivo: a week —, tra una settimana. —forth, —forward *avv.* da oggi in poi, per l'avvenire.

her (hûr) *pron.pers.f.* lei, la, le. *agg. poss.f.* suo, sua, suoi, sue *(di lei)*.

herald (hĕr'ăld) *n.* araldo, annunciatore; *(fig.)* precursore. *vt.* annunciare, proclamare.

herb (ûrb) *n.* erba.

herculean (hûr-kū'lē.ăn) *agg.* erculeo.

herd (hûrd) *n.* gregge, armento, mandra, branco, turba; mandriano: the common —, la plebaglia. *vt.* custodire, condurre una mandria, riunire in branco. *vi.* riunirsi in branco. —sman *n.* vaccaro, buttero; pastore.

here (hĕr) *avv.* qui, ecco: that is neither — nor there, questo non c'entra, questo è fuor di proposito; here's to you! alla vostra salute! —about, —abouts *avv.* qui vicino, nei dintorni. —after *n.* l'aldilà; *avv.* d'ora innanzi, in seguito, per l'avvenire. —by *avv.* con questo mezzo, con ciò, con la presente; qui vicino.

hereditary (hē-rĕd'ĭ-tĕr'ĭ) *agg.* ereditario.

heredity (hē-rĕd'ĭ-tĭ) *n.* ereditarietà.

herein (hĕr-ĭn') *avv.* qui dentro, in ciò; qui accluso.

heresy (hĕr'ĕ.sĭ) *n.* eresia.

heretic (hĕr'ĕ-tĭk) *n.* eretico.

hereto (hĕr'tŏō) *avv.* a tuttora, sin qui.

heretofore (hĕr'tŏō-fōr') *avv.* prima d'ora, sino ad ora, in passato.

hereupon (hĕr'ŭ-pŏn') *avv.* al che, dopo di che.

herewith (hĕr-wĭth') *avv.* con questo, unitamente, qui accluso.

heritage (hĕr'ĭ-tĭj) *n.* eredità, retaggio.

hermetic (hûr-mĕt'ĭk) *agg.* ermetico.

hermit (hûr'mĭt) *n.* eremita. —age *n.* eremitaggio, eremo.

hero (hĕr'ō) *n.* *(pl.* heroes) eroe, protagonista.

heroic (hē-rō'ĭk) *agg.* eroico.

heroine (hĕr'ō-ĭn) *n.* eroina, protagonista.

heroism (hĕr'ō-ĭz'm) *n.* eroismo.

heron (hĕr'ŭn) *n.* airone.

herring (hĕr'ĭng) *n.* aringa. —bone *n.* spina di pesce *(nei tessuti, ecc.)*.

hers (hûrz) *pron.poss.f.* il suo, la sua, i suoi, le sue *(di lei)*.

herself (hûr-sĕlf') *pron.rifl. f.* ella stessa, lei medesima: she said it —, lo disse lei stessa; by —, da sola.

hesitancy (hez'ĭ-tăn-sĭ) *n.* esitazione, indecisione.

hesitate (hĕz'ĭ-tāt) *vi.* esitare.

hesitation (hĕz'ĭ-tā'shŭn) *n.* esitazione.

heterogeneous (hĕt'ĕr-ō-jē'nē-ŭs) *agg.* eterogeneo.

hew (hū) *vt.* *(pass.* hewed, *pp.* hewn) tagliare, recidere, fendere: to — down, abbattere.

hewn (hūn) *pp. di* to hew.

hey (hā) *int.* ehi!, capital

heyday (hā'dā') *n.* rigoglio, freschezza; periodo felice.

hi (hī) *inter.* salve!, ehi!

hibernation (hī'bĕr-nā'shŭn) *n.* ibernazione.

hiccup (hĭk'ŭp) *n.* singhiozzo. *vi.* avere il singhiozzo.

hickory (hĭk'ō-rĭ) *n.* noce americano.

hid (hĭd) *pass. di* to hide.

hidden (hĭd'n) *pp. di* to hide. *agg.* nascosto, segreto, misterioso. —most *agg.* intimo, il più nascosto.

hide (hīd) (1) *vt.* *(pass.* hid, *pp.* hidden) nascondere. *vi.* nascondersi: —and-seek, rimpiattino.

hide (2) *n.* pelle d'animale, cuoio.

hideous (hĭd'ē-ŭs) *agg.* repellente, orribile.

hiding (hīd'ĭng) *n.* nascondiglio; *(fam.)* fustigazione.

hieroglyphic (hī'ĕr-ō-glĭf'ĭk) *n.* geroglifico.

hi-fi (hī'fī') *n.* alta fedeltà *(nella riproduzione dei suoni)*.

high (hī) *agg.* alto, elevato; grande; importante; forte; violento; brillo;

acceso (*di colorito*); frollo (*di carne*): — and low, dovunque; — fidelity, alta fedeltà (*nella riproduzione dei suoni*); — life, alta società; it's — time, è ormai tempo; to act with a — hand, commettere soprusi. — altar *n.* altar maggiore. —ball *n.* (*S.U.*) liquore con selz e ghiaccio; (*ferr.*) segnale di via libera, treno direttissimo; —born *agg.* di nobile nascita. —er *agg.comp.* più alto, superiore: — and —, sempre più in alto. —est *agg.superl.* supremo, (il) più alto. —handed *agg.* arbitrario, violento. —land *n.* regione montagnosa, altopiano. —lander *n.* montanaro. —light *n.* (*disegno, pitt. e fot.*) luce, zona più luminosa; (*fig.*) momento di fulgore *o* di grande interesse. *vt.* proiettare un fascio di luce su (*fig.*) mettere in risalto. —ly *avv.* altamente, sommamente, fortemente, molto. —most *agg.* altissimo, (il) più alto. —ness *n.* elevatezza, dignità; altezza (*titolo regale*). —road *n.* strada maestra. — school, scuola media. —sounding *agg.* pomposo, altisonante. —strung *agg.* coraggioso, ipersensibile. —tail *vi.* (*gergo*) squagliarsela in fretta; correre a tutta velocità. — water alta marea.

highway (hī'wā') *n.* strada maestra. —man *n.* predone, rapinatore.

hijack (hī'jăk') *vt.* (*gergo*) rubare, sottrarre; costringere con la prepotenza.

hike (hīk) *n.* passo pesante; gita *o* viaggio a piedi. *vt.* strappare, trascinare. *vi.* camminare con passo pesante; vagabondare; fare una gita *o* un viaggio a piedi.

hill (hĭl) *n.* colle, collina, poggio: up — and down dale, per monti e per valli. —ock *n.* collinetta. —y *agg.* collinoso, accidentato.

hilt (hĭlt) *n.* elsa, impugnatura.

him (hĭm) *pron.pers.m.* lui, lo, gli.

himself (hĭm-sĕlf') *pron.m.* egli stesso, lui stesso, si: he came —, venne lui stesso; he hurt —, si fece male; by —, da solo.

hind (hīnd) (1) *n.* cerva.

hind (hīnd) (2) *agg.* posteriore. —most *agg.* l'ultimo, il più arretrato.

hinder (hīn'dĕr) (1) *agg.* posteriore.

hinder (hĭn'dĕr) (2) *vt.* impedire, ritardare, ostacolare.

hindrance (hĭn'drăns) *n.* ostacolo, impedimento, intralcio.

hindsight (hīnd'sīt) *n.* senno di poi.

hinge (hĭnj) *n.* cardine, ganghero, cerniera, perno. *vt.* incardinare,

munire di cardini. *vi.* imperniarsi: everything hinges on his decision, tutto dipende dalla sua decisione.

hint (hĭnt) *n.* accenno, insinuazione, allusione: to take the —, capire l'antifona. *vt., vi.* alludere, accennare, insinuare.

hip (hĭp) *n.* anca, fianco: to have one's opponent on the —, trovarsi in vantaggio sull' avversario; to smite — and thigh, distruggere, annientare.

hippodrome (hĭp'ŏ-drōm) *n.* ippodromo.

hippopotamus (hĭp'ŏ-pŏt'à-mŭs) *n.* ippopotamo.

hire (hīr) *n.* nolo, affitto; salario; soldo. *vt.* noleggiare, prendere *o* dare in affitto; prendere in prestito; assoldare, assumere; corrompere.

hireling (hīr'lĭng) *n.* mercenario, servo prezzolato.

hiring (hīr'ĭng) *n.* noleggio.

his (hĭz) *agg., pron.poss.m.* suo, sua, di lui, suoi, sue, il suo, la sua, i suoi, le sue, il di lui: a friend of —, un suo amico.

hiss (hĭs) *n.* fischio, sibilo. *vt., vi.* sibilare, fischiare. —ing *n.* sibilo. *agg.* sibilante.

historian (hĭs-tō'rĭ-ăn) *n.* storico.

historic (hĭs-tŏr'ĭk) *agg.* storico.

history (hĭs'tō-rĭ) *n.* storia.

hit (hĭt) *n.* colpo; successo; idea, invenzione. *vt.* (*pass., pp.* hit) colpire, urtare, raggiungere (*un bersaglio*), toccare: — or miss, *o* va *o* spacca; to — it off well, andare d'accordo; to — on, upon, imbattersi in, trovare, scoprire.

hitch (hĭch) *n.* strappo; uncino, gancio, aggancio; difficoltà, ostacolo. *vt., vi.* muoversi a strattoni; impigliarsi; zoppicare; agganciare, afferrare; trascinare; dare uno strattone; attaccare (*un cavallo alla carrozza*); andar d'accordo.

hitch-hike *vi.* viaggiare con l'autostop.

hither (hĭth'ĕr) *agg.* il più vicino. *avv.* qui, qua: — and thither, qua e là. —to *avv.* sin qui, sino a questo momento.

hive (hīv) *n.* alveare, sciame (*anche di persone*); (*pl.*) eruzione cutanea, orticaria.

hoar (hōr) *n.* candore, vecchiaia. —frost *n.* brina.

hoard (hōrd) *n.* mucchio, cumulo, ammasso, tesoro. *vt., vi.* ammassare, accumulare, tesaurizzare, accaparrare, accumularsi.

hoarse (hōrs) *agg.* roco, rauco; flebile: — throat, raucedine. —ness *n.* raucedine, suono rauco.

hoary (hōr'ĭ) *agg.* bianco, biancastro, canuto; vecchio, venerabile.

hoax (hōks) *n.* mistificazione, trucco, scherzo, falsa notizia.

hobble (hŏb''l) *n.* zoppicamento, difficoltà, ostacolo, pastoia. *vt.* impastoiare, ostacolare. *vi.* zoppicare, incespicare.

hobby (hŏb'ĭ) *n.* passatempo favorito, mania: **to ride one's —**, trattare l'argomento favorito. **—horse** *n.* cavallino a dondolo.

hobo (hō'bō) *n.* (*S.U.*) vagabondo.

hock (hŏk) *n.* (1) garretto di cavallo.

hock (hŏk) (2) *vt.* (*gergo*) impegnare, dare in pegno.

hocus-pocus (hō'kŭs·pō'kŭs) *n.* gioco di prestigio, gherminella.

hodgepodge (hŏj'pŏj')*n.* guazzabuglio.

hoe (hō) *n.* zappa. *vt.*, *vi.* zappare, scavare.

hog (hŏg) *n.* maiale, porco: **to go whole —**, andare sino fondo. *vt.*, *vi.* arraffare. **—wash** *n.* beverone del porco.

hoist (hoist) *n.* paranco, montacarichi. *vt.*, sollevare, issare.

hold (hōld) *n.* presa, appoggio, sostegno; custodia, prigione; autorità, influenza; fortificazione, dominio; (*naut.*) stiva; (*aeron.*) scompartimento merci: **to get, to take — of**, prendere, afferrare, aggrapparsi a. *vt.* (*pass. pp.* **held**) tenere; mantenere; sostenere; possedere; detenere; trattenere; contenere; occupare; avere; considerare: **to — back**, trattenere, frenare; **to — forth**, porgere, esporre; concionare; **to — one's own**, conservare quel che si ha; mantenere la propria opinione; **to — off**, tenere a distanza; **to — up**, sollevare, esibire, arrestare; rapinare. *vi.* tenersi, durare, sopportare, persistere, attaccarsi: **to — back**, esitare; **to — on**, perseverare; **to — out**, resistere. **—er** *n.* possessore, detentore, locatario; impugnatura; astuccio; serbatoio. **—up** *n.* aggressione, rapina.

hole (hōl) *n.* buco, buca; antro, tana, spelonca: **to put in a —**, mettere in una situazione difficile. *vt.* bucare, perforare. *vi.* rintanarsi.

holiday (hŏl'ĭ·dā) *n.* festa, vacanza.

holiness (hō'lĭ·nĕs) *n.* santità.

hollow (hŏl'ō) *n.* cavo, cavità, caverna. *agg.* cavo, scavato, vuoto, profondo, infossato; sordo (*di suono*), falso. *vt.*, *vi.* scavare, incavare, incavarsi.

holly (hŏl'ĭ) *n.* agrifoglio.

holster (hōl'stĕr) *n.* fondina di pistola.

holy (hō'lĭ) *agg.* santo, sacro, benedetto.

homage (hŏm'ĭj) *n.* omaggio: **to do —**, rendere omaggio.

home (hōm) *n.* casa, focolare domestico, dimora, patria, asilo: **at —**, in casa; **to make oneself at —**, mettersi a proprio agio. *agg.* domestico, casalingo, nazionale: **— stretch** (*sport*) dirittura d'arrivo; **— rule**, autogoverno, autonomia; **— office**, sede centrale, casa madre. *avv.* **a o in casa**, a segno, efficacemente: **to strike —**, colpire nel vivo, cogliere nel segno. **—land** *n.* patria. **—less** *agg.* senza casa. **—liness** *n.* semplicità, domesticità, bruttezza. **—ly** *agg.* casalingo, semplice, brutto. **—made** *agg.* fatto in casa, di fabbricazione nazionale. **—sick** *agg.* nostalgico. **—sickness** *n.* nostalgia. **—stead** *n.* castello, fattoria. **—ward** *avv.* verso casa; verso la patria: **— voyage**, viaggio di ritorno. **—work** *n.* compiti di casa.

homicidal (hŏm'ĭ·sīd'ăl) *agg.* omicida.

homicide (hŏm'ĭ·sīd) *n.* omicidio, omicida.

homogeneous (hō'mō·jē'nē·ŭs) *agg.* omogeneo.

homologate (hō·mŏl'ō·gāt) *vt.* omologare.

hone (hōn) *n.* pietra da rasoio. *vt.* affilare.

honest (ŏn'ĕst) *agg.* onesto, sincero; genuino.

honesty (ŏn'ĕs·tĭ) *n.* onestà, sincerità.

honey (hŭn'ĭ) *n.* miele; dolcezza, tesoro, amore. **— bee**, ape. **—comb** *n.* favo. *agg.* a nido d'ape. **—ed** *agg.* melato. **—moon** *n.* luna di miele. **—suckle** *n.* caprifoglio.

honk (hŏngk) *n.* verso dell'oca; clacson. *vi.*, *vi.* sonare il clacson.

honor (ŏn'ĕr) *n.* onore, rispetto, dignità. *vt.* onorare, far onore a. **—able** *agg.* onorevole, onorabile. **—ableness** *n.* onorabilità.

hood (hŏod) *n.* cappuccio, mantice (*di veicolo*); cofano (*d'auto*); (*gergo*) bandito, teppista, sicario. *vt.* incappucciare.

hoodlum (hŏod'lŭm) *n.* (*S.U.*) giovane delinquente, teppista.

hoodwink (hŏod'wĭngk) *vt.* bendare gli occhi a, imbrogliare.

hoof (hŏof) *n.* zoccolo (*di quadrupede*).

hook (hŏok) *n.* gancio, uncino, amo: **by — or by crook**, con ogni mezzo, a qualunque costo; **on one's own —**, per conto proprio. *vt.* agganciare, uncinare, prendere all'amo. *vi.* agganciarsi, incurvarsi; svignarsela.

hooked *agg.* uncinato, curvo, adunco; *(gergo)* dedito agli stupefacenti.

hooky (hŏŏk′ĭ): **to play —**, marinare la scuola.

hooligan (hōō′lĭ.găn) *n.* furfante; teppista.

hoop (hōōp) *n.* cerchio, cerchietto, cerchione. *vt.* cerchiare.

hoot (hōōt) *n.* grido, schiamazzo, gracchio, sirena *(di fabbrica)*: **not to give a —**, infischiarsene. *vt.*, *vi.* urlare, schiamazzare, ululare.

hop ((hŏp) *n.* salto, balzo; *(bot.)* luppolo. *vt.*, *vi.* saltare, saltellare, svignarsela; salire *(su un treno, ecc.)*; *(aeron.)* decollare; trasvolare *(un oceano)*: **to — up** *(gergo)*, stimolare, eccitare *(spec. con stupefacenti)*.

hope (hōp) *n.* speranza. *vt.*, *vi.* sperare: **to — against —**, sperare l'impossibile. **—ful** *agg.* speranzoso; promettente. **—fully** *avv.* con speranza, con ottimismo. **—less** *agg.* disperato, inutile, irrimediabile. **—lessness** *n.* disperazione, inutilità, irrimediabilità.

horde (hôrd) *n.* orda.

horizon (hŏ.rī′z′n) *n.* orizzonte.

horizontal (hŏr′ĭ.zŏn′tăl) *agg.* orizzontale.

horn (hôrn) *n.* corno; antenna; cornetta; *(autom.)* tromba, segnale acustico: **— of plenty**, cornucopia. *vt.* dar cornate a, munire di corna. *vi.*: **to — in**, interloquire, intromettersi.

hornet (hôr′nĕt) *n.* calabrone: **hornets' nest**, vespaio.

hornpipe (hôrn′pīp′) *n.* cornamusa.

horny (hôr′nĭ) *agg.* calloso, corneo.

horoscope (hŏr′ō.skōp) *n.* oroscopo.

horrible (hŏr′ĭ.b'l) *agg.* orribile, atroce.

horribly (-blĭ) *avv.* orrendamente.

horrid (hŏr′ĭd) *agg.* orrido, odioso.

horrify (hŏr′ĭ.fī) *vt.* terrorizzare, far inorridire.

horror (hŏr′ẽr) *n.* orrore: **to strike with —**, orripilare; **— book**, romanzo nero.

horse (hôrs) *n.* cavallo; cavalletto; *(mil.)* cavalleria, soldato di cavalleria: **— chestnut**, ippocastano; **— opera** *(cinema)*, film western; **— sense**, fiuto, senso pratico; **— trade**, commercio di cavalli, *(fig.)* mercanteggiamento, compromesso. **—back** *n.* groppa: **on —**, in groppa, a cavallo. **—fly** *n.* mosca cavallina. **—laugh** *n.* risata grassa. **—man** *n.* cavaliere, cavallerizzo. **—manship** *n.* abilità equestre. **—power** *n.* cavallo vapore. **—shoe**

n. ferro da cavallo. **—woman** *n.* amazzone, cavallerizza.

hose (hōz) *n.* calza; uosa; tubo; idrante: **men's —**, calze da uomo.

hosier (hō′zhẽr) *n.* calzettaio.

hosiery (hō′zhẽr.ĭ) *n.* calze; commercio delle calze; calzetteria.

hospitable (hŏs′pĭ.tá.b'l) *agg.* ospitale.

hospital (hŏs′pĭt.ăl) *n.* ospedale, clinica; ricovero per vecchi.

hospitality (hŏs′pĭ.tăl′ĭ.tĭ) *n.* ospitalità.

host (1) (hōst) *n.* ospite *(chi ospita)*, albergatore.

host (2) *n.* turba, moltitudine, quantità.

Host (3) *n.* Ostia Consacrata.

hostage (hŏs′tĭj) *n.* ostaggio.

hostel (hŏs′tĕl) *n.* casa dello studente, albergo per la gioventù.

hostess (hōs′tĕs) *n.* ospite *(donna che ospita)*; ballerina stipendiata *(nei ritrovi)*; *(aeron.)* hostess.

hostile (hŏs′tĭl) *agg.* ostile.

hostility (hŏs.tĭl′ĭ.tĭ) *n.* ostilità.

hot (hŏt) *agg.* caldo, rovente, bollente; accaldato; appassionato; violento; frenetico; piccante; recentissimo, fresco, alla moda; travolgente, entusiasmante; scottante, pericoloso: **— from the press**, fresco di stampa; **— rod**, automobile da corsa; **— shot** *(gergo)*, persona dinamica, uomo in gamba; *agg.* dinamico, attivissimo, bravissimo; **— war**, conflitto armato. **—bed** *n.* vivaio; *(fig.)* focolaio. **—blooded** *agg.* ardente, sovreccitabile, focoso; *(di cavalli)* purosangue. **—headed** *agg.* violento, focoso. **—house** *n.* serra; postribolo.

hotel (hō.tĕl′) *n.* albergo: **— manager**, direttore d'albergo. **—keeper** *n.* albergatore.

hotly (hŏt′lĭ) *avv.* caldamente, vivacemente, con veemenza.

hotness (hŏt′nĕs) *n.* calore, veemenza.

hound (hound) *n.* cane, segugio; mascalzone; tifoso. *vt.* braccare, inseguire.

hour (our) *n.* ora: **an — ago**, un'ora fa. **—glass** *n.* clessidra. **— hand** *n.* lancetta delle ore *(nell' orologio)*. **—ly** *agg.* orario, frequente. *avv.* frequentemente, d'ora in ora.

house (hous) *n.* casa; famiglia, dinastia; albergo; teatro; aula *(parlamentare, ecc.)*: **full —** *(teat.)*, tutto esaurito. *vt.* alloggiare, ospitare, collocare. *vi.* abitare, ripararsi. **—breaker** *n.* ladro *(scassinatore)*. **—breaking** *n.* furto con scasso. **—coat** *n.* vestaglia *(femminile)*.

—hold *n.* famiglia, organizzazione domestica. *agg.* domestico, casalingo. —keeper *n.* governante di casa. —keeping *n.* governo della casa, faccende domestiche. —wife *n.* massaia. —wifery *n.* economia domestica. —work *n.* faccende domestiche.

housing (houz′ĭng) *n.* riparo, alloggio.

hove (hōv) *pass.* e *pp. di* to heave.

hovel (hŏv′ĕl) *n.* capanna, tugurio.

hover (hŭv′ẽr) *vi.* librarsi, gravitare; attardarsi; gironzolare; esitare.

how (hou) *avv.* come, in che modo, quanto, perchè; — are you? come state? — far? sino a qual punto?, a quale distanza? — long? quanto tempo? — much? quanto? — many? quanti? — beautiful! che bello! how nice of you! molto gentile da parte vostra!; — early (late, soon)? quando, a che ora?; — old are you? quanti anni avete?; no matter — much, per quanto, non importa quanto.

however *cong.* ciononostante, eppure. *avv.* per quanto, in qualunque misura: — he may do it, in qualunque modo lo faccia; — important it may be, per quanto importante sia; — that may be, comunque sia; — did you manage to do it? come diamine ci siete riuscito?

howl (houl) *n.* grido, ululato, gemito. *vi.* ululare, gemere.

howsoever (hou′sō·ĕv′ẽr) *avv.* comunque, per quanto.

hub (hŭb) *n.* centro, fulcro, mozzo (*di ruota*).

hubbub (hŭb′ŭb) *n.* tumulto, baccano.

huckster (hŭk′stẽr) *n.* venditore ambulante; imbroglione; (*S.U.*) agente di pubblicità radiofonica.

huddle (hŭd′′l) *n.* ammasso, confusione, folla; conciliabolo. *vt., vi.* ammassare, arruffare, raggomitolarsi, affollarsi.

hue (hū) (1) *n.* colore, sfumatura.

hue (hū) (2) *n.* clamore: — and cry, pandemonio, alzata di scudi.

huff (hŭf) *n.* collera; risentimento: to get into a —, andare in collera.

huffy (hŭf′ĭ) *agg.* arrogante, stizzito.

hug (hŭg) *n.* abbraccio. *vt.* abbracciare, stringere: to — oneself, compiacersi (*con se stesso*); to — the shore, costeggiare.

huge (hūj) *agg.* enorme, gigantesco. —ly *avv.* enormemente. —ness *n.* enormità, mole imponente.

hulk (hŭlk) *n.* carcassa di nave; pontone ammasso. —ing *agg.* goffo, corpulento.

hull (hŭl) *n.* (*naut.*) scafo; (*aeron.*) fusoliera; (*bot.*) guscio, buccia. *vt.* squarciare (*uno scafo*), sgusciare, sbucciare.

hum (hŭm) *n.* mormorio, ronzio. *vt., vi.* canticchiare, mormorare, ronzare; darsi da fare.

human (hū′măn) *agg.* umano.

humane (hū·mān′) *agg.* umanitario.

humanitarian (hū·măn′ĭ·târ′ĭ·ăn) *n., agg.* umanitario.

humanity (hū·măn′ĭ·tĭ) *n.* umanità; (*pl.*), materie classiche.

humanly (hū′măn·lĭ) *avv.* umanamente.

humble (hŭm′b′l) *agg.* umile. *vt.* umiliare, mortificare. —ness *n.* umiltà.

humbly (hŭm′blĭ) *avv.* umilmente.

humbug (hŭm′bŭg′) *n.* impostura, frode; impostore: —! frottole!

humdrum (hŭm′drŭm′) *agg.* monotono.

humiliate (hū·mĭl′ĭ·āt) *vt.* umiliare.

humiliating *agg.* umiliante.

humiliation (-ā′shŭn) *n.* umiliazione.

humility (hū·mĭl′ĭ·tĭ) *n.* umiltà.

humming (hŭm′ĭng) *n.* ronzio, mormorio. *agg.* ronzante; intenso, movimentato.

hummingbird (hŭm′ĭng·bûrd′) *n.* colibrì.

humorist (hū′mẽr·ĭst) *n.* umorista.

humorous (-ŭs) *agg.* umoristico, comico.

humor (hū′mẽr) *n.* umore, umorismo, spirito, capriccio: out of —, di cattivo umore. *vt.* assecondare, blandire.

hump (hŭmp) *n.* gibbosità; malumore. *vt., vi.* far la gobba, ingobbire, curvarsi. —back *n.* gobbo.

hunch (hŭnch) *n.* protuberanza, gibbosità; pezzo; (*S.U.*) sospetto, presentimento, intuizione. *vt.* curvare (*le spalle*). —back *n.* gobbo.

hundred (hŭn′drĕd) *n., agg.* cento, centinaio. —th *n.* la centesima parte. *agg.* centesimo.

hung (hŭng) *pass., pp.* di to hang.

hunger (hŭng′gẽr) *n.* fame, brama. *vt.* affamare. *vi.* aver fame: to — for, agognare, bramare.

hungrily (hŭng′grĭ·lĭ) *avv.* avidamente.

hungry (hŭng′grĭ) *agg.* affamato: to be —, aver fame.

hunk (hŭnk) *n.* grosso pezzo, blocco, massa.

hunt (hŭnt) *n.* caccia, inseguimento; muta di cani. *vt.* cacciare, inseguire, cercare accanitamente: to — down, perseguitare. *vi.* andare a caccia. —er *n.* cacciatore; cane da caccia. —sman *n.* cacciatore.

hurdle (hûr'd'l) *n.* ostacolo, siepe; (*pl.*) corsa a ostacoli.

hurl (hûrl) *vt.* lanciare, scagliare.

hurrah (hŏŏ·ra̅') *inter.* urrà, evviva. *vt., vi.* acclamare.

hurricane (hûr'ĭ·kăn) *n.* uragano, ciclone.

hurried (hûr'ĕd) *agg.* affrettato, frettoloso. —ly *avv.* frettolosamente, affrettatamente.

hurry (hûr'ĭ) *n.* fretta: to be in a —, aver fretta. *vt.* affrettare, precipitare, incalzare. *vi.* affrettarsi: to — away, allontanarsi in fretta; to — in (out); entrare (uscire) in fretta; to — up, far presto.

hurt (hûrt) *n.* male, danno, ferita. *vt.* (*pass., pp.* hurt) offendere, ferire, urtare, ledere; far male a: to — one's feelings, offendere, ferire, mortificare. *vi.* far male, nuocere, dolere. —ful *agg.* nocivo, doloroso.

hurtle (hûr't'l) *vt.* scaraventare. *vi.* cozzare; rovinare, precipitare.

hurtless (hûrt'lĕs) *agg.* innocuo; illeso.

husband (hŭz'bănd) *n.* marito, sposo.

hush (hŭsh) *n., inter.* silenzio. *vt.* far tacere, chetare; mettere in tacere: to — up a scandal, soffocare uno scandalo. *vi.* tacere, far silenzio.

husk (hŭsk) *n.* buccia, guscio, baccello, involucro. *vt.* sbucciare, sgusciare.

husky (hŭs'kĭ) *agg.* rauco; rude, vigoroso.

hussy (hŭz'ĭ) *n.* sgualdrina, insolente (*f.*).

hustle (hŭs'l) *n.* fretta; energia, spinta: — and bustle, andirivieni. *vt.* spingere. *vi.* affrettarsi.

hut (hŭt) *n.* capanna, tugurio, baracca.

hyacinth (hī'á·sĭnth) *n.* (*bot.*) giacinto.

hybrid (hī'brĭd) *n., agg.* ibrido.

hydraulic (hī·drô'lĭk) *agg.* idraulico.

hydrobomb (hī'drô·bôm') *n.* siluro sganciato da un aerosilurante.

hydrofoil (boat) (hī'drô·foil') *n.* aliscafo idroscivolante.

hydrogen (hī'drô·jen) *n.* idrogeno: — bomb, bomba all'idrogeno.

hydroplane (hī'drô·plān) *n.* idroscivolante; idroplano.

hyena (hī·ē'ná) *n.* (*zool.*) iena.

hygiene (hī'jēn) *n.* igiene.

hygienic (hī'jǐ·ĕn'ĭk) *agg.* igienico.

hymn (hĭm) *n.* inno.

hypertension (hī'pĕr·tĕn'shŭn) *n.* ipertensione.

hypertensive (-sĭv) *agg., n.* iperteso.

hyphen (hī'fĕn) *n.* trattino, lineetta di congiunzione.

hypnosis (hĭp·nō'sĭs) *n.* ipnosi.

hypnotic (-nŏt' k) *n., agg.* ipnotico, narcotico.

hypnotist (hĭp'nō·tĭst) *n.* ipnotizzatore.

hypocrisy (hĭ·pŏk'rĭ·sĭ) *n.* ipocrisia.

hypocrite (hĭp'ô·krĭt) *n.* ipocrita.

hypocritical (-krĭt'ĭ·kăl) *agg.* ipocrito.

hypodermic (hī'pô·dûr'mĭk) *n.* iniezione sottocutanea. *agg.* ipodermico, sottocutaneo.

hypothesis (hī·pŏth'ĕ·sĭs) *n.* ipotesi.

hysteria (hĭs·tĕr'ĭ·á) *n.* isterismo.

hysterical (-tĕr'ĭ·kăl) *agg.* isterico.

I

I (I) *pron.pers.nom.* io.

Iberian (I·bēr'ĭ·ăn) *n., agg.* iberico.

ice (Is) *n.* ghiaccio, gelo; gelato; zucchero cristallizzato. *vt., vi.* ghiacciare, gelare, glassare (*dolci*). —berg *n.* montagna di ghiaccio. —box *n.* ghiacciaia. —breaker *n.* nave rompighiaccio. —cream *n.* gelato: — parlor (*S.U.*) gelateria. —man *n.* venditore di ghiaccio.

Icelander (Is'lăn'dĕr) *n.* islandese.

icicle (I'sĭk·'l) *n.* ghiacciolo.

icterus (ĭk'tĕr·ŭs) *n.* itterizia.

icy (I'sĭ) *agg.* ghiacciato, gelido.

idea (I·dē'á) *n.* idea, concetto.

ideal (I·dē'ăl) *n., agg.* ideale. —ism *n.* idealismo. —ist *n.* idealista.

identical (I·dĕn'tĭ·kăl) *agg.* identico, stesso, medesimo.

identification (I·dĕn't'·fĭ·kā'shŭn) *n.* identificazione.

identify (I·dĕn'tĭ·fī) *vt.* identificare: to — oneself with, immedesimarsi con.

identity (I·dĕn'tĭ·tĭ) *n.* identità.

ideological (I'dē·ô·lŏj'ĭ·kăl) *agg.* ideologico.

ideology (I'dē·ŏl'ô·jĭ) *n.* ideologia.

idiocy (ĭd'ĭ·ô·sĭ) *n.* idiozia.

idiom (ĭd'ĭ·ŭm) *n.* idioma, idiotismo.

idiosyncrasy (ĭd'ĭ·ô·sĭng'krá·sĭ) *n.* idiosincrasia, peculiarità.

idiot (ĭd'ĭ·ŭt) *n.* idiota. —ic (-ŏt'ĭc) *agg.* insensato, da idiota.

idle (I'd'l) *n.* pigro, ozioso, inutile, inoperoso, morto (*di capitale*). *vt.* sprecare (*tempo*) in ozio. *vi.* oziare, impigrirsi; (*di motore*) andare al minimo, girare in folle. —ness *n.* pigrizia, ozio, inutilità.

idler (I'dlĕr) *n.* pigro, sfaccendato.

idly (I'dlĭ) *avv.* pigramente, oziosamente, vanamente.

idol (ī'dŭl) *n.* idolo. —ater (ī.dŏl'á·tẽr) *n.* idolatra.

idolize (ī'dŭl·īz) *vt.* idolatrare.

idyl, idyll (ī'dĭl) *n.* idillio.

if (ĭf) *cong.* se, qualora, sebbene, benchè: as —, come se; — anything, se mai; — so, in tal caso.

iffy (ĭf'ĭ) *agg.* (gergo) pieno di se e di ma, titubante.

ignite (ĭg·nīt') *vt.* accendere, incendiare. *vi.* prender fuoco.

ignition (ĭg·nĭsh'ŭn) *n.* accensione.

ignoble (ĭg·nō'b'l) *agg.* ignobile.

ignominy (ĭg'nō·mĭn·ĭ) *n.* ignominia.

ignoramus (ĭg'nō·rā'mŭs) *n.* ignorante.

ignorance (ĭg'nō·răns) *n.* ignoranza.

ignorant (-rănt) *agg.* ignorante.

ignore (ĭg·nōr') *vt.* ignorare.

ill (ĭl) *n.* male, malanno, sfortuna. *agg.* cattivo, malvagio; ammalato. *avv.* male: —advised, sconsiderato, imprudente; — at ease, inquieto, a disagio; —bred, maleducato; —favored, brutto; —mannered, scortese; — nature, malvagità, malanimo; —natured, malvagio; —starred, sfortunato; —timed, intempestivo; —will, malevolenza, ostilità.

illegal (ĭl·lē'gắl) *agg.* illegale.

illegible (ĭl·lěj'ĭ·b'l) *agg.* illeggibile.

illegitimacy (ĭl'lê·jĭt'ĭ·má·sĭ) *n.* illegittimità.

illegitimate (ĭl'lê·jĭt'ĭ·mĭt) *agg.* illegittimo, illegale.

illicit (ĭl·lĭs'ĭt) *agg.* illecito.

illiteracy (ĭl·lĭt'ẽr·á·sĭ) *n.* ignoranza; analfabetismo; errore.

illiterate (ĭl·lĭt'ẽr·ĭt) *agg.* illetterato.

illness (ĭl'nĕs) *n.* malattia.

illogical (ĭl·lŏj'ĭ·kăl) *agg.* illogico.

illuminate (ĭ·lū'mĭ·nāt) *vt.* illuminare, rischiarare; miniare, decorare.

illumination (-nā'shŭn) *n.* illuminazione; miniatura (*di un libro*).

illusion (ĭ·lū'zhŭn) *n.* illusione.

illusive (-sĭv), illusory (-sō·rĭ) *agg.* illusorio, ingannevole, fallace.

illustrate (ĭl'ŭs·trāt) *vt.* illustrare.

illustration (ĭl'ŭs·trā'shŭn) *n.* illustrazione.

illustrator (ĭl'ŭs·trā'tẽr) *n.* illustratore.

illustrious (ĭ·lŭs'trĭ·ŭs) *agg.* illustre.

I'm (īm) *contr. di* I am (*io sono*).

image (ĭm'ĭj) *n.* immagine. —ry *n.* raffigurazione; fantasia; iconografia

imaginary (ĭ·măj'ĭ·nẽr'ĭ) *agg.* immaginario.

imagination (ĭ·măj'ĭ·nā'shŭn) *n.* immaginazione, fantasia; concezione.

imaginative (ĭ·măj'ĭ·nā'tĭv) *agg.* immaginativo; fantasioso.

imagine (ĭ·măj'ĭn) *vt.* immaginare, figurarsi.

imbecile (ĭm'bê·sĭl) *n.*, *agg.* imbecille.

imbed (ĭm·bĕd') *vedi* embed.

imbibe (ĭm·bīb') *vt.*, *vi.* assorbire, imbeversi, assimilare (*idee*).

imbue (ĭm·bū') *vt.* imbevere, inculcare.

imitate (ĭm'ĭ·tāt) *vt.* imitare.

imitation (ĭm'ĭ·tā'shŭn) *n.* imitazione. *agg.* imitato, d'imitazione, finto.

imitator (ĭm'ĭ·tā'tŏr) *n.* imitatore.

immaculate (ĭ·măk'û·lĭt) *agg.* immacolato.

immaterial (ĭm'má·tẽr'ĭ·ăl) *agg.* insignificante, indifferente; incorporeo.

immature (ĭm'á·tūr') *agg.* immaturo, prematuro.

immeasurable (ĭ·mĕzh'ẽr·á·b'l) *agg.* incommensurabile, smisurato.

immediate (ĭ·mē'dĭ·ĭt) *agg.* immediato. —ly *avv.* immediatamente. *cong.* non appena.

immemorial (ĭm'mē·mō'rĭ·ăl) *agg.* immemorabile.

immense (ĭ·mĕns') *agg.* immenso.

immerse (ĭ·mûrs') *vt.* immergere; battezzare. *vi.* sommergersi, immergersi.

immersion (ĭ·mûr'shŭn) *n.* immersione.

immigrant (ĭm'ĭ·grănt) *n.*, *agg.* immigrante.

immigrate (ĭm'ĭ·grāt) *vi.* immigrare.

immigration (-grā'shŭn) *n.* immigrazione.

imminence (ĭm'ĭ·nĕns) *n.* imminenza.

imminent (ĭm'ĭ·nĕnt) *agg.* imminente.

immobility (ĭm'ō·bĭl'ĭ·tĭ) *n.* immobilità.

immobilize (ĭm·mō'bĭ·līz) *vt.* immobilizzare.

immoderate (ĭm·mŏd'ẽr·ĭt) *agg.* immoderato, smodato.

immodest (ĭm·mŏd'ĕst) *agg.* immodesto, impudico.

immodesty (-ĕs·tĭ) *avv.* immodestia, impudicizia.

immoral (ĭm·mŏr'ăl) *agg.* immorale. —ity (ĭm'mō·răl'ĭ·tĭ) *n.* immoralità.

immortal (ĭ·môr'tăl) *agg.* immortale. —ity (ĭm'ôr·tăl'ĭ·tĭ) *n.* immortalità.

immortalize (ĭ·môr'tăl·īz) *vt.* immortalare, perpetuare.

immovable (ĭm·mōōv'á·b'l) *agg.* immobile, inamovibile; impassibile; irremovibile.

immune (ĭ·mūn') *agg.* immune, esente.

immunity (ĭ·mū'nĭ·tĭ) *n.* immunità.

imp (ĭmp) *n.* diavoletto.

impact (ĭm'păkt) *n.* urto, collisione.

impair (ĭm·pâr') *vt.* diminuire, svalutare, indebolire, danneggiare, pregiudicare. *vi.* deteriorarsi. —ment *n.* danno, diminuzione, deterioramento.

impalpable (ĭm·păl′pȧ·b'l) *agg.* impalpabile.

impart (ĭm·pärt′) *vt.* impartire, comunicare, riferire; concedere.

impartial (ĭm·pär′shăl) *agg.* imparziale. —**ity** (ĭm′pär·shĭ·ăl′ĭ·tĭ) *n.* imparzialità.

impassable (ĭm·pȧs′ȧ·b'l) *agg.* impraticabile, insormontabile.

impassible (ĭm·păs′ĭ·b'l) *agg.* impassibile.

impassion (ĭm·păsh′ŭn) *vt.* appassionare, infiammare. —**ed** *agg.* appassionato, veemente, ardente.

impassive (ĭm·păs′ĭv) *agg.* impassibile.

impatience (ĭm·pā′shĕns) *n.* impazienza.

impatient (ĭm·pā′shĕnt) *agg.* impaziente; spazientito.

impeach (ĭm·pēch′) *vt.* incriminare, invalidare; mettere in stato d'accusa.

impecunious (ĭm′pē·kū′nĭ·ŭs) *agg.* povero.

impede (ĭm·pēd′) *vt.* impedire, ostacolare.

impediment (ĭm·pĕd′ĭ·mĕnt) *n.* impedimento, ostacolo.

impel (ĭm·pĕl′) *vt.* costringere, indurre.

impend (ĭm·pĕnd′) *vi.* minacciare, essere imminente, pendere (*sul capo*). —**ing** *agg.* imminente; minaccioso.

impenetrable (ĭm·pĕn′ē·trȧ·b'l) *n.* impenetrabile, inaccessibile.

imperative (ĭm·pĕr′ȧ·tĭv) *agg.* imprescindibile; imperioso; urgente, impellente, necessario; imperativo.

imperceptible (ĭm′pĕr·sĕp′tĭ·b'l) *agg.* impercettibile.

imperfect (ĭm·pûr′fĕkt) *n., agg.* imperfetto.

imperial (ĭm·pēr′ĭ·ăl) *n.* imperiale (*di veicolo*); mosca (*ciuffetto di barba*). *agg.* imperiale.

imperil (ĭm·pĕr′ĭl) *vt.* mettere in pericolo, compromettere.

imperious (ĭm·pēr′ĭ·ŭs) *agg.* imperioso; impellente.

imperishable (ĭm·pĕr′ĭsh·ȧ·b'l) *agg.* duraturo, non deperibile.

impersonal (ĭm·pûr′sŭn·ăl) *agg.* impersonale.

impersonate (ĭm·pûr′sŭn·āt) *vt.* impersonare, personificare, rappresentare.

impertinence (ĭm·pûr′tĭ·nĕns) *n.* impertinenza; incongruità.

impertinent (ĭm·pûr′tĭ·nĕnt) *agg.* impertinente; incongruo, futile.

impervious (ĭm·pûr′vĭ·ŭs) *agg.* impervio; impermeabile; ostinato; — **to reason**, sordo alla ragione.

impetuous (ĭm·pĕt′ū·ŭs) *agg.* impetuoso.

impetus (ĭm′pē·tŭs) *n.* impeto, impulso; (*fis.*) inerzia.

impinge (ĭm·pĭnj′) *vi.* sbattere: **to —upon**, urtare contro; interferire in.

impious (ĭm′pĭ·ŭs) *agg.* empio.

impish (ĭmp′ĭsh) *agg.* maligno, diabolico.

implacable (ĭm·plā′kȧ·b'l) *agg.* implacabile.

implant (ĭm·plȧnt′) *vt.* impiantare; inculcare.

implement (ĭm′plē·mĕnt) *n.* utensile. *vt.* compiere, eseguire; attuare.

implicate (ĭm′plĭ·kȧt) *vt.* implicare, sottintendere; aggrovigliare.

implication (-kā′shŭn) *n.* implicazione; sottinteso; cosa implicita; groviglio: **by —**, implicitamente.

implicit (ĭm·plĭs′ĭt) *agg.* implicito, sottinteso; assoluto.

implied (ĭm·plīd′) *agg.* sottinteso, tacito.

implore (ĭm·plōr′) *vt.* implorare.

imply (ĭm·plī′) *vt.* comportare, implicare; sottintendere, significare; insinuare.

impolite (ĭm′pō·līt′) *agg.* scortese.

import (ĭm′pōrt) *n.* portata, significato, senso, importanza; importazione. *vt.* significare, indicare, comportare; importare.

importance (ĭm·pōr′tăns) *n.* importanza.

important (ĭm·pōr′tănt) *agg.* importante. — **ly** *avv.* con importanza, con sussiego.

importation (ĭm′pōr·tā′shŭn) *n.* importazione.

importer (ĭm·pōr′tĕr) *n.* importatore.

importunate (ĭm·pōr′tū·nĭt) *agg.* importuno, insistente.

impose (ĭm·pōz′) *vt., vi.* imporre; (*tip.*) impaginare: **to — upon**, approfittare di, raggirare.

imposing *n.* impaginazione. *agg.* imponente.

imposition (ĭm′pō·zĭsh′ŭn) *n.* imposizione, gravame; frode; impaginazione.

impossibility (ĭm·pŏs′ĭ·bĭl′ĭ·tĭ) *n.* impossibilità.

impossible (ĭm·pŏs′ĭ·b'l) *agg.* impossibile; insopportabile.

impostor (ĭm·pŏs′tĕr) *n.* impostore.

imposture (-tūr) *n.* impostura.

impotence (ĭm′pō·tĕns) *n.* impotenza.

impotent (ĭm′pō·tĕnt) *agg.* impotente.

impoverish (ĭm·pŏv′ĕr·ĭsh) *vt.* impoverire, depauperare.

impracticable (ĭm·prăk′tĭ·kȧ·b'l) *agg.* impraticabile, inapplicabile; intrattabile.

impregnable (ĭm·prĕg′nȧ·b'l) *agg.* inespugnabile, invincibile.

impregnate (ĭm·prĕg′nāt) *vt.* impregnare; fecondare.

impress (ĭm·prĕs′) *n.* impressione, incisione, marchio. *vt.* imprimere; incidere; impressionare, far colpo. **—ion** *n.* impressione, impronta. **—ive** *agg.* impressionante, forte, convincente, suggestivo, imponente.

imprint (ĭm·prĭnt′) *n.* impronta, impressione. *vt.* imprimere, stampare, incidere.

imprison (ĭm·prĭz′'n) *vt.* imprigionare. **—ment** *n.* incarcerazione: false **—**, detenzione abusiva.

improbable (ĭm·prŏb′ȧ·b'l) *agg.* improbabile, inverosimile.

impromptu (ĭm·prŏmp′tū) *n.* improvvisazione. *agg.* improvvisato, estemporaneo. *avv.* estemporaneamente.

improper (ĭm·prŏp′ẽr) *agg.* sconveniente, scorretto; inadatto.

improve (ĭm·prōōv′) *vt.* migliorare, perfezionare, far progredire: **—** one's time, risparmiare tempo. *vi.* migliorare, perfezionarsi, far progressi. **—ment** *n.* miglioramento, progresso, evoluzione.

improvident (ĭm·prŏv′ĭ·dĕnt) *agg.* imprevidente.

improvise (ĭm′prŏ·vīz) *vt.* improvvisare.

imprudence (ĭm·prōō′dĕns) *n.* imprudenza.

imprudent (ĭm·prōō′dĕnt) *agg.* imprudente.

impudence (ĭm′pū·dĕns)*n.* impudenza.

impudent (ĭm′pū·dĕnt) *agg.* impudente.

impulse (ĭm′pŭls), **impulsion** (ĭm·pŭl′shŭn) *n.* impulso, slancio, spinta: to act on **—**, agire d'impulso.

impulsive (ĭm·pŭl′sĭv) *agg.* impulsivo.

impunity (ĭm·pū′nĭ·tĭ) *n.* impunità.

impure (ĭm·pūr′) *agg.* impuro.

impurity (-pū′rĭ·tĭ) *n.* impurità.

impute (ĭm·pūt′) *vt.* imputare.

in (ĭn) *agg.* interno. *avv.* dentro, in casa. *prep.* in, a; mentre; per; tra: **—** haste, in fretta, di premura; **—** writing, per iscritto; at two **—** the morning, alle due del mattino; come **—** a week, venite tra una settimana; come **—**, entrate, avanti; **—** spite of, nonostante, a dispetto di; to be **—**, essere in casa; to be the first **—**, arrivare per primo; to be all **—**, non poterne più, essere stanco morto; to have it **—** for someone, avercela con qualcuno; to put **—**, mettere; is the train **—**? è arrivato il treno?; to take **—**,

raggirare; to know all the ins and outs of, conoscere da cima a fondo, saperla lunga su.

inability (ĭn′ȧ·bĭl′ĭ·tĭ) *n.* inabilità, incapacità.

inaccessible (ĭn′ăk·sĕs′ĭ·b'l) *agg.* inaccessibile, inaccostabile.

inaccurate (ĭn·ăk′ū·rĭt) *agg.* inesatto, impreciso.

inaction (ĭn·ăk′shŭn) *n.* inerzia.

inactive (ĭn·ăk′tĭv) *agg.* inattivo, inerte; in ozio.

inactivity (ĭn′ăk·tĭv′ĭ·tĭ) *n.* inerzia.

inadequate (ĭn·ăd′ē·kwĭt) *agg.* inadeguato, insufficiente.

inadmissible (ĭn′ăd·mĭs′ĭ·b'l) *agg.* inammissibile.

inadvertent (-vûr′tĕnt) *agg.* disattento, sbadato; negligente; involontario. **—ly** *avv.* sbadatamente, inavvertitamente; involontariamente.

inanimate (ĭn·ăn′ĭ·mȧt) *agg.* inanimato; esanime; inerte.

inapproachable (ĭn′ȧ·prōch′ȧ·b'l) *agg.* inaccessibile, inaccostabile.

inappropriate (ĭn′ȧ·prō′prĭ·ĭt) *agg.* inadatto, inadeguato; improprio.

inapt (ĭn·ăpt′) *agg.* inadatto, inetto.

inarticulate (ĭn′är·tĭk′ū·lȧt) *agg.* inarticolato; muto.

inasmuch (ĭn′ăz·mŭch′) *avv.*: **—** as, visto che, in quanto, dato che.

inattentive (ĭn′ȧ·tĕn′tĭv) *agg.* disattento, distratto.

inaugurate (ĭn·ô′gū·rāt) *vt.* inaugurare.

inauguration (-rā′shŭn) *n.* inaugurazione.

inauspicious (ĭn′ôs·pĭsh′ŭs) *agg.* infausto, malaugurato.

inborn (ĭn′bôrn′) *agg.* innato, congenito.

inbred (ĭn′brĕd′) *agg.* innato, connaturato.

incandescent (ĭn′kăn·dĕs′ĕnt) *agg.* incandescente, rovente.

incapable (ĭn·kā′pȧ·b'l) *agg.* incapace.

incautious (ĭn·kô′shŭs) *agg.* incauto.

incense (ĭn′sĕns) *n.* incenso. *vt.* (-sĕns′) incensare; irritare, esasperare.

incentive (ĭn·sĕn′tĭv) *n.* incentivo, stimolo. *agg.* stimolante.

inch (ĭnch) *n.* pollice (misura=cm. 2,54): by inches, **—** by **—**, gradatamente; every **—**, completamente, da cima a fondo; within an **—** of, a un pelo da. *vi.* spostarsi gradatamente.

incident (ĭn′sĭ·dĕnt) *n.* incidente. *agg.* insito. **—al** *agg.* incidentale, fortuito, contingente. **—ally** *avv.* incidentalmente.

incinerator (ĭn·sĭn′ĕr·ā′tĕr) *n.* fornace per rifiuti.

incise (ĭn·sīz′) *vt.* incidere.

incite (ĭn·sīt′) *vt.* incitare, incoraggiare.

incivility (ĭn′sĭ·vĭl′ĭ·tĭ) *n.* scortesia.

inclination (ĭn′klĭ·nā′shŭn) *n.* inclinazione, pendio; propensione.

incline (ĭn·klīn′) *n.* pendio, piano inclinato. *vt.* inclinare. *vi.* propendere.

inclined (ĭn·klīnd′) *agg.* inclinato; incline, propenso.

inclose (ĭn·klōz′) *vedi* enclose.

include (ĭn·klōōd′) *vt.* includere, comprendere.

inclusive (ĭn·klōō′sĭv) *agg.* inclusivo, incluso, comprendente, compreso.

incoherent (ĭn′kō·hēr′ĕnt) *agg.* incoerente.

income (ĭn′kŭm) *n.* reddito. — tax, imposta sul reddito.

incoming (ĭn′kŭm′ĭng) *agg.* subentrante; in arrivo; prossimo.

incommensurate (ĭn′kŏ·mĕn′shŏō·rĭt) *agg.* sproporzionato; incommensurabile; inadeguato.

incommode (ĭn′kŏ·mōd′) *vt.* scomodare, disturbare.

incommodious (ĭn′kŏ·mō′dĭ·ŭs) *agg.* incomodo, scomodo; disadatto.

incommunicado (ĭn′kŏ·mū′nĭ·kä′dō) *agg.* isolato, segregato.

incomparable (ĭn·kŏm′pá·rá·b′l) *agg.* incomparabile.

incompatible (ĭn′kŏm·păt′ĭ·b′l) *agg.* incompatibile.

incompetent (ĭn·kŏm′pē·tĕnt) *agg.* incompetente, incapace, inadeguato.

incomplete (ĭn′kŏm·plēt′) *agg.* incompleto, monco.

incomprehensible (ĭn′kŏm·prē·hĕn′sĭ·b′l) *agg.* incomprensibile.

incongruence (ĭn·kŏng′grŏō·ĕns) *n.* incongruenza, discordanza; assurdità; sconvenienza.

incongruous (ĭn·kŏng′grŏō·ŭs) *agg.* incongruo, discordante, incongruente; assurdo; sconveniente.

inconsequence (ĭn′kŏn′sē·kwĕns) *n.* incoerenza, mancanza di logica.

inconsequent (-kwĕnt) *agg.* incoerente; illogico; che non c'entra.

inconsiderate (ĭn′kŏn·sĭd′ĕr·ĭt) *agg.* inconsiderato; poco riguardoso.

inconsistency (ĭn′kŏn·sĭs′·tĕn·sĭ) *n.* incoerenza, incompatibilità, disuguaglianza, contrasto.

inconsistent (ĭn′kŏn·sĭs′tĕnt) *agg.* incoerente, in contrasto (*con*).

inconspicuous (ĭn′kŏn·spĭk′ū·ŭs) *agg.* poco appariscente, sobrio, che non dà nell'occhio. —ly *avv.* discretamente, senza ostentazione.

inconstancy (ĭn·kŏn′stăn·sĭ) *n.* incostanza.

inconstant (ĭn·kŏn′stănt) *agg.* incostante, senza costanza.

inconvenience (ĭn′kŏn·vēn′yĕns) *n.* scomodità, disturbo; molestia, contrarietà. *vt.* incomodare, disturbare; molestare; ostacolare.

inconvenient (ĭn′kŏn·vēn′yĕnt) *agg.* inopportuno; scomodo, molesto.

incorporate (ĭn·kôr′pŏ·rāt) *agg.* consorziato; incorporato. *vt.* incorporare, consorziare. *vi.* incorporarsi, associarsi.

incorporated (ĭn·kôr′pŏ·rāt′ĕd) *agg.* incorporato; consorziato; (*di società*) anonima.

incorrect (ĭn′kŏ·rĕkt′) *agg.* inesatto.

incorrigible (ĭn·kŏr′ĭ·jĭ·b′l) *agg.* incorreggibile.

incorrupt (ĭn·kŏ·rŭpt′) *agg.* incorrotto, puro. —ible *agg.* incorruttibile.

increase (ĭn·krēs′) *n.* aumento, accrescimento. *vt.*, *vi.* accrescere, ingrandire; aumentare.

increasing *agg.* crescente. —ly *avv.* in modo crescente, sempre più.

incredible (ĭn·krĕd′ĭ·b′l) *agg.* incredibile; inverosimile.

incredulity (ĭn′krĕ·dū′lĭ·tĭ) *n.* incredulità.

incredulous (ĭn·krĕd′ū·lŭs) *agg.* incredulo.

increment (ĭn′krē·mĕnt) *n.* incremento. —al *agg.* che dà incremento, giovevole.

incriminate (ĭn·krĭm′ĭ·nāt) *vt.* incriminare; coinvolgere.

incriminating *agg.* incriminante; compromettente.

incubator (ĭn′kū·bā′tĕr) *n.* incubatrice.

inculcate (ĭn·kŭl′kāt) *vt.* inculcare.

incur (ĭn·kûr′) *vt.* incorrere in, esporsi a.

incurable (ĭn·kūr′á·b′l) *agg.* incurabile, inguaribile; irrimediabile.

indebted (ĭn·dĕt′ĕd) *agg.* indebitato; obbligato, grato. —ness *n.* debito.

indecency (ĭn·dē′sĕn·sĭ) *n.* indecenza, sconvenienza.

indecent (ĭn·dē′sĕnt) *agg.* indecente.

indecisive (ĭn′dē·sī′sĭv) *agg.* indeciso.

indecorous (ĭn·dē·kō′rŭs) *agg.* indecoroso, sconveniente, indecente.

indecorum (ĭn′dē·kō′rŭm) *n.* mancanza di decoro, indecenza.

indeed (ĭn·dēd′) *avv.* in verità, davvero, infatti, proprio, realmente, veramente; anzi.

indefatigable (ĭn′dē·făt′ĭ·gá·b′l) *agg.* instancabile. —ness *n.* instancabilità.

indefensible (ĭn'dĕ·fĕn'sĭ·b'l) agg. indifendibile, insostenibile.
indefinite (ĭn·dĕf'ĭ·nĭt) agg. indefinito,
illimitato. —ly avv. vagamente,
indefinitamente.
indelible (ĭn·dĕl'ĭ·b'l) agg. indelebile.
indelicate (ĭn·dĕl'ĭ·kĭt) agg. indelicato.
indemnification (ĭn·dĕm'nĭ·fĭ·kā'shŭn)
n. indennizzo, indennità.
indemnify (ĭn·dĕm'nĭ·fĭ) vt. indennizzare, risarcire.
indemnity (ĭn·dĕm'nĭ·tĭ) n. garanzia,
indennità.
indent (ĭn·dĕnt') vt., vi. intaccare,
dentellare; compiere una requisizione; stipulare un contratto;
legare con un contratto; rientrare
(andare   daccapo   rientrando).
—ation n. dentellatura, tacca. —ion
n. daccapo rientrato. —ure n.
contratto, documento legalizzato.
independence (ĭn'dĕ·pĕn'dĕns) n. indipendenza.
independent (ĭn·dĕ·pĕn'dĕnt) agg. indipendente.
ndescribable (ĭn'dĕ·skrĭb'ȧ·b'l) agg
indescrivibile.
indestructible (ĭn'dĕ·strŭk'tĭ·b'l) agg.
indistruttibile.
indeterminate (ĭn'dĕ·tûr'mĭ·nȧt) agg.
indeterminato, vago.
index (ĭn'dĕks) n. indice. vt. corredare d'indice, indicare; mettere in
ordine alfabetico.
Indian (ĭn'dĭ·ăn) n., agg. indiano: —
corn, granoturco.
India rubber n. gomma elastica.
indicate (ĭn'dĭ·kāt) vt. indicare, designare; far capire, accenare (a).
indication (ĭn'dĭ·kā'shŭn) n. indicazione, indizio; accenno.
indicative (ĭn·dĭk'ȧ·tĭv) agg. indicativo;
sintomatico.
indict (ĭn·dīt') vt. accusare; perseguire;
rinviare a giudizio. —ment n. accusa, atto d'accusa; rinvio a
giudizio.
indifference (ĭn·dĭf'ĕr·ĕns) n. indifferenza, apatia.
indifferent (ĭn·dĭf'ĕr·ĕnt) agg. indifferente, apatico; mediocre.
indigenous (ĭn·dĭj'ē·nŭs) agg. indigeno.
indigestion (ĭn'dĭ·jĕs'chŭn) n. indigestione.
indignant (ĭn·dĭg'nănt) agg. indignato.
—ly avv. sdegnosamente.
indignation (ĭn'dĭg·nā'shŭn) n. indignazione, sdegno.
indignity (ĭn·dĭg'nĭ·tĭ) n. oltraggio.
indigo (ĭn'dĭ·gō) n. indaco.
indirect (ĭn'dĭ·rĕkt') agg. indiretto;
tortuoso.
ndiscreet (ĭn'dĭs·krēt') agg. indiscreto;
imprudente.

indiscretion (ĭn'dĭs·krĕsh'ŭn) n. indiscrezione; imprudenza.
indiscriminate (ĭn'dĭs·krĭm'ĭ·nĭt) agg.
indiscriminato; confuso.
indiscrimination (-nā'shŭn) n. mancanza di discernimento.
indispensable (ĭn'dĭs·pĕn'sȧ·b'l) agg.
indispensabile.
indispose (ĭn'dĭs·pōz') vt. indisporre.
indisposed (ĭn'dĭs·pōzd') agg. indisposto, maldisposto.
indisposition (ĭn'dĭs·pō·zĭsh'ŭn) n. indisposizione; avversione.
indissoluble (ĭn·dĭs'ō·lû·b'l) agg. in-
dissolubile.
indistinct (ĭn'dĭs·tĭngkt') agg. indistinto.
indistinguishable (ĭn'dĭs·tĭng'gwĭsh-
ȧ·b'l) agg. indistinguibile.
individual (ĭn'dĭ·vĭd'û·ăl) n. individuo.
agg. individuale, singolo. —ity (-ăl'-
ĭ·tĭ) n. individualità.
individualize (-vĭd'û·ăl·īz) vt. indivi-
dualizzare.
indivisible (ĭn'dĭ·vĭz'ĭ·b'l) agg. indi-
visibile.
indoctrinate (ĭn·dŏk'trĭ·nāt) vt. ad-
dottrinare, istruire; fanatizzare.
indolence (ĭn'dō·lĕns) n. indolenza, pigrizia.
indolent (ĭn'dō·lĕnt) agg. indolente.
indomitable (ĭn·dŏm'ĭ·tȧb'l) agg. indomabile; indomito.
indoor (ĭn'dōr) agg. domestico, interno, da casa.
indoors (ĭn·dōrz') avv. in casa: to go
—, entrare (in casa).
indorse (ĭn·dôrs') vedi endorse.
induce (ĭn·dūs') vt. indurre. —ment n.
incentivo, esortazione; movente;
tentazione.
induct (ĭn·dŭkt') vt. introdurre; insediare; iniziare (istruire); (mil.)
arruolare, mobilitare.
inductee (ĭn'dŭk·tē') n. (mil.) recluta,
coscritto.
induction (ĭn·dŭk'shŭn) n. induzione;
(mil.) coscrizione, leva. — coil, bobina d'induzione.
inductive (ĭn·dŭk'tĭv) agg. induttivo.
indulge (ĭn·dŭlj') vt., vi. indulgere,
tollerare; favorire, appagare, viziare; adulare: to — in, abbandonarsi a, permettersi il lusso di.
indulgence (ĭn·dŭl'jĕns) n. indulgenza,
proroga; immoderatezza.
indulgent (ĭn·dŭl'jĕnt) agg. indulgente
compiacente.
industrial (ĭn·dŭs'trĭ·ăl) agg. industriale: — design, arte industriale,
estetica del prodotto. —ist n. industriale.
industrialize (-īz) vt. industrializzare.

industrious (ĭn-dŭs'trĭ-ŭs) *agg.* industrioso, attivo, diligente.

industry (ĭn'dŭs-trĭ) *agg.* industria; laboriosità, diligenza.

inebriate (ĭn-ē'brĭ-ăt) *n.*, *agg.* ubriaco, ebbro. *vt.* inebriare, ubriacare.

inebriation (-ā'shŭn) *n.* ubriachezza, ebbrezza.

ineffable (ĭn-ĕf'à-b'l) *agg.* ineffabile.

ineffective (ĭn'ĕ-fĕk'tĭv) *agg.* inefficace.

ineffectual (ĭn'ĕ-fĕk'tū-ǎl) *agg.* inutile, inefficace.

inefficacious (ĭn'ĕf-ĭ-kā'shŭs) *agg.* inefficace.

inefficiency (ĭn'ĕ-fĭsh'ĕn-sĭ) *n.* incapacità, inefficacia.

inefficient (ĭn'ĕ-fĭsh'ĕnt) *agg.* inefficace, incapace.

ineligible (ĭn-ĕl'ĭ-jĭ-b'l) *agg.* ineleggibile; disadatto.

inept (ĭn-ĕpt') *agg.* disadatto, incapace.

inequality (ĭn'ē-kwŏl'ĭ-tĭ) *n.* ineguaglianza, disparità; insufficienza; incompetenza.

inequitable (ĭn-ĕk'wĭ-tà-b'l) *agg.* ingiusto.

inert (ĭn-ûrt') *agg.* inerte. **—ia** (ĭn-ûr'shà) *n.* inerzia.

inestimable (ĭn-ĕs'tĭ-mà-b'l) *agg.* inestimabile, incalcolabile.

inevitable (ĭn-ĕv'ĭ-tà-b'l) *agg.* inevitabile; immancabile.

inexhaustible (ĭn'ĕg-zòs'tĭ-b'l) *agg.* inesauribile.

inexistent (ĭn'ĕg-zĭs'tĕnt) *agg.* inesistente; (*S.U.*) insito, innato.

inexpedience (ĭn'ĕks-pē'dĭ-ĕns) *n.* inopportunità; inefficacia.

inexpedient (-ĕnt) *agg.* inopportuno, inefficace.

inexpensive (ĭn'ĕks-pĕn'sĭv) *agg.* economico, modico, poco costoso.

inexperience (ĭn'ĕks-pē̠r'ĭ-ĕns) *n.* inesperienza.

inexperienced (-ĕnst) *agg.* inesperto.

inexplicable (ĭn-ĕks'plĭ-kà-b'l) *agg.* inesplicabile, incomprensibile.

inexpressible (ĭn'ĕks-prĕs'ĭ-b'l) *agg.* inesprimibile, indicibile.

inexpressibles *n.pl.* (*fam. scherz.*) calzoni.

inextinguishable (ĭn'ĕks-tĭng'gwĭsh-à-b'l) *agg.* inestinguibile.

infallible (ĭn-făl'ĭ-b'l) *agg.* infallibile.

infamous (ĭn'fà-mŭs) *agg.* infame, disonorato, infamante.

infamy (ĭn'fà-mĭ) *n.* infamia.

infancy (ĭn'făn-sĭ) *n.* infanzia.

infant (ĭn'fănt) *n.* infante; minorenne.

infantry (ĭn'făn-trĭ) *n.* fanteria. **—man** *n.* fante.

infect (ĭn-fĕkt') *vt.* infettare, contaminare, contagiare. **—ion** *n.* infezione, contagio. **—ious** *agg.* infettivo, contagioso.

infer (ĭn-fûr') *vt.*, *vi.* inferire, dedurre, arguire. **—ence** *n.* deduzione, illazione. **—ential** *agg.* deduttivo.

inferior (ĭnfĕr'ĭ-ẽr) *n.*, *agg.* inferiore. **—ity** (-ĭ-ŏr'ĭ-tĭ) *n.* inferiorità.

infernal (ĭn-fûr'nǎl) *agg.* infernale.

infest (ĭn-fĕst') *vt.* infestare. *vi.* incallire nel vizio.

infidel (ĭn'fĭ-dĕl) *n.*, *agg.* infedele, miscredente.

infiltrate (ĭn-fĭl'trāt) *vt.*, *vi.* infiltrare, infiltrarsi.

infinite (ĭn'fĭ-nĭt) *n.*, *agg.* infinito.

infinitive (ĭn-fĭn'ĭ-tĭv) *n.*, *agg.* (*gramm.*) infinito.

infinity (ĭn-fĭn'ĭ-tĭ) *n.* infinità, infinito.

infirm (ĭn-fûrm') *agg.* infermo; malfermo, irresoluto; malsicuro. **—ary** *n.* infermeria, dispensario. **—ity** *n.* infermità, debolezza.

inflame (ĭn-flām') *vt.* infiammare; infocare; infervorare. *vi.* infiammarsi; divampare.

inflammation (ĭn'flà-mā'shŭn) *n.* infiammazione.

inflate (ĭn-flāt') *vt.* enfiare, gonfiare; (*fin.*) inflazionare.

inflation (ĭn-flā'shŭn) *n.* gonfiatura; vanità; inflazione.

inflection (ĭn-flĕk'shŭn) *n.* inflessione; flessione, curvatura.

inflict (ĭn-flĭkt') *vt.* infliggere.

influence (ĭn'flŏo-ĕns) *n.* influenza, influsso. *vt.* influenzare, influire su.

influential (ĭn'flŏo-ĕn'shǎl) *agg.* influente.

influx (ĭn'flŭks) *n.* influsso, affluenza, fiotto, afflusso.

infold (ĭn-fōld') *vt.* abbracciare, avvolgere.

inform (ĭn-fôrm') *vt.* informare, ispirare. *vi.* deporre: **to — against**, deporre contro.

informal (ĭn-fôr'mǎl) *agg.* senza cerimonie: **— dinner**, pranzo intimo o alla buona; **— visit**, visita di confidenza; **— dress**, vestito di tutti i giorni. **—ity** (-măl'ĭ-tĭ) *n.* irregolarità, difetto di forma; semplicità. **—ly** *avv.* senza cerimonie, alla buona.

informant (ĭn-fôr'mǎnt) *n.* informatore.

information (ĭn'fŏr-mā'shŭn) *n.* informazione; deposizione; delazione.

informer (ĭn-fôr'mẽr) *n.* informatore, delatore.

infringe (ĭn-frĭnj') *vt.*, *vi.* infrangere, violare, trasgredire: **to — upon**, usurpare, violare. **—ment** *n.* violazione, usurpazione.

infuriate (ĭn·fū'rĭ·āt) *vt.* infuriare.

infuse (ĭn·fūz') *vt.* infondere, ispirare.

infusible (ĭn·fū'zĭ·b'l) *agg.* inculcabile; non fusibile, infusibile.

infusion (ĭn·fū'zhŭn) *n.* infusione.

ingenious (ĭn·jēn'yŭs) *n.* ingegnoso.

ingenuity (ĭn'jē·nū'ĭ·tĭ) *n.* ingegnosità.

ingenuous (ĭn·jĕn'yŭ·ŭs) *agg.* ingenuo.

ingoing (ĭn'gō'ĭng) *n.* ingresso. *agg.* entrante, in arrivo.

ingot (ĭng'ŏt) *n.* lingotto.

ingrain (ĭn·grān') *vt.* incorporare; istillare, infondere, permeare. —ed *agg.* inveterato, radicato.

ingrate (ĭn'grāt) *n.* ingrateful (ĭn·grāt'fŏŏl) *agg.* ingrato.

ingratiate (ĭn·grā'shĭ·āt) *vt.* ingraziarsi.

ingratitude (ĭn·grăt'ĭ·tūd) *n.* ingratitudine.

ingredient (ĭn·grē'dĭ·ĕnt) *n.* ingrediente.

ingrowing (ĭn'grō'ĭng) *agg.*: — nail, unghia incarnata.

ingulf (ĭn·gŭlf') *vt.* inghiottire; sopraffare.

inhabit (ĭn·hăb'ĭt) *vt.*, *vi.* abitare, dimorare, occupare. —ant *n.* abitante.

inhale (ĭn·hāl') *vt.* inalare, aspirare.

inharmonious (ĭn'här·mō'nĭ·ŭs) *agg.* disarmonico, stonato.

inherent (ĭn·hēr'ĕnt) *agg.* inerente, insito, intrinseco.

inherit (ĭn·hĕr'ĭt) *vt.*, *vi.* ereditare. —ance *n.* eredità.

inhibit (ĭn·hĭb'ĭt) *vt.* reprimere, inibire, impedire, proibire. —ion *n.* inibizione, proibizione.

inhospitable (ĭn·hŏs'pĭ·tá·b'l) *agg.* inospitale.

inhuman (ĭn·hū'măn) *agg.* inumano.

inimical (ĭn·ĭm'ĭ·kăl) *agg.* ostile.

inimitable (ĭn·ĭm'ĭ·tá·b'l) *agg.* inimitabile.

iniquitous (ĭ·nĭk'wĭ·tŭs) *agg.* iniquo; ingiusto.

iniquity (ĭ·nĭk'wĭ·tĭ) *n.* iniquità; ingiustizia.

initial (ĭ·nĭsh'ăl) *n.*, *agg.* iniziale. *vt.* mettere le iniziali, siglare. —ly *avv.* inizialmente, da principio.

initiate (ĭ·nĭsh'ĭ·āt) *vt.* cominciare; iniziare.

initiation (ĭ·nĭsh'ĭ·ā'shŭn) *n.* iniziazione.

initiative (ĭ·nĭsh'ĭ·á'tĭv) *n.* iniziativa. *agg.* iniziale.

inject (ĭn·jĕkt') *vt.* iniettare. —ion *n.* iniezione, clistere. —or *n.* iniettore.

injunction (ĭn·jŭngk'shŭn) *n.* ingiunzione.

injure (ĭn'jĕr) *vt.* nuocere a, danneggiare, ferire.

injurious (ĭn·jŏŏr'ĭ·ŭs) *agg.* nocivo; ingiurioso.

injury (ĭn'jĕr·ĭ) *n.* torto; danno; ferita; avaria.

injustice (ĭn·jŭs'tĭs) *n.* ingiustizia.

ink (ĭngk) *n.* inchiostro. *vt.* imbrattare d'inchiostro; inchiostrare.

inkling (ĭngk'lĭng) *n.* indizio, sentore.

inkstand (ĭngk'stănd') *n.* calamaio.

inkwell (ĭngk'wĕl') *n.* calamaio.

inky (ĭngk'ĭ) *agg.* nero come l'inchiostro; sporco di inchiostro.

inland (ĭn'lănd) *n.* interno (*di un territorio*). *agg.* interno. *avv.* verso l'interno, all'interno.

inlay (ĭn·lā') *n.* intarsio. *vt.* (*pass.*, *pp.* inlaid) intarsiare, decorare.

inlaid (ĭn·lād') *pass.* e *pp.* *di* to inlay: — work, lavoro d'intarsio.

inlet (ĭn'lĕt) *n.* accesso, piccola baia.

inmate (ĭn'māt) *n.* abitante, inquilino.

inmost (ĭn'mōst) *agg.* (*il*) più interno, (*il*) più intimo, (*il*) più profondo, (*il*) più segreto.

inn (ĭn) *n.* albergo, locanda, taverna: —keeper, oste, albergatore.

innate (ĭn'nāt) *agg.* innato, istintivo.

inner (ĭn'ĕr) *agg.* interiore, più interno, più segreto, più profondo. —most *agg.superl.* intimo, (*il*) più interno.

inning (ĭn'ĭng) *n.* occasione; turno; raccolto, bonifica; (*baseball*) ripresa, tempo; turno (*del battitore*).

innocence (ĭn'ō·sĕns) *n.* innocenza, candore.

innocent (ĭn'ō·sĕnt) *n.* innocente. *agg.* innocente; innocuo; lecito; privo (*di*); ignaro (*di*); immacolato.

innocuous (ĭ·nŏk'ū·ŭs) *agg.* innocuo.

innovate (ĭn'ō·vāt) *vt.* innovare.

innovation (ĭn'ō·vā'shŭn) *n.* innovazione.

innuendo (ĭn'ū·ĕn'dō) *n.* insinuazione, allusione, sottinteso.

innumerable (ĭ·nū'mĕr·á·b'l) *agg.* innumerabile, innumerevole.

inoculate (ĭn·ŏk'ū·lāt) *vt.* inoculare.

inoffensive (ĭn'ō·fĕn'sĭv) *agg.* innocuo.

inoperative (ĭn·ŏp'er·á'tĭv) *agg.* inefficace; non in vigore, non vigente.

inopportune (ĭn·ŏp'ŏr·tūn') *agg.* inopportuno, intempestivo.

inordinate (ĭn·ôr'dĭ·nĭt) *agg.* smodato.

inquest (ĭn'kwĕst) *n.* inchiesta, indagine, istruttoria preliminare.

inquire (ĭn·kwīr') *vt.*, *vi.* domandare, interrogare, indagare, informarsi, esaminare: to — after, chiedere notizie di; to — into, indagare.

inquiry (ĭn·kwīr'ĭ) *n.* ricerca, interrogazione, indagine: — office, ufficio informazioni.

inquisition (ĭn'kwĭ·zĭsh'ŭn) *n.* inchiesta, indagine, inquisizione.

inquisitive (ĭn·kwĭz'ĭ·tĭv) agg. inquisitivo, curioso.

inroad (ĭn'rōd') n. invasione, irruzione, infiltrazione; defalco; sottrazione, perdita (di tempo, denaro, ecc.): to make inroads upon a supply, intaccare una scorta; to make inroads on one's time, rubare tempo a qualcuno.

insalubrious (ĭn'să·lū'brĭ·ŭs) agg. insalubre.

insane (ĭn·sān') agg. pazzo: — asylum, manicomio.

insanity (ĭn·săn'ĭ·tĭ) n. pazzia.

insatiable (ĭn·sā'shĭ·à·b'l) agg. insaziabile.

inscribe (ĭn·skrĭb') vt. iscrivere; incidere; indirizzare.

inscription (ĭn·skrĭp'shŭn) n. iscrizione, dedica, titolo.

insect (ĭn'sĕkt) n. insetto.

insecure (ĭn'sē·kūr') agg. malsicuro, precario, incerto.

insecurity (ĭn'sē·kū'rĭ·tĭ) n. precarietà, incertezza.

insensate (ĭn·sĕn'sāt) agg. insensato; inconscio, inanimato; disumano, brutale.

insensible (ĭn·sĕn'sĭ·b'l) agg. insensibile; impercettibile; privo di sensi; inconsapevole; grossolano; insensato, stolto.

insensitive (ĭn·sĕn'sĭ tĭv) agg. insensibile; impassibile, indifferente.

inseparable (ĭn·sĕp'à·rà·b'l) agg. inseparabile.

insert (ĭn·sûrt') n. inserto, allegato. vt. inserire, introdurre. —ion n. inserzione, aggiunta.

inside (ĭn'sīd') n. interno, parte interna; (pl.) visceri. agg. interno. avv. internamente, dentro. prep. entro, dentro; nei limiti di: to turn — out, rovesciare, rivoltare.

insight (ĭn'sīt') n. conoscenza profonda, perspicacia, intuito.

insignia (ĭn·sĭg'nĭ·à) n.pl. distintivi, emblemi: collar —, mostrine, fiamme; — of rank, distintivi di grado.

insignificance (ĭn'sĭg·nĭf'ĭ·kǎns) n. futilità, scarsa importanza.

insignificant (ĭn'sĭg·nĭf'ĭ·kǎnt) agg. insignificante.

insinuate (ĭn·sĭn'û·āt) vt. insinuare; introdurre. vi. insinuarsi, penetrare.

insinuation (ĭn·sĭn'û·ā'shŭn) n. insinuazione.

insipid (ĭn·sĭp'ĭd) agg. insipido.

insist (ĭn·sĭst') vi. insistere, persistere. —ence n. insistenza, persistenza. —ent agg. insistente, persistente.

insnare (ĭn·snâr') vedi ensnare.

insociable (ĭn·sō'shà·b'l) agg. insocievole.

insolation (ĭn'sō·lā'shŭn) n. esposizione al sole; elioterapia; insolazione.

insolence (ĭn'sō·lĕns) n. insolenza.

insolent (ĭn'sō·lĕnt) agg. insolente.

insolvency (ĭn·sŏl'vĕn·sĭ) n. insolvenza.

insolvent (ĭn·sŏl'vĕnt) n. debitore insolvente. agg. insolvente.

insomuch (ĭn'sō·mŭch') avv. al punto che; posto che.

inspect (ĭn·spĕkt') vt. ispezionare, esaminare, verificare. —ion n. ispezione, esame. —or n. ispettore.

inspiration (ĭn'spĭ·rā'shŭn) n. ispirazione.

inspire (ĭn·spīr') vt., vi. ispirare.

inspirit (ĭn·spĭr'ĭt) vt. animare.

install (ĭn·stôl') vt. installare. —ation n. installazione, insediamento.

installment (ĭn·stôl'mĕnt) n. installazione; rata; puntata (di romanzo).

instance (ĭn'stǎns) n. istanza; esempio, occasione, caso, circostanza: for —, ad esempio; in the first —, da principio, in primo luogo.

instant (ĭn'stǎnt) n. attimo, istante. agg. urgente, immediato; insistente; corrente: the 5th —, il 5 corrente. —aneous agg. istantaneo. —ly avv. istantaneamente, urgentemente.

instead (n·stĕd'ĭ) avv. invece, anzichè.

instep (ĭn'stĕp) n. collo del piede.

instigate (ĭn'stĭ·gāt) vt. istigare.

instil (ĭn·stĭl') vt. istillare.

instinct (ĭn'stĭngkt) n. istinto, impulso. —ive agg. istintivo.

institute (ĭn'stĭ·tūt) n. istituto. vt. istituire, fondare.

institution (ĭn'stĭ·tū'shŭn) n. istituzione.

instruct (ĭn·strŭkt') vt. istruire, dare istruzioni a, incaricare. —ion n. istruzione, ordine. —ive agg. istruttivo. —or n. istruttore, insegnante.

instrument (ĭn'strōō·mĕnt) n. strumento. —al agg. strumentale; utile, adatto (allo scopo). —alist n. orchestrale, sonatore. —ality n. cooperazione, utilità.

insufferable (ĭn·sŭf'ĕr·à·b'l) agg. insopportabile, insoffribile.

insufficiency (ĭn'sŭ·fĭsh'ĕn·sĭ) n. insufficienza, deficienza; incapacità.

insufficient (ĭn'sŭ·fĭsh'ĕnt) agg. insufficiente; incapace.

insulate (ĭn'sû·lāt) vt. isolare.

insulation (ĭn'sû·lā'shŭn) n. isolamento.

insulator (ĭn'sû·lā'tĕr) n. isolatore, isolante.

insult (ĭn'sŭlt) n. insulto, affronto. vt. insultare.

insuppressible (ĭn'sŭ·prĕs'ĭ·b'l) *agg.* insopprimibile, irrefrenabile.

insurance (ĭn·shŏŏr'ăns) *n.* assicurazione: — broker, agente di assicurazione; life —, assicurazione sulla vita.

insure (ĭn·shŏŏr') *vt.* assicurare.

insurer (ĭn·shŏŏr'ĕr) *n.* assicuratore.

insurgence (ĭn·sûr'jĕns) *n.* insurrezione, rivolta.

insurgent (ĭn·sûr'jĕnt) *n.*, *agg.* insorto, ribelle, rivoltoso.

insurmountable (ĭn'sûr·moun'tá·b'l) *agg.* insuperabile, insormontabile.

insurrection (ĭn'sŭ·rĕk'shŭn) *n.* insurrezione, sommossa, rivolta.

intact (ĭn·tăkt') *agg.* intatto.

intake (ĭn'tāk') *n.* immissione, aspirazione; strozzatura.

integral (ĭn'tē·grăl) *n.* parte integrante, totalità. *agg.* integrale, integrante; essenziale.

integration (ĭn'tē·grā'shŭn) *n.* integrazione.

integrity (ĭn·tĕg'rĭ·tĭ) *n.* integrità.

intellect (ĭn'tē·lĕkt) *n.* intelletto. —ual *n.*, *agg.* intellettuale.

intelligence (ĭn·tĕl'ĭ·jĕns) *n.* intelligenza; intesa, accordo; informazione, notizia; spionaggio

intelligent (ĭn·tĕl'ĭ·jĕnt) *agg.* intelligente.

intemperance (ĭn·tĕm'pĕr·ăns) *n.* intemperanza.

intemperate (ĭn·tĕm'pĕr·ĭt) *agg.* intemperante.

intend (ĭn·tĕnd') *vt.* intendere, destinare, significare. *vi.* avere intenzione di, pensare.

intense (ĭn·tĕns') *agg.* intenso.

intensify (ĭn·tĕn'sĭ·fĭ) *vt.* intensificare. *vi.* intensificarsi.

intensity (ĭn·tĕn'sĭ·tĭ) *n.* intensità.

intensive (ĭn·tĕn'sĭv) *agg.* intensivo, indefesso: — course, corso accelerato.

intent (ĭn·tĕnt') *n.* intenzione, intento. *agg.* intento, attento, assorto.

intention (ĭn·tĕn'shŭn) *n.* intenzione. —al *agg.* intenzionale. —ally *avv.* intenzionalmente, di proposito.

intentness (ĭn·tĕnt'nĕs) *n.* attenzione.

inter (ĭn·tûr') *vt.* sotterrare.

intercede (ĭn'tĕr·sēd') *vi.* intercedere.

intercept (ĭn'tĕr·sĕpt') *vt.* intercettare, bloccare. —ion intercettazione. —or *n.* intercettore; (*aeron.*) caccia intercettore.

intercession (ĭn'tĕr·sĕsh'ŭn) *n.* intercessione.

interchange (ĭn'tĕr·chānj') *n.* scambio, alternazione. *vt.*, *vi.* scambiare, scambiarsi; succedersi; alternarsi.

—able *agg.* intercambiabile, sostituibile.

intercom *vedi* interphone.

intercourse (ĭn'tĕr·kōrs) *n.* relazione, rapporto.

interdiction (ĭn'tĕr·dĭk'shŭn)*n.*divieto.

interest (ĭn'tĕr·ĕst) *n.* interesse; interessamento; profitto. *vt.* interessare, destare interesse in; cointeressare. —ed *agg.* interessato: to be (*o* become) — in, interessarsi di *o* a. —ing *agg.* interessante.

interfere (ĭn'tĕr·fēr') *vt.* interferire, intromettersi: to — with, contrastare, ostacolare, frustrare.

interference (-fēr'ĕns) *n.* intromissione, intralcio; interferenza.

interim (ĭn'tĕr·ĭm) *n.* intervallo, interim. *agg.* temporaneo, interinale.

interior (ĭn·tēr'ĭ·ĕr) *n.*, *agg.* interno, interiore.

interjection (ĭn'tĕr·jĕk'shŭn) *n.* interpolazione; interiezione.

interlace (ĭn'tĕr·lās') *vt.*, *vi.* intrecciare, intrecciarsi.

interline (ĭn'tĕr·līn') *vt.* interlineare.

interlock (ĭn'tĕr·lŏk') *vt.*, *vi.* collegare, coordinare; incastrarsi; essere in collegamento.

interloper (ĭn'tĕr·lōp'ĕr) *n.* intruso; esercente abusivo.

interlude (ĭn'tĕr·lūd) *n.* intermezzo.

intermediate (ĭn'tĕr·mē'dĭ·ĭt) *agg.* intermedio.

interment (ĭn·tûr'mĕnt) *n.* sepoltura.

interminable (ĭn·tûr'mĭ·ná·b'l) *agg.* interminabile.

intermingle (ĭn'tĕr·mĭng'g'l) *vt.*, *vi.* mescolare, mescolarsi.

intermission (ĭn'tĕr·mĭsh'ŭn) *n.* intervallo, pausa.

intermittent (ĭn'tĕr·mĭt'ĕnt) *agg.* intermittente.

intern (ĭn'tûrn) *n.* medico ospitaliero, assistente interino. *vt.* internare, confinare.

internal (ĭn·tûr'năl) *agg.* interno.

international (ĭn'tĕr·năsh'ŭn·ăl) *agg.* internazionale.

internationalize (ĭn'tĕr·năsh'ŭn·ăl·īz) *vt.* internazionalizzare.

interphone (ĭn'tĕr·fōn') *n.* citofono.

interpolate (ĭn·tûr'pō·lāt) *vt.* interpolare.

interpose (ĭn'tĕr·pōz') *vt.*, *vi.* interporre, interloquire, interporsi.

interpret (ĭn·tûr'prĕt) *vt.* interpretare. —ation *n.* interpretazione. —er *n.* interprete.

interrogate (ĭn·tĕr'ō·gāt) *vt.* interrogare.

interrogation (ĭn·tĕr'ō·gā'shŭn) *n.* interrogazione: note of —, punto interrogativo.

interrogative (ĭn'tĕ·rŏg'á·tĭv) n., agg. interrogativo.

interrupt (ĭn'tĕ·rŭpt') vt. interrompere. —ion n. interruzione.

intersect (ĭn'tĕr·sĕkt') vt., vi. incrociare, incrociarsi, intersecare, intersecarsi. —ion n. intersezione; crocevia, incrocio.

intersperse (ĭn'tĕr·spûrs') vt. cospargere, disseminare.

intertwine (ĭn'tĕr·twīn') vt. intrecciare. vi. intrecciarsi, confondersi.

interval (ĭn'tĕr·vál) n. intervallo.

intervene (ĭn'tĕr·vēn') vi. intervenire; sopravvenire; esser situato; intercorrere.

intervention (ĭn'tĕr·vĕn'shŭn) n. intervento.

interview (ĭn'tĕr·vū) n. colloquio, intervista. vt. interpellare, intervistare. —er n. intervistatore.

intestine (ĭn·tĕs'tĭn) n., agg. intestino.

intimacy (ĭn'tǐ·má·sǐ) n. intimità.

intimate (ĭn'tǐ·māt) (1) n., agg. intimo.

intimate (ĭn'tǐ·māt) (2) vt. annunciare, far sapere, notificare.

intimately (ĭn'tǐ·mǐt·lǐ) avv. intimamente.

intimation (ĭn'tǐ·mā'shŭn) n. annuncio, avvisaglia, sentore.

intimidate (ĭn·tǐm'ǐ·dāt) vt. intimidire, minacciare.

intimidation (ĭn·tǐm'ǐ·dā'shŭn) n. intimidazione, minaccia.

into (ĭn'tōō) prep. entro, dentro, in.

intolerable (ĭn·tŏl'ĕr·á·b'l) agg. intollerabile.

intolerance (ĭn·tŏl'ĕr·ăns) n. intolleranza.

intolerant (-ănt) agg. intollerante.

intonation (ĭn'tō·nā'shŭn) n. intonazione, modulazione.

intone (ĭn·tōn') vt., vi. intonare, intonarsi.

intoxicate (ĭn·tŏk'sǐ·kāt) vt. ubriacare; esaltare, inebriare.

intoxicated agg. ubriaco, ebbro.

intoxicating agg. inebriante.

intoxication (ĭn·tŏk'sǐ·kā'shŭn) n. ubriachezza, esaltazione.

intractability (ĭn·trăk'tá·bĭl'ǐ·tǐ) n. intrattabilità.

intractable (ĭn·trăk'tá·b'l) agg. intrattabile.

intransigence (ĭn·trăn'sǐ·jĕns) n. intransigenza.

intransitive (ĭn·trăn'sǐ·tǐv) agg. intransitivo.

intravenous (ĭn'trá·vē'nŭs) agg. endovenoso.

intrench (ĭn·trĕnch') vedi entrench.

intrepid (ĭn·trĕp'ǐd) agg. intrepido.

intricacy (ĭn'trǐ·ká·sǐ) n. intrico, groviglio; complessità.

intricate (ĭn'trǐ·kǐt) agg. intricato complesso.

intrigue (ĭn·trēg') n. intrigo. vt. incuriosire, rendere perplesso. vi. intrigare, tramare.

intriguer (ĭn·trē'gĕr) n. intrigante.

introduce (ĭn'trō·dūs') vt. introdurre; presentare.

introduction (ĭn'trō·dŭk'shŭn) n. introduzione; presentazione.

intrude (ĭn·trōōd') vt. intrudere, imporre. vi. intrufolarsi; disturbare; to — on o upon, importunare, usurpare; to — oneself, imporre la propria presenza.

intruder (ĭn·trōōd'ĕr) n. intruso.

intrusion (ĭn·trōō'zhŭn) n. intrusione.

intrusive (ĭn·trōō'sǐv) agg. importuno.

intuition (ĭn'tû·ǐsh'ŭn) n. intuizione.

inundate (ĭn'ŭn·dāt) vt. inondare.

inundation (ĭn'ŭn·dā'shŭn) n. inondazione.

inure (ĭn·ūr') vt. assuefare; agguerrire.

invade (ĭn·vād') vt. invadere.

invader (ĭn·vād'ĕr) n. invasore.

invalid (ĭn'vá·lǐd) n. infermo. agg. (ĭn·văl'ǐd) invalido; non valido, nullo.

invalidate (ĭn·văl'ǐ·dāt) vt. invalidare, annullare.

invaluable (ĭn·văl'û·á·b'l) agg. inestimabile, prezioso.

invariable (ĭn·vâr'ǐ·á·b'l) agg. invariabile.

invariably (ĭn·vâr'ǐ·á·blǐ) avv. invariabilmente.

invasion (ĭn·vā'zhŭn) n. invasione.

inveigle (ĭn·vē'g'l) vt. sedurre, indurre, coinvolgere, adescare. —ment n. adescamento, allettamento.

invent (ĭn·vĕnt') vt. inventare. —ion n. invenzione. —ive agg. inventivo. —iveness n. inventiva. —or n. inventore.

inventory (ĭn'vĕn·tō'rǐ) n. inventario. vt. inventariare.

inverse (ĭn·vûrs') n., agg. inverso, contrario.

invert (ĭn·vûrt') vt. invertire; capovolgere.

invest (ĭn·vĕst') (1) vt. investire (in ogni accezione); rivestire, adornare.

invest (2) vt. avvolgere, rivestire; investire. —ment n. investimento (di capitale).

investigate (ĭn·vĕs'tǐ·gāt) vt. indagare, investigare, esaminare; ricercare.

investigation (ĭn·vĕs'tǐ·gā'shŭn) n. investigazione, indagine; ricerca.

investigator (ĭn·vĕs'tǐ·gā'tĕr) n. investigatore; ricercatore.

investor (ĭn·vĕs'tĕr) n. chi investe danaro, capitalista.

inveterate (ĭn·vĕt′ĕr·ĭt) *agg.* inveterato, radicato.

invidious (ĭn·vĭd′ĭ·ŭs) *agg.* ingiusto.

invigorate (ĭn·vĭg′ĕr·āt) *vt.* invigorire.

invigorating *agg.* energetico.

invincible (ĭn·vĭn′sĭ·b'l) *agg.* invincibile.

inviolable (ĭn·vī′ō·lá·b'l) *agg.* inviolabile.

invisible (ĭn·vĭz′ĭ·b'l) *agg.* invisibile.

invitation (ĭn′vĭ·tā′shŭn) *n.* invito.

invite (ĭn·vīt′) *vt.*, *vi.* invitare; provocare, indurre.

inviting *agg.* invitante, allettante, attraente.

invoice (ĭn′vois) *n.* fattura. *vt.* fatturare.

invoke (ĭn·vōk′) *vt.* invocare.

involuntary (ĭn·vŏl′ŭn·tĕr′ĭ) *agg.* involontario.

involve (ĭn·vŏlv′) *vt.* avvolgere; implicare, includere, complicare; coinvolgere: **to get —d**, impegolarsi.

invulnerable (ĭn·vŭl′nĕr·á·b'l) *agg.* invulnerabile.

inward (ĭn′wĕrd) *agg.* interno, interiore, intimo. *avv.* (*anche* **inwards**) internamente, verso l'interno, nell'intimo.

inwrought (ĭn·rôt′) *agg.* ornato, adorno, trapunto.

iodide (ī′ō·dĭd) *n.* ioduro.

iodine (ī′ō·dĭn) *n.* iodio.

I.O.U. (ī′ō′ū′) (*abbr. di* **I owe you**) cambiale.

I.Q. (ī′kū′) *n.* (*abbr.* di **intelligence quotient**) (*grado di*) intelligenza.

irascible (ī·răs′ĭ·b'l) *agg.* irascibile.

irate (ī′rāt) *agg.* adirato, incollerito.

ire (īr) *n.* ira. **—ful** *agg.* iracondo.

iridescent (ĭr′ĭ·dĕs′ĕnt) *agg.* iridescente.

iris (ī′rĭs) *n.* arcobaleno; (*bot.*) giaggiolo; (*anat.*) iride.

Irish (ī′rĭsh) *n.*, *agg.* irlandese.

irk (ûrk) *vt.* infastidire. **—some** *agg.* fastidioso.

iron (ī′ĕrn) *n.* ferro: **cast —**, ghisa; **— lung**, polmone d'acciaio. *agg.* ferreo, di ferro. *vt.*, *vi.* stirare; rivestire di ferro: **to — out a difficulty**, appianare una difficoltà. **—clad** *n.* corazzata (*nave*). *agg.* corazzato. **—ing** *n.* stiratura. **—monger** *n.* commerciante in ferramenta. **—work** *n.* lavoro in ferro; (*pl.*) ferriera.

ironical (ī·rŏn′ĭ·kăl) *agg.* ironico.

irony (ī′rō·nĭ) *n.* ironia.

irrecognizable (ĭr·rĕk′ŏg·nīz′á·b'l) *agg.* irriconoscibile.

irreconcilable (ĭr·rĕk′ŏn·sīl′á·b'l) *agg.* irreconciliabile, incompatibile.

irrecoverable (ĭr′rĕ·kŭv′ĕr·á·b'l) *agg.* irreparabile, irrecuperabile.

irredeemable (ĭr′rĕ·dēm′á·b'l) *agg.* irredimibile, irrimediabile.

irreducible (ĭr′rĕ·dūs′ĭ·b'l) *agg.* irriducibile.

irrefutable (ĭr·rĕf′ū·tá·b'l) *agg.* irrefutabile.

irregular (ĭr·rĕg′ū·lĕr) *n.*, *agg.* irregolare.

irrelevancy (ĭr·rĕl′ē·văn·sĭ) *n.* inconsistenza, scarsa importanza.

irrelevant (ĭr·rĕl′ē·vănt) *agg.* irrilevante; fuori luogo, estraneo all'argomento; inopportuno; non probatorio.

irreligious (ĭr′rĕ·lĭj′ŭs) *agg.* irreligioso, ateo.

irremediable (ĭr′rĕ·mē′dĭ·á·b'l) *agg.* irrimediabile, irreparabile.

irremovable (ĭr′rĕ·mōōv′á·b'l) *agg.* saldo, inamovibile.

irreparable (ĭ·rĕp′á·rá·b'l) *agg.* irreparabile.

irreplaceable (ĭr′rĕ·plās′á·b'l) *agg.* insostituibile.

irrepressible (ĭr′rĕ·prĕs′ĭ·b'l) *agg.* irrefrenabile; esuberante.

irreproachable (ĭr·rĕ·prōch′á·b'l) *agg.* irreprensibile, impeccabile.

irresistible (ĭr′rĕ·zĭs′tĭ·b'l) *agg.* irresistibile.

irresolute (ĭ·rĕz′ō·lūt) *agg.* irresoluto.

irresponsible (ĭr′rĕ·spŏn′sĭ·b'l) *n.*, *agg.* irresponsabile.

irretrievable (ĭr′rĕ·trēv′á·b'l) *agg.* irreparabile; irrecuperabile.

irreverence (ĭ·rĕv′ĕr·ĕns) *n.* irriverenza.

irreverent (-ĕnt) *agg.* irriverente.

irrigate (ĭr′ĭ·gāt) *vt.* irrigare.

irrigation (ĭr′ĭ·gā′shŭn) *n.* irrigazione.

irritability (ĭr′ĭ·tá·bĭl′ĭ·tĭ) *n.* irritabilità.

irritable (ĭr′ĭ·tá·b'l) *agg.* irritabile, irascibile.

irritate (ĭr′ĭ·tāt) *vt.* irritare.

irritation (ĭr′ĭ·tā′shŭn) *n.* irritazione.

irruption (ĭ·rŭp′shŭn) *n.* irruzione.

is (ĭz) 3a *pers.sing.pres. di* to be.

isinglass (ī′zĭng·glàs′) *n.* colla di pesce.

island (ī′lănd) *n.* isola. **—er** *n.* isolano.

isle (īl) *n.* isola.

islet (ī′lĕt) *n.* isoletta, isolotto.

isolate (ī′sō·lāt) *vt.* isolare, separare.

isolation (ī′sō·lā′shŭn) *n.* isolamento. **—ism** *n.* isolazionismo.

isotope (ī′sō·tōp) *n.* (*chim.*) isotopo.

Israeli (ĭz·rā′lĭ) *n.*, *agg.* israeliano.

issue (ĭsh′ū) *n.* uscita; esito; passaggio; fascicolo, numero, edizione; sfogo; distribuzione, emissione, spedizione, rilascio; scolo(*di acque*); eredi, progenie; (*med.*) secrezione: **to take — with**, dissentire da. *vt.*

pubblicare; emettere, diffondere, rilasciare. *vi.* uscire, scaturire; originare; concludersi.

isthmus (ĭs'mŭs) *n.* istmo.

it (ĭt) *pron.neutro* lo, la *(accusativo)*; *(introducibile in ital. se usato in forme impersonali)* esso, essa, ciò; *(col verbo in forma passiva)* si *(pron. indef.)*: — snows, nevica; who is —? chi è?; — is I, sono io; — is said, si dice; how goes —? come va?; to foot —, andare a piedi.

Italian (ĭ·tăl'yăn) *n., agg.* italiano.

Italic (ĭ·tăl'ĭk) *agg.* italico.

italics *n.pl.* corsivo.

italicize (ĭ·tăl'ĭ·sīz) *vt., vi.* comporre *o* stampare in corsivo, sottolineare.

itch (ĭch) *n.* scabbia, prurito; desiderio, voglia. *vi.* prudere, pizzicare; ardere dal desiderio. —y *agg.* scabbioso; pruriginoso: to feel —, avere prurito.

item (ī'tĕm) *n.* voce *(di fattura, catalogo, ecc.)*; paragrafo, articolo.

itemize (ī'tĕm·īz) *vt.* specificare, enumerare, elencare.

iterate (ĭt'ĕr·āt) *vt.* reiterare.

itinerary (ĭ·tĭn'ĕr·ĕr'ĭ) *n.* itinerario.

its (ĭts) *agg.poss.neutro* di esso, suo, sua, di ciò.

itself (ĭt·sĕlf') *pron.rifl.neutro* se stesso, esso stesso, se stessa, essa stessa, stesso, stessa: by —, da solo, isolato, in se stesso.

ivory (ī'vŏ·rĭ) *n.* avorio.

ivy (ī'vĭ) *n.* *(bot.)* edera.

J

jab (jăb) *n.* colpo, stoccata. *vt., vi.* colpire, punzecchiare.

jabber (jăb'ĕr) *vt.* mormorare. *vi.* balbettare.

jack (jăk) *n.* individuo, tizio; brocca, otre; maschio *(di alcuni animali)*; *(naut.)* marinaio; bandiera; *(ittiol.)* luccio; *(mecc.)* argano; verricello; *(auto.)* cric; *(carpent.)* cavalletto; *(carte da gioco)* fante; *(bocce)* pallino. *vt.* sollevare, issare: — of all trades, factotum; — pot, monte premi, premio massimo; successo; vincita.

jackknife (jăk'nīf) *n.* coltello a serramanico.

jackal (jăk'ôl) *n.* *(zool.)* sciacallo.

jackass (jăk'ăs') *n.* asino.

jackdaw (jăk'dô') *n.* cornacchia.

jacket (jăk'ĕt) *n.* giacca; involucro, buccia; sopraccoperta *(di libro)*.

jade (jād) (1) *n.* *(min.)* giada.

jade (jād) (2) *n.* ronzino; megera, donnaccia. *vt.* affaticare, opprimere. *vi.* logorarsi.

jaded *agg.* esausto; sazio.

jag (jăg) *n.* frastaglio, dentellatura, protuberanza. *vt.* frastagliare. —ged *agg.* dentellato, frastagliato.

jaguar (jăg'wär) *n.* *(zool.)* giaguaro.

jail (jāl) *n.* carcere. *vt.* incarcerare. —bird *n.* delinquente. —er *n.* carceriere.

jalopy (jȧ·lŏp'ĭ) *n.* *(gergo)* vecchia automobile, caffettiera *(fig.)*; *(aeron.)* vecchio aereoplano, carcassone.

... (jăm) (1) *n.* marmellata.

...(jăm) (2) *n.* ammasso, compresa..ne, accozzaglia; guaio; ingorgo: ...ession *(mus. jazz)* riunione di ...cisti per suonare improv-

visando; traffic —, ingorgo stradale. *vt.* comprimere, pigiare, ingombrare, stipare; inceppare; ingorgare: to — on the brakes, frenare di colpo; to — one's fingers, pestarsi le dita; *vi.* pigiarsi, ammassarsi; incepparsi. —pack *vt.* stipare; affollare.

jamb (jăm) *n.* stipite, pilastro.

jangle (jăng'g'l) *vt., vi.* risuonare, far risuonare sgradevolmente.

janitor (jăn'ĭ·tĕr) *n.* portiere, custode.

January (jăn'ū·ĕr'ĭ) *n.* gennaio.

japanese (jăp'ȧ·nēs) *n., agg.* giapponese.

jar (jär) (1) *n.* giara, brocca, boccale.

jar (jär) (2) *n.* vibrazione, dissonanza; urto; lite; spostamento: on the —, socchiuso. *vt.* far vibrare; contrariare; scuotere. *vi.* vibrare; stonare; urtare *(i nervi)*; ferire *(l'orecchio)*; urtarsi.

jargon (jär'gŏn) *n.* gergo, dialetto; *(min.)* zircone.

jasmine (jăs'mĭn) *n.* gelsomino.

jasper (jăs'pĕr) *n.* *(min.)* diaspro.

jaundice (jôn'dĭs) *n.* itterizia; prevenzione, pregiudizio.

jaunt (jônt) *n.* escursione, passeggiata. *vi.* fare una passeggiatina.

jaunty (jônt'ĭ) *agg.* gaio, vivace, sbarazzino; spavaldo; affettato, pretenzioso.

javelin (jăv'lĭn) *n.* giavellotto.

jaw (jô) *n.* mascella, mandibola; *(mecc.)* ganascia.

jawbone (jô'bōn') *n.* osso mascellare, mandibola.

jay (jā) *n.* *(ornit.)* ghiandaia; *(fig.)* donna perduta; *(S.U.)* gonzo. —walker *n.* pedone indisciplinato *o* distratto.

jazz (jăz) *n.* musica sincopata. *vt., vi.* sonare musica jazz, ballare musica jazz: to — up, sincopare; animare, rallegrare. —band n. orchestra jazz.

jealous (jĕl'ŭs) agg. geloso, invidioso.

jealousy n. gelosia, invidia.

jean (jēn) n. diagonale di cotone; (pl.) calzoni di tela, tuta.

jeep (jēp) n. camionetta, jeep.

jeer (jēr) n. scherno, beffa. vt. schernire, burlare. vi. farsi beffe (di).

jell (jĕl) vi. diventare gelatinoso; (fig.) cristallizzarsi, solidificarsi.

jelly (jĕl'ĭ) n. gelatina. vt., vi. mettere in gelatina, diventare gelatinoso. —fish n. (ittiol.) medusa.

jenny (jĕn'ĭ) n. filatoio.

jeopardize (jĕp'ẽr-dīz) vt. mettere a repentaglio, compromettere.

jeopardy (jĕp'ẽr-dĭ) n. repentaglio.

jerk (jûrk) n. scossa, urto, spinta, strappo, scatto; carne in conserva; gelataio, venditore di bibite analcoliche; (gergo) poco di buono, puzzone, lazzarone. vt. lanciare, spingere, scaraventare, scuotere, gettare; conservare (carni). vi. scattare, muoversi a scatti; traballare. —y agg. convulso, irregolare, traballante.

jersey (jûr'zĭ) n. lana pettinata; maglione, giubbetto di lana.

jest (jĕst) n. scherzo, burla, arguzia, derisione. vt., vi. beffare, scherzare. —er n. burlone, buffone.

Jesuit (jĕz'ū.ĭt) n. gesuita.

jet (jĕt) n. getto, sbocco, zampillo; becco (a gas); ambra nera. agg. d'ambra nera, nero; a reazione: —black, nerissimo; — motor, motore a reazione; — propulsion, propulsione a reazione; — plane, velivolo a reazione, aviogetto. vt., vi. lanciare, scaturire.

jetty (jĕt'ĭ) n. gettata, diga, argine.

Jew (jōō) n. ebreo, israelita. —ess n. ebrea. —ish n., agg. ebraico.

jewel (jōō'ĕl) n. gioiello, gemma. vt. ingioiellare, ingemmare. —er n. gioielliere. —ry n. gioielli, gioielleria (arte). —shop, gioielleria.

jib (jĭb) n. braccio di gru; (naut.) fiocco.

jiffy (jĭf'ĭ) n. attimo, istante: in a —, in men che non si dica.

jig (jĭg) n. giga (danza); (mecc.) maschera: —saw, sega da intaglio: — puzzle, rompicapo.

jiggle (jĭg'l) vi. camminare a scatti, camminare come gli ubriachi.

jilt (jĭlt) vt., vi. piantare (un innamorato).

jingle (jĭng'g'l) n. tintinnio; tiritera. vt. far tintinnare. vi. tintinnare.

jingo (jĭng'gō) n. guerraiolo, nazionalista fanatico: by —! perdiana! (pl.) allegria, chiasso.

jink (jĭngk) n. giravolta, piroetta;

job (jŏb) n. lavoro, opera, compito; impresa; impiego; affare; speculazione; prevaricazione; (gergo) colpo ladresco; un esemplare di qualunque cosa o essere: a blonde —, una bionda; to work by the —, lavorare a cottimo. vt. noleggiare. vi. lavorare a cottimo. —ber n. operaio cottimista; agente di cambio; noleggiatore. —holder n. impiegato, impiegato statale. —work n. lavoro a cottimo; (tip.) lavoro miscellaneo.

jock (jŏk) n. fantino: — strap (gergo S.U.), sospensorio.

jockey (jŏk'ĭ) n. fantino. vt., vi. montare (cavalli da corsa); ingannare, raggirare.

jocular (jŏk'ū.lẽr) agg. scherzoso.

jog (jŏg) n. scossa, urto; gomitata; asperità, sporgenza. vt. scuotere, spingere; dar di gomito. vi. procedere lentamente opp. ritmicamente: to — along, trotterellare; tirare avanti alla meglio, condurre vita monotona. — trot n. piccolo trotto; tran-tran.

John Doe (jŏn dō) n. (legge) persona fittizia.

join (join) vt., vi. unire, congiungere, allacciare; incrociare; raggiungere; unirsi, associarsi (a); partecipare; arruolarsi; essere contiguo, confinare (con): to — battle, iniziare la lotta, venire alle mani; to — issue, iniziare un dibattito.

joint (joint) n. congiunzione, giunto; grosso pezzo di carne; (anat.) articolazione; (bot.) nodo, connessura; (geol.) fessura: out of —, slogato, scompigliato; universal —, (mecc.) giunto cardanico. agg. aggiunto, unito, associato, collettivo: — action, azione collettiva; — committee, commissione mista; — session, seduta plenaria. vt. congiungere; tagliare alle giunture; unire; piallare. vi. unirsi. —ed agg. articolato, giuntato. —er o —ing plane n. pialla. —heir n. coerede. —ly avv. insieme, unitamente, di comune accordo. —stock n. capitale azionario. —stock company n. società anonima.

joke (jōk) n. arguzia, facezia, scherzo: a practical —, un tiro birbone; to crack a —, dire una spiritosaggine; vt. beffare, burlare. vi. celiare: no joking, scherzi a parte.

joker (jōk'ẽr) n. burlone; pagliaccio; (carte da poker, ecc.) 53a carta *(specie di "matta")* detta anche **jolly** joker.

jokingly (jōk'ĭng·lĭ) *avv.* per scherzo.

jolly (jŏl'ĭ) *agg.* allegro, spensierato, paffuto. *avv.* molto, grandemente. ——joker *vedi* joker.

jolt (jōlt) *n.* scossa, sobbalzo. *vt.* scuotere, far sobbalzare. *vi.* sobbalzare, traballare.

jostle (jŏs''l) *n.* urto; calca. *vt.* spingere, urtare. *vi.* spingersi, urtarsi; lottare.

jot (jŏt) *n.* jota, inezia. *vt.* (*gen.seg. da* **down**) annotare, scribacchiare.

journal (jûr'nāl) *n.* giornale, diario; (*naut.*) giornale di bordo; (*comm.*) libro giornale. ——ese *n.* gergo giornalistico. ——ism *n.* giornalismo. ——ist *n.* giornalista.

journey (jûr'nĭ) *n.* viaggio (*spec. terrestre*), tragitto, tappa: **by slow journeys,** a piccole tappe. *vi.* viaggiare.

jovial (jō'vĭ·ăl) *agg.* gioviale, allegro.

jowl (joul) *n.* guancia, mascella (*spec.inf.*); pappagorgia; bargigli.

joy (joi) *n.* gioia, allegria, felicità. ——ful *agg.* gioioso, contento. ——fully *avv.* gioiosamente, allegramente. ——less *agg.* afflitto, malinconico. ——ous *agg.* gioioso.

jubilant (jōō'bĭ·lănt) *agg.* giubilante, trionfante.

jubilation (jōō'bĭ·lā'shŭn) *n.* giubilo, trionfo.

jubilee (jōō'bĭ·lē) *n.* giubileo, anniversario; (*fig.*) festa.

judge (jŭj) *n.* giudice, arbitro, intenditore: **to be a — of,** intendersi di. *vt.*, *vi.* giudicare, credere, reputare; intendersene; distinguere; sentenziare. ——ment *opp.* **judgment** *n.* giudizio, sentenza; opinione: — **day,** giorno del giudizio.

judicial (jōō·dĭsh'ăl) *agg.* giudiziario, giuridico; sentenzioso.

judicious (jōō·dĭsh'ŭs) *agg.* giudizioso.

jug (jŭg) *n.* brocca, boccale, anfora; (*gergo*) carcere.

juggle (jŭg''l) *n.* gioco di prestigio; imbroglio. *vt.* ingannare, gabbare; manipolare. *vi.* fare giochi di prestigio; imbrogliare.

juggler (jŭg'lĕr) *n.* giocoliere; impostore.

juice (jōōs) *n.* sugo, succo; (*bot.*) linfa.

juiciness (jōōs'ĭ·nĕs) *n.* sugosità.

juicy (jōōs'ĭ) *agg.* sugoso, succoso; ricco di linfa; sostanzioso; piccante.

jujube (jōō'jōōb) *n.* (*bot.*) giuggiola.

jukebox (jook'bŏks) *n.* grammofono automatico *o* a gettone.

July (jōō·lī') *n.* luglio.

jumble (jŭm'b'l) *n.* confusione, guazzabuglio, mescolanza, congerie; ciambellina. *vt.* mescolare, confondere, gettare alla rinfusa. *vi.* confondersi, mescolarsi.

jump (jŭmp) *n.* salto, balzo; rialzo (*di prezzi*): **to be always on the —,** essere sempre in movimento *o* in agitazione. *vt.*, *vi.* saltare; superare; arrischiare; slanciarsi; sobbalzare; cadere; appropriarsi; accordarsi, coincidere: **to — about,** darsi d'attorno; **to — at,** balzare verso, affrettarsi ad accettare; **to — over,** scavalcare; **to — up,** sobbalzare, balzare in piedi; **to — to conclusions,** trarre conclusioni precipitose. ——er *n.* saltatore; casacchina; camiciotto. ——y *agg.* mai fermo; irrequieto, nervoso, teso.

junction (jŭngk'shŭn) *n.* congiunzione, giuntura, unione, diramazione; (*ferr.*) bivio.

juncture (jŭngk'tûr) *n.* articolazione, congiunzione; congiuntura, situazione.

June (jōōn) *n.* giugno.

jungle (jŭng'g'l) *n.* giungla.

junior (jōōn'yĕr) *n.*, *agg.* iuniore, minore; cadetto; figlio: — **college** (*S.U.*) corso inferiore dell' università; — **officer,** ufficiale subalterno.

juniper (jōō'nĭ·pĕr) *n.* (*bot.*) ginepro.

junk (jŭngk) *n.* giunca (*barca*); vecchio cordame; cianfrusaglie; carne salata.

jurisdiction (jōōr'ĭs·dĭk shŭn) *n.* giurisdizione.

jurisprudence (jōōr'ĭs·prōō'dĕns) *n.* giurisprudenza.

juror (jōōr'ĕr) *n.* giurato.

jury (jōōr'ĭ) *n.* giuria, collegio di giurati: **grand —,** gran giuri. — **box** *n.* banco dei giurati.

just (jŭst) *agg.* giusto, retto, imparziale; esatto; dovuto. *avv.* appunto, esattamente; solamente, solo, appena; quasi, un po'; or ora; giustamente: **he has — gone out,** è appena uscito; — **now,** ora, un momento fa; — **as,** nel momento in cui; — **out,** appena uscito, appena pubblicato; — **a little boy,** solo un bambino.

justice (jŭs'tĭs) *n.* giustizia; imparzialità; diritto; giudice.

justification (jŭs'tĭ·fĭ·kā'shŭn) *n.* giustificazione; assoluzione.

justify (jŭs'tĭ·fī) *vt.*, *vi.* giustificare, assolvere.

jut (jŭt) *n.* sporgenza; aggetto. *vi.* sporgere. ——ting *n.* sporgenza. *agg.* sporgente.

jute (jōōt) *n.* iuta.

juvenile (jōō'vē·nĭl) *n.* giovane, attor giovane; libro per ragazzi. *agg.* giovanile.

juxtaposition (jŭks'tá·pŏ·zĭsh'ŭn) *n.* contiguità; accostamento.

K

kale (kāl) cavolo arricciato.

kangaroo (kăng'gá·rōō') *n.* (*zool.*) canguro.

kayak (kī'ăk) *n.* sandolino.

keck (kĕk) *vi.* avere conati di vomito, avere nausea.

keel (kēl) *n.* chiglia; nave. *vt.*, *vi.* capovolgere, capovolgersi.

keen (kēn) *agg.* acuto; acuminato; pungente; tagliente; perspicace; ansioso.

keep (kēp) *n.* custodia; mantenimento; condizione: for keeps, per sempre. *vt.*, *vi.* (*pass.*, *pp.* kept) tenere; custodire; trattenere; mantenere; allevare; sostenere; rispettare; garantire; continuare a, persistere; conservarsi: to — from, astenersi; to — away from, tenere *o* tenersi lontano da; to — back, nascondere, dissimulare; trattenere; to — bad hours, fare le ore piccole; to — going, andare avanti, non fermarsi; to — off, allontanare; tenersi in disparte; to — on, continuare; to — silent, tacere; to — to, attenersi a. —er *n.* custode; conservatore: jail —, carceriere, secondino. —ing *n.* custodia; mantenimento, manutenzione; armonia: in —ing with, consono a. —sake *n.* ricordo, pegno.

keg (kĕg) *n.* barilotto.

kennel (kĕn'ĕl) *n.* canile, tana.

kept (kĕpt) *pass.*, *pp. di* to keep.

kerb (kûrb) (*Ingl.* = *S.U.* curb) *n.* cordone del marciapiede.

kerchief (kûr'chĭf) *n.* fisciù; fazzoletto.

kernel (kûr'nĕl) *n.* gheriglio (*di noce*); seme, grano, chicco; mandorla (*del nocciolo di pesco, ecc.*); nucleo.

kerosene (kĕr'ō·sēn') *n.* petrolio.

ketch (kĕch) *n.* (*naut.*) panfilio a due alberi, ketch.

ketchup (kĕch'ŭp) *n.* salsa di pomodoro aromatizzata.

kettle (kĕt'l) *n.* pentolino; cuccuma; teiera. —drum *n.* (*mus.*) timpano.

key (kē) *n.* chiave, chiavetta; tasto (*di strumento musicale o di macchina per scrivere*); tono: in — (*mus.*), a tono, intonato; out of —, fuori tono, stonato. *vt.* intonare, accordare: to — up, stimolare, eccitare; elevare il tono di. —board *n.* tastiera. —hole *n.* toppa. —note *n.* nota tonica; idea *o* principio fondamentale. —ring *n.* portachiavi. —stone. *n.* chiave di volta, fondamento, nota dominante.

khaki (kăk'ĭ) *n.*, *agg.* cachi, kaki.

kibitz (kĭb'ĭts) *vi.* (*gergo*) intromettersi, dare consigli non richiesti. —er *n.* ficcanaso, consigliere non richiesto.

kick (kĭk) *n.* pedata, calcio; rinculo (*di arma*); forza; protesta; stimolo; interesse, spasso. *vt.* dare un calcio a, prendere ‹ calci: to — out, scacciare a pedate; to — up a dust, sollevare polvere; to — up a row, fare una scenata; to — the bucket (*gergo*), morire. *vi.* scalciare, recalcitrare, rinculare: to — at, opporsi a. —back *n.* reazione violenta; rispostaccia; tassa clandestina pagata da un lavoratore per ottenere lavoro.

kid (kĭd) (1) *n.* tinozza.

kid (kĭd) (2) *n.* capretto; bimbo, ragazzo: — brother, fratellino, fratello minore. *vt.*, *vi.* (*gergo*) burlare, scherzare.

kidnap (kĭd'năp) *n.* ratto. *vt.* rapire. —per *n.* rapitore. —ping *n.* rapimento.

kidney (kĭd'nĭ) *n.* rene; rognone: — stones, calcoli renali; — bean, fagiolo.

kill (kĭl) *vt.* uccidere, ammazzare; distruggere; spegnere. *n.* preda, caccia. —er *n.* uccisore, assassino.

kiln (kĭln) *n.* forno, fornace.

kilogram (kĭl'ō·grăm) *n.* chilogrammo.

kilometer (kĭl'ō·mē'tĕr) *n.* chilometro.

kilt (kĭlt) *n.* gonnellino degli scozzesi.

kin (kĭn) *n.* parentela, stirpe, famiglia, parente: next of —, parente più prossimo.

kind (kīnd) (1) *n.* genere, specie; natura; razza; maniera: to pay in —, pagare in natura; — of, alquanto.

kind (kīnd) (2) *agg.* gentile, benevolo, garbato: — regards, ossequi, distinti saluti. —hearted, *agg.* di buon cuore, buono.

kindergarten (kĭn'dĕr·gär't'n) *n.* asilo infantile.

kindle (kĭn'd'l) *vt.* accendere, infiammare; eccitare, destare; incoraggiare. *vi.* infiammarsi, animarsi.

kindliness (kīnd'lĭ·nes) *n.* benevolenza, bontà.

kindly (kīnd'lĭ) *agg.* benevolo, bonario, buono. *avv.* amabilmente; favorevolmente; affettuosamente; di buon grado, volentieri.

kindness (kīnd'nĕs) *n.* gentilezza, bontà.

kindred (kīn'drĕd) *n.* parentela, parentado; affinità. *agg.* affine; imparentato.

kinetic (kĭ-nĕt'ĭk) *agg.* cinetico; (*fig.*) dinamico, energico, vivace.

king (kĭng) *n.* re. **—dom** *n.* regno. **—fisher** *n.* (*ornit.*) martin pescatore. **—ly** *agg.* regale; *avv.* regalmente. **—size** *agg.* (*di sigaretta*) lunga; (*fig.*) grosso, enorme, straordinario.

kink (kĭngk) *n.* nodo, garbuglio; riccio. **—y** *agg.* ricciuto, crespo.

kinsfolk (kĭnz'fōk') *n.* parenti, parentado.

kinsman (kĭnz'măn) *n.* parente.

kipper (kĭp'ẽr) *vt.* salare (*conservare sotto sale*). *n.* aringa salata.

kiss (kĭs) *n.* bacio. *vt.* baciare. *vi.* baciarsi.

kit (kĭt) *n.* equipaggiamento; armamentario, corredo, utensileria; astuccio; gattino: **medicine —,** cassetta dei medicinali; **repair —,** borsa *o* cassetta di attrezzi per riparazioni.

kitchen (kĭch'ĕn) *n.* cucina: **— garden,** orto; **— range,** cucina economica. **—ette** *n.* cucinino, stanza di cottura. **—ware** *n.* batteria di cucina.

kite (kīt) *n.* nibbio; aquilone (*cervo volante*); aliante; sfruttatore, imbroglione; (*comm.*) cambiale di favore.

kith (kĭth) *n.* cerchia di amici: **— and kin,** amici e parenti.

kitten (kĭt'n) *n.* gattino, micetto.

knack (năk) *n.* abilità, facoltà; abitudine; trucco.

knapsack (năp'săk') *n.* zàino.

knave (nāv) *n.* furfante; (*carte da giuoco*) fante.

knead (nēd) *vt.* impastare.

knee (nē) *n.* ginocchio: **on one's knees,** in ginocchio. **—cap** *n.* rotula; ginocchiera.

kneel (nēl) *vi.,* (*pass., pp.* knelt) inginocchiarsi.

knell (nĕl) *n.* rintocco funebre. *vi.* sonare a morto.

knelt (nĕlt) *pass.* e *pp. di* to kneel.

knew (nū) *pass. di* to know.

knickknack (nĭk'năk') *n.* gingillo; giocattolo; cianfrusaglia.

knife (nif) *n.* (*pl.* knives) coltello, lama; bisturi: **carving —,** trinciante;

clasp —, coltello a serramanico; **pen—,** temperino. *vt.* accoltellare.

knight (nīt) *n.* cavaliere; paladino; (*scacchi*) cavallo. *vt.* creare cavaliere: **—errant,** cavaliere errante.

knighthood (nīt'hŏod) *n.* cavalleria.

knit (nĭt) *vt., vi.* lavorare a maglia, sferruzzare; unire, congiungere; aggrottare (*le sopracciglia*); aggrottarsi; saldarsi (*di ossa*); contrarsi. **—ting** *agg.* lavoro a maglia. **—ting needle** *n.* ferro da calza.

knob (nŏb) *n.* protuberanza, nodo, nodulo; maniglia.

knock (nŏk) *n.* colpo, bussata: battito. *vt., vi.* bussare, battere, urtare, colpire: **to — about,** sballottare, malmenare; **to — down,** abbattere, rovesciare; smontare (*una macchina*); **to — in,** sfondare; **to — off,** smontare di lavorare, smettere il lavoro; ribassare (*un prezzo*); far saltare via; **to — out,** far uscire a colpi (*pugilato*) metter fuori combattimento; **—kneed,** sbilenco; che ha le ginocchia in dentro.

knocker (nŏk'ẽr) *n.* battaglio.

knockout (nŏk'out') *n.* colpo che abbatte; successore; (*pugilato*) fuori combattimento.

knoll (nōl) (1) *n.* altura, collina.

knoll (nōl) (2) *vt., vi.* sonare a morto.

knot (nŏt) *n.* nodo, nastro, vincolo, difficoltà, gruppo. *vt., vi.* annodare, annodarsi. **—ty** *agg.* nodoso, annodato; complesso.

know (nō) *n.* conoscenza: **—how,** conoscenza *o* esperienza del mestiere; **to be in the —,** saperla lunga. *vt., vi.* (*pass.* knew, *pp.* known) sapere; conoscere; riconoscere; capire: **to — how to swim,** saper nuotare; **to — the ropes,** saperla lunga; **to — better than,** guardarsi bene da, avere il buon senso di (*non fare una cosa*); **he should — better,** dovrebbe essere più saggio. **—ing** *agg.* perspicace, accorto. **—ingly** *avv.* accortamente; con l'aria di chi la sa lunga. **—ledge** *n.* conoscenza, cognizione.

known (nōn) *pp. di* to know.

knuckle (nŭk'l) *n.* nocca; giuntura, giunto. *vt.* battere con le nocche. *vi.* flettere le dita: **to — under,** sottomettersi; **— joint,** giunto a cerniera.

kudos (kū'dŏs) *n.* gloria, fama.

L

lab (lăb) *n.* laboratorio.

label (lā'bĕl) *n.* etichetta, cartellino. *vt.* mettere l'etichetta a, classificare.

labor (lā'bẽr) *n.* lavoro, fatica, travaglio; mano d'opera, la classe operaia: **— union,** sindacato operaio;

to be in —, avere le doglie; **hard** —, lavori forzati. *vt.*, *vi.* lavorare, elaborare; arrancare; angosciarsi, soffrire; avere le doglie. **—er** *n.* lavoratore.

labyrinth (lăb′ĭ-rĭnth) *n.* labirinto.

lace (lās) *n.* pizzo; spighetta, stringa da scarpe. *vt.* ornare di pizzi; allacciare, intrecciare.

lack (lăk) *n.* mancanza, scarsità. *vt.* mancare di. *vi.* mancare, scarseggiare.

lackadaisical (lăk′ȧ-dā′zĭ-kǎl) *agg.* languido, sdolcinato.

lacking *agg.* mancante (*di*), scarso, insufficiente: — **in**, privo di.

lackluster (lăk′lŭs′tẽr) *agg.* opaco.

lacquer (lăk′ẽr) *n.* lacca. *vt.* laccare.

lad (lăd) *n.* ragazzo.

ladder (lăd′ẽr) *n.* scala a piuoli; (*Ingl.*) smagliatura (*delle calze*).

lade (lād) *vt.* (*pass.* laded, *pp.* laden) caricare, imbarcare.

lading (lād′ĭng) *n.* carico: **bill of** —, polizza di carico.

ladle (lād′′l) *n.* mestolo. *vt.* versare col mestolo: **to** — **out**, distribuire.

lady (lā′dĭ) *n.* (*pl.* ladies) signora, gentildonna, nobildonna, donna (*come titolo di cortesia premesso al nome*). **—like** *agg.* da vera signora. **—love** *n.* innamorata.

lag (lăg) *n.* ritardo, rallentamento; galeotto. *vi.* tardare; restare indietro, muoversi con lentezza.

laggard (lăg′ẽrd) *n.* infingardo, persona lenta.

lagoon (lȧ-gōōn′) *n.* laguna.

laid (lād) *pass.*, *pp. di* to lay.

lain (lān) *pp. di* to lie (2).

lair (lâr) *n.* tana, rifugio.

lake (lāk) *n.* lago.

lam (lăm) *n.* (*gergo*) fuga.

lamb (lăm) *n.* agnello.

lambkin (lăm′kĭn) *n.* agnellino.

lame (lām) *agg.* zoppo; debole. *vt.* azzoppare. **—ly** *avv.* zoppicando; debolmente, poco plausibilmente.

lament (lȧ-ment′) *n.* lamento. *vt.*, *vi.* lamentare, lamentarsi. **—able** (lăm′ĕn-tȧ-b′l) *agg.* lamentevole, doloroso.

laminate (lăm′ĭ-nāt) *vt.* laminare; stratificare: **laminated plastic**, laminati plastici.

lamp (lămp) *n.* lampada, lanterna, fanale: **street** —, fanale, lampione; — **shade**, paralume. **—black** *n.* nerofumo. **—post** *n.* lampione.

lampoon (lăm-pōōn′) *n.* satira, libello.

lance (lăns) *n.* lancia, lanciere; (*chir.*) lancetta. *vt.* trafiggere con la lancia; incidere con la lancetta.

lancer (lăn′sẽr) *n.* lanciere.

lancet (lăn′sĕt) *n.* (*chir.*) lancetta.

land (lănd) *n.* terra, suolo, terreno; nazione. *vt.* sbarcare, collocare, tirare a riva; prender possesso di, prendere, guadagnare. *vi.* sbarcare, approdare, metter piede al suolo; (*aeron.*) atterrare. **—holder** *n.* proprietario terriero.

landing *n.* approdo, sbarco; pianerottolo; (*aeron.*) atterraggio: — **craft**, mezzo da sbarco; — **gear** (*aeron.*), carrello d'atterraggio; — **ground**, campo d'atterraggio; — **place**, sbarcatoio, pontile; — **strip**, pista di atterraggio.

landlady (lănd′lādĭ) *n.* albergatrice, affittacamere.

landlord (lănd′lôrd) *n.* albergatore, proprietario.

landmark (lănd′märk′) *n.* segno di confine, punto di riferimento; impronta, caratteristica.

landowner (lănd′ōn′ẽr) *n.* proprietario di terre, proprietario terriero.

landscape (lănd′skāp) *n.* paesaggio, panorama.

landslide (lănd′slīd′) **landslip** (-slĭp′) *n.* frana.

lane (lān) *n.* sentiero, vicolo; corsia (*di autostrada*).

language (lăng′gwĭj) *n.* linguaggio, lingua: **bad** —, turpiloquio.

languid (lăng′gwĭd) *agg.* languido.

languish (lăng′gwĭsh) *vi.* languire.

languor (lăng′gẽr) *n.* languore, stasi. **—ous** *agg.* languido.

lank (lăngk) *agg.* esile, allampanato.

lanky (lăngk′ĭ) *agg.* allampanato.

lantern (lăn′tẽrn) *n.* lanterna, faro.

lap (lăp) (1) *n.* grembo; lembo, falda (*di indumento, ecc.*), piega, sovrapposizione; giro di pista; riporto. *vt.* distendere, deporre; superare di un giro. *vi.* sovrapporsi.

lap (lăp) (2) *n.* sciacquio. *vt.*, *vi.* lambìre; bere rumorosamente.

lapel (lȧ-pĕl′) *n.* risvolto (*di giacca*).

lapse (lăps) *n.* errore, dimenticanza; caduta; lasso (*di tempo*); lacuna; scadenza. *vi.* sbagliare; scorrere, trascorrere; cadere, decadere, scadere.

larboard (lär′bôrd) *n.* (*naut.*) sinistra.

larceny (lär′sĕ-nĭ) *n.* furto.

larch (lärch) *n.* (*bot.*) larice.

lard (lärd) *n.* strutto. *vt.* lardellare.

larder (lär′dẽr) *n.* dispensa.

large (lärj) *n.* libertà, generalità: **at** —, in libertà, diffusamente, in generale; **in** —, su larga scala. *agg.* largo, ampio, spazioso, grande, grosso: **as** — **as life**, in bella vista.

—ly *avv.* ampiamente, prevalentemente.

largess (lär'jĕs) *n.* generosità, elargizione.

lark (lärk) *n.* allodola; (*fam.*) divertimento, beffa. *vi.* divertirsi, fare scherzi.

larynx (lăr'ĭngks) *n.* (*pl.* larynges) laringe.

lash (lăsh) *n.* frusta, frustata; ciglio. *vt.* frustare; legare, ormeggiare; insultare; incitare.

lass (lăs) *n.* fanciulla, donna.

lassitude (lăs'ĭ.tŭd) *n.* fiacchezza.

last (låst) *n.* ultimo; fine, conclusione; forma (*da scarpe*): at —, finalmente; to the —, fino alla fine. *agg.* ultimo, finale, scorso: — but one, penultimo; — night, ieri sera; — year, l'anno scorso. *avv.* ultimamente, da ultimo, l'ultima volta. *vi.* durare, resistere: to — out, sopravvivere, durare a lungo. —ing *agg.* durevole. —ly *avv.* in fine, in conclusione, da ultimo.

latch (lăch) *n.* saliscendi, serratura a scatto: on the —, chiuso con la sola maniglia (*di uscio*). *vt.* chiudere col saliscendi.

late (lāt) *agg.* tardo, in ritardo, ritardatario; ultimo, recente; defunto, ex: to be —, esser tardi, essere in ritardo; a — hour, un'ora avanzata; the — bishop, il defunto vescovo. *avv.* tardi, in ritardo, fino a tarda ora, tardivamente; recentemente; già (*un tempo*): — in the night, a notte tarda; — into the night, sino a notte tarda; — in the week, verso la fine della settimana; — of this firm, già appartenente a questa ditta; of —, recentemente; it is getting —, si fa tardi. —ly *avv.* ultimamente, recentemente.

later (lāt'ĕr) *agg.* posteriore, ulteriore. *avv.* più tardi: see you —! arrivederci!, a più tardi!

latest (lāt'est) *agg.* più recente, recentissimo, ultimo: at the —, al più tardi; — news, ultime notizie.

latent (lā'tĕnt) *agg.* latente, nascosto.

lateral (lăt'ĕr.ăl) *agg.* laterale.

lath (låth) *n.* corrente (*travicello per costruzione di tetti, ecc.*).

lathe (lāth) *n.* tornio.

lather (lăth'ĕr) *n.* schiuma, spuma. *vt.* insaponare, far spumeggiare. *vi.* spumeggiare, schiumare.

Latin (lăt'ĭn) *n.*, *agg.* latino.

latish (lāt'ĭsh) *agg.* alquanto tardivo.

latitude (lăt'ĭ.tŭd) *n.* latitudine; ampiezza; larghezza di vedute; libertà.

latter (lăt'ĕr) *agg.* ultimo, posteriore, recente; secondo (*di due*): I prefer the — to the former, preferisco il secondo al primo.

lattice (lăt'ĭs) *n.* grata, inferriata, graticcio.

laud (lôd) *n.* inno, salmo. *vt.* esaltare, lodare. —able *agg.* lodevole.

laugh (låf) *n.* risata, riso. *vi.* ridere: to — at, farsi beffe di; to — up one's sleeve, ridere sotto i baffi. —able *agg.* ridicolo, risibile.

laughing (låf'ĭng) *n.* ilarità, risa. *agg.* ridente: — gas gas esilarante. —stock *n.* zimbello.

laughter (låf'tĕr) *n.* ilarità.

launch (lônch) *n.* lancio, varo; lancia (*imbarcazione*). *vt.* lanciare, varare. *vi.* slanciarsi, tuffarsi.

launder (lôn'dĕr) *vt.*, *vi.* lavare e stirare; fare il bucato. —er *n.* lavandaio.

laundress (lôn'drĕs) *n.* lavandaia.

laundry (lôn'drĭ) *n.* biancheria; lavanderia.

laurel (lô'rĕl) *n.* alloro.

lava (lä'vä) *n.* lava.

lavatory (lăv'à.tō'rĭ) *n.* ritirata, latrina; lavatoio.

lavender (lăv'ĕn.dĕr) *n.* lavanda; *agg.* di lavanda; color lavanda.

lavish (lăv'ĭsh) *agg.* abbondante, sontuoso, prodigo, generoso. *vt.* elargire, sperperare: to — praise upon somebody, colmare qualcuno di lodi. —ly *avv.* abbondantemente, sontuosamente, prodigalmente.

law (lô) *n.* legge, diritto: criminal —, diritto penale; Law Courts, Palazzo di Giustizia: —abiding, ossequiente alle leggi. —breaker *n.* trasgressore. —ful *agg.* legale, legittimo. —less *agg.* illegale, sfrenato. —maker *n.* legislatore.

lawn (lôn) *n.* prato, tappeto erboso; rensa (*tessuto*): —mower *n.* falciatrice meccanica.

lawsuit (lô'sūt') *n.* causa, processo.

lawyer (lô'yĕr) *n.* avvocato, notaio.

lax (lăks) *agg.* molle, lento, rilassato, noncurante. —ative *n.*, *agg.* lassativo. —ity, —ness *n.* rilassamento, fiacca, sbadataggine.

lay (lā) (1) *n.* situazione, posizione. *vt.* (*pass.*, *pp.* laid) porre, deporre, collocare; spegnere; abbattere; tendere (*un trabocchetto*); calmare: to — a wager, fare una scommessa; to — the blame on, attribuire la colpa a; to — claim to, accampare diritti su; to — aside, mettere da parte; to — bare, mettere a nudo, scoprire; to — down, adagiare; stabilire (*un principio*); tracciare: to — hold of, impossessarsi di; to — open, esporre, mettere a nudo; to — out, distendere, esporre, preparare; sborsare. *vi.* fare le uova, scommettere.

lay (lā) (2) *pass. di* to lie.

lay (lā) (3) *agg.* laico.

layer (lā'ẽr) *n.* strato.

layman (lā'măn) *n.* laico; profano, inesperto.

layout (lā'out') *n.* disposizione; esposizione; situazione; piano, progetto; impaginazione, maestra (*facsimile*), menabò; armamentario.

lazily (lā'zĭ.lĭ) *avv.* pigramente.

laziness (lā'zĭ.nĕs) *n.* pigrizia.

lazy (lā'zĭ) *agg.* pigro, indolente.

lead (lĕd) (1) *n.* piombo, scandaglio; mina per matita; pallottole; (*tip.*) interlinea: red —, minio; white —, biacca. *vt.* piombare, impiombare; (*tip.*) interlineare.

lead (lēd) (2) *n.* direzione, comando, guida, posizione di testa, vantaggio; esempio; guinzaglio; esordio; primo attore. *vt., vi.* (*pass., pp.* led) condurre, guidare, capeggiare, precedere, indurre, far da guida: **to — an orchestra**, dirigere un'orchestra; **to — astray**, sviare, traviare; **to — the way**, precedere, fare strada.

leaden (lĕd'n) *agg.* di piombo, plumbeo, greve.

leader (lēd'ẽr) *n.* condottiero, guida; articolo di fondo; cavallo di punto. **—ship** *n.* comando, guida (*il guidare*), direzione.

leading (lēd'ĭng) *agg.* principale, primo: **— article**, articolo di fondo; **— man**, primo attore; **— strings**, dande.

leaf (lēf) *n.* (*pl.* leaves) foglia; foglio; pagina; battente, ribalta (*di tavola*): **to turn over a new —**, cambiar vita. *vt.* sfogliare. *vi.* fogliare. **—less** *agg.* senza foglie, sfogliato. **—let** *n.* fogliolina; foglietto; volante.

leafy (lēf'ĭ) *agg.* frondoso.

league (lēg) (1) *n.* lega, società.

league (lēg) (2) *n.* lega (*misura di lunghezza*).

leak (lēk) *n.* falla, fessura, perdita (*di liquido*), il trapelare (*di notizie riservate, ecc.*): **to spring a —**, fare acqua. *vi.* perdere, colare, far acqua, trapelare. **—age** *n.* perdita (*di liquido*), fuga (*di gas*), falla.

lean (lēn) (1) *n.* inclinazione, pendenza. *vt.* (*pass., pp.* leaned, leant) appoggiare, inclinare. *vi.* appoggiarsi; inclinarsi; propendere; pendere.

lean (lēn) (2) *agg.* magro, esile.

leaning *n.* propensione. *agg.* pendente.

leant (lĕnt) *pass., pp. di* to lean.

leap (lēp) *n.* salto, balzo. *vt.* (*pass., pp.* leaped, leapt) saltare, scaval-

care. *vi.* balzare, slanciarsi. **— year**, anno bisestile.

leapt (lĕpt) *pass., pp. di* to leap.

learn (lûrn) *vt., vi.* (*pass., pp.* learned, learnt) imparare; venire a sapere; istruirsi. **—ed** (*gen.* lûrn'ĕd) *agg.* dotto. **—er** *n.* allievo, principiante. **—ing** *n.* erudizione, sapere.

learnt (lûrnt) *pass., pp. di* to learn.

lease (lēs) *n.* affittanza, contratto d'affitto. *vt.* dare *o* prendere in affitto.

leash (lēsh) *n.* guinzaglio. *vt.* tenere al guinzaglio; tenere a freno.

least (lēst) *n.* quantità minima, minimo. *agg.* minimo, infimo, minore. *avv.* al minimo: **at —**, per lo meno; **not in the —**, nient'affatto; **to say the —**, a dir poco.

leather (lĕth'ẽr) *n.* pelle, cuoio: **patent —**, coppale. *vt.* rivestire di cuoio; staffilare.

leathern (lĕth'ẽrn) *agg.* di cuoio, coriaceo.

leathery (lĕth'ẽr.ĭ) *agg.* coriaceo; simile a cuoio.

leave (lēv) *n.* permesso, licenza, commiato: **on —**, in licenza; **sick —**, licenza di convalescenza; **to take French —**, filare all'inglese; **to take — of**, accomiatarsi da. *vt., vi.* (*pass., pp.* left) lasciare, abbandonare; andarsene, partire: **I have nothing left**, non mi resta nulla; **to — alone**, lasciare in pace; **to — off**, smettere.

leaven (lĕv'ĕn) *n.* lievito. *vt.* lievitare; impregnare.

leavings (lĕv'ĭngz) *n.pl.* residui; rifiuti.

lecherous (lĕch'ẽr.ŭs) *agg.* libertino, osceno.

lection (lĕk'shŭn) *n.* lezione.

lecture (lĕk'tûr) *n.* conferenza, lezione; ramanzina, predicozzo. *vt., vi.* tenere conferenze, istruire, rimproverare.

lecturer (lĕk'tûr.ẽr) *n.* conferenziere, docente.

led (lĕd) *pass., pp. di* to lead (2).

ledge (lĕj) *n.* davanzale, ripiano, bordo; strato; (*min.*) vena.

ledger (lĕj'ẽr) *n.* libro mastro.

lee (lē) *n.* riparo; (*naut.*) sottovento.

leech (lēch) *n.* sanguisuga; medico.

leer (lēr) *n.* occhiata obliqua. *vi.* guardare di traverso, sbirciare.

lees (lēz) *n.pl.* feccia, sedimento.

leeway (lē'wā') *n.* deriva; agio, margine; (*aeron.*) angolo di deriva.

left (lĕft) (1) *pass., pp. di* to leave.

left (lĕft) (2) *n.* sinistra: **at (on, to) the —**, a sinistra. *agg.* sinistro. *avv.* a sinistra. **—-handed** *agg.* mancino;

rotante da destra a sinistra; morganatico; ambiguo, goffo: — compliment, complimento ironico.

leftist (lĕft'ĭst) *n.* (*pol.*) persona di sinistra.

leftover (lĕft'ō'vĕr) *n.*, eccedenza. *agg.* eccedente.

leg (lĕg) *n.* gamba; piede (*di mobile*); zampa (*di animale*); asta (*di compasso*); tappa (*di viaggio o corsa*): to pull someone's —, prendere in giro qualcuno; to be on one's last —s, essere alle ultime risorse. *vi.* to — it (*gergo*), svignarsela.

legacy (lĕg'á·sĭ) *n.* legato, eredità.

legal (lē'gál) *agg.* legale, giuridico. —ity (lē·găl'ĭ·tĭ) *n.* legalità.

legalize (lē'gál.ĭz) *vt.* legalizzare, legittimare.

legate (lĕg'ĭt) *n.* legato, nunzio.

legatee (lĕg'á·tē') *n.* legatario, erede.

legation (lē·gā'shŭn) *n.* legazione, ambasciata.

legend (lĕj'ĕnd) *n.* leggenda.

legendary (lĕj'ĕn·dĕr'ĭ) *agg.* leggendario.

legerdemain (lĕj'ĕr·dē·mān') *n.* gioco di prestigio, gherminella.

leggings (lĕg'gĭngz) *n.pl.* uose.

legible (lĕj'ĭ·b'l) *agg.* leggibile.

legion (lē'jŭn) *n.* legione; moltitudine.

legislate (lĕj'ĭs.lāt) *vi.* legiferare.

legislation (lĕj'ĭs.lā'shŭn) *n.* legislazione.

legislative (lĕj'ĭs.lā'tĭv) *agg.* legislativo.

legislature (lĕj'ĭs.lā'tûr) *n.* legislatura.

legitimate (lē·jĭt'ĭ·mĭt) *agg.* legittimo.

legman (lĕg'măn') *n.* cronista; galoppino.

leisure (lē'zhĕr;lĕzh'ĕr) *n.* riposo, agio, comodo: at —, con comodo; to be at —, essere in ozio, non aver niente da fare; — hours, ore libere, ore di riposo. —ly *agg.* calmo, deliberato. *avv.* con comodo, senza fretta.

lemon (lĕm'ŭn) *n.* limone; *agg.* color limone. —ade *n.* limonata.

lend (lĕnd) *vt.*, *vi.* (*pass.*, *pp.* **lent**) prestare, fornire; conferire.

lender *n.* prestatore.

lending *n.* prestito: — **library**, biblioteca circolante.

lend-lease *n.* affitti e prestiti.

length (lĕngth) *n.* lunghezza; estensione; durata, lasso; punto, grado: at —, diffusamente, per esteso; finalmente, infine; to go the whole —, andare fino in fondo.

lengthen (lĕng'thĕn) *vt.* allungare, prolungare, estendere. *vi.* allungarsi, prolungarsi, protrarsi.

lengthwise (lĕngth'wĭz) *agg.* longitudinale. *avv.* longitudinalmente, per il lungo.

lengthy (lĕng'thĭ) *agg.* lungo, prolisso.

leniency (lē'nĭ·ĕn.sĭ) *n.* indulgenza, clemenza.

lenient (lē'nĭ·ĕnt) *agg.* clemente, indulgente.

lens (lĕnz) *n.* (*ott.*) lente; (*anat.*) cristallino.

lent (lĕnt) *pass.*, *pp. di* to lend.

Lent (lĕnt) *n.* quaresima.

lentil (lĕn'tĭl) *n.* (*bot.*) lenticchia.

leopard (lĕp'ĕrd) *n.* leopardo.

leper (lĕp'ĕr) *n.* lebbroso.

leprosy (lĕp'rŏ·sĭ) *n.* lebbra.

leprous (lĕp'rŭs) *agg.* lebbroso.

less (lĕs) *n.* meno. *agg.* meno, minore, più piccolo, inferiore. *avv.*, *prep.* meno: — and —, sempre meno.

lessee (lĕs·ē') *n.* affittuario.

lessen (lĕs''n) *vt.*, *vi.* diminuire.

lesson (lĕs''n) *n.* lezione.

lest (lĕst) *cong.* per paura che, a scanso di: I feared — he might fall, temevo che egli cadesse.

let (lĕt) *vt.*, *vi.* (*pass.*, *pp.* let) lasciare, permettere; affittare; causare; ostacolare: — me alone, — me be, lasciatemi in pace; — us go, andiamocene; to — down, piantare in asso, deludere; to — in, far entrare, lasciar entrare; to — loose, allentare, sciogliere, scatenare; to — know, far sapere; to — off, rilasciare.

lethargy (lĕth'ĕr.jĭ) *n.* letargo.

letter (lĕt'ĕr) *n.* lettera: — **of attorney**, procura. *vt.* contrassegnare con lettere, iscrivere. — **box**, cassetta per lettere.—**carrier** *n.* portalettere. —**head** *n.* intestazione (*di una lettera*). —**ing** *n.* iscrizione.

lettuce (lĕt'ĭs) *n.* lattuga.

levee (lĕv'ê) *n.* diga, argine.

level (lĕv'ĕl) *n.* livello, piano; (*tec.*) livella: to be on the —, agire rettamente, essere in buona fede, avere intenzioni oneste. *agg.* orizzontale, piano, levigato, uguale, a livello (*con*), al livello (*di*): to do one's — best, fare del proprio meglio. *vt.*, *vi.* livellare, spianare; dirigere, prendere di mira, puntare (*un'arma*); (*aeron.*) volare raso terra: to — with the dust, radere al suolo. —**headed** *agg.* equilibrato, assennato.

lever (lē'vĕr) *n.* leva: **control** —, asta di comando.

levy (lĕv'ĭ) *n.* coscrizione; esazione, requisizione. *vt.* mobilitare; esigere, requisire.

lewd (lūd) *agg.* osceno, spregevole. **—ness** *n.* oscenità, bassezza.

lexicon (lĕk'sĭ·kŏn) *n.* lessico, nomenclatura.

liability (lĭ'á·bĭl'ĭ·tĭ) *n.* obbligo, debito; pendenza, responsabilità; (*pl.*) passivo, passività.

liable (lī'á·b'l) *agg.* passibile, esposto (*a*), soggetto (*a*); proclive, suscettibile; profabile; impegnato, compromesso.

liar (lī'ẽr) *n.* bugiardo.

libel (lī'bĕl) *n.* libello, diffamazione. *vt.* diffamare.

liberal (lĭb'ẽr·ăl) *n.* (*pol.*) liberale. *agg.* liberale, generoso, abbondante. **—ity** (·ăl'ĭ·tĭ) *n.* liberalità, larghezza di vedute.

liberate (lĭb'ẽr.ăt) *vt.* liberare.

liberation (lĭb'ẽr·ā'shŭn) *n.* liberazione.

liberator (lĭb'ẽr·ā'tẽr) *n.* liberatore.

libertine (lĭb'ẽr·tēn) *n.* libertino. *agg.* licenzioso.

liberty (lĭb'ẽr·tĭ) *n.* libertà; facoltà: **at —**, in libertà; **at — to**, libero di, autorizzato a.

librarian (lĭ·brăr'ĭ·ăn) *n.* bibliotecario.

library (lī'brẽr'ĭ) *n.* biblioteca.

lice (līs) *n.* (*pl. di* louse) pidocchi.

license, licence (lī'sĕns) *n.* licenza, patente: **gun —**, porto d'armi; **driver's —**, patente di guida; **— plate**, targa di circolazione. *vt.* permettere, autorizzare.

licentious (lĭ·sĕn'shŭs) *agg.* licenzioso.

lick (lĭk) *n.* leccata. *vt.* leccare, lambire; malmenare, sopraffare, sconfiggere: **to — someone's boots**, leccare i piedi a qualcuno; **to — the dust**, mordere la polvere. **—ing** *n.* batosta.

licorice (lĭk'ō·rĭs) *n.* liquirizia.

lid (lĭd) *n.* coperchio; (*anat.*) palpebra.

lie (lī) (1) *n.* menzogna, smentita. *vi.* (*pass.*, *pp.* lied, *ppr.* lying) mentire.

lie (lī) (2) *n.* posizione, situazione. *vi.* (*pass.* lay, *pp.* lain, *ppr.* lying) giacere, coricarsi, trovarsi, riposare, stare; gravare; consistere: **it —s in my power**, dipende da me; **to — down**, coricarsi; **to — low**, star nascosto.

lief (lēf) *avv.* volontieri: **I had as —**, vorrei piuttosto, preferirei.

lieu (lū) *n.* luogo: **in — of**, invece di, a guisa di.

lieutenant (lû·tĕn'ănt) *n.* tenente: **first —**, tenente; **second —**, sottotenente.

life (līf) *n.* vita, esistenza: **from —**, dal vero; **to the —**, al naturale; **still —**, natura morta; **— imprisonment**, ergastolo; **— pension**, pensione a vita; **to come to —**,

rianimarsi; **to bring to —**, rianimare, dar vita a. **—belt** *n.* cintura di salvataggio. **—boat** *n.* scialuppa. **—buoy** *n.* salvagente. **—guard** *n.* bagnino. **— insurance**, assicurazione sulla vita. **—less** *agg.* inanimato, prostrato. **—like** *agg.* al naturale. **—long** *agg.* perpetuo, che dura tutta la vita *o* una vita. **—preserver**, salvagente; sfollagente.

lifer (līf'ẽr) *n.* ergastolo, ergastolano.

life-size *agg.* in grandezza naturale.

lifetime *n.* esistenza.

lift (lĭft) *n.* sollevamento, rialzo; montacarichi, ascensore; ponte aereo: **ski —**, **chair —**, seggiovia. **to give a —**, dare un passaggio (*a qualcuno, su un veicolo*). *vt.* alzare, sollevare, soppesare; (*fam.*) rubare; (*S.U.*) estinguere (*un'ipoteca*): **to — one's hat**, scappellarsi. *vi.* alzarsi (*salire*); innalzarsi; dissiparsi (*delle nubi*).

light (lĭt) (1) *n.* luce, giorno; faro, fanale, semaforo. *agg.* chiaro, luminoso. *vt.* (*pass.*, *pp.* lighted, lit) illuminare, rischiarare, accendere, *vi.* accendersi, splendere, illuminarsi.

light (lĭt) (2) *agg.* leggiero, lieve, frivolo, gaio: **to make — of**, prendere alla leggiera. **—headed** *agg.* stordito; frivolo, incostante; squilibrato. **—hearted** *agg.* allegro, spensierato.

lighten (lĭt''n) (1) *vt.* illuminare. *vi.* schiarirsi, rischiararsi, balenare.

lighten (lĭt''n) (2) *vt.* alleggerire, alleviare.

lighthouse (lĭt'hous') *n.* faro.

lighting (lĭt'ĭng) *n.* illuminazione.

lightly (lĭt'lĭ) *avv.* leggermente, facilmente; allegramente.

lighter (lĭt'ẽr) *n.* (*naut.*) chiatta; accendino.

lightning (lĭt'nĭng) *n.* fulmine, lampo. **—conductor**, **—rod** *n.* parafulmine.

likable (lĭk'á·b'l) *agg.* piacevole, simpatico, gradevole.

like (lĭk) *n.* l'uguale; gusto, preferenza, simpatia; pariglia: **our likes**, i pari nostri; **our likes and dislikes**, le nostre simpatie e avversioni. *agg.* simile a, somigliante a, pari a, uguale a, caratteristico. *avv.* similmente; probabilmente: **I feel — going**, ho voglia di andare; **to look —**, somigliare a, aver l'aria di. *prep.* come, alla maniera di. *cong.* come se. *vi.*, *vi.* voler bene a, piacere (*rifl.*), aver simpatia per, gradire, convenire, garbare, volere: **I —**

this, questo mi piace; to — better o best, preferire.

likelihood (lĭk'lĭ·hŏŏd), **likeliness** (-nĕs) n. probabilità.

likely (lĭk'lĭ) agg. probabile, conveniente: he is — to come, è probabile che egli venga. avv. probabilmente.

liken (lĭk'ĕn) vt. paragonare, confrontare.

likeness (lĭk'nĕs) n. somiglianza, apparenza, ritratto, aspetto.

likewise (lĭk'wĭz') avv. ugualmente, similmente, così; anche; lo stesso.

liking (lĭk'ĭng) n. inclinazione, gusto, simpatia, amicizia: to take a — to, prendere in simpatia.

lilac (lī'lăk) n., agg. lilla.

lily (lĭl'ĭ) n. giglio: —-of-the-valley, mughetto.

limb (lĭm) n. arto; ramo d'albero; alone; corolla; (pl.) membra.

limber (lĭm'bĕr) (1) n. avantreno.

limber (lĭm'bĕr) (2) agg. flessibile, agile. vt., vi. rendere o divenire flessibile.

lime (lĭm) n. calce; vischio; tiglio; limetta (agrume).

limelight (lĭm'lĭt') n. riflettore teatrale; notorietà: to be in the —, essere alla ribalta.

limestone (lĭm'stōn') n. pietra calcare.

limit (lĭm'ĭt) n. limite. vt. limitare. —**ation** n. limitazione; prescrizione. —**ed** agg. limitato, circoscritto: — company, società anonima.

limp (lĭmp) n. zoppicamento. agg. molle, fiacco, afflosciato. vi. zoppicare.

limpet (lĭm'pĕt) n. (ittiol.) patella.

limpid (lĭm'pĭd) agg. limpido.

linden (lĭn'dĕn) n. (bot.) tiglio.

line (lĭn) n. linea; corda, cordone; allineamento; contorno, limite; equatore; discendenza; campo (di attività), direzione; battuta (di commedia); assortimento (di merci); lenza: to bring into —, mettere in fila; to get in —, mettersi in fila. vt. bordare, foderare, rivestire; allineare. vi. allinearsi.

lineage (lĭn'ê·ĭj) n. lignaggio.

lined (lĭnd) agg. orlato (di); foderato (di).

linen (lĭn'ĕn) n. tela; biancheria. agg. di tela.

liner (lĭn'ĕr) n. piroscafo o velivolo di linea; opuscolo di accompagnamento (di un disco).

linger (lĭng'gĕr) vt. protrarre; passare (tempo) pigramente. vi. indugiare, soffermarsi, attardarsi, vagare; perdurare, prolungarsi.

lingo (lĭng'gō) n. gergo, frasario.

liniment (lĭn'ĭ·mĕnt) n. linimento.

lining (lĭn'ĭng) n. fodera, rivestimento interno.

link (lĭngk) n. vincolo, anello (di catena), collegamento; torcia, fiaccola: cuff links, gemelli per polsini. vt. collegare, unire, concatenare.

links (lĭngks) n. campo di golf.

linnet (lĭn'ĕt) n. (ornit.) fanello.

linseed (lĭn'sēd') n. seme di lino. — oil, olio di lino.

lint (lĭnt) n. filaccia per medicazioni.

lion (lī'ŭn) n. leone. —**ess** n. leonessa.

lip (lĭp) n. labbro; orlo; impertinenza: — service, fedeltà a parole; ipocrisia; conformismo.

lipstick (lĭp'stĭck') n. rossetto (per le labbra).

liquid (lĭk'wĭd) n., agg. liquido.

liquidate (lĭk'wĭ·dāt) vt. liquidare.

liquidation (lĭk'wĭ·dā'shŭn) n. liquidazione.

liquor (lĭk'ĕr) n. liquore.

lisp (lĭsp) n. pronuncia blesa. vt., vi. farfugliare, essere bleso.

list (lĭst) (1) n. lista, elenco. vt. elencare; arrolare. vi. arrolarsi.

list (lĭst) (2) n. orlo, vivagno, striscia, solco. vt. orlare, rigare, solcare.

list (lĭst) (3) n. inclinazione; (naut.) sbandamento. vi. inclinarsi, sbandare.

listen (lĭs''n) vt. ascoltare: to — in, ascoltare alla radio; orecchiare. —**er** n. ascoltatore.

listless (lĭst'lĕs) agg. disattento, svogliato, indifferente. —**ness** n. distrazione, indifferenza, svogliatezza.

lit (lĭt) pass., pp. di to light (1).

liter, litre (lē'tĕr) n. litro.

literal (lĭt'ĕr·ăl) agg. letterale. —**ly** avv. letteralmente.

literary (lĭt'ĕr·ĕr'ĭ) agg. letterario.

literature (lĭt'ĕr·á·tủr) n. letteratura.

lithograph (lĭth'ō·gráf) n. litografia (riproduzione).

lithography (lĭ·thŏg'rá·fĭ) n. litografia (arte).

litigant (lĭt'ĭ·gănt) n. contendente; parte in causa.

litigation (lĭt'ĭ·gā'shŭn) n. causa civile.

litter (lĭt'ĕr) n. lettiera, strame; lettiga; disordine; rifiuti. vt. sparpagliare, cospargere disordinatamente.

little (lĭt''l) n. poco, inezia. agg. piccolo, esiguo, poco: Little Bear, Orsa Minore; a — sugar, un po' di zucchero; a — while, un po' di tempo. avv. scarsamente, poco: they — knew that, non sapevano affatto che; — by —, a poco a poco.

live (lĭv) *agg.* vivo, ardente, acceso. (lĭv) *vt.*, *vi.* vivere, esistere; abitare; durare: to — from hand to mouth, vivere alla giornata; to — down, far dimenticare, cancellare (*il passato*). —lihood (lĭv'-) *n.* mezzi di sussistenza. —liness *n.* vivacità, animazione, vitalità. —ly *agg.* vivace, attivo, animato, brioso. *avv.* vivacemente, animatamente.

liver (lĭv'ẽr) (1) *n.* chi vive, abitante.

liver (lĭv'ẽr) (2) *n.* fegato.

livery (lĭv'ẽr.ĭ) *n.* livrea; governo dei cavalli: high —, alta tenuta; undress —, bassa tenuta; — stable, rimessa che noleggia cavalli e veicoli.

lives (lĭvz) *pl. di* life.

livestock (lĭv'stŏk') *n.* bestiame, mandrie.

livid (lĭv'ĭd) *agg.* livido, smorto.

living (lĭv'ĭng) *n.* vita, mezzi di sussistenza, rendita. *agg.* vivo, vivente, parlante (*di ritratti*).

lizard (lĭz'ẽrd) *n.* (*zool.*) lucertola.

llama (lä'mä) *n.* (*zool.*) lama.

load (lōd) *n.* carico, soma, fardello: loads of, mucchi di, montagne di. *vt.* caricare, opprimere, appesantire: loaded dice, dadi truccati.

loaf (lōf) *n.* (*pl.* loaves) panino, pagnotta; porzione. *vt.*, *vi.* oziare, bighellonare, sprecare (*tempo, ecc.*). —er *n.* bighellone; (*pl.*) mocassini (*tipo di scarpe*).

loan (lōn) *n.* prestito. *vt.* prestare. — shark, strozzino.

loath (lōth) *agg.* restio, avverso: to be — to, essere avverso a.

loathe (lōth) *vt.* aborrire.

loathing *n.* avversione, ripugnanza.

loathsome (lōth'sŭm) *agg.* repulsivo, odioso.

lobby (lŏb'ĭ) *n.* vestibolo, corridoio.

lobster (lŏb'stẽr) *n.* aragosta.

local (lō'kăl) *agg.* locale, regionale. —ity (lō-kăl'ĭ-tĭ) *n.* località.

localize (lō'kăl-īz) *vt.* localizzare.

locate (lō'kāt) *vt.* individuare, reperire, situare, collocare.

location (lō-kā'shŭn) *n.* posizione, collocamento, locazione; (*cinema*) esterni, luogo della ripresa.

lock (lŏk) *n.* serratura, lucchetto, chiusa (*di fiume, ecc.*); percussore, (*d'arma da fuoco*); fiocco (*di lana*); ciocca (*di capelli*). *vt.* chiudere a chiave, rinchiudere; abbracciare; bloccare; (*tip.*) chiudere (*una pagina*): to — up, rinchiudere, incarcerare. *vi.* chiudersi, unirsi saldamente: to — out, fare la serrata. —er *n.* ripostiglio. —et *n.*

medaglione. —out *n.* serrata (*di una fabbrica*). —smith *n.* fabbro.

locomotive (lō'kō-mō'tĭv) *n.* locomotiva: — engineer, macchinista.

locomotor (lō'kō-mō'tẽr) *n.*, *agg.* locomotore: — ataxy, atassia locomotrice.

locust (lō'kŭst) *n.* (*entom.*) locusta; (*bot.*) robinia.

lode (lōd) *n.* (*min.*) filone, vena.

lodestar (lōd'stär') *n.* stella polare.

lodge (lŏj) *n.* padiglione, baracca, portineria (*di villa*), loggia. *vt.* collocare, fissare, alloggiare: to — a complaint, sporgere querela. *vi.* abitare, essere alloggiato, incastrarsi, essere collocato.

lodger (lŏj'ẽr) *n.* inquilino.

lodging (lŏj'ĭng) *n.* alloggio.

loft (lŏft) *n.* granaio; soffitta; balconata.

lofty (lŏf'tĭ) *agg.* alto, elevato; altezzoso.

log (lŏg) *n.* ceppo, tronco; (*naut.*) solcometro; libro di bordo. *vt.*, *vi.* disboscare, tagliare alberi; (*naut.*) scrivere nel libro di bordo. —ger *n.* boscaiolo.

loggerhead (lŏg'ẽr·hĕd') *n.* stupido; (*zool.*) tartaruga marina: to be at loggerheads, essere in disputa.

logic (lŏj'ĭk) *n.* logica. —al *agg.* logico.

loin (loin) *n.* lombo.

loiter (loi'tẽr) *vt.* sprecare (*tempo*) in ozio. *vi.* oziare, attardarsi, bighellonare: to — behind, restare indietro. —er *n.* bighellone.

loll (lŏl) *vi.* penzolare, oscillare; sdraiarsi; afflosciarsi.

lone (lōn) *agg.* isolato, solitario, solo. —liness *n.* solitudine, desolazione. —ly *agg.* solitario, desolato, isolato. —some *agg.* solitario, solo, nostalgico.

long (lŏng) (1) *vi.* agognare, bramare: to — for, aspettare con impazienza.

long (lŏng) (2) *agg.* lungo, esteso, lento, noioso: — measure, misura di lunghezza; in the — run, alla lunga; all day —, tutto il santo giorno; two meters —, lungo due metri; to be — in coming, tardare a venire. *avv.* a lungo, lungamente, da (*o* per) molto tempo: before —, tra poco, in breve; — ago, molto tempo fa; so (*o* as) — as, fin tanto che; how—? quanto tempo ?; so—! ciao!, arrivederci! —suffering *agg.* tollerante. —winded *agg.* prolisso, noioso. —playing *agg.* a lunga durata.

longer (lŏng'gẽr) *agg.* più lungo, più esteso. *avv.* più a lungo, più ancora: no —, non più.

longest (lŏng'gĕst) *agg.* più lungo (*d'ogni altro*). *avv.* il più a lungo.

longevity (lŏn·jĕv'ĭ·tĭ) *n.* longevità.

longhair (lŏng'hâr') (*gergo*) *n.* artista, musicista, appassionato di musica classica. *agg.* teorico; sognatore; intellettuale.

longing (lŏng'ĭng) *n.* brama, smania. —ly *avv.* bramosamente.

longitude (lŏn'jĭ·tūd) *n.* longitudine.

longshoreman (lŏng'shŏr'măn) *n.* scaricatore del porto.

look (lŏŏk) *n.* sguardo; aspetto, apparenza: by the — of it, a quel che sembra; good looks, bell'aspetto. *vt., vi.* guardare; sembrare, aver l'aspetto, essere prospiciente: to — after, aver cura di, accudire a; to — alike, somigliare, sembrare uguali; to — down upon, guardare dall'alto in basso; to — for, cercare; to — forward to, non veder l'ora di, pregustare; to — into, esaminare; to — like, aver l'aria di, sembrare, somigliare a; to — out, cercare, stare in guardia; to — over, esaminare; to — up, alzare lo sguardo; cercare; to — up to, guardare a, guardare con ammirazione. —er *n.* chi guarda; persona bella: on looker, n. spettatore, astante. —ing glass, specchio.

lookout *n.* vigilanza; prospettiva; sentinella: that's my —, è affar mio; to be on the —, stare all'erta.

loom (lōōm) *n.* telaio (*per tessitura*); fusto del remo. *vt.* tessere al telaio. *vi.* apparire, delinearsi.

loony (lōōn'ĭ) *agg.* pazzo, pazzesco.

loop (lōōp) *n.* cappio, nodo scorsoio; occhiello, anello; circuito; (*aeron.*) cerchio della morte. *vt., vi.* annodare, allacciare; fare il cerchio della morte.

loophole (lōōp'hōl') *n.* feritoia; scappatoia.

loose (lōōs) *agg.* sciolto, sfrenato, allentato; dissoluto; libero; sconnesso: to break —, scappare, liberarsi; to let —, lasciar andare; — change, spiccioli. *vt., vi.* sciogliere, slegare, allentare, allentarsi; liberare, scatenare; disormeggiare; levar l'ancora. —ly *avv.* liberamente; dissolutamente; negligentemente; non strettamente; impropriamente.

loosen (lōōs''n) *vt.* slegare, allentare, smuovere. *vi.* allentarsi, sciogliersi.

looseness *n.* scioltezza, rilassatezza, trascuratezza, immoralità.

loot (lōōt) *n.* bottino, saccheggio. *vt., vi.* depredare, saccheggiare.

lop (lŏp) *vt., vi.* sfrondare, potare; penzolare.

loquacious (lō·kwā'shŭs) *agg.* loquace.

lord (lôrd) *n.* signore, padrone, sovrano, Pari d'Inghilterra: the Lord, Dio; Lord's Prayer, Padre Nostro. *vi.* signoreggiare. —ly *agg.* signorile, superbo, nobile, magnifico. *avv.* signorilmente, superbamente. —ship *n.* dominio, signoria, autorità.

lorry (lŏr'ĭ) *n.* (*Ingl.*) autocarro, carro matto; (*min.*) vagoncino.

lose (lōōz) *vt., vi.* (*pass., pp.* lost) perdere, smarrire, rimetterci: to — one's temper, andare in collera; to — sight of someone, perdere qualcuno di vista.

loser (lōōz'ĕr) *n.* perdente.

loss (lŏs) *n.* perdita, smarrimento: to be at a —, essere perplesso, non saper che pesci pigliare; to sell at a —, vendere in perdita; — leader, articolo venduto in perdita per scopi pubblicitari.

lost (lŏst) *agg.* (*e pass., pp. di* to lose) perduto, smarrito, sprecato: — in thought, soprappensiero, assorto; to get —, smarrirsi.

lot (lŏt) *n.* destino, sorte; spettanza, lotto, quantità, porzione; (*comm.*) partita: a —, una gran quantità, molto; to cast (*opp.* draw) lots, tirare a sorte; to fall to one's —, toccare in sorte a uno.

lotion (lō'shŭn) *n.* lozione.

lottery (lŏt'ĕr·ĭ) *n.* lotteria.

loud (loud) *agg.* sonoro, rumoroso; forte, sgargiante. —ly *avv.* a gran voce, sonoramente; vistosamente. —speaker *n.* altoparlante.

lounge (lounj) *n.* divano; atrio (*d'albergo, ecc.*). *vi.* oziare, bighellonare.

louse (lous) *n.* (*pl.* lice) pidocchio.

lousy (louz'ĭ) *agg.* pidocchioso; (*gergo*) spregevole, schifoso; pieno (*di*).

lout (lout) *n.* tanghero, villanzone.

lovable (lŭv'á·b'l) *agg.* amabile.

love (lŭv) *n.* amore, affetto, predilezione: to be in —, essere innamorato; to fall in — with, innamorarsi di; to make — to, fare la corte a; give my — to X, salutatemi affettuosamente X; there is no — lost between those two, quei due si detestano: — affair, relazione (*amorosa*). *vt.* amare: I — it, mi piace molto.

loveliness (lŭv'lĭ·nĕs) *n.* grazia, bellezza, amabilità, incanto.

lovely (lŭv'lĭ) *agg.* incantevole, grazioso, meraviglioso.

lover (lŭv'ĕr) *n.* amante, innamorato, appassionato (*di*).

loving (lŭv'ĭng) *agg.* amorevole, affettuoso. —**ly** *avv.* affettuosamente, amorevolmente; con amore.

low (lō) (1) *agg.* basso, profondo; debole; volgare; depresso, abbattuto: — **comedy**, farsa; — **gear** (*auto.*), prima; — **neck**, scollatura profonda; **in** — **spirits**, abbattuto, demoralizzato; **to be** — **on something**, essere a corto di qualcosa. *avv.* in basso; a bassa voce; profondamente; a buon mercato; bassamente, vilmente.

low (lō) (2) *n.* muggito. *vi.* muggire.

lower (lō'ĕr) (1) *agg.* più basso, inferiore. *vt.* abbassare, diminuire; adagiare. *vi.* scemare, scendere.

lower (lou'ĕr) (2) *vi.* rannuvolarsi, accigliarsi.

lowest (lō'ĕst) *agg.* (*il*) più basso, (*il*) più profondo, infimo.

lowland (lō'lănd) *n.* bassa, bassopiano.

lowliness (lō'lĭ·nĕs) *n.* umiltà.

lowly (lō'lĭ) *agg.* basso, umile, inferiore. *avv.* umilmente.

loyal (loi'ăl) *agg.* leale, fedele. —**ty** *n.* lealtà, fedeltà.

lube (lūb) (*gergo*) *n.* olio lubrificante.

lubricant (lū'brĭ·kănt) *n.* lubrificante.

lubricate (lū'brĭ·kāt) *vt.* lubrificare.

lubrication (lū'brĭ·kā'shŭn) *n.* lubrificazione.

lucid (lū'sĭd) *agg.* lucido, lucente, limpido.

luck (lŭk) *n.* fortuna, sorte, caso: **in** —, fortunato; **out of** —, sfortunato. —**ily** *avv.* fortunatamente.

lucky (lŭk'ĭ) *agg.* fortunato; favorevole, propizio.

lucrative (lū'krā·tĭv) *agg.* lucrativo, profittevole.

ludicrous (lū'dĭ·krŭs) *agg.* ridicolo.

lug (lŭg) *vt.* trascinare, issare.

luggage (lŭg'ĭj) *n.* bagaglio.

lukewarm (lūk'wôrm') *agg.* tiepido; indifferente.

lull (lŭl) *n.* tregua, pausa. *vt.* cullare, placare. *vi.* chetarsi, placarsi.

lullaby (lŭl'ā·bī') *n.* ninnananna.

lumber (lŭm'bĕr) *n.* legname, cianfrusaglie. *vt.* ammassare, ingombrare. *vi.* fare un rumore sordo, far legna, trascinarsi. — **room**, ripostiglio (*Ingl.*). —**yard**, *n.* magazzino legnami.

luminous (lū'mĭ·nŭs) *agg.* luminoso.

lump (lŭmp) *n.* massa, pezzo, zolla, protuberanza. *vt.* ammucchiare, raggruppare, mettere insieme; *vi.* ammucchiarsi; raggrupparsi; formare una massa; ingigantirsi; avanzare pesantemente. *agg.* **in** blocco; a zolle.

lumpy (lŭmp'ĭ) *agg.* bernoccoluto; a blocchi.

lunar (lū'nĕr) *agg.* lunare, a forma di luna; d'argento.

lunatic (lū'nà·tĭk) *n.*, *agg.* pazzo. — **asylum**, manicomio.

lunch (lŭnch), **luncheon** (lŭn'shŭn) *n.* seconda colazione; (*S.U.*) spuntino: —**room** *n.* saletta da pranzo. *vi.* desinare, fare uno spuntino.

lung (lŭng) *n.* (*anat.*) polmone.

lurch (lûrch) *n.* scarto, scossa, barcollone: **to leave in the** —, lasciare nelle peste. *vi.* scartare (*deviare*), barcollare.

lure (lūr) *n.* allettamento, esca, attrazione. *vt.* allettare, adescare.

lurid (lū'rĭd) *agg.* pallido, livido, spettrale; sgargiante, acceso; impressionante; efferato; sensazionale.

lurk (lûrk) *vi.* nascondersi, stare in agguato, incombere.

luscious (lŭsh'ŭs) *agg.* delizioso, voluttuoso.

lust (lŭst) *n.* brama, concupiscenza, libidine. *vi.*: **to** — **after**, bramare.

luster (lŭs'tĕr) *n.* splendore, lucentezza; lampadario a gocce, goccia di lampadario.

lustiness (lŭst'ĭ·nĕs) *n.* vigore.

lustrous (lŭs'trŭs) *agg.* luccicante, splendente.

lusty (lŭs'tĭ) *agg.* vigoroso, gagliardo.

lute (lūt) *n.* liuto.

luxuriant (lŭks·ū'rĭ·ănt) *agg.* lussureggiante, rigoglioso, esuberante.

luxurious (lŭks·ū'rĭ·ŭs) *agg.* lussuoso, sontuoso, comodo.

luxury (lŭk'shŏ·rĭ) *n.* lusso, dovizia.

lyceum (lī·sē'ŭm) *n.* circolo culturale.

lye (lī) *n.* ranno, liscivia.

lying (lī'ĭng) (1) *ppr. di.* to lie (1). *agg.* bugiardo, ingannevole, mendace.

lying (2) *ppr. di.* to lie (2). *agg.* giacente, orizzontale. —**in** *n.* puerperio.

lymph (lĭmf) *n.* (*fisiol.*) linfa.

lynch (lĭnch) *vt.* linciare.

lynx (lĭngks) *n.* (*zool.*) lince.

lyre (līr) *n.* (*astr., mus.*) lira.

lyric (lĭr'ĭk) *n.* lirica. —**al** *agg.* lirico.

M

macaroni (măk'à·rō'nĭ) *n.* maccheroni.

macaroon (măk'à·rōōn') *n.* amaretto, spumiglia.

machine (mȧ·shēn') *n.* macchina, meccanismo: — **gun**, mitragliatrice.

machinery (mȧ·shēn'ẽr·ǐ) *n.* meccanismo, macchinario.

machinist (mȧ·shēn'ǐst) *n.* macchinista, meccanico.

mackerel (măk'ẽr·ĕl) *n.* sgombro (*pesce*).

mackintosh (măk'ǐn·tŏsh) *n.* impermeabile.

mad (măd) *agg.* pazzo, pazzesco, furioso; idrofobo; adirato: **to drive** —, far impazzire; **to go** —, impazzire; **to get** —, adirarsi.

madam (măd'ăm) *n.* signora.

madcap (măd'kăp') *n.* scervellato. *agg.* temerario, avventato.

madden (măd''n) *vt.* far impazzire, esasperare. **—ing** *agg.* esasperante.

made (măd) *pass., pp. di* to make. *agg.* fatto, riuscito: **—up**, artificioso, falso, truccato.

madhouse (măd'hous') *n.* manicomio.

madly (măd'lǐ) *avv.* pazzamente.

madman (măd'măn) *n.* pazzo.

madness (măd'nĕs) *n.* pazzia.

madwoman *n.f.* pazza.

magazine (măg'ȧ·zēn') *n.* magazzino; arsenale, polveriera; caricatore; serbatoio; rivista, pubblicazione periodica.

magenta (mȧ·jĕn'tȧ) *n., agg.* cremisi.

maggot (măg'ŭt) *n.* larva.

magic (măj'ǐk) *n.* magia. *agg.* magico.

magician (mȧ·jǐsh'ăn) *n.* mago.

magistrate (măj'ǐs·trāt) *n.* magistrato.

magnanimous (măg·năn'ǐ·mŭs) *agg.* magnanimo.

magnet (măg'nĕt) *n.* magnete, calamita. **—ic, —ical** (-nĕt'-) *agg.* magnetico: **— recorder**, magnetofono.

magnetize (măg'nĕ·tīz) *vt.* magnetizzare.

magneto (măg·nē'tō) *n.* magnete.

magnificence (măg·nǐf'ǐ·sĕns) *n.* fasto, magnificenza.

magnificent (măg·nǐf'ǐ·sĕnt) *agg.* magnifico, splendido, generoso.

magnify (măg'nǐ·fī) *vt.* ingrandire, esagerare: **magnifying glass**, lente d'ingrandimento.

magnitude (măg'nǐ·tūd) *n.* grandezza, importanza, ampiezza.

magpie (măg'pī) *n.* gazza.

mahogany (mȧ·hŏg'ȧ·nǐ) *n.* mogano.

maid (măd) *n.* fanciulla; zitella; cameriera; **old** —, zitellona; **— of honor**, damigella d'onore.

maiden (măd''n) *n.* fanciulla, vergine. *agg.* di fanciulla, verginale, puro; inaugurale: **— name**, nome da ragazza; **— voyage**, viaggio inaugurale (*di una nave*).

mail (māl) (1) *n.* giaco (*armatura*).

mail (māl) (2) *n.* posta, corriere. *v* imbucare, spedire. **—box** *n.* casse ta delle lettere. **—man** *n.* portale tere. **— train**, treno postale.

maim (mām) *vt.* mutilare, storpiar menomare.

main (mān) *n.* condotto principa (*d'acqua, gas, ecc.*); (*la*) maggior p rte; forza; alto mare: **with might an** —, con tutta la forza. *agg.* princ pale, essenziale, primo; diretto.

mainland (mān'lănd') *n.* terraferma continente.

mainly (mān'lǐ) *avv.* principalment essenzialmente, per lo più.

maintain (mān·tān') *vt.* mantener conservare; sostenere, asserire.

maintenance (mān't'n·ăns) *n.* man tenimento, manutenzione.

maize (māz) *n.* granturco.

majestic (mȧ·jĕs'tǐk) *agg.* maestoso.

majesty (măj'ĕs·tǐ) *n.* maestà.

major (mā'jẽr) *n.* (mil.) maggiore (*legge*) maggiorenne; corso unive sitario di specializzazione. *agg.* mag giore, grave, più grande, più im portante. **—ity** (mȧ·jŏr'ǐ·tǐ) *n.* mag gioranza; età maggiore; (*mil.*) gra do di maggiore.

make (māk) *n.* foggia, forma; for mazione; fabbricazione; marca (*elett.*) contatto. *vt., vi.* (*pass., p* made) fare, creare, produrre, fab bricare, acquistare, raggiungere riuscire; dirigersi: **to — fast**, ormeg giare; **to — haste**, affrettarsi: **to — headway**, progredire; **to — light o** prendere alla leggera; **to — muc** of, dare gran peso a; **to — nothin** of it, non capirci nulla; **to — out** distinguere, capire, riuscire; **to — over**, cedere, trasferire; rifare, r modernare; **to — shift**, arrangiars **to — up**, completare; fare la pace accomodare; inventare; impag nare; **to — up for**, supplire a; com pensare di *o* per; rifarsi di; **to — i up**, riconciliarsi; **to — up one's mind** decidersi; **to — away with**, soppri mere, alienare; **to — for**, dirigers verso, contribuire a.

make-believe *n.* finzione.

maker (māk'ẽr) *n.* fabbricante, arte fice: **The Maker**, il Creatore.

makeshift (māk'shǐft') *n.* espediente *agg.* di fortuna, improvvisato.

make-up *n.* formazione, costituzione, natura; truccatura; (*tip.*) impagi nazione.

making *n.* formazione, creazione, fab bricazione; successo.

maladroit (măl'ȧ·droit') *agg.* goffo.

malady (măl'ȧ·dǐ) *n.* malattia.

malaria (mȧ·lâr'ǐ·ȧ) *n.* (med.) malaria.

male (măl) *n.* maschio. *agg.* maschio, maschile, mascolino.

malice (măl'ĭs) *n.* malizia, malevolenza, malignità; dolo: **to bear —**, avere del malanimo verso.

malicious (mȧ·lĭsh'ŭs) *agg.* malevolo, maligno.

malign (mȧ·līn') *n.* maligno, insidioso. *vt.* diffamare, malignare su.

malignant (mȧ·lĭg'nȧnt) *agg.* maligno, nocivo, pernicioso.

mallet (măl'ĕt) *n.* martello di legno.

mallow (măl'ō) *n.* (*bot.*) malva.

malmsey (măm'zĭ) *n.* malvasia.

malt (môlt) *n.* malto.

maltreat (măl·trēt') *vt.* maltrattare.

mamma, mama (mä'mȧ; mȧ·mä') (1) *n.* madre, mamma.

mamma (mä'mȧ) (2) (*anat.*) mammella.

mammal (măm'ăl) *n.* mammifero.

mammoth (măm'ŭth) *n.* mammut. *agg.* enorme.

man (măn) *n.* (*pl.* men) uomo, maschio; marito; servo, operaio, dipendente; soldato, (*scacchi*) pezzo, pedina: **— and wife**, marito e moglie; **enlisted —**, soldato, gregario. *vt.* fornire di uomini o di equipaggio, armare; fortificare.

manage (măn'ĭj) *vt.* dirigere, governare, amministrare, manipolare. *vi.* fare in modo (*di*), riuscire (*a*); cavarsela, destreggiarsi. **—able** *agg.* maneggevole, docile. **—ment** *n.* condotta, direzione, amministrazione.

manager (măn'ĭj·ẽr) *n.* amministratore, direttore.

mandate (măn'dāt) *n.* mandato.

mane (măn) *n.* criniera.

maneuver (mȧ·nōō'vẽr) *n.* manovra. *vt., vi.* manovrare.

manful (măn'fŏŏl) *agg.* virile, ardito, risoluto; da uomo.

mange (mānj) *n.* (*vet.*) rogna.

manger (măn'jẽr) *n.* mangiatoia.

mangle (măng'g'l) *n.* mangano, torchio. *vt.* maciullare, lacerare; manganare, torchiare; stirare.

mangy (măn'jĭ) *agg.* rognoso, spregevole.

manhole (măn'hōl) *n.* botola.

manhood (măn'hŏŏd) *n.* virilità, maturità; genere umano.

mania (mā'nĭ·ȧ) *n.* mania, pazzia.

maniac (mā'nĭ·ăk) *n., agg.* pazzo furioso.

manifest (măn'ĭ·fĕst) *n.* manifesto di carico. *agg.* manifesto, evidente. *vt.* manifestare. **—ation** *n.* manifestazione, dimostrazione.

manifesto (măn'ĭ·fĕs'tō) *n.* manifesto, proclama.

manifold (măn'ĭ·fōld) *agg.* molteplice, multiforme.

manikin (măn'ĭ·kĭn) *n.* nano, pigmeo; manichino, modello.

manila (mȧ·nĭl'ȧ) *n.* canapa di Manilla.

manipulate (mȧ·nĭp'ū·lāt) *vt.* manipolare, maneggiare, alterare.

manipulation (mȧ·nĭp'ū·lā'shŭn) *n.* manipolazione.

mankind (măn·kīnd') *n.* umanità (*genere umano*).

manliness (măn'lĭ·nĕs) *n.* virilità, coraggio.

manly (măn'lĭ) *agg.* virile, risoluto. *avv.* virilmente, risolutamente.

manner (măn'ẽr) *n.* modo, maniera, metodo; abitudine, stile; specie: **after the — of**, alla maniera di.

manners *n.pl.* modi, convenevoli, educazione: **to have no —**, essere maleducato.

mannish (măn'ĭsh) *agg.* mascolino.

manoeuvre (mȧ·nōō'vẽr) (*Ingl.*) *vedi* maneuver.

man-of-war *n.* nave da guerra.

manor (măn'ẽr) *n.* maniero, castello, feudo.

mansion (măn'shŭn) *n.* palazzo, castello; dimora.

manslaughter (măn'slô'tẽr) *n.* omicidio colposo *opp.* non premeditato.

mantel (măn't'l) *n.* mensola del camino.

mantis (măn'tĭs) *n.* mantide: **praying —**, mantide religiosa.

mantle (măn't'l) *n.* mantello, copertura; reticella per gas.

manual (măn'ū·ăl) *n., agg.* manuale.

manufactory (măn'ū·făk'tō·rĭ) *n.* fabbrica.

manufacture (măn'ū·făk'tŭr) *n.* manifattura, industria, fabbricazione. *vt.* fabbricare, produrre, confezionare.

manufacturer *n.* fabbricante.

manufacturing *n.* fabbricazione. *agg.* industriale.

manumission (măn'ū·mĭsh'ŭn) *n.* emancipazione (*di uno schiavo*).

manumit *vt.* emancipare.

manure (mȧ·nūr') *n.* concime, letame. *vt.* concimare.

manuscript (măn'ū·skrĭpt) *n., agg.* manoscritto.

many (mĕn'ĭ) *n.* molti, moltitudine. *agg.pl.* molti, numerosi, parecchi, diversi: **as — again**, due volte tanto; **how —?** quanti? **as — as**, tanti quanti; **too —**, troppi; **one too —**, uno di troppo; **a great —**, moltissimi; **— a time**, molte volte.

map (măp) *n.* mappa, carta geografica. *vt.* tracciare, delineare, progettare; pianificare.

maple (mā'p'l) *n.* acero.

mar (mär) *vt.* guastare, sfigurare, mutilare.

marauder (má·rôd'ĕr) *n.* predone, rapinatore.

marble (mär'b'l) *n.* marmo, statua; biglia, pallina. *agg.* marmoreo.

March (märch) (1) *n.* marzo.

march (märch) (2) *n.* marcia, corso, progresso. *vt.* far marciare. *vi.* marciare: to — in, entrare marciando.

marchioness (mär'shŭn·ĕs) *n.* marchesa.

mare (mâr) *n.* cavalla, giumenta: —'s nest, parto della fantasia, mistificazione.

margin (mär'jĭn) *n.* margine; bordo. —al *agg.* marginale; periferico.

marigold (mär'ĭ·gōld) *n.* fiorrancio, calendula.

marine (má·rēn') *n.* marina; fante di marina: merchant —, marina mercantile. *agg.* marino, marittimo.

mariner (mär'ĭ·nĕr) *n.* marinaio.

maritime (mär'ĭ·tĭm) *agg.* marittimo.

mark (märk) *n.* marca, segno, impronta; voto (*scolastico*); bersaglio; marco: to make one's —, distinguersi; to hit the —, cogliere nel segno; question —, punto interrogativo; trade —, marchio di fabbrica. *vt.* marcare, segnare, notare: to — down, annotare; — my words! senti bene quel che ti dico! —er *n.* contrassegno; segnatore, segnapunti.

market (mär'kĕt) *n.* mercato: — place, mercato; meat —, macelleria; stock —, borsa. *vt.*, *vi.* vendere e acquistare, commerciare: to go marketing, andare a far la spesa.

marking (märk'ĭng) *n.* marcatura, marchio.

marksman (märks'măn) *n.* tiratore esperto.

marmalade (mär'má·lād) *n.* composta (*spec. di arance*).

maroon (má·rōōn') (1) *agg.*, *n.* marrone (*colore*).

maroon (má·rōōn') (2) *vt.* abbandonare su un'isola deserta; (*fig.*) isolare.

marquee (mär·kē') *n.* pensilina, tettoia.

marquis (mär'kwĭs), marquess (-kwĕs) *n.* marchese.

marquise (mär·kēz') *n.* marchesa.

marriage (mär'ĭj) *n.* matrimonio.

married (mär'ĭd) *agg.* sposato, coniugale: — couple, coniugi, due sposi; to get —, sposarsi.

marrow (mär'ō) *n.* midollo, parte essenziale.

marry (mär'ĭ) *vt.*, *vi.* sposare.

marsh (märsh) *n.* palude, stagn — gas metano.

marshmallow (märsh'măl'ō) *n.* (bo altea.

marshal (mär'shăl) *n.* marescial prefetto, cerimoniere; sceriffo, ca celliere. *vt.* schierare, dirigere, sco tare.

marshy (mär'shĭ) *agg.* paludoso, p lustre.

marten (mär'tĕn) *n.* (*zool.*) martora.

martial (mär'shăl) *agg.* marziale.

martinet (mär'tĭ·nĕt') *n.* rigoris castigamatti.

martyr (mär'tĕr) *n.* martire. *vt.* ma tirizzare. —dom *n.* martirio.

marvel (mär'vĕl) *n.* meraviglia. stupirsi. —ous *agg.* meraviglios

mascot (mäs'kŏt) *n.* portafortuna.

masculine (mäs'kŭ·lĭn) *agg.* maschi virile.

mash (mäsh) *vt.* mescolare, ridurre polpa, impastare: mashed potato purea di patate.

mask (mȧsk) *n.* maschera. *vt.*, mascherare, mascherarsi: —ed ba ballo in maschera.

mason (mā's'n) *n.* muratore: Fre Mason, massone. —ry *n.* muratur arte muraria: Free Masonry, ma soneria.

masquerade (mäs'kĕr·ād') *n.* masch rata. *vi.* camuffarsi.

mass (mäs) (1) *n.* massa, ammass — meeting, riunione, adunata; production, produzione in mass *vt.* ammassare. *vi.* ammassarsi.

Mass (mäs) (2) *n.* santa messa.

massacre (mäs'á·kĕr) *n.* massacro. massacrare.

massage (má·säzh') *n.* massaggio. massaggiare.

massive (mäs'ĭv) *agg.* massiccio; ma sivo; pesante; consistente; vol minoso.

mast (mȧst) *n.* (*naut.*) albero.

master (mȧs'tĕr) *n.* maestro, padron capo; signorino; (*naut.*) capitan Master of Arts, laureato in letter band— *n.* direttore d'orchestra; — of ceremonies, gran cerimonier (*radio*) presentatore (*di uno spett colo*). *vt.* dominare, soggiogare, - padronirsi di, imparare. —ful *ag* autoritario. —ly *agg.* magistra *avv.* magistralmente. —piece capolavoro. —y *n.* maestria; pred minio, vittoria.

mastiff (mȧs'tif) *n.* cane mastino.

mat (măt) (1) *n.* treccia, stuoia, ste no; sacco; cornice di cartone, pass partout; (*tip.*) matrice. *vt.* intre ciare, tessere (*opp.* coprire di) stuoi *vi.* feltrarsi.

mat (măt) (2) *agg.* opaco, smerigliato.

match (măch) (1) *n.* fiammifero, miccia. —book *n.* bustina di fiammiferi.

match (măch) (2) *n.* eguale, compagno; oggetto gemello; coppia bene assortita; matrimonio; gara incontro, competizione; avversario di pari forza: to have no —, non aver l'uguale; to be a good —, accordarsi, intonarsi; essere un buon partito; to be a — for, tener testa a. *vt., vi.* uguagliare, accoppiare, far sposare; appaiarsi, intonarsi, corrispondere a. —less *agg.* incomparabile, senza pari.

mate (măt) *n.* compagno, amico; coniuge; (*naut.*) secondo; (*scacchi*) scaccomatto. *vt., vi.* unire, accoppiare, dare scaccomatto, accoppiarsi.

material (mȧ-tēr'ĭ-ăl) *n.* materiale, materia, stoffa; raw —, materia prima. *agg.* materiale, essenziale.

maternal (mȧ-tûr'năl) *agg.* materno.

maternity (mȧ-tûr'nĭ-tĭ) *n.* maternità.

mathematical (măth'ê-măt'ĭ-kăl) *agg.* matematico.

mathematician (măth'ê-mȧ-tĭsh'ăn) *n.* matematico.

mathematics (măth'ê-măt'ĭks) *n.* matematica.

matriculate (mȧ-trĭk'û-lāt) *vt.* matricolare. *vi.* iscriversi.

matriculation (mȧ-trĭk'û-lā'shăn) *n.* immatricolazione, iscrizione.

matrimony(măt'rĭ-mō'nĭ) *n.*sposalizio.

matrix (mā'trĭks) *n.* (*pl.* matrices [măt'rĭ-sēz]) matrice.

matron (mā'trŭn) *n.* matrona; capoinfermiera; sorvegliante, vigilatrice (*in collegi, carceri femminili, ecc.*).

matter (măt'ẽr) *n.* materia, sostanza, materiale, questione; pus: printed —, stampe; as a — of fact, effettivamente; as a — of course, come se niente fosse; no —, non importa; what is the — with you? che cosa vi prende?; what is the —? che cosa c'è? *vi.* importare, avere importanza.

matter-of-course *agg.* naturale.

matter-of-fact *agg.* pratico, positivo; banale; prosaico.

matting (măt'ĭng) *n.* stuoia.

mattress (măt'rĕs) *n.* materasso.

mature (mȧ-tūr') *agg.* maturo. *vt., vi.* maturare; scadere.

maturity (mȧ-tū'rĭ-tĭ) *n.* maturità; scadenza; maturazione.

maudlin (môd'lĭn) *agg.* sdolcinato, emotivo, piagnucoloso.

maul (môl) *n.* mazza, mazzuola. *vt.* martellare, malmenare.

mawkish (môk'ĭsh) *agg.* nauseante, sdolcinato.

maxim (măk'sĭm) *n.* massima, sentenza, norma, principio.

maximum (măk'sĭ-mŭm) *n., agg.* massimo.

may(mā)(1)*v.ausiliario.difettivo (pass.* might) potere, avere il permesso *o* la possibilità *o* la facoltà di: it — be true, può esser vero; be that as it —, comunque sia; — I go? posso andare? it — be that, può darsi che: he — be late, può darsi che arrivi in ritardo; I — go there, forse ci andrò.

May (mā) (2) *n.* maggio: — Day, primo maggio.

maybe (mā'bĕ) *avv.* forse.

mayhem (mā'hĕm) *n.* mutilazione, menomazione.

mayonnaise (mā'ŏ-nāz') *n.* maionese.

mayor (mā'ẽr) *n.* sindaco.

maze (māz) *n.* labirinto; confusione, disorientamento: to be in a —, essere confuso.

me (mĕ) *pron.pers.* me, mi, io: give it to —, datelo a me; look at —, guardatemi; it is —, sono io.

meadow (mĕd'ō) *n.* prato.

meager (mē'gẽr) *n.* magro, misero, scarso, povero.

meal (mēl) (1) *n.* pasto: —time *n.* l'ora del pasto.

meal (mēl) (2) *n.* farina.

mean (mēn) (1) *n.* punto intermedio, media; mezzo, strumento. *agg.* medio, intermedio: by all means, senza fallo, certamente; by no means, niente affatto; by means of, per mezzo di.

mean (mēn) (2) *agg.* basso, meschino, malvagio, losco.

mean (mēn) (3) *vt., vi.* (*pass., pp.* meant) significare, intendere, avere intenzione, destinare, predisporre: do you — it? dite sul serio? what does this —? che cosa significa ciò? to — well, avere buone intenzioni.

means *n.pl.* mezzi, rendite.

meaning (mēn'ĭng) *n.* significato; intenzione; importanza, valore. *agg.* significativo: well-— *agg.* ben intenzionato. —less *agg.* senza senso, insignificante.

meanly (mēn'lĭ) *avv.* meschinamente, ignobilmente.

meanness (mēn'nĕs) *n.* bassezza, meschinità, malvagità.

meant (mĕnt) *pass., pp. di* to mean.

meantime (mēn'tīm') meanwhile (mēn'hwīl') *avv.* nel frattempo, frattanto, intanto.

measles (mē'z'lz) *n.* (*med.*) rosolia, morbillo; (*vet.*) teniasi.

measly (mēz′lĭ) *agg.* insignificante, magro, spregevole.

measurable (mĕzh′ĕr.á·b'l) *agg.* misurabile, limitato.

measure (mĕzh′ĕr) *n.* misura; dimensione; moderazione; misurazione; tempo; ritmo, metro: **beyond —,** oltre misura. *vt.*, *vi.* misurare, distribuire, adattare, delimitare.

measured *agg.* misurato, moderato, ritmico.

measurement *n.* misurazione, misura, dimensione.

meat (mēt) *n.* carne; polpa; alimento: **— ball,** polpetta; **— market,** macelleria. **—y** *agg.* carnoso; polposo; sostanzioso.

mechanic (mē·kăn′ĭk) *n.*, *agg.* meccanico.

mechanical (mē·kăn′ĭ·kăl) *agg.* meccanico; macchinale.

mechanician (mĕk′á·nĭsh′ăn) *n.* meccanico.

mechanics (mē·kăn′ĭks) *n.* meccanica.

mechanism (mĕk′á·nĭz′m) *n.* meccanismo.

mechanize (mĕk′á·nĭz) *vt.* motorizzare; meccanizzare.

medal (mĕd′'l) *n.* medaglia.

meddle (mĕd′'l) *vi.* impicciarsi, immischiarsi.

meddler (mĕd′lĕr) *n.* intrigante.

meddlesome (mĕd′'l·sŭm) *agg.* inframmettente.

median (mē′dĭ·ăn) *n.* punto o linea o numero mediano. *agg.* mediano, di mezzo.

mediate (mē′dĭ·āt) *vt.* arbitrare, conciliare. *vi.* interporsi.

mediation (mē′dĭ·ā′shŭn) *n.* mediazione.

mediator (mē′dĭ·ā′tĕr) *n.* mediatore.

medical (mĕd′ĭ·kăl) *agg.* medico; medicinale: **— jurisprudence,** medicina legale.

medicinal (mē·dĭs′ĭ·năl) *agg.* medicinale.

medicine (mĕd′ĭ·sĭn) *n.* medicina; medicinale: **to take one's —,** rassegnarsi; **— man,** stregone.

medieval (mē′dĭ·ē′văl) *agg.* medievale.

mediocrity (mē′dĭ·ŏk′rĭ·tĭ) *n.* mediocrità.

meditate (mĕd′ĭ·tāt) *vt.* progettare. *vi.* meditare.

meditation (mĕd′ĭ·tā′shŭn) *n.* meditazione.

medium (mē′dĭ·ŭm) *n.* mezzo, strumento, tramite; elemento naturale; medium.

medlar (mĕd′lĕr) *n.* nespola, nespolo.

medley (mĕd′lĭ) *n.* mescolanza, miscuglio. *agg.* misto.

meek (mēk) *agg.* mite, mansueto. **—ness** *n.* mansuetudine, mitezza.

meerschaum (mēr′shŭm) *n.* schiuma di mare: **— pipe,** pipa di schiuma.

meet (mēt) *n.* riunione sportiva. *agg.* conveniente, adatto. *vt.*, *vi.* (*pass. pp.* met) incontrare, andare incontro a; far la conoscenza di; affrontare; rispondere a; soddisfare (*esigenze*); incontrarsi, riunirsi, far conoscenza: **to — one's engagements,** far fronte ai propri impegni.

meeting (mēt′ĭng) *n.* incontro, riunione: **to call a —,** indire una riunione.

megaphone (mĕg′á·fōn) *n.* megafono.

melancholic (mĕl′ăn·kŏl′ĭk) *agg.* malinconico.

melancholy (mĕl′ăn·kŏl′ĭ) *n.* malinconia. *agg.* triste.

mellow (mĕl′ō) *agg.* maturo, polposo, morbido, bonario; friabile (*di terreno*); brillo. *vt.* far maturare, ammorbidire, ammansire. *vi.* maturare, addolcirsi, ammorbidirsi.

melodious (mē·lō′dĭ·ŭs) *agg.* melodioso.

melodrama (mĕl′ō·drä′má) *n.* melodramma.

melody (mĕl′ō·dĭ) *n.* melodia.

melon (mĕl′ŭn) *n.* melone: **water —,** anguria.

melt (mĕlt) *vt.* (*pp.* melted, molten) fondere, liquefare; intenerire. *vi.* fondersi, liquefarsi; commuoversi; svanire.

member (mĕm′bĕr) *n.* membro; elemento; arto. **—ship** *n.* appartenenza, associazione; qualità o qualifica di socio o di membro; numero dei soci.

membrane (mĕm′brān) *n.* membrana.

memento (mē·mĕn′tō) *n.* memento, ricordo.

memoir (mĕm′wär) *n.* memoria, relazione, memoriale; biografia.

memorable (mĕm′ō·rá·b'l) *agg.* memorabile.

memorandum (mĕm′ō·răn′dŭm) *n.* memorandum; scrittura privata, distinta: **— book,** taccuino d'appunti.

memorial (mē·mō′rĭ·ăl) *n.* monumento; memoriale. *agg.* commemorativo: **Memorial Day,** giorno delle rimembranze.

memorize (mĕm′ō·rīz) *vt.* imparare a memoria.

memory (mĕm′ō·rĭ) *n.* memoria, ricordo.

men (mĕn) *pl. di* man.

menace (mĕn′ĭs) *n.* minaccia. *vt.* minacciare.

menacing *agg.* minaccioso.

mend (mĕnd) *n.* riparazione, miglioramento: on the —, in via di miglioramento. *vt.* riparare, rammendare, correggere, migliorare. *vi.* migliorare, emendarsi: past —ing, senza rimedio.

mending *n.* riparazione.

menial (mē'nĭ·ăl) *n.* domestico. *agg.* domestico, servile.

menstruation (mĕn'strŏo·ā'shŭn) *n.* mestruazione.

mental (mĕn'tăl) *agg.* mentale. —ity (·ăl'·) *n.* mentalità.

mention (mĕn'shŭn) *n.* menzione, allusione. *vt.* menzionare, citare: don't — it, non c'è di che (*in risposta a "grazie"*).

mephitic (mĕ·fĭt'ĭk) *agg.* mefitico.

mercenary (mûr'sĕ·nĕr'ĭ) *n.*, *agg.* mercenario.

merchandise (mûr'chăn·dīz) *n.* mercanzia: piece of —, articolo commerciale. *vt.* propagandare (*una merce*).

merchant (mûr'chănt) *n.* mercante; (nave mercantile.) *agg.* commerciale, mercantile. —man *n.* nave mercantile.

merciful (mûr'sĭ·fŏol) *agg.* pietoso, misericordioso, provvidenziale.

merciless (mûr'sĭ·lĕs) *agg.* implacabile, spietato.

mercury (mûr'kū·rĭ) *n.* mercurio.

mercy (mûr'sĭ) *n.* misericordia, pietà, clemenza: to be at the — of, essere alla mercé di; — killing, eutanasia.

mere (mēr) *agg.* mero, semplice, autentico: a — formality, una pura formalità; a — trifle, un nonnulla. —ly *avv.* puramente, semplicemente, soltanto.

merge (mûrj) *vt.* incorporare, fondere, assorbire, amalgamare. *vi.* amalgamarsi, essere assorbito, sparire.

merger (mûr'jĕr) *n.* (*comm.*) fusione.

meridian (mĕ·rĭd'ĭ·ăn) *n.*, *agg.* meridiano.

merit (mĕr'ĭt) *n.* merito, valore. *vt.* meritare. —orious (·tō'rĭ·ŭs) *agg.* meritorio, meritevole.

mermaid (mûr'mād') *n.* sirena.

merman (mûr'măn') *n.* tritone.

merrily (mĕr'ĭ·lĭ) *avv.* allegramente.

merry (mĕr'ĭ) *agg.* allegro, lieto, burlesco: Merry Christmas, buon Natale; to make —, divertirsi, fare baldoria. —go-round *n.* giostra. —making *n.* divertimento, festa. *agg.* allegro, festivo, festoso.

mesh (mĕsh) *n.* maglia, rete. *vt.* prendere nella rete; (*mecc.*) ingranare.

mess (mĕs) *n.* cibo, pasto; pasticcio, disordine; mensa: to be in a fine —,

essere in un bell'imbroglio; to make a — of, rovinare, guastare, insudiciare, mettere in disordine. *vt.* dar da mangiare a; impasticciare, mettere in disordine. *vi.* far mensa comune; far confusione.

message (mĕs'ĭj) *n.* messaggio.

messenger (mĕs'ĕn·jĕr) *n.* messaggero.

Messrs. (mĕs''rz) *n.pl.* signori (*vale:* "Spett. Ditta").

messy (mĕs'ĭ) *agg.* sudicio, disordinato.

met (mĕt) *pass. e pp. di* to meet.

metal (mĕt'l) *n.* metallo; breccia, pietrisco (*per fondo stradale*); (*ferr.*) rotaia. *vt.* metallizzare; selciare. —lic (·ăl'ĭk) *agg.* metallico. —lurgic (·ûrj'ĭk) *agg.* metallurgico. —lurgist (mĕt'-) *n.* metallurgico (*lavoratore*). —lurgy *n.* metallurgia.

metamorphosis (mĕt'à·môr'fŏ·sĭs) *n.* metamorfosi.

metaphor (mĕt'à·fĕr) *n.* metafora.

metaphysics (mĕt'à·fĭz'ĭks) *n.* metafisica.

mete (mēt) *vt.* misurare: to — out, distribuire.

meteor (mē'tĕ·ĕr) *n.* meteora. —ological (·ŏj'-) *agg.* meteorologico. —ologist (·ŏl'-) *n.* meteorologo. —ology *n.* meteorologia.

meter (mē'tĕr) *n.* metro; misuratore, contatore, tassametro.

method (mĕth'ŭd) *n.* metodo. —ical (·ŏd'ĭk·ăl) *agg.* metodico.

Methuselah (mĕ·thū'zĕ·là) *n.* Matusalemme.

metre *vedi* meter.

metrical (mĕt'rĭ·kăl) *agg.* metrico.

metropolis (mĕ·trŏp'ŏ·lĭs) *n.* metropoli.

metropolitan (mĕt'rŏ·pŏl'ĭ·tăn) *n.* metropolita. *agg.* metropolitano.

mettle (mĕt''l) *n.* coraggio, pertinacia: to put someone on his —, metter qualcuno di puntiglio.

mew (mū) *n.* miagolio. *vi.* miagolare.

mews (mūz) *n.pl.* scuderie.

mice (mīs) *pl. di* mouse.

microbe (mī'krŏb) *n.* microbo.

microgroove (mī'krŏ·grŏov') *n.*, *agg.* microsolco.

microphone (mī'krŏ·fŏn) *n.* microfono.

microscope (mī'krŏ·skŏp) *n.* microscopio.

microscopic (mī'krŏ·skŏp'ĭk) *agg.* microscopico.

mid (mĭd) *n.* mezzo, metà, centro. *agg.* medio, centrale, intermedio. *prep.* tra, in mezzo a: in —air, a mezz'aria.

midday (mĭd'dā') *n.* mezzodì. *agg.* meridiano, di mezzogiorno.

middle (mĭd''l) *n.* centro, mezzo, punto di mezzo. *agg.* medio, centrale, intermedio, mediano, mediocre: — age, mezza età; the Middle Ages, il Medioevo; — size, misura o statura media; in the — of, nel mezzo di, alla metà di. —aged agg. di mezza età. —man n. intermediario. —sized agg. di medie dimensioni.

middling (mĭd'lĭng) agg. medio, mediocre. avv. discretamente.

middy (mĭd'ĭ) n. (fam.) allievo guardiamarina: — blouse, camiciotto da marinaio.

midge (mĭj) n. moscerino.

midget (mĭj'ĕt) n. nano, pigmeo; piccola automobile da corsa.

midnight (mĭd'nīt') n. mezzanotte. agg. di mezzanotte.

midriff (mĭd'rĭf) n. (anat.) diaframma; (sartoria femminile) bustino.

midshipman (mĭd'shĭp'măn) n. allievo guardiamarina.

midst (mĭdst) n. mezzo, centro: in the — of, nel mezzo di, tra; in our —, tra noi. prep. fra.

midsummer (mĭd'sŭm'ĕr) n. solstizio d'estate.

midtown (mĭd'toun') n. centro della città.

midway (mĭd'wā') agg. situato a metà strada, intermedio. avv. a metà strada.

midwife (mĭd'wīf') n. levatrice.

mien (mēn) n. aspetto, cera.

might (mīt) (1) pass. di may.

might (mīt) (2) n. forza, potenza, potere: with — and main, con tutte le forze.

mighty (mīt'ĭ) agg. forte, potente. avv. molto.

migrate (mī'grāt) vi. migrare.

migration (mī-grā'shŭn) n. migrazione, emigrazione.

mike (mīk) n. (gergo) microfono.

mild (mīld) agg. mite, dolce, blando, moderato. —er agg. più dolce, più blando.

mildew (mĭl'dū) n. ruggine delle piante, muffa.

mildly (mīld'lĭ) avv. dolcemente, blandamente, moderatamente.

mildness (mīld'nĕs) n. dolcezza, mitezza, moderazione.

mile (mīl) n. miglio (misura = m. 1609,31): nautical —, miglio marino (=m. 1853). —age n. lunghezza o distanza in miglia; autonomia; (ferr.) prezzo per miglio. —stone n. pietra miliare.

military (mĭl'ĭ·tĕr'ĭ) n., agg. militare: the —, i militari, l'esercito.

militate (mĭl'ĭ·tāt) vi. (against o in favor of) militare (contro o a favore di), influire.

milk (mĭlk) n. latte. vt. mungere.

milkmaid (mĭlk'mād') n. lattaia.

milkman (mĭlk'măn) n. lattaio.

milky (mĭl'kĭ) agg. latteo, lattiginoso: the Milky Way, la Via Lattea.

mill (mĭl) (1) n. 1/1000 di dollaro.

mill (mĭl) (2) n. mulino; fabbrica: spinning —, filanda; sugar —, zuccherificio; textile —, fabbrica di tessuti. vt. macinare, polverizzare; sbattere; granire. —board n. cartone.

miller (mĭl'ĕr) n. mugnaio.

millet (mĭl'ĕt) n. (bot.) miglio.

milliner (mĭl'ĭ·nĕr) n. modista.

millinery (mĭl'ĭ·nĕr'ĭ) n. modisteria.

million (mĭl'yŭn) n. milione.

millionaire (mĭl'yŭn·âr') n. milionario.

millionth (mĭl'yănth) n., agg. milionesimo.

millstone (mĭl'stōn') n. macina da mulino.

mime (mīm) n. mimo.

mimeograph (mĭm'ē·ō·gráf') n. duplicatore, ciclostile. vt. ciclostilare.

mimic (mĭm'ĭk) agg. mimico, imitativo. n. mimo; parodista. vt. imitare, parodiare. —ry n. imitazione, parodia.

mince (mĭns) vt. tritare, sminuzzare; attenuare. vi. muoversi o parlare con affettazione: not to — words, parlare in tutta franchezza. —meat n. ripieno, ammorsellato.

mind (mīnd) n. mente, pensiero; intenzione; desiderio; opinione; intelligenza: to have a — to, avere intenzione di; to be out of one's —, essere pazzo; to make up one's —, decidersi; to change one's —, cambiar parere; to speak one's —, dire quel che si pensa; to give a piece of one's —, cantarle chiare; to my —, a mio modo di vedere. vt., vi. badare a, osservare, ascoltare, obbedire; preoccuparsi di; dispiacersi per; guardarsi da: I do not —, non mi preoccupo di, non m'importa di, non mi dà fastidio; — your own business, badate ai fatti vostri; never —, prego, non c'è di che; non disturbatevi; non fateci caso, lasciate perdere. —ful agg. circospetto, attento.

mine (mīn) (1) pron.poss. il mio, la mia, i miei, le mie: a friend of —, uno dei miei amici.

mine (mīn) (2) n. miniera, mina. vt. minare, scavare, estrarre (minerali). —layer n. posamine. —sweeper n. dragamine.

miner (mīn'ĕr) n. minatore.

mineral (mĭn'ĕr·ăl) n., agg. minerale.

mingle (mĭng'g'l) *vt.* mischiare, confondere. *vi.* mischiarsi.

miniature (mĭn'ĭ-á-tŭr) *n.* miniatura. *agg.* in miniatura, in sedicesimo.

minimize (mĭn'ĭ-mĭz) *vt.* minimizzare; cvilire, svalutare, sminuire.

minimum (mĭn'ĭ-mŭm) *n.* minimo.

mining (mĭn'ĭng) *n.* lavoro minerario, *agg.* minerario.

minister (mĭn'ĭs-tĕr) *n.* ministro; sacerdote. *vt.* somministrare, fornire. *vi.* dar aiuto, sopperire.

ministration (mĭn'ĭs-trā'shŭn) *n.* somministrazione; soccorso; cura.

ministry (mĭn'ĭs-trĭ) *n.* aiuto, soccorso; ministero; clero.

miniver (mĭn'ĭ-vĕr) *n.* (zool.) vaio.

mink (mĭngk) *n.* (zool.) visone.

minnow (mĭn'ō) *n.* avannotto.

minor (mī'nĕr) *n.* minorenne. *agg.* minore. —ity (mĭ-nôr'ĭ-tĭ; mĭ-) *n.* minoranza, minorità.

minstrel (mĭn'strĕl) *n.* menestrello.

mint (mĭnt) (1) *n.* menta.

mint (mĭnt) (2) *n.* zecca, tesoro: to have a — of money, avere un mucchio di danari. *vt.* coniare, fabbricare, inventare.

minus (mī'nŭs) *n.* meno (segno di sottrazione); prep. meno, diminuito di, privo di.

minute (mĭ-nūt') (1) *agg.* minuto, piccolo, minuzioso.

minute (mĭn'ĭt) (2) *n.* minuto (60a parte dell'ora), istante; abbozzo, minuta, verbale: — hand, lancetta dei minuti (dell'orologio).

minx (mĭngks) *n.* smorfiosa, civetta.

miracle (mĭr'á-k'l) *n.* miracolo.

miraculous (mĭ-răk'ū-lŭs) *agg.* miracoloso.

mirage (mĭ-räzh') *n.* miraggio.

mire (mĭr) *n.* fango, pantano. *vt.* infangare; porre in difficoltà. *vi.* infangarsi, impantanarsi.

mirror (mĭr'ĕr) *n.* specchio. *vt.* rispecchiare, riflettere.

mirth (mûrth) *n.* allegria, ilarità. —ful *agg.* ilare.

miry (mĭr'ĭ) *agg.* fangoso, sudicio.

misadventure (mĭs'ăd-vĕn'tŭr) *n.* disavventura.

misbehave (mĭs'bē-hāv') *vi.* comportarsi male.

misbehavior (mĭs'bē-hāv'yĕr) *n.* cattiva condotta.

misbelief (mĭs'bē-lēf') *n.* falsa credenza, incredulità.

misbelieve (mĭs'bē-lēv') *vt.* dubitare di, non credere a. *vi.* avere una falsa credenza.

miscalculate (mĭs·kăl'kū-lāt) *vt., vi.* calcolare male, sbagliare.

miscarriage (mĭs·kăr'ĭj) *n.* errore, disguido; aborto: — of justice, errore giudiziario.

miscarry (mĭs·kăr'ĭ) *vi.* fallire, smarrirsi; abortire.

miscellaneous (mĭs'ĕ-lā'nē-ŭs) *agg.* miscellaneo.

miscellany (mĭs'ĕ-lā'nĭ) *n.* miscellanea, zibaldone.

mischance (mĭs-chăns') *n.* sfortuna, disgrazia.

mischief (mĭs'chĭf) *n.* male, danno, torto, cattiveria: out of —, per cattiveria; — maker, seminatore di discordia, malvagio.

mischievous (mĭs'chĭ-vŭs) *agg.* malizioso; maligno, nocivo.

misconduct (mĭs-kŏn'dŭkt) *n.* cattiva condotta, scorrettezza; cattiva gestione. *vt.* (-dŭkt') ,dirigere o gestire male: to — oneself, comportarsi male.

misconstruction (mĭs'kŏn-strŭk'shŭn) *n.* falsa o errata interpretazione.

miscreant (mĭs'krē-ănt) *n., agg.* scellerato.

misdeed (mĭs-dēd') *n.* misfatto.

misdemeanor (mĭs'dē-mēn'ĕr) *n.* colpa, cattiva condotta, reato minore.

misdirect (mĭs'dĭ-rĕkt') *vt.* dirigere male, informare male.

miser (mī'zĕr) *n.* avaro.

miserable (mĭz'ĕr-á-b'l) *agg.* infelice; deplorevole, miserabile.

miserly (mĭz'ĕr-lĭ) *agg.* sordido, avaro.

misery (mĭz'ĕr-ĭ) *n.* infelicità, miseria, tormento.

misfire (mĭs'fīr') *vi.* far cilecca (di motore o arma).

misfortune (mĭs-fôr'tŭn) *n.* sfortuna, infortunio, disastro.

misgiving (mĭs-gĭv'ĭng) *n.* perplessità, diffidenza, dubbio, sospetto.

mishap (mĭs-hăp') *n.* incidente, disavventura.

misinterpret (mĭs'ĭn-tûr'prĕt) *vt.* fraintendere; interpretare erratamente.

misjudge (mĭs-jŭj') *vt., vi.* giudicare ingiustamente o erratamente.

mislay (mĭs-lā') *vt.* (pass., pp. mislaid) smarrire, metter fuori posto.

mislead (mĭs-lēd') *vt.* (pass., pp. misled) indurre in errore, sviare, forviare, corrompere; ingannare.

misleading *agg.* ingannevole, fallace.

mismanagement *n.* cattiva amministrazione.

mismatch *vt.* assortire male.

misplace (mĭs-plās') *vt.* collocar male, metter fuori posto.

misplaced *agg.* fuori di posto, mal riposto: — pride, orgoglio malinteso.

misprint (mĭs·prĭnt) *n.* refuso, errore di stampa.

mispronounce (mĭs'prō·nouns') *vt.* pronunziare scorrettamente.

misreckon (mĭs·rĕk'ŭn) *vt., vi.* calcolare erratamente.

misrepresent (mĭs'rĕp·rē·zĕnt') *vt., vi.* svisare, falsare, snaturare.

misrule (mĭs·rōōl') *n.* malgoverno.

miss (mĭs) (1) *n.* signorina, ragazza nubile: **Miss Calvert**, la signorina Calvert.

miss (mĭs) (2) *n.* omissione, errore; colpo mancato. *vt.* sbagliare, mancare, non raggiungere; dimenticare; sentire (*o* notare) la mancanza di, rimpiangere; perdere, lasciarsi sfuggire; schivare per un pelo: **to — the bus** *o* **the boat**, perdere l'autobus, (*fig.*), perdere un'occasione propizia. *vi.* mancare, non riuscire, essere assente; sbagliare il bersaglio.

misshapen (mĭs·shāp'ĕn) *agg.* deforme, malformato.

missile (mĭs'ĭl) *n.* proiettile, missile: **guided —**, missile telecomandato.

missing (mĭs'ĭng) *n.* mancante, scomparso, disperso: **a cup is —**, manca una tazza; **a man is —**, è scomparso un uomo.

mission (mĭsh'ŭn) *n.* missione. **—ary** *n., agg.* missionario.

missis (mĭs'ĭs), **missus** (mĭs'ŭs) *n.* (*fam.*) signora, padrona, moglie.

missive (mĭs'ĭv) *n.* missiva.

misspell (mĭs·spĕl') *vt., vi.* (*pass., pp.* **misspelled** *o* **misspelt**) scrivere (*o* pronunciare) erratamente, commettere errori d'ortografia.

misstate (mĭs·stāt') *vt.* esporre erratamente, svisare.

missus *vedi* **missis**.

mist (mĭst) *n.* nebbia, velo; pioggerella. *vi.* annebbiarsi, velarsi; piovigginare.

mistake (mĭs·tāk') *n.* errore, abbaglio. *vt.* (*pass.* **mistook**, *pp.* **mistaken**) sbagliare, confondere; capir male, fraintendere; scambiare (*una persona o una cosa per un'altra*). *vi.* errare.

mistaken (mĭs·tāk'ĕn) *agg.* erroneo, inesatto, frainteso: **to be —**, sbagliarsi, essere in errore. *pp. di* **to mistake**.

mister (mĭs'tĕr) *n.* signore, signor.

mistimed (mĭs·tīmd') *agg.* intempestivo.

mistletoe (mĭs''l·tō) *n.* (*bot.*) vischio.

mistook (mĭs·tŏŏk') *pass. di* **to mistake**.

mistreat (mĭs·trēt') *vt.* maltrattare.

mistress (mĭs'trĕs) *n.* signora, padrona, direttrice, istitutrice, maestra; amante: **head— —** *n.* direttrice di scuola.

mistrust (mĭs·trŭst') *n.* diffidenza, sfiducia. *vt., vi.* diffidare di, sospettare. **—ful** *agg.* diffidente.

misty (mĭs'tĭ) *agg.* nebbioso, nebuloso, velato, vago.

misunderstand (mĭs'ŭn·dēr·stănd')*vt., vi.* (*pass., pp.* **misunderstood**) fraintendere, equivocare.

misunderstanding *n.* incomprensione, malinteso, screzio.

misunderstood *agg.* frainteso, incompreso, malinteso.

misuse (mĭs·ūs') *n.* abuso; cattivo uso; maltrattamento. *vt.* (-ūz') fare un cattivo uso (*opp.* abusare) di; maltrattare.

mite (mīt) *n.* soldino, inezia, piccolo contributo; àcaro.

miter (mī'tĕr) *n.* mitra (*copricapo episcopale*); congiunzione ad angolo retto.

mitigate (mĭt'ĭ·gāt) *vt.* mitigare.

mitt (mĭt), **mitten** (mĭt''n) *n.* mezzo guanto, guanto a sacchetto; (*pugilato*) guantone.

mix (mĭks) *vt.* mischiare, unire, associare; confondere. *vi.* mischiarsi, associarsi. **—age** *n.* (*cinema*) missaggio. **—ed** (mĭkst) *agg.* misto, promiscuo, confuso. **—ture** *n.* miscuglio.

mizzen (mĭz''n) *n.* (*naut.*) vela di mezzana. **—mast** *n.* albero di mezzana.

moan (mōn) *n.* gemito, lamento. *vt., vi.* lamentare, lamentarsi, piangere, gemere.

moat (mōt) *n.* fosso, fossato.

mob (mŏb) *n.* folla, moltitudine, turba: **— law**, linciaggio. *vt.* assalire tumultuosamente *o* in massa.

mobile (mō'bĭl) *agg.* mobile, agile (*di mente*), versatile, incostante. *n.* parte mobile; macchina inutile (*tipo di soprammobile*).

mobilization (mō'bĭ·lĭ·zā'shŭn) *n.* mobilitazione.

mobilize (mō'bĭ·līz) *vt.* mobilitare.

mobster (mŏb'stĕr) *n.* tumultuante; gangster teppista.

moccasin (mŏk'à·sĭn) *n.* mocassino; (*zool.*) ancistrodonte.

mock (mŏk) *n.* canzonatura, parodia. *agg.* burlesco, ironico; falso, finto, fittizio, simulato. *vt.* beffare; parodiare; simulare, ingannare; frustrare: **to — at**, beffarsi di. **—er** *n.* burlone, impostore. **—ery** *n.* beffa, parodia, derisione.

mode (mōd) *n.* modo, forma, maniera, moda, metodo.

model (mŏd''l) *n.* modello, campione; modella; indossatrice. *agg.* esemplare. *vt.*, *vi.* modellare, plasmare; posare, fare la modella.

moderate (mŏd'ĕr·ĭt) *agg.* moderato, modico, modesto. *vt.* (-āt) moderare, temperare. *vi.* moderarsi.

moderation (mŏd'ĕr·ā'shŭn) *n.* moderazione.

modern (mŏd'ĕrn) *n.*, *agg.* moderno.

modernize (mŏd'ĕr·nīz) *vt.*, *vi.* modernizzare, modernizzarsi.

modest (mŏd'ĕst) *n.* modesto, moderato, castigato, pudico.

modesty (mŏd'ĕs·tĭ) *n.* modestia, moderazione; pudicizia.

modicum (mŏd'ĭ·kŭm) *n.* minima quantità, minimo.

modification (mŏd'ĭ·fĭ·kā'shŭn) *n.* modificazione.

modify (mŏd'ĭ·fĭ) *vt.* modificare. *vi.* modificarsi.

modish (mŏd'ĭsh) *agg.* elegante, di moda alla moda.

modulate (mŏd'ū·lāt) *vt.*, *vi.* modulare.

Mohammedan (mō·hăm'ĕ·dăn) *n.*, *agg.* maomettano.

moist (moist) *agg.* umido.

moisten (mois'n) *vt.* inumidire, umettare.

moisture (mois'tŭr) *n.* umidità.

molar (mō'lĕr) *n.*, *agg.* molare.

molasses (mō·lăs'ĕz) *n.* melassa.

mold (mōld) *n.* modello, stampo; modanatura; carattere; muffa; terriccio. *vt.* modellare, plasmare. *vi.* ammuffire. —**er** *n.* modellatore. *vi.* sgretolarsi.

moldy *agg.* muffoso.

mole (mōl) (1) *n.* neo.

mole (mōl) (2) *n.* molo; mole.

mole (mōl) (3) *n.* (*zool.*) talpa.

molecule (mŏl'ê·kūl) *n.* molecola.

molehill (mōl'hĭl) *n.* talpaia: **to make a mountain out of a —**, drammatizzare, esagerare.

molest (mō·lĕst') *vt.* molestare.

mollify (mŏl'ĭ·fĭ) *vt.* mollificare, ammansire, attenuare. *vi.* ammansirsi, commuoversi.

molten (mōl'tĕn) *agg.* fuso, liquefatto.

moment (mō'mĕnt) *n.* momento, istante; importanza, significato; impulso: **of little —**, di scarsa importanza. —**ary** *agg.* momentaneo; imminente. —**ous** (-mĕnt'-) *agg.* grave, importante, critico, decisivo.

momentum (mō·mĕn'tŭm) *n.* (*fis.*) momento, impulso.

monarch (mŏn'ĕrk) *n.* monarca.

monarchy (mŏn'ĕr·kĭ) *n.* monarchia.

monastery (mŏn'ăs·tĕr'ĭ) *n.* monastero.

Monday (mŭn'dĭ) *n.* lunedì: **Black Monday**, lunedì di Pasqua.

monetary (mŏn'ê·tĕr'ĭ) *agg.* monetario.

money (mŭn'ĭ) *n.* danaro, moneta: **ready —**, danaro contante; **earnest —**, caparra; **paper —**, carta moneta; **— broker**, **—changer** *n.* cambiavalute; **—lender** *n.* usuraio; **— order**, vaglia; **—making** *agg.* lucrativo, redditizio.

mongoose (mŏng'gōōs) *n.* (*zool.*) mangusta.

mongrel (mŏng'grĕl) *n.*, *agg.* bastardo, ibrido.

monitor (mŏn'ĭ·tĕr) *n.* ammonitore; ammonimento; (*scol.*) capoclasse; (*radio e T.V.*) monitor; (*naut.*) monitore.

monk (mŭngk) *n.* monaco.

monkey (mŭng'kĭ) *n.* scimmia; buffone; babbeo: **— wrench**, chiave inglese. *vt.* scimmiottare. *vi.* gingillarsi: **to — with** (gergo) manomettere; intromettersi in.

monocle (mŏn'ō·k'l) *n.* monocolo (*lente*).

monogamist (mō·nŏg'á·mĭst) *n.* monogamo.

monogamy (mō·nŏg'á·mĭ) *n.* monogamia.

monogram (mŏn'ō·grăm) *n.* monogramma.

monologue (mŏn'ō·lŏg) *n.* monologo.

monopolize (mō·nŏp'ō·līz) *vt.* monopolizzare.

monopoly (mō·nŏp'ō·lĭ) *n.* monopolio.

monotonous (mō·nŏt'ō·nŭs) *agg.* monotono.

monotony (mō·nŏt'ō·nĭ) *n.* monotonia.

monotype (mŏn'ō·tīp) *n.* monotipo (*f.*), monotype.

monotyper *n.* monotipista.

monster (mŏn'stĕr) *n.* mostro, prodigio. *agg.* mostruoso, enorme.

monstrosity (mŏn·strŏs'ĭ·tĭ) *n.* mostruosità.

monstrous (mŏn'strŭs) *agg.* mostruoso, prodigioso, enorme.

montage (mŏn·tăzh') *n.* montaggio; fotomontaggio.

month (mŭnth) *n.* mese. —**ly** *n.* pubblicazione mensile. *agg.* mensile. *avv.* mensilmente.

monument (mŏn'ū·mĕnt) *n.* monumento. —**al** *agg.* monumentale.

moo (mōō) *n.* muggito. *vi.* muggire.

mood (mōōd) *n.* umore, stato d'animo; modo (*del verbo*): **to be in a good —**, essere di buon umore; **to be in the —to**, essere in vena di; **to be in no — for**, non essere in vena di; **— swing**, sbalzi d'umore. —**iness** *n.* malumore, tristezza, mutevolezza, scontrosità.

moody (mōōd'ĭ) *agg.* triste, imbronciato; lunatico, mutevole; scontroso.

moon (mōōn) *n.* luna: once in a blue —, una volta ogni morte di vescovo. *vi.* vagare trasognato; incantarsi. —**light** *n.* chiaro di luna. —**shine** *n.* chiaro di luna; chimera; liquori di contrabbando. —**struck** *agg.* pazzo.

Moor (1) *n.* moro.

moor (mōōr) (2) *n.* landa, brughiera.

moor (mōōr) (3) *vt., vi.* ormeggiare, ormeggiarsi. —**ing** *n.* ormeggio.

Moorish (mōōr'ĭsh) *agg.* moresco.

moose (mōōs) *n.* alce americana.

moot (mōōt) *agg.* discutibile, controverso.

mop (mŏp) *n.* strofinaccio; tampone; (*naut.*) radazza: — of hair, zazzera. *vt.* strofinare, tamponare: to — one's brow, asciugarsi la fronte.

mope (mōp) *vt.* deprimere. *vi.* essere triste *o* apatico.

moral (mŏr'ăl) *n.* morale (*f.*); (*pl.*) moralità, costumi. *agg.* morale.

morale (mŏ·rál') *n.* morale (*f.*).; (*m.* = stato d'animo).

moralist (mŏr'ăl·ĭst) *n.* moralista.

morality (mŏ·răl'ĭ·tĭ) *n.* morale, moralità.

moralize (mŏr'ăl·īz) *vt.* moralizzare. *vi.* trarre la morale, moraleggiare.

morass (mŏ·răs') *n.* palude.

morbid (mŏr'bĭd) *agg.* morboso; macabro, spaventoso. —**ly** *avv.* morbosamente; in modo macabro.

more (mōr) *agg.* più, maggiore: — courage than strength, più coraggio che forza; the — we have the — we want, più si ha più si desidera; some —, ancora un po'. *avv.* più, di più, maggiormente, ancora: — and —, sempre di più; once —, ancora una volta; — or less, più o meno, suppergiù.

moreover (mōr·ō'vẽr) *avv.* inoltre, per giunta, anche.

morgue (mŏrg) *n.* obitorio; (*giornalismo*) archivio.

Mormon (mŏr'mŭn) *n.*, *agg.* mormone.

morning (mŏr'nĭng) *n.* mattino, mattina: tomorrow —, domattina; in the —, di mattina; good —! buongiorno! — star, stella del mattino. *agg.* mattutino.

morocco (mŏ·rŏk'ō) *n.* marocchino (*pelle*).

moron (mō'rŏn) *n.* deficiente mentale; scemo, imbecille.

morose (mŏ·rōs') *agg.* cupo, imbronciato, scontroso. —**ness** *n.* tristezza, scontrosità.

morphia (mŏr'fĭ·à) morphine (mŏr'fēn) *n.* morfina.

morrow (mŏr'ō) *n.* (*l'*)indomani: on the —, il giorno dopo.

morsel (mŏr'sĕl) *n.* frammento, boccone, pezzetto.

mortal (mŏr'tăl) *n.* mortale. *agg.* mortale, funesto; umano. —**ity** (-tăl'ĭ·tĭ) *n.* mortalità, natura umana. —**ly** *avv.* mortalmente, umanamente.

mortar (mŏr'tẽr) *n.* calcestruzzo; pestello; (*art.*) mortaio.

mortgage (mŏr'gĭj) *n.* ipoteca. *vt.* ipotecare.

mortician (mŏr·tĭsh'ăn) *n.* impresario di pompe funebri.

mortification (mŏr'tĭ·fĭ·kā'shŭn) *n.* mortificazione; (*med.*) necrosi.

mortify (mŏr'tĭ·fī) *vt.* mortificare; necrotizzare. *vi.* mortificarsi; andare in cancrena.

mortise (mŏr'tĭs) *n.* incavo, incastro.

mosaic (mŏ·zā'ĭk) *n.*, *agg.* mosaico.

mosque (mŏsk) *n.* moschea.

mosquito (mŭs·kē'tō) *n.* zanzara: — net, zanzariera.

moss (mŏs) *n.* (*bot.*) musco: —**grown**, coperto di musco. —**y** *agg.* muscoso.

most (mōst) *n.* la maggior parte, il più: to make the — of, trarre il miglior partito da; the — you can do, il massimo che tu possa fare; at the —, tutt' al più. *agg.* moltissimo, più, più grande, maggiore, preponderante: — people, il più della gente; for the — part, nella maggior parte; the — votes, la maggioranza dei voti. *avv.* grandemente, estremamente, prevalentemente, il più; (*gergo*) quasi: — of all, soprattutto. —**ly** *avv.* per la maggior parte, per lo più, principalmente.

motel (mō·tĕl') *n.* autostello, motel.

moth (mŏth) *n.* tarma; falena: — ball, palla di naftalina. —**eaten** *agg.* tarmato.

mother (mŭth'ẽr) *n.* madre. *agg.* materno, di madre; naturale, innato; natio: — country, madrepatria; — tongue, madrelingua. *vt.* dar vita a, far da madre a, proteggere.

motherhood *n.* maternità.

mother-in-law *n.* suocera.

motherly *agg.* materno. *avv.* maternamente.

mother-of-pearl *n.* madreperla.

motif (mō·tēf') *n.* motivo, tema.

motion (mō'shŭn) *n.* movimento, moto, mozione; cenno, segnale. *vt.*, *vi.* esortare col gesto, far cenno. —**less** *agg.* immobile. —**picture** *n.* film. *agg.* cinematografico.

motive (mō'tĭv) *n.* motivo, movente. *agg.* motore, causale, motrice.

motley (mŏt'lĭ) *n.* accozzaglia. *agg.* variegato, eterogeneo, multicolore.

motor (mō'tĕr) *n.*, *agg.* motore. *vi.* andare in automobile.

motorboat (mō'tĕr.bōt') *n.* motoscafo.

motorbus (mō'tĕr.bŭs') *n.* autobus.

motorcar (mō'tĕr.kär) *n.* automobile.

motorcade (mō'tĕr.kād) *n.* autocorteo.

motorcoach (mō'tĕr.kōch) *n.* autocorriera, pullman, torpedone.

motorcycle (mō'tĕr.sī'k'l) *n.* motocicletta.

motorist (mō'tĕr.ĭst) *n.* automobilista.

motorize (mō'tĕr.īz) *vt.* motorizzare.

mottle (mŏt''l) *vt.* screziare, venare, variegare, maculare.

motto (mŏt'ō) *n.* motto, massima.

mould (mōld) *vedi* mold.

mound (mound) *n.* terrapieno, collinetta, tumulo.

mount (mount) *n.* monte; monta; montaggio; ascesa; cavalcatura; incastellatura, affusto; montatura (*di foto, ecc.*). *vt.*, *vi.* montare; ascendere, salire; aumentare.

mountain (moun'tĭn) *n.* montagna. *agg.* montano. —**eer** *n.* montanaro, alpinista. —**eering** (-ēr'ing) *n.* alpinismo. —**ous** *agg.* montuoso; enorme.

mourn (mōrn) *vt.* piangere (*qualcuno*); rimpiangere. *vi.* addolorarsi; essere in lutto. —**er** *n.* persona in lutto, dolente. —**ful** *agg.* triste, lugubre, funebre, lamentoso.

mourning *n.* lamentazione, lutto: **deep** —, lutto stretto; **to go into** —, prendere il lutto. *agg.* di (*o* da) lutto.

mouse (mous) *n.* (*pl.* **mice**) topo, sorcio.

moustache *vedi* **mustache**.

mouth (mouth) *n.* bocca. *vt.* (th-) mettere in bocca, divorare; declamare; biascicare. —**ful** *n.* boccone. —**piece** *n.* bocchino, imboccatura (*di strumento mus.*), cornetto (*del telefono*); portavoce, (*gergo*) avvocato.

movable (mōōv'á.b'l) *n.* mobile: **movables,** *pl.* beni mobili. *agg.* movibile, mobile.

move (mōōv) *n.* mossa, movimento, trasloco. *vt.* muovere; commuovere; incitare, indurre; spostare, trasferire; proporre. *vi.* muoversi, mettersi in marcia; cambiare alloggio, traslocare; partire; fare una mossa: **to** — **for,** proporre; **to** — **away,** andarsene, spostarsi, appartarsi; **to** — **forward,** avanzare; **to** — **on,** avanzare, proseguire, camminare; **to** — **out,** andarsene, lasciare una casa, traslocare.

movement (mōōv'mĕnt) *n.* movimento.

mover (mōōv'ĕr) *n.* motore, movente.

movie (mōōv'ĭ) *n.* film, pellicola: **the movies,** il cinema.

moving (mōōv'ing) *agg.* commovente: — **power,** forza motrice.

mow (mō) *vt.*, *vi.* (*pass.* **mowed,** *pp.* **mowed, mown**) falciare, ammucchiare il fieno. —**er** *n.* falciatore; falciatrice (*macchina*).

Mr. (*abbr. di* **mister**) (mĭs'tĕr) signor, il signor. **Mrs.** (*vedi* **missis**) (mĭs'ĭz) signora, la signora.

much (mŭch) *n.*, *agg.*, *avv.* molto, tanto, assai, di gran lunga: **as** —, altrettanto; **as** — **as,** tanto quanto; — **as, per quanto; how** —? quanto? **too** —, troppo; **so** —, tanto, così, tutto questo; **so** — **that,** tanto che; **so** — **the better (the worse),** tanto meglio (peggio); **very** —, moltissimo; — **the same,** quasi lo stesso; **not** — **of a book,** non un gran che come libro; **to make** — **of,** dare molta importanza a.

muck (mŭk) *n.* letame, concime, sudiciume.

mucous (mū'kŭs) *agg.* mucoso: — **membrane,** mucosa.

mucus (mū'kŭs) *n.* muco.

mud (mŭd) *n.* fango.

muddle (mŭd''l) *n.* confusione, disordine, imbroglio. *vt.* confondere, abborracciare; intorbidare.

muddy (mŭd'ĭ) *agg.* torbido, fangoso, confuso, stordito. *vt.* oscurare, intorbidare, infangare; inebetire.

mudguard (mŭd'gärd') *n.* parafango.

muff (mŭf) *n.* manicotto (*di pelliccia*); sciocco. *vt.* impasticciare, lasciarsi sfuggire.

muffin (mŭf'ĭn) *n.* panino dolce.

muffle (mŭf''l) *n.* muffola. *vt.* imbaccucare; smorzare (*suoni*).

muffler (mŭf'lĕr) *n.* sciarpa; guantone (*da boxe*); silenziatore; (*mus.*) sordina.

mug (mŭg) *n.* boccale.

mulberry (mŭl'bĕr'ĭ) *n.* mora del gelso. — **tree** *n.* gelso.

mule (mūl) (1) *n.* mulo.

mule (mūl) (2) *n.* pantofola.

muleteer (mū'lĕ.tēr') *n.* mulattiere.

mull (mŭl) *vt.*, *vi.* macinare; faticare; rimuginare.

multiple (mŭl'tĭ.p'l) *n.*, *agg.* multiplo.

multiplication (mŭl'tĭ.plĭ.kā'shŭn) *n.* moltiplicazione; — **table,** tavola pitagorica.

multiplicity (mŭl'tĭ.plĭs'ĭ.tĭ) *n.* molteplicità.

multiply (mŭl'tĭ.plī) *vt.* moltiplicare. *vi.* moltiplicarsi.

multitude (mŭl'tĭ.tūd) *n.* moltitudine.

multitudinous (mŭl'tĭ-tū'dĭ-nŭs) agg. numeroso, sovrabbondante, affollato.

mum (mŭm) agg. silenzioso: to keep —, tenere acqua in bocca; —'s the word! acqua in bocca!

mumble (mŭm'b'l) n. borbottio. vt., vi. brontolare, borbottare.

mummy (mŭm'ĭ) n. mummia; poltiglia; cera per innesti.

mumps (mŭmps) n.pl. musoneria; (med.) orecchioni.

munch (mŭnch) vt., vi. biascicare, masticare rumorosamente.

municipality (mū-nĭs'ĭ-păl'ĭ-tĭ) n. municipio.

munificence (mū-nĭf'ĭ-sĕns) n. munificenza.

munificent (mū-nĭf'ĭ-sĕnt) n. munifico.

munitions (mū-nĭsh'ŭnz) n.pl. munizioni; equipaggiamento.

mural (mū'răl) n. pittura murale. agg. murale.

murder (mûr'dĕr) n. omicidio, assassinio. vt. assassinare. —er n. omicida, assassino. —ess n. assassina. —ing, —ous agg. omicida, feroce.

murk (mûrk) n. oscurità, tetraggine. —y agg. tenebroso, cupo, nebbioso.

murmur (mûr'mĕr) n. mormorio. vt., vi. mormorare.

muscle (mŭs'l) n. muscolo. vi. intrufolarsi.

muscular (mŭs'kū-lĕr) agg. muscolare.

Muse (mūz) (1) n. musa.

muse (mūz) (2) n. astrazione, meditazione. vt., vi. meditare, rimuginare.

museum (mū-zē'ŭm) n. museo.

mush (mŭsh) n. sorta di polenta, pappa; sentimentalismo.

mushroom (mŭsh'rōōm) n. fungo.

music (mū'zĭk) n. musica: to face the —, affrontare la situazione: — hall, caffè-concerto. — stand, leggio per musica, palco dell'orchestra.

musical agg. musicale n. (anche musical comedy) commedia musicale.

musician (mū-zĭsh'ăn) n. musicista.

musing (mūz'ĭng) n. meditazione. agg. meditabondo.

musk (mŭsk) n. muschio. —rat n. rat-misquè.

musket (mŭs'kĕt) n. moschetto. —eer (-tĕr) n. moschettiere.

musky (mŭs'kĭ) agg. muschiato.

muslin (mŭz'lĭn) n. mussolina.

muss (mŭs) vt. arruffare.

must (mŭst) (1) vi. difettivo ausil.

(mancante dell'inf. e pp.; pass. must) devo, devi, deve, dobbiamo, ecc.: it — be so, dev'essere così; something — be done, bisogna fare qualcosa. agg. da farsi assolutamente: a — book, un libro che si deve leggere.

must (mŭst) (2) n. mosto.

mustache (mŭs-tàsh') n. baffo, baffi.

mustard (mŭs'tĕrd) n. senape: — plaster, senapismo.

muster (mŭs'tĕr) n. esposizione, assembramento, adunata: to pass —, superare l'esame, esser passabile. vt., vi. adunare, riunire, riunirsi: to — up courage, prendere il coraggio a due mani.

musty (mŭs'tĭ) agg. muffito, muffoso.

mute (mūt) n. muto; (mus.) sordina. agg. muto. vt. mettere la sordina a.

mutilate (mū'tĭ-lāt) vt. mutilare.

mutilation (mū'tĭ-lā'shŭn) n. mutilazione.

mutineer (mū'tĭ-nēr') n. ammutinato.

mutinous (mū'tĭ-nŭs) agg. ribelle, turbolento, sedizioso.

mutiny (mū'tĭ-nĭ) n. ammutinamento. vi. ammutinarsi.

mutter (mŭt'ĕr) n. brontolio. vt., vi. brontolare, borbottare.

mutton (mŭt''n) n. montone: — chop, costoletta di montone.

mutual (mū'tū-ăl) agg. mutuo, reciproco.

muzzle (mŭz''l) n. bocca (d'arma da fuoco); muso (di animale); museruola. vt. metter la museruola a, far tacere, imbavagliare.

my (mī) agg.poss. mio, mia, miei, mie.

myriad (mĭr'ĭ-ăd) n. miriade.

myrtle (mûr't'l) n. (bot.) mirto.

myself (mī-sĕlf') pron.pers. io stesso, me stesso, mi: I went there —, ci andai di persona; I broke it —, lo ruppi io stesso; I hurt —, mi feci male: I was by —, ero solo; I talked to —, parlavo fra me.

mysterious (mĭs-tēr'ĭ-ŭs) agg. misterioso.

mystery (mĭs'tĕr-ĭ) n. mistero.

mystic (mĭs'tĭk) n., agg. mistico.

mystification (mĭs'tĭ-fĭ-kā'shŭn) n. mistificazione; perplessità, sconcerto.

mystify (mĭs'tĭ-fī) vt. mistificare; rendere perplesso, sconcertare, confondere.

myth (mĭth) n. mito. —ology (-ŏl'ŏ-jĭ) n. mitologia.

N

nab (năb) vt. afferrare, agguantare.

nabob (nā'bŏb) n. nababbo.

nacelle (nà-sĕl') n. navicella.

nacre (nā'kĕr) n. madreperla.

nag (năg) *n.* cavallino, ronzino. *vt.*, *vi.* tormentare, angariare; criticare.

naif (nă.ēf') *agg.* ingenuo.

nail (nāl) *n.* chiodo; unghia, artiglio: **on the —**, seduta stante. *vt.* inchiodare; concludere (*un affare*); cogliere a volo; smascherare; ribadire. **— file**, lima da unghie.

naive (nă.ēv') *n.*, *agg.* ingenuo.

naiveté (nă.ēv'tā') *n.* ingenuità.

naked (nā'kĕd) *agg.* nudo; crudo (*della verità*); manifesto; indifeso; spoglio: **stark —**, tutto nudo. **—ness** *n.* nudità, crudezza.

name (nām) *n.* nome; reputazione: **assumed —**, pseudonimo; **christian —**, nome di battesimo; **family —**, cognome; **to call someone names**, insolentire qualcuno; **to make a — for oneself**, farsi una fama; *vt.* chiamare, nominare, menzionare; scegliere. *agg.* di gran nome, famoso. **—less** *agg.* anonimo, senza nome.

namely (nām'lĭ) *avv.* cioè, vale a dire.

namesake (nām·sāk') *n.* omonimo.

nap (năp) *n.* peluria, lanuggine; pisolino: **to take a —**, schiacciare un pisolino. *vi.* sonnecchiare: **to catch somebody napping**, cogliere qualcuno alla sprovvista.

nape (nāp) *n.* nuca.

naphtha (năf'thà) *n.* nafta.

napkin (năp'kĭn) *n.* tovagliolo; pannolino.

narcissus (năr.sĭs'ŭs) *n.* (*bot.*) narciso.

narcotic (năr.kŏt'ĭk) *n.*, *agg.* narcotico.

narrate (nă.rāt') *vt.* narrare.

narration (nă.rā'shŭn) *n.* narrazione; trama, intreccio.

narrative (năr'à.tĭv) *n.* resoconto; narrativa. *agg.* narrativo.

narrow (năr'ō) *n.* stretto, strettoia; (*pl.*) stretti. *agg.* stretto, limitato; di misura; meschino: **— circumstances**, ristrettezze; **to have a — escape**, scamparla bella. *vt.* restringere, limitare, ridurre al minimo. *vi.* restringersi. **—ly** *avv.* strettamente; minuziosamente; dappresso; di stretta misura: **we — escaped falling**, per poco non cademmo. **—minded** *agg.* gretto. **—ness** *n.* strettezza; grettezza, ristrettezza.

nastiness (nàs'tĭ·nĕs) *n.* malvagità; volgarità, oscenità.

nasty (nàs'tĭ) *agg.* sudicio; osceno; malvagio; grossolano; ripugnante: **to smell —**, puzzare; **— wound**, ferita grave; **— disposition**, caratteraccio.

nation (nā'shŭn) *n.* nazione. **—al**

(năsh'-) *agg.* nazionale. **—ality** *n.* nazionalità.

nationalize (năsh'ŭn·ăl.īz) *vt.* nazionalizzare.

nationally (năsh'ŭn·ăl.lĭ) *avv.* su scala nazionale, in tutta la nazione.

native (nā'tĭv) *n.* indigeno. *agg.* nativo, indigeno, originario; naturale, innato: **to go —**, insabbiarsi.

nativity (nă.tĭv'ĭ.tĭ) *n.* natività, nascita; oroscopo.

natty (năt'ĭ) *agg.* inappuntabile.

natural (năt'ŭ.rắl) *n.* idiota; natura, carattere; (*fam.*) successo; (*mus.*) bequadro. *agg.* naturale, istintivo, spontaneo: **he is a — for that job**, ha un'inclinazione naturale per quel lavoro, è nato per fare quel lavoro. **—ism** *n.* naturalismo, verismo. **—ist** *n.* naturalista, verista. **—ization** *n.* naturalizzazione.

naturalize (năt'ŭ.rắl·īz) *vt.* naturalizzare; acclimare; adottare (*espressioni straniere, ecc.*).

naturally (năt'ŭ.rắl.lĭ) *avv.* naturalmente, spontaneamente.

naturalness (năt'ŭ.rắl.nĕs) *n.* naturalezza, spontaneità.

nature (nā'tŭr) *n.* natura, indole: **to copy from —**, copiare dal vero.

naught (nôt) *n.* nulla, zero: **to set at —**, disprezzare; **to come to —**, far fiasco. *agg.* nullo.

naughtiness (nô'tĭ·nĭs) *n.* perversità, cattiveria.

naughty (nô'tĭ) *agg.* cattivo.

nausea (nô'shē.à) *n.* nausea.

nauseate (nô'shē.āt) *vt.* nauseare, disgustare.

nauseating *agg.* nauseabondo, stomachevole.

nautical (nô'tĭ·kắl) *agg.* nautico, marittimo, marino.

naval (nā'vắl) *agg.* navale: **— officer**, ufficiale di marina.

nave (nāv) *n.* mozzo (*di ruota*); (*arch.*) navata.

navel (nā'vĕl) *n.* ombelico; centro.

navigable (năv'ĭ·gà·b'l) *agg.* navigabile.

navigate (năv'ĭ·gāt) *vt.*, *vi.* navigare, governare; (*aeron.*) pilotare.

navigation (năv'ĭ·gā'shŭn) *n.* navigazione: **— laws**, codice marittimo.

navigator (năv'ĭ·gā'tĕr) *n.* navigatore; ufficiale di rotta.

navy (nā'vĭ) *n.* marina; flotta: **— blue**, blu, turchino; **—yard**, arsenale.

nay (nā) *n.* diniego, voto negativo. *avv.* no, non solo, anzi.

Neapolitan *n.*, *agg.* napoletano: **— ice**, cassata.

near (nēr) *agg.* vicino, prossimo, intimo; esatto: **the — side of a car**

il lato sinistro di un'automobile; I had a — accident, per poco non mi succede un incidente; — silk, finta seta. *avv.* quasi, circa, vicino: to draw —, avvicinarsi; I came — forgetting to, per poco mi dimenticavo di; — at hand, a portata di mano; — by, vicinissimo. *prep.* accanto, presso: — the end of, verso la fine di. *vt.*, *vi.* avvicinarsi (*a*).

nearly *avv.* quasi, pressappoco; da vicino, strettamente: — related, parente stretto; it is — five o'clock, sono quasi le cinque; I — did it, stavo per farlo, poco mancò che non lo facessi.

nearness *n.* prossimità, vicinanza, intimità, avarizia.

nearsighted *agg.* miope.

neat (nēt) *agg.* netto; elegante; abile, accurato; puro. **—ly** *avv.* nettamente, abilmente, puramente, elegantemente. **—ness** *n.* lindezza, precisione, chiarezza.

necessaries *n.pl.* (*il*) necessario.

necessarily (nĕs′ĕ·sĕr′ĭ·lĭ) *avv.* necessariamente.

necessary (nĕs′ĕ·sĕr′ĭ) *agg.* necessario.

necessitate (nĕ·sĕs′ĭ·tāt) *vt.* necessitare, rendere necessario.

necessity (nĕ·sĕs′ĭ·tĭ) *n.* necessità.

neck (nĕk) *n.* collo; scollatura; manico (*di violino*); istmo, passo, gola (*di montagna*): — and —, alla pari; — or nothing, ad ogni costo. **—lace** *n.* collana. **—length** *n.* (*ippica*) incollatura.

necktie (nĕk′tī′) *n.* cravatta.

nectar (nĕk′tẽr) *n.* nettare.

need (nēd) *n.* bisogno; necessità; povertà: for — of, in mancanza di; if — be, se fosse necessario. *vt.*, *vi.* abbisognare di, mancare di, occorrere: he — not go, non occorre che egli vada. **—ful** *agg.* necessario, indispensabile; bisognoso.

needle (nē′d'l) *n.* ago; puntina (*da grammofono*); iniezione: the —, nervosismo. *vt.* cucire; pungere, punzecchiare; (*fig.*) dar colore, dar brio.

needless (nēd′lĕs) *agg.* inutile, superfluo.

needlework (nē′d'l·wûrk′) *n.* lavoro di cucito, ricamo.

needs (nēdz) *avv.* necessariamente, assolutamente: I must —, devo assolutamente.

needy (nēd′ĭ) *agg.* indigente, bisognoso.

ne'er (nâr) *avv.* (*contraz. di* never): **—-do-well**, buono a nulla.

negation (nē·gā′shŭn) *n.* diniego, negazione.

negative (nĕg′ȧ·tĭv) *n.* negazione;

negativa. *agg.* negativo. *vt.* smentire; respingere, votare contro.

neglect (nĕg·lĕkt′) *n.* negligenza, trascuratezza, abbandono. *vt.* trascurare, tralasciare, omettere. **—ful** *agg.* trascurato, negligente.

negligence (nĕg′lĭ·jĕns) *n.* negligenza.

negligent (nĕg′lĭ·jĕnt) *n.* negligente.

negligible (nĕg′lĭ·jĭ·b′l) *agg.* trascurabile.

negotiate (nē·gō′shĭ·āt) *vt.*, *vi.* negoziare; superare (*un ostacolo, una difficoltà, ecc.*).

negotiation (nē·gō′shĭ·ā′shŭn) *n.* negoziato, trattativa.

Negress (nē′grĕs) *n.* negra.

Negro (nē′grō) *n.*, *agg.* negro.

neigh (nā) *n.* nitrito. *vi.* nitrire.

neighbor (nā′bẽr) *n.* vicino; coinquilino: to love one's —, amare il prossimo. *agg.* vicino, adiacente. **—hood** *n.* vicinato, dintorni, vicinanza, quartiere. **—ing** *agg.* vicino, attiguo. **—ly** *agg.* di buon vicino, amichevole. *avv.* da buon vicino, socievolmente.

neither (nē′thẽr) *agg.*, *pron.* nè l'uno nè l'altro: I saw —, non vidi nè l'uno nè l'altro. *cong.* (*correlativo di* nor) nè, neppure: — my father nor my mother, nè mio padre nè mia madre; — will I, e neppure io. *avv.* in nessun caso.

nephew (nĕf′ū; nĕv′ū) *n.* nipote (*m.*).

nerve (nûrv) *n.* nervo; nervatura; coraggio, energia; impudenza: (*pl.*) nervi, nervoso: to get on one's —, dare ai nervi; to lose one's —, perdere le staffe;. *vt.* dar forza *o* coraggio.

nervous (nûr′vŭs) *agg.* nervoso; nerboruto; timoroso, timido; inquieto. **—ness** *n.* nervosità; inquietudine; timidezza.

nervy (nûr′vĭ) *agg.* nervoso; audace.

nest (nĕst) *n.* nido; tana, rifugio; wasp's —, vespaio. *vi.* nidificare, rifugiarsi. **—egg** *n.* endice; gruzzolo.

nestle (nĕs′'l) *vt.* ospitare; coccolare. *vi.* annidarsi, crogiolarsi.

net (nĕt) (1) *n.* rete, reticella. *vt.* coprire con (*opp.* prendere nella) rete.

net (nĕt) (2) *agg.* netto: — price, prezzo netto. *vt.* introitare come guadagno netto.

nether (nĕth′ẽr) *agg.* basso, inferiore.

netting (nĕt′ĭng) *n.* rete, reticolato.

nettle (nĕt′'l) *n.* (*bot.*) ortica. *vt.* pungere; irritare, indispettire.

network (nĕt′wûrk) *n.* rete, maglia: radio —, rete radiofonica; railroad —, rete ferroviaria.

neuralgia (nū·răl'jȧ) n. nevralgia.

neurasthenia (nū'rȧs·thḗnĭ·ȧ) n. nevrastenia.

neuritis (nū·rī'tĭs) n. (med.) nevrite.

neurosis (nū·rō'sĭs) n. nevrosi.

neurotic (nū·rŏt'ĭk) agg. nevrotico.

neuter (nū'tẽr) n., agg. neutro, neutrale.

neutral (nū'trăl) agg. neutrale, neutro, acromatico. —ity n. neutralità.

neutralize (nū'trăl·īz) vt. neutralizzare.

never (nĕv'ẽr) avv. mai, giammai: — mind, non importa. —ceasing agg. incessante. —ending agg. perpetuo, eterno.

nevermore (nĕv'ẽr·mōr') avv. mai più.

nevertheless (nĕv'ẽr·thḗ·lĕs') avv. ciononostante, tuttavia.

new (nū) agg. nuovo, recente, inesperto, fresco: as good as —, come nuovo; — look, linea nuova, nuovo corso. —born n. neonato. —comer n. nuovo venuto.

newel (nū'ĕl) n. albero della scala a chiocciola; colonnina di ringhiera.

newfangled (nū'făng'g'ld) agg. di nuovo conio o genere, di nuova invenzione.

newly (nū'lĭ) avv. di recente, da poco, di fresco. —wed n. sposino, sposina; (pl.) sposini.

newness (nū'nĕs) n. freschezza, novità.

news (nūz) n. novità, notizia, annuncio: a piece of —, una notizia, — agency, agenzia d'informazioni; — agent, agente d'informazioni, giornalista; giornalaio; — dealer, giornalaio.

newsboy n. strillone.

newscast n. notiziario radio, radiogiornale; telegiornale. —er n. annunciatore; radiocommentatore; telecommentatore.

newsman n. giornalista; giornalaio, strillone.

newspaper n. giornale.

newsprint n. carta da giornale.

newsreel n. cinegiornale.

newsstand n. edicola.

newsworthy agg. (giorn.) meritevole di essere pubblicato.

next (nĕkst) agg. vicino; prossimo; successivo, seguente; contiguo: — month, il mese venturo; — day, il giorno dopo; to be — in turn, essere (il prossimo) di turno; — best, il migliore subito dopo. avv. in seguito, subito dopo, quasi, accanto: — to impossible, quasi impossibile; what —? e poi?; — to me, accanto a me; — of kin, parente più prossimo.

nib (nĭb) n. becco (di uccello); punta (di penna), pennino.

nibble (nĭb'l) n. bocconcino, morso. vt., vi. rosicchiare, mordicchiare, sbocconcellare; brucare.

nice (nīs) agg. simpatico, buono, grazioso, piacevole, fine; preciso, accurato, scrupoloso. —ly avv. bene; amabilmente, piacevolmente, delicatamente; esattamente, scrupolosamente. —ty (nī'sḗ·tĭ) n. esattezza, raffinatezza, finezza, sfumatura; amabilità: to a —, esattamente, alla perfezione.

niche (nĭch) n. nicchia.

nick (nĭk) n. istante preciso; sbreccatura, tacca: in the — of time, al momento giusto, appena in tempo. vt. colpire giusto, cogliere, intaccare, sbreccare, troncare.

nickel (nĭk'ĕl) n. nichelio; moneta da 5 cents. —plating agg. nichelatura.

nicknack vedi knickknack.

nickname (nĭk'nām') n. nomignolo. vt. soprannominare.

niece (nēs) n. nipote (f.).

niggard (nĭg'ẽrd) n., agg. spilorcio. -liness n. spilorceria. -ly agg. spilorcio, misero. avv. avaramente.

nigger (nĭg'ẽr) n. (sprezz.) negro.

nigh (nī) agg. vicino, affine, prossimo. avv. quasi. prep. presso, vicino.

night (nīt) n. notte, sera: good —! buona notte! tomorrow —, domani sera, domani notte; at —, di notte; to make a — of it, fare nottata. —cap n. berretta da notte; bevanda che si beve prima di coricarsi; ultima gara di una giornata sportiva. —dress, —gown n. camicia da notte. —fall n. crepuscolo, imbrunire, calar della notte.

nightingale (nīt'ĭn·gāl) n. usignolo.

nightly (nīt'lĭ) agg. notturno. avv. nottetempo; tutte le notti.

nightmare (nīt'mâr') n. incubo.

nihilism (nī'ḷ·lĭz'm) n. nichilismo.

nihilist n. nichilista.

nimble (nĭm'b'l) agg. agile, lesto, leggiero. —ness n. agilità, sveltezza.

nincompoop (nĭn'kŏm·pōōp) n. stupido, sciocco.

nine (nīn) n., agg. nove. —pins n. birilli. —teen n., agg. diciannove. —teenth n., agg. diciannovesimo. —tieth n., agg. novantesimo. —ty n., agg. novanta.

ninth (nīnth) n., agg. nono.

nip (nĭp) n. pizzicotto, presa; morso; frizzo. vt., vi. pizzicare; mordere; strappare; frustrare; gelare; arraffare: to — away, svignarsela: to — in the bud, distruggere in germe.

—pers *n.pl.* pinza; tanaglie; manette.

nipple (nĭp′′l) *n.* capezzolo.

nit (nĭt) *n.* lendine.

nitrate (nī′trāt) *n.* (*chim.*) nitrato.

nitwit (nĭt′wĭt′) *n.* sciocco.

nix (nĭks) *n.* (*gergo*) niente. *avv.* no.

no (nō) *n.* no, negazione, voto contrario. *agg.* nessuno, non: have you — friends? non avete amici?; — doubt, senza dubbio; — one, nessuno; matter, non mporta; — matter how much I love you, per quanto io ti ami; I am — musician, non sono musicista; — smoking, vietato fumare; by — means, niente affatto; of — use, inutile. *avv.* non, no: — less, nientemeno; — more, non più; — longer, non più, non oltre.

nobility (nō-bĭl′ĭ-tĭ) *n.* nobiltà.

noble (nō′b′l) *n.*, *agg.* nobile —ness *n.* nobiltà.

nobody (nō′bŏd-ĭ) *n.* nessuno: — else, nessun altro; to be —, essere un illustre sconosciuto.

nocturne (nŏk′tûrn) *n.* (*mus.*) notturno.

noddle (nŏd′′l) *n.* (*fam.*) testa.

node (nōd) *n.* nodo; nodulo.

nohow (nō′hou′) *avv.* (*gergo*) in nessun modo, niente affatto.

noise (noiz) *n.* rumore, chiasso. *vt.* divulgare, strombazzare: it is noised that, corre voce che. —less *agg.* silenzioso.

noisily (noiz′ĭ-lĭ) *avv.* rumorosamente.

noisome (noi′sŭm) *agg.* molesto, nocivo; puzzolente; disgustoso.

noisy (noiz′ĭ) *agg.* rumoroso, chiassoso.

nominal (nŏm′ĭ-năl) *agg.* nominale.

nominate (nŏm′ĭ-nāt) *vt.* nominare, designare.

nomination (nŏm′ĭ-nā′shŭn) *n.* nomina, designazione; designazione di un candidato.

nonagenarian (nŏn′à-jê-nâr′ĭ-ăn) *n.*, *agg.* novantenne.

nonce (nŏns) *n.* occasione presente, momento attuale: for the —, per il momento.

nonchalance (nŏn′shà-lăns) *n.* disinvoltura, indifferenza.

nonchalant (nŏn′shà-lănt) *agg.* disinvolto, indifferente.

noncommissioned officer (nŏn′kŏ-mĭsh′ŭnd) *n.* sottufficiale.

noncommittal (nŏn′kŏ-mĭt′ăl) *agg.* evasivo, vago, generico.

nondescript (nŏn′dĕ-skrĭpt) *agg.* indefinibile, indefinito, scialbo, insignificante.

none (nŭn) *pron.*, *agg.* nessuno, nessuna, niente: I have —, non ne ho; — of that, niente di tutto ciò; that is — of your business, non sono affari tuoi; to be — the happier for that, non essere cosa che renda più felice; — the less, nondimeno; — but, nessuno all'infuori di, soltanto. *avv.* nientaffatto, in nessun modo, tutt'altro che.

nonentity (nŏn-ĕn′tĭ-tĭ) *n.* inesistenza, nullità, fattore ipotetico.

nonplus (nŏn′plŭs) *vt.* disorientare, sbalordire.

nonsense (nŏn′sĕns) *n.* sciocchezza, assurdità.

nonsensical (nŏn-sĕn′sĭ-kăl) *agg.* assurdo, illogico, stupido.

noodles (nōō′d′lz) *n.pl.* tagliatelle all'uovo.

nook (nŏŏk) *n.* angolo, recesso.

noon (nōōn) *n.* mezzogiorno. —day *n.* mezzogiorno. *agg.* meridiano. —tide, —time *n.* mezzogiorno.

noose (nōōs) *n.* nodo scorsoio, cappio; tranello. *vt.* annodare a scorsoio; prendere al laccio.

nor (nôr) *cong.* nè, nemmeno: neither I — he, nè io nè lui.

norm (nôrm) *n.* norma.

normal (nôr′măl) *agg.* normale; perpendicolare. —cy *n.* normalità.

north (nôrth) *n.* nord. *agg.* del nord: — pole, polo nord; — American, nordamericano. *avv.* al nord. —east *n.* nord-est. —ern *agg.* settentrionale: northern lights, aurora boreale. —erner *n.* settentrionale. —ward *avv.* verso nord. —west *n.* nord-ovest.

Norwegian (nôr-wē′jăn) *n.*, *agg.* norvegese.

nose (nōz) *n.* naso, muso; fiuto; prua: — dive (*aeron.*) pricchiata, tuffo. *vt.*, *vi.* fiutare; sporgere il naso o il muso; avanzarsi; insinuarsi; curiosare.

nosegay (nōz′gā′) *n.* mazzo di fiori.

nosewheel (nōz′hwēl′) *n.* (*aeron.*) ruota di prua (*del carrello triciclo*).

nosey (nōz′ĭ) *agg.* indiscreto, ficcanaso.

nostril (nŏs′trĭl) *n.* narice.

nosy (nōz′ĭ) *agg.* indiscreto.

not (nŏt) *avv.* non, no: — at all, niente affatto; non c'è di che (*risposta a* "thank you"); — even, neppure.

notable (nō′tá-b′l) *agg.* notevole.

notary (nō′tá-rĭ) *n.* notaio.

notation (nō-tā′shŭn) *n.* notazione.

notch (nŏch) *n.* tacca, intaccatura; gola (*di montagna*); grado. *vt.* intaccare.

note (nōt) *n.* nota, biglietto; punto, appunto; importanza: **bank —**, banconota; **— of exclamation**, punto esclamativo. *vt.* notare; annotare; denotare. **—book** *n.* taccuino, registro.

noted (nōt′ĕd) *n.* noto, cospicuo, famoso.

noteworthy (nōt′wûr′thĭ) *agg.* notevole, degno di nota.

nothing (nŭth′ĭng) *n.* niente, nulla: **next to —**, quasi niente; **to come to —**, finire in niente. *avv.* niente affatto, per nulla.

notice (nō′tĭs) *n.* notizia; notifica, disdetta; attenzione; avviso, preavviso; trafiletto; istruzione: **at short —**, a breve scadenza; **— to quit**, sfratto; **to come into —**, farsi conoscere; **to take — of**, fare caso a, badare a. *vt.* osservare; prendere nota di, badare a; notificare. **—able** *agg.* percettibile, notevole.

notify (nō′tǐ.fĭ) *vt.* notificare, avvertire, annunciare.

notion (nō′shŭn) *n.* nozione, idea, intenzione; (*S.U.*) aggeggio: **notions**, minuterie.

notorious (nō.tō′rǐ.ŭs) *agg.* notorio, famigerato.

notwithstanding (nŏt′wǐth.stăn′dǐng) *prep., cong., avv.* nonostante, sebbene, quantunque, benché, tuttavia.

nought (nòt) *vedi* **naught.**

noun (noun) *n.* nome, sostantivo.

nourish (nûr′ĭsh) *vt.* nutrire, alimentare. **—ing** *agg.* nutriente. **—ment** *n.* nutrimento, alimento.

novel (nŏv′ĕl) *n.* romanzo; racconto. *agg.* nuovo, novello. **—ette** *n.* romanzo breve. **—ist** *n.* romanziere.

novelty (nŏv′l.tĭ) *n.* novità.

November (nō.vĕm′bẽr) *n.* novembre.

novice (nŏv′ĭs) *n.* novizio, principiante, novellino.

now (nou) *avv.* ora, attualmente; allora; ebbene, dunque. *cong.* ora che, poiché, dal momento che: **— and then**, di tanto in tanto; **from — on**, d'ora in poi; **by —**, ormai, a quest'ora; **just —**, or ora, poco fa.

nowadays (nou′á.dāz′) *avv.* oggigiorno.

nowhere (nō′hwâr) *avv.* in nessun luogo: **to get —**, fare un buco nell'acqua, fallire.

nowise (nō′wǐz) *avv.* in nessun modo.

noxious (nŏk′shŭs) *agg.* nocivo.

nozzle (nŏz′'l) *n.* becco, boccaglio, ugello, iniettore; filiera.

nth (ĕnth) *agg.* ennesimo.

nuance (nū.äns′) *n.* sfumatura.

nuclear (nū′klē.ẽr) *agg.* nucleare.

nucleus (nū′klē.ŭs) *n.* nucleo.

nude (nūd) *n., agg.* nudo.

nudge (nŭj) *n.* gomitatina. *vt.* dare di gomito, toccare col gomito.

nugatory (nū′gá.tō′rǐ) *agg.* trascurabile, insignificante; vano, inefficace.

nugget (nŭg′ĕt) *n.* pepita.

nuisance (nū′săns) *n.* noia; molestia, seccatura; danno; seccatore.

null (nŭl) *agg.* nullo, non valido.

numb (nŭm) *agg.* torpido, tramortito: **to become —**, intorpidirsi. *vt.* intorpidire, tramortire.

number (nŭm′bẽr) *n.* numero, cifra; compagine, complesso (*di persone, ecc.*); persona; articolo di vendita: **odd —**, numero dispari; **even —**, numero pari; **a — of people**, un certo numero di persone o molte persone; **times without —**, innumerevoli volte; **—s pool**, lotteria clandestina. *vt.* contare, numerare, annoverare. **—less** *agg.* innumerevole.

numbness (nŭm′nĕs) *n.* intorpidimento, torpore, tramortimento.

numeral (nū′mẽr.ǎl) *n., agg.* numerale.

numerical (nū.mẽr′ĭ.kǎl) *agg.* numerico.

numerous (nū′mẽr.ŭs) *agg.* numeroso.

numskull (nŭm′skŭl′) *n.* stupido.

nun (nŭn) *n.* monaca, suora.

nuncio (nŭn′shĭ.ō) *n.* nunzio, delegato apostolico.

nunnery (nŭn′ẽr.ĭ) *n.* monastero.

nuptial (nŭp′shǎl) *agg.* nuziale. *n.pl.* nozze.

nurse (nûrs) *n.* nutrice, bambinaia; istitutrice; infermiera. *vt.* nutrire, allattare; allevare, curare, coltivare; covare (*rancori, ecc.*). **—maid** *n.* bambinaia.

nursery (nûr′sẽr.ĭ) *n.* stanza dei bambini; (*bot.*) vivaio: **— school**, asilo infantile. **—man** *n.* coltivatore.

nursing home *n.* convalescenziario.

nurture (nûr′tūr) *n.* allevamento; nutrimento; educazione. *vt.* nutrire; educare; allevare.

nut (nŭt) *n.* noce, mandorla, nocciuola, seme; (*mecc.*) dado; (*fig.*) problema, situazione difficile; (*gergo*) testa, sciocco: **a hard — to crack**, un osso duro da rodere; **to be nuts about** (*gergo*), avere il pallino di; **nuts!** frottole!; sciocchezze.

nutcracker (nŭt′krăk′ẽr) *n.* schiaccianoci; (*ornit.*) nucifraga.

nutmeg (nŭt′mĕg) *n.* noce moscata.

nutrition (nū.trĭsh′ŭn) *n.* nutrizione; nutrimento.

nutritious (nū·trĭsh′ŭs) *agg.* nutriente.

nutshell (nŭt′shĕl) *n.* guscio di noce: **in a —**, in poche parole.

nutty (nŭt′ĭ) *agg.* che abbonda di noci; che ha sapore di noce; (*gergo*) pazzo; entusiasta.

nylon (nī′lon) *n.* nylon, nailon.

nymph (nĭmf) *n.* ninfa; crisalide.

O

oaf (ōf) *n.* scemo, stupido.

oak (ōk) *n.* quercia. **—en** *agg.* di quer-

oakum (ō′kŭm) *n.* stoppa. [cia.

oar (ōr) *n.* remo. *vt.*, *vi.* remare. **—lock** *n.* scalmiera.

oasis (ō·ā′sĭs) *n.* (*pl.* **oases** [ō·ā′sēz]) oasi.

oat (ōt) *n.* (*gen.pl.*) avena: **to sow one's wild —s**, darsi alla pazza gioia, correre la cavallina.

oath (ōth) *n.* giuramento; bestemmia.

obdurate (ŏb′dū·rāt) *agg.* impeni-tente, ostinato.

obedience (ō·bē′dĭ·ĕns) *n.* ubbidienza.

obedient (ō·bē′dĭ·ĕnt) *agg.* ubbidiente.

obeisance (ō·bā′sāns) *n.* riverenza; os-sequio.

obese (ō·bēs′) *agg.* obeso.

obesity (ō·bēs′ĭ·tĭ) *n.* obesità.

obey (ō·bā′) *vt.*, *vi.* ubbidire.

obituary (ō·bĭt′ū·ĕr′ĭ) *n.* necrologio, necrologia.

object (ŏb′jĕkt) *n.* oggetto, scopo; (*gramm*). complemento oggetto. *vt.*, *vi.* (ŏb.jeckt′) obiett.r e, oppor-si, esser contrario.

objection (ŏb·jĕk′shŭn) *n* obiezione, contrarietà, disapprovazione.

objective (ŏb·jĕk′tĭv) *n.* obiettivo, scopo, mira. *agg.* oggettivo, obiet-tivo.

obligate (ŏb′lĭ·gāt) *vt.* obbligare.

obligation (ŏb′lĭ·gā′shŭn) *n.* obbligo, impegno, debito: **to be under — to,** avere un obbligo con.

obligatory (ŏb·lĭg′á·tō′rĭ) *agg.* ob-bligatorio.

oblige (ō·blīj′) *vt.* obbligare, fare un piacere a, favorire: **much obliged!** mille grazie!, obbligatissimo!

obliging (ō·blīj′ĭng) *agg.* compiacente, gentile, cortese.

oblique (ŏb·lēk′) *agg.* obliquo, tor-tuoso.

obliterate (ō·blĭt′ĕr·āt) *vt.* cancellare, distruggere.

oblivion (ŏb·lĭv′ĭ·ŭn) *n.* oblio: **act of —**, amnistia.

oblivious (ŏb·lĭv′ĭ·ŭs) *agg.* dimentico, ignaro.

oblong (ŏb′lŏng) *agg.* oblungo.

obnoxious (ŏb·nŏk′shŭs) *agg.* nocivo, molesto; odioso.

obscene (ŏb·sēn′) *agg.* osceno, abo-minevole.

obscenity (ŏb·sĕn′ĭ·tĭ) *n.* oscenità.

obscure (ŏb·skūr′) *agg.* oscuro. *vt.* oscurare, offuscare.

obscurity (ŏb·skū′rĭ·tĭ) *n.* oscurità.

obsequies (ŏb′sĕ·kwĭz) *n.* esequie.

obsequious (ŏb·sē′kwĭ·ŭs) *agg.* osse-quioso.

observance (ŏb·zûr′vāns) *n.* osser-vanza, rispetto; rito.

observant (ŏb·zûr′vănt) *n.* osservante, ligio; osservatore.

observation (ŏb′zēr·vā′shŭn) *n.* osser-vazione.

observatory (ŏb·zûr′vá·tō′rĭ) *n.* osser-vatorio.

observe (ŏb·zûrv′) *vt.*, *vi.* osservare.

observer (ŏb·zûr′vēr) *n.* osservatore.

obsess (ŏb·sĕs′) *vt.* ossessionare.

obsession (ŏb·sĕsh′ŭn) *n.* ossessione.

obsolete (ŏb′sō·lēt) *agg.* antiquato, in disuso.

obstacle (ŏb′stá·k'l) *n.* ostacolo.

obstetrics (ŏb·stĕt′rĭks) *n.* ostetricia.

obstinacy (ŏb′stĭ·ná·sĭ) *n.* ostinazione.

obstinate (ŏb′stĭ·nĭt) *agg.* ostinato.

obstruct (ŏb·strŭkt′) *vt.* ostruire, ostacolare. **—ion** *n.* ostruzione, im-pedimento. **—ionism** *n.* ostruzio-nismo.

obtain (ŏb·tān′) *vt.* ottenere, ricavare, procurarsi. *vi.* prevalere. **—able** *agg.* ottenibile.

obtuse (ŏb·tūs′) *agg.* ottuso.

obviate (ŏb′vĭ·āt) *vt.* ovviare a.

obvious (ŏb′vĭ·ŭs) *agg.* ovvio, evidente.

occasion (ō·kā′zhŭn) *n.* occasione, caso; causa. *vt.* dar luogo a, cau-sare. **—ally** *avv.* occasionalmente, sporadicamente, di quando in quando, a volte.

occident (ŏk′sĭ·dĕnt) *n.* occidente. **—al** *agg.*, *n.* occidentale.

occiput (ŏk′sĭ·pŭt) *n.* occipite.

occupant (ŏk′ū·pănt) *n.* occupante.

occupation (ŏk′ū·pā′shŭn) *n.* occu-pazione.

occupy (ŏk′ū·pī) *vt.* occupare, im-piegare, abitare.

occur (ō·kûr′) *vi.* accadere; venire in mente. **—rence** *n.* contingenza, av-venimento.

ocean (ō′shăn) *n.* oceano.

ochre (ō′kēr) *n.* ocra.

octane (ŏk′tān) *n.* (*chim*.) ottano.

October (ŏk·tō′bēr) *n.* ottobre.

octopus (ŏk′tō·pŭs) *n.* piovra.

ocular (ŏk′ū·lēr) *agg.* oculare.

oculist (ŏk′ū.lĭst) *n.* oculista.

odd (ŏd) *agg.* strano, singolare, bislacco; eccentrico; dispari; scompagnato; residuo; sporadico, avventizio: — shoe, scarpa scompagnata; — man, lavoratore avventizio: at — moments, a tempo perso; ten — dollars, dieci dollari e rotti. **—ity** *n.* stranezza. **—ly** *avv.* stranamente.

odds (ŏdz) *n.pl.* vantaggio concesso al più debole (*in una competizione*); disparità, differenza; probabilità; disputa: — and ends, cianfrusaglie; at —, in contrasto; the — are against me, la sorte mi è sfavorevole, non ho probabilità di vincere.

ode (ōd) *n.* ode.

odious (ō′dĭ.ŭs) *agg.* odioso.

odorous (ō′dĕr.ŭs) *agg.* odoroso, fragrante.

odor (ō′dĕr) *n.* odore; profumo. **—less** *agg.* inodoro.

oedipal (ĕd′ĭ.păl) *agg.* edipico.

o'er (ōr) *contraz. di* over.

of (ŏv) *prep.* di, del, della; a; in; da; per: very kind — you, molto gentile da parte vostra; — late, ultimamente; — course, naturalmente; a quarter — five, le cinque meno un quarto; as — today, a partire da oggi.

off (ŏf) *agg.* remoto, il più lontano; laterale, esterno; libero; destro (*di destra*): — day, giorno di libertà; — side, parte più lontana; to have one's hat —, essere a capo scoperto; the electricity is —, l'elettricità è interrotta; to be — to war, essere alla guerra. *avv.* via, fuori, a distanza, lontano; (*naut.*) al largo: to go —, spegnersi; to be well —, essere ricco; to put —, rimandare; to take a day —, prendersi un giorno di vacanza; ten miles —, a una distanza di dieci miglia; — and on, sporadicamente. *prep.* da; fuori di; giù da; davanti a; (*naut.*) al largo di.

offal (ŏf′ăl) *n.* rifiuti.

offbeat (ŏf′bēt′) *agg.* eterodosso, strano, originale.

offence *vedi* offense.

offend (ŏ.fĕnd′) *vt., vi.* offendere, molestare, dispiacere; violare; peccare. **—er** *n.* offensore, contravventore, peccatore, colpevole.

offense (ŏ.fĕns′) *n.* offesa, oltraggio; colpa, reato.

offensive (ŏ.fĕn′sĭv) *n.* offensiva, *agg.* offensivo, sgradevole; aggressivo; criminoso.

offer (ŏf′ĕr) *n.* offerta, proposta. *vt.* offrire, proporre, presentare: to —

violence, aggredire. *vi.* offrirsi, presentarsi. **—ing** *n.* offerta, sacrificio.

offhand (ŏf′hănd′) *avv.* sul momento, impensatamente, senza indugio, estemporaneamente. *agg.* (*anche* —ed) impensato, improvviso, improvvisato, estemporaneo.

office (ŏf′ĭs) *n.* ufficio; filiale, sede; mansione, carica, funzione; ministero: — building, palazzo commerciale; post —, ufficio postale; our Rome —, la nostra filiale (*o* sede) di Roma.

officer (ŏf′ĭ.sĕr) *n.* ufficiale; poliziotto; funzionario. *vt.* fornire di ufficiali; comandare.

official (ŏ.fĭsh′ăl) *n.* funzionario. *agg.* ufficiale.

officiate (ŏ.fĭsh′ĭ.āt) *vi.* officiare.

officious (ŏ.fĭsh′ŭs) *agg.* ufficioso; inframmettente, importuno.

offing (ŏf′ĭng) *n.* (*naut.*) largo: in the —, poco distante, all'orizzonte, probabile, imminente.

offset (ŏf′sĕt′) *n.* partenza; compensazione; germoglio; collaterale; deviazione; sperone (*di monte*); (*tip.*) contrastampa, fotolito. *vt.* compensare, bilanciare. *vi.* sporgere; germogliare.

offspring (ŏf′sprĭng′) *n.* risultato, conseguenza; progenie.

oft (ŏft) *vedi* often.

often (ŏf′ĕn) *avv.* spesso, frequentemente, in molti casi: how —? quante volte?

ogle (ō′g'l) *vt., vi.* adocchiare; fare l'occhio di triglia.

ogre (ō′gĕr) *n.* orco.

oil (oil) *n.* olio; petrolio: — field, giacimento *o* campo petrolifero; — painting, pittura a olio, dipinto a olio. — well, pozzo petrolifero. *vt.* oliare, lubrificare.

oilcloth *n.* tela incerata.

oilskin *n.* tela impermeabile; indumento di tela impermeabile.

oily (oil′ĭ) *agg.* oleoso.

ointment (oint′mĕnt) *n.* unguento.

O.K., okay (ō′kā′) *n.* approvazione, benestare. *avv.* bene, benissimo: it's —, sta bene. *vt.* approvare, sanzionare.

old (ōld) *agg.* vecchio; antiquato; usato: — maid, zitella; (*scherz.*) zitello; one's — man, il padre, il marito, il principale, il preside (*di una scuola*), il capitano (*di una nave*); of —, anticamente, una volta; how — are you? quanti anni avete? I am twenty years —, ho venti anni; to be — enough to, essere in età di; to be an — hand at, essere esperto in *o* di. — age vecchiaia. —clothesman *n.* rigattiere. —en *agg.* antico. —er *agg.* più vecchio, più anziano. —est *agg.* il più vecchio. —fashioned *agg.* antiquato; *n.* cocktail a base di rye whisky e angostura. —time *agg.* antico, vetusto, passato. —timer *n.* veterano; persona all'antica.

olive (ŏl'ĭv) *n.* ulivo, oliva: — grove, oliveto; — oil, olio d'oliva; — tree, olivo. *agg.* verde oliva.

omelette (ŏm'ĕ.lĕt) *n.* frittata.

omen (ŏ'mĕn) *n.* augurio, presagio.

ominous (ŏm'ĭ.nŭs) *agg.* sinistro, di malaugurio, minaccioso.

omission (ŏ.mĭsh'ŭn) *n.* omissione.

omit (ŏ.mĭt') *vt.* omettere.

omnipotence (ŏm.nĭp'ō.tĕns) *n.* onnipotenza.

omnipotent (ŏm.nĭp'ō.tĕnt) *agg.* onnipotente.

on (ŏn) *prep.* su, sopra; in; vicino a; verso; dopo, da: — arriving, all'arrivo; — board, a bordo, sul treno; — condition that, a patto che; — credit, a credito; — foot, a piedi; — horseback, a cavallo, in groppa; — Monday, il lunedì; — purpose, apposta; — sale, in vendita; — time, a tempo, puntualmente. *avv.* su, sopra; indosso; avanti: and so —, e così via; later —, più tardi, in sèguito; off and —, saltuariamente. *agg.* in corso, in azione: the light is —, la luce è accesa; to have one's hat —, avere il cappello in testa.

once (wŭns) *n.*, *avv.* una volta, un tempo: all at —, tutt'a un tratto; just this —, solo per questa volta; — and for all, una volta per tutte; — in a while, di tanto in tanto; — upon a time, una volta (*anticamente*); *cong.* una volta che, non appena.

oncoming (ŏn'kŭm'ĭng) *n.* l'avvicinarsi. *agg.* che si avvicina, prossimo; audace; promettente.

one (wŭn) *n.*, *agg.* uno, una, uno solo; un certo: — hundred, cento; — thousand, mille; my — chance, la mia unica occasione; his — and only, il suo solo e unico; — John Miller, un certo J.M. *pron. indef.* uno, uno solo; colui; quello; si (*impers.*): the blue pencil and the red —, la matita blu e quella rossa; the — who, quello *o* colui che, quella *o* colei che; — another, l'un l'altro; no —, nessuno; — by —, uno a uno; every—, ciascuno;

this —, questo; that —, quello; the beloved —, l'essere amato. — armed *agg.* monco; —eyed *agg.* guercio.

onerous (ŏn'ĕr.ŭs) *agg.* oneroso.

oneself (wŭn.sĕlf') *pron.rifl.* se stesso, si: by —, da solo; to wash —, lavarsi; to speak to —, parlare tra sè, ragionare con se stesso.

one-sided (wŭn'sīd'ĕd) *agg.* avente un solo lato, unilaterale; parziale.

onion (ŭn'yŭn) *n.* (*bot.*) cipolla.

onlooker (ŏn'lŏok'ẽr) *n.* spettatore.

only (ŏn'lĭ) *agg.* unico, solo. *avv.* solamente, unicamente. *cong.* solo che.

onrush (ŏn'rŭsh') *n.* impeto, assalto.

onset (ŏn'sĕt') *n.* attacco, assalto; esordio.

onslaught (ŏn'slŏt') *n.* aggressione, assalto impetuoso.

onto (ŏn'tŏo) *prep.* in cima a, sopra, su.

onward (ŏn'wẽrd) *agg.* avanzato, avanzante. *avv.* avanti, in avanti.

ooze (ōoz) *vi.* filtrare, fluire, colare; trapelare.

opal (ō'păl) *n.* (*min.*) opale.

opaque (ō.pāk') *agg.* opaco.

open (ō'pĕn) *n.* luogo (*campo, mare*) aperto, aria aperta. *agg.* aperto; scoperto, libero; accessibile; manifesto; esposto (*a*): — country, aperta campagna; — library, biblioteca aperta a tutti; — question, argomento non ancora risoluto; — teeth, denti radi; — town (*mil.*) città aperta; (*S.U.*) città senza restrizioni sugli alcolici; — to temptation, esposto alle tentazioni; — winter, inverno mite; wide —, spalancato. *vt.* aprire; inaugurare, iniziare. *vi.* aprirsi; esordire; confidarsi: to — into, dare in, affacciarsi in; to — one's heart, confidarsi; to — out, dischiudere, svelare; svolgere; allargare (*un foro*); to — up, dischiudere, aprire, scoprire, svelare; presentarsi; parlare apertamente. —handed *agg.* generoso. —hearted *agg.* buono, franco, spontaneo. —minded *agg.* di larghe vedute. —mouthed *agg.* a bocca aperta.

opening (ō'pĕn.ĭng) *n.* apertura; esordio, inaugurazione; radura; occasione; *agg.* primo, iniziale: — night, serata d'inaugurazione, prima.

openly (ō'pĕn.lĭ) *avv.* apertamente.

opera (ŏp'ẽr.à) *n.* opera: — glass, binocolo da teatro; — house, teatro dell'opera; — horse — film western; soap — (*radio e T.V.*) programma diurno di commedie a puntate dedicato alle massaie.

operate (ŏp'ĕr.āt) vt., vi. agire, operare, funzionare, manovrare, compiere.
operatic (ŏp'ĕr.ăt'ĭk) agg. d'opera,
lirico.
operation (ŏp'ĕr.ā'shŭn) n. operazione, manipolazione, azione; funzionamento. —al agg. di lavoro,
operativo; (mil.) da combattimento, strategico.
operative (ŏp'ĕr.ā'tĭv) n. agente;
mezzo; operaio; artigiano; investigatore. agg. operativo, ope-
rante; efficace; operatorio; attivo.
operator (ŏp'ĕr.ā'tĕr) n. operatore;
manovratore; speculatore: telegraph —, telegrafista; telephone —,
centralinista.
opiate (ō'pĭ.ĭt) n. narcotico.
opinion (ō.pĭn'yŭn) n. opinione, parere: — poll, referendum. —ated
agg. testardo; presuntuoso.
opium (ō'pĭ.ŭm) n. oppio.
opponent (ŏ.pō'nĕnt) n. oppositore,
avversario.
opportune (ŏp'ŏr.tūn') agg. opportuno.
opportunity (ŏp'ŏr.tū'nĭ.tĭ) n. occasione.
oppose (ŏ.pōz') vt. avversare; opporre;
combattere.
opposite (ŏp'ō.zĭt) n. (l') opposto, (il)
contrario. agg. opposto, contrario,
dirimpetto. prep. di fronte a.
opposition (ŏp'ō.zĭsh'ŭn) n. opposizione, resistenza, ostacolo.
oppress (ŏ.prĕs') vt. opprimere. —ion
(-shŭn) n. oppressione. —ive agg.
opprimente. —or n. oppressore.
opprobrious (ŏ.prō'brĭ.ŭs) agg. obbrobrioso.
opprobrium (ŏ.prō'brĭ.ŭm) n. obbro-
brio.
optical (ŏp'tĭ.kăl) agg. ottico.
optician (ŏp.tĭsh'ăn) n. ottico.
optics (ŏp'tĭks) n. ottica.
optimism (ŏp'tĭ.mĭz'm) n. ottimismo.
optimist (ŏp'tĭ.mĭst) agg. ottimista.
—ic agg. ottimistico.
option (ŏp'shŭn) n. opzione, scelta,
preferenza. —al agg. facoltativo.
opulence (ŏp'ū.lĕns) n. opulenza.
opulent (ŏp'ū.lĕnt) agg. opulento.
or (ŏr) cong. o, oppure: either this —
that, o questo o quello; — else, altrimenti.
oracle (ŏr'á.k'l) n. oracolo, profezia.
oral (ō'răl) agg. orale.
orange (ŏr'ĕnj) n. arancia: — grove,
aranceto; — tree, arancio; — blossom, fiore d'arancio. agg. arancio,
arancione; d'arancia. —ade n. aranciata.
oration (ō.rā'shŭn) n. discorso, orazione.

orator (ŏr'á.tĕr) n. oratore.
oratory (ŏr'á.tō'rĭ) n. oratoria; oratorio (cappella).
orb (ŏrb) n. orbe, sfera, orbita.
orbit (ŏr'bĭt) n. orbita.
orchard (ŏr'chĕrd) n. frutteto.
orchestra (ŏr'kĕs.trá) n. orchestra.
orchid (ŏr'kĭd) n. (bot.) orchidea.
ordain (ŏr.dān') vt. ordinare (conferire
gli ordini); decretare, designare.
ordeal (ŏr.dēl') n. prova, cimento.
order (ŏr'dĕr) n. ordine, decreto: in
— that, affinchè; in — to, per, allo
scopo di; out of —, in cattivo
stato, guasto (di meccanismo);
made to —, fatto su commissione
o su misura. vt., vi. ordinare;
ingiungere, comandare: to — away,
scacciare, espellere. —liness n.
ordine, metodicità, regolarità.
orderly (ŏr'dĕr.lĭ) n. ordinanza, attendente (soldato); inserviente (di
ospedale). agg. ordinato, metodico.
ordinance (ŏr'dĭ.năns) n. ordinanza
(decreto).
ordinarily (ŏr'dĭ.nĕr'ĭ.lĭ) avv. ordinariamente, generalmente.
ordinary (ŏr'dĭ.nĕr'ĭ) n. normalità;
locanda; pasto a prezzo fisso;
magistrato. agg. ordinario, comune,
usuale.
ordnance (ŏrd'năns) n. artiglieria.
ordure (or'dŭr) n. sterco; luridume.
ore (ōr) n. minerale metallico.
organ (ŏr'găn) n. organo: hand —,
organetto.
organic (ŏr.găn'ĭk) agg. organico.
organism (ŏr'găn.ĭz'm) n. organismo.
organist (ŏr'găn.ĭst) n. organista.
organization (ŏr'găn.ĭ.zā'shŭn) n. organizzazione.
organize (ŏr'găn.īz) vt. organizzare.
vi. organizzarsi.
organizer (ŏr'găn.īz'ĕr) n. organizzatore.
orgy (ŏr'jĭ) n. orgia.
orient (ō'rĭ.ĕnt) n. oriente, levante.
agg. orientale, sorgente; fulgido.
vt. volgere a oriente, orientare,
orientarsi. —al (-ĕn'-) n., agg. orientale.
orifice (ŏr'ĭ.fĭs) n. orifizio, apertura.
origin (ŏr'ĭ.jĭn) n. origine. —al (ō.rĭj'
ĭ.năl) agg. originale, originario.
—ality (-ăl'ĭ.tĭ) n. originalità. —ally
(-rĭj'-) avv. originariamente, origi-
nalmente.
originate (ō.rĭj'ĭ.nāt) vt. originare,
provocare. vi. derivare, provenire.
oriole (ō'rĭ.ōl) n. (ornit.) rigogolo.
ornament (ŏr'ná.mĕnt) n. ornamento.
vt. ornare. —al (-mĕnt'ăl) agg.
ornamentale, decorativo.

ornate (ôr·nāt') *agg.* ornato, sontuoso; fiorito (*di stile*).

ornithology (ôr'nĭ·thŏl'ō·jĭ) *n.* ornitologia.

orphan (ôr'făn) *n.*, *agg.* orfano. *vt.* rendere orfano. **—age** *n.* orfanotrofio.

orthodox (ôr'thō·dŏks) *agg.* ortodosso.

orthography (ôr·thŏg'rà·fĭ) *n.* ortografia.

oscillate (ŏs'ĭ·lāt) *vi.* oscillare; vacillare.

osier (ō'zhẽr) *n.* vimine.

ostentation (ŏs'tĕn·tā'shŭn) *n.* ostentazione.

ostentatious (ŏs'tĕn·tā'shŭs) *agg.* ostentatore.

ostrich (ŏs'trĭch) *n.* struzzo.

other (ŭth'ẽr) *agg.* altro, differente, ulteriore: every **—** day, a giorni alterni. *pron.* l'altro: any **—**, qualsiasi altro; each **—**, l'un l'altro; some day or **—**, un giorno o l'altro; some **—** time, un'altra volta; gifts **—** than flowers, regali che non siano fiori; natures **—** than ours, caratteri diversi dai nostri.

otherwise *avv.* altrimenti, diversamente, del resto. *cong.* se no.

otter (ŏt'ẽr) *n.* (*zool.*) lontra.

ought (ôt) *vi.irr.ausil.difett.* (*indica condiz. pres., pass.prossimo*) dovevo, dovevi, doveva, dovevamo, *ecc.*; dovrei, dovresti, dovrebbe, dovremmo, *ecc.*: we **—** to go, dovremmo andare; I **—** to have known it, avrei dovuto saperlo.

ounce (ouns) *n.* oncia.

our (our) *agg.poss.* nostro, nostri, nostra, nostre.

ours (ourz) *pron.poss.* il nostro, la nostra, i nostri, le nostre: a friend of **—**, un nostro amico.

ourselves (our·sĕlvz') *pron.rifl.pl.* noi stessi, ci: we will do it **—**, lo faremo noi stessi; by **—**, da soli.

oust (oust) *vt.* espellere; espropriare.

out (out) *n.* sporgenza; uscita; scappatoia; disaccordo. *agg.* spento; esterno, lontano; escluso; assente; errato; uscito, divulgato; terminato, disusato, fuori moda; spossato: **—** and **—** refusal, no chiaro e tondo; before the week is **—**, prima che termini la settimana; the book is just **—**, il libro è appena uscito; the secret is **—**, si è svelato il segreto. *avv.* fuori, al di fuori, via; completamente, esplicitamente: **—** of humor di malumore; **—** of money, senza soldi; **—** of touch with, isolato da; **—** of tune, stonato; to have it **—** with, farla fuori con; to speak **—**, parlare apertamente; to get **—**,

uscire; to find **—**, scoprire, smascherare; to be put **—**, essere malcontento.

out of *prep.* fuori di; privo di, senza; per, a causa di: **—** breath, senza respiro; **—** work, disoccupato; **—** charity, per carità; **—** print, esaurito (*di pubblicazione*); **—** date, antiquato.

outbalance (out·băl'ăns) *vt.* superare.

outboard (out'bōrd') *agg.*, *avv.* (*naut.*) fuoribordo: **—** motor, motore fuoribordo.

outbreak (out'brāk') *n.* esplosione, scoppio; insurrezione, tumulto; epidemia.

outburst (out'bûrst') *n.* esplosione, scoppio; slancio, accesso.

outcast (out'kàst') *n.*, *agg.* proscritto, reietto, abbandonato.

outcome (out'kŭm') *n.* risultato; conseguenza.

outcry (out'krī') *n.* grido, clamore.

outdo (out'dōō') *vt.* (*pass.* outdid, *pp.* outdone) superare.

outdoor (out'dōr') *agg.* esterno, all'aperto.

outdoors (out'dōrz') *avv.* all'aperto, fuori.

outer (out'ẽr) *agg.* esterno, esteriore.

outfit (out'fĭt') *n.* corredo, equipaggiamento; gruppo, unità. *vt.*, *vi.* equipaggiare, equipaggiarsi.

outgo (out'gō') *n.* uscita; spesa, esborso; risultato; prodotto. *vt.* (*pass.* outwent, *pp.* outgone) superare, sopravanzare. **—er** *n.* chi se ne va, l'uscente. **—ing** *agg.* che si allontana, uscente, in partenza; che spunta, sporgente; estrovertito, esuberante, espansivo. *n.* fuoriuscita; emanazione.

outgrowth (out'grōth') *n.* escrescenza.

outing (out'ĭng) *n.* passeggiata.

outlaw (out'lô') *n.* fuorilegge. *vt.* proscrivere, vietare, metter fuori legge, bandire.

outlay (out'lā') *n.* esborso.

outlet (out'lĕt) *n.* uscita, sbocco, sfogo, scarico.

outline (out'lĭn') *n.* contorno, profilo, abbozzo. *vt.* delineare, disegnare, abbozzare.

outlive (out·lĭv') *vt.* sopravvivere a.

outlook (out'lŏŏk')*n.* vedetta; prospettiva, visuale.

outlying (out'lī'ĭng) *agg.* periferico, esterno, distante.

outnumber (out·nŭm'bẽr) *vt.* superare in numero.

out-of-date *agg.* fuori di moda.

outpost (out'pōst') *n.* avamposto.

output (out'pŏŏt') *n.* produzione.

outrage (out'rāj) *n.* oltraggio, reato. *vt.* oltraggiare: to be —ed, sentirsi offeso; essere scandalizzato. — **ous** *agg.* oltraggioso; atroce; vergognoso, scandaloso.

outran (out·răn') *pass. di* to outrun.

outright (out'rīt') *agg.* completo; immediato, diretto. *avv.* immediatamente; completamente.

outrun (out·rŭn') *vt.* (*pass.* **outran**, *pp.* **outrun**) sorpassare, superare; battere in velocità.

outset (out'sĕt') *n.* inizio, partenza.

outshine (out·shīn') *vt.* (*pass.*, *pp.* **outshone**) eclissare, superare in splendore.

outside (out'sīd') *n.* esterno, parte esterna, margine: at the —, tutt'al più. *agg.* esterno, esteriore; superficiale. *avv.* esternamente; superficialmente, fuori. *prep.* fuori di, all'infuori di, oltre a.

outsider (out'sīd'ĕr) *n.* estraneo, forestiero; cavallo (*ecc.*) non favorito.

outsize (out'sīz') *n.* misura anormale. *agg.* fuori misura, sproporzionato.

outskirts (out'skŭrts') *n.pl.* margini; dintorni; sobborghi, periferia.

outsmart (out'smärt') *vt.* battere in astuzia.

outspoken (out'spō'kĕn) *agg.* chiaro, esplicito.

outstanding (out·stăn'dĭng) *agg.* insoluto (*non pagato*); sporgente; eminente: — bills, conti o fatture da pagare.

outstretch (out'strech') *vt.* protendere, tendere, allungare; stendere, tirare. —ed *agg.* teso, steso, proteso: with — arms, a braccia aperte.

outstrip (out·strĭp') *vt.* superare, lasciarsi alle spalle; eccellere (*su*) superare.

outward (out'wĕrd) *agg.* esterno, esteriore. *avv.* verso l'esterno, esternamente, esteriormente.

outweigh (out·wā') *vt.* superare in peso o importanza.

outwit (out·wĭt') *vt.* battere in astuzia, mettere nel sacco.

oval (ō'vặl) *agg.* ovale.

ovation (ō·vā'shŭn) *n.* ovazione.

oven (ŭv'ĕn) *n.* forno.

over (ō'vĕr) *agg.* finito; superiore; esterno; eccessivo. *prep.* su, sopra, al di sopra di oltre a, di là da; dalla parte opposta di; più di; a causa di: — the river, oltre il fiume; all — the country, per tutta la regione. *avv.* al di là; da una parte all'altra; da cima a fondo; d'avanzo; dalla parte opposta; al di sopra; troppo, attraverso; tutto, completamente:

all —, dappertutto, completamente; all — again, daccapo, di bel nuovo; — there, laggiù; — and —, ripetutamente; — again, di nuovo; to walk —, avvicinarsi.

overact (ō'vĕr·ăkt') *vt.*, *vi.* recitare (*una parte*) caricatamente, strafare.

over-all *agg.* totale, globale.

overall (ō'vĕr·ôl') *n.* spolverina; càmice.

overalls (ō'vĕr·ôlz') *n.* tuta.

overawe (ō'vĕr·ô') *vt.* intimidire, incutere rispetto a.

overbalance (ō'vĕr·băl'ặns) *vt.* superare (*in peso o importanza*); far perdere l'equilibrio a.

overbearing (ō'vĕr·bâr'ĭng) *agg.* tirannico, autoritario, prepotente.

overboard (ō'vĕr·bōrd') *avv.* (*naut.*) fuori bordo, in acqua: to go —, andare agli estremi; entusiasmarsi eccessivamente. *agg.* eccessivo.

overburden (ō'vĕr·bûr'd'n) *vt.* sovraccaricare.

overcast (ō'vĕr·kàst') *agg.* nuvoloso, cupo. *vt.*, *vi.* oscurare; rannuvolarsi; cucire a sopraggitto.

overcame (ō'vĕr·kām') *pass. di* to overcome.

overcharge (ō'vĕr·chärj') *vt.* sovraccaricare; chiedere un prezzo eccessivo.

overcoat (ō'vĕr·kōt') *n.* soprabito.

overcome (ō'vĕr·kŭm') *vt.*, *vi.* (*pass.* **overcame**, *pp.* **overcome**) superare, sopraffare, vincere.

overcrowd (ō'vĕr·kroud') *vt.* affollare eccessivamente, stipare.

overdo (ō'vĕr·dōō') *vt.*, *vi.* (*pass.* **overdid**, *pp.* **overdone**) esagerare, affaticare, cuocere troppo, strafare.

overdone (ō'vĕr·dŭn') *agg.* troppo cotto, esagerato.

overdose (ō'vĕr·dōs') *n.* dose eccessiva.

overdraft (ō'vĕr·dràft') *n.* (*banca*) prelevamento in scoperto; (*mil.*) leva esorbitante.

overdraw (ō'vĕr·drô') *vt.* (*pass.* **overdrew**, *pp.* **overdrawn**) tracciare attraverso; esagerare; (*banca*) prelevare allo scoperto.

overdue (ō'vĕr·dū') *agg.* scaduto, in ritardo.

overeat (ō'vĕr·ēt') *vt.*, *vi.* mangiare troppo, rimpinzarsi.

overestimate (ō'vĕr·ĕs'tĭ·māt) *vt.* sopravvalutare.

overexposure (ō'vĕr·ĕks·pō'zhĕr) *n.* (*fot.*) sovresposizione.

overflow (ō'vĕr·flō') *n.* inondazione; sovrabbondanza, eccedenza. *vt.*, *vi.* inondare, riempire troppo; traboccare, straripare, rigurgitare.

overgrown (ō'vĕr·grōn') *agg.* coperto (*di vegatazione*); troppo cresciuto: — boy, ragazzone.

overhang (ō'vĕr·hăng') *vt., vi.* (*pass., pp.* overhung) incombere; esser sospeso su; adornare; strapiombare, sovrastare.

overhaul (ō'vĕr·hôl') *vt.* ispezionare; guadagnar terreno su, raggiungere; (*naut.*) mollare; (*mecc.*) revisionare.

overhead (ō'vĕr·hĕd') *n.* spese generali. *agg.* superiore, di sopra, aereo. *avv.* in alto, sopra la testa.

overhear (ō'vĕr·hēr') *vt.* (*pass., pp.* overheard) udire per caso, sorprendere (*una conversazione*).

overlade (ō'vĕr·lād') *vt.* (*pp.* overladen) sovraccaricare.

overland (ō'vĕr·lănd') *agg.* terrestre. *avv.* per via di terra.

overlap (ō'vĕr·lăp') *vt., vi.* sovrapporre, sovrapporsi.

overload (ō'vĕr·lōd') *n.* sovraccarico. *vt.* sovraccaricare.

overlook (ō'vĕr·lŏŏk') *vt.* guardare (*dall'alto*); esaminare; sovrintendere; esser prospiciente a; passar sopra a, perdonare; omettere, trascurare.

overly (ō'vĕr·lĭ) *avv.* eccessivamente.

overmaster (ō'vĕr·más'tĕr) *vt.* sopraffare, dominare.

overmuch (ō'vĕr·mŭch') *n.* sovrappiù. *agg.* eccessivo. *avv.* eccessivamente.

overnight (ō'vĕr·nīt') *agg.* notturno, di una notte: — stop, pernottamento; — bag, valigetta per viaggi brevi. *avv.* durante la notte; dalla sera alla mattina; la sera precedente.

overpay (ō'vĕr·pā') *vt.* pagare troppo.

overpower (ō'vĕr·pou'ĕr) *vt.* sopraffare. **—ing** *agg.* irresistibile; eccessivo.

overproduction (ō'vĕr·prō·dŭk'shŭn) *n.* superproduzione.

overrate (ō'vĕr·rāt') *vt.* valutare troppo.

overreach (ō'vĕr·rēch') *vt., vi.* raggiungere; superare, sorpassare; ingannare; eccedere: to — oneself, passare i limiti.

override (ō'vĕr·rīd') *vt.* (*pass.* overrode, *pp.* overridden) affaticare (*un cavallo, ecc.*); trascurare; annullare; vincere (*un'opposizione*), superare (*ostacoli*).

overripe (ō'vĕr·rīp') *agg.* troppo maturo, arcimaturo.

overrule (ō'vĕr·rōōl') *vt., vi.* vincere, avere il sopravvento; respingere, invalidare, bocciare.

overrun (ō'vĕr·rŭn') *vt., vi.* (*pass.* overran, *pp.* overrun) invadere, dilagare, infestare; sorpassare, superare, travolgere; eccedere; (*tip.*) trasportare.

oversea (ō'vĕr·sē') *agg.* d'oltremare.

overseas (ō'vĕr·sēz') *avv.* oltremare.

oversee (ō'vĕr·sē') *vt.* ispezionare; sovrintendere.

overseer (ō'vĕr·sē'ĕr) *n.* sovrintendente; capofabbrica; critico.

overshadow (ō'vĕr·shăd'ō) *vt.* offuscare.

overshoe (ō'vĕr·shōō') *n.* soprascarpa.

oversight (ō'vĕr·sīt') *n.* sovrintendenza; svista, omissione, errore.

oversize (ō'vĕr·sīz') *n.* misura o mole eccessiva.

oversleep (ō'vĕr·slēp') *vt., vi.* (*pass., pp.* overslept) dormire oltre un'ora fissata *opp.* oltre il consueto.

overspread (ō'vĕr·sprĕd') *vt., vi.* (*pass., pp.* overspread) spandere, cospargere, spandersi.

overstate (ō'vĕr·stāt') *vt.* esagerare. **—ment** *n.* esagerazione.

overstep (ō'vĕr·stĕp') *vt.* oltrepassare: to — the bounds, superare i limiti.

overstock (ō'vĕr·stŏk') *n.* sovrabbondanza.

overstrain (ō'vĕr·strān') *n.* sforzo eccessivo, tensione eccessiva. *vt., vi.* tendere o sforzarsi troppo.

overt (ō'vûrt) *agg.* aperto, pubblico.

overtake (ō'vĕr·tāk') *vt.* (*pass.* overtook, *pp.* overtaken) raggiungere.

overtax (ō'vĕr·tăks') *vt.* tassare eccessivamente; mettere a troppo dura prova: to — one's strength, chiedere troppo alle proprie forze.

overthrow (ō'vĕr·thrō') *n.* sconvolgimento; disfatta. *vt.* (*pass.* overthrew, *pp.* overthrown) rovesciare, sconvolgere, sconfiggere.

overtime (ō'vĕr·tīm') *n.* ore straordinarie (*di lavoro*), straordinario.

overturn (ō'vĕr·tûrn') *vt.* rovesciare, capovolgere, sovvertire.

overweigh (ō'vĕr·wā') *vt.* superare nel peso; sopraffare, opprimere.

overweight (ō'vĕr·wāt') *n.* sovraccarico.

overwhelm (ō'vĕr·hwĕlm') *vt.* opprimere, sopraffare. **—ing** *agg.* opprimente, irresistibile.

overwork (ō'vĕr·wûrk') *n.* lavoro eccessivo. *vt., vi.* lavorare o far lavorare troppo; elaborare o adornare all'eccesso.

overwrought (ō'vĕr·rôt') *agg.* esausto; sovreccitato; troppo lavorato.

owe (ō) *vt.* dovere a, essere in debito con. *vi.* aver debiti.

owing (ō'ĭng) agg. dovuto, pendente (non pagato): — to, a causa di, in conseguenza di.

owl (oul) n. gufo, civetta, barbagianni.

own (ōn) agg. proprio, personale; caratteristico: of one's — accord, di propria iniziativa; on one's —, per conto proprio; a house of one's —, una casa propria; one's — people, la propria gente o famiglia; to come into one's —, entrare in

possesso del proprio; to hold one's —, restare della propria opinione. vt. possedere, essere proprietario di; riconoscere, ammettere, confessare.

owner (ōn'ĕr) n. proprietario. —ship n. proprietà.

ox (ŏks) n. (pl. oxen) bue.

oxide (ŏk'sĭd) n. ossido.

oxygen (ŏk'sĭ-jĕn) n. ossigeno.

oyster (ois'tĕr) n. ostrica.

ozone (ō'zōn) n. (chim.) ozono.

P

pace (pās) n. passo, andatura, ritmo. vt. misurare a passi; addestrare (cavalli, ecc.). vi. camminare, marciare, passeggiare, andare al passo.

pachyderm (păk'ĭ-dûrm) n. pachiderma.

pacific (pȧ-sĭf'ĭk) agg. pacifico.

pacify (păs'ĭ-fī) vt. pacificare, placare.

pack (păk) n. pacco, balla; mazzo (di carte da gioco); muta (di cani), turba; banchisa: — horse, cavallo da soma. vt., vi. imballare, impaccare, stipare; accalcarsi; fare i bagagli: to — off o away, andarsene a precipizio.

package (păk'ĭj) n. pacco, collo, balla.

packer (păk'ĕr) n. imballatore.

packet (păk'ĕt) n. pacchetto; vapore postale: — boat, piroscafo.

packing (păk'ĭng) n. imballaggio; (mecc.) guarnizione: — case, cassa d'imballaggio.

pact (păkt) n. patto, convenzione.

pad (păd) n. tampone, cuscinetto, imbottitura; blocco da annotazioni. vt. imbottire; ovattare. vi. camminare, andare a piedi. —ding n. imbottitura.

paddle (păd''l) n. pagaia, pala (di remo o ruota idraulica): — wheel, ruota a pale. vt., vi. remare, diguazzare, palpare, giocherellare.

paddock (păd'ŭk) n. prato annesso a una scuderia, recinto, paddock.

padlock (păd'lŏk') n. lucchetto. vt. chiudere col lucchetto.

pagan (pā'găn) n., agg. pagano. —ism n. paganesimo.

page (pāj) (1) n. pagina. vt. numerare le pagine di.

page (pāj) (2) n. paggio, valletto, inserviente d'albergo.

pageant (păj'ĕnt) n. corteo, carosello. —ry n. fasto, allegoria.

paid (pād) pass., pp. di to pay.

pail (pāl) n. secchio.

pain (pān) n. pena, sofferenza, dolore: to take —s to, prendersi il distur-

bo di. vt. affliggere, far soffrire. —ful agg. doloroso, penoso. —less agg. indolore; agevole.

painstaking (pānz'tāk'ĭng) agg. accurato, zelante, meticoloso.

paint (pānt) n. pittura, colore, vernice, belletto. vt., vi. dipingere, verniciare, truccare, imbellettarsi: to — the town red, farne di cotte e di crude. —brush n. pennello. —er n. pittore; (naut.) fune d'ormeggio. —ing n. pittura.

pair (pâr) n. paio, coppia. vt. accopiare, appaiare. vi. appaiarsi, accoppiarsi.

pajamas (pȧ-jä'mȧz) n.pl. pigiama.

pal (păl) n. amico, compagno.

palace (păl'ĭs) n. palazzo.

paladin (păl'ȧ-dĭn) n. paladino.

palatable (păl'ĭt-ȧ-b'l) agg. gustoso, gradevole; accettabile.

palate (păl'ĭt) n. palato; gusto.

palaver (pȧ-lăv'ĕr) n. conciliabolo, discussione. vi. confabulare.

pale (pāl) (1) n. palo, recinto; ambito. vt. cintare.

pale (pāl) (2) agg. pallido, scialbo, chiaro. vi. impallidire. —ness n. pallore.

palette (păl'ĕt) n. (pitt.) tavolozza.

paling (pāl'ĭng) n. palizzata.

palisade (păl'ĭ-sād') n. palizzata.

palisades n. pl. rupe, roccia.

pall (pôl) n. palio; drappo funebre. vt., vi. saziare, stancare, infastidire, disgustare, disgustarsi.

pallet (păl'ĕt) (1) n. tavolozza; paletta; ancora (d'orologio); (mecc.) dente d'arresto.

pallet (păl'ĕt) (2) n. pagliericcio.

palliate (păl'ĭ-āt) vt. attenuare, mitigare, alleviare.

pallid (păl'ĭd) agg. pallido, sbiadito.

palm (päm) n. palmo (della mano); palmizio; palma. vt. maneggiare; nascondere: to — something off on one, rifilare qualcosa a uno.

palmist (päm'ĭst) n. chiromante.

palmistry (päm'ĭs-trĭ) n. chiromanzia

palpable (păl'pá·b'l) *agg.* palpabile.
palpitate (păl'pĭ·tāt) *vi.* palpitare, pulsare.
palpitation (păl'pĭ·tā'shŭn) *n.* palpitazione.
palsied (pôl'sĭd) *agg.* intorpidito, paralizzato.
palsy (pôl'zĭ) *n.* paralisi.
paltry (pôl'trĭ) *agg.* meschino, esiguo.
pamper (păm'pĕr) *vt.* viziare, saziare.
pamphlet (păm'flĕt) *n.* opuscolo, libello.
pan (păn) *n.* padella; piatto (*di bilancia*); faccia; (*cinema*) panoramica. *vt.* cuocere in padella; ottenere, assicurarsi; vagliare; (*cinema*) muovere in panoramica. *vi.* riuscire, soddisfare; (*cinema*) carrellare.
pancake (păn'kāk') *n.* frittella.
pander (păn'dĕr) *n.* mezzano. *vt., vi.* fare da mezzano (*a*).
pane (pān) *n.* riquadro di vetro, vetro di finestra, pannello.
panel (păn'ĕl) *n.* pannello, riquadro; lista dei giurati; (*radio e T.V.*) gruppo di concorrenti a un quiz: — heating, riscaldamento a pannelli. *vt.* munire di pannelli; incorniciare.
pang (păng) *n.* dolore, trafittura, angoscia.
panic (păn'ĭk) *n., agg.* panico: — -stricken, atterrito. —ky *agg.* timoroso, atterrito.
pannikin (păn'ĭ·kĭn) *n.* pentolino.
pansy (păn'zĭ) *n.* viola del pensiero: (*gergo*) uomo effemminato; gagà; omosessuale.
pant (pănt) *n.* ansito, affanno. *vi.* ansare, palpitare.
panther (păn'thĕr) *n.* pantera; (*S.U.*) puma.
panties (păn'tĭz) *n. pl.* mutandine da donna *o* da bambino.
panting (păn'tĭng) *n.* ansito, affanno. *agg.* ansante, ansimante.
pantry (păn'trĭ) *n.* dispensa.
pants (pănts) *n.pl.* (*Ingl.*) mutande; (*S.U.*) calzoni.
papa (pä'pá) *n.* papà; vescovo.
papal (pā'pál) *agg.* papale.
paper (pā'pĕr) *n.* carta; documento; giornale; certificato; tema, saggio: — of pins, bustina di spilli; blotting —, carta assorbente; — knife, tagliacarte; — mill, cartiera; — money, carta moneta; — weight, fermacarte; on —, per iscritto. *agg.* di carta, cartaceo. *vt.* incartare, tappezzare con carta. —y *agg.* cartaceo.
papier-mâché (pā'pĕr·má·shä') *n.* cartapesta.

par (pär) *n.* parità, livello normale; tasso di scambio; valore, quotazione: — value, valore alla pari; at —, alla pari; on a — with, alla pari con; to feel above —, sentirsi superiore alla media.
parable (păr'á·b'l) *n.* parabola.
parachute (păr'á·shōōt) *n.* paracadute. *vt.* paracadutare. *vi.* lanciarsi col paracadute.
parachutist (păr'á·shōōt'ĭst) *n.* paracadutista.
parade (pá·rād') *n.* parata, esposizione, sfoggio, ostentazione. *vt., vi.* disporre in parata; esporre; sfilare; aggirarsi; ostentare, pavoneggiarsi.
paradise (păr'á·dīs) *n.* paradiso.
paradox (păr'á·dŏks) *n.* paradosso.
paraffin (păr'á·fĭn) *n.* paraffina.
paragon (păr'á·gŏn) *n.* paragone, modello, ideale.
paragraph (păr'á·gráf) *n.* paragrafo, trafiletto.
parallel (păr'ă·lĕl) *n.* parallelo; (*geom.*) parallela. *agg.* parallelo. *vt.* porre parallelamente; uguagliare; confrontare.
paralyze (păr'á·līz) *vt.* paralizzare.
paralysis (pá·răl'ĭ·sĭs) *n.* paralisi.
paramilitary (păr'á·mĭl'ĭ·tĕr'ĭ) *agg.* paramilitare.
paramount (păr'á·mount) *agg.* superiore, supremo, eminente, importantissimo.
paramour (păr'á·mŏŏr) *n.* amante.
parapet (păr'á·pĕt) *n.* parapetto.
parasite (păr'á·sīt) *n.* parassita.
parasol (păr'á·sŏl) *n.* parasole.
paratroop (păr'á·trōōp') *n.* corpo *o* scaglione di paracadutisti. —er *n.* (*mil.*) paracadutista.
parcel (pär'sĕl) *n.* parte, porzione; pacchetto; quantità: — post, servizio postale per pacchi. *vt.* spartire, dividere; involgere.
parch (pärch) *vt., vi.* disseccare, riardere, inaridirsi: —ed lips, labbra riarse.
parchment (pärch'mĕnt) *n.* pergamena.
pardon (pär'd'n) *n.* perdono; grazia: I beg your —, scusatemi. *vt.* perdonare, graziare. —able *agg.* perdonabile.
pare (pâr) *vt.* sbucciare; tosare, pelare; rifinire: to — down, ridurre.
parent (pâr'ĕnt) *n.* genitore, genitrice, origine: my parents, i miei genitori. —age *n.* parentado, stirpe. —al (-ĕnt'ăl) *agg.* dei genitori, paterno, materno.
parenthesis (pá·rĕn'thē·sĭs) *n.* (*pl.* **parentheses**) (-sēz) parentesi.
paring (pâr'ĭng) *n.* sbucciatura, scorza, buccia.

parish (păr'ĭsh) n. parrocchia, giurisdizione. —ioner (-ĭsh'-) n. parrocchiano.

Parisian (pȧ·rĭzh'ăn) n., agg. parigino.

park (părk) n. parco. vt. parcheggiare, posteggiare; collocare, depositare. —ing n. posteggio: — lot, posteggio per automobili, parcheggio; free —, posteggio gratuito; no —, vietato il posteggio, sosta vietata.

parlance (păr'lăns) n. linguaggio, terminologia, frasario.

parlay (păr'lā) vt., vi. rigiocare la puntata con relativa vincita in altra partita o in corsa successiva; ingrandire, ampliare; convertire; trasformare; sfruttare (qualcosa o qualcuno) per avere successo.

parley (păr'lĭ) n. trattativa, conferenza (spec. tra nemici). vi. parlamentare.

parliament (păr'lĭ·mĕnt) n. parlamento. —ary (-mĕnt'-) agg. parlamentare.

parlor (păr'lĕr) n. salotto: beauty —, salone di bellezza.

Parmesan (păr'mĕ·zăn') n., agg. parmigiano.

parochial (pȧ·rō'kĭ·ăl) agg. parrocchiale.

parody (păr'ô·dĭ) n. parodia. vt. parodiare.

parole (pȧ·rōl') n. parola d'onore, parola d'ordine; libertà condizionata: to put on —, concedere la libertà condizionata a.

paroxysm (păr'ŏk·sĭz'm) n. parossismo, accesso.

parquet (păr·kā') n. pavimento di legno; (S.U.) platea.

parrot (păr'ŭt) n. pappagallo. vt. scimmiottare; ripetere pappagallescamente.

parry (păr'ĭ) n. (sch.) parata. vt., vi. parare; eludere, evitare, sottrarsi.

parsley (părs'lĭ) n. prezzemolo.

parsnip (părs'nĭp) n. (bot.) pastinaca.

parson (păr's'n) n. parroco, curato.

parsonage (păr's'nĭj) n. canonica.

part (părt) n. parte; divisione; scriminatura; (pl.) dote (qualità): in foreign —s, all'estero; spare —s, pezzi di ricambio; do your —, fai il tuo dovere; for my —, per quel che mi riguarda; on my —, da parte mia; — and parcel of, parte integrante di. vt. dividere, spartire, separare. vi. separarsi, dividersi, fendersi: to — with, rinunciare a, abbandonare; to — from, separarsi da, allontanarsi da; to — company, separarsi, lasciarsi.

partake (păr·tāk') vt., vi. (pass. partook, pp. partaken) partecipare a,

comunicare, condividere, esser partecipe: to — of, prendere un po' di.

partial (păr'shăl) agg. parziale. —ity (ă-l'ĭ·tĭ) n. parzialità. —ly avv. parzialmente.

participant (păr·tĭs'ĭ·pănt) n., agg. partecipante.

participate (păr·tĭs'ĭ·pāt) vi. spartire, partecipare (a).

participation (păr·tĭs'ĭ·pā'shŭn) n. partecipazione.

participle (păr'tĭ·sĭ·p'l) n. participio.

particle (păr'tĭ·k'l) n. particella.

particular (pĕr·tĭk'û·lĕr) n. particolare, minuzia. agg. particolare, speciale; individuale; minuzioso, esigente, ricercato. —ly avv. particolarmente, particolareggiatamente.

parting (păr'tĭng) n. separazione, addio; scriminatura. agg. di commiato; divisorio; ultimo.

partisan (păr'tĭ·zăn) n., agg. partigiano.

partition (păr·tĭsh'ŭn) n. partizione, divisione, divisorio. vt. dividere, spartire, suddividere.

partly (părt'lĭ) avv. in parte, parzialmente.

partner (părt'nĕr) n. socio, compagno; cavaliere (ballerino), dama (ballerina); coniuge. —ship n. società.

partridge (păr'trĭj) n. pernice.

party (păr'tĭ) n. comitiva, partito, riunione, ricevimento; parte in causa; (mil.) distaccamento; (fam.) persona: shooting —, partita di caccia; — line, linea del partito.

parvenu (păr'vĕ·nū) n. villano rifatto, nuovo ricco.

pas (pä) n. passo di danza.

pass (pás) n. passo, passaggio; apertura; botta; salvacondotto, permesso, biglietto gratuito; punto, situazione. vt. (pass., pp. passed, past) attraversare, passare; trasmettere; approvare; promuovere (un esaminando, ecc.); tollerare. vi. passare; svenire; trascorrere; essere promosso: to come to —, accadere; to — away, svanire, sparire, morire; to — out, perdere conoscenza; distribuire; to — oneself off as, farsi passare per.

passable (pás'ȧ·b'l) agg. passabile; praticabile, navigabile, attraversabile.

passage (păs'ĭj) n. passaggio, traversata; corridoio, vestibolo; brano, passo.

passbook (pás'bŏŏk') n. libretto bancario.

passenger (păs'ĕn·jĕr) *n.* passeggiero, viaggiatore: — **pigeon,** piccione viaggiatore.

passer (pás'ĕr), **passer-by** *n.* (*pl.* passers-by) passante.

passion (păsh'ŭn) *n.* passione; collera: — **play,** sacra rappresentazione; **to fly into a —,** infuriarsi.

passionate (păsh'ŭn·ĭt) *agg.* appassionato.

passive (păs'ĭv) *n.*, *agg.* passivo.

passkey (pás'kē') *n.* chiave universale, comunella; grimaldello.

Passover (pás'ō'vĕr) *n.* Pasqua ebraica.

passport (pás'pōrt) *n.* passaporto.

password (pás'wûrd') *n.* parola d'ordine.

past (pást) *n.* passato. *agg.* passato, scorso, ultimo (*recente*): a — **master,** un intenditore, un maestro; — **tense,** passato remoto; **for some time —,** da un po' di tempo; **these — days,** in questi ultimi giorni. *prep.* dopo di; di là da; alla fine di; accanto a, davanti a: **half — twelve,** le dodici e mezzo; **it is — ten,** sono le dieci passate; — **all doubts,** fuori di dubbio; — **cure,** incurabile; — **bearing,** insopportabile; **to be — forty,** aver superato la quarantina. *avv.* oltre, innanzi.

paste (pást) *n.* colla; pasta: **alimentary —,** pasta alimentare. *vt.* incollare, appicciccare.

pasteboard (pást'bōrd') *n.* cartone.

pasteurize (păs'tĕr·ĭz) *vt.* pastorizzare.

pastime (pás'tĭm') *n.* passatempo.

pastor (pás'tĕr) *n.* pastore.

pastry (pás'trĭ) *n.* pasticceria: — **cook,** pasticciere; — **shop,** pasticceria.

pasturage (pás'tûr·ĭj) *n.* pascolo.

pasture (pás'tûr) *n.* pastura, pascolo. *vt.* pasturare. *vi.* pascolare.

pasty (păs'tĭ) *agg.* pastoso; flaccido, smorto.

P.A. system *vedi* Public-Address system.

pat (păt) *n.* colpetto, manata; panetto di burro. *agg.* pronto, adatto, opportuno: **to have a lesson —,** sapere una lezione a menadito; **to stand —,** restare immobile. *avv.* opportunamente. *vt.* dare un colpetto a, battere leggermente: **to — oneself on the back,** congratularsi da soli *o* con se stessi.

patch (păch) *n.* pezza, toppa; benda; neo artificiale; lembo di terra. *vt.* rattoppare, raffazzonare: **to — up a quarrel,** comporre una controversia.

patchwork (păch'wûrk') *n.* lavoro a toppe; raffazzonatura.

pate (păt) *n.* testa, zucca, cranio.

patent (păt'ĕnt) *n.* patente, brevetto, privilegio. *agg.* (pā'-) manifesto, patente; brevettato: —**leather shoes,** scarpe di vernice *o* di copale; — **medicine,** specialità medicinale. *vt.* brevettare.

paternal (pȧ·tûr'năl) *agg.* paterno.

paternity (pȧ·tûr'nĭ·tĭ) *n.* paternità.

path (páth) *n.* sentiero, percorso, via, traiettoria.

pathetic (pȧ·thĕt'ĭk) *agg.* commovente; patetico. *n.* espressione *o* gesto patetico.

pathos (pā'thŏs) *n.* patos.

pathway (páth'wā') *n.* sentiero.

patience (pā'shĕns) *n.* pazienza.

patient (pā'shĕnt) *n.*, *agg.* paziente.

patriarch (pā'trĭ·ärk) *n.* patriarca.

patrimony (pă'trĭ·mō'nĭ) *n.* patrimonio ereditario.

patriot (pā'trĭ·ŭt) *n.* patriota. —**ic** (-ŏt'ĭk) *agg.* patriottico. —**ism** *n.* patriottismo.

patrol (pȧ·trōl') *n.* pattuglia; agente. *vt.*, *vi.* perlustrare, pattugliare. —**man** *n.* poliziotto.

patron (pā'trŭn) *n.* patrono; sostenitore; cliente fedele: — **saint,** santo patrono. —**age** *n.* patronato, egida; protezione; clientela. —**ess** *n.* protettrice, patronessa.

patronize (pā'trŭn·ĭz) *vt.* proteggere, incoraggiare; trattare con condiscendenza; frequentare di preferenza (*un negozio, un ritrovo*), essere cliente abituale di.

patronizing *agg.* condiscendente, protettivo. —**ly** *avv.* con degnazione.

patter (păt'ĕr) *n.* chiacchiere, imbonimento; cantilena; crepitio, trepestio. *vt.*, *vi.* borbottare, recitare, picchiettare, camminare a passetti rapidi.

pattern (păt'ĕrn) *n.* modello, disegno, schema, motivo, campione, esempio: — **book,** campionario. *vt.* foggiare, decorare: **to — oneself after,** seguire l'esempio di, imitare; **to — something after,** modellare qualcosa a imitazione di. *vi.* comportarsi.

patty (păt'ĭ) *n.* pasticcino; polpetta.

paunch (pônch) *n.* pancia; rumine.

pauper (pô'pĕr) *n.* povero.

pause (pôz) *n.* pausa, interruzione, indugio. *vi.* fare una pausa, indugiare, sostare.

pave (pāv) *vt.* pavimentare, appianare: **to — the way,** appianare il terreno.

pavement (pāv'mĕnt) *n.* selciato; marciapiede.

pavilion (pȧ·vĭl'yŭn) *n.* padiglione, tenda.

paving (păv'ĭng) n. pavimentazione.

paw (pô) n. zampa. vt. dare zampate a; raspare con le zampe; maneggiare goffamente. vi. zampettare, scalpitare.

pawn (pôn) n. pegno, garanzia, ostaggio; (scacchi) pedina. vt. impegnare, dare in pegno. —broker n. prestatore su pegno. —shop n. monte di pegni. — ticket polizza di pegno.

pay (pā) n. paga, salario, retribuzione. vt. (pass., pp. paid) pagare, rimunerare, tributare; (naut.) mollare: to — attention, fare attenzione; to — back, restituire, rifondere; to — down, pagare in contanti; to — homage, rendere omaggio; to — one's respects, presentare i saluti; to — a visit, fare visita. vi. rendere, essere redditizio, valer la pena, pagare; (naut.) portarsi sottovento: to — off, liquidare; vendicarsi; rendere, essere proficuo; to — round, virare di bordo; to — the piper, pagare lo scotto. —able agg. pagabile. — day giorno di paga. —er n. pagatore. —master n. ufficiale pagatore. —ment n. pagamento. —off n. pagamento, liquidazione; conseguenza; rendita, compenso; apice, acme, soluzione; fattore decisivo. agg. risolutivo, decisivo; proficuo. —roll n. libro paga.

pea (pē) n. pisello.

peace (pēs) n. pace, calma, silenzio: to hold one's —, tacere. —able agg. pacifico. —ful agg. pacifico, quieto. —maker n. paciere.

peach (pēch) n. pesca: — tree, pesco.

peacock (pē'kŏk') n. pavone.

peak (pēk) n. picco, cima; punta, punto massimo; visiera. —ed agg. appuntito; a visiera; deperito.

peal (pēl) n. squillo: — of laughter, risata squillante; — of thunder, tuono. vt., vi. sonare, risonare.

peanut (pē'nŭt') n. arachide.

pear (pâr) n. pera: — tree, pero.

pearl (pûrl) n. perla, granulo.

pearly (pûrl'ĭ) agg. perlaceo.

peasant (pĕz'ănt) n. contadino. agg. campagnuolo.

pease (pēz) pl. di pea.

peat (pēt) n. torba: — bog, torbiera.

pebble (pĕb''l) n. ciottolo; sassolino.

peccadillo (pĕk'á·dĭl'ō) n. peccatuccio.

peck (pĕk) n. beccata; misura per cereali (circa 9 litri): a — of trouble, un mare di guai. vt., vi. beccare.

peculation (pĕk'ū·lā'shŭn) n. peculato, malversazione.

peculiar (pē·kūl'yēr) agg. peculiare, particolare. —ity (-ăr'ĭ·tĭ) n. particolarità, peculiarità.

pedagogue (pĕd'á·gŏg) n. pedagogo.

pedal (pĕd'ăl) n. pedale: — pushers, calzoni femminili alla pescatora. vi. pedalare, usare il pedale.

pedant (pĕd'ănt) n. pedante. —ic (-ănt'ĭk) agg. pedantesco.

peddle (pĕd''l) vt. vendere alla spicciolata. vi. fare il venditore ambulante.

peddler (pĕd'lēr) n. venditore ambulante.

pedestal (pĕd'ĕs·tăl) n. piedestallo.

pedestrian (pē·dĕs'trĭ·ăn) n. pedone, podista. agg. pedestre. —ism n. podismo.

pedicab (pĕd'ĭ·kăb') n. ciclotassì.

pedigree (pĕd'ĭ·grē) n. genealogia, albero genealogico.

pedlar (pĕd'lēr) vedi peddler.

peek (pēk) vedi peep.

peel (pēl) n. buccia, scorza; pala, paletta. vt. pelare, sbucciare, mondare. vi. spellarsi, squamarsi: to keep one's eyes peeled, vigilare, stare con gli occhi aperti.

peep (pēp) n. occhiata, sguardo furtivo; fessura; pigolìo. vi. sbirciare; sbucare, apparire; pigolare. —hole n. spioncino.

peer (pēr) (1) vi. apparire, spuntare, sbucare; sbirciare; fissare.

peer (pēr) (2) n. pari; Pari (d'Inghilterra). —less agg. impareggiabile.

peeve (pēv) vt. irritare, seccare: to get peeved, seccarsi.

peevish (pē'vĭsh) agg. petulante; stizzoso; di malumore.

peg (pĕg) n. cavicchio, piuolo, zipolo; (mus.) bischero: to come down a —, abbassare le arie; to take someone down a —, far abbassare la cresta, umiliare. vt. incavicchiare, incavigliare: to — away, lavorare senza sosta; to — out, morire.

pellet (pĕl'ĕt) n. pallina, pallottola, pallino, pillola.

pell-mell (pĕl'mĕl') agg. disordinato. avv. alla rinfusa, disordinatamente.

pellucid (pĕ·lū'sĭd) agg. limpido, trasparente.

pelt (pĕlt) (1) n. scroscio, colpo, velocità. vt. tempestare, scagliare. vi. scrosciare: to — with, tempestare di.

pelt (pĕlt) (2) n. cuoio grezzo.

pen (pĕn) (1) n. recinto, ovile, pollaio; prigione. vt. (pass., pp. penned, pent) rinchiudere, imprigionare, reprimere.

pen (pĕn) (2) n. penna, piuma: fountain —, penna stilografica; — name, pseudonimo. vt. vergare, redigere. —holder n. portapenne; cannuccia.

penal (pē'nắl) *agg.* penale: — servitude, lavori forzati. —ty *n.* punizione, multa, penalità; fio.

penance (pĕn'ắns) *n.* penitenza.

pence (pĕns) *vedi* penny.

penchant (pän'shän') *n.* propensione.

pencil (pĕn'sĭl) *n.* matita: — sharpener, temperamatite. *vt.* disegnare (*o* scrivere) a matita.

pendant (pĕn'dắnt) *n.* ciondolo, pendaglio; cosa gemella; stendardo.

pendent (pĕn'dĕnt) *agg.* pendente, sospeso.

pending (pĕnd'ĭng) *agg.* pendente, indeciso, in corso, incombente. *prep.* durante, fino a, in attesa di.

pendulum (pĕn'dụ̄·lŭm) *n.* pendolo, bilanciere.

penetrate (pĕn'ē·trāt) *vt.*, *vi.* penetrare, permeare, capire.

penetrating (pĕn'ē·trāt'ĭng) *agg.* penetrante, perspicace.

penetration (pĕn'ē·trā'shŭn) *n.* penetrazione, perspicacia.

penguin (pĕn'gwĭn) *n.* pinguino.

penicillin (pĕn'ĭ·sĭl'ĭn) *n.* penicillina.

peninsula (pĕn·ĭn'sụ̄·lá) *n.* penisola.

penitence (pĕn'ĭ·tĕns) *n.* pentimento, penitenza.

penitent (pĕn'ĭ·tĕnt) *n.*, *agg.* penitente.

penitentiary (pĕn'ĭ·tĕn'shá·rĭ) *n.*, *agg.* penitenziario.

penknife (pĕn'nīf') *n.* temperino.

penman (pĕn'măn) *n.* scrivano, autore. —ship *n.* scrittura.

pennant (pĕn'ắnt) *n.* pennone (*vessillo*), fiamma; (*naut.*) pennoncello.

penniless (pĕn'ĭ·lĕs) *agg.* povero, squattrinato.

penny (pĕn'ĭ) *n.* (*pl.* pennies *per indicare il numero di monete*, pence [*Ingl.*] *per indicare l'ammontare*) soldo (1/12 di scellino); (*S.U.*) un cent. di dollaro: a pretty —, una bella somma.

pension (pĕn'shŭn) *n.* pensione. *vt.* pensionare.

pensive (pĕn'sĭv) *agg.* pensieroso.

pent (pĕnt) *agg.* (*pass.*, *pp. di* to pen) chiuso, rinchiuso: —up feelings, sentimenti repressi.

penthouse (pĕnt'hous') *n.* tettoia, riparo; sopralzo; appartamento di lusso costruito sul tetto.

penurious (pē·nū'rĭ·ŭs) *agg.* avaro, meschino.

peon (pē'ŏn) *n.* bracciante.

people (pē'p'l) *n.* popolo; massa, gente; famiglia, parentela. *vt.* popolare.

pep (pĕp) *n.* vigore, vivacità. *vt.* rinvigorire.

pepper (pĕp'ẽr) *n.* pepe; peperone: — box, — caster, pepaiuola. *vt.* im-

pepare; tempestare (*di colpi*), crivellare.

peppercorn (pĕp'ẽr·kôrn') *n.* grano di pepe; inezia.

peppermint (pĕp'ẽr·mĭnt) *n.* menta piperina.

peppery (pĕp'ẽr·ĭ) *agg.* pepato, pungente; collerico.

peppy (pĕp'ĭ) *agg.* energico, vivace.

per (pẽr) *prep.* per, per ogni: — annum, all'anno, annualmente; — capita, a testa; — cent, per cento; ten cents — dozen, dieci centesimi la dozzina.

perambulator (pẽr·ăm'bụ̄·lā'tẽr) *n.* carrozzina per bambini.

perceive (pẽr·sēv') *vt.* percepire, scorgere, sentire, capire.

per cent (pẽr·sĕnt') per cento. —age *n.* percentuale, interesse, profitto.

perceptible (pẽr·sĕp'tĭ·b'l) *agg.* percettibile, sensibile.

perception (pẽr·sĕp'shŭn) *n.* percezione.

perch (pûrch) (1) *n.* pesce persico.

perch (pûrch) (2) *n.* trespolo, posatoio, palo, pertica. *vt.* mettere in bilico. *vi.* appollaiarsi, posarsi.

perchance (pẽr·chàns') *avv.* per caso, forse.

percolate (pûr'kō·lāt) *vt.*, *vi.* filtrare, colare.

percolator (pûr'kō·lā'tẽr) *n.* filtro.

percussion (pẽr·kŭsh'ŭn) *n.* percussione: — cap, percussore; — fuse, detonatore.

perdition (pẽr·dĭsh'ŭn) *n.* perdizione, rovina.

peremptory (pẽr·ĕmp'tō·rĭ) *agg.* perentorio.

perennial (pẽr·ĕn'ĭ·ắl) *n.* perenne.

perfect (pûr'fĕkt) *agg.* perfetto, completo. *n.* perfetto (*del verbo*). *vt.* perfezionare, completare. —ion (-fĕk'-) *n.* perfezione. —ly *avv.* perfettamente.

perfidious (pẽr·fĭd'ĭ·ŭs) *agg.* perfido, infido.

perfidy (pûr'fĭ·dĭ) *n.* perfidia.

perforate (pûr'fō·rāt) *vt.* perforare.

perforce (pẽr·fôrs') *avv.* necessariamente, per forza.

perform (pẽr·fôrm') *vt.* rappresentare, eseguire, compiere, adempire. *vi.* prodursi; funzionare. —ance *n.* esibizione, rappresentazione, esecuzione, prodezza; funzionamento, rendimento.

perfume (pûr'fūm) *n.* profumo. *vt.* profumare.

perfumery (pẽr·fūm'ẽr·ĭ) *n.* profumeria.

perfunctory (pẽr·fŭngk'tō·rĭ) *agg.* negligente, superficiale, macchinale.

perhaps (pĕr·hăps') *avv.* forse: — so, può darsi.

peril (pĕr'ĭl) *n.* pericolo. **—ous** *agg.* pericoloso.

perimeter (pĕ·rĭm'ê·tĕr) *n.* perimetro.

period (pēr'ĭ·ŭd) *n.* periodo, durata, termine; (*gramm.*) punto fermo. **—ic** (-ŏd'ĭk) *agg.* periodico. **—ical** *n.* periodico (*pubblicazione*). *agg.* periodico.

periscope (pĕr'ĭs·skōp) *n.* periscopio.

perish (pĕr'ĭsh) *vi.* perire; sparire; deteriorarsi. **—able** *agg.* mortale; caduco; deteriorabile.

peritonitis (pĕr'ĭ·tō·nī'tĭs) *n.* peritonite.

periwig (pĕr'ĭ·wĭg) *n.* parrucca.

perjure (pûr'jĕr) *vt.*, *vi.* spergiurare: to — oneself, giurare il falso.

perjurer (pûr'jĕr·ẽr) *n.* spergiuro (*chi spergiura*).

perjury (pûr'jĕr·ĭ) *n.* spergiuro (*giuramento falso*); falsa testimonianza.

perk (pûrk) *agg.* spavaldo, impudente; azzimato; orgoglioso. *vt.* agghindare. *vi.* darsi delle arie; tener alta la testa.

permanence (pûr'mȧ·nĕns) *n.* permanenza; durata.

permanent (pûr'mȧ·nĕnt) *agg.* permanente, immutabile.

permeate (pûr'mê·āt) *vt.* permeare, penetrare, saturare. *vi.* permearsi, diffondersi.

permissible (pĕr·mĭs'ĭ·b'l) *agg.* lecito.

permission (pĕr·mĭsh'ŭn) *n.* permesso.

permit (pĕr·mĭt') *n.* permesso, autorizzazione, licenza. *vt.*, *vi.* permettere.

pernicious (pĕr·nĭsh'ŭs) *agg.* pernicioso.

peroxide (pĕr·ŏk'sĭd) *n.* acqua ossigenata.

perpendicular (pûr'pĕn·dĭk'û·lẽr) *n.*, *agg.* perpendicolare.

perpetrate (pûr'pê·trāt) *vt.* perpetrare.

perpetual (pĕr·pĕt'û·ăl) *agg.* perpetuo.

perpetuate (pĕr·pĕt'û·āt) *vt.* perpetuare.

perplex (pĕr·plĕks') *vt.* confondere, render perplesso. **—ed** *agg.* perplesso, imbarazzato. **—ity** *n.* perplessità, imbarazzo.

perquisite (pûr'kwĭ·zĭt) *n.* incerto, gratifica; introito, reddito.

persecute (pûr'sê·kūt) *vt.* perseguitare.

persecution (pûr'sê·kū'shŭn) *n.* persecuzione.

perseverance (pûr'sê·vēr'ăns) *n.* perseveranza.

persevere (pûr'sê·vēr') *vi.* perseverare.

persevering *agg.* perseverante.

persiflage (pûr'sĭ·fläzh) *n.* superficialità, frivolezza (*di tono*); ironia, canzonatura.

persist (pĕr·sĭst') *vi.* persistere, perseverare; ostinarsi. **—ence** *n.* persistenza, tenacia; ostinazione. **—ent** *agg.* tenace, persistente; ostinato.

person (pûr's'n) *n.* persona, personaggio. **—able** *agg.* bello, presentabile. **—age** *n.* personaggio. **—al** *agg.* personale. **—ality** (-ăl'ĭ·tĭ) *n.* personalità.

personate (pûr'sŭn·āt) *vt.* impersonare.

personnel (pûr'sŏ·nĕl') *n.* personale; equipaggio: — director, capo del personale.

perspective (pĕr·spĕk'tĭv) *n.* prospettiva, veduta. *agg.* prospettico.

perspicacious (pûr'spĭ·kā'shŭs) *agg.* perspicace, sagace.

perspicacity (pûr'spĭ·kăs'ĭ·tĭ) *n.* perspicacia.

perspiration (pûr'spĭ·rā'shŭn) *n.* traspirazione.

perspire (pĕr·spīr') *vt.*, *vi.* sudare, traspirare, trasudare.

persuade (pĕr·swād') *vt.* persuadere: to — into, indurre a; to — from, dissuadere.

persuasion (pĕr·swā'zhŭn) *n.* persuasione, persuasiva; fede.

persuasive (pĕr·swā'sĭv) *agg.* persuasivo.

pert (pûrt) *agg.* vivace; insolente; spavaldo.

pertain (pĕr·tān') *vi.* appartenere, riferirsi, avere attinenza (*con*).

pertinacity (pûr'tĭ·năs'ĭ·tĭ) *n.* pertinacia.

pertinent (pûr'tĭ·nĕnt) *agg.* adeguato, pertinente, attinente, opportuno.

pertly (pûrt'lĭ) *avv.* vivacemente; insolentemente, spavaldamente.

pertness (pûrt'nĕs) *n.* vivacità; insolenza, spavalderia.

perturb (pĕr·tûrb') *vt.* perturbare.

perusal (pê·rōoz'ăl) *n.* esame, lettura.

peruse (pê·rōoz') *vt.* leggere, esaminare attentamente.

pervade (pĕr·vād') *vt.* pervadere, invadere, permeare.

perverse (pĕr·vûrs') *agg.* perverso, bizzarro, ostinato.

pervert (pĕr·vûrt') *vt.* pervertire, deformare. *n.* (pûr'vûrt) pervertito.

pesky (pĕs'kĭ) *agg.* noioso.

pessimism (pĕs'ĭ·mĭz'm) *n.* pessimismo.

pessimist (pĕs'ĭ·mĭst) *n.* pessimista.

pest (pĕst) *n.* peste, flagello.

pester (pĕs'tĕr) *vt.* tormentare, perseguitare, assillare.

pestilence (pĕs'tĭ·lĕns) *n.* pestilenza.

pestle (pĕs''l) n. pestello.
pet (pĕt) (1) n. stizza.
pet (pĕt) (2) n. beniamino, preferito, prediletto, coccolo, animale domestico. agg. caro, prediletto: — aversion, bestia nera; — name, vezzeggiativo. vt. prediligere, coccolare.
petal (pĕt''l) n. petalo.
peter (pē'tẽr) vi.: to — out (gergo) esaurirsi, affievolirsi; fare cilecca.
petition (pē·tĭsh'ŭn) n. petizione. vt. supplicare, presentare una petizione a. —er n. postulante, richiedente.
petrel (pĕt'rĕl) n. procellaria.
petrify (pĕt'rĭ·fī) vt. petrificare, pietrificare. vi. petrificarsi.
petrol (pĕt'rŏl) n. (Ingl.) benzina.
petroleum (pē·trō'lē·ŭm) n. petrolio naturale.
petticoat (pĕt'ĭkōt) n. gonnella, sottana.
pettifog (pĕt'ĭ·fŏg) vi. fare l'azzeccagarbugli; cavillare. —ger n. azzeccagarbugli, leguleio; novizio; incompetente, scagnozzo. —gery n. trucchi, cavilli. —ging agg. cavilloso, meschino; insignificante.
pettiness (pĕt'ĭ·nĕs) n. piccolezza, meschinità.
pettish (pĕt'ĭsh) agg. dispettoso, petulante.
petty (pĕt'ĭ) agg. piccolo, minimo; meschino, trascurabile; minore (di reato): — cash, piccola cassa; — officer, sottufficiale di marina.
petulance (pĕt' û.lᾰns) n. petulanza.
petulant (pĕt'û.lᾰnt) agg. petulante.
pew (pū) n. banco di chiesa.
pewter (pū'tẽr) n. peltro.
phalanx (fā'lᾰngks) n. falange.
phantom (fᾰn'tŭm) n. fantasma.
Pharaoh (fâr'ō) n. faraone.
Pharisee (fᾰr'ĭ·sē) n. fariseo.
pharmacist (fär'má·sĭst) n. farmacista.
pharmacy (fär'má·sĭ) n. farmacia.
pharynx (fär'ĭngks) n. faringe.
phase (fāz) n. fase.
pheasant (fĕz'ᾰnt) n. fagiano.
phenomenon (fē·nŏm'ē·nŏn) n. (pl. phenomena) fenomeno.
phial (fī'ᾰl) n. fiala.
philanthropist (fĭ·lᾰn'thrō·pĭst) n. filantropo.
philanthropy (fĭ·lᾰn'thrō·pĭ) n. filantropia.
philharmonic (fĭl'här·mŏn'ĭk) agg. filarmonico.
Philistine (fĭ·lĭs'tĭn) n., agg. filisteo.
philologist (fĭ·lŏl'ō·jĭst) n. filologo.
philology (fĭ·lŏl'ō·jĭ) n. filologia.
philosopher (fĭ·lŏs'ō·fẽr) n. filosofo.

philosophical (fĭl'ō·sŏf'ĭ·kᾰl) agg. filosofico.
philosophize (fĭ·lŏs'ō·fīz) vi. filosofeggiare.
philosophy (fĭ·lŏs'ō·fĭ) n. filosofia.
philter, philtre (fĭl'tẽr) n. filtro d'amore.
phlegm (flĕm) n. flemma; muco.
phlegmatic (flĕg·mᾰt'ĭk) agg. flemmatico.
phone (fōn) n. telefono. vt., vi. telefonare.
phoneme (fō'nēm) n. fonema.
phonemics (fō·nē'mĭks) n. fonematica, fonologia.
phonetic (fō·nĕt'ĭk) agg. fonetico.
phonetics n. fonetica.
phonogram (fō'nō·grᾰm) n. fonogramma.
phonograph (fō'nō·grᾰf) n. fonografo.
phonophile (fō'nō·fĭl) n., appassionato di dischi di alta fedeltà.
phony (fō'nĭ) (gergo) n. contraffazione, impostore. agg. contraffatto, fraudolento, falso, fasullo.
phosphorescence (fŏs'fō·rĕs'ĕns) n. fosforescenza.
phosphorescent (fŏs'fō·rĕs'ĕnt) agg. fosforescente.
phosphorus (fŏs'fō·rŭs) n. fosforo.
photo (fō'tō) n. foto, fotografia. agg. fotografico: — finish (sport), arrivo a fotografia.
photocell (fō'tō·sĕl') n. cellula fotoelettrica.
photofinishing n. (fot.) sviluppo e stampa.
photoflash lamp n. (fot.) lampada lampo.
photogenic (fō'tō·jĕn'ĭk) agg. fotogenico.
photograph (fō'tō·grᾰf) n. fotografia. vt. fotografare. —er (-ŏg'-) n. fotografo.
photography (fō·tŏg'rᾰ·fĭ) n. fotografia (arte).
photomontage (fo'tō·mŏn·täzh') n. fotomontaggio.
photomural (fō'tō·mū'rᾰl) n. pannello fotografico.
photoplay (fō'tō·plā') n. film, pellicola; copione.
phrase (frāz) n. frase. vt. formulare, esprimere.
phrenology (frē·nŏl'ō·jĭ) n. frenologia.
physic (fĭz'ĭk) n. medicina, rimedio, purgante. vt. curare, purgare. —al agg. fisico.
physician (fĭ·zĭsh'ᾰn) n. medico.
physicist (fĭz'ĭ·sĭst) n. fisico.
physics (fĭz'ĭks) n. fisica.
physiological (fĭz'ĭ·ō·lŏj'ĭ·kᾰl) agg. fisiologico.
physiologist (fĭz'ĭ·ŏl'ō·jĭst) n. fisiologo.
physiology (fĭz'ĭ·ŏl'ō·jĭ) n. fisiologia.

physique (fĭ·zēk') *n.* costituzione fisica.

pianist (pē'à·nĭst) *n.* pianista.

piano (pĭ·ăn'ō) *n.* pianoforte: **grand** —, piano a coda.

piazza (pĭ·ăz'à) *n.* piazza; portico; veranda.

pick (pĭk) *n.* piccone; grimaldello; scelta, diritto di scelta; fior fiore; raccolto: **ice** —, scalpello per il ghiaccio. *vt., vi.* cogliere, spiccare; scegliere; pulire, spennare; forzare (*una serratura*); togliere, separare (*con le dita*); pungere; rubacchiare: **to — a hole in somebody's coat,** trovare a ridire su qualcuno; **to — flaws,** trovare difetti; **to — a quarrel with,** attaccar briga con; **to — up,** raccogliere; captare; imparare; rimettersi; **to — up speed,** accelerare, acquistare velocità.

pickax (pĭk'ăks') *n.* piccone.

picket (pĭk'ĕt) *n.* piuolo, palo; picchetto, pattuglia avanzata; scioperante in servizio di guardia: **— boat,** lancia addetta alla vigilanza portuale. *vt., vi.* picchettare, legare a un palo, far la guardia a, esser di picchetto.

pickle (pĭk'l) *n.* sottaceto; posizione spiacevole: **to be in a fine —,** essere in un bel pasticcio. *vt.* mettere sotto aceto.

picklock (pĭk'lŏk') *n.* grimaldello; scassinatore.

pickpocket (pĭk'pŏk'ĕt) *n.* borsaiuolo.

pickup (pĭk'ŭp') *n.* raccolta, radunamento; scelta; miglioramento; ripresa (*di attività*); affare colto al volo; pasto improvvisato; conoscenza casuale, donna conosciuta per la strada; passeggiero raccolto a bordo; oggetto trovato o rubato; (*auto.*) ripresa o accelerazione; camioncino scoperto; fonorivelatore, pickup; (*giorn.*) piombo pronto per la stampa.

picnic (pĭk'nĭk) *n.* merenda all'aperto.

pictograph (pĭk'tō·gráf) *n.* pittogramma; diagramma a figure, schema grafico.

picture (pĭk'tŭr) *n.* quadro; illustrazione, immagine; pittura; ritratto; cinematografia: **— frame,** cornice; **— gallery,** pinacoteca; **— window,** finestrone panoramico. *vt.* dipingere, rappresentare, descrivere, immaginare.

pie (pī) *n.* timballo, pasticcio, torta ripiena: **to have a finger in the —,** avere le mani in pasta.

piece (pēs) *n.* pezzo; frammento: **— of advice,** consiglio; **— of money,** moneta; **— of news,** notizia; **— of**

nonsense, sciocchezza. *vt.* rappezzare, mettere insieme, unire. *vi.* mangiucchiare fuori dei pasti. **—meal** *agg., avv.* a pezzi, a poco a poco, gradatamente.

pier (pēr) *n.* gettata, molo, pontone, banchina; stipite, spalletta.

pierce (pērs) *vt., vi.* trafiggere, perforare, penetrare.

piercing (pēr'sĭng) *agg.* penetrante, pungente, lacerante (*di grido*).

piety (pī'ĕ·tĭ) *n.* pietà, devozione.

pig (pĭg) *n.* maiale; pane (*di metallo*): **guinea —,** cavia; **to buy a — in a poke,** comprare alla cieca.

pigeon (pĭj'ŭn) *n.* piccione: **carrier —,** piccione viaggiatore: **that's your —,** è affar vostro.

pigeonhole (pĭj'ŭn·hōl') *n.* nicchia di colombaia; casella. *vt.* archiviare, incasellare.

piggish (pĭg'ĭsh) *agg.* maialesco; cocciuto, ostinato.

pighead (pĭg'hĕd') *n.* ostinato, testa dura. **—ed** *agg.* testardo, cocciuto.

pigmy (pĭg'mĭ) *n.* pigmeo.

pigsty (pĭg'stī') *n.* porcile.

pigtail (pĭg'tāl') *n.* codino.

pike (pīk) *n.* picca, lancia, picco; (*ittiol.*) luccio.

pilchard (pĭl'chĕrd) *n.* (*ittiol.*) sardina.

pile (pīl) *n.* mucchio; rogo; catasta; edificio; pelo (*dei tessuti*); pila; gruzzolo, piuolo, palo: **— driver,** battipalo; **atomic —,** pila atomica. *vt., vi.* accumulare, ammonticchiare; ammassarsi, accumularsi.

piles (pīlz) *n.* emorroidi.

pilfer (pĭl'fĕr) *vt., vi.* rubacchiare. **—er** *n.* ladruncolo.

pilgrim (pĭl'grĭm) *n.* pellegrino.

pilgrimage (pĭl'grĭ·mĭj) *n.* pellegrinaggio.

pill (pĭl) *n.* pillola; (*gergo*) sigaretta; rompiscatole, persona asfissiante.

pillage (pĭl'ĭj) *n.* saccheggio, rapina. *vt., vi.* saccheggiare, depredare.

pillar (pĭl'ĕr) *n.* colonna, pilastro, sostegno: **from — to post,** da Erode a Pilato.

pillbox (pĭl'bŏks') *n.* scatoletta di pillole; carrozzella; (*mil.*) casamatta; cappellino a tamburello.

pillory (pĭl'ō·rĭ) *n.* gogna.

pillow (pĭl'ō) *n.* cuscino, guanciale, supporto: **—case,** — **slip,** federa.

pilot (pī'lŭt) *n.* pilota; timoniere; guida: **— plant,** cantiere pilota. *vt.* pilotare, guidare, condurre.

pimp (pĭmp) *n.* mezzano.

pimpernel (pĭm'pẽr·nĕl) *n.* primula.

pimple (pĭm'p'l) *n.* foruncolo, pustola.

pin (pĭn) *n.* spillo, spilla; zipolo (*di botte*); punzone; perno; catenaccio; bietta; bischero (*di strumento mus.*); birillo: **not to care a —**, infischiarsene; **— money**, spillatico; denaro per le piccole spese; **—wheel** *n.* girandola; mulinello. *vt.* agganciare, appuntare con gli spilli, immobilizzare: **to — on**, appioppare; **to — one's faith on**, fare affidamento su.

pinafore (pĭn'â·fōr') *n.* grembiulino per bambini.

pincers (pĭn'sĕrz) *n.pl.* pinze, tenaglie; (*mil.*) manovra a tenaglia.

pinch (pĭnch) *n.* pizzico; pizzicotto; strettoia, difficoltà; furto: **in a —**, in caso di bisogno; **— hitter**, sostituto, supplente. *vt.*, *vi.* pizzicare; stringere; affliggere; contrarre; rubare; arrestare.

pinchers *n. pl.* tenaglie.

pine (pĭn) (1) *n.* pino: **— cone**, pigna; **— grove**, pineto; **— nut**, pinolo.

pine (pĭn) (2) *n.* struggimento. *vt.* rimpiangere. *vi.* languire, deperire: **to — after**, spasimare per, agognare.

pineapple (pĭn'ăp''l) *n.* ananasso; (*mil.*) bomba a mano.

pinhead (pĭn'hĕd') *n.* capocchia di spillo.

pinion (pĭn'yŭn) *n.* penna; (*mecc.*) pignone. *vt.* immobilizzare.

pink (pĭngk) (1) *n.* rosso chiaro, (color) rosa; garofano: **in the — of condition**, nelle migliori condizioni. *agg.* roseo, rosso, imporporato.

pink (2) *vt.* pungere; frastagliare.

pinnacle (pĭn'â·k'l) *n.* pinnacolo; torretta; cima, apogeo.

pint (pĭnt) *n.* pinta (*circa mezzo litro*).

pin-up (girl) (pĭn'ŭp') *n.* foto di ragazza procace da appendere al muro.

pin-up lamp *n.* lampada a muro.

pioneer (pī'ō·nēr') *n.* pioniere; precursore. *vt.* scoprire, esplorare; guidare; essere il precursore di; aprire la strada a. *vi.* fare il pioniere.

pious (pī'ŭs) *agg.* pio, devoto.

pipe (pīp) *n.* pipa; tubo, condotto; voce; strumento a fiato; (*anat.*) faringe; (*bot.*) stelo; canna (*d'organo*). *vt.* convogliare con tubi, munire di tubature; eseguire con strumento a fiato. *vi.* sonare strumenti a fiato; fischiare; gridare, avere un suono acuto: **to — down**, abbassare la voce.

pipeline (pīp'līn') *n.* conduttura; oleodotto; (*fig.*) fonte di informazioni.

pipelines *n. pl.* zampogna.

piper (pīp'ĕr) *n.* zampognaro.

piping (pīp'ĭng) *n.* tubazione, tubatura; suono di strumento a fiato; cordoncino (*di seta, ecc.*). *agg.* stri-

dulo; morbido; tranquillo: **— hot**, caldissimo, scottante; recentissimo, caldo caldo.

pippin (pĭp'ĭn) *n.* specie di mela; seme.

piquant (pē'kănt) *agg.* piccante.

pique (pēk) *n.* puntiglio, picca. *vt.* offendere; provocare, piccare, stuzzicare; **to — oneself on**, piccarsi di.

piracy (pī'râ·sĭ) *n.* pirateria; (*fig.*) plagio.

pirate (pī'rĭt) *n.* pirata; plagiario. *vi.* pirateggiare; plagiare.

pirogue (pĭ·rōg') *n.* piroga.

pirouette (pĭr'ōō·ĕt') *n.* piroetta. *vi.* piroettare.

pistol (pĭs't'l) *n.* pistola.

piston (pĭs'tŭn) *n.* pistone: **— rod**, biella.

pit (pĭt) *n.* buca, pozzo, cava; ascella; buttero (*del vaiolo*); (*teat.*) platea: nocciolo: **— of the stomach**, bocca dello stomaco. *vt.*, *vi.* scavare, incavare; mettere alla prova; incavarsi.

pitch (pĭch) (1) *n.* punto; intensità; tonalità; lancio; pendenza; livello, immersione; distanza. *vi.* erigere, drizzare; scagliare, buttare, scaraventare; disporre, regolare: **to — into**, aggredire; rimproverare, strapazzare. *vi.* precipitare; immergersi; inclinarsi; allogarsi, posarsi; (*naut. e aeron.*) beccheggiare: **to — in**, mettersi al lavoro.

pitch (pĭch) (2) *n.* pece; resina: **—black** *agg.* nerissimo; **—dark** *agg.* scurissimo; buio pesto. *vt.* impeciare.

pitcher (pĭch'ĕr) (1) *n.* lanciatore.

pitcher (pĭch'ĕr) (2) *n.* brocca, boccale.

pitchfork (pĭch'fôrk') *n.* forca, forcone.

piteous (pĭt'ē·ŭs) *agg.* pietoso.

pitfall (pĭt'fôl') *n.* trappola, trabocchetto.

pith (pĭth) *n.* polpa; forza, vigore; parte essenziale.

pithy (pĭth'ĭ) *avv.* vigoroso, sostanzioso.

pitiable (pĭt'ĭ·áb'l) *agg.* pietoso.

pitiful (pĭt'ĭ·fōōl) *n.* pietoso, miserevole.

pitiless (pĭt'ĭ·lĕs) *agg.* spietato.

pittance (pĭt'ăns) *n.* alimenti; nonnulla.

pity (pĭt'ĭ) *n.* pietà, compassione, peccato: **what a —!** che peccato!; **for —'s sake!** per l'amor del cielo! *vt.*, *vi.* compiangere, impietosirsi.

pivot (pĭv'ŭt) *n.* perno. *vt.* imperniare. *vi.* far perno, imperniarsi, rotare.

pix (pĭks) *n.pl.* fotografie; illustrazioni; films.

pixilated (pĭk'sĭ.lāt'ĕd) *agg.* (*gergo*) stravagante, picchiatello; farsesco.

placard (plă'kärd) *n.* manifesto,cartellone, affisso. *vt.* affiggere, annunciare con manifesti.

placate (plă'kāt) *vt.* placare.

place (plās) *n.* luogo; posto; locale; dimora; posizione; impiego; dovere: **in the first —**, in primo luogo; **in — of**, in vece di; **out of —**, fuori di luogo; disoccupato; **to take —**, aver luogo; **to take one's —**, mettersi al proprio posto, prendere posto; *vt.* collocare, porre, situare.

placid (plăs'ĭd) *agg.* placido.

plagiarism (plā'jĭ.à.rĭz'm) *n.* plagio.

plagiarist (plā'jĭ.à.rĭst) *n.* plagiario.

plagiarize (plā'jĭ.à.rīz) *vt.*, *vi.* plagiare.

plague (plāg) *n.* piaga, flagello. *vt.* vessare, tormentare, appestare, assillare.

plaid (plăd) *n.* mantello scozzese, coperta da viaggio. *agg.* scozzese (*di tessuto a quadri*).

plain (plān) *n.* pianura. *agg.* semplice, puro, piano; brutto; esplicito; uniforme, a tinta unita; ordinario; evidente: **— fool**, perfetto cretino; **— woman**, donna brutta; **in — sight**, in piena vista; **—clothes man** *n.* agente in borghese; **—spoken**, *agg.* esplicito, franco. *avv.* (*anche* **—ly**) chiaramente, semplicemente; evidentemente; francamente.

plaint (plānt) *n.* lamento, lagnanza; istanza. **—iff** *n.* attore (*in causa*). **—ive** *agg.* lamentoso.

plait (plāt) *n.* piega, falda, treccia. *vt.* piegare, intrecciare.

plan (plăn) *n.* piano; progetto; metodo; pianta. *vt.*, *vi.* progettare, far progetti; pianificare: **planned economy**, economia pianificata. **—ner** *n.* progettista; pianificatore.

plane (plān) (1) *n.* piano, pianura, superficie piana, pialla; (*aeron.*) piano portante, aeroplano: **elevating —** (*aeron.*) timone di profondità. *agg.* piano. *vt.* piallare. *vi.* (*aeron.*) planare.

plane (2) **plane-tree** *n.* platano.

planer (plān'ẽr) *n.* (*mecc.*) piallatrice.

planet (plăn'ĕt) *n.* pianeta.

plank (plăngk) *n.* tavola, asse; piattaforma. *vt.* intavolare, coprire di assi; snocciolare (*danari*). **—ing** *n.* tavolato.

plant (plànt) *n.* (*bot.*) pianta; impianto; turlupinatura, tranello. *vt.* piantare, conficcare, fissare; stabilire; inculcare.

plantation (plăn.tā'shŭn) *n.* piantagione, colonia.

planter (plànt'ẽr) *n.* piantatore.

plaque (plăk) *n.* placca.

plasma (plăz'mà) *n.* plasma.

plaster (plăs'tẽr) *n.* intonaco, stucco, gesso; impiastro: **— cast**, modello in gesso; (*med.*) ingessatura. **— of Paris**, scagliuola, gesso; **court —**, cerotto. *agg.* falso. *vt.* ingessare, intonacare, cospargere; affiggere; mettere un impiastro a.

plastic (plăs'tĭk) *agg.* plastico. **—s** *n. sing.* plastica, materia plastica.

plat (plăt) *n.* appezzamento, progetto, mappa. *vt.* progettare, disegnare la pianta di.

plate (plāt) *n.* piatto; placca, piastra; targa; argenteria; incisione, lastra (*anche fot.*); illustrazione, tavola; catodo; (*sport*) trofeo, gara: **fashion —**, figurino; **license —**, targa di circolazione. *vt.* placcare, laminare, corazzare; patinare (*carta*); targare.

plateau (plă·tō') *n.* altipiano; placca; vassoio; (*fig.*) periodo di stabilità.

platen (plăt'n) *n.* (*tip.*) platina di pressione; rullo (*della macchina per scrivere*): **— press**, platina.

platform (plăt'fôrm') *n.* piattaforma; pianoro; (*ferr.*) banchina, marciapiede.

platinum (plăt'ĭ·nŭm) *n.* platino: **— blonde**, bionda platinata.

platitude (plăt'ĭ·tūd) *n.* banalità, luogo comune.

platoon (plă·tōōn') *n.* plotone.

platter (plăt'ẽr) *n.* piatto di portata.

plaudit (plô'dĭt) *n.* applauso.

plausible (plô'zĭ·b'l) *agg.* plausibile, persuasivo; specioso.

play (plā) *n.* gioco, scherzo, divertimento; dramma; libertà d'azione, esecuzione (*mus.*); commedia; manovra: **fair —**, condotta leale; **foul —**, dolo; (*sport*) fallo, scorrettezza; *vt.* giocare; far agire; sonare (*uno strumento*), eseguire (*mus.*); rappresentare. *vi.* divertirsi, scherzare; agire, comportarsi; funzionare; recitare: **to — cards**, giocare alle carte; **to — a joke**, combinare uno scherzo; **to — the fool**, far lo stupido; **to — truant**, marinare la scuola; **to — havoc**, con devastare; **to — on words**, equivocare, giocare sulle parole; **—ed out**, esaurito. **—er** *n.* giocatore; esecutore, attore: **— piano**, pianola; **piano —**, pianista. **—ful** *agg.* giocoso, scherzoso. **—ground** *n.* luogo di ricreazione, parco di giochi. **—mate** *n.* compagno di giochi. **—pen** *n.* recinto o box per poppanti. **—room** *n.* saletta da giuoco (*in una casa privata*). **—thing** *n.* trastullo. **—wright** *n.* commediografo, drammaturgo.

plea (plē) *n.* scusa, protesta; difesa, istanza, supplica.

plead (plēd) *vt.*, *vi.* addurre, difendere, perorare, dichiarare, invocare, argomentare, intercedere: **to — guilty,** dichiararsi colpevole.

pleasant (plĕz′ănt) *agg.* piacevole, gradevole, amabile, simpatico. **—ry** *n.* facezia; allegria.

please (plēz) *vt.*, *vi.* piacere, essere gradito, compiacere, accontentare, soddisfare, degnarsi: **if you —,** per cortesia, vi prego; **as you —,** come preferite; **— yourself,** fate come vi pare; **— do it,** per favore, fatelo; abbiate la cortesia di farlo.

pleased *agg.* contento, soddisfatto: **to be — to,** essere lieto di; **to be — with,** essere soddisfatto di, compiacersi di; **ill—** *agg.* malcontento.

pleasing (plēz′ĭng) *agg.* piacevole.

pleasurable (plĕzh′ĕr-á-b′l) *agg.* dilettevole, piacevole.

pleasure (plĕzh′ĕr) *n.* piacere; soddisfazione; piacimento: **at —,** a piacimento, a volontà; **during your —,** finchè vi piacerà; **what is your —?** che cosa desiderate?, che cosa preferite? **— trip,** viaggio di piacere.

pleat (plēt) *vedi* **plait.**

plebeian (plē-bē′(y)ăn) *n.*, *agg.* plebeo.

plebiscite (plĕb′ĭ-sĭt) *n.* plebiscito.

pledge (plĕj) *n.* garanzia, pegno, impegno, ostaggio: **as a — of,** in pegno di; **to take the —,** far voto di temperanza. *vt.* impegnare, depositare in garanzia, far giurare, garantire: **to — one's word,** dare la propria parola; **to — to secrecy,** impegnare al segreto.

plenipotentiary (plĕn′ĭ-pŏ-tĕn′shĭ-ĕr′ĭ) *n.*, *agg.* plenipotenziario.

plenteous (plĕn′tē-ŭs) *agg.* abbondante.

plentiful (plĕn′tĭ-fŏŏl) *agg.* abbondante, copioso.

plenty (plĕn′tĭ) *n.* abbondanza: **— of time,** tempo a volontà; **that is —,** ce n'è in abbondanza. *agg.* abbondante. *avv.* abbondantemente.

pleurisy (plŏŏr′ĭ-sĭ) *n.* pleurite.

plexus (plĕk′sŭs) *n.* (*anat.*) plesso.

pliable (plī′á-b′l) *agg.* pieghevole, adattabile, arrendevole.

pliant (plī′ănt) *agg.* flessibile, duttile, influenzabile, arrendevole.

pliers (plī′ĕrz) *n.pl.* pinze.

plight (plīt) *n.* stato, situazione critica; pegno; imbarazzo. *vt.* impegnare, promettere.

plod (plŏd) *vi.* camminare pesantemente; sgobbare.

plot (plŏt) *n.* mappa, appezzamento, macchia; complotto, piano; intreccio (*di romanzo, ecc.*). *vt.*, *vi.* trac-

ciare (il piano di); suddividere in lotti; complottare, tramare, macchinare. **—ter** *n.* cospiratore.

plough (plou) *vedi* **plow.**

plover (plŭv′ĕr) *n.* (*ornit.*) piviere.

plow (plou) *n.* aratro, spazzaneve. *vt.*, *vi.* arare, solcare, aprirsi un varco; (*gergo*) bocciare.

pluck (plŭk) *n.* strappo, strattone; frattaglie; coraggio. *vt.* cogliere, strappare, spennare; pizzicare (*le corde di uno strumento*); arraffare; bocciare: **to — asunder,** separarecon forza; **to — up,** svellere; raccogliere le forze (*o il coraggio*).

plucky (plŭk′ĭ) *agg.* coraggioso.

plug (plŭg) *n.* tappo, zaffo, tampone; spicchio; ronzino; libro che si vende poco; studente sgobbone; (*autom.*) candela; rubinetto; otturazione (*di un dente*); (*elett.*) spina; pubblicità insistente, pubblicità inserita in un programma radiofonico, pistolotto inserito in un discorso: **fire —,** idrante; **— hat,** cappello a cilindro. *vt.*, *vi.* tappare, tamponare; conficcare; colpire (*con un proiettile, in pugno, ecc.*); otturare (*un dente*); inserire (*una spina*); sgobbare; fare pubblicità intensa a.

plum (plŭm) *n.* susina; uva passa; il meglio: **— cake,** panfrutto; **— tree,** susino.

plumage (plŏŏm′ĭj) *n.* piumaggio.

plumb (plŭm) *n.* piombino, perpendicolo: **— bob,** piombino. *agg.* perpendicolare, verticale: **— crazy** (*gergo*) completamente pazzo. *avv.* a piombo, perpendicolarmente. *vt.* mettere a piombo, sondare, piombare.

plumber (plŭm′ĕr) *n.* idraulico.

plumbing (plŭm′ĭng) *n.* impianto idraulico; sondaggio.

plume (plŏŏm) *n.* penna, piuma, pennacchio. *vt.* impiumare: **to — oneself on,** vantarsi di, gloriarsi di.

plummet (plŭm′ĕt) *n.* piombino; scandaglio; (*fig.*) peso. *vt.* scandagliare. *vi.* cadere a piombo.

plump (plŭmp) (1) *n.* caduta, scroscio. *agg.* diretto, brusco. *avv.* pesantemente; improvvisamente; a perpendicolo. *vt.* far precipitare. *vi.* precipitare.

plump (plŭmp) (2) *agg.* grassoccio, paffuto. **—ness** *n.* grassezza, floridezza.

plunder (plŭn′dĕr) *n.* bottino, saccheggio. *vt.*, *vi.* saccheggiare, depredare. **—er** *n.* saccheggiatore.

plunge (plŭnj) *n.* tuffo, slancio: **to take the —,** rompere gli indugi. *vt.*

scaraventare, immergere. *vi.* tuffarsi, slanciarsi: to — headlong, buttarsi a capofitto.

plunger (plŭn′jĕr) *n.* tuffatore; (*mecc.*) pistone, stantuffo.

pluperfect (plōō′pŭr′fĕkt) *n.*, *agg.* piuccheperfetto.

plural (plōor′ăl) *n.*, *agg.* plurale.

plus (plŭs) *n.* più (+), sovrappiù. *agg.* più, addizionale, positivo. *prep.* più, più di, con: two — two, due più due.

plush (plŭsh) *n.* felpa. *agg.* felpato, di felpa; elegante all'eccesso; comodo; soffice.

plutocrat (plōō′tō̆·krăt) *n.* plutocrate.

ply (plī) *n.* piega; treccia. *vt.* piegare; usare, far buon uso di; percorrere, solcare; stimolare; ascillare: to — a trade, esercitare un commercio; to — with questions, tempestare di domande; to — oneself with, riempirsi di. *vi.* affrettarsi; lavorare assiduamente; fare la spola.

plyers (plī′ĕrz) *n.pl.* pinze.

pneumatic (nū·măt′ĭk) *n.*, *agg.* pneumatico.

pneumonia (nū·mō′nĭ·ȧ) *n.* polmonite.

poach (pōch) *vt.*, *vi.* cacciare di frodo; calpestare; trafiggere; impastare; intridersi; affogare (*le uova*). —er *n.* bracconiere.

pock (pŏk) *n.* pustola, buttero. *vt.* butterare.

pocket (pŏk′ĕt) *n.* tasca, taschino; cavità, sacca, buca (*del biliardo*). *vt.* intascare, sottrarre; sopportare (*un affronto*), rinfoderare (*l'orgoglio*): — battleship, corazzata tascabile. —book *n.* portafoglio, taccuino, libro tascabile. —knife *n.* coltello a serramanico.

pockmark (pŏk′märk′) *n.* buttero (*del vaiolo*). —ed *agg.* butterato.

pod (pŏd) *n.* baccello, guscio.

poem (pō′ĕm) *n.* poesia, poema.

poesy (pō′ĕ·sĭ) *n.* poesia (*arte*).

poet (pō′ĕt) *n.* poeta. —ess *n.* poetessa. —ic (-ĕt′ĭk) —ical *agg.* poetico. —ics *n.* poetica. —ry *n.* poesia.

poignant (poin′yȧnt) *agg.* piccante, intenso; drammatico, straziante.

point (point) *n.* punto; grado; punta; scopo, mira; argomento; costrutto; posizione: it is not to the —, it is beside the —, non c'entra, è fuori dell'argomento; at all points, sotto tutti i riguardi; in —, adatto, calzante; in — of, per quanto riguarda; in — of fact, effettivamente; to come to the —, venire al fatto; to make a — to, farsi un dovere di; to stretch a —, fare uno strappo alla regola. *vt.*, *vi.* appun-

tire, aguzzare; punteggiare; indicare, puntare: to — out, far notare. —blank *agg.* diretto, esplicito. *avv.* direttamente, a bruciapelo.

pointed (poin′tĕd) *agg.* acuto, appuntito; diretto, mordente, efficace.

pointer (poin′tĕr) *n.* indice, indicatore, lancetta; suggerimento; cane da punta, pointer.

poise (poiz) *n.* peso, gravità; equilibrio; portamento; sospensione. *vt.* bilanciare, equilibrare. *vi.* bilanciarsi, librarsi.

poison (poi′s'n) *n.* veleno. *vt.* avvelenare. —er *n.* avvelenatore.

poisonous (poi′z'n·ŭs) *agg.* velenoso.

poke (pōk) *n.* colpo, spinta, urto; sacco, tasca. *vt.*, *vi.* spingere; urtare; smuovere; rovistare; attizzare (*il fuoco*); intrufolarsi; andare a tastoni: to — into, ficcare, conficcare; to — out, sbucare, spuntare; to — fun at, prendersi gioco di.

poker (pōk′ĕr) *n.* attizzatoio; poker (*gioco di carte*).

polar (pō′lĕr) *agg.* polare: — bear, orso bianco; — lights, aurora boreale.

polarize (pōl′ĕr·īz) *vt.* polarizzare.

pole (pōl) (1) *n.* palo, pertica; timone (*di carro*): greased —, albero della cuccagna; — vault, salto con l'asta.

pole (pōl) (2) *n.* polo.

Pole (pōl) (3) *n.* polacco.

polecat (pōl′kăt′) *n.* puzzola.

polemic (pō·lĕm′ĭk) *agg.* polemico.

polemics *n.* arte polemica.

polestar (pōl′stär′) *n.* stella polare.

police (pō·lēs′) *n.* polizia: — state, stato poliziesco o totalitario; — station, commissariato di polizia. *agg.* poliziesco, piliziotto. *vt.* vigilare, mantenere l'ordine in.

policeman *n.* poliziotto, guardia.

policy (pŏl′ĭ·sĭ) *n.* politica; tattica, sistema; polizza assicurativa.

Polish (pō′ĭsh) (1) *agg.* polacco.

polish (pŏl′ĭsh) (2) *n.* lucido, lucidatura, lucentezza; stile, buone maniere. *vt.* lucidare, levigare, ingentilire. *vi.* diventar lucido, raffinarsi.

polite (pō·līt′) *agg.* cortese, garbato. —ness *n.* cortesia.

politic (pŏl′ĭ·tĭk) *agg.* sagace, diplomatico, prudente.

political (pō·lĭt′ĭ·kȧl) *agg.* politico.

politician (pŏl′ĭ·tĭsh′ȧn) *n.* uomo politico.

politics (pŏl′ĭ·tĭks) *n.* politica.

poll (pōl) *n.* testa, occipite; lista elettorale; scrutinio; referendum; urna elettorale. *vt.*, *vi.* cimare; rapare; scrutinare, votare, raccogliere voti; consultare (*in un referendum*).

pollen (pŏl'ĕn) n. polline.

pollster (pōl'stĕr) n. indagatore, scrutatore, addetto a un referendum.

pollute (pŏ·lūt') vt. corrompere, profanare, insudiciare, contaminare.

polo (pō'lō) n. (sport) polo: — coat, giacchettone di pelo di cammello; — shirt, camicia sportiva, camiciola, argentina.

polyclinic (pŏl'ĭ·klĭn'ĭk) n. policlinico.

polygamist (pŏ·lĭg'ȧ·mĭst) n. poligamo.

polygamy (pŏ·lĭg'ȧ·mĭ) n. poligamia.

polyglot (pŏl'ĭ·glŏt) n. poliglotta.

polyp (pŏl'ĭp) n. polipo.

pomade (pō·mād') n. pomata.

pomegranate (pŏm'grăn'ĭt) n. melagrana, melograno.

pomp (pŏmp) n. pompa, fasto.

pompous (pŏmp'ŭs) agg. pomposo.

pond (pŏnd) n. stagno, laghetto.

ponder (pŏn'dĕr) vt., vi. ponderare.

ponderous (pŏn'dĕr·ŭs) agg. ponderoso.

pontiff (pŏn'tĭf) n. pontefice.

pontoon (pŏn·tōōn') n. barcone, pontone; (aeron.) galleggiante: — bridge, ponte di barche.

pony (pō'nĭ) n. cavallo nano; bigino (vedi crib).

poodle (pōō'd'l) n. cane barbone.

pool (pōōl) n. stagno, pozza, sorgente; posta (di gioco); fusione, consorzio; fondo comune: swimming —, piscina. vt., vi. riunire in un fondo comune, contribuire a un fondo comune; consorziarsi.

poor (pōōr) agg. povero, misero; scarso, magro; scadente; debole. — house n. ospizio di mendicità. —ly agg. misero, malaticcio. avv. miseramente, malamente.

pop (pŏp) n. scoppio; sparo; colpo sordo. vt., vi. spingere, buttare; impegnare; entrare (o uscire) di colpo; far esplodere; lanciarsi; sparare, detonare; saltare (di tappo).

pope (pōp) n. papa.

popeyed (pŏp'īd') agg. con gli occhi sbarrati, stralunato.

popgun (pŏp'gŭn') n. fucile ad aria compressa.

poplar (pŏp'lĕr) n. (bot.) pioppo.

poppy (pŏp'ĭ) n. papavero.

populace (pŏp'ū·lĭs) n. popolino, plebe.

popular (pŏp'ū·lĕr) agg. popolare. —ity (-ăr'ĭ·tĭ) n. popolarità.

populate (pŏp'ū·lāt) vt. popolare. vi. popolarsi.

population (pŏp'ū·lā'shŭn) n. popolazione.

populous (pŏp'ū·lŭs) agg. popoloso.

porcelain (pōr'sĕ·lĭn) n. porcellana.

porch (pōrch) n. portico, veranda.

porcupine (pôr'kû·pĭn) n. porcospino.

pore (pōr) (1) n. (anat.) poro.

pore (pōr) (2) vi.: to — on, upon, over, esaminare, ponderare, leggere attentamente.

pork (pôrk) n. carne di porco: — pie, sformato di carne di maiale; cappello alla tirolese o a tronco di cono.

porpoise (pôr'pŭs) n. focena, delfino.

porridge (pŏr'ĭj) n. pappa d'avena (o di altra farina).

port (pōrt) (1) n. porto, scalo; (naut.) sinistra (della nave); boccaporto.

port (pōrt) (2) n. porto (vino d'Oporto).

portable (pōr'tȧ·b'l) agg. portabile, portatile.

portend (pôr·tĕnd') vt. presagire, significare, denotare.

portent (pôr'tĕnt) n. presagio; portento. —ous (-tĕnt'ŭs) agg. sinistro, sintomatico; importante, prodigioso.

porter (pōr'tĕr) n. facchino, portiere; birra forte; conduttore (di vagon letto).

portfolio (pōrt·fō'lĭ·ō) n. portafogli (ministeriale e comm.), portacarte.

porthole (pōrt'hōl') n. feritoia; (naut. portello, oblò.

portion (pōr'shŭn) n. porzione, parte vt. dividere, distribuire.

portliness (pōrt'lĭ·nĕs) n. portamento maestoso, corpulenza.

portly (pōrt'lĭ) agg. maestoso, corpulento.

portrait (pōr'trāt) n. ritratto.

portray (pōr·trā') vt. ritrarre, fare i ritratto a, descrivere. —al n. ritratto, descrizione.

Portuguese (pōr'tū·gēs) n., agg. portoghese.

pose (pōz) n. posa, atteggiamento. vt imbarazzare, confondere; metter in posa; formulare. vi. posare: t — as, posare a, fingersi.

poser (pōz'ĕr) n. rompicapo, domand imbarazzante; posatore.

position (pŏ·zĭsh'ŭn) n. posizione, si tuazione, tesi.

positive (pŏz'ĭ·tĭv) n. positiva (fot.) agg. positivo, assoluto; sicuro, con vinto. —ly avv. positivamente sicuramente, decisamente.

posse (pŏs'ē) n. forza pubblica; pat tuglia.

possess (pŏ·zĕs') vt. possedere; do minare.

possessed agg. invasato, pazzo.

possession (pŏ·zĕsh'ŭn) n. possesso possedimento.

possessive (pŏ·zĕs'ĭv) n., agg. posses sivo.

possibility (pŏs'ĭ·bĭl'ĭ·tĭ) n. possibilità probabilita.

ossible (pŏs'ĭ·b'l) *n*. probabile, possibile.

ossibly (pŏs'ĭ·blĭ) *avv*. forse, probabilmente; in alcun modo.

ossum (pŏs'ŭm) *n*. opossum: to play —, fare la marmotta.

ost (pōst) *n*. palo, pilastro; posta, corrispondenza; posto, carica; (*mil.*) presidio: — free, franco di porto; — office, ufficio postale; —-office box, casella postale; army —, guarnigione, distaccamento militare; — exchange (*mil.*), spaccio. *vt*. impostare, spedire; collocare; affiggere; ragguagliare; (*comm.*) riportare a mastro. *vi*. affrettarsi: to keep —ed, tenere *o* tenersi al corrente.

ostage (pōs'tĭj) *n*. affrancatura: — stamp, francobollo.

ostal (pōs'tăl) *agg*. postale: — order, vaglia postale.

ostcard *n*. cartolina postale.

oster (pōs'tẽr) *n*. cartellone, manifesto; attacchino.

oste restante (pōst'rĕs·tänt') *n*. fermo-posta.

osterior (pŏs·tẽr'ĭ·ẽr) *agg*. posteriore.

osterity (pŏs·tẽr'ĭ·tĭ) *n*. posterità.

osthaste (pōst'hāst') *avv*. frettolosamente.

osthumous (pŏs'tṳ·mŭs) *agg*. postumo.

ostman (pōst'măn) *n*. postino.

ostmark (pōst'märk') *n*. timbro postale.

ostmaster (pōst'mȧs'tẽr) *n*. ricevitore postale: — general *n*. ministro delle poste.

ost-mortem (pōst'môr'tĕm) *n*. autopsia.

ostpone (pōst·pōn') *vt*. rimandare, posporre, differire. —ment *n*. rinvio, posposizione.

ostscript (pōst'skrĭpt) *n*. poscritto.

osture (pŏs'tṳr) *n*. posa, atteggiamento, situazione. *vt*., *vi*. mettere (*o* mettersi) in posa.

osy (pō'zĭ) *n*. mazzo di fiori.

ot (pŏt) *n*. vaso, pentola, recipiente; premio.

otassium (pȯ·tăs'ĭ·ŭm) *n*. potassio.

otato (pȯ·tā'tō) *n*. patata: mashed potatoes, purè di patate; sweet —, patata dolce *o* americana.

otbellied (pŏt'bĕl'ĭd) *agg*. panciuto.

otency (pō'tĕn·sĭ) *n*. potenza, autorità; efficacia; capacità, potere.

otent (pō'tĕnt) *agg*. potente, efficace.

otential (pȯ·tĕn'shăl) *n*., *agg*. potenziale.

othook (pŏt'ho͝ok') *n*. catena del camino; scarabocchio.

potion (pō'shŭn) *n*. pozione, beveraggio.

potpourri (pō'po͞o'rē') *n*. accozzaglia, miscela.

potter (pŏt'ẽr) *n*. vasaio: —'s field, cimitero dei poveri.

pottery (pŏt'ẽr·ĭ) *n*. vasellame, fabbrica di vasellame, ceramica (*arte*).

pouch (pouch) *n*. borsa, tasca.

poultice (pōl'tĭs) *n*. cataplasma.

poultry (pōl'trĭ) *n*. pollame.

pounce (pouns) *n*. artiglio. *vt*., *vi*. artigliare: to — upon, ghermire, balzare su; to — into a room, irrompere in una stanza.

pound (pound) (1) *n*. libbra; lira sterlina.

pound (pound) (2) *vt*. battere, tempestare; polverizzare; ammaccare. *vi*. camminare pesantemente.

pour (pōr) *vt*. versare, riversare. *vi*. fluire, traboccare, diluviare: to — in, affluire.

pout (pout) *n*. broncio. *vi*. fare il broncio, imbronciarsi.

poverty (pŏv'ẽr·tĭ) *n*. povertà.

POW (pē'ō'dŭb'l·ū) *n*. (*sigla di* Prisoner Of War) prigioniero di guerra.

powder (pou'dẽr) *n*. polvere, polverina; cipria: — room, toilette per signore; to take a — (*gergo*) svignarsela. *vt*. polverizzare, cospargere, incipriare. *vi*. incipriarsi, andare in polvere.

power (pou'ẽr) *n*. potere, forza; potenza; facoltà, autorità; portata: — of attorney, procura (mandato); — plant, centrale elettrica; apparato motore; motive —, forza motrice. —ful *agg*. potente. —house *n*. centrale elettrica, (*fig.*) persona dinamica *o* attiva. —less *agg*. impotente.

practicable (prăk'tĭ·kȧ·b'l) *agg*. fattibile, praticabile.

practical (prăk'tĭ·kăl) *agg*. pratico: — joke, tiro birbone. —ly *avv*. praticamente, virtualmente.

practice (prăk'tĭs) *n*. pratica, prassi, procedura, abitudine, esercizio, uso; clientela *o* attività (*di professionista*). *vt*. praticare, studiare, esercitare. *vi*. esercitarsi.

practiced (prăk'tĭst) *agg*. addestrato, abile.

practise (prăk'tĭs) *vedi* practice.

practitioner (prăk·tĭsh'ŭn·ẽr) *n*. professionista, medico.

prairie (prâr'ĭ) *n*. prateria.

praise (prāz) *n*. lode, elogio. *vt*. lodare, elogiare, magnificare. —worthy *agg*. lodevole.

pram (prăm) *n*. (*abbr. di* perambulator) carrozzina per bambini.

prance (pràns) *vi.* caracollare; passeggiare con sussiego.

prank (prängk) *n.* stravaganza, scherzo, burla, tiro birbone.

prate (pràt) *n.* vaniloquio. *vi.* cianciare.

pratfall (prät'fôl') *n.* (*gergo*) capitombolo.

prattle (prät''l) *n.* ciancia, chiacchiera, balbettio. *vi.* cianciare, balbettare.

pray (prā) *vt.*, *vi.* pregare, supplicare.

prayer (prâr) *n.* preghiera: Lord's —, Padre Nostro.

preach (prēch) *vt.*, *vi.* predicare. —**er** *n.* predicatore. —**ing** *n.* predica, predicazione.

preamble (prē'ăm'b'l) *n.* preambolo.

prearrange (prē'á·rānj') *vt.* predisporre.

precarious (prē·kâr'ĭ·ŭs) *agg.* precario.

precaution (prē·kô'shŭn) *n.* precauzione.

precede (prē·sēd') *vt.*, *vi.* precedere.

precedence (prē·sēd'ĕns) *n.* precedenza.

precedent (prĕs'ē·dĕnt) *n.*, *agg.* precedente.

preceding (prē·sēd'ĭng) *agg.* precedente, previo.

precept (prē'sĕpt) *n.* precetto.

precinct (prē'sĭngkt) *n.* limite; distretto; giurisdizione: *pl.* dintorni, vicinanze.

precious (prĕsh'ŭs) *agg.* prezioso; adorato; ricercato. *avv.* molto: — **little**, ben poco.

precipice (prĕs'ĭ·pĭs) *n.* precipizio.

precipitate (prē·sĭp'ĭ·tāt) *n.* (*chim.*) precipitato. *agg.* precipitoso, avventato, improvviso. *vt.*, *vi.* precipitare.

precipitation (prē·sĭp'ĭ·tā'shŭn) *n.* precipitazione.

precipitous (prē·sĭp'ĭ·tŭs) *agg.* precipitoso; scosceso, impervio.

precis (prā·sē') *n.* riassunto, compendio.

precise (prē·sīs') *agg.* preciso, esatto.

precisian (prē·sĭzh'ăn) *n.* formalista.

precision (prē·sĭzh'ŭn) *n.* precisione, accuratezza.

preclude (prē·klōōd') *vt.* precludere, escludere, impedire.

precocious (prē·kō'shŭs) *agg.* precoce.

preconceived (prē'kŏn·sēvd') *agg.* preconcetto.

preconception (prē'kŏn·sĕp'shŭn) *n.* preconcetto, pregiudizio.

predecessor (prĕd'ē·sĕs'ĕr) *n.* predecessore.

predestine (prē·dĕs'tĭn) *vt.* predestinare.

predicament (prē·dĭk'á·mĕnt) *n.* situazione critica.

predicate (prĕd'ĭ·kāt) *n.* predicato.

predict (prē·dĭkt') *vt.* predire. —**ion** *n.* predizione.

predilection (prē'dĭ·lĕk'shŭn) *n.* predilezione.

predispose (prē'dĭs·pōz') *vt.* predisporre.

predominance (prē·dŏm'ĭ·nǎns) *n.* predominio, ascendente.

predominate (prē·dŏm'ĭ·nāt) *vt.*, *vi.* predominare, prevalere.

pre-empt (prē·ĕmpt') *vt.* acquistare la priorità su. —**ion** *n.* priorità, diritto di precedenza.

preen (prēn) *vt.* lisciarsi le penne; tirarsi a pomice; agghindarsi: **to — oneself upon**, gloriarsi di.

prefabricate (prē·făb'rĭ·kāt) *vt.* prefabbricare: **prefabricated smile**, sorriso stereotipato.

preface (prĕf'ĭs) *n.* prefazione. *vt.* fare una (*o* servire da) prefazione a.

prefect (prē'fĕkt) *n.* prefetto.

prefer (prē·fûr') *vt.* preferire; presentare (*querela, ecc.*); promuovere. —**able** (prĕf'ĕr·á·b'l) *agg.* preferibile. —**ably** *avv.* preferibilmente. —**ence** (prĕf'-) *n.* preferenza.

prefix (prē·fĭks') *n.* prefisso. *vt.* prefiggere, premettere, prestabilire.

pregnancy (prĕg'nǎn·sĭ) *n.* gravidanza.

pregnant (prĕg'nǎnt) *agg.* gravida, incinta, (*fig.*) gravido, significativo.

prehistoric (prē'hĭs·tŏr'ĭk) *agg.* preistorico.

prehistory (prē·hĭs'tō·rĭ) *n.* preistoria.

prejudge (prē·jŭj') *vt.* giudicare prematuramente *o* sommariamente.

prejudice (prĕj'ŏŏ·dĭs) *n.* pregiudizio, detrimento. *vt.* pregiudicare, influenzare.

prejudicial (prĕj'ŏŏ·dĭsh'ăl) *agg.* pregiudiziale.

prelate (prĕl'ĭt) *n.* prelato.

preliminary (prē·lĭm'ĭ·nĕr·ĭ) *n.*, *agg.* preliminare.

prelude (prĕl'ūd) *n.* preludio. *vt.*, *vi.* preludere a.

premature (prē'má·tūr') *agg.* prematuro, intempestivo.

premeditate (prē·mĕd'ĭ·tāt) *vt.* premeditare.

premier (prē'mĭ·ĕr) *n.* capo, primo ministro. *agg.* primo, principale.

premise (prĕm'ĭs) *n.* supposizione, premessa: —**s**, *pl.* beni immobili; terreni; on the —**s**, sul luogo. *vt.* premettere.

premium (prē'mĭ·ŭm) *n.* premio, aggio: **at a —**, sopra il valore nominale.

preoccupy (prē·ŏk'ū·pī) *vt.* occupare prima; preoccupare.

preordain (prē'ôr·dān') *vt.* preordinare.

prepaid 181 prevent

prepaid (prē·pād') agg. pagato anticipatamente: to send —, spedire
franco di porto.
preparation (prĕp'á·rā'shŭn) n. preparazione, preparativo.
preparatory (prē·păr'á·tō'rĭ) agg. pre-
paratorio, introduttivo.
prepare (prē·pàr') vt. preparare. vi.
prepararsi.
preposition (prĕp'ō·zĭsh'ŭn) n. preposizione.
prepossess (prē'pŏ·zĕs') vt. influenzare, impressionare favorevolmente. —ing agg. simpatico, attraente.
preposterous (prē·pŏs'tēr·ŭs) agg. assurdo.
prerequisite (prē·rĕk'wĭ·zĭt) n. requisito, condizione necessaria. agg. indispensabile.
prerogative (prē·rŏg'á·tĭv) n. prerogativa.
presage (prē·sāj') n. presagio. vt. presagire.
prescribe (prē·skrīb') vt. prescrivere.
prescription (prē·skrĭp'shŭn) n. prescrizione.
presence (prĕz'ĕns) n. presenza: — of
mind, prontezza di spirito.
present (prĕz'ĕnt) n. presente (il
tempo attuale); dono, regalo: at —,
ora, oggi; for the —, per ora, per
il momento. agg. presente, attuale:
— company excepted, esclusi i presenti. vt. (prē·zĕnt') presentare, esibire, regalare: to — someone with a
pen, regalare una penna a qualcuno.
—day agg. di oggi, odierno.
presentation (prĕz'ĕn·tā'shŭn) n. presentazione; dono, omaggio.
presentiment (prē·zĕn'tĭ·mĕnt) n. presentimento.
presently (prĕz'ĕnt·lĭ) avv. presentemente, ora; allora, in quel momento; immediatamente, tra poco, di
lì a poco; direttamente; di conseguenza.
preservation (prĕz'ēr·vā'shŭn) n. pre-
servazione, conservazione.
preserve (prē·zûrv') n. conserva; riserva (di caccia o pesca). vt. preservare, conservare, mettere in conserva, mantenere.
preside (prē·zīd') vt. presiedere: to —
at (o over) a meeting, presiedere a
un'assemblea.
presidency (prĕz'ĭ·dĕn·sĭ) n. presidenza.
president (prĕz'ĭ·dĕnt) n. presidente,
preside, rettore.
press (prĕs) n. pressa; stampa, stamperia; calca, folla; fretta; armadio.
vt.,vi. pressare, premere, spremere;
affrettare, incalzare, insistere; stirare; affrettarsi, accalcarsi: to —

one's point, insistere; to — through
the crowd, aprirsi un varco tra la
folla; hard-pressed by work, carico
di lavoro; to be hard-pressed for
money, avere bisogno impellente
di soldi.
pressing agg. urgente, pressante.
pressure (prĕsh'ēr) n. pressione, oppressione, coercizione, urgenza: —
gauge, manometro: — cooker, pentola a pressione.
pressurize (prĕsh'ēr·īz) vt. (aeron.)
pressurizzare.
prestige (prĕs·tēzh') n. prestigio.
presto (prĕs'tō) avv. subito, all'improvviso.
presumable (prē·zūm'á·b'l) agg. pre-
sumibile, probabile.
presume (prē·zūm') vt., vi. presumere;
agire con arroganza: to — to, permettersi di; to — on, upon, abusare
di, fare eccessivo affidamento su.
presuming agg. presuntuoso.
presumption (prē·zŭmp'shŭn) n. presunzione; supposizione.
presumptuous (prē·zŭmp'tū·ŭs) agg.
presuntuoso.
presuppose (prē'sŭ·pōz') vt. presupporre.
presupposition (prē'sŭp·ō·zĭsh'ŭn) n.
presupposizione.
pretence vedi pretense.
pretend (prē·tĕnd') vt., vi. fingere,
asserire, pretendere.
pretender (-dēr) n. simulatore; pretendente.
pretense (prē·tĕns') n. finzione, pretesto; ostentazione; asserzione,
pretesa: under — of, col pretesto di.
pretension (prē·tĕn'shŭn) n. pretesa,
diritto, presunzione.
pretentious (prē·tĕn'shŭs) agg. pretenzioso.
pretext (prē'tĕkst) n. pretesto.
prettily (prĭt'ĭ·lĭ) avv. graziosamente.
prettiness (prĭt'ĭ·nĕs) n. grazia, leg-
giadria.
pretty (prĭt'ĭ) agg. grazioso, bello, gentile; (fam.) considerevole. avv. discretamente, un po', abbastanza.
prevail (prē·vāl') vi. prevalere, predominare, riuscire: to — on, upon,
persuadere, vincere. —ing agg.
prevalente, comune, generale.
prevalence (prĕv'á·lĕns) n. prevalenza.
prevalent (prĕv'á·lĕnt) agg. prevalente, generale, diffuso.
prevaricate (prē·văr'ĭ·kāt) vi. cavillare, giocare sull'equivoco; mentire.
prevent (prē·vĕnt') vt. prevenire, evitare, ostacolare, impedire. —ion n.
prevenzione, precauzione, impedimento.

preview (prē'vū') *n.* visione privata, anteprima; il "prossimamente"; (*giorn.*) primizia; (*radio e T.V.*) prova generale.

previous (prē'vĭ·ŭs) *agg.* precedente, anteriore, previo. —**ly** *avv.* precedentemente.

prevision (prē·vĭzh'ŭn) *n.* previsione.

prey (prā) *n.* preda, bottino: birds of —, uccelli rapaci. *vi.* predare, saccheggiare; (*seg. da* on, upon) sfruttare, opprimere: to — on one's mind, angustiare, tormentare.

price (prīs) *n.* prezzo, valore, costo: at any —, a qualunque costo. *vt.* valutare, fissare il prezzo di.

priceless (prīs'lĕs) *agg.* inestimabile, impareggiabile.

prick (prĭk) *n.* punta, puntura, pungolo; puntino. *vt.* punzecchiare, pungere; drizzare (*le orecchie*); rimordere (*della coscienza*); spronare. *vi.* ergersi, drizzarsi, sentirsi pungere.

prickle (prĭk''l) *n.* pungiglione, aculeo, puntura, spina.

prickly (prĭk'lĭ) *agg.* spinoso, pungente: — heat, sudamina; — pear, fico d'India.

pride (prīd) *n.* orgoglio, fierezza. *vt.* inorgoglire: to — oneself, inorgoglirsi; vantarsi di, essere fiero di.

priest (prēst) *n.* prete. —**hood** *n.* sacerdozio, clero. —**ly** *agg.* sacerdotale.

prig (prĭg) *n.* saputello, pedante.

priggish (prĭg'ĭsh) *agg.* affettato; sostenuto; pedante; cattedratico.

prim (prĭm) *agg.* compito; affettato, sostenuto; pieno di sussiego.

primacy (prī'mȧ·sĭ) *n.* primato, supremazia.

primarily (prī'mĕr·ĭ·lĭ) *avv.* primariamente, originariamente.

primary (prī'mĕr·ĭ) *n.* primario; originario; principale, fondamentale; elementare.

prime (prīm) *n.* origine, principio; primavera, giovinezza, rigoglio, fior fiore; numero primo: to be in one's —, essere nel fiore degli anni. *agg.* primo; originale, primitivo; fondamentale, principale: — cost, costo di produzione. *vt., vi.* innescare, adescare; caricare; (*un'arma*); istruire tempestivamente.

primer (prĭm'ĕr) (1) *n.* sillabario.

primer (prĭm'ĕr) (2) *n.* detonatore.

primeval (prī·mē'vȧl) *agg.* primordiale.

priming (prīm'ĭng) *n.* esca, innesco.

primitive (prĭm'ĭ·tĭv) *n., agg.* primitivo.

primness (prĭm'nĕs) *n.* affettazione.

primp (prĭmp) *vt.* agghindare. *vi.* agghindarsi.

primrose (prĭm'rōz') *n.* primula.

prince (prĭns) *n.* principe. —**ly** *agg.* principesco.

princess (prĭn'sĕs) *n.* principessa.

principal (prĭn'sĭ·pȧl) *n.* principale; direttore; parte principale; mandante, responsabile; (*comm.*) capitale. *agg.* principale, essenziale.

principle (prĭn'sĭ·p'l) *n.* principio, regola, fondamento, base: on —, per principio; in —, in linea di massima.

prink (prĭngk) *vi.* agghindarsi.

print (prĭnt) *n.* stampa; giornale; impronta; stampo; tessuto stampato; incisione; (*fot.*) positiva: out of —, esaurito (*di libri*). *vt., vi.* imprimere; stampare; scrivere in stampatello. —**er** *n.* stampatore.

printing *n.* stampa, tiratura; stamperia: — press, torchio tipografico; — works, stamperia di tessuti.

prior (prī'ĕr) (1) *agg.* anteriore, precedente. *avv.* precedentemente: — to, prima di.

prior (prī'ĕr) (2) *n.* priore.

prioress (prī'ĕr·ĕs) *n.* madre superiora.

priority (prī·ŏr'ĭ·tĭ) *n.* priorità, precedenza.

priory (prī'ō·rĭ) *n.* convento.

prism (prĭz'm) *n.* prisma.

prison (prĭz''n) *n.* prigione, carcere. *vt.* imprigionare.

prisoner (prĭz''n·ĕr) *n.* prigioniero; detenuto, imputato.

privacy (prī'vȧ·sĭ) *n.* solitudine, intimità; segreto, segretezza: to have no —, non aver luogo dove appartarsi.

private (prī'vĭt) *n.* soldato semplice. *agg.* privato, particolare, personale, confidenziale, intimo: — eye (*gergo*) investigatore privato.

privation (prī·vā'shŭn) *n.* privazione, perdita.

privet (prĭv'ĕt) *n.* (*bot.*) ligustro.

privilege (prĭv'ĭ·lĭj) *n.* privilegio.

privileged *agg.* privilegiato: to be — to, avere il privilegio o la fortuna di.

privy (prĭv'ĭ) *n.* gabinetto; (*legge*) parte in causa. *agg.* segreto: — chamber, camera del consiglio; to be — to, essere a conoscenza di.

prize (prīz) *n.* premio, ricompensa, preda, bottino, vincita; stima, valutazione: — fight, incontro di pugilato; — fighter, pugile. *vt.* tenere in gran conto, valutare; (*mecc.*) azionare con una leva.

probability (prŏb'ȧ·bĭl'ĭ·tĭ) *n.* probabilità.

probable (prŏb´*a*·b'l) *agg.* probabile.

probably (prŏb´*a*·blĭ) *avv.* probabilmente.

probate (prō´bāt) *n.* omologazione. *vt.* omologare.

probation (prō·bā´shŭn) *n.* prova, noviziato, esame, tirocinio; (*legge*) libertà vigilata. **—er** *n.* candidato novizio.

probe (prōb) *n.* sonda. *vt.* sondare; sviscerare, scrutare, esaminare a fondo.

problem (prŏb´lĕm) *n.* problema.

procedure (prō·sē´d̬ŭr) *n.* procedura.

proceed (prō·sēd´) *n.* (*gen.pl.*) provento, ricavato. *vi.* procedere; disporsi (*a*); derivare, emanare; adire le vie legali.

proceeding (prō·sēd´ĭng) *n.* procedimento, azione; linea di condotta.

proceedings *pl.* resoconto, atti.

process (prŏs´ĕs) *n.* processo, procedimento, corso, ordine; citazione: **in the — of being made,** in via di preparazione; **in — of time,** col tempo; **to serve a —,** notificare una intimazione; **— printing,** tricromia, quadricromia; **—server,** ufficiale giudiziario. *vt.* lavorare (*un prodotto*), sottoporre a procedimento di lavorazione; addestrare (*attraverso un corso generale*).

procession (prō·sĕsh´ŭn) *n.* processione: **funeral —,** corteo fùnebre.

proclaim (prō·klām´) *vt.*, *vi.* proclamare, dichiarare, bandire.

proclamation (prŏk´l*a*·mā´shŭn) *n.* proclamazione, ordinanza.

procure (prō·kūr´) *vt.* procurare, procacciare, causare.

prod (prŏd) *n.* pungolo, stimolo. *vt.* stimolare, incitare.

prodigal (prŏd´ĭ·gål) *n.*, *agg.* prodigo.

prodigious (prō·dĭj´ŭs) *agg.* prodigioso.

prodigy (prŏd´ĭ·jĭ) *n.* prodigio.

produce (prō·dūs´) *n.* prodotto. *vt.*, *vi.* produrre.

producer (prō·dūs´ẽr) *n.* produttore; (*teat.*) impresario; (*cinema*) produttore, direttore di produzione. **— gas,** gas povero.

product (prŏd´ŭkt) *n.* prodotto.

production (prō·dŭk´shŭn) *n.* produzione, opera.

productive (prō·dŭk´tĭv) *agg.* produttivo.

profanation (prŏf´*a*·nā´shŭn) *n.* profanazione.

profane (prō·fān´) *agg.* profano. *vt.* profanare.

profanity (prō·făn´ĭ·tĭ) *n.* profanità, irriverenza, bestemmia.

profess (prō·fĕs´) *vt.* professare, dichiarare.

profession (prō·fĕsh´ŭn) *n.* professione.

professional (prō·fĕsh´ŭn·ål) *n.* professionista. *agg.* professionale.

professor (prō·fĕs´ẽr) *n.* professore.

proffer (prŏf´ẽr) *n.* offerta. *vt.* offrire.

proficiency (prō·fĭsh´ĕn·sĭ) *n.* abilità.

proficient (prō·fĭsh´ĕnt) *agg.* versato, abile, competente.

profile (prō´fīl) *n.* profilo.

profit (prŏf´ĭt) *n.* profitto, guadagno, vantaggio: **— and loss,** perdite e profitti; **net —,** guadagno netto. *vt.* giovare. *vi.* profittare, avvantaggiarsi: **to — by,** trarre profitto da.

profitable (prŏf´ĭt·*a*·b'l) *agg.* lucroso, vantaggioso.

profiteer (prŏf´ĭ·tẽr) *n.* profittatore, speculatore. *vi.* lucrare, speculare.

profligacy (prŏf´lĭ·g*a*·sĭ) *n.* dissolutezza.

profligate (prŏf´lĭ·gåt) *n.*, *agg.* dissoluto.

profound (prō·found´) *agg.* profondo.

profuse (prō·fūs´) *agg.* eccessivo, sovrabbondante; prodigo; esuberante.

progeny (prŏj´ĕ·nĭ) *n.* progenie.

program, programme (prō´grăm) *n.* programma.

progress (prŏg´rĕs) *n.* progresso, sviluppo, corso, avanzamento. *vi.* (prō·grĕs´) avanzarsi, progredire. **—ive** *n.* progressista. *agg.* progressivo.

prohibit (prō·hĭb´ĭt) *vt.* proibire.

prohibition (prō´ĭ·bĭsh´ŭn) *n.* proibizione.

project (prŏj´ĕkt) *n.* progetto, programma: **housing —,** piano edilizio, nuovo quartiere. *vt.* (prō·jĕkt´) progettare; proiettare. *vi.* sporgere, proiettarsi. **—ile** (-jĕkt´ĭl) *n.* proiettile, proietto. **—ion** *n.* proiezione; sporgenza. **—ionist** *n.* (*cinema*) operatore di cabina. **—or** *n.* riflettore; proiettore: **flame —,** lanciafiamme; **gas —,** lanciagas.

proletarian (prō´lē·târ´ĭ·ăn) *n.*, *agg.* proletario.

proletariat (prō´lē·târ´ĭ·ăt) *n.* proletariato.

prolix (prō·lĭks´) *agg.* prolisso.

prologue (prō´lŏg) *n.* prologo.

prolong (prō·lông´) *vt.* prolungare. **—ation** (-gā´shŭn) *n.* prolungamento, dilazione, propaggine.

promenade (prŏm´ē·nād´) *n.* passeggiata. *vi.* passeggiare.

prominence (prŏm´ĭ·nĕns) *n.* prominenza, preminenza.

prominent (prŏm´ĭ·nĕnt) *agg.* prominente, saliente, importante.

promiscuous (prō·mĭs´kū·ŭs) *agg.* promiscuo.

promise (prŏm'ĭs) *n.* promessa: **breach of —**, rottura di promessa (*matrimoniale*). *vt.*, *vi.* promettere.

promising *agg.* promettente.

promissory (prŏm'ĭ.sō'rĭ) *agg.* promissorio: **— note**, cambiale.

promontory (prŏm'ŭn.tō'rĭ) *n.* promontorio.

promote (prŏ.mōt') *vt.* promuovere, favorire, sviluppare, incoraggiare.

promoter (prŏ.mōt'ĕr) *n.* promotore.

promotion (prŏ.mō'shŭn) *n.* promozione, avanzamento, incoraggiamento; incremento.

prompt (prŏmpt) *n.* termine di pagamento. *agg.* pronto, alacre, immediato. *vt.* suggerire, istigare, incitare. **—er** *n.* suggeritore, consigliere, istigatore. **—ing** *n.* incitamento, suggerimento, impulso. **—ly** *avv.* prontamente. **—ness** *n.* prontezza, alacrità.

promulgate (prŏ.mŭl'gāt) *vt.* promulgare.

prone (prōn) *agg.* prono, incline; propenso, soggetto(*a*).

prong (prŏng) *n.* rebbio, corno. **—ed** *agg.* dentato, a rebbi.

pronoun (prō'noun) *n.* pronome.

pronounce (prŏ.nouns') *vt.*, *vi.* pronunziare; dichiarare, decretare.

pronounced (prŏ.nounst') *agg.* pronunziato: **— opinions**, opinioni precise.

pronto (prŏn'tō) *avv.* (*S.U.*) presto, fulmineamente.

pronunciation (prŏ.nŭn'sĭ.ā'shŭn) *n.* pronunzia.

proof (prōōf) *n.* prova, saggio; bozza di stampa; gradazione (*alcoolica*). *agg.* impenetrabile, impervio, resistente; probatorio: **— against**, a prova di; **bullet—**, a prova di proiettile; **galley —**, prima bozza, bozza in colonna; **—reader**, correttore di bozze; **—sheet**, bozza di stampa.

prop (prŏp) *n.* sostegno, appoggio; palo; (*teat. e cinema*) attrezzo scenico; (*aeron.*) elica. *vt.* puntellare, sostenere.

propagate (prŏp'à.gāt) *vt.* propagare, diffondere. *vi.* propagarsi.

propagation (prŏp'à.gā'shŭn) *n.* propagazione, trasmissione.

propel (prŏ.pĕl') *vt.* spingere avanti, azionare, lanciare. **—ler** *n.* propulsore, elica.

propensity (prŏ.pĕn'sĭ.tĭ) *n.* propensione.

proper (prŏp'ĕr) *agg.* proprio, vero e proprio; appropriato, adatto, giusto, conveniente, corretto: **— noun**, nome proprio; **the garden —**, il

giardino vero e proprio. **—ly** *avv.* propriamente, giustamente, correttamente, come si deve.

property (prŏp'ĕr.tĭ) *n.* proprietà, beni, possesso; (*teat.*) dotazione: **man of —**, possidente; **— man**, trovarobe.

prophecy (prŏf'ē.sĭ) *n.* profezia.

prophesy (prŏf'ē.sī) *vt.*, *vi.* profetizzare.

prophet (prŏf'ĕt) *n.* profeta. **—ical** (-ĕt'ĭk.ăl) *agg.* profetico.

prophylactic (prŏ'fĭ.lăk'tĭc) *agg.* profilattico.

propitiate (prŏ.pĭsh'ĭ.āt) *vt.* propiziare.

propitious (prŏ.pĭsh'ŭs) *agg.* propizio, favorevole.

prop-jet (engine) *n.*(*aeron.*)turboelica

proportion (prŏ.pōr'shŭn) *n.* proporzione: **out of —**, sproporzionato. *vt.* proporzionare.

proportionate (prŏ.pōr'shŭn.ĭt) *agg.* proporzionato.

proposal (prŏ.pōz'ăl) *n.* proposta.

propose (prŏ.pōz') *vt.* proporre. *vi.* fare una proposta di matrimonio; divisare, proporsi: **to — to do something**, ripromettersi di fare una cosa.

proposition (prŏp'ō.zĭsh'ŭn) *n.* proposta; proposizione.

propound (prŏ.pound') *vt.* sottoporre, proporre.

proprietary (prŏ.prī'ē.tĕr'ĭ) *agg.* padronale; esclusivo: **— classes**, classi abuienti; **— medicine**, specialità medicinale.

proprietor (prŏ.prī'ē.tĕr) *n.* proprietario. **—ial** (-tō'rĭ.ăl) *agg.* di padronanza.

propriety (prŏ.prī'ē.tĭ) *n.* proprietà, convenienza, correttezza, decoro.

prosaic (prŏ.zā'ĭk) *agg.* prosaico.

proscribe (prŏ.skrīb') *vt.* proscrivere, bandire.

prose (prōz) *n.* prosa. *agg.* di prosa; in prosa; prosaico.

prosecute (prŏs'ē.kūt) *vt.*, *vi.* perseguire, proseguire, querelare; fungere da pubblico ministero.

prosecution (prŏs'ē.kū'shŭn) *n.* prosecuzione; azione legale; parte civile, accusa.

prosecutor (prŏs'ē.kū'tĕr) *n.* pubblico ministero; querelante.

prospect (prŏs'pĕkt) *n.* vista, prospettiva, prospetto, aspettativa, speranza; probabile cliente, candidato acquirente. *vt.*, *vi.* esplorare (*in cerca di giacimenti*); fare ricerche (*spec.minerarie*). **—ive** *n.* prospettiva. *agg.* probabile, futuro.

prospector (prŏs'pĕk.tĕr) *n.* cercatore (*d'oro, ecc.*).

prosper (prŏs'pĕr) *vi.* prosperare. —**ity** (-pĕr'ĭ·tĭ) *n.* prosperità. —**ous** *agg.* prospero, prosperoso.

prostitute (prŏs'tĭ·tūt) *n.* prostituta. *vt.* prostituire.

prostitution (prŏs'tĭ·tū'shŭn) *n.* prostituzione.

prostrate (prŏs'trāt) *agg.* prosternato, prostrato, prono, supino. *vt.*, *vi.* prostrare, abattere, coricare, rovinare; prosternarsi.

prosy (prōz'ĭ) *agg.* prosaico; tedioso.

protect (prŏ·tĕkt') *vt.* proteggere. —**ion** *n.* protezione, garanzia; passaporto, salvacondotto; protezionismo. —**ive** *agg.* protettivo. —**or** *n.* protettore. —**orate** *n.* protettorato.

protégé (prŏ'tĕ·zhā) *m.*, **protégée** *f.* *n.* protetto, protetta.

protein (prŏ'tē·ĭn) *n.* proteina.

protest (prŏ·tĕst') *n.* protesta; protesto. *vt.*, *vi.* protestare; mandare in protesto; disapprovare.

Protestant (prŏt'ĕs·tănt) *n.*, *agg.* protestante.

Protestantism (prŏt'ĕs·tănt·ĭz'm) *n.* protestantesimo.

protestation (prŏt'ĕs·tā'shŭn) *n.* protesta.

protract (prŏ·trăkt') *vt.* protrarre.

protrude (prŏ·trōōd') *vt.*, *vi.* sporgere, proiettarsi.

protuberance (prŏ·tū'bĕr·ăns) *n.* protuberanza.

proud (proud) *agg.* orgoglioso, arrogante, superbo, grandioso.

prove (prōōv) *vt.* provare, dimostrare; verificare; omologare. *vi.* dimostrarsi, rivelarsi, risultare.

provender (prŏv'ĕn·dĕr) *n.* foraggio, vettovaglie.

proverb (prŏv'ûrb) *n.* proverbio.

provide (prŏ·vīd') *vt.*, *vi.* provvedere; fornire; prendere precauzioni; stipulare: **to** — **for**, prepararsi in previsione di; **to** — **with**, provvedere *o* fornire di.

provided (prŏ·vīd'ĕd) *cong.* purchè, a condizione che, sempre che.

providence (prŏv'ĭ·dĕns) *n.* provvidenza, previdenza, economia.

provident (prŏv'ĭ·dĕnt) *agg.* previdente, provvido, economo. —**ial** (-dĕn'shăl) *agg.* provvidenziale.

provider (prŏ·vīd'ĕr) *n.* fornitore: **to be a good** —, saper provvedere bene alla propria famiglia.

province (prŏv'ĭns) *n.* provincia; pertinenza, competenza: **it is not within my** —, non è di mia competenza.

provincial (prŏ·vĭn'shăl) *n.*, *agg.* provinciale.

provision (prŏ·vĭzh'ŭn) *n.* provvedimento; precauzione; preparativo; clausola: **provisions**, provviste. —**al**, —**ary** *agg.* provvisorio.

proviso (prŏ·vī'zō) *n.* condizione, clausola.

provocation (prŏv'ŏ·kā'shŭn) *n.* provocazione.

provoke (prŏ·vōk') *vt.* provocare, incitare; irritare.

provost (prŏv'ŭst) *n.* (*univ.*) rettore di facoltà: — **marshal**, capo della polizia militare.

prow (prou) *n.* prua.

prowess (prou'ĕs) *n.* prodezza, coraggio.

prowl (proul) *vt.*, *vi.* vagare in cerca di preda; aggirarsi furtivamente: — **car**, auto della polizia.

proximity (prŏks·ĭm'ĭ·tĭ) *n.* prossimità.

proxy (prŏk'sĭ) *n.* procuratore; procura: **by** —, per procura.

prude (prōōd) *n.* moralista.

prudence (prōō'dĕns) *n.* prudenza.

prudent (prōō'dĕnt) *agg.* prudente.

prudery (prōōd'ĕr·ĭ) *n.* austerità affettata.

prudish (prōōd'ĭsh) *agg.* moraleggiante, austero.

prune (prōōn) (1) *n.* prugna secca.

prune (prōōn) (2) *vt.* potare, sfrondare, mondare.

prurient (prōōr'ĭ·ĕnt) *agg.* smanioso, lascivo.

pry (prī) (1) *n.* indagatore; ficcanaso; curiosità indiscreta. *vt.*, *vi.* indagare; spiare; curiosare.

pry (prī) (2) *n.* leva, sbarra. *vt.* forzare (*con una leva, ecc.*): **to** — **apart**, separare con la forza; **to** — **open**, aprire con la forza; **to** — **up**, aprire con una leva; **to** — **a secret out of**, strappare un segreto a.

psalm (säm) *n.* salmo.

pseudonym (sū'dō·nĭm) *n.* pseudonimo.

psychiatrist (sī·kī'á·trĭst) *n.* psichiatra.

psychiatry (sī·kī'á·trĭ) *n.* psichiatria.

psychic (sī'kĭk) *agg.* psichico, telepatico.

psychoanalysis (sī'kō·á·năl'ĭ·sĭs) *n.* psicanalisi.

psychological (sī'kō·lŏj'ĭ·kăl) *agg.* psicologico.

psychologist (sī'kŏl'ō·jĭst) *n.* psicologo.

psychology (sī·kŏl'ō·jĭ) *n.* psicologia.

psychosis (sī·kō'sĭs) *n.* psicosi.

PT boat (pē'tē'bōt') *n.* (*naut.*) silurante.

ptomaine (tō'mān) *n.* ptomaina.

ptomaine (tō'mān) *n.* ptomaina.

pub (pŭb) *n.* (*gergo Ingl.*, *abb. di* public-house) taverna, bar.

public (pŭb'lĭk) *n.*, *agg.* pubblico: — **defender**, difensore d'ufficio;

— prosecutor, pubblico ministero; — domain, dominio pubblico; (*S.U.*) terre demaniali; — house, taverna, bar, albergo; — relations, rapporti col pubblico, relazioni pubbliche; — utility, azienda di servizi pubblici. —minded, —spirited *agg.* dotato di civismo. —minded-ness, —spiritedness *n.* civismo.

public-address system *n.* impianto di altoparlanti.

publication (pŭb'lĭ·kā'shŭn) *n.* pubblicazione.

publicist (pŭb'lĭ·sĭst) *n.* esperto di diritto internazionale; giornalista politico; agente pubblicitario.

publicity (pŭb·lĭs'ĭ·tĭ) *n.* pubblicità.

publicly (pŭb'lĭk·lĭ) *avv.* pubblicamente.

publish (pŭb'lĭsh) *vt.* pubblicare; divulgare. —er *n.* editore. —ing *agg.* editoriale; — house, casa editrice.

puck (pŭk) *n.* folletto; disco (*per hockey*).

pucker (pŭk'ĕr) *n.* piega, contrazione, grinza. *vt.* raggrinzare, contrarre. *vi.* raggrinzirsi, contrarsi.

pudding (pŏŏd'ĭng) *n.* torta, budino.

puddle (pŭd''l) *n.* pozzanghera.

pudgy (pŭj'ĭ) *agg.* tarchiato, grassoccio.

puff (pŭf) *n.* soffio, sbuffo; getto (*di vapore, ecc.*); protuberanza; piumino (*da cipria*); pistolotto, soffietto. *vt.* soffiar via; gonfiare; adulare. *vi.* soffiare, ansare; gonfiarsi; emetter fumo.

puffy (pŭf'ĭ) *agg.* gonfio, enfiato; tronfio; ventoso.

pug (pŭg) *n.* piccolo mastino; (*gergo*) pugile: — nose, naso camuso.

pugilism (pū'jĭ·lĭz'm) *n.* pugilato.

pugilist (pū'jĭ·lĭst) *n.* pugilista.

pugnacious (pŭg·nā'shŭs) *agg.* battagliero, combattivo.

puissance (pū'ĭ·sáns) *n.* potenza, forza.

puissant (pū'ĭ·sănt) *agg.* potente, forte.

puke (pūk) *vi.* vomitare.

pull (pŏŏl) *n.* trazione; strappo, strattone; impulso; attrazione; prestigio, autorità; sorsata; sforzo; vantaggio: to have —, avere prestigio, essere influente. *vt.*, *vi.* tirare, trascinare; strappare; arrancare; remare: to — a wry face, fare una smorfia; to — down, abbattere; tirar giù; to — up, trattenere; fermarsi; issare; to — one-self together, ricomporsi; to — somebody's leg, beffare qualcuno; to — through, riuscire, cavarsela, trarre d'impaccio; to — over to the right, portarsi alla destra; the

train —ed into the station, il treno si fermò in stazione.

pullet (pŏŏl'ĕt) *n.* pollastrella.

pulley (pŏŏl'ĭ) *n.* puleggia.

Pullman (car) (pŏŏl'măn) *n.* vettura salone, vagone letto.

pulmotor (pŭl'mō'tĕr) *n.* polmone d'acciaio.

pulp (pŭlp) *n.* polpa; pasta, impasto; libro *o* rivista di carta scadente; libraccio, giornale scandalistico; letteratura *o* giornalismo deteriore.

pulpit (pŏŏl'pĭt) *n.* pulpito.

pulpy (pŭlp'ĭ) *agg.* polposo, molle.

pulsate (pŭl'sāt) *vi.* pulsare.

pulse (pŭls) *n.* polso, pulsazione.

pulverize (pŭl'vĕr·ĭz) *vt.* polverizzare. *vi.* andare in polvere.

pumice (pŭm'ĭs) *n.* pomice.

pump (pŭmp) *n.* pompa: gasoline —, distributore della benzina; hand —, pompa a mano; tire —, pompa per i pneumatici. *vt.*, *vi.* pompare; gonfiare: to — someone, far cantare uno (*estorcergli un segreto*).

pumpkin (pŭmp'kĭn) *n.* (*bot.*) zucca.

pun (pŭn) *n.* gioco di parole. *vi.* fare giochi di parole.

punch (pŭnch) *n.* pugno; ponce; punzone; vigore, vitalità: — bowl, conca per ponce *o* liquori. *vt.* dare un pugno a; punzonare; forare; spronare: **punching bag** (*pugilato*), sacco.

puncheon (pŭn'chŭn) (1) *n.* grossa botte.

puncheon (2) *n.* punzone.

punctilious (pŭngk·tĭl'ĭ·ŭs) *agg.* preciso, formalista, scrupoloso, meticoloso.

punctual (pŭngk'tū·ăl) *n.* puntuale. —ity (-ăl'ĭ·tĭ) *n.* puntualità.

punctuate (pŭngk'tū·āt) *vt.* punteggiare.

punctuation (pŭngk'tū·ā'shŭn) *n.* punteggiatura.

puncture (pŭngk'tŭr) *n.* puntura; foratura (*di pneumatico*). *vt.* pungere; forare: to have a tire —, forare; to have a punctured tire, avere una gomma a terra.

punish (pŭn'ĭsh) *vt.* punire, castigare.

punishment (pŭn'ĭsh·mĕnt) *n.* punizione.

punt (pŭnt) *n.* chiatta.

puny (pū'nĭ) *agg.* debole, meschino, piccolo, insignificante.

pup (pŭp) *n.* cucciolo.

pupil (pū'p'l) (1) *n.* allievo, scolaro; pupillo, pupilla.

pupil (pū'p'l) (2) *n.* (*anat.*) pupilla.

puppet (pŭp'ĕt) *n.* bambola, marionetta: — show, spettacolo di marionette.

uppy (pŭp'ĭ) *n.* cucciolo.

urblind (pŭr'blĭnd') *agg.* debole di vista; ottuso.

urchase (pŭr'chĭs) *n.* compera, acquisto; presa sicura, appiglio, appoggio; (*mecc.*) leva, paranco: to get a — on, far presa su, trovare un punto| d'appoggio. *vt.* acquistare, comperare; sollevare (*con mezzi meccanici*).

urchaser (pŭr'chĭs·ẽr) *n.* acquirente.

ure (pŭr) *agg.* puro.

urely (pŭr'lĭ) *avv.* puramente.

urgative (pŭr'gá·tĭv) *agg.* purgativo.

urgatory (pŭr'gá·tō'rĭ) *n.* purgatorio.

urge (pŭrj) *n.* purga; epurazione. *vt.* purgare, espiare, purificare, epurare.

urify (pū'rĭ·fī) *vt.* purificare, depurare. *vi.* purificarsi.

urity (pū'rĭ·tĭ) *n.* purezza.

urloin (pŭr·loin') *vt.*, *vi.* rubare.

urple (pŭr'p'l) *n.* porpora. *agg.* purpureo; violetto; sgargiante.

urport (pŭr·pōrt') *n.* senso, significato, portata, intenzione. *vt.* indicare, significare, implicare.

urpose (pŭr'pŭs) *n.* scopo, proposito, mira, fine, funzione: to answer a —, servire a uno scopo; to no —, inutilmente; on —, a bella posta. *vt.*, *vi.* proporsi. —ful *agg.* deciso; intenzionale.

urr (pŭr) *n.* fusa (*del gatto*); borbottio. *vi.* fare le fusa; borbottare.

urse (pŭrs) *n.* borsa, borsetta, portamonete. *vt.* increspare, contrarre: to — one's lips, increspare le labbra.

urser (pŭr'sẽr) *n.* (*naut.*) commissario di bordo.

ursuant (pŭr·sū'ănt) *agg.* conforme: — to, in conseguenza di, conformemente a.

ursue (pŭr·sū') *vt.*, *vi.* perseguire, proseguire, inseguire, perseguitare; dedicarsi a.

ursuer (pŭr·sū'ẽr) *n.* inseguitore.

ursuit (pŭr·sūt') *n.* inseguimento, caccia; continuazione; pratica; ricerca; occupazione, esercizio (*di una professione*): — plane, velivolo da caccia; in — of, alla caccia di, alla ricerca di.

urulent (pū'rŏō·lĕnt) *agg.* purulento.

urvey (pŭr·vā') *vt.* procurare. *vi.* far provviste.

urveyor (pŭr·vā'ẽr) *n.* fornitore.

us (pŭs) *n.* (*med.*) pus.

ush (pŏōsh) *n.* urto, spinta, colpo; impulso, energia: — button, pul-

sante, bottone; (*agg.*) azionato a pulsante, automatico. *vt.*, *vi.* spingere, urtare, istigare: to be —ed for money, essere a corto di danaro; to — on, incalzare; to — through, aprirsi un varco a spintoni. —cart *n.* carretto a mano. —ing *agg.* intraprendente, energico.

pushmobile (pŏōsh'mō·bēl) *n.* automobilina a pedali.

pushover (pŏōsh'ō'vẽr) *n.* avversario facile da battere; ingenuo, credulone; sinecura, pacchia, giochetto.

puss (pŏōs) *n.* micio; (*gergo*) faccia.

put (pŏōt) *n.* posa; lancio; colpo; spinta; opzione; tentativo. *vt.*, *vi.* (*pass.*, *pp.* put) mettere, porre, deporre, collocare; sottoporre; presentare; forzare; applicare; lanciare; dirigersi: to — aside, away, by, mettere da parte; risparmiare; to — about, virare di bordo; to — a question, fare una domanda; to — across condurre a termine; far capire; to — before, presentare, prospettare; to — down, sopprimere, reprimere; annotare; to — forth, produrre, proporre, pubblicare; to — in writing, metter per iscritto; to — off, togliersi; sviare; frustrare; rimandare; salpare; to — on, indossare; to — on airs, darsi arie; to — out, spegnere; turbare; estromettere, espellere; to — to shame, svergognare; to — up, innalzare, montare; ospitare; alloggiare; affiggere; to — up with, sopportare; to — up for sale, mettere in vendita.

putrefaction (pū'trē·făk'shŭn) *n.* putrefazione.

putrefy (pū'trē·fī) *vt.*, *vi.* putrefare, putrefarsi.

putrid (pū'trĭd) *agg.* putrido.

puttee (pŭt'ĭ) *n.* mollettiera.

putty (pŭt'ĭ) *n.* stucco, mastice. *vt.* stuccare.

puzzle (pŭz''l) *n.* perplessità; rompicapo, enigma: cross-word —, cruciverba. *vt.* confondere; rendere perplesso: to — out, sciogliere (*un enigma*). *vi.* arzigogolare.

puzzling (pŭz'lĭng) *agg.* sconcertante, enigmatico.

PX (pē'ĕks') *abbr. di.* post exchange.

pygmy (pĭg'mĭ) *n.*, *agg.* pigmeo.

pyjamas (pĭ.jä'máz) *n.pl.* pigiama.

pyramid (pĭr'á·mĭd) *n.* piramide.

pyre (pīr) *n.* pira.

pyrotechnics (pī'rō·tĕk'nĭks) *n.pl.* pirotecnica.

python (pī'thŏn) *n.* (*zool.*) pitone.

Q

quack (kwăk) n. gracidio (dell'anatra); ciarlatano, medicastro. agg. ciarlatanesco, empirico. vi. anatrare; fare il ciarlatano. —ery n. ciarlataneria; empirismo.

quadruped (kwŏd'rŏo·pĕd) n., agg. quadrupede.

quadruple (kwŏd'rŏo·p'l) n., agg. quadruplo. vt. (kwŏd·rŏo'p'l) quadruplicare.

quaff (kwăf) vt., vi. tracannare.

quagmire (kwăg'mīr') n. palude.

quail (kwāl) (1) vi. sgomentarsi, tremar di paura.

quail (kwāl) (2) n. quaglia.

quaint (kwānt) agg. strano, bislacco, originale; caratteristico; abile.

quake (kwāk) n. tremito, scossa. vi. tremare; oscillare.

quaker (kwāk'ĕr) n. quacquero.

qualification (kwŏl'ĭ.fĭ·kā'shŭn) n. requisito, dote, attitudine; condizione; modifica, restrizione.

qualify (kwŏl'ĭ·fĭ) vt. qualificare, abilitare, rendere idoneo; modificare, condizionare, fissare; addolcire. vi. qualificarsi, rendersi idoneo.

quality (kwŏl'ĭ·tĭ) n. qualità.

qualm (kwäm) n. nausea, malore; apprensione; dubbio, scrupolo.

quandary (kwŏn'dá·rĭ) n. imbarazzo, dilemma, difficoltà.

quantity (kwŏn'tĭ·tĭ) n. quantità.

quarantine (kwŏr'ăn·tēn) n. quarantena. vt. mettere in quarantena.

quarrel (kwŏr'ĕl) n. disputa, litigio: to pick a —, attaccar briga. vi. litigare.

quarrelsome (kwŏr'ĕl·sŭm) agg. litigioso.

quarry (kwŏr'ĭ) (1) n. preda, selvaggina.

quarry (kwŏr'ĭ) (2) n. cava (di pietra, ecc.). vt. estrarre da una cava; vi. lavorare in una cava.

quart (kwôrt) n. quarto di gallone (liquidi: L. 0,9463; aridi: 1,1012).

quarter (kwŏr'tĕr) n. quarto; quarta parte; quarto d'ora; (scuola) bimestre; 25 centesimi di dollaro; parte, regione, distretto, quartiere; direzione; gruppo, cerchia, ambiente, sfera; (pl.) alloggio, caserma, quartiere: at close —s, a breve distanza, da vicino; from all —s, da tutte le parti; to come to close —s, venire alle mani; to give no —, non dar quartiere. vt. dividere in quarti; squartare; acquartierare, alloggiare. vi. acquartierarsi, alloggiarsi. agg. cor-

rispondente a un quarto: —day quarto di giornata; —moon, quart di luna; —year, trimestre.

quarterdeck n. (naut.) cassero.

quarterly (kwôr'tĕr·lĭ) n. pubblica zione trimestrale. agg. trimestrale avv. trimestralmente.

quartermaster (kwôr'tĕr·mȧs'tĕr) n quartiermastro; ufficiale d'ammi nistrazione; maresciallo d'alloggio — Corps, Intendenza Militare.

quartet (kwôr·tĕt') n. quartetto.

quartz (kwôrts) n. quarzo.

quash (kwŏsh) vt. schiacciare, an nientare.

quaver (kwā'vĕr) n. tremolo, tremito (della voce). vi. tremolare; cantar col tremolo.

quay (kē) n. molo, scalo.

queasy (kwē'zĭ) agg. nauseato; scon volto; sconvolgente.

queen (kwēn) n. regina. —ly agg. d regina.

queer (kwēr) agg. bizzarro, strano singolare, ambiguo: to feel —, a vere un malessere; to be in —, stree (Ingl.) essere nei guai. n. cosa persona bislacca. vt. (gergo) rovi nare, mandare a monte; mettere i ridicolo: to — oneself with some one, mettersi in disaccordo con qual cuno, attirarsi l'antipatia di qual cuno.

quell (kwĕl) vt. soffocare, stroncare reprimere.

quench (kwĕnch) vt. estinguere (sete fuoco, ecc.); soggiogare, reprimere

querulous (kwĕr'ū·lŭs) agg. querulo

query (kwē'rĭ) n. domanda, punt interrogativo. vt. indagare, do mandare, mettere in dubbio.

quest (kwĕst) n. inchiesta, ricerca richiesta.

question (kwĕs'chŭn) n. domanda dubbio; questione, discussione problema: — mark, punto inter rogativo; beyond all —, fuor d dubbio; out of the —, da escludersi vt., vi. interrogare, esaminare, do mandare, discutere, mettere in dub bio. —able agg. discutibile, dubbio —er n. interrogatore. —ing n interrogativo, sospetto, interroga zione. —naire n. questionario.

queue (kū) n. codino (di capelli); coda (di persone). vi. formare una coda

quibble (kwĭb''l) n. perifrasi; tergiver sazione, scappatoia, cavillo. vi. ter giversare, cavillare.

quick (kwĭk) n. vivo, carne viva, parte vitale: stung to the —, punto sul vivo. *agg.* rapido, lesto, agile, vivo, pronto, veloce: — **temper,** temperamento infiammabile, irascibilità; — **wit,** spirito pronto. *avv. vedi* quickly.

uicken (kwĭk'ĕn) *vt.* animare, acuire, accelerare, affrettare, stimolare. *vi.* animarsi, affrettarsi.

uickly (kwĭk'lĭ) *avv.* rapidamente, presto; vivamente.

uickness (kwĭk'nĕs) *n.* rapidità, prontezza.

uicksand (kwĭk'sănd') *n.* sabbia mobile.

uicksilver (kwĭk'sĭl'vĕr) *n.* mercurio.

uicky (kwĭk'ĭ) *n. (gergo)* cosa fatta in fretta e furia, cosa sbrigata alla svelta. *agg.* frettoloso, improvvisato, raffazzonato.

uid (kwĭd) *n.* cicca (*spec. di tabacco da masticare*).

uiet (kwī'ĕt) *n.* quiete, silenzio. *agg.* quieto, calmo; modesto, sobrio; silenzioso; immobile: be —! silenzio! on the —, clandestinamente. *vt.* chetare, calmare. *vi.* calmarsi, placarsi. —ly *avv.* quietamente, silenziosamente. —ness, —ude *n.* quiete, calma.

uill (kwĭl) *n.* penna; cannuccia; stuzzicadenti; aculeo (*di porcospino*); spola (*di telaio tessile*); (*mus.*) plettro.

uilt (kwĭlt) *n.* copripiedi, trapunta. *vt.* trapuntare, imbottire.

uince (kwĭns) *n.* cotogna.

uinine (kwĭ'nĭn) *n.* chinino.

uinsy (kwĭn'zĭ) *n.* tonsillite acuta.

uintet (kwĭn·tĕt') *n.* quintetto.

uip (kwĭp) *n.* frizzo, sarcasmo.

quirk (kwûrk) *n.* peculiarità; cavillo; guizzo; svolazzo; scanalatura.

quit (kwĭt) *vt.* (*pass., pp.* quit, —ed) lasciare, cessare, interrompere, rinunciare a: — laughing! smettila di ridere! *vi.* interrompersi, andarsene.

quite (kwīt) *avv.* completamente; notevolmente; realmente: — right, giustissimo; — so, proprio così; — a sight, una vista stupenda, un fior di panorama; to be — the fashion, essere l'ultimo grido della moda.

quits *agg.* pari: to be —, essere pari e patta.

quitter (kwĭt'ĕr) *n.* rinunziante, rinunciatario; vile; disertore.

quiver (kwĭv'ĕr) *n.* tremito, faretra. *vi.* tremare, fremere, vibrare.

quixotic (kwĭks·ŏt'ĭk) *agg.* donchisciottesco; idealistico.

quiz (kwĭz) *n.* enigma, indovinello; esame orale; occhialino; burlone, originale. *vt., vi.* burlare; esaminare, interrogare; mettere in imbarazzo. —zical *agg.* malizioso, beffardo.

quondam (kwŏn'dăm) *agg.* antico, ex, d'un tempo.

quorum (kwō'rŭm) *n.* numero legale (*che consente a un tribunale, ecc. di deliberare*), maggioranza.

quota (kwō'tà) *n.* quota.

quotation (kwō·tā'shŭn) *n.* citazione; quotazione: — marks, virgolette.

quote (kwōt) *vt.* citare; addurre; mettere tra virgolette; quotare: to — from, citare (da). *n.* citazione; (*pl.*) virgolette: in —s, tra virgolette.

quotient (kwō'shĕnt) *n.* quoziente.

R

bbi (răb'ĭ) *n.* rabbino.

bble (răb''l) *n.* marmaglia, plebe, canaglia.

bid (răb'ĭd) *agg.* furioso, fanatico, idrofobo, rabbioso.

bies (rā'bĭ·ĕz) *n.* idrofobia.

ccoon (ră·kōōn') *n.* (*zool.*) procione.

ce (răs) (1) *n.* razza, specie.

ce (răs) (2) *n.* corsa, gara; corrente, canale: — course, — track, campo di corse, pista; boat —, regata. *vt.* far correre; imballare (*un motore*); accelerare; sfidare (*nella corsa*). *vi.* correre.

cer (răs'ĕr) *n.* corridore; cavallo (*o* veicolo, *o* scafo) da corsa.

cial (rā'shăl) *agg.* razziale.

cing (răs'ĭng) *n.* corsa, il correre. *agg.* da corsa: — form, schedina del cism (răs'ĭz'm) *n.* razzismo. [Totip.

rack (răk) *n.* rastrelliera; reticella (*portabagagli*); scaffale; tormento, ruota (*di tortura*): cremagliera: to go to — and ruin, finire in rovina assoluta. *vt.* affaticare, torturare; travasare: to — one's brain, lambiccarsi il cervello.

racket (răk'ĕt) *n.* fracasso, schiamazzo; racchetta (*da tennis*); (*gergo*) associazione a delinquere, attività criminosa; trucco, raggiro.

racketeer (răk'ĕ·tēr) *n.* malfattore, imbroglione, bandito.

racy (rās'ĭ) *agg.* piccante, inebriante, aromatico, stimolante.

radar (rā'där) *n.* radiolocalizzatore, radar. —man *n.* radarista.

radial (rā'dĭ·ăl) *agg.* radiale.

radiance (rā'dĭ·ăns), radiancy *n.* splendore; irradiazione.

radiant (rā'dĭ.ănt) *agg.* raggiante, radioso.

radiate (rā'dĭ.āt) *vt.* irradiare. *vi.* raggiare, splendere.

radiator (rā'dĭ.ā'tĕr) *n.* radiatore.

radical (răd'ĭ.kăl) *n.*, *agg.* radicale.

radio (rā'dĭ.ō) *n.* radio, radiofonia: by —, per radio, alla radio. —active *agg.* radioattivo. —activity *n.* radioattività. — beacon *n.* radiofaro. — broadcast *n.* radiotrasmissione. —graph *n.* radiografia. —graphy (-ŏg'rā.fĭ) *n.* radiologia. — link *n.* ponte radio. — listener *n.* radioascoltatore. —location *n.* radiolocalizzazione. —locator *n.* radiolocalizzatore, radar.

radish (răd'ĭsh) *n.* ravanello.

radium (rā'dĭ.ŭm) *n.* (*min.*) radio.

radius (rā'dĭ.ŭs) *n.* raggio.

radome (rā'dōm) *n.* abitacolo dell'antenna radar.

raffle (răf''l) *n.* riffa (*lotteria*); cianfrusaglia. *vt.* sorteggiare.

raft (ràft) *n.* zattera.

rafter (ràf'tĕr) *n.* trave.

rag (răg) *n.* brandello, cencio, straccio, collera: — doll, bambola di pezza.

ragamuffin (răg'ā.mŭf'ĭn) *n.* pezzente.

rage (rāj) *n.* furore, collera; mania, entusiasmo: to fly into a —, andare sulle furie. *vt.*, *vi.* infuriare, imperversare.

ragged (răg'ĕd) *agg.* aspro, scabro; cencioso; frastagliato: — edge, orlo frastagliato; on the — edge, sull'orlo dell'abisso; nervoso, agitato.

ragout (ră.gōō') *n.* ragù.

ragtime (răg'tīm') *n.* musica sincopata.

raid (rād) *n.* razzia, incursione, irruzione: air —, incursione aerea. *vt.* compiere un'incursione su o in.

rail (rāl) *n.* sbarra; balaustra, cancellata; binario, rotaia: — fence, stecconata, recinto di paletti; by —, per ferrovia. *vt.* circondare con cancellata; spedire per ferrovia; redarguire; insolentire. —ing *n.* steccato, parapetto; rotaie; ingiurie.

raillery (rāl'ĕr.ĭ) *n.* beffa, scherzo.

railroad (rāl'rōd'), **railway** (rāl'wā') *n.* ferrovia, strada ferrata: — crossing, passaggio a livello.

raiment (rā'mĕnt) *n.* vestito, vestiario.

rain (rān) *n.* pioggia: — water, acqua piovana. *vt.* riversare (*come pioggia*). *vi.* piovere: it —s, piove; — or shine, che piova o faccia bel tempo; capiti quel che capiti.

rainbow (rān'bō') *n.* arcobaleno.

raincoat (rān'kōt') *n.* impermeabile

raindrop (rān'drŏp') *n.* goccia di pioggia.

rainfall (ran'fôl') *n.* precipitazione scroscio.

rainy (rān'ĭ) *agg.* piovoso.

raise (rāz) *n.* rialzo, aumento (*di paga*). *vt.* elevare, alzare, sollevare aumentare; allevare, coltivare; erigere; levare (*l'assedio*); evocare; raccogliere (*danaro*): to — a question, fare una domanda, proporre una questione.

raisin (rā'z'n) *n.* uva passa.

rake (rāk) (1) *n.* rastrello; inclinazione; sporgenza. *vt.*, *vi.* rastrellare raccogliere; cercare; raschiare; pulire; inclinare; far fuoco d'infilata to — up, coprire con detriti; riesumare, rivangare.

rake (rāk) (2) *n.* libertino, dissoluto

rake-off *n.* guadagno illecito, compenso illecito, "bustarella."

rally (răl'ĭ) (1) *n.* raccolta, adunata ripresa (*delle forze*). *vt.* raccogliere riorganizzare. *vi.* riorganizzarsi adunarsi; rimettersi in forze.

rally (răl'ĭ) (2) *n.* burla. *vt.*, *vi.* burlare.

ram (răm) *n.* battipalo; ariete. *vt* conficcare; stipare; battere, comprimere; urtare: to — it down one' throat, ingoiare la pillola.

ramble (răm'b'l) *n.* vagabondaggio passeggiata. *vi.* vagare, serpeggiare divagare.

ramp (rămp) *n.* rampa, balzo, pendio

rampart (răm'pärt) *n.* riparo, baluardo, bastione.

ramrod (răm'rŏd') *n.* calcatoio, scovolo.

ramshackle (răm'shăk''l) *agg.* sconquassato.

ran (răn) *pass. di.* to run.

ranch (rănch) *n.* fattoria american con grande allevamento di besti ame, ranch: — house, casa coloni ca, fattoria; villa o albergo di villeg giatura di modello rustico. —ma *n.* proprietario di ranch; buttero

rancid (răn'sĭd) *agg.* rancido.

rancor (răng'kĕr) *n.* animosità, ran core.

random (răn'dŭm) *agg.* a caso, casua le, irregolare; at —, a casaccio, vanvera.

rang (răng) *pass. di.* to ring (2).

range (rānj) *n.* fila; gita, giro, scorri banda; catena montuosa; classe ordine; gamma, varietà; distanz portata (*di armi, della voce, ecc.*) àmbito, cerchia; recinto; fornello cucina economica: gas —, cucina gas; shooting —, campo di tiro; target —, poligono di tiro; —finder, telemetro; — of vision, campo visivo, capacità visiva; in — with, in linea con; out of —, fuori di portata; within —, a portata. vt. allineare; disporre; classificare; percorrere; avere la portata di. vi. allinearsi; estendersi.

anger (rān'jĕr) n. guardia forestale; guastatore.

angy (răn'jĭ) agg. snello e con le gambe lunghe, allampanato.

ank (răngk) (1) n. ordine; schiera, fila; rango, classe; grado; dignità: — and file (mil.), truppa, bassa forza, ranghi. vt. schierare; classificare; (S.U.) essere superiore a. vi.schierarsi; essere classificato; to — above, essere superiore in grado a; to — high with, godere molta stima presso; to — with, essere alla pari con; to — below, essere inferiore di grado a.

ank (răngk) (2) agg. vigoroso, forte (di odore o sapore); lussureggiante; rancido, violento, acre.

anking n. classe, ordine. agg. (il) più anziano di grado; eminente, maggiore.

ankle (răng'k'l) vt. inasprire. vi. infiammarsi, essere fonte di rovello.

ansack (răn'săk) vt. frugare, perquisire, saccheggiare.

ansom (răn'sŭm) n. riscatto, prezzo del riscatto. vt. riscattare, redimere.

ant (rănt) vi. blaterare.

ap (răp) n.colpetto,colpo; (gergo) condanna, fio: not worth a —, privo d'ogni valore. vi. bussare.

apacious (rá·pā'shŭs) agg. rapace.

ape (răp) (1) n. ratto, violenza carnale. vt. rapire, violentare.

ape (2) n. vinaccia; (bot.) ravizzone.

apid (răp'ĭd) n. (gen.pl.) rapida. agg. rapido.

apier (rā'pĭ·ĕr) n. spada.

apt (răpt) agg. rapito, estatico.

apture (răp'tŭr) n. rapimento, estasi.

are (râr) agg. raro, rado, straordinario; poco cotto (di carni).

arefy (râr'ē·fī) vt. rarefare. vi. rarefarsi.

arely (râr'lĭ) avv. raramente, eccezionalmente.

areness (-nĕs) rarity (râr'ĭ·tĭ) n.rarità.

ascal (răs'kăl) n. briccone, farabutto.

ash (răsh) (1) n. eruzione cutanea.

ash (răsh) (2) agg. temerario, avventato, imprudente. —ness n. temerità, impulsività, imprudenza.

asp (răsp) n. raspa. vt. raspare; (fig.) irritare.

raspberry (răz'bĕr'ĭ) n. (bot.) lampone; (gergo S.U.) pernacchia.

rasping (răsp'ĭng) agg. stridente; esasperante.

raspy (răsp'ĭ) agg. rauco; stridente; irascibile.

rat (răt) n. topo; (fig.) rinnegato, traditore; crumiro: —race (fam.), trambusto; circolo vizioso. vi. fare il crumiro, tradire.

rate (răt) (1) vt. redarguire.

rate (răt) (2) n. prezzo; tasso; (Ingl.) aliquota; grado; ritmo; velocità; qualità: — of exchange, cambio; at the — of, in ragione di; at any —, in ogni caso; at this —, stando così le cose; first-— agg. di prim'ordine. vt. valutare; tassare; considerare; classificare. vi. essere classificato: he —s as the best, è considerato il migliore; he —s high, è molto stimato.

ratepayer (răt'pā'ĕr) (Ingl.) n. contribuente.

rather (răth'ĕr) avv. piuttosto; preferibilmente; alquanto: or —, o meglio; — than, piuttosto che; I would — die than, preferisco morire piuttosto che; I would — not go, preferirei non andare; to have —, preferire.

ratify (răt'ĭ·fī) vt. ratificare.

rating (răt'ĭng) n. estimo, valutazione; classificazione.

ratio (rā'shō) n. proporzione, ragione, rapporto.

ration (rā'shŭn; răsh'ŭn) n. razione. vt. razionare.

rational (răsh'ŭn·ăl) agg. razionale, ragionevole.

rationing (rā'shŭn·ĭng; ră'-) n. razionamento: gasoline —, razionamento della benzina.

ratline (răt'lĭn) n. (naut.) grisella.

rattle (răt''l) n. strepito; crepitio; nacchere; sonaglio; cicaleccio; rantolo: death —, rantolo della morte. vt. far risonare, scrollare rumorosamente; dire velocemente; (fam.) sconcertare, confondere. vi. crepitare; tintinnare; risonare, strepitare, rumoreggiare; rantolare.

rattlesnake (răt'l·snāk) n. serpente a sonagli, crotalo.

raucous (rô'kŭs) agg. rauco.

ravage (răv'ĭj) n. devastazione, rovina; saccheggio. vt. devastare; saccheggiare.

rave (răv) vi. delirare, farneticare; infuriare; agitarsi; entusiasmarsi, decantare, osannare. n. delirio, entusiasmo; infatuazione; lode sperticata. agg. laudatorio, osannante.

ravel (răv′ĕl) *n.* groviglio. *vt.* dipanare, sgrovigliare; chiarire.

raven (rā′vĕn) *n.* corvo. *agg.* corvino.

ravening (răv′ĕn·ĭng), **ravenous** (răv′ĕn·ŭs) *agg.* rapace, vorace.

ravine (rá·vēn′) *n.* burrone.

raving (rāv′ĭng) *n.* delirio. *agg.* farneticante, delirante; straordinario.

ravish (răv′ĭsh) *vt.* rapire; violentare; estasiare. —**ing** *agg.* meraviglioso, incantevole.

raw (rô) *n.* vivo, carne viva. *agg.* crudo, grezzo; inesperto; brutale; liscio (*non diluito*); vivo, infiammato: — **material**, materia prima: — **recruit**, recluta, cappellone; — **silk**, seta cruda.

rawboned (rô′bōnd′) *agg.* scarno.

rawhide (rô′hīd′) *n.* cuoio greggio; frustino di cuoio.

ray (rā) *n.* raggio; (*ittiol.*) razza.

rayon (rā′ŏn) *n.* raion, seta artificiale.

raze (rāz) *vt.* radere al suolo.

razor (rā′zĕr) *n.* rasoio: — **blade**, lametta per rasoio; **safety** —, rasoio di sicurezza.

reach (rēch) *n.* portata, distesa, limite: **beyond one's** —, fuori della portata di mano; **within one's** —, a portata di mano. *vt.* raggiungere; arrivare a; stendere, protendere, toccare, conseguire; mettersi in comunicazione con. *vi.* estendersi: **to** — **for**, allungare un braccio *o* la mano; **to** — **into**, infilare la mano; penetrare in.

react (rē·ăkt′) *vi.* reagire.

reaction (rē·ăk′shŭn) *n.* reazione: **chain** —, reazione a catena.

reactionary (rē·ăk′shŭn·ĕr′ĭ) *n.*, *agg.* reazionario.

reactivate (rē·ăk′tĭ·vāt) *vt.* ripristinare, riattivare.

reactive (rē·ăk′tĭv) *agg.* reagente, reattivo.

reactor (rē·ăk′tĕr) *n.* reattore, reagente.

read (rēd) *vt.*, *vi.* (*pass.*, *pp.* read [rĕd]) leggere; studiare; decifrare; registrare, segnare (*di contatori, manometri, ecc.*); insegnare; interpretare: **to be well** —, essere colto; **to** — **for the bar**, studiare legge; **a novel that** —**s well**, un romanzo di facile lettura; **his letter** —**s as follows**, la sua lettera dice quanto segue.

reader (rēd′ĕr) *n.* lettore; correttore. —**ship** *n.* (*giorn.*) numero dei lettori, diffusione.

readily (rĕd′ĭ·lĭ) *avv.* prontamente; volentieri; facilmente.

readiness (rĕd′ĭ·nĕs) *n.* prontezza; facilità: **in** —, pronto.

reading (rēd′ĭng) *n.* lettura; interpretazione; cultura. *agg.* da leggere; **che legge:** — **room**, sala di lettura.

readjust (rē′ă·jŭst′) *vt.* rassettare, rimettere in fase.

readmit (rē′ăd·mĭt′) *vt.* riammettere. —**tance** *n.* riammissione.

ready (rĕd′ĭ) *agg.* pronto, preparato; svelto; volenteroso, facile: **to get** —, prepararsi; —**made clothes**, abiti fatti; — **money**, pronta cassa.

real (rē′ăl) *agg.* vero, effettivo, reale, genuino: — **estate**, proprietà immobiliare.

realism (rē′ăl·ĭz′m) *n.* realismo.

realist (rē′ă·ĭst) *n.* realista.

realistic (rē′ăl·ĭs′tĭk) *agg.* realistico.

reality (rē·ăl′ĭ·tĭ) *n.* realtà.

realization (rē′ăl·ĭ·zā′shŭn) *n.* consapevolezza, comprensione (*il rendersi conto*); realizzazione.

realize (rē′ăl·ĭz) *vt.*, *vi.* rendersi conto di, capire, accorgersi di; realizzare.

really (rē′ăl·ĭ) *avv.* realmente, in realtà: —**? davvero?**

realm (rĕlm) *n.* reame, regno.

realtor (rē′ăl·tĕr) *n.* mediatore di immobili, agente immobiliare.

realty (rē′ăl·tĭ) *n.* beni immobili.

ream (rēm) (1) *n.* risma di carta.

ream (rēm) (2) *vt.* alesare.

reamer (rēm′ĕr) *n.* alesatrice.

reap (rēp) *vt.*, *vi.* mietere, raccogliere; guadagnare. —**er** *n.* mietitore.

reappear (rē′ă·pēr′) *vi.* riapparire.

rear (rēr) (1) *n.* retro, parte posteriore, ultima fila; retroguardia. *agg.* posteriore, ultimo: — **admiral**, contrammiraglio; —**guard** *n.* retroguardia.

rear (rēr) (2) *vt.* alzare; allevare; innalzare, erigere. *vi.* impennarsi, inalberarsi, ergersi.

rearm (rē·ärm′) *vt.* riarmare.

rearmament (rē·är′má·mĕnt) *n.* riarmo.

rearrange (rē′ă·rānj′) *vt.* riordinare.

reason (rē′z'n) *n.* ragione; causa, motivo: **by** —, **of**, a causa di; **it stands to** —, è logico. *vt.*, *vi.* ragionare, arguire, argomentare, discutere: **to** — **someone into**, persuadere qualcuno a; **to** — **someone out of**, dissuadere qualcuno da; **to** — **out**, discorrere, ragionare.

reasonable (rē′z'n·á·b'l) *agg.* ragionevole, moderato.

reasonably (rē′z'n·á·blĭ) *avv.* ragionevolmente; abbastanza.

reasoning (rē′z'n·ĭng) *n.* ragionamento, argomentazione.

reassemble (rē′ă·sĕm′b'l) *vt.*, *vi.* radunare (*o* radunarsi) nuovamente; (*mecc.*) rimontare.

assert (rē'ă·sûrt') vt. riaffermare, confermare.

assurance (rē'ă·shŏŏr'ăns) n. rassicurazione; riassicurazione.

assure (rē'ă·shŏŏr') vt. rassicurare; riassicurare.

bate (rē'bāt) vt. diminuire, ribassare. n. diminuzione, ribasso. —ment n. diminuzione, ribasso.

bel (rē·bĕl') vi. ribellarsi. n., agg. (rĕb'ĕl) ribelle. —lion n. ribellione, rivolta. —lious agg. ribelle.

birth (rē·bûrth') n. rinascita.

born (rē·bûrn') agg. rinato.

bound (rē·bound') n. rimbalzo, contraccolpo: on the —, di rimbalzo. vi. rimbalzare, ripercuotersi.

buff (rē·bŭf') n. rabbuffo; smacco; rifiuto. vt. respingere; infliggere un rabbuffo (o uno smacco) a.

build (rē·bĭld') vt. (pass., pp. rebuilt) ricostruire.

buke (rē·būk') n. rampogna, rimprovero. vt. rimproverare.

but (rē·bŭt') vt. confutare, respingere.

call (rē·kôl') n. richiamo, revoca. vt. richiamare, revocare; ricordare, rievocare.

cant (rē·kănt') vt. ritrattare.

cap (rē'kăp) abbr. di recapitulate e recapitulation.

capitulate (rē'kả·pĭt'û·lāt) vi. ricapitolare, riassumere.

capitulation (-lā'shŭn) n. ricapitolazione, riassunto.

cede (rē·sēd') vi. recedere, ritirarsi, esser sfuggente.

ceipt (rē·sēt') n. ricevuta, quietanza; ricevimento; ricetta; (pl.) entrate: on — of, dietro ricevuta di; we are in — of, siamo in possesso di. vt. quitanzare.

ceive (rē·sēv') vt. ricevere.

ceiver (rē·sēv'ẽr) n. ricevitore; ricettacolo; ricettatore; esattore;(radio) apparecchio ricevente; curatore, custode giudiziario.

cent (rē'sĕnt) agg. recente. —ly avv. recentemente: — married, sposato da poco o di fresco.

ceptacle (rē·sĕp'tȧ·k'l) n. ricettacolo.

ception (rē·sĕp'shŭn) n. ricevimento, ricezione; accoglienza.

ceptionist (-ĭst) n. impiegata che riceve (clienti, ecc.) in un ufficio, accoglitrice.

ceptive (rē·sĕp'tĭv) agg. ricettivo.

cess (rē·sĕs') n. recesso; ripostiglio, nicchia, rientranza; intervallo, tregua; ricreazione. vt. sospendere (un lavoro, una seduta, ecc.); aprire una nicchia.

recession (rē·sĕsh'ŭn) n. recessione, regresso, ritirazione, posizione arretrata; crisi.

recidivist (rē·sĭd'ĭ·vĭst) n. recidivo.

recipe (rĕs'ĭ·pē) n. ricetta.

recipient (rē·sĭp'ĭ·ĕnt) n. ricevente; recipiente. agg. ricettivo.

reciprocal (rē·sĭp'rō·kăl) agg. reciproco, mutuo.

reciprocate (rē·sĭp'rō·kāt) vt. ricambiare, riprocare. vi. contraccambiare; alternarsi, muoversi alternatamente.

reciprocity (rĕs'ĭ·prŏs'ĭ·tĭ) n. reciprocità.

recital (rē·sīt'ăl) n. enumerazione; recitazione; prova; resoconto, esposizione, descrizione; concerto.

recitation (rĕs'ĭ·tȧ'shŭn) n. recitazione.

recite (rē·sīt') vt., vi. recitare, enumerare, narrare.

reckless (rĕk'lĕs) agg. irriflessivo, temerario, avventato: — with one's money, spendaccione.

recklessness (-nĕs) n. temerità, imprudenza, irriflessività.

reckon (rĕk'ŭn) vt. contare, calcolare; reputare; valutare: to — up, addizionare. vi. far di conto: to — on, contare su; to — with, fare i conti con, tener conto di. —er n. calcolatore, contabile. —ing n. computo, calcolo, conto, regolamento (di conti): the day of —, il giorno del giudizio, la resa dei conti.

reclaim (rē·klām') vt. redimere, ricuperare; bonificare (terreni); (raro) reclamare.

reclamation (rĕk'lȧ·mā'shŭn) n. bonifica; redenzione, ricupero.

recline (rē·klīn') vt. reclinare,adagiare. vi. adagiarsi.

recluse (rĕk'lūs) n. eremita. agg. recluso, solitario.

recognition (rĕk'ŏg·nĭsh'ŭn) n. riconoscimento.

recognize (rĕk'ŏg·nīz) vt. riconoscere; ammettere.

recoil (rē·koil') n. il retrocedere, rimbalzo, rinculo; ripugnanza. vi. retrocedere, rinculare.

recollect (rĕk'ŏ·lĕkt') vt., vi. richiamare alla memoria, ricordare.

recollection (rĕk'ŏ·lĕk'shŭn) n. ricordo, reminiscenza.

recommence (rē'kŏ·mĕns') vt. ricominciare.

recommend (rĕk'ŏ·mĕnd) vt. raccomandare; consigliare. —ation n. raccomandazione; consiglio.

recompense (rĕk'ŏm·pĕns) n. ricompensa. vt. ricompensare.

reconcile (rĕk'ŏn·sīl) vt. riconciliare,

armonizzare, mettere d'accordo: **to — oneself to**, adattarsi a.

reconciliation (rĕk'ŏn·sĭl'ĭ·ā'shŭn) *n.* riconciliazione; armonizzazione; adattamento.

recondition (rē'kŏn·dĭsh'ŭn) *vt.* riparare, rimettere in efficenza.

reconnaissance (rē·kŏn'ĭ·sȧns) *n.* ricognizione; esame.

reconnoiter (rĕk'ŏ·noi'tẽr) *vt.* esplorare, ispezionare. *vi.* compiere una ricognizione.

reconsider (rē'kŏn·sĭd'ẽr) *vt.* riesaminare. *vi.* ripensarci.

reconstruct (rē'kŏn·strŭkt') *vt.* ricostruire. **—ion** *n.* ricostruzione.

record (rĕk'ẽrd) *n.* documentazione, verbale, copia autentica; registro; storia; registrazione; incisione fonografica, disco *(fonografico)*; precedenti personali; annale; *(sport)* primato, curriculum di un atleta: **a man with a —** *(legge)*, un uomo con la fedina sporca; **a man with no —**, un uomo incensurato; **this is off the —**, è una cosa detta in confidenza; **— player**, giradischi. *vt.* (rē·kôrd') registrare, annotare; mettere a verbale; incidere *(dischi)*.

recount (rē·kount') *vt.* raccontare, riferire; enumerare, elencare; ricontare. *n.* racconto; nuovo computo, nuovo conteggio.

recoup (rē·kōōp') *vi.* rifarsi (di una perdita).

recourse (rē·kōrs') *n.* ricorso; aiuto, fonte di aiuto; rifugio: **to have — to**, ricorrere a.

recover (rē·kŭv'ẽr) *vt.* ricuperare; riprendere; ritrovare; riconquistare; vincere *(una malattia)*; riparare *(una perdita)*; ottenere *(un indennizzo)*; guarire; salvare; restituire. *vi.* guarire, rimettersi; vincere una causa.

recovery (-ĭ) *n.* ricupero, ritrovamento; guarigione: **to be past —**, essere inguaribile.

recreate (rĕk'rē·āt) *vt.* ricreare; rianimare; distrarre; ristorare. *vi.* ricrearsi; ristorarsi.

recreation (-ā'shŭn) *n.* ricreazione; divertimento: **— room**, saletta da giuoco *(in una casa privata)*.

recruit (rē·krōōt') *n.* recluta; novellino, principiante; nuovo socio. *vt.* reclutare; rifornire, alimentare. *vi.* compiere un reclutamento; ristabilirsi. **—ing** *n.* reclutamento: **— depot**, centro di reclutamento.

rectangle (rĕk'tăng'g'l) *n.* rettàngolo.

rectification (rĕk'tĭ·fĭ·kā'shŭn) *n.* rettifica, correzione.

rectify (rĕk'tĭ·fī) *vt.* rettificare, correggere.

rectitude (rĕk'tĭ·tūd) *n.* rettitudine.

rector (rĕk'tẽr) *n.* parroco; *(univ.)* rettore.

rectum (rĕk'tŭm) *n.* intestino retto.

recumbent (rē·kŭm'bĕnt) *agg.* sdraiato, inclinato; inerte.

recuperate (rē·kū'pẽr·āt) *vt.* guarire, rimettere in salute. *vi.* guarire, rimettersi.

recuperation (rē·kū'pẽr·ā'shŭn) *n.* ricupero; guarigione.

recur (rē·kûr') *vi.* ricorrere, ritornare periodicamente, ripetersi; tornare alla mente. **—rence** *n.* ricorrenza, ritorno, ricorso.

red (rĕd) *n.*, *agg.* rosso: **Red Cross**, Croce Rossa; **— Cross nurse**, crocerossina; **— tape**, burocrazia, pratiche burocratiche. **—blooded** *agg.* sanguigno; coraggioso; energico. **—breast** *n.* pettirosso. **—cap** *n.* *(S.U.)* facchino di stazione; *(Ingl.)* poliziotto militare; *(ornit.)* cardellino. **—coat** *n.* giubbarossa, soldato inglese. **—handed** *agg.* in flagrante, con le mani nel sacco. **—hot** *agg.* rovente, incandescente, ardente; irato, infuriato; nuovissimo.

redden (rĕd''n) *vt.* arrossare. *vi.* arrossire, arrossarsi.

reddish (rĕd'ĭsh) *agg.* rossiccio.

redeem (rē·dēm') *vt.* ricuperare, riscattare *(un pegno)*; adempiere *(una promessa)*; redimere, ripristinare. **—er** *n.* redentore, liberatore.

redemption (rē·dĕmp'shŭn) *n.* redenzione, riscatto, ricupero.

redness (rĕd'nĕs) *n.* rossezza, rossore.

redouble (rē·dŭb''l) *vt.*, *vi.* raddoppiare, intensificare.

redoubtable (rē·dout'ȧ·b'l) *agg.* temibile.

redound (rē·dound') *vi.* ricadere, ripercuotersi, ridondare.

redress (rē·drĕs') *n.* riforma, emendamento, riparazione. *vt.* riformare, riparare, emendare.

redskin (rĕd'skĭn') *n.* pellerossa, indiano.

reduce (rē·dūs') *vt.* ridurre; costringere: **to — to the ranks**, degradare.

reduction (rē·dŭk'shŭn) *n.* riduzione.

redundancy (rē·dŭn'dăn·sĭ) *n.* ridondanza, sovrabbondanza.

redundant (rē·dŭn'dănt) *agg.* ridondante.

redwood (rĕd'wŏod) *n.* sequoia, legno di sequoia.

reed (rēd) *n.* canna; zampogna; ancia *(di strumenti a fiato)*.

reef (rēf) *n.* scogliera; *(min.)* vena

(*naut.*) terzaruolo. *vt.* fare i terza-ruoli.

reefer (rēf'ĕr) *n.* giacchettone; carro *o* camion frigorifero, nave frigorifera; (*gergo*) sigaretta alla marijuana.

reek (rēk) *n.* puzza. *vi.* puzzare.

reel (rēl) *n.* rocchetto, bobina, aspo; oscillazione; (*fot.*) rotolo. *vt.* av-volgere: to — off, svolgere, sroto-lare; raccontare senza inciampi, snocciolare. *vi.* vacillare, ronzare, girare.

re-elect (rē'ĕ·lĕkt') *vt.* rieleggere.

re-election (rē'ĕ·lĕk'shŭn) *n.* riele-zione.

re-enter (rē·ĕn'tĕr) *vt.*, *vi.* registrare di nuovo; rientrare.

re-establish (rē'ĕs·tăb'lĭsh) *vt.* ri-stabilire, restaurare.

reface (rē·fās') *vt.* rinnovare (la fac-ciata di).

refection (rē·fĕk'shŭn) *n.* refezione, pasto.

refectory (rē·fĕk'tō·rĭ) *n.* refettorio; tavolo da refettorio.

refer (rē·fûr') *vt.* riferire, indirizzare, rimandare, rimettere, attribuire. *vi.* riferirsi, alludere; rivolgersi, ricor-rere.

referee (rĕf'ĕr·ē') *n.* arbitro, giudice. *vt.*, *vi.* arbitrare.

reference (rĕf'ĕr·ĕns) *n.* referenza, riferimento, rapporto, allusione; (*pl.*) referenze, note personali. book of —, libro di consultazione; — mark, richiamo, asterisco; letter of —, lettera di raccomandazione, benservito; with — to, per quanto riguarda, rispetto a.

referendum (rĕf'ĕr·ĕn'dŭm) *n.* re-ferendum.

refill (rē·fĭl') *vt.* riempire di nuovo, rifornire. *n.* ricambio.

refine (rē·fīn') *vt.* raffinare, purificare. *vi.* raffinarsi, purificarsi.

refined (rē·fīnd') *agg.* raffinato; ri-cercato; purificato.

refinement (rē·fīn'mĕnt) *n.* raffinatez-za; raffinatura; ricercatezza.

refinery (rē·fīn'ĕr·ĭ) *n.* raffineria.

refit (rē·fĭt') *vt.* riparare, rimettere in sesto; (*naut.*) riarmare.

reflect (rē·flĕkt') *vt.*, *vi.* riflettere, rifrangere; rifrangersi; meditare: to — on, upon, andare a discapito di, incidere su.

reflection (rē·flĕk'shŭn) *n.* riflessione, rifrazione; discapito; biasimo.

reflex (rē'flĕks) *n.* riflesso, azione riflessa. *agg.* riflesso: — camera (*fot.*), macchina reflex.

reflexive (rē·flĕk'sĭv) *agg.* riflessivo.

reform (rē·fôrm') *n.* riforma. *vt.*, *vi.* riformare, migliorare; emendarsi.

—**ation** (rĕf'ŏr·mā'shŭn) *n.* riforma, emendamento. —**atory** (rē·fôr'mȧ·tō'rĭ) *n.* riformatorio. —**er** *n.* riformatore.

refract (rē·frăkt') *vt.* rifrangere. —**ion** *n.* rifrazione.

refractory (rē·frăk'tō·rĭ) *agg.* indocile, refrattario, ostinato.

refrain (rē·frān') (1) *vt.* reprimere, frenare. *vi.* trattenersi, astenersi (*da*).

refrain (rē·frān') (2) *n.* ritornello.

refresh (rē·frĕsh') *vt.* rinfrescare, ristorare. *vi.* ristorarsi, rianimarsi. —**er** *n.* cosa *o* persona che rianima; rinfresco, bibita; promemoria; corso di aggiornamento. —**ing** *agg.* rin-frescante; ristoratore; gradevole; consolante, rincuorante. —**ment** *n.* rinfresco, ristoro.

refrigerate (rē·frĭj'ĕr·āt)*vt.* refrigerare.

refrigeration (rē·frĭj'ĕr·ā'shŭn) *n.* re-frigerazione.

refrigerator (rē·frĭj'ĕr·ā'tĕr) *n.* frigori-fero.

refuge (rĕf'ūj) *n.* ricovero, rifugio, asilo.

refugee (rĕf'ū·jē') *n.* rifugiato, profu-go.

refund (rē·fŭnd') *vt.* rifondere, rim-borsare. *n.* rimborso.

refusal (rē·fūz'ăl) *n.* rifiuto; diritto di opzione.

refuse (rĕf'ūs) *n.* rifiuti, scorie, detriti. *vt.* (rē·fūz') rifiutare, respingere. *vi.* rifiutarsi, non volere.

refute (rē·fūt') *vt.* confutare.

regain (rē·gān') *vt.* riguadagnare, riacquistare.

regal (rē'găl) *agg.* regale.

regale (rē·gāl') *vt.*, *vi.* intrattenere, festeggiare, banchettare.

regalia (rē·gā'lĭ·ȧ) *n.pl.* insegne *o* prerogative regali; insegne di un ordine; pompa; alta tenuta.

regard (rē·gärd') *n.* sguardo, atten-zione; riguardo, considerazione; riferimento: in, with — to, rispetto a, per quanto riguarda; —**s**, complimenti, auguri; *vt.* guardare, considerare, valutare; riguardare, concernere: as —s this, quanto a questo.

regarding *prep.* riguardo a.

regardless *agg.* noncurante, negli-gente: — of, nonostante, a dispet-to di.

regatta (rē·găt'ȧ) *n.* regata.

regency (rē'jĕn·sĭ) *n.* reggenza.

regenerate (rē·jĕn'ĕr·āt) *agg.* rigene-rato. *vt.* rigenerare; emendare. *vi.* rigenerarsi; emendarsi.

regeneration (-ā'·shŭn) *n.* rigenera-zione; emendamento.

regent (rē'jĕnt) *n.* reggente.

regimen (rĕj'ĭ·mĕn) *n.* regime.

regiment (rĕj'ĭ·mĕnt) *n.* reggimento.

regimental (rĕj'ĭ·mĕn'tăl) *agg.* reggimentale. *n.pl.* uniforme militare.

region (rē'jŭn) *n.* regione.

register (rĕj'ĭs·tĕr) *n.* registro; protocollo, archivio, registrazione; *(mecc.)* regolatore. *vt.* registrare, iscrivere; raccomandare *(una lettera). vi.* iscriversi.

registered *agg.* registrato; raccomandato *(di posta).*

registrar (rĕj'ĭs·trär) *n.* cancelliere, archivista.

registration (rĕj'ĭs·trā'shŭn) *n.* registrazione; raccomandazione *(di lettere).*

registry (rĕj'ĭs·trĭ) *n.* registrazione, cancelleria, archivio.

regret (rē·grĕt') *n.* rammarico, rimpianto, dispiacere: **to send one's —s,** inviare le proprie scuse. *vt.* rammaricarsi di, rimpiangere, deplorare.

regretful ('-fŏŏl) *agg.* dolente.

regrettable (-á·b'l) *agg.* doloroso, deplorevole.

regular (rĕg'û·lĕr) *agg.* regolare, metodico, ordinato; autentico; completo: **a — fool,** un autentico cretino; **— price,** prezzo corrente. **—ity** (-är'ĭ·tĭ) *n.* regolarità.

regulate (rĕg'û·lāt) *vt.* regolare.

regulation (rĕg'û·lā'shŭn) regolamento; *(pl.)* regolamento, norme: **— uniform,** divisa d'ordinanza. *agg.* regolamentare.

regulator (rĕg'û·lā'tĕr) *n.* regolatore.

rehabilitate (rē'há·bĭl'ĭ·tāt) *vt.* riabilitare; ricostruire.

rehabilitation (rē·'há·bĭl'ĭ·tā'shŭn) *n.* riabilitazione; ricostruzione.

rehearsal (rē·hûr'săl) *n.* recitazione, narrazione; *(teat.)* prova: **dress —,** prova generale.

rehearse (rē·hûrs') *vt., vi.* ripetere, recitare, provare.

reign (rān) *n.* regno. *vi.* regnare.

reimburse (rē'ĭm·bûrs') *vt.* rimborsare.

reimbursement *n.* rimborso.

rein (rān) *n.* redine. *vt.* guidare con le redini; tenere a freno.

reincarnate (rē'ĭn·kär'nāt) *vt.* reincarnare.

reindeer (rān'dēr) *n.* renna.

reinforce (rē'ĭn·fōrs') *vt.* rinforzare, rafforzare: **—d concrete,** cemento armato.

reinforcement (rē'ĭn·fōrs'mĕnt) *n.* rafforzamento, rinforzo.

reinstate (rē'ĭn·stāt') *vt.* reintegrare.

reinsurance (rē'ĭn·shŏŏ'răns) *n.* riassicurazione.

reiterate (rē·ĭt'ĕr·āt) *vt.* reiterare.

reiteration (rē·ĭt'ĕr·ā'shŭn) *n.* ripetizione.

reject (rē·jĕkt') *vt.* rifiutare, scartare, respingere.

rejoice (rē·jois') *vt.* rallegrare. *vi.* esultare, gioire.

rejoicing (rē·jois'ĭng) *n.* giubilo, esultanza.

rejoin (rē·join') *vt., vi.* raggiungere, ricongiungere; riunirsi; rispondere.

rejoinder (rē·join'dĕr) *n.* replica, risposta.

rejuvenate (rē·jŏŏ've·nāt) *vt.* ringiovanire.

rekindle (rē·kĭn'd'l) *vt.* riaccendere.

relapse (rē·lăps') *n.* ricaduta. *vi.* ricadere.

relapser *n.* recidivo.

relate (rē·lāt') *vt.* raccontare, riferire; mettere in relazione. *vi.* riferirsi.

related (rē·lāt'ĕd) *agg.* connesso; imparentato: **to become —,** imparentarsi.

relation (rē·lā'shŭn) *n.* relazione, rapporto; parente. **—ship** *n.* parentela; rapporto, attinenza.

relative (rĕl'á·tĭv) *n.* parente, congiunto. *agg.* relativo.

relativity (rĕl'á·tĭv'ĭ·tĭ) *n.* relatività.

relax (rē·lăks') *vt.* rilassare, allentare, mitigare. *vi.* rilassarsi, afflosciarsi; distendere i nervi, abbandonarsi. **—ation** (=ā'shŭn) *n.* rilassamento, distensione, attenuazione.

relay (rē·lā') *n.* cambio; *(tecn.)* relais, relè: **— race,** corsa a staffetta. *vt.* dare il cambio a; trasmettere, ritrasmettere.

release (rē·lēs') *n.* liberazione, svincolo; sollievo, scarico. *vt.* liberare, rilasciare, svincolare; cedere; esonerare, alleviare; concedere: **to — a piece of news,** divulgare una notizia, comunicare una notizia alla stampa.

relegate (rĕl'ē·gāt) *vt.* relegare; assegnare, collocare; demandare, attribuire.

relent (rē·lĕnt') *vi.* impietosirsi, ammansirsi, cedere. **—less** *agg.* inflessibile, implacabile. **—lessly** *avv.* implacabilmente. **—lessness** *n.* inflessibilità, implacabilità.

relevance (rĕl'ē·văns), **relevancy** (-văn·sĭ) *n.* pertinenza, attinenza.

relevant (rĕl'ē·vănt) *agg.* pertinente, attinente.

reliability (rē·lī'á·bĭl'ĭ·tĭ)*n.* attendibilità, fondatezza, integrità.

reliable (rē·lī'á·b'l) *agg.* attendibile; leale; sicuro, degno di fiducia.

reliance (rē·lī'ăns) *n.* fiducia: **self—,** fiducia in sé.

relic (rĕl'ĭk) n. reliquia, ricordo.

relict (rĕl'ĭkt) n. vedova.

relief (rė·lēf') n. sollievo, soccorso, sussidio; cambio (della guardia, ecc.); rilievo: to be on —, vivere di sussidi.

relieve (rė·lēv') vt. alleviare, soccorrere, liberare; dare il cambio a; mettere in rilievo.

religion (rė·lĭj'ŭn) n. religione.

religious (rė·lĭj'ŭs) agg. religioso.

relinquish (rė·lĭng'kwĭsh) vt. abbandonare, rinunziare a.

relish (rĕl'ĭsh) n. gusto, fragranza; voluttà; condimento. vt. gustare, insaporire, godere. vi. aver sapore (di).

reload (rė·lōd') vt. ricaricare.

reluctance (rė·lŭk'tăns) n. riluttanza, ripugnanza.

reluctant (rė·lŭk'tănt) agg. rilluttante, restio. —ly avv. di malavoglia, con riluttanza, a malincuore.

rely (rė·lī') vi.: to — on, upon, fare affidamento su, fidarsi di.

remain (rė·mān') vi. restare, rimanere; spettare. —der n. rimanenza, residuo.

remains n. pl. resti; spoglie; scorie.

remake (rė·māk') n. rifacimento. vt. (pass., pp. remade) rifare.

remark (rė·märk') n. osservazione, commento, frase. vt. commentare, osservare: to — on, fare commenti su.

remarkable (rė·mär'kȧ·b'l) agg. notevole, considerevole.

remarkably (rė·mär'kȧ·blĭ) avv. notevolmente, spiccatamente.

remarry (rė·măr'ĭ) vt., vi. risposare.

remedial (rė·mē'dĭ·ăl) agg. riparatore.

remedy (rĕm'ė·dĭ) n. rimedio, cura: past —, irrimediabile. vt. rimediare.

remember (rė·mĕm'bẽr) vt., vi. ricordare, ricordarsi: — me to him, salutatelo da parte mia.

remembrance (rė·mĕm'brăns) n. ricordo, memoria.

remind (rė·mīnd') vt. ricordare a.

reminder (rė·mīn'dẽr) n. avvertimento, memorandum, memento, promemoria.

reminiscence (rĕm'ĭ·nĭs'ĕns) n. reminiscenza.

remiss (rė·mĭs') agg. negligente.

remission (rė·mĭsh'ŭn) n. remissione, perdono.

remit (rė·mĭt') vt. rimettere, condonare; trasmettere; rinunziare (a). —tal n. remissione, condono. —tance n. rimessa (di danaro). —tent agg. intermittente.

remnant (rĕm'nănt) n. rimanenza, avanzo, residuo, scampolo.

remodel (rė·mŏd''l) vt. rimodellare, rifare, rimodernare.

remonstrance (rė·mŏn'străns) n. rimostranza.

remonstrate (rė·mŏn'strāt) vi. rimostrare, protestare.

remorse (rė·môrs') n. rimorso. —ful agg. pentito. —less agg. spietato, senza rimorso.

remote (rė·mōt') agg. remoto, lontano, estraneo.

removal (rė·mōōv'ăl) n. rimozione; trasporto; destituzione; trasloco; eliminazione; estrazione.

remove (rė·mōōv') vt. rimuovere; sfrattare; destituire; togliere, eliminare, estirpare. vi. allontanarsi, trasferirsi.

removed agg. distante, separato.

remunerate (rė·mū'nẽr·āt) vt. rimunerare.

renaissance (rė·nā'säns) n. rinascimento.

rename (rė·nām') vt. ribattezzare.

rend (rĕnd) vt. (pass., pp. rent) squarciare, spaccare, lacerare. vi. spaccarsi, lacerarsi.

render (rĕn'dẽr) vt. rendere; rimborsare; tradurre; interpretare; purificare.

rendering (-ĭng) n. traduzione, interpretazione, versione.

rendez-vous (rän'dė·vōō) n. appuntamento, riunione.

rendition (rĕn·dĭsh'ŭn) n. resa, rendimento.

renegade (rĕn'ė·gād) n. rinnegato.

renew (rė·nū') vt. rinnovare, ripristinare. —al n. ripresa, rinnovamento; rinnovo, proroga.

rennet (rĕn'ĕt) n. caglio.

renounce (rė·nouns') vt. rinunziare a.

renovate (rĕn'ō·vāt) vt. rinnovare, ravvivare, rimettere a nuovo.

renown (rė·noun') n. rinomanza, fama.

renowned (rė·nound') agg. rinomato, famoso.

rent (rĕnt) (1) n. (pass., pp di to rend) squarcio, strappo, spaccatura.

rent (rĕnt) (2) n. rendita, affitto, pigione: for —, da affittare. vt. prendere (o dare) in affitto, affittare.

rental (rĕn'tăl) n. rendita, affitto.

renunciation (rė·nŭn'sĭ·ā'shŭn) n. rinunzia.

reopen (rė·ō'pĕn) vt. riaprire. vi. riaprirsi.

reorganization (rė·ôr'găn·ĭ·zā'shŭn) n. riorganizzazione.

reorganize (rė·ôr'găn·ĭz) vt. riorganizzare.

repair (rė·pâr') n. riparazione, condizione, rifugio: in good —, in buono stato. *vt.* riparare, rimediare a, restaurare. *vi.* andare spesso; recarsi (*a*); ritornare (*in salute*).

reparation (rĕp'á·rā'shŭn) *n.* riparazione.

repartee (rĕp'ẽr·tē') *n.*risposta pronta; frizzo.

repast (rĕ·påst') *n.* pasto.

repatriate (rĕ·pā'trĭ·āt) *vt.* rimpatriare.

repatriation (-ā'shŭn) *n.* rimpatrio.

repay (rĕ·pā') *vt.* (*pass., pp.* **repaid**) ripagare; rimborsare; contraccambiare. **—ment** *n.* rimborso; contraccambio.

repeal (rĕ·pēl') *n.* revoca, abrogazione. *vt.* revocare, abrogare.

repeat (rĕ·pēt') *vt., vi.* ripetere. *n.* ripetizione. **—ed** *agg.* ripetuto, reiterato. **—edly** *avv.* ripetutamente.

repel (rĕ·pĕl') *vt., vi.* respingere; ripugnare: it **—s** me, mi ripugna. **—lent** *agg.* repellente.

repent (rĕ·pĕnt') *vt.* pentirsi di, rimpiangere. *vi.* pentirsi. **—ance** *n.* pentimento. **—ant** *n., agg.* penitente.

repercussion (rē'pẽr·kŭsh'ŭn) *n.* ripercussione.

repertoire (rĕp'ẽr·twär) *n.* (*teat.*) repertoire.

repertory (rĕp'ẽr·tō'rĭ) *n.* magazzino, deposito; (*teat.*) repertorio: **— company**, compagnia stabile.

repetition (rĕp'ē·tĭsh'ŭn) *n.* ripetizione.

repine (rē·pīn') *vi.* (*gen.seg.da* at, against) dolersi.

replace (rĕ·plās') *vt.* ricollocare, reintegrare; sostituire. **—able** *agg.* ricollocabile; sostituibile. **—ment** *n.* ricollocamento; sostituzione.

replenish (rē·plĕn'ish) *vt.* riempire, colmare, rifornire.

replete (rĕ·plēt') *agg.* pieno; sazio.

replica (rĕp'lĭ·kå) *n.* copia, riproduzione, replica.

reply (rĕ·plī') *n.* risposta. *vt., vi.* rispondere.

report (rĕ·pōrt') *n.* rapporto, resoconto; diceria; detonazione, fragore: **news —**, notizia, notiziario. *vt.* riportare, riferire; denunziare: it is **—ed** that, si dice che. *vi.* fare un rapporto, fare il cronista; presentarsi, andare a rapporto.

reporter (rĕ·pōr'tẽr) *n.* cronista, giornalista; relatore.

repose (rē·pōz') *n.* riposo. *vt., vi.* riposare; posare: to **— one's confidence in**, fidarsi di, confidare in.

repository (rē·pŏz'ĭ·tō'rĭ) *n.* deposito; depositario.

reprehend (rĕp'rē·hĕnd') *vt.* biasimare, rimproverare, riprendere.

reprehensible (rĕp'rē·hĕn'sĭ·b'l) *agg.* reprensibile, riprovevole.

reprehension (rĕp'rē·hĕn'shŭn) *n.* riprovazione, biasimo.

represent (rĕp'rē·zĕnt') *vt.* esprimere, simboleggiare, rappresentare.

representation (rĕp'rē·zĕn·tā'shŭn) *n.* rappresentazione; rappresentanza; asserzione, istanza; protesta.

representative (rĕp'rē·zĕn'tá·tĭv) *n.* rappresentante, deputato. *agg.* rappresentativo.

repress (rĕ·prĕs') *vt.* reprimere.

repression (rē·prĕsh'ŭn) *n.*repressione.

reprieve (rē·prēv') *n.* tregua, sospensione. *vt.* accordare una proroga a; sospendere l'esecuzione capitale di.

reprimand (rĕp'rĭ·månd) *n.* rimprovero. *vt.* rimproverare.

reprint (rē·prĭnt') *n.* ristampa. *vt.* ristampare.

reprisal (rē·prīz'ăl) *n.* rappresaglia.

reproach (rē·prōch') *n.* rimprovero; vergogna, vituperio. *vt.* rimproverare, biasimare. **—ful** *agg.* di rimprovero, severo.

reprobate (rĕp'rō·bāt) *n.* reprobo, depravato.

reprobation (rĕp'rō·bā'shŭn) *n.* biasimo, riprovazione.

reproduce (rē'prō·dūs') *vt.* riprodurre.

reproduction (rē'prō·dŭk'shŭn) *n.* riproduzione.

reproof (rē·prōōf') *n.* rimprovero, biasimo.

reprove (rē·prōōv') *vt.* rimproverare, riprovare, biasimare.

reptile (rĕp'tĭl) *n.* rettile.

republic (rē·pŭb'lĭk) *n.* repubblica.

republican (rē·pŭb'lĭ·kǎn) *n., agg.* repubblicano.

republish (rē·pŭb'lĭsh) *vt.* ripubblicare.

repudiate (rē·pū'dĭ·āt) *vt.* ripudiare.

repugnance (rē·pŭg'năns) *n.* ripugnanza, avversione.

repugnant (rē·pŭg'nănt) *agg.* ripugnante, incompatibile.

repulse (rē·pŭls') *n.* ripulsa, rifiuto. *vt.* respingere.

repulsion (rē·pŭl'shŭn) *n.* repulsione; ripulsa.

repulsive (rē·pŭl'sĭv) *agg.* repulsivo.

reputable (rĕp'ú·tá·b'l) *agg.* rispettabile, stimato.

reputation (rĕp'ú·tā'shŭn) *n.* riputazione, fama.

repute (rē·pūt') *n.* fama, notorietà: **of ill —**, malfamato. *vt.* reputare, giudicare, ritenere.

reputed (rē·pūt'ĕd) *agg.* presunto.

request (rē·kwĕst') *n.* richiesta, istanza: **at the — of**, per richiesta di. *vt.* richiedere, esigere, pregare.

require (rĕ·kwīr') vt. richiedere, esigere, chiedere. —ment n. esigenza, richiesta, necessità, requisito.

requisite (rĕk'wĬ·zĬt) n. requisito. agg. richiesto, necessario.

requisition (rĕk'wĬ·zĬsh'ŭn) n. requisizione, richiesta. vt. requisire, mobilitare; richiedere.

requital (rĕ·kwĬt'ăl) n. ricompensa, contraccambio; rappresaglia.

requite (rĕ·kwĭt') vt. ricompensare, ripagare.

resale (rē·sāl') n. rivendita.

rescind (rĕ·sĬnd') vt. rescindere, annullare.

rescue (rĕs'kū) n. soccorso, salvamento, salvataggio: to go to the — of, andare in soccorso di, andare a salvare. vt. salvare, soccorrere.

research (rĕ·sûrch') n. ricerca, indagine. vi. fare ricerche.

resell (rē·sĕl') vt. (pass., pp. resold) rivendere.

resemblance (rĕ·zĕm'blăns) n. rassomiglianza.

resemble (rĕ·zĕm'b'l) vt. rassomigliare a.

resent (rĕ·zĕnt') vt. risentirsi di, infastidirsi per. —ful agg. sdegnato; offeso; permaloso, suscettibile. —ment n. risentimento, offesa.

reservation (rĕz'ẽr·vā'shŭn) n. riserva; riserbo; prenotazione: — of a room, prenotazione di una camera.

reserve (rĕ·zûrv') n. riserva; riservatezza, moderazione. vt. riservare.

reserved (rĕ·zûrvd') agg. riservato, circospetto, reticente.

reservoir (rĕz'ẽr·vwôr) n. serbatoio, cisterna, deposito.

reset (rē·sĕt') vt. (pass., pp. reset) rimontare (gemme, ecc.); (tip.) ricomporre.

reside (rē·zīd') vi. risiedere.

residence (rĕz'Ĭ·dĕns) n. residenza.

resident (rĕz'Ĭ·dĕnt) n., agg. residente.

residual (rĕ·zĭd'ū·ăl) n., agg. residuo, rimanente.

residuary (rĕ·zĭd'ū·ĕr'Ĭ) agg. residuale, rimanente.

residue (rĕz'Ĭ·dū) n. residuo, resto.

resign (rĕ·zīn') vt. rinunziare a, abbandonare: to — oneself, rassegnarsi. vi. dare le dimissioni; cedere.

resignation (rĕz'Ĭg·nā'shŭn) n. rassegnazione; dimissione; rinunzia.

resilience (rĕ·zĭl'Ĭ·ĕns), resiliency (rĕ·zĭl'Ĭ·ĕn·sĬ) n. elasticità, duttilità.

resilient (rĕ·zĭl'Ĭ·ĕnt) agg. elastico, duttile, facile a riprendersi.

resin (rĕz'Ĭn) n. resina.

resist (rĕ·zĭst') vt. resistere a, av-

versare. vi. resistere. —ance n. resistenza. —ant agg. resistente.

resolute (rĕz'ō·lūt) agg. risoluto.

resolution (rĕz'ō·lū'shŭn) n. risoluzione.

resolve (rĕ·zŏlv') n. risoluzione. vt. risolvere; sciogliere; indurre. vi. decidere, stabilire, risolversi: to — into, risolversi in; ridursi a; trasformarsi in; to — to, proporsi, risolversi a.

resonance (rĕz'ō·năns) n. risonanza.

resonant (rĕz'ō·nănt) agg. risonante.

resort (rĕ·zôrt') n. risorsa; affluenza; stazione climatica: summer —, luogo di villeggiatura; vice —, casa di malaffare; to have — to, ricorrere a; as a last —, come ultima risorsa. vi.: to — to, ricorrere a; affluire a. —er n. frequentatore: summer —, villeggiante.

resound (rē·zound') vi. risonare, ripercuotersi, rimbombare.

resource (rĕ·sôrs') n. risorsa; ingegnosità; prontezza: natural —s, ricchezze naturali. —ful agg. pieno di risorse, ingegnoso.

respect (rĕ·spĕkt') n. rispetto, considerazione, aspetto: in — of, with — to, riguardo a. vt. rispettare.

respectable (rĕ·spĕk'tá·b'l) agg. rispettabile, perbene.

respectful (rĕ·spĕkt'fŏŏl) agg. rispettoso.

respecting prep. riguardo a.

respective (rĕ·spĕk'tĬv) agg. rispettivo.

respiration (rĕs'pĬ·rā'shŭn) n. respirazione.

respirator (rĕs'pĬ·rā'tẽr) n. respiratore; maschera anti-gas.

respite (rĕs'pĬt) n. dilazione, tregua.

resplendent (rē·splĕn'dĕnt) agg. risplendente.

respond (rē·spŏnd') vt., vi. rispondere, reagire a, corrispondere.

response (rē·spŏns') n. risposta; responso; reazione, riflesso; rispondenza.

responsibility (rē·spŏn'sĬ·bĬl'Ĭ·tĬ) n. responsabilità.

responsible (rē·spŏn'sĬ·b'l) agg. responsabile; di responsabilità, di fiducia.

rest (rĕst) (1) n. riposo, pausa; appoggio, sostegno; quiete: at —, in riposo, in pace, tranquillo. vt. dar riposo a; posare; basare. vi. riposare, stare, adagiarsi; poggiare (su); fondarsi (su).

rest (rĕst) (2) n. resto, residuo: the —, il resto, tutto l'altro.

restaurant (rĕs'tō·rănt) n. ristorante; trattoria.

restful agg. quieto, riposante.

restitution (rĕs'tĭ·tū'shŭn) *n.* restituzione.

restive (rĕs'tĭv) *agg.* irrequieto, impaziente.

restless (rĕst'lĕs) *agg.* irrequieto, agitato, inquieto, turbolento.—**ness** *n.* inquietudine, nervosismo, agitazione, turbolenza.

restoration (rĕs'tŏ·rā'shŭn) *n.* restaurazione; restauro, restituzione.

restore (rĕ·stŏr') *vt.* ristabilire; restituire; restaurare; risanare.

restrain (rĕ·strān') *vt.* trattenere, reprimere; imprigionare.

restraint (rĕ·strānt') *n.* freno, ritegno, limitazione, moderazione; detenzione.

restrict (rĕ·strĭkt') *vt.* restringere, limitare. —**ion** *n.* restrizione.

result (rĕ·zŭlt') *n.* risultato, conseguenza: as a — of, come conseguenza di, in sèguito a. *vi.* risultare, risolversi (*in*), finire (*in*).

resume (rĕ·zūm') *vt.* riprendere, continuare, ricominciare.

resumé (rā'zū·mā') *n.* riassunto.

resurrect (rĕz'ŭ·rĕkt') *vt.*, *vi.* risuscitare. —**ion** *n.* risurrezione.

resuscitate (rĕ·sŭs'ĭ·tāt) *vt.*, *vi.* risuscitare.

retail (rē'tāl) *n.* vendita al minuto. *agg.* al minuto: — **dealer**, commerciante al minuto; — **price**, prezzo al minuto. *vt.* vendere al minuto; raccontare minuziosamente; ripetere, propalare.

retailer *n.* rivenditore, commerciante al minuto.

retain (rĕ·tān') *vt.* ritenere, servare; assicurarsi i servigi di; trattenere.

retainer (rĕ·tān'ẽr) *n.* seguace; domestico; caparra, anticipo (*spec. a un avvocato*).

retake (rĕ·tāk') *n.* (*cine*) seconda ripresa. *vt.* (*pass.* retook, *pp.* retaken) riprendere, riportare.

retaliate (rĕ·tăl'ĭ·āt) *vt.*, *vi.* fare rappresaglie, vendicarsi.

retaliation (rĕ·tăl'ĭ·ā'shŭn) *n.* rappresaglia, vendetta, ripicco.

retard (rĕ·tärd') *vt.*, *vi.* ritardare, rallentare.

retch (rĕch) *vi.* avere conati di vomito.

retention (rĕ·tĕn'shŭn) *n.* memoria; ritenzione, mantenimento.

retina (rĕt'ĭ·nȧ) *n.* (*anat.*) retina.

retinue (rĕt'ĭ·nū) *n.* seguito (*persone al seguito*).

retire (rĕ·tĭr') *vt.* ritirare; mettere a riposo. *vi.* ritirarsi.

retired (rĕ·tĭrd') *agg.* ritirato, appartato; a riposo, in ritiro.

retirement (rĕ·tĭr'mĕnt) *n.* ritiro, isolamento; collocamento a riposo.

retiring (rĕ·tĭr'ĭng) *agg.* riservato, timido.

retort (rĕ·tôrt') *n.* replica, risposta arguta; (*chim.*) storta. *vt.* ritorcere, ribattere; (*chim.*) distillare.

retouch (rĕ·tŭch') *vt.* ritoccare. *n.* ritocco.

retrace (rĕ·trās') *vt.* riandare; ricalcare: to — one's steps, ritornare sui propri passi.

retract (rĕ·trăkt') *vt.* ritirare, ritrattare, revocare. *vi.* ritirarsi, ritrattarsi. —**ion** *n.* ritrazione, ritrattazione.

retread (rē·trĕd') *vt.* (*autom.*) rinnovare il battistrada. *n.* (rē'trĕd) battistrada nuovo, gomma con battistrada nuovo.

retreat (rĕ·trēt') *n.* ritirata; eremo, ritiro. *vi.* ritirarsi, retrocedere.

retrench (rĕ·trĕnch') *vt.* ridurre, diminuire. *vi.* risparmiare.

retribution (rĕt'rĭ·bū'shŭn) *n.* ricompensa; punizione.

retrieval (rĕ·trēv'ăl) *n.* ricupero; riparazione.

retrieve (rĕ·trēv') *vt.* ricuperare, riparare.

retriever (-ẽr) *n.* cane da riporto.

retrospect (rĕt'rŏ·spĕkt) *n.* sguardo retrospettivo: in —, in retrospettiva.

return (rĕ·tûrn') *n.* ritorno; restituzione; guadagno, profitto; contraccambio; ricorrenza; elezione; rendiconto, rapporto; biglietto di ritorno: in — for, in cambio di; by — mail, a giro di posta; — game, — match (*sport*), rivincita; — ticket, biglietto di andata e ritorno; income tax —, dichiarazione dei redditi, modulo delle tasse; many happy —s! cento di questi giorni! *vt.* restituire; ricambiare; produrre; eleggere: to — a favor, ricambiare un favore. *vi.* ritornare; rispondere.

reunion (rĕ·ūn'yŭn) *n.* riunione, riconciliazione.

reunite (rē'ū·nīt') *vt.* riunire; riconciliare. *vi.* riunirsi, riconciliarsi.

rev (rĕv) *vt.* (*fam.*): to — up a motor, mandar su di giri un motore.

revamp (rē·vămp') *vt.* rimontare (*scarpe*); (*fam.*) rimettere a nuovo, rispolverare.

reveal (rĕ·vēl') *vt.* rivelare, svelare.

reveille (rĕv'ĕ·lĭ) *n.* sveglia, diana.

revel (rĕv'ĕl) *n.* festa, baldoria. *vt.* gozzovigliare, far festa: to — in, bearsi di.

revelation (rĕv'ĕ·lā'shŭn) *n.* rivelazione.

revelry (rĕv'ĕl·rĭ) *n.* baldoria, gozzoviglia, festa rumorosa.

revenge (rĕ·vĕnj') n. vendetta, rivincita. vt. vendicare. vi. vendicarsi. —ful agg. vendicativo.

revenue (rĕv'ĕ·nū) n. fisco; rendita, reddito: — cutter, guardacoste della finanza; — officer, funzionario delle imposte; — stamp, marca da bollo.

reverberate (rĕ·vûr'bĕr·āt) vt. ripercuotere. vi. ripercuotersi.

revere (rĕ·vēr') vt. venerare.

reverence (rĕv'ĕr·ĕns) n. venerazione; riverenza; rispetto. vt. venerare; rispettare.

reverend (rĕv'ĕr·ĕnd) n., agg. reverendo.

reverent (rĕv'ĕr·ĕnt) agg. riverente.

reverie (rĕv'ĕr·ĭ) n. sogno (a occhi aperti), fantasticheria.

reversal (rĕ·vûr'săl) n. revoca; capovolgimento; riforma (di sentenza).

reverse (rĕ·vûrs') n. inversione; tergo, dorso; rovescio, opposto, contrario; contrattempo. agg. inverso, invertito, contrario: — gear, retromarcia. vt. rovesciare, invertire; revocare; rivoltare.

reversion (rĕ·vûr'zhŭn) n. ritorno, reversione.

revert (rĕ·vûrt') vi. ritornare (a una condizione precedente opp. su un argomento); ricadere.

review (rĕ·vū') n. rivista; revisione; recensione, critica. vt. rivedere, riesaminare; recensire, criticare.

reviewer (-ēr) n. revisore; recensore, critico: film —, critico cinematografico.

revile (rĕ·vīl') vt., vi. insultare.

revise (rĕ·vīz') vt. rivedere, modificare.

revision (rĕ·vĭzh'ŭn) n. revisione.

revival (rĕ·vīv'ăl) n. ravvivamento, ripristino, riesumazione, ritorno, risveglio: religious —, risveglio religioso; — of a play, riesumazione di un lavoro teatrale; — of a film, ripresa o ritorno di un film.

revive (rĕ·vīv') vt. ravvivare, rinnovare; risuscitare, riesumare. vi. rivivere, rianimarsi.

revoke (rĕ·vōk') vt. revocare, annullare.

revolt (rĕ·vōlt') n. rivolta, insurrezione. vt. rivoltare, disgustare. vi. rivoltarsi; provar disgusto. —ing agg. rivoltante.

revolution (rĕv'ō·lū'shŭn) n. rivoluzione. —ary n., agg. rivoluzionario. —ist n. rivoluzionario.

revolve (rĕ·vŏlv') vt. ponderare; far rotare: to — in one's mind, rivolgere nella mente, riflettere (su). vi. rotare, girarsi.

revolver (rĕ·vŏl'vēr) n. rivoltella.

revolving agg. rotante, girevole.

revue (rĕ·vū') n. (teat.) rivista.

revulsion (rĕ·vŭl'shŭn) n. evoluzione improvvisa; revulsione.

reward (rĕ·wôrd') n. ricompensa; taglia. vt. ricompensare.

rewrite (rĕ·rīt') vt. (pass. rewrote, pp. rewritten) riscrivere.

rhapsody (răp'sŏ·dĭ) n. rapsodia.

rheostat (rē'ō·stăt) n. reostato.

rhetoric (rĕt'ō·rĭk) n. retorica, eloquenza.

rhetorical (rĕ·tŏr'ĭ·kăl) agg. retorico.

rheum (rōōm) n. catarro, muco.

rheumatism (rōō'mà·tĭz'm) n. reumatismo.

rheumy (rōōm'ĭ) agg. catarroso.

rhinoceros (rī·nŏs'ĕr·ŏs) n. rinoceronte.

rhubarb (rōō'bärb) n. rabarbaro; (gergo) tafferuglio, gazzarra.

rhyme (rīm) n. rima. vt., vi. rimare.

rhythm (rĭth'm) n. ritmo.

rib (rĭb) n. costa (di maglia); costola, nervatura; stecca (d'ombrello), sostegno; (aeron.) centina. vt. munire di costole o stecche; (fam.) canzonare, sfottere.

ribald (rĭb'ăld) agg. scurrile, volgare.

riband (rĭb'ănd) vedi ribbon.

ribbon (rĭb'ŭn) n. nastro; brandello.

rice (rīs) n. riso: — field, risaia.

ricer (rīs'ēr) n. schiacciapatate.

rich (rĭch) agg. ricco, fecondo; saporoso; ornato, costoso; abbondante; succulento; intenso: — color, colore vivo o intenso; — food, alimento sostanzioso.

riches (rĭch'ĕz) n.pl. ricchezza.

rick (rĭk) n. covone.

rickets (rĭk'ĕts) n. rachitismo.

rickety (rĭk'ĕ·tĭ) agg. rachitico; sgangherato, traballante.

ricochet (rĭk'ō·shā') n. rimbalzo (di proiettile). vi. (pass., pp. ricocheted (-shād') rimbalzare.

rid (rĭd) vt. (pass., pp. rid) sbarazzare, liberare, eliminare: to get — of, sbarazzarsi di.

ridden (rĭd''n) pp. di to ride.

riddle (rĭd''l) (1) n. crivello. vt. crivellare, vagliare: —d with bullets, crivellato di proiettili.

riddle (rĭd''l) (2) n. enigma, indovinello, problema.

ride (rīd) n. cavalcata; scorrazzata; corsa (su qualunque veicolo); percorso, pista. vt. (pass. rode, pp. ridden) montare, cavalcare, percorrere (a cavallo, ecc.); spronare, angariare: to — a bicycle, andare in bicicletta; to — a horse, andare a cavallo; to — someone, dominare una persona; prendersi gioco di una persona. *vi.* viaggiare; andare a cavallo (*in carrozza, in bicicletta, ecc.*); galleggiare, fluttuare; essere all'ancora: to — over a country, attraversare un paese (*in auto, in ferrovia, a cavallo, ecc.*).

rider (rīd′ẽr) *n.* cavaliere, fantino; ciclista; appendice (*a un documento*), codicillo.

ridge (rīj) *n.* catena o cresta (*di montagna*), dorso, cima, costura; (*agric.*) porca.

ridgepole (rīj′pōl′) *n.* trave maestra.

ridicule (rīd′ĭ·kūl) *n.* ridicolo, derisione. *vt.* deridere, beffare.

ridiculous (rĭ·dĭk′û·lŭs) *agg.* ridicolo; assurdo.

rife (rīf) *agg.* prevalente, diffuso, abbondante.

riffraff (rĭf′răf′) *n.* rifiuti; marmaglia, canaglia.

rifle (rī′f'l) *n.* carabina, fucile. *vt.* svaligiare.

rift (rĭft) *n.* crepa, squarcio.

rig (rĭg) *vt.* equipaggiare, armare (*navi*): to — oneself up, azzimarsi.

rigging (rĭg′ĭng) *n.* (*naut.*) sartiame, attrezzatura.

right (rīt) *n.* diritto; giusto, bene; destra (*lato destro, mano destra*): — of way, diritto di precedenza; by —, di diritto; from — to left, da destra a sinistra; to the —, a destra. *agg.* diritto, dritto, diretto; destro; giusto, retto: — angle, angolo retto; — side, lato destro; dritto (*di un tessuto, ecc.*); all —, va bene! to be all —, essere ineccepibile (*opp.* illeso); andare bene, star benissimo; to be —, aver ragione; that is —, è vero che; to be in one's — mind, essere sano di mente. *avv.* direttamente; in linea retta; giustamente, giusto; a destra; proprio: — away, — off, immediatamente; — now, proprio adesso; — there, proprio lì; to be — hungry, avere una fame da lupo; go — home! va direttamente a casa! it is — where you left it, è esattamente dove lo hai lasciato. *vt.* raddrizzare, correggere. *vi.* raddrizzarsi.

righteous (rī′chŭs) *agg.* giusto, virtuoso. —**ness** (rī′chŭs·nĕs) *n.* rettitudine, virtù.

rightful (rīt′fōōl) *agg.* legittimo, giusto.

right-hand *agg.* destro, di destra: he is my — man, egli è il mio braccio destro.

rightist (rīt′ĭst) *n.* (*pol.*) uomo di destra, conservatore.

rightly (rīt′lĭ) *avv.* rettamente, giustamente, esattamente.

rigid (rīj′ĭd) *agg.* rigido.

rigidity (rĭ·jĭd′ĭ·tĭ) *n.* rigidezza.

rigmarole (rĭg′mà·rōl) *n.* tiritera; frottole.

rigor (rĭg′ẽr) *n.* rigore, severità.

rigor mortis (rĭ′-) rigidità cadverica.

rigorous (rĭg′ẽr·ŭs) *agg.* rigoroso.

rile (rīl) *vt.* (*gergo*) irritare.

rill (rĭl) *n.* ruscello.

rim (rĭm) *n.* orlo, margine; cerchio (*di ruota*).

rime (rīm) (1) *n.* brina.

rime (rīm) (2) *n.* rima.

rind (rīnd) *n.* crosta, scorza, buccia.

ring (rĭng) (1) *n.* anello, cerchio; cricca; (*sport*) quadrato, pugilato: **wedding** —, fede nuziale. *vt.* cerchiare; accerchiare. —**shaped** *agg.* a forma di anello.

ring (rĭng) (2) *n.* suono, squillo; tono; tintinnio; telefonata: — of defiance, accento di sfida; — of shouts, urlio; — of a telephone, squillo di un telefono. *vt.* (*pass.* rang, *pp.* rung) sonare; far sonare; telefonare. *vi.* sonare; echeggiare; risonare: to — up, telefonare a; to — off (*telef.*), troncare la comunicazione; to — for something, sonare il campanello per farsi portare qualcosa.

rink (rĭngk) *n.* pista per pattinaggio.

rinse (rĭns) *vt.* (ri)sciacquare. *n.* (ri)sciacquo.

riot (rī′ŭt) *n.* tumulto, rivolta, gazzarra: — of colors, orgia di colori; to run —, scatenarsi. *vi.* tumultuare; ammutinarsi; far gazzarra.

riotous (rī′ŭt·ŭs) *agg.* tumultuoso.

rip (rĭp) *n.* scucitura, strappo, squarcio. *vt.* scucire, stracciare, strappare, squarciare. *vi.* stracciarsi, aprirsi.

ripe (rīp) *agg.* maturo: — for, maturo per, pronto per.

ripen (rīp′ĕn) *vt.*, *vi.* maturare.

ripeness (rīp′nĕs) *n.* maturità.

ripper (rĭp′ẽr) *n.* sventratore.

ripple (rĭp′'l) *n.* increspatura (*dell'acqua*). *vt.* increspare (*l'acqua*). *vi.* incresparsi.

rise (rīz) *n.* il sorgere (*del sole, ecc.*), levata; ascesa; salita, aumento; altura; miglioramento; origine, fonte: to give — to, dare origine a. *vi.* (*pass.* rose, *pp.* risen) sorgere, alzarsi, sollevarsi; salire; lievitare, gonfiarsi; aumentare; nascere, provenire; ribellarsi, insorgere.

risen (rĭz′'n) *pp. di* rise.

riser (rīz′ẽr) *n.:* to be an early —, essere mattiniero.

rising (rīz′ĭng) *n.* (*il*) sorgere; erta; lievitatura; ascesa, resurrezione; insurrezione; gonfiore. *agg.* crescente, nascente; promettente.

risk (rĭsk) *n.* rischio. *vt.* arrischiare.

isky (rĭs′kĭ) *agg.* rischioso.
ite (rīt) *n.* rito.
itual (rĭt′û.ăl) *n.*, *agg.* rituale.
ival (rī′văl) *n.*, *agg.* rivale, avversario. *vt.* compet erecon. *vi.* rivaleggiare. **—ry** *n.* rivalità, emulazione.
ive (rīv) *vt.* (*pass.* rived, *pp.* rived, riven) fendere. *vi.* fendersi.
iver (rĭv′ĕr) *n.* fiume; (*tip.*) sentiero, verme; **—head** *n.* sorgente. **—side** *n.* sponda di fiume. *agg.* ripario.
ivet (rĭv′ĕt) *n.* (*mecc.*) ribattino. *vt.* unire con ribattini; ribadire, fissare saldamente, consolidare.
ivulet (rĭv′û.lĕt) *n.* rivoletto, ruscello.
oach (rōch) *n.* scarafaggio; (*ittiol.*) carpa; baffo d'acqua (*provocato da idrovolante in corsa*).
oad (rōd) *n.* strada, stradone; itinerario; (*naut.*, *pl.*) ancoraggio: **—map**, carta stradale; **— police**, polizia stradale; **on the —**, lungo la strada, in cammino, in viaggio di affari. **—ability** *n.* (*autom.*) tenuta di strada. **—bed** *n.* fondo stradale, massicciata. **— block** blocco stradale, posto di blocco. **—house** *n.* autostello. **—man** *n.* cantoniere; commerciante girovago; commesso viaggiatore. **—side** *n.* ciglio della strada. **—stead** *n.* (*naut.*) ancoraggio. **—ster** *n.* cavallo da tiro; (*autom.*) due-posti. **—way** *n.* strada, carreggiata, parte (*di strada*) riservata ai veicoli.
oam (rōm) *vi.* vagare, aggirarsi.
oar (rōr) *n.* ruggito, mugghio; scroscio (*di risa*); urlo; rombo. *vi.* urlare; ruggire, mugghiare; tuonare; rombare; **to — with laughter**, sbellicarsi dalle risa.
oast (rōst) *n.* arrosto. *agg.* arrostito. **— beef**, rosbif, manzo arrosto. *vt.* arrostire; torrefare (*caffè*); abbrustolire; beffare, criticare.
ob (rŏb) *vt.* derubare, defraudare: **to — someone of something**, rubare qualcosa a qualcuno.
obber (rŏb′ĕr) *n.* ladro.
obbery (rŏb′ĕr·ĭ) *n.* furto, rapina.
obe (rōb) *n.* veste, tunica, manto; toga; abito talare.
obin (rŏb′ĭn) *n.* pettirosso.
obot (rō′bŏt) *n.* automa: **— bomb**, bomba volante, missile.
obust (rō·bŭst′) *agg.* robusto.
ock (rŏk) (1) *n.* roccia, rupe, baluardo; (*gergo*) gemma: **— alum**, allume di rocca; **— salt**, salgemma, sale. **to go on the —s**, finire in rovina. **— crystal**, cristallo di rocca.
ock (rŏk) (2) *n.* dondolo. *vt.* cullare, dondolare, scuotere: **to — to sleep**, cullare fino ad addormentare. *vi.* dondolarsi.
rocker (rŏk′ĕr) *n.* dondolo; sedia a dondolo.
rocket (rŏk′ĕt) *n.* razzo: **— launcher**, lanciarazzi. **—ry** *n.* studio o uso dei razzi; missilistica.
rocking (rŏk′ĭng) *n.* oscillazione, dondolio. *agg.* oscillante: **— chair**, sedia a dondolo; **— horse**, cavallo a dondolo.
rocky (rŏk′ĭ) *agg.* roccioso; instabile.
rod (rŏd) *n.* bacchetta, verga, canna; pertica (*misura di lunghezza = 5 metri circa*); (*mecc.*) albero, biella; (*gergo*) pistola: **fishing —**, canna da pesca; **hot —** (*gergo*), automobile col motore supercompresso.
rode (rōd) *pass.* di to ride.
roe deer (rō) *n.* capriolo.
Roger (rŏj′ĕr) *n.pr.* Ruggero. *inter.* (*radio*) ricevuto.
rogue (rōg) *n.* furfante.
roguish (rō′gĭsh) *agg.* bricconesco, malizioso.
roister (rois′tĕr) *n.* bontempone; gradasso. *vi.* fare il gradasso; far gazzarra.
role (rōl) *n.* parte (*di attore, ecc.*).
roll (rōl) *n.* rotolo, rullo; cilindro; panino; ruolo, lista; (*naut.*) rollio: **to call the —**, fare l'appello; **— call**, appello. *vt.* rotolare, arrotolare; avvolgere; roteare; spianare: **to — up one's sleeves**, arrotolarsi le maniche. *vi.* rotolare, ruzzolare, arrotolarsi, rotolarsi; rullare; rollare: **to — over in the snow**, rotolarsi nella neve.
roller (rōl′ĕr) *n.* rullo, cilindro rotante, laminatoio; ondata, maroso; rotolo (*di garza, ecc.*): **— bearing**, cuscinetto a sfere; **— coaster**, otto volante. **— skates** pattini a rotelle.
Roman (rō′măn) *n.*, *agg.* romano: **— nose**, naso aquilino.
romance (rō·măns′) *n.* racconto di cappa e spada, racconto fantastico; esagerazione, romanticheria; amore, idillio; (*mus.*) romanza. *vi.* raccontare storie fantasiose; **fantasticare**; fare il romantico.
romantic (rō·măn′tĭk) *agg.* romantico; romanzesco. **—ism** (=tĭ·sĭz′m) *n.* romanticismo. **—ist** *n.* romantico.
romp (rŏmp) *n.* monello, maschiaccio. *vi.* ruzzare.
rompers (rŏmp′ĕrz) *n.* tuta da bambino.
rood (rōōd) *n.* crocifisso, croce; ¼ di acro.
roof (rōōf) *n.* tetto, volta; imperiale (*di veicoli*); (*anat.*) palato: **— garden**, giardino pensile. *vt.* coprire con tetto, ricoverare.

rook (rŏŏk) *n.* cornacchia; (*scacchi*) torre; (*gergo*) baro.

room (rŏŏm) *n.* camera, stanza, sala; spazio, posto; possibilità: to give —, fare posto; ritirarsi; there is no — for, non c'è posto per. *vi.* alloggiare. —**er** *n.* pensionante. —**mate** *n.* compagno di stanza.

roominess (rŏŏm′ĭ·nĕs) *n.* spaziosità.

roomy (rŏŏm′ĭ) *agg.* vasto, spazioso.

roost (rŏŏst) *n.* pollaio, posatoio (*dei polli*). *vi.* appollaiarsi; riposare, pernottare.

rooster (rŏŏs′tẽr) *n.* gallo domestico.

root (rŏŏt) *n.* radice; origine. *vt.* piantare: to — up, out, sradicare. *vi.* radicarsi, attecchire; grufolare: to — for (*sport e fig.*) fare il tifo per.

rooted *agg.* radicato; inveterato.

rope (rōp) *n.* corda, fune: to be at the end of one's —, non saper più a che santo voltarsi; to give one —, lasciare che uno faccia; to know the —s, conoscere il mestiere, sapere il fatto proprio; — of sand, legame effimero, amicizia instabile. *vt.* legare (*o* delimitare) con una corda: to — in, adescare, coinvolgere; to — off, cintare *o* isolare con funi.

rosary (rō′zà·rĭ) *n.* rosario.

rose (rōz) (1) *pass. di* to rise.

rose (rōz) (2) *n.* rosa (*fiore e colore*). —**bud** *n.* bocciuolo di rosa. —**bush** *n.* roseto. —**mary** *n.* rosmarino.

rosin (rŏz′ĭn) *n.* resina.

roster (rŏs′tẽr) *n.* ruolo, lista.

rostrum (rŏs′trŭm) *n.* rostro; tribuna.

rosy (rōz′ĭ) *agg.* roseo, rosato: — future, roseo avvenire.

rot (rŏt) *n.* putrefazione, marciume; (*gergo*) sciocchezza. *vt.* far imputridire, macerare. *vi.* imputridire: to — away, off, andare in rovina.

rotary (rō′tà·rĭ) *agg.* rotatorio, rotante: — press, rotativa. *n.* (*traffico stradale*) rotonda.

rotate (rō′tāt) *vt.* rotare. *vi.* roteare, girare; voltarsi; procedere a rotazione.

rotation (rō·tā′shŭn) *n.* rotazione.

rote (rŏt) *n.* trantran; ripetizione macchinale: by —, macchinalmente.

rotor (rō′tẽr) *n.* rotore.

rotten (rŏt′'n) *agg.* putrido, corrotto cariato, malsicuro; ignobile.

rotter (rŏt′ẽr) *n.* farabutto; (*un*) poco di buono; scansafatiche.

rouge (rŏŏzh) *n.* rossetto, belletto. *vt.* imbellettare. *vi.* imbellettarsi, darsi il rossetto.

rough (rŭf) *n.* parte ruvida, terreno ineguale; gradasso; violento. *agg.* rude, rozzo, ruvido; ispido; aspro; ineguale; crudele, violento; approssimativo, grezzo; tempestoso: — diamond, diamante grezzo; — draft, brutta copia, minuta; — estimate, calcolo approssimato; — going, strada accidentata; corsa a sobbalzi; (*fig.*) difficoltà, ostacoli; — ground, terreno accidentato; — idea, idea approssimativa; — sea, mare grosso *o* agitato; — weather, tempaccio. *vi.*: to — it, adattarsi a tutto, vivere alla meglio.

roughen (rŭf′ĕn) *vt.*, *vi.* irruvidire, irruvidirsi.

roughhew (rŭf′hū′) *vt.* potare; abbozzare.

roughly (rŭf′lĭ) *avv.* duramente; rozzamente, ruvidamente; approssimativamente.

roughness (-nĕs) *n.* durezza, asprezza, ruvidezza; violenza.

round (round) *n.* tondo, cerchio, rotonda; giro; ciclo; turno; circonvallazione; distribuzione; piuolo (*di scala*); carica (*di cartucce*); ronda; (*pugilato*) ripresa: — of applause, scroscio di applausi; to go the —s, fare la ronda. *agg.* rotondo, circolare; completo; pingue: — trip, viaggio completo, viaggio di andata e ritorno; — numbers, cifre tonde. *avv.* intorno, all'intorno; all'incirca: all the year —, tutto l'anno; to come — again, tornare di nuovo, ritornare; — about, (tutt') intorno a; dalla parte opposta; indirettamente; all' incirca; in girotondo; to look —, voltarsi a guardare. *prep.* attorno a, ai margini di: — the corner, oltre la cantonata; — the clock, per ventiquatt'ore di seguito. *vt.*, *vi.* arrotondare, circondare; svoltare; fare il giro di; completare; arrotondarsi; (*naut.*) doppiare: to — off, arrotondare (*un orlo*); rifinire; completare; to — on, rivoltarsi contro; to — out, completare; rimettersi in salute; to — to, rimettersi in salute; tornare alle condizioni normali, riprendersi; to — up, radunare.

roundabout (round′à·bout′) *n.* giro vizioso; perifrasi; giostra; giro. *agg.* indiretto, tortuoso.

roundness (round′nĕs) *n.* rotondità.

roundup (round′ŭp′) *n.* raccolta (*del bestiame, ecc.*); retata.

rouse (rouz) *vt.* svegliare, destare; far alzare; infuriare. *vi.* alzarsi, svegliarsi, scuotersi.

roustabout (roust′à·bout′) *n.* scaricatore.

out (rout) *n.* folla, plebaglia; *(mil.)* rotta. *vt.* sbaragliare, mettere in fuga: to — out, scacciare, mettere in fuga.

oute (rōōt) *n.* via, percorso, itinerario. *vt.* instradare; smistare.

outine (rōō·tēn') *n.* trantran, andazzo; abitudine.

ove (rŏv) *vi.* vagare, vagabondare.

over (rŏv'ĕr) *n.* vagabondo; pirata.

ow (rou) (1) *n.* rissa, lite, tumulto. *vi.* litigare.

ow (rō) (2) *n.* fila, filare.

row (rō) (3) *n.* remata, gita in barca. *vt.* spingere a remi; trasportare in barca. *vi.* vogare.

owboat (rō'bōt') *n.* barca a remi.

owdy (rou'dĭ) *n.* briccone.

ower (rō'ĕr) *n.* rematore.

owlock (rō'lŏk') *n.* scalmiera.

oyal (roi'ăl) *agg.* reale, regio, regale.

oyalist (roi'ăl·ĭst) *n.* realista, legittimista.

oyalty (roi'ăl·tĭ) *n.* regalità, maestà, tributo; *(comm., gen.pl.* **royalties)** compartecipazione agli utili, diritti d'autore.

ub (rŭb) *n.* sfregamento, frizione; ostacolo, difficoltà; sarcasmo: there is the —! questo è il guaio! *vt.* strofinare, frizionare, spalmare; to — off, out, eliminare strofinando, cancellare; to — someone the wrong way, prendere uno di contropelo. *vi.* sfregarsi, fare attrito; irritare; logorarsi: to — along, tirare avanti.

rubber (rŭb'ĕr) *n.* strofinaccio; pulitore; gomma, cauccciù; gomma da cancellare; soprascarpa; *(bridge)* partita, *agg.* di gomma, elastico: — **band,** elastico; — **plantation,** piantagione di cauccciù; — **tree,** albero della gomma.

rubbish (rŭb'ĭsh) *n.* rifiuti; cianfrusaglie; sciocchezze.

rubble (rŭb'l) *n.* ciottoli, calcinacci, breccia; macerie; pietra grezza.

ruby (rōō'bĭ) *n.* rubino.

rucksack (rŭk'săk') *n.* sacco da montagna.

rudder (rŭd'ĕr) *n.* timone.

ruddy (rŭd'ĭ) *agg.* rubicondo, florido.

rude (rōōd) *agg.* rude, scortese, villano rozzo, aspro. **—ness** *n.* villania, rudezza, scortesia.

rudimentary (rōō'dĭ·mĕn'tȧ·rĭ) *agg.* rudimentale, primitivo.

rue (rōō) (1) *n.* (*bot.*) ruta.

rue (rōō) (2) *n.* pentimento, rimpianto. *vt.* pentirsi di, rammaricarsi di.

rueful (rōō'fŏŏl) *agg.* triste; doloroso; compassionevole.

ruffian (rŭf'ĭ·ăn) *n.* ribaldo, scellerato.

ruffle (rŭf''l) *n.* increspatura; balza pieghettata; turbamento. *vt.* spiegazzare; increspare; turbare, scompigliare. *vi.* incresparsi, spiegazzarsi; turbarsi.

rug (rŭg) *n.* tappeto, coperta.

rugged (rŭg'ĕd) *agg.* ruvido, scabro; rozzo; roccioso; solcato; severo; vigoroso; inclemente: a — **sport,** uno sport arduo; a — **individualist,** un individualista accanito.

ruin (rōō'ĭn) *n.* rovina: to go to —, finire in rovina. *vt.* rovinare. *vi.* andare in rovina.

ruinous (rōō'ĭ·nŭs) *agg.* rovinoso.

rule (rōōl) *n.* regola, regolamento; governo; metodo; legge; regolo, riga: as a —, generalmente. *vt.* regolare; governare; decretare; rigare: to — out, espellere, radiare. *vi.* regnare: to — over, governare, reggere.

ruler (rōōl'ĕr) *n.* governante, sovrano; regolo, riga.

ruling (-ĭng) *n.* regola, regolamento; decisione, governo; rigatura. *agg.* prevalente, dominante.

rum (rŭm) *n.* rum *(liquore).*

rumble (rŭm'b'l) *n.* rombo, brontolio: — **seat** *(autom.)* sedile posteriore scoperto *(delle spider).* *vi.* rombare, brontolare.

ruminate (rōō'mĭ·nāt) *vt., vi.* ruminare; meditare, rimuginare.

rummage (rŭm'ĭj) *n.* ricerca, rovistio; cianfrusaglie. — **sale** *n.* vendita di oggetti smarriti; fiera di beneficenza; liquidazione. *vt., vi.* rovistare, frugare.

rummy (rŭm'ĭ) *n.* ramino *(giuoco).*

rumor (rōō'mĕr) *n.* diceria. *vt.* propalare, divulgare: it is —ed that, si vocifera che.

rump (rŭmp) *n.* parte posteriore *(di animale),* deretano.

rumple (rŭm'p'l) *n.* grinza, piega. *vt.* sgualcire, arruffare.

rumpus (rŭm'pŭs) *n.* strepito, tumulto: — **room,** saletta da giuoco *(in una casa privata).*

run (rŭn) *n.* corsa; corso, andamento; classe, categoria; durata; direzione, gestione; recinto; conduttura; smagliatura *(di calza):* a — **for one's money,** compenso *(per uno sforzo fatto);* a — **of luck,** un periodo di fortuna; the common —, la gente comune; in the long —, alla lunga, col tempo; on the —, indaffarato, in trambusto; in fretta e furia, di corsa; in fuga; to get the — of, impadronirsi di *(un mestiere),* imparare il funzionamento di *(un meccanismo);* to have a long —

(*teat*.), tenere il cartellone a lungo.
vt. (*pass.* **ran**, *pp.* **run**) correre
(*un rischio*); far correre, condurre; gestire, dirigere; introdurre;
forzare (*un blocco*). *vi.* correre;
accorrere; scorrere; fuggire; passare; estendersi; fondersi *o* stingere
(*di colori*); funzionare; essere in
corso; diventare; suppurare; liquefarsi, grondare, colare: **to —
a fever**, avere la febbre; **to —
across**, imbattersi, incontrare; **to —
after**, inseguire; **to — against**, imbattersi; ostacolare, opporsi a; **to
— away**, fuggire; sfuggire al controllo di; **to — down**, dare la caccia
a; rintracciare, trovare; urtare, investire, travolgere; scaricarsi
(*di orologi, ecc.*); perdere
salute; guastarsi; finire in rovina;
scorrere, dare una scorsa a; **to —
dry**, asciugarsi, seccarsi; **to —
errands**, fare commissioni; **to —
for**, durare; essere candidato a;
(*teat.*) tenere il cartellone per; **to —
in**, rodare (*un motore*); arrestare;
fare una scappata da; **to — into**,
entrare di corsa; cozzare contro;
trasformare; imbattersi in; ammontare a; fare (*debiti*); **to — mad**,
impazzire; **to — off**, far fluire;
fluire, scaricarsi; fuggire; pubblicare; preparare *o* fare in fretta;
esaurirsi; **to — on**, parlare ininterrottamente; **to — out**, finire, esaurirsi; sperperare; scorrere; scacciare; protendersi; diffondersi; **to
— out of**, restare senza; **to — out
on**, abbandonare, piantare; **to —
over**, traboccare; dare un'occhiata
a, scorrere; travolgere, investire;
eccedere, superare; **to — risks**,
correre rischi; **to — short**, scarseggiare (*di*); **to — through**, trafiggere; scorrere, dare una scorsa
a; sperperare; correre per, pervadere; **to — to**, assommare a; **to —
to earth**, scovare, stanare; **to — up**,
innalzare; aumentare; costruire
in fretta; far crescere; **to — wild**,
crescere come un selvaggio; **to —
with**, frequentare, associarsi a;
andare d'accordo con, coincidere.
runabout (rŭn'à·bout') *n.* (*autom.*)
vetturetta.
runaround (rŭn'à·round') *n.*: **to give
someone the —**, far fare a una persona (*in cerca di informazioni, ecc.*)
il giro di tutti gli uffici.
runaway (rŭn'à·wā') *n.* fuggiasco;
fuga; cavallo imbizzarrito. *agg.*
fuggitivo; rapido; imbizzarrito.
rung (rŭng) (1) *pass., pp. di* to ring.
rung (rŭng) (2) *n.* piuolo, bastone.

runner (rŭn'ẽr) *n.* corridore; messaggiero; piazzista; spianatoio, cursore; contrabbandiere; passatoia;
lama (*di pattino*); pattino (*di slitta*);
smagliatura (*di calza*); (*bot.*) viticcio.
running (rŭn'ĭng) *n.* corso, corsa;
flusso; secrezione; gestione: **to be
out of the —**, essere fuori della battaglia. *agg.* corrente; in corso; dila-
gante; fluido; scorrente; continuo;
purulento: **— board**, predellino,
montatoio; **— expenses**, spese
giornaliere; **— knot**, nodo scorsoio; **— fire**, fuoco di fila; **— water**,
acqua corrente; **in — condition**,
in buono stato; **for ten days —**, per
dieci giorni di seguito.
runt (rŭnt) *n.* nanerottolo, omiciattolo.
runway (rŭn'wā') *n.* pista (*anche di
aeroporto*); sentiero; canale.
rupture (rŭp'tûr) *n.* rottura; scoppio;
disaccordo; (*med.*) ernia. *vt., vi.*
rompere; scoppiare (*di ascesso, ecc.*);
rompersi.
rural (rŏor'ăl) *agg.* rurale, rustico.
rurban (rûr'băn) *agg.* posto ai con-
fini tra città e campagna, periferico.
rush (rŭsh) (1) *n.* giunco: **— chair**,
sedia di vimini.
rush (rŭsh) (2) *n.* impeto, foga, furia,
urgenza; afflusso, affluenza: **— of
business**, forte movimento commerciale; **— of people**, afflusso *o*
ondata di gente. *agg.* urgente: **—
hours**, ore di punta; **— order**, ordine
urgente. *vt.* spingere (*o* trascinare)
con foga; trasportare d'urgenza;
prendere d'assalto; affrettare; sbrigare in fretta. *vi.* precipitarsi,
slanciarsi; affluire: **to — out**,
precipitarsi fuori; **to — past**, passare accanto (*a uno*) di corsa.
russet (rŭs'ĕt) *n.* color ruggine; mela
ruggine.
Russian (rŭsh'ăn) *n., agg.* russo.
rust (rŭst) *n.* ruggine. *vt., vi.* arrugginire.
rustic (rŭs'tĭk) *n., agg.* rustico.
rustle (rŭs''l) *n.* fruscio; bisbiglio. *vi.*
stormire, frusciare: **to — cattle**,
rubare bestiame.
rustler (rŭs'lẽr) *n.* ladro di bestiame.
rusty (rŭst'ĭ) *agg.* rugginoso, arrugginito; color ruggine; logoro; irrequieto, indocile.
rut (rŭt) *n.* solco; andazzo, tran-tran.
vt. solcare: **to be in a —**, seguire il
solito tran-tran.
ruthless (rōoth'lĕs) *agg.* spietato,
crudele. **—ness** *n.* crudeltà.
rutty (rŭt'ĭ) *agg.* solcato.
rye (rī) *n.* (*bot.*) segala: **spurred —**,
segala cornuta.

S

Sabbath (săb′áth) n. giorno del riposo; sabato ebraico.

saber (sā′bĕr) n. sciabola.

sable (sā′b′l) n. zibellino; (pl.) gramaglie, abito da lutto.

sabotage (săb′ō·täzh′) n. sabotaggio.

saboteur (săb′ō·tûr′) n. sabotatore.

sabre vedi saber.

saccharine (săk′á·rĭn) n. saccarina. agg. zuccherino.

sachem (sā′chĕm) n. capo pellirossa.

sack (săk) n. sacco, sacchetto; saccheggio; (gergo) licenziamento; (fam.) letto: to hit the —, andare a dormire; a sad —, un povero gonzo. vt. saccheggiare; insaccare; licenziare. —cloth n. tela di sacco, cilicio.

sacrament (săk′rá·mĕnt) n. sacramento.

sacred (sā′krĕd) agg. sacro, consacrato. —ness n. santità, inviolabilità.

sacrifice (săk′rĭ·fīs) n. sacrificio. vt. sacrificare.

sacrilege (săk′rĭ·lĕj) n. sacrilegio.

sacrilegious (săk′rĭ·lē′jŭs) agg. sacrilego.

sacrum (sā′krŭm) n. osso sacro.

sad (săd) agg. triste, pietoso, deplorabile.

sadden (săd′′n) vt. rattristare. vi. rattristarsi.

saddle (săd′′l) n. sella. vt. sellare: to — one with responsibilities, accollare responsabilità a uno.

sadiron (săd′ī′ĕrn) n. ferro da stiro.

sadism (săd′ĭz′m) n. sadismo.

sadist (săd′ĭst) n. sadico.

sadistic (sá·dĭs′tĭk) agg. sadico.

sadness (săd′nĕs) n. tristezza.

safe (săf) n. cassaforte. agg. salvo, sicuro, sano, fuori pericolo, certo, fidato: — and sound, sano e salvo. —conduct n. salvacondotto.

safeguard (sāf′gärd′) n. salvaguardia. vt. salvaguardare.

safely (sāf′lĭ) avv. sicuramente; felicemente, senza incidenti (o pericoli).

safety (sāf′tĭ) n. sicurezza, salvezza, garanzia, sicura (di arma): — pin, spilla di sicurezza; — belt, cintura di sicurezza; in —, con sicurezza, senza pericolo.

saffron (săf′rŭn) n. (bot.) zafferano. agg. giallo-zafferano.

sag (săg) n. incavo, depressione, cedimento, flessione. vi. piegarsi, abbassarsi, avvallarsi, cedere, afflosciarsi: his shoulders —, ha le spalle spioventi.

sagacious (sá·gā′shŭs) agg. sagace.

sagacity (sá·găs′ĭ·tĭ) n. sagacia.

sage (sāj) (1) n. (bot.) salvia.

sage (sāj) (2) n., agg. saggio, savio.

said (sĕd) pass., pp. di to say.

sail (sāl) n. vela, velame; viaggio o gita in barca a vela; veliero: to set —, salpare; at full —, a vele spiegate. vi. veleggiare, far vela, navigare, salpare: to — a kite, far volare un aquilone.

sailor (sāl′ĕr) n. marinaio: to be a bad —, soffrire il mal di mare.

saint (sānt) n. santo. agg. santo, san, sacro. vt. canonizzare, santificare.

sake (sāk) n. ragione, causa, scopo, fine, amore, riguardo: for God's —, per l'amor di Dio; for her (his) —, per amor suo; for the — of appearances, per salvare le apparenze; for love's —, per amore; for the — of argument, per amore di discussione.

salable (sāl′á·b′l) agg. vendibile.

salad (săl′ăd) n. insalata: — dressing, condimento per insalata.

salamander (săl′á·măn′dĕr) n. salamandra.

salaried (săl′á·rĭd) agg. salariato, stipendiato.

salary (săl′á·rĭ) n. salario, stipendio.

sale (sāl) n. vendita: goods on — or return, merce in deposito; — by auction, vendita all'asta; for (on) —, in vendita, da vendere.

saleable (sāl′á·b′l) vedi salable.

salesman (sālz′măn) n. venditore, commesso viaggiatore, piazzista.

saleswoman (sālz′wŏŏm′ăn) n. venditrice, commessa viaggiatrice.

salient (sāl′lĭ·ĕnt) n., agg. saliente.

saline (sā′lĭn) agg. salino, salso.

saliva (sá·lī′vá) n. saliva.

sallow (săl′ō) (1) agg. giallastro, olivastro, smorto.

sallow (2) n. salice.

sally (săl′ĭ) n. slancio, irruzione; capriccio; tratto di spirito, frecciata; (mil.) sortita. vi. sortire, fare una sortita.

salmon (săm′ŭn) n. salmone.

saloon (sá·lōōn′) n. salone; cabina di lusso; bar, taverna: dining —, salone da pranzo.

salt (sôlt) n. sale; spirito, acume: — mine, salina; the — of the earth, il fior fiore dell'umanità; smelling —s, sali da fiutare. agg. salato salino: — water, acqua salata, acqua di mare. vt. salare: to — away, down, conservare sotto sale; accumulare (ricchezze).

saltpeter (sòlt'pē'tĕr) *n.* (*chim.*) salnitro.

salty (sòlt'ĭ) *agg.* salato, salmastro; caustico, pungente.

salubrious (så·lū'brĭ·ŭs) *agg.* salubre.

salutary (săl'ū·tĕr'ĭ) *agg.* salutare.

salutation (săl'ū·tā'shŭn) *n.* saluto.

salute (så·lūt') *n.* saluto; salva. (*di artigl.*). *vt.* salutare.

salvage (săl'vĭj) *n.* salvataggio, ricupero, merci ricuperate (*da naufragio, incendio, ecc.*).

salvation (săl·vā'shŭn) *n.* salvezza, salvamento: **Salvation Army**, Esercito della Salvezza.

salve (săv) *n.* unguento, balsamo. *vt.* lenire, preservare.

salver (săl'vĕr) *n.* vassoio.

salvo (săl'vō) *n.* salva (*d'artiglieria*); scroscio (*d'applausi*), ovazione. *vt.*, *vi.* salutare con una salva.

samba (săm'bå) *n.* samba. *vi.* ballare la samba.

same (săm) *pron.* la stessa cosa (*o persona*), lo stesso: **all the —**, ciononostante; **just the —**, tuttavia; **at the — time**, nello stesso tempo, d'altronde; **it's all the — to me**, per me è la stessa cosa. *agg.* stesso, medesimo, uguale, anzidetto.

sample (såm'p'l) *n.* campione, esempio: **book of —s**, campionario. *vt.* prelevare un campione di, giudicare dal campione, assaggiare.

sampler (såm'plĕr) *n.* saggio (*spec. di ricamo*).

sanatorium (săn'å·tō'rĭ·ŭm) *vedi* sanitarium.

sanctify (săngk'tĭ·fī) *vt.* santificare.

sanctimonious (săngk'tĭ·mō'nĭ·ŭs) *agg.* bigotto, ipocrita.

sanction (săngk'shŭn) *n.* sanzione. *vt.* sanzionare, sancire.

sanctity (săngk'tĭ·tĭ) *n.* santità.

sanctuary (săngk'tū·ĕr'ĭ) *n.* santuario, asilo.

sanctum (săngk'tŭm) *n.* luogo sacro *o* privato; studio, ufficio personale.

sand (sănd) *n.* sabbia, rena. *vt.* coprire di sabbia; mescolare con sabbia; strofinare con la sabbia; smerigliare.

sandal (săn'dăl) *n.* sandalo. **—wood** *n.* legno di sandalo.

sandpaper (sănd'pā'pĕr) *n.* carta smerigliata.

sandstone (sănd'stōn') *n.* pietra arenaria.

sandwich (sănd'wĭch) *n.* panino imbottito. *vt.* mettere fra (*due cose*).

sandy (săn'dĭ) *agg.* sabbioso: **— hair**, capelli biondi.

sane (sān) *agg.* sano di mente, ragionevole, savio.

sang (săng) *pass. di* to sing.

sanguine (săng'gwĭn) *agg.* sanguigno; ardente; ottimista, fiducioso: **— hopes**, rosee speranze.

sanitarium (săn'ĭ·târ'ĭ·ŭm) *n.* casa di cura, convalescenziario.

sanitary (săn'ĭ·tĕr'ĭ) *agg.* sanitario, igienico.

sanitation (săn'ĭ·tā'shŭn) *n.* igiene.

sanity (săn'ĭ·tĭ) *n.* sanità mentale.

sank (săngk) *pass. di* to sink.

Santa Claus (săn'tå klôz) *n.* Babbo Natale.

sap (săp) *n.* succo, linfa, sangue; (*gergo*) stupido. *vt.* indebolire, fiaccare.

sapling (săp'lĭng) *n.* arboscello; giovanetto.

sapphire (săf'īr) *n.* zaffiro.

sarcasm (săr'kăz'm) *n.* sarcasmo.

sarcastic (săr·kăs'tĭk) *agg.* sarcastico.

sarcophagus (săr·kŏf'å·gŭs) *n.* sarcofago.

sardine (săr·dēn') *n.* sardina.

Sardinian (săr·dĭn'ĭ·ăn) *n.*, *agg.* sardo.

sarsaparilla (săr'så·på·rĭl'å) *n.* (*bot.*) salsapariglia.

sash (săsh) *n.* cintura, sciarpa; intelaiatura di finestra: **— window**, finestra a ghigliottina.

sat (săt) *pass.*, *pp. di* to sit.

Satan (sā'tăn) *n.* Satana, demonio.

satchel (săch'ĕl) *n.* cartella da scolaro, borsa da viaggio.

sate (sāt) *vt.* saziare, soddisfare.

sateen (så·tēn') *n.* satin (*tessuto*).

satellite (săt'ĕ·lĭt) *n.* satellite; stato satellite.

satiate (sā'shĭ·āt) *vt.*, *vi.* saziare; rimpinzare, rimpinzarsi.

satiety (så·tī'ĕ·tĭ) *n.* sazietà.

satin (săt'ĭn) *n.* raso.

satire (săt'īr) *n.* satira.

satirical (så·tĭr'ĭ·kăl) *agg.* satirico.

satirize (săt'ĭ·rīz) *vt.* satireggiare.

satisfaction (săt'ĭs·făk'shŭn) *n.* sodisfazione.

satisfactory (săt'ĭs·făk'tō·rĭ) *agg.* sodisfacente; convincente; esauriente.

satisfied (săt'ĭs·fīd) *agg.* sodisfatto; convinto.

satisfy (săt'ĭs·fī) *vt.*, *vi.* sodisfare; convincere: **to — oneself**, sincerarsi; convincersi. **—ing** *agg.* sodisfacente; convincente.

saturate (săt'û·rāt) *agg.* saturo. *vt.* saturare.

saturation (săt'ûrā'shŭn) *n.* saturazione.

Saturday (săt'ĕr·dĭ) *n.* sabato.

saturnine (săt'ĕr·nīn) *agg.* cupo, taciturno.

satyr (săt'ĕr) *n.* satiro.

sauce (sôs) *n.* salsa; impudenza; (*S.U.*) frutta cotta. *vt.* insaporire,

condire; dire impertinenze a. —boat
n. salsiera. —pan n. casseruola.

aucer (sô'sĕr) n. piattino.

aucily (sô'si-li) avv. sfacciatamente,
insolentemente; pepatamente.

auciness (sô'si-nĕs) n. sfacciataggine,
impertinenza; vivacità.

aucy (sô'si) agg. insolente, impertinente; piccante, pepato.

aunter (sôn'tĕr) n. passeggiata,
andatura calma. vi. bighellonare,
passeggiare.

ausage (sô'sij) n. salame, salsiccia.

avage (săv'ij) n. selvaggio. agg.
selvaggio, selvatico, feroce, violento, crudele. —ly avv.selvaggiamente,
ferocemente, villanamente, irosa-
mente. —ness, —ry n. ferocia, villania, brutalità, barbarie.

avant (să·vän') n. dotto.

ave (săv) prep. salvo, eccetto, tranne. vt. salvare, risparmiare, conservare, tenere in serbo. vi. fare
economia.

aver (săv'ĕr) n. salvatore, liberatore;
risparmiatore.

aving (săv'ing) n. risparmio, economia: —s, risparmi; —s bank,
cassa di risparmio. agg. economo,
economico, protettivo. prep. eccetto, salvo.

avior (săv'yĕr), saviour n. salvatore,
redentore.

avor (să'vĕr) n. sapore, gusto. vt. assaporare, gustare; insaporire. vi.
sapere (di).

avory (să'vĕr-i) agg. saporito.

aw (sô) (1) pass. di to see.

aw (sô) (2) n. proverbio, massima.

aw (sô) (3) n. sega: vt. (pass. sawed,
pp. sawn) segare. —dust n. segatura. —horse n. cavallo di frisia;
cavalletto. —mill n. segheria.

Saxon (săk'sŭn) n., agg. sassone.

saxophone (săk'sô-fôn) n. sassofono.

say (să) n. discorso, diritto di parola,
turno (per parlare): to have one's
—, dire la propria opinione; to
have a — in a matter, avere voce in
una questione; the final —, l'ultima parola. vt., vi. (pass., pp. said)
dire, affermare: it is said, si dice;
you don't —! che dite mai! that
is to —, vale a dire; I dare —, im-
magino; to — the least, a dir poco.
—ing n. detto, proverbio, massima:
as the —ing goes, come dice il
proverbio; it goes without —ing,
è ovvio, non occorre dire (che).

cab (skăb) n. crosta (di ferita); scabbia; crumiro. vi. formare la crosta,
coprirsi di croste.

scabbard (skăb'ĕrd) n. guaina, fodero
di spada.

scabby (skăb'i) agg. coperto di croste,
scabbioso.

scabrous (skā'brŭs) agg. scabro, scabroso; salace, osceno.

scaffold (skăf'ôld) n. palco, impalcatura, patibolo. —ing n. impalcatura.

scald (skôld) n. bruciatura, scottatura.
vt. scottare, ustionare, scaldare sino
all'ebollizione. —ing agg. scottante.

scale (skāl) (1) n. scaglia, squama. vt.
scrostare, togliere le scaglie a. vi.
sfaldarsi, squamarsi.

scale (skāl) (2) n. bilancia, piatto di
bilancia; gradazione, proporzione,
scala: a pair of —s, una bilancia;
platform —, basculla; sliding —,
scala mobile. vt., vi. pesare,
misurare, graduare; scalare, arrampicarsi: to — down, abbassare
gradatamente.

scallop (skŏl'ŭp) n. conchiglia, mollusco bivalve; dentellatura, smerlo.
vt. dentellare, smerlare; cucinare
al gratin.

scalp (skălp) n. cuoio capelluto,
capigliatura. vt. scotennare; rivendere (biglietti di teatro, ecc.) a prezzo
maggiorato.

scalpel (skăl'pĕl) n. (chir.) scalpello.

scalper (skăl'pĕr) n. scotennatore;
bagarino.

scaly (skāl'i) agg. squamoso.

scamp (skămp) n. furfante, scioperato.

scamper (skăm'pĕr) n. fuga frettolosa.
vi. correre, darsela a gambe.

scan (skăn) vt. scandire; scorrere frettolosamente, scrutare; (T.V.) esplorare.

scandal (skăn'dăl) n. scandalo, maldicenza, vergogna.

scandalize (skăn'dăl'iz) vt. scandalizzare, calunniare.

scandalmonger (skăn'dăl-mŭng'gĕr)
n.pettegolo, seminatore di scandali.

scandalous (skăn'dăl-ŭs) n. scandaloso, diffamatorio.

scant (skănt) agg. scarso, insufficiente,
esiguo. vt., vi. limitare, lesinare,
scarseggiare. —iness n. meschinità,
scarsezza.

scanty (skăn'ti) agg. scarso, meschino,
debole, insufficiente. scanties n.pl.
mutandine (da donna).

scapegoat (skāp'gōt') n. capro espiatorio.

scapegrace (skāp'grās') n. monello,
scapestrato.

scar (skär) n. sfregio, cicatrice. vt.
sfregiare. vi. cicatrizzarsi.

scarab (skăr'ăb) n. scarabeo.

scarce (skärs) agg. scarso, raro: to
make oneself —, eclissarsi. —ly
avv. a malapena, difficilmente,
raramente: — ever, quasi mai.

scarcity (skăr'sĭ·tĭ) *n.* scarsità, rarità, penuria.

scare (skâr) *n.* allarme, paura, panico. *vt.*, *vi.* spaventare, spaventarsi, allarmare, sgomentarsi: to — up, racimolare; to — away, mettere in fuga; to — easily, spaventarsi per ogni nonnulla.

scarecrow (skâr'krō') *n.* spauracchio, spaventapasseri.

scarehead (skâr'hĕd') *n.* (*S.U.*) titolo cubitale (*su quotidiano*).

scaremonger (skâr'mŭng'gĕr) *n.* allarmista.

scarf (skärf) *n.* sciarpa, fascia, cravatta; tappeto da tavola.

scarlet (skär'lĕt) *n.*, *agg.* rosso scarlatto: — fever, scarlattina.

scarred (skärd), **scarry** (skär'ĭ) *agg.* sfregiato, cosparso di cicatrici.

scary (skâr'ĭ) *agg.* allarmistico; timoroso.

scathing (skāth'ĭng) *agg.* caustico, aspro.

scatter (skăt'ẽr) *vt.* disperdere, disseminare, dissipare. *vi.* disperdersi, sparpagliarsi. —brain *n.* scervellato. —brained *agg.* scervellato.

scavenger (skăv'ẽn·jẽr) *n.* spazzino.

scene (sēn) *n* scena, spettacolo, panorama: to make a —, fare una scenata; — painter, scenografo.

scenery (sēn'ẽr·ĭ) *n.* scenario, panorama.

scent (sĕnt) *n.* odore, profumo; olfatto, odorato; pista, traccia: to put off the —, sviare; to be on the — of, essere sulle tracce di. *vt.* odorare, fiutare, profumare. *vi.* odorare (*di*).

scepter (sĕp'tẽr) *n.* scettro.

sceptic *vedi* skeptic

schedule (skĕd'ūl) *n.* lista, tabella; orario; programma: on —, in orario. *vt.* registrare, programmare, predisporre; assegnare un incarico (*da compiere in un determinato momento*).

scheme (skēm) *n.* schema, progetto, piano; ordine; disegno; macchinazione· color —, combinazione di colori. *vt.*, *vi.* progettare, complottare, macchinare.

schemer (skēm'ẽr) *n.* progettista; macchinatore, intrigante.

scheming (skēm'ĭng) *n.* macchinazioni. *agg.* intrigante, subdolo.

schism (sĭz'm) *n.* scisma.

schizophrenic (skĭz'ō·frĕn'ĭk) *n.*, *agg.* schizofrenico.

scholar (skŏl'ẽr) *n.* discepolo, erudito. —ly *agg.*, *avv* da erudito. —ship *n.* erudizione, scienza; (*univ.*) borsa di studio· to get a —, guadagnare una borsa di studio

scholastic (skŏ·lăs'tĭk) *n.*, *agg.* scolastico, pedante.

school (skōol) *n.* scuola, scolaresca, collegio, convitto; branco (*di pesci*). *vt.* istruire, ammaestrare disciplinare. —boy *n.* scolaro. —girl *n.* scolara. —house *n.* scuola edificio scolastico. —ing *n.* istruzione insegnamento, addestramento —master *n.* maestro di scuola —mate *n.* condiscepolo. —mistress *n.* maestra (*o direttrice*) di scuola —room *n.* aula, classe. —teacher *n* insegnante.

schooner (skōon'ẽr) *n.* (*naut.*) goletta (*gergo*) bicchierone: prairie —, carriaggio.

science (sī'ẽns) *n.* scienza, sapere.

scientific (sī'ẽn·tĭf'ĭk) *agg.* scientifico —ally *avv.* scientificamente.

scientist (sī'ẽn·tĭst) *n.* scienziato.

scintilla (sĭn·tĭl'à) *n.* scintilla, particella.

scion (sī'ŭn) *n.* rampollo, discendente (*bot.*) germoglio.

scissors (sĭz'ẽrz) *n.pl.* forbici.

scoff (skŏf) *n.* beffa, derisione. *vt.* deridere. *vi.*: to — at, ridersi di, far beffe di.

scold (skōld) *n.* brontolone, brontolona. *vt.*, *vi.* sgridare, rimproverare brontolare.

scolding *n.* sgridata. *agg.* brontolone

scone (skōn) *n.* focaccina.

scoop (skōop) *n.* ramaiuolo, paletta palettata; (*naut.*) gottazza; (*giornalismo*) notizia sensazionale, colpo giornalistico; (*comm.*) grosso colpo *vt.* scavare, vuotare; arraffare; (*giornalismo*) accaparrarsi una notizia prima degli altri.

scoot (skōot) *vi.* (*fam.*) filare, svignarsela.

scooter (skōot'ẽr) *n* monopattino; (*S.U.*) barca a vela anfibia.

scope (skōp) *n.* veduta, campo, portata, raggio d'azione.

scorch (skôrch) *vt.* bruciacchiare strinare, scottare; devastare, mettere a ferro e a fuoco. *vi.* scottarsi bruciacchiarsi: —ed earth, terra bruciata *o* devastata.

score (skōr) *n.* tocco, traccia, linea ventina; scotto, debito; punteggio segnatura; causa, ragione; (*mus.*) partitura; (*gergo*) (*la*) realtà dei fatti (*la*) situazione reale: on that —, a quel riguardo; on the — of, a causa di; to keep —, segnare il punteggio; to pay off old scores, liquidare un vecchio conto; to know what th — is, sapere come stanno le cose *vt.*, *vi.* intaccare, segnare, notare, ad debitare; tracciare, rigare; (*mus.*

orchestrare; segnare (*punti*); riportare (*un successo*).

scorer *n.* segnapunti.

scoring *n.* punteggio, tacca, solco.

scorn (skörn) *n.* scorno, disprezzo. *vt.* disprezzare, solegnare.

scornful (skörn'fŏŏl) *agg.* sprezzante.

scorpion (skôr'pĭ·ŭn) *n.* scorpione.

scot (skŏt) (1) *n.* scotto, tributo: **to go — free**, passarla liscia.

Scot (skŏt) (2) *n.* scozzese.

scotch (skŏch) *n.* whisky scozzese.

Scots (skŏts) Scottish (skŏt'ĭsh) *n.* lingua scozzese. *agg.* scozzese.

scoundrel (skoun'drĕl) *n.* mascalzone.

scour (skour) (1) *vt.* pulire, sgrassare, detergere, lustrare.

scour (skour) (2) *vt.* perlustrare.

scourge (skûrj) *n.* sferza, punizione. *vt.* sferzare, punire.

scout (skout) (1) *n.* esploratore; (*aeron.*) ricognitore: **— car** (*mil.*), camionetta da ricognizione. *vt., vi.* esplorare, perlustrare: **to — for**, andare in cerca di.

scout (skout) (2) *vt.* respingere con sdegno, beffare.

scowl (skoul) *n.* sguardo torvo, cipiglio. *vi.* accigliarsi, aggrottare le sopracciglia.

scrabble (skrăb''l) *n.* strisciamento, l'arrancare; scarabocchio. *vi.* arrancare, grattare, strisciare; scarabocchiare.

scraggy (skrăg'ĭ) *agg.* scarno, irregolare.

scram (skrăm) *vi.* (*gergo S.U.*) togliersi di mezzo, svignarsela: **—!** fila via!, filate via!

scramble (skrăm'b'l) *n.* scalata, arrampicata, corsa (*alla conquista di qualcosa*); mischia. *vt.* raccogliere alla rinfusa, arraffare; mischiare; strapazzare (*uova*). *vi.* arrampicarsi; gareggiare, lottare (*per il possesso di qualcosa*); affannarsi.

scrap (skrăp) (1) *n.* pezzetto, frammento, brano, ritaglio; *pl.* rimasugli: **— iron**, rottami di ferro. *vt.* scartare, gettar via.

scrap (2) *n.* zuffa. *vi.* azzuffarsi.

scrapbook *n.* album.

scrape (skrāp) *n.* raschiatura; difficoltà, perplessità: **to get into a —**, cacciarsi in un guaio. *vt., vi.* raschiare; cancellare; raggranellare; razzolare, grufolare: **to — acquaintance with**, insinuarsi presso; **to — along**, tirare avanti.

scraper (skrāp'ēr) *n.* raschiatoio, raschietto; avaro.

scratch (skrăch) *n.* graffio, scarabocchio; linea di partenza (*in una gara*); (*gergo*) baruffa: **from —**,

dal principio, dal niente; **— paper**, carta da minuta. *vt., vi.* grattare, graffiare, scalfire, strofinare; scribacchiare; cancellare; grattarsi.

scrawl (skrôl) *n.* scarabocchio. *vt., vi.* scarabocchiare.

scrawny (skrôn'ĭ) *agg.* scarno, ossuto.

screak (skrēk) *n.* grido, cigolio. *vi.* gridare, cigolare.

scream (skrēm) *n.* grido, strillo; (*gergo*) "asso," "cennone"; "cannonata"; spasso; cosa assurda. *vt., vi.* strillare, urlare. **—ing** *agg.* urlante, lacerante; scargiante; esilarante.

screech (skrēch) *n.* strido, stridore: *vi.* stridere. **— owl** *n.* allocco, gufo.

screen (skrēn) *n.* schermo; paravento, parafuoco; divisorio, riparo; vaglio, crivello. *vt.* riparare, coprire; schermare; vagliare; (*cinema*) proiettare, ridurre per lo schermo: **— door**, porta di rete metallica; **wire —**, rete metallica; **— writer**, scrittore cinematografico, sceneggiatore. **—ing** *u.* schermatura; vagliatura.

screw (skrōō) *n.* vite, elica: **to put the —s to somebody**, mettere qualcuno alle strette; **— bolt**, bullone a vite; **— nut**, dado; **— propeller**, propulsore a elica; **— wrench**, chiave inglese. *vt., vi.* avvitare, torcere, torcersi, avvitarsi: **to — a lid on**, avvitare un coperchio su. **to — up one's courage**, prendere il coraggio a due mani; **to — up one's face**, fare una smorfia.

screwball (skrōō'bôl') (*gergo*) *n., agg.* mattoide, "suonato."

screwdriver (skrōō'drīv'ĕr) *n.* cacciavite.

screwy (skrōō'ĭ) *agg.* prepotente; avaro; (*gergo*) brillo, alticcio; mattoide, "suonato": **— horse**, ronzino.

scribble (skrĭb''l) *n.* scarabocchio. *vt., vi.* scribacchiare, scarabocchiare.

scrimmage (skrĭm'ĭj) *n.* mischia.

scrimp (skrĭmp) *vt., vi.* restringere; lesinare, economizzare.

scrimpy (skrĭmp'ĭ) *agg.* esiguo; avaro.

script (skrĭpt) *n.* scrittura; (*tip.*) corsivo; (*teat., cinema, radio, T.V.*) copione, sceneggiatura.

Scriptures (skrĭp'tŭrz) *n. pl.* Sacre Scritture.

scroll (skrōl) *n.* rotolo di carta (*o pergamena*); ruolo, lista; cartiglio.

scrub (skrŭb) *n.* cespuglio, boscaglia. *agg.* di fortuna, improvvisato; stentato, inferiore. *vt.* strofinare energicamente, detergere. *vi.* sgobbare: **—woman** *n.* donna delle pulizie.

scruff (skrŭf) *n.* nuca, cervice.

scruple (skrōō'p'l) *n.* scrupolo. *vi.* aver scrupoli, esitare.

scrupulous (skrōō'pū·lŭs) *agg.* scruploso.

scrutinize (skrōō'tǐ·nīz) *vt.* scrutare, esaminare a fondo.

scrutiny (skrōō'tǐ·nǐ) *n.* esame scruploso, indagine.

scud (skŭd) *n.* nube. *vi.* correre velocemente.

scuffle (skŭf''l) *n.* zuffa, tafferuglio. *vi.* azzuffarsi, accapigliarsi; strascicare i piedi.

scull (skŭl) *n.* remo. *vt.*, *vi.* vogare con un remo, gondolare.

scullery (skŭl'ĕr·ǐ) *n.* retrocucina, acquaio.

sculptor (skŭlp'tĕr) *n.* scultore.

sculptress (skŭlp'trĕs) *n.* scultrice.

sculpture (skŭlp'tůr) *n.* scultura. *vt.* scolpire.

scum (skŭm) *n.* schiuma, scoria, rifiuto, feccia. *vt.*, *vi.* schiumare.

scupper (skŭp'ĕr) *n.* (*naut.*) ombrinale.

scurf (skûrf) *n.* squama, forfora.

scurrilous (skŭr'ǐ·lŭs) *agg.* scurrile.

scurry (skŭr'ǐ) *vi.* correre, affrettarsi.

scurvy (skûr'vǐ) *n.* scorbuto. *agg.* vile, spregevole.

scutcheon (skŭch'ŭn) *n.* scudo, blasone.

scuttle (skut''l) *n.* cesto; botola; passo rapido, corsa; (*naut.*) boccaporto. *vt.* aprire falle in (*uno scafo*), affondare (*uno scafo*). *vi.* correre, affrettarsi: to — away, fuggire; —butt *n.* (*gergo*) diceria, voce: — has it that, si vocifera che.

scythe (sīth) *n.* falce.

sea (sē) *n.* mare, onda, cavallone: to be at —, essere in alto mare *opp.* disorientato; to put to —, salpare; — biscuit, galletta; — gull, gabbiano; — level, livello del mare; — lion, otaria.

seaboard (sē'bōrd) *n.* costa, litorale. *agg.* costiero, litoraneo.

seafarer (sē·fâr'ĕr) *n.* navigatore, marinaio.

seal (sēl) (1) *n.* vitello marino, foca.

seal (sēl) (2) *n.* sigillo, suggello. *vt.* suggellare, sigillare, chiudere, stabilire.

sealing *n.* suggello: — wax, ceralacca.

seam (sēm) *n.* cucitura, giuntura, costura, solco, sutura; (*min.*) filone, vena. *vt.* cucire, suturare.

seaman (sē'măn) *n.* marinaio.

seamstress (sēm'strĕs) *n.* cucitrice.

seaplane (sē'plān') *n.* idrovolante.

seaport (sē'pōrt') *n.* porto di mare: — town, città marittima.

sear (sēr) *agg.* secco, avvizzito. *vt.* bruciacchiare, cauterizzare, inaridire.

search (sûrch) *n.* ricerca, perquisizione, investigazione: in — of, in cerca di, alla ricerca di. — warrant, mandato di perquisizione. *vt.*, *vi.* cercare; perquisire; ispezionare; sondare, scandagliare.

searchlight (sûrch'lit') *n.* faro.

seashore (sē'shōr') *n.* spiaggia.

seasick (sē'sǐk') *agg.* affetto da mal di mare: I got —, mi è venuto il mal di mare.

seasickness *n.* mal di mare.

seaside (sē'sīd') *n.* spiaggia, mare: to go to the —, andare al mare.

season (sē'z'n) *n.* stagione; epoca, tempo, momento opportuno: in good —, tempestivamente; out of —, a sproposito; opera —, stagione operistica *o* lirica. *vt.* maturare; assuefare; aromatizzare, condire; stagionare, salare; allenare, agguerrire.

seasoning (sē'z'n·ǐng) *n.* condimento; stagionatura.

seat (sēt) *n.* sedile, sedia; posto, sede; base, posizione; fondo dei calzoni, sedere: — of learning, centro di cultura. *vt.* insediare; collocare; far sedere, fornire di sedili: to — oneself, insediarsi; mettersi a sedere.

seaward (sē'wĕrd) *agg.*, *avv.* verso il mare *o* il largo.

seaweed (sē'wĕd') *n.* alga marina.

seaworthy (sē'wûr'thǐ) *agg.* atto a navigare.

sebaceous (sē·bā'shŭs) *agg.* sebaceo.

secede (sē·sēd') *vi.* compiere una scissione, scindersi, staccarsi.

seclude (sē·klōōd') *vt.* separare, isolare, rinchiudere: to — oneself, isolarsi.

secluded *agg.* ritirato, appartato, solitario.

seclusion (sē·klōō'shŭn) *n.* ritiro, solitudine, isolamento.

second (sĕk'ŭnd) *n.* minuto secondo; secondo (*in duello o incontro sportivo*); secondo arrivato; (*pl.comm.*) merci di seconda scelta. *agg.* secondo, inferiore; favorevole: every — day, ogni due giorni; on — thought, dopo averci ripensato. *vt.* assecondare, aiutare. —ary *agg.* secondario. —best *agg.* secondo (*in qualità*); mediocre: to come off —best, riuscire secondo (*in classifica*), essere sconfitto. — hand lancetta dei secondi (*nell'orologio*). —hand *agg.* d'occasione, di seconda mano. —ly *avv.* in secondo luogo. —rate *agg.* inferiore, di second'ordine.

secrecy (sē'krĕ.sĭ) *n.* segretezza, discrezione, reticenza.

secret (sē'krĕt) *n.* segreto. *agg.* segreto, occulto, reticente.

secretariat (sĕk'rē.târ'ĭ.ăt) *n.* segretariato, segreteria.

secretary (sĕk'rē.tĕr'ĭ) *n.* segretario; ministro, funzionario; scrivania.

secrete (sē.krēt') *vt.* celare, nascondere; (*fisiol.*) secernere.

secretion (sē.krē'shŭn) *n.* secrezione.

secretive (sē.krē'tĭv) *agg.* segreto, riservato; secretivo: — **gland,** ghiandola secretiva.

secretly (sē'krĕt.lĭ) *avv.* segretamente, privatamente, intimamente.

sect (sĕkt) *n.* setta. —**arian** (sĕk.târ'ĭ.ăn) *n.,* *agg.* settario.

section (sĕk'shŭn) *n.* sezione; suddivisione, parte, pezzo; spaccato; settore, tratto, regione. *vt.* suddividere, sezionare, fare lo spaccato di.

secular (sĕk'ū.lẽr) *n.* laico. *agg.* secolare, laico.

secure (sē.kūr') *agg.* sicuro, saldo, fiducioso: — **from,** al riparo da. *vt.* assicurare, mettere al sicuro, impadronirsi di, procurarsi. —**ly** *avv.* sicuramente, al sicuro, saldamente.

security (sē.kū'rĭ.tĭ) *n.* sicurezza, salvezza, protezione; garanzia, cauzione, pegno: **securities** *n. pl.* titoli, certificati azionari: **Security Council,** Consiglio di Sicurezza.

sedan (sē.dăn') *n.* guida-interna (*auto*).

sedate (sē.dāt') *agg.* calmo, tranquillo, sereno, equilibrato. —**ly** *avv.* posatamente, serenamente, con calma.

sedative (sĕd'à.tĭv) *n.,* *agg.* sedativo.

sedentary (sĕd'ĕn.tĕr'ĭ) *agg.* sedentario, inerte, stabile.

sediment (sĕd'ĭ.mĕnt) *n.* sedimento.

sedition (sē.dĭsh'ŭn) *n.* sedizione.

seditious (sē.dĭsh'ŭs) *agg.* sedizioso.

seduce (sē.dūs') *vt.* sedurre, allettare.

seducer (-ẽr) *n.* seduttore.

seduction (sē.dŭk'shŭn) *n.* seduzione.

seductive (sē.dŭk'tĭv) *agg.* seducente.

sedulous (sĕd'ū.lŭs) *agg.* diligente.

see (sē) (1) *n.* seggio (*o* giurisdizione) episcopale: **the Holy See,** la Santa Sede.

see (sē) (2) *vt., vi.* (*pass.* **saw,** *pp.* **seen**) vedere, scorgere; accompagnare; consultare; capire: **to — somebody home,** accompagnare qualcuno a casa; **to — a person off,** accompagnare alla stazione una persona; **to — somebody through a difficulty,** aiutare uno a superare una difficoltà; **to — through a**

person, indovinare le intenzioni di una persona; **to — to,** provvedere a, occuparsi di: — **that you do it,** ti raccomando di farlo.

seed (sēd) *n.* seme, semenza, granello, germe: **to run to —,** tallire, andare in decadenza. *vt.* seminare, disseminare, mondare dai semi. *vi.* produrre semi. —**ling** *n.* pianta nata da un seme, pianticella.

seedy (sēd'ĭ) *agg.* pieno di semi; logoro, male in arnese, malaticcio.

seeing (sē'ĭng) *cong.* visto che, dato che, tenuto conto di.

seek (sēk) *vt., vi.* (*pass., pp.* **sought**) cercare; perseguire; chiedere; indagare: **to be sought after,** essere cercato (*desiderato*).

seem (sēm) *vi.* sembrare, avere l'aria (*di*), apparire, aver l'impressione: **I — to,** mi par di; **it —s to me that,** mi sembra che. —**ing** *agg.* apparente. —**ingly** *avv.* apparentemente. —**ly** *agg.* decoroso, conveniente.

seen (sēn) *pp.* di **to see.**

seep (sēp) *vi.* filtrare, penetrare.

seer (sēr) *n.* veggente, indovino.

seesaw (sē'sô') *n.* altalena. *vi.* dondolare, altalenare.

seethe (sēth) *vt., vi.* bollire, schiumare; fremere (*di collera, ecc.*).

seething *agg.* bollente, fremente.

segment (sĕg'mĕnt) *n.* segmento.

segregate (sĕg'rē.gāt) *vt.* isolare. *vi.* isolarsi.

segregation (sĕg'rē.gā'shŭn) *n.* segregazione, isolamento.

seismic (sīz'mĭk) *agg.* sismico.

seize (sēz) *vt.* afferrare, catturare; impossessarsi di, sequestrare.

seizure (sē'zhẽr) *n.* confisca, cattura, presa di possesso; attacco, accesso.

seldom (sĕl'dŭm) *avv.* raramente.

select (sē.lĕkt') *agg.* scelto, speciale. *vt.* scegliere, preferire.

selectivity (sē.lĕk'tĭv'ĭ.tĭ)*n.*selettività.

self (sĕlf) *n.* la propria persona, l'io, personalità, egoismo: **for one's own —,** per se stesso; **one's better —,** il lato migliore del proprio io; **beside one's —,** fuori di sè; **to be one's —,** essere in piena coscienza. *agg.* proprio, personale, stesso. *pron.* (*pl.* **selves**) me stesso, se stesso: **payable to —,** pagabile all'ordine proprio.

self-acting *agg.* automatico.

self-addressed *agg.*: — **envelope,** busta già munita di indirizzo.

self-assurance *n.* sicumera.

self-centered *agg.* egocentrico.

self-command *n.* dominio di sè, sangue freddo.

self-complacent *agg.* tronfio, vanitoso.
self-conscious *agg.* imbarazzato, ipersensibile, schivo.
self-control *n.* padronanza di sè.
self-defense *n.* legittima difesa.
self-denial *n.* abnegazione.
self-educated *agg.* autodidatta.
self-esteem *n.* rispetto di se stesso, amor proprio.
self-evident *agg.* lampante.
self-explanatory *agg.* ovvio.
self-government *n.* autogoverno, autonomia.
self-importance *n.* presunzione, boria.
self-important *agg.* tronfio, borioso.
self-interest *n.* interesse personale, egoismo.
selfish (sĕl'fĭsh) *agg.* egoista. —ly *avv.* egoisticamente. —ness *n.* egoismo.
selfless (self'lĕs) *agg.* altruista.
self-love *n.* amore di sè.
self-made *agg.* che si è fatto da sè.
self-mailer *n.* modulo da spedire senza bisogno di busta.
self-possessed *agg.* equilibrato, padrone di sè.
self-reliant *agg.* autonomo; sicuro di sè.
self-respect *n.* rispetto di sè, dignità.
self-restraint *n.* dominio di sè.
self-sacrifice *n.* abnegazione.
selfsame (sĕlf'sām') *agg.* stesso, identico.
self-satisfied *agg.* soddisfatto di sè, vanitoso.
self-starter *n.* (*mecc.*) avviamento automatico.
self-styled *agg.* sedicente.
self-sufficient *agg.* autosufficiente, presuntuoso.
self-willed *agg.* ostinato.
sell (sĕl) *vt.*, *vi.* (*pass.*, *pp.* sold) vendere, smerciare; vendersi (*trovare smercio*): it —s well, si vende bene; to — out, vendere tutto, esaurire, liquidare. —er *n.* venditore: best —er, libro di grande vendita.
selvage, selvedge (sĕl'vĭj) *n.* vivagno, cimosa.
selves (sĕlvz) *pl. di* self.
semblance (sĕm'blăns) *n.* sembiante, apparenza; simulacro, parvenza.
semicircle (sĕm'ĭ·sûr'k'l) *n.* semicerchio.
semicolon (sĕm'ĭ·kō'lŏn) *n.* punto e virgola.
semimonthly (sĕm'ĭ·mŭnth'lĭ) *n.*, *agg.* quindicinale.
seminary (sĕm'ĭ·nĕr'ĭ) *n.* seminario.
semiweekly *agg.* bisettimanale.
sempstress (sĕm(p)'strĕs) *n.* cucitrice.
senate (sĕn'ĭt) *n.* senato.
senator (sĕn'á·tĕr) *n.* senatore.

send (sĕnd) *vt.* (*pass.*, *pp.* sent) mandare; spedire; inviare; lanciare; trasmettere; diffondere; (*gergo*) mandare in estasi, entusiasmare: to — for, mandar a chiamare; to — forth, spedire, inviare, emettere; esalare, emanare; to — word, mandare a dire; to — about one's business, mandare a quel paese. —er *n.* speditore, mittente; trasmettitore.
senility (sĕ·nĭl'ĭ·tĭ) *n.* senilità.
senior (sēn'yĕr) *n.* anziano, decano; studente dell'ultimo anno. *agg.* maggiore (*di età*), più anziano; (*mil.*) superiore: Mr. Brown, —, il signor Brown padre; he is my — by three years, è maggiore di me di tre anni. —ity (sēn·yŏr'ĭ·tĭ) *n.* anzianità, decanato: — in rank, anzianità in grado.
sensation (sĕn·sā'shŭn) *n.* sensazione, fatto sensazionale, scalpore.
sensational (sĕn·sā'shŭn·ăl) *agg.* sensazionale.
sense (sĕns) *n.* senso, significato, senso comune, sentimento, discernimento, ragione: common —, buon senso; to make —, avere senso, essere logico; senses, facoltà mentali; to be out of one's —s, sragionare. *vt.* sentire, avere la sensazione di, intuire, capire. —less *agg.* tramortito, svenuto; privo di significato, insensato, assurdo.
sensibility (sĕn'sĭ·bĭl'ĭ·tĭ) *n.* sensibilità, assennatezza.
sensible (sĕn'sĭ·b'l) *agg.* sensibile; ragionevole, assennato, conscio; percettibile.
sensibly (sĕn'sĭ·blĭ) *avv.* sensibilmente; ragionevolmente, assennatamente.
sensitive (sĕn'sĭ·tĭv) *agg.* sensibile, sensitivo, suscettibile, impressionabile. —ness, sensitivity *n.* sensitività, suscettibilità.
sensual (sĕn'shŏŏ·ăl) *agg.* sensuale.
sensuality (sĕn'shŏŏ·ăl'ĭ·tĭ) *n.* sensualità.
sent (sĕnt) *pass.*, *pp. di* to send.
sentence (sĕn'tĕns) *n.* sentenza; frase; (*gramm.*) proposizione: death —, condanna a morte. *vt.* condannare.
sentiment (sĕn'tĭ·mĕnt) *n.* sentimento, opinione. —al (sĕn'tĭ·mĕn'tăl) *agg.* sentimentale. —alist *n.* sentimentale. —ality (ăl'ĭ·tĭ) *n.* sentimentalità, sentimentalismo.
sentinel (sĕn'tĭ·nĕl) sentry (sĕn'trĭ) *n.* sentinella.
sentry-box *n.* garitta.
separate (sĕp'á·rĭt) *agg.* separato, disgiunto, diviso, singolo, a parte: under — cover, in plico a parte.

vt. (-rāt) separare, disgiungere, dividere. *vi.* separarsi, dividersi. —ly *avv.* separatamente.

separation (sĕp'á·rā'shŭn) *n.* separazione (*anche legale*).

September (sĕp·tĕm'bĕr) *n.* settembre.

septic (sĕp'tĭk) *agg.* settico.

septicemia (sĕp'tĭ·sē'mĭ·á) *n.* setticemia.

sepulchral (sē·pŭl'král) *agg.* sepolcrale.

sepulcher (sĕp'ŭl·kĕr) *n.* sepolcro.

sepulture (sĕp'ŭl·tŭr) *n.* sepoltura.

sequel (sē'kwĕl) *n.* sequela, seguito, conseguenza, continuazione.

sequence (sē'kwĕns) *n.* sequenza, serie, ordine, successione, conseguenza.

sequin (sē'kwĭn) *n.* zecchino.

seraphic (sē·răf'ĭk) *agg.* serafico, angelico.

serenade (sĕr'ē·nād') *n.* serenata. *vt.*, *vi.* fare la serenata (*a*).

serene (sē·rēn') *agg.* sereno, calmo.

serenity (sē·rĕn'ĭ·tĭ) *n.* serenità.

serge (sûrj) *n.* saia (*tessuto*).

sergeant (sär'jĕnt) *n.* sergente.

serial (sēr'ĭ·ál) *n.* periodico, pubblicazione a dispense (*o* puntate). *agg.* periodico; a dispense (*o* puntate): — **novel**, romanzo a puntate.

serialize (sēr'ĭ·ál·īz) *vt.* pubblicare a puntate.

series (sēr'ēz) *n. sing., pl.* serie, sequenza, successione.

serious (sēr'ĭ·ŭs) *agg.* serio; grave. —ly *avv.* seriamente; gravemente. —ness *n.* serietà; gravità.

sermon (sûr'mŭn) *n.* sermone, predica.

serpent (sûr'pĕnt) *n.* serpente.

serrate (sĕr'āt) *agg.* dentellato.

serried (sĕr'ĭd) *agg.* serrato, compatto.

serum (sēr'ŭm) *n.* siero.

servant (sûr'vánt) *n.* servitore, domestico, schiavo: **public** —, pubblico funzionario; —**girl**, —**maid**, domestica, cameriera.

serve (sûrv) *n.* (*tennis*) servizio. *vt.*, *vi.* servire, fungere (*da*); scontare (*una pena*): **to** — **as**, servire da; **to** — **one's purpose**, fare al caso proprio; **to** — **time**, scontare un periodo di reclusione; **to** — **a writ**, notificare una citazione; **it** —**s him right!** gli sta bene!

server (sûrv'ĕr) *n.* chi serve (*anche la messa*); vassoio: **process** —, ufficiale giudiziario.

service (sûr'vĭs) *n.* servizio: **at your** —, a vostra disposizione; **to be of** —, rendersi utile; **funeral** —, esequie; **mail** —, servizio postale; **table** —, servizio da tavola, vasellame; — **station**, stazione di ser-

vizio. *vt.* provvedere alla manutenzione di; fornire assistenza tecnica a; rivedere, revisionare, ripassare.

serviceable (sûr'vĭs·á·b'l) *agg.* utile, vantaggioso, pratico.

serviceman *n.* militare.

servicing (sûr'vĭs·ĭng) *n.* manutenzione; assistenza tecnica; revisione.

servile (sûr'vĭl) *agg.* servile.

servitude (sûr'vĭ·tūd) *n.* schiavitù: **penal** —, lavori forzati.

session (sĕsh'ŭn) *n.* sessione.

set (sĕt) *n.* assortimento, collezione, serie, complesso, servizio; accolita, gruppo; tendenza, posizione; (*teat., cinema*) scena; (*naut.*) direzione (*del vento*); partita (*di tennis*); (*radio*) apparecchio ricevente: — **of teeth**, dentiera. *agg.* fisso, stabile, determinato, rigido, ostinato; pronto (*a*): **deep**— **eyes**, occhi infossati *vt.* (*pass., pp.* set) posare, mettere, deporre; fissare, stabilire; regolare; apparecchiare; montare, incastonare; irrigidire; orientare; (*tip.*) comporre. *vi* tramontare, declinare; consolidarsi; covare; accingersi; tendere: **to** — **aside**, mettere da parte, annullare; **to** — **forth**, esporre, manifestare, mettere in valore, dar risalto a, partire, avviarsi; **to** — **in**, sopravvenire, calare; **to** — **off**, mettere in risalto; partire; far esplodere; **to** — **on fire**, incendiare; **to** — **out**, disporre; esporre, descrivere; assegnare, stabilire; progettare; avviarsi, partire; adornare; equipaggiare; **to** — **right**, rettificare; **to** — **sail**, spiegare le vele, salpare; **to** — **up**, fondare, avviare, rivendicare; (*tip.*) comporre; montare (*una macchina*).

setback (sĕt'băk') *n.* riflusso; scacco, ostacolo.

settee (sĕ·tē') *n.* divanetto.

setter (sĕt'ĕr) *n.* cane da ferma, setter; montatore.

setting (sĕt'ĭng) *n.* posa, adattamento, disposizione; incastonatura, montatura; scenario, ambiente; tramonto, declino; solidificazione. (*tip.*) composizione. *agg.*: — **sun**, sole al tramonto.

settle (sĕt'l) *n.* panca. *vt.* fissare, stabilire, assegnare; colonizzare; regolare, accomodare, risolvere; saldare (*un conto*); comporre (*una vertenza*); intestare (*beni*). *vi.* stabilirsi, fissarsi; consolidarsi; decidersi; posarsi, calmarsi; depositare; rimettersi al bello (*del tempo*): **to** — **a pension on**, assegnare una pensione a; **to** — **down**, accasarsi, stabilirsi,

darsi a una vita regolare; **to —
down to,** applicarsi a.

settlement (sĕt''l·mĕnt) *n.* accordo;
pagamento; saldo, liquidazione; assegnazione *o* trapasso (*di proprietà*);
colonia, colonizzazione; dote; sedimento; sistemazione; stabilimento;
rendita, pensione: **marriage —,**
dote; **— day,** giorno di liquidazione.

settler (sĕt'lẽr) *n.* colono, colonizzatore, pioniere; liquidatore: **— of
disputes,** arbitro; paciere.

settling (sĕt'lĭng) *n.* accomodamento,
regolamento (*di conti, ecc.*); sistemazione; deposito, sedimento.

setup (sĕt'ŭp') *n.* portamento; situazione; organizzazione; (*gergo S.U.*)
imbroglio (*in competizioni sportive*).

seven (sĕv'ĕn) *n.*, *agg.* sette.

seventeen (sĕv'ĕn·tēn') *n.*, *agg.* diciassette.

seventeenth (sĕv'ĕn·tēnth') *n.*, *agg.*
diciassettesimo.

seventh (sĕv'ĕnth) *n.*, *agg.* settimo.

seventieth (sĕv'ĕn·tĭ·ĕth) *n.*, *agg.*
settantesimo.

seventy (sĕv'ĕn·tĭ) *n.*, *agg.* settanta.

sever (sĕv'ẽr) *vt.* dividere, recidere,
troncare. *vi.* dividersi, scindersi.

several (sĕv'ẽr·ăl) *agg.* vari, parecchi,
svariati, distinti.

severe (sê·vẽr') *agg.* severo, rigoroso,
grave, austero; violento, aspro,
acuto (*di dolore*).

severity (sê·vẽr'ĭ·tĭ) *n.* severità, austerità, asprezza, gravità.

sew (sō) *vt.*, *vi.* (*pass.* sewed, *pp.*
sewed, sewn) cucire.

sewage (sū'ĭj) *n.* scolo di fogna.

sewer (sō'ẽr) (1) *n.* cucitore, cucitrice.

sewer (sū'ẽr) (2) *n.* cloaca, fogna.

sewerage (sū'ẽr·ĭj) *n.* fognatura.

sewing (sō'ĭng) *n.* cucitura, il cucire:
— machine, macchina per cucire.

sewn (sōn) *pp.* di to sew.

sex (sĕks) *n.* sesso: **— appeal,** attrazione sessuale, fascino carnale.

sextant (sĕks'tănt) *n.* sestante.

sextette (sĕks·tĕt') *n.* (*mus.*) sestetto.

sexton (sĕks'tŭn) *n.* sagrestano.

sexual (sĕk'shŏŏ·ăl) *agg.* sessuale.

shabbily (shăb'ĭ·lĭ) *avv.* sciattamente;
meschinamente; ignobilmente.

shabbiness (shăb'ĭ·nĕs) *n.* meschinità,
sciatteria; grettezza.

shabby (shăb'ĭ) *agg.* cencioso, logoro,
ignobile, gretto, vile, spregevole.

shack (shăk) *n.* capanna, baracca.

shackle (shăk''l) *n.* ostacolo, anello
del lucchetto, staffa; (*naut.*) maniglia: **shackles,** pastoie, ceppi, ferri.
vt. mettere le pastoie a, ostacolare.

shade (shād) *n.* ombra; ombreggiatura, sfumatura; paralume,

schermo, riparo; gradazione (*di
colore*); tendaggio: **a — longer,** un
tantino più lungo; **— of meaning,**
sfumatura di significato; **—s of
the schoolroom,** ricordi di scuola; **in
the — of,** all'ombra di. *vt.* ombreggiare, oscurare, riparare; adombrare.

shading (shād'ĭng) *n.* ombreggiatura,
chiaroscuro, sfumatura.

shadow (shăd'ō) *n.* ombra; (*S.U.*)
pedinatore: **under the — of,** al-
l'ombra di, col favore di. *vt.* ombreggiare, adombrare, oscurare;
spiare, pedinare.

shadowy (shăd'ō·ĭ) *agg.* ombroso,
oscuro, vago.

shady (shād'ĭ) *agg.* ombreggiato,
ombroso; (*fam.*) losco, ambiguo: **—
character,** individuo losco, poco di
buono.

shaft (shȧft) *n.* dardo; asta; fusto (*di
colonna*), gambo; stanga; biella;
manico; palo; tromba (*d'ascensore*);
pozzo (*di miniera*).

shaggy (shăg'ĭ) *agg.* peloso, irsuto,
villoso, ispido; **—dog story,** racconto insipido, barzelletta fiacca.

shagreen (shȧ·grēn') *n.* zigrino; pelle
di squalo.

shake (shāk) *n.* scossa; stretta (*di
mano*); tremito; scrollata. *vt.* (*pass.*
shook, *pp.* shaken) scuotere, scrollare, sconvolgere; (*gergo*) sbarazzarsi di. *vi.* tremare, agitarsi, tentennare, barcollare: **to — hands
with,** stringere la mano a; **to —
one's head,** tentennare il capo; **to —
with cold,** tremare di freddo.

shaky (shāk'ĭ) *agg.* tremante, vacillante, malfermo.

shale (shāl) *n.* (*geol.*) schisto.

shall (shăl) *v.aus.difettivo* (*pass.*
should; *mancano: inf., ppr., pp.*)
esprime il concetto di: dovere. Il
presente è l'ausiliare con cui si
forma il futuro (*predicente:* la pers.
sing. e pl.; *volitivo:* 2a e 3a sing. e
pl.): **I — go,** io andrò; **we — work,**
noi lavoreremo; **you — sing,** voi
canterete (*o* dovete cantare); **they
— obey,** essi obbediranno (*o* devono
obbedire). Il passato ha valore di
condizionale *opp.* di imperfetto soggiuntivo ed è l'ausiliare con cui si
forma il cond. degli altri verbi:
I — be glad, sarei lieto; **you
— have more sense,** dovreste
avere maggior prudenza; **— you
go to London,** se voi andaste a
Londra; **in case they — be
unable to come,** qualora essi fos-
sero nell'impossibilità di venire.

shallop (shăl'ŭp) *n.* barchetta.

shallow (shăl'ō) n. bassofondo. agg. poco profondo; superficiale; futile. **—ness** n. scarsa profondità; superficialità, frivolezza.

sham (shăm) n. finta, imitazione, impostura, finzione. agg. finto, contraffatto. vt., vi. fingere, simulare.

shamble (shăm'b'l) n. andatura goffa. vi. camminare goffamente, trascinarsi.

shambles (shăm'b'lz) n.pl. macello, mattatoio; carnaio, carneficina.

shame (shăm) n. vergogna, disonore, ignominia; pudore: to put to —, far vergognare; for —! vergogna! it's a —, è una vergogna; è un peccato. vt. svergognare, far arrossire, disonorare.

shamefaced (shăm'fāst') agg. vergognoso (che si vergogna), pudico; confuso; mortificato.

shameful (shăm'fŏŏl) n. infame, vergognoso.

shameless (shăm'lĕs) agg. spudorato, sfrontato.

shamelessness (-nĕs) n. sfrontatezza, spudoratezza.

shampoo (shăm-pōō') n. lavaggio dei capelli. vt. lavare (la testa).

shamrock (shăm'rŏk) n. trifoglio.

shanghai (shăng-hī') vt. (gergo) attirare con l'inganno; (naut.) imbarcare (un marinaio) con l'inganno.

shank (shăngk) n. gamba, tibia, stinco; gambo, fusto.

shan't (shànt) contr. di shall not.

shanty (shăn'tǐ) n. capanna, tugurio.

shape (shāp) n. forma, figura, sagoma: to be in bad —, stare male; to put into —, mettere in ordine, aggiustare. vt. formare, foggiare; adattare, regolare. vi. prendere forma, adattarsi: things are —ing well, le cose prendono una buona piega.

shapeless (-lĕs) agg. informe.

shapeliness (shāp'lǐ-nĕs) n. armonia di linee, bellezza.

shapely (shāp'lǐ) agg. bello, ben fatto.

share (shâr) n. parte, porzione, spartizione; (comm.) azione (titolo), dividendo, caratura; vomero (d'aratro): to go —s, dividere in parti uguali. vt., vi. dividere, spartire, avere in comune, condividere: to — in, essere cointeressato in, condividere. —cropper n. mezzadro.

shark (shärk) n. squalo; furfante, speculatore: loan —, usuraio, strozzino.

sharp (shärp) n. parte aguzza; (gergo) truffatore, esperto; (mus.) diesis. agg. acuto, aguzzo, affilato, tagliente, pungente; marcato; penetrante; perspicace; aspro; furbo; acre; squillante: — turn, svolta improvvisa, curva stretta; — ear, udito fine; — temper, carattere aspro. avv. in punto (dell'ora); puntualmente; bruscamente; (mus.) in tono maggiore.

sharpen (shär'pĕn) vt. affilare, aguzzare, arrotare; temperare (una matita); acuire, stimolare. vi. acuirsi, divenire aguzzo (o tagliente).

sharper (shär'pĕr) n. truffatore; baro.

sharply (shärp'lǐ) avv. acutamente; bruscamente; nettamente; puntualmente.

sharpness (shärp'nĕs) n. acume, acutezza; asprezza; intensità; filo (del rasoio).

shatter (shăt'ĕr) n. frammento: shatters, frantumi: to break into —s, mandare (o andare) in frantumi. vt. frantumare, sconquassare, devastare; distruggere. vi. frantumarsi.

shave (shāv) n. rasatura; pialla; scheggia, truciolo: to have a close —, scamparla bella. vt. (pass. shaved pp. shaved o shaven) radere; tosare; piallare; raschiare; sfiorare. vi. radersi, farsi la barba.

shaving (shāv'ǐng) n. rasatura; tosatura; scheggia; truciolo: — brush, pennello da barba; — soap, sapone da barba; wood —s, trucioli.

shawl (shôl) n. scialle.

she (shē) pron.f. ella, essa, colei: a —cat n. una gatta.

sheaf (shēf) n. (pl. sheaves) covone, fascio. vt., vi. legare in covoni, riunire in fascio.

shear (shēr) vt. (pass. sheared, shore, pp. sheared, shorn) tosare, tranciare; spogliare, potare; falciare.

shears (shērz) n.pl. cesoie.

sheath (shēth) n. guaina, fodero; membrana.

sheathe (shēth) vt. rivestire, inguainare.

sheave (shēv) n. ruota di puleggia.

sheaves pl. di sheaf.

shed (shĕd) (1) n. tettoia, riparo, capannone, baracca.

shed (shĕd) (2) vt. (pass., pp. shed) spandere; versare; emettere (suono, luce, ecc.); lasciar cadere, perdere (capelli, ecc.); spogliarsi di: to — leaves, sfogliarsi, perdere le foglie.

sheen (shēn) n. splendore. vi. risplendere, luccicare.

sheep (shēp) n. sing., pl. pecora, ovini: — dog, cane da pastore. —fold n. ovile, gregge. —skin n.

pelle di pecora, pergamena; (S.U.) diploma, laurea.

sheepish (shēp'ĭsh) agg. timido, smarrito; impacciato; melenso.

sheer (shēr) (1) agg. puro; semplice; fine, trasparente, diafano; ininterrotto; perpendicolare: — silk, seta trasparente o impalpabile; — stockings, calze velate.

sheer (shēr) (2) vt., vi. (naut.) deviare dalla rotta, virare.

sheet (shēt) n. lenzuolo; foglio, lastra, distesa; giornale; (naut.) scotta; teglia (per cibi): — anchor, ancora di salvezza; — lightning, lampo diffuso.

shelf (shĕlf) n. (pl. shelves) scaffale, mensola; strato di roccia, banco di sabbia.

shell (shĕl) n. guscio, conchiglia, involucro; tartaruga; barchetta; padiglione (dell'orecchio); mollusco; proiettile, pallottola, bossolo. vt. sgusciare, sgranare; bombardare.

shellac (shĕ·lăk') n. gommalacca, lacca. vt. laccare.

shellacking (shĕ·lăk'ĭng) n. (gergo) bastonatura, batosta.

shellfish (shĕl'fĭsh') n. mollusco, crostaceo.

shelter (shĕl'tĕr) n. riparo, ricovero, protezione, rifugio. vt. riparare, difendere, nascondere, proteggere. vi. ripararsi, ricoverarsi.

shelve (shĕlv) vt. scaffalare, mettere in disparte, archiviare. vi. digradare.

shelves pl. di shelf.

shepherd (shĕp'ĕrd) n. pastore: — dog, cane da pastore. vt. scortare, guidare, vigilare su.

shepherdess (shĕp'ĕr·dĕs) n. pastora, pastorella.

sherbet (shûr'bĕt) n. sorbetto.

sherry (shĕr'ĭ) n. vino di Xeres.

shield (shēld) n. scudo, difesa, protezione, riparo. vt., vi. difendere, riparare.

shift (shĭft) n. cambio, mutamento; espediente; sostituzione, spostamento; squadra (di operai, ecc.), turno; camicia (da donna): to make —, arrangiarsi, riuscire. vt. mutare, spostare, trasferire; (auto) cambiare (marcia): to — the blame on, addossare la colpa a. vi. trasferirsi, spostarsi; cambiarsi d'abito; ricorrere a espedienti, ingegnarsi.

shiftless (shĭft'lĕs) agg. indolente, inetto.

shifty (shĭft'ĭ) n. furbo, subdolo, evasivo.

shilling (shĭl'ĭng) n. scellino.

shimmer (shĭm'ĕr) vi. luccicare.

shin (shĭn) n. tibia, stinco, garretto. vi. arrampicarsi.

shine (shīn) n. splendore, lucentezza, lucidatura. vt. far risplendere; lucidare. vi. sfolgorare, brillare.

shingle (shĭng'g'l) n. ghiaia, embrice di legno, targhetta; capelli corti. vt. coprire di embrici di legno; tagliare (i capelli) corti.

shining (shīn'ĭng) n. splendore. agg. brillante, splendente, luminoso.

shiny (shīn'ĭ) agg. lucente, luccicanta, splendente, lucido.

ship (shĭp) n. nave, bastimento; aeronave, velivolo: on —board, a bordo. vt. imbarcare, caricare, trasportare su una nave. vi. imbarcarsi. —builder n. armatore navale. —master n. capitano di una nave. —mate n. compagno di bordo.

shipment (-mĕnt) n. imbarco, carico.

shipper (shĭp'ĕr) n. spedizioniere marittimo.

shipping (shĭp'ĭng) n. flotta; tonnellaggio; spedizione; caricamento, imbarco.

shipshape (shĭp'shāp') agg., avv. in perfetto ordine.

shipwreck (shĭp'rĕk') n. naufragio. vt. far naufragare. vi. naufragare.

shipyard (shĭp'yärd') n. cantiere navale.

shire (shīr; come suffisso: shĭr) n. contea.

shirk (shûrk) vt. schivare, evitare: —er n. scansafatiche; (mil.) renitente.

shirt (shûrt) n. camicia (da uomo): in —sleeves, in maniche di camicia; to keep one's — on, (gergo) reprimere la collera; —waist n. camicetta.

shiver (shĭv'ĕr) n. brivido, fremito; scheggia, frammento. vt. frantumare. vi. frantumarsi, tremare, rabbrividire.

shoal (shōl) n. branco di pesci; banco di sabbia, bassofondo; moltitudine.

shock (shŏk) n. colpo, scossa, urto, trauma, emozione; — of hair, ciuffo di capelli; — absorber, ammortizzatore; — troops, truppe d'assalto o d'urto; vt., vi. urtare, disgustare, spaventare, scandalizzare, colpire, cozzare.

shocking (shŏk'ĭng) agg. offensivo, repulsivo, sconveniente, scandaloso.

shod (shŏd) pass., pp. di to shoe.

shoe (shōō) n. scarpa, calzatura; ferro (da cavallo), zoccolo; copertone (d'auto); pattino (del freno): — polish, lucido da scarpe. vt. (pass., pp. shod) calzare; ferrare.

shoeblack n. lustrascarpe.

shoehorn n. calzascarpe.

shoelace n. stringa da scarpe.

shoemaker n. calzolaio.

shoestring n. stringa da scarpe; (*gergo*) somma esigua, capitale insufficiente.

shone (shōn) *pass., pp. di* to shine.

shook (shŏŏk) *pass. di* to shake.

shoot (shōōt) n. colpo, lancio, tiro; germoglio; cascata. *vt., vi.* (*pass., pp.* shot) sparare; fucilare; lanciare; emettere, cacciare; far brillare (*mine*); variegare; germogliare; dolorare; fotografare, riprendere *o* girare (*una scena*): to — forth, germogliare, scaturire; to — ahead, slanciarsi in avanti; to — by, passare rapidamente; to — the breeze (*gergo*), fare quattro chiacchiere.

shooter n. sparatore, cacciatore.

shooting n. sparatoria; caccia; il germogliare: — range, poligono, tiro al bersaglio. *agg.*: — pain, dolore acuto; — star, stella filante.

shop (shŏp) n. bottega, negozio; officina, laboratorio: to talk—, parlare di lavoro. *vi.* fare le compere.

shopkeeper n. negoziante.

shoplifter n. taccheggiatore, taccheggiatrice.

shopman n. commesso.

shopper (shŏp'ĕr) n. compratore, persona in giro per i negozi.

shopping (shŏp'ĭng) n. spesa, compere: to go —, andare in giro per i negozi; andare a far compere.

shop window n. vetrina.

shore (shōr) n. riva, spiaggia, costa, lido; puntello: to go a—, on shore, sbarcare; Shore Patrol (*mil.*), Polizia della Marina.*vt.* arenare; puntellare.

shorn (shōrn) *pp. di* to shear.

short (shŏrt) n. sommario, compendio; la parte corta (*di uno cosa*); (*cinema*) cortometraggio; *pl.* calzoncini; deficienze: —cut, scorciatoia; the long and — of, la conclusione di: in —, in breve. *agg.* corto, breve, scarso, piccolo, basso; a corto (*di*); brusco, conciso: to make — work of, liquidare per le spicce; in a — time, in poco tempo, tra poco. *avv.* bruscamente, di botto, laconicamente: to fall —, essere inadeguato; to fall — of, non riuscire a raggiungere; to be — of, essere a corto di; to run — of, restare a corto di; to cut — of, accorciare, interrompere bruscamente; to stop —, fermarsi di botto.

shortage (shŏr'tĭj) n. scarsità, carestia, ammanco.

shortcoming (shŏrt'kŭm'ĭng) n. deficienza, inconveniente.

shorten (shŏr't'n) *vt.* accorciare, abbreviare, contrarre. *vi.* accorciarsi.

shortening (shŏr't'n·ĭng) n. accorciamento, abbreviazione; (*pasticceria*) grasso.

shorthand (shŏrt'hănd') n. stenografia.

shortly (shŏrt'lĭ) *avv.* brevemente, bruscamente, fra poco, subito, di lì a poco.

shortness (shŏrt'nĕs) n. brevità, piccolezza (*di statura*); irascibilità.

shot (shŏt) (1) *agg.* variegato.

shot (shŏt) (2) *pass., pp. di* to shoot. n. sparo; lancio; mira; proiettile; pallini da fucile; tiratore; portata (*d'arma*); tentativo; fotografia; (*gergo*) iniezione, sorso: a dead —, un tiratore infallibile; not by a long —, niente affatto, per nulla; a big — (*gergo*) un pezzo grosso.

shotgun (shŏt'gŭn') n. fucile da caccia.

should (shŏŏd) *pass. di* shall.

shoulder (shōl'dĕr) n. spalla, prominenza, sostegno: — belt, bandoliera; — blade, scapola; to give the cold —, trattare freddamente; straight from the —, con tutta franchezza. *vt.* caricarsi sulle spalle, assumersi, addossarsi.

shout (shout) n. grido. *vt., vi.* gridare, acclamare.

shouting (shout'ĭng) n. urlio.

shove (shŭv) n. colpo, spinta, urto. *vt., vi.* sospingere, spingere, ficcare: to — off, spinger via una barca, portarsi al largo.

shovel (shŭv''l) n. pala, paletta. *vt.* spalare, scavare. —er n. spalatore.

show (shō) n. mostra, esposizione, spettacolo; indicazione, traccia; esibizione, ostentazione, pompa: dumb —, pantomima. *vt.* (*pass.* showed, *pp.* shown) mostrare, mettere in mostra, dimostrare, denotare, accompagnare. *vi.* apparire, esibirsi; affacciarsi, vedersi; (*gergo sport.*) arrivare piazzato: to — in, introdurre; to — out, condurre alla porta; to — off, mettere o mettersi in mostra; to — up, condurre di sopra; smascherare; comparire.

showcase (shō'kās') n. vetrinetta, teca.

shower (shou'ĕr) n. scroscio, gragnuola; doccia; abbondanza. *vt.* bagnare, inondare, riversare, elargire. *vi.* piovere a rovesci; fare la doccia. —bath n. doccia. —y *agg.* piovoso.

showman (shō'măn) n. presentatore, imbonitore, espositore.

shown (shōn) *pp. di* to show.

showy (shō'ĭ) *agg.* ostentato, sfarzoso, vistoso, appariscente.

shrank (shrăngk) *pass. di* to shrink.

shrapnel (shrăp'nĕl) *n. (art.)* granata.

shred (shrĕd) *n.* brandello, frammento, pezzetto: **to tear — —s**, fare a pezzetti *o* brandelli. *vt. (pass. pp.* shred, shredded) sminuzzare; sbrindellare.

shrew (shrōō) *n.* megera; *(zool.)* toporagno.

shrewd (shrōōd) *agg.* sagace, scaltro.

shriek (shrēk) *n.* strillo, sibilo, stridio. *vt., vi.* strillare, sibilare, stridere.

shrill (shrĭl) *agg.* acuto, penetrante, stridulo. *vi.* strillare.

shrimp (shrĭmp) *n.* gamberetto di mare; *(fig.)* omiciattolo.

shrine (shrīn) *n.* reliquiario, altare.

shrink (shrĭngk) *vt. (pass.* shrank, shrunk, *pp.* shrunk, shrunken) accorciare, contrarre, restringere. *vi.* ritrarsi, accorciarsi, restringersi, contrarsi. **—age** *n.* contrazione, accorciamento, calo.

shrivel (shrĭv''l) *vt.* contrarre, raggrinzire, far avvizzire. *vi.* raggrinzirsi, avvizzire.

shroud (shroud) *n.* sudario; *pl. (naut.)* sartie. *vt.* avvolgere in un sudario; coprire, riparare.

shrub (shrŭb) *n.* arbusto, cespuglio. **—bery** *n.* macchia d'arbusti.

shrug (shrŭg) *n.* alzata di spalle. *vt., vi.* scrollare *(le spalle)*; stringersi nelle spalle.

shrunk (shrŭngk) *pass., pp. di* shrink.

shrunken (shrŭngk'ĕn) *pp. di* shrink.

shudder (shŭd'ĕr) *n.* brivido, fremito. *vi.* tremare, rabbrividire, fremere.

shuffle (shŭf''l) *n.* andatura strascicata; mescolata; inganno, sotterfugio. *vt., vi.* strascicare; arruffare, mischiare *(le carte)*; tergiversare; ciabattare: **to — along**, camminare con passo strascicato; **to — in**, intrufolarsi; **to — out**, sgattaiolare fuori.

shun (shŭn) *vt.* evitare, schivare, scansare, sfuggire.

shunt (shŭnt) *n. (ferr.)* diramazione, scambio. *vt.* smistare. *vi.* far manovra.

shut (shŭt) *vt., vi. (pass., pp.* shut) chiudere, rinchiudere; chiudersi: **to — up**, confinare; tacere, far tacere; **to — out**, impedire l'accesso a; **to — off the light**, spegnere la luce; **to — off from**, isolare da, escludere da; **— up! silenzio!**

shutter (shŭt'ĕr) *n.* chiusura, sportello, persiana di finestra; *(fot.)*

otturatore. **— bug** *n. (gergo)* fotoamatore.

shuttle (shŭt''l) *n.* navetta, spoletta; *(S.U.)* treno locale. *vi.* andare avanti e indietro, fare la spola.

shy (shĭ) *agg.* timido; riservato; restio *(a):* **to be — on**, essere scarso di. *vi.* adombrarsi, fare uno scarto, imbizzarrirsi, ritrarsi *(da).*

shyly (shĭ'lĭ) *avv.* timidamente, timorosamente.

shyness *n.* timidezza, ritrosia, diffidenza.

shyster (shĭ'stĕr) *n.* imbroglione; avvocato equivoco, azzeccagarbugli.

Siamese (sī'á-mēs') *n., agg.* siamese: **— cat**, gatto siamese; **— twins**, fratelli siamesi; **the —**, i siamesi.

sibyl (sĭb'ĭl) *n.* sibilla.

sibylline *agg.* sibillino.

sick (sĭk) *agg.* ammalato; nauseato, stufo, disgustato: **to be —**, avere la nausea, vomitare *(Ingl.)*; **to be — at heart**, essere demoralizzato; **to grow —**, stufarsi; **to be — of**, essere stufo di; **— bay**, infermeria di bordo; **— leave**, licenza di convalescenza.

sicken (sĭk'ĕn) *vt.* far ammalare; disgustare, nauseare. *vi.* ammalarsi; disgustarsi, essere disgustoso.

sickening *agg.* disgustoso, stomachevole; di nausea *o* malessere.

sickle (sĭk''l) *n.* falcetto: **— and hammer**, falce e martello.

sickly (sĭk'lĭ) *agg.* malaticcio, malsano.

sickness (sĭk'nĕs) *n.* malattia, indebolimento; nausea.

side (sīd) *n.* lato, estremità; fianco, versante, pendio; campo, partito: **the wrong —**, il rovescio; **to take —s with**, schierarsi con,- parteggiare per; **— by —**, fianco a fianco; **to put on —** *(gergo)*, darsi delle arie; **— glance**, occhiata in tralice; **— issue**, questione secondaria; **— light**, luce laterale, ragguaglio incidentale. *agg.* laterale, indiretto. *vi.:* **to — with**, parteggiare per, schierarsi con.

sideboard (sīd'bōrd') *n.* credenza.

sidecar (sīd'kär') *n.* carrozzino di motociclo.

sideline (sīd'līn') *n.* attività secondaria; diramazione stradale, strada secondaria; *(sport.)* linea laterale.

sidetrack (sīd'trăk') *vt. (ferr.)* smistare su un binario morto; *(fig.)* sviare; mettere da parte.

sidewalk (sīd'wôk') *n.* marciapiedi.

sideways (sīd'wāz') **sidewise** (sīd'wīz') *avv.* obliquamente; lateralmente; di traverso; di fianco. *agg.* obliquo; laterale.

siding (sīd′ĭng) *n.* binario morto; binario di manovra.

sidle (sīd′l) *vi.* spostarsi lateralmente, sgattaiolare.

siege (sēj) *n.* assedio: **to lay — to,** assediare.

sieve (sĭv) *n.* staccio, vaglio. *vt.* vagliare.

sift (sĭft) *vt.* stacciare, vagliare, esaminare.

sigh (sī) *n.* sospiro. *vi.* sospirare.

sight (sīt) *n.* vista; visione, veduta; spettacolo; sguardo; mirino (*di arma da fuoco*): **at —,** a vista; **by —,** di vista; **to buy — unseen,** comprare alla cieca; **to catch — of,** avvistare, intravedere, adocchiare; **to lose — of somebody,** perdere di vista qualcuno; **to see the —s,** visitare i luoghi interessanti (*di una città*). *vt.* avvistare, prendere di mira. *vi.* mirare.

sightseeing (sīt′sē′ĭng) *n.* turismo: — **tour,** giro turistico, passeggiata turistica.

sightseer (sīt′sē′ĕr) *n.* turista, curioso.

sign (sīn) *n.* segno, cenno; insegna; indizio. *vt., vi.* firmare, segnare; scritturare; indicare: **to — up for a job,** firmare un contratto di assunzione.

signal (sĭg′năl) *n.* segnale, contrassegno, segnalazione. *agg.* segnalato, notevole, eminente. *vt., vi.* segnalare, far segnalazioni.

signature (sĭg′nȧ·tûr) *n.* firma; (*tip.*) segnatura; (*radio*) sigla.

signboard (sīn′bôrd′) *n.* insegna.

signer (sīn′ĕr) *n.* firmatario.

signet (sĭg′nĕt) *n.* sigillo: — **ring,** anello con sigillo.

significance (sĭg·nĭf′ĭ·kăns) *n.* significato, senso, importanza.

significant (sĭg·nĭf′ĭ·kănt) *agg.* sintomatico, significativo.

signify (sĭg′nĭ·fī) *vt., vi.* significare.

signpost (sīn′pōst′) *n.* cartello indicatore.

silence (sī′lĕns) *n.* silenzio. *vt.* far tacere, chetare, ridurre al silenzio.

silencer (sī′lĕn·sĕr) *n.* silenziatore.

silent (sī′lĕnt) *agg.* silenzioso, tacito; (*gramm.*) muto: — **partner,** socio che non figura, finanziatore; — **butler,** scatola raccoglirifiuti (*cenere, mozziconi, ecc.*).

silhouette (sĭl′ŏō·ĕt′) *n.* profilo, sagoma. *vt.,* proiettare, delineare. *vi.* profilarsi, delinearsi, stagliarsi (*contro*).

silk (sĭlk) *n.* seta: **raw —,** seta greggia; **sheer —,** seta trasparente *o* impalpabile. *agg.* di seta, serico.

silken (sĭl′kĕn) *agg.* serico, morbido.

silkworm (sĭlk′wûrm) *n.* baco da seta.

silky (sĭlk′ĭ) *agg.* setaceo, morbido.

sill (sĭl) *n.* basamento, soglia: **window —,** davanzale.

silly (sĭl′ĭ) *agg.* stupido, assurdo, insulso, sciocco.

silver (sĭl′vĕr) *n.* argento, argenteria. *agg.* d'argento, argenteo, argentino: — **plate,** —**ware,** argenteria; — **wedding,** nozze d'argento. *vt.* inargentare. *vi.* inargentarsi.

silversmith *n.* argentiere.

silvery *agg.* argenteo, inargentato, argentino.

similar (sĭm′ĭ·lĕr) *agg.* similare, analogo, simile. —**ity** (-ăr′ĭ·tĭ) *n.* somiglianza, analogia. —**ly** *avv.* similmente, analogamente.

simile (sĭm′ĭ·lē) *n.* paragone, similitudine.

similitude (sĭ·mĭl′ĭ·tūd) *n.* somiglianza.

simmer (sĭm′ĕr) *vi.* bollire a fuoco lento; schiumare (*di rabbia*).

simper (sĭm′pĕr) *n.* smorfietta, sorriso affettato. *vi.* sorridere affettatamente.

simple (sĭm′p'l) *n.* sciocco; erba medicinale. *agg.* semplice, puro; ignorante, ottuso: —**minded** *agg.* semplice, ingenuo, semplicione.

simpleton (sĭm′p'l·tŭn) *n.* sempliciotto.

simplicity (sĭm·plĭs′ĭ·tĭ) *n.* semplicità.

simplify (sĭm′plĭ·fī) *vt.* semplificare.

simply (sĭm′plĭ) *avv.* semplicemente, puramente, soltanto.

simulate (sĭm′ū·lāt) *vt.* simulare.

simulation (sĭm′ū·lā′shŭn) *n.* simulazione.

simulcast (sī′mŭl·kăst) *vt., vi.* trasmettere simultaneamente per radio e per televisione, radioteletrasmettere.

simultaneous (sī′mŭl·tā′nē·ŭs) *agg.* simultaneo.

simultaneity (sī′mŭl·tȧ·nē′ĭ·tĭ) *n.* simultaneità.

sin (sĭn) *n.* peccato. *vi.* peccare.

since (sĭns) *avv.* in seguito, dopo d'allora, prima d'ora, fa: **ever —,** da quell'epoca; **long —,** da molto tempo *prep.* da, dopo: **we have been here — four,** siamo qui dalle quattro. *cong.* dopo di, dacché, in seguito a, poiché, dal momento che, visto che.

sincere (sĭn·sēr′) *agg.* sincero. —**ly** *avv.* sinceramente: **yours —,** vostro devotissimo (*nella corrispondenza*).

sincerity (sĭn·sĕr′ĭ·tĭ) *n.* sincerità.

sinecure (sī′nē·kūr) *n.* sinecura.

sinew (sĭn′ū) *n.* tendine, nervo, vigore.

sinewy (sĭn'ŭ·ĭ) *agg.* nervoso; vigoroso.
sinful (sĭn'fŏŏl) *agg.* peccaminoso.
sing (sĭng) *vt.*, *vi.* (*pass.* sang, *pp.* sung) cantare: to — a child to sleep, addormentare un bimbo cantando; to — small, assumere un tono umile; to — out of tune, stonare.
singe (sĭnj) *n.* strinatura, scottatura. *vt.* strinare, bruciacchiare.
single (sĭng'g'l) *agg.* singolo, solo, unico, semplice, individuale; celibe (*m.*), nubile (*f.*): — blessedness, — life, celibato. *vt.* (*gen. seg. da* out) scegliere, prescegliere, isolare; esemplare.
singlehanded *agg.* con le proprie forze. *avv.* senza aiuto; con una sola mano.
singly (sĭng'glĭ) *avv.* a uno a uno, separatamente.
singsong (sĭng'sòng') *n.* cantilena.
singular (sĭng'gŭ·lẽr) *agg.* singolare, unico, individuale. —ity (-ǎr'ĭ·tĭ) *n.* singolarità.
sinister (sĭn'ĭs·tẽr) *agg.* sinistro.
sink (sĭngk) *n.* acquaio. *vt.* (*pass.* sank, *pp.* sunk) affondare, sommergere; diminuire, abbassare (*spec. la voce*); scavare; investire (*danaro*) in speculazioni: to — into one's mind, entrare in mente. *vi.* andare a fondo, sprofondare; decrescere; penetrare; affievolirsi. —er *n.* peso, piombino; (*min.*) sonda, escavatrice. —hole *n.* scarico. —ing *n.* depressione; escavazione: — fund, fondo d'ammortamento.
sinner (sĭn'ẽr) *n.* peccatore.
sinuous (sĭn'ŭ·ŭs) *agg.* sinuoso, tortuoso, indiretto.
sinus (sī'nŭs) *n.* insenatura; (*anat.*) seno (*cavità*).
sip (sĭp) *n.* sorso. *vt.*, *vi.* sorseggiare, centellinare.
siphon (sī'fŏn) *n.* sifone. *vt.*, *vi.* travasare con sifone, passare attraverso un sifone.
sir (sûr) *n.* signore.
sire (sīr) *n.* padre, genitore; sire, maestà.
siren (sī'rĕn) *n.* sirena.
sirloin (sûr'loin') *n.* lombo (*di bue*).
sirup (sĭr'ŭp) *vedi* syrup.
sis (sĭs) *n. fam.* sorella.
sissy (sĭs'ĭ) *n.*, *agg.* effeminato.
sister (sĭs'tẽr) *n.* sorella; suora; infermiera. *agg.* analogo: — ship, nave gemella.
sister-in-law *n.* cognata.
sit (sĭt) *vt.* (*pass.*, *pp.* sat) far sedere. *vi.* sedersi, sedere; appollaiarsi; stare; riunirsi; posare (*per un ritratto*); covare (*degli ovipari*); adattarsi (*d'indumenti*): to — tight,

aggrapparsi al sedile, tener duro; to — up, drizzarsi a sedere; vegliare; to — down, sedersi.
sit-down strike *n.* sciopero bianco.
site (sīt) *n.* posto, posizione, area.
sitting (sĭt'ĭng) *n.* seduta, sessione; posto da sedere; cova. *agg.* seduto; in cova: — room, salotto.
situate (sĭt'ŭ·āt) *vt.* collocare, situare; sistemare.
situation (sĭtŭ·ā'shŭn) *n.* situazione, posizione, impiego.
six (sĭks) *n.*, *agg.* sei.
sixteen (sĭks'tēn') *n.*, *agg.* sedici.
sixteenth (sĭks'tēnth') *n.*, *agg.* sedicesimo; (il) sedici del mese.
sixth (sĭksth) *n.*, *agg.* sesto; (il) sei del mese.
sixtieth (sĭks'tĭ·ĕth) *n.*, *agg.* sessantesimo.
sixty (sĭks'tĭ) *n.*, *agg.* sessanta.
sizable (sīz'á·b'l) *agg.* cospicuo, considerevole, voluminoso.
size (sīz) (1) *n.* glutine, appretto. *vt.* apprettare.
size (sīz) (2) *n.* grandezza, taglia, dimensioni, misura: full —, grandezza naturale. *vt.* misurare, proporzionare: to — up, giudicare, valutare.
sizeable *vedi* sizable.
sizzle (sĭz''l) *n.* sfrigolio. *vi.* sfrigolare.
skate (skāt) *n.* pattino; (*ittiol.*) razza: roller —s, pattini a rotelle. *vi.* pattinare.
skater (skāt'ẽr) *n.* pattinatore.
skedaddle (skĕ·dăd''l) *vi.* (*gergo*) svignarsela, sparpagliarsi nella fuga.
skein (skān) *n.* matassa, groviglio.
skeleton (skĕl'ĕ·tŭn) *n.* scheletro; intelaiatura, carcassa: — key, grimaldello, chiave universale.
skeptic (skĕp'tĭk) *n.*, *agg.* scettico. —al *agg.* scettico. —ism *n.* (-tĭ·sĭz'm) scetticismo.
sketch (skĕch) *n.* schizzo, abbozzo; (*teat.*) scenetta, numero. *vt.*, *vi.* schizzare, abbozzare. —ily *avv.* approssimativamente, affrettatamente.
sketchy *agg.* abbozzato, approssimativo.
skewer (skū'ẽr) *n.* spiedo.
ski (skē) *n.* sci.: — lift, seggiovia; — suit, costume da sciatore. *vi.* sciare.
skid (skĭd) *n.* slittata; sbandamento; freno a scarpa; piano inclinato; (*aeron.*) pattino di coda: — row, — road, via dei bassifondi; bassifondi. *vt.*, *vi.* frenare; scivolare; slittare, sbandare.
skiff (skĭf) *n.* schifo (*barca*).
skill (skĭl) *n.* abilità, capacità, intel-

ligenza, destrezza. **—ed** *agg.* abile, esperto; specializzato.

skillful (skĭl'fŏŏl) *agg.* abile, esperto.

skillet (skĭl'ĕt) *n.* casseruola.

skim (skĭm) *n.* schiuma, crema. *vt., vi.* schiumare, scremare; sfiorare; leggere superficialmente, scorrere: **to — over**, guardare di sfuggita.

skimp (skĭmp) *vt., vi.* lesinare, abborracciare, fare il taccagno, economizzare. **—y** *agg.* meschino, tirchio.

skin (skĭn) *n.* pelle; scorza, buccia; pergamena: **to save one's —**, salvare la pelle; **by the — of one's teeth**, per un pelo. *vt.* scorticare, pelare. **—deep** *agg.* a fior di pelle, epidermico, superficiale.

skinflint (skĭn'flĭnt) *n.* spilorcio.

skinny (skĭn'ĭ) *agg.* magro, scarno.

skip (skĭp) *n.* salto, balzo, omissione. *vt., vi.* saltare, sorvolare, omettere; sfuggire a, saltellare, rimbalzare: **— it!** sorvola!, lascia perdere!

skipper (skĭp'ẽr) (1) *n.* saltatore.

skipper (skĭp'ẽr) (2) *n.* (*naut.*) padron marittimo, capitano.

skirmish (skûr'mĭsh) *n.* scaramuccia.

skirt (skûrt) *n.* margine; falda; gonna. *vt., vi.* costeggiare, circondare, orlare, rasentare.

skit (skĭt) *n.* scherzo, burla, satira.

skulk (skŭlk) *vi.* appiattarsi, sgattaiolare.

skull (skŭl) *n.* cranio, teschio.

skunk (skŭngk) *n.* (*zool.*) moffetta.

sky (skī) *n.* (*pl.* skies) cielo: **— blue**, azzurro-cielo; **— train**, aereo per traino di alianti; **— truck**, aereo da trasporto, vagone volante.

skylark (skī'lärk') *n.* allodola.

skylight (skī'līt') *n.* lucernario.

skyscraper (skī'skrāp'ẽr) *n.* grattacielo.

slab (slăb) *n.* lastra, lastrone, fetta.

slack (slăk) *n.* polvere di carbone; inerzia, stasi; *pl.* calzoni sportivi. *agg.* allentato, lento, molle, pigro, fiacco, negligente, inerte: **— season**, stagione morta. *vt., vi.* (*anche* **slacken**) allentare, rilassare, diminuire, moderare; allentarsi, infiacchirsi, rilassarsi, rallentare. **—ness** (-nĕs) *n.* rilassatezza, lentezza, trascuratezza.

slag (slăg) *n.* scoria.

slain (slān) *pp.* di to **slay**.

slake (slāk) *vt.* saziare, placare, rallentare; allentare, spegnere (*la calce viva*). *vi.* placarsi, spegnersi.

slam (slăm) *n.* sbatacchiata; slam (*al bridge*). *vt.* sbatacchiare; scaraventare: **to — the door**, sbattere la porta.

slander (slăn'dẽr) *n.* calunnia, diffamazione. *vt.* calunniare, diffamare. **—er** *n.* calunniatore. **—ous** *agg.* calunnioso, diffamatorio.

slang (slăng) *n.* gergo. **—y** *agg.* di gergo, in gergo.

slant (slănt) *n.* declivio, inclinazione; punto di vista. *agg.* inclinato, obliquo. *vt.* inclinare; dare un particolare indirizzo a (*un giornale, uno spettacolo, ecc.*); addomesticare (*una notizia, ecc.*). *vi.* essere inclinato, inclinarsi, pendere.

slap (slăp) *n.* manata, ceffone; rabbuffo, umiliazione. *avv.* violentemente, di colpo. *vt.* schiaffeggiare; gettare con violenza; dare una manata a.

slash (slăsh) *n.* sfregio; squarcio, spacco. *vt.* tagliare; sfregiare, squarciare; sferzare; ridurre, falcidiare.

slat (slăt) *n.* striscia, stecca; lastra.

slate (slāt) *n.* ardesia, tegola d'ardesia; (*pol. S.U.*) lista dei candidati.

slattern (slăt'ẽrn) *n.* sciamannona. **—ly** *agg.* sciamannato.

slaughter (slô'tẽr) *n.* strage, carneficina, macellazione. *vt.* far strage di, trucidare, macellare. **—er** *n.* massacratore.

slave (slāv) *n.* schiavo; sgobbone: **— driver**, negriero, aguzzino. *vi.* lavorare come uno schiavo, sgobbare.

slaver (slāv'ẽr) (1) *n.* nave negriera; negriero.

slaver (slăv'ẽr) (2) *n.* bava, saliva. *vi.* sbavare, essere servile.

slavery (slāv'ẽr·ĭ) *n.* schiavitù.

slavish (slāv'ĭsh) *agg.* servile.

slay (slā) *vt.* (*pass.* slew, *pp.* slain) uccidere.

sleazy (slē'zĭ) *agg.* sottile, tenue.

sled (slĕd) *n.* slitta. *vt., vi.* trasportare (*o andare*) in slitta.

sledge (slĕj) (1) *n.* slitta, traino.

sledge (slĕj) (2) *n.* (*anche* **— hammer**) martello, mazza.

sleek (slēk) *agg.* liscio, lucente, levigato; ben pasciuto; inappuntabile; mellifluo. *vt.* lisciare, levigare.

sleep (slēp) *n.* sonno, letargo: **to go to —**, addormentarsi; **to put to —**, (far) addormentare. *vt., vi.* (*pass., pp.* slept) dormire, spirsi: **to — on it**, dormirci sopra (*detto di preoccupazioni, ecc.*). **—er** *n.* dormiente; (*ferr.*) traversina; vettura letto. **—ily** *avv.* sonnacchiosamente. **—iness** *n.* sonnolenza.

sleeping *n.* sonno, *agg.* dormiente, sopito: **— car**, vagone letto; **— draught**, sonnifero; **— sickness**, malattia del sonno, encefalite letargica.

sleepless *agg.* insonne.
sleeplessness *n.* insonnia.
sleepwalker *n.* sonnambulo.
sleepwalking *n.* sonnambulismo.
sleepy (slēp'ĭ) *agg.* assonnato; inattivo: **to be —**, aver sonno.
sleet (slēt) *n.* nevischio, neve mista a pioggia. *vi.* cadere neve mista a pioggia.
sleeve (slēv) *n.* manica; *(mecc.)* manicotto: **to laugh up one's —**, ridere sotto i baffi. **—less** *agg.* senza maniche; *(fig.)* futile.
sleigh (slā) *n.* slitta. *vi.* andare in slitta.
sleight (slīt) *n.* destrezza: **— of hand**, gioco di prestigio.
slender (slĕn'dẽr) *agg.* snello, sottile; tenue, vago, scarso.
slept (slĕpt) *pass., pp.* di to sleep.
sleuth (slōōth) *n.* segugio, investigatore.
slew (slōō) *pass.* di to slay.
slice (slīs) *n.* fetta, porzione, spicchio; spatola. *vt.* affettare.
slick (slīk) *agg.* liscio, disinvolto, astuto; viscido; *(gergo)* di prim'ordine: **— paper**, rivista raffinata, rivista di lusso. *vt.* lisciare, abbellire: **to — up**, agghindarsi, farsi bello. **—er** *n. (S.U.)* impermeabile; imbroglione.
slid (slīd) *pass., pp.* di to slide.
slide (slīd) *n.* slittamento, frana; piano inclinato, declivio; diapositiva; vetrino *(da microscopio); (mus.)* modulazione: **— fastener**, cerniera lampo; **— knot**, nodo scorsoio; **— rule**, regolo calcolatore; **— cover**, persiana avvolgibile, chiusura a serranda; **color —**, diapositiva a colori. *vt. (pass.* slid, *pp.* slid) far scorrere. far scivolare. *vi.* scivolare, sdrucciolare, slittare, scorrere: **to — in, out, away**, sgusciare dentro, fuori, via.
slight (slīt) *n.* indifferenza, insulto. *agg.* tenue, leggiero, insignificante. *vt.* denigrare, trascurare, disprezzare. **—ing** *agg.* offensivo, sprezzante. **—ly** *avv.* lievemente, scarsamente.
slim (slĭm) *agg.* snello, magro, scarso, misero.
slime (slīm) *n.* mucillagine, melma, bava.
slimy (slīm'ĭ) *agg.* viscoso, melmoso.
sling (slĭng) *n.* fionda; catena del verricello; cinghia; fascia *(per mettere il braccio al collo); (naut.)* braca. *vt. (pass., pp.* slung) lanciare; sospendere; appendere; legare: **to — a rifle over one's shoulder**, mettere il fucile a tracolla. **—shot** *n.* fionda, tirasassi.

slink (slĭngk) *vt., vi. (pass., pp.* slunk) sgattaiolare: **to — in**, sgusciar dentro.
slip (slĭp) *n.* scivolata; passo falso; fuga; foglietto, tagliando; germoglio; errore; indiscrezione; sottoveste, federa, mutandina; *(naut.)* calata: **to give the —**, piantare in asso; **to make a —**, fare una papera. *vt., vi.* far scorrere; infilare; rifilare; sbagliare; lasciarsi sfuggire; omettere; liberarsi di; eludere; sfuggire *(di mente);* scivolare; scorrere; sgattaiolare.
slipknot (slĭp'nŏt') *n.* nodo scorsoio.
slipper (slĭp'ẽr) *n.* pantofola.
slippery (slĭp'ẽr'ĭ) *agg.* sdrucciolevole, viscido; infido.
slipshod (slĭp'shŏd) *agg.* scalcagnato; scalcinato, trasandato.
slit (slĭt) *n.* fenditura, screpolatura, fessura. *vt. (pass., pp.* slit) fendere, stracciare, squarciare: **to — into strips**, tagliare a fette o strisce.
slither (slĭth'ẽr) *vt.* scivolare, strisciare.
sliver (slĭv'ẽr) *n.* scheggia.
slobber (slŏb'ẽr) *n.* bava. *vi.* sbavare; fare il sentimentale. **—ing** *agg.* bavoso; sentimentale.
sloe (slō) *n.* prugnola, prugnolo.
slogan (slō'găn) *n.* motto pubblicitario; parola d'ordine.
sloop (slōōp) *n.* specie di cutter, imbarcazione leggiera.
slop (slŏp) *n.* pozzanghera, risciacquatura di stoviglie, acqua sporca, brodaglia. *vt., vi.* versare, spandere, sbrodolare.
slope (slōp) *n.* pendio, inclinazione; versante. *vt.* inclinare. *vi.* pendere, inclinarsi, digradare.
sloping (slōp'ĭng) *agg.* in discesa, inclinato.
sloppy (slŏp'ĭ) *agg.* umido, melmoso, viscido; disgustoso, sciatto.
slot (slŏt) *n.* sbarra, catenaccio; scanalatura, fessura; buca *(per le lettere):* **— machine**, lotteria automatica; distributore automatico. *vt.* praticare una fessura in.
sloth (slōth; slŏth) *n.* indolenza. **—ful** *agg.* pigro, indolente.
slouch (slouch) *n.* andatura *(o persona)* goffa; scompostezza, portamento curvo: **— hat**, cappello a cencio. *vi.* camminare goffamente o curvo, pencolare.
slough (slou) (1) *n.* pozzanghera, pantano.
slough (slŭf) (2) *n.* spoglia *(di rettile),* squama. *vt.* spogliarsi di. *vi.* cadere, sfaldarsi, squamarsi.
sloven (slŭv'ĕn) *n.* sudicione, sciattone.

slovenliness n. sciatteria.

slovenly (slŭv'ĕn·lĭ) agg. sciatto, trasandato.

slow (slō) agg. lento, tardo, in ritardo, tardivo, indolente, ottuso, che ritarda (di orologio), tedioso. avv. lentamente. vt., vi. rallentare, indugiare, ritardare. —ly avv. lentamente, adagio, piano. —ness n. lentezza, indolenza; ottusità.

sludge (slŭj) n. fango, neve fangosa.

slug (slŭg) (1) n. (gergo) pallottola; pugno; sorso (di liquore). vt. percuotere, colpire.

slug (slŭg) (2) n. limaccia (specie di lumaca).

sluggard (slŭg'ĕrd) n. infingardo.

sluggish (slŭg'ĭsh) agg. pigro, lento.

sluice (slōōs) n. cateratta, scarico, canale, chiavica, chiusa: — gate, porta di chiusa. vt. far defluire, inondare. vi. defluire.

slum (slŭm) n. quartiere miserabile. vi. visitare i quartieri miserabili.

slumber (slŭm'bĕr) n. torpore, sonno. vi. sonnecchiare, dormire.

slump (slŭmp) n. caduta improvvisa, sprofondamento, crisi, tracollo, ribasso (dei prezzi). vi. stramazzare, sprofondare; ribassare, subire un tracollo.

slunk (slŭngk) pass., pp. di to slink.

slur (slŭr) n. onta, sfregio, calunnia; (mus.) legatura.

slush (slŭsh) n. neve fangosa, fanghiglia; morcia; sentimentalismo.

slut (slŭt) n. sciattona, sgualdrina.

sly (slī) agg. scaltro, sornione, insidioso: on the sly, di nascosto. slyness n. scaltrezza.

smack (smăk) n. schiocco, schiaffo; bacio schioccante; sapore. avv. di botto, in pieno. vt. far schioccare, sbattere violentemente; schiaffeggiare; baciare rumorosamente. vi. schioccar le labbra: to — of, sapere di. —ing agg. schioccante, sonoro.

small (smôl) agg. piccolo; basso; sottile; minuto; meschino: — change, spiccioli; — letter, lettera minuscola; — talk, chiacchiere; to feel —, sentirsi piccolo.

smallpox (smôl'pŏks') n. (med.) varicella.

smalltime (smôl'tīm') n. teatro di second' ordine. agg. scadente, di mezza tacca, misero, da poco.

smart (smärt) n. dolore, bruciore. agg. elegante; furbo, abile, intelligente; acuto; doloroso: — remark, osservazione acuta; the — set, il bel mondo, gli elegantoni. vi. dolere, soffrire.

smash (smăsh) n. fracasso, sconquasso, rovina; scontro, urto. vt. fracassare, sfondare, rovinare; vi. frantumarsi: to — against, into, andare a sbattere contro, cozzare contro.

smattering (smăt'ĕr·ĭng) n. infarinatura.

smear (smēr) n. macchia; vt. macchiare, impiastricciare; spalmare; (gergo) rovinare, mandare a monte; calunniare, diffamare: — campaign, campagna diffamatoria.

smell (smĕl) n. odore, profumo; odorato, fiuto. vt. (pass., pp. smelled o smelt) fiutare; (gergo) appestare. vi. odorare (di), puzzare: to — a rat, insospettirsi.

smelly agg. puzzolente.

smelt (smĕlt) (1) pass., pp. di to smell.

smelt (smĕlt) (2) vt. (metal.) fondere.

smile (smīl) n. sorriso. vi. sorridere.

smiling agg. sorridente. —ly avv. sorridendo, col sorriso sulle labbra.

smirch (smŭrch) vt. insudiciare.

smirk (smŭrk) n. sorriso affettato. vi. sorridere affettatamente.

smite (smīt) vt., vi. (pass. smote, pp. smitten) colpire, percuotere; angariare; rimordere; ferire.

smith (smĭth) n. fabbro, artigiano.

smithereens (smĭth'ĕr·ēnz') n.pl. frantumi. to smash to —, mandare in frantumi.

smithy (smĭth'ĭ) n. fucina.

smitten (smĭt'n) pp. di to smite.

smock (smŏk) n. camicia da donna; camiciotto, spolverina, camice.

smog (smŏg) n. caligine.

smoke (smōk) n. fumo, vapore. vt., vi. affumicare; fumare.

smoker (smōk'ĕr) n. fumatore; vagone per fumatori.

smoking (smōk'ĭng) agg. fumante: — carriage, scompartimento per fumatori; — room, sala per fumatori, fumoir (fr.).

smoky (smōk'ĭ) agg. fumoso, fumante.

smolder (smōl'dĕr) vi. ardere lentamente, covare sotto la cenere; fremere (di collera).

smooth (smōōth) agg. liscio, levigato; morbido; facile, regolare; blando, calmo. vt. lisciare, appianare; calmare; levigare; accarezzare. —en vt. levigare. —ly avv. pianamente, dolcemente; agevolmente. —ness n. dolcezza, levigatezza; agevolezza, scorrevolezza.

smote (smōt) pass. di to smite.

smother (smŭth'ĕr) vt., vi. soffocare.

smoulder (smōl'dĕr) vedi smolder.

smudge (smŭj) n. macchia, imbrattamento; fumo. vt., vi. affumicare;

imbrattare, macchiare, macchiarsi.

smug (smŭg) *agg.* tronfio.

smuggle (smŭg''l) *vt.* contrabbandare.

smuggler (smŭg'lĕr) *n.* contrabbandiere.

smut (smŭt) *n.* fuliggine, baffo (*di carbone*); carbone (*malattia dei cereali*); oscenità. *vt.* sporcare, annerire.

smutty (smŭt'ĭ) *agg.* sporco, annerito; osceno; (*bot.*) affetto dal carbone.

snack (snăk) *n.* spuntino, porzione, assaggio.

snaffle (snăf''l) *n.* morso semplice (*del cavallo*).

snafu (snă·fōō') (*gergo*) *n.* guazzabuglio, confusione. *vt.* ingarbugliare, scompigliare. *agg.* ingarbugliato, in uno stato di confusione.

snag (snăg) *n.* nodo; ramo conficcato sott'acqua; ostacolo; moncone. *vt.* ostruire, ostacolare.

snail (snāl) *n.* lumaca, chiocciola.

snake (snāk) *n.* serpente: — charmer, incantatore di serpenti. *vi.* serpeggiare.

snap (snăp) *n.* rottura, schianto; chiusura a scatto, scatto, schiocco; morso; vivacità, energia: not to care a —, infischiarsene. *vt.*, *vi.* addentare, tentare di mordere; scattare, chiudere con un colpo secco; spezzare, spezzarsi; schioccare (*le dita*); ribattere, redarguire: to — one's fingers at, ridersi di.

snapdragon (snăp'drăg'ŭn) *n.* (*bot.*) bocca di leone.

snappish (snăp'ĭsh) *agg.* brusco, secco, irascibile.

snappy (snăp'ĭ) *agg.* crepitante; mordace; rapido; vivace: make it —! sbrigati!

snapshot (snap'shŏt) *n.* (*fot.*) istantanea.

snare (snâr) *n.* trappola, agguato, insidia. *vt.* prendere in trappola, insidiare.

snarl (snärl) (1) *n.* groviglio; nodo (*del legno*); complicazione. *vt.* aggrovigliare, ingarbugliare. *vi.* aggrovigliarsi.

snarl (snärl) (2) *n.* ringhio. *vi.* ringhiare, brontolare.

snarling *agg.* ringhioso.

snatch (snăch) *n.* presa, strattone; brano, frammento; attimo. *vt.*, *vi.* afferrare, agguantare, ghermire; aggrapparsi a.

sneak (snēk) *n.* ladruncolo; spia; persona abietta. *vi.* strisciare, intrufolarsi, sgattaiolare; far la spia.

sneaker *n.* persona subdola.

sneakers *n.* *pl.* scarpe da ginnastica.

sneaky *agg.* subdolo, furtivo.

sneer (snēr) *n.* sogghigno, risata di scherno, sarcasmo. *vt.*, *vi.* irridere, deridere, sogghignare.

sneering *agg.* beffardo.

sneeze (snēz) *n.* starnuto. *vi.* starnutire.

snicker (snĭk'ĕr) *vedi* snigger.

sniff (snĭf) *n.* fiutata, zaffata (*di profumo, ecc.*). *vt.*, *vi.* aspirare rumorosamente, fiutare, tirare su col naso; piagnucolare: to — at, annusare; disprezzare.

sniffle (snĭf''l) *vi.* moccicare; piagnucolare; tirar su col naso.

snigger (snĭg'ĕr) *n.* risatina soffocata. *vi.* ridacchiare.

snip (snĭp) *n.* taglio, forbiciata; pezzetto, ritaglio; persona insignificante. *vt.*, *vi.* tagliare, tagliuzzare.

snipe (snĭp) *n.* beccaccino. *vi.* sparare in appostamento.

snitch (snĭch) (*gergo*) *n.* spia, traditore. *vt.* rubare. *vi.* fare la spia.

snivel (snĭv''l) *n.* moccio; singhiozzo. *vi.* moccicare; piagnucolare; tirar su col naso.

snob (snŏb) *n.* snob, villano rifatto. —bish *agg.* da snob, pretenzioso. —bery, —bishness *n.* snobismo.

snoop (snōōp) *n.* spia, ficcanaso. *vi.* spiare, curiosare.

snoot (snōōt) *n.* (*gergo*) naso.

snooze (snōōz) *n.* sonnellino: to take a —, fare un pisolino. *vi.* sonnecchiare.

snore (snōr) *n.* (il) russare. *vi.* russare.

snort (snôrt) *n.* sbuffata. *vi.* sbuffare.

snout (snout) *n.* muso, proboscide; naso; beccuccio (*di recipiente*).

snow (snō) *n.* neve. *vi.* nevicare: it is snowing, nevica; to be snowed under, essere sommerso dalla neve.

snowball (snō'bôl') *n.* palla di neve. *vt.* colpire con palle di neve. *vi.* fare alle palle di neve; (*S.U.*) aumentare a ritmo accelerato.

snowdrift (snō'drift') *n.* bufera (*o* cumulo) di neve.

snowfall (snō'fôl') *n.* nevicata.

snowflake (snō'flāk') *n.* fiocco di neve.

snowplow (snō'plou') *n.* spazzaneve.

snowstorm (snō'stôrm') *n.* bufera di neve.

snowy (snō'ĭ) *agg.* nevoso; candido, niveo.

snub (snŭb) *n.* affronto, rimprovero, rabbuffo. *agg.* camuso; all'insù: — nose, naso camuso. *vt.* rimproverare, umiliare, mortificare; frenare.

snuff (snŭf) *n.* tabacco da naso, fiutata; presa (*di tabacco*); zaffata; smoccolatura (*di candela*). *vt.*, *vi.* smoccolare (*la candela*); fiutare.

snuffbox (snŭf'bŏks') n. tabacchiera.

snuffle (snŭf''l) n. fiutata. vt., vi. respirare (o fiutare) rumorosamente; naseggiare.

snug (snŭg) agg. comodo; nascosto; compatto; riparato. vi. rannicchiarsi, accomodarsi.

snuggle (snŭg''l) vi. rannicchiarsi.

snugly (snŭg'lĭ) avv. comodamente, a proprio agio.

snugness (snŭg'nĭs) n. comodità, agio.

so (sō) avv., cong. così, quindi, di modo che, perciò; talmente, tanto: and — on (opp. forth), e così via; — as to, in modo da; — much, tanto; — many, tanti; — far, sin qui, sinora;——, così così, passabilmente; Mr. — and —, il signor Taldei-Tali; — much the better, tanto meglio; — that, di modo che; an hour or —, un'ora circa; I think —, credo di sì; is that —? ah, sì?, ma davvero?

soak (sōk) n. imbibizione, bagnata, immersione; (gergo) pugno; beone, bevuta; pegno; costo eccessivo. vt. inzuppare, assorbire, immergere; (gergo) ubriacare, bere all'eccesso; percuotere; far pagare; impregnare. vi. inzupparsi, filtrare: to be soaked through, essere bagnato sino al midollo.

soap (sōp) n. sapone: — bubble, bolla di sapone; — dish, portasapone; — opera, (radio, TV) commedia a puntate (offerta da una ditta commerciale). vt. insaponare.

soapbark (sōp'bärk') n. saponaria.

soapstone (sōp'stōn') n. steatite.

soapsuds (sōp'sŭdz') n. pl. saponata.

soapy (sōp'ĭ) agg. saponoso.

soar (sōr) vi. prendere lo slancio; librarsi; salire, prender quota.

sob (sŏb) n. singhiozzo, singulto: — -stuff, scritto (o film) lacrimogeno; vi. singhiozzare.

sober (sō'bĕr) agg. sobrio, moderato; lucido; serio, calmo; non ubriaco: to be —, avere la mente lucida, non essere ubriaco. vt. far passare l'ubriachezza a; calmare, placare; disilludere. vi. rinsavire, calmarsi; divenir serio o lucido; smaltire la sbornia. —ly avv. sobriamente, seriamente, con calma.

sobriety (sō·brī'ĕ·tĭ) n. sobrietà, calma, moderazione, serietà, lucidità.

sobriquet (sō'brĭ·kā) n. soprannome.

so-called agg. cosiddetto.

soccer (sŏk'ĕr) n. (giuoco del) calcio.

sociable (sō'shá·b'l) n. riunione. agg. socievole, cordiale.

social (sō'shăl) n. riunione. agg. sociale, di società; socievole.

socialism (sō'shăl·ĭzm) n. socialismo.

socialist (-ĭst) n. socialista.

socialite (-īt) n. (S.U.) persona del bel mondo.

society (sō·sī'ĕ·tĭ) n. società.

sociology (sō'sĭ·ŏl'ō·jĭ) n. sociologia.

sock (sōk) (1) n. calzino, calzettone.

sock (sōk) (2) n. (gergo) pugno. vt. dare un pugno a.

socket (sŏk'ĕt) n. alveolo, cavità; portalampada; orbita (dell'occhio).

sod (sŏd) n. zolla, tappeto erboso. vt. coprire di zolle.

soda (sō'dá) n. soda: — fountain, spaccio di bibite; — water, acqua gasata; baking —, bicarbonato di soda; — jerk (gergo). gelataio, venditore di bibite analcooliche.

sodden (sŏd''n) agg. inzuppato, impregnato; ubriaco, tumefatto; ebete, ottuso.

sodium (sō'dĭ·ŭm) n. (chim.) sodio.

sofa (sō'fá) n. sofà, divano: — bed, divano-letto.

soft (sŏft) agg. molle, morbido, tenero; debole, dolce, sommesso: — drink, bibita analcoolica; — water, acqua dolce; —boiled egg, uovo à la coque. avv. vedi softly.

soften (sŏf'ĕn) vt. addolcire, ammorbidire, lenire, ammansire; fiaccare, indebolire. vi. ammorbidirsi, rammollirsi, addolcirsi, placarsi, intenerirsi.

softening n. ammorbidimento, indebolimento, intenerimento: — of the brain, rammollimento cerebrale.

softly (sŏft'lĭ) avv. mollemente, dolcemente, sommessamente; adagio.

softness (sŏf'nĕs) n. morbidezza, delicatezza, dolcezza; facilità.

soft-pedal n. pedale del piano, sordina. vt., vi. attenuare, moderare; abbassare il tono.

soft-soap n. adulazione. vt. adulare.

soft-spoken agg. blando, persuasivo.

soggy (sŏg'ĭ) agg. inzuppato.

soil (soil) n. macchia, sudiciume; fango; letame; terra, suolo, terreno. vt. sporcare, infangare, profanare; concimare.

sojourn (sō'jûrn) n. soggiorno. vi. soggiornare.

solace (sŏl'ĭs) n. consolazione, sollievo. vt. consolare, confortare.

solar (sō'lĕr) agg. solare.

sold (sōld) pass., pp. di to sell: to be — on, essere convinto di.

solder (sŏd'ĕr) n. saldatura. vt., vi. saldare, saldarsi.

soldier (sōl'jĕr) n. soldato.

sole (sōl) (1) *agg.* solo, unico, singolo; esclusivo; non coniugato.

sole (sōl) (2) *n.* sogliola.

sole (sōl) (3) *n.* pianta (*del piede*), suola (*di scarpa*); fondo, base. *vt.* solare, risolare.

solely (sōl'lĭ) *avv.* solamente, esclusivamente, puramente.

solemn (sŏl'ĕm) *agg.* solenne, serio. **—ity** (sŏ·lĕm'nĭ·tĭ) *n.* solennità; ricorrenza.

solicit (sŏ·lĭs'ĭt) *vt.*, *vi.* sollecitare, importunare; far la piazza.

solicitor (sŏ·lĭs'ĭ·tẽr) *n.* propagandista; (*ingl.*) procuratore, avvocato.

solicitous (sŏ·lĭs'ĭ·tŭs) *agg.* sollecito; desideroso, ansioso.

solicitude (sŏ·lĭs'ĭ·tūd) *n.* sollecitudine; ansia.

solid (sŏl'ĭd) *n.* solido. *agg.* solido, intiero; massiccio, compatto, concreto; unanime; serio; solvibile: **— red,** rosso unito; **— gold,** oro massiccio; **for one — hour,** per un'ora intiera.

solidarity (sŏl'ĭ·dăr'ĭ·tĭ) *n.* solidarietà.

solidify (sŏ·lĭd'ĭ·fĭ) *vt.* solidificare. *vi.* solidificarsi.

solidity (sŏ·lĭd'ĭ·tĭ) *n.* solidità.

soliloquy (sŏ·lĭl'ō·kwĭ) *n.* soliloquio.

solitaire (sŏl'ĭ·târ') *n.* solitario (*brillante e giuoco di carte*).

solitary (sŏl'ĭ·tẽr'ĭ) *agg.* solitario, isolato; unico, solo: **— confinement,** segregazione cellulare.

solitude (sŏl'ĭ·tūd) *n.* solitudine.

solo (sō'lō) *n.* (*mus.*) assolo.

soloist (sō'lō·ĭst) *n.* (*mus.*) solista.

Solomonic (sŏl'ō·mŏn'ĭk) *agg.* salomonico.

solstice (sŏl'stĭs) *n.* solstizio.

soluble (sŏl'ū·b'l) *agg.* solubile.

solution (sŏ·lū'shŭn) *n.* soluzione.

solvable (sŏl'vá·b'l) *agg.* solubile.

solve (sŏlv) *vt.* risolvere, spiegare; sciogliere.

solvency (sŏl'vĕn·sĭ) *n.* solvibilità.

solvent (sŏl'vĕnt) *n.* (*chim.*) solvente; *agg.* solvente; (*comm.*) solvibile.

somber, sombre (sŏm'bẽr), *agg.* fosco, scuro, tenebroso, cupo.

some (sŭm) *agg.*, *pron. partitivo* qualche, qualcuno, alcuni; ne, un po' di, del, della, delle, dei: **— thirty years ago,** circa trent'anni fa. *avv.* circa, all'incirca.

somebody (sŭm'bŏd'ĭ) *n.*, *pron.* qualcuno: **— else,** qualcun altro.

somehow (sŭm'hou) *avv.* chissà come, in qualche modo, in certo qual modo: **— or other,** in un modo o nell'altro, per questo o quel motivo.

someone (sŭm'wŭn) *n.*, *pron.* qualcuno.

somersault (sŭm'ẽr·sŏlt) *n.* capriola, salto mortale: **to turn somersaults,** far salti mortali.

something (sŭm'thĭng) *n.* qualche cosa, qualcosa: **— else,** qualcos'altro; *avv.* alquanto, piuttosto, un po'.

sometime (sŭm'tīm') *agg.* passato, già, ex, d'altri tempi: **my — general,** il mio ex generale. *avv.* un tempo, una volta o l'altra, a qualche ora, uno di questi giorni.

sometimes (sŭm'tīmz') *avv.* a volte, qualche volta, di quando in quando.

somewhat (sŭm'hwŏt') *n.* qualche cosa. *avv.* alquanto, un poco.

somewhere (sŭm'hwâr') *avv.* da qualche parte, in qualche luogo: **— else,** altrove; **— about,** all'incirca.

somnolence (sŏm'nō·lĕns) *n.* sonnolenza.

somnolent (sŏm'nō·lĕnt) *agg.* sonnolente.

son (sŭn) *n.* figlio.

son-in-law *n.* genero.

song (sŏng) *n.* canto, canzone: **to buy something for a —,** comprare qualcosa a prezzo irrisorio.

sonnet (sŏn'ĕt) *n.* sonetto.

sonorous (sŏ·nō'rŭs) *agg.* sonoro.

soon (sōōn) *avv.* presto, ben presto, subito: **as — as,** non appena; **as — as possible,** il più presto possibile; **how —?** quando?; **— after,** subito dopo.

sooner *avv.* più presto: **— or later,** presto o tardi; **— than,** piuttosto che.

soot (sōōt) *n.* fuliggine.

soothe (sōōth) *vt.* placare, alleviare, blandire.

soothing (sōōth'ĭng) *agg.* calmante, dolce, consolante; adulatore.

soothsayer (sōōth'sā'ẽr) *n.* profeta, indovino.

sooty (sōōt'ĭ) *agg.* fuligginoso, nero.

sop (sŏp) *n.* pezzo di pane (*ecc.*) inzuppato; dono (*per placare o corrompere*). *vt.* inzuppare, assorbire; *vi.* inzupparsi: **sopping wet,** bagnato sino alle ossa.

sophomore (sŏf'ō·mōr) *n.* (*univ.*) studente del secondo anno.

soporific (sō'pō·rĭf'ĭk) *agg.* soporifero.

sopping (sŏp'ĭng) *agg.* inzuppato.

soprano (sŏ·prä'nō) *n.* soprano; parte per soprano; voce da soprano.

sorcerer (sôr'sẽr·ẽr) *n.* stregone, mago.

sorceress (sôr'sẽr·ĕs) *n.* strega; maga.

sorcery (sôr'sẽr·ĭ) *n.* sortilegio, magia.

sordid (sôr'dĭd) *agg.* sordido, abietto.

sore (sōr) *n.* piaga, ulcera; male, dolore. *agg.* infiammato, doloroso, dolente, indolenzito; offeso, sdegnato, imbronciato; grave, violento: — eyes, male agli occhi; — throat, mal di gola; to be — at, essere risentito con; to make —, irritare; a sight for — eyes, una vista rincuorante. —ly avv. dolorosamente, gravemente; fortemente: you are sorely mistaken, vi sbagliate di grosso. —ness n. indolenzimento, dolore; amarezza, rancore.

sorrel (sŏr'ĕl) n. cavallo sauro; agg. sauro.

sorrow (sŏr'ō) n. angoscia, pena, tristezza, rincrescimento. vi. affliggersi, affannarsi, addolorarsi. —ful agg. triste, afflitto, doloroso. —fully avv. penosamente, tristemente, dolorosamente.

sorry (sŏr'ĭ) agg. dolente, triste, meschino, doloroso; miserabile, deplorevole: I am —, scusatemi, mi dispiace; I am — for him, mi rincresce per lui, mi fa pena.

sort (sôrt) n. sorta, specie, genere, classe: of sorts, mediocre, di genere imprecisato; out of sorts, indisposto; di malumore; all sorts of people, gente di ogni genere. vt. scegliere, classificare, selezionare, riordinare.

sot (sŏt) n. ubriacone.

sought (sôt) pass., pp. di to seek.

soul (sōl) n. anima: All Soul's Day, il giorno dei morti; not a —, neppure un'anima.

soulful (sōl'fŏŏl) agg. ascetico, spirituale.

sound (sound) (1) n. stretto, braccio di mare; (med.) sonda. vt., vi. sondare, scandagliare, indagare.

sound (sound) (2) n. suono, rumore: — track (cinema), colonna sonora; — wave (radio), onda sonora; — barrier (aeron.), muro del suono. vt., vi. sonare; proclamare; risonare; sembrare; avere il tono di.

sound (sound) (3) agg. solido, sano, saldo; saggio, logico, fondato: safe and —, sano e salvo; — sleep, sonno profondo.

soundless agg. silenzioso, muto.

soundness n. saldezza, solidità; rettitudine, giustezza, saggezza; salute.

soundproof (sound'prŏŏf') agg. antisonoro.

soup (sŏŏp) n. minestra, zuppa.

sour (sour) agg. agro, acido, acerbo, aspro; arcigno: to turn —, inacidire. vt. rendere agro, far inacidire, inasprire, irritare. vi. inacidire; inasprirsi, irritarsi.

source (sŏrs) n. fonte, origine.

sourness (sour'nĕs) n. acidità; acrimonia.

souse (sous) n. salamoia, viveri in salamoia. vt. marinare, immergere, inzuppare.

south (south) n. sud, mezzogiorno. agg. del sud, meridionale, australe: the South Sea, l'Oceano Pacifico; the — pole, il polo sud.

southeast (south''ĕst') n. sud-est. agg. di sud-est.

southeastern (south'ĕs'tĕrn) agg. sud-orientale.

southern (sŭth'ĕrn) agg. meridionale, del sud: the Southern Cross, la Croce del Sud.

southward (south'wĕrd) avv. a sud, verso sud.

southwest (south'wĕst') n., agg. sud-ovest, di sud-ovest.

southwestern (south'wĕs'tĕrn) agg. sud-occidentale.

souvenir (sŏŏ've-nêr') n. pegno, ricordo.

sovereign (sŏv'ĕr-ĭn) n., agg. sovrano.

sovereignty (sŏv'ĕr-ĭn-tĭ) n. sovranità.

soviet (sō'vĭ-ĕt) agg. sovietico: the Soviet, la Repubblica Sovietica.

sow (sou) (1) n. scrofa.

sow (sō) (2) vt., vi. (pass. sowed, pp. sowed o sown) seminare, disseminare, sparpagliare.

soy (soi) n. (bot.) soia.

spa (spä) n. sorgente minerale.

space (spās) n. spazio, intervallo. vt. spazieggiare, spaziare. agg. spaziale, interspaziale: — station, stazione spaziale; — ship, astronave.

spacious (spā'shŭs) agg. spazioso, vasto.

spade (spād) n. vanga, pala: spades, spade o picche (nelle carte da giuoco); to call a — a —, dir pane al pane; vt. vangare.

span (spăn) n. spanna, palmo; portata; apertura (di un arco); apertura d'ala; luce (di ponte); lasso di tempo; pariglia: life —, durata della vita. vt. misurare a spanne, abbracciare, attraversare.

spangle (spăng'g'l) n. pagliuzza, lustrino. vt. ornare di lustrini; vi. luccicare: the Star-Spangled Banner, la Bandiera Stellata, la Bandiera degli S.U.

Spaniard (spăn'yĕrd) n. spagnuolo.

spaniel (spăn'yĕl) n. spaniel (cane da caccia).

Spanish (spăn'ĭsh) n., agg. spagnuolo.

spank (spăngk) n. sculacciata; vt. sculacciare.

spanker n. (naut.) vela di randa.

spanking n. sculacciatura. agg. vigoroso; straordinario; sferzante.

spanner (spăn'ĕr) *n.* chiave inglese.

spar (spär) *n.* palo, stanga; (*naut.*) albero, pennone; (*aeron.*) longarone. *vi.* fare la box, battersi; discutere.

spare (spâr) *n.* pezzo di ricambio. *agg.* disponibile, superfluo, di avanzo; scarso; frugale; magro; economo; di ricambio: — **time,** ritagli di tempo; — **parts,** pezzi di ricambio. *vt.* risparmiare; tralasciare; tenere in serbo; esentare; riservare: **I cannot — another dollar,** non posso spendere un altro dollaro; **I cannot — my car today,** oggi non posso restare senza la macchina; **to — no expense,** non badare a spese; *vi.* fare economia: **to have no time to —,** non aver tempo da perdere; **enough and to —,** più che a sufficienza.

sparing (spâr'ĭng) *agg.* economo, frugale.

spark (spärk) *n.* scintilla, favilla; luccichio: — **plug** (*auto.*), candela. *vi.* scintillare, mandar faville.

sparkle (spär'k'l) *n.* scintilla, scintillio; vivacità; effervescenza. *vi.* scintillare; essere effervescente; luccicare.

sparkling *agg.* scintillante; spumeggiante; vivace: — **wine,** vino spumante.

sparrow (spăr'ō) *n.* passero, passerotto.

sparse (spärs) *agg.* raro, rado; scarso; sparpagliato.

spasm (spăz'm) *n.* contrazione, accesso, spasmo spasimo.

spat (spăt) (1) *pass., pp. di* to **spit.**

spat (spăt) (2) *n.* uova di mollusco.

spat (spăt) (3) *n.* battibecco; colpo; schiaffetto, scappellotto. *vt., vi.* scappellottare, bisticciare.

spat (spăt) (4) *n.* ghetta.

spatial (spā'shăl) *agg.* spaziale.

spatter (spăt'ĕr) *n.* spruzzo, schizzo; picchiettio. *vt.* spruzzare, aspergere; picchiettare.

spatula (spăt'ū.lá) *n.* spatola.

spawn (spôn) *n.* uova di pesce; progenie.

speak (spēk) *vt., vi.* (*pass.* spoke, *pp.* spoken) dire, denotare, parlare: **to — one's mind,** dire il proprio parere; **so to —,** per così dire; **to — up** (*o* out), parlare ad alta voce, parlare francamente; **to — up for,** parlare in favore di; **to — for,** parlare a nome di.

speaker *n.* chi parla; interlocutore; oratore; (*radio*) annunziatore.

spear (spēr) (1) *n.* germoglio, stelo.

spear (spēr) (2) *n.* lancia, giavellotto;

fiocina. *vt.* trafiggere; arpionare, fiocinare.

spearfish (spēr'fĭsh') *vi.* fare pesca subacquea. **—ing** *n.* pesca subacquea.

speargun *n.* fucile subacqueo.

spearhead (spēr'hĕd') *n.* punta di lancia; (*fig.*) araldo. *vt.* mettersi all'avanguardia di.

spearmint (spēr'mĭnt') *n.* (*bot.*) menta.

special (spĕsh'ăl) *n.* cosa (*o* persona *o* treno) speciale; edizione straordinaria. *agg.* speciale, particolare straordinario.

specialist (spĕsh'ăl.ĭst) *n.* specialista

speciality (spĕsh'ĭ.ăl'ĭ.tĭ) *n.* specialità particolarità; (*pl.*) particolari.

specialize (spĕsh'ăl.īz) *vi.* specializzarsi.

specially (spĕsh'ăl.lĭ) *avv.* specialmente, particolarmente, soprattutto.

specialty (spĕsh'ăl.tĭ) *n.* specialità carattere distintivo, particolarità

specie (spē'shĭ) *n.* valuta metallica.

species (spē'shĭz) *n.* (*pl.* species) specie sorta, classe, genere.

specific (spē.sĭf'ĭk) *n.* specifico, rimedio. *agg.* specifico, particolare preciso, caratteristico: — **gravity** peso specifico. **—ally** *avv.* specificamente, particolarmente.

specify (spĕs'ĭ.fĭ) *vt., vi.* specificare.

specimen (spĕs'ĭ.mĕn) *n.* campione esemplare, saggio, modello.

speck (spĕk) *n.* macchiolina, puntino bruscolo. *vt. vedi* **speckle.**

speckle (spĕk'l) *n.* chiazza, segno macchiolina. *vt.* chiazzare, macchiettare.

speckled *agg.* chiazzato, macchiettato: — **with freckles,** lentigginoso.

spectacle (spĕk'tá.k'l) *n.* spettacolo vista: **spectacled,** occhialuto; **spectacles,** occhiali.

spectacular (spĕk.tăk'ū.lĕr) *agg.* spettacoloso; teatrale; sensazionale.

spectator (spĕk.tā'tĕr) *n.* spettatore

spectral (spĕk'trăl) *agg.* spettrale.

spectre (spĕk'tĕr) *n.* spettro.

spectrum (spĕk'trŭm) *n.* (*fis.*) spettro

speculate (spĕk'ū.lāt) *vi.* speculare meditare.

speculation (spĕk'ū.lā'shŭn) *n.* speculazione, meditazione.

speculative (spĕk'ū.lā'tĭv) *agg.* speculativo; meditativo; teorico.

speculator (spĕk'ū.lā'tĕr) *n.* speculatore.

sped (spĕd) *pass., pp. di* to **speed.**

speech (spēch) *n.* discorso; linguaggio, eloquio, parlata.

peechless *n.* ammutolito, muto. **—ly** *avv.* senza parola, mutamente.

peed (spēd) *n.* velocità, rapidità; fretta, prontezza: **at full —,** a tutta velocità; **— limit,** velocità massima. *vt., vi.* (*pass., pp.* sped) affrettare, accelerare; incrementare; affrettarsi, passare in fretta, correre; eccedere in velocità.

peedily (spēd′ĭ.lĭ) *avv.* velocemente, alacremente, prontamente.

peeding (spēd′ĭng) *n.* eccesso di velocità.

peedometer (spēd.ŏm′ē̇.tēr) *n.* tachimetro.

peedway (spēd′wā′) *n.* autostrada.

peedy (spēd′ĭ) *agg.* rapido, svelto; spiccio.

pell (spĕl) *n.* incantesimo, magia, incanto; periodo; accesso; intervallo, turno di lavoro. *vt., vi.* (*pass., pp.* spelled *o* spelt) rimpiazzare, dare il cambio a; compitare, sillabare; significare; preannunziare: **how do you — it?** come si scrive? **— it,** please, ditemi come si scrive, per favore; **to — out,** spiegare chiaramente.

pellbinder (spĕl′bĭn′dēr) *n.* (*S.U.*) affascinatore.

pellbound (spĕl′bound′) *agg.* incantato, affascinato; ammutolito.

peller (spĕlēr) *n.* chi compita; sillabario.

pelling *n.* compitazione, ortografia: **— book,** sillabario; **the — of this word is . . .,** questa parola si scrive così . . .

pelunker (spē̇.lŭngk′ēr) *n.* (*fam.*) speleologo.

pend (spĕnd) *vt., vi.* (*pass., pp.* spent) spendere, sprecare; esaurire; consumare; trascorrere, impiegare; consumarsi, esaurirsi.

pendthrift (spĕnd′thrĭft′) *n.* prodigo, scialacquatore.

pent (spĕnt) *pass., pp. di* to spend; *agg.* esaurito, esausto.

pew (spū) *vt., vi.* vomitare.

phere (sfēr) *n.* sfera; àmbito.

pherical (sfēr′ĭ.kăl) *agg.* sferico.

phinx (sfĭngks) *n.* sfinge.

pice (spīs) *n.* spezie, droga, aroma. *vt.* condire con spezie, aromatizzare.

picy (spīs′ĭ) *agg.* pepato, aromatico, piccante.

pick-and-span (spĭk′ănd.spăn′) *agg.* nuovo di zecca; in perfetto ordine; lustro e ordinato.

pider (spī′dēr) *n.* ragno. **—web** *n.* ragnatela.

pigot (spĭg′ŭt) *n.* zipolo, rubinetto.

pike (spīk) *n.* punta, aculeo, chiodo;

spiga. *vt.* inchiodare, chiodare; trafiggere; frustrare, stroncare.

spill (spĭl) *n.* versamento, zampillo, spruzzo; sfioratore (*di diga, ecc.*); caduta; zipolo. *vt.* (*pass., pp.* spilled *o* spilt) versare, spandere; disarcionare, buttar giù; (*gergo*) confessare, rivelare. *vi.* rovesciarsi, riversarsi; confessare, "cantare."

spin (spĭn) *n.* rotazione, corsa; (*aeron.*) vite. *vt., vi.* (*pass. pp.* spun) filare; far la tela (*dei ragni*); arrotolare, attorcigliare; far girare, girare, torcersi, roteare; passare velocemente: **to — a yarn,** farla lunga.

spinach (spĭn′ĭch) *n.* spinaci.

spinal (spī′năl) *agg.* spinale: **— column,** colonna vertebrale; **— cord,** midollo spinale.

spindle (spĭn′d'l) *n.* fuso, perno.

spine (spīn) *n.* spina, aculeo; spina dorsale.

spinet (spĭn′ĕt) *n.* (*mus.*) spinetta.

spinner (spĭn′ēr) *n.* filatore, filatrice (*macchina*).

spinning (spĭn′ĭng) *n.* filatura: **— jenny,** filatoio; **— mill,** filanda; **— top,** trottola; **— wheel,** filatoio.

spinster (spĭn′stēr) *n.* zitella.

spinstress (spĭn′strĕs) *n.* filatrice.

spiral (spī′răl) *n.* spirale. *agg.* a spirale: **— staircase,** scala a chiocciola.

spire (spīr) *n.* cima, cuspide; guglia, campanile; stelo.

spirit (spĭr′ĭt) *n.* spirito, forza, vigore, coraggio; alcool; vivacità: **low spirits,** malumore, abbattimento; **good spirits,** buon umore; **to be out of spirits,** essere di malumore. *vt.:* **to — off** (*o* away), portar via, aspire.

spirited (spĭr′ĭ.tĕd) *agg.* coraggioso, brioso.

spiritless (spĭr′ĭt.lĕs) *agg.* scoraggiato, abbattuto.

spiritual (spĭr′ĭ.tū.ăl) *n.* canto mistico (*spec. dei negri am.*). *agg.* spirituale.

spiritualism (spĭr′ĭ.tū.ăl.ĭz′m) *n.* spiritismo.

spirituous (spĭr′ĭ.tū.ŭs) *agg.* alcoolico.

spit (spĭt) (1) *n.* penisoletta, capo; spiedo. *vt.* infilzare sullo spiedo, trafiggere.

spit (spĭt) (2) *n.* sputo, saliva, spruzzo di pioggia, breve nevicata. *vt., vi.* (*pass.* spat, *pp.* spit) sputare, sputacchiare; piovigginare.

spite (spĭt) *n.* dispetto, rancore, astio: **in — of,** a dispetto di, nonostante; **out of —,** per dispetto. *vt.* indispettire, vessare, contrariare.

spiteful (spĭt'fŏŏl) agg. astioso, dispettoso, ostile.

spittoon (spĭ·tŏōn') n. sputacchiera.

splash (splăsh) n. chiazza, pillacchera,
spruzzo; tonfo. vt. schizzare, chiazzare, inzaccherare. vi. diguazzare,
spruzzare.

splay (splā) agg. sguancio; sbilenco.
vt. sguanciare; slogare.

spleen (splēn) n. (anat.) milza; malinconia, umor nero.

splendid (splĕn'dĭd) agg. splendido.

splendor (splĕn'dẽr) n. splendore.

splice (splīs) n. (naut.) impiombatura;
(carp.) calettatura. vt. impiombare;
calettare.

splint (splĭnt) n. stecca, asticciola. vt.
steccare.

splinter (splĭn'tẽr) n. scheggia, stecca.
vt. scheggiare, ridurre in schegge.
vi. scheggiarsi, frantumarsi.

split (splĭt) n. fessura, fenditura;
scissione, separazione: splits, spac-
cata (movimento coreografico). agg.
diviso, spaccato; sdoppiato. vt.
(pass., pp. split) fendere, dividere;
sdoppiare, scindere; staccare; distribuire. vi. spaccarsi, fendersi,
separarsi: to — hairs, sottilizzare;
to — asunder, spaccare in due; to
— the difference, dividere il male a
metà; to — one's sides with laughter, sbellicarsi dalle risa; —ting agg.
lacerante, violento.

splotch (splŏch) n. chiazza.

splurge (splûrj) n. (gergo) ostentazione, sfarzo.

splutter (splŭt'ẽr) vedi sputter.

spoil (spoil) n. bottino, preda. vt.
(pass., pp. spoiled o spoilt) spogliare, rovinare, guastare, viziare;
vi. deperire, guastarsi, sciuparsi.

spoke (spōk) (1) pp. di to speak.

spoke (spōk) (2) n. razza (o raggio) di
ruota; piuolo.

spoken (spō'kĕn) pp. di to speak; agg.
orale, parlato: English is — here,
(qui) si parla l'inglese.

spokesman (spōks'măn) n. oratore,
portavoce, relatore.

spoliation (spō'lĭ-ā'shŭn) n. spogliazione, saccheggio.

sponge (spŭnj) n. spugna, spugnatura: — cake, torta Margherita.
vt., vi. assorbire (o lavare) con la
spugna; scroccare, vivere a scrocco.

sponger (spŭn'jẽr) n. beone; parassita, scroccone.

spongy (spŭn'jĭ) agg. spugnoso, poroso.

sponsor (spŏn'sẽr) n. padrino, madrina; garante; patrocinatore, promotore; cliente abituale; (S.U.)
ditta che offre trasmissioni radio-
foniche (per pubblicità). vt. patro-

cinare, promuovere; garantire pe
essere cliente assiduo di.

spontaneity (spŏn'tá·nē'ĭ·tĭ) n. spc
taneità.

spontaneous (spŏn·tā'nē·ŭs) agg. spc
taneo.

spoof (spōōf) vt. (gergo) imbrogliare.

spook (spōōk) n. fantasma.

spool (spōōl) n. rocchetto, bobir
vt. incannare (filati).

spoon (spōōn) n. cucchiaio, cucch
ino. vt., vi. raccogliere col cucchia
pescare col cucchiaino.

spoonful (spōōn'fŏŏl) n. cucchiaiata.

sporadic (spō·răd'ĭk) agg. sporadico.

sport (spōrt) n. sport, giuoco; svag
piacere, passatempo; scherz
(fam.) bontempone; amico; (bio
anomalia: to be a good —, esse
condiscendente, prenderla con sp
rito; to make — of, prende
giuoco di; to be the — of, essere
zimbello di. vt., vi. divertire; oste
tare, sfoggiare; divertirsi, sche
zare, dedicarsi allo sport: to —
new hat, sfoggiare un cappe
nuovo; to — a roll of money, oste
tare ricchezza.

sports agg. sportivo: — clothes, ab
sportivi, abbigliamento sportivo.

sportsman (spōrts'măn) n. sportiv
buon giocatore; vero signore.

sportswoman (spōrts'wŏŏm'ăn) n
sportiva.

sporty (spōr'tĭ) agg. sportivo, da spc
tivo; spendaccione; volgare, app
riscente, ricercato.

spot (spŏt) n. macchia, punto, pu
tino, chiazza; luogo; goccia, sors
on the —, immediatamente; o
luogo. vt. macchiare, chiazzar
scoprire, individuare, scorgere.

spotless agg. immacolato.

spotted agg. macchiato, chiazzato.

spouse (spous) n. sposo, sposa.

spout (spout) n. condotto, tubo
scarico, fontana, grondaia; bec
(di brocca, ecc.). vt., vi. versare, i
scaturire; declamare, concionar
sgorgare, zampillare.

sprain (sprān) n. storta, distorsior
vt. storcere, slogare: to — one
ankle, slogarsi una caviglia.

sprang (sprăng) pass. di to spring.

sprawl (sprôl) n. scarabocchio; po
scomposta. vi. sdraiarsi (o seder
scompostamente; scarabocchiar
to send someone sprawling, ma
dare qualcuno lungo disteso.

spray (sprā) n. frasca, ramoscell'
spruzzo (dei marosi), spuma (
mare); raffica (di proiettili); spru
zatore. vt., vi. spruzzare, anna
fiare; vaporizzare.

spread (sprĕd) *n.* distesa, estensione; festa, festino; coperta da letto, tappeto da tavola; diffusione; sostanza da spalmare; sfoggio; (*aeron.*) apertura alare. *vt.*, *vi.* (*pass.*, *pp.* spread) estendere, spandere; spalmare; divulgare, diffondere; stendere, spiegare (*una vela*), allargare; estendersi; spalmarsi; diffondersi: to — apart, aprirsi, divaricarsi; to — butter, spalmare burro; to — out the tablecloth, stendere la tovaglia; to — with, spalmare di, ungere di.

spree (sprē) *n.* orgia, scappata, baldoria: to go on a —, andare in bagordi.

sprig (sprĭg) *n.* ramoscello.

sprightly (sprīt′lĭ) *agg.* vivace, animato, allegro, brioso.

spring (sprĭng) *n.* primavera; fonte, sorgente; elasticità; slancio, salto; causa, origine; molla. *vt.*, *vi.* (*pass.* sprang o sprung, *pp.* sprung) far sorgere; far esplodere; saltare, far saltare; molleggiare; scavalcare; far scattare; germogliare, scaturire; scagliarsi, balzare; provenire (*da*), sorgere, aprirsi, fendersi: to — at, slanciarsi contro; to — a leak, avere una falla; to — a piece of news, dare una notizia di sorpresa; to — to one's feet, balzare in piedi.

springboard (sprĭng′bôrd′) *n.* trampolino.

springtide (sprĭng′tĭd), **springtime** (sprĭng′tĭm′) *n.* primavera.

springy (sprĭng′ĭ) *agg.* elastico.

sprinkle (sprĭng′k′l) *n.* aspersorio; spruzzata; pioggerella. *vt.* spruzzare, aspergere, cospargere. *vi.* piovigginare.

sprint (sprĭnt) *n.* scatto, slancio; gara di velocità su breve percorso. *vi.* correre a tutta velocità.

sprinter *n.* velocista.

sprite (sprĭt) *n.* spirito.

sprout (sprout) *n.* germoglio, gemma: Brussels sprouts, cavolini di Bruselle; *vi.* germogliare.

spruce (sprōōs) (1) *n.* (*bot.*) abete.

spruce (sprōōs) (2) *agg.* lindo, inappuntabile, affettato. *vt.*, *vi.*: to — up, mettere (*o* mettersi) in ghingheri.

sprung (sprŭng) *pp. di* to spring.

spry (sprī) *agg.* agile, vivace.

spud (spŭd) *n.* zappetta; (*fam.*) patata.

spume (spūm) *n.* spuma, schiuma.

spun (spŭn) *pass.*, *pp. di* to spin. *agg.* filato, ritorto.

spunk (spŭngk) *n.* coraggio, foga.

spunky (spŭngk′ĭ) *agg.* coraggioso.

spur (spûr) *n.* sperone, sprone; artiglio; puntello: on the — of the moment, d'acchito, impulsivamente; to win one's spurs, far buona prova. *vt.* spronare, incitare.

spurious (spū′rĭ-ŭs) *agg.* spurio, falso.

spurn (spûrn) *vt.* respingere con sdegno, disprezzare, ripudiare.

spurt (spûrt) *n.* getto; vampata; schizzo; impeto momentaneo; scatto, volata. *vt.*, *vi.* schizzare, scaturire; compiere uno sforzo; fare una volata.

sputter (spŭt′ẽr) *n.* spruzzo; scoppiettio; balbettamento; *vt.*, *vi.* sbavare, spruzzare; balbettare, farfugliare.

sputum (spū′tŭm) *n.* sputo.

spy (spī) *n.* spia, delatore. *vt.*, *vi.* spiare, scrutare; scorgere. —glass *n.* cannocchiale.

squab (skwŏb) *n.* piccioncino.

squabble (skwŏb′′l) *n.* bisticcio, disputa. *vi.* bisticciare.

squad (skwŏd) *n.* squadra; plotone: — car, auto radio-comandata (*della polizia*).

squadron (skwŏd′rŭn) *n.* squadrone; squadra navale; (*aeron.*) stormo.

squalid (skwŏl′ĭd) *agg.* squallido.

squall (skwŏl) *n.* raffica, scroscio. *vi.* soffiare a raffiche.

squalor (skwŏl′ẽr) *n.* squallore.

squander (skwŏn′dẽr) *vt.* profondere, scialacquare.

square (skwâr) *n.* quadrato, piazza; squadra da disegno; (*gergo*) gonzo, minchione, semplicotto: on the —, in buona fede, onestamente. *agg.* quadrato, ad angolo retto; giusto, leale, esatto; saldato (*di un conto*): to get —, pareggiare i conti; — root, radice quadrata; a — refusal, un no chiaro e tondo; a — deal, un trattamento onesto, un comportamento leale; a — meal, un pasto sostanzioso. *avv.* vedi squarely. *vt.* squadrare, quadrare, regolare, pareggiare; corrompere; (*mat.*) elevare al quadrato. *vi.* quadrare, concordare; to — one's shoulders, raddrizzare le spalle. —ly *avv.* equamente, onestamente; precisamente, in pieno; direttamente.

squash (skwŏsh) *n.* polpa, poltiglia; urto (*dei corpi molli*); caduta; (*bot.*) zucca. *vt.* schiacciare, ridurre in polpa; *vi.* spiaccicarsi.

squat (skwŏt) *agg.* tozzo, tarchiato; allargato; accoccolato. *vi.* accoccolarsi, accucciarsi, sedersi alla turca; (*S.U.*) installarsi senza diritto su un terreno. —ter *n.* pioniere.

squaw (skwô) *n.* donna (*o* sposa) dei pellirossa.

squawk (skwôk) n. gracchio, gracidio. vi. gracchiare.

squeak (skwēk) n. grido rauco, stridore, gracchio. vi. gridare raucamente, stridere, gracchiare.

squeal (skwēl) n. strillo; delazione. vt., vi. strillare; rivelare, farsi delatore.

squeamish (skwēm'ĭsh) agg. delicato, schizzinoso.

squeeze (skwēz) n. spremitura; strizzata, abbraccio; (gergo) estorsione. vt. strizzare, stringere; spremere; abbracciare strettamente; introdurre a forza. vi. incunearsi, insinuarsi: to — through, aprirsi faticosamente un varco.

squelch (skwĕlch) vt. sfracellare, annientare; tacitare: to — a revolt, soffocare una rivolta. vi. diguazzare.

squint (skwĭnt) n. occhiata obliqua, sbirciata; inclinazione; strabismo. agg. obliquo; strabico. vt., vi. guardare con gli occhi socchiusi, guardare in cagnesco, sbirciare; essere strabico.

squint-eyed agg. strabico.

squire (skwīr) n. scudiero, signorotto. vt. scortare.

squirm (skwûrm) vi. contorcersi.

squirrel (skwûr'ĕl) n. scoiattolo.

squirt (skwûrt) n. spruzzo; siringa; (fam.) omiciattolo. vt., vi. siringare; schizzare, zampillare.

stab (stăb) n. pugnalata, coltellata, stoccata. vt. pugnalare, accoltellare, trafiggere; punzecchiare.

stability (stá-bĭl'ĭ-tĭ) n. stabilità.

stabilize (stă'bĭ-līz) vt. stabilizzare.

stabilizer (stă'bĭ-līz'ĕr) n. stabilizzatore.

stable (stā'b'l) (1) n. stalla, scuderia; vt. mettere (o tenere) nella stalla.

stable (stā'b'l) (2) agg. stabile.

stack (stăk) n. fascio, catasta, covone, mucchio; camino, ciminiera. vt. affastellare, ammucchiare; preparare (le carte) per barare.

staff (stăf) n. (pl. staffs o staves) bastone, asta; puntello, palo; manico; (mus.) pentagramma; personale (di ufficio, ecc.), corpo (diplomatico); (mil.) stato maggiore: editorial —, corpo redazionale; teaching —, corpo insegnante; — college, scuola militare; — officer, ufficiale di stato maggiore; — of life, sostegno della vita.

stag (stăg) n. cervo maschio; (S.U.) uomo solo. agg. per uomini soli.

stage (stāj) n. palco, palcoscenico, teatro, scena; stadio (grado); tappa: to go on the —, darsi alle scene; by easy stages, a piccole tappe, con calma; landing —, pontile d'approdo; — box, palco di proscenio —coach, diligenza, corriera; — director, regista teatrale; — door, entrata al palcoscenico; — hand (teat.) attrezzista; — manager, direttore di scena. vt. inscenare.

stagger (stăg'ĕr) n. barcollamento, vacillamento. vt. far vacillare scuotere, sconcertare, sbalordire. vi. barcollare, esitare, vacillare.

stagnant (stăg'nănt) agg. stagnante: to become —, stagnare.

stagnate (stăg'nāt) vi. stagnare, ristagnare.

staid (stād) agg. posato, serio.

stain (stān) n. macchia, chiazza; tintura, sostanza colorante, tinta. vt. macchiare; colorire; tingere. vi. macchiarsi: stained glass, vetro colorato (o istoriato).

stainless agg. immacolato; inossidabile.

stair (stâr) n. gradino; pl. scala, scale, gradinata.

staircase (stâr'kās') n. scala.

stairway (stâr'wā') n. scalinata.

stake (stāk) n. palo, steccato; rogo; premio, posta (di scommessa): at —, in giuoco o a repentaglio. vt. rischiare, scommettere; palettare, puntellare.

stale (stāl) agg. stantio, raffermo; inacidito; vecchio, ritrito; caduto in prescrizione. vt. rendere stantio; vi. invecchiare, inacidire.

stalk (stôk) n. stelo; sostegno; ciminiera; inseguimento; pedinamento. vt. braccare, pedinare. vi. camminare rigidamente; appostarsi.

stall (stôl) (1) n. palo (complice di un ladro); trucco, finzione. vt., vi. ingannare; tergiversare: quit stalling! smettila di tergiversare!

stall (stôl) (2) n. stallo, scanno, palchetto; edicola, chiosco. vt. chiudere in uno stallo; rallentare, bloccare. vi. fermarsi, perdere velocità: to be stalled in the mud, essere bloccato dal fango.

stallion (stăl'yŭn) n. stallone.

stalwart (stôl'wêrt) agg. robusto, aitante; risoluto.

stamina (stăm'ĭ-ná) n. resistenza fisica.

stammer (stăm'ĕr) n. balbettamento, balbuzie. vt., vi. balbettare, essere balbuziente.

stammerer n. balbuziente.

stammering n. balbettamento. agg. balbettante, balbuziente.

stamp (stămp) n. stampo, marchio; francobollo, timbro; punzone, sigillo; trancia: **postage** —, francobollo; **revenue** —, marca da bollo; — **collector**, filatelico. *vt.* stampare, marcare, timbrare; punzonare; affrancare; calpestare, battere (*il piede*); caratterizzare. *vi.* pestare i piedi, scalpitare.

stampede (stăm-pēd') *n.* fuga precipitosa e disordinata, fuggifuggi. *vt.* mettere in fuga disordinata. *vi.* fuggire in disordine.

stanch (stänch) *agg.* forte, resistente, solido; fido, costante; stagno. *vt.* stagnare (*il sangue, ecc.*).

stanchion (stăn'shŭn) *n.* puntello.

stand (stănd) *n.* fermata, sosta; luogo; tribuna; piedestallo, leggio, appoggio, sostegno; posteggio, banco, edicola; posizione; resistenza: **to make a** —, opporre resistenza; **to take one's** —, prendere posizione. *vt.* (*pass., pp.* stood) posare, collocare; sopportare, subire, resistere a. *vi.* trovarsi; stare in piedi, rizzarsi; fermarsi; resistere, sussistere; esitare: **to** — **one's ground**, mantenere le proprie posizioni; **to** — **a chance of**, avere la probabilità di; **it stands to reason**, è ovvio; **to** — **an expense**, sostenere una spesa; **to** — **aside**, appartarsi, tirarsi da parte; **to** — **by**, assistere, difendere; stare all'erta; **to** — **for**, prendere le parti di, sostituirsi a; significare; **to** — **in the way**, ostacolare; **to** — **off**, tenersi al largo; **to** — **out**, sporgere, spiccare; **to** — **up**, alzarsi; **to** — **up for**, prendere le difese di; **to** — **six feet in one's stockings**, essere alto un metro e ottanta.

standard (stăn'dĕrd) *n.* palo, asta, sostegno; stendardo, insegna; modello, misura; base monetaria; norma, criterio, tipo uniforme; livello: — **of life**, tenore di vita; **to be up to** —, essere soddisfacente, rispondere ai criteri. *agg.* classico, tipico, regolamentare, usuale, basilare, uniformato; di serie, standardizzato, uniformato.

standardization (stăn'dĕr-dĭ-zā'shŭn)*n.* standardizzazione, uniformazione.

standardize (stăn'dĕr-dĭz) *vt.* standardizzare, uniformare.

stand-in *n.* (*cinema, teat.*) controfigura; (*fam.*) sostituto.

standing (stăn'dĭng) *n.* posizione, situazione; durata, anzianità: **twenty years'** —, vent'anni di servizio; **of long** —, di antica data. *agg.* in piedi, eretto; fisso, fermo: — **account**, conto corrente; — **pool**, stagno (*acqua stagnante*); — **room**, posto in piedi.

standpoint (stănd'point') *n.* punto di vista.

standstill (stănd'stĭl') *n.* fermata, sosta, punto morto, vicolo cieco.

stank (stăngk) *pass. di* to stink.

stanza (stăn'zà) *n.* strofa.

staple (stā'p'l) (1) *n.* prodotto principale; merce di consumo; fibra tessile; mercato; materia prima; *pl.* articoli di prima necessità. *agg.* principale, indispensabile; corrente, di normale produzione (*o* consumo).

staple (stā'p'l) (2) *n.* chiodo ricurvo a due punte; anello (*o* bocchetta) di chiavistello; punto metallico (*per quaderni, ecc.*). *vt.* cucire a punto metallico.

stapler (stā'plĕr) *n.* cucitrice a punto metallico.

star (stär) *n.* stella, astro; asterisco; primo attore, prima attrice: — **-spangled**, stellato. *vt.* ornare di stelle, costellare; segnare con asterisco; avere come protagonista (*detto di film, ecc.*). *vi.* brillare, splendere; essere il primo attore.

starboard (stär'bŏrd) *n.* dritta. *agg.* destro; *avv.* a dritta.

starch (stärch) *n.* amido, fecola. *vt.* inamidare.

starchy (stär'chĭ) *agg.* amidaceo, rigido, inamidato.

stare (stär) *n.* sguardo fisso. *vi.* sbarrare gli occhi; restare attonito: **to** — **at**, guardare fissamente.

starfish (stär'fĭsh') *n.* stella di mare.

stark (stärk) *agg.* rigido, stecchito; vero e proprio; desolato; assoluto. *avv.* assolutamente, completamente: — **naked**, completamente nudo; — **raving mad**, pazzo da legare.

starlet (stär'lĕt) *n.* stellina (*anche di cinema*).

starlight (stär'lit') *n.* luce stellare.

starry (stär'ĭ) *agg.* stellare; stellato; lucente come le stelle; a forma di stella; stellante.

start (stärt) *n.* sobbalzo; impulso; partenza, avviamento, principio, punto di partenza; vantaggio: **by fits and starts**, saltuariamente; **to wake with a** —, svegliarsi di soprassalto. *vt.* far trasalire; far partire, mettere in moto, avviare, iniziare. *vi.* trasalire, riscuotersi; cominciare, avviarsi, partire: **to** — **out on a trip**, mettersi in viaggio. — **er** *n.* iniziatore; (*mecc.*) messa in moto; (*sport*) mossiere.

startle (stär't'l) *vt.* far trasalire, allarmare. *vi.* trasalire, allarmarsi.

startling (stär'tling) *agg.* sconcertante, allarmante, sensazionale.

starvation (stär·vā'shŭn) *n.* inedia, fame.

starve (stärv) *vt.* far morire di fame, affamare. *vi.* morire di fame.

state (stāt) *n.* stato; condizione, rango. *agg.* statale, di stato; solenne. *vt.* dichiarare, stabilire, formulare.

stateliness (stāt'lĭ·nĕs) *n.* pompa, solennità.

stately (stāt'lĭ) *agg.* imponente, grandioso, solenne.

statement (stāt'mĕnt) *n.* dichiarazione; rapporto; affermazione, testimonianza: — of account, estratto conto.

stateroom (stāt'rōōm') *n.* cabina riservata (*su navi, treni, ecc.*).

Stateside (stāt'sīd') *agg.* diretto a o proveniente da o caratteristico degli Stati Uniti. *avv.* dagli, negli, verso gli Stati Uniti.

statesman (stāts'mŭn) *n.* statista, uomo politico.

static (stăt'ĭk) *agg.* statico *n.* (*radio*) scarica, disturbo.

statics *n.* (*fis.*) statica.

station (stā'shŭn) *n.* stazione; posto, posteggio; posizione, condizione, rango; commissariato; (*mil.*) presidio: broadcasting —, stazione trasmittente; police —, commissariato di polizia; service —, stazione di servizio; — wagon, giardinetta; weather —, osservatorio meteorologico. *vt.* mettere (di stanza), dislocare; collocare. *vi.* essere di stanza.

stationary (stā'shŭn·ĕr'ĭ) *agg.* stazionario; fisso, fermo, immobile.

stationer (stā'shŭn·ĕr) *n.* cartolaio.

stationery (stā'shŭn·ĕr'ĭ) *n.* cancelleria, articoli di cartoleria.

statistics (stá·tǐs'tǐks) *n.* statistica.

statuary (stăt'ū·ĕr'ĭ) *n.* collezione di sculture, statuaria.

statue (stăt'ū) *n.* statua.

status (stā'tŭs) *n.* stato, condizione, rango, figura giuridica.

statute (stăt'ūt) *n.* statuto, decreto, legge, regolamento.

statutory (stăt'ū·tō'rĭ) *agg.* statutario.

staunch (stônch) *vedi* stanch.

stave (stāv) *n.* doga (*di botte*); piuolo, stecca; (*mus.*) pentagramma, strofa. *vt.* sfondare, fendere, fracassare: to — off, tenere a distanza, evitare, respingere.

stay (stā) (1) *n.* fermata, sosta, permanenza, soggiorno; proroga; ostacolo, freno; sostegno; *pl.* busto (*da donna*). *vt.* (*pass., pp.* stayed) fermare, sospendere, trattenere; sostenere. *vi.* stare, sostare, rimanere, soggiornare, abitare, fer-

marsi; resistere: to — up, restare alzato, vegliare.

stay (stā) (2) *n.* (*naut.*) straglio.

stead (stĕd) *n.* luogo, servizio, vece: in his —, in sua vece; to stand in good — to, essere molto utile a.

steadfast (stĕd'fást) *agg.* saldo, costante, fisso, fermo; risoluto; fedele.

steadily (stĕd'ĭ·lĭ) *avv.* fermamente saldamente; regolarmente, ininterrottamente.

steadiness (stĕd'ĭ·nĕs) *n.* fermezza, costanza, saldezza; uniformità, regolarità, solidità.

steady (stĕd'ĭ) *agg.* fermo, saldo; coerente, uniforme, regolare; fisso, continuo; sicuro. *vt.* appoggiare; mettere in equilibrio; sorreggere rinfrancare. *vi.* rimettersi in equilibrio, rinfrancarsi, calmarsi.

steak (stāk) *n.* braciuola, bistecca.

steal (stēl) *vt., vi.* (*pass.* stole, *pp.* stolen) rubare, derubare, carpire: to — in (out), sgusciare dentro (fuori); to — a glance, lanciare un'occhiata furtiva; to — away, svignarsela.

stealth (stĕlth) *n.* segretezza; azione subdola: by —, in segreto, furtivamente. —ily *avv.* di nascosto, furtivamente, subdolamente.

stealthy (stĕl'thǐ) *agg.* segreto, furtivo, subdolo, clandestino.

steam (stēm) *n.* vapore. *agg.* di vapore; a vapore: — boiler, caldaia a vapore; — engine, macchina a vapore; — roller, rullo compressore. *vt.* esporre al vapore, vaporizzare; cuocere a vapore. *vi.* fumare, emettere vapore: to — in, entrare in porto; to — off, dileguarsi.

steamboat (stēm'bōt') *n.* battello a vapore.

steamer (stēm'ĕr) *n.* piroscafo.

steamship (stēm'shǐp') *n.* bastimento a vapore.

steamy (stēm'ĭ) *agg.* fumante, pieno di vapore.

steed (stēd) *n.* destriero, corsiero.

steel (stēl) *n.* acciaio, lama. *agg.* d'acciaio: — works, acciaierie. *vt.* rivestire d'acciaio; rendere inflessibile, indurire: to — one's heart, fare il cuore duro; to — oneself, prepararsi l'animo, prepararsi a combattere, corazzarsi. —y *agg.* d'acciaio; duro, inflessibile.

steelyard (stēl'yärd) *n.* stadera.

steep (stēp) (1) *vt.* immergere, imbevere, saturare. *vi.* imbeversi.

steep (stēp) (2) *n.* precipizio, pendio, scarpata. *agg.* ripido, inclinato; arduo, impraticabile; eccessivo, esorbitante.

steeple (stē'p'l) *n.* campanile, torre, guglia.

steeplechase (stē'p'l·chās') *n.* corsa a ostacoli; corsa campestre.

steepness (stēp'nĕs) *n.* ripidezza.

steer (stēr) (1) *n.* manzo.

steer (stēr) (2) *n.* (*gergo*) suggerimento. *vt.*, *vi.* guidare, pilotare, sterzare, orientare, dirigersi: to — clear of, girar largo da; this car —s easily, questa macchina ha un buono sterzo.

steerage (stēr'ĭj) *n.* governo (*di nave, ecc.*), guida; terza classe (*sulle navi*).

steering wheel *n.* ruota del timone; (*auto.*) volante, sterzo.

stem (stĕm) *n.* gambo, stelo; cannello o bocchino (*di pipa*); ceppo (*di famiglia*); prua; (*gramm.*) radice: from — to stern, da poppa a prua; da cima a fondo. *vt.* risalire (*una corrente*); resistere a; arginare, stagnare (*un'emorragia*); tappare. *vi.* provenire (*da*).

stench (stĕnch) *n.* puzzo, fetore.

stencil (stĕn'sĭl) *n.* stampino.

stenographer (stĕ·nŏg'rá·fĕr) *n.* stenografo.

stenography (stĕ·nŏg'rá·fĭ) *n.* stenografia.

stentorian (stĕn·tō'rĭ·ăn) *agg.* stentoreo.

step (stĕp) *n.* passo, orma; gradino, scalino, piuolo, predellino; andatura: — by —, passo passo, gradualmente; to be in — with, marciare di pari passo con; essere consono a; to take —s, prendere provvedimenti. *vi.* fare un passo, camminare, andare, salire, scendere: to — aside, tirarsi da parte; to — back, retrocedere; to — in, entrare, intervenire; to — out, uscire; to — on, calpestare, salire su; to — on the gas (*auto.*), premere l'acceleratore, dare gas; to — over, attraversare.

stepbrother *n.* fratellastro.

stepchild *n.* figliastro.

stepdaughter *n.* figliastra.

stepfather *n.* patrigno.

stepladder *n.* scala a piuoli.

stepmother *n.* matrigna.

steppe (stĕp) *n.* steppa.

stepsister *n.* sorellastra.

stepson *n.* figliastro.

stereoscope (stĕr'ē·ō·skōp') *n.* stereoscopio.

stereotype (stĕr'ē·ō·tīp') *n.* stereotipia.

sterile (stĕr'ĭl) *agg.* sterile.

sterility (stĕ·rĭl'ĭ·tĭ) *n.* sterilità.

sterilize (stĕr'ĭ·līz) *vt.* sterilizzare.

sterling (stûr'lĭng) *n.* (*metall.*) titolo. *agg.* puro, genuino, di buona lega: — qualities, doti preclare: pound —, lira sterlina.

stern (stûrn) (1) *agg.* rigido, severo, duro, austero.

stern (stûrn) (2) *n.* poppa.

sternness (stûrn'nĕs) *n.* severità, durezza, austerità.

stethoscope (stĕth'ō·skōp) *n.* stetoscopio.

stevedore (stē'vĕ·dōr) *n.* stivatore.

stew (stū) *n.* stufato, umido: to be in a —, essere sossopra, essere preoccupato. *vt.* cuocere a fuoco lento. *vi.* cuocersi lentamente; (*gergo*) agitarsi, preoccuparsi.

steward (stū'ĕrd) *n.* dispensiere, fattore, economo, amministratore; (*sport*) commissario; cameriere di bordo, inserviente. —ess *n.* cameriera di bordo.

stick (stĭk) *n.* bastone, randello, bacchetta; bastoncino; dynamite —, tubo di dinamite; control — (*aeron.*), barra di comando; walking —, bastone da passeggio. *vt.* (*pass., pp.* stuck) ficcare, conficcare; appiccicare; ferire, trafiggere; appuntare; appioppare; affiggere; (*fam.*) sopportare. *vi.* appiccicarsi; incepparsi; essere conficcato, restare; attenersi, ostinarsi; radicarsi (*nella mente*); restar fedele; sporgere, spuntar fuori; persistere: to — at, arretrare davanti a; to — close, tenersi vicino; to — up, alzarsi; assaltare, rapinare; to — up for, difendere, proteggere; to — out, sporgere, essere evidente; to — to a job, perseverare in un lavoro; — to it! tieni duro!, continua così! —er *n.* persona pertinace; attacchino; scioperante; etichetta (*cartellino*) (*fam.*) problema.

stickler (stĭk'lĕr) *n.* formalista, intransigente; ostinato.

stick-up *n.* rapinatore; rapina a mano armata: — man, rapinatore; — collar, colletto duro, colletto troppo alto.

sticky (stĭk'ĭ) *agg.* appiccicoso.

stiff (stĭf) *n.* (*gergo*) cadavere. *agg.* rigido, duro; intirizzito; faticoso, difficile; impacciato; elevato (*di prezzi*): scared —, paralizzato dalla paura; — neck, torcicollo; ostinazione, cocciutaggine.

stiffen (stĭf'ĕn) *vt.* indurire, irrigidire. *vi.* indurirsi, irrigidirsi.

stiffly (stĭf'lĭ) *avv.* rigidamente, ostinatamente; con sussiego.

stiffness (stĭf'nĕs) *n.* rigidezza, inflessibilità, irrigidimento; sussiego.

stifle (stī'f'l) vt., vi. soffocare, estinguere, reprimere: to — a yawn, soffocare uno sbadiglio; to — a revolt, reprimere una rivolta.

stifling (stī'flĭng) agg. soffocante.

stigma (stĭg'mă) n. marchio d'infamia; pl. stigmata, stimmate, stimma.

stile (stīl) n. gradino, gradinata; arganello (cancelletto a ruota).

still (stĭl) (1) n. alambicco.

still (stĭl) (2) avv. ancora, tuttora; tuttavia: — less, ancor meno; — more, ancor più; cong. nondimeno.

still (stĭl) (3) n. quiete, silenzio; (fot.) fotografia a posa; (cine) foto di lavorazione. agg. immobile, tranquillo, silenzioso, calmo: — life, natura morta. vt. calmare, sedare, far tacere. vi. calmarsi.

stillborn (stĭl'bôrn') agg. nato morto.

stillness (stĭl'nĕs) n. tranquillità, silenzio, immobilità.

stilt (stĭlt) n. trampolo; palafitta.

stilted (stĭl'tĕd) agg. ricercato, sostenuto, pomposo.

stimulant (stĭm'û·lănt) n., agg. stimolante.

stimulate (stĭm'û·lāt) vt. stimolare.

stimulating agg. stimolante.

stimulation (stĭm'û·lā'shŭn) n. stimolo.

stimulus (stĭm'û·lŭs) n. (pl. stimuli) stimolo.

sting (stĭng) n. aculeo, pungiglione; pungolo; puntura, dolore; bruciore; asprezza; ironia. vt., vi. (pass., pp. stung) pungere, dolere, bruciare; punzecchiare, irritare: stung to the quick, punto sul vivo.

stinginess (stĭn'jĭ·nĕs) n. meschinità, avarizia.

stingy (stĭn'jĭ) agg. avaro, meschino.

stink (stĭngk) n. puzza, fetore. vt., vi. (pass. stank o stunk, pp. stunk) puzzare, appestare; avere cattiva reputazione.

stint (stĭnt) n. restrizione, limite. vt. limitare, lesinare. vi. limitarsi, economizzare; to — oneself, lesinarsi il necessario. —er n. avaro.

stipulate (stĭp'û·lāt) vt., vi. stipulare, pattuire.

stipulation (stĭp'û·lā'shŭn) n. stipulazione; condizione, clausola.

stir (stûr) (1) n. (gergo) carcere.

stir (stûr) (2) n. movimento, trambusto, fermento. vt. (spesso seg. da up) muovere, scuotere, rimescolare; destare, risvegliare, commuovere, istigare, agitare, fomentare. vi. muoversi, affaccendarsi, scuotersi, agitarsi, stormire.

stirring (stûr'ĭng) agg. emozionante, eccitante, commovente.

stirrup (stĭr'ŭp) n. staffa.

stitch (stĭch) n. punto; maglia, puntura, trafittura. vt., vi. cucire, suturare.

stoat (stōt) n. ermellino d'estate.

stock (stŏk) n. blocco, tronco; palo, manico; ceppo; stirpe; fusto (dell'ancora); calcio (d'arma da fuoco); materia prima; provviste, assortimento, riserve; (teat.) repertorio; live—, bestiame; — company, società anonima; (teat.) compagnia di repertorio; — exchange, borsa valori; — in trade, assortimento di merci; armamentario; repertorio; — market, mercato finanziario; —room n. magazzino; sala di esposizione. to take — of, fare l'inventario di, stimare. vt. fornire, provvedere, riempire; fornire di bestiame; immanicare; immagazzinare; mettere in ceppi.

stocks n.pl. (naut.) tacchi; (finanza) titoli azionari, capitale (di società).

stockade (stŏk·ăd') n. palizzata; vt. munire di palizzata.

stockbroker (stŏk'brō'kĕr) n. agente di cambio.

stockholder (stŏk'hōl'dĕr) n. azionista.

stocking (stŏk'ĭng) n. calza.

stockjobber (stŏk'jŏb'ĕr) n. speculatore; agente di cambio.

stock-still agg. immobile.

stocky (stŏk'ĭ) agg. tarchiato, massiccio.

stockyard (stŏk'yärd') n. parco per il bestiame.

stodgy (stŏj'ĭ) agg. pesante, noioso.

stoic ((stō'ĭk) n., agg. stoico.

stoke (stōk) vt. attizzare; alimentare (una fornace).

stoker (stōk'ĕr) n. fochista.

stole (stōl) (1) n. stola.

stole (stōl) (2) pass. di to steal.

stolen (stō'lĕn) pp. di to steal.

stolid (stŏl'ĭd) agg. stolido, impassibile.

stomach (stŭm'ăk) n. stomaco; vt. digerire, tollerare.

stone (stōn) n. sasso, pietra, lapide; nocciolo (di frutto); (med.) calcolo, calcolosi; within a stone's throw, a due passi, vicinissimo. agg. di pietra, di sasso: Stone Age, età della pietra; — blind, completamente cieco; — dead, morto stecchito; — deaf, sordo come una talpa. vt. lapidare; acciottolare; levare il nocciolo a.

stony (stōn'ĭ) agg. di pietra; duro, insensibile, impassibile.

stood (stŏŏd) pass., pp. di to stand.

stooge (stōōj) *n.* (*teat.*) spalla; (*fig.*) fantoccio, tirapiedi, sicario.

stool (stōōl) *n.* sgabello; posatoio (*per uccelli*); gabinetto di decenza; evacuazione (*di escrementi*): — **pigeon**, piccione da richiamo (*anche fig.*); (*gergo S.U.*) spia, confidente (*della polizia*).

stoop (stōōp) *n.* inclinazione, portamento curvo; sostegno; gradinata, porticato; condiscendenza; **to walk with a** —, camminare ricurvo. *vi.* chinarsi, abbassarsi, curvarsi, essere curvo; umiliarsi; accondiscendere. **—-shouldered** *agg.* con le spalle curve o spioventi.

stop (stŏp) *n.* fermata, sosta, scalo; interruzione, impedimento; tappo, zipolo; fermo; (*mus.*) tasto, registro (*d'organo*); punto (*segno d'interpunzione*): —**watch**, cronometro. *vt.* fermare, impedire, ostacolare; turare, otturare; sospendere; sopprimere; interrompere; (*sport*) bloccare, parare. *vi.* fermarsi, sostare, desistere, cessare, smettere; **to — short**, fermarsi di colpo; **to — at nothing**, non avere scrupoli, essere capace di tutto; **to — over at**, fare tappa a; **to — somebody from**, impedire a qualcuno di.

stoppage (stŏp'ĭj) *n.* interruzione, fermata, arresto; ostruzione, occlusione.

stopover (stŏp'ō'vẽr) *n.* tappa, fermata, scalo.

stopper (stŏp'ẽr) *n.* chiusura, tappo.

storage (stōr'ĭj) *n.* deposito, magazzino; magazzinaggio; **to keep in** —, immagazzinare, conservare; **in cold** —, in refrigerante; — **battery**, accumulatore.

store (stōr) *n.* magazzino, deposito, negozio; riserva; assortimento, provvista: **department** —, grandi magazzini, emporio; **grocery** —, drogheria; **shoe** —, calzoleria; **in** —, in serbo; **to set little (great)** — **by**, tenere in scarsa (grande) considerazione. *vt.* fornire, rifornire; immagazzinare, far provvista di: **to — up,** accumulare; **to — away,** mettere in serbo.

storehouse (stōr'hous') *n.* magazzino.

storekeeper (stōr'kēp'ẽr) *n.* magazziniere; negoziante.

storeroom (stōr'rōōm') *n.* magazzino; dispensa.

stork (stôrk) *n.* cicogna.

storm (stôrm) *n.* uragano, bufera, tempesta, gragniuola; assalto, tumulto; scroscio (*d'applausi*): **hail** —, grandinata; **snow** —, tormenta (*di neve*); **wind** —, tempesta

di vento; — **troops,** reparti d'assalto, truppe d'urto; **to take by** —, prendere d'assalto. *vt.* assaltare. *vi.* scatenarsi, infuriare, imperversare; riversarsi.

stormy (stôr'mĭ) *agg.* burrascoso, tempestoso.

story (stō'rĭ) (1) *n.* piano (*di un edificio*).

story (stō'rĭ) (2) *n.* storia, racconto; favola; articolo, resoconto; (*cinema*) trama, soggetto, vicenda; versione; frottola; diceria.

storyteller (stō'rĭ-tĕl'ẽr) *n.* narratore.

stout (stout) *n.* birra forte (*nera*). *agg.* forte, robusto; grasso, tarchiato; energico. **—ly** *avv.* risolutamente. **—ness** *n.* risolutezza; corpulenza.

stove (stōv) (1) *pass., pp. di* to stave.

stove (stōv) (2) *n.* stufa, fornello da cucina, cucina (*a gas o elettrica*).

stow (stō) *vt.* colmare; riporre; (*naut.*) stivare.

stowaway (stō'à-wā') *n.* passeggiero clandestino.

straddle (străd''l) *vt.* inforcare; mettersi a cavalcioni su. *vi.* divaricare le gambe; tenere il piede in due staffe.

straggle (străg''l) *vi.* staccarsi (*da un gruppo*), sparpagliarsi, scompigliarsi; vagare; smarrirsi.

straggler (străg'lẽr) *n.* disperso, sbandato, vagabondo.

straight (strāt) *n.* dirittura; linea retta; (*poker*) scala. *agg.* dritto, diretto; onesto; puro, liscio (*non diluito*); attendibile: **to let someone have it** —, dire a qualcuno il fatto suo: — **flush**, scala reale; — **face**, faccia seria; — **hair**, capelli lisci; *avv.* dritto, direttamente; immediatamente; francamente, onestamente; **in linea retta**: — **from the shoulder**, esplicitamente; **for two hours** —, per due ore di fila.

straightaway (strāt'à-wā') *n.* dirittura. *agg.* dritto, rettilineo. *avv.* immediatamente.

straighten (strāt''n) *vt.* raddrizzare; appianare, accomodare, riordinare. *vi.* raddrizzarsi.

straightforward (strāt'fôr'wẽrd) *agg.* dritto, diretto; rettilineo; esplicito, onesto, franco. *avv.* in linea retta, direttamente; schiettamente.

straightness (strāt'nĕs) *n.* dirittura, rettitudine.

straightway (strāt'wā') *avv.* direttamente, immediatamente.

strain (strān) *n.* sforzo; tensione; strappo (*muscolare*); suono, tono, motivo (*mus.*); razza, ramo. *vt.*

tendere (*anche l'orecchio*); stiracchiare, forzare, tirare; spremere, filtrare; costringere; aguzzare (*gli occhi*). *vi.* sforzarsi, tendere i muscoli: to — one's wrist, storcersi un polso; to — a point, fare un'eccezione, fare l'impossibile. —ed *agg.* forzato, non spontaneo. —er *n.* colatoio, filtro; tirante.

strait (străt) *n.* (*spesso pl.*) stretto (*di mare*); difficoltà, imbarazzo, ristrettezze finanziarie; strettoia. *agg.* stretto, disagevole: — **jacket**, camicia di forza.

straiten (străt'n) *vt.* stringere, restringere; mettere in difficoltà.

strand (strănd) (1) *n.* riva, spiaggia. *vt.* arrenare; abbandonare, lasciare **nelle peste.** *vi.* arrenarsi: **to be stranded**, essere arrenato.

strand (strănd) (2) *n.* fibra, filaccia, corda; filo (*di perle*); treccia (*di capelli*). *vt.* attorcigliare, intrecciare; sfilacciare; rammendare.

strange (strānj) *agg.* strano, bizzarro; spaesato; straniero, sconosciuto; inusitato.

strangeness (strānj'nĕs) *n.* stranezza.

stranger (strān'jĕr) *n.* straniero, forestiero, estraneo, sconosciuto.

strangle (străng'g'l) *vt.,vi.* strangolare, soffocare.

strangler (străng'glĕr) *n.* strangolatore.

strap (străp) *n.* cinghia, correggia; cinturino; maniglia; coramella (*da rasoio*); spallina; metal —, cinturino di metallo. *vt.* assicurare con cinghie; staffilare; cingere; affilare.

strapping (străp'ĭng) *agg.* bello, aitante.

stratagem (străt'á-jĕm) *n.* stratagemma.

strategic (strá·tē'jĭk) *agg.* strategico.

strategist (străt'ē·jĭst) *n.* stratega.

strategy (străt'ē·jĭ) *n.* strategia.

stratosphere (străt'ō·sfĕr) *n.* stratosfera.

stratovision (străt'ō·vĭzh'ŭn) *n.* ritrasmissione televisa da aerei in volo nella stratosfera, stratovisione.

straw (strô) *n.* paglia, pagliuzza, fuscello; inezia: **not to be worth a —**, non valere nulla; **not to care a —**, infischiarsene; — **color**, giallo paglierino.

strawberry (strô'bĕr'ĭ) *n.* fragola.

stray (strā) *n.* animale sperduto; vagabondo. *agg.* sperduto, smarrito; sviato; sporadico. *vi.* smarrirsi, girovagare; divagare; sviarsi.

streak (strēk) *n.* striscia, striatura, linea, traccia; vena. *vt.* rigare, striare.

stream (strēm) *n.* corrente; flusso, corso d'acqua, fiume; fiotto; getto (*di vapore*); fascio (*di luce*): **against the —**, controcorrente. *vt.* inondare; *vi.* scorrere, riversarsi; filtrare, irradiarsi; sfilare (*di processione,ecc.*); fluire; sventolare: **to — out of,** sgorgare da, fluire da.

streamer (strēm'ĕr) *n.* nastro svolazzante, banderuola; testata (*di giornale*).

streamline (strēm'līn') *n.* linea aerodinamica. *vt.* dare una linea aerodinamica a.

streamlined *agg.* aerodinamico.

street (strēt) *n.* via, strada: **in queer —**, nell'imbarazzo; **in poverty —**, in ristrettezze.

streetcar (strēt'kär') *n.* (*S.U.*) tram.

strength (strĕngth) *n.* forza, potenza, resistenza: **on the — of**, in base a.

strengthen (strĕng'thĕn) *vt.* rafforzare, fortificare, rinfrancare. *vi.* rafforzarsi, rinfrancarsi.

strenuous (strĕn'ū·ŭs) *agg.* energico; strenuo, accanito.

stress (strĕs) *n.* forza, risalto; pressione; urgenza; importanza; (*mecc.*) sforzo; accento: **to lay — upon,** dare grande rilievo a. *vt.* accentare; accentuare, mettere in risalto; ribadire, sottoporre a uno sforzo.

stretch (strĕch) *n.* stiramento; estensione; tensione, sforzo; periodo, portata; rettifilo: **at a —,** difilato; **home —,** dirittura d'arrivo. *vt.* tendere, estendere; spiegare, stendere; sforzare; (*naut.*) tesare. *vi.* stendersi; estendersi, allungarsi; allargarsi; sforzarsi: **to — oneself,** stiracchiarsi; **to — out one's hand,** porgere la mano.

stretcher (strĕch'ĕr) *n.* telaio; barella; tenditore, tenditoio: — **bearer**, portaferiti.

strew (strōō) *vt.* (*pass.* strewed, *pp.* strewed *o* strewn) sparpagliare, spargere, disseminare.

strewn (strōōn) *pp. di* to strew: — **with,** cosparso di.

stricken (strĭk'ĕn) *pp. di* to strike.

strict (strĭkt) *agg.* stretto, ristretto; rigido, scrupoloso, severo. —**ness** *n.* strettezza, esattezza, rigorosità. —**ure** *n.* critica, censura, stroncatura; (*med.*) strozzatura, restringimento.

stridden (strĭd''n) *pp. di* to stride.

stride (strīd) *n.* passo lungo, andatura, lunghezza del passo: **to take in one's —,** affrontare con disinvoltura. *vi.* (*pass.* strode, *pp.* stridden) camminare a gran passi.

strife (strīf) *n.* lotta, contesa.

strike (strĭk) *n.* sciopero; scoperta di un giacimento: **— breaker** *n.* crumiro; **air —**, attacco aereo. *vt.* (*pass.* **struck**, *pp.* **stricken** *o* **struck**) colpire, percuotere, battere; sonare (*delle ore*); imprimere; strofinare (*un fiammifero*); sembrare, coniare; assumere (*un atteggiamento*); scoprire (*giacimenti*); (*naut.*) ammainare: **to — off**, tagliar via, cancellare; diffalcare; far uscire, eliminare; **to — down**, abbattere; **to — one's attention**, richiamare l'attenzione di; **to — one's fancy**, colpire la fantasia di; **to — up a friendship**, stringere un'amicizia; **to — with terror**, terrorizzare; **how does the boy — you?** che impressione ti fa quel ragazzo?. *vi.* urtare, battere, cozzare; bussare; prendere una direzione; scioperare; attecchire: **to — on, upon,** colpire, rifrangersi in, ripercuotersi su; imbattersi in, scoprire; **to — at,** assalire, colpire; **to — home,** colpire nel segno; **to — a light,** accendere un fiammifero; **to — a bargain,** concludere un affare; **to — dumb,** far ammutolire; **to — oil,** scoprire un giacimento di petrolio; far fortuna.

triker *n.* battitore; percussore; scioperante.

triking *agg.* notevole, impressionante; netto.

tring (strĭng) *n.* fettuccia, funicella, fibra, laccio, cordoncino; fila, filza; (*mus.*) corda: **strings**, strumenti a corda, archi. *vt.* (*pass.*, *pp.* **strung**) fornire di corde; infilare (*perle, ecc.*); tendere; rinforzare; adornare di festoni; mondare dei fili (*p.es.i fagiuolini*); impiccare; (*mus.*) accordare: **to — out,** allungarsi, dipanarsi; **to — up,** innervosire; impiccare.

tringbean *n.* fagiuolino.

tringy (strĭng'ĭ) *agg.* fibroso, elastico.

trip (strĭp) *n.* striscia, fascia; lembo (*di terra*); (*aeron.*) pista (di decollo *o* di atterraggio): **comic strips,** fumetti. *vt.* privare, spogliare, denudare, mondare; spanare (*una vite*). *vi.* spogliarsi, svestirsi: **to — off,** strappare. **—tease** *n.* (*teat.*), spogliarello.

tripe (strĭp) *n.* sferzata, staffilata; striscia, riga; tipo; *pl.* galloni. *vt.* rigare, listare, variegare.

triped (strĭpt) *agg.* rigato, a striscie.

trive (strīv) *vi.* (*pass.* **strove**, *pp.* **striven**) sforzarsi, gareggiare, lottare; mirare.

trode (strōd) *pass. di* **stride**.

troke (strōk) (1) *n.* colpo, percossa; tratto; accesso (*attacco*); bracciata (*al nuoto*); lampo (*di genio*); tocco; corsa (*di stantuffo*); (*naut.*) vogata, capovoga: **— of a bell,** tocco di campana; **brush —,** spazzolata; **— of the pen,** tratto di penna; **on the — of two,** allo scoccar delle due. *vt.* segnare; cancellare (*con un tratto di penna, ecc.*); essere capovoga in.

stroke (2) *n.* carezza, lisciata. *vt.* accarezzare, lisciare, sfiorare.

stroll (strōl) *n.* passeggiata. *vi.* passeggiare, gironzolare.

strong (strŏng) *agg.* forte, solido, resistente; energico, risoluto; impetuoso: *avv.* fortemente, intensamente.

strongbox *n.* forziere.

stronghold *n.* fortilizio, roccaforte.

strongly *avv.* fortemente, intensamente.

strong room *n.* camera blindata (*di banca, ecc.*)

strop (strŏp) *n.* coramella (*per rasoio*). *vt.* affilare sulla coramella.

strove (strōv) *pass. di* **strive**.

struck (strŭk) *pass.*, *pp. di* **to strike**: **— with a disease,** colpito da una malattia.

structural (strŭk'tŭr.đl) *agg.* strutturale.

structure (strŭk'tŭr) *n.* struttura, edificio.

struggle (strŭg''l) *n.* lotta, sforzo. *vi.* lottare, dibattersi; affaticarsi.

strum (strŭm) *vt.*, *vi.* strimpellare.

strumpet (strŭm'pĕt) *n.* prostituta.

strung (strŭng) *pass.*, *pp. di* **to string**.

strut (strŭt) *n.* andatura pettoruta. *vi.* camminare pettoruto, pavoneggiarsi.

strychnine (strĭk'nĭn) *n.* stricnina.

stub (stŭb) *n.* ceppo, moncone; mozzicone; matrice (*di ricevuta, ecc.*) *vt.* sbattere.

stubble (stŭb''l) *n.* stoppia; pelame ispido, barba ispida.

stubborn (stŭb'ẽrn) *agg.* ostinato, testardo, inflessibile, caparbio.

stubbornness *n.* caparbietà, ostinazione; inflessibilità.

stucco (stŭk'ō) *n.* stucco, lavoro a stucco. *vt.* ornare con stucco.

stuck (stŭk) *pass.*, *pp. di* **to stick**.

stud (stŭd) (1) *n.* borchia, chiodo; bozza; bottone per polsino. *vt.* costellare; fissare con borchie; disseminare.

stud (stŭd) (2) *n.* scuderia, allevamento di cavalli da corsa; stallone: **— horse,** stallone.

student (stū'dĕnt) *n.* studente; studioso.

studied (stŭd'ĭd) *agg.* studiato.

studio (stū'dĭ.ō) *n.* studio (*d'artista*); (*radio*) auditorium; (*cinema*) teatro di posa.

studious (stū'dĭ.ŭs) *agg.* studioso; studiato, elaborato.

study (stŭd'ĭ) *n.* studio; cura, attenzione, diligenza; ufficio, gabinetto di lavoro. *vt.*, *vi.* studiare.

stuff (stŭf) *n.* stoffa, tessuto; roba, materia, sostanza: that liquor was good —, quel liquore era roba buona; sob —, roba lagrimogena; — and nonsense! tutte sciocchezze! *vt.* riempire, imbottire, rimpinzare; ammucchiare; tappare; impagliare. *vi.* rimpinzarsi. —ing *n.* borra, imbottitura, ripieno.

stuffy (stŭf'ĭ) *agg.* afoso, soffocante; noioso; retrogrado, codino; compassato.

stultify (stŭl'tĭ.fī) *vt.* mettere in ridicolo; infirmare.

stumble (stŭm'b'l) *n.* inciampata, passo falso, errore. *vt.* far incespicare, rendere perplesso. *vi.* inciampare, incespicare; impappinarsi; esitare: to — on, upon, across, imbattersi in, trovare per caso.

stumbling (stŭm'blĭng) *n.* inciampo: — block, ostacolo, scoglio.

stump (stŭmp) *n.* ceppo, moncone; torsolo; radice (*di dente*); moncherino; mozzicone. *vt.* troncare; confondere, disorientare. *vi.* camminare pesantemente; concionare.

stumpy *agg.* tozzo.

stun (stŭn) *vt.* stordire, sbalordire; assordare; tramortire.

stung (stŭng) *pass.*, *pp. di* to sting.

stunk (stŭngk) *pass.*, *pp. di* to stink.

stunning (stŭn'ĭng) *agg.* sbalorditivo, meraviglioso; che tramortisce.

stunt (stŭnt) (1) *n.* (*gergo*) esibizione, prodezza. *vi.* esibirsi.

stunt (stŭnt) (2) *vt.* impedire la crescita di, far intristire; ostacolare.

stunted *agg.* nano, mal sviluppato.

stupefy (stū'pē.fī) *vt.* intorpidire; stupire; intontire, abbrutire.

stupendous (stū.pĕn'dŭs) *agg.* prodigioso.

stupid (stū'pĭd) *agg.* stupido. —ity (-ĭd'ĭ.tĭ) *n.* stupidità.

stupor (stū'pẽr) *n.* stordimento, abbrutimento: in a —, stordito.

sturdy (stûr'dĭ) *agg.* vigoroso, forte.

sturgeon (stûr'jŭn) *n.* storione.

stutter (stŭt'ẽr) *n.* balbuzie, balbettamento. *vt.*, *vi.* balbettare, essere balbuziente. —er *n.* balbuziente. —ing *n.* balbettamento. *agg.* balbuziente.

sty (stī) (1) *n.* (*med.*) orzaiuolo.

sty (stī) (2) *n.* porcile.

style (stīl) *n.* stile, maniera; stilo gnomone (*di meridiana*); (*comm.* ragione sociale. *vt.*, *vi.* denominare decorare; foggiare (*secondo l stile di moda*).

stylish (stīl'ĭsh) *agg.* elegante, ricercato.

stymie (stī'mĭ) *vt.* ostacolare, bloccare

suave (swäv) *agg.* blando, mellifluo.

subaltern (sŭb.ôl'tẽrn) *n.*, *agg.* subalterno.

subcommittee (sŭb'kŏ.mĭt'ĭ) *n.* sotto comitato.

subconscious (sub.kŏn'shŭs) *n.* subcosciente. *agg.* del subcosciente, in conscio: the — self, il subcosciente

subcutaneous (sŭb'kû.tā'nē.ŭs) *agg* sottocutaneo.

subdivide (sŭb'dĭ.vīd') *vt.* suddividere

subdivision (sŭb'dĭ.vĭzh'ŭn) *n.* sud divisione.

subdue (sŭb.dū') *vt.* reprimere; attenuare; soggiogare, sottomettere ammansire; abbassare (*la voce*).

subdued (sŭb.dūd') *agg.* ammansito attenuato; sommesso; docile, mo derato: — light, luce attenuata luce tenue.

subeditor (sŭb.ĕd'ĭ.tẽr) *n.* vice-redattore.

subject (sŭb'jĕkt) *n.* argomento, materia, tema; suddito; (*gramm.*) soggetto. *agg.* soggetto, esposto (*a*) suscettibile (*di*); sottomesso: — matter, sostanza, essenza; argomento (*di una discussione, ecc.*) dati essenziali (*di un argomento ecc.*). *vt.* (sŭb.jĕkt') assoggettare soggiogare; sottoporre (*a*); esporr (*a*).

subjection (sŭb.jĕk'shŭn) *n.* sottomissione.

subjective (sŭb.jĕk'tĭv) *agg.* soggettivo.

subjugate (sŭb'jŏŏ.gāt) *vt.* soggiogare

subjunctive (sŭb.jŭngk'tĭv) *agg.* soggiuntivo.

sublease (sŭb'lēs') *n.* subaffitto. *vt* subaffittare (*prendere o dare i subaffitto*).

sublet (sŭb.lĕt') *vt.* (*pass.*, *pp.* sublet subaffittare (*a*).

sublime (sŭb.līm') *agg.* sublime.

submachine gun (sŭb'mȧ.shēn') *n* fucile mitragliatore, mitra.

submarine (sŭb'mȧ.rēn') *n.* sotto marino, sommergibile.

submerge (sŭb.mûrj') *vt.* sommergere *vi.* inabissarsi, tuffarsi.

submission (sŭb.mĭsh'ŭn) *n.* sotto missione, umiltà; rassegnazione.

submissive (sŭb.mĭs'ĭv) *agg.* sotto messo, umile; rassegnato.

submit (sŭb·mĭt′) *vt.* sottomettere, sottoporre; presentare. *vi.* sottomettersi, assoggettarsi.

subordinate (sŭ·bôr′dĭ·nĭt) *n.*, *agg.* subordinato, inferiore, subalterno. *vt.* (-āt) subordinare.

suborn (sŭb·ôrn′) *vt.* subornare.

subpoena (sŭb·pē′nà) *n.* citazione di testimone. *vt.* citare a testimone.

subscribe (sŭb·skrīb′) *vt.*, *vi.* sottoscrivere; firmare; abbonarsi; impegnarsi, aderire (*a*).

subscriber (sŭb·skrīb′ẽr) *n.* sottoscrittore, abbonato.

subscription (sŭb·skrĭp′shŭn) *n.* sottoscrizione, abbonamento.

subsequent (sŭb′sē·kwĕnt) *agg.* susseguente. —**ly** *avv.* successivamente, conseguentemente.

subservient (sŭb·sûr′vĭ·ĕnt) *agg.* subordinato, sussidiario; servile.

subside (sŭb·sīd′) *vi.* decrescere, attenuarsi; calar di livello; calmarsi; smetter di parlare; cessare.

subsidiary (sŭb·sĭd′ĭ·ẽr′ĭ) *n.*, *agg.* sussidiario, sussidiario, accessorio; tributario (*di corso d'acqua*).

subsidize (sŭb′sĭ·dīz) *vt.* sovvenzionare, sussidiare.

subsidy (sŭb′sĭ·dĭ) *n.* sovvenzione, sussidio.

subsist (sŭb·sĭst′) *vt.* mantenere. *vi.* sussistere, esistere; consistere; sopravvivere, vivere (*di*). —**ence** *n.* sussistenza; esistenza; sopravvivenza; mezzi di sussistenza. —**ent** *agg.* sussistente, esistente, inerente.

subsoil (sŭb′soil′) *n.* sottosuolo.

substance (sŭb′stàns) *n.* sostanza, essenza.

substantial (sŭb·stăn′shăl) *agg.* sostanziale, cospicuo; solido, concreto: **to be in** — **agreement**, essere d'accordo in linea di massima.

substantiate (sŭb·stăn′shĭ·āt) *vt.* comprovare, suffragare.

substantive (sŭb′stăn·tĭv) *n.* sostantivo.

substitute (sŭb′stĭ·tūt) *n.* sostituto; surrogato; ripiego; supplente. *vt.* sostituire.

substitution (sŭb′stĭ·tū′shŭn) *n.* sostituzione.

subterfuge (sŭb′tẽr·fūj) *n.* sotterfugio.

subterranean (sŭb′tĕ·rā′nē·ăn) *agg.* sotterraneo; subdolo, segreto.

subtitle (sŭb′tī′t′l) *n.* sottotitolo.

subtle (sŭt′′l) *agg.* scaltro, sottile. —**ness**, —**ty** *n.* sottigliezza, astuzia.

subtract (sŭb·trăkt′) *vt.* sottrarre.

subtraction (sŭb·trăk′shŭn) *n.* sottrazione.

suburb (sŭb′ûrb) *n.* suburbio, sobborgo.

suburban (sŭb·ûr′băn) *agg.* suburbano, periferico.

subversive (sŭb·vûr′sĭv) *agg.* sovversivo, sovvertitore.

subvert (sŭb·vûrt′) *vt.* sovvertire.

subway (sŭb′wā′) *n.* sottopassaggio; (*S.U.*) ferrovia sotterranea.

succeed (sŭk·sēd′) *vt.* succedere a, seguire; subentrare a. *vi.* succedere, seguire; riuscire, aver successo.

success (sŭk·sĕs′) *n.* successo, riuscita; **a man of** —, un uomo affermato. —**ful** *agg.* fortunato, riuscito, felice: **to be a** —, avere successo, riuscire, avere esito felice. —**fully** *avv.* vittoriosamente, felicemente, con successo.

succession (sŭk·sĕsh′ŭn) *n.* successione.

successive (sŭk·sĕs′ĭv) *agg.* successivo.

successor (sŭk·sĕs′ẽr) *n.* successore.

succor (sŭk′ẽr) *n.* soccorso; *vt.* soccorrere.

succulent (sŭk′û·lĕnt) *agg.* succulento.

succumb (sŭ·kŭm′) *vi.* soccombere.

such (sŭch) *agg.* tale, simile: — **a good man**, un uomo tanto buono; — **as**, quale, quali; chi, coloro; **at** — **an hour**, a un'ora simile; **at** — **and** — **a place**, nel tal posto; **and** —**like**, e altre cose del genere; *pron.* colui, colei, quello, quelli, quelle, coloro, tale, tali.

suck (sŭk) *n.* succhiata, poppata, sorsata; risucchio; gorgo. *vt.*, *vi.* succhiare, poppare; aspirare.

sucker (sŭk′ẽr) *n.* poppante; parassita; ventosa; (*mecc.*) pistone di pompa aspirante; (*S.U.*) credulone, stupido, gonzo, "fesso."

suckle (sŭk′′l) *vt.*, *vi.* allattare.

suckling (sŭk′lĭng) *n.* lattante.

suction (sŭk′shŭn) *n.* aspirazione, assorbimento, succhiamento: *agg.* aspirante: — **pump**, pompa aspirante.

sudden (sŭd′′n) *agg.* improvviso, inatteso; precipitoso: **all of a** —, tutt'a un tratto.

suddenly *avv.* improvvisamente, repentinamente.

suddenness *n.* subitaneità.

suds (sŭdz) *n.pl.* saponata.

sue (sū) *vt.*, *vi.* richiedere; corteggiare; citare, perseguire: **to** — **for damages**, citare per danni.

suède (swād) *n.* pelle scamosciata.

suet (sū′ĕt) *n.* grasso, sugna.

suffer (sŭf′ẽr) *vt.*, *vi.* tollerare; soffrire, subire; permettere: **he was suffered to go**, lo lasciarono andare. —**er** *n.* vittima; paziente. —**ing** *n.*

sofferenza, dolore. *agg.* sofferente; ammalato (*di*).

suffice (sŭ·fīs′) *vt.*, *vi.* bastare, soddisfare.

sufficiency (sŭ·fīsh′ĕn·sĭ) *n.* sufficienza.

sufficient (sŭ·fīsh′ĕnt) *agg.* sufficiente, bastante. —**ly** *avv.* abbastanza, sufficientemente.

suffix (sŭf′ĭks) *n.* (*gramm.*) suffisso.

suffocate (sŭf′ō·kāt) *vt.*, *vi.* soffocare, asfissiare.

suffocation (sŭf′ō·kā′shŭn) *n.* soffocazione, asfissia.

suffrage (sŭf′rĭj) *n.* suffragio.

suffragette (sŭf′rá·jĕt′) *n.* suffragetta.

sugar (shŏŏg′ẽr) *n.* zucchero: lump —, zucchero in zollette; — **bowl**, zuccheriera. *agg.* di zucchero, zuccherino: — **beet**, barbabietola da zucchero; — **cane**, canna da zucchero. *vt.* inzuccherare. *vi.* cristallizzarsi. —**y** *agg.* zuccherino, zuccheroso.

suggest (sŭg·jĕst′) *vt.* proporre, suggerire, ispirare, indicare.

suggestion (sŭg·jĕs′chŭn) *n.* proposta, suggerimento; traccia.

suggestive (sŭg·jĕs′tĭv) *agg.* suggestivo; indicativo; allusivo.

suicidal (sū′ĭ·sĭd′ăl) *agg.* suicida.

suicide (sū′ĭ·sĭd) *n.* suicidio; suicida: to commit —, togliersi la vita.

suit (sūt) *n.* assortimento; vestito (*da uomo*); petizione, corteggiamento; (*legge*) causa, azione; seme (*di carte da gioco*), colore (*al poker*): to bring a — against, intentare causa a; to follow —, seguire l'esempio. *vt.* adattare; convenire a, piacere a, far comodo a: it suits me, mi conviene; — yourself, fate come vi pare.

suitable (sūt′á·b′l) *agg.* conveniente, adatto, opportuno.

suitably (sūt′á·blĭ) *avv.* acconciamente, opportunamente, convenientemente.

suitcase (sūt′kās′) *n.* valigia.

suite (swēt) *n.* serie, collezione; infilata; seguito (*codazzo*); appartamento: — of furniture, ammobiliamento; — of rooms, appartamento.

suitor (sūt′ẽr) *n.* richiedente; corteggiatore, pretendente; querelante.

sulfa, sulpha (sŭl′fá) *agg.* sulfamidico: — drugs, sulfamidici.

sulk (sŭlk) *n.* malumore, broncio. *vi.* tenere il broncio, essere di malumore.

sulkiness (sŭlk′ĭ·nĕs) *n.* scontrosità, malumore.

sulky (sŭl′kĭ) *agg.* arcigno, imbronciato, scontroso.

sullen (sŭl′ĕn) *agg.* tetro, scontroso, torvo, imbronciato, taciturno.

sully (sŭl′ĭ) *vt.* sporcare. *vi.* sporcarsi.

sulphate (sŭl′fāt) *n.* solfato.

sulphide (sŭl′fĭd) *n.* solfuro.

sulphite (sŭl′fĭt) *n.* solfito.

sulphur (sŭl′fẽr) *n.* zolfo.

sulphuric (sŭl·fū′rĭk) *agg.* solforico.

sultan (sŭl′tăn) *n.* sultano.

sultriness (sŭl′trĭ·nĕs) *n.* afa, umidità.

sultry (sŭl′trĭ) *agg.* afoso, soffocante, opprimente; umido.

sum (sŭm) *n.* somma, cifra; sommario; quantità, essenza, sostanza; addizione, problema. *vt.* (*spesso seg. da* up) sommare; riassumere, ricapitolare.

summarize (sŭm′á·rīz) *vt.* riassumere, compendiare.

summary (sŭm′á·rĭ) *n.* sommario, compendio, riassunto. *agg.* sommario, sbrigativo, conciso.

summer (sŭm′ẽr) *n.* estate. *agg.* estivo: — resort, stazione estiva, luogo di villeggiatura. *vi.* passare l'estate.

summit (sŭm′ĭt) *n.* cima, sommità, apice, vetta.

summon (sŭm′ŭn) *vt.* citare, convocare, adunare, chiamare, raccogliere.

summons (sŭm′ŭnz) *n.* chiamata, convocazione, citazione.

sumptuous (sŭmp′tū·ŭs) *agg.* suntuoso.

sun (sŭn) *n.* sole: — porch, — parlor, solario. *vt.* esporre al sole. *vi.* esporsi al sole: to — oneself, crogiolarsi al sole.

sunbeam (sŭn′bēm′) *n.* raggio di sole.

sunburn (sŭn′bûrn′) *n.* scottatura da sole; abbronzatura. *vt.*, *vi.* bruciare esponendo al sole; abbronzare, abbronzarsi, crogiolarsi al sole.

sunburnt (sŭn′bûrnt′) *agg.* scottato dal sole; abbronzato.

sundae (sŭn′dē) *n.* cassata.

Sunday (sŭn′dĭ) *n.* domenica.

sunder (sŭn′dẽr) *vt.* separare; *vi.* separarsi, scindersi.

sundial (sŭn′dĭ′ăl) *n.* meridiana.

sundown (sŭn′doun′) *n.* tramonto del sole.

sundries (sŭn′drĭz) *n.pl.* miscellanea, oggetti diversi.

sundry (sŭn′drĭ) *agg.* separati, diversi, parecchi.

sunflower (sŭn′flou′ẽr) *n.* girasole.

sung (sŭng) *pp. di* to sing.

sunk (sŭngk) *pass.*, *pp. di* to sink. *agg.* affondato; incavato, sprofondato; sommerso; infossato.

sunlamp (sŭn′lămp′) *n.* lampada solare.

sunlight (sŭn′līt′) *n.* luce solare, sole.

sunlit (sŭn′līt′) *agg.* soleggiato.

sunny 245 surety

sunny (sŭn'ĭ) agg. soleggiato, assolato; solatio; radioso, felice: — day, giornata di sole; — disposition, carattere allegro.
sunrise (sŭn'rīz') n. levar del sole, alba.
sunset (sŭn'sĕt') n. tramonto del sole.
sunshade (sŭn'shād') n. parasole.
sunshine (sŭn'shīn') n. luce del sole, sereno.
sunstroke (sŭn'strōk') n. colpo di sole.
sup (sŭp) vt. centellinare. vi. cenare.
superabundant (sū'pēr·à·bŭn'dănt) agg. sovrabbondante.
superannuate (sūp'ēr·ăn'ū·āt) vt. mandare in pensione.
superb (sū·pûrb') agg. superbo; eccellente, splendido.
supercargo (sū'pēr·kär'gō) n. (naut.) sovraccarico (sovrintendente al carico).
supercharger (sū'pēr·chär'jēr) n. (mecc.) turbocompressore.
supercilious (sū'pēr·sĭl'ĭ·ŭs) agg. altezzoso, sprezzante, arrogante.
superficial (sū'pēr·fĭsh'ăl) agg. superficiale.
superficies (sū'pēr·fĭsh'ĭ·ēz) n. superficie.
superfine (sū'pēr·fīn') agg. sopraffino. n.pl. merci sopraffine.
superfluous (sū·pûr'floō·ŭs) agg. superfluo.
superhighway (sū'pēr·hī'wā') n. superautostrada.
superhuman (sū'pēr·hū'măn) agg. sovrumano.
superimpose (sū'pēr·im·pōz') vt. sovrapporre.
superintend (sū'pēr·ĭn·tĕnd') vt. sovrintendere a, dirigere.
superintendent (sū'pēr·ĭn·tĕn'dĕnt) n. sovrintendente; direttore; ispettore.
superior (sū·pēr'ĭ·ēr) n., agg. superiore: a — air, un'aria di superiorità.
superiority (sū·pēr'ĭ·ŏr'ĭ·tĭ) n. superiorità.
superlative (sū·pûr'lá·tĭv) n., agg. superlativo.
superman (sū'pēr·măn') n. superuomo.
supermarket (sū'pēr·mär'kĕt) n. supermercato.
supernatural (sūp'ēr·năt'ū·răl) n., agg. soprannaturale.
supernumerary (sū'pēr·nū'mēr·ēr'ĭ) n. impiegato in soprannumero; (teat.) comparsa. agg. soprannumerario.
supersede (sū'pēr·sēd') vt. soppiantare, sostituire.
supersonic (sū'pēr·sŏn'ĭk) agg. ultrasonoro; (aeron.) supersonico.
superstition (sū'pēr·stĭsh'ŭn) n. superstizione.

superstitious (sū'pēr·stĭsh'ŭs) agg. superstizioso.
supervise (sū'pēr·vīz) vt. sovrintendere a, sorvegliare, dirigere.
supervision (sū'pēr·vĭzh'ŭn) n. controllo, direzione, sovrintendenza.
supervisor (sū'pēr·vī'zēr) n. sovrintendente.
supine (sū·pīn') agg. supino, inerte, indifferente.
supper (sŭp'ēr) n. cena.
supplant (sŭp·lánt') vt. soppiantare.
supple (sŭp'l) agg. flessibile, elastico, duttile, docile, cedevole.
supplement (sŭp'lē·mĕnt) n. supplemento; vt. completare, integrare; aggiungere a.
suppliant (sŭp'lĭ·ănt), supplicant (sŭp'lĭ·kănt) n., agg. postulante.
supplicate (sŭp'lĭ·kāt) vt. supplicare.
supplication (sŭp'lĭ·kā'shŭn) n. supplica.
supplier (sŭ·plī'ēr) n. fornitore.
supply (sŭp'lĭ) (1) avv. elasticamente, docilmente, cedevolmente.
supply (sŭ·plī') (2) n. (spesso usato al pl.: supplies) provvista; fornitura, rifornimento; viveri. agg. di riformimento. vt., vi. (gen.seg. da with) fornire, rifornire, provvedere, soddisfare; sostituire.
support (sŭ·pōrt') n. sostegno, appoggio, puntello; mantenimento, sostentamento; (teat.) attore secondario. vt. reggere, sostenere; difendere; mantenere; appoggiare.
supporter n. sostenitore, difensore, fautore; fascia elastica, giarrettiera.
suppose (sŭ·pōz') v. supporre, immaginare: it is supposed, si presume.
supposed (sŭ·pōzd') agg. presunto, ipotetico. —ly (-ĕd·lĭ) avv. presumibilmente, ipoteticamente.
supposition (sŭp'ō·zĭsh'ŭn) n. supposizione, ipotesi.
suppress (sŭ·prĕs') vt. sopprimere; reprimere, soffocare; nascondere. —ed agg. soppresso; represso, soffocato. —ion n. soppressione; repressione.
suppurate (sŭp'ū·rāt) vi. suppurare.
supremacy (sŭ·prĕm'á·sĭ) n. supremazia.
supreme (sŭ·prēm') agg. supremo.
surcharge (sŭr·chärj') n. sovraccarico; stampigliatura.
sure (shōōr) agg. sicuro, certo, stabile: to make —, assicurare, assicurarsi; to be —! certo!; avv. (anche —ly) sicuramente, indubbiamente. —ness n. sicurezza, certezza.
surety (shōōr'tĭ) n. sicurezza; pegno, garanzia; garante: to stand — for, farsi garante di.

surf (sûrf) *n.* risacca, spuma.

surface (sûr'fĭs) *n.* superficie. *agg.* di superficie; superficiale. *vt.* lisciare, spianare, rifinire; far emergere. *vi.* emergere, affiorare.

surfeit (sûr'fĭt) *n.* eccesso, sazietà, disgusto. *vt.* saziare, disgustare.

surge (sûrj) *n.* maroso, ondata; tumulto. *vi.* gonfiarsi, sollevarsi, tumultuare.

surgeon (sûr'jŭn) *n.* chirurgo.

surgery (sûr'jĕr-ĭ) *n.* chirurgia; ambulatorio; sala operatoria.

surly (sûr'lĭ) *agg.* sgarbato, burbero, arcigno.

surmise (sûr·mīz') *n.* supposizione, congettura. *vt.*, *vi.* arguire, intuire, dedurre.

surmount (sûr·mount') *vt.* sormontare, superare, valicare.

surname (sûr'nām') *n.* cognome.

surpass (sẽr·pás') *vt.* superare, sorpassare. **—ing** *agg.* eccellente, superiore, straordinario.

surplice (sûr'plĭs) *n.* (*eccles.*) cotta.

surplus (sûr'plŭs) *n.* soprappiù, eccedenza; residuo (*attivo*), maggior utile. *agg.* in soprappiù, eccedente.

surprisal (sẽr·prīz'ăl) *n.* sorpresa.

surprise (sẽr·prīz') *n.* sorpresa, stupore. *vt.* cogliere alla sprovvista, meravigliare, stupire.

surprising (sẽr·prīz'ĭng) *agg.* sorprendente.

surrender (sŭ·rĕn'dẽr) *n.* resa, capitolazione; consegna; rinunzia. *vt.*, *vi.* consegnare; abbandonare; arrendersi; rinunziare (*a*); sottomettersi, costituirsi.

surreptitious (sûr'ĕp·tĭsh'ŭs) *agg.* fraudolento, clandestino, furtivo.

surrogate (sûr'ŏ·gât) *n.* sostituto, interino, supplente; surrogato.

surround (sŭ·round') *vt.* circondare, cingere, attorniare.

surrounding *n.* accerchiamento. *agg.* circostante.

surroundings *n.pl.* dintorni; ambiente; circostanze.

surtout (sûr·tōōt') *n.* finanziera, soprabito.

surveillance (sûr·vāl'ăns) *n.* vigilanza.

survey (sẽr·vā') *n.* veduta generale; esame, ispezione, estimo, perizia; planimetria. *vt.* osservare, ispezionare; stimare (*terreni*, *ecc.*); esaminare, contemplare.

surveyor (sẽr·vā'ẽr) *n.* ispettore (*della dogana, ecc.*); agrimensore.

survival (sẽr·vīv'ăl) *n.* sopravvivenza; residuo (*o* superstite) di tempi passati.

survive (sẽr·vīv') *vt.* sopravvivere a. *vi.* sopravvivere.

survivor (sẽr·vī'vẽr) *n.* superstite.

susceptibility (sŭ·sĕp'tĭ·bĭl'ĭ·tĭ) *n.* suscettibilità.

susceptible (sŭ·sĕp'tĭ·b'l) *agg.* suscettibile, sensibile, ricettivo.

suspect (sŭs'pĕkt) *n.* sospetto; persona sospetta, indiziato. (sŭs·pĕkt') *vt.* sospettare, diffidare di. *vi.* avere dei sospetti.

suspend (sŭs·pĕnd') *vt.* appendere; sospendere: **suspended animation**, morte apparente.

suspenders (sŭs·pĕn'dẽrz) *n.pl.* bretelle; giarrettiere.

suspense (sŭs·pĕns') *n.* incertezza, ansia, dubbio; sospensione: **to keep in —**, tenere con l'animo sospeso.

suspension (sŭs·pĕn'shŭn) *n.* sospensione: **— bridge**, ponte sospeso.

suspicion (sŭs·pĭsh'ŭn) *n.* sospetto, diffidenza; traccia.

suspicious (sŭs·pĭsh'ŭs) *agg.* sospettoso; sospetto, losco.

sustain (sŭs·tān') *vt.* sostenere, sorreggere; sopportare, subire; sostentare; prolungare.

sustenance (sŭs'tĕ·năns) *n.* alimento; mantenimento, mezzi di sussistenza.

swab (swŏb) *n.* straccio per pavimenti; scovolo da cannone; (*med.*) tampone; (*naut.*) radazza.

swaddle (swŏd'l) *vt.* fasciare.

swaddling (swŏd'lĭng) *n.* fasciatura: **— clothes**, fasce per neonato.

swag (swăg) *n.* fardello; (*gergo*) bottino, refurtiva.

swage (swāj) *n.* (*mecc.*) punzone.

swagger (swăg'ẽr) *n.* bravata, fanfaronata; andatura spavalda. *vi.* fare il rodomonte, pavoneggiarsi.

swain (swān) *n.* innamorato (*spec. campagnuolo*); giovanotto.

swallow (swŏl'ō) (1) *vt.* inghiottire, tranguiare. *vi.* deglutire.

swallow (swŏl'ō) (2) *n.* rondine.

swam (swăm) *pass.* di to swim.

swamp (swŏmp) *n.* palude, marcita. *vt.*, *vi.* inondare, impantanare; (*naut.*) riempire d'acqua; affondare; imbarcare acqua: **swamped with work**, sommerso dal lavoro. *agg.* paludoso.

swan (swŏn) *n.* cigno.

swank (swăngk) *n.* (*gergo*) vanteria, esagerazione; *agg.* (*anche* **swanky**) pretenzioso, vistoso, ricercato; snello, flessibile.

swap (swŏp) *n.* baratto. *vt.* barattare.

swarm (swôrm) *n.* sciame, moltitudine. *vt.*, *vi.* invadere, affollare, sciamare, pullulare, accalcarsi, brulicare.

swarthy (swôr'thĭ) *agg.* scuro (*di pelle*), olivastro.

swash (swŏsh) *n.* canale, sciacquio. *vt., vi.* diguazzare, guazzare; turbinare, sferzare; far roteare.

swat (swŏt) *n.* colpo violento.

swath (swŏth) *n.* falciata; solco.

swathe (swāth) *vt.* fasciare, bendare.

sway (swā) *n.* ondeggiamento; potere, potenza, preponderanza. *vt.* sballottare, dominare, far dondolare, influenzare. *vi.* ondeggiare, bilanciarsi, barcollare; propendere; predominare.

swear (swâr) *vt., vi.* (*pass.* swore, *pp.* sworn) giurare, far giurare, testimoniare; imprecare, bestemmiare: **to — at,** imprecare contro.

sweat (swĕt) *n.* sudore, traspirazione. *vt.* (*pass., pp.* sweat *o* sweated) far sudare; trasudare; far sgobbare. *vi.* sudare; sfacchinare.

sweater (swĕt'ẽr) *n.* sudatore; maglione; aguzzino.

sweaty (swĕt'ĭ) *agg.* sudato; faticoso.

Swede (swēd) *n., agg.* svedese.

Swedish (swēd'ĭsh) *n.* lingua svedese: **the —,** gli svedesi. *agg.* svedese.

sweep (swēp) *n.* spazzata; spazzatura; colpo; curva; gesto (*o* moto) circolare; strascico; spazzacamino; (*pl.*) remi: **to make a clean —,** fare un repulisti. *vt., vi.* (*pass., pp.* swept) scopare, spazzar via; strisciare; sfiorare; dragare; passare rapidamente; camminare con portamento eretto; sfilare; estendersi: **to — down on,** piombare su.

sweeper *n.* spazzino; spazzola.

sweeping *n.* spazzata: sweepings, immondizia. *agg.* rapido; ampio; generale, completo: **— victory,** vittoria assoluta.

sweet (swēt) *n.* dolce, dolcezza; *agg.* dolce, zuccherino, fragrante, piacevole, fresco: **to be — on,** essere innamorato di: **to have a — tooth,** essere ghiotto di dolciumi; **— bay,** alloro, magnolia virginiana; **— pea,** pisello odoroso; **— potato,** patata americana.

sweetbread (swēt'brĕd') *n.* animella.

sweeten (swēt'n) *vt.* addolcire, inzuccherare, ammansire.

sweetheart (swēt'härt') *n.* innamorato, innamorata.

sweetish (swēt'ĭsh) *agg.* dolciastro.

sweetly (swēt'lĭ) *avv.* dolcemente, soavemente; melodiosamente.

sweetmeat (swēt'mēt') *n.* dolciume.

sweetness (swēt'nĕs) *n.* dolcezza, soavità.

swell (swĕl) *n.* protuberanza, gonfiore; aumento; monticello; caval-lone (*onda*); crescendo. *agg.* grandioso; elegante; magnifico. *vt.* (*pass.* swelled, *pp.* swelled *o* swollen) enfiare, gonfiare; accrescere; insuperbire. *vi.* gonfiarsi, aumentare; espandersi; sollevarsi; intensificarsi; insuperbirsi.

swelling *n.* protuberanza, gonfiore; piena (*di fiume*). *agg.* gonfio, tronfio, crescente.

swelter (swĕl'tẽr) *n.* afa. *vt., vi.* opprimere; soffocare dal caldo.

swept (swĕpt) *pass., pp. di* to sweep.

swerve (swûrv) *n.* scarto, svolta, deviazione. *vt.* sviare. *vi.* deviare, svoltare; fare uno scarto.

swift (swĭft) *n.* rapida (*di fiume*); mulinello; rondone. *agg.* rapido, svelto, leggiero, pronto. **—ly** *avv.* velocemente, prontamente. **—ness** *n.* rapidità, prontezza.

swig (swĭg) *n.* lunga sorsata. *vt.* tracannare.

swill (swĭl) *n.* lunga sorsata (*di liquore*); beverone del maiale; rifiuti. *vt.* tracannare avidamente; lavare, risciacquare.

swim (swĭm) *n.* nuotata. **— suit,** costume da bagno. *vt.* (*pass.* swam, *pp.* swum) far galleggiare. *vi.* nuotare, galleggiare; essere inondato (*o* inzuppato); girare (*della testa*), avere le vertigini.

swimmer *n.* nuotatore.

swindle (swĭn'd'l) *n.* truffa, frode. *vt., vi.* truffare, abbindolare.

swindler (swĭn'dlẽr) *n.* truffatore.

swine (swĭn) *n.* maiale, porco; maiali, porci.

swing (swĭng) *n.* oscillazione, dondolamento; altalena; impulso, propulsione, slancio: **in full —,** in piena attività, al colmo; **— door,** porta a molle. *vt.* (*pass., pp.* swung) dondolare, far oscillare; appendere; brandire, far rotare. *vi.* oscillare, rotare; girare (*sui cardini*); voltarsi; ondeggiare, bilanciarsi; svoltare; penzolare, morire impiccato.

swipe (swĭp) *n.* (*gergo*) manata, colpo violento; *vt.* colpire violentemente; (*gergo*) rubacchiare, rubare.

swirl (swûrl) *n.* turbine, gorgo; ricciolo; guizzo; *vt.* prillare, far turbinare; *vi.* turbinare, guizzare.

swish (swĭsh) *n.* fruscio.

Swiss (swĭs) *n., agg.* svizzero.

switch (swĭch) *n.* bacchetta, verga; cambiamento; treccia posticcia; (*ferr.*) scambio; (*elett.*) interruttore, commutatore; *vt., vi.* sviare, sferzare; deviare, mutare: **to — on,** accendere (*la luce*); **to — off,** spegnere, interrompere.

switchboard (swĭch'bôrd') *n.* quadro elettrico, centralino telefonico.

switchblade knife (swĭch'blād') *n.* coltello a serramanico.

swivel (swĭv''l) *n.* perno, gancio girevole. *vt.* far rotare. *vi.* rotare, girare.

swollen (swōl'ĕn) *pp. di* to swell. *agg.* gonfio, tronfio, turgido.

swoon (swōōn) *n.* svenimento. *vi.* svenire.

swoop (swōōp) *n.* calata (*del rapace*); assalto. *vt.* ghermire. *vi.* piombare sulla preda: **to — down upon,** piombare addosso a.

sword (sôrd) *n.* spada: **— cane,** bastone animato.

swordsman (sôrdz'măn) *n.* schermidore, spadaccino; soldato.

swore (swôr) *pass. di* to swear.

sworn (swôrn) *pp. di* to swear.

swum (swŭm) *pp. di* to swim.

swung (swŭng) *pass., pp. di* to swing.

sycophant (sĭk'ō-fănt) *n.* adulatore.

syllable (sĭl'á-b'l) *n.* sillaba.

syllabus (sĭl'á-bŭs) *n.* sommario.

sylph (sĭlf) *n.* silfo, silfide.

symbol (sĭm'bŭl) *n.* simbolo; sigla. **—ic, —ical** (-bŏl'ĭk-ăl) *agg.* simbolico. **—ism** *n.* simbolismo.

symmetrical (sĭ-mĕt'rĭ-kăl) *agg.* simmetrico.

symmetry (sĭm'ĕ-trĭ) *n.* simmetria.

sympathetic (sĭm'pá-thĕt'ĭk) *agg.* comprensivo, compassionevole, solidale.

sympathize (sĭm'pá-thīz) *vi.* provare (*o* esprimere) comprensione: **to —with,** compiangere, fare le condoglianze a; approvare, condividere l'opinione di; comprendere.

sympathy (sĭm'pá-thĭ) *n.* comprensione, compassione, solidarietà; condoglianze.

symphonic (sĭm-fŏn'ĭk) *agg.* sinfonico.

symphony (sĭm'fō-nĭ) *n.* sinfonia: **— orchestra,** orchestra sinfonica.

symptom (sĭmp'tŭm) *n.* sintomo, indizio. **—atic** (-măt'ĭk) *agg.* sintomatico.

synagogue (sĭn'á-gŏg) *n.* sinagoga.

synchronism (sĭng'krō-nĭz'm) *n.* sincronismo.

synchronize (sĭng'krō-nīz) *vt.* sincronizzare. *vt.* coincidere; essere sincrono.

synchronous (sĭng'krō-nŭs) *agg.* sincrono.

syncopate (sĭng'kō-pāt) *vt.* sincopare.

syncopation (sĭng'kō-pā'shŭn) *n.* sincopatura.

syndicalism (sĭn'dĭ-kăl-ĭz'm) *n.* sindacalismo.

syndicate (sĭn'dĭ-kāt) *n.* sindacato, consiglio, società, consorzio. *vt.* consorziare; pubblicare simultaneamente in vari periodici; *vi.* consorziarsi.

synonym (sĭn'ō-nĭm) *n.* sinonimo. **—ous** (-ŏn'ĭ-mŭs) *agg.* sinonimo, equivalente.

synopsis (sĭ-nŏp'sĭs) *n.* sintesi, sunto.

syntax (sĭn'tăks) *n.* sintassi.

synthesis (sĭn'thĕ-sĭs) *n.* sintesi.

synthetic (sĭn-thĕt'ĭk) *agg.* sintetico.

syntony (sĭn'tō-nĭ) *n.* sintonia.

syphilis (sĭf'ĭ-lĭs) *n.* (*med.*) sifilide.

syphon *vedi* siphon.

syringe (sĭr'ĭnj) *n.* siringa. *vt.* siringare, iniettare.

syrup (sĭr'ŭp) *n.* sciroppo.

syrupy (sĭr'ŭp-ĭ) *agg.* sciropposo.

system (sĭs'tĕm) *n.* sistema; (*gergo*) organismo; (*ferr.*) rete. **—atic** (-ăt'ĭk) *agg.* sistematico.

systematize (sĭs'tĕm-á-tīz) *vt.* metodizzare, ridurre a sistema.

T

tab (tăb) *n.* linguetta, aletta; etichetta, talloncino: **to keep tabs on,** vigilare; tenersi al corrente di.

tabby (tăb'ĭ) *n.* gatto; (*tess.*) moire.

tabernacle (tăb'ĕr-năk''l) *n.* tenda, tabernacolo; (*naut.*) pozzo dell'albero.

table (tāb''l) *n.* tavola; tabella, lapide; indice: **multiplication —,** tavola pitagorica; **— cover,** tappeto da tavola. *vt.* ordinare in tabella; porre sulla tavola; rinviare (*una discussione, ecc.*)

tableau (tăb-lō') *n.* quadro.

tablecloth (tā'b'l-clŏth') *n.* tovaglia.

tableland (tā'b'l-lănd') *n.* altipiano.

tablespoon (tā'b'l-spōōn') *n.* cucchiaio da minestra. **—ful** *n.* cucchiaiata.

tableware (tā'b'l-wâr') *n.* vasellame, servizio da tavola.

tablet (tăb'lĕt) *n.* tavoletta; pastiglia, compressa; blocco per annotazioni, taccuino.

tabloid (tăb'loid) *n.* pasticca; giornale a formato ridotto.

tabulate (tăb'ū-lāt) *vt.* ridurre a sinossi, catalogare.

tachometer (tá-kŏm'ĕ-tĕr) *n.* tachimetro.

tacit (tăs'ĭt) *agg.* tacito, implicito. [tro.

taciturn (tăs'ĭ-tûrn) *agg.* taciturno.

tack (tăk) *n.* chiodo, bulletta, puntina da disegno; (*naut.*) mura (*fune che* *fissa l'angolo di una vela*), bordata, virata, rotta, bordeggio: **to be on the right —**, essere sulla buona via; **to change —**, cambiar rotta. *vt.*, *vi.* inchiodare, attaccare, imbastire; *(naut.)* andar di bolina, bordeggiare, virare.

tackle (tăk''l) *n.* carrucola; armamentario; *(naut.)* paranco; sartiame; attrezzatura; *(calcio)* carica, attaccante: **fishing —**, attrezzi per la pesca. *vt.* impugnare, afferrare; affrontare; avvinghiarsi a; bardare; *(calcio)* ostacolare, attaccare.

tact (tăkt) *n.* tatto, diplomazia.

tactful (tăkt'fŏŏl) *agg.* accorto, diplomatico: **— man**, uomo di tatto.

tactics (tăk'tĭks) *n.sing.* tattica.

tactile (tăk'tĭl) *agg.* tattile.

tactless (tăkt'lĕs) *agg.* privo di tatto, indelicato.

tadpole (tăd'pōl') *n.* *(zool.)* girino.

taffrail (tăf'rāl) *n.* *(naut.)* parapetto di poppa.

taffy (tăf'ĭ) *n.* caramella.

tag (tăg) *n.* pendaglio, appiccagnolo; punta ferrata *(di stringa, ecc.)*; etichetta *(da appendere al bagaglio, ecc.)*; estremità; *(teat.)* battuta: **to play —**, giocare a rincorrersi. *vt.* mettere l'etichetta a; attaccare, appendere; *(fam.)* pedinare.

tail (tāl) *n.* coda; estremità; seguito; rovescio *(di moneta)*; *(fam.)* pedinatore; *pl.* marsina. *vt.* metter la coda a; mettere in fila; *(gergo)* pedinare. *vi.* formare una coda: **to — off** (out, away, down), diminuire, affievolirsi, disperdersi **—light** *n.* fanale di coda. **—spin** *n.* *(aeron.)* caduta in vite.

tailor (tā'lēr) *n.* sarto. **—ing** *n.* sartoria *(arte)*.

tailpiece (tāl'pēs') *n.* aggiunta; trave.

taint (tānt) *n.* infezione; magagna, macchia; discredito. *vt.* contaminare, insozzare, guastare. *vi.* guastarsi.

take (tāk) *n.* presa; pesca; *(cinema)* ripresa; *(gergo)* incasso, introito. *vt.*, *vi.* *(pass.* took, *pp.* taken*)* prendere; impadronirsi di; condurre, guidare, portare; credere; attrarre; contenere; subire; chiedere *(un prezzo)*; attecchire; riuscire bene *(in fotografia)*: **to — aback**, cogliere di sorpresa; **to — after**, somigliare a; **to — amiss**, prendere in mala parte; **to — apart**, smontare, scomporre; **to — away**, togliere, privare, sottrarre, portare via; **to — back**, riprendere, ritirare; **to — back one's word**, rimangiarsi la parola; **to — down**, annotare; de-

molire; smontare; mandare giù, inghiottire; umiliare; **to — for**, prendere per, scambiare per; **to — for granted**, avere la certezza che; **to — from**, prendere a, prendere da, portare via a; **to — in**, comprendere; includere; accogliere; contenere; ingannare, imbrogliare; stringere *(un vestito)*; **to — off**, togliere, togliersi; distogliere; dedurre; cessare; partire; *(aeron.)* decollare; parodiare; **to — (oneself) off**, andarsene; **to — on**, prendere; assumere; accogliere; addossarsi *(una responsabilità)*; accettare *(un avversario)*; agitarsi, eccitarsi; **to — out**, togliere, portare via; asportare; separare; sottrarre; omettere; portare a, condurre a; **to — over**, subentrare a, prendere la direzione di; **to — to**, darsi a; affezionarsi a; correre a, buttarsi a; **to — up**, occupare, portare via *(tempo)*; raccogliere *(passeggieri)*; assorbire; interrompere, correggere *(uno che parla)*; darsi a, intraprendere; riprendere *(un discorso)*; adottare; accollarsi; fare onore a *(un impegno)*; **to — to one's heels**, darsela a gambe; **to — to heart**, prendere a cuore; **to — to pieces**, fare a pezzi; **to — to task**, richiamare all'ordine; **to — a chance**, correre un rischio; **to — a fancy to**, incapricciarsi di, innamorarsi di; **to — a jump**, spiccare un salto; **to — a look at**, dare un'occhiata a; **to — a notion to**, mettersi in testa di; **to — an oath**, prestare un giuramento; **to — a trip**, fare un viaggio; **to — advantage of**, approfittare di; **to — care**, stare attento; **to — care of**, aver cura di; **to — charge of**, incaricarsi di, assumere la direzione di; **to — effect**, avere effetto; fare effetto; **to — exercise**, fare esercizio; **to — leave**, congedarsi, salutare; **to — offense**, offendersi; **to — place**, aver luogo, avverarsi, capitare; **to — stock in**, avere stima di, avere fiducia in; **to — stock of**, fare l'inventario di; prendere visione di; **to — the floor**, prendere la parola; **to — one's time**, fare con comodo *o* con calma; **— it easy!** calma!, non agitatevi!, non prendetevela!, andateci piano!

taken (tāk'ěn) *pp. di* to take: **to be — ill**, cadere ammalato, ammalarsi.

takeoff (tāk'ŏf') *n.* caricatura, parodia; *(aeron.)* decollo, involo.

talc, talcum (tăl'kăm) *n.* talco.

tale (tāl) *n.* racconto, favola, storiella; bugia; pettegolezzo; resoconto:

the — of years, la somma degli anni.

talebearer (tāl'bâr'ĕr) n. propalatore, malalingua.

talent (tăl'ĕnt) n. ingegno, propensione, abilità, talento. —ed agg. abile, intelligente, di ingegno.

talk (tôk) n. conversazione, discorso, colloquio; eloquio; diceria: small —, chiacchiere insulse; the — of the town, l'argomento di cui tutti parlano. vt. parlare di, dire. vi. parlare, chiacchierare: to — nonsense, dire sciocchezze; to — someone out of, dissuadere qualcuno da; to — someone into, persuadere qualcuno a; to — over, discutere. —ative (-á.tĭv) agg. loquace, ciarliero. —er n. parlatore; chiacchierone. —ing agg. parlante: — picture, film sonoro o parlato.

tall (tôl) agg. alto, grande: a — order, un compito arduo, una richiesta eccessiva; a — story, una storia incredibile.

tallow (tăl'ō) n. sego.

tally (tăl'ĭ) n. tacca; conto; spunta; etichetta, talloncino; duplicato. vt. spuntare; registrare; calcolare; munire d'etichetta. vi. fare la spunta; corrispondere, collimare.

talon (tăl'ŭn) n. artiglio.

tame (tām) agg. domestico, addomesticato, mansueto, docile; insulso, fiacco. vt. domare, addomesticare.

tamely avv. docilmente, passivamente.

tamer (tăm'ĕr) n. domatore.

tamper (tăm'pĕr) vi. immischiarsi; armeggiare: to — with, adulterare; manomettere; tentar di forzare.

tan (tăn) n. tannino, concia; abbronzatura; marrone (colore). vt. conciare; abbronzare; (fam.) malmenare. vi. abbronzarsi.

tang (tăng) n. sapore violento, aroma; codolo (di lama).

tangent (tăn'jĕnt) n., agg. tangente: to go off on a —, partire per la tangente.

tangerine (tăn'jĕ·rēn') n. mandarino.

tangible (tăn'jĭ.b'l) agg. tangibile.

tangle (tăng'g'l) n. groviglio, complicazione, imbroglio. vt. aggrovigliare, ingarbugliare, complicare. vi. ingarbugliarsi.

tangly (tăng'glĭ) agg. aggrovigliato.

tank (tăngk) n. serbatoio, cisterna; carro armato.

tankard (tăngk'ĕrd) n. boccale.

tanker (tăngk'ĕr) n. nave cisterna.

tanner (tăn'ĕr) n. conciatore.

tannery (tăn'ĕr·ĭ) n. conceria.

tannin (tăn'ĭn) n. (chim.) tannino.

tanning (tăn'ĭng) n. concia; abbronzatura; (fam.) bastonatura.

tantalization (tăn'tá·lĭ·zā'shŭn) n. supplizio di Tantalo, tormento.

tantalize (tăn'tá·līz) vt. sottoporre al supplizio di Tantalo, tormentare.

tantamount (tăn'tá·mount') agg. equivalente.

tantrum (tăn'trŭm) n. accesso di collera; bizze, capricci.

tap (tăp) n. colpetto, segnale; rubinetto, zipolo, spina; banco di mescita, bar; (elett.) presa, inserimento: (pl., mil.) silenzio: — dance, tip-tap; beer on —, birra spillata. vt., vi. battere, bussare; spillare; forare; inserirsi (su una linea elett. o telef.).

tape (tăp) n. fettuccia, nastro, striscia; nastro magnetico: — line, — measure, metro a nastro; — recorder, magnetofono. vt. misurare (o legare) con nastro; incidere su nastro.

taper (tā'pĕr) n. assottigliamento; candela, cero. vt., vi. assottigliare, assottigliarsi, diminuire, affusolare, affusolarsi, rastremare.

tapering agg. affusolato; rastremato.

tapestry (tăp'ĕs·trĭ) n. arazzo, tappezzeria.

tapeworm (tāp'wûrm') n. tenia.

taproom (tăp'rōōm') n. sala di taverna.

tapster (tăp'stĕr) n. barista.

tar (tär) n. pece; catrame. vt. impeciare; incatramare.

tardy (tär'dĭ) agg. lento, tardivo: to be —, arrivare in ritardo.

tare (tär) n. (comm.) tara.

target (tär'gĕt) n. bersaglio; obiettivo.

tariff (tär'ĭf) n. tariffa.

tarn (tärn) n. lago di montagna.

tarnish (tär'nĭsh) vt. macchiare; opacare; annerire; ossidare; inquinare. vi. annerirsi, ossidarsi. n. opacità; annerimento; ossidazione; macchia.

tarpaulin (tär'pô'lĭn) n. tela incerata (o catramata).

tarry (tär'ĭ) (1) agg. incatramato.

tarry (tär'ĭ) (2) vi. sostare, indugiare, attardarsi.

tart (tärt) (1) n. crostata, pasticcio; (gergo) sgualdrina.

tart (tärt) (2) agg. agro, aspro. —ly avv. aspramente.

task (tăsk) n. mansione, compito, fatica; (mil.) missione: to take to —, redarguire; — force, contingente destinato a una missione. vt. assegnare (un compito) a; caricare (di); mettere alla prova; accusare (di).

tassel (tăs''l) n. fiocco, nappa.

taste (tāst) *n.* gusto, sapore, assaggio, buon gusto. *vt.* assaggiare, gustare. *vi.* sapere (*di*). **—ful** *agg.* elegante, di buon gusto. **—less** *agg.* insipido, insapore; privo di buon gusto.

tasty *agg.* saporito; elegante, di buon gusto.

tatter (tăt'ĕr) *n.* brandello, straccio.

tatterdemalion (tăt'ĕr·dē·māl'yŭn) *n.* straccione.

tattered (tăt'ĕrd) *agg.* lacero, cencioso.

tattle (tăt'l) *n.* chiacchierio. *vi.* cicalare, chiacchierare.

tattoo (tă'tōō') (1) *n.* tatuaggio. *vt.* tatuare.

tattoo (2) *n.* rullo di tamburo, stamburamento; (*mil.*) segnale di ritirata; battito ritmato.

taught (tòt) *pass., pp. di* to teach.

taunt (tònt) *n.* punzecchiatura, sarcasmo; sfida. *vt.* beffare, punzecchiare; sfidare.

taut (tòt) *agg.* rigido, teso; lindo.

tauten (tòt'n) *vt.* tendere, irrigidire. *vi.* tendersi, irrigidirsi.

tavern (tăv'ĕrn) *n.* taverna, locanda.

taw (tò) *n.* biglia, pallina.

tawdry (tò'drĭ) *agg.* pacchiano, vistoso.

tawny (tò'nĭ) *agg.* bruno, bronzeo, fulvo.

tax (tăks) *n.* tassa, imposta; compito, gravame: income **—**, tassa sul reddito. *vt.* tassare, imporre; mettere a dura prova; tacciare, accusare.

taxi (tăk'sĭ), taxicab (tăk'sĭ·kăb') *n.* tassì, autopubblica. *vi.* andare in tassì; (*aeron.*) rullare.

taxidermist (tăk'sĭ·dûr'mĭst) *n.* imbalsamatore.

taximeter (tăk'sĭ·mē'tĕr) *n.* tassametro.

taxpayer (tăks'pā'ĕr) *n.* contribuente.

tea (tē) *n.* tè: beef **—**, brodo di carne; **— kettle**, cuccuma per tè. **—cup**, *n.* tazza da tè. **—pot** *n.* teiera. **—spoon** *n.* cucchiaino da tè.

teach (tēch) *vt., vi.* (*pass. pp.* taught) insegnare, istruire. **—er** *n.* insegnante. **—ing** *n.* insegnamento.

team (tēm) *n.* tiro (*a due, a quattro, ecc.*); coppia; gruppo, squadra (*anche sport.*). *vt.* aggiogare; raggruppare; accoppiare.

teamster (tēm'stēr) *n.* guidatore.

teamwork (tēm'wûrk') *n.* lavoro di squadra.

tear (tēr) (1) *n.* lagrima, pianto.

tear (tēr) (2) *n.* strappo, lacerazione; impeto: wear and **—**, logorio. *vt.* strappare, stracciare, lacerare. *vi.* stracciarsi, lacerarsi; andare a precipizio; infuriare: **to — apart**, smontare; separare, staccare; dilaniare; strappare; **to — down**, abbattere, demolire; smontare; **to — into**, entrare precipitosamente; **to — oneself away**, andarsene a malincuore.

tearful (tēr'fŏŏl) *agg.* lagrimoso, piangente.

tease (tēz) *n.* tormentatore, tormento. *vt.* stuzzicare, importunare, tormentare.

teasel (tē'z'l) *n.* (*bot.*) cardo; (*mecc.*) cardatrice.

teat (tēt) *n.* capezzolo.

technical (tĕk'nĭ·kăl) *agg.* tecnico.

technicality (tĕk·nĭ·kăl'ĭ·tĭ) *n.* particolare tecnico.

technician (tĕk·nĭsh'ăn) *n.* tecnico.

technic (tĕk'nĭk) *n.* tecnica.

technique (tĕk·nēk') *n.* tecnica, metodo.

technology (tĕk·nŏl'ŏ·jĭ) *n.* tecnologia.

tedious (tē'dĭ·ŭs) *agg.* tedioso. **—ness** *n.* tediosità.

tedium (tē'dĭ·ŭm) *n.* tedio.

teem (tēm) *vi.* essere fecondo, abbondare: to **— with**, abbondare di.

teen (tēn) *agg.* dell' adolescenza: **— age**, età dell'adolescenza, età dai 13 ai 19 anni.

teen-age *agg.* caratteristico dell'adolescenza; da adolescente.

teen-ager *n.* adolescente; giovanetto; fanciulla.

teens (tēnz) *n.pl.* età dai 13 ai 19 anni: to be in one's **—**, avere fra i 13 e 19 anni, essere adolescente.

teeny (tēn'ĭ) *agg.* minuscolo.

teeth (tēth) *pl. di* tooth: by the skin of one's **—**, per il rotto della cuffia; in the **—** of, a dispetto di.

teethe (tēth) *vi.* mettere i denti.

teething *n.* dentizione.

teetotal (tē·tō't'l) *agg.* astemio.

teevee (tē'vē') *n.* televisione, TV.

telecast (tĕl'ē·kàst') *n.* trasmissione televisiva. *vt.* teletrasmettere, trasmettere per televisione.

telegenic (tĕl'ē·jĕn'ĭk) *agg.* telegenico.

telegram (tĕl'ē·grăm) *n.* telegramma.

telegraph (tĕl'ē·grăf) *n.* telegrafo. *vt., vi.* telegrafare.

telegraphic *agg.* telegrafico.

telegraphy (tē·lĕg'rå·fĭ) *n.* telegrafia.

telemeter (tē·lĕm'ē·tĕr) *n.* telemetro.

telepathy (tē·lĕp'å·thĭ) *n.* telepatia.

telephone (tĕl'ē·fōn) *n.* telefono: **— booth**, cabina telefonica; **— directory**, guida telefonica; **— exchange**, centralino telefonico; **— operator**, telefonista. *vt., vi.* telefonare.

teleprinter (tĕl'ē·prĭn'tĕr) *n.* telescrivente.

telescope (tĕl'ē·skōp) *n.* telescopio; cannocchiale. *vi.* (*di oggetti*) infilarsi uno nell'altro.

teletype (tĕl'ê·típ) *n.* telescrivente.
teleview (tĕl'ê·vū') *vt.* vedere al televisore. —er *n.* telespettatore.
television (tĕl'ê·vĭzh'ŭn) *n.* televisione:
— set, televisore.
tell (tĕl) *vt.* (*pass.*, *pp.* told) dire, rac-
contrare; indicare, denotare, rive-
lare; distinguere, giudicare. *vi.* parlare; essere efficace; fare effetto:
the hard work told on him, lo strenuo lavoro lo ha logorato; to — one
from the other, distinguere l'uno
dall'altro; to — somebody off, cantarle chiare a qualcuno.
teller (tĕl'ẽr) *n.* narratore; computista, cassiere; (*pol.*) scrutatore.
telling (tĕl'ĭng) *agg.* efficace.
telltale (tĕl'tāl) *n.* informatore. *agg.*
significativo, rivelatore.
telpher (tĕl'fẽr) *n.* teleferica.
temerity (tê·mĕr'ĭ·tĭ) *n.* temerità.
temper (tĕm'pẽr) *n.* umore, indole;
malumore, collera; tempera; tempra (*di metallo*): in a good —, di
buon umore; out of —, fuori dei
gangheri; to keep one's —, dominarsi; to lose one's —, perdere
la pazienza. *vt.* temperare, temprare, attenuare.
temperament(tĕm'pẽr·à·mĕnt) *n.* temperamento, personalità. —al *agg.*
eccitabile, emotivo; collerico.
temperance (tĕm'pẽr·ăns) *n.* temperanza.
temperate (tĕm'pẽr·ĭt) *agg.* tempe-
rato; temperante, moderato.
temperature (tĕm'pẽr·à·tûr) *n.* temperatura; febbre.
tempest (tĕm'pĕst) *n.* tempesta, uragano.
tempestuous (tĕm·pĕs'tū·ŭs) *agg.* tempestoso; turbolento.
temple (tĕm'p'l) (1) *n.* tempio.
temple (tĕm'p'l) (2) *n.* (*anat.*) tempia.
temporal (tĕm'pō·rắl) *agg.* temporale.
temporarily (tĕm'pō·rẽr'ĭ·lĭ) *avv.* tem-
poraneamente, provvisoriamente.
temporary (tĕm'pō·rẽr'ĭ) *agg.* provvisorio, temporaneo, momentaneo.
tempt (tĕmpt) *vt.* allettare, tentare,
provocare, indurre. —ation (-ā'-
shŭn) *n.* tentazione. —er *n.* tentatore. —ing *agg.* allettante. —ress
n. tentatrice.
ten (tĕn) *n.*, *agg.* dieci.
tenable (tĕn'à·b'l) *agg.* sostenibile,
resistente.
tenacious (tê·nā'shŭs) *agg.* tenace;
adesivo.
tenacity (tê·năs'ĭ·tĭ) *n.* tenacia; adesi-
vità.
tenancy (tĕn'ăn·sĭ) *n.* locazione.
tenant (tĕn'ănt) *n.* locatario, inquilino.
tench (tĕnch) *n.* (*ittiol.*) tinca.

tend (tĕnd) *vt.* curare, vegliare su,
badare a, servire; custodire. *vi.*
tendere (*avere tendenza*).
tendency (tĕn'dĕn·sĭ) *n.* tendenza.
tendentious (tĕn·dĕn'shŭs) *agg.* tendenzioso, capzioso, interessato: —
writings, scritti tendenziosi, interessati, partigiani.
tender (tĕn'dẽr) (1) *n.* offerta, proposta. *vt.* offrire, porgere.
tender (tĕn'dẽr) (2) *n.* custode, servitore; (*naut.*) nave ausiliaria; scialuppa a rimorchio; (*ferr.*) tender,
carro scorta.
tender (tĕn'dẽr) (3) *agg.* tenero, sensibile, delicato, debole, immaturo,
affettuoso: —hearted *agg.* sensibile, di cuore tenero.
tenderloin (tĕn'dẽr·loin') *n.* filetto.
tenderness (tĕn'dẽr·nĕs) *n.* tenerezza,
delicatezza, morbidezza.
tendon (tĕn'dŭn) *n.* (*anat.*) tendine.
tendril (tĕn'drĭl) *n.* (*bot.*) viticcio.
tenement (tĕn'ê·mĕnt) *n.* abitazione,
possesso, casa d'affitto: — house,
casa popolare.
tenet (tĕn'ĕt) *n.* principio, precetto,
canone, dogma.
tenfold (tĕn'fōld') *agg.* decuplo. *avv.*
dieci volte tanto.
tennis (tĕn'ĭs) *n.* tennis: — court,
campo da tennis.
tenon (tĕn'ŭn) *n.* incastro.
tenor (tĕn'ẽr) *n.* tenore; tono, livello.
tenpins (tĕn'pĭnz') *n.* giuoco dei birilli.
tense (tĕns) *n.* tempo (*del verbo*). *agg.*
teso, contrario, rigido.
tension (tĕn'shŭn) *n.* tensione.
tent (tĕnt) *n.* tenda. *vt.* (*chir.*) sondare.
vi. attendarsi.
tentacle (tĕn'tá·k'l) *n.* tentacolo.
tentative (tĕn'tá·tĭv) *agg.* di prova, di
sondaggio, sperimentale. —ly *avv.*
sperimentalmente, a titolo di indagine, per tastare il terreno.
tenter (tĕn'tẽr) *n.* tenditoio.
tenterhook (-hŏŏk') *n.* uncino di tenditoio: on tenterhooks, sulle spine.
tenth (tĕnth) *n.*, *agg.* decimo.
tenuous (tĕn'ū·ŭs) *agg.* tenue.
tenure (tĕn'ûr) *n.* gestione, occupazione; periodo (*di carica, ecc.*).
tepid (tĕp'ĭd) *agg.* tiepido.
term (tûrm) *n.* termine, durata, limite
(*di tempo*), periodo, sessione; pl.
trattative, condizioni, prezzi: on
good terms, in buoni rapporti; to
come to terms, venire a patti. *vt.*
definire, nominare.
termagant (tûr'má·gănt) *n.* megera.
terminal (tûr'mĭ·nắl) *n.* estremità,
limite; (*elett.*) collegamento, innesto; stazione di testa, capolinea,
agg. terminale, finale, confinario.

terminate (tûr′mĭ·nāt) *vt.*, *vi.* terminare, delimitare, concludere.

termination (tur′mĭ·nā′shŭn) *n.* termine, conclusione; desinenza.

terminology (tûr′mĭ·nŏl′ō·jĭ) *n.* terminologia.

terminus (tûr′mĭ·nŭs) *n.* limite, confine; scalo, stazione di testa, capolinea.

terrace (tĕr′ĭs) *n.* terrazza, altura, terrapieno. *vt.* terrazzare.

terrapin (tĕr′á·pĭn) *n.* tartaruga acquatica.

terrestrial (tĕr·ĕs′trĭ·ăl) *agg.* terrestre, terragno.

terrible (tĕr′ĭ·b'l) *agg.* terribile, atroce; formidabile.

terribly (tĕr′ĭ·blĭ) *avv.* terribilmente; estremamente, straordinariamente.

terrier (tĕr′ĭ·ĕr) *n.* cane terrier.

terrific (tĕ·rĭf′ĭk) *agg.* terribile; fenomenale, sbalorditivo, vertiginoso.

terrify (tĕr′ĭ·fī) *vt.* atterrire.

territory (tĕr′ĭ·tō′rĭ) *n.* territorio.

terror (tĕr′ĕr) *n.* terrore.

terrorism (tĕr′ĕr·ĭz'm) *n.* intimidazione, terrorismo.

terrorist (tĕr′ĕr·ĭst) *n.* terrorista.

terrorize (tĕr′ĕr·īz) *vt.* terrorizzare.

terse (tûrs) *agg.* terso, chiaro; conciso, elegante.

tessellate (tĕs′ĕ·lāt) *vt.* lavorare a mosaico, tessellare.

test (tĕst) *n.* prova, saggio, collaudo, esperimento, esame, test: — tube, provetta; to undergo a —, essere sottoposto a una prova; — pilot, pilota collaudatore. *vt.* esaminare, collaudare, mettere alla prova, analizzare.

testament (tĕs′tá·mĕnt) *n.* testamento.

testator (tĕs·tā′tĕr) *n.* testatore.

tester (tĕs′tĕr) (1) *n.* sperimentatore, collaudatore.

tester (tĕs′tĕr) (2) *n.* baldacchino.

testify (tĕs′tĭ·fī) *vt.*, *vi.* testimoniare, attestare.

testimonial (tĕs′tĭ·mō′nĭ·ăl) *n.* attestato.

testimony (tĕs′tĭ·mō·nĭ) *n.* testimonianza.

testiness (tĕs) *n.* petulanza.

testy (tĕs′tĭ) *agg.* petulante, stizzoso.

tetanus (tĕt′á·nŭs) *n.* (*med.*) tetano.

tether (tĕth′ĕr) *n.* catena, cavezza, limite, risorse: the end of one's —, allo stremo delle proprie risorse. *vt.* legare con la cavezza.

text (tĕkst) *n.* testo: — edition, edizione normale o corrente.

textbook (tĕkst′bŏŏk′) *n.* libro di testo.

textile (tĕks′tĭl) *n.* tessuto, fibra tessile. *agg.* tessile: — mill, fabbrica di tessuti.

texture (tĕks′tū̆r) *n.* tessitura; struttura, trama, grana.

than (thăn) *cong.* che, di, che non, di quello che, di quanto: older — I am, più vecchio di me; less — a hundred, meno di cento; rather —, piuttosto di: more — once, più d'una volta; more — he knows, più di quanto egli non sappia.

thank (thăngk) *vt.* ringraziare: — God, grazie a Dio; I will — you to explain, abbiate la compiacenza di spiegare; thanks, grazie, ringraziamenti; — you! grazie!

thankful *agg.* riconoscente. —ly *avv.* con riconoscenza. —ness *n.* riconoscenza.

thankless *agg.* ingrato; non apprezzato. —ness *n.* ingratitudine.

thanksgiving (thăngks′gĭv·ĭng) *n.* ringraziamento, preghiera di ringraziamento: — Day, giorno del ringraziamento (*S.U.*, *l'ultimo giovedi di novembre*).

that (thăt) *agg.*, *pron. dimostrativo* (*pl.* those) quello, quella; ciò; lo: —'s right, è giusto, proprio così; — one, quello, quella. *pron.rel.* che, il quale, la quale, le quali, i quali. *cong.* che, se. *avv.* così, a tal segno, in tal modo (*o* misura), tanto: — is, cioè, ossia; — much, così, tanto; — far, così lontano, sino a quel punto; he was — weak he could not stand, era così debole da non potersi reggere; so —, sicchè, in modo da, affinchè.

thatch (thăch) *n.* paglia (*per tetti*); stoppie. *vt.* coprire di paglia: thatched roof, tetto di paglia o di stoppie.

thaw (thô) *n.* disgelo. *vt.*, *vi.* disgelare; ammansire, ammansirsi.

the (thē) *art.determ.* il, lo, gli, i, la, le: of —, del, della, dei, delle; to —, al, allo, agli, alle; from —, dal, dallo, dalla, dagli, dalle. *avv.* tanto: — more so, tanto più; — more I see it, — less I like it, quanto più lo vedo, tanto meno mi piace.

theater, **theatre** (thē′á·tĕr) *n.* teatro: — of war, teatro di guerra; arena —, teatro a pista centrale.

theatrical (thē·ăt′rĭ·kăl) *agg.* teatrale; istrionico; esagerato; melodrammatico.

theatricals *n.pl.* rappresentazioni di prosa (*spec. di filodrammatici*); pose teatrali.

thee (thē) *pron.pers.* te, ti.

theft (thĕft) *n.* furto.

their (thâr) *agg.* il loro, la loro, i loro, le loro.

theirs (thârz) *pron.poss.* il loro, la loro,

i loro, le loro: **a friend of —,** un
loro amico.

them (thĕm) *pron.pers.* essi, esse, loro,
li, quelli, quelle, coloro: **give me —
books** (*forma dialett.*), datemi quei
libri.

theme (thēm) *n.* tema, argomento;
(*radio, TV*) sigla.

themselves (thĕm·sĕlvz′) *pron.rifl.pl.*
essi stessi, esse stesse, se stessi, se
stesse, si, se, sè: **they wash —,** essi
si lavano; **by —,** da se stessi, da soli.

then (thĕn) *avv.* poi, in seguito, indi;
allora, in quell'epoca, in tal caso:
now and —, di tanto in tanto;
and there, seduta stante; **since —,**
dopo di allora, da quel tempo; **by
—,** a quell'ora, ormai; **now —!**
dunque, allora!; **well —!** bene,
allora! *cong.* dunque, perciò, cosic-
chè. *agg.* di allora, di quell'epoca:
the — president, il presidente di
allora.

thence (thĕns) *avv.* dopo d'allora, successivamente, da quel luogo, di là,
donde, perciò.

thenceforth (thĕns′fôrth′), **thencefor-
ward** (thĕns′fôr′wĕrd) *avv.* d'allora
in poi, in seguito.

theologian (thē′ō·lō′jǐ·ăn) *n.* teologo.

theological (thē′ō·lŏj′ǐ·kăl) *agg.* teo-
logico.

theology (thē·ŏl′ō·jǐ) *n.* teologia.

theorem (thē′ō·rĕm), *n.* teorema.

theoretical (thē′ō·rĕt′ǐ·kăl) *agg.* teorico, ipotetico.

theory (thē′ō·rǐ) *n.* ipotesi, teoria.

therapeutic (thĕr′à·pū′tǐk) *agg.* tera-
peutico.

therapeutics (thĕr′à·pū′tǐks) *n.* tera-
peutica.

therapy (thĕr′à·pǐ) *n.* terapia.

there (thâr) *avv.* là, colà, vi, ci; ecco:
— is, c'è; **— are,** ci sono; **down —,**
laggiù; **here and —,** qua e là; **—
and then,** immediatamente; **— he
is,** eccolo là; **— you are!** ecco!,
ecco qua!; qui ti volevo!, visto?;
— are many people, c'è molta
gente.

thereabouts (thâr′à·bouts′) *avv.* là
intorno, nei dintorni; all'incirca.

thereafter (thâr·àf′tĕr) *avv.* dopo di
che, in seguito, da allora in poi.

thereat (thâr·ăt′) *avv.* al che, in quel
luogo, dopo di che.

thereby (thâr·bī′) *avv.* con ciò; all'incirca; in conseguenza di ciò; con
tale mezzo.

therefor (thâr·fôr′) *avv.* in cambio, a
causa di ciò, per cui.

therefore (thâr′fōr) *avv.* di conseguenza, quindi, per questo (*o* quello), perciò.

therein (thâr·ǐn′) *avv.* in questo (*o*
quel) luogo, entro quel lasso di
tempo, là dentro.

thereof (thâr·ŏv′) *avv.* di quello, di
ciò, da ciò.

thereon (thâr·ŏn′) *avv.* su quello, su
ciò, al che, successivamente.

thereupon (thâr′ǔ·pŏn′) *avv.* al che,
dopo di che, in seguito.

therewith (thâr·wǐth) *avv.* con ciò,
oltre a ciò.

therewithal (thâr′wǐth·ôl′) *avv.* per
soprammercato, per giunta.

thermal (thûr′măl) *agg.* termale.

thermometer (thĕr·mŏm′ê·tĕr) *n.* ter-
mometro.

thermonuclear (thûr′mō·nū′klê·ĕr)
agg. termonucleare.

Thermos (*marca*) **bottle** (thûr′mŏs) *n.*
termos.

thermostat (thûr′mō·stăt) *n.* ter-
mostato.

thesaurus (thē·sò′rŭs) *n.* lessico,
raccolta, compendio.

these (thēz) *pron.dimostrativo, agg.* (*pl.
di* this) questi, queste.

thesis (thē′sǐs) *n.* (*pl.* theses) tesi.

Thespian (thĕs′pǐ·ăn) *n.* attore drammatico *agg.* di Tespi, dram-
matico.

they (thā) *pron.pers.* essi, esse, coloro:
— say, si dice, dicono.

thick (thǐk) *n.* fitto, folto: **through —
and thin,** a dispetto di tutto; **in the
— of the fight,** nel folto della
mischia. *agg.* denso, spesso, folto,
fitto; grosso, massiccio; stupido;
confuso; (*fam.*) stretto, intimo: **as
— as thieves,** amici inseparabili.
—headed *agg.* stupido. **—skinned**
agg. coriaceo, insensibile. **—witted**
agg. tardo, ottuso; *avv. vedi* thickly.

thicken (thǐk′ĕn) *vt., vi.* inspessire,
aumentare, infittire; inspessirsi;
complicarsi.

thicket (thǐk′ĕt) *n.* boschetto, macchia.

thickly (thǐk′lǐ) *avv.* fittamente,
densamente; confusamente; strettamente.

thickness (thǐk′nĕs) *n.* spessore,
densità, consistenza; difficoltà (*di
pronunzia*); torbidezza.

thickset (thǐk′sĕt′) *agg.* massiccio,
tarchiato.

thief (thēf) *n.* (*pl.* thieves) ladro.

thieve (thēv) *vt., vi.* rubare.

thigh (thī) *n.* (*anat.*) coscia: **— bone,**
femore.

thimble (thǐm′b'l) *n.* ditale.

thin (thǐn) *agg.* magro, sottile; rado;
leggiero, inconsistente; smilzo, scarso; debole, rarefatto; trasparente:
— broth, brodo leggiero, brodino;
— hair, capelli radi. *vt.* assotti-

gliare, dimagrare, ridurre; diradare, rarefare. *vi.* dimagrire, assottigliarsi, diradarsi, rarefarsi.

thine (thīn) *pron.poss.* il tuo, la tua, i tuoi, le tue.

thing (thǐng) *n.* cosa; faccenda: **not a — to eat**, niente da mangiare; **the things of the mind**, le qualità spirituali *o* morali; **the —s of the body**, le necessità del corpo; **of all —s!** incredibile!, inaudito! **poor —!** povera creatura! **taking one — with another**, tutto considerato; **for one —**, innanzi tutto; **the very — for me**, proprio quel che mi ci vuole; **to be quite the —**, essere molto di moda; **to feel quite the —**, sentirsi bene.

think (thǐngk) *vt.*, *vi.* (*pass.*, *pp.* thought) pensare; credere; immaginare; giudicare; supporre: **to — better of it**, cambiar parere; **to — nothing of**, non dar peso a; **to — of**, pensare a, pensare di; **to — up an excuse**, inventare *o* trovare una scusa; **to my way of thinking**, a mio modo di vedere, secondo me.

thinker *n.* pensatore.

thinking *n.* pensiero: **to my —**, secondo me. *agg.* pensante, ragionante.

thinly (thǐn'lǐ) *avv.* scarsamente, radamente; leggermente.

thinness (thǐn'něs) *n.* sottigliezza, magrezza; trasparenza, inconsistenza.

third (thûrd) *n.*, *agg.* terzo: **—rate** *agg.* di terz'ordine.

thirst (thûrst) *n.* sete, brama. *vi.* aver sete: **to — for, after**, bramare.

thirsty (thûrs'tǐ) *agg.* assetato: **to be —**, aver sete.

thirteen (thûr'tēn') *n.*, *agg.* tredici.

thirteenth (thûr'tēnth') *agg.* tredicesimo.

thirtieth (thûr'tǐ.ěth) *agg.* trentesimo.

thirty (thûr'tǐ) *n.*, *agg.* trenta.

this (thǐs) *agg.*, *pron.* (*pl.* these) questo, questa: **like —**, così; **by — time**, a quest'ora, ormai.

thistle (thǐs'l) *n.* (*bot.*) cardo.

thither (thǐth'ẽr) *avv.* .là, da quella parte, a quella volta.

tho *vedi* though.

thole (thōl) *n.* (*naut.*) scalmo.

thong (thǒng) *n.* correggia, striscia di cuoio.

thorax (thō'rǎks) *n.* (*anat.*) torace.

thorn (thôrn) *n.* spina, pruno; tormento.

thorny (thôr'nǐ) *agg.* spinoso.

thorough (thûr'ō) *agg.* intero, completo, perfetto, approfondito; meticoloso; radicale.

thoroughbred (thûr'ō·brěd') *n.* purosangue. *agg.* di pura razza, ben nato.

thoroughfare (thûr'ō·fâr') *n.* arteria stradale: **no —**, passaggio vietato.

thoroughly (thûr'ō·lǐ) *avv.* completamente, fino in fondo; radicalmente, minuziosamente.

those (thōz) *agg.*, *pron.* (*pl. di* that) quei, quegli, quelli, coloro, quelle: **— who, — which**, quelli che, quelle che.

thou (thou) *pron.pers.* tu.

though (thō) *cong.* benchè, anche se, quantunque, però, nonostante. *avv.* tuttavia, ciononostante: **as —**, come se; **even —**, ancorchè, quand'anche, anche se.

thought (thôt) (1) *pass.*, *pp. di* to think.

thought (thôt) (2) *n.* pensiero, idea, ispirazione, opinione, concetto, intenzione: **on second —**, ripensandoci; **lost in —**, assorto, sopprappensiero.

thoughtful *agg.* pensieroso; riflessivo; premuroso; previdente. **—ly** *avv.* pensosamente; premurosamente, previdentemente. **—ness** *n.* attenzione, sollecitudine, previdenza; raccoglimento.

thoughtless *agg.* irriflessivo, sbadato, trascurato. **—ly** *avv.* sbadatamente; spensieratamente; trascuratamente. **—ness** *n.* spensieratezza; sbadataggine, trascuratezza, negligenza.

thousand (thou'zǎnd) *n.*, *agg.* mille: **by the —**, al mille; **by thousands**, a migliaia.

thrall (thrô) *n.* schiavo; schiavitù.

thrash (thrǎsh) *vt.*, *vi.* trebbiare (grano, *ecc.*); bastonare, malmenare: **to —out**, dibattere, sceverare. **—er** *n.* trebbiatore.

thread (thrěd) *n.* filo, filetto (anche di vite); filamento, vena. *vt.*, *vi.* infilare; filettare; aprirsi un varco, procedere a fatica, serpeggiare; (cucina) filare.

threadbare (thrěd'bâr') *agg.* spelato, logoro, liso; misero.

threat (thrět) *n.* minaccia.

threaten (thrět''n) *vt.*, *vi.* minacciare.

threatening *agg.* minaccioso, incombente.

three (thrē) *n.*, *agg.* tre.

three-dimensional *agg.* tridimensionale.

thresh (thrěsh) *vedi* to thrash.

threshold (thrěsh'ōld) *n.* soglia, limitare.

threw (thrōō) *pass. di* to throw.

thrice (thrīs) *avv.* tre volte.

thrift (thrǐft) *n.* risparmio; frugalità.

thrifty *agg.* economo, frugale; prospe-roso.

thrill (thrĭl) *n.* fremito, brivido, emo-zione. *vt.* far fremere, elettrizzare, procurare un'emozione a. *vi.* fre-mere, emozionarsi, commuoversi, eccitarsi.

thriller (thrĭl'ĕr) *n.* racconto *o* ro-manzo *o* dramma del brivido.

thrilling (thrĭl'ĭng) *agg.* emozionante, elettrizzante, eccitante.

thrive (thrĭv) *vi.* (*pass.* throve, *pp.* thriven) prosperare.

thriving *agg.* fiorente, prosperoso.

throat (thrōt) *n.* gola: to have a sore —, avere il mal di gola.

throaty *agg.* gutturale.

throb (thrŏb) *n.* battito, palpito, pulsazione. *vi.* battere, pulsare, palpitare. —bing *agg.* pulsante.

throe (thrō) *n.* angoscia; travaglio, doglie; agonia.

throne (thrōn) *n.* trono.

throng (thrŏng) *n.* moltitudine, folla. *vt.* affollare, stipare. *vi.* affollarsi.

throttle (thrŏt''l) *n.* trachea, gola; (*mecc.*) valvola a farfalla, ac-celeratore. *vt.* strangolare, sof-focare; (*mecc.*) strozzare: to — down, rallentare, diminuire la velocità.

through (thrōō) *agg.* completo; diret-to, continuo; finito: — train, treno diretto, direttissimo: — ticket, biglietto per treno diretto. *prep.* durante, attraverso, per, fra, in mezzo a; per mezzo di, mediante; a causa di. *avv.* da parte a parte; fino in fondo, dal principio alla fine; a buon fine; completamente: to be — with, non aver più nulla a che fare con; wet —, bagnato fradicio; to carry —, attuare, eseguire, portare a compimento; to fall —, far fiasco, andare a monte.

throughout (thrōō-out') *prep.* in ogni punto di; durante; dal principio alla fine di. *avv.* da ogni parte; a ogni momento; completamente.

throve (thrōv) *pass. di* to thrive.

throw (thrō) *n.* lancio, colpo, tiro; portata. *vt.*, *vi.* (*pass.* threw, *pp.* thrown) gettare, scagliare; ritor-cere (*filati*) disarcionare; far girare; abbattere, travolgere: to — off, disfarsi di, rinunciare a; to — open, spalancare; to — about, dis-seminare, sparpagliare; sperperare; agitare (*le braccia*); to — away, buttar via; sprecare; to — down, buttare a terra, abbattere, rove-sciare; to — in, dare in aggiunta; buttare lì (*una frase*); arrendersi; to — in gear, ingranare (*una*

marcia); to — off, sbarazzarsi di, liberarsi di; rinunciare a; to — out, emettere, buttar fuori; respin-gere; aggiungere (*un'ala a un edificio*); distrarre, far perdere il filo; to — over, abbandonare; to — overboard, buttare a mare; to — up, issare, rinunziare a; vomitare.

throwaway (thrō'á-wā') *n.* (*S.U.*) volantino pubblicitario.

thrown (thrōn) *pp. di* to throw.

thrum (thrŭm) *vt.* *vi.* strimpellare.

thrush (thrŭsh) *n.* tordo.

thrust (thrŭst) *n.* colpo, urto, pres-sione; botta, stoccata; (*mecc.*) forza di propulsione. *vt.*, *vi.* (*pass.*, *pp.* thrust) spingere, sospingere, ficcare; imporre; trafiggere, colpi re; insinuarsi; dare una botta: to — away, respingere; to — in, inserire, cacciar dentro, introdurre di forza; to — something upon, imporre qualcosa a.

thud (thŭd) *n.* tonfo, colpo sordo. *vt.* colpire. *vi.* risonare sordamente.

thug (thŭg) *n.* brigante, furfante.

thumb (thŭm) *n.* dito pollice: under the — of, dominato da. *vt.* sporcare; sfogliare (*un libro*) alla svelta; chiedere un passaggio con l'auto-stop. *vi.* viaggiare con l'autostop.

thumbtack (thŭm'tăk') *n.* puntina da disegno.

thump (thŭmp) *n.* colpo, tonfo. *vt.* colpire (*o cadere*) con un tonfo; percuotere; bussare. *vi.* palpitare; camminare pesantemente.

thunder (thŭn'dĕr) *n.* tuono, uragano. *vt.*, *vi.* tuonare, minacciare: it thunders, tuona. —bolt *n.* fulmine. —clap *n.* colpo di tuono. —ing *agg.* tonante; (*fam.*) straordinario, enor-me. —ous *agg.* tonante, bur-rascoso. —storm *n.* temporale, uragano.

Thursday (thûrz'dĭ) *n.* giovedì.

thus (thŭs) *avv.* così, come segue, nel modo seguente, in questo (*o* quel) modo: — far, fin qui (*o* là); a tal segno; fino ad ora.

thwart (thwôrt) *vt.* attraversare; ostacolare, sventare, frustrare.

thy (t̸hī) *agg.poss.* tuo, tua, tuoi, tue.

thyme (tĭm) *n.* (*bot.*) timo.

thymus (thī'mŭs) *n.* (*anat.*) timo.

thyroid (thī'roid) *n.* (*anat.*) tiroide.

thyself (t̸hī·sĕlf') *pron.rifl.* te stesso (*o* stessa), tu stesso (*o* stessa).

tick (tĭk) *n.* ticchettio, tocco leg-giero; traliccio; puntino; segno della spunta; attimo; (*entom.*) zec-ca, acaro. *vt.*, *vi.* ticchettare, fare tictac, battere: to — off, spuntare, fare la spunta.

ticket (tĭk'ĕt) *n.* biglietto, tagliando, bolletta, scheda, cartellino; lista elettorale: **return** —, biglietto di andata e ritorno; **season** —, abbonamento; **mileage** —, biglietto circolare; **single** (*opp.* **one-way**) —, biglietto di corsa semplice; — **office**, biglietteria.

tickle (tĭk'l) *n.* solletico, titillamento. *vt.* solleticare, stuzzicare; lusingare; divertire. *vi.* sentire solletico: **to be** —**d to death**, essere lusingatissimo; divertirsi un mondo.

ticklish (tĭk'lĭsh) *agg.* sensibile al solletico; delicato, precario, difficile.

tidbit (tĭd'bĭt) *vedi* titbit.

tide (tīd) *n.* marea, flusso, corrente; tempo, stagione, epoca, periodo; corso, andamento; occasione, festa. *vt.*: **to** — **someone over a crisis**, aiutare qualcuno a superare una crisi.

tidings (tī'dĭngz) *n.pl.* novità, notizie.

tidy (tī'dĭ) *agg.* ordinato, lindo: **a** — **sum**, una buona sommetta. *vt.*, *vi.* riordinare, pulire, riassettare, riassettarsi.

tie (tī) *n.* nodo, vincolo, legame; cravatta; pareggio (*in gare, ecc.*); (*pol.*) parità di voti; (*ferr.*) traversina. *vt.*, *vi.* legare, allacciare, vincolare, annodare; pareggiare: **to** — **up**, avvolgere in pacco e legare; vincolare; bloccare, ostruire.

tier (tēr) *n.* ordine (*di posti a teatro*); fila, filare.

tiff (tĭf) *n.* stizza; bisticcio.

tiger (tī'gẽr) *n.* tigre: **American** —, giaguaro; **red** —, puma; — **cat**, gattopardo.

tight (tīt) *agg.* stretto; attillato; scarso; tirchio; difficile; teso; chiuso, ermetico, stagno; (*gergo*) alticcio: **to be in a** — **spot**, essere in grande imbarazzo. *avv.* strettamente; ermeticamente: **to sit** —, tener duro.

tighten (tīt''n) *vt.* stringere, restringere, serrare; tendere, tirare. *vi.* stringersi; tendersi.

tightness (tīt'nĕs) *n.* tensione, strettezza, aderenza; tirchieria.

tights (tīts) *n.pl.* maglia da palcoscenico, calzamaglia.

tigress (tī'grĕs) *n.* tigre (*femmina*).

tile (tīl) *n.* tegola, embrice; piastrella; *vt.* coprire di tegole, piastrellare.

till (tĭl) (1) *prep.* fino a. *cong.* finchè.

till (tĭl) (2) *n.* cassetto del danaro, cassa (*di negozio*).

till (tĭl) (3) *vt.*, *vi.* arare, coltivare.

tillage (tĭl'ĭj) *n.* coltivazione, aratura.

tiller (tĭl'ẽr) *n.* agricoltore; (*naut.*) barra del timone.

tilt (tĭlt) *n.* inclinazione, pendio; contesa, disputa. *vt.* inclinare, far pendere. *vi.* pendere, inclinarsi; capovolgersi.

timber (tĭm'bẽr) *n.* legname da costruzione; bosco; trave, tronco; (*naut.*) costola.

time (tīm) *n.* tempo; orario; ora, momento; epoca; ritmo; volta (*occasione*): **at most** —**s**, generalmente; **as** — **s go**, coi tempi che corrono; **to have a wonderful** —, spassarsela; **against** —, a ritmo accelerato; **at** —**s**, ogni tanto, certe volte; **behind** —, in ritardo; **from** — **to** —, di tanto in tanto; **in no** —, in quattro e quatt'otto, all'istante; **in** —, in tempo; col tempo, a suo tempo; a tempo (*mus.*); **on** —, puntualmente, in orario; **al momento giusto**; **out of** —, troppo presto; troppo tardi; **for the** — **being**, per il momento; — **and again**, ripetutamente; **what** — **is it?** che ora è? *vt.* regolare, far coincidere; cronometrare; fissare l'ora (*o* la durata) di; scegliere il momento per; sincronizzare.

timeliness (tīm'lĭ·nĕs) *n.* opportunità, tempestività.

timely (tīm'lĭ) *agg.* opportuno, tempestivo. *avv.* opportunamente, tempestivamente.

timepiece (tīm'pēs) *n.* orologio.

timetable (tīm'tā'b'l) *n.* orario.

timid (tĭm'ĭd) *agg.* timido, timoroso.

timidity (tĭ·mĭd'ĭ·tĭ) *n.* timidezza.

timing (tīm'ĭng) *n.* sincronizzazione, calcolo dei tempi; ritmo.

timorous (tĭm'ẽr·ŭs) *agg.* timoroso.

tin (tĭn) *n.* stagno (*metallo*); latta, barattolo di latta; *agg.* di stagno, di latta: — **foil**, foglio di stagno (*o* latta); — **plate**, latta stagnata. *vt.* stagnare; mettere in scatola (*conserve*).

tincture (tĭngk'tûr) *n.* tintura; tinta; traccia. *vt.* tingere; mescolare.

tinder (tĭn'dẽr) *n.* acciarino, esca.

tinge (tĭnj) *n.* tinteggiatura; sapore; parvenza, pizzico; pizzico. *vt.* tinteggiare: **to** — **with**, dare una sfumatura di.

tingle (tĭng'g'l) *n.* formicolio; puntura; *vt.* punzecchiare. *vi.* fremere, formicolare.

tinker (tĭngk'ẽr) *vt.*, *vi.* rattoppare; abborracciare.

tinkle (tĭng'k'l) *n.* tintinnio. *vi.* tintinnare.

tinsel (tĭn'sĕl) *n.* orpello. *agg.* falso; vistoso.

tinsmith (tĭn'smĭth') *n.* lattonaio.

tint (tĭnt) *n.* tinta; sfumatura, tratteggio. *vt.* colorire; sfumare, tratteggiare.

tiny (tī'nĭ) *agg.* minuscolo.

tip (tĭp) *n.* punta, cima, apice; puntale; (*fam.*) mancia; informazione confidenziale, consiglio. *vt., vi.* appuntire; dare la mancia a; dare un consiglio (*o* un'informazione) a; inclinare. *vi.* inclinarsi; ribaltarsi, capovolgersi: to — off, mettere al corrente, avvertire: to — one's hat, toccarsi il cappello.

tipple (tĭp'l) *vt., vi.* bere all'eccesso; sorseggiare.

tipsy (tĭp'sĭ) *agg.* ubriaco; instabile.

tiptoe (tĭp'tō') *n.* punta dei piedi: on —, in punta di piedi. *vi.* camminare in punta di piedi.

tire (tīr) (1) *n.* pneumatico (*di ruota*); cerchione. *vt.* munire di pneumatici (*o* cerchioni).

tire (tīr) (2) *vt.* stancare, annoiare. *vi.* stancarsi, annoiarsi.

tired (tīrd) *agg.* stanco; annoiato: — out, esausto, sfinito.

tiredness (tīrd'nĕs) *n.* stanchezza.

tireless (tīr'lĕs) *agg.* instancabile.

tiresome (tīr'sŭm) *agg.* faticoso; noioso.

tissue (tĭsh'ū) *n.* tessuto: — paper, carta velina, tovagliolino di carta (*per cremesi*)

titbit (tĭt'bĭt') *n.* bocconcino prelibato, leccornia; notiziola prelibata.

tithe (tĭth) *n.* decima.

title (tī't'l) *n.* titolo: — page, frontespizio. *vt.* intitolare.

titmouse (tĭt'mous') *n.* cincia.

titter (tĭt'ĕr) *n.* risolino. *vi.* ridacchiare.

tittle (tĭt''l) *n.* particella, iota.

tittle-tattle (tĭt''l-tăt''l) *n.* pettegolezzi, chiacchiere.

to (tōō; tōŏ) *prep.* a, al, alla, alle, agli; per, al fine di; verso in, nel, nello, nella, negli, nelle; fino a; a paragone di: a quarter — four, le quattro meno un quarto; — my surprise, con mio stupore; — ten — one, con dieci probabilità contro una; — this day, fino ad oggi, ancor oggi; from house — house, di casa in casa; you have — go, devi andare. *avv.* accosto, addosso: to come —, rinvenire (*riprendere i sensi*); to push the door —, accostare la porta; — and fro, avanti e indietro.

toad (tōd) *n.* (*zool.*) rospo.

toadstool (tōd'stōōl') *n.* fungo velenoso.

toady (tōd'ĭ) *n.* parassita; piaggiatore, adulatore. *agg.* orribile, repellente.

toast (tōst) *n.* crostino, pane abbrustolito; brindisi. *vt.* abbrustolire; brindare a. *vi.* abbrustolirsi. —er *n.* chi brinda; tostatore, tostino.

tobacco (tṓ·băk'ṓ) *n.* (*bot.*) tabacco.

tobacconist (tṓ·băk'ṓ·nĭst) *n.* tabaccaio.

toboggan (tṓ·bŏg'ăn) *n.* toboga.

tocsin (tŏk'sĭn) *n.* segnale d'allarme; campana a martello.

today (tṓŏ·dā') *avv.* oggi, oggigiorno.

toddle (tŏd''l) *vi.* vacillare.

to-do (tṓŏ·dōō) *n.* trambusto, tumulto.

toe (tō) *n.* dito del piede; punta (*di piede, calza o scarpa*). *vt.* toccare (*o* smuovere) con la punta del piede: to — in, camminare con i piedi in dentro.

toenail (tō'nāl') *n.* unghia del piede.

together (tṓŏ·gĕth'ĕr) *avv.* insieme, unitamente; a raccolta; contemporaneamente; — with, insieme con; all —, tutti insieme; to bring —, mettere a contatto, riunire.

togs (tŏgz) *n.pl.* indumenti.

toil (toil) *n.* fatica, lavoro; pena, travaglio, lotta. *vi.* faticare, affannarsi.

toilet (toi'lĕt) *n.* toletta, gabinetto di decenza: — paper, carta igienica.

toilsome (toil'sŭm) *agg.* penoso, faticoso, gravoso.

token (tō'kĕn) *n.* segno, pegno; indizio; ricordo; gettone, contrassegno. *agg.* simbolico, nominale: — payment, pagamento simbolico.

told (tōld) *pass., pp. di* to tell.

tolerance (tŏl'ĕr·ăns) *n.* tolleranza.

tolerant (tŏl'ĕr·ănt) *agg.* tollerante.

tolerate (tŏl'ĕr·āt) *vt.* tollerare, sopportare.

toleration (tŏl'ĕr·ā'shŭn) *n.* tolleranza.

toll (tōl) (1) *n.* rintocco. *vt.* sonare (*le campane*). *vi.* rintoccare.

toll (tōl) (2) *n.* tributo, pedaggio: — bridge, ponte a pedaggio; — call (*S.U.*), telefonata interurbana; — gate, barriera di pedaggio; — line, linea interurbana; — road, strada a pedaggio.

tomato (tṓ·mā'tō) *n.* (*bot.*) pomodoro.

tomb (tōōm) *n.* tomba.

tomboy (tŏm'boi') *n.* maschietta, sbarazzina, maschiaccio (*detto di bambina*).

tombstone (tōōm'stōn') *n.* lapide sepolcrale.

tomcat (tŏm'kăt') *n.* gatto (*maschio*).

tome (tōm) *n.* tomo, volume.

tommy (tŏm'ĭ) *n.* pagnotta; soldato inglese: — gun, fucile mitragliatore, mitra.

tomorrow (tṓŏ·mŏr'ṓ) *n., avv.* domani: — morning, domani mattina; —

night, domani sera *o* notte; **the day after** —, dopodomani; — **week** (*Ingl.*) domani a otto.

ton (tŭn) *n.* tonnellata.

tone (tōn) *n.* tono, accento, timbro. *vt.* intonare; colorire; modificare il tono di. *vi.* intonarsi, armonizzare; (*fot.*) sottoporre a viraggio: **to — down**, smorzare, attenuare; **to — up**, accentuare, rinforzarsi.

tongs (tŏngz) *n.pl.* pinze, molle.

tongue (tŭng) *n.* lingua, linguaggio; linguetta; adiglione (*di fibbia*); timone (*di carro*); ancia (*di strumento a fiato*); ago (*di scambio ferr.*): **—tied** *agg.* impacciato (*nell'eloquio*), ammutolito.

tonic (tŏn'ĭk) *n.* tonico; acqua gasata. *agg.* tonico.

tonight (tŏō·nīt') *avv.* questa sera; questa notte.

tonnage (tŭn'ĭj) *n.* tonnellaggio.

tonneau (tŭn·ō') *n.* (*auto*) compartimento posteriore con sedile.

tonsil (tŏn'sĭl) *n.* tonsilla.

too *avv.* anche, inoltre, per giunta; troppo, di troppo: **he will come —**, verrà anche lui; — **much**, troppo; — **many**, troppi; **one — many**, uno di troppo; **you were none —** early, sei arrivato appena appena in tempo; **you are really — kind!** molto gentile da parte vostra! **I shall be only — glad to**, sarò lietissimo di; **that's — bad!** che peccato! **mi rincresce tanto! to go — far**, esagerare, eccedere.

took (tŏōk) *pass. di* to take.

tool (tŏōl) *n.* utensile, attrezzo, strumento.

toot (tŏōt) *n.* squillo; fischio; suono di tromba; urlo (*di sirena*). *vt., vi.* sonare, strombettare.

tooth (tŏōth) *n.* (*pl.* teeth) dente: **to fight — and nail**, lottare con tutte le proprie forze; **to have a sweet —**, essere goloso di cose dolci. **—ache** *n.* odontalgia, mal di denti. **—brush** *n.* spazzolino da denti. **—less** *agg.* sdentato. **—paste** *n.* dentifricio. **—pick** *n.* stuzzicadenti. **—some** *agg.* gustoso, buono, saporito, appetitoso.

top (tŏp) *n.* cima, sommità; estremità; coperchio; colmo, apice, cocuzzolo; testa; trottola; superficie; imperiale (*di autobus*); (*naut.*) coffa: **to be at the — of**, essere il primo di; **at the — of one's voice**, a squarciagola; **filled up to the —**, pieno sino all'orlo; **from — to bottom**, da cima a fondo; **from — to toe**, da capo a piedi. *agg.* superiore, primo; massimo; sommo; princi-

pale; estremo: — **hat**, cappello a cilindro; — **speed**, velocità massima; — **secret**, segreto assoluto. *vt.* sovrastare; coprire; coronare; sormontare; sorpassare; completare; cimare. *vi.* elevarsi, eccellere.

topcoat (tŏp'kōt') *n.* soprabito.

topflight (tŏp'flīt') *agg.* di altissimo grado; eminente; massimo.

topmast (tŏp'màst') *n.* (*naut.*) albero di gabbia.

topmost (tŏp'mōst) *agg.* (*il*) più in alto.

topee (tō·pē') *n.* casco coloniale.

toper (tōp'ẽr) *n.* ubriacone.

topic (tŏp'ĭk) *n.* argomento, tema.

topical (tŏp'ĭ·kǎl) *agg.* attuale, di attualità; pertinente.

topography (tō·pŏg'rả·fĭ) *n.* topografia.

topper (tŏp'ẽr) *n.* cimatore (*di piante*); smoccolatoio; baro (*ai dadi*); casacchino da donna; (*gergo*) coperchio, strato superiore, cappa; campione, fuoriclasse.

topping (tŏp'ĭng) *agg.* (*gergo*) superiore, eccellente.

topple (tŏp''l) *vt., vi.* ribaltare.

topsail (tŏp'sāl') *n.* vela di gabbia.

topsy-turvy (tŏp'sĭ·tûr'vĭ) *n.* scompiglio. *agg.* capovolto, sovvertito. *avv.* sottosopra.

torch (tôrch) *n.* torcia, fiaccola.

tore (tōr) *pass. di* to tear.

torment (tôr'měnt) *n.* tormento, supplizio. *vt.* (tôr·měnt') tormentare.

tormentor (tôr·měn'tẽr) *n.* tormentatore; (*teat.*) quinta.

torn (tôrn) *pp. di* to tear.

tornado (tôr·nā'dō) *n.* uragano, ciclone.

torpedo (tôr·pē'dō) *n.* siluro, torpedine: — **boat**, torpediniera; — **boat destroyer**, cacciatorpediniere. *vt.* silurare.

torpid (tôr'pĭd) *agg.* torpido, inerte.

torpor (tôr'pẽr) *n.* torpore, inerzia.

torrent (tôr'ĕnt) *n.* torrente. *agg.* torrenziale, impetuoso.

torrid (tôr'ĭd) *agg.* torrido.

torsion (tôr'shŭn) *n.* torsione.

tortoise (tôr'tŭs) *n.* tartaruga.

tortuous (tôr'tū·ŭs) *agg.* tortuoso.

torture (tôr'tûr) *n.* tortura, tormento. *vt.* torturare, tormentare.

toss (tŏs) *n.* lancio, colpo, scossa, moto brusco; beccheggio. *vt.* gettare, lanciare, sballottare, scuotere; alzare bruscamente; esaminare. *vi.* agitarsi, rivoltolarsi, slanciarsi, dimenarsi; becheggiare: **to — off**, tracannare; **to — up**, giocare a testa o croce.

tot (tŏt) *n.* bimbo; bicchierino.

total (tō'tăl) *n.*, *agg.* totale.

totalitarian (tō·tăl'ĭ·târ'ĭ·ăn) *agg.* totalitario. **—ism** *n.* totalitarismo.

tote (tōt) *vt.* (*S.U.*) portare, trasportare.

totter (tŏt'ẽr) *vi.* vacillare, traballare, barcollare.

touch (tŭch) *n.* tocco, tatto; contatto; leggiero attacco; sfumatura, pizzico; to keep in — with, mantenersi in comunicazione con; a — of fever, un po' di febbre; a — of the sun, una lieve insolazione. *vt.* toccare, sfiorare, raggiungere; concernere; commuovere; maneggiare. *vi.* combaciare, toccarsi, essere a contatto: to — at, fare scalo a; to — on, upon, accennare a, fare allusione a; to — off, accendere la miccia di (*un cannone*); (*fig.*) far esplodere.

touch-and-go *n.* situazione precaria o delicata. *agg.* precario, rischioso; incerto.

touchiness (tŭch'ĭ·nĕs) *n.* suscettibilità.

touching (tŭch'ĭng) *agg.* commovente. *prep.* riguardo a.

touchstone (tŭch'stōn') *n.* pietra di paragone.

touchwood (tŭch'wōōd') *n.* esca; persona irascibile.

touchy (tŭch'ĭ) *agg.* permaloso, suscettibile.

tough (tŭf) *n.* (*gergo*) furfante; violento. *agg.* duro, coriaceo, resistente, tenace, inflessibile, ostinato; violento; coercitivo, minaccioso; difficile: a — customer, un tipaccio; — policy, politica di forza.

toughen (tŭf'ĕn) *vt.* indurire. *vi.* indurirsi.

toughness (tŭf'nĕs) *n.* durezza, tenacia; difficoltà; ostinazione; violenza.

tour (tōōr) *n.* giro (*turistico o artistico*), escursione, viaggio. *vt.*, *vi.* visitare (*una regione, ecc.*); compiere un giro (*turistico o artistico*).

tourism (tōōr'ĭz'm) *n.* turismo.

tourist (tōōr'ĭst) *n.* turista. *agg.* turistico: — class, classe turistica.

tournament (tōōr'nà·mĕnt) *n.* torneo, concorso, competizione.

tousle (tou'z'l) *vt.* scompigliare, arruffare.

tow (tō) (1) *n.* filaccia, stoppa.

tow (tō) (2) *n.* rimorchio: in —, a rimorchio. *vt.* rimorchiare.

toward (tō'ẽrd), **towards** (tō'ẽrdz) *prep.* verso; alla volta di; nei confronti di; a favore di; in previsione di: — midnight, verso la mezzanotte.

towboat (tō'bōt') *n.* rimorchiatore.

towel (tou'ĕl) *n.* asciugamano.

tower (tou'ẽr) *n.* torre; rocca. *vi.* torreggiare, innalzarsi. **—ing** *agg.* torreggiante, elevato.

towline (tō'līn') *n.* cavo di rimorchio.

town (toun) *n.* città, cittadina, borgata; cittadinanza (*popolazione*): — hall, municipio.

township (toun'ship) *n.* comune; unità primaria di governo; area demaniale di sei miglia quadrate.

towpath (tō'páth') *n.* alzaia.

toxic (tŏk'sĭk) *agg.* tossico.

toxicology (tŏk'sĭ·kŏl'ō·jĭ) *n.* tossicologia.

toxin (tŏk'sĭn) *n.* tossina.

toy (toi) *n.* giocattolo. *agg.* che ha forma di giocattolo; minuscolo: — dog, cane giocattolo, cagnolino. *vi.* giocare, giocherellare, gingillarsi.

trace (trās) (1) *n.* tirella (*di carrozza*).

trace (trās) (2) *n.* traccia, indizio; pizzico, parvenza; grafico. *vt.* tracciare; rintracciare, risalire alle origini di; ricalcare, delineare; attribuire.

tracing (trās'ĭng) *n.* tracciato; ricalco, copia a lucido.

track (trăk) *n.* traccia, orma, solco; scia; cammino, carreggiata; pista; (*ferr.*) linea, binario: race —, pista da corsa; cinder —, pista di cenere; to be on the — of, essere sulla pista di; to follow in somebody's —, seguire le orme di; the beaten —, il sistema invalso, il solito tran-tran; to keep — of, tenersi al corrente di; to go off the —s, deragliare; divagare. *vt.* tracciare; braccare, seguire la pista di: to — down, catturare.

tract (trăkt) (1) *n.* tratto; spazio: digestive —, apparato digerente.

tract (trăkt) (2) *n.* opuscolo (*spec. religioso*).

traction (trăk'shŭn) *n.* trazione; attrito; forza motrice.

tractor (trăk'tẽr) *n.* trattore, trattrice; (*aeron.*) elica traente.

trade (trād) *n.* commercio, traffico, scambio; arte, mestiere, occupazione, professione; clientela. *agg.* commerciale; sindacale; di categoria: — agent, agente di commercio; — agreement, accordo sindacale; — association, associazione di categoria; — goods, merci; — paper, giornale o organo di categoria; — name, nome commerciale; — school, scuola d'arti e mestieri; — edition, edizione di lusso. *vt.*, *vi.* commerciare, barattare, negoziare: **to — upon**, speculare su.

trademark (trăd'märk') *n.* marchio di fabbrica, marca.

trader (trād'ẽr) *n.* mercante; nave mercantile.

tradesman (trādz'măn) *n.* negoziante.

trade union (trād'ūn'yŭn), **trades union** (*Ingl.*) (trādz'ūn'yŭn), sindacato, camera del lavoro.

trade unionism (trād'ūn'yŭn·ĭz'm) sindacalismo.

trade winds venti alisei.

tradition (trȧ·dĭsh'ŭn) *n.* tradizione.

traditional (trȧ·dĭsh'ŭn·ăl) *agg.* tradizionale.

traduce (trȧ·dūs') *vt.* diffamare, calunniare.

traffic (trăf'ĭk) *n.* traffico, commercio; circolazione stradale, movimento. *vt.*, *vi.* (*pass.*, *pp.* **trafficked**, *ppr.* **trafficking**) commerciare, barattare, trafficare.

tragedian (trȧ·jē'dĭ·ăn) *n.* autore (*o* attore) drammatico.

tragedienne (trȧ·jē'dĭ·ĕn') *n.f.* attrice drammatica.

tragedy (trăj'ẽ·dĭ) *n.* tragedia.

tragic (trăj'ĭk) *agg.* tragico.

trail (trāl) *n.* solco, traccia, pista, sentiero; strascico; seguito. *vt.*, *vi.* strascinare, seguire la pista di; trascinarsi: **to — off**, affievolirsi, dispersi.

trailer (trāl'ẽr) *n.* rimorchio; roulotte (*fr.*).

train (trān) *n.* treno, convoglio; seguito, corteo; serie, andamento; strascico (*di vestito*); (*mecc.*) trasmissione. *vt.* istruire, allenare, addestrare; puntare (*un'arma, ecc.*). *vi.* esercitarsi, allenarsi.

trainee (trān·ē') *n.* allievo, novizio; (*mil.*) recluta.

trainer *n.* istruttore, allenatore.

training *n.* addestramento, allenamento: **— ship**, nave scuola.

trait (trāt) *n.* tratto, caratteristica.

traitor (trā'tẽr) *n.* traditore.

traitorous (trā'tẽr·ŭs) *agg.* insidioso, infido, sleale.

trajectory (trȧ·jĕk'tō·rĭ) *n.* traiettoria.

tram (trăm) *n.* tram, carrello; (*mecc.*) messa a punto.

trammel (trăm'ĕl) *n.* tramaglio; ellissografo; *pl.* pastoie, ostacolo. *vt.* ostacolare, impastoiare.

tramp (trămp) *n.* vagabondaggio, viaggio a piedi; rumor di passi; vagabondo; (*fam.*) prostituta; (*naut.*) mercantile. *vt.*, *vi.* percorrere a piedi; calpestare; vagabondare; camminare pesantemente.

trample (trăm'p'l) *n.* calpestio. *vt.* calpestare. *vi.* camminare pesantemente: **to — on, upon, opprimere, inferire su.**

tramway (trăm'wā') *n.* tram; teleferica.

trance (trȧns) *n.* ipnosi, estasi: **to be in a —**, essere in stato di ipnosi, essere come ipnotizzato.

tranquil (trăng'kwil) *agg.* tranquillo.

tranquillity (trăn·kwĭl'ĭ·tĭ) *n.* tranquillità.

transact (trăns·ăkt') *vt.*, *vi.* negoziare, trattare, portare a termine. **—ion** *n.* trattativa, affare; operazione (*bancaria*); accordo.

transatlantic (trăns'ăt·lăn'tĭk) *agg.* transatlantico.

transcend (trăn·sĕnd') *vt.* trascendere, superare. *vi.* eccellere.

transcontinental (trăns'kŏn·tĭ·nĕn'tăl) *agg.* transcontinentale.

transcribe (trăn·skrīb') *vt.* trascrivere.

transcript (trăn'skrĭpt) *n.* trascrizione, copia.

transfer (trăns'fûr) *n.* trasporto, trasferimento; cessione, trapasso; trasbordo; (*S.U.*) biglietto cumulativo (*tramviario, ecc.*). *vt.*, *vi.* trasportare; trasferire; cedere; riprodurre (*un disegno*); trasferirsi; trasbordare.

transfigure (trăns·fĭg'ûr) *vt.* trasfigurare.

transform (trăns·fôrm') *vt.* trasformare. *vi.* trasformarsi.

transformation (trăns'fôr·mā'shŭn) *n.* trasformazione, metamorfosi.

transformer (trăns·fôr'mẽr) *n.* trasformatore.

transfuse (trăns·fūz') *vt.* trasfondere, infondere; iniettare, fare una trasfusione di.

transfusion (trăns·fū'zhŭn) *n.* trasfusione.

transgress (trăns·grĕs') *vt.*, *vi.* trasgredire; oltrepassare; violare; peccare.

transgression (trăns·grĕsh'ŭn) *n.* trasgressione, abuso, violazione.

transgressor (trăns·grĕs'ẽr) *n.* trasgressore.

transistor (trăn·zĭs'tẽr) *n.* transistor.

transient (trăn'shĕnt) *n.* ospite di passaggio. *agg.* transitorio, provvisorio, di passaggio.

transit (trăn'sĭt) *n.* transito: **in —**, in transito, di passaggio.

transition (trăn·zĭsh'ŭn) *n.* transizione.

transitive (trăn's*l*·tĭv) *n.* verbo transitivo. *agg.* transitivo.

transitory (trăn's*l*·tō'rĭ) *agg.* transitorio.

translate (trăns·lāt') vt. tradurre; trasferire; (teleg.) ritrasmettere.

translation (trans·lā'shŭn) n. traduzione; (teleg.) ritrasmissione.

translator (trăns·lā'tẽr) n. traduttore.

translucent (trăns·lū'sĕnt) agg. traslucido, diafano.

transmission (trăns·mĭsh'ŭn) n. trasmissione.

transmit (trăns·mĭt') vt. trasmettere.

transmitter (trăns·mĭt'ẽr) n. trasmettitore.

transom (trăn'sŭm) n. lunetta (di porta); (naut.) traversa di poppa.

transparence (trăns·pâr'ĕns) n. trasparenza.

transparency (trăns·pâr'ĕn·sĭ) n. trasparenza; effigie su lastra trasparente, vetrino; diapositiva.

transparent (trăns·pâr'ĕnt) agg. trasparente.

transpire (trăn·spīr') vt., vi. traspirare, trasudare; trapelare.

transplant (trăns·plănt') vt. trapiantare.

transport (trăns·pōrt') n. trasporto, impeto; nave (o aereo) da trasporto. vt. trasportare, deportare; rapire in estasi; mandare in collera: to be transported with, essere trasportato da.

transportation (trăns'pŏr·tā'shŭn) n. trasporto; mezzi di trasporto; biglietto di viaggio; deportazione.

transpose (trăns·pōz') vt. trasporre, invertire.

transship (trăns·shĭp') vt., vi. trasbordare.

transverse (trăns·vûrs') agg. traversale.

trap (trăp) n. trappola, insidia; sifone; calesse; (S.U.) bocca: — door, botola. vedi traps. vt. intrappolare.

trapeze (tră·pēz') n. trapezio.

trapper (trăp'ẽr) n. trappolatore.

trappings (trăp'ĭngz) n.pl. ornamenti, fronzoli; vestiario; gualdrappa.

traps (trăps) n.pl. bagaglio, effetti personali; (mus.) batteria.

trash (trăsh) n. rimasugli, scorie; cianfrusaglie, robaccia; stupidaggini; marmaglia.

travail (trăv'āl) n. travaglio, fatica; doglie del parto.

travel (trăv'ĕl) n. viaggio; (mecc.) corsa. vt., vi. percorrere; viaggiare, muoversi.

traveler n. viaggiatore: —'s check, assegno turistico, assegno per viaggiatori.

traveling n. il viaggiare. agg. viaggiante: — salesman, commesso viaggiatore.

traverse (trăv'ẽrs) n. traversa. agg. obliquo, trasversale: — rod (opp.

track), rotaia per tendaggi, riloga. vt. attraversare; pattugliare; ostacolare.

travesty (trăv'ĕs·tĭ) n. farsa, parodia. vt. parodiare.

trawl (trôl) n. strascino (rete).

tray (trā) n. vassoio.

treacherous (trĕch'ẽr·ŭs) agg. infido, proditorio, sleale; precario.

treachery (trĕch'ẽr·ĭ) n. tradimento.

treacle (trē'k'l) n. melassa.

tread (trĕd) n. passo, andatura; suola; pianta (del piede e del gradino); battistrada (del pneumatico). vt. (pass. trod, pp. trodden) percorrere, calpestare. vi. camminare: to — on, upon, calpestare.

treadle (trĕd''l) n. pedale.

treason (trē'z'n) n. tradimento.

treasonable (trĕz'n·à·b'l) agg. proditorio, sleale.

treasure (trĕzh'ẽr) n. tesoro. vt. accantonare; far tesoro di, custodire gelosamente, tesaurizzare.

treasurer (trĕzh'ẽr·ẽr) n. tesoriere.

treasury (trĕzh'ẽr·ĭ) n. erario, tesoro, tesoreria.

treat (trēt) n. festa, trattenimento, piacere. vt. trattare, curare; offrire.

treatise (trē'tĭs) n. trattato (libro).

treatment (trēt'mĕnt) n. trattamento; cura; (lett.) adattamento.

treaty (trē'tĭ) n. trattato, patto.

treble (trĕb''l) n. (mus.) soprano; suono acuto; squillo; vocetta, voce sottile. agg. triplice; di soprano, acuto. vt., vi. triplicare, triplicarsi.

tree (trē) n. albero; palo, asta; forma da scarpe: to be up a —, essere nei guai.

treeless agg. senz'alberi.

trefoil (trē'foil) n. trifoglio.

trellis (trĕl'ĭs) n. graticolo.

tremble (trĕm'b''l) n. tremito; trepidazione, timore. vi. tremare, fremere.

trembling (trĕm'blĭng) n. tremito agg. tremante.

tremendous (trê·mĕn'dŭs) agg. terribile; straordinario, fenomenale.

tremor (trĕm'ẽr) n. tremito.

tremulous (trĕm'û·lŭs) agg. tremulo tremolante.

trench (trĕnch) n. fossato, solco trincea.

trend (trĕnd) n. direzione, andamento, tendenza.

trepan (trê·păn') n. (chir.) trapano vt. trapanare (spec. il cranio).

trephine (trê·fĭn') n. (chir.) trapano vt. trapanare.

trepidation (trĕp'ĭ·dā'shŭn) n. trepidazione.

trespass (trĕs'pás) n. sconfinamento trasgressione; peccato. vi. scon

finare; trasgredire; abusare; peccare: no —ing, vietato l'accesso.

tress (trĕs) *n.* treccia; ricciolo.

trestle (trĕs'l) *n.* cavalletto.

trial (trī'ăl) *n.* prova, collaudo; avversità; tentativo; processo: on —,
in prova; — flight, volo di prova.

triangle (trī'ăn'g'l) *n.* triangolo.

triangular (trī-ăng'gū-lĕr) *agg.* tri-
angolare.

tribe (trīb) *n.* tribù, famiglia.

tribulation (trĭb'ū-lā'shŭn) *n.* tribolazione.

tribunal (trī-bū'năl) *n.* tribunale.

tributary (trĭb'ū-tĕr'ĭ) *n.* affluente;
agg. tributario.

tribute (trĭb'ūt) *n.* tributo; omaggio.

trice (trīs) *n.* attimo, istante.

trick (trĭk) *n.* trucco, artificio, frode,
gherminella; ticchio, vezzo; abitudine; malizia; (*gergo*) ragazzina: a
dirty —, uno scherzo di cattivo
genere; **to do the** —, risolvere il
problema. *vt.* burlare, gabbare,
ingannare: **to** — **somebody into
doing something** indurre con un
trucco qualcuno a fare qualcosa.

trickery (trĭk'ĕr·ĭ) *n.* astuzia, disonestà.

trickle (trĭk''l) *n.* sgocciolio, stillicidio. *vi.* colare, sgocciolare.

tricky (trĭk'ĭ) *agg.* furbo, disonesto;
malsicuro; difficile.

tricot (trē'kō) *n.* tessuto a maglia,
lavoro a maglia; maglia; calzamaglia nera (*per ballerini*).

tricycle (trī'sĭk·'l) *n.* triciclo.

tried (trīd) *pass., pp. di* to **try.** *agg.*
provato, sperimentato.

triennial (trī-ĕn'ĭ-ăl) *agg.* triennale.

trifle (trī'f'l) *n.* bagattella, frivolezza,
gingillo, inezia. *vi.* scherzare,
gingillarsi: **to** — **with,** prendere alla
leggiera; amoreggiare con; **to** —
away, sprecare.

trifling (trī'flĭng) *agg.* insignificante,
frivolo.

trig (trĭg) *agg.* lindo, ordinato.

trigger (trĭg'ĕr) *n.* grilletto. *vt.*: **to** —
off, far scattare.

trigonometry (trĭg'ō·nŏm'ē·trĭ) *n.*
trigonometria.

trill (trĭl) *n.* trillo. *vt., vi.* trillare;
canticchiare: **to** — **one's r,** parlare
con la erre moscia.

trillion (trĭl'yŭn) *n.* trilione (*Ingl.*: un
milione alla terza potenza; *S.U.*: un
milione di milioni).

trilogy (trĭl'ō·jĭ) *n.* trilogia.

trim (trĭm) *n.* stato, assetto; condizione, ordine; ornamento; equilibrio; rifinitura; **to be in — form,**
essere in forma per. *agg.* lindo,

ordinato, curato, elegante; at-
trezzato. *vt.* attrezzare; mettere in
ordine, decorare; potare, sfrondare;
rifinire; (*naut., aeron.*) equilibrare
il carico di, stabilizzare; (*fam.*)
sconfiggere. *vi.* barcamenarsi, orientarsi.

trimming *n.* allestimento, fronzolo,
guarnizione, rifinitura; lezione,
sconfitta; *pl.* ritagli; contorno (*di
vivande*); cascami; fronzoli; guadagni disonesti: **the truth without
—,** la verità senza fronzoli *opp.*
nuda e cruda.

Trinity (trĭn'ĭ·tĭ) *n.* Trinità.

trinket (trĭng'kĕt) *n.* bagattella,
gingillo, aggeggio.

trip (trĭp) *n.* viaggio, viaggetto;
sgambetto, inciampo. *vt.* fare lo
sgambetto a; urtare; cogliere in
fallo; (*mecc.*) sganciare, mettere in
moto. *vi.* inciampare, mettere il
piede in fallo; sbagliare, commettere una indiscrezione; saltellare.

tripe (trīp) *n.* trippa; (*gergo*) sciocchezze.

triple (trĭp''l) *agg.* triplo, triplice.
vt. triplicare.

triplicate (trĭp'lĭ·kăt) *agg.* triplicato,
triplice. *vt.* triplicare.

tripod (trī'pŏd) *n.* tripode, treppiede.

triptych (trĭp'tĭk) *n.* trittico.

trite (trīt) *agg.* trito, banale, comune.

triumph (trī'ŭmf) *n.* trionfo. *vi.*
trionfare, esultare. —**al** (-ŭm'făl)
agg. fale.

triumphant (trī-ŭm'fănt) *agg.* trionfante, esultante. —**ly** *avv.* con
esultanza, trionfalmente.

trivet (trĭv'ĕt) *n.* treppiede.

trivial (trĭv'ĭ·ăl) *agg.* insignificante,
trascurabile, banale; triviale.

trod (trŏd) *pass., pp. di* to **tread.**

trodden (trŏd''n) *pp. di* to **tread.**

trolley (trŏl'ĭ) *n.* carrello; asta di
presa (*del tram*), pantografo (*del
treno elettrico*); rotella scanalata: —
bus, filovia, filobus.

trollop (trŏl'ŭp) *n.* sudiciona, prostituta.

troop (trōop) *n.* truppa; branco,
frotta; (*teat.*) compagnia. *vt.* raggruppare. *vi.* intrupparsi; affluire;
sfilare. —**er** *n.* soldato di cavalleria; poliziotto a cavallo.

trophy (trō'fĭ) *n.* trofeo.

tropic (trŏp'ĭk) *n.* tropico.

tropical (trŏp'ĭ·kăl) *agg.* tropicale.

trot (trŏt) *n.* trotto. *vt.* far trottare.
vi. trottare.

trouble (trŭb''l) *n.* disturbo, briga;
afflizione, malanno; preoccupazione; turbolenza; guaio; guasto,
avaria: **heart —,** disturbo di cuore;

it is not worth the —, non ne vale la pena; to get into —, mettersi nei pasticci. *vt.* disturbare, turbare, importunare, affliggere. *vi.* turbarsi; prendersi la briga (*di*): may I — you to? posso pregarvi di?

troubled (trŭb'l'd) *agg.* turbato, inquieto; torbido.

troublemaker (trŭb'l·māk'ẽr) *n.* agitatore, facinoroso, provocatore, indisciplinato.

troublesome (trŭb''l·sŭm) *agg.* noioso, molesto; turbolento; penoso; complicato, faticoso.

troublous (trŭb'lŭs) *agg.* irrequieto, sconvolto; torbido; molesto.

trough (trôf) *n.* truogolo; condotto; solco, avvallamento.

troupe (trōōp) *n.* (*teat.*) compagnia.

trousers (trou'zẽrz) *n.pl.* calzoni.

trousseau (trōō·sō') *n.* corredo (*da sposa*).

trout (trout) *n.* (*ittiol.*) trota.

trowel (trou'ĕl) *n.* cazzuola, appianatoia.

troy weight (troi-) *n.* peso troy.

truant (trōō'ănt) *n.* infingardo; chi marina la scuola. *agg.* svogliato, ozioso, trascurato: to play —, marinare la scuola.

truce (trōōs) *n.* tregua, armistizio.

truck (trŭk) (1) *n.* carro; carrello, piattaforma di carico; autocarro; (*ferr.*) carrello (*di vagone*): — trailer, rimorchio di autocarro. *vt.*, *vi.* trasportare (o caricare) su autocarro.

truck (trŭk) (2) *n.* baratto; commercio; rapporti; mercanzia: to have no — with, non aver nulla da spartire con; garden —, frutta e verdura; — garden, orto. *vt.*, *vi.* barattare, commerciare.

trucker (trŭk'ẽr) *n.* autotrasportatore; camionista.

truckle (trŭk''l) *n.* puleggia. *vi.* sottomettesi.

trudge (trŭj) *vi.* camminare faticosamente, arrancare. *n.* camminata, maratona.

true (trōō) *agg.* vero, onesto, fedele, genuino, fidato; conforme (*a*), esatto. *vt.* rendere conforme (*a*), rettificare.

truffle (trŭf''l) *n.* (*bot.*) tartufo.

truism (trōō'iz'm) *n.* assioma.

truly (trōō'lĭ) *avv.* veramente, onestamente, esattamente, fedelmente: yours — (*nella corrispondenza*), vostro devotissimo.

trump (trŭmp) *n.* (*carte da giuoco*) trionfo, briscola. *vt.*, *vi.* battere con la briscola, giocar di briscola: to — up, inventare, falsificare.

trumpet (trŭm'pĕt) *n.* registro d'organo, tromba; cornetto acustico; barrito. *vt.* strombazzare, proclamare. *vi.* sonare la tromba; barrire.

truncheon (trŭn'chŭn) *n.* randello, sfollagente.

trundle (trŭn'd'l) *vt.* far rotolare. *vi.* rotolare.

trunk (trŭngk) *n.* tronco, fusto; condotto, tubo; proboscide; baule; (*telef.*) linea interurbana; *pl.* mutandine (*da bagno, atletica, ecc.*); — line, linea principale.

truss (trŭs) *n.* balla, fascio; cinto erniario; bendaggio; armatura (*costruzione*). *vt.* legare; imballare; immobilizzare.

trust (trŭst) *n.* fiducia, fede; custodia; credito; monopolio; consorzio; cura: breach of —, abuso di fiducia. *vt.* fidarsi di, affidarsi a, far affidamento su, far credito a. *vi.* fidare, confidare: to — somebody with, affidare a qualcuno.

trustee (trŭs·tē') *n.* depositario, curatore, fidecommissario.

trustful (trŭst'fŏŏl) *agg.* fiducioso.

trustworthy (trŭst'wûr'thĭ) *agg.* fidato, attendibile.

trusty (trŭs'tĭ) *agg.* sicuro, fidato, leale. *n.* prigioniero cui si concedono certi privilegi per buona condotta.

truth (trōōth) *n.* verità, realtà; sincerità, fedeltà, rettitudine. —ful *agg.* veritiero. —fulness *n.* veracità.

try (trī) *n.* prova, tentativo. *vt.*, *vi.* provare, tentare; mettere alla prova, stancare; sforzarsi, sperimentare; verificare, saggiare; processare, giudicare: to — to, cercare o tentare di; to — on a suit, provarsi un vestito; to — one's luck, tentare la fortuna; to — somebody's patience, mettere alla prova la pazienza di qualcuno.

trying (trī'ĭng) *agg.* difficile, penoso faticoso, critico.

T-shirt (tē'shûrt') *n.* maglietta estiva (*senza collo e con le maniche corte*).

tub (tŭb) *n.* tino, tinozza, vasca, bagno; (*fam.*) barca.

tube (tūb) *n.* tubo; galleria (o ferrovia) sotterranea; (*anat.*) tromba, canale; (*S.U., radio*) valvola: inner —, camera d'aria; test —, provetta.

tuber (tū'bẽr) *n.* (*bot.*) tubero.

tubercular (tû·bûr'kû·lẽr) *agg.* tubercolare.

tuberculosis (tû·bûr'kû·lō'sĭs) *n.* (*med.*) tubercolosi.

tuberculous (tû·bûr'kû·lŭs) *agg.* tubercoloso.

tubing (tūb'ĭng) n. tubatura, tubi.

tubular (tū'bů·lẽr) agg. tubolare.

tuck (tŭk) n. piega, basta (d'indumento); (S.U.) energia, vita. vt. piegare, ripiegare; ficcare; rimboccare: **to — away**, mangiare con gusto; **to — in the bedclothes**, rimboccare le coltri.

Tuesday (tūz'dĭ) n. martedì.

tuft (tŭft) n. ciocca, ciuffo, nappa, batuffolo; cespuglio.

tug (tŭg) n. sforzo, strattone, strappo; (naut.) rimorchiatore: **— of war**, tiro della fune. vt., vi. tirare con forza, trascinare, rimorchiare; faticare.

tugboat (tŭg'bōt') n. rimorchiatore.

tuition (tū·ĭsh'ŭn) n. insegnamento; tassa scolastica.

tulip (tū'lĭp) n. tulipano.

tumble (tŭm'b'l) n. ruzzolone, capitombolo; disordine, ammasso. vt. rovesciare, scompigliare; far capitombolare. vi. rotolare, capitombolare, far capriole o acrobazie: **— to** (gergo), intuire; **to — into someone**, incontrare qualcuno per caso.

tumbledown (tŭm'b'l·doun') agg. diroccato, in rovina.

tumbler (tŭm'blẽr) n. acrobata; bicchiere cilindrico; nasello (di serratura), cane.

tumor (tū'mẽr) n. tumore.

tumult (tū'mŭlt) n. tumulto.

tumultuous (tů·mŭl'tů·ŭs) agg. tumultuoso, agitato.

tun (tŭn) n. botte, tino.

tuna (tōō'ná) n. tonno; (bot.) fico d'India.

tune (tūn) n. tono; melodia, motivo, aria; (radio) sintonia: **in —**, d'accordo; **out of —**, in contrasto. vt., vi. accordare, intonare, sincronizzare: **to — in** (radio), sintonizzare, sintonizzarsi; **to — up a motor**, mettere a punto un motore.

tungsten (tŭng'stĕn) n. tungsteno.

tunic (tū'nĭk) n. tunica; (mil.) giubba.

tuning (tūn'ĭng) n. accordo, accordatura: **— fork**, diapason.

tunnel (tŭn'ĕl) n. galleria sotterranea, traforo; (fam.) ciminiera. vt., vi. perforare, scavare una galleria.

tunny (tŭn'ĭ) n. tonno.

turban (tûr'băn) n. turbante.

turbine (tûr'bĭn) n. (mecc.) turbina.

turbojet (tûr'bō·jĕt') n. turbogetto.

turbopropeller (tûr'bō·prŏ·pĕl'ẽr), **turboprop** n. turboelica.

turbulent (tûr'bů·lĕnt) agg. turbolento.

tureen (tů·rēn') n. zuppiera.

turf (tûrf) n. prato, piota; ipp ippodromo.

turgid (tûr'jĭd) agg. turgido.

Turk (tûrk) n. turco, turca.

Turkey (tûr'kĭ) (1) n. Turchia.

turkey (tûr'kĭ) (2) n. tacchino; (g teatr.) fiasco.

turmoil (tûr'moil) n. tumulto, ag zione.

turn (tûrn) n. giro, turno; svol curva; rotazione; piega; servig direzione; (fam.) sussulto, sgom to, smarrimento: **to a —**, alla p fezione; **by turns**, a rotazione intervalli; **a bad —**, un brutto tir a good —, un buon servigio. voltare, girare, rivoltare; cambia tramutare, tradurre; tornire; volgersi; voltarsi, deviare; tr sformarsi; dirigersi, accingersi: **— adrift**, mandare alla deriva; **— aside**, deviare; distogliere il visо **to — back**, mandare (o tornare indietro; **to — down**, respingere **to — in**, entrare, coricarsi; **to — into**, trasformarsi (o trasformare) in **to — off**, chiudere (il gas, l'acqua) spegnere (la luce); **to — out**, espellere; porre in vendita; rivelarsi **to — over**, sfogliare; rigirare; esa minare; consegnare; **to — round**, volgersi; **to — sour**, inacidire; **to — up**, comparire; **to — upside down**, capovolgere, rivoltare, capovolgersi.

turnaround (tûrn'á·round') n. spiazzo per girare (con l'automobile, ecc.); voltafaccia; tempo totale di un viaggio di andata e ritorno (di una nave, un aereo, ecc.).

turncoat (tûrn'kōt') n. voltagabbana.

turner (tûr'nẽr) n. tornitore.

turning (tûr'nĭng) n. giro, rotazione, svolta; tornitura: **— point**, svolta decisiva, fulcro; **— lathe**, tornio.

turnkey (tûrn'kē') n. carceriere.

turnout (tûrn'out') n. tenuta, vestiario; utile netto; riunione; produzione; (ferr.) raccordo.

turnover (tûrn'ō'vẽr) n. movimento di danaro (o d'affari); rovesciamento; **labor —**, rotazione di personale operaio; **apple —**, torta di mele. agg. rovesciabile, rivoltato.

turnpike (tûrn'pĭk') n. cancello a ruota di strada a pedaggio; (S.U.) strada a pedaggio; autostrada.

turnscrew (tûrn'skrōō') n. cacciavite.

turnstile (tûrn'stĭl') n. arganello (cancelletto a ruota).

turntable (tûrn'tā'b'l) n. piatto girevole (del grammofono), giradischi; piattaforma girevole.

turnip (tûr'nĭp) n. (bot.) rapa.

turpentine (tûr'pĕn·tĭn) *n*. trementina.

turpitude (tûr'pĭ·tūd) *n*. turpitudine.

turquoise (tûr'koiz) *n*. turchese.

turret (tûr'ĕt) *n*. torretta.

turtle (tûr't'l) *n*. tartaruga: **to turn —**, capovolgersi.

turtledove (tûr't'l·dŭv') *n*. tortora.

tusk (tŭsk) *n*. zanna; (*mecc*.) dente.

tussle (tŭs''l) *n*. zuffa, rissa. *vi*. rissare, azzuffarsi.

tutor (tū'tẽr) *n*. istitutore, precettore; tutore. *vt*., *vi*. istruire, educare, fare il precettore.

tutu (tōō'tōō) *n*. tutù, gonnellino da ballerina.

tuxedo (tŭk·sē'dō) *n*. (*S.U.*) smoking, abito nero.

tuyère (twēr) *n*. (*metall*.) ugello.

twaddle (twŏd''l) *vi*. cianciare.

twang (twăng) *n*. suono vibrato, tono nasale; sapore violento. *vt*. far vibrare. *vi*. emettere un suono vibrato; parlare con voce nasale.

tweak (twēk) *n*. tirata, strattone. *vt*. pizzicare, tirare (*le orecchie*), torcere.

tweed (twēd) *n*. panno di lana, tweed: **— suit**, abito di tweed.

tweezers (twēz'ẽrz) *n.pl*. pinzette.

twelfth (twĕlfth) *n*., *agg*. dodicesimo.

twelve (twĕlv) *n*., *agg*. dodici.

twelve-tone *agg*. (*mus*.) dodecafonico: **— system**, dodecafonia.

twentieth (twĕn'tĭ·ĕth) *n*., *agg*. ventesimo.

twenty (twĕn'tĭ) *n*., *agg*. venti.

twerp (twûrp) *n*. (*gergo*) persona insignificante *o* spregevole, balordo, gonzo, povero stupido, babbeo.

twice (twīs) *avv*. due volte: **— as much**, due volte tanto; **— as big**, grosso il doppio.

twiddle (twĭd''l) *vt*. rigirare oziosamente, giocherellare con. *vi*. roteare, piroettare; oziare: **to — one's thumbs**, rigirarsi i pollici.

twig (twĭg) *n*. rametto, ramoscello.

twilight (twī'līt') *n*. crepuscolo, semioscurità.

twill (twĭl) *n*. diagonale (*tess*.)

twin (twĭn) *n*., *agg*. gemello. *vt*. accoppiare. *vi*. accoppiarsi; avere un parto gemellare.

twine (twīn) *n*. attorcigliamento, groviglio; funicella, spago. *vt*. intrecciare, attorcigliare, avvolgere, legare. *vi*. attorcigliarsi, avviticchiarsi, aggrovigliarsi, serpeggiare.

twinge (twĭnj) *n*. spasimo, fitta. *vt*. pungere, trafiggere.

twinkle (twĭng'k'l) *n*. scintillio, ammicco, balenio, attimo; *vi*. ammiccare, scintillare, tremolare.

twinkling (twĭng'klĭng) *n*. balenio; ammicco: **in the — of an eye**, in un batter d'occhio.

twirl (twûrl) *n*. rotazione, evoluzione, voluta, spira; piroetta. *vt*., *vi*. roteare, rigirare, avvolgere; piroettare.

twist (twĭst) *n*. torcitura, attorcigliamento, torsione; propensione; contorsione; corda, cordoncino, treccia; capriccio; curva, tortuosità; **to give a —**, torcere; attorcigliare; **to give a humorous — to a novel**, dare a un romanzo un piglio umoristico. *vt*. torcere, attorcigliare, ritorcere, avvolgere; deformare, pervertire, snaturare. *vi*. attorcigliarsi, contorcersi; serpeggiare; voltarsi; intrecciarsi.

twisted *agg*. attorcigliato, contorto, ritorto; pervertito, snaturato.

twister (twĭs'tẽr) *n*. torcitore; bugiardo; bugia; piroetta; turbine.

twitch (twĭch) *n*. fitta, contrazione, spasimo, guizzo; strattone. *vt*. tirare bruscamente, muovere di scatto, pizzicare. *vi*. contrarsi spasmodicamente, guizzare.

twitter (twĭt'ẽr) *n*. cinguettio; risatina; orgasmo. *vt*., *vi*. cinguettare; ridacchiare; essere in orgasmo.

two (tōō) *n*., *agg*. due.

twofold (tōō'fōld') *agg*. doppio, duplice.

two-master *n*. (*naut*.) due-alberi.

two-time (tōō'tīm') *vt*. (*gergo*) tradire, ingannare, fregare; fare le corna a.

two-timing *agg*. falso, traditore, ipocrita, infedele.

two-seater *n*. automobile a due posti.

tycoon (tī·kōōn') *n*.(*S.U.*) magnate.

tympanum (tĭm'pá·nŭm) *n*. (*anat*., *zool*., *arch*.) timpano; (*elett*.) diaframma.

type (tīp) *n*. tipo, modello; (*tip*.) carattere: **in —**, composto. *vt*., *vi*. simboleggiare; scrivere a stampatello; dattilografare.

typesetter (tīp'sĕt'ẽr) *n*. (*tip*.) compositore.

typewrite (tīp'rīt') *vt*., *vi*. dattilografare.

typewriter (tīp'rīt'ẽr) *n*. macchina per scrivere; dattilografo.

typewriting (tīp'rīt'ĭng) *n*. dattilografia.

typewritten (tīp'rīt''n) *pp. di* **typewrite**, dattiloscritto, scritto a macchina.

typhoid (tī'foid) *n*. tifoidea. *agg*. tifoide.

typhoon (tī'fōōn) *n*. tifone, ciclone.

typhus (tī'fŭs) *n*. (*med*.) tifo.

typical (tĭp'ĭ·kǎl) *agg*. tipico.

typist (tǐp'ǐst) *n.* dattilografo, dattilo-grafa.

typography (tǐ·pǒg'rȧ·fǐ) *n.* arte gra-fica.

tyrannical (tǐ·rǎn'ǐ·kǎl) *agg.* tirannico.

tyrannize (tǐr'ȧ·nǐz) *vt.*, *vi.* tiranneg-giare.

tyrannous (tǐr'ȧ·nǔs) *agg.* dispotico.

tyranny (tǐr'ȧ·nǐ) *n.* tirannia.

tyrant (tī'rȧnt) *n.* tiranno, despota.

tyre (tīr) (*Ingl.*) *n.* pneumatico (*di ruota*).

tyro (tī'rō) *n.* novizio, principiante.

Tyrolean (tǐ·rō'lē·ȧn) *agg.* tirolese.

Tyrrhenian (tǐ·rē'nǐ·ȧn) *n.*, *agg.* etru-sco: the — Sea, il Mar Tirreno.

U

ubiquitous (û·bǐk'wǐ·tǔs) *agg.* onni-presente.

udder (ǔd'ẽr) *n.* (*zool.*) ghiandola mammaria.

ugliness (ǔg'lǐ·něs) *n.* bruttezza, bas-sezza, viltà; caparbietà; gravità, pericolosità.

ugly (ǔg'lǐ) *agg.* brutto, odioso; pre-occupante, pericoloso; caparbio.

ukulele (û'kû·lā'lē) *n.* chitarra ha-waiana.

ulcer (ǔl'sẽr) *n.* ulcera.

ulterior (ǔl·tẽr'ǐ·ẽr) *agg.* ulteriore, re-condito.

ultimate (ǔl'tǐ·mǐt) *agg.* ultimo, estre-mo; definitivo, finale. —**ly** *avv.* finalmente, definitivamente.

ultimo (ǔl'tǐ·mō) *agg.* scorso. *avv.* nel mese scorso.

ultra (ǔl'trȧ) *agg.* estremo, eccessivo.

ultramarine (ǔl'trȧ·mȧ·rēn') *n.* oltre-mare (*colore*). *agg.* d'oltremare, oltremarino.

ultramontane (ǔl'trȧ·mǒn'tān) *n.*, *agg.* oltremontano.

ultramundane (ǔl'trȧ·mǔn'dān) *agg.* oltremondano.

ululate (ǔl'û·lāt) *vi.* ululare.

umber (ǔm'bẽr) *n.* terra d'ombra.

umbrage (ǔm'brǐj) *n.* ombra; foglia-me; accenno; offesa: to take —, adombrarsi.

umbrella (ǔm'brěl'ȧ) *n.* ombrello, parapioggia.

umpire (ǔm'pīr) *n.* arbitro. *vt.*, *vi.* arbitrare.

un- (ǔn) *pref. negativo* non, senza, in-, dis-.

unabashed (ǔn'ȧ·bǎsht') *agg.* imper-territo, disinvolto, spavaldo.

unable (ǔn·ā'b'l) *agg.* incapace, im-possibilitato, impotente, inetto: I am — to do it, non so farlo, non posso farlo, non riesco a farlo.

unabridged (ǔn'ȧ·brǐjd') *agg.* inte-grale, completo.

unaccountable (ǔn'ȧ·koun'tȧ·b'l) *agg.* inesplicabile; non responsabile.

unaccounted-for *agg.* inspiegato; in-giustificato.

unaccustomed (ǔn'ȧ·kǔs'tǔmd) *agg.* non abituato, inusitato, insolito.

unacquainted (ǔn'ȧ·kwān'těd) *agg.* ignaro, estraneo, insolito.

unadorned (ǔn'ȧ·dôrnd') *agg.* disa-dorno.

unadvised (ǔn'ȧd·vīzd') *agg.* sconsi-derato, imprudente, inopportuno.

unaffected (ǔn'ȧ·fěk'těd) *agg.* non influenzato; indifferente, imper-territo; naturale, spontaneo.

unafraid (ǔn'ȧ·frād') *agg.* intrepido.

unaided (ǔn·ād'ěd) *agg.* senza aiuto.

unalloyed (ǔn'ȧ·loid') *agg.* puro, non mescolato.

unalterable (ǔn·ôl'tẽr·ȧ·b'l) *agg.* in-alterabile.

un–American (ǔn'ȧ·mẽr'ǐ·kȧn) *agg.* (*S.U.*) antiamericano.

unanimity (û'nȧ·nǐm'ǐ·tǐ) *n.* unani-mità.

unanimous (û·nǎn'ǐ·mǔs) *agg.* unani-me.

unannealed (ǔn'ȧ·nēld') *agg.* (*metal.*) dolce.

unannounced (ǔn'ȧ·nounst') *agg.* in-aspettato, non annunziato, inopi-nato.

unanswerable (ǔn·ȧn'sẽr·ȧ·b'l) *agg.* inconfutabile; inesplicabile.

unanswered (ǔn·ȧn'sẽrd) *agg.* incon-futato; inevaso; insoluto; non ricambiato.

unapproachable (ǔn'ȧ·prōch'ȧ·b'l) *agg.* impareggiabile; inavvicinabile, in-accessibile.

unarm (ǔn·ärm') *vt.* disarmare, ren-dere innocuo.

unarmed (ǔn·ärmd') *agg.* inerme, di-sarmato.

unashamed (ǔn'ȧ·shāmd') *agg.* spu-dorato, imperterrito.

unasked (ǔn·àskt') *agg.* spontaneo, non richiesto; non invitato.

unassuming (ǔn'ȧ·sům'ǐng) *agg.* mo-desto, senza pretese.

unattached (ǔn'ȧ·tacht') *agg.* separa-to, indipendente; esterno (*di stu-dente univ.*).

unattainable (ǔn'ȧ·tān'ȧ·b'l) *agg.* inac-cessibile; irraggiungibile.

unattended (ǔn'ȧ·těn'děd) *agg.* solo, senza scorta (*o* cure); privo di udi-torio.

unattractive (ŭn'ắ·trăk'tĭv) *agg.* brutto, sgradevole.

unauthorized (ŭn·ô'thĕr·īzd) *agg.* abusivo, arbitrario, illegale.

unavailing (ŭn'á·vāl'ĭng) *agg.* inefficace, inutile.

unavoidable (ŭn'á·void'á·b'l) *agg.* inevitabile.

unaware (ŭn'á·wâr') *agg.* inconscio, ignaro. *avv.* (*anche* **unawares**) alla sprovvista, inópinatamente, inavvertitamente.

unbalanced (ŭn·băl'ắnst) *agg.* sbilanciato, instabile; squilibrato; precario: **— account,** conto scoperto.

unbearable (ŭn·bâr'á·b'l) *agg.* insopportabile.

unbeaten (ŭn·bēt''n) *agg.* imbattuto, indenne; non frequentato (*di strada, ecc.*)

unbecoming (ŭn'bē·kŭm'ĭng) *agg.* disadatto, indecoroso: **an — dress,** un vestito che sta male.

unbelief (ŭn'bē·lēf') *n.* incredulità, scetticismo.

unbelievable (ŭn'bē·lēv'á·b'l) *agg.* incredibile.

unbeliever (ŭn'bē·lēv'ĕr) *n.* miscredente, scettico.

unbelieving *agg.* incredulo.

unbend (ŭn·bĕnd') *vt.* (*pass.*, *pp.* **unbent**) allentare; raddrizzare; mettere a proprio agio; (*naut.*) mollare. *vi.* allentarsi; raddrizzarsi; ammansarsi.

unbending *agg.* inflessibile, risoluto, rigido.

unbiased, unbiassed (ŭn'bī'ắst) *agg.* imparziale, senza prevenzioni.

unbind (ŭn·bĭnd') *vt.* (*pass.*, *pp.* **unbound**) slegare, sciogliere, liberare.

unblemished (ŭn·blĕm'ĭsht) *agg.* immacolato, senza macchia; perfetto.

unblushing (ŭn·blŭsh'ĭng) *agg.* impudente, sfrontato.

unborn (ŭn·bôrn') *agg.* non ancora nato, inesistente, futuro, increato.

unbosom (ŭn·bŏŏz'ŭm) *vt.* confidare, rivelare: **to — oneself,** sfogarsi, confidarsi.

unbound (ŭn·bound') *pass.*, *pp. di* to unbind, *agg.* slegato, sciolto, libero, non rilegato.

unbreakable (ŭn·brāk'á·b'l) *agg.* infrangibile.

unbridled (ŭn·brī'd'ld) *agg.* sfrenato, sbrigliato.

unbroken (ŭn·brō'kĕn) *agg.* ininterrotto, continuo; intiero, intatto; indomo; uniforme.

unburnt (ŭn·bûrnt') *agg.* incombusto, senza bruciature, crudo.

unbusinesslike (ŭn·bĭz'nĕs·līk') *agg.* malpratico, anticommerciale.

unbutton (ŭn·bŭt''n) *vt.* sbottonare.

uncalled (ŭn·kôld') *agg.* non chiamato, non invitato: **— for,** inopportuno, inutile; ineducato, impertinente.

uncanny (ŭn·kăn'ĭ) *agg.* magico, fantastico, soprannaturale.

unceasing (ŭn·sēs'ĭng) *agg.* incessante. **—ly** *avv.* incessantemente.

uncertain (ŭn·sûr'tĭn) *agg.* incerto, malsicuro, vago.

uncertainty (ŭn·sûr'tĭn·tĭ) *n.* incertezza.

unchallenged (ŭn·chăl'ĕnjd) *agg.* incontestato, indisturbato, non sfidato.

unchangeable (ŭn·chān'já·b'l) *agg.* immutabile, invariabile.

unchanged (ŭn·chānjd') *agg.* immutato.

unchanging (ŭn·chān'jĭng) *agg.* invariabile, costante.

uncharitable (ŭn·chăr'ĭ·tá·b'l) *agg.* severo, poco caritatevole.

uncivil (ŭn·sĭv'ĭl) *agg.* scortese, sgarbato, villano.

uncivilized (ŭn·sĭv'ĭ·līzd) *agg.* incivile, barbaro.

unclasp (ŭn·klåsp') *vt.* lasciare la presa di; slacciare; sgrovigliare, sciogliere.

uncle (ŭng'k'l) *n.* zio; (*gergo*) prestatore su pegno: **— Sam,** gli (*S.U.*); **to talk like a Dutch —,** catechizzare.

unclean (ŭn·klēn') *agg.* sudicio, peccaminoso, losco. **—ness** *n.* sporcizia; impudicizia.

unclouded (ŭn·kloud'ĕd) *agg.* senza nubi.

uncoil (ŭn·koil') *vt.* svolgere, srotolare, dipanare.

uncomely (ŭn·kŭm'lĭ) *agg.* brutto, sgraziato; sconveniente.

uncomfortable (ŭn·kŭm'fĕrt·á·b'l) *agg.* scomodo, molesto, inquietante, spiacevole, imbarazzante.

uncomfortably (ŭn·kŭm'fĕrt·á·blĭ) *avv.* a disagio, scomodamente, inquietamente, molestamente.

uncommon (ŭn·kŏm'ŭn) *agg.* poco comune, insolito, raro. **—ly** *avv.* insolitamente, eccezionalmente.

uncommunicative (ŭn'kŏ·mū'nĭ·kā'tĭv) *agg.* non communicativo, taciturno.

uncomplaining (ŭn'kŏm·plān'ĭng) *agg.* rassegnato, paziente.

uncomplimentary (ŭn'kŏm·plĭ·mĕn'tá·rĭ) *agg.* non lusinghiero, offensivo.

uncompromising (ŭn·kŏm'prŏ·mīz'ĭng) *agg.* inflessibile, ostinato.

unconcern (ŭn'kŏn·sûrn') *n.* disinteresse, indifferenza.

unconcerned (ŭn'kŏn·sûrnd') *agg.* indifferente, imperterrito.

unconditional (ŭn'kŏn·dĭsh'ŭn·ăl) agg. incondizionato, assoluto.

unconformable (ŭn'kŏn·fôr'må·b'l) agg. incompatibile.

uncongenial (ŭn'kŏn·jēn'yăl) agg. incompatibile; sgradevole, antipatico.

unconnected (ŭn'kŏ·nĕk'tĕd) agg. staccato; estraneo (a), senza rapporti, non imparentato, indipendente (da); vago, slegato.

unconquerable (ŭn·kŏng'kēr·å·b'l) agg. invincibile, indomabile, insormontabile.

unconquered (ŭn·kŏng'kērd) agg. invitto, indomito, inespugnato.

unconscionable (ŭn·kŏn'shŭn·å·b'l) agg. irragionevole, eccessivo; non coscienzioso; smisurato.

unconscious (ŭn·kŏn'shŭs) n. (psic.) inconscio. agg. inconscio, ignaro, inconsapevole; svenuto; involontario. —ness n. stato di incoscienza; automatismo.

unconstrained (ŭn'kŏn·strānd') agg. spontaneo, libero, disinvolto.

unconstraint (ŭn'kŏn·strānt') n. disinvoltura, spontaneità, libertà.

uncontrollable (ŭn'kŏn·trōl'å·b'l) agg. incontrollabile, irresistibile.

unconventional (ŭn'kŏn·vĕn'shŭn·ăl) agg. non convenzionale, semplice, schietto, alla buona.

unconvinced (ŭn'kŏn·vĭnst') agg. incredulo, scettico.

uncork (ŭn·kôrk') vt. sturare, stappare.

uncorrupted (ŭn'kŏ·rŭp'tĕd) agg. incorrotto; genuino; non putrefatto.

uncounted (ŭn·koun'tĕd) agg. innumerevole, incalcolabile.

uncouple (ŭn·kŭp''l) vt. disgiungere, sganciare; spaiare; disinnestare.

uncouth (ŭn·kōōth') agg. goffo, rozzo, sgraziato, grottesco, strano.

uncover (ŭn·kŭv'ĕr) vt. scoprire, scoperchiare; rivelare; esporre. vi. scoprirsi (il capo).

unction (ŭngk'shŭn) n. unzione, santità, grazia divina, fervore; balsamo.

unctuous (ŭngk'tṳ·ŭs) agg. untuoso, oleoso; insinuante, mellifluo.

uncultivated (ŭn·kŭl'tĭ·vāt'ĕd) agg. incolto (di terreno).

uncultured (ŭn·kŭl'tṳrd) agg. incolto (ignorante).

uncurl (ŭn·kûrl') vt. raddrizzare, svolgere, spianare. vi. raddrizzarsi (spec. da una posa raggomitolata).

uncut (ŭn·kŭt') agg. non tagliato, intero, intonso, grezzo (di diamante).

undamaged (ŭn·dăm'ĭjd) agg. indenne, intatto, in buono stato.

undaunted (ŭn·dôn'tĕd) agg. imperturbato, intrepido, pertinace.

undeceive (ŭn'dē·sēv') vt. disingannare, aprire gli occhi a.

undecided (ŭn'dē·sīd'ĕd) agg. indeciso, incerto.

undelivered (ŭn'dē·lĭ'vērd) agg. non recapitato, giacente.

undeniable (ŭn'dē·nī'å·b'l) agg. innegabile.

under (ŭn'dēr) agg. inferiore, subordinato. prep. sotto, al di sotto di, meno di, dipendente da: — sail, in navigazione; — way, in corso, in viaggio; — age, minore di età; — cover of, col favore di, al riparo di; — pretense of, col pretesto di; to be — obligation to, essere in debito con. avv. sotto, al di sotto, in grado inferiore, in soggezione: to go —, fallire, far fiasco.

underact (ŭn'dēr·ăkt') vt., vi. recitare in maniera fiacca; recitare in maniera sobria o scarna (per dar maggior vigore alla parte).

underbred (ŭn'dēr·brĕd') agg. maleducato; bastardo.

underbrush (ŭn'dēr·brŭsh') n. sottobosco.

undercarriage (ŭn'dēr·kăr'ĭj) n. (auto) telaio; (aeron.) carrello d'atterraggio.

undercharge (ŭn'dēr·chärj') vt. fare un prezzo di favore a; applicare un prezzo ridotto a.

underclothes (ŭn'dēr·klōthz) n.pl. biancheria personale.

undercurrent (ŭn'dēr·kûr'ĕnt) n. corrente subacquea; influenza (o tendenza) segreta.

undercut (ŭn'dēr·kŭt') vt., vi. vendere (o lavorare) a prezzo minore.

underdog (ŭn'dēr·dŏg') n. (fam.) diseredato; chi ha la peggio, vinto, perdente.

underdone (ŭn'dēr·dŭn) agg. poco cotto.

underdose (ŭn'dēr·dōs') n. dose scarsa.

underestimate (ŭn'dēr·ĕs'tĭ·māt) vt. sottovalutare.

underexposed (ŭn'dēr·ĕks·pōzd') agg. (fot.) sottesposto.

underfed (ŭn'dēr·fĕd') agg. malnutrito.

underfoot (ŭn'dēr·fŏŏt') avv. sotto i piedi; sul terreno.

undergarment (ŭn'dēr·gär'mĕnt) n. indumento intimo.

undergo (ŭn'dēr·gō') vt. (pass. underwent, pp. undergone) subire, sottostare a, sopportare.

undergraduate (ŭn'dēr·grăd'ū·åt) agg. laureando.

underground (ŭn'dĕr·ground') *n.* sottosuolo; passaggio sotterraneo; metropolitana (*ferrovia*); (*pol.*) resistenza partigiana. *agg.* sotterraneo, clandestino. *avv.* sotterra; clandestinamente.

underhand (ŭn'dĕr·hănd') **underhanded** *agg.* segreto, tortuoso, subdolo.

underlie (ŭn'dĕr·lī') *vt.* (*pass.* **underlay**, *pp.* **underlain**) sottostare a, essere passibile di; essere sotto a; essere alla base di; formare il substrato di.

underline (ŭn'dĕr·līn') *vt.* sottolineare.

underling (ŭn'dĕr·lĭng) *n.* subalterno.

underlying (ŭn'dĕr·lī'ĭng) *agg.* fondamentale, sottostante, inferiore.

undermine (ŭn'dĕr·mīn') *vt.* minare alle fondamenta; pregiudicare, insidiare.

undermost (ŭn'dĕr·mōst) *agg.sup.* imo, infimo, più basso.

underneath (ŭn'dĕr·nēth') *prep.* sotto a, al di sotto di. *avv.* sotto, di sotto.

undernourished (ŭn'dĕr·nûr'ĭsht) *agg.* denutrito.

undernourishment (ŭn'dĕr·nûr'ĭsh·mĕnt) *n.* denutrizione.

underpaid (ŭn'dĕr·pād') *agg.* mal pagato.

underpay (ŭn'dĕr·pā') *vt.* pagare inadeguatamente.

underproof (ŭn'dĕr·proof') *agg.* a bassa gradazione alcoolica.

underrate (un'dĕr·rāt') *vt.* sottovalutare.

underscore (un'dĕr·skōr') *vt.* sottolineare.

under secretary (ŭn'dĕr sĕk'rĕ·tĕr·ĭ) vicesegretario; sottosegretario.

undersell (ŭn'dĕr·sĕl') *vt.* (*pass.*, *pp.* **undersold**) svendere; vendere più a buon mercato di.

undershirt (ŭn'dĕr·shûrt') *n.* maglietta; camicetta.

underside (ŭn'dĕr·sīd') *n.* parte inferiore.

undersign (ŭn'dĕr·sīn') *vt.* sottoscrivere.

undersigned (un'dĕr·sīnd') *n.*, *agg.* sottoscritto.

undersized (ŭn'dĕr·sīzd') *agg.* in miniatura, di misura minima.

underskirt (ŭn'dĕr·skûrt') *n.* sottana, sottoveste.

understand (ŭn'dĕr·stănd') *vt.*, *vi.* (*pass.*, *pp.* **understood**) capire, afferrare; rendersi conto di; sentir dire, essere informato di; sottintendere: **I — that he is coming**, mi risulta che egli verrà; **it is understood that**, resta inteso che; **to make oneself understood**, farsi capire.

understandable (ŭn'dĕr·stăn'dá·b'l) *agg.* comprensibile.

understanding *n.* intelligenza, comprensione; intesa; competenza, discernimento; *agg.* competente, comprensivo.

understate (ŭn'dĕr·stāt') *vt.* esporre inefficacemente, sminuire.

understatement (ŭn'dĕr·stāt'mĕnt) *n.* esposizione inadeguata, attenuazione.

understood (ŭn'der·stŏŏd') *pass.*, *pp. di* **to understand**. *agg.* inteso, convenuto, stabilito, sottinteso.

understudy (ŭn'dĕr·stŭd'ĭ) *n.* attore sostituto. *vt.*, *vi.* studiare una parte per sostituire un attore.

undertake (ŭn'dĕr·tāk') *vt.*, *vi.* (*pass.* **undertook**, *pp.* **undertaken**) intraprendere, tentare; assumersi, impegnarsi (*a*); prendere in appalto.

undertaker (ŭn'dĕr·tāk'ĕr) *n.* impresario di pompe funebri.

undertaking (ŭn'dĕr·tāk'ĭng) *n.* impresa, compito, impegno.

undertone (ŭn'dĕr·tōn') *n.* tono sommesso, susurro, sfumatura.

undertook (ŭn'dĕr·tŏŏk') *pass. di* **to undertake**.

undervalue (ŭn'dĕr·văl'ū) *vt.* sottovalutare, sminuire, deprezzare.

underwear (ŭn'dĕr·wâr') *n.* biancheria personale.

underwent (ŭn'dĕr·wĕnt') *pass. di* **to undergo**.

underwood (ŭn'dĕr·wŏŏd') *n.* sottobosco.

underworld (ŭn'dĕr·wûrld') *n.* malavita, bassifondi, delinquenza; inferno; antipodi.

underwrite (ŭn'dĕr·rīt') *vt.* (*pass.* **underwrote**, *pp.* **underwritten**), sottoscrivere, assicurarsi (*contrarre un'assicurazione*). *vi.* fare l'assicuratore.

undeserved (ŭn'dĕ·zûrvd') *agg.* immeritato, ingiusto.

undeserving *agg.* immeritevole.

undesirable (ŭn'dĕ·zīr'á·b'l) *n.*, *agg.* indesiderabile, inauspicabile.

undetected (ŭn'dĕ·tĕkt'ĭd) *agg.* inavvertito, inosservato, non scoperto.

undeveloped (ŭn'dĕ·vĕl'ŭpt) *agg.* non sviluppato.

undignified (ŭn'dĭg'nĭ·fīd) *agg.* non dignitoso, incomposto, indecoroso.

undiluted (ŭn'dĭ·lūt'ĭd) *agg.* puro, non diluito.

undiminished (ŭn'dĭ·mĭn'ĭsht) *agg.* costante, non diminuito, implacato.

undine (ŭn·dēn') *n.* ondina, ninfa.

undisciplined (ŭn·dĭs'ĭ·plĭnd) *agg.* indisciplinato.

undiscovered (ŭn'dĭs·kŭv'ẽrd) *agg.* non scoperto, nascosto, sconosciuto.

undisguised (ŭn'dĭs·gīzd') *agg.* senza travestimento; aperto, sincero, genuino, esplicito.

undismayed (ŭn'dĭs·mād') *agg.* imperterrito.

undisputed (ŭn'dĭs·pūt'ĕd) *agg.* incontestato.

undistinguishable (ŭn'dĭs·tĭng'gwĭsh·á·b'l) *agg.* indistinguibile, confuso, irriconoscibile.

undistinguished (ŭn'dĭs·tĭng'gwĭsht) *agg.* indistinto, oscuro; privo di distinzione.

undisturbed (ŭn'dĭs·tûrbd') *agg.* indisturbato, imperturbato.

undivided (ŭn'dĭ·vīd'ĕd) *agg.* indiviso.

undo (ŭn·dōō') *vt.* (*pass.* undid, *pp.* undone) disfare, sciogliere, snodare; annullare; distruggere, rovinare: to — one's hair, sciogliersi i capelli.

undoing (ŭn·dōō'ĭng) *n.* rovina; annullamento; distruzione.

undone (ŭn·dŭn') *pp. di* to undo, *agg.* disfatto, distrutto, incompiuto; omesso; annullato: it is still —, è ancora da farsi; to come —, disfarsi, sciogliersi.

undoubted (ŭn·dout'ĕd) *agg.* indubitato, certo.

undress (ŭn·drĕs') *n.* (*mil.*) bassa tenuta. *vt.* svestire, sbendare. *vi.* svestirsi.

undue (ŭn·dū') *agg.* superfluo, eccessivo, abusivo, indebito.

undulate (ŭn'dū̆·lāt) *vt.* ondulare, far ondeggiare. *vi.* ondeggiare, vibrare.

undulation (ŭn'dū̆·lā'shŭn) *n.* ondulazione, ondeggiamento.

undulatory (ŭn'dū̆·lȧ·tō'rĭ) *agg.* ondulatorio.

unduly (ŭn·dū'lĭ) *avv.* indebitamente, abusivamente; eccessivamente.

undying (ŭn·dī'ĭng) *agg.* immortale.

unearned (ŭn·ûrnd') *agg.* immeritato.

unearth (ŭn·ûrth') *vt.* dissotterrare; stanare, rintracciare.

uneasily (ŭn·ēz'ĭ·lĭ) *avv.* a disagio, penosamente, inquietamente.

uneasiness (ŭn·ēz'ĭ·nĕs) *n.* disagio, ansia, inquietudine, imbarazzo.

uneasy (ŭn·ēz'ĭ) *agg.* gravoso, molesto, imbarazzante; imbarazzato, preoccupato, inquieto: to feel —, sentirsi a disagio.

uneatable (ŭn·ēt'á·b'l) *agg.* immangiabile.

uneducated (ŭn·ĕd'ū·kāt'ĕd) *agg.* ignorante.

unembarrassed (ŭn'ĕm·băr'ăst) *agg.* libero da impacci; imperturbato, disinvolto.

unemotional (ŭn'ē·mō'shŭn·ăl) *agg.* non emozionante; non emotivo; calmo, imperturbabile.

unemployed (ŭn'ĕm·ploid') *agg.* inutilizzato; disoccupato.

unemployment (ŭn'ĕm·ploi'mĕnt) *n.* disoccupazione.

unending (ŭn·ĕn'dĭng) *agg.* interminabile, infinito.

unendurable (ŭn'ĕn·dūr'á·b'l) *agg.* insopportabile.

unequal (ŭn·ē'kwăl) *agg.* ineguale; sproporzionato; inferiore (*non all'altezza di*), impari: to be — to one's task, non essere all'altezza del proprio compito.

unequivocal (ŭn'ē·kwĭv'ō·kăl) *agg.* palese, chiaro, schietto.

unerring (ŭn·ûr'ĭng) *agg.* infallibile.

unessential (ŭn'ĕ·sĕn'shăl) *agg.* superfluo.

uneven (ŭn·ē'vĕn) *agg.* ineguale; scabroso; dispari (*di numero*).

uneventful (ŭn'ē·vĕnt'fŏŏl) *agg.* quieto, monotono, senza incidenti.

unexceptionable (ŭn'ĕk·sĕp'shŭn·á·b'l) *agg.* ineccepibile, irreprensibile.

unexpected (ŭn'ĕks·pĕk'tĕd) *agg.* inatteso, imprevisto; —ly *avv.* inaspettatamente, improvvisamente.

unexpensive (ŭn'ĕks·pĕn'sĭv) *agg.* economico, a buon mercato.

unexperienced (ŭn'ĕks·pēr'ĭ·ĕnst) *agg.* inesperto.

unexplained (ŭn'ĕks·plānd') *agg.* inesplicato.

unexplored (ŭn'ĕks·plōrd') *agg.* inesplorato.

unexpressed (ŭn'ĕks·prĕst') *agg.* inespresso, sottinteso.

unexpurgated (ŭn'ĕks'pēr·gāt'ĕd) *agg.* integrale, non espurgato.

unextinguished (ŭn'ĕks·tĭng'gwĭsht) *agg.* inestinto.

unfailing (ŭn·fāl'ĭng) *agg.* infallibile, immancabile.

unfair (ŭn·fâr') *agg.* ingiusto, sleale, disonesto. —ly *avv.* ingiustamente, slealmente.

unfaithful (ŭn·fāth'fŏŏl) *agg.* infedele.

unfaltering (ŭn·fôl'tẽr·ĭng) *agg.* fermo, impassibile; risoluto; immutabile.

unfamiliar (ŭn'fá·mĭl'yẽr) *agg.* non familiare, inusitato, nuovo, sconosciuto: to be — with, non intendersi di, non sapere.

unfashionable (ŭn·făsh'ŭn·á·b'l) *agg.* inelegante, fuori moda: to be —, non essere di moda.

unfasten (ŭn·fàs''n) *vt.* slegare, slacciare, sganciare, aprire. *vi.* sganciarsi, slegarsi.

unfathomable (ŭn·făth'ŭm·á·b'l) *agg.* insondabile.

unfathomed (ŭn·făth'ŭmd) *agg.* insondato.

unfavorable (ŭn·fā'vẽr·á·b'l) *agg.* sfavorevole, contrario.

unfeeling (ŭn·fēl'ĭng) *agg.* insensibile, crudele.

unfeigned (ŭn·fānd') *agg.* genuino, sincero.

unfetter (ŭn·fĕt'ẽr) *vt.* liberare dalle pastoie.

unfinished (ŭn·fĭn'ĭsht) *agg.* incompleto, incompiuto, mal rifinito.

unfit (ŭn·fĭt') *agg.* disadatto, inidoneo, indegno (*di*). *vt.* rendere disadatto, inabilitare, squalificare.

unfledged (ŭn·flĕjd') *agg.* implume, inesperto.

unflinching (ŭn·flĭn'chĭng) *agg.* risoluto, imperterrito.

unfold (ŭn·fōld') *vt.* aprire, spiegare, esporre, sviluppare, rivelare. *vi.* espandersi, dispiegarsi, aprirsi.

unforced (ŭn·fôrst') *agg.* non forzato, spontaneo, naturale.

unforeseen (ŭn'fōr·sēn') *agg.* imprevisto.

unforgettable (ŭn'fŏr·gĕt'á·b'l) *agg.* indimenticabile.

unforgivable (ŭn'fŏr·gĭv'á·b'l) *agg.* imperdonabile.

unformed (ŭn·fôrmd') *agg.* informe, embrionale.

unfortunate (ŭn·fôr'tū·nĭt) *n.* sventurato; donna perduta. *agg.* sfortunato, deplorevole. **—ly** *avv.* sfortunatamente; deplorevolmente; purtroppo.

unfounded (ŭn·foun'dĕd) *agg.* non fondato, infondato.

unfrequented (ŭn'frē·kwĕn'tĕd) *agg.* poco frequentato, solitario.

unfriendly (ŭn·frĕnd'lĭ) *agg.* scontroso; malevolo, ostile.

unfruitful (ŭn·frōōt'fŏŏl) *agg.* improduttivo, vano, sterile.

unfulfilled (ŭn·fŏŏl·fĭld') *agg.* non adempiuto, incompiuto.

unfurl (ŭn·fûrl') *vt.* srotolare, svolgere; (*naut.*) spiegare. *vi.* distendersi.

unfurnished (ŭn·fûr'nĭsht) *agg.* smobiliato, sprovvisto.

ungainly (ŭn·gān'lĭ) *agg.* rozzo, goffo.

ungenerous (ŭn·jĕn'ẽr·ŭs) *agg.* ingeneroso; taccagno.

ungentle (ŭn·jĕn't'l) *agg.* aspro, scortese, sgarbato.

ungentlemanly (ŭn·jĕn't'l·măn·lĭ')*agg.* indegno di un gentiluomo, riprovevole.

unglazed (ŭn·glāzd') *agg.* senza vetri.

ungodly (ŭn·gŏd'lĭ) *agg.* empio, irreligioso.

ungovernable (ŭn·gŭv'ẽr·ná·b'l) *agg.* ingovernabile, sfrenato, sregolato.

ungraceful (ŭn·grās'fŏŏl) *agg.* goffo, sgraziato.

ungracious (ŭn·grā'shŭs) *agg.* scortese, scompiacente; spiacevole.

ungrateful (ŭn·grāt'fŏŏl) *agg.* ingrato.

unguarded (ŭn·gär'dĕd) *agg.* improtetto; disattento, incauto.

unhallowed (ŭn·hăl'ōd) *agg.* profano, empio.

unhappiness (ŭn·hăp'ĭ·nĕs) *n.* infelicità.

unhappy (ŭn·hăp'ĭ) *agg.* infelice, sfortunato, inopportuno.

unharmed (ŭn·härmd') *agg.* illeso, intatto, incolume.

unhealthful (ŭn·hĕlth'fŏŏl) *agg.* insalubre, malsano, cagionevole.

unhealthy (ŭn·hĕl'thĭ) *agg.* malsano, insalubre, pernicioso.

unheard (ŭn·hûrd') *agg.* non udito, inascoltato, inesaudito: **— of,** inaudito, sconosciuto.

unheeded (ŭn·hēd'ĕd) *agg.* negletto, ignorato, inascoltato.

unhesitating (ŭn·hĕz'ĭ·tāt'ĭng) *agg.* risoluto. **—ly** *avv.* risolutamente.

unhinge (ŭn·hĭnj') *vt.* togliere dai cardini, sgangherare, sbilanciare, sconvolgere, staccare.

unhitch (ŭn·hĭch') *vt.* disincagliare, sganciare, distaccare.

unholy (ŭn·hō'lĭ) *agg.* empio, profano.

unhook (ŭn·hŏŏk') *vt.* sganciare, sfibbiare.

unhorse (ŭn·hôrs') *vt.* disarcionare, far smontare da cavallo.

unhurried (ŭn·hûr'ĭd) *agg.* calmo, comodo, senza fretta. **—ly** *avv.* con calma, con comodo, senza fretta.

unhurt (un·hûrt') *agg.* incolume.

unhygienic (ŭn'hī·jĭ·ĕn'ĭk) *agg.* anti-igienico.

unification (ū'nĭ·fĭ·kā'shŭn) *n.* unificazione.

uniform (ū'nĭ·fôrm) *n.* uniforme, divisa. *agg.* uniforme, regolare. *vt.* uniformare.

uniformity (ū'nĭ·fôr'mĭ·tĭ) *n.* uniformità.

unify (ū'nĭ·fī) *vt.* unificare.

unimaginative (ŭn'ĭ·măj'ĭ·ná'tĭv) *agg.* prosaico; privo di fantasia.

unimpaired (ŭn'ĭm·pârd') *agg.* inalterato, intatto, in pieno vigore.

unimpeachable (ŭn'ĭm·pēch'á·b'l) *agg.* irreprensibile; incontestabile, inattaccabile; inaccusabile.

unimportant (ŭn'ĭm·pôr'tănt) *agg.* trascurabile, insignificante.

uninformed (ŭn'ĭn·fôrmd') *agg.* non informato, ignaro, ignorante.

uninhabitable (ŭn'ĭn·hăb'ĭ·tá·b'l) agg. inabitabile.

uninhabited (ŭn'ĭn·hăb'ĭ·tĕd) agg. disabitato.

uninjured (ŭn·ĭn'jẽrd) agg. incolume, intatto.

unintelligent (ŭn'ĭn·tĕl'ĭ·jĕnt) agg. ottuso, stupido.

unintelligible (ŭn'ĭn·tĕl'ĭ·jĭ·b'l) agg. inintelligibile, incomprensibile.

unintentional (ŭn'ĭn·tĕn'shŭn·ăl) agg. involontario.

uninterested (ŭn·ĭn'tẽr·ĕs·tĕd) agg. indifferente.

uninteresting (ŭn·ĭn'tẽr·ĕs·tĭng) agg. privo di interesse, insulso, tedioso.

uninterrupted (ŭn'ĭn·tẽ·rŭp'tĕd) agg. ininterrotto.

uninvited (ŭn'ĭn·vĭt'ĕd) agg. non invitato, indesiderato; inopinato.

union (ūn'yŭn) n. unione; matrimonio, combinazione; sindacato; confederazione; tessuto misto; (mecc.) giunto: trade —, sindacato di categoria; — leader, capo di sindacato, sindacalista.

unique (ū·nēk') agg. unico.

unison (ū'nĭ·sŭn) n. unisono: in —, all'unisono.

unit (ū'nĭt) n. unità, quantità fissa.

unite (ū·nīt') vt. unire, riunire. vi. unirsi, riunirsi.

unity (ū'nĭ·tĭ) n. unità, concordia.

universal (ū'nĭ·vûr'săl) agg. universale.

universe (ū'nĭ·vûrs) n. universo.

university (ū'nĭ·vûr'sĭ·tĭ) n. università.

unjust (ŭn·jŭst') agg. ingiusto.

unkempt (ŭn·kĕmpt') agg. arruffato; trasandato; spettinato.

unkind (ŭn·kīnd') agg. scortese; malvagio, crudele. —liness n. scortesia; malvagità. —ly agg. sgarbato, malvagio; inclemente (del tempo). avv. sgarbatamente, crudelmente: to take something —, prendere qualcosa in mala parte. —ness n. scortesia, durezza, crudeltà.

unknowing (ŭn·nō'ĭng) agg. ignaro; ignorante.

unknown (ŭn·nōn') agg. sconosciuto, ignoto; — quantity, incognita.

unlace (ŭn·lās') vt. slacciare.

unlade (ŭn·lād') vt. scaricare.

unlatch (ŭn·lăch') vt. aprire la serratura di.

unlawful (ŭn·lô'fŏŏl) agg. illegale, illecito, illegittimo.

unlearn (ŭn·lûrn') vt. disimparare.

unlearned (ŭn·lûrnd') agg. ignorante; uon imparato, intuito, istintivo.

unleash (ŭn·lēsh') vt. sguinzagliare.

unleavened (ŭn·lĕv'ĕnd) agg. non lievitato, azzimo.

unless (ŭn·lĕs') cong. a meno che, se non, fuorchè, eccetto che. prep. eccetto.

unlike (ŭn·līk') agg. dissimile, diverso, non somigliante. prep. diversamente da, a differenza di.

unlikelihood (ŭn·līk'lĭ·hŏŏd), unlikeliness (ŭn·līk'lĭ·nĕs) n. inverosimiglianza, improbabilità.

unlikely (ŭn·līk'lĭ) agg. improbabile, inv32erosimile. avv. improbabilmente.

unlimited (ŭn·lĭm'ĭ·tĕd) agg. illimitato.

unlit (ŭn·lĭt') agg. spento.

unload (ŭn·lōd') vt., vi. scaricare; (S.U.) smaltire, liquidare.

unlock (ŭn·lŏk') vt. aprire (una porta chiusa a chiave, ecc.).

unlooked-for (ŭn·lŏŏkt·fôr') agg. inatteso, imprevisto.

unloose (ŭn·lōōs') vt.sciogliere, slegare, allentare (un nodo), liberare, mollare.

unlucky (ŭn·lŭk'ĭ) agg. sfortunato, sinistro, malaugurato, funesto.

unman (ŭn·măn') vt. abbattere, scoraggiare, snervare; rammollire; evirare; (naut.) disarmare.

unmanageable (ŭn·măn'ĭj·á·b'l) agg. ingovernabile, indomabile, intrattabile, ribelle.

unmanly (ŭn·măn'lĭ) agg. molle, effeminato, debole, vile, infantile.

unmannerly (ŭn·măn'ẽr·lĭ) agg. maleducato, sgarbato, grossolano. avv. villanamente, sgarbatamente.

unmarked (ŭn·märkt') agg. non marcato (o contrassegnato); illeso; inosservato.

unmarried (ŭn·măr'ĭd) agg. celibe; nubile; non sposato.

unmask (ŭn·mask') vt. smascherare. vi. gettare la maschera.

unmatched (ŭn·măcht') agg. incomparabile, senza pari; scompagnato.

unmeaning (ŭn·mēn'ĭng) agg. privo di significato; insignificante.

unmeasured (ŭn·mĕzh'ẽrd) agg. incommensurato, illimitato; irregolare.

unmentionable (ŭn·mĕn'shŭn·á·b'l) agg. innominabile, indegno di menzione. n. pl. (scherz.) calzoni.

unmerciful (ŭn·mûr'sĭ·fŏŏl) agg. inesorabile, crudele.

unmindful (ŭn·mīnd'fŏŏl) agg. immemore, noncurante.

unmistakable (ŭn'mĭs·tāk'á·b'l) agg. inconfondibile, evidente.

unmitigated (ŭn·mĭt'ĭ·gāt'ĕd) agg. non mitigato, implacato: — impudence, sfrontatezza senza pari; — liar, bugiardo fatto e finito; — ass, asino calzato e vestito; — fraud, truffa bella e buona.

unmolested (ŭn·mŏ·lĕs'tĕd) agg. indisturbato.

unmoor (ŭn·mōōr') vt. (naut.)disormeggiare. vi. levare l'ancora.

unmovable (ŭn·mōōv'á·b'l) agg. saldo, inamovibile, inflessibile.

unmoved (ŭn·mōōvd') agg. immoto; freddo, indifferente.

unmusical (ŭn·mū'zi·kál) agg. disarmonico, stridente.

unnamed (ŭn·nāmd') agg. anonimo, innominato.

unnatural (ŭn·năt'ū̆·rál) agg. innaturale, anormale, snaturato, artificioso, eccessivo: — mother, madre snaturata.

unnecessary (ŭn·nĕs'ĕ·sĕr'ĭ) agg.superfluo, inutile.

unnerve (ŭn·nûrv') vt. togliere forza a, togliere fermezza a, togliere coraggio a.

unnerved (ŭn·nûrvd') agg. privato di forza o di fermezza o di coraggio.

unnoticed (ŭn·nō'tĭst) agg. inosservato, inavvertito.

unnumbered (ŭn·nŭm'bĕrd) agg. non numerato; innumerevole.

unobliging (ŭn'ô·blīj'ĭng) agg. scompiacente.

unobserved (ŭn'ŏb·zûrvd') agg. inosservato.

unobstructed (ŭn'ŏb·strŭk'tĕd) agg. libero, non ostruito, non ostacolato.

unobtainable (ŭn'ŏb·tān'á·b'l) agg. introvabile; non ottenibile.

unobtrusive (ŭn'ŏb·trōō'sĭv) agg. modesto, timido, discreto.

unoccupied (ŭn·ŏk'ū·pīd) agg. disoccupato, ozioso; disabitato, vacante, libero.

unoffending (ŭn'ô·fĕn'dĭng) agg. innocuo, innocente.

unofficial (ŭn'ô·fĭsh'ál) agg. non ufficiale.

unopened (ŭn·ō'pĕnd) agg. chiuso, sigillato, non aperto.

unorganized (ŭn·ôr'gán·īzd) agg. non organizzato, inorganico.

unorthodox (ŭn·ôr'thô·dŏks) agg. eterodosso.

unostentatious (ŭn'ŏs·tĕn·tā'shŭs) agg. sobrio, semplice, privo d'ostentazione.

unpack (ŭn·păk') vt. disimballare, scaricare, disfare (valigie, ecc.). vi. disfare i bagagli.

unpaid (ŭn·pād') agg. non pagato, insoluto: — bills, conti da pagare.

unpalatable (ŭn·păl'ĭt·á·b'l) agg. sgradevole al gusto; (fig.) ostico.

unparalleled (ŭn·păr'ǎ·lĕld) agg. senza pari, ineguagliabile, unico.

unpardonable (ŭn·pär'd'n·á·b'l) agg. imperdonabile.

unpaved (ŭn·pāvd') agg. non pavimentato.

unperceived (ŭn'pĕr·sēvd') agg. inosservato, inavvertito.

unperturbed (ŭn'pĕr·tûrbd') agg. imperturbato.

unpleasant (ŭn·plĕz'ănt) agg. sgradevole, villano. —ly avv. sgradevolmente, villanamente. —ness n. spiacevolezza; villania; disaccordo; complicazione; incidente, dissapore.

unpolished (ŭn·pŏl'ĭsht) agg. rozzo, grezzo, non rifinito.

unpopular (ŭn·pŏp'ū·lĕr) agg. impopolare.

unpracticed (ŭn·prăk'tĭst) agg. inesperto.

unprecedented (ŭn·prĕs'ĕ·dĕn'tĕd) agg. senza precedenti, nuovo.

unpredictable (ŭn'prē·dĭk'tá·b'l) agg. imprevedibile; (fam.) capriccioso, balzano.

unprejudiced (ŭn·prej'ŏŏ·dĭst) agg. imparziale, senza pregiudizi.

unpremeditated (ŭn'prē·mĕd'ĭ·tāt'ĕd) agg. impremeditato.

unprepared (ŭn'prē·pârd') agg. impreparato.

unprepossessing (ŭn'prē·pô·zĕs'ĭng) agg. sgradevole, antipatico.

unpretentious (ŭn'prē·tĕn'shŭs) agg. sobrio, non pretenzioso.

unpreventable (ŭn'prē·vĕn'tá·b'l) agg. inevitabile.

unprincipled (ŭn·prĭn's ĭ·p'ld) agg. amorale.

unprintable (ŭn·prĭn'tá·b'l) agg. non stampabile.

unprofitable (ŭn·prŏf'ĭt·á·b'l) agg. non redditizio, poco proficuo, inutile.

unpromising (ŭn·prŏm'ĭs·ĭng) agg. poco promettente.

unpronounceable (ŭn'prô·noun'sá·b'l) agg. impronunziabile.

unprotected (ŭn'prô·tĕk'tĕd) agg. non protetto.

unprovided (ŭn'prô·vĭd'ĕd) agg. sprovvisto; impreparato.

unprovoked (ŭn'prô·vōkt') agg. non provocato, gratuito.

unpublished (ŭn·pŭb'lĭsht) agg. inedito; segreto.

unpunished (ŭn·pŭn'ĭsht) agg. impunito.

unqualified (ŭn·kwŏl'ĭ·fīd) agg. inidoneo; incondizionato, assoluto.

unquenchable (ŭn·kwĕn'chá·b'l) agg. inestinguibile.

unquestionable (ŭn·kwĕs'chŭn·á·b'l) agg. incontestabile.

unquote (ŭn′kwōt′) *vt.* (*S.U.*) chiudere una citazione, chiudere le virgolette.

unravel (ŭn·răv′ĕl) *vt.* districare, sbrogliare, sciogliere, dipanare, chiarire, risolvere. *vi.* sciogliersi, districarsi.

unread (ŭn·rĕd′) *agg.* non letto; illetterato, ignorante, incolto.

unreal (ŭn·rē′ăl) *agg.* irreale, fantastico.

unreasonable (ŭn·rē′z′n·à·b′l) *agg.* irragionevole, eccessivo, assurdo.

unrecognizable (ŭn·rĕk′ŏg·nīz′à·b′l) *agg.* irriconoscibile.

unreconcilable (ŭn·rĕk′ŏn·sīl′à·b′l) *agg.* irreconciliabile, incompatibile.

unrecorded (ŭn′rē·kôr′dĕd) *agg.* non registrato; dimenticato, ignorato.

unreel (ŭn·rēl′) *vt.* svolgere (*dalla bobina*).

unrefined (ŭn′rē·fīnd′) *agg.* non raffinato, grezzo, grossolano.

unregretful (ŭn′rē·grĕt′fŏŏl) *agg.* senza rimpianti, rassegnato.

unregretted (ŭn′rē·grĕt′ĭd) *agg.* non rimpianto.

unrehearsed (ŭn′rē·hûrsd′) *agg.* (*teat.*) senza prove; improvvisato.

unrelated (ŭn′rē·lāt′ĕd) *agg.* senza rapporto (*con*), non imparentato, non attinente (*a*), indipendente.

unrelenting (ŭn′rē·lĕn′tĭng) *agg.* inesorabile.

unreliable (ŭn′rē·lī′à·b′l) *agg.* che non dà affidamento, inattendibile, dubbio; insolvibile; precario.

unremitting (ŭn′rē·mĭt′ĭng) *agg.* pertinace, incessante.

unrequested (ŭn′rē·kwĕst′ĭd) *agg.* non richiesto, spontaneo.

unrequited (ŭn′rē·kwīt′ĕd) *agg.* non ripagato, non ricambiato, inulto.

unreserved (ŭn′rē·zurvd′) *agg.* non riservato; assoluto, completo; comunicativo, franco.

unresisting (ŭn′rē·zĭs′tĭng) *agg.* acquiescente, sottomesso.

unrest (ŭn·rĕst′) *n.* inquietudine, agitazione.

unresting *agg.* perseverante, indefesso.

unrestrained (ŭn′rē·strānd′) *agg.* sfrenato, scatenato.

unrestraint (ŭn′rē·strānt′) *n.* sfrenatezza, abbandono.

unrestricted (ŭn′rē·strĭk′tĕd) *agg.* non limitato.

unrig (ŭn·rĭg′) *vt.* disarmare (*un veliero*); (*fam.*) spogliare, svestire.

unripe (ŭn·rīp′) *agg.* immaturo, acerbo.

unrivaled (ŭn·rī′văld) *agg.* unico, senza pari.

unroll (ŭn·rōl′) *vt.* srotolare, svolgere. *vi.* srotolarsi, svolgersi.

unruffled (ŭn·rŭf′l′d) *agg.* tranquillo, calmo, liscio, imperturbato.

unruly (ŭn·rōōl′ĭ) *agg.* indisciplinato, turbolento, ribelle.

unsaddle (ŭn·săd′′l) *vt.* dissellare, disarcionare.

unsafe (ŭn·sāf′) *agg.* malsicuro, pericoloso.

unsaid (ŭn·sĕd′) *agg.* non detto: **to leave —**, sottacere.

unsalable, unsaleable (ŭn·sāl′à·b′l) *agg.* invendibile. **—ness** *n.* invendibilità.

unsatisfactory (ŭn′săt·ĭs·făk′tō·rĭ) *agg.* non soddisfacente, insufficiente.

unsavory (ŭn·sā′vĕr·ĭ) *agg.* insipido; disgustoso, rivoltante.

unscathed (ŭn·skāthd′) *agg.* incolume, illeso.

unscientific (ŭn′sī·ĕn·tĭf′ĭk) *agg.* non scientifico, empirico.

unscrew (ŭn·skrōō′) *vt.* svitare.

unscrupulous (ŭn·skrōō′pū·lŭs) *agg.* disonesto, senza scrupoli.

unseal (ŭn·sēl′) *vt.* dissigillare, aprire.

unseasonable (ŭn·sē′z′n·à·b′l) *agg.* intempestivo, fuori stagione.

unseat (ŭn·sēt′) *vt.* sloggiare, disarcionare, destituire.

unseeing (ŭn·sē′ĭng) *agg.* che non vede, cieco.

unseemly (ŭn·sēm′lĭ) *agg.* sconveniente, deplorevole, disdicevole. *avv.* sconvenientemente, deplorevolmente.

unseen (ŭn·sēn′) *agg.* invisibile, non visto, inosservato.

unselfish (ŭn·sĕl′fĭsh) *agg.* disinteressato, altruista. **—ness** *n.* disinteresse, altruismo.

unsettle (ŭn·sĕt′′l) *vt.* scompigliare, scuotere, smuovere, rendere precario.

unsettled *agg.* non stabilito; sconvolto; pendente (*di conto*); precario, squilibrato: **— weather**, tempo instabile; **— liquid**, liquido torbido.

unshakable (ŭn·shāk′à·b′l) *agg.* incrollabile.

unshaken (ŭn·shāk′ĕn) *agg.* fermo, imperturbato, inconcusso, saldo.

unshaven (ŭn·shāv′ĕn) *agg.* non rasato.

unsheathe (ŭn·shēth′) *vt.* sguainare.

unsheltered (ŭn·shĕl′tĕrd) *agg.* senza riparo, scoperto.

unshorn (ŭn·shōrn′) *agg.* non tosato, non tagliato.

unshrinkable (ŭn·shrĭngk′à·b′l) *agg.* irrestringibile.

unsightly (ŭn·sīt′lĭ) *agg.* brutto, spiacevole a vedersi.

unsigned (ŭn·sīnd′) *agg.* non firmato.

unsinkable (ŭn·sĭngk'á·b'l) *agg.* inaffondabile.

unskillful (ŭn·skĭl'fŏŏl) *agg.* inabile, goffo.

unskilled (ŭn·skĭld') *agg.* inesperto, non specializzato.

unslaked (ŭn·slākt') *agg.* insaziato, inestinto: — lime, calce viva.

unsociable (ŭn·sō'shá·b'l) *agg.* scontroso, riservato, rustico.

unsold (ŭn·sōld') *agg.* invenduto.

unsought (ŭn·sôt') *agg.* non richiesto.

unsound (ŭn·sound') *agg.* malfermo; squilibrato; disonesto; difettoso, guasto; precario, fallace; insolvibile.

unsparing (ŭn·spâr'ĭng) *agg.* generoso, prodigo.

unspeakable (ŭn·spēk'á·b'l) *agg.* indicibile, inesprimibile; inqualificabile.

unspoiled (ŭn·spoild') *agg.* non rovinato, non sciupato; incorrotto, non viziato; intatto; puro.

unstable (ŭn·stā'b'l) *agg.* instabile, precario.

unstained (ŭn·stānd') *agg.* non macchiato, non colorato, non tinto.

unsteadily (ŭn·stĕd'ĭ·lĭ) *avv.* precariamente, irresolutamente; con passo malfermo; irregolarmente.

unsteadiness (ŭn·stĕd'ĭ·nĕs) *n.* precarietà, irresolutezza, irregolarità, scarsa solidità, incertezza.

unsteady (ŭn·stĕd'ĭ) *agg.* precario, malfermo, irresoluto, incerto; irregolare, vacillante.

unsubdued (ŭn'sŭb·dūd') *agg.* indomato, indomito.

unsuccessful (ŭn'sŭk·sĕs'fŏŏl) *agg.* vano, mancato, infruttuoso: to be —, non avere successo, andare male. —ly *avv.* senza successo, infruttuosamente, vanamente.

unsuitable (ŭn·sūt'á·b'l) *agg.* disadatto, sconveniente, inopportuno.

unsuited (ŭn·sūt'ĕd) *agg.* disdicevole, disadatto.

unsullied (ŭn·sŭl'ĭd) *agg.* incontaminato, immacolato, puro.

unsupported (ŭn·sŭ·pôr'tĕd) *agg.* non sostenuto, non aiutato, non suffragato.

unsure (ŭn·shŏŏr') *agg.* incerto, malsicuro.

unsurpassed (ŭn'sẽr·pȧst') *agg.* insuperato, non sorpassato.

unsuspected (ŭn'sŭs·pĕk'tĕd) *agg.* insospettato, ignorato.

unsuspecting (ŭn'sŭs·pĕk'tĭng) *agg.* non sospettoso, impreparato.

untainted (ŭn·tān'tĕd) *agg.* incorrotto, immacolato, puro.

untalented (ŭn·tăl'ĕn·tĕd) *agg.* inetto, privo di doti (o d'ingegno).

untamed (ŭn·tāmd') *agg.* indomato.

untarnished (ŭn·tär'nĭsht) *agg.* non appannato, pulito, lucente; puro; non denigrato; non annerito, non ossidato.

untenable (ŭn·tĕn'á·b'l) *agg.* indifendibile, insostenibile.

unthankful (ŭn·thăngk'fŏŏl) *agg.* ingrato.

unthinkable (ŭn·thĭngk'á·b'l) *agg.* inconcepibile, impensabile.

unthinking (ŭn·thĭngk'ĭng) *agg.* irriflessivo, sconsiderato.

untidy (ŭn·tī'dĭ) *agg.* disordinato, sudicio, trasandato, sciatto.

untie (ŭn·tī') *vt.* slegare, sciogliere (*un nodo*).

until (ŭn·tĭl') *prep.* sino (a). *cong.* finchè, fintantochè, non prima di: — now, — this day, fino a oggi, finora; — then, fino allora.

untimely (ŭn·tīm'lĭ) *agg.* intempestivo, inopportuno, prematuro. *avv.* intempestivamente, prematuramente.

untiring (ŭn·tīr'ĭng) *agg.* costante, pertinace; infaticabile.

unto (ŭn·tōō) *prep.* a, verso, nei confronti di, sino a.

untold (ŭn·tōld') *agg.* non detto, non raccontato, inespresso, sottaciuto, sottinteso; innumerevole, immenso, incalcolabile.

untouched (ŭn·tŭcht') *agg.* intatto; non menzionato; non commosso: to leave —, non toccare, lasciare intatto.

untoward (ŭn·tō'ẽrd) *agg.* sfavorevole, malauguroso; indocile, goffo, perverso.

untrained (ŭn·trānd') *agg.* non addestrato, inesperto, indisciplinato.

untrammeled (ŭn·trăm'ĕld) *agg.* senza intralci.

untried (ŭn·trīd') *agg.* intentato; inesperto; non provato; non processato.

untrod (ŭn·trŏd'), **untrodden** (ŭn·trŏd'n) *agg.* deserto, non battuto, non calpestato.

untroubled (ŭn·trŭb''ld) *agg.* imperturbato, calmo, limpido.

untrue (ŭn·trōō') *agg.* falso, inesatto; insincero, sleale.

untruth (ŭn·trōōth') *n.* menzogna, falsità.

unturned (ŭn·tûrnd') *agg.* non voltato: to leave no stone —, non lasciar nulla di intentato.

untutored (ŭn·tū'tẽrd) *agg.* non istruito, ignorante.

untwine (ŭn·twīn'), **untwist** (ŭn·twĭst')

vt. disfare (*ciò che è ritorto*), districare. *vi.* disfarsi (*detto di fune, ecc.*).

unused (ŭn·ūzd′) *agg.* non usato, nuovo; non abituato.

unusual (ŭn·ū′zhŏŏ·ăl) *agg.* insolito, eccezionale, raro, straordinario.

unutterable (ŭn·ŭt′ẽr·à·b'l) *agg.* inesprimibile, indicibile.

unvalued (ŭn·văl′ūd) *agg.* non valutato, inestimabile.

unvarnished (ŭn·vär′nĭsht) *agg.* non verniciato; (*fig.*) non artefatto, semplice, naturale, puro, schietto.

unvarying (ŭn·vâr′ĭ·ĭng) *agg.* invariabile, costante, invariato.

unveil (un·vāl′) *vt.* svelare, scoprire.

unverified (ŭn·vẽr′ĭ·fĭd) *agg.* non verificato.

unwanted (ŭn·wŏn′tĕd) *agg.* indesiderato; superfluo.

unwarranted (ŭn·wŏr′ăn·tĕd) *agg.* abusivo; ingiustificato; non garantito.

unwary (ŭn·wâr′ĭ) *agg.* incauto.

unwashed (ŭn·wŏsht′) *agg.* non lavato, sporco.

unwavering (ŭn·wā′vẽr·ĭng) *agg.* saldo, risoluto, pertinace.

unwearied (ŭn·wẽr′ĭd) *agg.* inesausto, infaticabile.

unwelcome (ŭn·wĕl′kŭm) *agg.* sgradito, inopportuno, malaugurato.

unwell (ŭn·wĕl′) *agg.* malato, indisposto.

unwholesome (ŭn·hōl′sŭm) *agg.* malsano, insalubre, nocivo, repulsivo.

unwieldy (ŭn·wēl′dĭ) *agg.* difficile a maneggiarsi, pesante, ingombrante, voluminoso.

unwilling (ŭn·wĭl′ĭng) *agg.* maldisposto, restio, riluttante: to be — to, non essere disposto a, non avere voglia di. **—ly** *avv.* malvolentieri, a malincuore. **—ness** *n.* riluttanza, avversione.

unwind (ŭn·wĭnd′) *vt.* (*pass., pp.* unwound) sbrogliare, svolgere, dipanare. *vi.* svolgersi, disfarsi.

unwise (ŭn·wīz′) *agg.* insensato, incauto, malaccorto.

unwitting (ŭn·wĭt′ĭng) *agg.* ignaro, inconsapevole, avventato. **—ly** *avv.* inconsapevolmente, avventatamente, involontariamente.

unwonted (ŭn·wŏn′tĕd) *agg.* insolito, straordinario.

unworthy (ŭn·wûr′thĭ) *agg.* indegno, immeritevole; sconveniente.

unwrap (ŭn·răp′) *vt.* svolgere, disfare (*un involto*).

unwritten (ŭn·rĭt′'n) *agg.* non scritto, orale, tradizionale: — law, legge naturale, tradizione.

unyielding (ŭn·yēl′dĭng) *agg.* non cedevole, inflessibile, duro, ostinato.

unyoke (ŭn·yōk′) *vt.* sciogliere dal giogo, liberare.

up (ŭp) *n.*: the ups and downs of life, gli alti e bassi della vita. *agg.* ascendente; alto; ritto, eretto; inferiore; informato; terminato, scaduto; in vantaggio: to be one point —, essere in vantaggio di un punto. *avv.* su, sopra, in alto, in aria, in piedi, in posizione eretta, in rivolta, alla fine, in rialzo: to be —, essere in piedi; essere alzato; essere aumentato; to be — terminato; to get —, alzarsi; time is —, è ora, è venuto il momento, è scaduto il termine; — to date, alla moda; sino al momento attuale; aggiornato; to be — against, dover affrontare; — to, all'altezza di, fino a; to be — to, essere intento a, essere pronto a, essere capace di; it is — to him, dipende da lui, spetta a lui decidere (*o agire*); what's —? che cosa succede? *prep.* su per, al disopra di, in cima a: to go — the stairs, salire le scale. *vt.* (*fam.*) aumentare, elevare; issare. *vi.* saltar su; salire, alzarsi.

up-and-down *agg.* completo. *avv.* verticalmente; su e giù; qua e là.

upbraid (ŭp·brād′) *vt., vi.* sgridare, redarguire, rimproverare.

upbringing (ŭp′brĭng′ĭng) *n.* allevamento, educazione.

update (ŭp·dāt′) *vt.* aggiornare; ammodernare, modernizzare.

upgrade (ŭp·grād′) *vt.* migliorare; promuovere, portare a un grado superiore.

upheaval (ŭp·hēv′ăl) *n.* sollevamento.

upheld (ŭp·hĕld′) *pass., pp. di* to uphold.

uphill (ŭp′hĭl′) *agg.* erto, ripido; difficile, improbo. *avv.* in salita, in su.

uphold (ŭp·hōld′) *vt.* (*pass., pp.* upheld) sostenere; sollevare.

upholster (ŭp·hōl′stẽr) *vt.* tappezzare, imbottire. **—er** *n.* tappezziere. **—y** *n.* tappezzeria, tendaggi.

upkeep (ŭp′kēp) *n.* mantenimento; manutenzione.

upland (ŭp′lănd′) *n.* altipiano, altura. *agg.* alto, elevato, montuoso.

uplift (ŭp·lĭft′) *n.* sollevamento, innalzamento, incoraggiamento. *vt.* sollevare, innalzare, incoraggiare, esaltare.

upon (ŭ·pŏn′) *prep.* su, sopra, al disopra di, nell'atto di: to take — oneself, assumersi, accollarsi; to call —, far visita (*o rivolgersi*) a; depend — it, contateci, statene certo; — **his arrival**, al momento del suo arrivo.

upper (ŭp'ẽr) *n.* tomaia; cuccetta superiore; *pl.* ghette; tomaia: **on one's** —**s**, al verde, a terra. *agg.* superiore, più elevato, più alto: **to have the** — **hand**, avere il sopravvento.

uppercut (ŭp'ẽr·kŭt') *n.* pugno dal basso all'alto.

uppermost (ŭp'ẽr·mōst) *agg.* sommo, il più elevato, il più alto, il primo.

upraise (ŭp·rāz') *vt.* sollevare, elevare.

upright (ŭp'rīt') *n.* pianoforte verticale; pilastro, montante. *agg.* dritto, perpendicolare, eretto; giusto, leale, onesto. *avv.* (*anche* —**ly**) verticalmente; lealmente, rettamente. —**ness** *n.* perpendicolarità; rettitudine.

uprising (ŭp·rīz'ĭng) *n.* levata, ascesa; sollevazione, rivolta.

uproar (ŭp'rōr') *n.* tumulto, gazzarra, strepito, clamore.

uproarious (ŭp·rōr'ĭ·ŭs) *agg.* chiassoso, tumultuoso.

uproot (ŭp·rōōt') *vt.* sradicare, estirpare.

upset (ŭp·sĕt') *n.* rovesciamento, sconvolgimento; disordine; indisposizione. *agg.* rovesciato, capovolto; sconvolto; preoccupato: — **price**, prezzo iniziale. *vt.* (*pass.*, *pp.* **upset**) rovesciare, sconvolgere, scompigliare, turbare. *vi.* capovolgersi, rovesciarsi.

upsetting *n.* capovolgimento, sconvolgimento. *agg.* sconvolgente.

upshot (ŭp'shŏt') *n.* risultato, conclusione, esito, sostanza.

upside (ŭp'sĭd') *n.* parte superiore. *avv.* sopra: — **down**, sottosopra; **to turn** — **down**, capovolgere.

upstairs (ŭp'stârz') *n.* piano superiore. *agg.* del piano superiore. *avv.* di sopra, al piano superiore; (*aeron.*) ad alta quota.

upstanding (ŭp·stăn'dĭng) *agg.* eretto; onesto.

upstart (ŭp'stärt') *n.* nuovo ricco, villano rifatto.

upstream (ŭp'strēm') *avv.* a monte, contro corrente: **to go** —, risalire il fiume.

uptake (ŭp'tāke') *n.*: **to be quick on the** —, capire al volo.

up-to-date *agg.* aggiornato; moderno.

uptown (ŭp'toun') *avv.* nella parte alta di una città, alla periferia.

uptrend (ŭp'trĕnd') *n.* tendenza (*spec. dell'economia*) verso una situazione migliore, sintomi di miglioramento.

upturn (ŭp·tûrn') *n.* rialzo, ripresa. *vt.* voltare all'insù, rivoltare.

upward (ŭp'wẽrd) *agg.* rivolto vers l'alto, ascendente. *avv.* (*anche* **upwards**) verso l'alto, all'insù, oltre; **upwards of**, più di, al disopra di.

uranium (û·rā'nĭ·ŭm) *n.* (*min.*) uranic

urban (ûr'băn) *agg.* urbano, cittadino

urbane (ûr·bān') *agg.* urbano, cortese

urchin (ûr'chĭn) *n.* monello: **sea** — riccio di mare.

urge (ûrj) *n.* impulso, brama, stimolo *vt.*, *vi.* addurre, sostenere, spingere urgere, sollecitare, incitare, stimo lare, incalzare, caldeggiare; affret tarsi.

urgency (ûr'jĕn·sĭ) *n.* urgenza, insi stenza, pressione.

urgent (ûr'jĕnt) *agg.* urgente, incal zante, insistente, imperioso.

urine (û'rĭn) *n.* orina.

urn (ûrn) *n.* urna; bricco, cuccuma **coffee** —, caffettiera, macchina pe il caffè (*nei bar*).

us (ŭs) *pron.pers.* noi; ci.

usable (ûz'á·b'l) *agg.* servibile.

usage (ûz'ĭj) *n.* uso, usanza, consuetu dine; trattamento: **to meet wit hard** —, essere maltrattato.

use (ûs) *n.* uso, impiego; utilità, van taggio; trattamento; abitudine; ser vizio; scopo: **it is no** —, è inutile non c'è rimedio; **to have no** — for non aver bisogno di, non saper ch farsene di; **what is the** —? a ch serve? *vt.* (ûz) usare, adoperare abituare, servirsi di, fare uso di *vi.* solere: **to** — **up**, consumare, lo gorare.

used (ûst) *agg.* usato, abituato, abi tuale: **to get** — **to**, abituarsi; **to be** — **to**, essere abituato a, aver fatt l'abitudine a; **he** — **to do it**, er solito farlo, lo faceva sempre.

useful (ûs'fŏŏl) *agg.* utile. —**ly** *avv.* util mente, proficuamente. —**ness** *n* utilità.

useless (ûs'lĕs) *agg.* inutile. —**ly** *avv* inutilmente. —**ness** *n.* inutilità.

user (ûz'ẽr) *n.* utente, consumatore

usher (ŭsh'ẽr) *n.* usciere; maschera (*inserviente di teatro, ecc.*). *vt.* introdurre, annunziare: **to** — in **into**, far entrare; **to** — **out**, fa uscire, accompagnare alla porta.

usherette (ŭsh'ẽr·ĕt') *n.f.* maschera mascherina (*inserviente di teatro ecc.*).

usual (û'zhŏŏ·ăl) *agg.* abituale, solito frequente: **as** —, come al solito —**ly** *avv.* solitamente, abitualmente

usurer (û'zhŏŏ·rẽr) *n.* usuraio.

usurious (û·zhŏŏr'ĭ·ŭs) *agg.* esoso, esor bitante.

usurp (û·zûrp') *vt.* usurpare.

usurper (û·zûr'pẽr) *n.* usurpatore.

usury (ū′zhŏŏ·rĭ) *n.* usura, strozzinaggio.

utensil (ū·tĕn′sĭl) *n.* utensile, arnese.

uterus (ū′tĕr·ŭs) *n.* utero.

utility (ū·tĭl′ĭ·tĭ) *n.* utilità, servizio, profitto: public —, servizio di pubblica utilità; — man, uomo a tutto fare; (*teat.*) generico; — room, lavanderia, stanzino della caldaia, ripostiglio.

utilize (ū′tĭl·īz) *vt.* utilizzare.

utmost (ŭt′mōst) *n.* estremo, (*il*) meglio, massimo grado, massimo: at the —, tutt'al più; to the —, sino a non poterne più; to do one's —, fare del proprio meglio. *agg.* estremo, (il) più lontano; ultimo; massimo, sommo.

utter (ŭt′ĕr) (1) *agg.* estremo, completo, totale, assoluto, massimo, perfetto.

utter (ŭt′ĕr) (2) *vt.* esprimere, proferire, dire, emettere.

utterance (ŭt′ĕr·ăns) *n.* espressione, pronunzia, suono vocale, emissione; to give — to, manifestare.

utterly (ŭt′ĕr·lĭ) *avv.* completamente.

uttermost (ŭt′ĕr·mōst) *n.* massimo, limite estremo, sommo grado. *agg.* estremo, ultimo, (il) più remoto, (il) più lontano: to the —, all'estremo.

uvula (ū′vū·lá) *n.* ugola.

V

V (vē), Vittoria (*nella 2a guerra mondiale*): V-sign, segno della vittoria (*anulare e medio divaricati*); V-E Day, Giorno della Vittoria in Europa (8 *maggio* 1945); V-J Day, Giorno della Vittoria sul Giappone (14 *agosto* 1945).

vacancy (vā′kăn·sĭ) *n.* vacanza (*l'esser vacante*), disponibilità; posto vacante; lacuna, vuoto.

vacant (vā′kănt) *agg.* vacante, vuoto, libero, disponibile; vacuo, distratto, ebete.

vacate (vā′kāt) *vt.* lasciar libero, abbandonare, sgomberare; annullare.

vacation (vā·kā′shŭn) *n.* vacanza (*ferie*); sgombero, sospensione.

vaccinate (văk′sĭ·nāt) *vt.* vaccinare.

vaccination (văk′sĭ·nā′shŭn) *n.* vaccinazione.

vaccine (văk′sēn) *n.* vaccino.

vacillate (văs′ĭ·lāt) *vi.* vacillare.

vacuous (văk′ū·ŭs) *agg.* vacuo, ebete.

vacuum (văk′ū·ŭm) *n.* vuoto, vuoto pneumatico. *agg.* vuoto, a vuoto, nel vuoto; pneumatico: — bottle, termos; — cleaner, aspirapolvere; — tube, valvola termoionica.

vagabond (văg′á·bŏnd) *n.*, *agg.* vagabondo, nomade.

vagary (vá·gâr′ĭ) *n.* stravaganza.

vagrancy (vā′grăn·sĭ) *n.* vagabondaggio.

vagrant (vā′grănt) *n.*, *agg.* vagabondo.

vague (vāg) *agg.* vago, incerto, impreciso. —ly *avv.* vagamente.

vain (vān) *agg.* vano, infruttuoso; vanitoso: in —, invano.

vainglorious (văn′glō′rĭ·ŭs) *agg.* vanaglorioso.

vainglory (văn′glō′rĭ) *n.* vanagloria.

vale (vāl) *n.* valle, valletta.

valedictory (văl′ē·dĭk′tō·rĭ) *agg.* d'addio, di commiato.

valence (vā′lĕns) *n.* (*chim.*) valenza.

valentine (văl′ĕn·tīn) *n.* dono *opp.* cartoncino decorato e contenente una dichiarazione, che ie giorno di S. Valentino si invia alla persona amata; innamorata o innamorato (*scelto il giorno di S. Valentino*): to my —, al mio amore.

valet (văl′ĕt) *n.* cameriere, domestico. *vt.*, *vi.* servire.

valetudinarian (văl′ē·tū′dĭ·nâr′ĭ·ăn) *n.*, *agg.* infermo.

valiant (văl′yănt) *agg.* valoroso, coraggioso.

valid (văl′ĭd) *agg.* valido, valevole.

validity (vá·lĭd′ĭ·tĭ) *n.* validità.

valise (vá·lēs′) *n.* valigia.

valley (văl′ĭ) *n.* valle, vallata.

valor (văl′ẽr) *n.* valore, ardimento.

valorous (văl′ẽr·ŭs) *agg.* valoroso.

valuable (văl′ū·á·b'l) *agg.* prezioso, costoso, valutabile; *pl.* preziosi, oggetti di valore.

valuation (văl′ū·ā′shŭn) *n.* valutazione.

value (văl′ū) *n.* valore, pregio, significato. *vt.* stimare, valutare, apprezzare.

valued (văl′ūd) *agg.* valutato, stimato, pregiato.

valueless (văl′ū·lĕs) *agg.* privo di valore; da poco insignificante.

valve (vălv) *n.* valva; valvola: safety —, valvola di sicurezza.

vamoose (vá·mōōs′) *vi.* (*gergo*) svignarsela, sparire.

vamp (vămp) (1) *n.* tomaia, rimonta. *vt.* rimontare (*scarpe*), rimettere a nuovo.

vamp (vămp) (2) *n.* (*gergo*) donna fatale. *vt.* irretire. *vi.* far la donna fatale.

vampire (văm′pīr) *n.* vampiro.

van (văn) *n.* furgone; (*mil.*) avanguardia.

vandal (văn'dăl) *n.* vandalo.

vane (văn) *n.* banderuola, ventaruola; pala (*d'elica o mulino*).

vanguard (văn'gärd') *n.* avanguardia.

vanilla (vȧ·nĭl'ȧ) *n.* (*bot.*) vaniglia.

vanish (văn'ĭsh) *vi.* svanire, sparire.

vanity (văn'ĭ·tĭ) *n.* vanità: — case, portacipria, trousse (*fr.*); — table, pettiniera, toilette (*fr.*).

vanquish (văng'kwĭsh) *vt.* vincere, sopraffare, soggiogare.

vantage (văn'tĭj) *n.* vantaggio: — point, posizione di vantaggio; punto d'osservazione.

vapid (văp'ĭd) *agg.* insipido, insulso.

vaporizer (vā'pēr·īz·ēr) *n.* vaporizzatore, atomizzatore.

vapor (vā'pēr) *n.* vapore, esalazione.

variable (vâr'ĭ·ȧ·b'l) *n.*, *agg.* variabile.

variance (vâr'ĭ·ăns) *n.* discrepanza, divergenza, disaccordo: at —, in contrasto.

variation (vâr'ĭ·ā'shŭn) *n.* variazione.

varied (vâr'ĭd) *agg.* vario, variāto.

variety (vȧ·rī'ĕ·tĭ) *n.* varietà.

various (vâr'ĭ·ŭs) *agg.* vario, diverso, variabile, molteplice; vari, parecchi, diversi.

varnish (vär'nĭsh) *n.* vernice. *vt.* verniciare.

varsity (vär'sĭ·tĭ) *n.* (*fam.*) università.

vary (vâr'ĭ) *vt.*, *vi.* variare, modificare, trasformare; differire. **—ing** *agg.* mutevole.

vase (vās; văz) *n.* vaso.

vassal (văs'ăl) *n.* vassallo.

vast (våst) *agg.* vasto, esteso, abbondante. **—ly** *avv.* vastamente; molto; immensamente; in gran parte. **—ness** *n.* vastità, immensità.

vat (văt) *n.* serbatoio, tino.

vaudeville (vōd'vĭl) *n.* commedia musicale; (*spettacolo di*) varietà.

vault (vôlt) *n.* volta; sotterraneo; camera di sicurezza (*di banca*); cripta, tomba; salto, volteggio: pole —, salto con l'asta. *vt.* coprire con una volta, costruire a volta; scavalcare con un volteggio. *vi.* volteggiare; saltare l'ostacolo, saltare con l'asta.

vaulted *agg.* a volta, arcuato.

vaunt (vônt) *n.* vanto, vanteria. *vt.* millantare, ostentare. *vi.* gloriarsi.

veal (vēl) *n.* carne di vitello.

veep (vēp) *n.* (*fam.*) vicepresidente.

veer (vēr) *n.* virata. *vt.*, *vi.* voltare, orientare; (*naut.*) poggiare, mollare; cambiare direzione.

vegetable (vĕj'ê·tȧ·b'l) *n.*, *agg.* vegetale; *pl.* verdura, ortaggi; **— garden**, orto.

vegetate (vĕj'ê·tāt) *vi.* vegetare.

vegetation (vĕj'ê·tā'shŭn) *n.* vegetazione.

vehemence (vē'ê·mĕns) *n.* veemenza, ardore, impeto.

vehement (vē'ê·mĕnt) *agg.* veemente, impetuóso.

vehicle (vē'ĭ·k'l) *n.* veicolo.

veil (vāl) *n.* velo. *vt.* velare.

vein (vān) *n.* vena; nervatura; filone; umore. *vt.* venare. **—ed** *agg.* venato.

vellum (vĕl'ŭm) *n.* pergamena.

velocity (vê·lŏs'ĭ·tĭ) *n.* velocità.

velvet (vĕl'vĕt) *n.* velluto. *agg.* vellutato, di velluto.

velveteen (vĕl'vê·tēn') *n.* velluto di cotone; *pl.* calzoni di velluto.

velvety (vĕl'vê·tĭ) *agg.* vellutato.

vendor (vĕn'dŏr) *n.* venditore.

veneer (vê·nēr') *n.* impiallacciatura, rivestimento; apparenza superficiale. *vt.* impiallacciare, rivestire.

venerable (vĕn'ēr·ȧ·b'l) *n.*, *agg.* venerabile; venerando.

venerate (vĕn'ēr·āt) *vt.* venerare.

veneration (vĕn'ēr·ā'shŭn) *n.* venerazione.

venereal (vê·nēr'ê·ăl) *agg.* venereo; carnale.

Venetian (vê·nē'shăn) *n.*, *agg.* veneziano: — **blind**, (persiana alla) veneziana.

vengeance (vĕn'jăns) *n.* vendetta: **with a —**, violentemente; all'eccesso.

vengeful (vĕnj'fŏŏl) *agg.* vendicativo.

venison (vĕn'ĭ·z'n) *n.* cacciagione, selvaggina (*spec. carne di cervo*).

venom (vĕn'ŭm) *n.* veleno; astio.

venomous (vĕn'ŭm·ŭs) *agg.* velenoso; astioso.

venous (vē'nŭs) *agg.* venoso.

vent (vĕnt) *n.* apertura, sfiatatoio, condotto, sbocco, sfogo; focone (*d'arma da fuoco*): **to give — to**, dar libero corso a. *vt.* manifestare, sfogare, dar sfogo a.

ventilate (vĕn'tĭ·lāt) *vt.* ventilare.

ventilation (vĕn'tĭ·lā'shŭn) *n.* ventilazione.

ventilator (vĕn'tĭ·lā'tĕr) *n.* ventilatore.

ventriloquism (vĕn·trĭl'ô·kwĭz'm) *n.* ventriloquio.

ventriloquist (vĕn·trĭl'ô·kwĭst) *n.* ventriloquo.

venture (vĕn'tŭr) *n.* ventura, impresa, rischio; posta: **business —**, speculazione, impresa rischiosa. *vt.*, *vi.* tentare, arrischiare, osare, avventurarsi.

venturesome (vĕn'tŭr·sŭm), **venturous** (vĕn'tŭr·ŭs) *agg.* avventuroso; rischioso; audace.

Venus (vē'nŭs) *n.* Venere.

veracious (vĕ·rā'shŭs) *agg.* verace, autentico.

veracity (vĕ·răs'ĭ·tĭ) *n.* veracità.

veranda (vĕ·răn'dá) *n.* veranda.

verb (vûrb) *n.* verbo.

verbal (vûr'băl) *agg.* verbale.

verbatim (vûr·bā'tĭm) *avv.* testualmente.

verbiage (vûr'bĭ·ĭj) *n.* verbosità.

verbose (vûr·bōs') *agg.* verboso.

verdant (vûr'dănt) *agg.* verdeggiante; (*fam.*) ingenuo, inesperto.

verdict (vûr'dĭkt) *n.* sentenza, verdetto: — of not guilty, assoluzione.

verdigris (vûr'dĭ·grēs) *n.* verderame.

verdure (vûr'dŭr) *n.* verzura, freschezza, rigoglio.

verge (vûrj) *n.* bordo, limite, margine, orlo; verga: on the — of, sul punto di. *vi.* tendere, propendere: to — on, upon, rasentare, costeggiare.

verify (vĕr'ĭ·fĭ) *vt.* verificare, attestare, comprovare, confermare.

verily (vĕr'ĭ·lĭ) *avv.* veramente, sinceramente.

verisimilitude (vĕr'ĭ·sĭ·mĭl'ĭ·tūd) *n.* verosimiglianza.

veritable (vĕr'ĭ·tá·b'l) *agg.* vero, autentico.

verity (vĕr'ĭ·tĭ) *n.* verità.

vermifuge (vûr'mĭ·fūj) *n.*, *agg.* vermifugo.

vermilion (vẽr·mĭl'yŭn) *agg.* vermiglio.

vermin (vûr'mĭn) *n. sing., pl.* parassita; gentaglia, feccia.

vermouth (vẽr·mōōth') *n.* vermut.

verse (vûrs) *n.* verso, strofa.

versed (vûrst) *agg.* versato, dotto.

version (vûr'shŭn) *n.* versione.

verso (vûr'sō) *n.* tergo, rovescio; (*tip.*) pagina pari.

versus (vûr'sŭs) *prep.* contro.

vertex (vûr'tĕks) *n.* vertice, apice.

vertical (vûr'tĭ·kăl) *n.*, *agg.* verticale.

vertigo (vûr'tĭ·gō) *n.* (*med.*) vertigine.

very (vĕr'ĭ) *agg.* stesso, vero, reale; solo: this — day, oggi stesso; the — man who ..., proprio l'uomo che, lo stessissimo uomo che; the — thought of ..., il semplice pensiero di ... *avv.* molto, grandemente, estremamente: — many, moltissimi; — much, moltissimo; — good, buonissimo; benissimo; — cold, freddissimo, molto freddo.

Vesper (vĕs'pĕr) *n.* vespro.

vessel (vĕs'l) *n.* nave, bastimento; velivolo; recipiente; (*anat., bot.*) condotto, vaso.

vest (vĕst) *n.* panciotto; maglia. *vt.* conferire, devolvere. *vi.* vestirsi; essere devoluto: to — an estate in,

assegnare una proprietà a; to — with powers, investire di poteri.

vesta (vĕs'tá) *n.* cerino, fiammifero.

vestibule (vĕs'tĭ·būl) *n.* vestibolo; piattaforma (*di vagone*).

vestige (vĕs'tĭj) *n.* vestigio, traccia.

vestment (vĕst'mĕnt) *n.* vestito, abito sacerdotale, paramento.

vestry (vĕs'trĭ) *n.* sagrestia, consiglio parrocchiale, fabbriceria.

veteran (vĕt'ĕr·ăn) *n.*, *agg.* veterano, reduce: Veterans Day (*S.U.*), Anniversario dei Veterani (11 *novembre*).

veterinarian (vĕt'ĕr·ĭ·nâr'ĭ·ăn) *n.* veterinario.

veterinary (vĕt'ĕr·ĭ·nĕr'ĭ) *n.*, *agg.* veterinario.

veto (vē'tō) *n.* veto, divieto. *vt.* porre il veto a, proibire.

vex (vĕks) *vt.* vessare, infastidire, preoccupare, affliggere.

vexation (vĕks·ā'shŭn) *n.* vessazione; irritazione; contrarietà.

via (vī'á) *prep.* via, per, attraverso: — air mail, per via (*o* posta) aerea.

viable (vī'á·b'l) *agg.* vitale.

viaduct (vī'á·dŭkt) *n.* viadotto.

vial (vī'ăl) *n.* fiala.

viand (vī'ănd) *n.* commestibili, vivande.

vibrate (vī'brāt) *vt.* far vibrare; scagliare, misurare, scandire. *vi.* vibrare, oscillare.

vibration (vī·brā'shŭn) *n.* vibrazione, oscillazione.

vicar (vĭk'ĕr) *n.* delegato; vicario.

vicarage (vĭk'ĕr·ĭj) *n.* vicariato, presbiterio.

vicarious (vī·kâr'ĭ·ŭs) *agg.* sostitutivo, indiretto.

vice (vīs) (1) *n.* vizio; imperfezione.

vice (vīs) (2) *prep.* in luogo di. *pref.* vice.

viceroy (vīs'roi) *n.* vicerè.

vice versa (vī'sĕ·vûr'sá) *avv.* viceversa.

vicinity (vĭ·sĭn'ĭ·tĭ) *n.* vicinanza, dintorni, vicinato.

vicious (vĭsh'ŭs) *agg.* vizioso; malvagio, nocivo; maligno; violento; fallace.

vicissitude (vĭ·sĭs'ĭ·tūd) *n.* vicissitudine.

victim (vĭk'tĭm) *n.* vittima.

victor (vĭk'tĕr) *n.* vincitore.

victorious (vĭk·tō'rĭ·ŭs) *agg.* vittorioso.

victory (vĭk'tō·rĭ) *n.* vittoria.

victrola (vĭk·trō'lá) *n.* (*S.U.*) grammofono.

victuals (vĭt''lz) *n.pl.* viveri, vettovaglie.

vicuña (vĭ·kōōn′yȧ) *n.* vigogna (*animale e tessuto*).

video (vĭd′ē·ō) *n.* televisione; video (*parte visiva della TV*). *agg.* video: — **channel**, canale video.

videogenic (vĭd′ē·ō·jĕn′ĭk) *agg.* telegenico.

vie (vĭ) *vi.* (*pass.* **vied**, *ppr.* **vying**) competere, gareggiare.

view (vū) *n.* vista, veduta, panorama; ispezione; prospettiva, aspetto; opinione, intenzione, proposito: **field of** —, campo visivo; **in** — **of**, in vista di; **on** —, esposto al pubblico; **with a** — **to**, allo scopo di; — **finder** (*fot.*), mirino. *vt.* considerare, esaminare, contemplare.

viewpoint (vū′point′) *n.* punto di vista.

vigil (vĭj′ĭl) *n.* veglia, vigilia; vigilanza: **to keep** —, vigilare.

vigilance (vĭj′ĭ·lȧns) *n.* vigilanza, cautela.

vigilant (vĭj′ĭ·lȧnt) *agg.* vigile, cauto.

vigor (vĭg′ẽr) *n.* vigore.

vigorous (vĭg′ẽr·ŭs) *agg.* vigoroso.

vile (vīl) *agg.* spregevole, ignominioso, pessimo, odioso.

vilify (vĭl′ĭ·fī) *vt.* vilipendere, diffamare.

village (vĭl′ĭj) *n.* paese, villaggio.

villager (vĭl′ĭj·ẽr) *n.* villico, paesano.

villain (vĭl′ĭn) *n.* furfante, colpevole, malvagio.

villainous (vĭl′ĭn·ŭs) *agg.* infame, scellerato.

villainy (vĭl′ĭn·ĭ) *n.* infamia, misfatto, scelleratezza.

vim (vĭm) *n.* vigore, energia.

vindicate (vĭn′dĭ·kāt) *vt.* giustificare, difendere, sostenere; riscattare, rivendicare.

vindication (vĭn′dĭ·kā′shŭn) *n.* rivincita, difesa, rivendicazione.

vindictive (vĭn·dĭk′tĭv) *agg.* vendicativo.

vine (vīn) *n.* vigna, vite.

vinegar (vĭn′ē·gẽr) *n.* aceto.

vinegarish (vĭn′ē·gẽr·ĭsh) *agg.* acetoso, che sa di aceto; (*fig.*) aspro, acido, caustico, sarcastico.

vineyard (vĭn′yẽrd) *n.* vigna.

vintage (vĭn′tĭj) *n.* vendemmia; annata (*vinicola*).

violate (vī′ō·lāt) *vt.* violare.

violation (vī′ō·lā′shŭn) *n.* violazione.

violence (vī′ō·lĕns) *n.* violenza.

violent (vī′ō·lĕnt) *agg.* violento.

violet (vī′ō·lĕt) *n.* viola mammola, violetta; color viola. *agg.* violetto.

violin (vī′ō·lĭn′) *n.* violino.

violinist (vī′ō·lĭn′ĭst) *n.* violinista.

VIP (vīp, vē′ī′pē′) *n.* (*gergo*) pezzo grosso, alto papavero (*sigla di* **v**ery **i**mportant **p**erson).

viper (vī′pẽr) *n.* vipera.

virgin (vûr′jĭn) *n.* vergine. *agg.* vergine, virginale.

virginal *agg.* virgineo.

virosis (vī·rō′sĭs) *n.* virosi.

virtu (vûr·tōō′) *n.* amore per l'arte: **articles of** —, soggetti d'arte.

virtual (vûr′tū·ȧl) *agg.* virtuale, potenziale.

virtue (vûr′tū) *n.* virtù; rettitudine; pregio, dote, valore, merito; castità; efficacia.

virtuoso (vûr′tū·ō′sō) *n.* collezionista di opere d'arte.

virtuous (vûr′tū·ŭs) *agg.* virtuoso.

virulence (vĭr′ū·lĕns), **virulency** (vĭr′ū·lĕn·sĭ) *n.* virulenza, acrimonia.

virus (vī′rŭs) *n.* virus.

visa (vē′zȧ) *n.* visto, vidimazione. *vt.* vidimare.

visage (vĭz′ĭj) *n.* faccia, aspetto.

vis-à-vis (vē·zȧ·vē′) *n.* dirimpettaio. *avv.* a faccia a faccia.

viscose (vĭs′kōs) *n.* viscosa.

viscosity (vĭs·kŏs′ĭ·tĭ) *n.* viscosità.

viscous (vĭs′kŭs) *agg.* viscoso, tenace.

visé (vē′zā) *vedi* **visa**.

visible (vĭz′ĭ·b'l) *agg.* visibile.

visibly (vĭz′ĭ·blĭ) *avv.* visibilmente.

vision (vĭzh′ŭn) *n.* vista, visione, visuale, campo visivo.

visionary (vĭzh′ŭn·ĕr′ĭ) *n.*, *agg.* visionario.

visit (vĭz′ĭt) *n.* visita, soggiorno: **to pay a** —, fare una visita. *vt.* visitare, andare a trovare, ispezionare: **to** — **punishment upon**, infliggere un castigo a.

visitation (vĭz′ĭ·tā′shŭn) *n.* visitazione, visita; castigo divino.

visitor (vĭz′ĭ·tẽr) *n.* visitatore, ospite.

visor (vī′zẽr) *n.* visiera.

vista (vĭs′tȧ) *n.* panorama, prospettiva, visuale.

visual (vĭzh′ū·ȧl) *agg.* visivo, ottico.

visualize (vĭzh′ū·ȧl·īz) *vt.* prospettare; figurarsi.

vital (vī′tȧl) *agg.* vitale, essenziale.

vitals *n.pl.* parti vitali, organi vitali.

vitamin (vī′tȧ·mĭn) *n.* vitamina.

vitriol (vĭt′rĭ·ŭl) *n.* vetriolo.

vivacious (vī·vā′shŭs) *agg.* vivace, animato.

vivacity (vī·văs′ĭ·tĭ) *n.* vivacità.

vivid (vĭv′ĭd) *agg.* vivido, intenso.

vivisection (vĭv′ĭ·sĕk′shŭn) *n.* vivisezione.

vixen (vĭk′s'n) *n.* volpe femmina; megera.

vocabulary (vō·kăb′ū·lĕr′ĭ) *n.* vocabolario.

vocal (vō′kȧl) *n.* vocale; *agg.* vocale; parlante; eloquente; sonoro.

vocalist (vō′kȧl·ĭst) *n.* cantante.

---

vocation (vō·kā′shŭn) *n.* vocazione, professione, occupazione. **—al** *agg.* professionale: **—al** school, scuola d'arti e mestieri.

vocative (vŏk′á·tĭv) *n.*, *agg.* vocativo.

vociferous (vō·sĭf′ĕr·ŭs) *agg.* clamoroso, vociferante.

vogue (vōg) *n.* voga, moda.

voice (vois) *n.* voce, suono, voto: with one **—**, all'unanimità. *vt.* esprimere, manifestare; intonare (*strumenti*).

voiceless (vois′lĕs) *agg.* afono, muto; **—** consonant, consonante sorda.

void (void) *n.* lacuna, vuoto. *agg.* vuoto; privo (*di*); inconsistente, nullo. *vt.* vuotare, annullare.

volatile (vŏl′á·tĭl) *agg.* volatile; incostante.

volcanic (vŏl·kăn′ĭk) *agg.* vulcanico.

volcano (vŏl·kā′nō) *n.* vulcano.

volition (vō·lĭsh′ŭn) *n.* volizione, volontà.

volley (vŏl′ĭ) *n.* raffica, scarica; (*tennis*) volata. *vt.*, *vi.* sparare a raffica; (*tennis*) ribattere: **—ball** *n.* palla a volo.

volplane (vŏl′plān′) *n.* volo planato. *vi.* librarsi, planare.

volt (vōlt) *n.* (*elett.*) volta.

voltage (vōl′tĭj) *n.* voltaggio.

voltameter (vŏl·tăm′ē·tẽr) *n.* voltametro.

voltammeter (vōlt′ăm′mē·tẽr) *n.* voltamperometro.

voltmeter (vōlt′mē′tẽr) *n.* voltmetro.

voluble (vŏl′û·b'l) *agg.* sciolto, loquace.

volume (vŏl′ûm) *n.* volume; massa; libro; quantità.

voluminous (vō·lū′mĭ·nŭs) *agg.* voluminoso.

voluntary (vŏl′ŭn·tẽr′ĭ) *agg.* volontario, spontaneo, intenzionale.

volunteer (vŏl′ŭn·tẽr′) *n.*, *agg.* volontario. *vt.*, *vi.* offrire, offrirsi spontaneamente, offrire i propri servigi; arruolarsi volontario.

voluptuous (vō·lŭp′tū̯·ŭs) *agg.* voluttuoso.

vomit (vŏm′ĭt) *n.* vomito. *vt.*, *vi.* vomitare.

voracious (vō·rā′shŭs) *agg.* vorace, ingordo.

vortex (vôr′tĕks) *n.* turbine, vortice.

votary (vō′tá·rĭ) *n.* devoto, seguace.

vote (vōt) *n.* voto, suffragio. *vt.*, *vi.* votare.

voter (vōt′ẽr) *n.* votante, elettore.

vouch (vouch) *vt.*, *vi.*: to **—** for, convalidare; garantire per, rispondere di.

voucher (vouch′ẽr) *n.* garante; garanzia, pezza giustificativa, ricevuta.

vouchsafe (vouch·sāf′) *vt.* concedere, sancire.

vow (vou) *n.* voto, promessa solenne. *vt.* votare, consacrare, promettere solennemente. *vi.* fare un voto.

vowel (vou′ĕl) *n.* vocale.

voyage (voi′ĭj) *n.* viaggio (*per mare o in aereo*), traversata. *vi.* viaggiare, navigare.

vulcanization (vŭl′kăn·ĭ·zā′shŭn) *n.* vulcanizzazione.

vulcanize (vŭl′kăn·īz) *vt.* vulcanizzare.

vulgar (vŭl′gẽr) *agg.* volgare, comune.

vulgarian (vŭl·gâr′ĭ·ăn) *n.* zoticone.

vulgarity (vŭl·găr′ĭ·tĭ) *n.* volgarità.

vulgarization (vŭl′gẽr·ĭ·zā′shŭn) *n.* volgarizzazione.

vulnerable (vŭl′nẽr·á·b'l) *agg.* vulnerabile.

vulture (vŭl′tṳr) *n.* avvoltoio.

W

wabble (wŏb′'l) *n.* vacillamento, oscillazione. *vi.* vacillare, traballare, tentennare, oscillare.

WAC (wăk) *n.* Ausiliaria dell' Esercito Americano.

wacky (wăk′ĭ) *agg.* (*gergo*) pazzo, tocco, svanito, suonato.

wad (wŏd) *n.* stoppaccio, batuffolo, tampone, imbottitura; rotolo (*di banconote*); (*gergo*) gruzzolo. *vt.* imbottire, tamponare, appallare, ovattare. **—ding** *n.* imbottitura, ovatta.

waddle (wŏd′'l) *n.* andatura ciondolante. *vi.* camminare a passetti ciondolando.

wade (wād) *vt.*, *vi.* guadare, fendere; avanzare penosamente: to **— into** (*gergo*), attaccare vigorosamente.

WAF (wăf) *n.* Ausiliaria dell' Aviazione Americana.

wafer (wā′fẽr) *n.* ostia, cialda; sigillo (*di carta gommata, ecc.*).

waffle (wŏf′'l) *n.* galletta.

waft (wăft) *n.* zaffata, folata, segnalazione. *vt.* trasportare sui flutti (*o attraverso l'aria*), sospingere. *vi.* fluttuare.

wag (wăg) *n.* burlone; dimenamento, scotimento. *vt.* dimenare, scuotere. *vi.* dimenarsi: to have a wagging tongue, avere la lingua troppo lunga; to **—** the tail, scodinzolare.

wage (wāj) *n.* (*anche pl.*) salario, paga: **—earner** *n.* salariato. *vt.*, *vi.* intraprendere (*una guerra*), impegnarsi in (*una competizione*).

wager (wā'jĕr) *n.* scommessa. *vt.*, *vi.* scommettere.

waggish (wăg'ĭsh) *agg.* scherzoso.

waggle (wăg''l) *vt.* dimenare.

wagon (wăg'ŭn) *n.* furgone, carro.

wagoner (wăg'ŭn·ĕr) *n.* carrettiere.

wagonette (wăg'ŭn·ĕt') *n.* giardiniera (*carrozza*).

wail (wāl) *n.* gemito, lamento. *vt.* deplorare, rimpiangere. *vi.* gemere, lamentarsi.

wain (wān) *n.* carro.

wainscot (wăn'skŭt), **wainscoting** *n.* rivestimento in legno; zoccolo (*di parete*).

waist (wāst) *n.* cintola, cinta, vita, parte centrale; corpetto, blusa: —band *n.* cintura.

waistcoat (wăs(t)'kōt') *n.* panciotto.

wait (wāt) *n.* attesa; imboscata. *vt.*, *vi.* aspettare: to — for somebody, aspettare qualcuno; to lie in — for someone, appostare qualcuno; to — at table, servire a tavola; to — on, upon, assistere, servire.

waiter (wāt'ĕr) *n.* cameriere; vassoio.

waiting (wāt'ĭng) *n.* attesa; servizio: — room, sala d'aspetto.

waitress (wāt'rĕs) *n.* cameriera (*di ristorante*).

waive (wāv) *vt.* abbandonare, rinunziare a.

waiver (wāv'ĕr) *n.* rinunzia.

wake (wāk) (1) *n.* scia, solco: in the — of, nel solco di.

wake (wāk) (2) *n.* veglia (*anche funebre*). *vt.*, *vi.* svegliare, destare, vegliare; svegliarsi.

wakeful (wāk'fōōl) *agg.* sveglio, vigilante, insonne.

waken (wāk'ĕn) *vt.* svegliare, risvegliare. *vi.* svegliarsi.

wale (wāl) *n.* riga, striscia, costa.

walk (wôk) *n.* passeggiata; andatura; percorso, cammino; passo; sentiero: a ten-minute —, una passeggiata di dieci minuti; — of life, sfera di azione, carriera. *vt.* far camminare, percorrere. *vi.* camminare, passeggiare, andare a piedi: to — back home, tornare a casa a piedi; to — down, scendere; to — in, entrare; to — off, svignarsela; to — out, uscire, andarsene; far sciopero; to — the streets, girare per le strade, andare in giro.

walkie-talkie (wôk'ĭ·tôk'ĭ) *n.* (*radio*) trasmittente-ricevente portatile.

walking (wôk'ĭng) *n.* marcia, andatura. *agg.*: at — pace, al passo; — stick, bastone da passeggio.

walkout (wôk'out') *n.* sciopero.

walkover (wôk'ō'vĕr) *n.* facile vittoria.

walk-up (wôk'ŭp) *n.* (*S.U.*) casa senza ascensore.

wall (wôl) *n.* muro, muraglia, parete: to go to the —, soccombere; to drive to the —, mettere con le spalle al muro. *vt.* cingere con muro, fortificare; murare.

wallet (wôl'ĕt) *n.* borsa; portafoglio.

walleyed (wôl'ĭd') *agg.* dagli occhi scialbi; strabico; sbieco (*di sguardo*).

wallflower (wôl'flou'ĕr) *n.* violacciocca; persona che fa tappezzeria (*a un ballo*).

wallop (wôl'ŭp) *n.* (*gergo*) pugno, sgrugnone. *vt.* colpire con violenza.

wallow (wôl'ō) *vi.* diguazzare, rotolarsi (*nel fango*); crogiolarsi.

wallpaper (wôl'pā'pĕr) *n.* tappezzeria.

walnut (wôl'nŭt) *n.* noce.

walrus (wôl'rŭs) *n.* tricheco.

waltz (wôlts) *n.* valzer. *vi.* ballare il valzer.

wan (wŏn) *agg.* pallido, scialbo, languido, malaticcio.

wand (wŏnd) *n.* verga, bacchetta magica, bastone di comando.

wander (wŏn'dĕr) *vi.* vagare; sviarsi; divagare; deviare; distrarsi; vaneggiare. —er *n.* vagabondo. —ing *n.* peregrinazione; vaneggiamento. *agg.* errante, nomade; vaneggiante.

wane (wān) *n.* declino, diminuzione: on the —, in decadenza. *vi.* diminuire.

want (wŏnt) *n.* bisogno, necessità, mancanza, deficienza, indigenza: to stand in — of, aver bisogno di; — ad, offerta di lavoro o impiego (*sul giornale*). *vt.*, *vi.* aver bisogno di, desiderare, scarseggiare di; difettare, mancare, essere bisognoso.

wanting *agg.* mancante, assente, insufficiente. *prep.* in mancanza di, senza, meno.

wanton (wŏn'tŭn) *n.* libertino, persona lasciva, donnaccia. *agg.* sregolato; ingiustificato; spietato; licenzioso, lascivo; folle.

war (wôr) *n.* guerra: to be at —, essere in guerra; War Office, Ministero della Guerra: — of nerves, guerra dei nervi, guerra psicologica; cold —, guerra fredda. *vi.* guerreggiare, combattere.

warble (wôr'b'l) *n.* gorgheggio. *vt.*, *vi.* cantare, gorgheggiare.

warbler (wôr'blĕr) *n.* gorgheggiatore, uccello canoro.

ward (wôrd) *n.* guardia, custodia, tutela; pupillo, pupilla; rione, quartiere; reparto (*d'ospedale*); raggio (*di carcere*). *vt.*, *vi.* custodire, proteggere, parare, stare in guardia:

to — off, respingere, parare, schivare.

warden (wôr'd'n) n. custode; guardiano; governatore (di carcere, ecc.); direttore (di collegio).

warder (wôr'dēr) n. custode, carceriere.

wardrobe (wôrd'rōb') n. guardaroba.

ware (wâr) n. (gen.pl.) merce; mercanzia, articolo.

warehouse (wâr'hous') n. magazzino, deposito.

warfare (wôr'fâr') n. guerra, lotta.

warlike (wôr'lik') agg. bellicoso, guerriero, guerresco, militare.

warm (wôrm) agg. caldo, caloroso, animato, violento, accalorato; cordiale; recente, scottante: —hearted agg. di buon cuore, imbarazzante; to be—, avere caldo; it is —, fa caldo. vt., vi. scaldare, scaldarsi: to — over, riscaldare; to — up, scaldare, scaldarsi, accalorare, accalorarsi, entusiasmarsi. —ly avv. caldamente, calorosamente, cordialmente, concitatamente. —ness n. tepore, calore.

warmth (wôrmth) n. ardore, calore.

warn (wôrn) vt. avvertire, ammonire, mettere in guardia, prevenire: to — off, diffidare; allontanare.

warning n. avvertimento, ammonimento, diffida; preavviso; licenziamento.

warp (wôrp) n. ordito; torsione, incurvatura, deformazione; prevenzione (preconcetto), fissazione; (naut.) gherlino. vt. ordire; falsare, deformare, snaturare; (naut.) tonneggiare. vi. torcersi, incurvarsi, deformarsi.

warrant (wôr'ănt) n. autorizzazione, garanzia, mandato, citazione, ordine; brevetto: — officer, sottufficiale. vt. garantire, giustificare, sanzionare, certificare, autorizzare.

warren (wôr'ĕn) n. conigliera; tana; casa popolare.

warrior (wôr'ĭ-ĕr) n. guerriero.

warship (wôr'shĭp') n. nave da guerra.

wart (wôrt) n. porro, verruca.

wary (wâr'ĭ) agg. circospetto, cauto: to be — of, diffidare di.

was (wŏz) 1a e 3a pers.sing. pass. di to be.

wash (wŏsh) n. lavatura, bucato; sciacquio; corrente; risucchio; scoria; pantano; beverone, brodaglia; placcatura: mouth —, sciacquo per la bocca, dentifricio liquido. vt. lavare, purificare, bagnare; placcare. vi. lavarsi, fare il bucato, scorrere, essere lavabile, frangersi: to — away, off, eliminare lavando, scomparire; to — out, mondare, pulire, togliere (lavando); sfinire, stremare; escludere, scartare, espellere, eliminare; bocciare; scolorirsi.

washable (wŏsh'á-b'l) agg. lavabile.

washed-out (wŏsht'out') agg. mondo, lavato; sbiadito; esausto, sfinito; escluso, scartato, eliminato; bocciato.

washer (wŏsh'ĕr) n. lavatore, macchina per lavare; (mecc.) ranella, guarnizione. —woman n. lavandaia.

washing (wŏsh'ĭng) n. lavaggio, bucato, lavatura: — machine, macchina per lavare.

washout (wŏsh'out') n. erosione prodotta dall'acqua; stasatura; (gergo) fallito; fallimento, fiasco; bocciato; bocciatura.

washy (wŏsh'ĭ) agg. acquoso, fiacco.

wasp (wŏsp) n. vespa.

Wasp (wŏsp) n. Ausiliaria Aviatrice dell' Aviazione Americana.

waspish (wŏsp'ĭsh) agg. irascibile, pungente.

wastage (wăs'tĭj) n. logorio, consumo.

waste (wăst) n. perdita, sciupio; rovina, devastazione; deperimento; regione incolta, deserto, distesa; rifiuti: to run to —, andare in rovina. agg. devastato, sterile, incolto; sprecato, inutile, di scarto: — land, distesa; deserto; regione incolta. vt. sprecare, sciupare, devastare, deteriorare, consumare. vi. sciuparsi, deperire, logorarsi.

wastebasket n. cestino dei rifiuti.

wasteful (wăst'fŏŏl) agg. prodigo, dispendioso, rovinoso, devastatore.

wastepaper n. carta straccia.

wastrel (wăs'trĕl) n. rifiuto; buono a nulla.

watch (wŏch) n. orologio; veglia, vigilanza; guardia, sentinella, pattuglia: on the —, all'erta, di guardia. vt., vi. osservare, sorvegliare, aspettare, vegliare, vigilare: to — out for, stare attento a; — out! attento!, attenti!

watchdog (wŏch'dŏg') n. cane da guardia.

watcher (wŏch'ĕr) n. sorvegliante, osservatore.

watchful (wŏch'fŏŏl) agg. vigilante, attento, circospetto.

watchmaker (wŏch'māk'ĕr) n. orologiaio.

watchman (wŏch'măn) n. guardiano.

watchtower (wŏch'tou'ĕr) n. torre di vedetta.

watchword (wŏch'wûrd') n. parola d'ordine.

water (wô'tĕr) n. acqua. agg. d'acqua, da acqua, ad acqua, acquatico, idraulico: — color, acquerello; — power, forza idraulica; — sports, sport acquatici. *vt.* inumidire, irrigare, irrorare. abbeverare, annacquare; marezzare (*tessuti*). *vi.* fare acqua, rifornirsi d'acqua, abbeverarsi, secernere: to make one's mouth —, far venire l'acquolina in bocca; my eyes —, mi piangono gli occhi.

waterfall (wŏ′tĕr·fôl′) *n.* cascata.

watering (wô′tĕr·ĭng) *n.* anaffiamento, irrigazione; marezzatura; abbeveramento, rifornimento d'acqua: — place, stazione balneare *o* termale.

watermark (wô′tĕr·märk′) *n.* livello delle acque; filigrana.

watermelon (wô′tĕr·mĕl′ŭn) *n.* anguria.

waterproof (wô′tĕr·prōōf′) *n.*, *agg.* impermeabile. *vt.* impermeabilizzare.

watershed (wô′tĕr·shĕd′) *n.* spartiacque, versante.

waterside (wô′tĕr·sīd′) *n.* riva. *agg.* rivierasco.

waterspout (wô′tĕr·spout′) *n.* tromba d'acqua, grondaia.

watertight (wô′tĕr·tīt′) *agg.* stagno, ermetico.

waterway (wô′tĕr·wā′) *n.* idrovia, canale navigabile.

waterworks (wô′tĕr·wûrks′) *n.pl.* impianto idrico; fontana ornamentale.

watery (wô′tĕr·ĭ) *agg.* acqueo, acquatico, acquoso, bagnato.

watt (wŏt) *n.* (*elett.*) watt.

wattle (wŏt′l) *n.* ramoscello, cannicciata, vimine; (*zool.*) bargiglio.

wave (wāv) *n.* onda, ondata; ondulazione; ondeggiamento; cenno (*della mano*): permanent —, ondulazione permanente. *vt.* far ondeggiare, sventolare, agitare, ondulare. *vi.* ondeggiare, fluttuare; far cenno con la mano: to — away, allontanare con un cenno; to — one's hand, agitare la mano; to — hair, ondulare capelli.

WAVE (wāv) *n.* Ausiliaria della Marina Americana.

waver (wā′vĕr) *vi.* ondeggiare; vacillare; titubare. *n.* ondeggiamento; vacillamento; titubanza.

wavy (wāv′ĭ) *agg.* ondulato, ondoso, ondeggiante.

wax (wăks) (1) *vi.* svilupparsi, aumentare, trasformarsi; essere in fase crescente (*della luna*).

wax (wăks) (2) *n.* cera, cerume, pece, ceralacca. *vt.* incerare: — paper, carta cerata.

waxen (wăk′sĕn) *agg.* cereo, di cera.

waxy (wăk′sĭ) *agg.* cereo; molle; adesivo.

way (wā) *n.* via, cammino, passaggio; direzione; mezzo, metodo; stato, condizione, modo; (*naut.*) rotta: a long — off, molto lontano; by the —, a proposito; by — of, a guisa di, a titolo di; to be in the —, ingombrare; to make one's —, avanzarsi; to be in the family —, essere incinta; to have one's own —, fare a modo proprio; out of the —, fuori mano, fuori del comune; this —, da questa parte; to be in a bad —, essere in una brutta situazione; to get into the — of, prendere l'abitudine di; the — in, l'ingresso; the — out, l'uscita; a — through, un passaggio; under —, in corso, in rotta.

wayfarer (wā′fâr′ĕr) *n.* viandante.

waylay (wā′lā′) *vt.* tendere un agguato a, aggredire; sequestrare (*una persona*).

wayside (wā′sīd′) *n.* ciglio della strada.

wayward (wā′wĕrd) *agg.* capriccioso; ostinato; perverso; irregolare, zigzagante.

we (wē) *pron.pers.* noi.

weak (wēk) *agg.* debole; leggiero (*di tè, brodo, liquore, ecc.*); fiacco, malaticcio: —headed *agg.* tardo, ottuso; —sighted *agg.* debole di vista.

weaken (wēk′ĕn) *vt.* indebolire, affievolire, diluire. *vi.* indebolirsi, attenuarsi.

weakling (wēk′lĭng) *n.*, *agg.* debole, inetto.

weakly (wēk′lĭ) *agg.* debole, malaticcio. *avv.* debolmente.

weakness (wēk′nĕs) *n.* debolezza.

weal (wēl) *n.* lividura.

wealth (wĕlth) *n.* ricchezza, prosperità, abbondanza.

wealthy (wĕl′thĭ) *agg.* ricco, opulento.

wean (wēn) *vt.* svezzare, slattare, disabituare.

weapon (wĕp′ŭn) *n.* arma.

wear (wâr) *n.* uso, logorio; durevolezza; vestiario, moda: — and tear, usura, logorio; to be the worse for —, essere in pessime condizioni; men's —, abbigliamento maschile. *vt.* (*pass.* wore, *pp.* worn) portare, indossare, logorare, corrodere, consumare, stancare. *vi.* consumarsi, logorarsi; resistere, durare; passare (*del tempo*): to — out, esaurire, consumare; to — away, logorare, logorarsi; to — off, cancellare, sparire; to — well, resistere, conservarsi bene; as the day wore on, col passare della giornata.

wearied (wẽr′ĭd) *agg.* stanco, annoiato.

wearily (wẽr′ĭ·lĭ) *avv.* stancamente, tediosamente, fiaccamente.

weariness (wēr′ĭ·nĕs) *n.* stanchezza, tedio.

wearing (wâr′ĭng) *agg.* logorante, faticoso: — **apparel**, indumenti.

wearisome (wēr′ĭ·sŭm) *agg.* fatocosi, gravoso, monotono, tedioso.

weary (wēr′ĭ) *agg.* annoiato, stanco; tedioso, gravoso. *vt.* affaticare, annoiare. *vi.* stancarsi.

weasel (wē′z′l) *n.* donnola.

weather (wĕth′ĕr) *n.* tempo (*atmosferico*): — **bureau**, ufficio meteorologico; — **conditions**, condizioni atmosferiche; **it is fine** —, c'è bel tempo, fa bel tempo; **under the** —, indisposto, ubriaco. *agg.* (*naut.*) di sopravvento. *vt.* resistere a (*una burrasca, ecc.*); esporre alle intemperie; stagionare (*o* far seccare) all'aria; (*naut.*) passare sopravvento, doppiare. *vi.* superare una burrasca; stagionarsi.

weather-beaten *agg.* battuto dalle intemperie, logoro, agguerrito.

weathercock (wĕth′ĕr·kŏk′) *n.* girotta.

weatherglass (wĕth′ĕr·glăs′) *n.* barometro.

weatherproof (wĕth′ĕr·proof′) *agg.* resistente alle intemperie.

weave (wēv) *n.* tessitura. *vt., vi.* (*pass.* **wove**, *pp.* **woven**) intrecciare, tessere, intessere.

weaving *n.* tessitura.

web (wĕb) *n.* tessuto, tela, rete, ragnatela, trama; membrana interdigitale (*dei palmipedi*).

wed (wĕd) *vt.* (*pass.* **wedded**, *pp.* **wedded**, **wed**) sposare, unire, legare. *vi.* sposarsi.

wedded (wĕd′ĕd) *agg.* sposato; coniugale; legato.

wedding (wĕd′ĭng) *n.* matrimonio: — **card**, partecipazione di nozze; — **day**, giorno di nozze, anniversario del matrimonio; — **ring**, fede nuziale.

wedge (wĕj) *n.* cuneo, bietta. *vt.* incuneare, spaccare (*o* allargare) con un cuneo. *vi.* incunearsi.

wedlock (wĕd′lŏk) *n.* matrimonio.

Wednesday (wĕnz′dĭ) *n.* mercoledì.

wee (wē) *agg.* piccolo, minuscolo.

weed (wēd) (1) *n.* fascia di lutto; *pl.* gramaglie.

weed (wēd) (2) *n.* erbaccia, zizzania; (*fam.*) tabacco, sigaro. *vt.* sarchiare, ripulire, epurare. —**y** *agg.* pieno di erbacce.

week (wēk) *n.* settimana: **this day** —, oggi a otto; **a** — **of Sundays**, un'eternità; — **day**, giorno feriale; — **end**, fine-settimana.

weekly (wēk′lĭ) *n.* pubblicazione set-timanale. *agg.* settimanale. *avv.* settimanalmente.

weep (wēp) *vt., vi.* (*pass., pp.* **wept**) piangere; secernere: **to** — **one's eyes out**, piangere disperatamente.

weeping *agg.* piangente: — **willow**, salice piangente. *n.* pianto, lagrime.

weevil (wē′v′l) *n.* gorgoglione.

weft (wĕft) *n.* trama (*di tessuto*).

weigh (wā) *vt., vi.* pesare; soppesare, ponderare; levare (*l'ancora*); aver peso (*o importanza*); gravare: **to** — **down**, opprimere.

weight (wāt) *n.* peso, gravità; importanza. *vt.* appesantire, gravare; valutare.

weighty (wāt′ĭ) *agg.* pesante, gravoso; efficace, importante.

weir (wēr) *n.* chiusa, cateratta, diga.

weird (wērd) *agg.* magico, soprannaturale, sconcertante, fatale.

welcome (wĕl′kŭm) *n.* benvenuto, accoglienza. *agg.* benvenuto, gradito, opportuno, tempestivo: — **home!** bentornato! **to be** — **to**, esser libero di; **you are** —, (in risposta a "**thank you**") non c'è di che, prego. *vt.* dare il benvenuto a, accogliere bene, gradire.

weld (wĕld) *n.* saldatura, sutura. *vt.* saldare, unire. *vi.* saldarsi.

welder (wĕl′dĕr) *n.* saldatore.

welfare (wĕl′fâr′) *n.* benessere, bene, prosperità.

well (wĕl) (1) *n.* pozzo, serbatoio, sorgente, fonte, tromba (*di scala, ecc.*); (*naut.*) sentina. *vi.* scaturire, sgorgare: **tears welled up in her eyes**, le sgorgarono le lagrime.

well (wĕl) (2) *agg.* in buona salute; fortunato; in buone condizioni: **to be** —, star bene; **to get** —, ristabilirsi. *avv.* bene; giustamente; molto; pienamente: **everything is going** — **with me**, sto bene, vado bene, tutto mi sta andando bene; **to do oneself** —, vivere bene, vivere negli agi; **to stand** — **with**, godere la simpatia di; **he ought to be** — **beaten**, meriterebbe proprio una lezione coi fiocchi; **he must be** — **over fifty**, deve avere cinquant'anni sonati da un pezzo; **you may** — **be surprised**, hai ben ragione di meravigliarti; **we may as** — **begin at once**, ci conviene cominciare subito; **you might just as** — **throw away your money**, tanto vale che tu butti il denaro dalla finestra; **he gave me advice and money as** —, non solo mi ha dato consigli, ma anche denaro. *int.* dunque, ebbene, bene. —**behaved** *agg.* cortese, corretto. —**being** *n.* benessere. —

born *agg.* bennato. —bred *agg.* di buona razza, beneducato. —meaning *agg.* benintenzionato. —meant *agg.* a fin di bene. —nigh *avv.* quasi. —off *agg.* benestante, in buone condizioni. —read *agg.* colto. — to-do *agg.* agiato.

welsh (wĕlsh) (1) *vt.*, *vi.* (*gergo*) truffare, svignarsela senza pagare.

Welsh (wĕlsh) (2) *n.*, *agg.* gallese.

welt (wĕlt) *n.* orlo, guàrdolo (*di scarpa*). *vt.* orlare, munir di guàrdolo.

welter (wĕl'tĕr) *n.* tumulto, confusione. *vi.* tumultuare, sguazzare, avvoltolarsi (*nel fango, ecc.*).

welterweight (wĕl'tĕr·wāt') *n.* medioleggiero (*pugile*).

wen (wĕn) *n.* natta.

wench (wĕnch) *n.* ragazza, cameriera.

went (wĕnt) *pass. di* to go.

wept (wĕpt) *pass., pp. di* to weep.

were (wŭr) *pass.* (*nel pl. e nella 2a pers. sing.dell'indic.*), *cong.imperfetto di* to be: if I — you, se fossi al posto tuo.

werewolf, werwolf (wĕr'wŏolf') *n.*lupo. mannaro, licantropo.

west (wĕst) *n.* ovest, ponente, occidente. *agg.* occidentale, dell'ovest. *avv.* all'ovest: to go —, (*gergo*) andare al Creatore.

westerly (wĕs'tĕr·lĭ) *agg.* occidentale.

western (wĕs'tĕrn) *n.* (*S.U.*) racconto (*o film*) sull'ovest degli U.S.A.. *agg.* occidentale.

westerner (wĕs'tĕr·nĕr) *n.* occidentale (*degli S.U.*).

Westwall (wĕst'wŏl') *n.* Linea Sigfrido (*2a guerra mondiale.*)

westward (wĕst'wĕrd) *agg.* diretto (*o rivolto*) a ovest. *avv.* verso ovest.

wet (wĕt) *n.* umidità, pioggia; (*S.U.*) antiproibizionista. *agg.* umido, bagnato, piovoso; — blanket, guastafeste; — dock (*naut.*), bacino; — nurse, nutrice. *vt.* (*pass.*), *pp.* wet, —ted) inumidire, umettare, bagnare. *vi.* bagnarsi.

wether (wĕth'ĕr) *n.* montone castrato.

wetness (wĕt'nĕs) *n.* umidità.

whack (hwăk) *n.* pacca, colpo; (*gergo*) tentativo. *vt.*, *vi.* battere, menar pacche; (*gergo*) spartire.

whale (hwāl) *n.* (*zool.*) balena. *vt.* (*gergo*) malmenare, percuotere. *vi.* andare alla pesca della balena.

whalebone (hwāl'bōn') *n.* stecca di balena.

whaler (hwāl'ĕr) *n.* baleniera, baleniere.

wharf (hwôrf) *n.* molo, banchina. *vt.* attraccare, ormeggiare.

what (hwŏt) *agg.interr.* di quale specie?, quanto?, quale? *pron.rel.*

ciò che, quello che. *pron.interr.* che?, che cosa?, quale? *avv.* come?, perchè? *cong.* che, tanto che: and — not, eccetera; — for? perchè?, a che scopo? — of that? che importa? to know —'s —, saperla lunga; —'s up? che succede? —'s the matter with you? che avete?; — a car! che automobile!

whatever (hwŏt·ĕv'ĕr) *agg.*, *pron.* tutto cio che, qualunque, qualsiasi cosa, quel poco di. *agg.* di nessuna specie: of no use —, assolutamente inutile; — happens, accada quel che accada.

whatnot (hwŏt'nŏt') *n.* scaffale; (*fam.*) qualunque cosa.

whatsoever (hwŏt'sō·ĕv'ĕr) *vedi* whatever.

wheat (hwēt) *n.* frumento, grano.

wheedle (hwē'd'l) *vt.*, *vi.* carpire; adulare, adescare: to — somebody into, persuadere qualcuno a.

wheel (hwēl) *n.* ruota; volante; ciclo; girandola; cerchio; rotazione, conversione; (*fam.*) bicicletta: driving —, ruota motrice; cog —, ruota dentata; steering —, volante di guida; ruota del timone; — chair, poltrona a rotelle *o* ruote. *vt.* far girare, trasportare su ruote. *vi.* rotare, girare; cambiare direzione, voltarsi; girare in bicicletta: to — around, voltarsi, fare un voltafaccia.

wheelbarrow (hwēl'băr'ō) *n.* carriola.

wheeze (hwēz) *n.* respiro affannoso, sibilo; artificio, dispositivo; (*gergo*) luogo comune, banalità. *vi.* ansimare.

wheezy (hwēz'ĭ) *agg.* asmatico.

whelp (hwĕlp) *n.* cucciolo.

when (hwĕn) *avv.*, *cong.* quando, mentre, allorchè; qualora; benchè: since—? da quando in qua?

whence (hwĕns) *avv.*, *cong.* donde, dal che, per cui.

whenever (hwĕn·ĕv'ĕr) *cong.* ogni volta che, quando, in qualunque momento.

where (hwâr) *avv.*, *cong.* dove; a quale punto; in quale situazione; in che senso.

whereabout (hwâr'à·bout'); whereabouts *n.* luogo, posto, località in cui qualcuno si trova, ubicazione: I don't know her whereabouts, non so dove ella si trovi. *avv.*, *cong.* ove, in qual luogo, in quali paraggi.

whereas (hwâr·ăz') *cong.* mentre, invece, in considerazione di, stante che, poichè.

whereat (hwâr·ăt') *avv.*, *cong.* al che.

whereby (hwâr·bī') *avv.*, *cong.* per il

quale, per cui; per mezzo del quale; attraverso cui; secondo cui.

wherefore (hwâr'fōr) *n.* causa, motivo. *avv.*, *cong.* ragione per cui, perciò; *(interr.)* perchè?

wherefrom (hwâr·frŏm') *avv.* donde, da cui.

wherein (hwâr·ĭn') *avv.* in cui, nel quale, nei quali; *(interr.)* in che cosa?, dove?

whereof (hwâr·ŏv') *avv.*, *cong.* del quale, di cui; *(interr.)* di che?

whereon (hwâr·ŏn') *avv.* su cui; *(interr.)* su che cosa?

wheresoever (hwâr'sō·ĕv'ĕr) *avv.*, *cong.* dovunque.

whereupon (hwâr'ŭ·pŏn') *avv.* *(interr.)* su che cosa?. *cong.* al che, dopo di che.

wherever (hwâr·ĕv'ĕr) *avv.* *(interr.)* dove?, dove mai? *cong.* dovunque, in qualunque luogo; in ogni caso.

wherewith (hwâr·wĭth') *avv.*, *cong* con cui, col quale, per mezzo del quale: —? con che cosa?

wherewithal (hwâr'wĭth·ôl') *n.* mezzi, fondi, soldi.

whet (hwĕt) *vt.* aguzzare, affilare, stimolare.

whether (hwĕth'ĕr) *cong.* se; sia; sia che: — ... or, se ... oppure; we do not know — he will pay (or not), non sappiamo se egli pagherà (o no); — we stay or — we go, sia che restiamo, sia che ce ne andiamo; I doubt —, dubito che.

whetstone (hwĕt'stōn') *n.* cote.

whey (hwā) *n.* siero del latte.

which (hwĭch) *agg.* qualunque; *(interr.)* quale? *pron.rel.* che, il quale, la quale, i quali, le quali, il che: I cannot tell — is —, non so distinguerli l'uno dall'altro; — way? da quale parte?, da che parte?

whichever (hwĭch·ĕv'ĕr) *agg.*, *pron.* chiunque, qualunque; quello che, quella che: —? quale?, quali?; take — road you like, prendete la strada che volete.

whiff (hwĭf) *n.* zaffata, ondata, soffio, scatto. *vt.*, *vi.* sbuffare, aspirare, fumare.

while (hwīl) *n.* momento, tempo, lasso: in a little —, in breve, tra poco; for a short —, per un po', per poco, poco tempo; a short — ago, poco fa, da poco. once in a —, una volta tanto; to be worth —, valere la pena. *cong.* mentre, intanto che, nello stesso tempo che. *vt.* trascorrere (*il tempo*): to — away time, ammazzare il tempo.

whilst (hwīlst) *vedi* while.

whim (hwĭm) *n.* capriccio, ubbia.

whimper (hwĭm'pĕr) *n.* piagnisteo, lamento. *vi.* lamentarsi, piagnucolare.

whimsical (hwĭm'zĭ·kăl) *agg.* fantastico, capriccioso, comico.

whine (hwīn) *n.* piagnisteo, lamento, gemito. *vi.* piagnucolare, lagnarsi piagnucolando.

whiner *n.* piagnone.

whinny (hwĭn'ĭ) *n.* nitrito. *vi.* nitrire.

whip (hwĭp) *n.* frusta, sferza, scudiscio, staffile; sferzata; *(naut.)* paranco. *vt.* frustare; criticare, stimolare; sbattere, frullare (*uova*, *panna*, *ecc.*); *(fam.)* sopraffare, vincere. *vi.* guizzare, slanciarsi: to — out, tirar fuori fulmineamente.

whippet (hwĭp'ĕt) *n.* levriere inglese.

whipping (hwĭp'ĭng) *n.* frustata, flagellazione.

whir (hwûr) *n.* ronzio, fruscio. *vi.* ronzare, frusciare.

whirl (hwûrl) *n.* turbine, rotazione, vortice; voluta, spirale (*di fumo*); confusione. *vt.*, *vi.* far turbinare, roteare; turbinare, girare: my head whirls, mi gira la testa.

whirligig (hwûr'lĭ·gĭg') *n.* giostra; trottola.

whirlpool (hwûrl'pōōl') *n.* gorgo.

whirlwind (hwûrl'wĭnd') *n.* tromba d'aria, bufera.

whish (hwĭsh) *vi.* sibilare.

whisk (hwĭsk) *n.* spazzolata; movimento rapido; spazzola, scopa, frullino. *vt.* spazzar via, portar via, arraffare; sbattere, frullare (*uova*, *ecc.*). *vi.* fuggire rapidamente, guizzare: to — away, far sparire, trascinar via.

whisker (hwĭs'kĕr) *n.* pelo di barba, baffo *pl.* basette; barba.

whisky, whiskey (hwĭs'kĭ) *n.* whisky, uischi (*acquavite di cereali*).

whisper (hwĭs'pĕr) *n.* mormorio, susurro; ronzio; diceria. *vt.*, *vi.* bisbigliare, mormorare; confabulare; insinuare; ronzare, stormire: it is whispered that ..., si mormora che.

whispering *n.* bisbiglio, mormorio, diceria. *agg.* mormorante, frusciante.

whistle (hwĭs''l) *n.* fischietto, fischio, sibilo; *(fam.)* gola: paesucolo. *vt.*, *vi.* fischiare, zufolare, sibilare.

whit (hwĭt) *n.* inezia, iota.

white (hwīt) *n.*, *agg.* bianco; puro, innocente, onesto, leale: to show the — feather, mostrarsi vigliacco; — hot, rovente; — lie, bugia perdonabile (o pietosa); —livered, *agg.* codardo, vigliacco.

whiten (hwīt''n) *vt.*, *vi.* imbiancare.

whiteness (hwīt′něs) *n.* bianchezza, candore; pallore; purezza.

whitewash (hwīt′wŏsh′) *n.* calce da imbianchino, pittura bianca. *vt.* imbiancare a calce; passare la spugna su (*errori, colpe*); scagionare (*senza giustizia*),mandare impunito.

whither (hwĭth′ẽr) *avv.* dove, nella quale direzione; (*interr.*) dove?, in quale direzione?

whitish (hwīt′ĭsh) *agg.* biancastro.

whitlow (hwĭt′lō) *n.* patereccio.

Whitsunday (hwĭt′sŭn′dĭ) *n.* Domenica della Pentecoste.

Whitsuntide (hwĭt′sŭn-tīd′) *n.* Pentecoste.

whittle (hwĭt′′l) *vt.*, *vi.* temperare, truciolara; far la punta a (*un lapis*); assottigliare; ridurre (*spese, ecc.*).

whiz (hwĭz) *n.* sibilo; passaggio rapido; (*gergo*) affare; persona (*o cosa*) straordinaria. *vt.* centrifugare. *vi.* fischiare, sibilare; *vi.* sfrecciare.

whizzer *n.* centrifuga.

who (hōō) *pron.rel.* chi, il quale, la quale, i quali, le quali, che; (*interr.*) chi?: he —, colui che; — is it? chi è?

whodunit (hōō′dŭn′ĭt) *n.* (*gergo*) racconto poliziesco.

whoever (hōō·ĕv′ẽr) *pron.rel.* chiunque; (*interr.*) chi mai?

whole (hōl) *n.* totalità, tutto, totale: on the —, in complesso, tutto considerato; as a —, come una cosa unica, nel complesso; the — of us, tutti noi. *agg.* tutto, intero, completo, integrale, sano, intatto: the — day, tutto il giorno; —-hearted *agg.* cordiale, sincero, leale; —-heartedly *avv.* cordialmente, lealmente.

wholesale (hōl′sāl′) *n.* vendita all'ingrosso. *agg.*, *avv.* all'ingrosso, in grande quantità: — dealer, grossista; — slaughter, carneficina, ecatombe.

wholesaler *n.* grossista.

wholesome (hōl′sŭm) *agg.* sano, salutare.

wholly (hōl′lĭ) *avv.* interamente, completamente.

whom (hōōm) *pron.rel. e interr.* che, chi, il quale, la quale, i quali, le quali: to —, cui, a chi; — did you give it to? a chi lo hai dato?

whoop (hōōp) *n.* urlo; ululato (*della tosse canina*). *vt.*, *vi.* gridare, ululare; esultare (*o protestare*) clamorosamente.

whooping cough (hōōp′ĭng) *n.* tosse canina.

whore (hōr) *n.* prostituta.

whorl (hwôrl) *n.* spirale, spira.

whose (hōōz) *pron.rel.* di cui, del quale, della quale, dei quali, delle quali; (*interr.*) di chi?: — book is this?, di chi è questo libro?

why (hwī) (1) *n.* (il) perchè, causa, motivo. *avv.* (*anche interr.*) perchè, per quale ragione, per cui: the reason —, la ragione per cui.

why! (2) *inter.* diamine!, suvvia!, ma guarda!, ma come!, oh bella!, perbacco!, caspita!: —, of course! ma naturale!

wick (wĭk) *n.* lucignolo, stoppino (*di candela, ecc.*).

wicked (wĭk′ĕd) *agg.* malvagio, tristo; molesto; indocile.

wickedness *n.* malvagità; indocilità.

wicker (wĭk′ẽr) *n.* vimine. *agg.* di vimini.

wicket (wĭk′ĕt) *n.* sportello; usciolo; cancelletto; porta (*del cricket*); archetto (*del croquet*); cateratta (*di chiusa*).

wide (wīd) *agg.* ampio, largo, aperto, esteso, lontano: —open, spalancato; — of the mark, lontano dal segno. *avv.* largamente, lontano, a distanza: far and —, in lungo e in largo; — apart, distanziati.

wide-awake (wīd′à·wǎk′) *n.* cappello floscio. *agg.* completamente sveglio, pronto, vigile.

widely (wīd′lĭ) *avv.* largamente, ampiamente; prevalentemente.

widen (wīd′n) *vt.* allargare, ampliare, estendere, dilatare. *vi.* aprirsi, allargarsi, estendersi, dilatarsi.

widespread (wīd′sprĕd′) *agg.* diffuso.

widow (wĭd′ō) *n.* vedova.

widower (wĭd′ō·ĕr) *n.* vedovo.

widowhood (wĭd′ō·hŏŏd) *n.* vedovanza.

width (wĭdth) *n.* larghezza, ampiezza; (*tess.*) altezza.

wield (wēld) *vt.* esercitare (*autorità*); maneggiare; brandire.

wife (wīf) *n.* (*pl.* wives) moglie, sposa.

wig (wĭg) *n.* parrucca.

wiggle (wĭg′′l) *vedi* wriggle.

wigwag (wĭg′wǎg′) *n.* (*naut.*) segnalazione con bandierine.

wigwam (wĭg′wŏm) *n.* capanna dei pellirosse; (*gergo*) sala di comizi.

wild (wīld) *n.* deserto, selva, luogo selvaggio, solitudine. *agg.* selvaggio; silvestre; violento, feroce, incontrollato, selvatico, irruento, ribelle, indomato, irragionevole, stravagante, incauto, pazzo, furioso; (*fam.*) entusiasta: a — goose chase, un'impresa vana, l'impossibile. *avv. vedi* wildly.

wildcat (wīld′kǎt′) *n.* gatto selvatico;

(*S.U.*) locomotiva di manovra; impresa sballata.

wilderness (wĭl'dẽr·nĕs) *n.* selva, deserto.

wildly (wĭld'lĭ) *avv.* selvaggiamente, impetuosamente, disordinatamente, furiosamente, a vanvera.

wildness (wĭld'nĕs) *n.* selvatichezza, ferocia, sregolatezza, furore, irruenza.

wile (wĭl) *n.* astuzia, raggiro. *vt.* raggirare; adescare.

wilful (wĭl'fōōl) *vedi* willful.

will (wĭl) (1) *verbo aus. difettivo (pass.* would); *esprime il concetto di volere: il pres.* (will) voglio, *ecc.*; vogliamo, *ecc.*, è l'aus. con cui si forma il futuro (predicente: 2a e 3a pers. sing. e pl.; volitivo: 1a pers. sing. e pl.): I — go, io andrò (*voglio andare*); we — work, noi lavoreremo (*vogliamo lavorare*); you — sing, voi canterete; they — obey, essi obbediranno. *Il pass.* (would) *ha valore di condizionale:* vorrei, *ecc.*; vorremmo, *ecc.*; *opp. d'imperfetto soggiuntivo:* (io) volessi, *ecc.*; volessimo, *ecc.*; *indica spesso azione abituale, ed è un aus. con cui si forma il condizionale degli altri verbi:* I would refuse if, rifiuterei se; he would work from morning to night, lavorava giorno e notte.

will (wĭl) (2) *n.* volontà, volere, arbitrio; testamento: at —, a volontà, a discrezione; free —, libero arbitrio; ill—, malavoglia, malevolenza; to have one's —, spuntarla; with a —, con entusiasmo, di lena. *vt.*, *vi.* ordinare, ingiungere, deliberare, imporre; lasciare per testamento, disporre; costringere a: the king willed that, il re dispose che; to — oneself to, imporsi di.

willful (wĭl'fōōl) *agg.* intenzionale, doloso; ostinato, caparbio.

willing (wĭl'ĭng) *agg.* disposto, compiacente, volonteroso, spontaneo, volontario.

willingly *avv.* volontariamente, spontaneamente, volontieri.

willingness *n.* spontaneità, compiacenza, propensione, buon volere.

willow (wĭl'o) *n.* salice; (*tess.*) cardatrice meccanica.

willy-nilly (wĭl'ĭ·nĭl'ĭ) *avv.* volente o nolente.

wilt (wĭlt) *vt.* far avvizzire. *vi.* avvizzire, languire, deprimersi.

wily (wĭl'ĭ) *agg.* astuto.

wimble (wĭm'b'l) *n.* succhiello.

wimple (wĭm'p'l) *n.* soggolo.

win (wĭn) *vt.*, *vi.* (*pass.*, *pp.* won) vin-

cere, trionfare; ottenere, conquistare; sedurre; accattivarsi; persuadere, indurre: to — back, riguadagnare; to — out, vincere, trionfare; to — over, persuadere; conquistare.

wince (wĭns) *vi.* ritrarsi, trasalire, fare una smorfia dolorosa; imbizzarrirsi (*di cavallo*).

winch (wĭnch) *n.* manovella, arganello.

wind (wĭnd) (1) *n.* svolta, curva; (*elett.*) avvolgimento. *vt.* (*pass.*, *pp.* wound) avvolgere; caricare (*orologi, ecc.*); issare. *vi.* serpeggiare, mutare direzione, avvolgersi, attorcigliarsi, arrotolarsi; caricarsi; insinuarsi: to — up, caricare; concludere, terminare.

wind (wĭnd) (2) *n.* vento, soffio, respiro, respirazione, flatulenza; sentore, notizia; vaniloquio: to get — of, venire a sapere; to get the — up, agitarsi, montarsi. *vt.* (*pass.*, *pp.* winded) esporre al vento, arieggiare; sfiatare; fiutare; far riprender fiato.

windbag (wĭnd'băg') *n.* (*gergo*) parolaio, chiacchierone.

wind cone (*o* sleeve *o* sock), manica a vento.

windfall (wĭnd'fōl') *n.* vento improvviso; frutta abbattuta dal vento; colpo di fortuna; eredità insperata.

winding (wĭn'dĭng) *n.* svolta, curva, sinuosità, avvolgimento. *agg.* sinuoso, serpeggiante, a chiocciola: — engine, argano; — sheet, sudario.

windlass (wĭnd'lăs) *n.* argano.

windmill (wĭnd'mĭl') *n.* mulino a vento.

window (wĭn'dō) *n.* finestra; finestrino (*di auto, ecc.*); sportello (*di banca, ecc.*); vetrina: show —, vetrina; — dresser, vetrinista; — sash, telaio di finestra; — sill, davanzale. —pane *n.* vetro di finestra.

windpipe (wĭnd'pĭp') *n.* trachea.

wind-screen, **windshield** *n.* (*auto*) parabrezza: — wiper, tergicristallo.

windup (wĭnd'ŭp') *n.* conclusione.

windy (wĭn'dĭ) *agg.* ventoso, tempestoso, battuto dal vento; vaniloquente: it is —, tira vento.

wine (wĭn) *n.* vino: — cellar, cantina; — stone, tartaro.

wing (wĭng) *n.* ala; volo; (*teat.*) quinta; *pl.* distintivo di pilota militare, distintivo d'una specializzazione nell'aviazione militare: on the —, in volo; to take —, spiccare il volo, fuggire; under the — of, sotto la protezione di. *vt.* munire di ali, sorvolare; colpire in un'ala, ferire in un braccio. *vi.* volare.

winged (wĭngd) *agg.* alato.

wingspread (wĭng'sprĕd') *n.* apertura d'ala.

wink (wĭngk) *n.* strizzata d'occhio, ammicco; istante: **not to sleep a —,** non chiudere occhio. *vt., vi.* battere (*gli occhi, le palpebre*), ammiccare; vacillare; brillare a intermittenza, lampeggiare: **to — at,** chiudere un occhio su, fingere di non vedere; strizzare l'occhio a.

winner (wĭn'ĕr) *n.* vincitore.

winning (wĭn'ĭng) *n.* vittoria; *pl.* guadagni, vincita. *agg.* vincitore, vincente, cattivante: **— post,** palo d'arrivo.

winsome (wĭn'sŭm) *agg.* incantevole, affascinante.

winter (wĭn'tĕr) *n.* inverno. *agg.* da inverno, invernale. *vt.* riparare per l'inverno. *vi.* svernare.

wintry (wĭn'trĭ) *agg.* invernale, freddo, triste.

wipe (wīp) *vt.* asciugare, pulire: **to — away, off, out,** cancellare; spazzare via; eliminare; annientare, distruggere; asciugare.

wiper (wīp'ĕr) *n.* pulitore; strofinaccio; (*gergo*) fazzoletto; (*elett.*) spazzola; (*auto*) tergicristallo.

wire (wīr) *n.* filo metallico; reticolato; cavo (*telegrafico, ecc.*); (*fam.*) telegrafo, telegramma: **barbed —,** filo spinato; **— recorder,** magnetofono; **to pull wires,** esercitare influenze. *vt., vi.* legare con (*o* munire di, *o* infilare su) filo metallico; fare un impianto elettrico; telegrafare.

wiredraw (wīr'drô') *vt.* (*pass., pp.* wiredrawn) trafilare.

wire-glass *n.* vetro armato.

wireless (wīr'lĕs) *n.* radiotelegrafia (*o* telefonia); apparecchio radio; radiotelegramma. *agg.* senza fili, radiotelegrafico, radiofonico.

wirephoto (wīr'fō'tō) *n.* radiofoto.

wiry (wīr'ĭ) *agg.* di (*o* simile a) filo metallico; robusto, segaligno; agile.

wisdom (wĭz'dŭm) *n.* saggezza, prudenza: **— tooth,** dente del giudizio.

wise (wīz) *n.* maniera, modo. *agg.* saggio, prudente, giudizioso; edotto: **to be — to,** essere informato di.

wiseacre (wīz'ā'kĕr) *n.* sapientone.

wisecrack (wīz'krăk') *n.* (*S.U.*) spiritosaggine, battuta.

wisely (wīz'lĭ) *avv.* saggiamente, prudentemente.

wish (wĭsh) *n.* augurio, desiderio, richiesta. *vt., vi.* desiderare, augurare, augurarsi: **I — I could go,** vorrei poter andare; **I — it were true!** magari fosse vero! **I — I had not struck him,** rimpiango di averlo colpito; **to — for,** desiderare. **—ful** *agg.* desideroso: **— thinking,** pio desiderio, illusione.

wisp (wĭsp) *n.* ciuffo.

wistful (wĭst'fŏŏl) *agg.* nostalgico; pensoso; malinconico, mesto.

wit (wĭt) *n.* (*spesso pl.*) acume, ingegno; arguzia; sagacia; lucidità; persona sagace: **to be at one's —'s end,** non saper più dove battere la testa; **out of one's —s,** fuor di senno; **to live by one's —s,** vivere di espedienti; **to —,** cioè, vale a dire.

witch (wĭch) *n.* maga, strega: **— doctor,** stregone.

witchcraft (wĭch'kráft') *n.* stregoneria, magia.

with (wĭth) *prep.* con; per mezzo di; insieme con; presso; alle dipendenze di: **what do you want — her?** che volete da lei?; **— a view to,** con l'intenzione di; **to begin —,** innanzi tutto; **filled —,** pieno di; **ill —,** malato di.

withdraw (wĭth·drô') *vt.* (*pass.* withdrew, *pp.* withdrawn) ritirare, ritrarre, ritrattare. *vi.* ritirarsi, arretrare, andarsene.

withdrawal (wĭth·drô'ăl) *n.* ritirata, ritiro, ritrattazione.

withdrawn (wĭth·drôn') *pp. di* to withdraw. *agg.* ritirato, appartato; (*di carattere*) chiuso, schivo.

withdrew (wĭth·drŏŏ') *pass. di* to withdraw.

wither (wĭth'ĕr) *vt.* disseccare, far avvizzire; (*fig.*) annientare (*con lo sguardo*). *vi.* avvizzire, disseccarsi, deperire.

withers (wĭth'ĕrz) *n.pl.* garrese (*del cavallo*).

withhold (wĭth·hōld') *vt.* (*pass., pp.* withheld) trattenere, frenare; negare, rifiutare. *vi.* astenersi.

within (wĭth·ĭn') *prep.* entro, fra nell'ambito di, in, nel: **— a year of my arrival,** entro un anno dal mio arrivo; nemmeno un anno dopo il mio arrivo; **— five miles,** entro un raggio di cinque miglia; **it is not — my power,** non ne ho la facoltà, non ho la facoltà *o* possibilità di; **— an ace of,** a un pelo da. *avv.* dentro, in casa: **from —,** dall'interno.

without (wĭth·out') *prep.* senza; fuori di, all'esterno di; oltre. *avv.* fuori, all'esterno, esteriormente.

withstand (wĭth·stănd') *vt.* (*pass., pp.* withstood) subire, sopportare, affrontare. *vi.* opporsi, resistere.

witless (wĭt'lĕs) *agg.* stupido, insulso.

witness (wĭt'nĕs) *n.* testimonio, testimonianza. *vt.* testimoniare; assistere a; convalidare; firmare come testimone.

witticism (wĭt'ĭ-sĭz'm) *n.* arguzia, spiritosaggine, freddura.

witty (wĭt'ĭ) *agg.* intelligente, arguto.

wives (wīvz) *pl. di* wife.

wizard (wĭz'ẽrd) *n.* mago, stregone.

wizardry (wĭz'ẽrd·rĭ) *n.* stregoneria, magia.

wizened (wĭz''nd) *agg.* dissecato, raggrinzito, avvizzito.

wobble (wŏb''l) *vedi* wabble.

woe (wō) *n.* dolore, pena; sventura. *int.* guai (*a*), sventura!: — is me! oh, me infelice!

woebegone (wō'bĕ·gŏn') *agg.* afflitto, sconsolato.

woke (wōk) *pass. di* to wake.

wolf (wŏolf) *n.* (*pl.* wolves) lupo; (*fam.*) donnaiolo, gallo, "pappagallo"; *vt.* (*fam.*) divorare. **—'s bane** *n.* (*bot.*) aconito.

wolfram (wŏol'frăm) *n.* tungsteno.

woman (wŏom'ăn) *n.* (*pl.* women) donna: **— writer,** scrittrice.

womanhood (wŏom'ăn·hŏod) *n.* femminilità; il sesso femminile, le donne.

womanish (wŏom'ăn·ĭsh) *agg.* femminile; effeminato.

womankind (wŏom'ăn·kīnd') *n.* il sesso femminile, le donne.

womanly (wŏom'ăn·lĭ) *agg.* femminile. *avv.* femminilmente.

womb (wŏom) *n.* utero, matrice; ventre, cavità.

women (wĭm'ĕn) *pl. di* woman.

won (wŭn) *pass., pp. di* to win.

wonder (wŭn'dẽr) *n.* meraviglia, miracolo, stupore, ammirazione, prodigio: **to work —s,** fare prodigi; **no — that,** non c'è da meravigliarsi che. *vt., vi.* meravigliarsi; domandarsi; meditare: **I — at you,** mi meraviglio di voi; **I — what happened,** mi domando che cosa è successo; **I should not — if,** non mi stupirei se.

wonderful (wŭn'dẽr·fŏol) *agg.* meraviglioso, prodigioso. **—ly** *avv.* meravigliosamente, prodigiosamente.

wondering (wŭn'dẽr·ĭng) *agg.* stupito, perplesso.

wondrous (wŭn'drŭs) *agg.* mirabile, prodigioso, incredibile.

wont (wŏnt) *n.* usanza, abitudine. *agg.* abituato, avvezzo: **to be — to,** essere solito, solere.

wonted (wŏn'tĕd) *agg.* abituato, abituale.

woo (wŏo) *vt.* corteggiare, circuire; chiedere in matrimonio; sollecitare, cercare.

wood (wŏod) *n.* bosco, foresta; elgno,

legname; *pl.* bosco, foresta, selva: **— engraving,** incisione in legno. *vt.* piantare ad alberi; fornire di legna. *vi.* far legna.

woodcut (wŏod'kŭt') *n.* incisione su legno.

woodcutter (wŏod'kŭt'ẽr) *n.* legnaiuolo, taglialegna; incisore in legno.

wooded (wŏod'ĕd) *agg.* boscoso, alberato.

wooden (wŏod''n) *agg.* di legno, legnoso; rigido, impassibile.

woodland (wŏod'lănd) *n.* terreno boscoso, foresta.

woodman (wŏod'măn) *n.* (*pl.* —men) boscaiuolo; guardia forestale.

woodpecker (wŏod'pĕk'ẽr) *n.* (*ornit.*) picchio.

woodshed (wŏod'shĕd') *n.* baracca della legna.

woodsman (wŏodz'măn) *n.* uomo dei boschi.

woodwork (wŏod'wûrk') *n.* lavoro in legno; rivestimento in legno.

woody (wŏod'ĭ) *agg.* boscoso, legnoso.

wooer (wŏo'ẽr) *n.* corteggiatore, pretendente.

woof (wŏof) *n.* (*tess.*) trama.

wool (wŏol) *n.* lana, fibra, lanugine. *agg.* di lana, capelli crespi.

woolen, woollen (wŏol'ĕn) *n.* tessuto di lana. *agg.* di lana: **— mill,** fabbrica di tessuti di lana.

woolly (wŏol'ĭ) *agg.* lanoso; arruffato.

word (wûrd) *n.* parola, vocabolo; promessa; notizia, ambasciata, messaggio: **by — of mouth,** a viva voce; **to be as good as one's —,** essere di parola. *vt.* formulare, esprimere.

wore (wōr) *pass. di* to wear.

work (wûrk) *n.* lavoro, opera, fatica; impiego; azione, effetto, funzionamento; movimento; *pl.* fabbrica, officina; meccanismo; fortificazioni: **to make short — of,** sbrigare alla svelta; **to give the —s to** (*gergo*) dare il fatto suo a. *vt., vi.* (*pass., pp.* worked *o* wrought) lavorare, elaborare, produrre, ottenere, far lavorare, far funzionare, manovrare, maneggiare, manipolare; causare; operare, funzionare, agire; riuscire: **to — out,** sfruttare; risolvere, escogitare, calcolare; **to — one's way,** procedere a fatica, aprirsi un varco; **it didn't —,** non ha funzionato, non è riuscita, non è andata bene; **it —ed well,** è andata bene, è riuscita.

workbook (wûrk'bŏok') *n.* manuale; diario di lavoro; libro di esercizi.

workday (wûrk'dā') *n.* giorno lavorativo, giorno feriale.

worker (wûr'kẽr) *n.* lavoratore.

working (wûr'kĭng) n. lavoro, funzionamento, lavorazione, elaborazione; fermentazione. agg. operaio; lavorativo; operoso; da lavoro; in vigore: **in — order**, in perfetto stato di funzionamento; — **class**, classe lavoratrice; — **hours**, orario di lavoro.

workman (wûrk'măn) n. operaio, artigiano.

workmanship (wûrk'măn-shĭp) n. lavoro, abilità manuale, fattura, esecuzione.

workshop (wûrk'shŏp) n. officina, bottega; corso di specializzazione (basato su metodi pratici).

workwoman (wûrk'wŏom'ăn) n. operaia.

world (wûrld) n. mondo: **all over the —**, in tutto il mondo; **World War I (II)**, la prima (seconda) guerra mondiale.

worldly (wûrld'lĭ) agg. mondano, terreno, umano, materialistico.

worm (wûrm) n. verme; baco, lombrico; filetto (di vite). vt. ottenere tortuosamente, strappare (un segreto, ecc.). vi. strisciare, serpeggiare: **to — one's way**, insinuarsi; **to — oneself out**, sgattaiolare fuori; **to — oneself into**, insinuarsi; **to — a secret out of somebody**, strappare un segreto a qualcuno.

wormeaten agg. tarlato; decrepito.

worn (wôrn) pp. di **to wear**. agg. logoro, consumato: **—out** agg. molto logoro, esausto.

worried (wûr'ĭd) agg. ansioso, preoccupato, tormentato.

worry (wûr'ĭ) n. preoccupazione, ansietà, tormento. vt. tormentare, preoccupare; straziare. vi. preoccuparsi, tormentarsi: **don't —!** non preoccupatevi!, non abbiate paura!

worrying (wŭr'ri'ĭng) agg. tormentoso, preoccupante.

worrywart (wûr'ĭ-wôrt') n. (gergo) pessimista; cacadubbi.

worse (wûrs) n. (il) peggio (di): **to change for the —**, cambiare in peggio. agg. peggiore, meno buono, più cattivo. avv. peggio: **— and —**, di male in peggio; **to get —**, peggiorare; **so much the —**, tanto peggio.

worsen (wûr's'n) vt., vi. peggiorare.

worship (wûr'shĭp) n. venerazione, adorazione, culto: **his —**, sua signoria, sua eccellenza. vt., vi. adorare, venerare.

worshiper n. adoratore, fedele.

worst (wûrst) n. (il) peggio (in senso assoluto). agg. pessimo, (il) peggiore (di tutti). avv. nel peggior modo possibile, peggio: **at the —**, alla peggio. vt. sopraffare, sconfiggere. vi. peggiorare.

worsted (wŏos'tĕd) n. tessuto (di lana) pettinato.

worth (wûrth) n. valore, prezzo, pregio, merito, importanza: **two cents — of**, due soldi di; **to get one's money's —**, ricevere una cosa pari alla spesa, spendere bene il proprio denaro. agg. del valore di, degno di: **to be — ten millions**, possedere dieci milioni; **it is not — while**, non ne vale la pena.

worthless (wûrth'lĕs) agg. privo di valore, indegno, spregevole, inutile.

worthy (wûr'thĭ) n. valentuomo; personaggio illustre. agg. meritevole, degno, stimabile, conveniente.

would (wŏod) pass., cong. di **will**: **we — go if it weren't raining**, noi andremmo se non piovesse; **they said they — come**, dissero che sarebbero venuti; **— you do it?** lo faresti? **that's just what you — say**, è proprio quel che avresti detto; è proprio quel che prevedevo di sentirti dire; **he —n't help me**, non voleva opp. non volle aiutarmi; **he — say that**, diceva sempre che, era solito dire che; **I — rather go**, preferirei andarmene; **— to God I had not gone**, mai ci fossi andato!

wound (wound) (1) pass., pp. di **to wind**.

wound (wŏond) (2) n. ferita, lesione. vt. ferire.

wove (wōv) pass. di **to weave**.

woven (wō'vĕn) pp. di **to weave**.

wow (wou) n. deformazione della voce o dei suoni riprodotti da un grammofono, magnetofono, ecc., dovuta a imperfetto funzionamento dell'apparecchio. inter. accipicchia!, caspita! vt. entusiasmare, mandare in visibilio.

wraith (rāth) n. fantasma.

wrangle (răng'g'l) n. disputa, rissa. vt., vi. disputare, discutere, litigare; (S.U.) imbrancare (il bestiame).

wrap (răp) n. sciarpa; coperta; involucro; mantello; (pl.) segreto, censura: **under military —s**, protetto dal segreto militare. vt. avvolgere, avviluppare, nascondere: **to — up**, involtare, avvolgere, avvolgersi: **to be —ped up in**, essere avvolto in (o assorto in).

wrapper (răp'ĕr) n. spolverina, vestaglia; sopraccoperta (di libro); foglia esterna del sigaro.

wrapping (răp'ĭng) *n.* involucro, confezione, imballaggio, copertura: — **paper**, carta da pacchi.

wrath (răth) *n.* ira, indignazione, furore.

wrathful (răth'fŏŏl) *agg.* adirato, furibondo.

wreak (rēk) *vt.* sfogare (*collera*) su: **to — vengeance on**, vendicarsi su.

wreath (rēth) *n.* ghirlanda, corona, anello: — **of smoke**, spirale di fumo.

wreathe (rēth) *vt.* intrecciare, inghirlandare, cingere.

wreck (rĕk) *n.* naufragio; relitto, rudere, rottame; distruzione, rovina, devastazione. *vt.* far naufragare; distruggere, rovinare: **to — a train**, far deragliare un treno. *vi.* naufragare, andare in rovina.

wreckage (rĕk'ĭj) *n.* distruzione; relitto.

wrecker (rĕk'ĕr) *n.* demolitore; ricuperatore di relitti; carro attrezzi *o* di soccorso.

wren (rĕn) *n.* (*ornit.*) scricciolo.

WREN (rĕn) *n.* Ausiliaria della Marina Britannica.

wrench (rĕnch) *n.* torsione violenta, slogatura, storta; (*mecc.*) chiave fissa: **monkey —**, chiave inglese. *vt.* torcere, strappare torcendo, slogare.

wrest (rĕst) *n.* torsione, strappo. *vt.* torcere, strappare, forzare, falsare.

wrestle (rĕs''l) *n.* lotta; colluttazione. *vi.* lottare, far la lotta, colluttarsi, arrabattarsi.

wrestler (rĕs'lĕr) *n.* lottatore.

wrestling (rĕs'lĭng) *n.* (*sport.*) lotta.

wretch (rĕch) *n.* sciagurato, sventurato, scellerato, miserabile.

wretched (rĕch'ĕd) *agg.* pietoso, sfortunato, infelice; doloroso; ignobile, abominevole, disgraziato: **this aching tooth makes me feel —**, questo mal di denti mi riduce a uno straccio; **a — life**, una vita miseranda; **— weather**, tempaccio; **his — stupidity**, la sua colossale stupidaggine.

wriggle (rĭg''l) *vt.* torcere, contorcere. *vi.* torcersi, contorcersi, dimenarsi, strisciare: **to — in**, intrufolarsi; **to — out**, scapolarsela, cavarsela, sgusciar fuori.

wring (rĭng) *n.* torsione, strizzatura. *vt.* torcere; stringere, spremere, strizzare; estorcere, *vi.* torcersi: **to — the truth out of**, estorcere la verità a; **to — somebody's hand**, stringere la mano a qualcuno; **to — linen**, strizzare la biancheria; **to — anything from**, estorcere qualcosa a.

wrinkle (rĭng'k'l) (1) *n.* trovata, novità; congegno; suggerimento; bernoccolo, tendenza.

wrinkle (rĭng'k'l) (2) *n.* ruga, grinza, increspatura, sgualcitura. *vt.* contrarre; corrugare, raggrinzire, increspare, spiegazzare. *vi.* spiegazzarsi, incresparsi, raggrinzirsi.

wrinkly (rĭng'klĭ) *agg.* rugoso, grinzoso, facile a sgualcirsi.

wrist (rĭst) *n.* polso: **— band**, polsino; **— watch**, orologio da polso.

writ (rĭt) *n.* decreto, mandato, ordinanza: Holy **—**, Sacra Scrittura.

write (rīt) *vt., vi.* (*pass.* wrote, *pp.* written) scrivere: **to — down**, registrare, annotare; **to — off**, scrivere speditamente; cancellare (*un addebito*), annullare; **to — out**, scrivere per esteso; **to — up**, scrivere il resoconto di, descrivere, redigere, aggiornare.

writer (rīt'ĕr) *n.* scrittore, autore; scrivente: **woman —**, scrittrice.

writhe (rīth) *vt.* torcere. *vi.* contorcersi, divincolarsi.

writing (rīt'ĭng) *n.* scrittura, scritto; produzione letteraria; stile, forma: **— desk**, scrivania; **— paper**, carta per scrivere; **to put in —**, mettere per iscritto.

written (rĭt''n) *pp. di* to write.

wrong (rŏng) *n.* torto, ingiustizia, male, danno, reato, sopruso: **to be in the —**, avere torto, essere dalla parte del torto; **to do —**, fare torto a, offendere. *agg.* falso, sbagliato, erroneo; disadatto; in errore, scorretto; spostato; ingiusto; illegittimo; rovescio; (*mecc.*) guasto: **to be —**, aver torto; essere guasto; **something is — with this dress**, questo vestito ha qualcosa che non va; **what's — with you?** che hai?, che c'è?, qualcosa che non va?; **to take the — train**, sbagliare treno; **to go the — way**, andare di traverso; **the — side**, il rovescio. *avv.* male, a torto, ingiustamente, erroneamente; a rovescio; al contrario: **to go —**, andar male, sbagliare, traviarsi. *vt.* far torto a, danneggiare, ledere, offendere, accusare ingiustamente.

wrongdoer (rŏng'dŏŏ'ĕr) *n.* malfattore, peccatore.

wrongful (rŏng'fŏŏl) *agg.* ingiusto, illegittimo, illegale; nocivo; iniquo.

wrongly (rŏng'lĭ) *avv.* male, ingiustamente, a torto, erroneamente.

wrote (rōt) *pass. di* to write.

wroth (rŏth) *agg.* adirato, iracondo.

wrought (rŏt) *pass., pp. di* to work. *agg.* lavorato, operato, elaborato: **— iron**, ferro battuto.

wrung (rŭng) pass., pp. di to wring.
wry (rī) agg. storto, di traverso, obliquo, contorto; snaturato, falso:

to make a — face, fare una smorfia.
wryneck (rī'nĕk') n. torcicollo.

X

xanthous (zăn'thŭs) agg. giallo.
xebec (zē'bĕk) n. (naut.) sciabecco.
xenogenesis (zĕn'ō·jĕn'ē·sĭs) n. (biol.)
eterogenesi.
xenomania (zĕn'ō·mā'nĭ·à) n. estero-
filia.
xenophobia (zĕn'ō·fō'bĭ·à) n. xeno-
fobia.

xylograph (zī'lō·gráf) n. silografia
(opera). —er (-ŏg'-) silografo.
xylography (zī·lŏg'rá·fĭ) n. silografia
(arte).
xyloid (zī'loid) agg. xiloide, ligneo.
xylophone (zī'lō·fōn) n. (mus.) silo-
xylophonist (-ĭst) n. silofonista. [fono.
xyster (zĭs'tĕr) n. (chir.) raschiatoio.

Y

yacht (yŏt) n. (naut.) panfilio. vi. navigare su un panfilio.
yank (yăngk) (1) n. (fam.) strattone.
vt., vi. strappare, tirare violentemente, dare uno strattone.
Yank (yăngk) (2) (gergo) vedi Yankee.
Yankee (yăng'kė) n., agg. americano
del nord degli S.U.; (fam.) statu-
nitense, americano.
yap (yăp) n. latrato; (gergo) chiacchiera rumorosa. vi. abbaiare; blaterare.
yard (yärd) n. corte, cortile; cantiere;
iarda (misura di lunghezza); (ferr.)
parco di smistamento; (naut.) pennone: navy —, cantiere navale.
yardstick (yärd'stĭk') n. asta di una
iarda (per misurare); misura, norma, metro.
yarn (yärn) n. filo, fibra tessile, filato;
storia, racconto.
yaw (yô) vi. (naut.) straorzare; (aeron.)
deviare dalla rotta.
yawl (yôl) n. (naut.) iole, scialuppa.
yawn (yôn) n. sbadiglio; apertura,
voragine. vi. sbadigliare; aprirsi.
yea (yā) n. assenso, voto affermativo.
avv. sì, già.
year (yėr) n. anno, annata: leap —,
anno bisestile; by the —, per anno,
annualmente. —book n. annuario.
yearly (yėr'lĭ) agg. annuale. avv. annualmente, ogni anno.
yearn (yûrn) vi. intenerirsi; anelare: to — for, agognare, sospirare
per, avere la nostalgia di.
yearning (yûr'nĭng) n. brama; nostalgia. agg. bramoso, nostalgico.
yeast (yėst) n. lievito, fermento;
schiuma. vi. fermentare, lievitare.
yell (yĕl) n. urlo. vt., vi. urlare, strillare.
yellow (yĕl'ō) n. giallo; tuorlo d'uovo.
agg. giallo; vile, vigliacco; infido;
sensazionale, scandalistico: the —

press, la stampa scandalistica; —
jack, febbre gialla; (naut.) bandiera
gialla. vt., vi. ingiallire, ingiallirsi.
yellowish (yĕl'ō·ĭsh) agg. giallastro.
yelp (yĕlp) n. guaito, latrato, grido.
vi. guaire, latrare, gridare.
yen (yĕn) n. (gergo) passione, desiderio,
nostalgia.
yes (yĕs) n., avv. sì: — man, persona
ossequiosa, tirapiedi, servo.
yesterday (yĕs'tĕr·dĭ) n., avv. ieri:
the day before —, l'altro ieri.
yet (yĕt) avv., cong. ancora, di più,
finora, eppure, però; prima o poi,
in ogni caso; tuttora, ma, d'altronde: as —, finora; not —, non ancora.
yew (yōō) n. (bot.) tasso.
yield (yēld) n. prodotto, produzione,
rendimento, reddito. vt., vi. produrre, rendere, fruttare, cedere,
concedere, emettere, rassegnare,
rinunciare: to — oneself up, costituirsi, arrendersi.
yoke (yōk) n. giogo; basto; coppia (di
animali aggiogati). vt. aggiogare, appaiare.
yolk (yōk) n. tuorlo d'uovo; lanolina.
yonder (yŏn'dĕr) agg. di laggiù, il più
lontano, quello, quelli, quella,
quelle. avv. laggiù.
yore (yōr) n. (il) passato: of —, di un
tempo; passato (agg.).
you (yōō) pron.pers. voi, a voi, vi, tu,
te, ti, lei, le: I gave it to —, l'ho
dato a voi; as I said to you, come
vi dissi.
young (yŭng) n. piccolo; piccoli o
cuccioli (di animali); (i) giovani.
agg. giovane, immaturo, fresco,
inesperto: — lady, signorina; —
man, giovane, giovanotto; — people, i giovani.
younger (-gĕr) agg. più giovane (di),
cadetto.

youngest (-gĕst) *agg.* il più giovane.

youngster (yŭng'stĕr) *n.* bambino, giovanetto, giovinotto.

your (yŏor) *agg.poss.* vostro, vostra, vostri, vostre, tuo, tua, tuoi, tue.

yours (yŏorz) *pron.poss.* il vostro, la vostra, i vostri, le vostre, il tuo, ecc. a friend of —, un vostro amico; — truly, vostro devotissimo.

yourself (yŏor·sĕlf') *pron.* (*pl.* yourselves) voi stesso, voi stessa, vi, tu stesso, te stesso, ti.

youth (yŏoth) *n.* giovinezza, gioventù; adolescenza; adolescente, giovane.

youthful (yŏoth'fŏol) *agg.* giovane, giovanile.

youthfulness *n.* gioventù, aspetto giovanile, freschezza.

yowl (youl) *n.* ululato, gemito. *vi.* ululare, gemere.

yule (yŏol) *n.* Natale.

yuletide (yŏol'tīd') *n.* periodo natalizio.

Z

zany (zā'nĭ) *n.* buffone,

zeal (zēl) *n.* zelo, entusiasmo, fervore.

zealot (zĕl'ŭt) *n.* fanatico.

zealous (zĕl'ŭs) *agg.* zelante, fervente.

zenith (zē'nĭth) *n.* zenit; apogeo, apice.

zephyr (zĕf'ĕr) *n.* zefiro, brezza; (*tess.*) zefir.

zero (zē'rō) *n.* zero, nulla.

zest (zĕst) *n.* gusto, sapore, aroma, interesse, ardore.

zigzag (zĭg'zăg') *n.* zigzag, serpeggiamento. *agg.*, *avv.* a zigzag. *vi.* andare a zigzag, serpeggiare.

zinc (zĭngk) *n.* zinco: — white, ossido di zinco, biacca. *vt.* zincare.

Zionism (zī'ŭn·ĭz'm) *n.* Sionismo.

zip (zĭp) *n.* sibilo (*di proiettile*); (*fam.*) forza, energia.

zipper (zĭp'ĕr) *n.* chiusura lampo.

zodiac (zō'dĭ·ăk) *n.* zodiaco.

zone (zōn) *n.* zona, area, fascia: time —, fuso orario. *vt.* cingere, dividere in zone.

zoo (zōo) *n.* giardino zoologico.

zoological (zō'ō·lŏj'ĭ·kăl) *n.* zoologico.

zoologist (zō·ŏl'ō·jĭst) *n.* zoologo.

zoology (zō·ŏl'ō·jĭ) *n.* zoologia.

zoophilist (zō·ŏf'ĭ·lĭst) *n.* zoofilo.

zoophily (zo·ŏf'ĭ·lĭ) *n.* zoofilia.

zoophyte (zō'ō·fīt) *n.* (*zool.*) zoofito.

zooplasty (zō'ō·plăs'tĭ) *n.* trapianto di tessuto animale.

?????

_____43883 QUESTIONS YOU ALWAYS WANTED TO ASK
            ABOUT ENGLISH But Were Afraid to Raise
            Your Hand, Maxwell Nurnberg $2.50

_____43572 THE QUICK AND EASY WAY TO EFFECTIVE
            SPEAKING $2.75

_____44739 SHORT CUTS TO EFFECTIVE ENGLISH,
            Harry Shefter $2.95

_____43140 6 MINUTES A DAY TO PERFECT SPELLING,
            Harry Shefter $2.50

_____44837 6 WEEKS TO WORDS OF POWER, Wilfred Funk $2.75

_____45675 30 DAYS TO A MORE POWERFUL VOCABULARY $2.95

_____42286 WORDS MOST OFTEN MISSPELLED AND
            MISPRONOUNCED, Gleeson & Colvin $2.50

POCKET BOOKS
Department REF
1230 Avenue of the Americas
New York, N.Y. 10020

Please send me the books I have checked above. I am enclos-
ing $_____ (please add 50¢ to cover postage and handling,
N.Y.S. and N.Y.C. residents please add appropriate sales tax).
Send check or money order—no cash or C.O.D.s please. Allow
six weeks for delivery.

NAME_____

ADDRESS_____

CITY_____ STATE/ZIP_____

221

Look for these popular titles from Washington Square Press at your bookseller now

Look for these popular titles from Washington Square Press at your bookseller now

Graham Greene
THE END OF THE AFFAIR

"One of the best, most true and moving novels of my time, in anybody's language"—William Faulkner.
44535-9/$2.95/240 pp.

THE HONORARY CONSUL

A compelling tale of political intrigue and heartfelt passion by "the finest living novelist, bar none, in our language"—Harper's.
42881-0/$3.95/320 pp.

ORIENT EXPRESS

A stunning novel of violence and psychological intrigue.
43514-0/$2.75/256 pp.

Joan Didion
PLAY IT AS IT LAYS

At the center of this powerful novel is Maria, a young actress caught off balance by Hollywood, her husband, her hopelessly retarded daughter—and most of all, herself.
43596-5/$2.75/266 pp.

RUN RIVER

An unforgettable novel from one of America's most elegant and brilliant writers.
44258-9/$2.95/256 pp.

WSP

WASHINGTON SQUARE PRESS
Published by Pocket Books